World Literature and Its Times

VOLUME 1

Latin American Literature and Its Times

World Literature and Its Times

Profiles of Notable Literary Works and the Historical Events That Influenced Them

Joyce Moss • Lorraine Valestuk

Detroit
San Francisco
London
Boston
Woodbridge, CT

LIBRARY
COLBY-SAWYER COLLEGE
NEW LONDON, NH 03257

#41273102

World Literature and Its Times

Profiles of Notable Literary Works and the Historical Events That Influenced Them

VOLUME 1

Latin American Literature and Its Times

JOYCE MOSS • LORRAINE VALESTUK

STAFF

Lawrence J. Trudeau, *Production Editor*
Maria Franklin, *Permissions Manager*
Kimberly F. Smilay, *Permissions Specialist*

Mary Beth Trimper, *Production Director*
Evi Seoud, *Production Manager*

Cynthia Baldwin, *Art Director*
Pamela Galbreath, *Cover and Page Designer*

Barbara J. Yarrow, *Graphic Services Supervisor*
Randy Bassett, *Image Database Supervisor*
Robert Duncan, *Scanner Operator*
Pamela Hayes, *Photography Coordinator*

∞™The paper used in this publication meets the minimum requirements of American National Standard for Information Sciences—Permanence Paper for Printed Library Materials, ANSI Z39.48-1984.

This publication is a creative work fully protected by all applicable copyright laws, as well as by misappropriation, trade secret, unfair competition, and other applicable laws. The authors and editors of this work have added value to the underlying factual material herein through one or more of the following: unique and original selection, coordination, expression, arrangement, and classification of the information.

All rights to this publication will be vigorously defended.

Copyright © 1999
Joyce Moss

All rights reserved including the right of reproduction in whole or in part in any form.

ISBN 0-7876-3726-2

Printed in the United States of America
10 9 8 7 6 5 4 3 2 1

Library of Congress Cataloging-in Publication Data

Moss, Joyce, 1951–
Latin American literature and its times: profiles of notable literary works and the historical events that influenced them / Joyce Moss, Lorraine Valestuk
p. cm.—(World literature and its times)
Includes bibliographical references and index.
ISBN 0-7876-3726-2 (hardcover)
1. Latin American literature—History and criticism. 2. Literature and history—Latin America. 3. Latin America—History Miscellanea. I. Valestuk, Lorraine, 1963- II. Title. III. Series.
PQ7081 .M625 1999
860.9'98—dc21

99-29292
CIP
Rev.

LIBRARY
COLBY-SAWYER COLLEGE
NEW LONDON, NH 03257

Contents

General Preface

The world at the turn of the twenty-first century is a shrinking sphere. Innovative modes of transmission make communication from one continent to another almost instantaneous, encouraging the development of an increasingly global society, heightening the urgency of the need for mutual understanding. At the foundation of *World Literature and Its Times* is the belief that within a people's literature are keys to their perspectives, their emotions, and the formative events that have brought them to the present point.

As manifested in their literary works, societies experience phenomena that are in some instances universal and in other instances tied to time and place. T. S. Eliot's poem *The Wasteland,* for example, is set in Europe in the early 1920s, when the region was rife with the disenchantment of the post-World War I era. Coincidentally, Juan Rulfo's novel *Pedro Páramo,* set in Latin America over a spread of decades that includes the 1920s, features a protagonist whose last name means "bleak plain" or "wasteland." The two literary works, though written oceans apart, conjure a remarkably similar atmosphere. Likewise, Joaquim Maria Machado de Assis's *Dom Casmurro* has sometimes been called Brazil's *Othello,* since both the novel and Shakespeare's play feature men driven by an overpowering jealousy. In this case, the two works are set three centuries apart, suggesting that time as well as place is of little consequence. A close look at the two men, however—and the two wastelands referred to above—exposes illuminating differences, which are in fact tied to the particular times and places in which the respective works are set.

World Literature and Its Times regards both fiction and nonfiction as rich mediums for understanding the differences, as well as the similarities, among people and societies. In its view, full understanding of a literary work demands attention to events and attitudes of the period in which a work takes place and of the one in which it is written. The series therefore examines a wide range of novels, short stories, biographies, speeches, poems, and plays by contextualizing a work in these two periods. Each volume covers some fifty literary works that span a mix of centuries and genres. The literary work itself takes center stage, with its contents determining which issues—social, political, psychological, economic, or cultural—are covered in a given entry. Every entry discusses the relevant issues apart from the literary work, making connections to it when merited, and allowing for comparisons between the literary and the historical realities. Close attention is given as well to the literary work itself, in the interest of extracting historical understandings from it.

Of course, the function of literature is not necessarily to represent history accurately. Nevertheless the images and ideas promoted by a powerful literary work—be it Miguel de Cervantes's *The Adventures of Don Quixote* (Spain), Nadine Gordimer's *Burgher's Daughter* (South Africa), or Salman Rushdie's *Midnight Children* (India)—

leave impressions that are commonly taken to be historical. In taking literature as fact, one risks acquiring a mistaken notion of history. The gaucho of Argentina is a case in point, having inspired a collection of poetry by non-gauchos whose verse conveys a highly romantic image of these cowboylike nomads, albeit one that includes some realistic details (see *The Gaucho Martín Fierro* in *Latin American Literature and Its Times*). To adjust for such discrepancies, this series distinguishes between historical fact and its literary reworkings.

On the other hand, literary works can broaden our understanding of history. They are able to convey more than the cut-and-dried record, by portraying events in a way that captures the fears and challenges of a period or by drawing attention to groups of people who are generally left out of standard histories. This is well illustrated with writings that concern the position of women in different societies—for example, Flora Nwapa's novel *Efuru* (Nigeria) or Mary Wollstonecraft's essay *A Vindication of the Rights of Women* (England). Literature, as illustrated by these works, engages in a vigorous dialogue with other forms of communication. It often defies stereotypes by featuring characters or ideas that are contrary to preconceptions. In fact, many of the literary works covered in this series feature characters and ideas that attack or upset deeply ingrained stereotypes, from Friar Bartolomé de las Casas's *A Short Account of the Destruction of the Indies* (mid-1500s Latin America) to Mongo Beti's *Mission to Kala* (mid-1900s Cameroun Republic).

Even nonfiction must be anchored in its place and times to derive its full value. Octavio Paz's essay *The Labyrinth of Solitude* explains the character of contemporary Mexicans as a product of historical experience; the entry on the essay amplifies this experience. A second entry, on Albert Memmi's *Pillar of Salt,* uses the less direct genre of biography to describe the life of a Tunisian Jew during the Nazi occupation of North Africa. A third entry, on Frantz Fanon's essays in *The Wretched of the Earth,* about the merits of violence, considers his views as an outgrowth of the ravages in colonial Algeria.

The task of reconstructing the historical context of a literary work can be problematic. An author may present events out of chronological order, as Carlos Fuentes does in *The Death of Artemio Cruz* (Mexico), or may create works that feature legendary heroes who defy attempts to fit them neatly into an exact time slot (such as the warrior Beowulf of Denmark, glorified in England's epic poetry; or the emperor Sunjata of Mali in Western Sudan). In the first case, *World Literature and Its Times* unscrambles the plot, providing a linear rendering of events and associated historical information. In the second, the series profiles customs particular to the culture in which the epic is set, arming the reader with details that inform the hero's adventures. The approach sheds light on the relationship between fact and fiction, both of which are shown to provide insight into a people and their epics. As always, the series takes this approach with a warm appreciation for the beauty of the literary work independent of historical facts, but also in the belief that ultimate regard is shown for the work by placing it in the context of pertinent events.

Beyond this underlying belief, the series is founded on the notion that a command of world literature bolsters knowledge of the writings produced by one's own society. Long before the present century, fiction and nonfiction writers from different locations influenced one another through trends and strategies in their literatures. In our postcolonial age, such cross-fertilization has quickened. Latin American literature, having been influenced by French and Spanish trends, among others, itself influences Chinese writers of today. Likewise, Africa's literary tradition has affected and been affected by France's, and the same relationship holds true for the writings of India and Great Britain. The degree of such literary intermixture promises only to multiply given our increasingly global society. In the process, world literature and its landmark texts gain even greater significance, attaining the potential to promote understanding not only of others, but also of ourselves.

The Selection of Literary Works

The works chosen for *Latin American Literature and Its Times* have been carefully selected by professors in the field at the universities detailed in the Acknowledgments. Keeping the literature-history connection in mind, the team made its selections based on a combination of factors: how frequently a literary work is studied, how closely it is tied to pivotal events in the past or present, and how strong and enduring its appeal has been to readers in and out of the society that produced it. Attention has been paid to contemporary as well as to classic works that have met with critical and/or popular acclaim. There has also been a careful effort to include a balance from both Spanish-speaking Latin America and Brazil, to represent female as well as male authors, and to include a mix of genres. Selections were limited to those literary works currently available in English; fortuitously much of the finest literature from the region has been translated, though a great many works still await such a transformation. Recognizing that political borders belie cultural boundaries, the series includes in its purview a number of entries on Latino works produced in the United States. In selecting which Latino works to include, the team invoked additional considerations—representation of literature by Caribbean expatriates as well as by Mexican Americans, of nonfiction as well as fiction, and of works created in various regions of the nation.

Format and Arrangement of Entries

The volumes in *World Literature and Its Times* are arranged geographically. Within each volume, entries are arranged alphabetically by title of the literary work. The time at which the work is set appears at the beginning of an entry.

Each entry is organized as follows:

1. **Introduction**—identifying information in three parts:

   The literary work—specifies the genre, the place and time period in which the work is set, the year it was first published, and, if applicable, the year in which it was first translated; also provided, for translations, is the title of the literary work in its original language.

   Synopsis—summarizes the storyline or contents of the work.

   Introductory paragraph—introduces the literary work in relation to the author's life.

2. **Events in History at the Time the Literary Work Takes Place**—describes social and political events that relate to the plot or contents of the literary work. The section may discuss background information as well as relevant events during the period in which the work is set. Subsections vary depending on the literary work. Taking a deductive approach, the section starts with events in history and telescopes inward to events in the literary work.

3. **The Literary Work in Focus**—summarizes in detail the plot or contents of the work, describes how it illuminates history, and identifies sources used by the author. After the summary of the work comes a subsection focusing on an aspect of the literature that illuminates our understanding of events or attitudes of the period. This subsection takes an inductive approach, starting with the literary work, and broadening outward to events in history. It is followed by a third subsection specifying sources that inspired elements of the work and discussing its literary context, or relation to other works.

4. **Events in History at the Time the Literary Work Was Written**—describes social, political, and/or literary events in the author's lifetime that relate to the plot or contents of a work. Also discussed in this section are the reviews or reception accorded the literary work.

5. **For More Information**—provides a list of all sources that have been cited in the entry as well as sources for further reading about the different issues or personalities featured in the entry.

If the literary work is set and written in the same time period, sections 2 and 4 of the entry on that work ("Events in History at the Time the Literary Work Takes Place" and "Events in History at the Time the Literary Work Was Written") are combined into the single section "Events in History at the Time of the Literary Work."

Additional Features

Whenever possible, primary source material is provided through quotations in the text and material in sidebars. There are also sidebars with historical details that amplify issues raised in the text, and with anecdotes that provide a fuller understanding of the temporal context. Timelines appear in various entries to summarize intricate periods of history. Finally, historically relevant illustrations enrich and further clarify information in the entries.

Comments and Suggestions

Your comments on this series and suggestions for future editions are welcome. Please write: Editors, *World Literature and Its Times,* The Gale Group, 27500 Drake Road, Farmington Hills, Michigan 48331-3535.

Acknowledgments

Latin American Literature and Its Times is a collaborative effort that evolved through several stages of development, each of which was monitored by a team of experts in Spanish American, Brazilian, and Latino literatures. A special thank you goes to Professors Randal Johnson and Efraín Kristal of the University of California at Los Angeles for their enthusiastic guidance at every stage in the development process.

For their incisive participation in selecting the literary works to cover in the volume, the editors extend deep appreciation to the following professors:

Robert Aguirre, Wayne State University, Department of English

Roberto Díaz, University of Southern California, Department of Spanish and Portuguese

David William Foster, Arizona State University, Department of Languages and Literatures

Lucille Kerr, University of Southern California, Department of Spanish and Portuguese

Gwendolyn Kirkpatrick, University of California at Berkeley, Department of Spanish and Portuguese

Efraín Kristal, University of California at Los Angeles, Department of Spanish and Portuguese

Randal Johnson, University of California at Los Angeles, Chair, Department of Spanish and Portuguese

Doris Sommer, Harvard University, Department of Romance Languages and Literatures

Warm gratitude is extended to the following professors for their careful review of the entries to insure accuracy and completeness of information:

Robert Aguirre, Wayne State University, Department of English

Roberto Castillo, Haverford College, Department of Spanish

Roberto Díaz, University of Southern California, Department of Spanish and Portuguese

Jennifer Eich, Loyola Marymount University, Modern Languages

David William Foster, Arizona State University, Department of Languages and Literatures

Jean Graham-Jones, Florida State University, Department of Modern Languages and Linguistics

Efraín Kristal, University of California at Los Angeles, Department of Spanish and Portuguese

Randal Johnson, University of California at Los Angeles, Chair, Department of Spanish and Portuguese

Lucille Kerr, University of Southern California, Department of Spanish and Portuguese

José Luis Passos, University of California at Berkeley, Department of Spanish and Portuguese

Jacobo Sefami, University of California at Irvine, Department of Spanish and Portuguese

Michael Schuessler, United States International University, Mexico, Head, Liberal and Global Studies

Doris Sommer, Harvard University, Department of Romance Languages and Literatures

Gwendolyn Kirkpatrick, University of California at Berkeley, Department of Spanish and Portuguese

For their painstaking research and composition, the editors thank the contributors whose names appear at the close of the entries that they wrote. A complete listing follows:

Robert Aguirre, Assistant Professor, Wayne State University

Soraya Alamdari, Ph.D. candidate, University of California at Los Angeles

Kimberly Ball, M.A. candidate, University of California at Berkeley

Thomas O. Beebee, Associate Professor, Pennsylvania State University

Gilberto M. Blasini, Ph.D. candidate, University of California at Los Angeles

Terence Davis, B. A., University of California at Los Angeles; Professional writer

Amy Garawitz, M.A., University of Southern California; Professional writer

Kristine Ibsen, Associate Professor, University of Notre Dame

Randal Johnson, Professor and Chair, Department of Spanish and Portuguese, University of California at Los Angeles

Sabrina Karpa-Wilson, Assistant Professor; Director of Portuguese Studies, Indiana University

Deborah Kerney, Ph.D. candidate, University of California at Los Angeles

Jacob Littleton, Ph.D. candidate, University of California at Los Angeles

Pamela S. Loy, Ph.D., University of California at Santa Barbara; Professional writer

Barbara Lozano, B.A., University of California at Los Angeles; Professional writer

Anna Moschovakis, M.F.A., Bard College; Professional writer

Emerson Spencer Olin, M.A., University of Southern California; Professional writer

Anthony Miles Potter, Ph.D. candidate, University of California at Los Angeles

John W. Roleke, M.A., Indiana University; Professional writer

Victoria Sams, Ph.D. candidate, University of California at Los Angeles

Michael Schuessler, Associate Professor; Head, Liberal and Global Studies, United States International University, Mexico

Jennifer Garson Shapiro, Ph.D., University of California at Los Angeles; Professional writer

Diane R. Sneva, B.A., University of California at Los Angeles; Professional writer

Vincent Spina, Associate Professor; Chair, Department of Modern Languages and Cultures, Clarion University

Olivia Treviño, Ph.D. candidate, University of California at Los Angeles

Carolyn Turgeon, Ph.D. candidate, University of California at Los Angeles

Renata R. Mautner Wasserman, Professor, Wayne State University

Allison Weisz, M.Phil, Cambridge University; teacher, Convent of the Sacred Heart

Deep appreciation is extended to Larry Trudeau of Gale Research for his deft editing of the entries and his painstaking research and compilation of the illustrations. Anne Leach indexed the volume with great sensitivity to both readers and subject matter. Finally, the editors extend a hearty note of gratitude to Peter Kline for his photographic research, and to Autumn Mayfield for her proficient word processing and organizational management.

Introduction to Latin American Literature and Its Times

Latin American literature attracted unprecedented global attention in the 1960s, a volatile period in the region, one in which many of its residents were upset or challenged by the success of revolution in Cuba. Debate raged furiously across national borders, calling into question relationships long regarded as inviolable, with writers factoring themselves into the political and social dialogue through the literary works they produced. Of course, authors had already engaged in such dialogue for decades. For them, as for many Latin Americans, literature has long been as legitimate a medium as any to explore the most compelling political, social, and spiritual concerns of the past and the present.

In keeping with this conviction, *Latin American Literature and Its Times* arises out of the notion that a grasp of historical events is fundamental to understanding Latin America's literary works. Such knowledge is, in some cases, necessary to decipher the meaning of the works; in others, it enhances or illuminates one's reading of them. By the same token, the literary works can elucidate history when one has a grounding in its particulars. Latin America has vibrant traditions in poetry, the short story, the novel, nonfiction (essays, biographies, and epistles), drama, and a hybrid genre, the testimonial, all of which relate to history. There are even narratives (Brazil's *Rebellion in the Backlands* by Euclides da Cunha and Argentina's *Facundo* by Domingo F. Sarmiento) that defy classification, yet share with other works a relation to events in the region.

There have been several transfiguring events in Latin America, which vary in their particulars depending on location. Among these events are conquest by European powers; the colonial experience; environmental encounters with the jungle, grasslands, plains, and in Brazil the drought-ridden sertão; a mystical/spiritual dimension that affects everyday life; the incessant struggle for political control and economic survival; and ethnic clashes among European immigrants, indigenous Americans, Africans, and mixed-race offspring.

Details about these transformative experiences surface in the literary works covered in this volume. Out of the Conquest, for example, comes the philosophical question of civilization versus barbarism, which rears its confounding head in Domingo F. Sarmiento's essay *Facundo* (set in Argentina), Rómulo Gallegos's novel *Doña Barbara* (Venezuela), and Pablo Neruda's poem *The Heights of Macchu Picchu* (Peru). From the mystical/ spiritual dimension incorporated into various novels comes the perception that boundaries are blurred; there are no clear distinctions between life and death, or humans and the rest of the animate and inanimate world. Illustrating this perception is Juan Rulfo's *Pedro Páramo* (Mexico), which features souls of the dead lingering on earth. A postman is transformed into a coyote in Miguel Ángel Asturias's *Men of Maize* (Guatemala) and a woman into a statue in Elena Garro's *Recollections of Things to Come* (Mexico). Another factor that finds its way into such novels is the unrestrained power of the local strongman (the *cacique* in Mexico, the *coronel* in Brazil, the *caudillo* in Argentina and elsewhere), a figure who emerges out of genuine struggles for political control in the 1800s and early 1900s. Other common factors manifest themselves in the region's literary works too:

• **Dictatorship experience**—*Santa Evita* (set in Argentina); *I the Supreme* (Paraguay); *In the Time of the Butterflies* (Dominican Republic); *The Celebration* (Brazil)

• **Revolution at the national and local levels**—*Rebellion in the Backlands* (Brazil); *Like Water for Chocolate* (Mexico); *A House in the Country* (Chile)

• **Geography and its effect on humanity**—*The Decapitated Chicken and Other Stories* (Argentina); *Barren Lives* (Brazil); *. . . and the earth did not part* (southwestern United States)

• **Ethnic and social disparity**—Indians and ladinos in *I, Rigoberta Menchú* (Guatemala); Afro-Caribbeans and Europeans in *The Kingdom of This World* (Cuba); Jews and Catholics in *The Fragmented Life of Don Jacobo Lerner* (Peru); haves and have-nots in *The Hour of the Star* (Brazil)

• **Mythical foundations**—*Men of Maize* (Guatemala); *The Gaucho Martín Fierro* (Argentina); *Iracema, the Honey-Lips* (Brazil)

• **Impact of popular culture**—Cinema in *Kiss of the Spider Woman* (Argentina); music in *Macho Camacho's Beat* (Puerto Rico); folklore in *Macunaíma* (Brazil)

• **Search for individual or national identity**—*The Labyrinth of Solitude* (in Mexico); *Days of Obligation* (by Mexican Americans); *The Devil to Pay in the Backlands* (in Brazil)

Beyond such related concerns, Latin American literature shows a longstanding streak of rebelliousness that surfaces in works written at home and abroad. As early as 1542 Friar Bartolomé de las Casas wrote the polemical *A Short Account of the Destruction of the Indies,* directed at the colonizing Spaniards in defense of Latin America's indigenous peoples. In 1691 Sor Juana Inés de la Cruz, playwright, poet, and essayist who challenged the sexist assumptions of her times, penned a tract in defense of a woman's right to learn, producing the first feminist writing in the Western Hemisphere. Two centuries later, from New York, expatriate poet and essayist José Martí wrote tirelessly to embed an independence of thought in Cubans, in the process arguing for a distinct Latin American literature whose foundations he helped lay. Martí also contributed to the origin of a subset of Latin American literature, the writings of expatriates and their descendants from the Caribbean and from Central and South America in the United States. In the twentieth century, the Latino writers who followed Martí aimed likewise to influence popular thought through their works. Tomás Rivera, for example, upset stereotypes of Mexicans in the United States by portraying migrant laborers as ambitious, hard-working, humane, and intelligent (*. . . and the earth did not part*). On both sides of the border, in the tradition of Sor Juana, writers crafted tales that portrayed the defiant rather than the compliant female, as demonstrated by Sandra Cisneros's *Woman Hollering Creek and Other Stories* (the U.S. Southwest) and by Rosario Ferré's "The Youngest Doll" (Puerto Rico).

Literary works written from the end of the nineteenth to the end of the twentieth century would go far in developing the distinct Latin American literature that Martí foresaw. Innovation in language and narrative style have been key building blocks in the process. Incorporated into groundbreaking stories is the vernacular used by the people portrayed. Unfortunately the dexterity of an author in infusing a text with nuanced localisms—the Spanish spoken by Mexican peasants or the Portuguese characteristic of various regions of Brazil—is often lost in translation. Authors have nonetheless taken major strides by writing such localisms into the original editions of their works (see Mário de Andrade's *Macunaíma*). Other authors, such as Guillermo Cabrera Infante in *Three Trapped Tigers* (Cuba) and João Guimarães Rosa in *The Devil to Pay in the Backlands* (Brazil), have experimented daringly with language, coining words of their own invention to inspire new levels of understanding. There has also been tremendous originality in narrative style. Juan Rulfo's *Pedro Páramo,* for example, uses not one straightforward narrator but a series of narrative voices, who tell the tale in the first-person and the third-person, and in discontinuous fragments of time.

Given its focus on the connections between literary works and historical events, *Latin American Literature and Its Times* does not cover some well-known Latin American works. It does not, for example, feature poetry by the Nicaraguan master Rubén Darío, whose formal achievements can hardly be accounted for in translation; there is, however, discussion of Darío's impact on other literary works when relevant. Moreover, the volume does include works that are representative of various literary movements in Latin America—for example, the naturalist novel with its scientific bent (*A Brazilian Tenement*), the regionalist novel that features one or another of the major landscapes of the area (*Doña Barbara*), and the so-called "Boom" novel of the 1960s, when Latin American literature became a worldwide rage. There are two writers whose works defy this sort of categorization—Brazil's Joaquim Maria Machado de Assis (1839–1908) and Argentina's Jorge Luis Borges (1899–1986). Machado (see *Dom Casmurro*) took the Latin American novel to new heights, writing tales that can be read on different levels with a skill that many have described as still unsurpassed. Borges excelled in briefer genres (see the short story "The South"), becoming a model for other writers, his works fusing the past with the present, the local with the universal, fantasy with reality, and fiction with nonfiction.

In the 1960s a number of Spanish-speaking writers would fuse fiction with nonfiction to create a new genre, the testimonial novel, of which Elena Poniatowska's *Massacre in Mexico* is a prime example. The '60s in general featured technical virtuosity from novelists such as Carlos Fuentes, who told a tale out of chronological time and through an amalgam of points of view in *The Death of Artemio Cruz,* and Gabriel García Márquez, who encapsulated a century in a few hundred pages in *One Hundred Years of Solitude,* and brought to the fore the mix of registers (human, historical, magical, allegorical) that figures into everyday life in Spanish-speaking Latin America.

Muzzled to a large extent by a military dictatorship in the 1960s, Brazilian letters flowed more freely in the '70s, a decade in which Latin American literature on the whole began to show a renewed concern for the politics of the moment. Two of the decade's novels—José Donoso's *A House in the Country* and Isabel Allende's *The House of the Spirits*—alluded to the coup in Chile against the Western World's first democratically elected socialist president, Salvador Allende. Other novels began for the first time to infuse popular culture into their storylines, which gave greater voice to the masses, acknowledging the importance, for example, of popular music in Puerto Rico (Luis Rafael Sanchez's *Macho Camacho's Beat*), and film in Argentina (Manuel Puig's *Kiss of the Spider Woman*).

As the century neared its close, Latin American literature would continue to serve as an instrument through which to communicate about current events. At the same time, these latest literary works would show a loyalty to a longstanding perception of them as separate entities, apart from the events they happen to portray. This perception of literature as more than a reflection of events is evident in classic stories with unreliable narrators (by Machado or Borges) and in recent novels with self-conscious or multiple narrators. Ivan Ângelo's *The Celebration,* in part about a violent incident near a Brazilian train station, inserts into its narrative "Author's Notes," which turn the novelist into a character. Similarly, Mario Vargas Llosa's *The Storyteller,* which focuses on an indigenous people of the Peruvian jungle, includes multiple narrators, who become a conspicuous part of the action. These strategies, like others in earlier works, call into question standard ways of viewing events, infusing Latin American literature with no easy answers but with an exhilarating, exploratory edge that expands the reader's comprehension and consciousness.

Chronology of Relevant Events

Latin American Literature and Its Times

FROM CONQUEST TO COLONIZATION

Latin American civilizations evolved over thousands of years, experiencing conquest and domination before the arrival of the Europeans. Beginning in 1492 with Christopher Columbus's first voyage to the Caribbean, Europeans insinuated themselves into the region, lured largely by the promise of economic rewards. Within roughly 100 years the Spaniards and Portuguese had destroyed every important New World civilization and had established a colonial infrastructure. To a large extent, they succeeded in imposing Christianity on the region.

	Historical Events	Related Literary Works
1500 B.C.	1500 B.C. Olmec civilization, the mother culture of Mesoamerica, develops on Mexico's Gulf Coast	
500 C.E.	500 C.E. Rise of the Mayans in the Yucatán peninsula, southern Mexico, and Guatemala	
	600–900 Height of the Mayan Empire	
	972 Toltecs from central Mexico begin to dominate Mayan civilization	
1000		
1300	1324 Aztecs build capital city of Tenochtitlan on site of present-day Mexico City	
1400	1400s Inca civilization rises in modern-day Peru	*The Heights of Macchu Picchu* by Pablo Neruda
	1492 Sponsored by Spain, Christopher Columbus lands on Bahama island of San Salvador, on Cuba, and on Hispaniola (Haiti and the Dominican Republic)	
	1493 Pope Alexander VI signs the papal bull *Inter caetera,* which decrees that Spain can colonize the New World, as long as it conquers in the name of Jesus Christ; on his second voyage, Columbus claims Puerto Rico (originally called Borikén) for Spain	

	Historical Events	Related Literary Works
	1494 Treaty of Tordesillas splits the newly discovered world between Portugal and Spain	
1500	1500 Pedro Álvares Cabral lands in Brazil	
	1502 Queen Isabella of Spain signs proclamation authorizing the governor of Hispaniola to "compel and force" the natives to grow crops, construct buildings, and mine gold for a fair wage	
	1507 An account of Amerigo Vespucci's travels uses *America* to designate South America and the West Indies; the term is soon applied to the whole New World	
	1511 Diego Velásquez conquers Cuba	
	1512 Hatuey, leader of Cuban Indians, is burned at the stake for leading an uprising against the Spanish	
	1519 Spanish take Panama and Costa Rica	
	1521 Hernán Cortés conquers capital city of the Aztec Empire, Tenochtitlan—Empire falls to Spaniards; amid violence, Friar Bartolomé de las Casas tries to establish peaceful, noncoercive settlements of natives and priests	*A Short Account of the Destruction of the Indies* by Friar Bartolomé de las Casas
	1522 Malintzin, Indian translator and mistress of Hernán Cortés, gives birth to their son, Martín, who will become known as the first mestizo; Spanish take Nicaragua	*The Labyrinth of Solitude* by Octavio Paz *Woman Hollering Creek* by Sandra Cisneros
	1524 Spanish take Guatemala	
	1525 Spanish take Ecuador	
	1527 Spanish take Venezuela and Yucatán; Bartolomé de las Casas begins to write his *History of the Indies*	
	1528 Spanish take Florida	
	1531 Virgin of Guadalupe is said to have appeared on a hilltop in Mexico to Juan Diego, a young Indian boy	*Days of Obligation* by Richard Rodríguez
	1533 Francisco Pizarro conquers the Incas in Peru	
	1539 French attack Havana	
	1545–60 Bartolomé de las Casas again tries to establish noncoercive settlements of natives and priests	
	1555 French establish a colony in Guanabara Bay, Brazil	
	1567 Portuguese expel French from Guanabara Bay	
	1570 Spanish Inquisition sets up court in Lima, Peru	*The Fragmented Life of Don Jacobo Lerner* by Isaac Goldemberg
	1572 The emperor Túpac Amaru is executed in Cuzco, ending Inca rebellion in the Andes	
	1580 Portugal and Spain are unified under Spanish Crown	
	1588 England defeats Spain's Invincible Armada, causing widespread political and economic chaos in Spain	
1600		
	1604 Tabajara Indians in northeastern Brazil are conquered by Portuguese soldier Pero Coelho de Sousa	*Iracema, the Honey-Lips* by José de Alencar
	1609 Garcilaso de la Vega writes *Comentarios reales de los Incas* (Royal Commentaries of the Incas)	
	1615 Portuguese expel French from Maranhão, Brazil; first exports of Caribbean sugar reach Spain	
	1624 Dutch invade Brazil	
	1638 Spanish Inquisition in Peru burns 11 Jews at the stake	

	Historical Events	Related Literary Works
	1640 Portugal reasserts independence from Spain	
	1654 Portuguese and mestizo forces repel the Dutch in Brazil	
	1670 Spain cedes Jamaica and Cayman Islands to England	
	1695 Spain cedes western Hispaniola to France in Treaty of Ryswijk	
1700	1780 Túpac Amaru II (José Gabriel Condorconqui) leads unsuccessful Indian revolt in Peru	
1800	1805 Spanish navy is decimated by the English at the Battle of Trafalgar	
	1808 Portugal's Prince Regent João (the future João VI) flees the French forces of Napoleon Bonaparte, moves Portuguese court to Brazil; opens Brazil's ports to world trade	
	1808 Napoleon places his brother Joseph on Spanish throne, ousting King Ferdinand VII	
	1814 Ferdinand VII returns to Spanish throne	
	1821 João VI returns from Brazil to Portugal	

SLAVERY

In their new Latin American colonies, the Spanish and Portuguese found immensely rich natural resources. To exploit these resources, they exacted forced labor from the Indians, then imported hundreds of thousands of Africans and enslaved them on sugar and other plantations. Slavery across the region ended in the second half of the nineteenth century when European public opinion turned against the practice, and when modern industrialization made it preferable to rely on wage labor.

	Historical Events	Related Literary Works
1500	1500 Inca Empire reaches its height, extracting forced labor from conquered peoples	*The Heights of Macchu Picchu* by Pablo Neruda
	early 1500s *Encomienda* system is established—Spanish Crown gives control of a region to a designated Spaniard, whose natives owe him labor and goods in return for protection and religious instruction	
	1503 Sugar is first produced on Hispaniola	
	1512 Laws of Burgos regulate how much work slaves can be forced to do and how they can be punished; laws also define the slaveowners' obligation to provide food, rest, and religious education	
	1513 *Requerimiento* clarifies the conditions under which the Spanish can make war on and enslave native peoples	
	1518 Spanish government grants permission for 4,000 Africans to be sent as slaves to the West Indies	
	1523 Sugar mills start up in Jamaica	
	1528 Spanish government sends 700 additional Africans as slaves to Cuba	
	1530s Portuguese Crown makes massive land grants in Brazil to military men and members of the nobility	

	Historical Events	Related Literary Works
	1534 Africans are first brought to Argentina as slaves	
	1537 Pope Paul III issues the bull *Sublimis Deus,* which declares that Indians were created by God with human souls	
	1542 New Laws enact sweeping reform of encomienda system throughout Spanish colonies (repealed 1545)	*A Short Account of the Destruction of the Indies* by Friar Bartolomé de las Casas
	1550s–1600 Encomiendas decline; haciendas, or private estates, grow increasingly common	*Deep Rivers* by José María Arguedas
	1550s–1850 Africans are shipped to Brazil as slaves	
1600		
	1685 The *Code Noir,* or Black Code, is passed by Louis XIV of France; establishes legal conditions for treatment of slaves, defined as property	
1700		
	1727 Europeans introduce coffee into Brazil	
	1793 Slavery abolished in Saint-Domingue (Haiti)	*The Kingdom of This World* by Alejo Carpentier
1800		
	1808 United States and Great Britain abolish slave trade	
	1813 Revolutionary government in Buenos Aires, Argentina, discontinues slave trade	
	1817 Cuban slave trade is made illegal by treaties between Spain and Great Britain	
	1833 August 26—Britain passes Emancipation Act, abolishing slavery in all British lands	
	1845 Spain passes anti-slavery measure	
	1850 Brazil bans import of African slaves	
	1854 Peru abolishes slavery	
	1856–69 90,000 Africans are taken to Cuba as slaves	
	1861 Argentina abolishes slavery	
	1865 Last slave ship arrives in Cuba; slavery ends here 21 years later, in 1886	*Biography of a Runaway Slave* by Miguel Barnet
	1871 September 28—Law of the Free Womb frees Brazilians born to slaves	
	1879 Spanish Prime Minister Arsenio Martínez Campos frees all Cuban slaves without compensation to the owners	
	1888 Brazil abolishes slavery	*A Brazilian Tenement* by Aluísio Azevedo
	1880s–1920s During Peru's short-lived rubber boom, Machiguenga Indians are enslaved and forced to tap rubber trees	

	Historical Events	Related Literary Works

INDEPENDENCE AND REVOLUTION

In 1804, Haiti (formerly Saint-Domingue) declared independence. Starting in 1810, other Latin American countries followed suit, taking advantage of Spain's weakened position as a victim of Napoleon Bonaparte's invading armies. The swiftness of the transition between colony and independent nation encouraged economic and political instability. Beginning a political tradition that extends to the present, individual strongmen rose to assume the absolute power once enjoyed by the European colonizers. Soon the new nations were at war with themselves and one another to assert autonomy, and to ensure economic power.

	Historical Events	Related Literary Works
	1794 Revolution begins in Saint-Domingue	
1800		
	1804 Haiti (Saint-Domingue) becomes first independent black country in the world; French troops are driven from Brazil	*The Kingdom of This World* by Alejo Carpentier
	1806 Argentines begin conscripting gauchos to fight in wars; they will continue to do so into the 1870s	*The Gaucho Martín Fierro* by José Hernández
1810	1810 In the absence of Spanish King Ferdinand VII (who had been dethroned by Napoleon Bonaparte), a local council claims temporary autonomy for Viceroyalty of La Plata—a region including present-day Argentina, Paraguay, Uruguay, and Bolivia	
	1811 Spanish forces quash Venezuelan independence movement under Simón Bolívar; Paraguayan creole officers stage coup against Spanish governor Bernardo de Velasco	
	1813 Paraguay becomes first independent republic in South America; Mexico declares independence; Simón Bolívar returns to Venezuela and earns title of "The Liberator"	
	1815 José María Morelos, a priest and leader of Mexico's pro-agrarian reform, anti-Spanish contingent, is executed	
	1816 La Plata region declares complete independence from Spain; fighting continues until 1824, when Spain finally cedes the point; José Gaspar Rodríguez de Francia becomes Supreme Dictator for life of Republic of Paraguay	*I the Supreme* by Augusto Roa Bastos
	1818 Chile declares independence	
	1819 Simón Bolívar takes control of Venezuela	
1820		
	1821 Peru and Guatemala declare independence from Spain; Mexico gains independence	
	1822 Under Pedro I, Brazil becomes independent monarchy	
	1824 Peruvian forces under Bolívar defeat Spanish at Battle of Junín in Peru; Francia nationalizes Church lands and takes fiscal control of Catholic wealth in Paraguay	
	1825 Upper Peru establishes itself as Bolivia (in honor of Simón Bolívar)	
	1826 Unionists and federalists fight civil war in Argentina	
	1828 Cisplantine War results in creation of Uruguay	
	1829 Juan Manuel de Rosas becomes governor of Buenos Aires; deposed 1852	*Facundo* by Domingo F. Sarmiento

	Historical Events	Related Literary Works
1830		
	1837 Peasant and Indian revolt in Guatemala	
1840	1840 15-year-old Pedro II takes the throne in Brazil; Gaspar Rodríguez de Francia dies, Carlos Antonio López (1840–62) becomes new dictator in Paraguay	
1850		
	1858–63 In Colombia, Liberals win civil wars against Conservatives, who will wrest power back in 1885	*One Hundred Years of Solitude* by Gabriel García Márquez
1860		
	1861–65 Spain occupies Dominican Republic	
	1862 The French Army invades Mexico, establishes empire with Mexican conservatives in 1864	
	1865–70 Argentina, Brazil, and Uruguay wage War of the Triple Alliance against Paraguay	
	1866 Spanish fight naval war against Peru and Chile	
	1868–78 Ten Years' War in Cuba fails to gain independence	
	1869 Spain officially recognizes Peru's independence	
1870		
	1873–85 Under President Justo Rufino Barrios in Guatemala, the army becomes a tool for oppressing the Indians	
	1876 Argentina returns to Paraguay the lands to the east of the River Paraná	*Men of Maize* by Miguel Ángel Asturias
	1879–83 Chile fights Bolivia and Peru in the War of the Pacific	
1880		
	1889 Brazilian emperor Pedro II is exiled; Brazil becomes a Republic	
	1889–1930 Arid backlands in northeastern Brazil are plagued by constant warfare between competing landowners	*The Devil to Pay in the Backlands* by João Guimarães Rosa
1890		
	1891 Chile fights civil war	
	1895 U.S. president Grover Cleveland helps establish border between Brazil and Argentina; José Martí dies at Battle of Dos Ríos in Cuban war of independence	"Our America," by José Martí
	1897 Federal army of Brazil conducts Siege of Canudos to rout a religious enclave in northeastern Brazil	*Rebellion in the Backlands* by Euclides da Cunha
	1898 Manuel Estrada Cabrera becomes president, then dictator, in Guatemala; he is deposed in 1920; Cuba wins independence	

MODERNIZATION AND URBAN MIGRATION

For centuries the wealth of Latin America was concentrated in its countryside, where slaves labored for Europeans to raise crops and work mines. Peasants also labored as peons on vast haciendas, or private estates. In the mid-to-late nineteenth century, industrialization began to transform the basic economic and social patterns of much of Latin American society; slavery ended; the landed oligarchy, though it would continue to wield power, began to decline; a new professional urban class emerged; and thousands of settlers, including huge waves of European immigrants, made their way into urban centers. Tenements and shantytowns sprang up in the city, which had long been considered the bastion of civilization in contrast to the countryside, which was viewed as the seat of barbarism. While urban migration was to persist over the next century, many would be disappointed in their hopes for a better life.

	Historical Events	Related Literary Works
1825		
	1827 Central government dissolves in Argentina as Federalists, who favor autonomy for the provinces, and Unitarians, who favor hegemony for Buenos Aires city, vie for power	*Facundo* by Domingo F. Sarmiento
	1845 Ranchers in Argentina begin to fence their lands, in an effort to tame the frontier for their personal benefit	*The Gaucho Martín Fierro* by José Hernández
1850		
	1850s Telegraphs, railroads, banking systems, and factories begin to appear in Brazil	
1875		
	1880s Along with internal migrants, Europeans immigrate in droves to Brazil's cities, mainly to Rio de Janeiro	*A Brazilian Tenement* by Aluísio Azevedo
	1890s Boom-and-bust cycle in Brazil shakes confidence of the new republic	*Dom Casmurro* by Joaquim Maria Machado de Assis
1900	1900–10 Railroad lines, ports, schools, and a newspaper appear in the frontier jungle of Misiones, Argentina	*The Decapitated Chicken and Other Stories* by Horacio Quiroga
	1910s–30s Contrasts between urban and rural areas sharpen with the growth of cities; illiteracy remains as high as 71 percent in the *llanos* (plains) of Venezuela in 1936	*Macunaíma* by Mário de Andrade; *Doña Barbara* by Rómulo Gallegos
	1918–25 Murderous pogroms in Eastern Europe drive tens of thousands of Jews to immigrate to Latin America, primarily to Argentina	*The Fragmented Life of Don Jacobo Lerner* by Isaac Goldemberg
	1920–30s A series of devastating droughts blight the sertão in Brazil; in the '20s rubber industry collapses in the Amazon, adding to the urban migration	*Barren Lives* by Graciliano Ramos
	1924 Victor Raúl Haya de la Torre founds APRA (*Alianza Popular Revolucionaria Americana*), a nationalist political party that favors modernization of Peru and its Indians	*Deep Rivers* by José María Arguedas
1925		
	1930s–40s Depression and drought drive hundreds of thousands of Northeastern Brazilians to the nation's cities; peasants and miners migrate to cities in Chile	*The Hour of the Star* by Clarice Lispector
	1937–43 About 70,000 per year migrate from rural areas, mostly from the pampas or grasslands, to cities in Argentina; industry becomes more valuable than agriculture in the Argentine economy	"The South" by Jorge Luis Borges

	Historical Events	Related Literary Works
	1942–52 Rural dwellers from northern Mexico migrate to Texas and the Midwest under Bracero Program; Latinos of the U.S. Southwest migrate to its urban centers	*. . . and the earth did not part* by Tomás Rivera *Bless Me, Ultima* by Rudolfo A. Anaya
1950		
	1951 Juan Perón wins a second term as president in Argentina, amid growing disenchantment with his rule; the author Julio Cortázar emigrates from Argentina to begin three decades of self-imposed exile in France	*Blow-Up and Other Stories* by Julio Cortázar
	1956 Juscelino Kubitschek promises "fifty years of progress in five" and is elected Brazilian president	*Gabriela, Clove and Cinnamon* by Jorge Amado
	1961 Brasília, Brazil's futuristic capital city, is completed	
	1960s Inequitable land tenure in Brazil's Northeast inspires continued migration and the formation of peasant leagues to struggle actively for change	*The Celebration* by Ivan Ângelo
1975		
	1980 Puerto Rican population in cities reaches 67 percent	*Macho Camacho's Beat* by Luis Rafael Sánchez

TWENTIETH-CENTURY DICTATORSHIPS

Economic strife (caused in part by the worldwide depression of the 1930s) exerted immense pressure on Latin American governments. As communism and fascism gained ground in Europe, civilian governments were commonly replaced by military dictatorships in twentieth-century Latin America. Countries experimented with socialism as well as fascism, with the military governments exercising control for long stretches in certain areas. Under the auspices of these dictatorships, governments sometimes committed tremendous travesties of human rights—a great many citizens lost their political voice and their lives.

	Historical Events	Related Literary Works
1910	1908–35 Juan Vicente Gómez is dictator in Venezuela	*Doña Barbara* by Rómulo Gallegos
1920		
	1928 Venezuelan students protest Gómez regime; Gómez closes universities	
1930	1930 Getúlio Vargas comes to power in Brazil; Rafael Leonidas Trujillo comes to power in the Dominican Republic, beginning three decades of brutal oppression (1930–61)	
	1934 On January 14 Fulgencio Batista becomes Cuban dictator, ousting leftist Ramón Grau San Martín	
	1935 Death of Juan Vincente Gómez; riots, arson, and looting ensue in Caracas, Venezuela	
	1936–39 Right-wing military officers defeat left-wing government in civil war in Spain	*The Death of Artemio Cruz* by Carlos Fuentes
	1937 On November 10 Getúlio Vargas proclaims *Estado Novo* (New State), assumes dictatorial powers in Brazil to deal with "communist threat"	
1940		
	1945 Getúlio Vargas is removed from power in Brazil; Pablo Neruda joins the Communist Party in Chile	*The Heights of Macchu Picchu* by Pablo Neruda

	Historical Events	Related Literary Works
	1946 Juan Perón becomes president of Argentina; Miguel Ángel Asturias's novel *El Señor Presidente,* about the typical Latin American dictator, is published	"The South" by Jorge Luis Borges
	1947 Novelist Rómulo Gallegos (*Doña Barbara*) is elected president of Venezuela in a brief respite from military dictatorship; he is overthrown in a military coup in 1948	
	1948 General Manuel A. Odría seizes power in Peru	
1950		
	1951–54 Getúlio Vargas is elected president of Brazil	
	1952 Fulgencio Batista overthrows Cuban president Carlos Prío; death of Eva ("Evita") Perón	*Santa Evita* by Tomás Eloy Mart¡nez
	1953 On July 26 Fidel Castro leads failed assault on Moncada barracks in Havana, Cuba	
	1954 General Alfred Stroessner becomes military dictator of Paraguay—he rules until 1989; Brazil's Getúlio Vargas commits suicide in face of growing scandal	
	1956 Free elections are held in Peru—Manuel Prado, a former president (1949–45), wins	*The Storyteller* by Mario Vargas Llosa
	1955 Argentine dictator Juan Perón is ousted in a bloodless military coup	
	1957 François ("Papa Doc") Duvalier becomes Haitian president; his rule devolves into brutal dictatorship	
	1959 Cuban Revolution occurs; the dictator Fulgencio Batista flees (December 31, 1958); Fidel Castro assumes power	*Three Trapped Tigers* by Guillermo Cabrera Infante *Before Night Falls* by Reinaldo Arenas
1960	1960 On November 25 three women who take action to unseat the dictator Rafael Leonidas Trujillo—Patricia Mercedes Mirabal, Minerva Mirabal, and María Teresa Mirabal are assassinated in the Dominican Republic	*In the Time of the Butterflies* by Julia Alvarez
	1961 Rafael Leonidas Trujillo is assassinated in the Dominican Republic; Fidel Castro declares Cuba to be a communist country	*The Mambo Kings Play Songs of Love* by Oscar Hijuelos
	1964–85 On March 31 Brazilian military overthrows President João Goulart; two-decade-long military rule begins; civil rights and elections are suspended	*The Celebration* by Ivan Ângelo
	1966 Under right-wing General Juan Carlos Onganía, "Argentine Revolution" begins; ushers in decades of state-sponsored violence and guerilla reprisals	
	1968 On October 2 military cracks down on student protestors at demonstration in Mexico City, killing 43 by the government's count, at least 400 by other sources' count	*Massacre in Mexico* by Elena Poniatowska
	1969 Mario Vargas Llosa's *Conversación en la Catedral* (Conversation in the Cathedral), on the regime of Peru's dictator Manuel Odría (1948–56), is published	
1970		
	1971 "Papa Doc" Duvalier dies, leaves Haiti in the hands of his son Jean-Claude ("Baby Doc") Duvalier	
	1973 Salvador Allende, the first popularly elected socialist president, in the Western Hemsiphere is deposed in a coup led by General Augusto Pinochet	*A House in the Country* by José Donoso *The House of the Spirits* by Isabel Allende

	Historical Events	Related Literary Works
	1974 In Argentina, President Juan Perón sets out to repress left-wing groups; Perón dies; his wife and vice-president María Estela (Isabel) Martínez Perón becomes president; three more novels on dictators are published—Alejo Carpentier's *El recurso del método* (Reasons of State); Ernesto Sábato's *Abbadón el exterminador* (Abbadón the Exterminator); and Roa Bastos's *Yo el Supremo* (I the Supreme)	*Kiss of the Spider Woman* by Manuel Puig
	1975 Gabriel García Márquez's *The Autumn of the Patriarch,* about a fictional dictator, is published	
	1976–83 "Dirty War" ravages Argentina under military dictatorship; at least 10,000 people are unaccounted for and presumed dead	
	1977 Brazilian students riot for social justice, protest military government's brutally repressive regime	*The Hour of the Star* by Clarice Lispector
	1977–78 Amnesty International records more than 300 cases of "disappeared" Guatemalans	
	1978–82 General Fernando Romeo Lucas García assumes power in Guatemala; in 1979, Amnesty International documents 5,000 "disappearances" and extrajudicial killings; in 1980 protestors occupy the Spanish embassy in Guatemala City; although the Spanish ambassador wishes to protect the protestors, the Guatemalan army sets fire to the place and 39 die	*I, Rigoberta Menchú* by Rigoberta Menchú
1980		
	1982 On March 23 right-wing politicians and dissident army officers stage a military coup in Guatemala; president Lucas García is forced to resign and General José Efraín Ríos Montt assumes power as the head of a military dictatorship	
	1989 Chilean regime of Augusto Pinochet passes amnesty law stating that no member of regime can be held accountable for civil rights violations; military coup ousts Paraguayan dictator Alfred Stroessner; Patricio Aylwin unseats Augusto Pinochet in Chile	*Death and the Maiden* by Ariel Dorfman
1990		
	1991 Rettig Report documents thousands of cases of death and torture under the regime of Augusto Pinochet	
	1998 Augusto Pinochet is detained in London, England, and charged by the Spanish government with human rights abuses	

	Historical Events	Related Literary Works

MEXICO: REVOLUTION

The Mexican Revolution turned into a lengthy, drawn-out military and political process; some historians argue that it continues to this day. The height of the fighting, however, took place from 1910–24. Afterwards there were ancillary conflicts, such as the Church–state *Cristero* Rebellion of the late 1920s. The Revolution itself, which began as a political and agrarian reform movement, has meant many things to soldiers and civilians alike—education and land reform, religious reform, universal suffrage, and Indian rights, among others.

	Historical Events	Related Literary Works
1875		
	1876 Porfirio Díaz becomes president of Mexico	
1900		
	1910 Under Francisco Madero, Mexican Revolution begins	*Pedro Páramo* by Juan Rulfo
	1911 May—Porfirio Díaz resigns presidency and leaves the country; November—Francisco Madero becomes elected president of Mexico; December—Emiliano Zapata issues Plan de Ayala, calling for restoration of ancestral Indian lands taken by the government	
	1913 In February Francisco Madero overthrown and killed by General Adolfo de la Huerta	
	1914 The rebels fight among themselves, with Venustiano Carranza and Álvaro Obregón pitted against Emiliano Zapata and Pancho Villa; Carranza becomes president; divorce is legalized in Mexico	*The Death of Artemio Cruz* by Carlos Fuentes *Like Water for Chocolate* by Laura Esquivel
	1915 Mexican president Venustiano Carranza approves decree allowing villages to buy back some of the land confiscated earlier by the government	
	1917 Mexican Law of Domestic Relations allows married women to enter into contracts and legal suits and to maintain child custody; government under President Carranza writes new constitution; Church powers are limited and peasant land rights recognized (although very minimally realized)	
	1919 Emiliano Zapata is assassinated	
	1920 Venustiano Carranza is assassinated	
	1920–24 Under presidency of Álvaro Obregón, an artistic revolution flourishes, in which Indian and mestizo themes are privileged over European ones	
	1924–28 Plutarco Calles becomes President	
1925		
	1926 Archbishop of Mexico, José Mora y del Río, states that Roman Catholics should not accept the new, anticlerical constitution; leads to wide-ranging revolt on behalf of the Church called the *Cristiada* (1926–29)	*Recollections of Things to Come* by Elena Garro
	1928 A Church rebel assassinates Mexico's President Álvaro Obregón	
	1934 Under President Lázaro Cárdenas, land reform finally materializes	
	1938 Cárdenas nationalizes the oil business in Mexico	
	1946 Under President Miguel Alemán Valdés, Mexico's national focus shifts from agrarian reform to urbanization	

	Historical Events	Related Literary Works
1950		
	1953 Mexican women achieve national suffrage; President Adolfo Ruiz Cortines admits that Mexico remains a poor country, with 19 million peasants subsisting in dire poverty	*Days of Obligation* by Richard Rodriguez
	1958 Government breaks strikes held by railway workers	
	1962 Agrarian revolt in the South of Mexico	
	1964 Archconservative Gustavo Díaz Ordaz becomes Mexican president	
	1968 Olympic Games are held in Mexico City; August 27—500,000 students participate in the most massive antigovernment demonstration in Mexico's history; October 2—massacre of students at Plaza of the Three Cultures in Tlatelolco, Mexico City	*Massacre in Mexico* by Elena Poniatowska
1975		
	1994 Mexico suffers a severe economic crisis; an uprising of the Zapatista Army of National Liberation erupts in Chiapas in the South over the lack of land reform	

LATIN AMERICA AND THE UNITED STATES

The United States has demonstrated constant economic and political interest in Latin America since the turn of the nineteenth century. This interest has ranged from investment in Latin American businesses and governments to outright military occupation. After the 1959 Cuban Revolution, which eventually brought a communist government to power, the United States cast a wary eye on leftist movements throughout the region and participated actively in their downfall.

	Historical Events	Related Literary Works
1800		
	1808 U.S. president Thomas Jefferson suggests that the United States buy Cuba from Spain	
	1823 U.S. president James Monroe asserts "Monroe Doctrine," signaling U.S. desire to exercise economic and ideological control over the Americas	
1825		
	1848 Treaty of Guadalupe Hidalgo ends Mexican-American War; United States annexes Texas and takes most of what is now the U.S. Southwest from Mexico	
1850		
	1854 Ostend Manifesto declares that if Spain will not sell Cuba to the United States, the United States will be justified in seizing the island by force	
1875		
	1889 Inaugural Pan-American Congress held in Philadelphia and Washington D.C. to discuss common systems of law and commerce	
	1891 International Monetary Conference held in Washington D.C.; United States attempts to have Latin American nations accept monetary standard of bimetallism	"Our America" by José Martí
	1895 May 18—José Marté dies at Battle of Dos Ríos in Cuban war for independence; U.S. President Grover Cleveland helps demarcate border between Brazil and Argentina	

	Historical Events	Related Literary Works
	1898 Cuba fights Spanish-American War for independence from Spain; U.S. President William McKinley pledges not to annex Cuba, sends troops to fight war	
	1899 Treaty of Paris is signed; Spain cedes Puerto Rico, the Philippine Islands, and Guam, as well as authority over Cuba, to the United States; U.S. United Fruit Company forms to dominate the banana industry	
	1899–1902 United States occupies Cuba	
1900	1900 Puerto Rico becomes a U.S. territory	
	1901 Platt Amendment authorizes the United States to intervene in Cuba to preserve Cuban independence and to ensure that the Cuban government protects the life, property, and liberty of its citizens	
	1902 Official Languages Act states that both English and Spanish can be used as official languages in all official and public activities in Puerto Rico	
	1906 Guatemalan President Manuel Estrada Cabrera makes critical concessions to United Fruit Company so that it will bring its business to Guatemala; among other benefits, he grants them the exclusive right to operate Guatemala's central railway line	
	1913 U.S. Ambassador Henry Lane Wilson is involved in the overthrow and assassination of Mexican president Francisco Madero by General Adolfo de la Huerta	
	1914 Panama Canal opens	
	1915–34 U.S. forces occupy Haiti	
	1916–22 U.S. forces occupy the Dominican Republic	
	1918–34 Colombian banana workers stage major strikes against United Fruit Company; government sides with company	*One Hundred Years of Solitude* by Gabriel García Márquez
1925		
	1942 Bracero Program begins, encouraging Mexicans to migrate to the United States for farmwork	*. . . and the earth did not part* by Tomás Rivera
	1943 Zoot-Suit riots in Los Angeles pit U.S. servicemen and police against Mexican American teenagers, known as *pachucos*	*The Labyrinth of Solitude* by Octavio Paz
	1946 Puerto Rico has its first native governor, Jesús T. Piñero, who is nevertheless appointed by the U.S. president	
	1947 Through a special amendment to the Jones Act approved by the U.S. Congress, Puerto Ricans are allowed to choose their own governor	
	1948 Nations of the Western Hemisphere form the Organization of American States (OAS); Luis Muñoz Marín (1898–1980) becomes Puerto Rico's first elected governor, inaugurating Operation Bootstrap program to attract U.S. businesses to the island	
1950	1950 U.S. Congress approves Law 600 authorizing Puerto Ricans to be governed by their own constitution, which must be submitted to the U.S. president and Congress for approval	
	1950–54 More than 100,000 Puerto Ricans move to the U.S. mainland, capitalizing on the favorable labor conditions caused by the departure of men to fight in the Korean War	*The Mambo Kings Play Songs of Love* by Oscar Hijuelos

	Historical Events	Related Literary Works
	1951 A referendum confirms Puerto Ricans' acceptance of Law 600, which also establishes Puerto Rico's status as an associate territory of the United States	
	1952 Puerto Rico is given commonwealth status within United States	
	1954 U.S. Central Intelligence Agency helps oust Guatemalan president Jacobo Arbenz Guzmán; handpicks his successor, Colonel Carlos Castillo Armas; CIA and the "Committee Against Communism" compile blacklist of 70,000 opponents to the new regime	
	1960–61 U.S. emissaries urge Rafael Leonidas Trujillo to change his methods in the Dominican Republic; U.S. agents withdraw support for plans to assassinate him	
	1961 January 3—U.S. president Dwight D. Eisenhower breaks off diplomatic relations with Cuba; April 17—Bay of Pigs: United States sponsors Cuban counter-revolutionaries whose invasion of Cuba fails; March 30—Dominican dictator Leonidas Trujillo is assassinated by his own people, without the help of U.S. agents, who withdrew from the plot	
	1962 The United States and Soviet Union come to the brink of war in the Cuban Missile Crisis	
	1964 Bracero Program ends	
	1967 Puerto Ricans vote to remain a U.S. commonwealth	
	1968–72 Luis Ferré is elected governor of Puerto Rico, whose economy is in shambles; U.S. president Richard Nixon extends the food stamp program to Puerto Ricans	"The Youngest Doll" by Rosario Ferré *Macho Camacho's Beat* by Luis Rafael Sánchez
	1970–73 U.S. Central Intelligence Agency helps destabilize the economy of Chile to hasten 1973 downfall of Marxist president Salvador Allende	*A House in the Country* by José Donoso *The House of the Spirits* by Isabel Allende
1975		
	1980–90 Total U.S. Latino population rises from 14 million to 22 million; controversy rages over Mexican Americans, due to high number of illegal immigrants	
	1980 Mariel boatlift brings Cuban refugees to United States	*Before Night Falls* by Reinaldo Arenas
	1994 Californians pass "Save Our State" initiative, banning undocumented workers from public benefits, including education and health care	*Days of Obligation* by Richard Rodriguez

	Historical Events	Related Literary Works

HUMAN RIGHTS

Long periods of rule by strongmen, from the first Spanish conquistadors to contemporary military dictators, have created a Latin American human rights record that is among the worst in the world—from the denial of education and suffrage to women, to the outright slaughter of Indians, to the clandestine massacre of government opponents. Travesties have been visited on assorted ethnic and political groups. With few exceptions, such abuses have gone unpunished, although the people themselves have risen up to protest injustice. Aside from slavery, which is detailed in a timeline above, many more human rights abuses and protest movements occurred than those included here.

	Historical Events	Related Literary Works
1500	1500–1550 Conquest and encomienda system of the Spaniards showers abuses on the native Indian populations	*A Short Account of the Destruction of the Indies* by Friar Bartolomé de las Casas
1600		
	1691 Colonial women are limited to becoming wives and mothers or nuns; famous letter from the Bishop of Puebla, alias "Sor Philotea," admonishes Sor Juana Inés de la Cruz for her secular studies	"Reply to Sor Philotea"by Sor Juana Inés de la Cruz
1700		
	1781 Spaniards draw and quarter the Inca leader Túpac Amaru II in Cuzco, Peru, for revolting against them in protest of the abuses heaped upon his people	*Deep Rivers* by José María Arguedas
1800		
	1854 Peru abolishes the head tax on Indians	
	1877 *Reglamento de Jornaleros* permits Guatemalan coffee growers to recruit Indians against their will	
	1897 Federal army of Brazil conducts Siege of Canudos to rout a religious enclave in northeastern Brazil	*Rebellion in the Backlands* by Euclides da Cunha
1900		
	1919 January 7–13—*Semana Trágica* (Tragic Week) occurs in Argentina—mobs attack Jews in Buenos Aires, accusing them of being revolutionary communists	*The Fragmented Life of Don Jacobo Lerner* by Isaac Goldemberg
	1923 Argentina restricts Jewish immigration	
1925		
	1926–29 Women participate greatly in the Cristero Rebellion on the side of the Church against the government of Mexico; human abuses are committed by both sides	*Recollections of Things to Come* by Elena Garro
	1932 Brazilian working women achieve suffrage (by 1945 all Brazilian women have the vote)	*Gabriela, Clove and Cinnamon* by Jorge Amado
	1934 Tension between ladinos and Indians continues in Guatemala; under President Jorge Ubico, unemployed Indians are subject to periods of enforced labor	*Men of Maize* by Miguel Ángel Asturias
	1944 Guatemalan laborers strike in protest of President Ubico's policies—as a result, Ubico is deposed	
	1945–50 Guatemalan President Juan José Arévalo Bermejo supports a program of labor reform that protects the rights of all workers in Guatemala	
	1947 Community Service Organization sets out to register Mexican American voters	

	Historical Events	Related Literary Works
	1949 Chilean women achieve suffrage	
1950		
	1952 Guatemalan President Jacobo Arbenz Guzmán (1950–54) sponsors agrarian reform act redistributing large tracts of public and privately owned land; women achieve suffrage in Chile	
	1953 Women achieve suffrage in Mexico	
	1955 Women achieve suffrage in Peru	
	1960 On January 25 Church leaders in the Dominican Republic read the first of several pastoral letters stating the human rights do not exist in the Dominican Republic	*In the Time of the Butterflies* by Julia Alvarez
	1960–70 Number of Mexican American women in the U.S. work force rises from 24 to 35 percent	*Woman Hollering Creek* by Sandra Cisneros
	1964–68 Brazil's military government passes five institutional acts, allowing it to eliminate political parties, disband Congress, and abolish human and political rights like habeas corpus	*The Celebration* by Ivan Ângelo
	1968 Olympic Games are held in Mexico City; August 27—500,000 students participate in the most massive antigovernment demonstration in Mexico's history; October 2—massacre of students at Plaza of the Three Cultures in Tlatelolco, Mexico City	*Massacre in Mexico* by Elena Poniatowska
	mid-1960s–1973 New Song movement of protest music spreads in Chile; the death of Pablo Neruda prompts a funeral protest march against the military coup in Chile	*The House of the Spirits* by Isabel Allende
	late 1960s–1975 Cuban Cultural Council adopts resolution that encourages authorities to harass homosexuals	*Before Night Falls* by Reinaldo Arenas
1975		
	1976–83 "Dirty War" ravages Argentina under military dictatorship; at least 10,000 people are unaccounted for and presumed dead; mothers of the disappeared keep marching in the Plaza de Mayo demanding to know the whereabouts of their loved ones	*Kiss of the Spider Woman* by Manuel Puig
	1977 Brazilian students demonstrate for social justice, protest military government's brutal regime	*The Hour of the Star* by Clarice Lispector
	1977–78 Amnesty International records more than 300 cases of "disappeared" Guatemalans	
	1978 *Unified Black Movement to Combat Racial Discrimination* organizes on behalf of blacks in Brazil; General Morales Bermúdea issues law barring Peru's indigenous people from full title to lands suitable for forestry or agriculture; Kechi Indians are massacred in Guatemala	
	1979 Amnesty International documents 5,000 "disappearances" and extrajudicial killings in Guatemala	
	1980 Guatemalan students, laborers, and peasant leaders stage protest in Guatemala City; although the protestors are peaceful, the Guatemalan army sets fire to the embassy that they occupy, and 39 die	*I, Rigoberta Menchú* by Rigoberta Menchú
	1991 Rettig Report documents thousands of cases of death and torture under the regime of Augusto Pinochet in Chile	*Death and the Maiden* by Ariel Dorfman
	1998 Former Chilean dictator Augusto Pinochet is detained in London, England, and charged by the Spanish government with human rights abuses	

Contents by Title

Contents by Title

Contents by Author

Contents by Author

Photo Credits

Bracero farm workers on a truck, photograph. UPI/Corbis-Bettmann. Reproduced by permission. —César Chávez, photograph. Corbis-Bettmann. Reproduced by permission. —Man carrying water buckets during drought, 1998, Serra Talhada, Brazil, photograph. AP/Wide World Photos/Agencia Lumiar. Reproduced by permission. "Green Shirts" giving a fascist salute, 1938, Rio de Janeiro, Brazil, photograph. Corbis/Bettmann. Reproduced by permission. — Cuban dictator Fulgencio Batista, 1953, Cuba, photograph. AP/Wide World Photos. Reproduced by permission. —Tugboat *Dr. Daniels* delivering Cuban refugees during the Mariel boatlift, 1980, photograph. AP/Wide World Photos. Reproduced by permission. — Cuban insurgents, 1869, illustration. Corbis/ Bettmann. Reproduced by permission. —Spanish troops in Cuba, photograph. The Library of Congress. —Cowboys branding cattle, 1939, G. W. Evans ranch, Gila National Forest, New Mexico, photograph by Fred L. McCament. Corbis. Reproduced by permission. —Reies Tijerina, photograph. AP/Wide World Photos. Reproduced by permission. — People celebrating the ouster of Juan Perón, December, 1955, Buenos Aires, Argentina, photograph. Corbis/Bettmann. Reproduced by permission. —Charlie Parker, photograph. Archive Photos, Inc. Reproduced by permission. —Slaves mining diamonds in eighteenth century Brazil, color print. Iconografico SA, Archivo. Reproduced by permission. —Slum in Rio de Janeiro, Brazil, photograph by Morton Beebe. Corbis/Morton Beebe, S. F. Reproduced by permission. —Citizens in a street cheering rebel troops in Rio de Janeiro, Brazil, 1930, photograph. Corbis/ Bettmann. Reproduced by permission. —Soldiers and tanks surrounding the War Ministry in Rio de Janeiro, Brazil, 1964, photograph. Corbis/Bettmann. Reproduced by permission. —Moctezuma and Hernán Cortés, lithograph. Corbis-Bettmann. Reproduced by permission. —Supporters of gay and lesbian rights in an annual parade, 1983, San Francisco, California, photograph. Corbis/Bettmann. Reproduced by permission. —Salvador Allende in Santiago, Chile, 1973, photograph. Corbis/ Bettmann. Reproduced by permission. —Movie still with Ben Kingsley and Sigourney Weaver, from the adaptation of *Death and the Maiden,* by Ariel Dorfman, 1994, photograph by Francois Duhamel. Fine Line. Courtesy of The Kobal Collection. Reproduced by permission.

Francisco "Pancho" Villa and Emiliano Zapata in Mexico City, Mexico, c. 1916, photograph by Agustin Cassola. Archive Photos. Reproduced by permission. —Diego Rivera, 1936, photograph. AP/Wide World Photos. Reproduced by permission. —Rio Iguazú waterfall, photograph. Susan D. Rock. Reproduced by permission. Horacio Quiroga, photograph. —Peruvian holding a painting of Tupac Amaru II, photograph. Daniel Laine/ Corbis. Reproduced by permission. — Flute player leaning against an Inca stone wall in Cuzco, Peru, photograph. Corbis/Nevada Wier. Reproduced by permission. —Bandits' heads on display, Maceio, Brazil, 1938, photograph. Corbis/Hulton-Deutsch Collection. Reproduced by permission. —Brazilian cowboy, 1985, photograph by Stephanie Maze. Corbis/Stephanie Maze. Reproduced by permission. —House at Fazenda Campo Alto, São Paulo, Brazil, photograph by Francesco Venturi. Corbis/Francesco Venturi; Kea Publishing Service. Reproduced by permission. —Sebastian District of Rio de Janeiro, color illustration from Atlante dell' America del Sud, by Giulio Ferrario. Iconografico SA, Archivo. Reproduced by permission. — Llanero on a horse herding cattle, Hato Pinero, Llanos, Venezuela, 1992, photograph. Corbis/ Kevin Schafer. Reproduced by permission. — Juan Vicente Gómez, painting. The Library of Congress. — Juan Manuel Rosas, painting. The Library of Congress. —Domingo F. Sarmiento, reproduction of a painting. The Library of Congress. —Jewish pogrom in Russia, 1905, photograph. Corbis/Hulton-Deutsch Collection. Reproduced by permission. —Jewish immigrants, 1937, photograph. Corbis/Austrian Archives. Reproduced by permission. —Emperor Dom Pedro II, steel engraving. Corbis/Bettmann. Reproduced by permission. —The National Congress Building, Brasília, Brazil, photograph by Julia Waterlow. Corbis/Julia Waterlow; Eye Ubiquitous. Reproduced by permission. —Four gauchos on the pampas, c. 1900–20, Argentina, photograph. Corbis/Hulton-Deutsch Collection. Reproduced by permission. —Gauchos on the pampas, Argentina, photograph by Fulvio Roiter. Corbis/Fulvio Roiter. Reproduced by permission.

Machu Picchu, Peru, photograph by Roman Soumar. Corbis/Roman Soumar. Reproduced by permission. —Pablo Neruda, photograph by Jerry Bauer. (c) Jerry Bauer. Reproduced by permission. —Slums in Rio de Janeiro, Brazil, photograph. Corbis/Vittoriano Rastelli. Reproduced by permission. —Crowd of demonstrators marching through downtown São Paulo, Brazil, 1964, photograph. Corbis/Bettmann. Reproduced by permission. —Armed riot police surrounding Moneda Palace in Santiago, Chile, 1973, photograph. Corbis/Bettmann. Reproduced by permission. —Mapuche weaver, Bio Bio River area, Chile, 1993, photograph by Chris Rainier. Corbis/Chris Rainier. Reproduced by permission. —Salvador Allende, photograph. Corbis-Bettmann. Reproduced by permission. — People being held in in the National Stadium, Santiago, Chile, 1973, photograph. Corbis/ Bettmann. Reproduced by permission. —Rafael Leonidas Trujillo, photograph. The Library of Congress. "A Song to Liberty" memorial, Santo Domingo, Dominican Republic, 1997, photograph John Riley. AP/Wide World Photos. Reproduced by permission. "Natives Attacking Colonial Villages During the Early French and Portuguese Colonization of Brazil," color engraving by Theodor de Bry, 1562. Iconografico SA, Archivo. Reproduced by permission. —Tupi Indian family, engraving, sixteenth century. — Quiché woman weaving on backstrap loom, c. 1980, Guatemala, photograph. Corbis/ Jack Fields. Reproduced by permission. —Rigoberta Menchú, at a Truth Commission presentation, Guatemala City, Guatemala, photograph. Corbis/Bettmann. Reproduced by permission. — Young Guaraní women in Brazil, 1998, photograph by Douglas Engle. AP/Wide World Photos. Reproduced by permission. —Alfredo Stroessner, photograph. The Library of Congress. — Toussaint L'Ouverture, engraving. Fisk University. Reproduced by permission. —Grouping of Vodou religious articles, photograph. Archive Photos/Express. Reproduced by permission. — Youths fleeing tear gas during a protest in Buenos Aires, Argentina, 1969, photograph. Corbis/ Bettmann. Reproduced by permission. —Crowd of supporters gathered outside Juan Perón's villa in Vicente Lopez, Argentina, 1972, photograph. Corbis/Bettmann. Reproduced by permission.

Sor Juana Inés de la Cruz, painting. Arte Publico Press Archives, University of Houston. Reproduced by permission of Arte Publico Press. —Father Miguel Hidalgo y Costilla, illustration. The Library of Congress. —Women on flatbed train car cooking for the rebel army during the Mexican Revolution, November, 1913, photograph. Corbis/Bettmann. Reproduced by permission. —Mexican kitchen, painting by Manuel Serrano. Iconografico SA, Archivo. Reproduced by permission. —Young men in jail after a student uprising at the University of Puerto Rico, San Juan, 1948, photograph. Corbis/Bettmann. Reproduced by permission. —Slum district in San Juan, Puerto Rico, photograph. Corbis/Tony Arruza. Reproduced by permission. —Borra Indians near the Amazon River, photograph by Wolfgang Kaehler. Corbis/Wolfgang Kaehler. Reproduced by permission. —Dona Vitoria Umbarana dos Santos, macumba priestess, 1985, Salvador, Brazil, photograph. Corbis/Stephanie Maze. Reproduced by permission. —Desi Arnaz, photograph. Archive Photos, Inc. Reproduced by permission. —Movie still with Antonio Banderas and Armand Assante, from the adaptation of *The*

Mambo Kings Play Songs of Love by Oscar Hijuelos, 1991, photograph. The Kobal Collection. Reproduced by permission. —Tommie Smith, John Carlos, and Peter Norman at the 1968 Mexico City Olympics, photograph. Corbis/Bettmann. Reproduced by permission. —Aerial view of student protest along Reforma Boulevard, Mexico City, Mexico, 1968, photograph. Corbis/Bettmann. Reproduced by permission. —Adelu Cho, Chicacnab, Guatemala, 1992, photograph. Corbis/Natalie Fobes. Reproduced by permission. —Manuel Estrada Cabrera, c.1910, photograph. Corbis. Reproduced by permission. —Colombian troops, 1902, photograph. Corbis. Reproduced by permission. —Colombian troops in Bogota, Colombia, 1949, photograph. Corbis/Bettmann. Reproduced by permission. —José Martí, photograph. The Bettmann Archive. Reproduced by permission. —Simón Bolivar, painting. The Library of Congress. —Francisco "Pancho" Villa and Álvaro Obregon, 1914, photograph. Corbis-Bettmann. Reproduced by permission. —Celebration of the Day of the Dead festival, Michoacan, Mexico, photograph. Corbis/Charles & Josette Lenars. Reproduced by permission.

Statue of Antonio Maciel, "Conselheiro," Monte Santo, Brazil, photograph by Thomas Beebe. Reproduced by permission. —Submerged site of Canudos, Brazil, place of Antonio Maciel's rebellion, photograph by Thomas Beebe. Reproduced by permission. —Brigadas Femininas, 1911, photograph. Corbis. Reproduced by permission. —Aztec emissaries making a treaty with Hernán Cortés illustration. Corbis-Bettmann. Reproduced by permission. —Church of Santo Domingo, Oaxaca, Mexico, photograph by Thomas A. Kelly and Gail Mooney. Corbis/Kelly-Mooney Photography. Reproduced by permission. —Sor Juana Inés de la Cruz, painting. The Granger Collection. Reproduced by permission. —Juan Perón and Eva Perón, Buenos Aires, Argentina, 1950, photograph. AP/Wide World Photos. Reproduced by permission. —Eva Perón, photograph. Library of Congress. —Spaniards beating Indians, illustration from a sixteenth-century edition of *A Short Account of the Destruction of the Indies*. The Library of Congress. —Bartolomé de las Casas, illustration. The Library of Congress. —Argentine pampas, photograph by Fulvio Roiter. Corbis/Fulvio Roiter. Reproduced by permission. —Gaucho on a horse during a cattle roundup near Quilmes, Argentina, photograph. Corbis/ Hubert Stadler. Reproduced by permission. —Machiguenga woman, photograph by Allen and Orna Johnson. Reproduced by permission. —Mario Vicente, Machiguenga storyteller, photograph by Glenn Shepard, Jr. Reproduced by permission. —Poster promoting tourism in Cuba, c. 1941, photograph. Corbis/Lake County Museum. Reproduced by permission. —Casino Español, Matanzas, Cuba, photograph by Paul Seheult. Corbis/Paul Seheult; Eye Ubiquitous. Reproduced by permission. —Virgin of Guadalupe, painting by Juan de Villegas. Arte Publico Press. Reproduced by permission. —Emiliano Zapata, photograph. Corbis-Bettmann. Reproduced by permission. —Governor Luis Muñoz Marín, 1950, San Juan, Puerto Rico, photograph. Corbis/Bettmann. Reproduced by permission. —Men leading oxen pulling carts of sugar cane, Puerto Rico, photograph. Corbis/Underwood & Underwood. Reproduced by permission.

. . . *and the earth did not part*

by
Tomás Rivera

Tomás Rivera was born in Crystal City, Texas, in 1935 to Mexican American parents. Migrant laborers, they traversed the South and Midwest each year in search of enough work to support the family. Rivera later wanted to relate his experiences growing up as a migrant worker but felt reluctant to write in English—a language he did not consider fully expressive of his emotions. His dilemma was solved by Quinto Sol Publications, one of the first companies to publish in Spanish and English. "When I learned that Quinto Sol accepted manuscripts in Spanish, it liberated me. I knew that I could fully express myself as I wanted" (Rivera in Lomelí and Shirley, p. 207). Rivera submitted . . . *and the earth did not part* to a literary contest sponsored by Quinto Sol and was awarded first prize. The company published the work in Spanish that year (1970), then issued a bilingual edition in 1971. The novel managed for the first time to portray the overlooked experience of Mexican and Mexican American migrants in the United States.

THE LITERARY WORK

A novel set in Texas and the midwestern United States in the 1940s and '50s; published in Spanish (as . . . *y no se lo tragó la tierra*) in 1970, in English in 1971.

SYNOPSIS

Comprised of 12 vignettes, the novel exposes the racial, social, and economic obstacles faced by Mexican and Mexican American migrants in their daily lives in a hostile country.

Events in History at the Time the Novel Takes Place

Migrant labor. During World War II, Mexico and the United States entered into an unprecedented agreement that would endure for 22 years (1942–64). Called the Bracero Program, it sanctioned the contracting of temporary migrant laborers from Mexico to the United States under certain conditions. These conditions, insisted on largely by Mexico, aimed to protect migrants from past abuses in the United States, of which Mexican authorities were well aware. There was to be a written labor contract for the migrant workers; employers or the U.S. government would pay expenses incurred for travel from Mexico to the work site; and public places could not refuse the workers service on account of their ethnicity. In the event that a state permitted such discrimination, it would be banned from participating in the program. Rivera's novel focuses on Texas, where anti-Mexican discrimination was so rampant that the state was ineligible for the Bracero Program from 1942 to 1946. Instead its growers hired undocumented (illegal) migrants, who were called "wetbacks" (because they crossed the Rio Grand river from Mexico into the United States).

In hindsight, the Bracero Program encouraged legal and illegal emigration from a half dozen states in north-central Mexico. The arrangement, which had been initiated because of the dearth of workers in the United States during World War II, stimulated even greater migration after the war, as reflected by records from the program's first decade:

Year	Braceros	Illegal Migrants*
1942	4,203	not available
1943	52,098	8,189
1944	62,170	26,689
1945	49,454	63,602
1946	32,043	91,456
1947	19,632	182,986
1948	35,345	179,385
1949	107,000	278,538
1950	67,500	458,215
1951	192,000	500,000
1952	197,100	543,538

*Number apprehended

(Adapted from Gutiérrez, p. 49)

CREW LEADERS: FRIEND OR FOE?

While some crew leaders worked diligently to find steady work, good wages, and decent living conditions for a worker, others took advantage of the worker's dependence on them. In the novel, a worker worries about the way his crew leader has exploited him:

> He loaned me two hundred dollars, but by the time one pays for the trip almost half is gone, what with this business of having to pay half fare for children. And when I get back I have to pay back double the amount. Four hundred dollars! Interest is too high, but there's no way out of it, one can't fool around when one is in need. I've been told to turn him in because the interest rates are too high, but the fact is that he even has the Trust Deed to my house already.
>
> (Rivera, *. . . and the earth did not part,* p. 158)

How would a U.S. employer recruit braceros? Mexico's government would accept candidates, then turn them over to the U.S. Department of Labor, whose representatives selected those fit for agricultural work. The candidates were next transported to the United States, where another official took their fingerprints and prepared documents for them, after which they were sent to labor contract centers near the border. They would be screened by a health official, then considered for hire by visiting employers or their agents. This was more or less the official procedure, though in some years it slackened—government officials were bypassed and employers or their agents dealt directly with the workers.

Often migrants, be they braceros or wetbacks, found jobs through an agent or crew leader who would contract with farmers to provide labor for the harvest. Unfortunately, these crew leaders frequently abused their power. They charged workers exorbitant fees for transportation, garnished wages for food and supplies, and advanced money at 50 percent interest rates. As a result of these unethical practices, many migrant workers ended the harvest season deeply in debt.

Even when harvests were abundant and migrant workers found steady jobs, their wages remained far below U.S. poverty levels. In 1941 a Texas state study revealed an average annual income of $350 for a 6-7 member family in agricultural labor, compared to $480 for a 4-5 member family on relief, or welfare (Kibbe, p. 89). The continual influx of new migrants made it possible for farmowners to keep wages miserably low. If a laborer refused to work under abysmal conditions for unbearably low wages, ten others were ready to fill his or her place. The consequent fear of losing one's job, along with brutal employment practices, kept migrants working for hours on end under a blistering sun, often winding up with heat stroke or worse. It was not until union organization in the 1960s that the migrant laborers would become formidable enough to overcome such exploitation.

Not only the workday but also the work year was harsh. Given the different harvest seasons and locations of crops, migrants were on the move practically year-round to keep their families clothed and fed. Migrants from Texas typically left the state from December through October:

December–March: Trek to Florida for the orange harvest.
April–June: Harvest asparagus across the country in Washington State.
July–August: Trek back thousands of miles to New York to pick onions.
August-September: Truck over to Virginia to harvest tomatoes.
September–October: Return to New York to pick strawberries.

Other stops included sugar beet and onion farms in Iowa, Michigan and Minnesota; some migrant workers even crossed over into Canada. In November they would head back to Texas or perhaps home to Mexico until the process began anew.

Braceros on their way to the fields.

Miserable conditions. In addition to poor wages, sporadic work, and unscrupulous crew leaders, migrant workers faced countless dangers in the fields and poor living conditions in their temporary quarters away from home. Rafael Guerra, a third-generation migrant from Texas who spent his early childhood working in the fields with his parents, remembers their miserable housing on the farms:

> We lived in terrible places when we were working in the fields, sometimes chicken coops, really. No windows, no plumbing, no water, swarms of mosquitoes every night in some places. The walls were like paper, and you could hear everything, babies crying all night. My mother used to douse the floors with kerosene where we stayed, to kill the bugs.
>
> (Guerra in Ashabranner, p. 53)

It is hardly surprising, given these conditions and the grueling labor, that the average farm worker's lifespan was 49 years, compared with the national average of 74 years.

While some farms provided clean, comfortable housing, most failed to do so. As a rule, like Rafael Guerra, the laborers found themselves herded into poorly kept living quarters that lacked basic conveniences. The unsanitary environment put them at risk for preventable infections—tuberculosis, flu, pneumonia, and intestinal parasites. But the work itself posed the greatest danger. Falls from ladders in orchards were common, as was injury and maiming from equipment. Since their wages depended on how much they picked, many workers kept up a rapid pace, focusing more on filling their bags or buckets than on safety. There was also danger from pesticides sprayed on fields; as many as 1,000 workers died each year from exposure to these chemicals.

In the title vignette, ". . . and the earth did not part," a young boy feels hate and anger for the first time when he thinks about the conditions in which his family is forced to work. His aunt dies from tuberculosis and his father and brother are incapacitated by sunstroke from working too long in the heat. The boy vents his frustration to his mother: "Either the germs eat us from the inside or the sun from the outside. . . . Why should we always be tied to the dirt, half buried in the earth like animals without any hope of any kind?" (*. . . and the earth,* pp. 75-76).

Education and migrant children. The constant moving of migrant families had disastrous effects on the education of migrant children. Not only was their schooling constantly interrupted, but in many cases the children were kept out of school to work in the fields for pay. One study estimated that only 42.5 percent of the state's

Latino (mostly Mexican) children enrolled in Texas public schools in 1944–45 (Kibbe, p. 86). A U.S. Labor Department study of 1941 provided many case studies of families who simply could not afford to have children attend school rather than work. Oralia Leal recalls her family being faced with this dilemma in her childhood:

> I went to school a little bit but not much, maybe two months a year. My parents knew it was important, but the money I could make in the fields when we had a chance to work was more important. I couldn't get much out of school anyway because I didn't speak any English then, just Spanish.
>
> (Leal in Ashabranner, p. 63)

COMPETITION FOR LABOR

Between 1940 and 1950 the United States Immigration Service apprehended more than 800,000 illegal Mexican immigrants. It estimates that at least three times as many escaped detection and remained working as migrant laborers during this period. With so many farmhands in need of jobs and without sufficient labor and wage regulations to stop them, farmers and large agricultural conglomerates deflated the wages they paid and still found laborers willing to work. A farm worker in McAllen, Texas, summed up a common attitude: "[The farmers] prefer to get people from Mexico because if [the workers] have an accident . . . they just throw them back to Mexico, and that will be the end of it. No responsibility. If you're more hungry than me, you got to work more cheap" (Dunbar and Kravitz, p. 15).

When migrant children did attend school, they often felt unwelcome and found themselves segregated from the rest of the students. With this segregation came an inferior education, as acknowledged by a Texas state survey: "In some instances segregation has been used for the purpose of giving the Mexican children a shorter school year, inferior buildings and equipment, and poorly paid teachers" (Reynolds in Mirande, p. 98). Segregated or not, the children were encouraged to abandon their heritage and language. Many schools had rules against speaking Spanish and failed to include lessons on Mexico's history—even though for three centuries the territory now comprising Texas was governed by Spain and Mexico, and the region's people had spoken Spanish. There were relevant lessons to learn, too, about Mexico's influence on the United States. Texas, for example, was one of the first states to enact women's property rights (in 1845), adopting this policy from Mexican law. Rather than acknowledge such contributions, the U.S. mainstream alienated migrant children of the 1940s and '50s and subjected them to intimidating treatment in some schools. The first class often began with the nurse searching a migrant child for lice, as a young boy reports in *. . . and the earth did not part*:

> They pulled me out of the classroom as soon as I arrived and they took me to the nurse who was all dressed in white. They made me take off all my clothes and they examined me all over. . . . But where they took the longest was on my head. . . . After a while they let me go, but I was very embarrassed because I had to take off my pants and even my shorts in front of the nurse.
>
> (*. . . and the earth,* p. 31)

When the same boy gets into a fight with a white student, the principal talks about what to do with him. The principal makes an assumption about how the boy's parents will react, "They could care less if I expel him . . . they need him in the fields" (*. . . and the earth,* p. 33). Rivera's own case demonstrates how false the first part of this assumption is. Though they could have benefited from his work in the fields, his parents enrolled him in schools wherever they traveled, even after he graduated from high school. "My parents were still working in Iowa, but I would only work three months and then I had to return to complete the year at the college" (Rivera in Lomelí and Shirley, p. 207).

Discrimination in South Texas. In the early 1940s Texans themselves began objecting in force to anti-Mexican discrimination. It is true that they were in part pushed to do so because they wanted to qualify for the Bracero Program, but in any case U.S. citizens here and elsewhere started to take action. Cartoons depicting blatant anti-Mexican discrimination by Texans appeared in *Time* magazine and the state formed an independent commission to investigate allegations of wrongdoing. Conducting a survey in 1943, the Good Neighbor Commission received 117 complaints. Most of them involved the refusal to serve Mexicans in public places. Others involved segregated schools and unequal working or housing conditions. The majority of complaints originated in West Texas, in rural cotton-growing communities that relied on migrant labor. In

South Texas, too, complaints stemmed from rural communities.

McAllen, Texas, was not deemed by the Commission to be a discriminatory community, yet an incident there exposed prejudice in the small farming town. In the mid-1940s the local Young Men's Christian Association (YMCA) began raising funds to buy the city swimming pool. Donations poured in until rumors surfaced that the YMCA intended to allow Mexican Americans into the pool. When the YMCA confirmed that they were considering such a policy, many patrons demanded refunds and donations slowed. During an emergency meeting, YMCA directors considered three alternatives: allow no Mexican Americans; allow Mexican Americans if they belonged to Anglo organizations renting the pool; or allow no Mexican Americans Tuesday through Sunday, permit them to use the pool on Monday when it was closed, then drain and scrub it Monday night. Hearing this news, Mexican Americans responded with outrage and the YMCA agreed to adopt a nonsegregated policy, after which donations from Anglos slowed even further. In the end, the owner of the pool decided not to sell it to the YMCA because of the nonsegregation policy.

In Rivera's novel, similar discriminatory attitudes appear in the vignettes "It is Painful" and "Christmas Eve." The stories feature attempts to keep Mexican Americans out of school and out of a white shopping area because they are believed to be dirty and prone to petty thievery. In contrast to these stereotypes, Rivera's novel reveals the dignity, ambition, perseverance, and frustrations of the Mexican migrants:

> My poor husband, he must be very tired by now. . . . And there's no way I can help him, burdened as I am with the two children I'm holding. . . . I wish I could help him out in the fields this year. . . . At least I can help him along now so he won't feel the strain so much. . . . That husband of mine, from the time the kids are still small he already wants them to be in school. I hope I can help him. May God grant that I be able to help him.
>
> (. . . *and the earth*, p. 159)

The Novel in Focus

Plot summary. Written as 12 vignettes, . . . *and the earth did not part* portrays the Mexican migrant worker experience in various facets and forms. "El Año Perdido (The Lost Year)," the prologue that opens the work, introduces a protagonist trapped in a cycle of memories that he equates to a lost year. The 12 vignettes that follow evoke a series of recollections; together they represent the 12 months lost to everyone in this cycle of struggle and hardship. Each vignette paints a vivid and emotionally charged portrait of life in the Mexican American community. Each is told in a different voice, from a different perspective.

"The Children Were Victims" begins with a stark portrait of a migrant boy, killed for daring to drink water out of turn. The overseer fires his rifle just to scare him, but the shot ends up killing the boy.

"A Prayer" describes a mother praying to God to watch over her son, who is a soldier fighting in the Korean War.

"It Is Painful" depicts a migrant boy's first day at a new school. When he gets into a fight with another boy in his class, the school principal expels him, expecting that it won't matter much to his parents.

"His Hand in His Pocket" concerns a young boy who has to live with an older couple in order to finish the school year after his parents leave for the summer harvest. An eyewitness to their acts of murder and theft, he is forced to do some morally repugnant dirty work for the "respectable" couple.

"It Was A Silvery Night" features a boy who tries to summon the devil and then questions the existence of God.

LETTER TO THE GOVERNOR

In February of 1945 Governor Coke R. Stevenson of Texas received a letter from Sergeant Ramon Espinosa, a decorated soldier fighting in World War II.

> Dear Sir:
>
> I was born in Texas 23 years ago. I have been in the Service for 3 years. I was on furlough and on my way home stopped at a Highway Cafe to eat supper. I was very hungry. So the manager says, "You are Mexican." I said yes. He said for me to get out. . . I am sure this is very wrong. I am sure that you can, and will help me, and I will fight harder, so that this war may end sooner. In the front lines we do not ask the next man what race he is. Nor does my Commanding Officer.
>
> Yours truly,
> Sgt. Ramon Espinosa
> (Espinosa in Kibbe, p. 212)

". . . and the earth did not part" portrays a boy contemplating the cruelties of life when his father is stricken with sunstroke. He curses God for his family's misery and is astonished when the earth does not part to swallow him.

"First Holy Communion" follows a boy on the way to church for his first communion. He peers into a window and witnesses a man and a woman having sexual relations. Believing he has committed a sin of the flesh by seeing them, the boy finds it difficult to go through with the communion. But once it is over, he begins viewing the world in a new light and determines to learn more about sin and human nature.

"Little Children Burned" centers on a couple whose lives are torn apart when their children are killed in a fire because the parents had to leave them alone and go to work.

"The Night of the Blackout" focuses on a migrant laborer who returns home from working in the Midwest and discovers that his girlfriend has been unfaithful in his absence. Sinking into depression, the young man walks to the power plant and electrocutes himself, causing a power outage in the town.

"Christmas Eve" portrays a timid Mexican mother. Afraid of the bewildering white world around her, she ventures downtown to buy Christmas presents for her children. She is disoriented by the crowds in the department store and, in her confusion, flees with some unpurchased toys. She is arrested for being a thief and vows never to go downtown again when talking over the experience with a sympathetic person.

> "In Mexico it isn't Santa Claus who brings toys, but the Reyes Magos [three kings]. And they don't come until the sixth of January."
>
> ". . . I'll tell [the boys] there is no Santa Claus so they won't bother you with [not getting presents] anymore."
>
> "No . . . tell them that if they didn't get anything for Christmas, it's because the Reyes Magos will bring them something."
>
> "But . . . well, whatever you say. I guess it's always best to have hope."
>
> (*. . . and the earth,* pp. 129, 133)

"The Portrait" focuses on the reaction of a couple almost swindled by a portrait salesman who plays on their love for their dead son, who served as a U.S. soldier in Korea.

"When We Arrive" shares the experiences of a truckload of migrant laborers traveling across country to find work.

"Under the House" concludes the novel with the character from the prologue emerging from his hiding place. It first appears that he skipped school and crawled under the house. But when he emerges, he is a man, not the boy he believes himself to be. A neighbor pities him: "Poor family. First the mother, and now him. Maybe he is going crazy. I think he's losing his mind. He has lost his sense of time. He's lost track of the years" (*. . . and the earth,* p. 177).

With the realization that all the novel's harsh situations have happened to this one character, the grimness of the migrant experience is revealed. As the man shuffles away, the reader realizes that the lost year, suggested by the preceding 12 vignettes, is actually all the lost years of the man's life.

Alienation of Mexican Americans. Throughout the novel, the Mexican American characters come into very little contact with white American society. Whenever contact is made, there are always negative consequences for the Mexican Americans: the white overseer accidentally kills a young Mexican American; the white principal kicks a boy out of school; the white portrait salesman cheats the entire Mexican American community. These painful interactions expose prevalent attitudes toward Mexican Americans at the time; they were regarded as either animals good only for work, violent thugs who posed a threat to white children, or stupid victims who made easy targets. Certainly they were perceived as inferior.

The stereotype harked back to the 1920s, a decade in which the mainstream population in the United States thought of Mexican immigrants as Indian peons. Descriptions of the decade identified the Mexicans as "docile, indolent, and backward" (Gutiérrez, p. 25). Since they were Indians, people argued, they had little sense of cleanliness or of saving for the future; once they had some money, they would be inclined to quit work and take it easy, so it was best to keep wages low.

Meanwhile, the Mexican immigrants developed divergent attitudes within their own community. The attitudes of the mainstream promoted a sense of alienation from the rest of American society. Feelings of isolation and alienation from the white community surface in the novel, from the prologue in which the protagonist hides under the house, to "Christmas Eve," in which a young mother feels terrified of downtown, much preferring the rural environment she knows. When she forces herself to make a shopping trip, the downtown district overwhelms and disorients her. She feels alone and afraid despite the teeming streets. Her sense of separation reflects an emotion experienced by many Mexican Americans at this time. A young migrant woman described a similar experience: "Sometimes someone asks me if I was envious of people I saw in towns who had good homes and good clothes and big new cars. No, I wasn't. They belonged to another world, a world I didn't know anything about" (Ashabranner, p. 63).

Meanwhile, leaders in the Mexican American community shared divergent opinions about relations to mainstream society in the United States. Opinions were broadcast in daily newspapers—*La Prensa* in San Antonio, Texas, and *La Opinión* in Los Angeles, California. *La Opinión* set the tone for immigrants in the first few decades of the twentieth century, advising against Americanization. Perhaps we are exploited here, the newspaper admitted, but life is, after all, better than in Mexico. We should not try to gain equal rights by joining labor unions, for membership requires us to become U.S. citizens. We would lose our cultural integrity and to no avail, for the mainstream would still treat us as if we were inferior aliens. American ways (in architecture and music, for example) have already spilled over onto the Mexican side of the border and begun to savage our culture, to make it less civilized. We should guard against the corruption of our culture during our sojourn in the United States, developing self-reliant communities here, cultural enclaves of our own.

The 1930s saw the advent of other, contrary opinions, published in the weekly *El Espectador* by Ignacio L. López of Pomona, California. Instead of self-induced segregation, it promoted integration while maintaining Mexican ethnic ways. *El Espectador* encouraged both attendance at U.S. public schools and bilingual education, for example. (*La Opinión* had called for a separate Mexican school system in the United States.) Over the years, then, there was heated debate among Mexicans about how to address the sense of alienation that surfaces in the novel and that characterized much of the migrant population before and during the decades in which it is set.

Sources and literary context. Rivera's own experiences as a child in a migrant laborer family inspired him to write *. . . and the earth did not part*. As he explains, "I saw a lot of suffering and much isolation of the people. Yet they lived through the whole thing, perhaps because they had no choice. I saw a lot of heroic people and I wanted to capture their feelings" (Rivera in Lomelí and Shirley, p. 210).

The publication of *. . . and the earth did not part* marks an important milestone in Mexican American literature. The Mexican American novel before the 1970s was typically a work of social protest or a fictionalized account of personal experiences. While Rivera's novel is in a way both these things, its stark realism and fragmented structure set it apart and influenced a whole new generation of writers. By presenting the grim realities of migrant life in a way that also celebrated Mexican American culture, Rivera encourage other writers to follow suit.

ORAL LEGACY: STORIES AND POEMS

Rivera uses small anecdotes to set the tone for each of the chapters. Most of these introductions focus on details of migrant life, the tragedies and small triumphs.

> The teacher was astonished with the youngster when, upon learning that the class needed a button with which to designate the button industry on a poster, he tore one off his shirt and gave it to her . . . because she knew that it was probably the only shirt he owned.
>
> (*. . . and the earth*, p. 99)

These introductions were inspired by the oral tradition Rivera encountered while working among migrant workers in his early life. In retrospect, Rivera describes the tales as a type of balm, that is, as soothing relief from the daily grind. "There was always someone who knew the old traditional stories. . . . People find refuge . . . sitting in a circle, listening, telling stories and, through words, escaping to other worlds as well as inventing them" (Rivera in Lomelí and Shirley, p. 209).

Events in History at the Time the Novel Was Written

The turbulent '60s. There was a cultural explosion in the 1960s, a profound new commitment to the social transformation of the disadvantaged in U.S. society and to the acquisition by minorities of the rights they were owed by law. Migrant workers benefited from the ferment, joining labor unions like César Chávez's National Farm Workers Association in California. Chávez's union, later called United Farm Workers (UFW), mounted a strike against table-grape growers in 1965. The nonviolent strike, staged largely to combat low wages, grew into a national cause, a

César Chávez

"crusade for human dignity and civil rights" (Meier and Ribera, p. 210). Among the strikers were Filipino as well as Mexican American farm workers, who politicized their cause in 1966 with a 250-mile march to the state capital (Sacramento), in 1967 with a 25-day fast by Chávez, and from 1968 to 1970 with a national table-grape boycott. The strike ended successfully in 1970, the year the novel appeared, undoubtedly leaving the strikers feeling satisfied about their ability to improve conditions through direct action. Most of the grape growers entered into new three-year contracts that were favorable to the migrant workers. For the time being, in California at least, conditions had improved.

Chávez tried to expand the union to Texas, the base for the migrant farm workers in . . . *and the earth did not part*. However, the union fared less well here. Texas farm workers staged strikes of their own from 1966 to 1969 but failed to gain widespread support. In the end, these strikes did little for Texas's migrant workers, though they did rivet attention on Mexican American civil rights groups in the state.

The plays of Luis Valdez publicized the plight of migrant workers too. Working with Chávez in California, Valdez had founded El Teatro Campesino, "the farm workers' theater," and developed a type of play called the acto to inspire workers to try to rectify the injustices they suffered. A typical acto showed a wicked grower (bearing a sign that designated his profession) thrown to the ground by an upstanding worker who would release the tyrant only after he had signed a labor contract. In 1967 Valdez took El Teatro Campesino across the country and by 1971 his plays had expanded from the evils of farm labor to other subjects touched on by Rivera's novel, like the failure to meet the needs of Mexican American students or to teach about the contributions of their culture in public schools.

La Raza Unida. Texas's Mexican American community contributed to the ferment of the era by founding a third political party, an alternative to the Democrats and Republicans that promised to improve life for its members. The formation of the party was closely bound up with conditions in Texas schools. When the community of Crystal City, Texas, was first established, there was no school for Mexican American students. They were gradually integrated into the school system, with limited success. In 1951 a mere 9 percent of Mexican American first graders had gone on to graduate from high school. By 1958 the figure had climbed only to 17 percent. The average amount of school completed by Spanish-surnamed students in Crystal City was just 2.3 years, compared to the 11.2 years of Anglo students. Even though the community was 80 percent Mexican American, the school board and local government were completely controlled by Anglos. Racist policies prevailed, with many of the teachers showing prejudice. According to one source, these teachers "precipitated many incidents in their classrooms, occasionally lashing out at all Mexicans, telling them they 'should feel privileged to sit next to whites,' and in general doing their best to make the Mexicans feel insecure and inferior" (Shockley in Mirande, p. 99).

In 1963 Mexican Americans began to mobilize against the local government and succeeded in taking control of the Cystal City city council. The takeover lasted only two years, and conditions at the school and in the local community remained as before. But in 1969 the Mexican American community rallied again and carried out a successful school boycott, which led to the establishment of the political party *El Partido de la Raza Unida.* The political party organized local Mexican Americans and gave them the power to regain control of the city council and the school board. Similar conflicts were occurring at the same time in California's barrio schools as Mexican Americans realized the power that institutes of learning held in each community:

> Schools had become the no man's land of the cultural conflict. They are the most visible, best known, and most exposed institutions of the Anglo society in the barrios. On the inside they are the bastions where the language, philosophy, and goals of the conqueror are taught; but to those outside they are the bastions that the conquered can most easily besiege, with common cause, so that their children may be taught the language, philosophy, and goals of La Raza.
>
> (Steiner in Mirande, p. 100)

Rivera was certainly aware of this conflict; he was born and spent much of his early life in Crystal City. Moreover, he taught Spanish and English in Crystal City from 1958 to 1960 and would have known many of the school boycott's central figures. The school in his novel mirrors the problems of the Crystal City public school system.

In the end, all the ferment would produce mixed results. Some Mexican Americans were elected to political office, unionization stimulated wage increases, and bilingual education took root, but eventually the activism died down. The hard-core activists, say some historians, failed to perceive the conservative nature of most Mexican Americans. Some balked at joining a farmworkers' union, the union's membership declined, and La Raza Unida lost ground, gaining a reputation for being too radical. However, in the early 1970s, when Rivera wrote his novel, activism was still on the rise, fanning the hope—which surfaces in *. . . and the earth did not part*—that Mexicans would come from under the house, so to speak, and gain rights and proper remuneration in U.S. society.

Reviews. From the moment of its publication, Rivera's first novel, *. . . and the earth did not part,* received praise. Critics were struck by the tragic tones of the novel, and moved by Rivera's ability to tell the stories of the migrant workers in the American Southwest. Daniel Testa wrote of the novel: "With a free and flexible narrative technique, the author blends abrupt exchanges of dialogue, shifts of perspective, and internal monologue into the account of an external action or series of actions" (Testa in Lesniak,

p. 369). Other critics also recognized the dynamic nature of the storytelling. Juan Bruce-Novoa praised the realism achieved by Rivera's style: "It is a measure of Rivera's talent that the reader thinks that s/he has read a detailed depiction of reality, so much so, that many have used the book as an accurate sociological statement of the migrants' condition" (Bruce-Novoa in Lesniak, p. 369). Reviewers were also impressed by the novel's success in showing how the inner strength of the migrants prevails, despite the bleakness of their lives and the continual tragedies they suffer. "What Rivera achieves is the evocation of an environment with a minimum of words, and within that environment the migratory farmworkers move with dignity, strength, and resilience" (Bruce-Novoa in Lesniak, p. 369). While critics continued to praise Rivera's narrative dexterity, it was his depiction of the migrant life that made the greatest impact. Ralph Grajeda focused on this element of the novel in his review: "Rivera has a clear eye for the cruel ironies of life. In the world his characters inhabit, people are often victimized by the very hopes they nurture, hopes that spring from the positions in life which they endure" (Grajeda in Lesniak, p. 369). This is perhaps the way Rivera would prefer the novel be remembered. He has claimed that the novel was not meant to be political, but rather a testament to the way in which migrant workers have lived. As a former migrant worker himself, Rivera wanted to "document, somehow, the strength of those people that I had known" (Rivera in Lomelí and Shirley, p. 210).

—Terence Davis

For More Information

Ashabranner, Brent. *Dark Harvest: Migrant Farmworkers in America.* New York: Dodd, Mead, & Co., 1985.

Dunbar, Tony, and Linda Kravitz, eds. *Hard Traveling: Migrant Farm Workers in America.* Cambridge: Ballinger Publishing, 1976.

Gutiérrez, David G. *Between Two Worlds: Mexican Immigrants in the United States.* Wilmington, Del.: Scholarly Resources, 1996.

Kibbe, Pauline R. *Latin Americans in Texas. Albuquerque: University of New Mexico Press,* 1946.

Lesniak, James G., ed. *Contemporary Authors New Revision Series.* Vol. 32. Detroit: Gale Research, 1991.

Lomelí, Francisco A., and Carl R. Shirley, eds. *Chicano Writers.* 1st series. Dictionary of Literary Biography. Vol. 82. Detroit: Gale Research, 1989.

Mirande, Alfredo. *The Mexican American Experience: An Alternative Perspective.* Notre Dame, Ind.: University of Notre Dame Press, 1985.

Meier, Matt S., and Feliciano Ribera. *Mexican Americans—American Mexicans: From Conquistadors to Chicanos.* New York: Hill and Wang, 1993.

Rivera, Tomás. *. . . and the earth did not part.* Berkeley: Quinto Sol Publications, 1971.

Barren Lives

by

Graciliano Ramos

Born in the Brazilian state of Alagoas in 1892, Graciliano Ramos spent his first years in the *sertão,* the semiarid northeastern interior where *Barren Lives* takes place. One of his earliest recollections, recorded in his memoirs of youth, *Infância* (1945), is of a parched, burnt landscape seared into memory by a feeling of unquenchable thirst. The author's later personal history informs *Barren Lives*'s concern with the profound social inequities of the region. Ramos wrote the novel shortly after his release from prison in 1937. Two years earlier the increasingly despotic government of Getúlio Vargas unleashed a campaign of mass persecutions in response to a communist uprising. Although he was not a member of the Communist Party at the time and was never formally accused of anything, Ramos was swept up in Vargas's repressive campaign and spent ten months in prison, experiencing the perversions brought on by an unjust dictatorial regime. The novel's moving representation of extreme deprivation and the unequal distribution of power in Brazilian society can thus be read as a vehement indictment rooted in the author's own intimate understanding of social and political oppression.

THE LITERARY WORK

A novel set in the back country of northeastern Brazil some time in the late nineteenth or early twentieth century; published in Portuguese (as *Vidas Secas*) in 1938, in English in 1965.

SYNOPSIS

A downtrodden cattleman and his family struggle to survive in a region plagued by drought and deep-rooted social injustice.

Events in History at the Time the Novel Takes Place

The other Northeast. Neither time nor place are explicitly indicated in *Barren Lives*. Certain details, such as the use of kerosene lamps, suggest that the events narrated take place sometime in the late nineteenth or the early twentieth century. Regional terminology and a focus on particular economic activities reveal the novel's setting to be somewhere in the northeastern cattle-raising interior. In 1937 the northeastern scholar Djacir Menezes published a book entitled *The Other Northeast*. As he explains in his preface, his book is not about the Northeast featured in the renowned works of his contemporaries, sociologist Gilberto Freyre and novelist José Lins do Rego. It does not concern the coastal Northeast of sugarcane plantations and African cadences—but rather the "other," inland Northeast, of "ranch hands and corrals" and a stronger Amerindian presence (Menezes, p. 15).

When Portuguese colonizers arrived in Brazil in the sixteenth century, they founded their settlements along the coast where they soon set up prosperous sugarcane plantations. The interior held little interest for them during this early stage, and it was only in the late seventeenth century that they began full-scale exploration and colonization of the sertão. Penetration into the backlands came largely as a response to the need for more land on which to raise the cattle that provided plantations with work animals, meat, and leather. The Portuguese Crown encouraged the exploration of the interior by donating immense land grants or *sesmarias* to those who could prove they had sufficient assets to successfully carry out the arduous enterprise.

Unlike the plantation system, cattle-raising as practiced in the northeastern interior was not labor-intensive and thus did not require large numbers of slaves. The labor force consisted mostly of a *mestizo* or mixed-race population that arose through European contact with various Amerindian groups. White men, however, at times also occupied the lower rungs of sertão society, as we see in the case of Fabiano, the red-haired, blue-eyed protagonist of *Barren Lives*. Although they were not based primarily on African slave labor like those of the coast, the sertão's social structures were—and still are—quite stratified. Sharp distinctions were drawn between those who owned land and those who did not. The owners of the huge sesmaria properties, forerunners of the modern large landowners or *latifundistas*, were at the top of the hierarchy and possessed almost unlimited authority during the early stages of colonization. Such authority was due to their isolation from the colony's administrative centers. Although eventually the Portuguese—and after independence in 1822 the Brazilian—government attempted to rein in the power of these backlands strongmen, the early colonization pattern established authoritarian social relations that became deeply ingrained and would prove difficult to change. In *Barren Lives*, the internalization and passive acceptance of authoritarianism surfaces again and again. It comes to the fore in many of the characters' thoughts and actions, as when Fabiano, after being arbitrarily thrown in jail by a belligerent petty police officer, is reminded of words of consolation he used to offer those in similar situations: "Don't worry. It's no disgrace to take a beating from the law" (Ramos, *Barren Lives,* p. 30).

SERTÃO

The word *sertão* has more than one meaning in Brazil. Kempton E. Webb describes its "open-ended connotation" well: "One definition is geographic, referring to the dry lowland interior of Northeast Brazil; the other definition means sparsely populated backlands, hinterlands . . . the 'outback' of the Australians" (Webb, p. 112). The subject of Graciliano Ramos's novel is the specifically indicated northeastern sertão of the first definition, although the novel's setting is, in many senses, a universal space.

Working for the sesmeiros and later the latifundistas were the cattlemen, the *vaqueiros* who oversaw much of the work on the ranch. Their payment usually consisted of one out of every four calves and foals born under their management; a division of the herd was made at the time of payment. While at first some cattlemen managed to save up the resources to rent land from their bosses and establish their own smaller-scale cattle-raising businesses, such social mobility became increasingly rare over time. Traditionally the vaqueiro was allowed to raise his own animals alongside the landowner's herd. Absentee landlords later modified this tradition, forcing vaqueiros to sell their animals soon after the division of the herd, out of fear that their own animals might be neglected in their absence. Any possibility that the vaqueiro would someday become a cattle-raiser in his own right was thus removed. In *Barren Lives,* this situation is depicted in Fabiano's hopeless predicament:

> In the division of stock at the year's end, Fabiano received a fourth of the calves and a third of the kids, but as he grew no feed, but merely sowed a few handfuls of beans and corn on the river flat . . . he disposed of the animals. . . . Once the beans had been eaten . . . there was no place to go but the boss's cash drawer. He would turn over [to the boss] the animals that had fallen to his lot for the lowest of prices. . . .
>
> (*Barren Lives,* p. 93)

Other classes composing sertão society were the ranchhands, wage earners who were allowed to cultivate small plots on the rancher's land, and tenant farmers, who also lived on the landowner's property and cultivated subsistence crops, paying rent in money, crop yield, or labor. Smallholders or *minifundistas,* owners of their own, miniscule plots, hardly fared better than tenant farmers, for their small holdings barely allowed them to produce enough for their own subsistence. None of these other classes appear prominently in Ramos's novel, which is focused primarily on the figure of the vaqueiro. The harsh living conditions faced by the cattleman Fabiano and his family, however, seem to encompass the difficulties faced by all the lower classes of sertão society.

Brazil's Northeast continues to suffer from recurrent droughts. This scene from a 1998 drought in the state of Pernambuco shows a man carrying water through the parched land.

A barren land. At one level, the title of Ramos's novel refers to the problem of drought in the northeastern backlands. *Barren Lives* opens with Fabiano and his family crossing a bleak landscape of dry riverbeds and thorny brushland dotted with heaps of bones. Starved and exausted, they are fleeing the latest drought and have reached the end of their strength when they spot gathering clouds in the sky. It eventually rains and Fabiano is hired at a local ranch, but the cyclical nature of the drought in the sertão will not let them rest for long.

The drought zone of northeastern Brazil covers a large area, spread across eight states. While the region is often depicted as a barren desert, it is in fact topographically and climatically quite diverse, and includes six major river systems and a number of fertile upland zones. *Barren Lives* is set in the *caatinga,* the part of the sertão that is more properly defined as semi-arid. The word *caatinga* is an indigenous term meaning "white forest," an evocative image for the drought-resistant vegetation that characterizes this landscape: cacti, thorny shrubs, and small trees, many of which shed their leaves during the summer months to minimize water loss.

Droughts of catastrophic proportions occur in the sertão about once every century; milder droughts occur more frequently, at varying intervals that can be as short as two years. During the early period of colonization, the human impact on the sparse population was small. It was greatly exacerbated, however, by a population growth brought on by the introduction of drought-resistant cotton in the late nineteenth century. A cotton boom ensued and other crops were sacrificed to make way for the profitable cotton business. By the early 1870s, however, prices had declined, and when drought hit the region in 1877, not only subsistence crops but even the drought-resistant cotton crops failed, and a huge, starving population was forced to emigrate. It is estimated that 500,000 drought refugees, or *retirantes*, perished from hunger and disease in the 1877-79 drought (Hall, p. 4). This disaster was followed by others, prompting successive waves of emigration from the sertão to coastal cities and other areas, in a movement that has become a notorious feature of northeastern—and national—reality in the twentieth century. When Fabiano and his wife decide to try their luck in the city at the end of *Barren Lives*, they are doing what millions of other *sertanejos*, or sertão dwellers, have done since the late nineteenth century.

The proportions of the 1877 calamity finally led to direct government intervention, but the projects devised were largely focused on water-supply issues. Reservoir-building became the centerpiece of drought-relief action for the next several decades, a strategy that tended to benefit large landowners but had little if any impact on the predicament of the lower-income population. Of course, the landowners managed to control the reservoirs and therefore water distribution in the region. In times of drought, they could keep the water from reaching pockets of the population and sell it at high prices. The ineffectiveness of government policy in the sertão underscores the fact that the harsh climate is not sufficient to explain the calamitous extent of the damage provoked by recurring droughts. As Anthony L. Hall notes, the roots of the problem lie elsewhere, in unequal social and economic structures (Hall, p. 15).

BALEIA

The English translation of Ramos's novel inexplicably omits the dog's name. However, the fact that the dog is given a name (*Baleia,* which means "whale") in the original text while Fabiano and Vitória's children remain nameless—referred to simply as "the older boy" and "the younger boy"—is not a gratuitous act on the author's part. This apparently odd narrative gesture highlights the human characters' dehumanization, while it privileges Baleia's perspective as a full-fledged character. By not naming the boys, the text emphasizes their lack of status and power, their facelessness in a society that devours poor people like them. While in real life human beings generally have names, this is not necessarily the case with animals. The novel, however, reverses this truism. Humans and dog are placed on the same level in the story: they are all animals struggling to survive in an unjust, brutal world. Many parallels are set up between Baleia's experience as a dog, subject to her masters' whims, and the characters' positions within sertão social and familial hierarchy.

The lower-income rural population of the backlands is particularly vulnerable to drought effects because it has no economic safety nets of any kind. The legacy of the colonial sesmaria system was one of profoundly unequal land distribution: in 1950 less than one percent of northeastern property holders owned over one-third of available land area, a situation that was probably worse when Ramos wrote *Barren Lives* and that to this day has not changed in any significant way. A majority of the sertão population thus has access to but a tiny fraction of the area's resources and cannot produce and save the necessary food stocks to survive in times of crisis. It is this underlying social and economic inequity that Ramos sought to expose in writing his novel. Drought is not the primary agent of his characters' deprived existence; rather, it is the skewed distribution of wealth that keeps both the land and people barren, stripped of even the most basic necessities.

The Novel in Focus

Plot summary. *Barren Lives* is composed of 13 chapters that can be read independently of one another. Many of them, in fact, were initially written and published in newspapers as short stories, a strategy Ramos used to earn more money from his writings. The composite, loosely structured character of the novel has prompted at least one critic to call it a "modular novel" (*romance desmontável*), and indeed, the order of most of the chapters could be rearranged without significantly affecting the text's overall meaning or impact (Rubem Braga in Candido, p. 45). The first and last chapters are an exception, for they mark the cyclical movement of the characters' lives, trapped in the endless recurrence of drought and its social consequences. The other chapters describe various events in the lives of a typical sertanejo family. Several chapters focus on the perceptions of an individual character, viewing events from his or her particular perspective.

"A New Home." The novel opens with the vaqueiro Fabiano, his wife Vitória, their two young sons—who remain nameless throughout the narrative—and their dog, Baleia, crossing an inhospitable desert landscape. Fleeing the latest drought, they have already eaten their parrot and are on the brink of starvation. Significantly, Vitória justifies the parrot's sacrifice "by telling herself the bird was quite useless—it didn't even talk" (*Barren Lives,* p. 6). The bird's silence, a product of the family's silence (he has no one to imitate), is the first manifestation of the central theme of language in the novel. Coming upon an abandoned ranch, its owners and cattle driven away by the lack of water, the family stops to rest. As they gaze up at a thickening cloud and eat a cavy that Baleia has caught, Fabiano feels a surge of hope and decides to stay on at the ranch.

"Fabiano." We listen in on the vaqueiro's thoughts as he goes about his daily work on the ranch. He has been working at the ranch for some time, hired by the absentee ranch owner who returned briefly to reclaim his property after the first thunderstorms. While he tracks down a missing heifer, superstitiously intoning a prayer he believes has magical powers to cure the heifer's sores, Fabiano ponders his new life. His pride at having survived the drought and finding a job is tempered by a consideration of his lowly social status. The perspectives of the third-person omniscient narrator and of the character Fabiano are intermingled here, as they are throughout the novel, allowing for the emergence of important issues that Fabiano himself only confusedly understands. Among them are his dehumanized status as a landless worker, the authoritarian behavior of the landed gentry, and his belief that as a mere cattleman he has no "right" to ask questions and to aspire to knowledge that is a privilege of the wealthy folk (*Barren Lives,* p. 18).

"Jail." Fabiano has gone into town to buy household provisions and is roped into playing a card game with a local policeman. When Fabiano, having lost all his money, abandons the game in frustration, the policeman feels insulted and provokes a scuffle that ends in Fabiano's arrest. In jail, the vaqueiro laments his fate, vacillating between anger at the policeman's injustice, frustration at his own ignorance and consequent impotence, and acceptance of such abuse as his lot in life.

"Vitória." The perspective shifts to Fabiano's wife, Vitória, whose thoughts revolve around her desire for a leather-bottomed bed, a "real bed" to replace the tree-branch bed she and Fabiano sleep on (*Barren Lives,* p. 44). As she goes about her household chores, her thoughts return obsessively to the object of her desire. Her yearning for a "bed on which a Christian [can] stretch his bones" encapsulates a general longing for a stability and dignity that seem perpetually out of reach (*Barren Lives,* p. 43).

"The Younger Boy." The omniscient narrator adopts the point of view of the younger son, focusing on the child's awe of his father. Having watched Fabiano break a horse, the boy attempts to ride a billy-goat to emulate his father's feat. Within the realm of the child's experience, Fabiano appears as a powerful figure and the highest model he can aspire to. The narrator's perspective, however, implicitly conveys the bleakness of the child's future prospects: a repetition of the pattern of poverty and ignorance in which his father and forefathers have been caught for centuries.

"The Older Boy." Having encountered a word with which he is unfamiliar—"hell"—the older son questions his parents as to its meaning. He receives no reply from his father. Vitória gives him a curt, vague explanation that does not satisfy him, for it seems to have little to do with the world he knows. When he questions her further, she strikes him, punishing the child for his curiosity, whereupon he takes refuge with Baleia. There is more than an ironic touch here in the fact that the meaning of the word (*inferno* in Portuguese) whose sound enchants him—"a word with so musical a ring"—eludes his understanding, for he and his family may be said to live in a "hell" far more real than the place "full of red-hot spits and bonfires" his mother describes (*Barren Lives,* pp. 59, 56).

"Winter." The family huddles around the fireplace on a rainy winter night. A nearby river has flooded and is creeping towards the ranch, a common event in the caatinga, where the rivers often flood in the rainy season. With the threat of an immediate drought removed, Fabiano expresses his contentment by telling a "tall tale" in which he appears as the main hero (*Barren Lives,* p. 68). He has trouble making himself understood, however, and the other characters pursue their own fragmented thoughts.

"Feast Day." Dressed in their best clothes, the family heads into town for the Christmas festivities. They are uncomfortable in shoes and clothes they are not used to wearing and feel out of place in the bustling town atmosphere: "The two boys stared at the street lamps. . . . They were afraid, rather than curious. . . . How could there be so many houses and so many people?" (*Barren Lives,* p. 74). Feeling inferior to the city folk, Fabiano gets drunk and grows increasingly aggressive. He has fantasies of revenge against the officer who threw him in jail, makes incoherent threats, and finally collapses on the pavement.

"The Dog" ("Baleia" in the Portuguese original). This was the first chapter Ramos wrote and published as a short story, and might be considered the original starting point of the novel. It narrates Baleia's death, seen partially from the dog's perspective. She is terribly sick, and Fabiano, suspecting rabies, decides to kill her with his flintlock rifle. As Vitória restrains the children in the house, the vaqueiro goes after the dog, shooting her in the hindquarters. She dies slowly, and her last moments are narrated in moving detail, conveying her innocent, uncomprehending perceptions as she struggles to make sense of what has happened to her.

"Accounts." Fabiano goes into town to receive his payment from the ranch owner. As traditional payment for his services, he is entitled to a quarter of the calves born under his care during the year. In order to make ends meet, however, he has already sold his share of the animals back to the ranch owner and has even had to borrow money from him. Utterly befuddled by accounts, he is certain he is being cheated, but cannot grasp the idea of interest on money he has borrowed. Although he knows Vitória's accounting is different from the ranch owner's, he withdraws his protest and capitulates to the owner after being threatened with the loss of his job. Once again Fabiano is left vacillating between rage against authority, self-recrimination, and a fatalistic acceptance of his lot.

"The Policeman in Khaki." While tracking down an animal in the caatinga, Fabiano unexpectedly encounters the policeman who jailed him. The vaqueiro instinctively raises his machete to kill the man before the policeman even recognizes him, but manages to stay his hand. He realizes he has the trembling policeman utterly in his power, but after struggling with opposing impulses he finally lets the man go, concluding, "The law is the law" (*Barren Lives,* p. 108).

"The Birds." Signs of an imminent drought are everywhere, most visibly in large flocks of birds of passage. In an attempt to pinpoint a concrete cause for the impending tragedy that looms over her family, Vitória blames the "cursed birds [who] drank up what was left [of the water], trying to kill the stock" (*Barren Lives,* p. 109). Fabiano marvels at his wife's logic and shoots at the birds, giving vent to his rage. The birds are too many, however, and he cannot fight them or his fate. He decides to store some for food to take on the long trip he knows is ahead of them.

"Flight." No longer able to deny that the drought has arrived and unable to settle their debt to the ranch owner, Fabiano and his family flee under cover of night, setting out across the barren caatinga. Desperate and fearful, Fabiano and Vitória wonder what will become of them. Vitória asks if they might not go back to being what they were before the drought. They finally agree it would be fruitless, or impossible, to return to their old selves. The couple discuss their possible future, as well as that of their children. They try to imagine a better life in the city, even though they are ignorant of what it might hold for them. The narrator's voice takes over in the final, concluding lines:

> They were on their way to an unknown land, a land of city ways. They would become its prisoners. And to the city from the backlands would come ever more and more of its sons, a never-ending stream of strong, strapping brutes like Fabiano, Vitória, and the two boys.
>
> (*Barren Lives,* p. 131)

A note about the translation. The translation of Ramos's novel conveys some misimpressions when compared to the original *Vidas Secas.* In the English translation above, Fabiano and his family are, for example, described as "strong, strapping brutes." However, *brutos,* from the original, refers to their ignorance, not their physical appearance; moreover, the translation's addition of "strapping"—no such word appears in the Portuguese original—connotes a physical robustness that contradicts the rest of the novel.

Barren tongues. The title of Ramos's novel is richly suggestive, and can be read as a reference to multiple forms of barrenness. One of the central preoccupations of the narrative is education or the lack of access to it. Fabiano, his wife, and his children are illiterate. They do not know how to read or write, and can barely express themselves in speech. With only the most rudimentary linguistic tools at their disposal, they struggle at a basic cognitive level: they cannot even articulate fully-formed thoughts because they do not possess the vocabulary and hence the conceptual framework with which to give shape to complete ideas. This fundamental lack is a grave handicap that keeps them at the margins of society, unable to understand or communicate with the world around them and therefore unable to defend themselves from it because they do not control one of the most crucial instruments of power: language. When Fabiano is unjustly imprisoned, he is confusedly aware that his lack of linguistic knowledge is largely to blame for his situation:

> He had never seen a school. That was why he couldn't defend himself. . . . Sometimes he came out with a big word, but it was all fake. . . . He didn't know how to set his thoughts in order. If he did, he would go out and fight policemen in khaki uniforms who beat up harmless people.
>
> (*Barren Lives,* pp. 32-33)

The deficiencies and inequities of the Brazilian educational system have a long and tortuous history. The original Constitution of 1824, while paying lip service to universal education as a civil right, failed to establish a system of free public education because of public disinterest and a lack of resources. Access to education remained extremely limited: throughout the nineteenth century the rate of illiteracy did not fall below 85 percent (Haussman and Haar, p. 32). Brazil's shift from a monarchy to a republican state in 1889 brought the development of a public network of primary, secondary, and post-secondary educational institutions. Access to public education, however, was largely limited to urban centers; the quality of education in rural areas remained extremely poor.

An 1883 report on educational progress in Ramos's native state of Alagoas identifies obstacles:

> It is truly cause for surprise that, while it is calculated that the province has a school-age population of 80,000 . . . little over one-twentieth of this population attends the public schools. The causes of this fact are complex . . . a) the lack of resources of parents who are dayworkers [or] who eke out scarce resources for subsistence from small crop cultivation . . . b) the dissemination of the population across a vast territory and the lack of roads . . . to the towns where the schools are located.
>
> (Moacyr, pp. 615-16)

When *Barren Lives* was published, this situation had not seen significant change. A 1949 study on education in the interior of the northeastern state of Ceará affirms that 80 percent of the school-age population in the 1940s did not attend school at all (Barreira, p. 57). Even today, the illiteracy rate in the rural Northeast as a whole is shockingly high. Data collected in 1982 indicates that at that time fully two- thirds of the northeastern rural population remained illiterate, and almost as many of the region's inhabitants had less than one year of schooling. Outside the Northeast one-fifth of the population was illiterate (Harbison and Hanushek, p. 31).

In making the question of language and literacy a core problem in his novel, Ramos thus touches on an issue that is still highly relevant and urgent today. As a writer, and most notably as the former Director of Public Instruction of Alagoas, he would have been painfully aware of the problem. The poignant force of *Barren Lives* does not derive solely or even primarily from a technical knowledge of the issue, however. Rather, it is the product of a narrative exploration that manages to render, by way of the written word, the impoverished reality of an existence without knowledge of words.

Sources and literary context. As he admits in his memoirs, Ramos's image of the natural and human devastation caused by the periodic northeastern droughts is informed as much by habitual, generalized notions as by personal memory. When Ramos wrote *Barren Lives,* there was already a considerable body of literature on drought and hardship in the northeastern backlands; this literature may have shaped his own narrative vision as much as personal experience did.

Barren Lives is a classic of what has been called "the Northeastern Novel," the term used for a body of politically oriented regionalist novels that exploded onto the Brazilian literary scene in the 1930s and 1940s. Generally, Ramos is placed alongside Jorge Amado (see ***Gabriela, Clove and Cinnamon,*** also covered in *Latin American Literature and Its Times*), José Lins do Rego, and Rachel de Queiroz. All are northeastern writers who purportedly used realist narrative techniques and focused on northeastern themes to denounce social ills endemic to the region. Ramos's novel fits specifically in a body of works on the drought problem, among which one of the most well-known is de Queiroz's 1930 novel *O Quinze* (*Fifteen*).

Most of Ramos's work, however, does not fit comfortably under this rubric, for it tends to focus more on the complex psychological workings of its characters and less on overt descriptions of regional settings and problems. Of his four novels, *Barren Lives* may be said to be his most regionalist work, focused as it is on the perennial problem of drought and emigration and on the specific geographic and human space of the sertão. Even this novel is somewhat anomalous in relation to other Northeastern Novels of the period, however, in its use of narrative techniques such as indirect free-style discourse to convey its ignorant characters' psychological processes. In *Barren Lives,* as in his other novels, Ramos is most concerned with exploring the effects of a given social reality on the individual psyche.

Aside from its association with the northeastern regionalism of the 1930s, *Barren Lives* has been read as culling from an older tradition of writings about the Northeast; most notably, a number of critics have identified parallels between Ramos's novel and Euclides da Cunha's ***Rebellion in the Backlands*** (*Os Sertões*; also covered in *Latin American Literature and Its Times*), a 1902 account of the sertão and its inhabitants that became tremendously influential in shaping subsequent writings on the region. Such a comparison should be undertaken with caution, however, for there are significant stylistic and ideological differences between the two texts. Da Cunha's style, for example, is dense—full of adjectives and terminology—while Ramos's style is deliberately sparse. He prided himself on cutting his writing down to the bare minimum.

Aside from literary influences, Ramos's personal and political plight in the 1930s can also shed light on the novel. He wrote *Barren Lives* shortly after being released from jail, and much of the novel can be read through the prism of this grueling personal experience. During his ten-month incarceration, the writer witnessed and was victimized by the excesses of an authoritarian regime. Ignorant of what he was being accused of, awaiting a trial that never came, he was sent from one prison to the next, and at one point was confined to a "correctional colony" for end-of-the-road criminals that took away every last shred of his dignity. *Barren Lives*'s focus on power and its abuse, seen perhaps most clearly in the chapter "Jail" but present in all the major interactions between the novel's various characters, comes into razor-sharp focus when viewed within this personal context.

Events in History at the Time the Novel Was Written

Political change and the sertão. The early decades of the twentieth century were a tumultuous period in Brazilian socio-political history. By the beginning of the century the republican government established in 1889 was riddled with corruption, controlled by coffee politics and a handful of rural oligarchs who governed solely with their own interests in mind. Indignation with this state of affairs grew throughout the 1920s, most visibly among the middle ranks of the military, who promoted several unsuccessful revolts. This rebellious movement, known as the *tenente,* or lieutenant movement, expressed a more general dissatisfaction on the part of those who felt marginalized by the republican political system, most notably the growing urban middle groups (Burns, p. 340). Although attempts were made to stir up feeling in the countryside, the rural population remained largely uninvolved in the revolts of the 1920s. In fact, as Bradford Burns notes, during this period "[t]he masses, rural and urban, fatalistically accepted their menial position" (Burns, p. 343).

Political discontent within the army and among the urban middle classes deepened further with the 1929 worldwide economic crisis and eventually led to the successful Revolution of 1930 that placed Getúlio Vargas in power. During the early years of his administration, Vargas attempted to create a power base but formulated no clear political ideology. He did nonetheless introduce some significant political and social laws: among these were the extension of suffrage to working women, the guarantee of voting by secret ballot, the lowering of the voting age from 21 to 18, and a host of labor reform laws. The repercussions of these laws were largely limited to urban centers, however. Rural Brazil saw little change in traditional social relations.

In 1934 the Constituent Assembly promulgated a new constitution, expanding the powers of the executive and promptly electing Vargas to office. However, pressures on the president were mounting, coming both from politicians linked to the pre-1930 regime and from emerging extremist political doctrines: fascism and communism. Fascism appeared in Brazil in 1932 in the guise of the Integralist Party (*Ação Integralista Brasileira*), a frank imitation of European fascist parties. In the mid-1930s Vargas forged a temporary alliance with the Integralistas, which ended in 1938, when the fascists were shut out of Vargas's newly minted *Estado Novo* (New State) dictatorship. Meanwhile, the Communist Party, founded in 1922, gained ground steadily in the early 1930s. In 1934 one of its factions began to organize a popular front to combat fascism, the National Liberation Alliance (*Aliança Nacional Libertadora*). Most supporters of the ANL did not consider themselves communists but saw certain social changes as necessary for modernization and development. In 1935 the ANL was outlawed by Vargas, after the organization's honorary president called for the defeat of the Vargas regime and the establishment of a popular revolutionary government. This was followed some months later by three communist uprisings in the capitals of the northeastern states of Rio Grande do Norte and Pernambuco, and in Rio de Janeiro. The uprisings produced outrage among the general population and, because of the violence, discredited the Communist Party. Riding on the wave of public anger, Vargas used the situation to his advantage, strengthening his power. From 1935 to 1937 he pursued a virulent anticommunist campaign, in which anyone rumored to harbor communist sympathies was threatened with imprisonment. Ramos, then the Director of Public Instruction of Alagoas, was

A group of fascist *Integralistas,* or "green shirts," in Rio de Janeiro at the time of the attempted coup against Getúlio Vargas.

swept up in the campaign, despite his lack of involvement with the ANL or the Communist Party. Politically, Ramos at this point remained unaffiliated, an independent thinker.

The repressive crescendo of the Vargas government culminated in a coup in 1937. Presidential elections were cancelled, Congress was dismissed, and Vargas proclaimed his authoritarian regime, the Estado Novo, which would last until 1945. It was in this repressive political climate that the recently released Ramos wrote *Barren Lives.* Small wonder then that the novel should be so profoundly concerned with power and its victims. While it does not openly refer to the Vargas regime and the political convulsions of the period, its portrayal of the radically dispossessed of Brazil indirectly denounces the contemporary political scene and questions Vargas's promise of change, progress, and advancement for all in a "New State."

Reviews. The initial critical response to *Barren Lives* ran the gamut from enthusiastic acclaim to a more tempered and even openly negative assessment of the novel's value. Lúcia Miguel Pereira, for instance, a well-respected critic of the period, praised *Barren Lives* for the structural originality of its modular chapters and for its ability to convey the humanity and "hidden [psychological] wealth" of those occupying the lowest rungs of society (Pereira in Candido, p. 104). On the other end of the spectrum, Olívio Montenegro criticized the novel for endowing "rustic" characters with an unrealistic psychological depth (Montenegro, p. 221). Adopting a more moderate position, one of the most prominent critics of the period, Alvaro Lins, praised the book for its moments of "poetry" and for its Brazilianness, but echoed Montenegro's view in his reservations regarding the novel's structure and the "excess[ive]" psychological introspection of its "primitive" characters (Lins, pp. 151-53). Critical opinion has since shifted overwhelmingly toward Miguel Pereira's positive position. Among the general reading public in Brazil, *Barren Lives* remains Ramos's best-known and most popular novel. The fact that it has become a household name is perhaps the most significant confirmation of its enduring social and poetic value.

—Sabrina Karpa-Wilson

For More Information

Barreira, Américo. *A Escola Primária no Ceará.* Fortaleza: Clã, 1949.

Burns, E. Bradford. *A History of Brazil.* 3rd ed. New York: Columbia University Press, 1993.

Candido, Antonio. *Ficção e Confissão: Ensaios sobre Graciliano Ramos.* Rio de Janeiro: Editora 34, 1992.

Hall, Anthony L. *Drought and Irrigation in North-East Brazil.* Cambridge: Cambridge University Press, 1978.

Harbison, Ralph W., and Eric A. Hanushek. *Educational Performance of the Poor: Lessons from Rural Northeast Brazil.* Oxford: Oxford University Press, 1992.

Haussman, Fay, and Jerry Haar. *Education in Brazil.* Hamden, Conn.: Archon, 1978.

Lins, Alvaro. "Valores e Misérias das Vidas Secas." In *Vidas Secas* by Graciliano Ramos. Rio de Janeiro: Record, 1992.

Menezes, Djacir. *O Outro Nordeste. Formação Social do Nordeste.* Rio de Janeiro: José Olympio, 1937.

Moacyr, Primitivo. *A Instrução e as Províncias (Subsídios para a historia da Educação no Brasil) 1834-1889.* Vol. 1. São Paulo: Companhia Editora Nacional, 1939.

Montenegro, Olívio. *O Romance Brasileiro.* 2nd ed. Rio de Janeiro: José Olympio, 1953.

Ramos, Graciliano. *Barren Lives.* Trans. Ralph Edward Dimmick. Austin: University of Texas Press, 1965.

Webb, Kempton E. *The Changing Face of Northeast Brazil.* New York: Columbia University Press, 1974.

Before Night Falls

by
Reinaldo Arenas

> **THE LITERARY WORK**
>
> An autobiographical memoir set in Cuba and in the United States from 1945 to 1990; published posthumously in Spanish (as *Antes que anochezca*) in 1992, in English in 1993.
>
> **SYNOPSIS**
>
> The author reexamines his life in 70 short sections that progress from his childhood (age two) in Cuba to his death in exile (at age 47) in the United States.

Reinaldo Arenas was born on July 16, 1943, in the province of Oriente, Cuba. An illegitimate child in a fatherless household, Arenas was raised in a poor, rural town. He lived with his mother's family, developing an intimate connection with his grandmother. After Fidel Castro's rise to power in 1959 Arenas moved to Havana where he published his first novel, *Celestino antes del alba* (Singing from the Well), which won him both First Mention in the Cuban Writers and Artists Union literary contest and the distrust of the Revolutionary government on account of the novel's irreverence and critical stance towards the regime. After years of political persecution for his beliefs and his homosexuality, Arenas left Cuba for the United States, where he recorded his autobiography on audiocassettes before committing suicide in 1990. (Arenas had actually started to write his memoir in Cuba but it was confiscated and destroyed by the government.) Beyond the sociopolitical specifics that it provides about life under Castro's regime, *Before Night Falls* is a vivid testament of what it means to be part of a minority fighting for freedom and self-expression in any repressive society.

Events in History at the Time the Memoir Takes Place

Political struggles under Batista's dictatorship. On March 10, 1952, Fulgencio Batista led a successful coup d'état against Cuban President Carlos Prío. Although Batista attempted to invigorate Cuba's economy by focusing on the sugar industry and foreign trade, this strategy, among other effects, resulted in an increase in the number of the unemployed and underemployed in the nation. It also promoted a widening disparity in living conditions between Cuba's urban and rural areas. While, for example, color television was available in Havana in the 1950s, education, health services, and housing were scarce and inferior in rural areas. "Most of the new housing consisted of multiple-dwelling units and suburban residences in and around Havana" (Suchlicki, p. 136).

Batista failed to build an economic or political foundation that won the confidence of Cubans, resorting to violence and repression as his strategy to remain in power. His main opposition came from student movements and from the youth of the Orthodox Party, who were led by Fidel Castro. On July 26, 1953, Castro led an attack on the Moncada military barracks located

Batista addresses Cuban army troops the day after the attack on the Moncada military barracks.

in Santiago de Cuba. The attackers aimed to weaken Batista's power to the point that he would be forced to resign from Cuba's presidency. Castro synchronized his attack to coincide with the popular Santiago carnival of Oriente province, hoping that security would not be as tight as usual on the army installations. Unfortunately, security was not as lax as originally expected and Batista's army defeated Castro's men. The Moncada assault failed, ending in numerous casualties and Castro's imprisonment. Castro estimated that 70 of his men were tortured and executed; a lawyer as well as a rebel, he defended himself at his trial. Find me guilty, he challenged the judges in a now-famous warning; history will absolve me. Ironically the failure at Moncada brought national recognition to those associated with Castro's "July 26 Movement" and its ideals.

The struggle between Batista and his opponents escalated during the rest of the 1950s. A failed assassination attempt in 1957 by members of the student movement brought with it more repression and violence. Meanwhile, Castro organized a second uprising, this time from Mexico, where he was living in exile. This second Santiago de Cuba uprising, which took place November 30, 1956, also ended in failure. After the uprising, Castro and some of his allies returned to Cuba, where the unwelcome lot sought shelter in the remote mountains of the Sierra Maestra located in Oriente province.

Among Oriente's peasants, the July 26 Movement found support for its anti-Batista cause. Like other members of society, the peasants had grown tired of their impoverished living conditions and governmental neglect of their needs, and also of the unjustified violent abuses inflicted on them by Batista's Rural Guards. From the pool of local peasants, the anti-Batista cause drew new soldiers who were very knowledgeable about the Sierra Maestra's geography and who helped Castro defeat two Rural Guard stations by mid-1957. As a result, Batista intensified his military presence in rural areas and forced numerous families to relocate to detention camps, treating those who refused to relocate as enemies. This failed to discourage Castro sympathizers. In fact, Batista's relocation policy had quite the opposite effect—more peasants joined Castro in what became known as the "Rebel Army."

Along with the Rebel Army's growing power, Batista faced other formidable pockets of resistance. The dictator found himself in a precarious situation when the U.S. government and the Catholic Church, among many other powers, withdrew their support for his government. On December 31, 1958, Batista and some of his allies escaped to the Dominican Republic. That same day, Castro and the July 26 Movement took charge of Cuba's government.

Castro swung quickly into action. His government organized a literacy campaign that would result in 96 percent of the nation being able to read and write within a couple of years. The government also initiated reforms that divided up large landholdings in rural areas and lowered rents paid in the cities. By 1961, though, the economic situation was perilous; Cuba did not have enough food to feed its people, its consumer goods were being depleted, and it was buying more from foreign countries than it was selling to them. Castro looked to communism for the solution.

Homosexuality in communist Cuba. In 1961 Castro declared Marxism-Leninism to be the Cuban Republic's official ideology and fused the July 26 Movement with Cuba's Communist Party. The adoption of this ideology looked to rectify all the bourgeois wrongs said to have been plaguing Cuba for decades, including, for example, homosexuality and art for art's sake. Homosexuality became a main target partly because Soviet communists, with whom Castro allied Cuba's communists, described the preference for same-sex partners as a decadent bourgeois phenomenon (Lumsden, p. 65). In 1967 the government instituted camps, called Military Units to Aid Production, where male homosexuals (along with other citizens who were considered "unproductive" or counter-revolutionary, such as Jehovah's Witnesses and Seventh-day Adventists) were sent to be "rehabilitated." These camps involved forced labor, wages lower than those paid to other Cubans for similar work, and military surveillance (workers could leave the camps only with military escorts). The camps were closed by 1968, thanks to the efforts of different national and international groups.

In the late 1960s the Cuban Cultural Council adopted a resolution that encouraged the authorities to harass homosexuals involved with the arts, education, and culture. This resolution was "used to fire homosexual artists from their jobs and force them to do manual labor," and continued to plague homosexuals until 1975 when Cuba's Supreme Court abolished it and remunerated financially those who had been affected by it (Lumsden, p. 71). In 1971 the government held a National Congress on Education and Culture. At this Congress, homosexuality was publicly denounced as an "antisocial" behavior that needed to be contained. Formally, the Congress "resolved that 'notorious homosexuals' should be denied employment in any institution that had an influence upon youth . . . [and that] homosexuals should not be allowed to represent Cuba in cultural activities abroad" (Lumsden, p. 73). The Congress also suggested that homosexuals involved in the corruption of minors should be severely punished. Any adult who engaged a minor under the age of 16 in homosexual relations could be sentenced to five years in prison, a law that was most likely to be used against gay men in Cuban society. In the memoir, Arenas's arrest for alleged molestation of young boys can be understood as part of Cuba's intense intolerance for homosexuals.

The 1980 Mariel boatlift of exiles from Cuba constituted an opportunity for many homosexuals to escape persecution by leaving the country. Although there are no exact statistics about the number of homosexual exiles, it is significant that "they were numerous enough to be singled out as targets in the mass demonstrations directed against those who had opted to leave" (Lumsden, p. 78). Arenas, who himself escaped this way, adds that "a large number of gays were able to leave the Island in 1980" (Arenas, *Before Night Falls*, p. 281).

Cuban artists and the Revolution, 1959-71. Under Castro's leadership new social, political, and cultural reforms were implemented in order to improve the chaos left behind by Batista. As John Spicer Nichols explains, this included "a swift takeover of the country's mass media," which had been in Batista's pocket, until all of them were owned or controlled by Castro's government (Nichols, p. 219). Under Batista, the government paid large sums of money in monthly bribes to some journalists and forced other, uncooperative newspapers out of business (Nichols, p. 220).

Although Castro's government helped eradicate these problems, it also established different ways of controlling information and personal expression that included not only mass media, but other forms of cultural manifestations, such as literature, as well. This control emanated from the government's renewed interest in generating and monitoring cultural activities. Since the Revolution was facilitating artistic productions, it expected artists to create works that would reflect its ideologies. There was a short spurt of cultural vitality during the first years of the post-Revolutionary Cuban republic, due principally to the institution of various organizations such as the literary supplement *Lunes de revolución* (*Mon-*

day of Revolution) and the Cuban Institute of Cinematographic Arts and Industries. By 1961 this energetic burst of cultural activity had come to a halt; the government banned the short film about Cuban night life called *P.M.* and *Lunes de revolución* ceased publication. These two events led to a series of meetings among artists, intellectuals, and government officials that climaxed with Fidel Castro's famous address, "Words to the Intellectuals."

In this address Castro acknowledges that the rapidity of the Revolution had not permitted its leaders to foresee a number of future questions, such as what role culture should play in the post-Revolutionary republic (Castro, p. 5). When it comes to cultural manifestations, Castro explains, artists must keep in mind that their driving force should be the ideals of the Revolution. According to Castro, to be considered a revolutionary artist, one must be willing to sacrifice his or her own artistic calling in the name of the Revolution (Castro, p. 8). He summarized his position with the now famous words: "Inside the Revolution, everything; against the Revolution, nothing. Since the Revolution encompasses the interests of the people, since the Revolution represents the interests of the whole Nation, nobody should go against it" (Castro, p. 11; trans. G. Blasini). From 1961 onwards, these words became the model to follow in acceptable cultural creations. The state would eventually became more and more rigid in its dealings with artists and writers until 1971 when the infamous "Padilla case" took place.

The Padilla case. Born January 20, 1932, the poet Heberto Padilla is one of the most renowned Cuban writers of the twentieth century. Although he was supportive of the 1959 Revolution, his attacks against revolutionary writer Lisandro Otero and his defense of dissident writer Guillermo Cabrera Infante in 1967 put him in a precarious position with Castro's government. In 1968 Padilla won first prize in the Cuban Writers and Artists Union's literary contest for a book of poems entitled *Fuera del juego* (*Out of the Game*). Some of the poems were critical both of Cuba's relationship with the Soviet Union and of the island's contemporary sociopolitical situation, especially of the role that writers were expected to play within the Revolution. Around three years after the book's publication, in 1971, Padilla was arrested and detained for 28 days for his counter-revolutionary views. Ultimately, the poet was forced to deliver a public apology at a Cuban Writers and Artists Union assembly. Padilla's incarceration prompted an international intellectual debate: writers from all over the world drafted a letter that denounced the situation as unjust and degrading. Along with prominent international writers, Latin American signatories to the letter included Carlos Fuentes, Octavio Paz, Mario Vargas Llosa, and Gabriel García Márquez. The Padilla case became "a turning point in relations between the Cuban government and intellectuals, Cubans or otherwise" and led to the irremediable division of Latin America's literary world between those who supported Castro and those who did not (Valero, p. 261). Like Arenas, Padilla left Cuba in 1980 to settle in the United States.

The Memoir in Focus

Contents summary. *Before Night Falls* starts with an introduction written in August 1990 that is paradoxically entitled "The End." In it, Arenas recounts the sufferings he has undergone since 1987 when he discovered he had AIDS. "The End" also provides a brief overview of Arenas's life while hinting at three of the main issues that informed his days and his literary production (and that reappear through the memoir): his homosexuality, his anti-Castro political views, and the ominous presence of death in life.

After the introduction the memoir proceeds chronologically, beginning with Arenas's reminiscence of hungrily eating dirt at age two. He describes the material poverty of his surroundings, the *bohío* (a hut with a thatched roof and dirt floor) on the farm where he lived with his mother and her family (parents, sisters, brothers-in-law, grandmother), who welcomed them after his mother was impregnated and abandoned by her fiancé. Arenas sees his father just once, while at the river with his mother, and it is only after the short encounter that he discovers the man's identity.

At age five Arenas contracts meningitis and, against all odds, survives it. He starts to attend Rural School 91 in the area of Perronales at age six, where he learns to read and write. Although his childhood is steeped in poverty, Arenas identifies this as the most wonderful period of his life. The absolute freedom of these years allows him to explore his natural surroundings as well as his own sexual desires. For him, nature and sexuality go hand in hand since "in the country, sexual energy generally overcomes all prejudice, repression, and punishment. That force, the force of nature, dominates" (*Before Night Falls,* p. 19).

At this point, the text focuses on Arenas's early explorations of his erotic desires, which include having sexual encounters with boys, girls, animals—and even a tree.

The deteriorating living conditions on the farm force Arenas's family to move to the city of Holguín with the hope of improving their financial situation. Although Arenas dislikes the town, a place that thoroughly bores him in comparison to his previous rural surroundings, Holguín introduces him to the magic of movies, which eventually inspire him to start writing novels. In Holguín, Arenas attends a junior high school where he is called a "faggot" for the first time (*Before Night Falls,* p. 38).

The boredom of life in Holguín as well as the town's insufferable living conditions under Fulgencio Batista's dictatorship—the town had little food and no electricity—inspire Arenas to join the Revolutionary guerrilla groups commanded by Fidel Castro. Even though Arenas never fights directly against Batista's men, he becomes a hero in Holguín after Castro and his followers defeat the dictator Batista and establish the Revolutionary government in 1959.

At age 16 Arenas wins a scholarship to study in a polytechnic institute from which he will graduate as an agricultural accountant. While at the institute, he comes to two realizations. First, he must hide any homosexual proclivity since this variety of desire is severely punished by the Revolutionary government. Second, the "free" educational opportunities provided by the state actually do have a price: communist indoctrination. His 16th year is also marked by two major events: for the first time, he visits Havana (the city where he will later live in his aunt's house) and he takes his first male lover, Raúl, with whom he lives for approximately four months.

After entering a storytelling competition in 1963 and impressing the jury with his literary talent, Arenas obtains a job at the National Library in Havana, thanks to the director, María Teresa Freyre de Andrade. This job proves to be a turning point in his life; Arenas not only has the opportunity to expand his knowledge by reading the materials available in the National Library, but he also starts to develop friendships and alliances with other artists and intellectuals who live in Havana. While working at the library he writes his first novel, *Celestino antes del alba* (published in English in 1987 as *Singing from the Well*). Arenas submits this novel to the 1965 competition sponsored by the Cuban Writers and Artists Union (UNEAC) and wins First Honorable Mention.

In 1966 Arenas enters the UNEAC competition again, this time with his second novel, *El mundo alucinante* (published in English in 1987 as *The Ill-Fated Peregrinations of Fray Servando*). Once again he wins First Honorable Mention, but this time the jury—which consists of Virgilio Piñera, Alejo Carpentier, José Antonio Portuondo, and Félix Pita Rodríguez—decides not to award any First Prize. During the awards ceremony, Arenas meets Piñera, who tells the young novelist that he was robbed of the First Prize by Carpentier and Portuondo. Piñera offers to help Arenas polish *El mundo alucinante* so that it can be published. From that day on, Piñera becomes Arenas's mentor, friend, and inspiration: Piñera, also a homosexual, speaks his mind without thinking about political consequences. Arenas also establishes a close friendship and literary affinity with another Cuban writer—José Lezama Lima. One of Latin America's most renowned novelists, Lima wrote *Paradiso,* a controversial novel with a chapter on homosexuality.

Arenas's literary recognition enables him to land a job at the Cuban Book Institute. He meets new friends, some homosexual, and attends literary soirees at which everyone writes poems or

ARENAS'S OTHER NOVELS

Celestino antes del alba (*Singing from the Well*) is a novel about a mentally challenged boy growing up in one of Cuba's many poor rural areas. *El mundo alucinante* (*The Ill-Fated Peregrinations of Fray Servando*) uses a historical figure, Mexican monk Fray Servando Teresa de Mier, to create a fictionalized narrative that examines issues of anticolonialism and freedom of expression in eighteenth-century Mexico. Cuban authorities considered both of these novels irreverent, anti-revolutionary, and critical of the regime. In fact, *El mundo alucinante* was banned on the island (it was eventually published in Mexico). Arenas became a controversial figure not only because he had smuggled his manuscript out of Cuba, but also because he had it published abroad without the consent of Nicolás Guillén, president of the Writers and Artists Union. In 1969 *El mundo alucinante,* along with Gabriel García Márquez's *One Hundred Years of Solitude,* shared first prize as the best foreign novel in France.

A U.S. Coast Guard ocean-going tugboat heads for Key West with an estimated 700 to 900 Mariel refugees, May 6, 1980.

chapters of books and shares stories about erotic adventures.

While the 1960s constitute an intense period of creativity and sexual activity in his life, they also see the beginning of State Security's harassment of Arenas for his ideas and work. His award-wining novel, *Celestino antes del alba,* is banned in Cuba after being published abroad without the consent of Nicolás Guillén, UNEAC's president at the time. In 1967 Arenas meets the renowned Cuban painter Jorge Camacho and his wife, Margarita, now living in Europe but visiting Cuba's *Salón de Mayo* international painting exhibition. Through the Camachos, who would become loyal friends until his death, Arenas manages to smuggle his manuscripts out of Cuba.

According to the memoir, a period of "Super-Stalinism" starts for writers during the early 1970s; they face forced "voluntary" work on labor camps established in 1969 (*Before Night Falls,* pp. 124, 126). This kind of environment does not weaken Arenas's creativity, however; he deliberately meets every Sunday with his friends to read poetry, novels, and plays in Lenin Park. The beginning of the '70s also marks the intensification of the persecution of intellectuals in Cuba, which reaches a critical point with the Padilla case.

Around the same time, Castro's government organizes the First Congress of Education and Culture. One of the main purposes of this Congress, says Arenas, is to target homosexuals as enemies. It starts the system of *parametraje,* in which writers or artists known to be gay receive a telegram informing them that their behavior does not fall within the political and moral parameters necessary for their job and that therefore they must either be fired or relocated to a forced-labor camp.

In the summer of 1973 Arenas and his friend Pepe Malas are arrested for having sexual relations with two young men. Even though these young men agreed to have sex, they now accuse both Arenas and Malas of sexual molestation in order to cover up the fact that they have stolen Arenas's and Malas's bags. After being released on bail, Arenas discovers from his lawyer that his case goes beyond the alleged sexual crime to include counter-revolutionary charges. Resolving to flee before his trial, Arenas attempts to escape Cuba through Guantánamo Bay (a U.S. base on Cuba) as a friend has advised him. After this attempt fails, he returns to Havana with a fake identification card and, for ten days, manages to evade the police. Upon his capture, Arenas is immediately transferred to Morro Castle, a Spanish-built colonial fortress that has become one of Cuba's worst prisons.

While in the Morro, Arenas suffers the atrocities of life as a prisoner: hunger, sickness, violence, loneliness, lack of sanitary facilities. He tries to commit suicide, but fails. A short time later, the authorities transfer him to Villa Marista, the headquarters of State Security, where he is subjected to constant threats from the government. After four months in isolation, Arenas agrees to write a confession in which he apologizes for his counter-revolutionary views (just as Padilla had done some years earlier). This forced action makes Arenas feel like he has nothing left in life: "I had lost my dignity and my rebellious spirit" (*Before Night Falls,* p. 207). He is then returned to the Morro to await his trial. A reversal in the testimony of the young men who had originally accused Arenas makes the sexual molestation charges invalid; they now say that Arenas never attempted to seduce them. In the end, Arenas receives a two-year sentence of jail time for lascivious abuses.

Released from prison in early 1976, Arenas must pretend constantly to be a supporter of Cuba's Revolutionary agenda; otherwise, he will have to face jail again. During the late 1970s his mentors and close friends, Piñera and Lezama Lima, both die. In 1980 history and luck help Arenas leave Cuba in the Mariel boatlift.

Arenas departed from the port of Mariel on a small boat, the *San Lázaro,* carrying more than 30 refugees. A few miles out to sea the boat broke down, unable to support so much weight. The voyagers drifted for three days without food or water before being rescued by the U.S. Coast Guard. "There were thousands of us wanting to come to [Key West] and kiss the earth," said Arenas. "That day we became human beings" (Arenas in García, p. 62).

In May 1980 Arenas reaches the United States. Although he finally has the opportunity of tasting the freedom that he has been fighting for most of his life, the experience turns somewhat bitter. His impression is that the exiled Cuban community in Miami cares almost exclusively about generating money and not necessarily about helping others. At this point, he declares that "the difference between the communist and capitalist systems is that, although both give you a kick in the ass, in the communist system you have to applaud, while in the capitalist system you can scream. And I came here to scream" (*Before Night Falls,* p. 288). Nevertheless, Arenas finds friends in Miami: Reinaldo Sánchez, who offers him a position as visiting professor at the Florida International University, as well as the highly respected writers Lydia Cabrera and Enrique Labrador Ruiz. In December, after an invitation to speak at Columbia University, Arenas decides to move to New York City. In New York he continues to denounce the injustices he has experienced in Cuba, in part by founding, along with other Cubans living in exile, the *Mariel* literary magazine. This magazine not only serves to vindicate some of the literary figures marginalized by the Castro regime (such as Lezama Lima) but also to attack the bourgeois morality so prevalent in Miami.

THE MARIEL BOATLIFT

In 1980 more than 125,000 Cubans left the island between the months of April and September in an unprecedented mass migration, heading especially, but not exclusively, for the United States. This 159-day exodus, known as the Mariel Boatlift, started when six Cubans drove a bus through the gates of the Peruvian Embassy in search of political asylum. After the embassy's gates were demolished and Cuban guards left the place, thousands of Cubans gradually entered the embassy in an attempt to leave their country. Once the initial turmoil subsided, Castro authorized the departure of all those who wished to leave Cuba. The port of Mariel became the point of departure for Cubans who emigrated in boats that were allowed to carry dissidents to the United States. This authorization caught by surprise U.S. president Jimmy Carter who, after initially refusing to admit legally any Cuban migrating through the port of Mariel, "was forced to change his policy and announce that the U.S. would accept all Cuban refugees" (Powelson, p. 524).

By the end of the 1980s Arenas discovers that he has contracted AIDS (Acquired Immune Deficiency Syndrome). After three years of living with the disease and its complications, the writer commits suicide. He leaves a note explaining that since he feels too weak to continue fighting for Cuba's freedom, it is better for him to end his life. Yet he wants his suicide to be understood not "as a message of defeat but of continued struggle and of hope" (*Before Night Falls,* p. 317).

> You are the heirs of all my terrors, but also of my hope that Cuba will soon be free. I am satisfied to have contributed, though in a very small way, to the triumph of this freedom. I end

> my life voluntarily because I cannot continue working. . . . There is only one person I hold accountable: Fidel Castro. The sufferings of exile, the pain of being banished . . . the loneliness, and the diseases contracted in exile would probably never have happened . . . in my country.
>
> (*Before Night Falls,* p. 317)

Homosexuality and Cuban society. In his tribute to Arenas, Guillermo Cabrera Infante (see ***Three Trapped Tigers,*** also covered in *Latin American Literature and Its Times*) states that "three passions ruled the life and death of Reinaldo Arenas: literature not as a game but as a flame that consumes, passive sex and active politics. Of the three, the dominant passion was sex" (Cabrera Infante, p. 412). The notion of "passive sex" might be confusing without an understanding of how Cuban society views homosexuality.

CUBAN HOMOSEXUALITY IN FILM

In *Before Night Falls* Reinaldo Arenas talks enthusiastically about his participation as an interviewee in the 1984 documentary *Improper Conduct* by Néstor Almendros and Orlando Jiménez Leal. The film denounces the injustices perpetrated against homosexuals in Cuba and includes 26 interviews that address different homophobic policies instituted by the Cuban government after the Revolution and up to the early 1980s. Produced with French financial support, this documentary presents the point of view of artists who lived in exile and pitted themselves against Castro's government.

Arenas humorously proposes four categories of gays in Cuban society: the "dog collar gay" (a boisterous homosexual who was continually being arrested and who lived under constant surveillance by the government), the "common gay" (a homosexual who never takes great risks and has relations with other men who think of themselves as gays), the "closeted gay" (a homosexual whom nobody knows is gay), and the "royal gay" (those who can afford to be openly gay because of their close connections to Castro's government) (*Before Night Falls,* pp. 77-78). Even though he proposes these categories, Arenas does not define homosexuality as a preference for relations with someone of the same gender. In fact, for many Cubans, a man who has sex with another man is not necessarily regarded as a homosexual. In order to be considered a homosexual in Cuba a man has to play the passive role in the sexual act. It is not the norm there, explains Arenas, "for one queer to go to bed with another queer" but rather for a "queer" to go to bed with a "real macho" man (*Before Night Falls,* p. 108). On the other hand, some Cuban men are suspected of being gay if they do not behave in a macho way—that is, if they do not like rough sports or are not physically strong or aggressive.

Literary context. Arenas wrote vigorously in exile, producing novels, short stories, essays, and a long poem, as well as his autobiography. The suicide note at the end of *Before Night Falls* suggests that he wrote his memoir because literature constitutes a powerful weapon to convey his experiences (in his words, "los terrores") as someone who does not conform to the norm. More specifically, Arenas wants to provide insight into what it means to be an anti-Castro, homosexual writer living in Cuba (although he also addresses how those same characteristics can make him a pariah in exile).

Leaving Cuba in 1965, novelist Cabrera Infante was one of the most renowned Cuban writers in the first wave of post-Revolution exiles. Arenas emigrated in the next wave, distinguishing himself, in Cabrera Infante's estimation, as "the only Cuban novelist who could be called a child of the Revolution" (Cabrera Infante, p. 78). In his memoir, though, Arenas gives the impression that there could have been others:

> What did happen to most of the talented young men of my generation? Nelson Rodríquez, for example, author of *El regalo* [*The Gift*], was executed. Delfín Prats, one of the best poets among us, became a dehumanized alcoholic; Pepe el Loco, the bold chronicler, ended up killing himself; Luis Rogelio Nogueras, a talented poet, recently died under suspicious circumstances, it being unclear whether from AIDS or at the hands of Castro's police. . . . Guillermo Rosales, an excellent novelist, is wasting away in a home for the handicapped in Miami.
>
> (*Before Night Falls,* pp. 88–89)

Events in History at the Time the Memoir Was Written

Cuban exiles. Like prior Cuban immigrants to the United States, the Mariel newcomers included enterprising writers who founded publications. In 1983, along with Roberto Valero and

Juan Abreau, Arenas began publishing in New York the journal *Revista Mariel* (which later, under different ownership, became *Mariel Magazine*). The journal provided a forum for well-known emigré authors as well as for Latin American and European writers. It also published pieces by writers who had been censored or silenced back in Cuba and so had never enjoyed the readership their work merited.

Ever since the arrest of Padilla in 1971 writers had become more outspoken about human rights abuses and political and economic developments in Cuba. They formed the *Comité de Intelectuales por la Libertad de Cuba* (Committee of Intellectuals for the Liberty of Cuba), holding meetings in Paris (1979), New York (1980), and Caracas (1987) to discuss Cuban affairs. In 1991, when intellectuals back in Cuba were imprisoned for issuing a declaration that called for democratic reforms, more than 100 emigrés rushed to their defense with a letter praising them for working within the system to effect change and urging outside nations to keep a close watch on the prisoners' future.

Meanwhile, Cuban writers living in the United States complained of being treated poorly by mainstream publishers. They also complained of being denied academic positions because of their anti-Castro (equated to anticommunist) views, arguing that some liberal-minded institutions looked askance at them for this reason (García, p. 193). In his collection of essays, *Necesidad de libertad,* Arenas observed,

> The Cuban intellectual is forced to disappear two times. First the Cuban State erases him from the literary map of his own country; afterward, the preponderant and mighty Left, installed, of course, in capitalist countries, condemns him to silence. . . . [In certain circles] being anticommunist is in bad taste. . . .
>
> (Arenas in García, p. 193)

Other emigrés vocalized their support for Castro's government. The pro-Castro contingent founded a journal of their own, *Areíto,* which Arenas dubbed "the official organ of the Cuban state police in New York" (Arenas in García, p. 203). It numbered among the more conservative publications put out by Cuban exiles. Arenas's own *Revista Mariel* (1983-85), which gave voice to anti-Castro intellectuals, occupied the other end of the spectrum. Through these and other journals, the exiles engaged in vigorous dialogue about issues particular to their homeland, status, and identity. They also produced novels, poems, testimonies, and autobiographies (like *Before Night Falls*) that convey the experience of the more than one million emigrés who attempted, with greater or lesser success, to settle in the United States from 1959 to 1994. In Arenas's case, the writer continued to feel like an alien:

> I have realized that an exile has no place anywhere . . . because the place where we started to dream . . . is always the world of our dreams. . . . I ceased to exist when I went into exile.
>
> (*Before Night Falls,* p. 293)

Homosexuality in the 1980s—from Cuba to the United States. By the 1980s the perception of homosexuals in Cuba started to change for the better. Although homophobia was not eradicated, more liberal philosophies towards sexuality emerged, fostering a different understanding of homosexuals. As Ian Lumsden points out, part of this shift had to do with changes in the government's institutionalized homophobic practices. More exactly, the 1979 Penal Code "decriminalized homosexuality per se" to the extent that "it is . . . perfectly legal for consenting adults to engage in homosexual acts in private." However, other repressive statutes in the Penal Code, such as the prohibition of "private homosexual acts inadvertently seen by third parties," remained intact until 1987 (Lumsden, pp. 81, 82).

By 1990 the worldwide AIDS epidemic was entering its second decade. That year the United States reported 43,352 AIDS victims, more than half from homosexual/bisexual contact. It was common knowledge that the infection occurs through HIV, the human immunodeficiency virus, which travels from one body to another, often through blood or semen. In most cases, HIV slowly destroys the immune system and leaves victims at the mercy of opportunistic illnesses.

A number of drugs have been developed to battle AIDS. In 1987 the Food and Drug Administration officially approved AZT (azidothymidine) as a therapeutic treatment against AIDS. But the drug had multiple side-effects, such as anemia and impotence. By 1990 Arenas was experiencing some of AZT's side-effects and so he committed suicide by taking pills. As many as 165 other AIDS victims are known to have opted for suicide by the end of the 1980s. Almost all were men, and 35 percent killed themselves, as Arenas did, through some form of drug poisoning.

Reviews. Literary critics from Latin America and the United States have unanimously praised *Before Night Falls,* calling it "one of the great books of our times" (Manrique, p. 17) as well as "one of the most explosive, liberating texts to come from Latin America . . . a classic that readers of the future will not resist" (Stavans, p. 797). Some critics note that to some degree the book is a combination of different literary styles and categories; at the same time, reviews generally praise it for its straightforwardness. In *World Literature Today,* Ilan Stavans compliments Arenas's memoir for its moving content: *Before Night Falls* is "a testament of Arenas's indomitable spirit and his confrontational attitude towards the world . . . a rare, disturbing book with a message that refuses to fade away long after the last breathtaking page is read" (Stavans, p. 797).

—Gilberto M. Blasini

For More Information

Arenas, Reinaldo. *Before Night Falls.* Trans. Dolores M. Koch. New York: Penguin Books, 1993.

Cabrera Infante, Guillermo. *Mea Cuba.* Trans. Kenneth Hall and Guillermo Cabrera Infante. London: Faber & Faber, 1994.

Castro, Fidel. *Palabras a los intelectuales.* La Habana: Ediciones del Consejo Nacional de Cultura, 1961.

Cote, Timothy R., Robert J. Biggar, and Andrew L. Dannenberg. "Risk of Suicide among Persons with AIDS." *Journal of the American Medical Association* 268, no. 15 (October 21, 1992): 2066-68.

García, Maria Cristina. *Havana USA: Cuban Exiles and Cuban Americans in South Florida, 1959-1994.* Berkeley: University of California Press, 1996.

Lumsden, Ian. *Machos, Maricones, and Gays: Cuba and Homosexuality.* Philadelphia: Temple University Press, 1996.

Manrique, Jaime. "An Exile from All Conventions." *Lambda Book Report* 4, no. 1 (November-December 1993): 16-17.

Nichols, John Spicer. "The Press in Cuba." In *The Cuba Reader: The Making of a Revolutionary Society.* Eds. Philip Brenner, et. al. New York: Grove Press, 1989.

Powelson, Michael. "Mariel Boatlift." *Encyclopedia of Latin American History and Culture.* Vol. 3. New York: Macmillan Library Reference, 1996.

Stavans, Ilan. Review of *Before Night Falls. World Literature Today* 68, no. 2 (Autumn 1994): 797.

Suchlicki, Jaime. *Cuba: From Columbus to Castro.* 2nd ed. Washington: Pergamon-Brassey's International Defense, 1986.

Valero, Roberto. "Heberto Padilla." *Encyclopedia of Latin American History and Culture.* Vol. 4. New York: Macmillan, 1996.

Biography of a Runaway Slave

by
Miguel Barnet

Miguel Barnet was born in 1940 and raised in Havana, Cuba. In the late 1950s he became interested in Afro-Cuban religion and trained as a folklorist under the direction of Fernando Ortiz, a pioneer in the study of Afro-Cuban culture. The Cuban Revolution (1959) had a tremendous impact on Barnet's life and outlook, and fueled his passion to learn about the people of Cuba. In 1963 he first heard of Esteban Montejo, who was then 103 years old. Interviews with the former slave and runaway evolved into *Biography of a Runaway Slave*, which is considered the first Latin American testimonial novel. Barnet has continued to experiment with this form in *La Canción de Rachel* (1969) and *Gallego* (1981). Although his international reputation rests on his testimonial novels, his poetry has won Cuban and international awards.

THE LITERARY WORK

A biography of Esteban Montejo set in Cuba from his birth in 1860 to the turn of the century; published in Spanish (as *Biografía de un cimarrón*) in 1966, in English in 1968 under the title *Autobiography of a Runaway Slave*, and in 1994 as *Biography of a Runaway Slave*.

SYNOPSIS

Written by Barnet in the first-person voice of Montejo, the biography recounts Montejo's life as a slave, runaway, plantation worker, and rebel soldier in the Cuban War of Independence.

Events in History at the Time the Biography Takes Place

Sugar is made out of blood. Sugar has held paramount importance in Cuba's economy and society since the nineteenth century, during which sugar plantations expanded considerably in size and number. By the 1860s so much land and energy were devoted to sugarcane that the colony—Spain's last major possession in Latin America—had to import food from Spain, the United States, and elsewhere. Cuba depended greatly upon the success of the sugarcane harvest, and on the labor of slaves in the cane fields and sugar mills.

Working on the sugar plantations, the slaves cleared virgin forest, planted the sugarcane, and harvested it. White overseers directed the work, often resorting to violent punishments to discipline the slaves, including public whippings and shacklings and even murder if the slaves resisted. The hardest season for the slaves was the harvest, which lasted for six months and demanded as many as 20 hours a day of labor in the fields.

Sugarcane had to be processed in the plantation's mill, or *trapiche*. Directed by a white overseer (at times an American or Englishman), called the "sugarmaster," slaves transformed the cane—by crushing, boiling, crystallizing, and draining it—into cane syrup, *muscovado* (unrefined sugar), molasses, and white sugar. Work in the sugar mills, though less arduous than in the fields, was still backbreaking, and fatal accidents with machinery were not uncommon. Beginning in the 1850s the increasing use of centrifuges allowed dry white sugar to be separated easily from the muscovado. Improvements in machinery throughout the nineteenth century allowed larger and larger mills to operate. The slaves continued to fill unskilled positions; blacks, it was believed, did not have the intelligence to direct the extraction process or handle the steam engines used in the mill.

The planter, or owner of the plantation, rarely appeared in the mill or the fields. Many did not even live on the plantation, but resided in the capital, Havana, or in another city or town. Occupying the upper echelons of Cuban society, the planters consisted of two groups: they were either members of oligarchic and interrelated families that had been in Cuba since before the nineteenth century, or self-made immigrant men from Spain and elsewhere in Europe. The established families tended to be old-fashioned and slow to change, in contrast to the immigrants, who spearheaded the mechanical innovations in sugar production.

Slaves. In the nineteenth century increasing numbers of African slaves entered Cuba. The expansion of the sugar plantations generated a growing need for field hands that the existing slave population could not meet. There was a low rate of childbirth among these slaves, explainable by the fact that more male slaves had been brought over than female because women were considered inferior for sugarcane labor. The infant mortality rate and the death rate from accident, overwork, or epidemic were also high. Other factors contributed to the decrease in the domestic slave population, too. Cuban slaves could purchase their own freedom, and many took the less costly course of simply running away. A typical sugar plantation had to replace 8 to 10 percent of its slaves annually.

Whereas in the United States the slave population expanded steadily over several generations, in Cuba slaves arrived in huge numbers during a short span of time. This explains why in 1870, during the time of the biography, as many as 75 percent of slaves in Cuba had been born in Africa. Most of these people came from the Atlantic coast of Africa, where they lived in nations that were broadly defined by ethnicity, culture, or geography. The two largest nations were the Lucumí (Yoruba) and the Congo (people from the Congo River area). Some of the smaller nations included the Carabalí, the Fanti, and the Ebros. Once in Cuba the slaves became homogenized into large categories. It was common practice for whites and blacks in Cuba to stereotype slaves and free blacks according to their nation. For example, Congos were said to be short, Carabalí proud, and Lucumí industrious.

Slaves lived in *barracoons*, small, hot, cramped quarters that had only one entrance, which was locked at night. With only a small hole or barred window for air, the rooms grew stiflingly hot. Fleas and ticks were a constant nuisance in the barracoons, whose conditions incubated disease and ill health. Next to their quarters, slaves grew small fruit and vegetable gardens to supplement their monotonous diet of beans, rice, and beef jerky.

Children began working at five or six years old. They progressed from chores around the mill and fields to full-time labor in the fields before they were teenagers. Some children were trained to become servants and nurses in the owner's house. As in other slave societies, the easier life indoors caused envy and distrust between the household servants and field hands.

Afro-Cuban culture. Slaves sustained much of their former African culture in Cuba. Food, games, language, music, divination, magic, and religion from many regions of Africa continued and merged with one another and with European cultural forms in Cuba. In contrast to the whites, who mostly imported their culture wholesale from Europe, the slaves fused or syncretized African and European sources to develop their own spiritual and material dimensions of life, which helped to sustain them under the brutality of slavery.

Santería, a Yoruba-derived religion that mixed African and European sources and remained hidden from the surface of the society, is a case in point. Lucumí slaves brought the worship of *orishas*, or African gods, to Cuba. There the orishas acquired the names and likenesses of Catholic saints, since the colonial authorities would not permit the open worship of African deities. For example, slaves fused or syncretized Oshún, the Yoruba divinity that controls love, marriage, and children, with Our Lady of La Caridad del Cobre, the Catholic patron saint of Cuba. Oshún's love of copper facilitated her syncretization with this Virgin of Copper (the Spanish word *cobre* means "copper"). The island's resources prompted modifications, too. Coconuts became the symbols of the orisha, replacing the kola nut used in Africa.

Although they were expected to be baptized and to convert to the Catholic faith, most rural slaves had very limited contact with the Church beyond a rudimentary baptism, which meant little to the participants besides payment to the officiating priest. Barnet explains that "the plantation bell calling [the slave] to the implacable chores of the day had much greater significance than the bell on the chapel; the work-bell was resonant and cruel, the worship-bell dull and hollow" (Barnet, "The Culture that Sugar Created," p. 43). In contrast, the continuing belief in African gods brought solace and meaning to the slaves' lives.

The *santeros*, or Santería priests, worshiped their gods under the gaze of plantation overseers, the Catholic Church, and other authorities by keeping secret the African identity of the saint to which they ostensibly prayed. At fiestas for a certain Catholic saint, the blacks joined the parades and celebrations that outwardly expressed their devotion to the saint, and held their own separate and private celebrations for their version of the saint. In the cities, *cabildos*, or fraternal clubs of blacks and mulattos, were important incubators of Santería and Afro-Cuban culture. The practice of Santería and other African lore became a badge of identity that distinguished its practitioners from Cuba's Spaniards, Creoles, and Chinese.

Although Santería and other African cultural expressions began exclusively with blacks, elements of this culture spread throughout Cuba among the lower classes of all colors. White overseers learned some aspects of Afro-Cuban belief and culture through their black mistresses and through daily contact with slaves. White children reared by black and mulatto nurses were taught African-derived beliefs while still in the cradle. Yet, because of class consciousness and racism, upper-class and, later, middle-class Cubans did their best to reject or ignore the African roots of Cuban society.

The end of slavery. On August 26, 1833, Great Britain passed the Emancipation Act, abolishing slavery in all British lands, including colonies; for humanitarian reasons and to protect their economic interests in the West Indies, the English pressured Spain to abolish slavery in Cuba. If abolition were achieved, Cuba's industries would not have an unfair economic advantage. Planters, of course, felt threatened by the prospect of abolition since this would seriously cut into their efficiency and profits. Neither the poor white farmers, called *guajiros*, nor the significant number of free blacks and mulattos on the island would deign to do the work of the slaves in the cane fields, preferring starvation to such labor. The planters feared that without slavery there would not be enough workers to harvest the sugarcane. A failed harvest would devastate them economically. The Spanish authorities exploited the planters' fear by threatening to free the slaves if the planters agitated for independence. The worldwide pressure to end the slave trade ironically prompted one of the largest importations of slaves ever into Cuba: between 1856 and 1860 some 90,000 African slaves were brought to the island. The movement to end the trade drove up the price of slaves, leading to further debate about the costs and benefits of slavery.

CIMARRONES

Since the earliest colonial days, slaves in Cuba managed to escape from their masters and live as runaways (or *cimarrones*) in the woods and mountains. Groups of cimarrones formed communities and built *palenques,* well hidden and easily defended dwellings. Some palenques became platforms for resisting Spanish authority. There were also individuals and small groups of runaways who lived independently of any fixed palenque. The cimarrones aided other runaways, pirates, and the French attack on Havana in 1539. Their members raided plantations, killed whites, stole food and guns, and freed slaves. The Cuban Office for the Capture of Maroons (another word for cimarrones) reported thousands of runaways between 1795 and 1846. A few palenques survived into the 1860s, but their existence was threatened by the expansion of sugar plantations. Also, the rise in slave prices made the capture of runaways a more lucrative trade and the existence of palenques, which often traded with guajiros and free blacks, perilous. Many guajiros became devoted slave hunters. Cimarrones like Montejo lived alone in fear of betrayal, even by other runaways.

In the 1860s a group of wealthy planters formed a Reformist party that advocated greater political representation for Cuba in Spain. These men foresaw the end of slavery—Spain itself had passed an anti-slavery measure in 1845. Their plan was to gain political control and then seek the best means of abolition; they wanted to be

LIBRARY
COLBY-SAWYER COLLEGE
NEW LONDON, NH 03257

An 1869 illustration of the Cuban rebellion against Spain led by Carlos Manuel de Céspedes. Here the rebels are shown setting fire to the cane fields and houses of a sugar plantation.

compensated for the emancipation of their slaves. Other groups sought annexation by the United States, where, until January 1, 1863, slavery was still legal and thriving.

In the mid-1800s an alternate source of labor was found: Indians from the Yucatan and Chinese workers—125,000 Chinese by the early 1870s—came to Cuba with eight-year contracts that bound them to sugar plantations, as slaves in all but name. They were treated even worse than slaves, since their value to the plantation owner ceased at the end of their contracts, and many of them perished.

In 1865 the last ship carrying slaves arrived in Cuba. The end of the trade caused the price of slaves to skyrocket. Only the wealthiest planters could afford to buy more slaves. The economics of slavery became much harder to sustain. Three years later the planter Carlos Manuel de Céspedes rebelled against Spain's control of Cuba and slavery, calling for gradual abolition in Cuba. In 1879, the Prime Minister of Spain, General Arsenio Martínez Campos, freed all Cuban slaves without compensation to the owners. He did, however, stipulate that the freed slaves serve eight years for their master as *patronatos,* which meant they remained in the same barracoons, and did the same work for food, lodging, and a small wage. In order to avoid the expenses of providing for workers outside of the harvest season, many masters freed their slaves outright and then hired them to work only for the harvest. The patronato system as a temporary compromise between slavery and free labor failed, and by general consensus it ended two years early.

The end of slavery in 1886 did not bring great change to the lives of most blacks, a theme that is treated by Montejo in the biography. The freedmen continued working in the cane fields and mills, often for the same master they had served as slaves.

> There were masters, or rather, owners, who believed that blacks were made for locking up and whipping. So they treated them the same as before. To my mind many blacks didn't realize things had changed because they kept on saying: "Your blessing Master."
>
> (Barnet, *Biography of a Runaway Slave,* p. 62)

Educational opportunities were limited for the ex-slaves, as was entrance to other occupations. Only literate men could gain the vote, a qualification that held back almost all blacks. Racism replaced slavery as the system separating whites from blacks.

Ten Years' War. The desire of the planters for independence from Spain blossomed during the 1860s. Reform-minded Cuban planters felt burdened by the inefficient overseas Spanish

LIBRARY COLBY-SAWYER COLLEGE NEW LONDON, NH 03257

bureaucracy, and resented the preferential treatment given to *peninsulares* (Spanish-born residents of Cuba) by bureaucrats and judges. Many felt that they could guide their own destiny better than Madrid did.

In 1867 the Spanish government exacerbated the Cubans' resentment by levying an extra property tax during an economic recession. The next year the Glorious Revolution in Madrid, which toppled the Spanish monarchy, brought more political turbulence to Cuba, and gave the rebellious planters in Oriente, the eastern province of the island, a chance to rise. On October 10, 1868, Carlos Manuel de Céspedes took up arms against the colonial government, declaring the independence of Cuba and freeing his own slaves. (As noted, he called for gradual abolition of all slavery on the island.) Many flocked to join his army, which initially succeeded by capturing two towns. Céspedes's revolt swelled as whites and blacks, slaves and the free, joined the ranks of the rebels, who were led almost exclusively by men from the wealthy planter families.

The Spanish army, backed by the ferocious volunteers—peninsulares who fought for Spain—launched a vicious campaign of mass murder and repression against the rebels. Rebel sympathizers—most notably the future revolutionary José Martí (author of **"Our America"** [also covered in *Latin American Literature and Its Times*])—were exiled or imprisoned. Pressed back by the superior numbers and resources of the Spanish, the rebels retreated to the hills and woods and waged a guerilla war.

The rebellion, however, could not be squelched quickly, and the war dragged on for years. The rebels succeeded only in the limited engagements of guerilla warfare. The skilled rebel commanders Maximo Gómez and Antonio Maceo wanted to bring the war to the western, and more prosperous, provinces of Cuba and destroy the plantations, which would cripple the island, but their plans were handicapped by the conservative leaders of the rebellion. Switching from guerilla warfare to pitched battles, rebel generals twice defeated larger Spanish forces, but these victories proved costly since they depleted the rebels' ammunition and resources.

In 1877, with the Spanish king back on his throne, the reinforced Spanish army launched a successful offensive against a dwindling rebel force. In February 1878 the war almost ended with the Pact of Zanjón, which granted the rebels amnesty, and gave Cuba increased political representation in Spain, equal to that of Puerto Rico. Maceo would not agree to end the war without full independence and returned to battle, but his small force could not hold out. In May 1878 he was defeated and sent into exile.

The War of Independence. The dream of independence did not die in 1878. Cuban exiles began to organize, plan, and raise funds for a successful revolution. José Martí, an exile living in New York, led the efforts of Cubans abroad. An indefatigable writer, speaker, and organizer, Martí united the various exile groups interested in liberating Cuba. He envisioned a new Cuba that would be racially and socially egalitarian, politically and economically independent of Spain and the United States, and a true democracy, unlike the republics ruled by petty tyrants throughout Latin America. Cubans everywhere caught the passion of Martí's message.

DESCRIPTION OF SPAIN'S DESTRUCTIVE CAMPAIGN BY A FOREIGN TRAVELER

"I traveled by rail from Havana to Matanzas. The country outside the military posts was practically depopulated. Every house had been burned, banana trees cut down, cane fields swept with fire, and everything in the shape of food destroyed. . . . I did not see a house, man, woman, or child, a horse, mule, or cow, nor even a dog. I did not see a sign of life, except an occasional vulture or buzzard sailing through the air. The country was wrapped in the stillness of death and the silence of desolation."

(Simons, p. 162)

Martí put his plans into action in 1895; while rebellions broke out across the island, a small force led by him and Maximo Gómez invaded eastern Cuba. In a skirmish with the Spanish, tragedy struck and Martí was killed. Gómez reunited with Maceo to lead the rebel army. Unlike the upper-class leadership of the Ten Years' War, men from a broader span of society spearheaded this revolution. Despite the Spanish army's superior numbers, the war did not turn in its favor. The Spaniards were fighting not just a war but a revolutionary army that commanded support throughout Cuba. Under Gómez, revolutionaries burned plantations and brought the entire economy under their control. Bandits, such as Manuel García, who had vague political motives before the war, joined the rebel cause.

Spanish troops at an ordnance depot in Havana during the Spanish-American War.

They formed small, undisciplined bands, separate from the trained forces under Gómez. Staying in the hills and woods, living off the land and local farms, the rebels had spread across Cuba to the western provinces by October of 1895.

Nonetheless, rebel successes slowed as counter-insurgents of Spanish descent joined the Spanish forces. By mid-1896 war had engulfed the entire country, and almost all males had joined one side or the other. General Valeriano Weyler, the Spanish commander, had his troops viciously drive more than 300,000 rural civilians into the Spanish-controlled cities, thereby depriving the rebels of their support network. His destructive campaign converted many previously neutral Cubans into new rebels against him.

Although in 1896 Gómez and fellow commander Calixto García controlled the center and east of the island, they lacked the resources to launch an offensive. After the Spanish trapped Maceo's army and killed him in battle, desertion from the rebel forces increased dramatically. By the end of 1896 the western provinces were firmly back in Spanish control.

The U.S. intervenes. On the evening of February 15, 1898, the U.S.S. *Maine*—an American battleship anchored in Havana's port—blew up and sank, killing most of the crew. Although the cause of the explosion could not be proved, many Americans believed—or were eager to believe—that the Spanish caused the destruction. Already there existed a great deal of American public antipathy toward the Spanish in Cuba, an attitude instigated in part by the war-mongering of William Randolph Hearst's *New York Journal*. The *Maine* tragedy led directly to the United States's declaring war on Spain in April. Known as the Spanish-American War, the conflict pitted Spain against the United States in a contest that spread from Cuba to Puerto Rico and the Philippines.

A U.S. force of 6,000 men led by General William Rufus Shafter invaded eastern Cuba on June 22, 1898. At the Battle of San Juan Hill, their only major conflict in Cuba, U.S. soldiers forced the Spanish to retreat, and took the outer defenses of the city of Santiago. The U.S. Navy further defeated the Spanish fleet outside Santiago. By mid-July the city had surrendered. This U.S. victory along with others in the Philippines and Puerto Rico led to the capitulation of Spanish forces. Cuba gained its independence in 1902, while Puerto Rico and the Philippines became U.S. possessions.

Postwar relations with the United States. Despite a troubling history of American imperialist ambition in the Caribbean basin, for much of the nineteenth century many Cubans looked upon the United States positively as an example in their own struggle for liberty against colonial oppression. This attitude shifted dramatically into a negative one, beginning with the Cuban War of Independence.

Although the United States invaded Cuba on the side of the rebels, tensions developed between the U.S. forces and the rebels. Racist U.S. soldiers, overwhelmingly white, disparaged the blacks that comprised the majority of the rebel forces. The U.S. soldiers considered the Cubans incompetent, and lavished more praise upon the chivalrous actions of the Spanish enemy. Major William Schafter even contemptuously suggested to the rebel commander Calixto García that his local forces serve as laborers instead of soldiers.

The United States governed Cuba from 1899 until 1902, during which the Cuban rebel army did not receive the honors earned by its long struggle. The U.S. occupiers believed that their own army and navy deserved all the credit for the victory. Neither the rebel army, nor its commander, Gómez, was invited to attend the formal withdrawal of Spanish forces from Havana in December 1898. During the occupation, tensions between Cuban and U.S. soldiers boiled over into street fighting in Havana and Cienfuegos.

The island was in ruins after the war; the population, plantations, and sugar mills had been decimated. U.S. companies and investors received the lion's share of opportunities in rebuilding the island's infrastructure. Tariffs in the United States gave Cuban sugar an advantage over beet sugar from Europe, which encouraged the re-dedication of the island to sugar cane production. U.S. investors assumed control of a large amount of the sugar industry, and took their profits out of the nation.

During the drafting of the Cuban Constitution, the U.S. government demanded that the Cubans accept the Platt Amendment as part of the constitution. Cuban politicians initially opposed this amendment because it granted the United States the right to intervene in Cuban affairs whenever it believed the island's independence to be in question. The amendment also gave the United States the right to maintain naval bases in Cuba, and—the most patronizing of all—to intervene if Havana was literally not kept clean. But the Cuban drafters of the constitution were forced to abandon their protest when General Leonard Wood, the leader of the U.S. occupation, made it clear that his army would not leave the island until the amendment had been passed. Thereafter, politics in Cuba would hinge on the approval or disapproval of the United States, squelching the dream of true political and economic independence as envisioned by José Martí and his fellow liberators.

The Biography in Focus

Plot summary. *Biography of a Runaway Slave* recounts Esteban Montejo's actions over the course of 40 years, along with his observations on Cuban society and the political events through which he lived. His descriptions of cultural life include sections on magic, religion, social and sexual relations, festivals, African slaves and *criollo* slaves (those born in Cuba), and sugarmaking. His observations are as important as the narrative of his life and adventures, for they provide an eyewitness account of a culture otherwise little known or documented.

Barnet organizes Montejo's life into three sections:

> **Slavery:** Montejo describes his childhood and young adulthood as a slave, and then his years—it is unclear how long—as a cimarrón or runaway. The section begins with some of the details of his birth in late 1860, and ends with the abolition of slavery in 1881.
>
> **Abolition of Slavery:** From approximately 1881 until 1895, Montejo works as a laborer in sugarcane fields and in sugar mills on plantations throughout the countryside. He conveys a picture of the emerging Afro-Cuban culture and the building tensions within colonial Cuba.
>
> **The War of Independence:** This section details Montejo's career as a rebel soldier in the War of Independence, beginning with his enlistment in December 1895. The section ends soon after the end of the war and includes Montejo's observations on the post-war Cuba.

Montejo was born on December 26, 1860. On the Catholic calendar, this is St. Stephen's Day, from which he attained the name Esteban (Spanish for "Stephen"). He is a *criollito* (a slave child born in Cuba); his father hails from Africa (a Lucumí); his mother, from Haiti. Since his original master sold him as a baby, he meets his parents for the first time as an adult.

When he is ten, Montejo works with a pick and shovel on the *bagazo,* the remains of the cane after cutting. He notes that "ten years of age then was like saying thirty now because children worked like oxen" (*Runaway Slave,* p. 22).

Montejo details life in the barracoons (slave quarters), describing the crowded, inadequate housing, as well as the slaves' games, fiestas, dances, and religion. "Strange as it may seem, blacks had fun in the barracoons," he asserts (*Runaway Slave,* p. 26). Despite the emerging slave culture, life in the barracoons takes its toll physically and spiritually: "it didn't take much to get tired of living that life. The ones who got used to it didn't have much spirit. Life in the woods was healthier. In the barracoons you caught a lot of diseases" (*Runaway Slave,* p. 41). Montejo decides to run away. Even as a child he always had "the spirit of a cimarrón in [him]" (*Runaway Slave,* p. 44). Although his first escape attempt fails, he later succeeds.

MAMBISES

At the start of the War of Independence the Spanish soldiers nicknamed black Cuban rebels *Mambises* (singular *Mambí*), which means the children of a monkey and buzzard. The rebels, however, accepted the derogatory name as a term for their ferocity and courage. The machete, the tool of the sugarcane laborer, became a weapon in the hands of the Mambises—and their symbol. Many lacked rifles and carried machetes into battle against the Spanish. In his first combat, at the Battle of Mal Tiempo, Montejo took the guns of cowardly Spanish soldiers after capturing them with just his machete from the sugar fields. He and other Mambises supplied the rebel troops with food by raiding farms for pigs and other supplies. Blacks and mulattos comprised between 75 and 85 percent of the Cuban rebel forces. About 40 percent of the rebel officers were blacks, in contrast to the Ten Years' War, in which whites dominated the leadership positions.

As a cimarrón (runaway slave), Montejo lives in a cave and then in the woods, where he travels constantly and covers his trail to avoid capture by slave-hunting guajiros. He keeps to himself, avoiding even other runaways, since "cimarrón with cimarrón sells cimarrón" (*Runaway Slave,* p. 47). He lives off the land, taking animals and plants in the forest, and stealing pigs from the farms of guajiros. In the woods he lacks for nothing, it would seem, except for the companionship of a woman. His solitary days in the woods are a defining time in Montejo's life. They established his lifelong desire for independence, and an inclination to avoid social entanglements. He lives by his hands and by his wits. After abolition, Montejo, unlike other freed slaves, does not crave the security of life on a plantation.

Montejo learns about the abolition of slavery by overhearing the celebrations of freed slaves, and he leaves his idyllic life in the forest. After wandering the land for a while, he finds a job cutting cane at a plantation in Las Villas. Life and work on plantations remains much the same as before abolition. While the barracoons no longer have locks, and the overseers do not "hit you like during slavery" (*Runaway Slave,* p. 61), the work and living conditions remain dismal. Montejo establishes a pattern of living and working at a single plantation for a couple years, and then moving to another for employment in the fields or sugar mills.

Despite having many lovers, Montejo neither lives in a family, nor knows his children. His relationships are temporary arrangements. After the War of Independence he will enter into an informal marriage, which he prefers to a permanent arrangement.

Montejo participates in social and cultural life. For example, he attends the annual fiesta celebration of San Juan in the town of Calabazar, and describes the three competing or overlapping sets of activities that occur there. During the day he sees the official Catholic ceremonies, and the accompanying secular celebrations that include music, dancing, drinking, and gambling. At night he attends the celebration of the Santería god, Oggún, who is associated with the saint. Although Montejo respects all religions, he believes that the African gods are stronger than the Christian god and dislikes the weak Catholic priests.

Montejo joins in the War of Independence in December 1895, leaving behind his life and work at a sugar mill. He provides an eyewitness account of the next three years of fighting. Montejo serves under three commanders during the course of the war. The first two were bandits before the war, and lead small, informal bands of men. The first, Tajó, he describes as "a horse thief in a liberator's uniform," and the second, Cayito, is no better (*Runaway Slave,* p. 169). Both men attempt to desert their commands and surrender to the Spanish. Tajó successfully switches his allegiances back and forth throughout the war, always searching for personal gain; but Cayito's attempt fails when his men discover his plan to go over to the Spanish, and murder him.

Montejo's third commander, Brigadier Higinio Esquerra, is a true revolutionary. Under his command, Montejo joins part of the main rebel army. He fights in the large battle of Arroyo Prieto, and serves as a soldier in a disciplined regiment.

When the war finally ends, Montejo compares his shock and disbelief to that which he felt when slavery ended. The victory finally strikes him when he reaches Havana, where he joins in the victory celebrations that continue for weeks. In Montejo's view the city is a crazy place full of women, drunks, dancing, violence, and chaotic merrymaking. He sees the U.S. soldiers taking control of the city and disrespecting Cuban women. In 1899 he joins a group of Mambises that clash with Yankee soldiers in Cienfuegos. In the end Montejo despairs of the corrupt city and returns to the countryside and the life of a sugarcane worker.

Magic and belief. Throughout Montejo's biography, there are descriptions of magic that at first glance may appear unbelievable to unaccustomed modern eyes. Montejo identifies two types of African-derived religion: Santería from the Lucumí, and magic from the Congo. He learns some magic from an older Congo man, including how to make and keep a tiny devil to do his bidding. Montejo also refers to stories about the supernatural and the magical, like men returning from the dead, as well as folk beliefs and tales about headless horsemen and ghosts. Although these stories and beliefs may sound fantastic, it is important not to dismiss them as nonsense.

For centuries stereotypes about African "witchdoctors" have inaccurately portrayed traditional healers in Africa and the New World as evil witches or quacks who rely on fear and superstition. These stereotypes are misguided. Traditional healers in Africa and Cuba had extensive, highly valued knowledge of medicinal herbs and plants, the properties of which form the basis of many Western medicines. The same knowledge of herbs and medicines was also used for malevolent purposes, such as providing poison for the tips of daggers used by black rebels in the Ten Years' War. Montejo tells of slaves who wielded magic to control or kill their masters. Regardless of the actual success of such magic, the belief that it was effective is significant, since it raised the slave, the least powerful person in society, over his master. This inversion through magic must have secured a modicum of self-respect and confidence among men and women at the mercy of a brutal system.

Along with the folktales and beliefs that Montejo relates, magic helped form for Africans and Afro-Cubans a separate identity and culture amid that of Spaniards, creoles, and Chinese. To dismiss Montejo's discussions of magic as nothing more than fantasies is to fail to recognize the beliefs that enabled slaves to create a viable Afro-Cuban culture while physically shackled.

Barnet/Montejo. When *Biography of a Runaway Slave* was first printed in English, the translator rendered the title *Autobiography of a Runaway Slave.* This misnomer gave the impression that Montejo had been the author of the work, and neglected Barnet's role in its creation, which was significant.

Barnet interviewed, arranged, edited, wrote, and rewrote the account. He questioned Montejo for several tape-recorded sessions over the course of several days. The questions that jogged Montejo's memory are not included in the text. Barnet took the transcripts from the sessions and arranged them into the biography's three major sections and smaller subsections. He edited Montejo's words, eliminating some incidents and phrasing, and adding other phrases that he found appropriate. Barnet's goal was neither pure replication of testimony nor pure fiction. He wanted to give a voice to the common people of Cuba by combining the anthropological and the literary. His work strove to challenge the notion that slaves and other marginal people had no history, or any connection to the history or consciousness of their times.

Sources and literary context. One of Barnet's major sources of inspiration was the work of his mentor, Fernando Ortiz, who had introduced the term "Afro-Cuban" in the 1910s. Ortiz's studies of Afro-Cuban culture were groundbreaking and opened the eyes of many middle-class Cubans to the reality and prominence of African-derived culture in Cuba.

In the 1950s Oscar Lewis, an anthropologist in the United States, started a movement to compile and relate the life-stories of individuals. In his *La Vida: A Puerto Rican Family in the Culture of Poverty—San Juan and New York,* Lewis strove to write according to his informants' wishes. Barnet followed Lewis's philosophy in general, but believed that the writer must also use his or her own imagination and not rely completely on informants.

Barnet wrote *Biography of a Runaway Slave* during an exciting period in Cuban literature. Initially the Cuban Revolution had inspired Cuban writers to experiment with styles in order to find a new form that expressed the emerging realities of a society undergoing radical change. Much of the Cuban literature of the 1960s, including Barnet's testimonial biography, shares certain themes: a critical view of pre-Revolutionary society; attempts to reconcile oneself with personal and social pasts; and a drive to capture the authentic language of the Cuban people.

Events in History at the Time the Biography Was Written

The Cuban Revolution. In 1959 Fidel Castro overthrew the dictator Fulgencio Batista in a revolution that enjoyed broad public support. The liberators were national heroes who had come to fulfill the promise of an independent Cuba cherished by Martí and others. Castro, the sole source of political power and the director of the Revolution, intended to reinvent Cuban society. He aimed to end the sugar industry's domination of the economy, so that Cuba would no longer be subject to foreign competition and the whims of the world markets for sugar. Castro planned to develop other industries and agricultural products, which would make Cuba less dependent upon the United States for food and manufactured goods. In 1960 he nationalized the sugar industry despite the protests of the U.S. government.

The next year Castro declared himself a communist. The United States broke off diplomatic relations, made attempts to remove Castro from power, and imposed an economic embargo on the island, which remains in effect (although relaxed to some degree in January 1999) 40 years later. That same year an army of Cuban exiles, trained and supported by the U.S. Central Intelligence Agency, attempted to invade Cuba at the Bay of Pigs, but suffered a humiliating defeat from Castro's army. Later in 1962 the world almost saw nuclear war when U.S. President John F. Kennedy confronted Soviet Premier Nikita Krushchev over the presence of Soviet missiles in Cuba. The United States set up a naval blockade of the island, whereupon the Soviets backed down and removed the missiles. These U.S. attempts to control events in Cuba followed the pattern of intervention that had been established during the Spanish-American War, antagonizing Cubans.

These conflicts, on the other hand, bolstered many Cubans' enthusiasm for Castro, and garnered the respect and admiration of other Latin Americans. It appeared that Castro was raising a prostrate Cuba from generations of U.S. political, economic, and cultural hegemony. At the same time, his Revolution improved the living conditions for the poorest Cubans, raising their standards of literacy, health, housing, education, and sanitation.

Cuban intellectuals. For three days in June 1961 Castro addressed a prominent group of intellectuals at the National Library in Havana. In his speeches he outlined the Revolution's goals for artists and writers, establishing the official policy of the government toward the arts until 1968. The Revolution did not limit the freedom of the true artist, he claimed, but rather gave him or her the opportunity to serve the people whose freedom had been denied for so long. Artists must be willing, said Castro, to dedicate their abilities to the Revolution. They should help form a cultural revolution in addition to the socioeconomic one. The art they produced should not be for personal prosperity but for the benefit of their contemporaries, the people of Cuba.

Those intellectuals and artists whose work did not reflect the ideals of the Revolution received cold rebukes from the government. Their jobs were terminated, their books were not published, and their art was not displayed. In one renowned case, the poet Heberto Padilla was imprisoned for verse that was critical of the government. A number of artists, including Padilla, ultimately fled the island to pursue their art in exile.

Although Castro's new Cuba caused some artists to flee, others answered the call to celebrate the popular culture of Cuba, and experimented with styles to complement its new society. Genres such as the novel were transformed to accommodate revolutionary concerns and beliefs, and the testimonial novel—oral testimony told to a transcriber—was born. Barnet wrote that "with a brush stroke we became the spokesmen of an all-knowing view of the world and our role in the life of our country" (*Runaway Slave,* p. 204).

The closing section from Castro's "Words to the Intellectuals" has particular relevance for Barnet's *Biography of a Runaway Slave*:

> We recently had the experience of meeting an old woman, 108 years old, who had just learned to read and write, and we proposed to her that she write a book. She had been a slave, and we wanted to know what the world looked like to her as a slave, what her first impressions were, of her masters, of her fellow slaves. I believe that this old woman can write something more

interesting than any of us could about that era. . . . Things like these are the fruit of the Revolution! Who can write about what the slave endured better than she, and who can write about the present better than you?

(Castro, p. 298)

Castro is here calling for a new history that includes the voices of oppressed participants. Barnet was a student in Havana at that time. Then and later, he would have had the opportunity to hear or read accounts of Castro's words, and be influenced by the message.

As early as 1959, two months after his victory, Castro counseled "public condemnation against any people so filled with old vices and prejudices that they would discriminate against Cubans over questions of lighter and darker skin" (Castro in Cannon, p. 114). On the heels of this antiracist declaration came advances in civil rights for black Cubans. An adviser to Castro's government recalls how its new leaders "opened up the beaches, they opened up the hotels . . . they put the weight of the society . . . against racism. . . . The whole thing took place with surprising speed, with surprisingly little opposition" (Boorstein in Cannon, p. 114). Certainly Cuba did not rid itself of racism—to a large extent a legacy of the slavery featured in the 1966 biography of Esteban Montejo. But Castro's stance meant the government was attaching a negative value to prejudice against blacks in Cuba, making the biography a timely publication indeed.

Reviews. By 1980 *Biografía de un cimarrón* had sold better than any other Cuban book published since the Castro Revolution (Sklodowska in Luis and González, p. 61). It has been translated into many European languages, adapted into two films, and transformed into a year-long radio serial in Cuba. Early reviewers of the English translation, which bore the title *Autobiography of a Runaway Slave,* considered the book in light of its importance to the study of Cuban history. Pritchard Flynn wrote that it "will prove invaluable" for its detailed accounts of Afro-Cuban life (Flynn, p. 100). In contrast Paul Bailey said the book "has little value as a historical document" because Montejo's understanding of the War of Independence is "naive and one-sided, a matter of heroes and villains" (Bailey, p. 587). Another review considered the biography's importance to understanding Cuba in the 1960s: "Anyone seeking to view the Cuban social and political events of the past decade in the deeper perspective of a centenarian . . . may find it here" (*Times Literary Supplement,* p. 501).

—John Roleke

For More Information

Bailey, Paul. "Slave Talking." *New Statesman* 75 (May 3, 1968): 587-88.

Barnet, Miguel. *Biography of a Runaway Slave.* Trans. W. Nick Hill. Willimantic, Conn.: Curbstone Press, 1994 (1966).

———. "The Culture that Sugar Created." *Latin American Literary Review* 8, no. 16 (1981): 38-46.

Brandon, George. *Santería from Africa to the New World: The Dead Sell Memories.* Bloomington: Indiana University Press, 1993.

Cannon, Terence. *Revolutionary Cuba.* New York: Thomas Y. Crowell, 1981.

Castro, Fidel. "Words to the Intellectuals." In *Radical Perspectives in the Arts.* Baltimore: Penguin, 1972.

Flynn, Pritchard. Review of *Autobiography of a Runaway Slave. Newsweek,* September 16, 1968, 100.

Luis, William, and Ann González, eds. *Modern Latin-American Fiction Writers.* 2nd series. Dictionary of Literary Biography. Vol. 145. Detroit: Gale Research, 1994.

Simons, Geoff. *Cuba: From Conquistador to Castro.* New York: St. Martin's Press, 1996.

Sklodowska, Elzbieta. "Spanish American Testimonial Novel: Some Afterthoughts." In *The Real Thing.* Ed. Georg M. Gugelberger. Durham, N. C.: Duke University Press, 1996.

Thomas, Hugh. *Cuba: The Pursuit of Freedom.* New York: Harper & Row, 1971.

Review of *Autobiography of a Runaway Slave. Times Literary Supplement,* May 16, 1968, 501.

Bless Me, Ultima

by
Rudolfo A. Anaya

THE LITERARY WORK

A novel set in a small New Mexico town in the 1940s; published in English in 1972.

SYNOPSIS

Through his relationship with Ultima, a mystical healer, a Mexican American boy learns to reconcile the seemingly conflicting elements of his heritage, and to forge his own future in 1940s New Mexico.

Rudolfo Alfonso Anaya was born in 1937 in New Mexico, and his family history mimics that of the region. His father was a *vaqueros*, one of the free-spirited horsemen who began working the cattle and sheep ranches of the *llanos* or wild plains before the arrival of the American cowboy; his mother belonged to a farming family with ties to settled village life. "Those are the two halves of my nature," Anaya observes. "Much is in the blood, because the blood has memory . . . the whispers of the blood are stories" (Anaya in Clark, p. 41). Other legacies from Anaya's and New Mexico's past concern the Hispano-Catholic and pre-Catholic traditions of the region. These several legacies converge in *Bless Me, Ultima* and are at the heart of the dilemma faced by the novel's young hero.

Events in History at the Time the Novel Takes Place

Northwest Mexico or the U.S. Southwest? By the turn of the twentieth century, New Mexico had become an amalgamation of cultures. Native tribes had inhabited the region for millenia. These tribes were joined in the mid-1500s by Spanish conquistadors and their *mestizo* (Indian-Spanish) descendants, and, beginning in the mid-1800s, by a rising number of Americans from the United States. Meanwhile, the region changed political hands: Mexico won independence from Spain in 1821 and so gained control of the area, then lost it to the United States in the Mexican War of 1848. Mexico's defeat was cemented by the Treaty of Guadalupe Hidalgo, in which it ceded to the United States all claims to Texas and, for $15 million, forfeited the territories of New Mexico and California (present-day New Mexico, Arizona, California, Nevada, Utah, and half of Colorado). Suddenly territories shifted from being northwestern Mexico to forming the southwestern United States. Still the area's Mexican and Indian populations remained constant, comprising, despite U.S. newcomers to the region, the basis of Southwest society.

Vaqueros and farmers. From the arrival of the Spaniards (mid-1500s) to the time of the novel (mid-1900s), the Southwest gave rise to mining towns, fortresses, missions, haciendas, and ranches. Because 90 percent of New Mexico's terrain is unfit for crops, grazing became the most logical use for much of its open land, first by sheep (in flocks of about 2,000 head), then by cattle. Ten million square acres of New Mexico comprise the Llano Estacado, or staked plains—flat, parched stretches of land that became home to the vaqueros who roamed the open range. Spread over the llanos were great ranches, of 30 or 40 square miles each, whose herds required tending by these free-spirited vaqueros.

COMANCHE GHOSTS

The Comanche Indians were relative latecomers to the region that became New Mexico. When they appeared in 1746, the Spanish were more or less content to let them stay, despite their violent raiding parties; they proved a useful buffer between New Mexico and French-controlled Louisiana to the east. When, in 1762, Louisiana became Spanish rather than French territory, the Comanche were no longer so useful. The Spanish began to strike at them, launching a century of warfare that ended with significant Comanche losses to the Spanish and their U.S. successors, culminating in a final foray in 1874. "Several large units . . . converged on the Llano Estacado from all directions, catching the Indians within the jaws of a giant trap" (Beck, p. 198).

In the novel, Ultima is called to the neighboring Téllez ranch to lift a curse that involves the manipulation of three Comanche ghosts, or *bultos*, by the evil Trementina sisters. Ultima explains what is wrong:

> "A long time ago," she began, "the llano of the Agua Negra was the land of the Comanche Indians. Then the comancheros [traders who dealt with the Comanches] came, then the Mexican with his flocks—many years ago three Comanche Indians raided the flocks of one man, and this man was the grandfather of Téllez. Téllez gathered the other Mexicans around him and they hanged the three Indians. They left the bodies strung on a tree; they did not bury them according to their custom. Consequently, the three souls were left to wander on that ranch."
>
> (*Bless Me, Ultima,* p. 227)

After she performs a proper burial ceremony, the Comanche ghosts are freed of their endless wandering.

Despite the unfettered beauty of the plains, the life of a vaquero was far from easy. He was almost always too poor to educate his children, a difficult proposition in any case because of the remoteness of most vaquero villages. Long periods of drought could be devastating to a herd. Brushfires sometimes burned the dry grass for weeks on end, threatening the livestock as well as the men who tended them. During the winter, freezing cold and heavy snowfall took their toll. The invention of barbed wire led to the fencing of most of the open range by 1890, and, along with the migration of more farmers to the region, heralded its disappearance. Despite these changes, cattle would retain their importance in the region, as shown by their consistent numbers despite the increase in human population. In 1890 New Mexico claimed 1.3 million head of cattle, and in the 1950s the figure was about the same. But the industry had by then become more the concern of businessmen than adventurers. In the novel, Tony's father laments the changes that have impinged on vaquero life. His relatives and friends now earn income as itinerant farmhands, moving around the West, helping harvest crops, a consequence, thinks Tony, of their vaquero heritage:

> My father had been a vaquero all his life, a calling as ancient as the coming of the Spaniard to Nuevo Mejico. Even after the big rancheros and the tejanos [American Texans] came and fenced the beautiful llano, he and those like him continued to work there, I guess because only in that wide expanse of land and sky could they feel the freedom their spirits needed.
>
> (Anaya, *Bless Me, Ultima*, p. 2)

While sheep and cattle raising dominated the economy, farming was also traditional in New Mexico, and it too changed greatly over the years. On the 10 percent of land suitable for raising crops, people labored as small farmers or as part of the *patrón* system, in which a large landowner employed hundreds of peasants under exploitative conditions. The patrón system endured until World War II, although many more small farmers entered the region from 1879 to 1882, after the railroad appeared. In any case, farmers of all types faced mostly dismal conditions in the early-to-mid 1900s.

The long drought of 1909-12 wreaked havoc in agriculture, and many dusty farms reverted to grazing land once again. Another drought devastated the area in the 1930s, contributing to the Great Depression. Some tenacious farmers—such as Tony's Luna uncles in the novel—hung onto their land, learning dry farming and prospering in the late 1930s and 1940s. But lurking around the bend was another devastating drought, which ruined many New Mexico farming communities in the 1950s. Rural dwellers had in the previous decade begun moving to the area's urban centers. The new drought increased this trend, adding to a major population shift that

Scene from a New Mexico cattle ranch at about the time *Bless Me, Ultima* is set.

involves the family in the novel. This shift, along with much of twentieth-century Mexican American history, merits further scrutiny, according to scholar Ernesto Galarza. Galarza points to a great vacuum in our knowledge of the farming and vaquero experiences as well as the rural-urban migration:

> We have yet to study and understand more thoroughly two important chapters of history [of Mexicans in the Southwest] which between them divide the last seventy years [1900-70]. Up to the early 1940's, the story is principally that of the Mexican landworker, locked into an exploitative wage system by mob violence, police power, and legal process. After the 1940's, the story is mainly that of the displacement of these same people toward the cities, with still another cycle of drastic changes such as the shift from agrarian to urban vocations, the dissolution of the family as an economic unit, the loss of the communitarian sense of the rural colonia.
>
> (Galarza in Spicer, p. 273)

Agents of change—urbanization and World War II. In *Bless Me, Ultima,* the Gabriel Márez family has moved from the tiny llanos village of Las Pasturas to the larger town of Guadalupe. Tony's father, Gabriel, has given up the free-spirited life of the vaquero to build highways for the government. Such migration was widespread at the time of the novel. During the Great Depression of the 1930s U.S. president Franklin D. Roosevelt instituted the Works Progress Administration (WPA), which gave thousands of unemployed Americans jobs creating a national infrastructure—dams, bridges, and highways such as that on which Gabriel works. Later, from 1939 to 1942, about 50 percent of New Mexico's working-class males migrated to urban areas to take advantage of wartime opportunities to become welders, mechanics, or electricians through government-sponsored training programs.

Two years into World War II, on December 8, 1941, the United States finally joined the fight. The war leaves its imprint on the novel, from the restlessness of Tony's now worldly brothers, to the madness of Lupito, who has come home with severe psychological trauma, to the bells that toll the funeral masses for yet another son of the Guadalupe area. In some respects "war sickness" was a general malady suffered by soldiers of various ethnic backgrounds. The cause has something to do with the difference between the public perception of the World War II experience in the United States and the reality of fighting for soldiers who labored under handicaps the public back home had no knowledge of—poorer weaponry than the Germans, the dismembered body parts thrown into the soldier's path by modern warfare, a pervasive uncertainty about exactly what he was fighting for, given the fact that unconscionable atrocities were committed on both sides. All these factors contributed to a silence on the part of veterans, whose experience of the war was so far afield from what the public conceived it to be.

> What annoyed the troops and augmented their sardonic, contemptuous attitude toward those who viewed them from afar was in large part [the] public innocence about the bizarre damage suffered by the human body in modern war. . . . You can't take much of that sort of thing [encountering dismembered body parts] without going mad. . . . In war it is not just the weak soldiers, or the sensitive ones, or the highly imaginative or cowardly ones, who will break down. Inevitably all will break down if in combat long enough.
>
> (Fussell, pp. 270, 272, 281)

BEYOND HELL

In the novel, the healer Ultima travels to the Téllez ranch to undo the work of the Trementina sisters, witches (or *brujas*) who have manipulated three Comanche ghosts into victimizing the Téllez family: their house is pounded with rock and a huge cloud settles over it. To this latest demonstration of Trementina witchery, Anaya ties the effects of the thermonuclear bomb. The connection is not direct; that is, the sisters are not held personally responsible for the nuclear blast, but, as one critic points out, the characters in the novel "are aware of the resemblance between the events of Téllez's ranch and the explosion of the first atomic bomb" (Sáldivar, p. 121). Tony wonders whether the bomb is not responsible for the sandstorms and harsh winds that now blow across the llano:

> Many grown-ups blame[d] the harsh winter and the sandstorms of spring on the new bomb that had been made to end the war. "The atomic bomb," they whispered, "a ball of white heat beyond the imagination, beyond hell—" And they pointed south, beyond the green valley of El Puerto.
>
> (*Bless Me, Ultima,* p. 190)

In the early part of the novel, Tony worries about his three older brothers, Gene, León, and Andrew, who are serving overseas. When they return, they are restless and haunted by their memories of the fighting. They spend their nights out drinking and their days sleeping and will say nothing of their experiences during the war. "We knew," says Tony, "the war-sickness was in them" (*Bless Me, Ultima,* p. 65).

In other respects, the war had a distinctive effect on Mexican Americans. About 350,000 Mexican Americans fought in World War II, winning 17 Medals of Honor, incontrovertible evidence of Mexican American patriotism. Upon their return, under the G.I. Bill the veterans qualified for U.S. housing loans and education programs that promised social and economic advancement to a degree not yet experienced by Mexican Americans in U.S. society. The benefits encouraged assimilation, as did the war itself, weakening the tight-knit Mexican American family, a reality reflected in the novel when two of Tony's brothers choose to go their separate ways. They perhaps expect to suffer less discrimination than before the war, when Mexican Americans were regularly and blatantly refused service in public establishments, and relegated to substandard education, housing, and healthcare. Unhappily, the general population re-relegated Mexican Americans to second-class status after the war; however, there was a profound shift in terms of Mexican American reactions to such injustice—the veterans now thought of themselves as fully American. They had sacrificed lives and limbs, had confirmed with their blood their entitlement to civil rights. No longer willing to tolerate being deprived of them, a number of these veterans helped form Mexican American or Chicano rights groups, such as the 1947 Community Service Organization, which set out to register Mexican American voters.

World War II had a local impact on New Mexico, too. In the desert near Los Alamos, New Mexico (about 90 miles from Albuqerque), U.S. military scientists were building—and on July 15, 1945, would test—the world's first atomic bomb. The blast blew a hole in the desert floor 1,200 feet in diameter, and altered New Mexico's landscape in other ways as well. To protect the secrecy of the project, which had been developing since 1943, the federal government withdrew from public domain and private ownership hundreds of thousands of acres in rural New Mexico. Postwar defense projects attracted hundreds of people from other states, while New Mexico's own residents shifted localities to work in the uranium mines powering the projects.

Curanderismo. *Curanderismo* is an age-old system of supernatural belief and herbal remedies still invoked in the Southwest to cure illness and disease. The tradition has some of its roots in Moorish culture, that of the Arabic people who conquered Spain in the Middle Ages. Knowledge about medicinal plants came to the New World with the Spanish and mingled with similar knowledge held by America's indigenous people. As Tony says: "[Ultima] spoke to me of the common herbs and medicines we shared with the Indians of the Rio del Norte. She spoke of the ancient medicines of other tribes, the Aztecas, Mayas, and even of those in the old, old country, the Moors" (*Bless Me, Ultima,* p. 42). Many people will turn to *curanderas* or *curanderos* (female or male healers, respectively) rather than to modern medicine if they believe that a particular illness has been caused by a curse laid upon them by brujas (evil witches) or by the inadvertent actions of someone with whom they have associated.

The curandera makes remedies from leaves, bark, roots, and flowers that have various curative powers. These ingredients may be mixed with oils to prepare salves that can be directly applied to the body part causing the sickness or pain. Sometimes poultices of lard and turpentine, or pastes made from chiles, are applied. In the novel, the healer Ultima concocts such remedies. Some of her favorite herbs are orégano, which she uses for coughs and fever, and oshá, which can be used to cure "colds, cuts and bruises, rheumatism and stomach troubles," and to ward off snakes: "the old sheepherders used it to keep poisonous snakes away from their bedrolls by sprinkling them with oshá powder" (*Bless Me, Ultima,* p. 40). Ultima's powers in the novel exceed those of most curanderas. While she appears to have the ability to foresee the future, most curanderas are simply folk healers with a knowledge of herbal remedies and the desire to help others.

The Novel in Focus

Plot summary. The summer in which Antonio (Tony) Márez turns seven, an old woman, Ultima, arrives to live with his family. Ultima comes from the village of Las Pasturas, where Tony's family lived among his father's people until his mother convinced her husband to move to the larger town of Guadalupe, where the children could attend school. World War II has emptied the llanos village where Ultima has been living. In return for the old woman's lifetime of service as midwife and healer to the Márez family and other llanos residents, Tony's parents decide to invite her into their home. Tony's sisters are initially wary of Ultima's arrival and so, too, is Tony's father, Gabriel; although he loves and respects the old woman, he knows that bringing her into his family could have unfortunate consequences, since Ultima, also called La Grande, is a curandera, a folk healer renowned for her herbal remedies and her power to dispel curses. There are connections between her powers and those associated with the evils of witchcraft. Tony understands his father's fear:

> I knew why he expressed concern for me and my sisters. It was because Ultima was a curandera, a woman who knew the herbs and remedies of the ancients, a miracle-worker who could heal the sick. And I had heard that Ultima could lift the curses laid by brujas, that she could exorcise the evil the witches planted in people to make them sick. And because a curandera had this power she was misunderstood and often suspected of practicing witchcraft herself.
>
> (*Bless Me, Ultima,* p. 4)

That night, Tony has the first of many dreams that surface in the novel. He dreams of his own birth and the battle between the Lunas, his mother's people (whose name means "moon"), and his father's, the Márezes (whose name means "sea"), over what his destiny is to be. The Lunas wish him to be a farmer like them, or a priest, like their first ancestor, while the Márez's wish him to be a vaquero, like they are. The two families squabble over the afterbirth, the ritual disposal of which is thought to affect an infant's fate. Suddenly the old woman who delivered the child halts the argument: "Cease! she cried, and the men were quiet. I pulled this baby into the light of life, so I will bury the afterbirth and the cord that once linked him to eternity. Only I will know his destiny" (*Bless Me, Ultima,* p. 6). Tony understands that this dreamed figure of authority is Ultima, and the next morning he discovers that his dream was true—Ultima did defuse just such a fight between the Lunas and the Márezes. Thus, a powerful bond links him with the healer:

> She took my hand, and I felt the power of a whirlwind sweep around me. Her eyes swept the surrounding hills and through them I saw for the first time the wild beauty of our hills and the magic of the green river. . . . The four directions of the llano met in me and the white sun shone on my soul.
>
> (*Bless Me, Ultima,* p. 12)

Ultima takes Tony with her on her quests for potent herbs and she begins to teach him about the peace, beauty, and spiritual power of the land. Her teachings complement, and sometimes contradict, the spiritual instruction of his mother, who hopes he will one day be a Catholic priest.

Ultima has an owl that is her kindred spirit. One night the owl calls out a warning, after which the neighbor Chávez rushes in with terrible news: his brother, the sheriff, has been shot to death by Lupito, who has returned from World War II with severe psychological trauma. Some of the local men have gathered to hunt down the madman, and they want Tony's father to join them. Tony slips out behind them and hides in the bushes along the river; he witnesses the shooting of Lupito. Badly wounded but not yet dead, Lupito staggers past Tony, who thinks he hears him say "Bless me" (*Bless Me, Ultima,* p. 22). Tony prays for Lupito, wonders why his mother wishes him to be a priest who must deal with such horrifying things all the time, and worries that Lupito's blood will never be washed from his beloved river. Racing home, Tony hears Ultima's owl hooting and takes comfort. When he arrives at the house, Ultima is waiting for him, apparently aware of all that he has experienced.

Shortly after Tony begins school, his three brothers—Andrew, León, and Eugene—return safely from the war. Tony's mother, María, attributes their return to the intercession of the Virgin of Guadalupe, patron saint of the town and of her family, the Lunas (the Virgin of Guadalupe is figured in Catholic tradition as standing on the horned moon), to whom she has been praying constantly. Soon, however, the brothers grow restless with small-town life: "It's hell to have seen half the world then come back to this," says León (*Bless Me, Ultima,* p. 66). Tony overhears their plans to leave and agrees that it is their Márez blood, so much like the restless sea, that drives them all. Breaking their father's heart—Gabriel has long fantasized about moving with his sons to California—León and Eugene take off in search of a better life, while Andrew gets a job at a grocery store in town.

One summer day Tony and his friend Samuel go fishing in the river that winds through the town. Samuel recounts an Indian legend in which he believes. Once, though they had been warned by the gods not to, some starving natives ate the carp from the river. As punishment they were turned into carp themselves. One of the gods took pity and, to protect them, had himself changed into a golden carp, which still lives in the river. This information shakes Tony. "If the golden carp was a god, who was the man on the cross? The Virgin? Was my mother praying to the wrong God?" (*Bless Me, Ultima,* p. 81).

The rhythm of everyday life is broken by news that Tony's uncle Lucas is gravely ill. His family believes his illness has been caused by the Trementina sisters, evil brujas who laid a curse on him after he witnessed one of their secret ceremonies. The local doctor, priest, and even a specialist have been unable to cure Uncle Lucas. Afraid that Lucas will die if the curse is not lifted, the family asks Ultima for help. She consents, insisting on taking Tony along with her. First Ultima confronts Tenorio, demanding that he make his daughters lift the curse, but Tenorio refuses and threatens to kill Ultima for the shame she has brought on his family when she publicly accuses his daughters of being witches. Unconcerned by the death threat, Ultima warns Tenorio that she will use her own magic to lift the curse. Ultima concocts and administers to Lucas a powerful remedy, then makes three small dolls, each of which she stabs with a pin; gradually, over the course of the novel, the dolls slump, signifying the efficacy of her magic. Ultima uses the young, healthy, and empathetic Tony as a channeller of her healing power: "He [Lucas] was across the room from me, but our bodies did not seem separated by the distance.

KINDRED SPIRITS

Still vital in New Mexico at the time of the novel was a cultural belief of the Aztecs and their descendants. Practitioners of magic were associated with animals. Those who practiced "good" magic, such as that of Ultima, shared a special relationship with a *tona*:

> A magic link between a man and an animal . . . causes that the wounds and the fortunes of one are shared by the other. *Tonalism* implies that these individuals have a *tona*; a mystical relationship between one man and just one animal; that both share the same luck; but that there is no ability for either to change himself into the other.
>
> (López Austin in Bauder, p. 47)

In *Bless Me, Ultima* Ultima is constantly attended by her owl, an owl that looks after her safety and that of Tony's family, and that mysteriously does her bidding. When the madman Tenorio shoots and kills the bird, Ultima too declines and dies the same night.

We dissolved into each other, and we shared a common struggle against the evil within, which fought to repulse Ultima's magic" (*Bless Me, Ultima,* p. 100). Her cure is triumphant; Lucas fully recovers.

Shortly thereafter, one of Tenorio's daughters dies. Narciso, the town drunk, comes to the house and warns Ultima that Tenorio has gathered a group of men who are on their way to kill her. Tenorio accuses Ultima of being a witch and the men with him, frightened of Ultima's power, demand that Tony's father hand her over. Ultima faces them down by successfully passing a test: supposedly no witch can pass beneath the sign of the cross. As one man pushes crossed needles into the doorway, Ultima's owl attacks Tenorio, tearing out one of his eyes. In the confusion they notice that Ultima has successfully passed over the threshold—she is thus proved to the men not to be a witch. Bleeding, a humiliated Tenorio is dragged away; he vows revenge. Tony later discovers the two crossed needles on the ground—"whether someone had broken the cross they made, or whether they had fallen, I would never know" (*Bless Me, Ultima,* p. 135).

Later that summer Tony learns more about the golden carp when another boy, Cico, takes him to a hidden pond where they see the magnificent fish. Knowledge of the fish-god is reserved for a select few who have a special relationship with the land and its power. When Tony reminds Cico that "Márez" means "sea," Cico immediately connects this to the prophesy that the golden carp will one day rule again; the town of Guadalupe, which is surrounded by water, will one day sink beneath the waves, weighted down by its sins. That night, Tony has a dream in which his mother and father tell him, respectively, that "the water the Church chooses to make holy and place in its font" runs through his veins, and that "the salt water of the oceans" is the water that "binds you to the pagan god of Cico, the golden carp!" (*Bless Me, Ultima,* p. 120). Against their competing voices rises that of Ultima, who tells them it is all the same water: "You have been seeing only parts . . . and not looking beyond into the great cycle that binds us all" (*Bless Me, Ultima,* p. 121).

Several months later, Tony witnesses a brutal fight between Narciso and Tenorio. Another of Tenorio's daughters is dying and the enraged father insists that Ultima is to blame. He swears to kill her and leaves. Narciso stumbles off through the heavy snow, determined to warn Ultima of Tenorio's murderous intent, unaware that Tony is following him. Suddenly a shot rings out, and Tony sees Tenorio kill Narciso. Tenorio also aims at Tony but his gun fails. Once again, Tony prays for a dying man. Because the authorities would never believe a child's testimony about what occurred, Tenorio goes unpunished for the murder. That night, Tony dreams of the golden carp, which swallows the town and everyone in it, and then becomes "a new sun to shine its good light upon a new earth" (*Bless Me, Ultima,* p. 176).

In the summer Tony again sees the golden carp. He is on his way to initiate one of his friends, Florence, into the secret knowledge of the fish-god when he comes upon the drowning scene of that same boy. For the third time, Tony prays over a corpse. Tony has for the past year been questioning the truth and power of his mother's conventional Catholicism, and has recently been disappointed in the sacrament of Communion, which he expected would enable him to know the mysteries of the Catholic God; Florence's death now shatters Tony's belief in God and ruins his health. His parents send him to his Luna uncles to recuperate.

THE SIGN OF THE CROSS

In the late 1930s and 1940s Lorin Brown, a fieldworker with the Federal Writers' Project, recorded the following tale told him by a New Mexico resident:

> José Chávez's wife claimed . . . that Teodorita was trying to bewitch her or her baby and swore that she had proved her a witch. She testified that she had tested Teodorita once when she called at her home. After Teodorita was inside she had secretly placed two needles in the shape of a cross over the door-frame. Teodorita tried to leave the house several times, but she would get only as far as the door and return. She tried this several times and became desperate at her inability to go through that door.
>
> (Brown, pp. 147-48)

Working in the fields, Tony and Uncle Pedro learn from Uncle Juan that Tenorio's second daughter has died and that Tenorio has gone mad. Pedro instructs the boy to return to the farm in preparation for going back to his own home to warn Ultima, but Tony is waylaid by Tenorio who tries to ride over him on his black horse and then leaves him for dead beside the road.

Luckily Tony is unhurt, and runs the ten miles home to warn Ultima. Upon his arrival, Tony spots Tenorio with a rifle and screams a warning to his family. Tenorio aims at him, but is attacked by Ultima's owl. Managing to kill the bird, Tenorio cries out gleefully that now Ultima will die. Uncle Pedro arrives and, as Tenorio is again taking aim at Tony, shoots Tenorio dead. The madman's prediction, however, is borne out: Ultima, her soul connected to the owl's, lies dying. Before taking her last breath, she blesses Tony, who himself has been blessing dead and dying people throughout the novel. He buries the owl with Ultima's final words echoing in his mind: "I bless you in the name of all that is good and strong and beautiful, Antonio. Always have the strength to live. Love life" (*Bless Me, Ultima,* p. 261).

Curanderas vs. brujas. In the novel, when Uncle Lucas is cursed by the Trementina sisters, Ultima tells their father, Tenorio: "I know when and where the curse was laid, I know when Lucas came to your shop for a drink and to have his hair clipped by your evil shears. I know that your daughters gathered the cut hair, and with that they worked their evil work!" (*Bless Me, Ultima,* p. 94). Sure enough, when Lucas is cured, a writhing ball of hair is found to have been in his stomach.

The bruja or "black curandera" is thought to derive her power from a pact with the devil or with a more powerful bruja. The pact gives her supernatural abilities that she invokes by using magical words and gestures. It is said that to create their curses, some brujas obtain the hair, blood, or saliva of their enemies, cast evil magic upon it, and then bring it into contact with the victim, as in Lucas's case. Supposedly brujas also have the ability to change shapes. In the novel, the Trementina sisters shape-shift into coyotes that howl and paw at the walls of the house in which Ultima is curing Uncle Lucas of their curse.

To prevent curses and protect oneself from the spells of a bruja, curanderas advise several courses of action: pray to God; throw dust in the direction of the bruja or pour water on the ground where the bruja will walk; write a prayer on tree bark or paper and wear the written prayer around the neck; make certain herbs into amulets and wear them. In the novel, Ultima gives Tony a pouch filled with oshá and other herbs to wear around his neck. She tells him the amulet will protect him from Tenorio and the evil magic of his daughters.

Sources and literary context. According to one literary historian, *Bless Me, Ultima,* "stood in stark contrast to the shrill polemics that emerged from . . . the 1960s and attempted to pass for literature" (Márquez in Vassallo, p. 34). Along with Tómas Rivera's ***. . . and the earth did not part*** (also covered in *Latin American Literature and Its Times*), it diverged from the social protest stories of the period to inaugurate a new, richly textured fiction. Both novels contradicted stereotypes that construed Mexican Americans as simple, fun-loving, non-achievers (Márquez in Vassallo, p. 35). Unique to *Bless Me, Ultima,* is the concentration on myth and foundational traditions. At least one scholar has explained the novel's myth of the golden carp as a reflection of ethnic religious history:

> [I]n the myth of the golden carp, Anaya presents the Indian rendering of European Christianity. The parallel between the golden carp story and the Biblical stories demonstrates the Mexican cultural and mythical assimilation. As the Spanish conquerors attempted to Christianize the Indians, the natives merely translated the Biblical stories into their folklore. Thus the golden carp represents the naïve and somewhat confused version of the missionaries' religious teachings.
> (Ray, p. 27)

While various explanations may be offered for myths and traditions in the novel, its acknowledgement of their importance is unmistakable. *Bless Me, Ultima* claims certain legacies of the Mexican American past with pride, from the vaquero and farming lifestyles to the skills of the curandera. At the same time, the novel is the first in a trilogy by Anaya that fictionalizes twentieth-century Mexican American history in the Southwest. After *Bless Me, Ultima* (1972), which captures the rural-to-urban movement, came *Heart of Aztlán* (1976), which portrays labor exploitation and the breakup of the family in the city, and *Tortuga* (1979), which depicts the group's new dependency on modern technology.

Beyond the United States, *Bless Me, Ultima* resembles other Latin American literature of the era in notable ways: "In its tone *Ultima* is not too far removed from the magical realism of . . . Latin American writers . . . also sharing with several Latin American authors perception of landscape—Southwestern landscape in this case—as a key to the primeval American world" (González Echevarría and Pupo-Walker, p. 570).

Events in History at the Time the Novel Was Written

From the 1940s to the 1970s. The central irony of *Bless Me, Ultima* is that neither of the choices over which Tony agonizes—whether he should be a farmer or a vaquero—were promising possibilities in 1940s New Mexico. The population, as mentioned, was moving in the other direction, from rural to urban lifestyles. This potentially made available vacated lands, but then the government was buying up hundreds of thousands of acres for the nuclear bomb project.

By the time the novel was written, in the early 1970s, the population shift had been achieved. Farmhands no longer formed the most sizable portion of the Latino labor force. In 1970 in New Mexico only 4.7 percent of Mexican American men and a scant 0.5 percent of Mexican American women were farm laborers. Meanwhile, in the urban centers, Mexican Americans held low-ranking positions and their earnings tended to be less than those of Anglos. The incipient activism of the post-World War II years proliferated in the 1960s and early 1970s. Mexican Americans organized into labor unions such as the United Farm Workers organization led by California's César Chávez and demonstrated against low wages and difficult working conditions. In New Mexico, another land-related movement erupted. Led by Reies Tijerina, an organization called *Alianza* (*Alianza de los Pueblos Libres*—Alliance of Free City States) set out to regain land grants, amounting to 4 million acres, that Mexicans had owned before the region became part of the United States (1848). The Treaty of Guadalupe Hidalgo promised that Mexicans in the Southwest would retain their property, yet many had been deprived of it. A Federal Land Grant Act of 1851 had required all Spanish and Mexican land grants to be verified within two years or they would be null and void. Since most of the grants had never been recorded, this requirement posed insurmountable difficulties and the majority of the properties had to be forfeited to the U.S. government. Tijerina attributed the problems of his people to the loss of these lands, claiming this rightful heritage in a way that recalls Tony's acknowledgement of the importance of the land in the novel. His group Alianza threatened to seize some federal lands in the area, then to form an independent republic. In 1967 Tijerina staged an insurrection of sorts in Tierra Amarilla in northwest New Mexico. His supporters stormed into the courthouse to achieve the release of some fellow activists who had been arrested. A shootout ensued. Tijerina and his supporters freed 11 prisoners and left town with two hostages, then became the targets of a fierce manhunt, involving

Reies Tijerina, leader of *Alianza de los Pueblos Libres.*

helicopters, tanks, state troopers, and the National Guard. Captured, the fugitives were charged with kidnapping and attempted murder as well as other crimes. Defending himself in court, Tijerina emerged victorious. He was cleared of kidnapping and lesser offenses but later served a two-year prison term based on other charges.

Literary activism. Young Mexican Americans of the period showed similar activism when they were conscripted to fight in the Vietnam War of the 1960s and early 1970s. As in World War II, Mexican American soldiers distinguished themselves with valor in this conflict, but this time they were fighting and dying in numbers completely out of proportion to their ethnic group's share of the U.S. population. To protest the inequity, Mexican Americans staged a huge demonstration in California in 1972, the year *Bless Me, Ultima* appeared. Thus, Anaya wrote his novel in an environment replete with protests from segments of the Mexican American population. These activists, explained the scholar Galarza in 1972, were starting to respond to limitations imposed on Mexican Americans by the Anglo. Their response would also involve the destruction of invalid stereotypes attached to them and the reconstruction of a legitimate image:

> A character type that historically belonged to the Mexican because he created it—the vaquero—was rustled and retouched as a gringo hero, the 'good guy' cowboy. Another character type that grew out of the Mexican's typical economic roles of farm and section hand was perverted into a picture of the peasant dozing by a cactus. . . . Stereotypes of a more subtle kind have pervaded novels and textbooks by Anglo authors.
>
> (Galarza in Spicer and Thompson, pp. 286–87)

The remaking of the Mexican American self-image, adds Galarza, is basic to all other expressions of the protest culture. "However grandiloquent the Chicanos may sound when they identify themselves with their Indian ancestors . . . they are in this respect moving with a significant effort at historical reinterpretation. No one writer has yet put all its pieces together, but several are beginning to try" (Galarza in Spicer and Thompson, pp. 287–88).

The effort, he continues, requires some leaps backward in time to achieve a sense of common history, especially since much of the 1900s experience of Mexican Americans has gone unrecorded. It will, Galarza warns, be slow work, this remaking of the image from false stereotypes to honest representation. In light of this 1972 warning, Anaya's *Bless Me, Ultima* can be positioned as a novel that helped give this general cultural task a running start.

Reviews. *Bless Me, Ultima* has been recognized as one of the most important literary works by a Mexican American, and has taken its place among the classics of American literature. Upon publication, critics praised the novel "for its communication of tender emotion and powerful spirituality without being mawkish or haughty; for its eloquent presentation of Chicano consciousness in all its intriguing complexity; finally, for being an American novel which accomplishes a harmonious resolution, transcendent and hopeful" (Wood in Gunton and Stine, p. 22). The novel has since been faulted by some. A number of critics have argued that Anaya wasted his voice by not incorporating a more contemporary political attitude into his novels. "Necesitamos un mito más racional que confronte las necesidades contemporáneas" [We need a more rational myth that confronts contemporary necessities] (Alurista in Vassallo, pp. 38-39). Undaunted, Anaya has observed that storytellers must remain independent from outside whims. Like a curandera, a storyteller is a kind of mediator who must work alone (Anaya in Lomelí and Shirley, p. 25).

—Terence Davis

For More Information

Anaya, Rudolfo. *Bless Me, Ultima.* New York: Warner, 1994.

Bauder, Thomas A. "The Triumph of White Magic in Rudolfo Anaya's *Bless Me, Ultima.*" *Mester* 14, no. 1 (spring 1985): 41-54.

Beck, Warren A. *New Mexico: A History of Four Centuries.* Norman: University of Oklahoma Press, 1962.

Brown, Lorin, with Charles L. Briggs and Marta Weigle. *Hispano Folklife of New Mexico: The Lorin W. Brown Federal Writers' Project Manuscripts.* Albuquerque: University of New Mexico Press, 1978.

Clark, William. "Rudolfo Anaya: 'The Chicano Worldview.'" *Publishers Weekly* 242, no. 23 (June 5, 1995): 41-42.

Fussell, Paul. *Wartime: Understanding and Behavior in the Second World War.* New York: Oxford University Press, 1989.

González Echevarría, Roberto, and Enrique Pupo-Walker. *The Cambridge History of Latin American Literature.* Vol. 2. Cambridge: Cambridge University Press, 1996.

Gunton, Sharon R., and Jean C. Stine, eds. *Contemporary Literary Criticism.* Vol. 23. Detroit: Gale Research, 1983.

Lomelí, Francisco A., and Carl R. Shirley, eds. *Chicano Writers.* 1st series. Dictionary of Literary Biography. Vol. 82. Detroit: Gale Research, 1989.

Ray, Karen J. "Cultural and Mythical Archetypes in Rudolfo Anaya's *Bless Me, Ultima.*" *New Mexico Humanities Review* 1, no. 3 (September 1978): 23–28.

Sáldivar, Ramón. *Chicano Narrative: The Dialectics of Difference.* Madison: University of Wisconsin Press, 1990.

Spicer, Edward H., and Raymond H. Thompson, eds. *Plural Society in the Southwest.* New York: Weatherhead Foundation, 1972.

Vassallo, Paul, ed. *The Magic of Words: Rudolfo A. Anaya and His Writings.* Albuquerque: University of New Mexico Press, 1982.

Blow-Up and Other Stories

by
Julio Cortázar

THE LITERARY WORK

A collection of 15 short stories set in various times and places; first published in Spanish in the volumes *Bestiario* (1951), *Final del juego* (1956), and *Las armas secretas* (1959); published in English in 1967 as *End of the Game and Other Stories,* in 1968 as *Blow-Up and Other Stories.*

SYNOPSIS

The 15 stories include realistic or fantastic plot lines, ranging from a photographer's investigation of an adolescent boy's bizarre seduction, to the final days in the life of a talented but self-destructive jazz musician, to an illuminating game of charades by three young Argentines.

Born in Brussels, Belgium, to Argentine parents, Julio Cortázar (1914-84) moved with his family to Banfield, a suburb of Buenos Aires, when he was four years old. Soon after, his father abandoned the family and young Julio became interested in *literatura fantástica* (fantastic literature), which he viewed as a genre that blends the believable with the supernatural to broaden human understanding of the surrounding world. Later in life, Cortázar taught in the secondary schools of Bolívar and Chivilcoy and at the University of Cuyo (from which he resigned in protest against Juan Domingo Perón, an army officer who became president of Argentina in 1946). Subsequently Cortázar worked as a manager for the Argentine Publishing Association and then passed examinations to become a freelance translator for the United Nations Educational, Scientific, and Cultural Organization (UNESCO). Frustrated with Perónian repression, he moved to France in 1951, where he composed a number of short stories, novels, and essays. His success in Europe was impressive. It can be measured in part by the fact that filmmakers made features based on his stories—for example, Michelangelo Antonioni's *Blow Up,* adapted from the story of the same name.

Events in History at the Time of the Stories

Switching icons: from Perón to Guevara. Once the South American leader in cultural and democratic advances, from 1946-55 Argentina was ruled by the dictator Juan Domingo Perón. These years were marked by a shift in power from the traditional bourgeois oligarchy (a middle-class ruling elite preoccupied with private property and commercial interests) to a single, charismatic leader (Perón) whose authority was anchored in the popular support of the working class (*los descamisados,* or "the shirtless ones"). To solidify his power, Perón promised workers economic and cultural liberation in the form of increased wages, freedom from foreign capital, increased military strength, and renewed commitment to the precepts of the Catholic Church (such as the

Crowds in Buenos Aires celebrate Juan Perón's fall, 1955.

traditional two-parent family). Having risen to leadership in the wake of World War II, Perón was influenced by fascism, a right-wing political philosophy exalting nation and race over the individual and operating under the leadership of a military-backed dictator. Many Argentine workers—and to a lesser degree the middle-class nationalists who advocated national solidarity but without military tyranny—saw in Perón's fascism an effective resistance against foreign imperialism and control by the domestic bourgeoisie. However, Perón was never truly committed to a national, grass-roots revolution; instead he used the language and symbols of working class revolt to secure his successive elections. As early as September 1951 the nationalist Rodolfo Irazusta attacked the Perónian "reformation":

> Instead of the truly national revolution we wanted . . . we have class struggle; instead of a national consciousness, we have a strengthening of the mentalities of class; instead of citizen participation, we have iron discipline; instead of prosperity, we have poverty; instead of liberty, we have popular tyranny.
>
> (Irazusta in Rock, p. 175)

The growing conviction among nationalists, strangely enough, was that in Peronism, a movement influenced by right-wing fascism, lay the seeds of communism (the political system of the radical left, advocating collective economic ownership and characterized by a state-run bureaucracy). By the mid-1950s, the nationalist Mario Amadeo asserted that the communists intended to take over the Perónist movement, "since the Marxist Left only objects to Perón himself, but looks at his movement as a powerful weapon against imperialism" (Amadeo in Rock, p. 182). Peronism's apparent fascist-to-communist metamorphosis became even more blurred when Perón changed his earlier promise to workers and opened up the Argentine economy to global sources of capital, an unheard-of move for proponents of either ultra-right-wing or ultra-left-wing persuasions. Such political incongruity eventually led to Perón's demise, and when he finally fell in September 1955, the nationalist wing of the Argentine army vowed to prevent *Perónistas* (who, in its view, now simultaneously represented sellouts to global capital and ineffectual leaders of the national revolution) from regaining power.

A number of changes in Argentine society resulted from Perón's collapse. Among them was a heightened awareness (and, some have argued, a dash of paranoia) among nationalists regarding a global communist menace. Nationalists asserted a new doctrine of national security that, in effect, called for resistance to the "subversive hidden enemy" and the "world conspiracy" of communists against the West (Rock, p. 195). Interestingly, considering Julio Cortázar's residence in France at this time, much of this possibly paranoiac geopolitical perspective came from French military specialists who instructed Argentine officers that:

> The nuclear age had produced a military stalemate between East and West . . . [and communists would be] taking control of key institutions like the trade unions, the political parties, the mass media and the universities. . . . Thus, "a new form of war, lateral war, revolutionary war," had begun which would determine the future course of the world.
>
> (Rock, p. 196)

By the late 1950s Argentine politics was largely a fight between two factions: liberal nationalists who sought a strong military rule that would usher in a return to a conservative, bourgeois tradition and undo working class gains; and leftist radicals who favored state initiative in industry, anti-imperialism, working class solidarity, and the 1958 presidential election of Arturo Frondizi. The following year, Fidel Castro's Cuban Revolution would decidedly influence this volatile debate.

Argentina's Marxist left wing found in Castro and Castro's charismatic third-in-command, the Argentine expatriate Ernesto "Che" Guevara, significant new leaders for the revolution that Perón had not delivered. Whereas Perón had actually suppressed a proletarian revolution through spurious claims that he would transfer power from the bourgeoisie to the working class, Fidel Castro seemed to be making good on that promise.

Though they never met, Julio Cortázar and Che Guevara were in many respects kindred spirits. Both men were idealistic seekers who challenged the status quo, and actualized in their own lives a level of personal and collective freedom typically curtailed by tyrannical men of power (such as Argentina's Juan Perón and Cuba's Fulgencio Batista). And, of course, they were both Argentines who did the bulk of their life's work outside their native country. Although Cortázar was at first apolitical, years after the Cuban Revolution he began to sympathize with the rebels. As one observer noted, "Cortázar has become increasingly political in his pronouncements, and through hindsight has tended to interpret his entire oeuvre as a political gesture, as though his questing characters were faltering prototypes for Che Guevara's New Man" (Riley and Mendelson, p. 128).

On January 1, 1959, a little more than three years after Perón's fall, Castro and his force of 5,000 guerrillas deposed Cuban dictator Fulgencio Batista. As a Marxist-Leninist (a term derived from the names of communism's early architects, the German Karl Marx and the Russian Vladimir Lenin), Castro called for workers to liberate themselves from imperialistic capital interests. During the 1960s, the decade in which *Blow-Up and Other Stories* was translated into English, Castro's (and, for that matter, Guevara's) revolution reverberated strongly throughout Latin America. The left in Argentina used the Cuban Revolution as a source of inspiration and guidance for its own radicalization, especially as it grappled with its ongoing, if not always clearly delineated, fight with the nationalists. By the end of the decade, the line between these two opposing groups was almost indistinguishable. In May 1968 Sánchez Sorondo, editor of the nationalist publication *Azul y Blanco,* prophesied "that a [leftist/nationalist] popular insurrection would match the recent explosion in Paris"—a significant claim, given the serious unrest ignited in that city during a leftist student-led protest (Rock, p. 212). The communist explosion was in full force around the globe, and the once-fascist Argentina appeared to be under its sway.

"¡CHE!"

Ernesto "Che" Guevara was born June 14, 1927, in Argentina to middle-class parents. He received his medical degree in 1953 and immediately set off to experience life abroad in Venezuela. Guevara met the Cuban revolutionary Fidel Castro for the first time in Mexico City in the summer of 1954. Renowned for his skill in guerrilla warfare, Guevara would go on to help lead the Cuban Revolution, which toppled the Batista dictatorship and ushered in a decade of global left-wing revolutionary activity. In the process, he showed a strong sense of camaraderie, calling his guerrillas *che* ("pal" or "buddy"), which prompted them to dub him with the nickname.

***Sur* versus *Contorno:* A battle between the generations.** If leftist/nationalist relations colored politics in late 1950s and 1960s Argentina, then the contributors to *Sur* (high-society publisher Victoria Ocampo's literary magazine) and *Contorno* (the literary magazine of Buenos Aires' university students) waged the primary battle in the field of cultural criticism. Though other publications (such as *Annales de Buenos Aires, Verbum,*

Conducta, and later *Primera Plana, Casa de las Américas,* and *Mundo Nuevo*) offered observers a lens through which to observe and discuss significant events of the day, *Sur* and *Contorno* most clearly illustrated a shift in literary commitment, style, and purpose among Argentine writers.

From the early 1930s through the mid-1950s *Sur* dominated Argentine literary life. Its contributors included international writers such as T. S. Eliot, Jean-Paul Sartre, Simone de Beauvoir, Albert Camus, Aldous Huxley, Graham Greene, D. H. Lawrence, George Orwell, William Faulkner, and André Breton, along with Latin American writers such as Cortázar, Jorge Luis Borges, Guillermo Cabrera Infante, Octavio Paz, Carlos Fuentes, Miguel Angel Asturias, Gabriel García Márquez, and Mario Vargas Llosa. With such contributors (and subscribers), *Sur* was unsurpassed among literary magazines in Latin America. Catering to an affluent, educated audience that desired in its literary diet European sophistication and bourgeois sensibility, the magazine offered an alternative to the worldview promoted by Argentina's succession of dictatorial leaders.

However, as the younger writers of *Contorno* would begin to point out, *Sur* represented an elite sector of Argentine society, as disinterested in cultural revolution as was Perón himself. The *Contorno* writers acknowledged that the authors revered by the *Sur* audience were indeed technically excellent, but also saw a certain impotence in them:

> Writers such as [Eduardo] Mallea and Borges had demonstrated more than adequately their mastery of words and procedures: they were doctors of technique. But their writing lacked vital substance, a result of their own lack of interaction with the reality in which they lived. . . . The fanciful escape into dreams, playful intrigues, and conceptual labyrinths . . . typified [by] the *Sur* group . . . [was more] a negative factor when it confused the reader's comprehension of history and worked against his advancement of consciousness.
>
> (Katra, pp. 57, 61)

Contorno writers such as Adolfo Prieto, Juan Carlos Portantiero, Noé Jitrik, and León Rozitchner emerged largely from the universities; they instigated a new cultural criticism that championed the writer as social activist. Their aim was to discern "how the intellectual, through his writing and moral example, could best influence and hopefully guide society's active forces in the creation of a more just order" (Katra, p. 27). The Cuban Revolution inspired, and possibly legitimized, this position.

On the other hand, true to its own character and evolution, *Sur* turned its back on Cuba, "thus rejecting much that was innovative in Latin American culture in the 1960s . . . [while] the younger generation of critics . . . [became] increasingly . . . 'third-worldist' and socialist" (King, p. 167). *Sur*'s anti-Cuban stance reduced its influence in defining the Argentine nation. By the end of the decade, unable to effectively comment or act upon such developments as Marxist guerrilla violence, a radicalized middle class, and a combative trade union movement, Victoria Ocampo stopped publishing the magazine. *Contorno,* on the other hand, continued to flourish, providing a significant voice for the period's Marxian revolution.

Following the repression of Perón's decade-long dictatorship, the 1960s were also considered the "boom" years in Argentina. In economic terms this meant an increase in commercialization and consumption; in cultural terms, it meant widespread public revolt and experimentation. *Contorno* writers contributed to this atmosphere by reassessing the Marxian vision of social justice. They were inspired by French intellectual Jean-Paul Sartre, who insisted that Man is not merely an abstract being to be manipulated within a global class struggle, but is distinctly human and therefore is able to have an intentional impact on his destiny. In keeping with this philosophy, *Contorno* writers sought through literature and criticism to raise the consciousness of the working class in order to improve its material circumstances.

The surreal socialist. Cortázar sought a socialist destiny for Latin America that would permit individuals their personal liberties, but he believed that Peronism would prevent such a reality from ever coming true. In 1951 Cortázar fled Argentina and moved to France. From Jean-Paul Sartre's native country he would argue: "My idea of socialist man is a man in a more just society where no one is exploited or is an exploiter, but a man who doesn't lose any of his individual capabilities. [Up] to now, no society has achieved that" (Cortázar in Garfield, p. 9).

During his more than three-decade stay in France, Cortázar continued to pursue two childhood loves—jazz music and surrealism—and added to these an interest in psychology and consciousness. Surrealism, a movement in 1920s art, literature, and film, featured startling combinations that resulted in fantastic images, designed to challenge and disrupt the everyday, conventional understanding of reality. By the "boom" years of the late 1960s and early 1970s, Cortázar came to feel that intellectuals had a duty to unite with the repressed and lead them toward their goals of revolution. His unique literary style suited this belief; he had developed a *literatura fantástica* that attempted to subvert all known structures of reality in the name of personal and collective liberation. Also in keeping with this belief, Cortázar became in 1968 a writer "committed to socialism" and began to produce work that was "scattered among everyday concerns" (Vargas Llosa, pp. 251–52).

The Collection in Focus

Plot summaries. *Blow-Up and Other Stories* is a collection of 15 short stories written primarily while Cortázar was living in France in the 1950s. "Blow-Up," the title story, deals with one of Cortázar's favorite subjects: the creative process and its relationship to life. The story begins with the musings of Roberto Michel, a French-Chilean translator and amateur photographer living in Paris:

> It'll never be known how this has to be told, in the first person or in the second, using the third person plural or continually inventing modes that will serve for nothing. If one might say, I will see the moon rose; or: we hurt me at the back of my eyes, and especially: you the blond woman was the clouds that race before my your his our yours their faces. What the hell.
> (Cortázar, *Blow-Up and Other Stories,* p. 114)

It is a November day and, during a stroll through Paris, Michel comes upon a woman who seems to be trying to seduce an adolescent boy. Michel empathizes with the boy and compares his nervous innocence to a "terrified bird, a Fra Filippo angel, rice pudding with milk" (*Blow-Up,* p. 120). Michel senses the woman's power over the boy—"her laugh, all at once, a whip of feathers, crushing him just by being there, smiling, one hand taking a stroll through the air"—and at first imagines the final seduction in her apartment (*Blow-Up,* pp. 122-23). But then he has a strange intuition that she is actually engaging in this cruel game as if she were exciting "herself for someone else, someone who in no way could be that kid" (*Blow-Up,* p. 124). Next, Michel notices a man who is wearing a gray hat and sitting in his parked car on the dock. When the woman sees Michel taking a photograph of her strange seduction and demands the film be given to her, the boy breaks away from her grasp, "disappearing like a gossamer filament of angel-spit in the morning air" (*Blow-Up,* p. 125). The original Spanish title of the story, "Las Babas del Diablo," (The Devil's Spittle) is taken from this scene, in which the boy-angel escapes and the man in the gray hat—the devil—appears. When the man menacingly approaches to retrieve the film, Michel refuses to give it up and leaves. Days later, after developing and examining his pictures, Michel concludes that his intervention permitted the boy's escape. He then concludes that the woman was not propositioning the boy for her own pleasure, but instead for the homosexual man in the gray hat. The seduction scene begins to repeat itself in his head like an ongoing film with Michel screaming at its participants to stop. Unable to assist the boy, he finally moves forward *into* the photograph. The man and the woman turn toward Michel and once again the boy runs off. Michel closes his eyes and when he opens them he is seated at his windowsill, watching the clouds and the pigeons, relating his story to us, the readers.

The creative process and its relationship to life is also a central issue in "The Pursuer," which features a jazz artist from New York. Inspired by the life of saxophonist and drug addict Charlie Parker, "The Pursuer" focuses on two characters: Johnny Carter, one-time brilliant musician and now tortured soul, and Bruno, jazz critic, analytical spectator, and confidante to the artist. The story opens as Bruno checks up on Johnny and his girlfriend Dédée, who are holed up in a seedy hotel, even though Johnny has just completed a fairly successful European tour. Bruno has recently finished a biography on the tormented saxophonist, and is upset to find out just how disconnected his anguished friend has become: "Every time, it was getting more difficult to get him to talk about jazz, about his memories, his plans, to drag him back to reality" (*Blow-Up,* p. 217).

Plagued by a personal anguish that accompanies his double life as a heroin addict and a genius, Johnny yearns for an authenticity that will fill the disturbing gaps he perceives in conventional reality. But each time he gets a fleeting glimpse of such authenticity through his transcendent music, the desire for it on a permanent basis grows even stronger. And so he lives his days swinging from one extreme (creative bliss) to another (existential torment). However, as Bruno acknowledges, Johnny is no victim: "I know now . . . that Johnny pursues and is not pursued, that all the things happening in his life

Jazz saxophonist Charlie Parker, the model for Johnny Carter in "The Pursuer."

are the hunter's disaster, not the accidents of the harassed animal" (*Blow-Up*, p. 221).

Obsessed by this pursuit of the real, Johnny enters into his music as if compressing all experience—-past, present, and future—-into a soothing "now." He despises self-assuredness and easy answers, coldly dismissing Bruno's comparison of his music to a communion with God: "On top of everything, I don't buy your God. . . . I'm never going to pray to him, because I don't wanna know nothing about that . . . opener of doors in exchange for a goddamned tip . . ." (*Blow-Up,* p. 243). Bruno, the critic, admits that he could never forgo the security of his everyday "coffee and cigarettes" to pursue a life that cannot exist unless everyone goes crazy. And yet he empathizes with Johnny's attempts "to move forward with his decapitated sentences," pursuing such a dangerous path (*Blow-Up,* p. 189). But Johnny's heroin addiction and alcoholism will not permit the pursuit to go on any longer. During Johnny's final days, Bruno simply keeps a watchful eye on his disintegrating friend, accompanying him to the few remaining jazz clubs willing to pay him, holding him up in back alleys so he can vomit away his pain. After Johnny dies, a conflicted Bruno eulogizes the man whom he both respected and pitied. He concludes that, although Johnny was valiant and brave in his quest, he was also a helpless "hunter with no arms and legs" (*Blow-Up,* p. 221).

Finally, in "End of the Game," Cortázar turns his attention to adolescence and the issues of otherness and alienation. Letitia, Holanda, and an unnamed youngest sister (the story's narrator) live above Palermo (an upper-class section of metro Buenos Aires), near the Argentine Central railroad tracks, the "capital city of the kingdom, the wilderness city and the headquarters of our game" (*Blow-Up,* p. 137).

Letitia, according to the narrator, "was the luckiest and most privileged of the three of us," which means that she rules the kingdom in their game. Performed out by the willows in front of all the strangers passing by in trains, the game is a kind of charades consisting of two categories: Attitudes and Statues. The former requires expressiveness and acting ability (baring teeth and clenching fists for Envy, or making an angelic face and turning eyes to the sky for Charity), while the latter is achieved through costuming and ornamentation. After several days of game-playing, a note drops from one of the trains: "The Statues are very pretty. I ride in the third window of the second coach. Ariel B" (*Blow-Up,* p. 140). The blond Ariel, whom the girls decide is 18 and a student at some private English school (though more likely he is 16 and learning a craft at a local trade school), continues to drop notes off for the next few days. Finally, one note announces that he is going to get off at a nearby station the next day to meet the girls. For the first time, the game has been disrupted by an intruder, something the younger two sisters find upsetting, and the older sister finds exhilarating. But Letitia suffers from a partial paralysis, noticeable when she isn't completely still. That evening she says that she does not feel well and will not be attending the rendezvous with Ariel. She writes a note to her admirer and seals it in a lilac envelope. The next day the other two sisters meet up with Ariel to deliver Letitia's letter. He pockets it and departs. That night, when the girls are going to sleep, Holanda whispers to the youngest sister, "The game's finished from tomorrow on, you'll see" (*Blow-Up,* p. 147). Sure enough, the following day the three sisters again play Attitudes and Statues out by the train tracks, but this time Letitia brings their mother's pearl collar and all of her rings. When her sisters inquire about the fine jewels, Letitia brushes them off, saying, "I would like you to leave it to me today" (*Blow-Up,* p. 148). She then bends her body backwards, assuming an incredible pose, "the most regal statue she'd ever done," and waits for the train (*Blow-Up,* p. 148). When it zooms by, Ariel just looks at Letitia, who now has tears streaming from her closed eyes, without saying a word. He of course has read Letitia's letter, the contents of which Cortázar keeps secret. The following day Letitia stays home and the other two sisters once again go out to the willows. "When the train came by," the youngest sister reports, "it was no surprise to see the third window empty, and while we were grinning at one another, somewhere between relief and being furious, we imagined Ariel riding on the other side of the coach, not moving in his seat, looking off toward the river with his gray eyes" (*Blow-Up,* p. 149).

Psychology, jazz, and the tango. With the highest number of psychiatrists per capita in the world, Argentines have, not surprisingly, gained a reputation for being brooding and introspective to the extent that many of them fall prey to a particular form of depression: "*El mufarse* . . . involves bitter introspection, but Argentines add to this emotion a clear sense of self-indulgence when they give in to a *mufa.* It is a depression, but with a cynicism about the depression itself, an awareness that it can feel good to throw practicalities aside . . . and contemplate one's bad luck and its universal implications" (Taylor, p. 4). A mufa, then, is a type of self-indulgent depression common in Argentine society. This deep current of melancholy can be attributed to a variety of causes:

- Lack of roots in a pre-conquest indigenous civilization;
- The post-1880 wave of immigration that left three foreign-born people for every native Argentine;
- The continually high proportion of men to women that contributed to Buenos Aires' position as a world-renowned depot of the white slave trade;
- The nostalgia and resentment of newcomers when dreams of owning land became impossible to realize and other forms of success remained elusive.

(Adapted from Taylor, p. 2)

Whatever the reasons, Cortázar's lifelong appreciation of psychology is in many respects a product of such a cultural heritage. So, too, is his passion for jazz, which he once described as "the only surrealistic music" (Garfield, p. 8). Both disciplines can be found in his short stories: in Michel's frenetic imagination in "Blow-Up," the self-absorbed destruction of the jazz musician Johnny in "The Pursuer," or the dreamy introspection of Letitia in "End of the Game."

RAILROADS, URBAN GROWTH, AND FOREIGN CAPITAL

The population boom from the early twentieth century, when metropolitan Buenos Aires was a dusty, sparsely populated *pampas* region, to the mid-1950s, when the area boasted upwards of 3 million people, necessitated a more diverse public transportation system. From its inception, the railroad industry—which, in fact, included the story's Argentine Central tracks—had been largely funded by foreign capital and labor. The first Argentine railroad, for example, was built with locomotives, rolling stock, and tracks imported from England, and was constructed with the aid of 160 British laborers. In 1928 Argentine taxi drivers began a *colectivo* service (minivan-type vehicles holding 25-30 people), which threatened the railways' viability to such an extent that within four years, one-quarter of the train passengers had switched to colectivos. A few years later Argentine President Roberto Ortíz responded by advocating the complete nationalization of the railroad network: "As far as the public is concerned, they must be given the idea that they [have] an interest in the railways and be induced to cherish them, as it were, as part of a necessity vital to the country's existence" (Randall, p. 184). By the end of World War II, however, the deteriorating railway system had accumulated a deficit of 40 million pesos and no longer served as an effective rallying cry. With the fall of President Juan Perón in 1955, any hope of nationalizing the railroad system came to an end.

Cortázar discovered in improvisational jazz and dream psychology insights that complemented his interest in challenging literary conventions and societal norms. He once argued that his short stories "oppose that false realism that [is] . . . part of a world ruled . . . by a system of laws [and] principles, of cause and effect relationships or defined psychologies, of well-mapped geographies" (Cortázar in Garfield, p. 12). Save for *literatura fantástica,* he rarely found in Argentine culture a comparable irreverent spirit. The controlled and self-conscious artists who danced the tango, for instance, seemed a far cry from the jazz musicians so spontaneous in their disregard for rules and procedures.

Nonetheless, one Argentine who did embrace Cortázar's love of jazz—and, by extension, personal and artistic freedom—was the tango composer Astor Piazzolla. Once all the rage in 1930s Paris and New York, the tango (primarily an Argentine invention) declined in later years as young people heeded the rebellious spirit of rock-and-roll. But this all changed when, after an extended stay in Paris during the 1950s, Piazzolla introduced an updated version of the tango (*El Tango Nuevo*) that was a hybrid mix of jazz and classical music. As Piazzolla put it: "It swaggered back and forth between instinct and reason, pitting harmony against dissonance. It was complex and contradictory, the struggle of modern life set to music" (Piazzolla in Bach, p. 14). By the 1960s Piazzolla had a devoted following and by the end of the decade he was creating "tango-operitas" based upon the work of the Argentine writer Jorge Luis Borges (see **"The South,"** also covered in *Latin American Literature and Its Times*), a collaboration that gave him a stamp of approval within the cultural establishment.

Sources and literary context. "What I like about the snail is that he doesn't have to return to his nest like spiders and other insects. He carries his nest with him and travels all over the world" (Cortázar in Garfield, p. 5). Cortázar traveled extensively throughout his career, relishing the textures and flavors of the cultures he encountered. He considered himself an international writer and his traveling perhaps contributed to a certain universality in his work, one that reflects a search for personal contentment. Like his contemporaries, Cortázar to some degree eschewed Spanish literature, and preferred French and English authors. Speaking of William Shakespeare and the English Romantics, Cortázar said, "For me, English is the language of poetry" (Cortázar in Garfield, p. 7). He is said to have been influenced by the Romantic poet John Keats, about whom he wrote a sizeable book. On French Surrealism, Cortázar commented: "It undeniably constituted the most intensive motivating force of all or nearly all of my books, something which can't please me enough" (Cortázar in Garfield, p. 7). Like many of his Latin American contemporaries who were interested in *literatura fantástica,* Cortázar attempted in his fiction to apply a heightened awareness to daily reality in order to discover the extraordinary in the ordinary: "In my case, the suspicion of another more secret and less communicable order . . . [has] oriented me in my personal search for a literature on the outskirts of a realism that is far too ingenuous" (Cortázar in Garfield, p. 12).

Despite his European sensibilities, Cortázar was influenced by two major Argentine writers: essayist and short story writer Jorge Luis Borges, with his intellectualism and universality; and fiction writer Roberto Arlt, with his sensuality, eroticism, and earthiness. From the former he learned to be demanding and "ethically implacable with himself as a writer"; from the latter he "sensed an enormously intuitive creative force" (Garfield, p. 6). However, Cortázar himself professes not to have consciously employed their techniques:

> I never register influences consciously. In my case, the critics must point them out. . . . I learn a lot about myself because actually there are many interpretations that I believe to be either completely or partially accurate. Thus they show pieces of my own mosaic, or my unknown unconscious. They show me my nocturnal self, nocturnal in the psychological sense, and in that sense I'm very grateful for that kind of interpretation.
>
> (Cortázar in Garfield, pp. 7-8)

Cortázar influenced other Latin American writers of the mid- to late-twentieth century, encouraging the works, for example, of Gabriel García Márquez and Mario Vargas Llosa, reading and correcting their manuscripts before they became famous. In fact, Cortázar's fiction helped forge the path for the "New Novel" of the 1950s and the "Boom Novel" of the 1960s in Latin America. Unlike their predecessors, the New Novelists approached fiction not as a mirror with which to reflect reality but as a universe of the imagination in which it was appropriate to indulge in fantasy. Not only did Cortázar's stories engage in fantasy, but they also prefigured other elements in later Latin American fiction, such as the treatment of popular culture (like jazz music, in "The Pursuer"). In the 1960s Cortázar wrote a novel, *Hopscotch* (1963), about a jazz-loving Argentine exile who lives in Paris and the novelist himself, who instructs his audience to jump forward to this chapter and backward to that one, calling for an unconventional reading of his story. *Hopscotch* ushered in the tradition of the Boom Novel, which stressed the interconnectedness of all time, included "flights of fantasy," and carried with it "the conviction that it is possible [for Latin American authors] to write new literature and that this will have a purifying effect on [their] society" (González Echevarría and Pupo-Walker, p. 232).

Reviews. Unlike some of Cortázar's other works, *Blow-Up and Other Stories* received a warm reception when first published (as *End of the Game and Other Stories*). In the *Times Literary Supplement,* critic Daniel Stern wrote:

> In [*End of the Game and Other Stories*] the shorter form allows no time for the merely tricky. Yet what magnificent tricks Cortázar does play. . . . [Cortázar manipulates the absurd and the mysterious] with sufficient skill to make the contrived seem impressively natural. . . . Cortázar writes with all the ambiguity, irony and attention to objects common to [certain other current authors]. . . . The difference is that Cortázar, in [his] stories, knows precisely when to stop.
>
> (Stern in Nasso, p. 196)

Donald A. Yates noted that, "His genius here lies in the knack for constructing striking, artistically 'right' subordinate circumstances out of which his fantastic and metaphysical whimsies appear normally to spring" (Yates in Nasso, p. 197). Neil Millar suggested poetically that "The very young accept the world's mystery. . . . To us older children the world is no less mysterious, and if we forget that fact our mornings come stale and too easy upon us . . . our perceptions drowse behind their dusty windows. Cortázar stings them alert again . . . he engulfs us in his dreams of Earth" (Millar in Nasso, p. 197).

—Emerson Spencer Olin

For More Information

Bach, Caleb. "Astor Piazzolla: A New-Age Score for the Tango." *Americas* 43, nos. 5-6 (September-October 1991): 14.

Cortázar, Julio. *Blow-Up and Other Stories.* Trans. Paul Blackburn. New York: Pantheon, 1967.

Gonzáles Echevarría, Roberto, and Enrique Pupo-Walker. *Cambridge History of Latin American Literature.* Vol. 2. Cambridge: Cambridge University Press, 1996.

Garfield, Evelyn Picon. *Julio Cortázar.* New York: Frederick Ungar, 1975.

Katra, William H. *Contorno: Literary Engagement in Post-Perónist Argentina.* Toronto: Associated University Presses, 1988.

King, John. *Sur: A Study of the Argentine Literary Journal and Its Role in the Development of a Culture, 1931-1970.* Cambridge: Cambridge University Press, 1986.

Nasso, Christine, ed. *Contemporary Authors.* Vols. 21-24. Detroit: Gale Research, 1977.

Randall, Laura. *An Economic History of Argentina in the Twentieth Century.* New York: Columbia University Press, 1978.

Riley, Carolyn, and Phyllis Carmel Mendelson, eds. *Contemporary Literary Criticism.* Vol. 5. Detroit: Gale Research, 1976.

Rock, David. *Authoritarian Argentina: The Nationalist Movement, Its History and Its Impact.* Berkeley: University of California Press, 1993.

Taylor, Julie. *Paper Tangos.* Durham, N.C.: Duke University Press, 1998.

Vargas Llosa, Mario. *Making Waves.* Trans. John King. New York: Penguin, 1998.

A Brazilian Tenement

by
Aluísio Azevedo

Brazilian writer Aluísio Tancredo Gonçalves de Azevedo was born in São Luis do Maranhão in 1857, when Brazil was still a monarchy. An immigrant from Portugal, his mother, Emília Amália Pinto de Magalhães, was, unlike many of the people around her, literate. She was also unconventional. First she shocked the townspeople by leaving her husband, a philanderer who mistreated her. Her second husband, David Gonçalves de Azevedo, was a vice-consul of Portugal. Again she scandalized the city, this time by moving into his townhouse without marrying him. The couple had three sons, including Aluísio, who were all illegitimate until their father acknowledged them as his offspring and heirs in 1864. Moving to Rio de Janeiro in 1876, Aluísio Azevedo studied at the Imperial Academy of Fine Arts, worked as a cartoonist for political and humor magazines, and began his writing career there. Initially he wrote unrealistic romantic tales, but then transitioned into naturalist novels that concentrated on telling stories in all their often grim detail. With the 1881 publication of *O mulato,* Rio critics began to recognize Azevedo as a premier writer of Brazilian naturalism. His masterpiece, *A Brazilian Tenement,* is recognized as one of the republic's foremost nineteenth-century novels. Serving as a historical document of sorts, the story provides a window into lower-class life in Brazil during the tumultuous 1870s.

THE LITERARY WORK

A novel set in Rio de Janeiro, Brazil, in the 1870s; first published in Portuguese (as *O cortiço*) in 1890, in English in 1926.

SYNOPSIS

Set in a Rio de Janeiro tenement, the novel focuses on the daily lives of its residents and its owner, as well as the owner's relationship with some higher-class neighbors.

Events in History at the Time of the Novel

Brazilian naturalism. Azevedo grew up in his father's comfortable tile-faced townhouse, with a strong ambition to profit from the books he wrote. When naturalism came into vogue in Brazil (1880 to 1895), he shifted from writing romantic potboilers to this more realistic genre, which invoked scientific terms in the telling of a story. Like other writers in Brazil at the time, Azevedo based his naturalist stories on three fundamental suppositions:

1) Change is either impossible or has negative consequences;

2) The sexual drive is the most significant in human life;

3) Environment and genetics determine a

person's actions and character; human will is of little consequence.

(Haberly, p. 337)

These were certainly grim suppositions. The question is, why at this point in time was Brazil ripe for such pessimism? If one keeps in mind that the few readers in late 1800s Brazil belonged to the upper class, there is a reasonable explanation. These upper-class readers lived in a tumultuous decade, in which events threatened to upset the stable empire of Brazil, which for so long had been a monarchy dominated by the upper class and a slave society. Upper-class Brazilians were full of fear, worried about the imminent abolition of slavery, about heightened competition from all the immigrants flooding the nation from Europe, and about the emergence of fresh "progressive" ways of working and living, as reflected in the rise of new tenements in Azevedo's novel.

Political backdrop. *A Brazilian Tenement* takes place in the late nineteenth century, a time of transition in Brazilian politics. At the beginning of the century (1808), to escape the invading French conqueror Napoleon Bonaparte, the monarch Dom João VI moved his court from Portugal to Rio de Janeiro, Brazil. Once there, he transformed Rio into a more powerful city politically and economically, opening its ports to international trade. The king returned to Portugal in 1816, and a few years later (1822) Brazil declared independence, becoming a separate monarchy for 67 years. Its final ruler, Dom Pedro II, enjoyed a long stable reign (1840–89), which ended a year before Azevedo's novel appeared. In 1889 Brazil replaced its monarchy with a republic, but enthusiasm for the change was far from universal. In many ways a monarchist mentality still prevailed. Back in 1808 Dom João VI had brought with him to Brazil thousands of courtiers, setting the stage for a society based on notions of aristocracy that still held sway at the end of the century. To be sure, Brazil's aristocracy was not purely hereditary—patents of nobility were bought and sold. In the novel, the tenement owner João Romão dreams of buying the title of count, while Miranda, his neighbor, becomes a baron, thanks to his social success. "He began," says the novel, "to dream of a baronetcy, this ambition . . . would cost money" (Azevedo, *A Brazilian Tenement,* p. 27).

Slavery. Society's hierarchy rested on a foundation of slavery, which began after the Portuguese arrived in 1500 and converted Brazil into an overseas colony that supplied Portugal with raw materials such as wood, cotton, sugar, coffee, gold, and diamonds. Slavery would endure for the next 400 years, involving brutal 15- to 18-hour workdays during harvest time, along with whippings, brandings, and other harsh punishments. Around 90 percent of Brazil's slaves still lived in rural areas at the time of the novel. Conditions were somewhat better for the minority of city slaves. They often went unnoticed, due to their co-existence with the free black population in cities. Also, the cities offered more opportunities for slaves to earn income in their spare time, and public whipping was prohibited in urban centers.

Slaves in Brazil could hire themselves out for a fee on the frequent Catholic holidays, and then use their accumulated money to purchase their own freedom. By 1860 the free black population had grown so large that slaves numbered less than 17 percent of a population that was primarily black, mulatto, and mestizo. The white sector formed less than 40 percent of the population. It was not uncommon for white masters to free their slave mistresses, their children from these unions, and their elderly slaves. Meanwhile, Brazil began to emancipate its slaves, in stages, from the termination of the slave trade in 1850, to the Law of the Free Womb in 1870, which proclaimed that blacks would no longer be born into slavery, to complete abolition in 1888. In the novel, an old Brazilian laments the demise of slavery: "[H]e vented his spleen on the times, the customs and the changes, all for the worse, as he was ever ready to point out. . . . The old man hit upon the subject of the abolition agitation" (*A Brazilian Tenement,* pp. 31–32).

The agitation stemmed from foreign ideas—such as the growing global disdain for slavery—and from changes within Brazil itself. After mid-century, many Brazilians began to view slavery as "backward" and incompatible with progress. The enforcement in the 1850s of the ban on the international slave trade encouraged this point of view, as did abolition in other Latin American countries and the United States in the mid-to-late nineteenth century. Meanwhile, within Brazil, sons of the rural elite were moving away from their homes into cities and becoming professionals rather than planters. Distanced from their heritage, they began to turn a critical, reformist eye on the institutions from which they descended.

Immigration and internal migration. Once slavery's collapse appeared imminent, Brazil's doors opened wider to immigrants from Europe

Eighteenth-century depiction of Brazilian slaves mining diamonds. For nearly 400 years Brazil's social hierarchy rested on a foundation of slavery.

in an attempt to find cheap labor. The first immigrant schemes were developed in the 1820s in Brazil, but it was not until the second half of the nineteenth century that immigration occurred on a mass scale. In order to supply labor to the booming coffee regions of southern Brazil, many slaves were transferred from the declining Northeastern sugar regions. However "even if every slave in the Northeast had moved south they could not have furnished the labor needed in the coffee economy" (Skidmore and Smith, p. 146). The acute demand for labor made immigration a top priority. Most of these immigrants came from Portugal, Italy, and Spain, to the coffee regions of southern Brazil, in hopes of someday acquiring land. They are represented in the novel by Jerônimo, a native of Portugal, who immigrates to Brazil as a *colono,* or hired plantation worker, but finds himself forced to migrate with his wife and child to the city because of the poor return on his hard labor. For a time, he fares better there, finding work as a granite blaster and rising to the position of foreman.

> [Jerônimo] had come to Brazil contracted as a farm hand, and had labored like a beast on a plantation for two years. There he lived among the slaves and endured the hardest life he ever had known. His contract finished, finding himself with nothing accumulated for all this intense effort and with no future for his wife and little girl, he refused to continue longer and came to the city, where he found employment in a quarry, breaking stone for a miserable wage. By dint of Piedade's poorly paid laundry work, they managed to keep a roof over their heads and not go hungry.
>
> (*A Brazilian Tenement,* p. 66)

RIO'S TENEMENT POPULATION, 1867-88

	Tenements	Inhabitants	Brazilians	Immigrants
1869	642	21,929	9,630	12,299
1875	876	33,255	13,863	19,392
1888	1,331	46,680	—	—

(Hahner, *Poverty and Politics,* pp. 7, 26)

In the 1870s, the decade in which the novel takes place, there was a huge influx of immigrants (200,000 entered Brazil between 1872 and 1880). One consequence of all this immigration was increased competition for jobs in the southern cities. Though industrialization was increasing, there were not enough positions for the rising urban population, so that many residents felt compelled to enter the informal economy as peddlers, laundresses, and the like. Meanwhile, blessed with an abundant labor pool, employers aggravated the tensions between native Brazilians and immigrants by keeping wages low and otherwise contributing to much of the anti-immigrant resentment depicted in the novel

Reform and the lower classes. Azevedo's novel is set in Rio tenements in an era when they housed increasing numbers of the city's working population. As indicated, it was also an era of reform, in which progressive ideas such as the abolition of slavery, the promotion of mass immigration, the separation of church and state, and educational and political change dominated discussion. Though Brazil was still an empire in the 1870s, the emperor moved into the political background and gave more power to his ministers, property qualifications were lowered for voters, and the judicial branch grew more independent. These and other reforms were capped in 1888 with the abolition of slavery and in 1889 with the elimination of the emperor and the transformation of the country into a republic. But its power structure remained largely intact, and Brazil's population "continued to be exploited as it always had been" (Bethell, p. 726). Little, for example, was done to alter the appalling living conditions that are vividly rendered in *A Brazilian Tenement.*

Problems only escalated as the end of the century approached. The population grew from 3.8 million in 1822, to more than 10 million in 1872, to 14 million in 1889 (Bethell, p. 728). Hoping for positions in Brazil's railways, banks, and industries, immigrants continued to pour into the cities. Some 70 percent of these immigrants settled in Rio, which nearly doubled in population between 1872 and 1890, from 274,972 to 522,651 inhabitants (Bethell, p. 728). In *A Brazilian Tenement,* the male protagonists are mostly immigrants while Brazilians play minor roles, a dynamic that reflects the population in Rio and its tenements at the time.

Tenement life. While immigration continued apace, conditions improved in cities—in water, sewage, housing, and transportation services. At the same time, however, the swelling population stimulated the growth of tenement buildings to house the new urban masses, whose presence "raised new questions and created problems of social control, which an elite habituated to dis-

A shantytown overlooking Rio de Janeiro. Such slums began springing up in the hills around Rio in the nineteenth century.

ciplined slaves still did not know how to deal with" (Bethell, p. 733).

Rio's workers lived in sharp contrast to the elite strata of society, whose members enjoyed dining in downtown Rio cafes, shopping on the elegant Rua Ouvidor, and attending the theater and upscale parties. Because of the high cost of homes in Rio, only the middle and upper classes could afford to live in comfort; rents escalated to such a degree that the only housing affordable to the urban poor became tenement dwellings. Workers would often pay a quarter of their salaries to live in these places, while tenement owners grew rich with profit. Annual rents might generate as much as 50 percent profit for the owners over the buildings' original cost (Hahner, *Poverty and Politics,* p. 25). Often tenements were "carelessly constructed in violation of all rules of hygiene, just to have as many rooms as possible in order to produce more revenue for their owners" (Sousa in Hahner, *Poverty and Politics,* p. 25). In other words, tenement owners grew rich by cramming Rio's workers into substandard, disease-ridden housing. Luckier residents might occupy a small apartment in the tenement, with a living room, kitchen, and bedroom. The less fortunate were relegated to "narrow and dark cubicles packed with people" (Costa in Hahner, *Poverty and Politics,* p. 25). In the midst of several of these cubicles was an interior patio, which contained latrines, water spigots, tubs, and space for drying clothes, until, in time, much of this space was replaced by additional rooms for rent. In the novel, the tenement owner, João Romão, shares with his neighbor plans to rebuild the dwelling after a fire:

> [H]e explained his project. The courtyard was wider than was really necessary. He intended to extend the line of houses farther toward the front on the left-hand side, against the wall toward Miranda. The burned part would be rebuilt and a second story added to the whole. . . . Then, instead of a hundred tenants, he expected the new construction would enable him to accommodate at least four hundred. . . .
>
> (*A Brazilian Tenement,* p. 251)

Yellow fever. As more tenements were built in damp and diseased areas, overcrowding created even less sanitary conditions for the urban poor. Such conditions contributed to the reappearance in 1870s Rio of yellow fever, a disease that had been almost absent in the 1860s and that would not leave the city until the successful eradication campaign of the early twentieth century. Extremely serious outbreaks of the yellow fever occurred in 1873 and 1876, causing more than 7,000 fatalities between them. After the 1873 outbreak, Pereira Rego, president of the Board of Health, determined that the disease had two main causes: clogged sewers and the filthy tenements housing the poor. As Sidney Chalhoub maintains, "the identification of the [tenements] as the cooking pots for the germs of yellow fever was of enormous symbolic and political significance" (Chalhoub, p. 456). Once tenements were identified as a main source of the yellow fever, public officials began to define "tenements" as broadly as possible, concluding that Rio's entire downtown area was filled with them. City planners, dreaming of demolishing all of Rio's tenements, began gradually to shut them down. As many critics have noted, city officials were also motivated by fear of the lower classes, including the many ex-slaves who inhabited the tenements. Because nobody made any serious effort to provide alternative housing, the former tenement dwellers began moving to the hills of Rio, where they started building the shantytowns that have been prominent throughout the twentieth century.

Yellow fever proved fatal to European immigrants more often than to native Brazilians. In Azevedo's novel an Italian tenement dweller dies of the disease. The affliction threatened the rich as well as the poor, and unsurprisingly the city's most urgent concerns were for its upper-class citizens. The alleged lower-class origins of the disease brought to the forefront the position of servants. During the 1870s about 71 percent of all working women and 15 percent of all working men labored as servants: wet-nurses, seamstresses, laundresses, water carriers, cooks, and maids (Graham, pp. 4-5). Domestic servants provided the link between upper-class homes and the tenement slums in which the servants themselves lived. Suddenly these urban masses became the problem of the society at large, which was filled with a dread of contagion. Families grew fearful of laundresses, many of whom washed and hung clothes around the tenements' communal tubs; in 1891 the city council would finally prohibit tenement dwellers from washing any but their own clothing in these tubs (Graham, p. 117). Wet-nurses in particular were seen as carriers of disease. While various proposals attempted to regulate domestic servants, the unsanitary, overcrowded tenements, as well as cases of yellow fever, continued through the end of the nineteenth century.

The Novel in Focus

Plot summary. The novel concerns the growth of an urban Rio de Janeiro tenement, built by the Portuguese immigrant João Romão with the help of a slave woman, Bertoleza. João enriches his tenement by exploiting the slave woman, who becomes his partner and lover, and by cheating both customers and residents. His initial thriftiness is soon replaced by a burning desire (fueled by a competitive jealousy of his higher-class neighbor, Miranda) to attain not only economic wealth, but to rise socially as well.

João's neighbor, Miranda, is a Portuguese merchant with a business in downtown Rio. Married to Dona Estella because of her dowry, Miranda must rely on this dowry for the security of his business, though he and his wife despise each other. João owns not only the tenement but also a store and restaurant frequented by the tenants, as well as a nearby quarry. Miranda lives in a townhouse next door to João's growing tenement complex and the two quickly lock horns. Jealous of his Portuguese neighbor's financial success, Miranda, a Portuguese immigrant himself, decides to get even by acquiring an aristocratic title for himself. Living with Miranda is the aged Botelho, an old "parasite" who had been a slave broker in his youth, and who speaks of "a voyage he once made to Africa for a cargo of negroes" (*A Brazilian Tenement,* p. 31). He subsequently suffered from bad luck and now depends on Miranda for his sustenance.

In full naturalist detail, the novel describes the residents of the tenement, discussing their ethnicity, their occupations, and often their physical characteristics: one female resident, for instance, is described as "an aggressive Portuguese much given to shouting, with thick, hairy arms and the general build of a draft horse" (*A Brazilian Tenement,* p. 41). The novel promotes an animalistic view of the residents, who "lived herded together like cattle and toiled from sun to sun with no ideals or ambitions other than to eat and sleep and procreate" (*A Brazilian Tenement,* p. 216). Peddlers, a carpenter, laundresses, a policeman, Italian immigrants, and other types are described by the third-person narrator, who contrasts the immigrants to the Brazilians. For example, the narrator speaks of how "the Portuguese women wore bright silk handkerchiefs and the Brazilians a spray of flowers in their elaborately dressed hair" (*A Brazilian Tenement,* p. 71).

With his wife and child, the hard-working Portuguese immigrant Jerônimo is hired as foreman at the quarry and moves with his family into the tenement. As João Romão experiences his economic and social ascent, Jerônimo experiences his concomitant descent. He abandons his wife,

Piedade, for a beautiful, charming mulatta, Rita, whom he first encounters at a Sunday dance session in the tenement. Rita has a lover, Firmo, who "enjoyed the distinction of having been born at court, where his father was one of the Emperor's stable-hands" (*A Brazilian Tenement,* p. 83).

Before Jerônimo abandons Piedade for Rita, the two women have a physical fight, during which Piedade insults Rita's black origins and Rita insults Piedade's foreign origins. Piedade attributes most of her bad luck to the climate and to the tropical sun of Brazil. "In moments of desperation she raised her clenched hands, not against the man she awaited, but in impotent rage against the bright sunlight, this tropic glare that causes men's blood to boil and their senses to overcome their reason" (*A Brazilian Tenement,* p. 236). As the two women fight, tenement dwellers cheer and take sides according to ethnicity—immigrant against Brazilian. The fight is cut short when a fire erupts in the tenement, and all tenement dwellers unite to extinguish the flames.

After eliminating his competitor, Firmo, by clubbing him to death, Jerônimo leaves the tenement to live with Rita. Piedade suffers a moral decline, taking refuge in alcohol. Because Jerônimo has not paid for their daughter's tuition, the daughter leaves school to live in the tenement, where she catches the eye of Pombinha. A prostitute, Pombinha has abandoned her husband and joined company with Leonie, a French prostitute who is godmother to the child of one of the tenement residents. The narrator describes Pombinha's entry into the world of prostitution as nothing less than an inevitable consequence of the tenement environment: "the tenement tree had borne its fruit," as it promises to do with Jerônimo's neglected daughter (*A Brazilian Tenement,* p. 309).

Meanwhile, João Romão, in his eagerness to rise socially, arranges to marry the fair-skinned, educated daughter of his neighbor, Miranda, who is now a baron. An obstacle is the slave woman Bertoleza (his lover), who has toiled at João's side for years and whose labor in fact elevated him to his current position as capitalist and socialite.

> "Oh, yes," remonstrates Bertoleza in self defense. "[N]ow you can ridicule me—now that I am not necessary to you any longer. But back in the days when you did need me, then my black body did very nicely for you, and you built your fortune on the sweat of my labor."
>
> (*A Brazilian Tenement,* p. 298)

With the former slaver-trader who lives at Miranda's, João devises the plan of locating Bertoleza's original owners—he has misled her into believing that he already purchased her freedom. When the owners arrive to take her away, Bertoleza commits suicide rather than return to a life of slavery.

Laundresses and prostitutes. Most of the novel's female characters do laundry for patrons, conducting their labor on the grounds of the tenement. In mid-to-late nineteenth century Brazil, laundresses washed and ironed outside their patrons' homes. Around the middle of the century they performed this labor at public streams and fountains; when the tenements appeared they began conducting business in their interior patios. As one foreign visitor observed, "the workman leaves his house for his work, and the wife passes the whole day washing and ironing. The health of these women often breaks down from overwork" (Hahner, *Emancipating the Female Sex,* p. 98). There were, however, few other choices for lower-class women at the time, and their income was generally critical to family survival. A large number were unschooled; few could even read or write.

SOCIAL MOBILITY THROUGH MARRIAGE

As elsewhere in the world, it was not uncommon in nineteenth-century Brazil for marriages to be arranged by the parents, in order to guarantee a union that would economically or socially benefit the interested parties. In the novel the socially mobile and increasingly wealthy João arranges to marry the daughter of his higher-status neighbor, Miranda. Miranda's own social status was attained by marrying into money; as the novel explains, unwilling to leave his adulteress wife, he was now "mortgaging himself to a she-devil who had brought him eighty thousand milreis and also incalculable shame and humiliation. He had an easy life, but he was eternally tied to a woman he loathed" (A Brazilian Tenement, p. 25).

Brazil's literacy rate never climbed higher than 15 percent before 1889. In the novel pretty young Pombinha is a laundry-list and letter writer for the older tenement dwellers, who correspond through her to their loved ones. Exposed to their anxieties and arguments, she hears the harsh realities that give the lie to her mother's ideal of escape from tenement life through Pombinha's forthcoming marriage to a man of better fortune.

Marriage in late 1800s Brazil, understands Pombinha, does not guarantee happiness and can bring quite the reverse.

Actually a few of the novel's female characters regard marriage as a foolhardy institution in light of the fact that a woman's husband "was her master, he owned her. He had all the rights" (Hahner, *Emancipating the Female Sex,* p. 88). In the novel one of the female tenement dwellers rails at husbands and denigrates marriage in general:

> They're all alike. . . . If a woman is fool enough to try to please them, they get sick of her; and if she realizes that marriage is a joke and proceeds accordingly [sees other men], she's treated to kicks and cuffs. . . .
>
> (*A Brazilian Tenement,* p. 114)

For some women prostitution appeared to be a viable avenue of escape, from both male domination and economic misfortune. Never legalized but long tolerated in Brazil, prostitution included a luxury, high-class strata, called *cocotes,* who are represented in the novel by Leonie and later by Pombinha herself. They were finely dressed, self-employed prostitutes, who moved with discretion through theaters and other public places, garbed in silk, feathers, and jewels. Either French or pretending to be so, they catered to the Brazilian elite's admiration for France and plied their trade with success. Burgeoning cities like Rio swarmed with unmarried men who paid prices that often brought prostitutes more income than laundresses or factory workers. While the genuine elite scorned these cocotes, they were accorded a measure of respect in the tenements:

> Leonie, with the gaudy and exaggerated clothing usually affected by French cocotes, aroused much interest and admiration on her visits to [the tenement]. Her gown of steel-colored silk, trimmed with ox-blood, was short and saucy, exposing slippers the height of whose heels filled the laundresses with awe. Her twenty-button gloves reached almost to her armpits. A red parasol foaming with a sea of pink lace . . . and with a wonderfully carved handle was an acknowledged work of art. And her hat—not a woman in all of the ninety-five households could behold that hat without emotion. It was a large one, with two enormous wings and a nest of red velvet, over which hovered a whole bird, though a small bird.
>
> (*A Brazilian Tenement,* p. 136)

Ethnic friction. In the novel, when Rita, a native Brazilian, battles with the Portuguese woman Piedade, a fire in the tenement ends the fight, and all the observers, who had initially taken sides according to ethnicity, join to put out the common aggressor, nature. The tenement dwellers share other common problems—such as alcohol abuse, the high number of single-mother households, and promiscuity. The immigrant Piedade degenerates into a promiscuous alcoholic after her husband rejects her for Rita; Florinda, the mulatta daughter of a native Brazilian, becomes pregnant out of wedlock.

The novel reflects real-life tensions between Brazilians and immigrants, based largely on attitudes and stereotypes of the day. Often, the immigrants received preferential treatment over native Brazilians in the labor market. Because of the late-nineteenth-century scientific theory of Darwinism, which taught that the fittest survive, and because of racial prejudices that considered the white race to be the most highly evolved, many believed that whitening the country would lead to progress. In the novel the seductive Rita fascinates Jerônimo, and she is likewise drawn to him, partly, says the novel, because of race: "He fascinated her with his strength and his seriousness, and the instinctive attraction of the male of a superior race immediately awakened a response in her mulatta blood" (*A Brazilian Tenement,* p. 226).

Another prejudice in Brazil at the time held that the white immigrants from Europe were harder workers than native Brazilians. Many plantation owners and capitalists held "a firm and unshakable belief in the innate laziness and irresponsibility of the black and racially mixed Brazilian masses" (Andrews, p. 89). In *A Brazilian Tenement* the once-industrious immigrant Jerônimo undergoes a transformation: "The Portuguese was thoroughly Brazilianized. He had become lazy and loved ease and luxury" (*A Brazilian Tenement,* p. 263). One reason for such stereotyping was the lingering effect of bondage; people tended to resist work conditions similar to those of slavery. "Experiences of slavery had produced a deep determination among all Brazilians, and particularly black ones, to avoid conditions of employment at all reminiscent of the slave regime" (Andrews, p. 112). On the other hand, European immigrants, often driven by a desire to earn their fortune in Brazil and then return home, were more accepting of harsh working conditions. Such factors increased racial tensions, and "those hatreds were further exacerbated by the discontent and resentment of Brazilians locked out of the labor market" (Andrews, p. 92). A 1893 census of the city of São Paulo showed that 79 percent of its factory workers, for example, were foreign born (Andrews, p. 97). The situation in Rio was not as extreme, for São Paulo subsidized immigration, but competition nevertheless existed.

Though it acknowledges this racial resentment, the novel portrays the Brazilian environment as even more powerful and debilitating. The seductress Rita represents Brazil in the novel: "She was the brilliant glare at midday, the red heat of the plantation field; she was the aroma of the vanilla tree, filling the Brazilian forest; she was the virgin palm which lifts its head aloft and scorns contact with another living thing; she was poisonous and marvelously sweet" (*A Brazilian Tenement,* p. 100). The Brazilian environment dooms even the industrious, suggests the novel; there is no escape.

Sources and literary context. Aluísio Azevedo is credited with introducing Brazil to naturalism, a genre that included detailed descriptions of places, characters, and the sexual exploits of these characters to substantiate the "scientific validity of the larger truths they were expounding" (Haberly, p. 336). In contrast to naturalism in France, where hopeful aspects entered into the genre, naturalism in Brazil was thoroughly pessimistic. Also, the novel was more explicit in its descriptions of sexuality than French novels of the day. Naturalist writers saw their function as comparable to that of a scientist: they placed their characters in certain volatile situations, then observed and recorded the outcomes in all their realism, no matter how grotesque or unappealing. In Azevedo's case, this meant focusing on the filthy, disease-ridden tenements of Rio. Such a focus was at the time shocking to an audience accustomed to more "elevated" literature. A popular philosophy of the day, positivism, taught that the scientific method was the only way to acquire real knowledge. In keeping with this philosophy, Azevedo conducted "experiments" before writing *A Brazilian Tenement.* Disguised as a laborer, he visited tenements and even rented a room in one, living there only briefly because some of the neighbors became suspicious when he questioned them. Along with this firsthand research, Azevedo perused official papers and news articles that concerned tenements, which contributed to the documentary value of the novel.

Personally Azevedo was an abolitionist, and also harbored strong feelings about immigrants in his era, criticizing the fact that most of the tenements springing up in the city were owned and operated by foreigners. He attempted nevertheless to report his observations in neutral, scientific fashion. There was no ulterior motive here; he was not agitating for urban improvements. "His novel is, above all, a rationalization for inaction: environmentally and genetically maimed, the inhabitants of the tenement are largely beyond redemption" (Haberly, p. 339).

POPULAR PHILOSOPHIES

Though Azevedo did not have a political agenda in mind, his writing was influenced by philosophies of the day. In vogue in late-nineteenth-century Brazil was a set of scientifically based ideas that became known as "positivism." Based largely on the teachings of Auguste Comte (the French father of sociology), positivism was a belief that the scientific method could create conditions of social progress. Positivists regarded society not as a collection of individuals but as a developing organism. In his novel, Azevedo describes the tenement as a growing entity that appears to have a life of its own, that seems to move and breathe.

> The tenement was now in full activity and the confused sounds of the awakening neighborhood had given way to the steady din of normal movement. Individual voices no longer were distinguished, but instead was heard the compact roar of the entire populace. . . . There could be felt in that human fermentation, like the damp black loam that feeds the roots of a fragrant rambler, the source of vigorous life.
>
> (*A Brazilian Tenement,* p. 39)

Another philosophy of the day, "determinism," taught that people were products of habit and instinct, affected by adaptation to their environment, and that human will had little impact. The philosophy furthermore taught that race determined someone's character, psychology, and potential. Given that the majority of Brazil's population was black and mestizo or mulatto by 1890, such thinking encouraged a desire for white (allegedly more highly evolved) immigrants from Europe in the belief that the racial composition of Brazil would determine its progress. Unwilling to point to a history of slavery and landed estates as the root of its underdevelopment (which would place the blame on the elite), people looked for other culprits. Along with the tropical climate, which was believed to affect a person's genetic makeup, people blamed the ethnic balance in Brazil.

Reviews. Initially some conservative reviewers hesitated to praise *A Brazilian Tenement*—in part because it included language and scenes considered scandalous and grotesque. However, the novel was generally well received by the more liberal Rio critics, and in reviews of the English translation (although much of the scandalous content was censored out of the translation). Acknowledging Azevedo's objectivity, the *Boston Transcript* declared that he "set down implacably the slice of life that he has seen, that he knows as he knows himself. He does not interpret. Neither does he write with the conscious artistry of the author who would rather frame a neat sentence than create a real character" (*Boston Transcript* in Knight and James, p. 27). A *New York Times* book review praised Azevedo's mastery of "the difficult art of progressing from the specific to the universal," noting that Romão "is a recognizable individual" connected to his time and locale, yet the tenement owner "might almost stand as a personification of ruthless greed for possessions and material power" (*New York Times Book Review,* p. 22). Even now the novel's setting and characters are called "powerful and convincing," although today, a century after its initial release, the plot has been characterized as "far more melodramatic than realistic" (Haberly in González Echevarría and Pupo-Walker, p. 149).

—Olivia Treviño

For More Information

Andrews, George Reid. "Black and White Workers: São Paulo, Brazil, 1888-1928." In *The Abolition of Slavery and the Aftermath of Emancipation in Brazil.* Ed. Rebecca J. Scott. Durham, N. C.: Duke University Press, 1988.

Azevedo Aluísio. *A Brazilian Tenement.* Trans. Harry W. Brown. New York: Robert M. McBride, 1926.

Bethell, Leslie, ed. *The Cambridge History of Latin America.* Vol. 5. Cambridge: Cambridge University Press, 1986.

Chalhoub, Sidney. "The Politics of Disease Control: Yellow Fever and Race in Nineteenth Century Rio de Janeiro." *Journal of Latin American Studies* 25, no. 3 (October 1993): 441.

González Echevarría, Roberto, and Enrique Pupo-Walker. *The Cambridge History of Latin American Literature.* Vol. 3. Cambridge: Cambridge University Press, 1996.

Graham, Sarah Lauderdale. *House and Street: The Domestic World of Servants and Masters in Nineteenth-Century Rio de Janeiro.* Cambridge: Cambridge University Press, 1988.

Haberly, David T. "Aluísio Azevedo." In *Latin American Writers.* Vol. 2. Eds. Carlos A. Solé and Maria Isabel Abreu. New York: Charles Scribner's Sons, 1989.

Hahner, June E. *Poverty and Politics: The Urban Poor in Brazil, 1870-1920.* Albuquerque: University of New Mexico Press, 1986.

———. *Emancipating the Female Sex: The Struggle for Women's Rights in Brazil, 1850–1940.* Durham, N. C.: Duke University Press, 1990.

Knight, Marion A., and Mertice M. James, eds. *The Book Review Digest, 1926.* New York: H. W. Wilson, 1927.

Review of *A Brazilian Tenement. The New York Times Book Review,* May 23, 1926, 17.

Skidmore, Thomas E., and Peter H. Smith. *Modern Latin America.* 3rd ed. New York: Oxford University Press, 1997.

The Celebration

by
Ivan Ângelo

Ivan Ângelo (b. 1937) was part of an important intellectual generation that formed in Belo Horizonte, Brazil, in the 1950s, and that included such notable writers as Fernando Gabeira, Affonso Romano de Sant'Anna, and Silviano Santiago. A practicing journalist throughout his literary career, Ângelo began writing short stories in the 1950s. His first volume of short stories, *Homem sofrendo no quarto*, won the City of Belo Horizonte Award in 1959. Other works include *Duas faces* (1961), *A casa de vidro* (1979; *The Tower of Glass*, 1986), *A face horrível* (1986), all of which are collections of short stories, and the novella *Amor?* (1995). He has also published numerous works of fiction for young people. *The Celebration*, his only novel to date, concerns Brazilian society at the time—or very shortly before—Ivan Ângelo wrote the work.

THE LITERARY WORK

A novel set in the city of Belo Horizonte, Brazil, in March 1970; published in Portuguese (as *A Festa*) in 1976, in English in 1982.

SYNOPSIS

Organized loosely around events that take place on a single day, the novel presents a series of texts, documents, episodes, vignettes, and stories that paint a mural of the situation and historical antecedents of Brazilian society under post-1964 military rule.

Events in History at the Time of the Novel

The Celebration deals with fictional events that take place in the city of Belo Horizonte on the evening of March 30 and the early morning of March 31, 1970. But it is much more than a snapshot of such a brief moment. By including episodes set in different time frames as well as multiple historical, political, and cultural references, Ângelo's work offers a succinct and incisive background of the social and historical genesis of the problems depicted: the poverty of Brazil's Northeast and its attendant causes and consequences, including the authoritarianism, violence, and repressive tactics of the Brazilian military government; migration from the countryside to the cities; the student movement; and the oppositional role of intellectuals. The novel, in short, deals with the social, political, cultural, and personal implications of authoritarianism and injustice in modern Brazil.

The authoritarian legacy. The novel's concern with authoritarianism is made clear in the first two of its four epigraphs, from Nicolo Machiavelli's *The Prince* and W. H. Auden's "Herod," respectively. Machiavelli's affirmation that the "appellation of cruel, however, should not matter to a prince striving to maintain the unity and faith of his subjects" suggests that repression in the name of order is justified (Machiavelli in Ângelo, *The Celebration*, p. 6). Auden's citation refers to the difficulty of forcing "the masses to

Citizens welcome rebel troops to Rio de Janeiro during the Revolution of 1930, which brought Getúlio Vargas to power.

be sensible" when vital forces at work in human beings do not always fit into the rationalist designs of authoritarian leaders (*The Celebration*, p. 6). The words of both Machiavelli and Auden's Herod find significant resonances within Ângelo's novel, particularly in the actions of the police—both in the streets and in later interrogations—and in the figure of the police commissioner, who echoes Machiavelli's words and Herod's perspective: "The time has come to unleash the means of crushing all disorder, though the future may judge me cruel. For I have learned: the appellation of 'cruel' should not trouble a prince striving to maintain unity and order" (*The Celebration*, pp. 110-11).

Brazil has a long history of authoritarian government. From 1500 until 1822, the country was a colony of Portugal, and its inhabitants had limited political rights. From Independence in 1822 until the declaration of the Republic in 1889, it was ruled by a monarchy that was often enlightened, but autocratic nonetheless. The nation was defined not by the totality of its population, but rather by those eligible to vote: male—and usually white—landowners.

During the First Republic (1889-1930), Brazil had a formal democracy, but in reality the ideals of political liberalism were never able to overcome the forms of clientelism (the exchange of political support for tangible benefits) that resulted in fraudulent and corrupt electoral processes. By the end of the 1920s, democratic liberalism was largely discredited, since the reality did not conform to the ideal, and political extremes of the left and right (communism and fascism) had tremendous appeal. The Revolution of 1930, which carried Getúlio Vargas to power, initiated a 15-year period of authoritarian rule that hardened in 1937 into what is known as the *Estado Novo*, or New State, which indelibly marked Brazilian culture and society through its institution building. A new labor code in 1943, for example, permitted unions to organize at the local level, though they were prohibited at the state and federal levels. After a democratic interregnum starting in 1945, which saw such remarkable accomplishments as the construction of a new federal capital—Brasília—a military coup d'état in 1964 initiated a 21-year period of military rule.

Authoritarianism is not just a political system or mode of government—it permeates the very foundations of society. A rigidly hierarchical system limits upward mobility and sustains itself through complex mechanisms such as clientelism, the exchange of favors, and the various myths of national identity. In a very influential essay, Robert Schwarz discusses mechanisms of domination in nineteenth-century Brazil, when both slavery and patron-client relations contradicted liberal ideas. The granting of favors by the powerful, for example, placed the grantee in a dependent relationship in which he or she had to repay the favor in accordance with the interests of the grantor (Schwarz, p. 22). The persistent myth of racial democracy in fact sustains racism by suppressing debate on the issue. The legacy of slavery has been reconfigured in relations between the privileged and their domestic servants, as in the case of lawyer Jorge Paulo de Fernandes and his maid Maria in *The Celebration*. The tradition of patriarchy, with its inherent intolerance and violence, continues in marital relations—such as those between Candinho and Juliana, Cléber and Lenice, or Jorge Paulo and Mônica—and through the objectification of women such as Andrea. Unequal power relations are embedded in the social relations of everyday life.

Prelude to dictatorship. *The Celebration* is set almost six years to the day after the Brazilian military overthrew the democratic government of João Goulart, initiating 21 years of military dictatorship. Events leading up to the coup d'état are multiple and complex. In 1945 Getúlio Vargas, who had ruled Brazil in authoritarian fashion since 1930, was removed from power, and the country returned to a democratic form of government. Vargas regained the presidency through electoral processes in 1951 as a populist reformer. He was not well liked by the military and other conservative sectors of Brazilian society. In August 1954 an assassination attempt was made on the life of conservative politician and Vargas opponent Carlos Lacerda, and it was soon learned that the head of Vargas's security detail was involved. In the midst of a growing political scandal, Vargas committed suicide. Interim presidents held power from then until January 1956, when Juscelino Kubitschek took office.

Kubitschek promised 50 years of progress in his five years in office, and he embarked on an ambitious plan of industrial development and economic expansion. He was one of only two presidents between 1930 and 1964 to remain in office legally through his designated term, partially because of his ability to rally the Brazilian people around his plans. Brasília, with its ultramodern architecture, is perhaps the most perfect symbol of Kubitschek's views. His brand of developmentalism, however, was fraught with contradiction: although it was indeed a means of mobilizing support and guaranteeing the system's stability, it was also an effective tool for controlling social and political tensions. It toyed with the people's nationalist sentiments, for example, yet based its program of industrialization on foreign investment.

Kubitschek was succeeded by former São Paulo governor Jânio Quadros, another populist leader who campaigned against political corruption. Quadros took office as president in January 1961, only to resign on August 25, a mere eight months later. His vice president, Vargas protegé and former Minister of Labor, João Goulart, was out of the country on an official visit to communist China. Because of Goulart's absence, the president of the Chamber of Deputies was sworn in as acting president. Goulart returned quickly to assume his constitutionally guaranteed position, but he found himself in the midst of a political crisis brought on by the fact that the military and conservative political sectors thought that he was too closely aligned with leftist forces. Congress approved a change in the Constitution, creating a parliamentary form of government, in which the president was to share the executive position with a council of ministers, and Goulart took office with weakened presidential powers on September 7, Brazil's Independence Day.

Goulart faced numerous serious problems while in office, such as high inflation, a growing foreign debt, and an increasing cost of living for the Brazilian people. A plebiscite held on January 7, 1963, returned the country to a presidential system of government, and Goulart finally gained the powers that had been denied him in 1961. Supported by political parties of the left, labor unions, students, and other progressive social sectors, Goulart sought to implement large-scale social reforms, including agrarian reform and the nationalization of foreign enterprises, particularly in the impoverished Northeast. Conflicts between his government and the opposition—both military and civilian—increased rapidly.

A number of events unleashed the military's move against Goulart. At a large rally held in front of Rio de Janeiro's central train station on March 13, 1964, Goulart signed two decrees, one nationalizing all private petroleum refineries in the country, and the other creating a government agency to advance the process of agrarian reform. Both of these measures further displeased the conservative opposition. On March 19, some 500,000 people, organized by women's religious groups, marched through the streets of São Paulo in a counter-demonstration to Goulart's rally of the 13th. Opposition continued to grow, including the governors of Brazil's largest and most powerful states, such as Magalhães Pinto from Minas Gerais, in whose capital, Belo Horizonte, *The Celebration* is set.

On March 20 the Association of Sailors and Marines (a labor union of enlisted men), in a clear violation of military hierarchy, demanded the firing of the Minister of the Navy, Sílvio Mota, who had attempted to discipline one of the organizers of this illegal association. Goulart conceded to the demand and replaced the minister with an admiral who met the approval of labor leaders. This agitated officers in the military and increased fears among them that Goulart was using the armed forces for his own radical political ends. The generals warned the president that he would have to choose between the support of the armed forces and that of the labor unions and that they would no longer tolerate breakdowns in discipline. The army took action against Goulart on March 31, 1964, and easily removed him from office.

VICTIM OF THE 1958 DROUGHT

"[W]herever we traveled we found him starving, ragged, sad-eyed, and skeletal, in search of help that is not forthcoming. Already without hope, though his only ambition be the smallest provision of manioc flour, to ease the hunger which day by day devours his system. . . . Here in Brazil, where we seem quite proud of ourselves, singing out with paeans of self-praise . . . , it is estimated that more than two million people live in the most abject state of malnutrition and poverty possible to human beings. . . ."
(Colonel Orlando Gomes Ramagem . . . personal observer for President Juscelino Kubitschek of the drought of 1958. His report . . . was suppressed by the Kubitschek government. . . .)
(*The Celebration,* pp. 19-20)

Agrarian reform and internal migration. One of the most volatile issues in Brazil during the Goulart period—and one that is as yet unresolved—was that of agrarian reform, particularly in the northeastern part of the country. The Northeast is one of the most impoverished regions in Brazil. Often called the country's "drought polygon," the region comprises three distinct ecological zones: the humid coastal zone known as the *zona da mata,* the intermediate or transitional zone called the *agreste,* and the arid backlands or *sertão.* The zona da mata, which includes coastal cities and state capitals such as Maceió (Alagoas), Recife (Pernambuco), and João Pessoa (Paraíba), cultivates one major crop: sugar. The cheap labor that has sustained sugar production has contributed to the wealth of a few Brazilians, namely plantation owners, while doing little to improve the workers' standard of living. The agreste is dryer than the zona da mata, and it is dominated economically by cotton and livestock. Although inhabitants of the zone, and particularly small farmers, may often be better off than those who live in slums along the coast, they are still quite poor. The sertão, which is covered by a thin, scrub forest called the *caatinga* ("white forest," in indigenous terms), has low and variable precipitation and suffers cycles of torrential rain and devastating drought. The dry season, which generally persists from July to January, may last for more than a year in periods of drought, which have been recorded since early in the colonial period (it is said that the drought of 1877-79 may have killed upwards of 500,000 people).

Not only do the poor face harsh climatic conditions in the Northeast but also an economic system characterized by an extreme concentration of land ownership that dates from the colonial period. The lack of land has led to an exploitative system of agricultural labor in which tenant farmers and menial farmhands work to earn subsistence or low wages from a landowner who has them trapped in a cycle of debt. This situation, combined with periodic droughts, often prompts peasants to flee toward the coastal cities of the Northeast or to the South in search of a better life. Such is the case with the Northeastern migrants in *The Celebration.*

Banditry and peasant leagues. The rural poor in the Northeast are not always passive victims of an unjust socio-economic system and a harsh climate. They have resisted in many ways, including participation in millenarian movements such as that which surrounded Antônio Conselheiro at Canudos in the late nineteenth century and which is the subject of two very important books—Euclides da Cunha's ***Rebellion in the Backlands*** (1902; also covered in *Latin American Literature and Its Times*) and Mario Vargas Llosa's *War at the End of the World* (1981). The character Marcionílio de Mattos in *The Celebration* embodies two other forms of resistance: the social banditry that existed in the Northeast up until the 1940s, and the peasant leagues that were organized to struggle actively against the region's system of land tenure in the 1960s.

Tanks surround the War Ministry in Rio de Janeiro on April 1, 1964, during the military's overthrow of João Goulart.

In his youth, says the novel, Marcionílio had been an outlaw or *cangaceiro,* "but that was at a time when to be an outlaw was the only means of survival in the drought-beleaguered lands" of the Northeast (*The Celebration,* p. 21). Cangaceiros operated in the Northeastern sertão during the nineteenth and early twentieth centuries and represented a threat to local political bosses and landowners. Since the most famous of such bandits, Lampião, was killed in 1938, cangaceiros have taken on almost legendary dimensions in Brazilan literature and film.

Later in his life the novel's Marcionílio joins the peasant leagues and takes part in the seizure of a sugar refinery. Peasant leagues began to form in the late 1940s to defend the interests of small farmers and rural workers. In the 1950s the peasant movement acquired a new vigor under the leadership of Francisco Julião, who mobilized students and politicians along with rural workers. The movement gained national notoriety when it forced the government of the state of Pernambuco to divide the lands of a large sugar plantation—Galiléia—among peasants. Clearly the peasant leagues represented a threat to the traditional power structure in the Northeast. In fact, partially because of the leagues U.S. president John F. Kennedy's Alliance for Progress made the region a test case for policies designed to counter the threat of revolution. The peasant movement was brutally repressed by the military after the coup d'état of 1964.

The military in power. After seizing power the military moved quickly to squash social reforms then underway in the country and also to repress those sectors—labor unions, peasant leagues, progressive political parties, students, intellectuals—actively involved in the process of social transformation. To override the constitution and increase their control over the nation, the military invoked special decrees or "institutional acts." The initial *Ato Institucional* or First Institutional Act (known as AI-1; April 9, 1964) suspended job security in civil service for six months, thus allowing the government to dismiss "subversive" employees; the act also authorized the military president to suspend the political rights of citizens for ten years and to cancel the electoral mandate, or term in office, of public officials. This decree resulted in a purge of the leadership of the political opposition as well as of labor unions and peasant leagues. It also affected many intellectuals and military officers who had supported the previous democratic administration, who had not backed the coup d'état, or who had criticized the military regime. Such measures would eventually extend to intellectuals, such as sociologist Fernando Henrique Cardoso (a future President of Brazil, elected in 1994). In the wake of the overthrow of Goulart and the implementation of the First Institutional Act, more than 10,000 people were called for interrogation, over 6,000 were indicted, and around 4,500 were forced to retire from civilian and military government service.

The Second Institutional Act (October 27, 1965) abolished all existing political parties and determined that Congress would henceforth choose the country's presidents. A supplementary act issued the following month established guidelines for forming new parties, resulting in the creation of the pro-government ARENA (National Renovating Alliance), and the opposition party, the MDB (Brazilian Democratic Movement). Given the limited space for political action, these artificially established parties were often referred to jokingly as the parties of "Yes" and "Yes, sir!"

Doing away with the popular vote, the Third Institutional Act (February 5, 1966) required the indirect selection of state governors by state legislatures, and eliminated elections for mayors of capital cities. They would henceforth be chosen by the military regime.

From the beginning of the dictatorship, hard-liners and moderates within the military disagreed about the necessity of working within a legal framework and about the degree of repression needed to attain their goals. The first two military presidents, Marechal Humberto de Alencar Castelo Branco (1964-67) and General Arthur da Costa e Silva (1967-69), were seen as relatively moderate. Between April 1964 and 1968 the hard-liners increasingly gained the upper hand, resulting in the decree of the AI-5, or Fifth Institutional Act, on December 13, 1968.

The AI-5 gave the president the authority to disband Congress and legislative bodies throughout the country, to cancel elective mandates and remove individuals' political rights, and to suspend legal guarantees of civil service tenure. It also abolished basic human and political rights, such as habeas corpus. Repression and censorship intensified, and torture of political prisoners became common. Brazil entered a dark and brutal period of authoritarian rule during which thousands of people were arrested, and many were tortured, killed, or exiled under the watchful eye of hard-line general Emílio Garrastazu Médici, who held the reins of power from 1969 until 1974. *The Celebration* is set precisely during this period, and it is within this context that the novel's violent repression of the Northeasterners outside the train station and other interrogations and abusive actions by police and military officials must be seen.

From student power to armed resistance. Prior to the military coup d'état, university students throughout the country were mobilized in such organizations as the National Students' Union, the Center for Popular Culture in Rio de Janeiro, and the Movement for Popular Culture in the Northeast. All of these student organizations developed alliances with the political left—unions, peasant leagues, and progressive political parties—in an attempt to transform Brazilian society and end the violence, injustice, and exploitation that had long characterized class relations in the country.

The 1964 coup presented activist students with few options: divert energies from politics to other areas of activity, forget politics and go back to the classroom, sell out to the right wing that had supported the move against democracy, or join forces with the political resistance being mounted by parties of the left. This was a moment in which vigorous discussions about the viability of armed struggle against the regime were underway, resulting, in 1962, in a split in the Brazilian Communist Party and the formation of other splinter parties, such as the Marxist Revolutionary Organization, which is referred to as "Radical Action" in the novel (*The Celebration,* p. 57). Many students and intellectuals joined such movements and participated in the armed struggle against the military regime, a struggle that was particularly active in the period between 1968 and 1971. The actions of Carlos Bicalho and Samuel Aparecido Fereszin in *The Celebration* are suggestive of such involvement.

The Novel in Focus

Plot summary. *The Celebration* has no central plot line, no main character, and no single narrative voice or perspective. Indeed, its very genre is ambiguous. The bibliographical information included in the volume's front matter refers to it as a *romance, contos* (novel, short stories). The work consists of nine chapters or sections, ranging from four to 85 pages in length in the English translation. The first seven may be read as a group of relatively autonomous short stories that often seem to have little connection to one another. Some contain references to characters in other sections, but in no case does one section determine or necessarily lead into the next. The eighth chapter brings the events and characters of the previous sections together, at least to the extent that it explains how some of those events develop and what the characters are doing at different moments of the same day. The final section, printed on blue paper in the first edition and with black borders in the English translation, offers an explanatory index of the characters mentioned throughout the text, providing a fictional contextualization and background and informing the reader about subsequent turns in their lives. This section fills in some of the gaps in episodes related in previous segments.

The novel revolves around two events, neither of which is directly narrated. The first is a violent disturbance that takes place near the train station in downtown Belo Horizonte, capital of the Brazilian state of Minas Gerais. The violence erupts as the police and military try to force poor migrants from Brazil's impoverished Northeast to return to their homeland on the same train that had just brought them to the city in search of a better life. The second is the party, or "celebration," that gives the novel its title. Although references to it occur throughout and we eventually learn of certain things that take place at the party or in its wake, none of the chapters has the party as its setting. In fact, the novel's last two sections are titled "Prior to the Celebration" and "After the Celebration," respectively. Through not fully developed in narrative terms, the party and the violent disturbance give the novel coherence by linking some of its seemingly disparate elements.

Although *The Celebration* is set at a precise moment in time—March 30-31, 1970—its different perspectives and its insistence on historical contextualization offer a broad panorama of modern Brazilian society. The novel, therefore, does not simply narrate events that take place in 1970; it also provides the historical and social elements necessary for understanding Brazilian society and culture at a particularly critical moment in history—when the country was suffering the darkest days of the repressive military dictatorship that had been in power since March 31-April 1, 1964. The fact that the novel takes place precisely six years to the day after the military coup d'état is certainly not coincidental. The work's title may even be understood as a bitterly ironic comment on the sixth anniversary of the coup. The sections or chapters are as follows:

"A Short Documentary (the city and the interior, 1970)." Through real and fictional texts, the initial section of *The Celebration* documents the disturbances of March 30, 1970, and their aftermath, as well as the historical background necessary for understanding those events. The section compiles fragments of newspaper reports, books, almanacs, journalistic dispatches, official documents, police interrogation reports, songs, leaflets, business association reports, and presidential speeches. It also includes a brief section composed entirely of names of towns in Brazil's impoverished Northeast.

Four broad, interwoven narrative lines can be identified in the chapter. The first, largely made up of newspaper articles and police reports about the interrogation of Marcionílio de Mattos, the leader of the Northeastern migrants who have arrived in the city, provides "documentary" information about the disturbance that took place on March 30: "The turmoil began at 1:45 a.m. . . . A riot truck . . . had been sent there to quell any disturbance . . ." (*The Celebration,* p. 11). The second narrative line offers information about Mattos's background in the Northeast, including his involvement with the cangaceiro Lampião and the peasant leagues. A third line provides social and historical background information about the Northeast. A final line concerns the history of resistance and revolt in the Northeast.

"Thirtieth Anniversary: Pearls (of love in the '30s)." The novel's second part is divided into two subsections—one from the perspective of the husband, the other from that of the wife—providing two views of a marriage that began with passion but has degenerated into mistrust, betrayal, suspicion, and madness. The husband, a university professor named Candinho, believes that it is time for the couple to fulfill their youthful promise to die together. The wife, Juliana, relates her husband's previous attempts to kill her (and presumably himself). She is having an affair with a younger man named Carlos. On their anniversary, the married couple shares a cake that Candinho had made for the occasion. Juliana takes the first bite of the delicious cake, notices Candinho hesitating before eating his, and braces "for the onslaught of its poison" (*The Celebration,* p. 46). Her lover Carlos turns out to be Carlos Bicalho, who is involved in the violent events outside the train station.

"Andrea (a girl of the '50s)." *The Celebration*'s third section is described as a "BIOGRAPHY: discovered by the author among the papers belonging to one of the characters in the book, who should perhaps be identified at some point later on" (*The Celebration,* p. 47). The chapter consists of ten sections tracing Andrea's life from her teens in the 1950s until the evening of March 30, 1970.

Andrea was an attractive, middle-class Catholic girl raised in Rio de Janeiro. Her one desire is to be completely in love, yet that desire is continually frustrated. In Belo Horizonte she becomes involved in high society, which uses her for its own ends, and later mixes with journalists and intellectuals, who find her amusing but a bit "dense upstairs" (*The Celebration,* p. 56). She leaves the city for several years, and when she returns, she starts going out with the "latest young painter of the city," Roberto Miranda, who is described as vain, egotistical, mannered, and quite possibly homosexual. At one point they believe themselves to be marriageable, but in a game of "To Tell the Truth" at Roberto's infamous party (the "celebration"), he publicly humiliates her by revealing, among other secrets, her sexual problems.

"Corruption (of a triangle in the '40s)." The triangle to which the subtitle of this chapter refers is not a traditional love triangle, but rather a triangle that develops between a father, mother, and their son who is born in 1941. The corruption is not political but personal, as father and son increasingly marginalize the mother from their relationship. Ângelo structures the chapter with alternating narrative voices that present the diverse perspectives in a chronology of the five-year period from 1941 to 1946. The father's segments are relayed in the third person; the mother and son's in the first. The son is Roberto Miranda, who hosts the celebration on the evening of March 30, 1970.

"Sanctuary (insecurity, 1970)." The "sanctuary" is the apartment of one Jorge Paulo de Fernandes, "age thirty-one, successful young lawyer, former budding author until age twenty-five, whereupon the defect was wholly corrected by a law degree" (*The Celebration,* p. 77). Narrated largely in the third person, this chapter describes Jorge Paulo de Fernandes's thoughts and actions from the time he arrives home until he leaves to go to the celebration several hours later. The portrait is one of a vain, selfish, uncouth, and politically reactionary individual who thinks of little but his own image. Shortly before he leaves for the party, he receives a phone call about the arrest of Carlos. "Carlos who? . . . Yes, I know him. What's the problem? . . . Arrested for what? . . . Friend nothing. Look, you want to know something? It's just as well, it'll get rid of him for a while" (*The Celebration,* p. 89).

"Class Struggle (vignette, 1970)." This brief section, only four pages long (including the title page), draws a contrast between two characters, the working-class Ataíde, and the middle-class Fernando. A brief confrontation between the two occurs at the Plaza Station, where both of them had gone after work to have a drink at the bar. Ataíde inadvertently knocks over Fernando's glass. Fernando insults him, and Ataíde slugs Fernando.

"Preoccupations (obsessions, 1968)." This part is divided into two subsections, the first narrated by the worried mother of a college student (Carlos), the second by a commissioner of the political police (DOPS—Departamento de Ordem Política e Social), which played a key role in the political repression of the late 1960s and early 1970s. The two discourses, although from different perspectives, are ultimately similar in their moralism and conservatism. They both long for hierarchy and order. The widowed mother casts her lament in personal, emotional, and religious terms, constantly evoking the name of God in her desire to protect her son from the evils he faces on the street, from the police, and from the counterculture and girls with loose morals in miniskirts. She is particularly concerned about her son's involvement in student politics and potential conflicts with the police. She sees danger everywhere, but she does not truly understand the underlying causes for the turmoil in which her son is caught up. All of the social problems youth confront could have been avoided, in her mind, if there had been more repression and censorship.

The police commissioner's section is an answer to appeals such as that of Carlos's mother. In contrast to her emotionalism, his discourse is based on reason, much like that of Machiavelli's *Prince* and Auden's "Herod" of *The Celebration*'s epigraphs. His belief in reason and order justify, in his mind, any measure he may need to take against those who threaten that order. He is the novel's incarnation of the authoritarian military regime. "From the very heart of my people," he thinks, "I can sense a growing cry: protect us; for our own sakes do what must be done to dispel this mounting anguish, this new fanaticism, this mystic madness among the younger generations" (*The Celebration,* p. 109).

"Prior to the Celebration (victims of the '60s)." This section, one of the longest of the novel, consists of multiple textual fragments that narrate actions by different people on the evening of March 30 and the early morning of March 31. Each fragment is identified by the time and place the action takes place—for example, "New Moon Bar and Restaurant, 7:00 p.m." (*The Celebration,*

p. 115)—but they are not arranged in spatial or chronological order. In addition to these fragments, brief texts in parentheses and italics, titled "Author's notes," are interspersed throughout the section. The most important segments of this chapter trace the movements of journalist Samuel Aparecido Fereszin from 6:00 p.m.—when, in front of a bookshop, someone tells him that he will like "the crowd" who will be at the party later on that evening—until shortly after 1:00 a.m.—when he decides that he must do something to help the Northeastern refugees and he readies himself "for what will have to be done" (*The Celebration,* p. 148).

"After the Celebration (index of their fates)." The final section of *The Celebration* is described as "a cross-index of the characters, in order of appearance or reference, with additional* information regarding the fate of those who were alive during the events of the night of March 30" (*The Celebration,* p. 149). The asterisk remits to the following list of questions: "necessary? surprising? useful? corroborative? unnecessary? useless?" (*The Celebration,* p. 149). The chapter ties up loose ends and provides further information about characters in the novel's previous chapters. It also clarifies the sometimes obscure connections between segments presented earlier.

For example, in this section we learn that the professor, Candinho, of "Thirtieth Anniversary: Pearls," had been Carlos Bicalho's teacher and that he is one of the people whom Samuel Aparecido Ferezsin called in his efforts to get the student out of jail. Candinho's wife's affair is with this same Carlos Bicalho. We also learn that the fictional biography that constitutes "Andrea" was apparently written by her fiancé, Roberto Miranda, in order to help his friend Samuel write a novel about her. Parts of Samuel's sexually explicit novel were confiscated by the police, leading to Andrea's humiliating interrogation in the aftermath of the disturbances outside the train station. Ataíde, the working-class character from "Class Struggle," was arrested during the disturbance near the train station and held for a month and ten days, although he had no direct involvement. During his imprisonment the police extorted sex from his wife in exchange for promises to release him. In one of the most curious segments, the novel offers a popular version of the life of the leader of the Northeastern migrants, Marcionílio, in which he has been transformed into the devil.

On writers and writing. A salient feature of much of Ivan Ângelo's fiction is the infusion of the author into the story—or at least a fictional author—who comments on the work in the process of composition. *The Celebration* does this in a number of ways, particularly through "Author's notes" and conversations among writers and intellectuals who have gathered at the New Moon Bar and Restaurant in the chapter "Before the Celebration" and in segments of "After the Celebration." The "Author's notes" are entirely outside the fictional frame developed through the narrative, while the writers and intellectuals are fictional characters. Authorial interventions and the insistent presence of writers draw attention to the artificiality of narrative conventions; they also bring the social role and function of writers and intellectuals to the foreground.

The "Author's notes" provide commentaries not about the action narrated in the novel, but rather about the work's structure or process of composition. One of them, in fact, talks about the "Author's notes" themselves:

> *Include in 'Before the Celebration' various 'author's notes' (including this one). Projects, phrases, ideas for stories, literary problems, quick sketches, preoccupations. In that way, the author would become, together with Samuel [the journalist], the other main protagonist of the story he's writing.*
>
> (*The Celebration,* p. 127)

Unlike traditional realist novels, which create an illusion of reality, *The Celebration* breaks down reader expectations of realism while at the same time providing ample information about the motivation, strategies, and processes of the narrative's construction. One such note outlines the research undertaken to describe the phases of Roberto's childhood from birth until the age of five or six. The note also provides an indication of the author's compositional strategy: *"In italics or parentheses, place concepts that cannot as yet be grasped by his intellective sphere; by the end of the story, the italicized words are reduced to a minimum, because by then he has mastered language"* (*The Celebration,* pp. 122-23).

This technique causes the reader to reflect on the process of novelistic creation and perhaps to situate that creation in a specific historical time frame. Beyond its aesthetic and narrative dimensions, the novel becomes a symbolic form of intervention in the social and historical circumstances that gave it birth. It is intentional, and it was written with a specific purpose in mind. The same may well be said of all novels, but whereas *The Celebration* foregrounds its intentions and its motivations, most traditional novels seek to hide or efface their intentionality through their narrative strategies. By being forced to consider the author's choices in the construction of his text, readers must also consider questions of choice and responsibility in a broader sense.

The Celebration's use of writers as characters offers, on the one hand, an ironic perspective of writers' self-importance; on the other, it raises questions of intellectual commitment and limitations in unjust and repressive political situations such as that of post-1964 Brazil. Writers are, above all else, writers, and sometimes they react virulently to pressures to be politically engagé or to adopt the "appropriate" stance of cultural nationalism. Thus, in the novel's New Moon Bar and Restaurant, one writer complains, "Literature isn't economics. You can't go and establish national priorities for literary investment . . ." (*The Celebration,* p. 133). The fact of the matter is that writers are not always free to choose their subjects. Social and historical circumstances inevitably shape the concerns of the literary field at a given moment in time, despite the creative freedom writers may assert. This has been a particularly salient issue in Brazil, where writers and intellectuals have often proclaimed their crucial role in processes of national construction.

Prior to *The Celebration,* Ivan Ângelo had published several books of short stories. He has explained that before 1964 he had another idea in mind for the novel. After the coup d'état, however, he stopped writing fiction for ten years. When he resumed work on the novel in 1974, he modified the original project. According to Ângelo, at that time writers and other artists had several different possible attitudes concerning the political situation:

> 1) Political oppression and social injustice exist, and they represent a good theme for my work;
>
> 2) Political oppression and social injustice exist, but they are subjects for politics, not art;
>
> 3) Political oppression and social injustice do not exist;
>
> 4) Political oppression exists, but only for the purpose of doing away with social injustice;
>
> 5) Yes they exist, but worrying about it is only for squares, so what's the big deal?
>
> (Ângelo, "Nós que amávamos tanto a literatura," p. 71; trans. R. Johnson)

Ângelo himself clearly adopted the first attitude. His novel deals with political oppression and social injustice even as it implicates the reader in the circumstances described, transforming him or her into an accomplice.

Sources and literary context. *The Celebration* is one of several novels published in the mid- to late-1970s that discuss the period of military rule in Brazil. In 1971, during the most repressive period of dictatorship, Antônio Callado wrote *Bar Don Juan,* which deals with the tragedy of the young students and intellectuals who became engaged in the armed struggle. That same year, João Ubaldo Ribeiro presented a fascinating and brutal portrait of authoritarianism in his *Sargento Getúlio.* Between 1977 and 1979 a number of fictional works dealt with issues related to the armed resistance against the military regime. Notable among the novels in this current are Renato Tapajós's *Em Câmara Lenta* (1977), Antônio Callado's *Reflexos do Baile* (1978), and Márcio Souza's *Operação Silêncio* (1979). *The Celebration* shares with all of these works a concern with reassessing the impact of military rule through a fragmented, self-reflexive narrative style. Ivan Ângelo apparently decided to resume his novel, which had been suspended since shortly after the 1964 military coup d état, during a trip to Europe in 1972 in which he was able to get away from Brazil's stifling political climate and have renewed contact with freedom of expression and creation. That experience gave him a new sense of hope that, despite military repression, he could find a way to say what he felt was necessary to say (Medina, p. 9). This attitude resulted in *The Celebration.*

Reviews. *The Celebration* has been very well received in Brazil, the United States, and Europe. Writing in *Chasqui,* Katherine Delos refers to *The Celebration* as "a complex, multiform novel" whose diverse segments "are carefully positioned for cumulative effect" (Delos, pp. 106, 107). Critic Emir Rodríguez Monegal writes that Ângelo's novel is a "model of seriousness and suggestion"; its "somewhat elaborate construction makes the reader complete the puzzle and reconstruct the celebration himself" (Rodríguez Monegal, p. 40; trans. R. Johnson). Nelson Vieira has described it as "a tour-de-force of language and narrative structure as well as a mirror of the fear, injustice, and repression of Brazil of the early 1970s" (Vieira in Stern, p. 29). Robert DiAntonio suggests that the novel, "through its skillful use of mythic and narrative impulses, portrays the underlying quotidian realities that evoke and define true history" (DiAntonio, p. 15).

—Randal Johnson

For More Information

Ângelo, Ivan. *The Celebration.* Trans. Thomas Colchie. New York: Avon, 1982.

———. *A Festa.* 3rd ed. São Paulo: Summus, 1978.

———. "Nós, que amávamos tanto a literatura." In *Brasil: O Trânsito da Memória.* Ed. Saúl Sosnowski and Jorge Schwarz. College Park/São Paulo: University of Maryland/EDUSP, 1994.

Delos, Katherine. "A Festa." *Chasqui* VI, no. 2 (February 1977): 106-07.

DiAntonio, Robert E. *Brazilian Fiction: Aspects and Evolution of the Contemporary Narrative.* Fayetteville: The University of Arkansas Press, 1989.

Medina, Cremilda. "Literatura, a maneira de Ivan Ângelo entender o seu poro." *Minas Gerais, Suplemento Literário,* no. 967 (April 20, 1985): 9.

Page, Joseph A. *The Brazilians.* Reading, Mass.: Addison-Wesley, 1995.

Rodríguez Monegal, Emir. "Escribir bajo los ojos de la censura (Tres novelas brasileñas)." *Vuelta* 4, no. 28 (January 1980): 37-40.

Schneider, Ronald M. *"Order and Progress": A Political History of Brazil.* Boulder, Colo.: Westview Press, 1991.

Schwarz, Roberto. *Misplaced Ideas: Essays on Brazilian Culture.* Ed. John Gledson. London: Verso, 1992.

Skidmore, Thomas E. *Politics in Brazil, 1930-1964: An Experiment in Democracy.* New York: Oxford University Press, 1967.

———. *The Politics of Military Rule in Brazil, 1964-85.* New York: Oxford University Press, 1988.

Stern, Irwin, ed. *Dictionary of Brazilian Literature.* New York: Greenwood Press, 1988.

Days of Obligation: An Argument with My Mexican Father

by
Richard Rodriguez

> **THE LITERARY WORK**
>
> A densely interwoven collection of ten essays, set in California and Mexico, ranging in historical purview from 1521 to the late 1980s; published in English in 1992.
>
> **SYNOPSIS**
>
> Placed within the broad context of California's position as a border state adjoining Mexico, these essays explore the often paradoxical contradictions of personal identity, ethnic politics, religion, homosexuality, and U.S./Mexican relations.

Born in 1944, Richard Rodriguez spent his youth in Sacramento, California, where his parents settled after emigrating from Mexico. He recounts his struggle to master the English language and assimilate into American society in his acclaimed, though controversial, autobiography, *Hunger of Memory* (1981). The book, which among other discussions argues against affirmative action and bilingual education, drew praise from conservatives and scorn from many Latinos, establishing Rodriguez as a formidable presence on the American literary scene. In subsequent years, his regular Sunday columns in the *Los Angeles Times* and his appearances on Public Broadcasting Service's (PBS's) *The NewsHour* further broadened his role as an important commentator on subjects relating to Latinos, ethnic politics, Catholicism, California, and the West. Rodriguez's second book, *Days of Obligation*, takes his readers on a series of journeys back and forth across the U.S./Mexican border, exploring the imaginatively fertile zone born from the clash of cultures, languages, histories, and traditions. The tensions of this mediating place, Rodriguez implies, are contained and embodied within himself, and his book is an attempt to work them through. Its settings encompass a wide range of historical contexts, from Spain's conquest of Mexico in the sixteenth century; to the founding of missions in California in the eighteenth century; to the growth of a homosexual community in San Francisco, California, in the 1970s; and to the ravages of the AIDS disease in the 1980s.

Events in History at the Time of the Essays

The conquest of Mexico. Rodriguez is deeply interested in the long and tangled history of the Americas, both before and after Christopher Columbus's landfall in 1492. In order to tell his story, Rodriguez refers to events far back in the historical record, such as the conquest of Mexico in the 1520s. For him, these events exert a

Moctezuma welcomes Cortés to Tenochtitlán.

pressing force on the present, welling up at unexpected moments to shape contemporary reality. Rodriguez's essays make strategic use of this perspective on history, as they shuttle back and forth between the present and the past.

A central event in the social history of the Americas, the conquest of Mexico by the Spanish gave birth to an entirely new culture, formed from the violent union of the so-called Old and New Worlds. (A European historian, Peter Martyr, coined the term "New World" in a 1516 account of the discovery of the Americas.) Within a few years of Columbus's voyages, rumors circulated among the Spanish of splendid civilizations thriving in the interior of the new land. In 1518, at the behest of Diego Velásquez, the governor of Cuba, the Spanish explorer Hernán Cortés sailed with a large army to the Yucatán Peninsula and along the eastern coast of Mexico. He encountered and battled several groups of indigenous peoples, defeating some and forging alliances with others. He also took a native woman, Malinche, as his mistress and interpreter. Her ability to translate and act as a go-between would later play a critical role in the conquest of the Aztecs, who ruled the region.

Cortés sailed further south and landed with his men at a spot he named Veracruz, located due east of the famed Aztec capital, Tenochtitlán. To prevent his men from deserting and returning to Cuba, Cortés ordered his ships to be sunk in the harbor. Skillful in war and a master of deceit, Cortés created alliances with Indian nations, such as the Tlaxcalans, who resented the dominance of Tenochtitlán. With the aid of these new allies and Malinche, his translator, the conquistador marched into the Aztec capital, imprisoning the emperor Moctezuma after he had received Cortés in the city. Cortés then drew back from the city and marched to Veracruz to fight an expedition sent after him by the now-hostile Velásquez, who had grown suspicious of Cortés's growing power and ambitions in Mexico. Taking advantage of this opportunity, the Aztecs struck back, driving the Spaniards from Tenochtitlán in what the Spaniards would later call *La noche triste*, or "night of sorrow."

Upon his return to the Valley of Mexico, Cortés regrouped his army and laid siege to the Aztec capital, now led by Cuahtémoc. Over a period of 75 days, the Spaniards blockaded the city, which was set in the midst of a vast lake and could be entered only by narrow causeways. In August 1521, weakened by thirst and starvation, the Aztecs finally succumbed to Cortés. The king of Spain, Charles V, rewarded Cortés with the titles of governor and captain of the territory, which the conquerors called New Spain.

Despite the ruthlessness and devastation of the Conquest, many Mexicans and U.S. Latinos have come to view it less as a story of military defeat than as a profound symbol of the union of two hemispheres, peoples, and cultures. In subjugating the indigenous peoples of the Americas, the Spaniards were also forced to embrace and incorporate them, and, as a result, to bond with them in the creation of a wholly new culture. From the union of Cortés and Malinche (also called Malintzin or Doña Marina), in particular, Mexico traces the origins of the *mestizo*, the person of mixed Indian and European heritage. Throughout Latin America, and especially in Mexico, the influence of *mestizaje* (mixture) is evident, not only in the commingling of genes but in hybrid religious forms, language, and other social conventions. In the United States, the Indian population was depleted and driven onto reservations that were removed from the larger population. By contrast, the presence of indigenous Mexican peoples continues to weigh heavily upon the conscience and consciousness of Mexicans and U.S. Latinos alike. As Rodriguez notes, "In New England the European and the Indian drew apart to regard each other with suspicion over centuries. . . . In Mexico the European and the Indian consorted" (Rodriguez, *Days of Obligation*, p. 13)

The Virgin of Guadalupe and the conversion of Mexico. Though divided by a political border, Mexicans and Mexican Americans participate in many varieties of cultural expression that defy and transcend arbitrary national boundaries. Among the most significant of these is the shared tradition of Catholicism, brought originally by the Spanish and subsequently fused to the pre-Columbian religious traditions of the indigenous peoples. Indeed, one may attribute the success of Latin American Catholicism to its extraordinary ability to assimilate within itself the existing forms of native belief. This syncretism, in effect another kind of mestizaje, is perhaps most striking in the cult of the Virgin of Guadalupe, patron saint of Mexico and the most revered symbol of Catholic veneration for both Mexicans and Mexican Americans.

According to Catholic legend, the Virgin of Guadalupe first appeared in December 1531 on a hilltop outside Mexico City called Tepeyac. She had dark skin, Indian features, and spoke in Nahuatl, the Aztec tongue. The place she chose for this epiphany, Tepeyac, is itself significant, for it had once served as a temple to the Aztec goddess Tonantzín. The apparition, however, was at first disbelieved, because its witness was not a priest, nor even a Spaniard of high rank, but a young Indian boy, Juan Diego. Upon hearing the miraculous story of the appearance of the Virgin, who requested that a church be erected in her name, the Spanish bishop to whom Juan Diego reported his vision requested that the boy bring proof of her existence. The Virgin directed Juan Diego to a place nearby and instructed him to gather the red Castilian roses she had caused to bloom there, in the middle of winter, and to bring them to the bishop. When Juan Diego once again approached the authorities, he unfurled his cloak to reveal the miracle of the red roses. As he spoke, the image of the Virgin herself was miraculously emblazoned on his cloak, sealing the authority of his vision. This cloak, many Catholics believe, is the very one now displayed in one of three churches built on the site of the miracle. Each December, millions of Mexican (and Mexican American) Catholics make a pilgrimage to the site, to worship at the Shrine of the Virgin of Guadalupe.

The legend illustrates the adaptive power of Spanish Catholicism in the Americas. Though thousands of the indigenous were forcibly converted to the Catholic faith in the years just after the Conquest, many continued to cling to their ancestral religions. The appearance of the Virgin signified that the Church would not minister only to those of European descent, but also to Indians and to mestizos. Her dark skin and Indian features symbolize the transplanting of Catholicism to the Americas, and her association with the Aztec goddess Tonantzín demonstrates the in-between position that she occupies. As Rodriguez observes, "The joke is that Spain arrived with missionary zeal. . . . But Spain had no idea of the absorbent strength of Indian spirituality" (*Days of Obligation*, p. 20). The Church quickly publicized the Virgin's appearance to Juan Diego, which led to the rapid conversion of many indigenous people, who felt a strong connection with *La Morenita*, or the beloved dark lady. Today, throughout Mexico, her image is everywhere, and it is impossible to understand the conversion of Mexico without telling her story.

Latinos in California during the 1980s and 1990s. As late as 1848 California was part of Mexico. It was called *Alta* (upper) *California*, and its inhabitants were known as *Californios*. This changed with the defeat of Mexico by the United States in the Mexican War, which is known in

Mexico as the War of the North American Invasion (1846-48). As a result of the defeat, which ended with the capture of Mexico City by General Winfield Scott, the northern half of Mexico's territory was ceded to the United States. The Treaty of Guadalupe Hidalgo laid out the terms of the surrender, stipulating that Mexico would receive $15 million in exchange for this land, which included Texas, California, large parts of Arizona and New Mexico, and portions of Nevada, Colorado, and Utah. At the stroke of a pen, these territories were joined to the United States. Those who lived in the territories were told they could choose either Mexican or U.S. citizenship and keep their land, but in the aftermath of the war, many of these promises were broken. The land was wrested from people of Mexican descent, who suddenly became second-class citizens on their own home ground.

LATINO POPULATION IN CALIFORNIA AND THE UNITED STATES

1. Between 1980 and 1990 the total U.S. Hispanic population rose from 14 to 22 million. Of all states, California's Hispanic population was the largest, growing from 4.5 million in 1980 to 7.7 million in 1990.

2. By the year 2000 the total U.S. Hispanic population is projected to swell to 31 million. By 2025, the Census Bureau predicts, it will rise to 51 million, and by 2050 to 88 million. Once again, California will lead all states in Hispanic population, with Texas, Florida, New York, and Illinois following behind.

(Hornor, p. 3)

Newcomers nevertheless continued to emigrate northward from Mexico to *el otro lado* (the other side), drawn by the promise of steady work and improved economic conditions. While the population of Latinos increased across the Southwest, California has shown particularly strong gains. In fact, in California, Latinos will soon once again form the majority of the population, not by forcible re-conquest, but by the irresistible power of demographic change. By the 1980s Latinos comprised more than 40 percent of the population of Los Angeles, the largest city in California and the second largest, after New York, in the nation. According to the U.S. Census Bureau, the population of "Hispanics" (its name for Latinos) will continue to grow at a rapid rate.

Yet, despite the growth of the Latino population, or perhaps in reaction to it, Latinos continue to struggle for equal opportunity. In California, especially, Latinos often find themselves the scapegoat for large-scale social ills. Most recently, Californians passed three ballot initiatives that were widely viewed as anti-Latino. The first, dubbed the "Save Our State Initiative" (Proposition 187), banned undocumented immigrants from receiving public education and public benefits, such as welfare and health care, except in an emergency. This proposition passed in 1994 with 59 percent of the vote. In 1996 a related measure (Proposition 229) was passed, prohibiting California from using "race, sex, color, ethnicity, or national origin as a criterion for either discriminating against or granting preferential treatment to any individual or group in the operation of the State's system of employment, public education or public contracting." As a result, minority enrollments plummeted at the University of California's undergraduate, graduate, and professional schools. And finally, in 1998, Californians passed the "Unz initiative," which severely restricted the practice of bilingual education in the state's public schools. Since the large majority of bilingual students are Latino, the initiative was strongly opposed by state Latino leaders. Taken together, these initiatives, and the demographic and political climate that brought them into law, illuminate the growing tensions faced by Latinos in California during the late 1980s and early 1990s—precisely the period in which Rodriguez wrote *Days of Obligation.*

Latinos, gays, and the AIDS crisis in California. Given the strong Catholic influence in Latino life, a powerfully patriarchal culture, and the norms of masculinity bequeathed by the ethic of machismo, Latino homosexuals have always occupied a problematic position on the margins of the culture. The Latino male, according to traditional formulas at least, should be *feo, fuerte, y formal,* or "rugged, strong, and decorous." Latino popular culture is shot through with jokes and caricatures ridiculing the feminized man, who serves as a negative foil for the strong, silent type long enshrined in the public consciousness. According to Rodriguez himself, "The macho holds his own ground. There is sobriety in the male, and silence, too—a severe limit on emotional range. The male isn't weak" (*Days of Obligation,* p. 57). The gay Latino male thus finds himself doubly disadvantaged, standing outside the dominant culture by virtue of his ethnicity and outside the subculture by virtue of his sexuality.

In the 1980s gays, influenced by the civil rights movement and responding to the AIDS epidemic, increasingly became politically active, as seen in this gay pride march in the Castro district of San Francisco, June 26, 1983.

The Chicano movement of the 1960s drew its inspiration from the broad agenda of the U.S. civil rights movement, which arose in protest over the unequal treatment, in law and culture, of black Americans. These struggles for political rights rested on the argument that the U.S. Constitution, which had promised equal rights to all Americans, constituted an unfulfilled mandate, since many Mexican Americans and blacks continued to suffer discrimination in the courts, the workplace, and in public venues.

Following this logic, gay Latinos have argued that Latino culture must itself come to terms with the demands of homosexuals for basic civil rights: to express themselves openly, to seek political representation, and to lay claim to their dual identities as Latinos and homosexuals. The AIDS crisis (or *SIDA,* as it is known in Spanish) has served to focus attention on such larger issues as access to health care and the stigmatization of those with communicable diseases. As a phenomenon of the 1980s and 1990s, the period between *Hunger of Memory* and *Days of Obligation,* AIDS also plays a particularly important role in Rodriguez's development as a writer. Based in San Francisco during this period, Rodriguez saw firsthand the flowering of a Latino homosexual community in the city's Castro District. Playing off the meanings of domestic architecture, Rodriguez describes the scene in the Castro: "Two decades ago, some of the least expensive sections of San Francisco were wooden Victorian sections. It was thus a coincidence of the market that gay men found themselves living within the architectural metaphor for family. . . . In those same years—the 1970s—and within those same Victorian houses, homosexuals were living rebellious lives to challenge the foundations of domesticity" (*Days of Obligation,* p. 30).

Long celebrated for its laissez-faire, sometimes lawless, and certainly unconventional lifestyles, San Francisco has been a haven for homosexuals for nearly 30 years. According to one critically acclaimed history: "Between 1969 and 1973, at least 9,000 gay men moved to San Francisco, followed by 20,000 between 1974 and 1978. By 1980, about 5,000 homosexual men were moving to the Golden Gate every year. The immigration now made for a city in which two in five adult males were openly gay" (Shilts, p. 15). Thus, the city was hit hard by the tragedy of AIDS as the disease ravaged members of its homosexual population.

Just how many of these men were also Latino is hard to discern, especially given the cultural prohibitions against homosexuality and the unwillingness of many gays, Latino or otherwise, to be counted as such. Yet it is safe to say, given the proportion of Latinos to the overall population in California—1 in 5 in 1980, 1 in 4 in 1990—that the gay renaissance of San Francisco involved a sizable number of Latinos. It is known that the AIDS crisis, especially during the late 1970s and early '80s, when information about the disease was not widely available, struck hard among Latinos. In any case, no statistics can adequately measure the loss of individual lives, nor the grief felt by those who are diminished by the victims' passing.

The Essays in Focus

Contents summary. *Days of Obligation* comprises an Introduction and ten interwoven essays. The Introduction finds Rodriguez in Mexico, on assignment with the British Broadcasting Corporation (BBC), searching for his parents' village. The opening of this section is striking and emblematic of Rodriguez's method:

> I am on my knees, my mouth over the mouth of the toilet, waiting to heave. It comes up with a bark. All the badly pronounced Spanish words I have forced myself to sound during the day, bits and pieces of Mexico spew from my mouth, warm, half-understood, nostalgic reds and greens dangle from long strands of saliva.
>
> (*Days of Obligation,* p. xv)

This image literally embodies Rodriguez's alienation from the homeland he seeks to explain to his television audience. Being in Mexico reminds Rodriguez that he is a stranger there. The food and water do not agree with him. He is an outsider in the land of his parents, and, like many visitors, he suffers from what Mexicans call, with a wink, *turista,* a temporary sickness that is a sign of being out of place. Of course, the food and water do not make them ill, for they are at home in their own country. Rodriguez, though, imagines that he vomits not only the contents of his stomach, but also Mexico's version of words. Like the food he cannot keep down, the language is foreign to him. It is unfamiliar. His return to the fatherland is occasioned, at least at first, by alienation.

The stories told in *Days of Obligation* rely, as the Introduction does, on paradox and irony. Its essays do not apprehend experience from a safe, objective distance; rather they involve the musculature and nervous system of the author himself.

Chapter One, "India," explores the mestizo legacy of the Spanish Conquest of Mexico, viewed in the author's divided selfhood and in Mexican/Mexican-American culture at large. Central to this essay is the pivotal story of Juan Diego's vision of the Virgin of Guadalupe.

Chapter Two, playfully entitled "Late Victorians," combines an elegy over the loss of a friend to AIDS with a broader meditation on the fate of the gay community in the aftermath of that disease. Though the careful reader may infer that the chapter constitutes the author's "coming out," or declaration of his homosexuality, the essay in fact offers no such simple statement. As is characteristic, the writing employs careful irony and subject-less grammatical constructions to suggest, rather than proclaim, his position: "To grow up homosexual is to live with secrets and within secrets" (*Days of Obligation,* p. 30). Readers familiar with Rodriguez's earlier *Hunger of Memory* will recall that one of its chapters was entitled "Mr. Secrets," and that it, too, offered suggestive clues to the story outlined here. Recently, Rodriguez has more openly declared his homosexuality, delivering a lengthy personal essay on the subject as part of his regular stint on PBS's *The NewsHour* (September 15, 1998).

The third chapter, "Mexico's Children," examines certain paradoxes in the life of Mexican immigrants to the United States, some of whom choose to assimilate, many of whom do not. The essay moves outward here to consider the various identities that result from a population at once settled and on the move.

The subject of the fourth chapter, "In Athens Once," is the increasingly porous zone of the U.S./Mexican border, where cities such as San Diego and Tijuana, despite their important differences, are becoming inexorably joined by transnational cultural practices (language, media, cross-border migration) and the economic imperatives of free trade. According to Rodriguez's essay, the growing interface along the border, where cultures and persons flow back and forth virtually unimpeded, promises to transform ideas of nationalism, personal identity, and political culture in ways that few have imagined.

Chapter Five, "The Missions," takes the reader on a journey long familiar to every California child: the examination of the mission system and the legacy of its founder, Junípero Serra. As in the other essays, this one ranges far beyond its local theme. It takes up, for instance, the weighty question of how the status of the Indian differed between Spanish Catholicism and English Protestantism, the two religious-cultural world views that dominate and inform the history of the American West.

Chapter Six tells the story of Joaquin Murietta, a nineteenth-century Mexican whose exploits and death are the inspiration for a series of mythic tales about old California. On the trail of this mysterious figure, Rodriguez examines the myth-making quality of California itself.

"Sand," the title of Chapter Seven, turns to more overtly autobiographical themes—Rodriguez's vexed relationship with the two leading cities in California, San Francisco and Los Angeles, each of which reflects facets of the state and of the author himself.

Chapter Eight, entitled "Asians," treats the growing influence and presence of the Asian American population in California. Once again mixing personal reflection with cultural analysis, Rodriguez's essay ponders the future of California as it becomes the American focus of a new economic and political entity, the "Pacific Rim."

"The Latin American Novel," Chapter Nine, returns to questions of religion, proposing the conflict between Catholicism and Protestantism as a useful lens through which to view U.S./Mexican relations.

The final chapter, "Nothing Lasts a Hundred Years," circles back to questions raised at the start of the text. Rodriguez returns home to Sacramento, California's capital, and in this "end" that is also a beginning, considers yet again his dual identities, his mixed heritage, and the peculiar journeys of his adult life.

The question of language. In his first work, *Hunger of Memory,* Rodriguez meditated long and lovingly on language itself: "I was a student of language. Obsessed by the way it determined my public identity. The way it permits me here to describe myself, writing" (*Hunger of Memory,* p. 7). As a graduate student of Renaissance literature at UC Berkeley during the 1970s, Rodriguez would have studied theoretical accounts of language that describe it in just this way. Language is both a force that shapes identities and a tool that allows or "permits" one to shape the world. In *Days of Obligation,* Rodriguez further explores such issues, with a renewed emphasis on language as a social, rather than merely a personal, medium. In "Mexico's Children," for example, Rodriguez takes up a favorite theme, the conflict between public and private. In *Hunger of Memory* he describes his upbringing as torn between the private discourse of Spanish, spoken as it was only in the home, and the public world of English, which he encountered in institutions such as the school and the university. Here, he points out that Spanish itself is structured along a division of private and public. Its forms of address vary according to the social context: "*Tú* belongs within the family. . . . *Usted,* the formal, the bloodless, the ornamental you, is spoken to the eyes of strangers" (*Days of Obligation,* p. 54). The distinction between public and private is familiar in much social analysis, yet Rodriguez's discussion of it suggests an inter-generational change as well as larger shifts. His parents, immigrants from Mexico, brought with them the Spanish grammar of both intimacy and formality. This becomes a key paradigm for Rodriguez, a legacy of Mexico, though as a U.S. Latino educated and writing in English, he is forced to employ a tongue that largely ignores the distinction. The inter-generational change results from a historical overlay of English and Spanish.

AN ARGUMENT WITH MY MEXICAN FATHER

The work's subtitle, "An Argument with My Mexican Father," hints at the text's geographical and cultural orientation, for it suggests a conflict-driven dialogue between the U.S.-born Rodriguez and the Latin American world of his father. As a Latino, Rodriguez is acutely conscious of his difference from Latin Americans proper. Though he can visit Mexico, he is not Mexican. Yet he can no more ignore Mexico, and beyond that Latin America, than he can deny his dark skin, Indian features, and cultural memory. However problematic it may be, his connection to Latin America—its traditions, cultural assumptions, and history—is undeniable. The subtitle also suggests that for Rodriguez historical change is, at least in part, a conflict between generations, with his father representing Mexico and the claims of the Old World with its customary ways, and the son arguing for inexorable changes both in the fabric of Mexico and in the United States.

Latin American history is unintelligible apart from a consideration of the shaping force of language. Cortés and his armies brought not only the sword and cross, but also a new tongue, and hence a new grammar for consciousness and social relations. The change has been all but complete; the indigenous tongues of Latin America survive principally in such remote areas as the state of Chiapas in southern Mexico or in the Guatemalan highlands. With the exception of

Brazil, which is Portuguese-speaking, Spanish is as dominant in Latin America as is English in the United States. In both regions, power is exercised through the dominant language. And in both regions, of course, history teaches us that the dominant language is also an imposed language, brought by European conquerors and settlers to the newfound lands.

SPANGLISH

"*Vamos a lunchar*" [We are going to have lunch]. "*El quiere parquear el carro*" [He wants to park the car]. "I am going dancing with *las girlfriends.*" Horrific to language purists, such everyday Latino expressions illustrate the dissolving border between Spanish and English. Dictionaries and grammar books specify *almorzar* for the English verb "to have lunch" and *estacionar* for "to park a car." *Las girlfriends,* as a hybrid formulation, defies categorization. Such expressions are known as Spanglish, an increasingly pervasive blend—a linguistic mestizaje—of two languages that conjoin and overlap in everyday usage. English words flow into Spanish, and Spanish grammatical forms pervade English. The combinations are unpredictable and lawless, obeying no rules. Sometimes, like *rock en español* ("rock-and-roll"), they come to seem inevitable, almost untranslatable. The marriage of English and Spanish might even suggest a more extensive interweaving of the tongues to come, though, given the history of English, it is more likely that English will simply absorb new expressions without a fundamental change in its structure or grammar.

Straddling the English-Spanish divide, Latinos are extraordinarily sensitive to the historical conditions that have produced the dominant tongues of the Americas: conquest, domination, demographic shifts, patterns of immigration, and changing political geographies. The effects of these shaping conditions are evident all around us. California, for example, with its Disneyland mascots, eight-lane freeways, and Hollywood dreamscapes, seems at first a familiar, "American" place. To look more closely, however, is to discover that beneath this rather thin veneer exists a rich Hispanic heritage, evidenced in patterns of settlement, the mission system, and, not least, in language. No Californian can avoid the public discourse that names its largest cities (Los Angeles, San Francisco, San Jose, San Diego), mountain ranges (Sierra Nevada), and valleys (San Joaquin, Santa Clara). These names are all of Spanish origin, bequeathed by the historical legacy of a California that until 1848 was part of Mexico. To pronounce them in Spanish is to remind oneself of this Mexican past. By contrast, to pronounce them in English, to Anglicize them, is to voice the historical change that replaced the once dominant tongue of Spain with the now official language of the United States, English.

Historical forces continue to shape the question of language in the United States and in the border zone between the United States and Mexico. Periodically, groups concerned over the increased use of Spanish as the lingua franca of Latinos have lobbied state legislatures for limits to and controls on the use of Spanish in schools, law courts, and the marketplace. Bilingual education is a hotly contested issue, with opponents arguing that its continuing practice in the schools does a disservice to the prospects of those it intends to help. Proponents answer that language and identity cannot be divorced, and that in the case of Spanish, the drive toward the all-English classroom is a thinly veiled attack on the historical significance of Spanish as the bedrock of Latino cultural cohesion.

The theme of language recurs throughout the essays in *Days of Obligation,* both overtly and more implicitly, in the personal experience of the author and in the larger historical events he examines. La Malinche, for example, is a go-between, the translator who makes the indigenous world of the Americas readable for Cortés. The Virgin of Guadalupe, Rodriguez reminds us, spoke to Juan Diego in his native tongue, Nahuatl, not in Spanish. San Diego and Tijuana, as the essay "In Athens Once" makes clear, are in effect one city, married by common economic interests and, perhaps more importantly, an increasingly shared culture grounded in the mutuality of English and Spanish, and in their hybrid creation—"Spanglish." In San Diego *telenovelas* (Spanish soap operas) share the TV schedule with reruns of "Bonanza." In Tijuana, English is as useful a currency for business as Spanish. The border is daily trammeled by forces it cannot contain: language and culture.

Rodriguez's discussion of homosexuality also relies upon an understanding of language as an instrument that conceals and reveals, brands and affirms. Driven underground, homosexual culture, Rodriguez suggests, gradually sought refuge in irony, decoration, and verbal wit. His essay on homosexual life in San Francisco, therefore, takes as its central metaphor the richly decorated Victorian house, beautified by lace and whimsy. Taking refuge in pure style, the homosexual plays around the edges of language, as does Rodriguez. Long noted for its ellipses, gaps, and paradoxes, Rodriguez's literary style is perfectly attuned to the task of discussing homosexuality without really discussing it. As noted above, nowhere does he declare his sexual orientation. Instead, the essay suggests, nudges, and implies. This may be viewed not as a failing, but rather as an embodiment of the argument the essay is making—that as a result of social repression, gays have had to master indirection. Granted, Rodriguez has subsequently ventured more publicly direct utterances, as in his aforementioned essay for *The News Hour* on PBS. Yet even here, the theme remains, for the essay is entitled "Language and Silence."

Sources and literary context. Contributing to the slippery texture of Rodriguez's prose is the literary genre he chooses as his vehicle, the essay. The form arose during the European Renaissance, and was practiced by such masters as Michel de Montaigne (1533-92) and Francis Bacon (1561-1626), writers Rodriguez surely studied while pursuing his doctoral degree at Berkeley. Latin American literature, however, also has its own tradition of the essay, a genre invoked by such prominent writers as Octavio Paz (1914-98), Carlos Fuentes (1928-), and Carlos Monsiváis (1938-). Indeed, one suspects that at least part of Rodriguez's intent is to reply to Paz, and especially to the famous essay in ***The Labyrinth of Solitude*** (also covered in *Latin American Literature and Its Times*) entitled "The Pachuco and other Extremes," published in 1961. In this much-discussed piece, Paz, like other Mexican intellectuals after him, portrays Mexican Americans as "ashamed of their culture," persons who are "wearing disguises," suffering from a "lack of spirit" (Paz, p. 13). The essay marks their distance from their Mexican roots and heritage.

Rodriguez's collection replies to Paz, not through overt refutation, but through a counterstrategy of celebrating the dissolving boundary between Mexicans and Mexican Americans. To work this subversive magic, Rodriguez goes back to the root meaning of the word *essay,* which stems from the French word *essai,* meaning a "trial" or "attempt." Rich, allusive, ebullient in the play of language itself, the essay is fundamentally an exploratory genre, written with no predetermined end in mind. It does not prove a thesis, but sifts and sorts several. Freewheeling, open to contradiction and paradox, the essay "enjoys an idea like a fine wine; it thumbs through things. It turns round and round upon its topic, exposing this aspect and that; proposing possibilities, reciting opinions, disposing of prejudice and even of the simple truth itself—as too undeveloped, not yet of an interesting age" (Gass, p. 25).

While a predilection for fluid prose was evident in *Hunger of Memory,* it has become pronounced in *Days of Obligation.* Its essays are filled with gaps, discontinuities, ruptures, and ellipses. Not everything can be told, Rodriguez implies, even if one desires to do so. Language, although the chosen medium of the writer, inevitably falls short. And the subjects of his essays are themselves contradictory, making the task all the more difficult. Yet in his willingness to skate at the edge of meaning, to explore the ineffable, Rodriguez proves himself worthy of addressing the complex matters that stand at the center of *Days of Obligation.*

Reviews. With *Days of Obligation,* Rodriguez appears to have crafted a work that will take him, finally, out of the narrow category of the minority writer who opposes affirmative action and bilingual education. Given his prominence, the work has been reviewed in many major journals and newspapers, and has drawn the attention of cultural critics and literary scholars in the academy. Not all the notices have been positive. In his review of *Days of Obligation,* Jonathan Yardley objects to the apparent obscurantism of Rodriguez's elliptical style. The work, he claims, "never states in sufficiently clear terms either the nature of the argument or the author's own line of reasoning" (Yardley, p. 3). David L. Kirp, by contrast, finds Rodriguez's elusiveness a source of great appeal: "*Days of Obligation* reveals the writer as a tightrope walker who balances pessimism and the defeat of predictable expectations against the discovery of the profoundly unanticipated" (Kirp, p. 42). Perhaps most significantly, Latino intellectuals on the left have found in the work important imperatives for the ongoing critique of border consciousness, now a major area of inquiry in literary and cultural study of Latinos. José David Saldívar, in his acclaimed book on this subject, *Border Matters,* acknowledges that Rodriguez is "one of the fascinating new geocultural chroniclers of North-South interactions," who is at the forefront of a new vision—that "the future of California is in its Latinoization" (Saldívar, p. 151).

—Robert Aguirre

For More Information

Anzaldua, Gloria. *Borderlands/La Frontera: The New Mestiza.* San Francisco: Spinsters/Aunt Lute Press, 1987.

Gass, William H. "Emerson and the Essay." In *Habitations of the Word: Essays.* New York: Simon and Schuster, 1985.

Hornor, Louise L. *Hispanic Americans: A Statistical Sourcebook.* Palo Alto, Calif.: Information Publications, 1996.

Kirp, David L. Review of *Days of Obligation. The New York Times Book Review,* November 22, 1992, 42.

Moraga, Cherríe. *Loving in the War Years: lo que nunca pasó por sus labios.* Boston: South End Press, 1983.

Paz, Octavio. *The Labyrinth of Solitude and Other Writings.* Trans. Lysander Kemp, Yara Milos, and Rachel Phillips Belash. New York: Grove Press, 1985.

Rodriguez, Richard. *Days of Obligation: An Argument with My Mexican Father.* New York: Viking, 1992.

———. *Hunger of Memory: The Education of Richard Rodriguez.* Boston: David R. Godine, 1981.

———. "Language and Silence." *The NewsHour.* September 15, 1998.

Saldívar, José David. *Border Matters: Remapping American Cultural Studies.* Berkeley: University of California Press, 1977.

Shilts, Randy. *And The Band Played On: Politics, People, and the AIDS Epidemic.* New York: Penguin, 1987.

Yardley, Jonathan. Review of *Days of Obligation. Washington Post Book World,* November 15, 1992, 3.

Death and the Maiden

by
Ariel Dorfman

Ariel Dorfman was born in Argentina in 1942, and two years later moved with his family to the United States. His father relocated the family to Chile in 1954 and Dorfman became a naturalized Chilean citizen in 1967. Like many Chilean artists and writers, Dorfman supported the Marxist president Salvador Allende and was forced into exile after a successful 1973 military coup under General Augusto Pinochet, in which Allende died. During his exile, Dorfman lived in Argentina, France, the Netherlands, and eventually the United States. He continued to write about the atrocities that were being committed by the Chilean dictatorship in his poetry and novels. In 1983 Dorfman was officially allowed to return to Chile, but he would not move back to his country until Pinochet left office and a democratic government was restored under elected President Patricio Aylwin in 1990. A year later Dorfman wrote *Death and the Maiden,* a play that dramatizes Chile's struggle to heal from the human rights violations perpetrated by the Pinochet regime.

THE LITERARY WORK

A play set in Chile in 1990; published in Spanish (as *Muerte y la Doncella*) and in English in 1991; first performed in Santiago, Chile, in 1991.

SYNOPSIS

A chance encounter brings a woman face to face with the man who tortured her 15 years earlier.

Events in History at the Time of the Play

A history of political factions. In the 1950s and 1960s Chile experienced a severe recession and overall economic instability. The gap between the rich and the poor widened, and industrial production dropped to an all-time low. Wages for agricultural workers plummeted 38 percent between 1953 and 1960. The per capita income for an average Chilean in 1954 was less than $150, compared to $2000 in the United States. By contrast, school and university enrollments were on the rise during this period. While Chileans had one of the best educated populations and one of the most democratic countries in South America, millions of lower-class workers were left mired in poverty, which put increasing pressure on the government for more radical economic reforms. In 1952 Chilean women were given full voting privileges and became, along with the growing middle class and the rural workers, another popular constituency. The newly formed *Partido Democrata Cristiano* (PDC), or the Christian Democrats, appealed to these constituencies but had strong competition from the growing Socialist party, whose members formed an electoral alliance known as the *Frente de Acción Popular* (FRAP). A third prominent political organization was an assortment of labor unions; controlled

Salvador Allende

mainly by communists, the unions called for improved working conditions and equality for workers with other members of Chilean society. By 1957 the socialist factions increased membership and FRAP threw its support behind Salvador Allende in the 1958 presidential campaign. Allende came in a close second to businessman Jorge Alessandri. Alessandri, however, proved unable to improve several glaring economic problems, including the unequal distribution of land and the overwhelmingly foreign ownership of Chilean copper mines and industries, which bled revenues out of the country. The poorer classes, especially in rural areas, suffered from lack of food and medical attention. A wide disparity in wages among social classes would continue to be reported in the 1960s.

Allende. In the 1970 elections Salvador Allende represented the newly formed *Unidad Popular* (UP) party, a combination of six socialist factions. Allende ran once again against Jorge Alessandri, now a candidate for the National Party, but this time Allende won by a narrow margin. He became the first socialist to be elected president in the Western Hemisphere.

The problems that riddled Chile when Allende took office were formidable. Inflation plagued the country and the overall annual economic growth rate per capita from 1960 to 1970 was only 2.6 percent. Agricultural development lagged behind the increasing population growth and Chile found itself importing an ever-increasing amount of foodstuffs. The cost of these imports also rose steadily from the mid-1950s to the early 1970s. Meanwhile, as demonstrated by his narrow victory, Allende did not enjoy overwhelming support, given all the different political factions in Chile at that time. The six socialist parties that combined to form Allende's own party, Unidad Popular, each had a different agenda in respect to what particular problems the government should address first. There was intense ideological and political polarization throughout the country, and outside opposition complicated the situation. The United States opposed Allende's Marxist government and U.S. interference in Chilean affairs—"passing dollars . . . to conservative groups and subsidizing anti-Allende strikes"—further frustrated Allende's attempts to establish better living conditions for his people (Skidmore and Smith, p. 142).

Allende worked to redistribute national income in favor of the economically depressed classes and stepped up government spending on education, health, and housing. By the end of 1972 all rural properties greater than 200 acres had been appropriated by the government to help give the poorer factions of the population land on which to live and work. Allende set out to nationalize industry and bought out the foreign owners of Chile's copper mines. This buyout was fiercely contested by many companies and caused problems for Chile's international trade. During 1971 the average price of copper, Chile's most important resource, fell by 27 percent and the value of copper exports fell by 16.5 percent. As inflation continued to rise, opposition parties encouraged poor Chileans to take matters into their own hands and to seize large estates and factories before official government decrees were issued allowing this to happen in an organized, lawful fashion. Citizens mounted strikes and boycotts in opposition to Allende's failing strategies. Economically indebted to the United States, Chile suffered when U.S. companies did all they could to stifle Allende's socialist administration. The United States reportedly spent $8 million on Central Intelligence Agency (CIA) actions to prevent Allende's election in the first place and then, once he was in power, to run him out of office. The CIA plan, according to declassified documents, had been to "make Chile ungovernable under Allende, provoke social chaos, and bring about a military coup" (Anderson, p. 50).

The Pinochet regime. General Augusto Pinochet was appointed commander of the Chilean armed forces by President Allende in 1973. Pinochet voiced no political opinions in public, and it is believed that this ostensible neutrality persuaded Allende that Pinochet was the perfect choice to lead the Chilean military. Until 1973 the Chilean military rarely intervened in the political process, nor did the government, under any party, interfere in the institutional concerns of the military. However, because the intense polarization of the people during Allende's presidency began to cause small outbreaks of violent protest, the military emerged from its historically neutral position. On September 11, 1973, the military staged a brutal overthrow of the government. Salvador Allende and at least 3,000 other Chileans—male and female—died in the process (Anderson, p. 46).

The Pinochet regime acted decisively and severely in letting the Chilean people know that the result of active socialist and/or communist practices would be torture and death. The Chilean military made men and women who supported any kind of socialist element "disappear" by abducting, torturing, and murdering them. The victims were mostly left-wing members of trade union, student, and worker groups. All political and trade union activity was banned. Military officers were drafted to take over all the main industries and universities, and the media was brought under strict control.

In 1980 Pinochet drew up a new national constitution that weakened the power of political parties, and he appointed himself Chile's leader for the next few years. The United States had a history of supporting any regime, whether brutal or not, that would oust a socialist government, but it did not continue to back Pinochet. His blatant human rights violations were exposed internationally and by the mid-1980s U.S. president Ronald Reagan finally abandoned his support of the Chilean dictatorship and stated that the United States would prefer Pinochet to step down from office. In 1986 there was a failed assassination attempt on Pinochet and, following this incident, a series of strikes and protests that shook Pinochet's regime. Pinochet retaliated by unleashing more repression and torture against opposition leaders, sparing not even Catholic priests in his program of intimidation.

PROCLAMATION NO. 7 (WARNING)

"The Junta of the Military Government hereby advises the population:

1) All persons resisting the new Government should be aware of the consequences.

2) All industries, housing units, and businesses shall cease resistance immediately or the Armed Forces shall proceed with the same energy and decision evident in its attack on La Moneda, the Presidential Palace.

3) The Junta of the Military Government hereby announces that, while having no intention to destroy, if public order is in any way disrupted by disobedience to its decrees, it will not hesitate to act with the same energy and decision which the citizenry has already had occasion to observe."

(Meiselas, pp. 2-3)

Torture. When democracy was restored in Chile in 1990 with the election of Patricio Aylwin, who unseated Pinochet as president, many acts of torture that took place in Chile during the dictatorship were finally documented and publicly criticized not only in Chile, but worldwide. Chile's human rights record under Pinochet was condemned by the United Nations as one of the world's worst. As Dorfman and fellow artists continued to refer in their work to the terror that their homeland endured under Pinochet, Chile published the 1991 Rettig Report, which documented thousands of cases of death and torture at the hands of the Chilean military. Up and down the coast of Chile, detention centers had been established; the National Stadium in Santiago had also been used to hold detainees. A young woman, an Allende supporter, recounts the following experience after an arrest, during which she was questioned about illegal gun smuggling. Her hands were tied behind her back and her head covered with a hood.

> Quickly I replied I knew nothing of such activities. But before I finished the sentence I was suddenly thrown out of the chair and my captor's fists were pounding my back, chest, and breasts to the accompaniment of curses and obscenities. . . . I don't know how long this assault continued because I lost consciousness. . . . I remember coming back to reality and my tormentors were at it once more, telling me that this was only a foretaste of what was to come.
> (Chavkin, p. 181)

Another report describes a woman whose hands were tied to her legs and who was left hanging from a bar for three days. Her circulation was permanently damaged and her bones were dislocated and broken. A third woman was raped in front of her husband, then thrown into a vat of human excrement where she nearly choked to death. Amnesty International has collected reports from various torture victims, male and female, as well as state agencies about the types of torture used in Chile during the Pinochet regime. The most common were beatings, electric shock, rape, sleep deprivation, near drowning, and non-therapeutic use of drugs. Although most of the reported incidents of torture by the military in Chile came from political prisoners, allegations of torture and ill-treatment from those accused of ordinary crimes were also reported.

Exile. Sectors of Chilean society fell apart immediately after the military coup of 1973. Those who had supported Allende's socialist regime now found themselves without work, and even non-socialists who simply opposed the actions of the dictatorship under Pinochet were ostracized. In addition, like Paulina in *Death and the Maiden,* many students were forbidden to return to the university and continue their education. As a result, several hundred thousand Chileans went into exile after Pinochet seized power. This mass exodus brought international attention to the atrocities being committed in Chile, as did their exposure by poets (Pablo Neruda; see ***The Heights of Macchu Picchu,*** also covered in *Latin American Literature and Its Times*), novelists (Isabel Allende; see ***The House of the Spirits)***, and playwrights (Ariel Dorfman). Their writings brought to the forefront themes of repression and torture.

Forcing Pinochet out of office. Opposition parties realized that in order to relieve Pinochet of his position as leader of Chile they would have to operate within the framework of the dictator's own constitution. The three main parties, the Christian Democrats, the Socialists, and the Radicals, joined forces and voted to terminate Pinochet's rule in 1988. In 1989 Christian Democrat candidate Patricio Aylwin became the first elected president in Chile in nearly 20 years. Although he was not pleased with the result, Pinochet resigned as president, but arranged the laws so that he would remain commander-in-chief of the Chilean military until 1998. He also appointed nine senators for life, to ensure himself a continuing influence in Chilean politics. In March 1998 he finally removed himself as commander-in-chief and settled into his new post as senator, a role that his 1980 constitution guaranteed to a former president for life.

Lack of accountability. There is overwhelming evidence that the Chilean military violated human rights by declaring states of "seige" or "emergency" and arresting people deemed enemies of the government. Including teachers, students, peasants, doctors, lawyers, trade unionists, workers, and shantytown dwellers, these victims came from a broad spectrum of society. People were arrested and held for weeks in secret detention centers, where they were kept incommunicado and were tortured to obtain information. The torturers didn't even bother to charge many detainees with any offense or to bring them to trial if they were charged. Records show that military personnel against whom detainees filed charges were typically dealt with by military tribunals that consistently failed to charge or convict anyone in the military. In spite of this, President Aylwin refused to put Pinochet and his military officers on civilian trial. Some Chileans have severely criticized Aylwin for this stance, while others point out that his position with the military is precarious as long as Pinochet retains power. Moreover, Pinochet's military regime passed an amnesty law in 1978 to insure that there be no future retaliation against them. Under this law, neither Pinochet nor anyone who was in the regime can be held accountable for violations committed upon the Chilean people during the military reign. There are, nevertheless, victims like Paulina in *Death and the Maiden,* who insist on holding the culprits accountable. Lawsuits for human rights violations, though often dropped, have continued to plague some of the leaders in Pinochet's military regime. Pinochet himself would be arrested in England in 1998 and charged by the government of Spain with torture and murder.

The Play in Focus

Plot summary. Set in 1991, the play takes place in a country (implied to be Chile although not specifically designated as such) that is currently in transition from a military dictatorship to a democratic government. The play opens as Gerardo Escobar, a lawyer and former political activist, is dropped off at his beach house by a man who spotted him on the roadside with a flat tire. Gerardo is greeted by his wife, Paulina Salas, whom we have just seen arm herself with a gun as she hears male voices, and then put the weapon away when she recognizes Gerardo. Gerardo tells her he has invited the good Samaritan who drove him home, Dr. Roberto Miranda, to dinner the following Sunday.

We learn that Gerardo has just been appointed to a national commission that will investigate human rights violations committed in their country under the previous military regime and then issue a public report about them. This is a sensitive subject for Paulina who 15 years ago was a victim of torture herself. She had been arrested for questioning about the political activities of her then-boyfriend, Gerardo. Mindful of this, Gerardo lies at first, saying he has not yet agreed to serve on the commission because he wants to make sure Paulina can handle what is to come if he does.

Pinochet had enacted the 1978 Amnesty Law, which prevented military officers from being brought to trial for any human rights violations committed between September 11, 1973, and March 10, 1978, the period of the worst human rights infringements. Aylwin felt that the Amnesty Law should be overturned, but the Chilean Supreme Court refused to do so. Therefore, Aylwin's new democratic regime was unable to bring any of the torturers to justice. Also, many judges who had been appointed under Pinochet were reluctant to prosecute any military officer as long as Pinochet remained leader of the armed forces in Chile. In the play, Paulina reminds her husband of the essential toothlessness of his new commission:

> PAULINA: Find out what happened. Find out everything. Promise me that you'll find everything that . . .
>
> GERARDO: Everything. Everything we can. We'll go as far as we . . . (*Pause.*) As we're . . .
>
> PAULINA: Allowed.
>
> (Dorfman, *Death and the Maiden,* p. 6)

An hour later, Roberto Miranda drives back to the Escobar home. He returns Gerardo's damaged flat, but his real motive is to talk with Gerardo about the new commission on which Gerardo is going to sit. Roberto and Gerardo discuss the trouble the commission will have finding the names of those who perpetrated crimes; Roberto seems eager to talk about the probable results of the investigation. The two men agree that moral condemnation is probably all that can be done. The hour is late, so Gerardo invites Roberto to stay the night rather than drive home. While Roberto is sleeping, Paulina, who has been eavesdropping on their conversation, knocks him out, ties him to a chair in the spare room, and gags him. She then leaves with his car.

THE RETTIG COMMISSION

Because of the bitterness and resentment among the Chilean people about the human rights violations carried out under the Pinochet regime, the *Comisión Nacional de Verdad y Reconciliación* (National Commission for Truth and Reconciliation) was formed in Chile to document these crimes against the people. Headed by former senator Paul Rettig, the commission investigated executions and also cases of torture that led to death. (Paulina's own case would have gone uninvestigated by the Rettig Commission, since she lived through her ordeal.) Its findings were announced on television by President Aylwin on March 4, 1991, and later published in two volumes (887 pages in all). The Commission confirmed 979 disappearances and 1,319 deaths by torture or execution.

When Roberto awakens, Paulina is pointing a gun at him. She alludes to a past they have shared and plays a tape of Schubert's *Death and the Maiden* that she has taken from his car. She relates that Schubert was once her favorite composer but that the sound of his work now makes her physically ill: "he's still my favorite composer, such a sad, noble sense of life. But I always promised myself a time would come to recover him, bring him back from the grave, so to speak, and just sitting here listening to him with you I know that I was right, that I'm—so many things are going to change from now on, right?" (*Death and the Maiden,* p. 15).

FROM POETIC VERSE TO CLASSIC SONG TO DRAMATIC LINCHPIN

Franz Schubert composed *Der Tod und das Mädchen* (*Death and the Maiden*) in 1817; published in 1821, it proved immediately popular. The song set to music the poem of the same name by Matthias Claudius:

The Poem "Der Tod und das Mädchen"

THE MAIDEN: Pass by! ah, pass by!
You wild man of bones!
I am still young, go, dear sir!
And touch me not.

DEATH: Give me your hand, you lovely delicate thing!
I'm a friend and do not come to punish.
Be of good cheer, I am not wild.
You shall sleep softly in my arms.

(Erickson, p. 204)

When Gerardo stumbles upon this scene, he is horrified. He demands that Paulina drop the gun immediately, but she refuses, explaining that, although she was blindfolded at the time, she recognizes Roberto's voice—the way he laughs, phrases he uses—as that of her rapist torturer from 15 years ago. When her husband moves to untie Roberto, Paulina fires. As Act One closes, she tells her husband: "We're going to put him on trial, Gerardo, this doctor. Right here. Today. You and me. Or is your famous Investigating Commission going to do it?" (*Death and the Maiden,* p. 18).

Act Two opens with Paulina talking to Roberto. She has never been quite the same after her release from captivity, during which her torturers tried to extract information about Gerardo. "But I never gave them Gerardo's name. . . . If I had mentioned Gerardo, he wouldn't have been named to any Investigating Commission, but would have been one of the names that some other lawyer was investigating" (*Death and the Maiden,* p. 19). Working underground at the time, Gerardo had been helping to smuggle people out of the country to save them from execution. Paulina was finally released only to find that Gerardo had taken up with another woman.

Most poignantly, Paulina remembers that the doctor who tortured her played a recording of Franz Schubert's *Death and the Maiden* before brutally and repeatedly raping her. Although she has entertained violent fantasies of revenge, Paulina feels that obtaining a confession from Roberto will resolve her lingering emotional torment. She convinces Gerardo that her treatment of Roberto will not jeopardize his position with the commission—she and Gerardo will tape Roberto's confession and make it public if he ever exposes her. Uncertain of his wife's sanity and confused himself—he exhibits rage toward Roberto at the same time that he entertains the possibility that the man is innocent—Gerardo has no choice but to go along with Paulina's scheme. He does, however, follow a suggestion of Roberto's and asks his wife to first repeat exactly what happened to her under torture. Gerardo then relates this information to Roberto so that he can make a convincing confession. Although Roberto vehemently denies Paulina's accusations from the start, Gerardo convinces him to go along with the confession so that he can be released. Gerardo does not want this to go any further, regardless of the potential truth of the accusations.

After Roberto confesses, Gerardo, thinking that Paulina has gotten all she wants and the ordeal is over, leaves to pick up Roberto's car. The "ordeal" is not over, however. Paulina tells Roberto that she is now convinced of his guilt and is going to kill him. Roberto protests that the confession is false and that he only confessed the details that Gerardo fed him. However, Paulina tells him that she knew what Gerardo was doing so she purposely gave him little bits of altered detail in her story. In his "false" confession, Roberto regurgitated the story but corrected these little bits of information with the right facts, thus giving himself away as the man who tortured her.

Roberto drops to his knees, begging for his life. He asks his victim, Paulina, to sacrifice her own personal revenge to end the cyclical acts of retaliation.

ROBERTO: Oh Paulina—isn't it time we stopped?
PAULINA: And why does it always have to be people like me who have to sacrifice, why are we

Sigourney Weaver as Paulina and Ben Kingsley as Roberto, in a scene from the 1994 film adaptation of *Death and the Maiden.*

> always the ones who have to make concessions when something has to be conceded, why always me who has to bite her tongue, why? . . . What do we lose by killing one of them? What do we lose? What do we lose?
>
> (*Death and the Maiden,* p. 44)

The play concludes with Paulina and Gerardo at a concert. Gerardo speaks of the success of his Investigating Commission, which has just published its final report. As Franz Schubert's *Death and the Maiden* is performed, Paulina exchanges a glance with Roberto, who is also in the concert hall, and then, deliberately, looks away

Sources and literary context. Dorfman claims that he first outlined the plot of *Death and the Maiden* while Pinochet was still in power in the early 1980s. Each of his main characters would be representative of the Chilean population as it experienced life under the Pinochet regime. Dorfman had trouble developing the character of Gerardo and figuring out how he would fit into the plot as a representative of political ideologies directly opposed to those of the Pinochet regime. When Chile was restored to democracy in 1990, Dorfman returned there to live and was inspired by the formation of the Rettig Commission to have Gerardo sit on a similar board.

Representing a divided Chile. The characters in *Death and the Maiden* represent the healing factions of the Chilean people: Paulina, a survivor of torture by the military; Roberto, one of those who inflicted the torture; and Gerardo, who represents the current government, which is trying to satisfy the need for justice while avoiding a recurrence of forceful military intervention in the country.

Paulina. Chilean women participated prominently in the political struggles in the early 1970s. They had been granted the right to vote in 1952, becoming a legitimate constituency to which political parties now catered; still, they remained largely underrepresented on the national political scene, even though they began to grow prominent by entering such professions as law and medicine. After Pinochet essentially banned trade unions and political parties, new grassroots movements emerged that were spearheaded by women. They formed shantytown organizations and soup kitchens to help the poor.

Because women also participated in what the Pinochet regime considered to be subversive organizations, they were subjected to the same kind of torture used to punish men. At particular risk were women who favored labor unions and maintained support for Allende's former government. Paulina is representative of such a woman, as she was a medical student who helped smuggle subversives out of the country. In *Death and the Maiden* we are privy to the torture—the cigarette burns, the beating, and the rape—that Paulina endured when she was brought in for questioning about Gerardo's identity as a subversive activist. According to the testimony of Chilean women who in real life were held for questioning by the military during the first years of the Pinochet regime, they had mistakenly believed that only men would be tortured and that women would be spared harsher treatment. This was not the case. Paulina represents the collective survivors of such torture as they strive for justice that is denied them in 1990 because Pinochet still heads the armed forces and cannot be held accountable for any human rights violations committed by the military.

Gerardo. Gerardo represents the Chilean government's attempt to appease those who were directly violated, or whose loved ones were tortured and killed during the military regime. In the play, Gerardo is a lawyer and political activist who once helped to smuggle other political activists out of his country to avoid arrest and possibly torture and death. Now that a democratic government has been restored in Gerardo's country, he is appointed to a commission that will investigate the human rights violations committed by the former regime. However, because the military remains powerful in his country he can offer only a report on the crimes, not punishment to those found guilty of them.

> GERARDO: . . . For starters, the Army is going to fight the Commission all the way. They've told the president this investigation was an insult, and dangerous, yes, dangerous, for the new government to be opening old wounds. But the president went ahead anyway, thank God, for a moment I thought he'd get cold feet, but we all know these people are ready to jump on us at the slightest mistake we make. . . .
>
> (*Death and the Maiden,* p. 11)

Paulina holds a gun to Roberto's head and is willing to kill him for all she believes he has done to her, but Gerardo cannot—or will not—do the same. A career lawyer and budding politician, Gerardo expresses his desire for justice yet must act within the confines of the law, which will not hold men such as Roberto officially accountable for their crimes, nor punish them. Gerardo seems to be in the same position as Patricio Aylwin when he unseated Pinochet as president of Chile. Aylwin could do nothing to bring the military criminals to justice, but he commissioned the Rettig Report to document the human rights violations that were committed during Pinochet's rule.

Roberto. Amnesty International published a report in 1983 entitled *Chile: Evidence of Torture.* This report was based on findings of an Amnesty International delegation to Chile in 1982 that included two doctors who examined people based on their allegations of specific tortures. The doctors found medical evidence consistent with what the victims claimed had happened to them while detained by the military police. A disturbing finding in this report was that medically trained personnel, probably doctors,had taken part in the torture of detainees. Dr. Roberto Miranda represents such a person. Roberto claims that he started working for the dictatorship for humanitarian reasons, but he slowly changed. "At first I told myself it was a way of saving lives. . . . I ordered them to stop [the torture] or the prisoner would die. But afterwards I began to—bit by bit, the virtue I was feeling turned into excitement. . . . By the time Paulina Salas was brought in it was already too late" (*Death and the Maiden,* p. 39). Although Roberto is accused by Paulina of committing acts of torture and rape against her, he seems to be living a carefree life in the aftermath of the government changeover to democracy. Roberto represents those military personnel who live and work side-by-side with the victims of their own crimes but are not held accountable or punished for them.

Reviews. While *Death and the Maiden* opened to mixed reviews abroad, in his own country Dorfman was seen as opening wounds that were still healing and was thus criticized as exploiting the country's pain rather than contributing to its recovery. Dorfman answers such critics in his afterword to *Death and the Maiden*:

> I . . . knew I would be savagely criticised by some in my own country for "rocking the boat" by reminding everyone about the long-term effects of terror and violence on people precisely at a time when we were being asked to be notably cautious.
>
> I felt, however, that . . . as an artist I had to answer the wild mating call of my characters and break the silence which was weighing upon so many of my self-censored compatriots, fearful of creating "trouble" for the new [post-Pinochet] democracy. It was then and is now more than ever my belief that a fragile democracy is strengthened by expressing for all

> to see the deep dramas and sorrows and hopes that underlie its existence and that it is not by hiding the damage we have inflicted on ourselves that we will avoid its repetition.
>
> (*Death and the Maiden,* p. 48)

Outside of Chile, some critics felt that the play minimized such serious issues by portraying them via a troubled married couple. John Simon, for example, who reviewed the play for *New York Magazine,* agreed with the Chilean critics who felt that Dorfman trivialized torture and suffering; Simon said that the play had a "basic insufficiency of reducing a national and individual tragedy to a mere whodunit" (Simon, p. 88).

However, many other critics felt that Dorfman's play raised poignant questions about the all-too-real issues that Chile was facing in 1991. In the *Times Literary Supplement,* John Butt praised Dorfman for delivering the message of how a country struggles back to democracy after years of living under a military dictatorship; the play, he argued, offered "no easy answers to the question of how the new democracies should deal with the criminals in their midst without either sinking back into violence or sweeping hideous crimes under the carpet" (Butt, p. 22).

—Barbara Lozano

For More Information

Amnesty International. *Torture in the Eighties: An Amnesty International Report.* London: Amnesty International, 1984.

Anderson, Jon Lee. "Profile: The Dictator." *New Yorker* LXXIV, no. 32 (October 19, 1998): 44–57.

Bethell, Leslie, ed. *Chile Since Independence.* New York: Cambridge University Press, 1993.

Butt, John. Review of *Death and the Maiden. The Times Literary Supplement,* February 28, 1992, 22.

Chavkin, Samuel. *Storm Over Chile: The Junta under Seige.* Westport, Conn.: Lawrence Hill & Company, 1982.

Constable, Pamela, and Arturo Valenzuela. *Chile under Pinochet: A Nation of Enemies.* New York: W. W. Norton & Company, 1991.

Dorfman, Ariel. *Death and the Maiden.* New revised edition. London: Nick Hern, 1994.

Erickson, Raymond. *Schubert's Vienna.* New Haven, Conn.: Yale University Press, 1997.

Meiselas, Susan, ed. *Chile from Within, 1973–1988.* Photographs by Paz Errazuriz and others. Texts by Marco Antonio de la Parra and Ariel Dorfman. New York: W. W. Norton, 1990.

Skidmore, Thomas E., and Peter H. Smith. *Modern Latin America.* 4th ed. New York: Oxford University Press, 1997.

Simon, John. Review of *Death and the Maiden. New York* Magazine 25, no. 13 (March 30, 1992): 87–88.

The Death of Artemio Cruz

by
Carlos Fuentes

Born in Mexico City in 1928 to a diplomat father, Carlos Fuentes grew up primarily in Mexico and the United States. He was living in Mexico in the 1950s, when his first two novels were published (*Where the Air is Clear* [1958] and *The Good Conscience* [1959]). His third novel, *The Death of Artemio Cruz,* established him as an author of world renown. Fuentes began writing it in 1960 in Cuba, after Fidel Castro's revolution there. At the time "almost the entire intellectual world of Latin America shared a fervor—or at least a sympathy—for the Cuban Revolution" (Krauze, p. 653). It especially touched Mexicans in Fuentes's generation, who had been struggling to define their national essence and were disturbed by the course onto which their own revolution had veered.

THE LITERARY WORK

A novel set in Mexico from 1889 to 1959; published in Spanish as *La Muerte de Artemio Cruz* in 1962, in English in 1964.

SYNOPSIS

On his deathbed, a millionaire tycoon reviews twelve momentous days of his life.

Events in History at the Time the Novel Takes Place

Dual legacy. Fuentes's novel begins during the reign of President Porfirio Díaz, first a fighter for reform but then a dictator who monopolized power for his own sake. In the 1870s Díaz seized control of the government from the legitimate president, going on to "win" reelection seven times. He governed for 34 years (1876-80 and 1884-1911) of painful poverty but also blessed peace. Before Díaz, Mexico had endured a century of armed disputes—the War of Independence (1821), the War of the North American Invasion (otherwise known as the Mexican American War [1848]), and the War of the French Intervention (1862). In collusion with conservative Mexicans, France had seized control briefly, but then internal tensions exploded into more armed conflict: led by Benito Juárez, liberal Mexicans wrested power from the conservatives and threw out the French in the War of the Reform (1867).

Díaz fought under Juárez. By the time Díaz himself was in power, two contrary traditions had emerged—a spirit of reform and a tenacious spirit of dictatorship. The 1800s had been dominated by military strongmen, or *caudillos*, which boded well for dictatorship. Preeminent among the strongmen was Antonio López de Santa Anna, who was president 11 times between 1833 and 1855. Owner of a vast *hacienda* (landed estate) in Veracruz, Santa Anna grew so enamored with power during his decades of rule that he had his minions call him "His Most Serene Highness."

In 1857 the spirit of reform took over, and the liberals drafted a new constitution, a vain at-

A meeting of Pancho Villa and Emiliano Zapata in the Presidential Palace, Mexico City, around 1916.

tempt to break the hold that a small minority of hacienda owners, army leaders, and the Catholic Church had over the nation's wealth. At the time the Church controlled close to one half of all the land, and earned enormous income from rents and loans to its allies, the hacienda owners. The liberals tried but failed to loosen the Church's grip. They auctioned off only a fifth of Church lands, and to little effect. The upper class grew slightly, enlarged by the few Mexicans who, like Artemio's father-in-law, old Gamaliel Bernal, in *The Death of Artemio Cruz,* had the cash to buy the auctioned parcels.

Not at all happy about the 1857 reforms, which infringed on their monopoly of the country's riches, the conservatives attacked the liberals, and Mexico descended into nearly 20 years of civil war. Meanwhile and afterward, the bulk of the nation remained impoverished. In fact, people grew poorer during Díaz's reign, many of them losing their lands because of legal maneuvering, cause enough for revolution. Of 11 million rural dwellers, fewer than 3 percent of them owned any land by 1910. Hacienda owners let vast areas lie fallow year after year, while peasants went hungry and their lives were made even more miserable by *rurales* (rural police), who charged them "for living, for the hens, for the pigs" (García in Krauze, p. 284). In cities and in the countryside, illiteracy was rampant: 75 percent of the Mexican population could neither read nor write.

Again the spirit of reform reared its stubborn head, or, in this case, hand. The spark that lit the Mexican Revolution came not from a rifle or a torch but from a book by a member of the educated elite—*The Presidential Succession of 1910* by Francisco I. Madero. Madero declared Mexico's problem to be the concentration of power in one man, and he prescribed a solution—a return to the Constitution of 1857, along with the principle of "Valid Voting, No Reelection." A president, counseled Madero, should serve as head of the nation for only one term.

Díaz thought Madero's ideas outrageous and proceeded to engineer an eighth reelection for himself and his deputies. Madero mounted an antireelection campaign against Díaz that attracted thousands of supporters, so in 1910 Díaz's government decided to arrest Madero. From prison, Madero wrote the *Plan de San Luis,* calling for revolution: "Fellow citizens, do not hesitate, even for a moment! Take up arms, throw the usurpers out of power, recover your rights as free men!" (Madero in Krauze, p. 255). Released from prison, Madero took up arms. Díaz started his eighth term, but scattered uprisings and Madero's capture of Ciudad Juárez convinced him to resign. Afterward, Madero became temporary president, demobilizing his own troops, and leaving Díaz's federal army and congress in place. The strife had hardly begun.

The Mexican Revolution—an overview. Mexico's was the first of the momentous revolutions of the twentieth century. Lasting more than a decade (1910–24), the Revolution led to subsequent Mexican upheavals, from civil conflicts in the 1920s to radical economic changes in the 1930s. During the war years, the number of men-in-arms at any one time was never great. In 1915, the most factious year, fewer than 100,000 soldiers fought in a nation of over 15 million. Still, the overall human and economic costs of the Revolution were astronomical—240,000 dead in combat and 750,000 dead from related diseases, plus destruction to mines, factories, haciendas, and railroads. And there was also an untabulated cost—the dissolution and betrayal of burgeoning democratic ideals, as reflected in the novel by Artemio and his fellow army officers.

Madero served as president for less than a year. Within months of his victory, federal soldiers, under Victoriano Huerta, staged a counterrevolution that included Madero's assassination (February 22, 1912). Huerta became president until pro-Madero rebels and trouble with the United States drove him into exile in 1914. Three caudillos emerged among the pro-Madero rebels—Francisco "Pancho" Villa, General Álvaro Obregón, and Governor Venustiano Carranza. In the south, a fourth caudillo, Emiliano Zapata, promoted his *Plan de Ayala*, calling for restitution of land to its rightful, deed-carrying owners. These four caudillos took on distinct personae: Zapata became champion of the landless; Villa, though not concerned with land, won renown as a Robin Hood-style fighter out to ravage the rich for the benefit of the poor; Carranza was the landowner-reformer; Obregón was the military genius.

Villa, Obregón, and Carranza met at the Convention of Aguascalientes to hammer out a future government for Mexico, but there was an ominous break between Carranza and Villa. Remaining uncommitted for the moment, Obregón finally sided with Carranza. It was a politically astute choice, since Governor Carranza operated under an aura of legitimacy, in contrast to the renegade Villa.

Exercising his military prowess, Obregón went on to defeat Villa. The great battles of 1915 were fought in the Bajío, the fertile central basin north of Mexico City. A fierce warrior and an expert horseman, Villa's fame spread all the way to the movie capital of the world—Hollywood. Needing the $25,000 that was offered him, Villa allowed the Mutual Film Corporation to film his División del Norte (Northern Division) in action. For the sake of the camera, he fought during the daytime and postponed executions from 5 a.m. to 7 a.m. Villa was clearly preoccupied with fighting, but there were idealists in his camp, too—men like Felipe Ángeles, who promoted the spread of education and democracy.

The 1915 campaign in the Bajío proved fatal to Villa's forces. Against Ángeles's advice, Villa insisted on frontal cavalry charges. He sent one cavalry charge after another against Obregón's soldiers, who had entrenched themselves in ditches surrounding the battleground. In a fateful battle, Obregón's troops fought a defensive war from the trenches, then faked a retreat, after which their reserve forces rushed at the enemy in an offensive attack. The statistics speak for themselves. Obregón's losses totaled 200 dead, wounded, or captured; Villa's totaled 10,000, and his men began deserting in droves. Villa continued fighting, but with a shrunken force of 3000. Wiping out Villa's strongholds in the state of Sonora at the end of 1915, Obregón's troops reduced Villa to guerrilla warfare thereafter. Villa's forces continued to plague the north for years (during which time Carranza served as president). In 1920 the renegade Villa finally surrendered—only to be assassinated in 1923, along with a car full of unfortunate bysitters.

AN ELECTORAL SHOWDOWN

The contest was the 1928 election, not a military campaign, but guns still figured into the equation. An attempt was made on General Álvaro Obregón's life in 1927. President earlier in the decade (1920–24), Obregón ran for reelection in 1928. This not only threatened the right of the sitting president (Plutarco Elias Calles) to designate his own successor, but it also violated the Revolution's commitment to "Valid Voting, No Reelection." As the contest approached, the number of murders escalated, including 25 generals and 150 others. Obregón was elected, only to be assassinated a few months later (July 17, 1928). Subsequently Calles met with Mexico's 30 most notable generals to request their support, a gathering that is mirrored in *The Death of Artemio Cruz* by the meeting of Artemio's war cronies at a whorehouse. Artemio persuades them to switch loyalties to the new man in power, after which they appear at the new man's offices to profess loyalty to him.

Villa's 1915 defeat spelled disaster for Zapata in the south, whose own movement dwindled. He himself retained a religious zeal for his cause—the return of Mexican land to its rightful owners—but the federal army killed 508 of his followers in 1915 and 1916, and finally tricked Zapata into a 1919 meeting that resulted in his murder. Zapata's movement has been described as an independent rebellion, a cause apart from the others, though he briefly joined with Villa. Yet Zapata was bent on justice for his whole village and other pueblos like it. In contrast, after the first assassination—the killing of Madero—most of the Revolution's strongmen seemed out for themselves. In *The Death of Artemio Cruz,* the protagonist winds up in jail with Gonzalo Bernal. Bernal warns him that one day he will have to choose between Carranza and Obregón, foreseeing that their alliance will not last. Artemio makes it clear that Obregón is his man. A few years later, as the 1928 election approaches, a police officer threatens Artemio's life unless he switches his allegiance from General Obregón. Now a congressman, Artemio recalls the oath of loyalty he swore to the general in years past but then dismisses it and behaves like the opportunist he has become, a man loyal, above all, to himself. He agrees to switch allegiances, aligning himself, as always, with the strongest scoundrel, siding with "the emerging leader against the fading leader" (Fuentes, *The Death of Artemio Cruz,* p. 129).

Civil strife in the 1920s. In 1917 the civilian caudillo Carranza oversaw the drafting of a new constitution, a document that turned out to be far more radical than he himself anticipated. There was widespread hostility toward the Church, whose property had been desecrated in the 1910s by Obregón's troops. Soldiers "drank out of chalices, paraded wearing priestly vestments, built fires in confessionals, shot up sacred images, converted churches into barracks, carried out mock executions of the statues of the saints" (Krauze, p. 356). The hostility found its way into the new Constitution. Article 130 required all priests to register with the government, authorized each state to limit its number of priests, and prohibited clerics from criticizing the law of Mexico.

But the movement to punish the Church was far from universal. In 1926, when President Calles set out to apply Article 130, a portion of the population rose up in defense of the priests. The conflict escalated, breaking out into a savage three-year war between the federal army and Church defenders, known as the *Cristeros.* "*Viva Cristo Rey!*" (Long Live Christ the King!) they shouted in the *Cristiada* (War for Christ; also referred to as the "Cristero rebellion" [1926–29]), which spread to 13 states and claimed more than 70,000 lives. Cristeros were hanged, villages burned, and priests killed. In the novel an official informs Artemio, "Tomorrow they shoot the priests" (*Artemio Cruz,* p. 122). Altogether 90 priests were executed during the Cristiada. The Cristeros, in turn, burned government buildings, blew up trains, and brutally killed teachers and other government workers.

Another internal conflict of the 1920s involved the Yaqui Indians. In the novel, Villa's troops capture a daring Yaqui along with Artemio. Tobias, the Yaqui, demonstrates a courage that reflects the real-life reputation of these Indians, who fought for Obregón with such bravery that, according to some historians, they enabled him to defeat Villa. The Yaquis expected afterward to be rewarded with restitution of their land in Sonora, as promised. Instead, a decade after the Yaquis helped him defeat Villa, Obregón led 15,000 soldiers in a campaign against these

Indians (October 1926–April 1927), betraying his revolutionary debt to them.

Radical economic change and war abroad. President Calles (1924–28) became less of a reformer and more of a dictator over the years.

> Hundreds of his enemies were jailed . . . and a large number were reported to have "committed suicide." Moreover, he and his close associates became . . . millionaires. Their lavish estates in the Lomas district of the capital [where Catalina lives in the novel] were referred to as "palaces of Ali Baba and the Forty Thieves."
>
> (Miller, p. 314)

The spirit of reform resurfaced in the 1930s during the presidency of Lázaro Cárdenas (under whom Fuentes's own father was a diplomat). As president, Cárdenas distributed 44 million acres to Mexican peasants, mostly to *ejidos*—communal landholding units—which was not always to the liking of the peasants themselves, as Cárdenas later admitted. Still he distributed far more land than his predecessors had, destroying the oppressive class of *hacendados* (hacienda owners) in Mexico. Article 27 of the new Constitution identified the nation, not private property holders, as the owner of all minerals and oil beneath Mexico's lands. In 1938 Cárdenas invoked this article to appropriate the subsurface oil that foreign, mostly United States, companies had been exploiting.

Wild with enthusiasm, Mexicans banded together to help the government compensate the oil companies for their losses. Of course, not all Mexicans welcomed such change. From 1914 to 1920 General Manuel Peláez had profited from the old laws, charging foreign oil companies a combined $15,000 a month to protect them from the central government. Peláez's kind would soon find their way around new laws. A mineral edict of 1934 declared that concessions would go to applicants with the most economic and technical resources, provided that the applicants were Mexican; this anti-foreigner emphasis continued in 1935, when terms for concessions to foreigners became so stiff that, to set up operations, they needed front men who were Mexican. In the novel Artemio serves as such a front man for a pair of U.S. sulfur miners and, in the tradition of the real-life oil-mogul Peláez, charges them $2,000 just to arrange the concession.

Global affairs exploded during Cárdenas's presidency, beginning with the Spanish Civil War (1936–39). There was a leftist government in power in Spain at the time (the Second Spanish Republic), and some right-wing officers set out to topple it. Mexico backed not the army officers but the legitimate government, as did Spain's liberal citizens. Thousands of Spanish intellectuals sought refuge from the war in Mexico. Traveling in the other direction, 330 Mexicans enlisted to fight on the side of the Spanish Republic. Only 59 would survive the war, so the chances of someone like Artemio's son, Lorenzo, coming out alive were slim. The volunteers sailed to Spain from Veracruz, as Lorenzo does in the novel, on freighters called *Magallanes, Motomar,* and *Mar Cantábrico.*

FROM A FOLK SONG CELEBRATING CÁRDENAS'S AUDACITY

On the eighteenth of March, the day of the great sensation!
He nationalized the oil then! The Chief of our Nation!

(Krauze, p. 475)

In winter 1939 the Spanish Republic was losing the war to the army insurgents under Francisco Franco, who seized the city of Barcelona in January. Madrid fell to them in March, ending the civil war. In the novel Lorenzo leaves for Spain in February, when the fighting is nearly over. Germany, supporting Franco, has been using Spain as a kind of testing ground for World War II, trying out night and bad-weather bombing. It is a gray, dismal day when Lorenzo confronts a barely visible German bomber, and, in one of the novel's most gripping scenes, goes down fighting like a "real macho," while his Spanish companion Miguel rants about the craziness of Lorenzo's courage.

There is sense to Lorenzo's action, however, in light of how the Mexican male regards death. "*La vida no vale nada!*" (Life is worth nothing!) is a familiar cry before mortal combat, meaning that the way one dies is worth everything. The idea is to *hombrearse con la muerte* (face death like a man), which is what Lorenzo has done, and also what Artemio does in the novel by reviewing his whole life—even the painful memories that until now he has repressed—at the moment of his death.

Official betrayal—1940–1950s. Much has been made of the fact that a democratic revolution that was begun to overthrow Díaz's dictatorship ended up creating an equally autocratic government. The president became all-powerful in post-Revolutionary Mexico, handling public property as if it were his own, doling out funds and favors as he chose. Meanwhile, senators and deputies like Artemio Cruz rubber-stamped his decisions, failing to represent their districts yet invoking revolutionary rhetoric. Public officials tried to disguise selfish motivations as benevolent gestures for the good of the people. But no one was fooled. The peasants, an aide informs Artemio in the novel, "realize that you gave them land only good for dry-farming and kept the watered land for yourself. That you go on charging interest on the loans you made them, just like . . . before" the Revolution, but they do not complain because "as bad as things are, these people are better off now" (*Artemio Cruz,* p. 90).

Murals by two Mexicans—Diego Rivera and José Clemente Orozco—depicted the promise and betrayal of the Revolution. Rivera's murals portrayed the promise; Orozco's, the reality of sacrifice and betrayal. Businessmen and politicians invoked Rivera's images, using them as a flimsy cover for the abuse of power that raged through society, especially during the presidency of Miguel Alemán Valdés (1946–52). Alemán managed to protect private property from being redistributed to peasants, amending legislation that had been passed by Cárdenas. Committed to industrializing the nation, Alemán also adopted a policy of replacing imported with Mexican goods. The upper and middle classes grew wealthier as a result; meanwhile, "the scale of corruption attained by [the president's own circle of friends] was something that had never been seen before" (Krauze, p. 556). After becoming public officials, businessmen sold their goods to the government at prices they themselves deemed fit. They learned of upcoming construction projects and purchased nearby land, whose value was sure to rise. And everyone bribed government workers. Life in Mexico seemed splendid at first glance. The newly rich "raised mansions like Hollywood film sets, held bacchanalian parties, poured out rivers of money," but Alemán failed to put anything over on the poor who, like the painter Orozco, perceived the grim reality of ongoing inequity in society (Krauze, p. 556). A post-Alemán poem by Jorge Hernández Campos captures this reality: "I'm the most excellent Mr. President Don So and So of Something / and when . . . I shout Viva Mexico! / what I really mean is Viva me!" (Krauze, p. 564). The industrialization had not brought general progress, but a limited variety, of benefit to a few small pockets of the population.

The Novel in Focus

Plot summary. The novel opens on April 10, 1959, the day of Artemio Cruz's death. Prostrate in bed, the ailing multimillionaire has visitors—his estranged wife, Catalina; his embittered daughter, Teresa; his son-in-law, Gerardo; and his devoted secretary, Padilla. A priest enters, and Artemio's granddaughter, Gloria, appears. Doctors come and go.

Meanwhile, Artemio muses about 12 pivotal days in his life, out of chronological order. His story emerges slowly, like a jigsaw puzzle, whose pieces are laid out in the following sequence:

July 6, 1941: Cruz negotiates a partnership in Mexican sulfur mining with some U.S. investors.

May 20, 1919: A veteran soldier, Artemio insinuates himself into the family of a dead wartime acquaintance, Gonzalo Bernal.

December 4, 1913: Artemio's first love, Regina, is hanged by enemy soldiers.

June 3, 1924: Artemio and his wife, Catalina, an uncommunicative couple, have a pivotal argument; he takes a young mistress, Lilia.

November 23, 1927: Artemio, now a congressman, switches allegiance from his wartime superior to the new powerholder.

September 11, 1947: A middle-aged Artemio brings his mistress, Lilia, to the honeymoon spot of the '40s—Acapulco; she cheats on him with a fellow vacationer, but Artemio takes her back.

October 22, 1915: Villa's retreating troops capture Captain Artemio Cruz and his fellow-in-arms, a Yaquis Indian; after meeting a third prisoner, Gonzalo Bernal, Artemio parleys with the enemy in a way that allows him to save himself from a firing-squad fate.

August 12, 1934: Artemio's lover, Laura, gives him an ultimatum that he turns down, opting to stay in his unfulfilling marriage.

February 3, 1939: Artemio's beloved son, Lorenzo, perishes in the Spanish Civil War.

December 31, 1955: The aged Artemio throws a lavish New Year's Eve party at his home in Coyoacán, where he lives with Lilia.

January 18, 1903: A neighboring landowner threatens to separate 13-year-old Artemio from his guardian/uncle, Lunero; Artemio murders a man to prevent the separation.

April 9, 1889: Artemio is born to a peasant mother who has been raped by the hacendado Atanasio Menchaca.

Diego Rivera at work on one of his murals, 1936.

The novel alternates among three voices and tenses, with Artemio employing the first-person *I* and present tense for thoughts about his physical deterioration on his deathbed; the second-person *you* and future tense to judge his past actions and entertain alternate choices he could have made; and the third person *he* and past tense to narrate the course of his life events. His own voice is interrupted occasionally by his wife's thoughts and by a chapter on his son's experiences in Spain.

BEHIND THE FRONTLINES

Without a commissary or medical corps, the armies of the Mexican Revolution depended on women to forage for their food, wash their clothes, and nurse their wounds. Loosely speaking, a *soldadera* was any woman who followed her man when he left home and joined an army. Soldaderas anticipated the troops' movements, waiting for their arrival at the next campsite with refreshments at the ready. "In the abandoned battlefield they carr[ied] water to their wounded masters and despoil[ed] the dead of their clothing" (Macías, p. 41). They did not, as a rule, wage war themselves. Nonetheless, all the movement often put them in harm's way. Rape followed by murder was commonplace.

Born in Veracruz in 1889 on a hacienda called Cocuya, Artemio is the child of a wealthy hacendado who raped Artemio's mulatta mother and, after the birth, ran her off the estate. Rescuing the infant, her mulatto brother, Lunero, raises the green-eyed boy until he is 13. The uncle and nephew remain in their shed on the decaying hacienda, crafting and selling candles and canoes. Artemio's father, the hacendado Atanasio Menchaca, has been killed and the surviving Menchacas have fallen on hard times. They lead listless, unproductive lives in the main house.

One day a neighboring tobacco grower threatens to take Lunero away. To prevent this, 13-year-old Artemio kills a man. Before he and his uncle can rendezvous to escape, Lunero is shot dead. The boy flees northward utterly alone, then enters into another emotionally important relationship with Sebastián, who teaches the unschooled Artemio how to read, write, and count. Sebastián inspires Artemio, at age 21, to join the Mexican Revolution. He fights in Sonora and Sinaloa, where Artemio one day rapes an unwary young woman, as he and fellow soldiers have done so many times before. This time the lustful encounter grows into love. The young woman, Regina, weaves a fiction about how they met to spare Artemio the shame of it and he plays along with her, in one of the many deceptions that will riddle his lifetime. For seven months, Regina is Artemio's soldadera, anticipating the movements of his troops, meeting him in this town or that, so that the two of them can grasp a few precious moments together.

In 1913 Artemio is fighting Huerta's federal soldiers. He abandons an unknown wounded mate on the battlefield to save himself for Regina's love, then finds that she and nine others have been hanged by Huerta's *federales* as punishment for a town's having supported the rebels.

Two years later the rebels are fighting among themselves. Artemio has been promoted to captain under General Obregón. Pursuing the retreating troops of Pancho Villa, Captain Artemio Cruz and a fellow soldier, a Yaqui Indian named Tobias, are caught. The Yaqui daringly helps Artemio try to effect an escape, but to no avail. Both end up in prison, alongside a young lawyer, Gonzalo Bernal, who feels that the Revolution has been lost no matter who wins because the rebels, the supposed "good guys," have sold out to their own self-interests. Bernal reveals a few details about his life—he has a sister, Catalina, and a father, Don Gamaliel, who inhabit a hacienda of their own in Puebla. Outside the jail cells, the enemy offers Artemio a deal; he can escape the firing squad if he reveals his troops' plans. Opting to relay some bogus plans and save his skin, after trying in vain to save his fellow soldier Tobias, Artemio watches as Bernal and Tobias are executed.

In 1919 the army discharges Artemio who, now a colonel, finds his way to the home of Gonzalo Bernal. On the flimsy strength of having shared Gonzalo's final moments, he latches onto the father's dwindling fortune. The Bernal hacienda has lost control of its workers and is in decline. Employing shrewd, if ruthless, business tactics, Artemio loans money to the workers at low interest and collects debts owed to old Bernal for a share of the take. He marries Catalina, with whom he has fallen in love. Pushed into the marriage, a vengeful Catalina reciprocates his love but does not allow herself the luxury of showing it to a man she believes deserves her wrath, a man she suspects is somehow involved in the death of her brother and whom she blames for the ruin of her father. Artemio shrewdly convinces old Don Gamaliel that it would be to their advantage in revolutionary Mexico to turn over some of his unfertile plots to the peasants on his hacienda. Thereafter, Artemio is regarded as a hero of Mexico's agrarian-reform program.

Five years later Don Gamaliel has died and left his estate to Catalina and Artemio. She reflects on their passion by night and their lack of communication by day, still refusing to reveal her affection for him. Artemio is elected to congress, largely on the strength of his supposed "contribution" to agrarian reform. There is a rift in the marriage when Catalina fails to stick by his side during the election, and Artemio takes a mistress, a young Indian girl, Lilia. Yet Catalina remains with Artemio, because, he thinks, of his money. He and Catalina have two children—a daughter, Teresa, and a beloved son named Lorenzo.

Teresa grows up away at school and later by her mother's side, far from Artemio. At age 12 Lorenzo, to whom Catalina is devoted, is taken from her by Artemio. He rebuilds for his son the hacienda in Veracruz where he himself was born. The boy grows up with a passion for horses and an enjoyment of the countryside. At 19 he ships out for Spain's Civil War, invoking his father's originally pure ideals at the outset of the earlier Mexican Revolution. This touches Artemio deeply and also becomes one of his most haunting memories, as demonstrated by a refrain that crops up repeatedly throughout the novel: "That morning I waited for him with pleasure. We crossed the river on horseback" (*Artemio Cruz,* p. 82).

In Spain, after a defeat, Lorenzo and a fellow soldier named Miguel encounter some young women also fleeing the area. Lorenzo and the young woman Lola dare to lead their small group across a possibly mined bridge. Thankfully, they survive and share a night of passion before joining a long line of France-bound refugees. Lorenzo and his companions fall in step with women carrying mattresses, men hauling mirrors, and carts lumbering toward the border. They are trudging along when a Nazi bomber suddenly fires on them. Instead of putting his own survival first, Lorenzo tries to shoot his rickety old rifle at the menacing bomber. But the worn-out weapon fails to fire, and Lorenzo is killed.

Back in Mexico, Artemio, blocking out his feelings as best he can, goes on to increase his fortune through various means, which include sulfur domes, logging concessions, interest on railroad loans, his take as a front man on behalf of U.S. miners, a daily newspaper of his own, and assorted real-estate investments. He owns some vacant lots, his reward for switching allegiance from Obregón to the current power brokers in government, and he also has a cool $15 million stashed away in U.S. and European banks.

NEWSPAPERS AND LABOR UNIONS

In the novel Artemio owns a Mexico City newspaper and has a vested interest in the nation's railroads, to which he has made loans. He therefore orders his employees to make sure not a single line about police repression gets into his paper during a 1959 railroad strike. There actually was strife in Mexico's railroad industry in 1959. Labor leader Demetrio Vallejo inspired work stoppages to press for higher wages and new union elections to replace corrupt officers. The unrest led to a 16.66 percent pay increase for all but two companies, whose workers proceeded to go on strike. It was Easter week, a time of increased travel, and the government quickly quashed the strike, arresting its leaders and firing 13,000 workers. A few days later all Mexican railroads went on a sympathy strike, and 10,000 more workers were arrested. When a leading rebel, Román Guerra Montamayor, died at the scene of a protest, authorities painted his lips and nails red to brand him a communist, then threw his corpse across a railroad track.

Revolution was very much on everyone's mind, since Fidel Castro had just staged a successful one in Cuba (January 1, 1959). Information about it filtered into Mexico, with people relying on word-of-mouth rather than newspapers. It was generally known that paper owners slanted the news to suit their purposes. They were more concerned with not offending the current strongmen than with reporting facts. So readers could find trustworthy details about parties, bullfights, religious gatherings, and crimes of the heart, but not about hard news. A paper's "news" was affected also by business interests. Mexico City papers grew into rich enterprises, and their owners into tycoons because of advertising, not the number of papers sold. All the large businesses "had to pay up in one way or another or else they might read 'Coca-Cola is bad for your health'" (Revel in Krauze, p. 598).

Artemio's marriage has become meaningless—he and his wife live in separate residences.

Five years before Lorenzo's death, while traveling abroad, Artemio began an affair with Laura, a woman of refined taste who cared little for his money. Their affair continued in Mexico, but one day Laura gave him an ultimatum—Artemio must choose his wife (and current life) or her. Artemio forgoes Laura's love, returning to his mistress, Lilia, and pursuing an empty but convenient relationship with her. The by-now aging congressman takes Lilia on a trip to Acapulco, where she has a brief affair with a younger man. Artemio notices but ignores the betrayal. She is with him in 1955 when he throws a New Year's Eve party at his mansion in Coyoacán, a remodeled convent furnished in the finest of taste. The "Mummy of Coyoacán," they call Artemio, a fact of which he is well aware as he sits regally at the party without letting any of his guests get too close. Surrounding the "mummy" are his hard-won possessions—"my paintings, my wines, my comforts, which I control the same way I control all of you" (*Artemio Cruz,* p. 259).

LAS LOMAS VS. COYOACÁN

In the novel Artemio complains that he is dying at the "wrong" house, the one in Las Lomas, where his wife lives, not at his own house in Coyoacán. Mexican social history recounts the flight of upper-class residents from downtown Mexico City in the 1920s and '30s to suburban *colonias* (communities) like Las Lomas. Distinctly modern, these colonias contrasted sharply with old Spanish-built towns like Coyoacán, which was located farther outside the city in the Valley of Mexico.

Four years later, physically ill, his insides exploding, Artemio lies on his deathbed, reviewing the course of his life, justifying and blaming himself, reflecting on his marriage, recognizing in these final feeble moments that Catalina does love him after all, mourning his son, and ignoring his daughter but mentally thanking her for bringing his granddaughter to his deathbed. He acknowledges his all-consuming quest for power and takes responsibility for having disregarded his effect on others. The multimillionaire Mummy of Coyoacán tells himself that he is who he is because he knew how to violate other people before they could violate him. In retrospect, he realizes that over the years this approach to life has made him betray significant relationships and cheat himself of love. It is too much for a body to take, and Artemio dies, ostensibly, according to the doctors, of mesentery infarct.

National search for an elusive identity. "Is there a single Mexican who believes in me?" wonders Artemio as he negotiates with U.S. sulfur miners. "If the gringos were the only ones willing to finance the explorations, what was he supposed to do?" (*Artemio Cruz,* p. 20). A shrewd businessman, a capitalist through and through, he cements his partnership with the U.S. investors, telling himself,

> You turned your eyes northward and lived with the regret that a geographical error kept you from being part of them in everything. You admire their efficiency, their comforts, their hygiene, their power, and you look around you and the incompetence, the misery, the filth, the languor, the nakedness of this poor country that has nothing, all seem intolerable to you.
>
> (*Artemio Cruz,* pp. 26–27)

Artemio, however, is not to be taken at his word. His actions and feelings speak louder. He chooses to live not in modern Las Lomas but in Coyoacán, a Spanish-built town from Mexico's colonial past. He represses feelings of indebtedness to Sebastián (the teacher who inspired him with revolutionary ideals), of shame at abandoning a wounded soldier in 1913, and of guilt for not facing the firing squad with his fellow prisoners in 1915. Artemio kills their murderer, but this does not, in his own eyes, atone for his failure. In hindsight, he admits wronging other Mexicans, building his fortune on their decline, facilitating the exploitation of Mexico's resources by Americans, and having his newspaper defend brutal dictators like the Dominican Republic's General Rafael Trujillo. Yet Artemio is not a clear-cut villain. Though merciless and cruel, he is also "endearing, admirable, [and] pitiable"; the man "cheats, but catches himself at it" (Harss and Dohmann, p. 300). A product of complex circumstances and fateful choices, he suffers remorse on his deathbed, spending his last moments in desperate search of himself, a task in which the reader must also engage. "I am not going to say everything I have to say," warns Fuentes. "I am going to leave a door open, so that the reader can complete and collaborate with me in the creation of the novel" (Fuentes in Gazarian Gautier, p. 104).

The flitting between three voices—the *I,* the *you,* and the *he*—underscores Artemio's struggle to find himself. In fact, his (and the novel's) concern for self-definition reflects a real-life preoccupation of intellectuals in mid-20th-century Mexico. In 1950 Octavio Paz published ***The Labyrinth of Solitude*** (also covered in *Latin American Literature and Its Times*), a landmark essay positing that the average Mexican disguises the person that he really is. He remains distant from everyone, including himself. This proposition had been tendered before. Paz's essay, however, took it a step further, arguing that the Mexican man prefers not even to acknowledge the existence of the person behind the mask, the reality that he disguises.

At the root of this reality is the conquest of Mexico by Hernán Cortés, the Spaniard who received as a gift from the Indians one of their own, a princess named Malintzin, alias Marina (her Christian name), alias La Malinche (her legendary title). She became Cortés's mistress, gaining folkloric stature over the centuries, growing into a symbol of violation and betrayal because she is said to have gone into Cortés's arms willingly. In 1522 Malintzin and Cortés had a son, Martín. Regarded as the first mestizo, Martín would become the symbolic ancestor of contemporary Mexico. People thought of him as a child of violation and betrayal. Preferring to have no legacy rather than this one, argues Paz, the Mexican male denies his past and breaks with tradition. He is left adrift in this broken state, a fragmented being, as reflected in the novel by the three-way split of Artemio Cruz. Paz speaks also of a word derived from La Malinche, *malinchista,* used in modern Mexico to denounce anyone corrupted by foreign influences, the way Artemio is.

Blocking out the past, the average mid-twentieth-century Mexican male aspired to a masculine ideal. Society steered him into becoming the *macho,* the strongman who retreated into himself and remained a private being. The ideal encouraged him not to share his true feelings with his wife or anyone else. Women too negated their true selves to play a role prescribed for them by society, acting stoical, denying their own desires to fulfill the feminine ideal—absolute service to the needs of everyone else in the family. Even mothers showed disappointment at the birth of a daughter, prompted by the widespread belief that a baby girl was worth less and would surely grow up to suffer more than a boy.

In the novel both parents fawn over their son, Lorenzo, and even Catalina ignores their daughter, Teresa, until she matures. This mother-daughter dynamic is consistent with a real-life syndrome of the time: "As the girl grows older," explains one social historian, "she is drawn into a conscious and highly verbal complicity with her mother against her father" (Barber, p. 27). So hostile are Teresa's outbursts against the dying Artemio that they drive even her mother to distraction.

Living up to the male and female ideals made genuine communication between a man and woman difficult, if not impossible. The ideals militated against a mutually satisfying love relationship, so that Artemio and Catalina were not as atypical as a reader might assume. The result was loneliness for the woman, who took refuge in her children, and for the man, who gravitated to extramarital relationships. Since his macho behavior continued, these relationships often failed too. The man who divulged his true feelings opened himself up to possible scorn, too great a risk in a society whose highest value was manliness—the ability to impose one's will on others. "To the Mexican," says Paz, "there are only two possibilities in life: either he inflicts the actions implied by *chingar* [to violate] on others, or else he suffers them at the hands of others" (Paz in Barber, p. 64). Artemio, who has lived by this principle, dies a powerful but lonely man, having attained the Mexican ideal.

Sources and literary context. Fuentes's novel centers on the betrayal of the initially high values of Artemio and of the Mexican Revolution itself. In the long line of stories that have been written about the Revolution, his novel is not the first to speak of betrayal. Most prior sagas, however, combined fiction with reportorial-style narrative, producing chronicles of local warfare and its combatants. In contrast, Fuentes's novel belongs to a new wave of Latin American fiction that transcends this regional focus. *The Death of Artemio Cruz* also reaches beyond the earlier novels by extending into mid-twentieth-century Mexico, exploring the Revolution's aftereffects and their impact on the Mexican character. In doing so, *Artemio Cruz* coincides with the attempts of other mid-century works, like Paz's essay cited above, to sift out and define the essence of being Mexican. The novel, furthermore, follows the lead of stories such as Leo Tolstoy's *The Death of Ivan Ilich* by placing its protagonist at the end of his life, a vantage point from which he reviews and weighs the value of his days. Among other influences on *The Death of Artemio Cruz* is Orson Welles's *Citizen Kane,* a film in fragmentary style about the death of a newspaper tycoon who became a symbol of his nation.

Events in History at the Time the Novel Was Written

Return to the goals of the Revolution. Fidel Castro's 1959 Cuban Revolution inspired self-reflection in Mexico, especially among intellectuals. Many believed that even though the democratic intentions of their own revolution had been extinquished, they could be reignited. In 1962, when *The Death of Artemio Cruz* was published, Fuentes wrote an article for *Siempre!* Much to the chagrin of Mexico's government (which pulled its advertising from the magazine), the article described the recent murder of Rubén Jaramillo, a peasant who, like the war hero Zapata, had pressed for redistribution of land to the thousands of Mexicans with legal claims to it. The killers, as Fuentes's report shows, murdered not only Jaramillo but also his wife and sons, "certainly with the agreement of the President" (Krauze, p. 642).

> They pushed him down. Jaramillo . . . threw himself at the party of murderers; he was defending his wife and his children, and especially the unborn child; they brought him down with their rifle butts, they knocked out an eye. . . . [A son] cursed at them. . . . While he was still alive, they opened his mouth . . . and laughing filled it with earth. After that . . . the submachine guns spat on the five fallen bodies. The squad waited for them to stop breathing. But they went on living. They put their pistols to the foreheads of the woman and the four men. They fired the finishing shots.
>
> (Fuentes in Krauze, p. 642)

Intellectuals of mid-twentieth-century Mexico spoke out against this and other outrages. They decided that it was time to get back on an ethical track, to call attention to betrayals of their ideals and to resume the genuine revolution, with the help of works like *Artemio Cruz*.

Reviews. *The Death of Artemio Cruz* was favored by critics in Mexico and abroad, though not without some reservations. Various reviewers complimented the rounded portrait of Artemio. There is something "irresistibly heroic" about this "complex, witty, divided" man, declared one such critic (Eberstadt, p. 158). Others applauded the effect achieved by the shifting points of view and use of past, present, and future tenses, although the novel's fragmented style troubled at least two scholars: "Fuentes is at his best in 'straight' narration. The most effective passages in *Artemio Cruz* are linear" (Harss and Dohmann, p. 301).

These and other critics nevertheless deemed *The Death of Artemio Cruz* to be a novel that approaches masterpiece status. Reviewing it for Mexico's *Siempre!* Fernando Benitez would at times have liked to see some themes more fully developed ("*a veces . . . no desarrolla los temas*"), but he praised the rhythmic prose and profound force of a novel described as courageous and exceptionally beautiful (Benitez, p. II). The consensus is perhaps best reflected by the conclusion of one of England's reviewers—"This is a difficult book, but an enormously powerful and rich one, well worth the reading" (Bradbury, p. 359).

—Joyce Moss

For More Information

Barber, Janet. "Mexican Machismo in Novels by Lawrence, Sender, and Fuentes." Ph.D. diss., University of Southern California, 1972.

Benitez, Fernando. Review of *The Death of Artemio Cruz*. *Siempre!* no. 465 (May 23, 1962): II.

Bradbury. Malcolm. Review of *The Death of Artemio Cruz*. *Punch* (September 1964): 359

Eberstadt, Fernanda. *Montezuma's Literary Revenge*. *Commentary* 81, no. 5 (May 9, 1986): 35–40.

Fuentes, Carlos. *The Death of Artemio Cruz*. Trans. Alfred MacAdam. New York: Noonday, 1991.

Gazarian Gautier, Marie Lise. *Interviews with Latin American Writers*. Elmwood Park, Ill.: Dalkey Archive Press, 1989.

Harss, Luis, and Barbara Dohmann. *Into the Mainstream: Conversations with Latin American Writers*. New York: Harper and Row, 1967.

Krauze, Enrique. *Mexico: Biography of Power*. Trans. Hank Heifetz. New York: HarperCollins, 1997.

Macías, Anna. *Against All Odds: The Feminist Movement in Mexico to 1940*. Westport, Conn.: Greenwood, 1982.

Miller, Robert Ryal. *Mexico: A History*. Norman: University of Oklahoma Press, 1985.

Powell, T. G. *Mexico and the Spanish Civil War*. Albuquerque: University of New Mexico Press, 1981.

The Decapitated Chicken and Other Stories

by
Horacio Quiroga

Horacio Quiroga (1878-1937) was born in Salto, Uruguay, to an Uruguayan mother and an Argentine father. In 1901 Quiroga published his first book, *Coral Reefs*, and went on to publish more than 200 stories throughout his career. The writer divided his adult life between the tropical jungle area of Misiones in northeastern Argentina—near the River Plate region where Brazil, Uruguay, and Paraguay meet—and the urban center of Buenos Aires, Argentina. Many of his short stories are set in the tropical borderlands of Misiones, where he lived and wrote for many years. Not only is Quiroga considered a master of the Latin American short story, but throughout his career he wrote renowned technical and instructional essays about the short story as a genre; his most famous is the "Decalogue of the Perfect Short Story Writer." Recurring throughout his stories is the issue of human mortality, often, as in "Drifting" and "The Dead Man," in relation to the Misiones environment to which he felt so closely bound.

THE LITERARY WORK

Featured here are two short stories, "Drifting" ("A la deriva") and "The Dead Man" ("El Hombre muerto"), set in Misiones, a tropic rural region of northeastern Argentina in the early 1900s; first published in Spanish in 1912 and 1920, respectively; anthologized in English in *The Decapitated Chicken and Other Stories* in 1976.

SYNOPSIS

The protagonists of "Drifting" and "The Dead Man" are wounded in sudden, fatal accidents, and in their final moments are forced to confront death.

Events in History at the Time the Short Stories Take Place

Argentina in the early twentieth century. In 1903 Quiroga traveled on a photographic expedition to the frontier zones of Misiones, a virgin territory populated by natives and immigrant *colonos* (farmer colonists). A large number of European immigrants had entered Argentina in the late nineteenth and early twentieth centuries, many of whom settled in these rural agricultural areas, working as colonos, tenant farmers, and rural laborers. This colonization of rural frontier lands is an important backdrop to the two short stories addressed here. In "The Dead Man" the dying man is a colono who cleared the land "that was a thicket when he came, and virgin bush before that" (Quiroga, "The Dead Man," in *The Decapitated Chicken and Other Stories,* p. 125). In "Drifting" the dying protagonist remembers his former employer, who had made his living exporting and selling timber—thus contributing to the beginnings of deforestation.

Argentina enjoyed economic success in the period between 1880 and 1914, largely because it was exporting agricultural goods to the industrializing and rapidly growing northern European and North American markets. Two principal exports, meat and grain, flourished on the immensely fertile Argentine grassland called the *pampas*. The export economy's further development was stifled, however, by a lack of capital and labor, and Argentina was forced to seek aid from its largest importer, England: "Virtually the entire infrastructure of the export sector was financed by the British," most notably the train network that funneled exports to major port cities such as Buenos Aires (Skidmore and Smith, p. 72).

The labor needed to fuel the export industry also came from Europe, especially from southern Europe. By 1914, 30 percent of Argentines were foreign born: over 3 million immigrants entered in the latter half of the nineteenth century and in the early twentieth, increasing the population from 1.7 million in 1869 to nearly 8 million in 1914. Many of these newly arrived laborers went to work as colonos.

The rapid growth of the import-export sector brought riches to the pampas and Buenos Aires, but for the most part the nation's interior remained underdeveloped. The only exceptions were the wine- and sugar-producing provinces of Mendoza, Tucumán, and Córdoba, all of which avoided the rampant social and economic decay suffered by the rest of the interior. Along with massive immigration, such economic inequities fueled cultural tensions and blurred attempts to define national identity, a struggle that preoccupied many young South American writers and intellectuals of the time.

Misiones. The two short stories, "Drifting" and "The Dead Man," are set in the Misiones frontier region off the River Paraná, where Quiroga resided and wrote for many years. Bounded by Brazil and Paraguay, Misiones is a subtropical region, home to a population of about 40,500 (1914) around the time of the short stories. Its beauty left travelers of the era awestruck, particularly its breathtaking Iguazú Falls. The travelers described thick groves of flowers and fruit as well as palm trees, noting also the numerous streams and the mountain range of Iman dividing the region from southwest to northeast. Called a hothouse by day, relieved by cool, refreshing nights, the area yielded a mix of wild and domesticated products: sugar cane, wheat, maize, tobacco, pine and rosewood, oranges, bananas, pineapples, guavas, ground nuts, and especially *maté,* or Paraguayan tea. The chief means of communication was the Paraná River; there were few roads. Several towns existed, chief among them the capital Posadas, to which the Argentine Railway had a line.

Impressed by the rugged beauty of Misiones, Quiroga purchased a ranch there in 1906, where he lived with his wife from 1910 to 1916, and he often returned to the region throughout his life. "Quiroga was enthralled with what he found in Misiones: the broad expanse of the Paraná River, the tropical forest, the exotic animals (including deadly serpents). He became an integral part of this land and its people, its mighty rivers and treacherous jungle" (Schade in Solé and Abreu, p. 552).

Misiones—named for the Jesuit missions established during Spanish rule—was disputed territory in the early nineteenth century. Argentina, Paraguay, and Brazil all struggled for control of the area. The region became a province of Argentina in the mid-nineteenth century. At the time *yerba maté* (from a native evergreen tree, Ilex paraguariensis, whose dried leaves are used to prepare tea) was the principal crop in Misiones, whose inhabitants also began to raise sugar in the 1860s following the Paraguay War. Initial projects for the exploitation of wood began in the 1860s as well, when immigrants from neighboring countries and from Europe started to arrive in large numbers. Their arrival initiated a period of official, government-planned colonization.

In 1876 Argentina resolved border disputes with Paraguay, returning to that nation control of the lands to the west of the River Paraná, in the Tacurú-Pucú zone mentioned in "Drifting." These negotiations established the Paraná River as the definitive border between the two countries. At the time, the zone was largely populated by Argentine colonos harvesting yerba maté. Having secured the more remote regions of the Upper Paraná from resident indigenous groups, new settlers now took control of the coast along the Paraná River in order to exploit yerba maté and to develop commercial trade. As late as the 1880s Misiones territory was still being disputed between Argentina and its eastern neighbor, Brazil. United States President Grover Cleveland stepped in to help establish the border and in 1895 the lines between Brazil and Argentina were demarcated, finally designating as part of Argentina the Misiones frontier lands that Quiroga would visit and describe only a few years later.

At the turn of the century, the region's principal industries continued to be yerba maté and wood. Buenos Aires was becoming a large city

Cataratas de Iguazú.

and needed Misiones wood for construction. An 1882 Act of the National Congress allowed Misiones land plots to be sold at two pesos per hectare. By the late 1890s there were few plots left, such was the absorption of lots by arriving colonos from neighboring countries and from Europe. Official colonization soon ended, but not before the creation of a number of planned colonies by local leader Juan José Lanusse, who distributed animals and tools to European families arriving at the *Hotel de Inmigrantes* (Immigrants Hotel). By 1901 more than 650 new families were living in just one of the Lanusse agricultural colonies.

"GREAT WATERS"

In 1883 the first foreign expedition, organized by a German scientific commission searching for lands suitable for immigration, arrived at the *Cataratas de Iguazú,* waterfalls which are not far from where the Iguazú meets the Paraná. Cascading along a 2.5 mile crescent-shaped bluff, about 275 separate falls roar down 270 feet and can be heard miles away. (By comparison, Niagara Falls has a height of about 150 feet.) When visiting at the turn of the century, U.S. President Theodore Roosevelt's wife was so impressed with the falls that she uttered the now famous phrase: "Poor Niagara!" The Iguazú Falls are commonly heralded as one of the wonders of the natural world.

In these early years of the century, Misiones began to be "modernized"—or cleared and developed for capitalist commercial extraction—at an accelerated pace. What was once virgin jungle now saw the appearance of railroad lines, new ports, large navigation companies, schools, and a first newspaper (founded in 1908). In 1908 Adán Luchessi, who organized the exploitation of newly discovered virgin maté by local indigenous workers, gave the name Puerto Esperanza to a popular locale used for the loading of yerba maté and wood; *Puerto Esperanza* appears in "Drifting" as the place in which the protagonist's ex-employer sells his timber.

Growing tensions between implacable nature and an encroaching civilization are a recurring theme in Quiroga's tales, including the two stories examined here. Other characteristics of life in Misiones find their way into these short stories as well. The two protagonists appear to be farmers, or colonos, making their living off the land: one of them grows bananas and the other sugar. "The Dead Man" depicts a possibly immigrant, landowning colono (a banana planter), and makes reference to a new port on the River Paraná. The banana planter has lived in his cleared plot of Misiones bushland, which "he himself spaded up during five consecutive months . . . the work of his hands alone," for only 10 years ("The Dead Man," p. 123). In "Drifting," the protagonist has a small ranch and a sugar-cane press. This story refers to the ominous Paraná River, the Iguazú River, and the proximity of Brazil and Paraguay. Both of these stories attest to a clash between civilization and nature that is far from harmonious; death takes the two protagonists by surprise in these unforgiving natural settings.

The *cuento* in Quiroga's day. One of Quiroga's many contributions to Latin American literature was his role in developing the short story as a legitimate and respected Latin American genre. In his famous essay "La crisis del cuento nacional" (The Crisis of the Argentine Short Story), Quiroga wrote that the artistic production of the short story had become decadent, due to the demands of the media and to the publications and journals that solicited and published short stories. Quiroga complained that for years these daily publications and newspapers had been stubbornly soliciting short novels rather than short stories. He lamented that because of the demands of these publications, which desired to fill space with the more prestigious short novel, many writers needlessly and recklessly elongated entries that were meant to be short stories.

According to Quiroga, this elongation and expansion of a short story serves only to weaken it, because a good short story is one that is efficient, brief, and devoid of *relleno*, or superfluous "stuffing." Quiroga goes so far as to insist, perhaps facetiously, that a good short story must not exceed 1,250 words. Quiroga proposed that a good *cuento* (short story) writer should be exact, have precise discipline, and never use one unnecessary word. The short story writer should be able to suggest more than is written, winding precisely chosen words into an energetically brief yet intense tale aimed like an arrow to create the desired impression—which, in his case, was often horror.

Quiroga's contribution to Latin American literature thus included not only his many masterful stories, but also theories on the narrative form that were widely read and had a direct impact on many writers of his day.

The Short Stories in Focus

Plot summary. Nine of the 12 tales that comprise *The Decapitated Chicken and Other Stories* are set in the rural, tropical frontier lands near the river border of Argentina, Brazil, and Paraguay. They share common themes: man's struggle to survive in an imposing, ominous natural environment (Quiroga consistently depicts nature as an aggressive force), as well as madness, monstrosity, and death. The two celebrated stories "The Dead Man" and "Drifting" take place in the jungle regions of the Upper Paraná River and depict man as the weaker party in his confrontation with an untamable and deadly nature.

"Drifting" opens with a simple phrase: "the man stepped on something soft and yielding and immediately felt the bite on his foot" (Quiroga, "Drifting," in *The Decapitated Chicken and Other Stories*, p. 69). The narrator reveals that the man has been bitten by a *yararacusú* snake, which the man kills with his machete. Immediately he feels a sharp pain in his leg, so he follows the trail back to his small ranch. The victim, Paulino, throws his arms over the wheel of a sugar-cane press and calls to his wife, Dorotea. Paulino asks Dorotea to bring him some rum, but his mouth is so numb by now that the rum tastes like water when he drinks it. At this point he makes a somber realization: "Well, this is getting bad" ("Drifting," p. 70). Paulino does not want to die, and, after climbing into his canoe, he rides down the Paraná River in hope of making it to Tacurú-Pacú in time for help. He stops on the river's neighboring Brazilian shore, crawls out of the canoe, and calls for his friend Alves to help. He soon realizes, however, that there is no help in sight. He returns to his canoe and continues floating down the Paraná, in a setting the narrator describes as "funereal," "black," "lugubrious," "menacing," and "sombre" ("Drifting," p. 71). Slowly the weakening Paulino begins to feel better, and he remembers his friends and his former employer, Mr. Dougald, wondering if he will see Mr. Dougald in town. Then he notices a pair of birds flying overhead towards Paraguay, and remembers the man who bought Mr. Dougald's timber in Port Esperanza. Suddenly Paulino stops breathing altogether and dies.

"The Dead Man" concerns a colono who lives in the frontier land near the Iguazú River border of Argentina/Brazil/Paraguay. He owns a sugar-cane press, and has in the past labored for the (presumably) British Mr. Dougald, who runs a timber business and directs the goods to port for sale—most likely to Uruguay's industrializing and growing urban centers. Having just finished clearing his banana grove, this colono slips and lands on his machete as he attempts to cross a wire fence. The entire account is told in the third-person and speaks of the man's resistance and stupefaction as he realizes he is dying. The man lies on his side, dying slowly and pondering his death, while everyday routines continue around him. He watches his banana grove, thinks of the new port and of the Paraná River nearby, and remembers how he had cleared his plot in this Misiones bushland with his own hands: "How many times, at mid-day like this, on his way to the house, has he crossed this clearing that was a thicket when he came, and virgin bush before that?" ("The Dead Man," p. 125).

EXCERPTS FROM QUIROGA'S "DECALOGUE OF THE PERFECT SHORT-STORY WRITER"

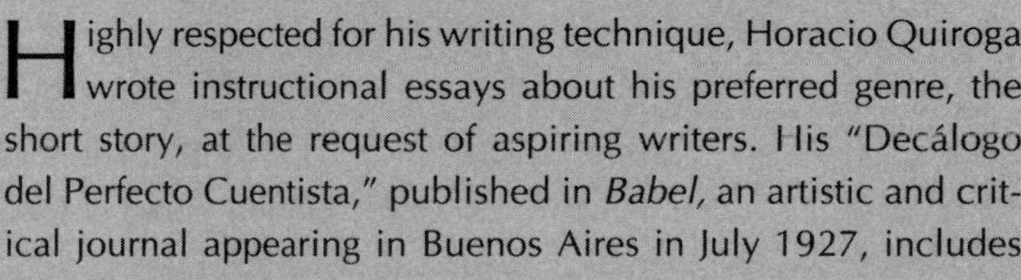

Highly respected for his writing technique, Horacio Quiroga wrote instructional essays about his preferred genre, the short story, at the request of aspiring writers. His "Decálogo del Perfecto Cuentista," published in *Babel*, an artistic and critical journal appearing in Buenos Aires in July 1927, includes the following advice:

- Believe in a master—Poe, Maupassant, Kipling, Chejov [Chekhov]—as you would in God. . . .
- Have blind faith not in your capacity to succeed, but in the ardor with which you desire to. Love your art as you would your girlfriend, giving to it your whole heart. . . .
- Take your characters by the hand and lead them firmly until the end, looking at nothing but the path you have traced. Do not distract yourself by looking at that which they can not, or care not to, observe. Do not abuse the reader. . . .

(Quiroga, *Todos los Cuentos,* pp. 1194-95; trans. O. Treviño)

The protagonist cannot believe that after so many years of toiling he could be dying in this way, by his own machete. Unable to come to grips with the fact that he is dying, "The man resists—such an unforeseen horror! And he thinks: it's a nightmare: that's what it is!" ("The Dead Man," p. 122). He thinks of his banana grove, hears a boy whistling as he walks, listens to his son calling out to him, and dies. The final words, which state that the fallen man "has rested now," carry double meaning if the reader considers that the dead man, who "was always tired" can now finally rest from the brutal work of clearing his grove ("The Dead Man," p. 125).

Regionalism. Horacio Quiroga played an important role in developing the literary movement known as "regionalism," which attempted to define Latin America by describing its unique regional traits, nature, and character types. Many of Horacio Quiroga's short stories speak of the duel between man and nature, focusing primarily on the horrors and tragedies associated with man's attempts to tame nature, always depicted as a wild force. This theme of the struggle against an ominous environment became prevalent in the regionalist movement of early twentieth-century Latin American fiction.

RUBÉN DARÍO

Modernism in Spanish America was primarily a poetic movement, and without question the Nicaraguan poet Rubén Darío was its leader. In fact, modernism was recognized as a new artistic movement upon the 1888 publication of Darío's *Azul* (*Blue*) in Santiago de Chile. Darío himself coined the term *modernismo* to describe this new literary current, considered by many to be Spanish America's first important contribution to world literature. His poetry was highly literary and technically innovative, filled with allusions to antiquity and mythology, and usually centered around themes of loss and poetic and spiritual crisis. His impact on Latin American literature has been enormous. As Jorge Luis Borges wrote,

> Darío renovated everything: subject matter, vocabulary, meter, the magic of certain words, the poet's sensibility and that of the reader. Its flavor has not ceased and never will cease. Those of us who at some point rejected him now understand that we are his followers. We can call him the liberator.
>
> (Borges in García Pinto, p. 251)

Many young writers at the turn of the century, including Quiroga, noted a changing social reality, a historic transition: the replacement of traditional Latin American society and lifestyles (tied to the rural oligarchy and nature) by the modern bourgeoisie (tied to industry and the city). It has been argued (by Leonida Morales) that the theme of ominous nature so prevalent in Latin American regionalist fiction was a result of contemporary development and industrialization. In the early twentieth century, industry led to both urbanization and a new bourgeoisie (including writers) who abandoned their reclusive way of life and took to the streets. As nature began its historical retreat, regionalist writers sought to capture the changes taking place around them. The Spanish American War (1898) and increasing North American intervention in Latin America also contributed to the interest in defining Latin American national identity by way of its landscape and environment. In short, Quiroga's *cuentos misioneros* are affected by what the country was experiencing: a revolutionary *ruptura* brought on by its own explosive economic development and international integration.

Regionalist literature often focused on the theme of a potentially dangerous nature in all its forms. Many regionalists set their literary works in rural zones, depicting "types" that were considered more authentically representative of Latin America (such as rural peasants, the Indian) than characters one might find in other types of literature. Regionalist fiction also tended to pit man against an aggressive nature as part of the tension between *civilización* and *barbarie* (civilization and barbarism). The outcome of this battle was often death, as is the case in many of Quiroga's works.

Spanish American regionalism was preceded by the modernist movement, which promoted the project of conquering rural savage space, of carrying civilization into the outback. A transitional figure between the two literary movements (modernism and regionalism), Quiroga pointed to the failure of this project. Its promoters, in his view, could only expect to be beaten down by nature, which absorbed those who tried to dominate it. The attempt to Europeanize the countryside was unwise. Quiroga, in short, found fault with the belief that nature, whether environmental or human, could be tamed. While "The Dead Man" and "Drifting" deal with a threatening environment, the collection's title story, "The Decapitated Chicken," about four "idiot" brothers and the revenge they exact on their normal sister, concerns the overpowering drives of human nature: "From the moment of the first poisonous quarrel Mazzini and Berta [the parents] had lost respect for one another, and if there is anything to which man feels himself drawn with cruel fulfillment it is, once begun, the complete humiliation of another person" (Quiroga, "The Decapitated

Chicken," in *The Decapitated Chicken and Other Stories,* p. 61).

Lasting in Spanish America from roughly 1888 to 1911, modernism began to seem artificial to younger writers, who, like Quiroga, turned to a more brutal reality that grew out of the environment and its people as subjects for their prose. Quiroga met Nicaragua's great modernist, Rubén Darío, in Paris in 1900, and actually began his career by writing modernist works, such as the poetry collection *Los Arrecifes de Cora* (1901); he also participated in the modernist literary circles of Montevideo, Uruguay. After his move to Buenos Aires and visits to the northeastern Argentine frontier lands, however, Quiroga began writing in the regionalist style that he helped introduce to Latin America. Set in the ominous jungles of Misiones, his short stories introduced new themes in literature to a Latin American reading public that was still mostly accustomed to modernist works.

Quiroga and violence. Probably the most dramatic aspects of Quiroga's fiction are its violence, fatalism, and unrelenting concern with death. In story after story man confronts a fierce, implacable nature, and usually meets his death as a result. The two stories featured here focus on two men's last moments, after they have been absurdly and mortally wounded. In the title story referred to earlier, "The Decapitated Chicken," the four "idiot" sons one day mimic the killing of a chicken by decapitating their sister; the tale ends with the horrified parents approaching "a sea of blood on the floor" of the kitchen ("The Decapitated Chicken," p. 66). Almost every story in the collection includes one tragic event or death.

Quiroga's own life was filled with tragic accidents and casual violence. His father's death in a hunting accident made a huge impression on the young Quiroga. Then, when he was 17, he came upon his stepfather's dead body and was the first to find that the man had shot himself. When Quiroga was 24 he himself accidentally shot and killed one of his best friends. Thirteen years later his wife, unable to bear life in Misiones, poisoned herself to death, leaving Quiroga with two young children to raise on his own. Finally, Quiroga poisoned himself after discovering that he had an incurable cancer. As George D. Schade points out, the "singular amount of violence marring the writer's personal life cannot be overly stressed, for it explains a great deal about his obsession with death, which is so marked in his work" (Schade, p. x). In

Horacio Quiroga

Quiroga's fiction, then, death is "just as pervasive, protean and arbitrary" as it was in his life, and serves finally "to portray human life as a preordained struggle that, however valiant, affirms inglorious destiny and the futility of individual action" (Borgeson, p. 697).

Literary sources and context. Horacio Quiroga drew much of the content for his stories from life experiences in urban Buenos Aires and in the frontier region of Misiones where he lived and worked as a colono. As noted, Quiroga became one of the prime initiators of regionalism, which strove to "rediscover" Latin America and its authentic identity, depicting its unique types and landscapes. Quiroga found these ingredients in Misiones, which provided the themes, settings, and characters for his stories. Many of those set in the tropical jungles of Misiones include references to real-life places, rivers, and ports (such as the Paraná, the Iguazú, Tacurú-Pacú, and Puerto Esperanza in "Dead Man" and "Drifting"). The story "The Incense Tree Roof," for example (also anthologized in *The Decapitated Chicken*), describes the tribulations of a recently arrived government official who keeps poor records and is always distracted by a leaky roof that fails to shelter him from the torrential tropical rains. The story is based on Quiroga's real-life experiences.

Quiroga is also considered a precursor of the concentration on the fantastic in Latin American fiction. In the horrific, often unsettling content of some of his stories, he shows a tendency to depict reality as interrupted by the supernatural (as in the story "The Feather Pillow," also anthologized in *The Decapitated Chicken*).

Horacio Quiroga did not write with an explicitly social or political agenda. Yet his stories contain some of the most powerful social criticism of the day, especially in regard to their analysis of the transformations of the land effected by the process of modernization. Without being didactic, Quiroga's stories offer testimony to the social injustices common in his time, such as the violent exploitation of laborers by bosses. *The Decapitated Chicken*'s "A Slap in the Face," for instance, tells of an indigenous man's revenge on the arrogant ex-boss who beat him.

Reviews. Quiroga's regionalist work enjoyed favorable reception by critics early in his career, especially in Buenos Aires, where he had already established a reputation in the first decade of the century. Many of his short works, including "Drifting" and "The Dead Man," were originally published in periodicals that brought them to the attention of relatively small audiences. With the 1917 publication of the book collection *Cuentos de amo, de locura y de muerte* (Stories of Love, Madness, and Death), which included the cuentos misioneros, "Quiroga achieved widespread popularity and critical acclaim" (Poupard, p. 206).

The Decapitated Chicken, which anthologizes and publishes for the first time in English the two short stories "Drifting" and "The Dead Man," received favorable reviews in U.S. journals, which took note of the bizarre quality to the stories. A reviewer in *Library Journal* concluded that the "telling is so vibrantly and surely done that the reader is captivated by method and universality of meaning more than content" (Dougherty in Mooney and Klaum, p. 1091). The *New Yorker* (August 9, 1976) called the stories "lucid and written with great economy," and went on to compare Quiroga to Edgar Allan Poe (*New Yorker* in Mooney and Klaum, p. 1092). With its perfect combination of technique and content, "The Dead Man" is commonly considered Quiroga's masterpiece.

—Olivia Treviño

For More Information

Barreyro, Julio G. *Breve historia de Misiones.* Buenos Aires: Editorial Plus Ultra, 1979.

Borgeson, Paul W., Jr. "Horacio Quiroga, 1878-1937." In *Encyclopedia of Latin American Literature.* Ed. Verity Smith. Chicago: Fitzroy Dearborn Publishers, 1997.

García Pinto, Magdalena. "Rubén Darío, 1867-1916." In *Encyclopedia of Latin American Literature.* Ed. Verity Smith. Chicago: Fitzroy Dearborn Publishers, 1997.

Mooney, Martha T., and Robert E. Klaum, eds. *The Book Review Digest, 1978.* New York: H. W. Wilson, 1979.

Morales, Leonida. "Historia de una ruptura: el tema de la naturaleza en Quiroga." *Revista Chilena de Literatura* 22, 1983.

Poupard, Dennis, ed. *Twentieth-Century Literary Criticism.* Vol. 20. Detroit: Gale Research, 1986.

Quiroga, Horacio. *The Decapitated Chicken and Other Stories.* Trans. Margaret Sayers Peden. Austin: University of Texas Press, 1976.

———. *Todos los cuentos.* Edición crítica de Napoleón Baccino Ponce de Leon and Jorge Lafforgue. Madrid: Colección Archivos, 1993.

Schade, George D. "Introduction." In *The Decapitated Chicken and Other Stories.* Trans. Margaret Sayers Peden. Austin: University of Texas Press, 1976.

Skidmore, Thomas E., and Peter H. Smith. *Modern Latin America.* 4th ed. Oxford: Oxford University Press, 1997.

Solé, Carlos A., and Maria Isabel Abreu, eds. *Latin American Writers.* Vol. 2. New York: Charles Scribner's Sons, 1989.

Ziman, Ladislao, and Alfonso Scherer. *La selva vencida; crónica del Departamento Iguazú.* Buenos Aires: Marymar Ediciones, 1976.

Deep Rivers

by
José María Arguedas

José María Arguedas was born in 1911 in Peru's south-central highlands, an area in which the culture of the Quechua Indians has remained vital despite the Spanish Conquest and subsequent exploitation of the native peoples. Though Arguedas's family belonged to the white Hispanic upper class, they were poor. His mother died when Arguedas was two years old, and his father, an itinerant lawyer whose clients were mostly Indians and mestizos, remarried shortly thereafter. According to Arguedas, his stepmother and her family despised him and relegated him to the Indian kitchen of the household, where he was welcomed and loved by the Indian servants and where he learned the Quechua language. For the rest of his life, Arguedas felt a filial attachment to the Quechua that helped shape his work. Arguedas was a professor of anthropology and, aside from novels, short stories, and poetry, wrote important ethnographic monographs on the Quechua of Peru's highlands. Frustrated by the discrimination they endured, and suffering clinical depression, Arguedas committed suicide in 1969.

THE LITERARY WORK

A novel set in Peru around the mid-1920s; published in Spanish (as *Los ríos profundos)* in 1958, in English in 1978.

SYNOPSIS

The main character and narrator of the novel recounts some of the events of his adolescent years, focusing on his experiences in a Catholic boarding school in the Andean city of Abancay, Peru.

Events in History at the Time the Novel Takes Place

Inca ruins. Ernesto, the narrator of *Deep Rivers,* is steeped in the traditions of the Quechua Indians and surrounded by the ruins of their once mighty Inca Empire. Since the 1300s, highly organized agricultural societies had existed in the highlands and coastal regions of Peru. In the 1400s a relatively new culture emerged in the southern highlands, centered at Cuzco. Its members came to be known as the Incas (a term now used variously for the culture itself, for its upper-class noble families, or for its supreme ruler). The Incas, like neighboring societies, wove beautiful cloth, constructed monuments and residences of stone and adobe, and planted dozens of crops. Unlike these neighbors, however, the Incas rose to a position of dominance in the area. They forged into a single empire the many agricultural societies of Peru, Ecuador, Bolivia, and parts of Chile and Argentina, forming a civilization that rivaled in size that of the Romans.

Inca civilization left behind some of the world's most impressive archaeological sites. Among these are the Inca walls of Cuzco, which so impress Ernesto, and the fortress Sacsayhuamán, described in the *Royal Commentaries of the Incas,* an invaluable account of the origin, growth, and fall of the Inca empire written by Inca Garcilaso de La Vega (1539–1616). His account places the fortress at Cuzco's northern outskirts on a high hill, called "Sacsahuana." The commentaries also mention Machu Picchu, a fortress city 54 miles northwest of Cuzco that was rediscovered by Hiram Bingham in 1911, not long before *Deep Rivers* is set (and that would soon after be celebrated in Pablo Neruda's 1946 poem, ***The Heights of Macchu Picchu*** [also covered in *Latin American Literature and Its Times*]).

FROM THE *ROYAL COMMENTARIES OF THE INCAS*

The *Royal Commentaries of the Incas* reports that the Incas modeled their architecture on structures from the period before them, building the fortress of Cuzco in imitation of these structures. The *Royal Commentaries* includes a description of the walls of such fortresses:

> There are stones of immense size, and one cannot conceive how they were cut, carried, and set in their places. . . . They did not use mortar and had no iron or steel for cutting and working the stone, nor engines or instruments for shifting it, yet the surface of the wall is often so smooth that in many places the joint is scarcely visible. And many of the stones used are so large. . . . In Tiahuanaco I measured a stone thirty-eight feet long and eighteen broad, and it must have been six feet thick. The wall of the fortress at Cuzco . . . contains many stones that are even larger. The most remarkable thing is that though the stones in the wall . . . are extremely irregular in size and shape, they nevertheless fit together with incredible exactitude.
>
> (Acosta in de La Vega, pp. 138, 464–65)

Despite such remarkable achievements, the Inca empire was short-lived. Already weakened because of a civil war, by 1533 the Incas fell to Francisco Pizarro, a handful of Spaniards under his command, and some of his Indian allies—rivals of the Incas. This Inca defeat laid the groundwork for a system of Indian exploitation that has begun to change only within recent times.

From encomiendas to haciendas. The social and political conditions that affect the characters in Arguedas's novel are rooted in Peru's colonial past. Before the Conquest the native population of Peru lived in cities or, for the most part, in small farming communities. These communities were subdivided into *ayllus*, a word from the Quechua language that primarily refers to an extended family and the land that they cultivate communally. *Ayllu* land was separated into three parts. All produce from the first part was reserved for use by the community, the *ayllu* itself. A second part was stored in community warehouses to be used in case of crop failure or famine within the community itself or in other communities. A third part was owed to the Inca, and used by the army, the empire's administrators, and the numerous male and female priests.

The Spanish monarchy immediately took advantage of the native social structure, modifying it to their needs as a colonizing nation that lacked mineral resources, agricultural products, and, of course, gold to finance the wars occurring in Europe during this period. The most productive and geographically accessible ayllus were turned into *encomiendas,* royal land grants administrated by an *encomendero,* a Spaniard in charge of a certain area. The land was not allocated to the Spaniard; rather the natives in a given area were entrusted to him. They owed him tribute in the form of labor or goods, and in return he owned them protection and religious instruction. Meanwhile, the land, formerly the property of the Indian community as a whole, now belonged to the Spanish Crown. The natives were expected to work the soil as before. Stripped of their fundamental source of income (their farm produce), they became de facto slaves, forced by the encomendero to work for others on land that was formerly theirs.

In exchange for Indian labor, the encomendero was obligated to insure the physical and spiritual well-being of the Indians; insuring their spiritual health meant he had to provide them with instruction in the Catholic faith. The Indians had little choice in the matter of becoming Catholic, Spain's conviction being that native beliefs emanated from the devil and must be condemned. There was nevertheless some tolerance. While certain native practices—such as human sacrifice—were outlawed, others were adapted into the natives' observance of the Catholic faith.

The new situation was particularly onerous for native women. Before the European invasion, women of the Andean regions enjoyed privileges. In contrast to European women of the time, some Andean women owned and inherited property, served on governing councils, and became ordained priests. In *Deep Rivers,* the *chicheras,* female venders of the corn beer, *chicha,* lead a small revolt to secure salt for themselves and the ha-

SYNCHRONISM

In *The Virgin of the Andes,* Carol Damian describes how Andean Indian artists, unwilling to abandon their veneration for the earth deity Pachamama, secretly incorporated symbols and characteristics attributed to her into the paintings of the Blessed Virgin that the Catholic priests of the sixteenth and seventeenth centuries commissioned them to execute. These paintings generally depict the Virgin in elaborately decorated and flowing gowns that resemble a mountain in the way they flare out from the waist to the feet. Many of the designs on the gowns themselves, such as flowers and other vegetation, correlate to symbols associated with the Pachamama. The blurring between the Blessed Virgin and the Pachamama makes it difficult to decide which of the two was actually being venerated. Considering the Indians' tolerance for other religions, the Blessed Virgin and Pachamama were likely held in equal esteem. In any case, the works of these artists became world-famous. Painters in this style are known as the Cuzco School; their practice of combining elements of two or more religions is called "synchronism." The novel's non-Indian schoolboys exhibit this same religious combination when they show faith in both Catholicism and the mountain spirits.

cienda workers, bringing to mind the prominent role of women in Andean society.

Some ayllus—a minority—survived relatively unscathed, through the period of the encomienda system and even into contemporary times. These, however, were located in the least desirable of Andean regions, where agricultural production was severely limited because of poor soil or because of the altitude. Though close to the equator, the higher regions of the Andes can become very cold, which limits crops to potatoes and other roots.

Although, from time to time, the Spanish monarchy passed laws to respect the dignity of and improve conditions for the indigenous peoples, life for them was appalling. Desperate to make a fortune and return to Spain as rich men, encomenderos exploited Indian labor to the ultimate degree. Men, women, and children were forced to work in any capacity the landowner deemed fit. Labor, often performed without compensation, sometimes exceeded physical endurance. Protest or insubordination was punished in the cruelest ways imaginable, including mutilation, drawing and quartering, and burning at the stake. According to one report, natives who managed to gain access and complain to high authorities "got their heads cut off" (Fisher, p. 14). Such practices, along with exposure to European diseases like smallpox, decimated the native population by 90 percent in this and other sectors of the Americas. The Indians would hardly fare better under the subsequent system of private estates after the encomiendas began to decline in the mid-to-late sixteenth century.

The hacienda was a system of large privately owned estates on which peasants labored for wages. They might be paid with advances of food and clothing, for which they became indebted, or with land leased to them for their own cultivation, as often happened in Peru. In any case, under the hacienda system the Spanish Crown lost authority over the peasants and the mandate to protect them fell by the wayside.

Arguedas made a considerable effort to rectify the view that the native Andean people passively accepted the abuses of the hacienda system, an assumption that Ernesto makes about the colonos living near him in the novel. This view is not true. Revolts were frequent during all phases of the colonial and republican periods while the hacienda system was in existence. The most famous was the revolt of Tupac Amaru II, whose Christian name was José Gabriel Condorcanqui. Born during the colonial period, Tupac Amaru belonged to a noble Inca family. Reacting to the abuse of his people, he led a revolt that nearly succeeded in driving the Spanish colonists from Cuzco and Peru. However, because his army lacked weapons and he himself was reluctant to attack the capital of the former Inca Empire, he was defeated and captured by the Spanish. Tupac Amaru was tried by a Spanish tribunal, found guilty, and drawn and quartered in the plaza of Cuzco in 1781. The rest of his family was also executed, putting an end to the last vestiges of native leadership in the Andes.

Independence. With the exceptions of Cuba and Puerto Rico, by the early 1800s all the Spanish-speaking countries of the Americas had gained their independence. Peru won its independence on July 28, 1821, beginning a turbulent Republican period. It soon became clear that "independence" would apply only to the upper class, known as the *criollos,* and, to some extent, to the *mestizos,* or mixed-race Peruvians. During the colonial period, the term criollos referred to persons of Spanish parentage who were born in Peru. Suspected of disloyalty to Spain by virtue of their birthplace, the criollos could own land but could not hold the highest government positions, which were occupied exclusively by Spaniards born in Spain. After independence the criollos became the ruling class of the country. From their ranks were drawn the nation's government officials, professionals, and landed gentry. It is important to understand that land distribution was not substantially affected after independence. The transition from encomiendas to haciendas became finalized, with control shifting from the encomendero to the *hacendado*, or hacienda owner. These hacendados, now unrestricted even by the weak laws that Spain had passed to protect Indian rights, confiscated more and more of the land held by comuneros (Quechua people living on communal lands). Meanwhile, working conditions on the haciendas became even grimmer. The hacendado became known as the *gamonal,* a word referring either to a parasitic insect or plant. The "Old Man" depicted in the first chapter of *Deep Rivers* exemplifies the Andean *gamonales,* whose dominance over the Indian population on their haciendas is vividly described. They could have an Indian whipped for the slightest offense, for perhaps just looking them directly in the eye.

In defense of the Indian. Other Peruvians attempted to better the lot of the Quechua as they saw fit. In 1924 Victor Raúl Haya de la Torre founded APRA: the *Alianza Popular Revolucionaria Americana* (Popular American Revolutionary Alliance). A nationalist party, APRA strove to integrate the three classes of Peruvian society—whites, mestizos, and Indians. It also attempted to make Peru more independent of the economic dominance of Great Britain and the United States. Although APRA demonstrated an appreciation of native Andean society, "its goals implied the modernization of the country, the advancement of capitalism, and the disappearance of the routine world of country folk" (Flores Galindo, p. 285; trans. V. Spina). APRA appealed mainly to the small landowners and the middle class of the coast; its policies clashed with the communal and other traditions of the Andean Quechua and so it failed to attract much of their support. Communist movements of the decade also tried to make inroads among the native populations of the Andes, but like APRA, they attracted few Indian followers. The Quechua instead resisted injustice in their own way.

At the time of the novel, the region in which it takes place consisted mostly of haciendas, Indian villages, and scattered Spanish towns. Even in the towns, with their separate criollo and Indian neighborhoods, the Indians comprised the majority and resisted authority. Their unrest continued a tradition that harks back earlier than the Inca rebellion of Tupac Amaru, to the Conquest itself. However, these incidents of unrest went largely undocumented, since the hacendados and the upper classes of Peruvian Andean society were in firm control of the news media. In recent years, this situation has been changing as more and more "unofficial" oral histories come to light (for example, *Andean Lives* by Ricardo Valderrama Fernández and Carmen Escalante Gutiérrez). These oral histories, recollections of the Quechua people themselves, stand in contrast to "official" histories,

COMUNEROS AND *COLONOS*

In *Deep Rivers* Ernesto mentions both the free Indians of the ayllus among whom he was raised—the *comuneros—and* the Indians attached to the haciendas—the *colonos.* These groups are the modern descendants of the ancient ayllus and of the colonial encomiendas respectively. The spirit of the free Indians working and living on communal land becomes the source of Ernesto's most positive memories. On the other hand, the living conditions of the colonos factors in the depression that besets him at the boarding school. Lowest among workers, a colono lived on the hacienda. He received the use of a small portion of its land in exchange for his labor, which involved working four to six days a week for the hacendado. On the small parcel he worked for himself, the colono had to give 50 percent of everything that he raised to the hacendado.

A modern-day Peruvian proudly displays a painting of Tupac Amaru II (1738–1781), demonstrating the lasting influence of the eighteenth-century Inca rebel.

the version that those in power—military dictators or oligarchs—wish the world to know.

The Novel in Focus

Plot summary. *Deep Rivers* is a novel about an adolescent, Ernesto, in Peruvian Andean society in the 1920s. Apart from the pressures of growing up, Ernesto must come to terms with the antagonism between the dominant white society to which he belongs racially, and the Quechua society in which he was raised.

The novel opens at night as Ernesto and his father, an impoverished, itinerant lawyer, enter Cuzco, the ancient capital of the Inca Empire. They are bound for Abancay, another Andean city, where Ernesto will enter a boarding school run by Catholic priests. Stopping at Cuzco, they plan to settle an old debt with a hated relative of Ernesto's father, a local hacendado, identified only as the "Old Man." Ernesto is immediately enthralled with the historic city of which he has heard so much. On their way to the Old Man's house, whose architecture dates to the colonial period, they pass one of Cuzco's famous Inca walls.

To the young boy the Inca walls are magical. The Incas quarried many-sided stones of varying sizes, then fit them together to construct the walls. The junctures between the stones were so precisely carved that, even now, a knife blade cannot fit between them. To the impressionable and sensitive Ernesto, the zigzag patterns created by the junctures between the uneven stones make the walls seem to move and flow. Their apparent motion reminds him of the rivers of the many Indian towns and villages in which he has lived. Ernesto does not fully understand at this moment exactly what the walls and other Andean symbols will come to mean for him, but the experience reveals a paradox that is key to Quechua thinking: two apparently unrelated phenomena can be identified as a single process—in this case, the stillness associated with rocks and the movement associated with water. There is an allusion here to the essential oneness of Indian cosmology: all things are related or share the same essence. Stillness gives rise to movement and, without movement, the concept of stillness evaporates.

Ernesto's father's plan to confront the Old Man results in his own humiliation, when the hacendado sends him and the boy to sleep in the servants' quarters. Ernesto and his father are infuriated by the insult. Despite this humiliation, however, it is harder for Ernesto to accept or comprehend the appalling conditions of the Indian people of Cuzco. As we learn, he has been raised by comuneros, Quechua people living on their own communal lands. They were dignified, brave, and gentle people willing to give him love after the death of his mother and his father's remarriage to a woman who, Ernesto explains, hated him. How the Indians can accept their humiliation at the hands of the whites within the very confines of their ancient capital is beyond him.

Life in the boarding school proves difficult for Ernesto. He had thought that his father would settle down in Abancay and they could at last be together. These plans become impossible, though, because there is no work in Abancay. The father's former clients were mestizos and free Indians, not hacienda dwellers. But Abancay is surrounded by haciendas. The hacendados have no need of a lawyer. As for the colonos—they have no legal rights anyway.

Ernesto is profoundly moved by the suffering and humiliation of the colonos on the haciendas, but he is even more disturbed by their apparent acceptance of the conditions under which they live. Men, women, and children are dressed in rags. Music and dancing, the most popular forms of entertainment for the Quechua people, are prohibited to them. Since Abancay is situated in a tropical valley of the Andes, where the climate is warm enough, the haciendas grow sugarcane. This aggravates conditions in that the colonos live close to the juice extracting plants, and breathe air that reeks of rotting cane and swarms with flies and other vermin. The people seem en-

PONGOS

In *Deep Rivers* Ernesto is deeply troubled by the behavior of the *pongo* (domestic servant) in the Old Man's house, who does not dare even look white people in the eye, and who whimpers like a child when he must address them. Pongos were normally selected from among the colono population living and working on a hacienda. They were expected to work as household servants for a certain amount of time each year. The obligation rotated within the colono population so that the same men and women were not chosen year after year. Their service went unpaid and did not relieve them from their work obligations as colonos.

A Quechua flute player beside one of Cuzco's famous Inca walls.

tirely passive about these conditions and are even afraid to accept the adolescent Ernesto into their homes when he attempts to visit, which is indeed disturbing, since hospitality toward strangers is all but obligatory within Quechua culture.

At school in the evening, the older boys retreat to an inner courtyard where a demented mestizo woman, brought to the school by one of the priests, awaits them. She offers them sex, and if she is unwilling to do so, they rape her. Ernesto himself, who has reached puberty, experiences for the first time the power of the sexual urge. At the same time, he is thoroughly repulsed by the scenes of sexual violence taking place in the courtyard, a few feet from latrines and open sewers. He becomes alienated from his peers and also from the land, which, as a child raised among Indians, he revered and felt was his. Only the nearby Pachachaca River and the bridge that crosses it can cleanse him of what he is forced to witness each night in the very place in which he is supposed to learn and to become a moral human being. "Both of them [the river and the bridge] cleansed my soul. . . . All of the . . . evil memories were erased from my mind" (Arguedas, *Deep Rivers,* pp. 62–63). Little by little, however, the incongruity between the idealized life of his childhood and the present reality cannot be suppressed by images of the river. All his romantic notions regarding women, all his fantasies and the "crushes" he has experienced in his journeys with his father, crumble before the sexual fury of his older schoolmates and the demented women. Simultaneously, all his notions concerning the Indian community—their bravery and kindness—seem no more than chimeras in view of the brutalized existence of the colonos and their inability to react against it.

Then another boy at school, Antero, introduces Ernesto to the Andean top, called *zumbayllu* in Quechua because of the humming sound it makes when it is thrown. The top in motion and its noise reminds Ernesto of the Indian concepts of *illa* (which refers to the visual world) and *yllu* (which refers to the aural); in both these realms forces that seem to oppose each other, like good and evil or life and death, are united (a river, for example, may ravage a land, yet it also brings mud and debris to fertilize the flooded area). At a deep psychological level, Ernesto begins to intuit the oneness and connectedness of the universe. He throws the top down onto the inner courtyard, feeling that the violence done to the demented woman there is somehow related to the spinning top.

As they mature, the friendship between Antero and Ernesto deepens. Both boys take the first tentative steps toward having girlfriends. The friendship between the boys deteriorates, though, as the plight of the poor hacienda workers becomes more critical and the first violent reaction against their conditions takes place. The reaction comes from the *chicheras,* the mestizo bar owners and waitresses, *chicha* being a popular fermented corn mash drink. When the government fails to deliver salt to the town and local haciendas, the chicheras take it upon themselves to break into the government warehouse and distribute it among the colonos of the surrounding haciendas. Doña Felipa, the female leader of the revolt, takes rifles from the local police and runs off into the mountains to escape the army sent in to crush this "rebellion."

Ernesto and Antero react differently to the rebellion. Ernesto is exhilarated by the assertive women and follows them to the haciendas. For him, theirs is a welcome first reaction of the people against the oppression they endure, although he wishes that such a demonstration had come from the colonos. Antero looks upon the rebellion with trepidation. A member of the propertied class himself, he cannot condone a revolt against the system.

The day after the insurrection, the school's rector, Father Linares, goes to the hacienda Patibamba with Ernesto to preach to the colonos that they are not to follow the lead of the chicheras; it is God's will that they be poor and they must accept their lot. The rhetoric of his sermon, combined with the colonos' naive belief that the priest's words are God's, soon reduces his listeners to a weeping mass, kneeling in the muck of the hacienda. Considering the rector's words wrong and hypocritical, Ernesto begins to understand the Church's role in oppressing the Indians.

The rift between Ernesto and Antero widens when Gerardo, the son of the commander sent to put down the chichera revolt, appears on the scene. Gerardo represents another type of Peruvian, a white Hispanic from the coastal area of the country. In contrast to the Andes where, despite all the racial discrimination, white Hispanics are intimately associated with Indian culture, coastal Peruvians have little or no contact with it. They speak only Spanish and consider themselves culturally superior to all *serranos* (any person, white or Indian, from the mountains). By coastal standards Gerardo is a decent enough individual, athletic and loyal to his male friends.

Antero decides to follow Gerardo's lead and "conquer" as many young women as possible. Ernesto, appalled by the changes in his friend, stops calling him by his Quechua nickname, Markask'a, using instead his Spanish given name. Overall, the incident increases Ernesto's alienation from white society and confirms more deeply his adhesion to the Indian.

The excitement surrounding the arrival of army troops from the coast is overshadowed by the threat of a typhus epidemic and the growing fear that the colonos, among whom it seems to have begun, will march as a group into the city demanding that the rector of the boarding school say a mass to deliver them from the threat. One of the first to succumb to the disease is the demented woman, but not before she undergoes a kind of spiritual transformation. Shortly after the chichera rebellion, she retrieves a shawl left by the rebel doña Felipa on a cross placed on the Pachachaca Bridge as a warning to the soldiers not to follow the rebels. As though aware of the significance of the shawl, the demented woman stops visiting the inner courtyard. Now she lies dying in the kitchen of the boarding school, where Ernesto witnesses a transformation as her face loses its deformity and becomes beautiful. In the name of all humanity and of all those who have tormented her, he asks for her forgiveness.

Abancay and the boarding school reach a state of near chaos as the plague enters the city and as rumors spread that the colonos are approaching. Ernesto, who has lost all faith in the courage of the colonos, does not believe that they will dare challenge the police and soldiers who are guarding the entrances to the city. Fearing that he may have contracted the disease from the demented woman, he is in a panic and is almost at the point of hallucinating. He decides that he will go to meet the plague and challenge it. His wanderings bring him to Patibamba.

The Indian quarters of the hacienda have been abandoned except by the children. The adults have begun their march on the city. Ernesto sees a child lying on her stomach on the floor, while her older sister picks out with a needle a nest of parasitic insects embedded in the flesh of her buttock. "I lay my head on the ground; I smelled the stench coming from the hut and waited there for my heart to stop, for the sun's light to be extinguished, for torrents of rain to fall and wash away the earth" (*Deep Rivers,* pp. 227-28).

The colonos arrive at midnight and the rector says the mass for them. Their arrival is like that of a river; nothing has been able to stop them, not even armed guards. They are the deep rivers of the novel, triumphantly chasing the plague out of the city with valor and song. Despite their seeming passivity, Ernesto realizes that, when motivated, the colonos are capable of great deeds.

The next morning Ernesto gets ready to leave the school and return to Cuzco and the Old Man until the epidemic subsides. He starts in the direction of the Old Man's house but, remembering the treatment of the Indians there, and their toleration of it, he changes direction. The novel does not reveal Ernesto's final destination. He is merely bound for the surrounding countryside, the home of the Quechua people, where the plague cannot find him.

The warring faces of Peruvian society. *Deep Rivers* is not only about a boy growing up and the exploitation of the Indian people around him. Its characters represent different classes and facets of Peruvian society. First, the novel introduces characters of Ernesto's youth, the Indians of the free ayllus, Don Maywa and Don Victor Pusa. Though unable to equal the glory of the ancient Inca Empire, they represent Indian resistance to the occupation of their lands and inhabit one end of a scale in Peruvian society.

In the school, the only Indian student, Palacios, is scorned for his innocence and Indian beliefs. On the other hand, the boys who feel a kinship for Quechua culture respect him, despite his youth, for what he knows about Indian customs. In this way, the novel begins to inform us of many Peruvians' ambivalence about the Inca past. On the one hand, they admire the lofty former empire, but on the other, they believe that Indians are inherently inferior to whites, an attitude shared by people in real life.

The concept of valuing Andean Quechua culture and attempting to integrate it, along with the Quechua people themselves, into a broader national culture long ran as a powerful countercurrent to the hacienda system and to the assumption of Indian inferiority upon which this system was based. Manuel González Prada (1848–1918), a progressive social philosopher whose ideas would prove influential among later Peruvian intellectuals, called out "to Peru's enlightened minority to struggle against the tyranny of the unenlightened whites and educate the Indians in order to integrate them into Peruvian society" (Kristal, p. 114). González Prada urged these "enlightened" whites to join with the nation's Indians in overthrowing the status quo. Describing the judge, the governor, and the priest as the principle sources of Indian exploitation, he condemned all three, conferring on them the title "the trinity of brutalization" (Kristal, p. 114).

Clorinda Matto de Turner (1854–1905), a native of Cuzco who was influenced by González Prada, became one of Peru's first writers to deal with relations between the white Hispanic ruling class of her birthplace and the native population. Her *Aves sin Nido* (*Birds without a Nest*) is a vivid account of the exploitation and brutalization of the Indians forced to work on highland haciendas. Matto de Turner admired Indian culture, spoke the Quechua language fluently, translated the gospel of Saint Luke into that language, and vigorously defended the language's richness of expression at a time before modern linguistics, when European languages were considered superior to non-European ones. Nevertheless, she was convinced, as were most progressive thinkers at the turn of the twentieth century, that advancement for native peoples depended on Westernization. To become fully integrated into Peruvian society, the native people would have to abandon their own culture. Such thinking was congruent with the positivist philosophy dominant in most of Hispanic America around this time, which taught, among other things, that education was the key to material progress. Positivists wanted to educate the Indians in order to integrate them into Peru's population; education, they believed, would solve what became known as the "Indian problem," that is, the problem of fitting the Indian populations into modern Peruvian society.

On the other hand, José Carlos Mariátegui (1894–1930), a socialist and one of Peru's foremost social philosophers, advocated preserving the native economy. He firmly believed that a socialist system founded on the ancient ideas of communal lands would provide answers to the country's serious economic problems:

> He believed that despite centuries of attack, it [the concept of the ayllu] had survived with a vitality which protected the Indians . . . that only by destroying the huge estates and returning that land to the Indians could Peru throw off the shackles of feudalism and truly progress. Thus, the uplifting of the Indian race depended solely on land reform. . . .
>
> (Davies, p. 95)

Arguedas's writings reveal the extent to which he believed that the answer to his country's problems—including the "Indian problem"—lay in the thought of Mariátegui. Though never a member of Peru's communist party, Arguedas firmly espoused the kind of communal landownership that had been the cornerstone of Inca society. Like Mariátegui, he believed that contemporary communism was compatible with the Indians' propensity to communal land ownership.

Literary context. *Deep Rivers* was the third of Arguedas's narrations to deal with relations between Indians and whites in the Andes. His book of short stories, *Agua,* and the novel *Yawar Fiesta* preceded it. It was immediately realized that these were not the usual *indigenista* stories, which combined realism and naturalism to manifest to the world the exploitation of the Indian people of the Andes. It is true that certain familiar elements of indigenista stories, such as the exploitative hacienda owner and hypocritical Church official, appear in *Deep Rivers,* and Arguedas includes episodes that make clear the suffering of the Quechua people; however, in a way never seen before, he delved into the Indian mind and spirit. His descriptions of the concept of illa/yllu introduced to readers a system of cognition and interpretation of the universe as complex as that offered by any of the world's religions. In this sense he put to rest the notion that Indian cosmology was a world of magic, superstition, and folklore. Indians were no longer "quaint" or "picturesque": Arguedas humanized them and made their problems real. As others have noted, this aspect of the novel was particularly remarkable for its time. *Deep Rivers* replaces the "abstract and subjective Indians" created in earlier fiction with "the Indian as he is in reality, a complex being" (Vargas Llosa in Gunton, p. 9)

Arguedas also diverged from other indigenista writers by championing the right of Indian culture to exist side-by-side with Hispanic culture. He advocated an Indian culture that, while retaining its own integrity, would take advantage of some developments of non-Indian Western society. In retrospect, Arguedas's literary works surpass others of his day by focusing not only on Indians learning white cultures but on whites learning Indian culture as well.

Events in History at the Time the Novel Was Written

Mid-century upheaval. In the 1950s Peru was experiencing a social upheaval that still has not come to an end. The Indian populations had begun to demand their basic human rights in ways not experienced before. At last there were a sufficient number of persons of Indian origin who had received basic education, knew about laws, and demanded protection under them. Arguedas was well aware of these movements. Indeed, he was a friend of Hugo Blanco who was, at the time, leading a guerrilla movement in the sierra.

With the success of the Cuban revolution of 1959, one year after the publication of *Deep Rivers,* agitation for social change in Peru became even more demanding. The strikes and rebellions of the Indian miners of Cerro de Pasco, chronicled in the fiction of the Peruvian writer Manuel Scorza, would go on to benefit Indian societies in general. In time, programs of agrarian reform were introduced that, at least, eliminated the hacienda system.

As for Arguedas himself, though he pushed for many of the reforms initiated by Peru's socialist and communist parties, he refrained from joining them because he felt that they were based too much on European models of history and were not adapted enough to the Andean reality. He has consequently been criticized for advocating a return to an "Inca utopia." But a careful reading of his works shows that this was not really the case. His conviction was rather that before the peoples of Peru could come together they had to learn to respect one another's culture and beliefs.

The Indian in literature. José Carlos Mariátegui, a social philosopher and political activist, made an essential contribution to the understanding of literature dealing with Native American themes:

> Mariátegui distinguishes three types of stories about the Indian. The first, a narrative in which the Indian appears as an exotic motif or a source of nostalgia, can be called *indianista* for convenience. Mariátegui designates the second type with the term *indigenista,* meaning a literature written by non-Indian writers committed to the vindication of the Indian. The third type, *indígena,* does not yet exist [in Mariátegui's time], but if it did, it would be written by the Indians themselves and would present their reality and spirit.
>
> (Kristal, p. 3)

Today there are stories of the "indígena" type, that is, stories written by the Indians themselves that are based on their native reality and way of envisioning the world. In any case, however, Arguedas's novel fits into none of Mariátegui's types.

Though not an Indian himself, Arguedas's understanding of the world was founded in native beliefs; at the same time, he was a university professor, fully integrated into the intellectual community of Latin America. His work thus confounds Mariátegui's clearcut divisions. It reflects Arguedas's own vision—his defense of a pure Indian culture that would take advantage of contact with the non-Indian West but not be damaged by it. For example, Arguedas, a lover of music, believed that European instruments in Indian hands were no longer European; the Indians used them differently and made them emit different sounds. Arguedas, then, believed that the Indians should adapt whatever the world had to offer as long as the integrity of the Indian world was respected.

Deeply respectful of this world himself, Arguedas debated whether to write *Deep Rivers* in Quechua or Spanish, deciding to employ the latter in the interest of reaching the widest possible audience. However, he constructed the grammar of his Spanish sentences in a way that echoed Quechua grammar—positioning the verb, for example, toward the end rather than the middle of a thought. When describing the rebellion of the chicheras, Arguedas wrote, "*Frente a las chicherías bailban*" (In front of the chicha shops, they were dancing). By repeatedly invoking such sentence structure—unusual for Spanish (or English)—the novel creates a cumulative effect reminiscent of the Quechua language (*Los ríos profundos,* p. 108; trans. V. Spina).

Reviews. From its first publication *Deep Rivers* received favorable reviews. It is today considered one of the classics of Peruvian literature. This is not to say that the book's episodic nature and lack of one central plot have gone unnoticed by critics, but they have also recognized the "intensity" of the novel and "the rare force of its authenticity" (Ortega in Gunton, p. 7). "[Arguedas] is the first Latin American writer to render a legitimate vision of indigenous culture . . . vindicating the distorted and defamed world of the Peruvian Indian, who appears in his beautiful books with an unending spiritual force and with dazzling magic" (Lévano, p. 103; trans. V. Spina).

—Vincent Spina

For More Information

Arguedas, José María. *Deep Rivers.* Trans. Frances Horning Barraclough. Austin: University of Texas Press, 1989.

———. *Los Ríos Profundos.* Buenos Aires: Editorial Losada, 1968.

Damian, Carol. *The Virgin of the Andes.* Miami Beach: Grassfield Press, 1995.

Davies, Thomas M., Jr. *Indian Integration in Peru.* Lincoln: University of Nebraska Press, 1974.

De la Vega, Inca Garcilaso. *Royal Commentaries of the Incas.* Vol. 1. Trans. Harold V. Livermore. Austin: University of Texas Press, 1966.

Fisher, Lillian Estelle. *The Last Inca Revolt, 1780–1783.* Norman: University of Oklahoma Press, 1966.

Flores Galindo, Alberto. *Buscando un Inca: Identidad y Utopía en los Andes.* Lima: Instituto de Apoyo Agrario, 1987.

Gunton, Sharon R., ed. *Contemporary Literary Criticism.* Vol. 18. Detroit: Gale Research, 1981.

Kristal, Efraín. *The Andes Viewed from the City.* New York: Peter Lang, 1987.

Lévano, César. *Arguedas: Un Sentimiento Trágico de la Vida.* Lima: César Lévano, 1969.

Matto de Turner, Clorinda. *Birds without a Nest.* Trans. J. G. Hudson (1904), emended by Naomi Lindstrom (1996). Austin: University of Texas Press, 1996.

Spina, Vincent. *El Modo Epico en José María Arguedas.* Madrid: Editorial Pliegos, 1986.

Valderrama Fernández, Ricardo, and Carmen Escalante Gutiérrez, eds. *Andean Lives.* Trans. Paul H. Gelles and Gabriela Martínez Escobar. Austin: University of Texas Press, 1996.

The Devil to Pay in the Backlands

by
João Guimarães Rosa

João Guimarães Rosa was born in 1908 in the rural interior of the Brazilian state of Minas Gerais, where many of his works, including *The Devil to Pay in the Backlands,* are set. Although his intellectual and professional pursuits took him far from his rural beginnings, he never severed his ties to his home state, particularly to its central and northern cattle-raising regions. Rosa always considered himself to be at heart a cowboy and a man of the backlands, the Brazilian hinterland known in Portuguese as the *sertão.* He started his literary career in 1946, after pursuing by turns medical, military, and diplomatic careers, and participating briefly in a political rebellion. Through these experiences, he enriched his understanding of human nature and therefore his writing: "As a doctor I became acquainted with the mystical value of suffering; as a rebel, the value of conscience; as a soldier, the value of the proximity of death" (Rosa in Lorenz, p. 67). But the most important force in shaping his writing were his roots in the rural backlands of Minas Gerais, where he learned the value of storytelling, for "what else can a person do [there] with his free time besides tell stories?" (Rosa in Lorenz, p. 69). In *The Devil to Pay in the Backlands* the sertão is both a concrete geographic area, where real men and women struggle to survive and make sense of their lives, and a symbolic space in which a universal drama of conscience, love, and metaphysical doubt is movingly enacted.

THE LITERARY WORK

A novel set in the interior of Brazil around the turn of the twentieth century; published in Portuguese (as *Grande sertão: veredas*) in 1956, in English in 1963.

SYNOPSIS

In his old age, a former backlands gunman spends three days telling a stranger the story of his adventures on the road, in an attempt to understand his violent past as well as a world caught between the forces of good and evil.

Events in History at the Time the Novel Takes Place

The development of backlands society and the roots of violence. The main character and narrator of *The Devil to Pay in the Backlands,* Riobaldo, identifies himself early on in his story as a former *jagunço.* In the context of Riobaldo's narration, a jagunço is a member of a band of gunmen hired by backlands political bosses who warred against each other and against government forces at the turn of the twentieth century. Violence was an integral part of life in the Brazilian sertão from the earliest days of colonization. When the Portuguese arrived in Brazil in 1500, they were primarily interested in its coastal regions, where they first set up trading posts and then prosperous sugar plantations. The interior of the country remained largely unexplored until the late seventeenth century, when adventurers began organizing an increasing number of inland expeditions. The march to the interior was driven by the needs of the expanding cattle industry. As the sugar economy grew, so did the internal demand for meat and other food products, as well as for draft animals and leather goods. There was an increasing population to feed and clothe, and, with coastal land being devoted to sugar, there was less land here for cattle raising. So to provide for cattle ranches, the Portuguese Crown began handing out immense land grants to those willing to endure the inevitable hardships of frontier life in the hinterland, thus laying the foundation for a system of large estates or *latifundia* that mirrored the system already established on the coast. In central and northeastern Brazil, the "leather civilization," an economic and social system based on cattle-raising, followed the course of the São Francisco River and its tributaries.

The civilization of the São Francisco River valley, where *The Devil to Pay in the Backlands* is set, developed particular social patterns shaped by economic activity and geographic isolation. Unlike the coastal plantation economy, the cattle industry was for the most part not based on slave labor. Nonetheless society was still highly stratified in a hierarchy that made clear distinctions between landowners and the landless. The social structure was patriarchal, with the cattle baron occupying the uppermost rung of the hierarchy as the leader of a clan composed of extended family, workers, other dependents, and associates. He exercized tremendous authority, for Portugal did not have the demographic or financial means to govern the Brazilian hinterland effectively and left the government largely in the hands of local strongmen. Working for the cattle baron were cowboys, who had a right to one out of four calves born on the ranch and could therefore aspire to some social mobility, and ranch hands, itinerant wage earners who were given a small plot of land to cultivate and were less likely to climb the social ladder. A tenant class, composed of those whom the landowner allowed to live on his land and eke out an income through subsistence agriculture, made up the lowest rung of society.

In exchange for their loyalty, those who worked for the landowner or who lived on his lands were guaranteed protection. Such bonds were necessary in a world in which violent conflict was the norm. Besides attacks from indigenous tribes and the threat from escaped black slaves, the settlers faced conflicts with their neighbors as well as within their own families. Disputes over property boundaries, conflicts over questions of honor, and battles over inheritance created a climate of instability and war. Families competing for scarce resources often resorted to violence to defend their interests, and at times entire regions became war zones, as disputes between extended families and those living on their lands expanded to the general population, creating huge factions. Such battles could last decades.

After Brazil gained its independence from Portugal in 1822, the clan wars in the sertão intensified in response to the raised political stakes. Clan leaders fought to gain control of their regions and to present themselves as legitimate political representatives. Once they achieved such political status, they could perpetuate it by getting cronies elected, thereby controlling regional and national policies. Gaining access to power was often a matter of imposing one's will by force, and the landowners therefore frequently maintained private militias.

Such militias were usually composed of three different elements. Family members were, of course, involved, but so were jagunços and *cabras*. The former functioned as the landowner's bodyguards, which was appropriate, since they were bandits. They often had a criminal past or were professional gunmen who lived under the landowner's protection in exchange for military services. This is the case of some of the jagunços in *The Devil to Pay in the Backlands*, although not of Riobaldo, for as we shall see, he has other reasons for joining a jagunço band. The cabras were male tenants or ranch hands who lived and worked on the landowner's property and who were required to take up arms to defend their boss when necessary.

Progress and instability in the Old Republic. In the second half of the nineteenth century, backlands society experienced both economic and political changes. The economy became more diversified, commerce expanded, and a small measure of progress came to the sertão, in the form of railroads and telegraph and postal services. At the beginning of his story, Riobaldo mentions a train ride he took, a sign of rapidly changing times. These economic transformations were related to significant political changes. The overthrow of the Brazilian monarchy in 1889 initiated a new political era, that of the first republican period, otherwise known as the Old Republic. Not only did the Republic accelerate economic innovations that had been introduced during the monarchy; it also inaugurated a federalist system that gave more autonomy to regional elites. Now state governors could be elected directly, and the states acquired an important source of revenue through import taxes. Increased autonomy led to the formation of state oligarchies that maintained themselves in power through the politics of corruption and favor. This, in turn, resulted in even fiercer political competition in the sertão as rural landowners fought to establish their local leadership and to make profitable alliances with the reigning oligarchy. During the period 1889-1930—that is, for the duration of the Old Republic—the backlands were plagued by constant warfare between patriarchal leaders competing for regional control. The level of conflict was exacerbated further by a development in land ownership: land had become increasingly fractionalized since the colonial period. That is, the original land grants had been divided up into smaller properties, splintering the power base and increasing the number of political players competing for local power.

The second half of the nineteenth century also saw the formation and proliferation of independent outlaw bands. While the rural elite enjoyed relative economic prosperity and the promise of greater political power, the lower classes experienced harsher living conditions. Life had never been easy for the Brazilian peasantry, but as the economy grew, land became more valuable and many tenants who had been living on the landowner's property in exchange for small services were now forced to pay rent. In addition the backlands population had multiplied, which aggravated the problem of drought that plagued the northeastern hinterland and also led to mass migrations. In short, conditions grew more difficult and unstable. The result was dissatisfaction and social upheaval, which led to the formation of outlaw bands that for the first time were independent of the landowners' militias.

The members of such independent bands became known as *cangaceiros*. The first entirely independent cangaceiro groups appeared during a great drought in the 1870s, and the last such group was destroyed in 1940. Cangaceiros resorted to banditry for a number of reasons. Most often, they became outlaws to avenge an injustice they believed they had suffered. After committing a first act of violence, they were forced to go into hiding, which led to a continuing pattern of criminal behavior. They joined bands or formed their own and wandered through the sertão, stealing and imposing their own notions of justice. In the popular imagination, cangaceiros became romantic figures, Robin Hood types who crisscrossed the backlands righting various wrongs. This image was not entirely unfounded, for certain bandits did perform occasional acts of generosity, as in the case of Jesuíno Brilhante, who, during the 1870s drought, stole food to distribute among the poor.

In fact, the cangaceiro was an ambiguous figure, capable of terrible violence but also of acts of kindness. Other famous bandits followed Brilhante, the most notorious being Lampião, who became renowned more for his extreme cruelty than for his generous impulses. The feats and adventures of such bandits were celebrated in a popular literature that helped to shape their legendary status among the lower classes. On the other hand, when unable to enlist these bandits in the service of their own political interests, many of the landowners viewed them as a nuisance or a threat. After the 1870s drought the rural elite pressured the government to wage war on the outlaws. Auxiliary police forces were formed for the specific purpose of fighting the independent bandit groups. Often, however, the state's organized campaigns against banditry were, in truth, targeting the private armies of landowners who were perceived as threats to the political status quo. Thus, throughout the Old Republic period there were clashes between government forces and various armed groups, both the independent ones and those allied to particular landowning interests.

It is during this extremely turbulent period in Brazilian history that *The Devil to Pay in the Backlands* is set. While Riobaldo identifies himself as a jagunço, the term is used somewhat loosely and the distinctions and motivations of the various warring parties in the novel often remain vague or unexplained. Riobaldo and the other jagunço characters are perhaps best seen as archetypes that combine elements of the jagunço and the cangaceiro to evoke a warrior figure out of Brazil's not-so-distant past. This blurring of distinctions is part of a larger historical indetermination in the novel. Despite the indication of a general time frame—the Old Republic—the events that Riobaldo narrates are never precisely dated, nor are the characters' actions provided with a concrete political context. This indetermination is a central component of the novel's structure, which, while it purposefully blurs the specific historical parameters of the story, nonetheless refers to the warring sertão of the first republican period as an evocative framework for a host of psychological and philosophical considerations.

Codes of behavior in jagunço and cangaceiro bands. The private armies of powerful landown-

A gruesome display of the heads of the notorious cangaceiro Lampião and members of his band, after their capture and execution in 1938.

ers as well as the cangaceiro groups functioned according to a particular set of values and code of behavior. Hierarchy was as important as in the rest of Brazilian patriarchal society, with the leader of a band exercising absolute authority over its members. As shown in *The Devil to Pay in the Backlands,* the members of any given army or band were known by the name of their leader; in the novel the jagunços identify themselves as "zébebelos" (after Zé Bebelo), "hermógenes" (after Hermógenes), and so forth, according to their chieftains. Nonetheless, bands offered a certain "democratic" path toward social ascension through individual merit, as in the case of Riobaldo, who rises to a position of leadership thanks to his superb marksmanship and his eloquent way with words.

In order to be respected and admired within the band, members had to display "manly" characteristics, not the least of which was courage. This bandit sociology mirrored Brazilian patriarchal society's values as a whole, and particularly those of the sertão, where being a *cabra-macho*—a "real man"—was extremely important. The need to affirm individual strength within the band can also be understood in the context of a society that consistently dehumanized the lower classes. As one historian suggests, bandit groups may have developed a violent ethos of individual power and valor at least partly in order to compensate for this dehumanization (Dória, p. 86). There were many ways to display courage, from daredevil acts to fierceness in battle. The practice of the *gritada,* for example, required that bandits yell out their names and place of origin when fighting with the police. Since this information might later be used against them, such behavior was considered a daring act of courage. Valued as a way of spreading one's fame, the gritada also made it more difficult for members to desert the band, for once their names were known, they were branded as criminals and could not easily return to normal life. In Rosa's novel, the jagunços often shout out their names as they make their way into battle. Some of them also groom themselves to accentuate their fierceness, such as when the men in Hermógenes's band sharpen their teeth to a point. Such practices were widespread and served to set the warrior apart and to provide an outward and physical sign of courage. It is small wonder that in *The Devil to Pay in the Backlands* Riobaldo should be so concerned with the nature of courage and true manliness.

Religion in the backlands—reign of the supernatural. Brazil is well-known for its eclectic range of religious practices. Although officially a Roman Catholic country, other traditions, including other European, African, and Amerindian practices, have enriched and complicated the Brazilian religious scene. In nineteenth-century backlands society, Catholicism, sprinkled liberally with ancient European and Amerindian beliefs, formed the core of a religious system in which the supernatural was ever-present and in intimate contact with the natural world. Dealings with the supernatural were possible, at times advisable, and often unavoidable, since its forces were perceived to permeate and control the rhythms of the visible world. As one historian has put it, backlands Catholicism's major premise was "the appeasement or manipulation of supernatural forces . . . for one's protection and enhancement" (Chandler, p. 206).

Some examples of this belief system can be found in the practices of famous backlands bandits. Lampião, the brutal cangaceiro who roamed the northeastern countryside in the early twentieth century, wore small bags around his neck in which were kept prayers thought to have magical powers. Among other things, he believed they had the power to shield his body from harm, that is, to make it invulnerable to bullets or any weapon. Before one of his many battles, Riobaldo is given such an amulet by another jagunço to protect him from harm.

In the novel, the main villain, Hermógenes, is also believed to have a shielded body. His apparent invulnerability, however, is attributed to his having made a pact with the devil. The devil, as is clear from the book's title, features prominently in Rosa's novel. Riobaldo himself is obsessed with the question of whether he made such a pact. Beliefs in the devil fit into the general framework of backlands belief in the supernatural, and their origins reach far back into European history. Likewise the idea of a pact with the devil has a very long tradition, both in popular belief and in erudite literature. There are documented cases of such pacts in the sixteenth and seventeenth centuries. Riobaldo's own attempt at making a contract with the devil contains many features of the European tradition, such as the crossroads, the hour of midnight, the presence of a tree and of wind. In accordance with popular tradition, he calls out to the devil at the crossroads, expecting him to appear in some animal form. The novel departs from tradition, however, in the absence of the visible evil entity and the anguished doubt this generates in Riobaldo's mind, doubt about the devil's existence and about whether or not he has allied himself with such evil.

The Novel in Focus

Plot summary. *The Devil to Pay in the Backlands* is constructed as a conversation between two men: the retired jagunço Riobaldo and an unknown interlocutor, whom we are given to understand is an outsider—an educated city man who is travelling through the backlands taking notes on what he sees and hears. It is a one-sided conversation, almost a monologue, in which for three days Riobaldo narrates momentous events in his life as a gunman. His listener occasionally makes comments that are recorded only indirectly, through the reactions they elicit in the narrator.

It becomes clear early in the novel that there is an urgency to Riobaldo's story, a need to understand the meaning of his past actions and make sense of certain pivotal events and emotions. As he moves deeper into the past, two central preoccupations constitute the obsessive shaping forces of his narrative: the existence or nonexistence of the devil and the nature of his relationship with a fellow jagunço named Diadorim. The events are not told in strict chronological order, for Riobaldo moves through his tale by association, weaving back and forth in time according to the processes of his memory and the rhythm of his personal search for understanding. "You can only relate things straight through . . . when they are things of minor import," he explains to his listener (Rosa, *The Devil to Pay in the Backlands,* p. 81).

Rearranged chronologically, the story begins when Riobaldo is a youth of 14 and carries him through to his present old age. At 14 he meets a mysterious boy to whom he is strangely and disturbingly attracted, and goes through a transformative experience during a river crossing in which the boy's extraordinary lack of fear causes him to lose his own. The boy disapppears but will turn up years later as a decisive force in Riobaldo's life. After the death of his mother, Riobaldo is taken in by his godfather, a wealthy landowner who loves telling jagunço stories. At his godfather's house, he gets his first glimpse of a real bandit, Joca Ramiro, whose band he will later join.

A new phase in Riobaldo's life begins when he finds out that his godfather is in fact his father. Shamed and angered, he runs away and takes up a teaching job at a distant ranch. His pupil is Zé Bebelo, a politically ambitious man who wants to bring progress to the backlands by ridding it of banditry. In order to do so, he forms his own army and invites Riobaldo to come along as his secretary. Ribaldo is initially stimulated by the freedom and excitement of constant travel but becomes disturbed by the violence he witnesses. Seeing little sense in the brutality of war, and riddled with feelings of doubt and compassion, he flees once again, only to run into members of the enemy camp. Among the men, he recognizes the boy from the river crossing, now a handsome young jagunço and, overwhelmed by emotion, feels that he can never again be separated from the boy. Reinaldo (who also has a secret name, Diadorim, revealed only to Riobaldo) is just as moved to see Riobaldo, and welcomes him unhesitatingly into Joca Ramiro's band.

A series of battles between Zé Bebelo and Joca Ramiro and his lieutenants ensue. Riobaldo fights under one of Joca Ramiro's lieutenants, Hermógenes, a cruel man whom he finds both repulsive and oddly fascinating. During the fighting, Riobaldo experiences a renewed conflict of conscience. He is also tormented by his feelings for Diadorim, an intense love that clashes with accepted ideas of manhood. Nonetheless he garners respect as an excellent sharpshooter and is given the nickname of Tatarana, or "Fire Caterpillar." Eventually Zé Bebelo is beaten and, in an unusual move, calls for a trial. During the trial, Joca Ramiro and his lieutenants disagree on the verdict. Hermógenes and the lieutenant Ricardão demand Zé Bebelo's execution, but the other lieutenants, and Riobaldo himself, who gives an eloquent speech, argue that he should be allowed to live. Ramiro finally decides on banishment.

The band disperses into smaller groups, preparing to fight against government forces that have been pursuing them all along. While resting at an idyllic spot, however, Riobaldo, Diadorim, and others are informed that Joca Ramiro has been killed, betrayed by Hermógenes and Ricardão. The leader must be avenged, and they go off to fight a new war, but are cursed with bad luck, as one thing after another goes wrong. Feeling indebted to the murdered Ramiro for the earlier decision not to execute him, Zé Bebelo returns and takes up leadership of the band, but things only get worse. In what might be described as a descent into hell, they get lost in an unknown, unmapped backlands region where they find an archaic, destitute people near a village decimated by the plague. Stopping at a place called the "Dead Paths," Zé Bebelo seems to have all but given up, and Riobaldo grows increasingly frustrated. It is rumored that Hermógenes's success is due to his having made a pact with the devil, which has shielded his body and made him invulnerable. Driven by a complex set of desires and fears, among which are ambition, and a need to affirm his manhood and repress his love for Diadorim, Riobaldo decides he too will make a pact. At the "Dead Paths," he goes to the crossroads at midnight and calls out to the devil. Although the devil does not make an appearance and he is unsure of whether or not he has really entered a pact, Riobaldo feels himself transformed. He becomes self-assured to the point of arrogance and soon wrests control from Zé Bebelo. As a leader, now known as White Rattlesnake, he is capricious, as though drunk on power. At the same time, he is tortured by his compassionate conscience and his passion for Diadorim. Meanwhile, Diadorim has revealed that he is Joca Ramiro's son and is obsessed with avenging his father. After a series of bizarre actions, Riobaldo decides on a daring tactic to defeat Hermógenes: he leads his band with amazing ease across a terrible desert that had defeated them before, and in a surprise attack destroys Hermógenes's ranch and kidnaps his wife.

In an escalating string of battles, Riobaldo beats back Hermógenes and kills Ricardão. But Hermógenes is not defeated so easily and, in a final apocalyptic scene, he traps Riobaldo and his men in a hamlet. After hours of fighting, Riobaldo watches helplessly from the second floor of a building as the two opposing forces agree to hand-to-hand combat. Diadorim and Hermógenes charge each other and Hermógenes is killed. Diadorim disappears, whereupon Riobaldo loses consciousness. Riobaldo wakens to learn that Diadorim is dead. When the body is being prepared for burial, Riobaldo discovers what had been hinted at throughout the narrative: Diadorim was a beautiful woman in disguise. In utter despair, Riobaldo abandons the bandit life. After a deathly illness, he inherits his father's properties, marries his second love, Otacília, and settles down to a farmer's life.

As his retrospective narrative reveals, Riobaldo is still tormented by the past and wracked with guilt. What is the nature of good, the nature of evil? What makes up courage and fear? Is the courage to love more valuable than the courage to hate? These are some of the questions that fuel Riobaldo's need to tell and retell his story.

Women in nineteenth-century Brazil. Diadorim, whose real name Riobaldo discovers is Maria Deodorina, disguises herself as a boy at a young age at her father's bidding—"My father told me that I had to be different, very different"

A twentieth-century Brazilian cowboy. The experiences of such figures provided Rosa with inspiration and material for writing *The Devil to Pay in the Backlands.*

(*Devil to Pay in the Backlands,* p. 91)—presumably so that at some future time she might avenge his death. The need for the disguise might be explained in terms of women's status in nineteenth-century Brazil. Women, and particularly upper-class women, led sheltered lives, guarded by protective fathers and husbands. Seldom allowed out of the house unaccompanied, they had little freedom of movement and little control over their own lives. Diadorim herself obliquely comments on women's subjugated condition when she laments: "Women are such poor wretches" (*Devil to Pay in the Backlands,* p. 145). Widows of rural landowners, some of whom took over their husbands' roles and became formidable matriarchs, were the exception to the rule. In the course of his story, Riobaldo mentions some of these matriarchs. Frequently lower-class women also moved more freely between house and street, for they had to go where their work took them. Making a living could be very difficult, however. As the novel illustrates, some poor women, such as young Nhorinhá whom Riobaldo encounters in his travels, were forced into occasional or long-term prostitution due to the lack of other employment opportunities.

In the early twentieth century a number of women joined the band of the notorious bandit Lampião. Maria Bonita, Lampião's famous partner, started the trend, allegedly asking to join the band because she was attracted by the bandit's legendary fame. Other women followed. However, such women did not join as warriors but fulfilled stereotypical female tasks like cooking, cleaning, and darning clothes. They carried only small weapons for self-defense, and their male companions were expected to defend them.

Therefore Diadorim's disguise is probably not historically inspired but is rather a literary device. The theme of the warrior maiden is present in folk tales all over the world, from China to the Celtic isles. Rosa modifies the theme, however, for in the traditional story the maiden takes up the warrior disguise only for a limited period of time, in order to perform a specific task, and then returns to her former female condition. By contrast, Diadorim is made to disguise herself as a boy when very young and is trapped in her male role, so much so that when Riobaldo makes inquiries in her home town he can find no trace of her former female self except for a baptismal certificate.

Sources and literary context. Despite his many travels and years of residence abroad, Rosa never lost touch with the sertão of his childhood. Summarizing its significance for his writing, he once described it as "the symbol, I would even say the model of my universe" (Rosa in Lorenz, p. 66). He returned to it multiple times for renewal and research, replenishing his contact with the life and ways of the backlands and gathering concrete material for his texts. One of these many trips was made in 1952, when he travelled on horseback with a group of cowboys and their herd for ten days across Minas Gerais, covering a distance of 150 miles. During the trip he took copious notes in booklets he wore tied to his neck while he rode. This journey is believed to have provided much of the concrete geographic and linguistic material reworked in *The Devil to Pay in the Backlands.* According to one of the cowboys with whom he travelled, Rosa requested to meet an old woman storyteller, traditional musicians, and other elders acquainted with the old ways, with "what was real and in the beginning" (Manuelzão in Granato, p. 14).

THE WRITER IN THE TEXT

The man who listens to Riobaldo's story in *The Devil to Pay in the Backlands* is identified as an urban intellectual type who takes abundant notes as the gunman spins his tale. Rosa uses this narrative device in several other texts, making his narrators tell their stories to a silent, educated interlocutor. Could this unnamed listener be a stand-in for the writer himself? In his many trips to the sertão, Rosa, like his silent characters, took notes that were used as raw material for his fiction. He considered his travels so central to his writing that when he entered his first book of short stories, *Sagarana,* in a literary contest, he used the pseudonym "Viator," Latin for "traveller." While the urban listener in *The Devil to Pay in the Backlands* and other stories should not be seen as literally representing the writer, the presence of this character suggests something about Rosa's conception of his own work. Rather than presenting it as a direct picture of rural life, he conceives of it as a dialogue between urban perception and rural experience.

While his roots in rural Minas and his research expeditions to the region provide the most immediate and palpable sources for the setting of *The Devil to Pay in the Backlands,* the novel also culls from many literary traditions. Readers have found parallels between its plot and traditions such as the Greek epic, medieval chivalric romance, the French *chanson de geste,* courtly literature, and the quest of the Holy Grail, among others (Vincent, p. 77).

Within Brazilian literature, *The Devil to Pay in the Backlands* is clearly affiliated with a regionalist fiction that begins in the nineteenth century, reaches a high point in the 1930s, and continues into the 1950s and beyond. Unlike most of this fiction, however, Rosa's work is not based on documenting the "typical" way of life of a specific region through realist pictorial reproductions. It introduces daring stylistic and linguistic innovations and explores philosophical questions in a way that has prompted more than one critic to identify his writing as a kind of globalizing regionalism. His wording is unique in that he takes idiosyncrasies of the Portuguese spoken in rural areas and transforms them into his own invented, literary language. Philosophically, the plot raises questions about the nature of good and evil, courage and fear, and death and desire. In short, the novel's focus on a concrete geographic and human landscape—Minas Gerais—achieves a broad universal resonance.

Events in History at the Time the Novel Was Written

Democracy and development. The period 1945-64 was characterized by experiments in democracy and a significant amount of economic growth in Brazil. The Old Republic had been brought to a close with the Revolution of 1930, which put the strongman Getúlio Vargas in power. United by their dissatisfaction with the corrupt politics of the Old Republic and the political dominance of the rural oligarchies, particularly the powerful southeastern coffee planters, a coalition of different interest groups joined forces to topple the government and institute change. A significant fraction of these groups was driven by a modernizing impetus, viewing the abolition of an archaic and rigid political system as the first step in bringing the nation fully into the twentieth century. Vargas governed from 1930 to 1945, instituting some of the changes that the revolutionary forces had clamored for, trimming the power of the rural oligarchies and strengthening the position of urban groups, modernizing and industrializing. But these transformations were felt mostly in the South and Southeast, and had little impact on the rest of Brazil. Ultimately Vargas developed into a dictator.

In 1945, as many Brazilians pressed for a return to democracy, Vargas was removed from power. The country had not seen the last of him, however, for in 1951 he returned, this time as a constitutional president elected by the people. His government (1951-54), as well as the one that followed it (Juscelino Kubitschek, 1956-61), continued to foster economic growth, but this did not necessarily lead to real development. Although the pace of industrialization quickened, the government failed to reform Brazil's institutions. The result was an exacerbation of social inequality and injustice, with the dominant groups benefitting from economic growth at the expense of the poor. Kubitschek's government promised "fifty years of development in five" and indeed during this period Brazil saw unparalleled economic and industrial growth. As part of this developmentalist vision, Kubitschek decided to move the capital from Rio de Janeiro, on the coast, to Brasília, located in the central-western state of Goiás. Vargas had often spoken of plans to develop the immense potential of the Brazilian interior, what he dubbed the "March to the West." The construction and inauguration of Brasília in 1961 was meant to be the first momentous step in uniting coast and interior and tapping the resources of the neglected hinterlands.

Nonetheless the sertão remained at the margins of change in the 1950s. Although their power was diminished, the rural bosses still retained a significant hold on local political processes. By the 1950s the level of violence in the sertão had diminished considerably and clan and family wars were increasingly rare. Rural landowners continued to exert their influence through political means, by regimenting the local vote in favor of their preferred candidates. While electoral reforms were implemented to ensure freedom at the polls and accurate vote count, in more remote rural areas charges of fraud were not infrequent. A study of life in the sertão of the São Francisco River valley in the '50s sums up the socio-political structures of the region well:

> Ambushes, armed conflicts and pillages are now almost entirely a thing of the past, although the relation between "protector" and "protected" continues. . . . [T]he old obligations of the "protected" were partially or entirely replaced by the invariable obligation to accompany the landowner in his political convictions and action, and in particular, to vote with him in elections. Currently [1950] this situation still prevails in a number of places.
>
> (Pierson, p. 254)

The violent conflagrations at the center of *The Devil to Pay in the Backlands* were thus receding into the past when Rosa wrote his novel, but in other ways the backlands had not changed markedly in the 50 or 60 years between the novel's setting and its writing. Social inequality, grinding poverty, ignorance, and superstition continued to characterize backlands existence.

EXPERIMENTING WITH LANGUAGE

In *The Devil to Pay in the Backlands* as well as in his other works, Rosa creates a startlingly new literary language. Working with forms and processes already existent in Portuguese, he generates an unfamiliar language that exists nowhere but in his writing. Rosa believed that language lost its power to express meaning fully as it became familiar and automatic, and so he was continually on the lookout for ways of defamiliarizing common usage. The English translation of *The Devil to Pay in the Backlands* does not, for the most part, attempt to imitate Rosa's linguistic play. An example from the text, placing a translation that attempts to capture some of the strangeness of the original below the published one, illustrates this difference:

> I saw many a man knocked off his horse. We let riderless horses escape, but we picked off the men on the ground, one by one.
>
> (*Devil to Pay in the Backlands,* p. 209)

> I saw men fallen too much [or too many], the horses hoofing it hoovesback. Given the disorder. Only horses alone could escape, but the men on the ground, in the picking off, picking off.
>
> (Rosa, *Grande sertão: veredas,* p. 218; trans. S. Karpa-Wilson)

Reviews. When the novel came out in 1956 it was greeted with an ecstatic rush of critical praise. Rosa's earlier work had already received significant acclaim for its startling stylistic and linguistic innovations, but nothing could compare to the reception given *The Devil to Pay in the Backlands.* The words of one respected Brazilian critic may be taken as representative of the general sentiment: "In a literature of little imagination . . . this navigation of the high seas, this outpouring of creative imagination in language, composition, plot, psychology is dazzling" (Candido, p. 294; trans. S. Karpa-Wilson).

A few critics voiced reservations, largely in regard to the difficulty of the work. The English translation of *Grande sertão: veredas* has mostly eliminated the linguistic density of the original, but one of the major characteristics of the text in Portuguese is its daring experimental use of the language. Some felt the novel was simply unintelligible; others, while acknowledging the value of Rosa's experiment, worried that it might be detrimental to Brazilian letters, "tying up traffic" in a manner akin to James Joyce's *Ulysses* (Casais Monteiro in Vincent, p. 64).

In the long run, such reservations have not prevailed or interfered with the book's receiving a number of prizes, including the prestigious Machado de Assis Prize, comparable to the U.S. National Book Award (Vincent, p. 65). Critics at the Brazilian National Book Institute showed an almost unprecedented degree of consensus when they unanimously voted to award *Grande sertão: veredas* this coveted prize.

—Sabrina Karpa-Wilson

For More Information

Burns, E. Bradford. *A History of Brazil.* New York: Columbia University Press, 1980.

Candido, Antônio. "O Homem dos Avessos." In *João Guimarães Rosa.* Rio de Janeiro: Civilização Brasileira, 1983.

Chandler, Billy Jaynes. *The Bandit King: Lampião of Brazil.* College Station: Texas A&M University Press, 1978.

Dória, Carlos Alberto. *O Cangaço.* São Paulo: Brasiliense, 1981.

Granato, Fernando. *Nas Trilhas do Rosa: Uma Viagem pelos Caminhos de Grande Sertão: Veredas.* São Paulo: Scritta, 1996.

Hahner, June E. *Emancipating the Female Sex: The Struggle for Women's Rights in Brazil, 1850-1940.* Durham, N. C.: Duke University Press, 1990.

Lorenz, Günter. "Diálogo com Guimarães Rosa." In *João Guimarães Rosa.* Rio de Janeiro: Civilização Brasileira, 1983.

Pierson, Donald. *O Homem no Vale do Rio São Francisco.* Vol. 3. Rio de Janeiro: SUVALE, 1972.

Rosa, João Guimarães. *The Devil to Pay in the Backlands.* Trans. James L. Taylor and Harriet de Onís. New York: Alfred A. Knopf, 1963.

———. *Grande sertão: veredas.* 26th ed. Rio de Janeiro: Nova Fronteira, 1988.

Vincent, Jon S. *João Guimarães Rosa.* Boston: Twayne Publishers, 1978.

Dom Casmurro

by
Joaquim Maria Machado de Assis

THE LITERARY WORK

A novel set in Rio de Janeiro, Brazil, from 1857 to the turn of the century; published in Portuguese in 1899, in English in 1953.

SYNOPSIS

A retired, aristocratic lawyer writes a jaded and ironic account of his teenage courtship, marriage, and later abandonment of his apparently unfaithful wife.

Joaquim Maria Machado de Assis was born in Rio de Janeiro, in 1839. His parents—his father was a mulatto and his mother a Portuguese immigrant from the Azores—lived as dependents, or *agregados*, in the household of a wealthy family. Machado himself worked as a journalist, editor, and typesetter before taking a position as a civil servant at the age of 27. He spent his whole life in Rio de Janeiro—then the capital and largest city of Brazil—where he took an active part in the fledgling cultural life. For over 40 years Machado produced a steady stream of poems, criticism, short stories, newspaper columns, translations from English and French, and nine novels. His intellectual peers praised his voluminous work, and elected him the first President of the Brazilian Academy of Letters in 1897, a post that he held until his death in 1908. Machado wrote *Dom Casmurro* during the 1890s, when he had already established his literary reputation and Brazil was in its first decade of existence as an independent republic rather than an empire.

Events in History at the Time the Novel Takes Place

Imperial Brazil. The novel opens in 1857, during a prosperous period in the reign of Emperor Pedro II (1840-89). Although Brazil was slowly beginning to transform itself, the nation's mid-nineteenth-century society was still traditional and patriarchal, depending on slaves to raise sugar and coffee for export to Europe. White Brazilian male owners of vast *fazendas* (plantations) were the patriarchs who dominated society; they directed their families and slaves, as well as Brazil's political and cultural landscape. Dom Pedro II ruled as the primary father-figure of all the heads of families. (Used most often for people of nobility, *Dom* is a title of respect in Brazilian society.) The last surviving empire based in the New World, Brazil was a constitutional monarchy with a two-party political system and representative legislature. Its "representative nature was a farce," however; the Emperor retained ultimate control, and the legislature was elected and filled by a minuscule segment of the population, Brazil's male landowners (Gledson, p. 4).

Dom Pedro II's rule ushered in a period of political stability and economic expansion, during which Brazil's modernization began. The intellectual and cultural life of Rio de Janeiro and the other cities of Brazil grew to unprecedented proportions. However, while the Emperor encouraged the country's modernization and urbanization, Brazil

An example of a Brazilian fazenda.

under his reign failed to keep up with the pace of change set by European nations at the time. To what degree this failure can be attributed to the emperor is open to question. According to one of the baronesses of the day, "[Pedro II's] palace seemed a graveyard to all lively people, especially to young men and women" (Ortigão in Freyre, *Order and Progress,* p. 62). But hers was by no means a unanimous opinion; others regarded Pedro II as an enlightened, charismatic leader.

Fazendas and the ruling class. For centuries, as both a Portuguese colony and an independent nation, Brazilian society consisted of an upper class of wealthy European rulers and an underclass of African, mulatto, and mestizo slaves. There was also a diverse middle segment of government officials, merchants, artisans, doctors, lawyers, teachers, priests, and army officers; from the 1850s to the 1890s, this middle segment would become large enough to influence developments in Brazil and to challenge the rural upper class.

The upper class connected with the underclass on the fazendas of the patriarchal families. While upper-class males oversaw the agricultural operations involved in raising sugar and coffee, the actual work was done by the slaves. A fazenda formed a self-sufficient community that fed the master's family as well as the slaves with the food grown on its land. The landowners comprised an oligarchic elite, whose members controlled the national economy and society, just as they did their families and slaves. An aristocratic group, the landowners held titles such as Viscount, Baron, and Duke. The protagonist of *Dom Casmurro,* Bento Santiago, grew up in a ruling-class family, though without an aristocratic title. His father owned a fazenda in Itaguaí, a town 40 miles west of Rio de Janeiro.

Gender relations. Within the ruling families, the patriarchal regime strove to distinguish women from men as much as possible. While men were conceived of as active, mobile, and strong, women were regarded as passive, domestic, and weak. Only sons had the opportunity to receive an education; daughters were raised solely to serve their husbands and male relatives. Accordingly, in *Dom Casmurro* Bento studies both theology and law, while his female playmate, Capitu, stays home, helping his mother, who is herself dedicated to her son.

Women's communication with males outside the family occurred rarely and was restricted to subtle gestures. Marriage outside the same class (and race) was not permitted, nor could the bride freely choose her husband-to-be. Familial obligations and alliances took precedence over love or attraction. The society condoned a double standard of sexual morality that condemned women for extramarital affairs, but turned a blind eye to men's extramarital sexual relations with their slaves or with prostitutes. Although there were cases of women who took on a masculine role and actively directed plantations, the vast majority of upper-class Brazilian women were restricted to their homes and their roles as wives and mothers.

Many women channeled their energy into devotion to the Catholic Church. Religion allowed them to leave their homes for Mass, and gave them the opportunity to go to confession, which one historian credits with preserving the sanity of Brazilian women in such a patriarchal society. Confession provided an outlet for "many anxieties, many repressed desires" (Freyre, *Mansions,* p. 74) . Dona Gloria, the mother of the novel's Bento Santiago, necessarily has some business dealings, yet she still plays a passive role; she collects income from real-estate investments made after the sale of her deceased husband's plantation. Remaining secluded in her home, Dona Gloria devotes her life to the Catholic Church, her adolescent son, and the memory of her dead husband.

THE CATHOLIC CHURCH IN NINETEENTH-CENTURY BRAZIL

Although the Brazilian Constitution of 1824 guaranteed religious liberty, it also made Roman Catholicism the state religion. "The emperor continued to exercise royal patronage over the Church within his domains, as his Portuguese ancestors had done for centuries," which means that Pedro II controlled the most important Church decisions (Burns, p. 183). The Church and the ruling class were thus intertwined, with sons of the ruling class filling the ranks of priests and bishops. Individual priests served ruling-class families in private chapels and as tutors more often than the priests served their bishops. Priests enjoyed the privileges of their high position in the social hierarchy, as does *Dom Casmurro*'s Father Cabral, who tutors young Bento in Latin and has a taste for gourmet foods. In the cities, the Church at first played important roles in education and in government—in the early nineteenth century, taking holy orders was a means for a young man of the upper class to reach a position of intellectual or political importance. However, the Church's power waned as modernization decreased the attraction of gifted men to its ranks. When Bento and his friend Escobar enter the seminary in the late 1850s, the number of seminarians is decreasing because of greater interest in commerce, law, and medicine. In the 1870s the Brazilian Church began to reform itself by recruiting priests and other clergy from overseas and by systematically replacing the native-born clergy.

The ruling class in the cities. During the nineteenth century, the cities of Brazil experienced an economic boom that attracted increasing migration of the aristocratic class from the countryside. In the city the hierarchy and structure of the countryside was repeated in miniature: the ruling families brought their slaves into the cities and settled into mansions on large properties. The Santiago family of *Dom Casmurro* joins this tide in the 1840s, moving from the countryside to a mansion on the Rua de Matacavalos, an exclusive area near the center of Rio de Janeiro.

Smaller in scale than their country estates, the urban mansions of the elite still attempted to create an enclosed world. A typical mansion stood three or four stories high, and was built of stone, like a fortress, to safeguard the owner's valuables and women from thieves of various sorts. Women were limited to household contacts and to whatever sights and sounds of the street they could glean from the verandah or garden—not that the street afforded much excitement. Upper-class families disdained traveling by foot through the dirty and poorly lit city streets; instead, they rode in enclosed carriages that protected them from the gaze and "affronts" of the common people. A French visitor who bemoaned the lack of street life wrote, "Compared to that of Spanish-American cities, the private life of Rio de Janeiro is confined to the home" (Radiguet in Freyre, *Order and Progress,* p. 64). Despite the restricted access of young women in upper-class society, they nevertheless managed to be courted by young men. The young women flirted with gestures and fans, making seemingly innocuous movements that were magnified in significance by women's confinement. At one point in the novel, for example, Capitu meets the glance of a passerby, a gesture that Bento jealously interprets as an overt flirtation.

In the city, the space devoted to slaves' quarters was reduced and often renamed "servants' quarters." The slaves cared for the mansion's inhabitants, rooms, and gardens (a source of food in the larger mansions), tended the horses and other animals, and drove the family's carriage. Many slaves worked away from the mansion as physical laborers, hired out by their owners. Any wages found their way into the master's pocket. The novel's Dona Gloria derives part of her income in this way.

Agregados. Between the status of slave and master, another category of people developed in Brazil: that of the dependents, or agregados. Men and women who were neither wholly free, nor wholly bound, agregados worked for the ruling-class families, but not for wages. The principle that governed their lives was the reciprocity of favors. In return for their services, the family provided for their needs. The dependent might care for and educate the children, or engage in clerical or domestic duties. For example, José Dias, the Santiagos' dependent in *Dom Casmurro,* serves the family as a scribe, an adviser, a would-be doctor, and a companion. With the waning of slavery, urbanites favored the use of European immigrants as live-in dependents.

The agregados embodied some of the contradictions of Brazil's changing society. They enabled the rich to avoid having slaves at a time when slavery came under criticism, but, like slaves, they received no wages for their labor. The agregados had more freedom than slaves, but they lacked true independence because they could be dismissed at any time. They had to show absolute deference to the family and especially to the patriarch in all matters. The dependents lived as if they were extended members of families, yet could neither forget their role nor their lower class. Despite the close physical proximity between an aristocratic family and their dependents, marriage across the class divide was forbidden; a number of Machado's earlier novels centered on the dilemma of agregados who fell in love with a social superior. Furthermore, there was no great cohesion among the agregados, for the importance of remaining in the good graces of the wealthy made rivals of dependents and other favor seekers. In *Dom Casmurro,* José Dias makes subtle power plays against his main rivals for access to the Santiagos' privilege.

Urbanization and modernization. During the reign of Pedro II, the middle class expanded while the upper and lower classes shrank. Developments in European society, thought, and economy resounded in Brazil, leading to a gradual transformation of its society.

One of the first signals (and instigators) of change was the demise of the slave trade. Although slavery itself would not be outlawed in Brazil until 1888, the government banned the importation of slaves from Africa in 1850. The internal and external pressures to end the slave trade came from the same source: Europe. While Brazil's slave-driven economy exported tropical goods to Europe, the nation imported from Europe the notion that slavery was a corrupt, outdated system. In Europe progressive thinkers decried the cruelties of slavery, while capitalists regarded it as an inferior economic system to wage-earning that locked up the owner's capital, since a slave could not be fired. Loathing the idea of appearing backwards and culturally inferior in the eyes of Europeans, educated, urban Brazilians formed an abolition movement. They exerted internal pressure that, along with the demands of England, Brazil's largest trading partner, terminated the slave trade.

The end of the slave trade had two major effects on the development of modern Brazil. The demise of the extensive trading enterprise freed a great deal of capital for investments in trade and infrastructure, which helped the economy to boom; and the drying up of the slave labor pool encouraged European immigration. The combined effects would propel changes in the economy and urban environment. Meanwhile, the dominant agricultural export shifted from sugar to coffee, which moved the wealth of the nation from the north to the coffee-producing southern regions around the cities of Rio de Janeiro and São Paulo. The expanding coffee plantations turned to Italian immigrants, instead of slaves, for labor. In the 1850s the increase in capital and the influx of Europeans encouraged the beginnings of industrialization, a transformation supported by the educated Emperor. Telegraphs and railroads were constructed, a banking system was developed, and factories opened. However, the pace of industrialization was slow in comparison to that of other nations, since slave labor persisted to a degree. Using slaves was still considered cheaper than buying and maintaining machinery.

Along with industrial and technological developments, the arts and education flourished in Rio de Janeiro, the first city of Brazil and, by the 1850s, also the largest in South America, with a population of over 600,000 (Burns, p. 164). The city became a thriving metropolis during the 1850s, complete with gas lighting and paved streets for the mule-driven omnibuses, carriages, and coaches that transported people to public events. Theaters opened, and European opera companies toured the major cities. Local newspapers hired writers like Machado de Assis to report on events, and education for the professions became more popular. Instead of running the fazendas, the sons of wealthy landowners chose to study medicine and law in Rio de Janeiro and São Paulo—or even at universities in Europe. There they learned the latest European ideas and trends.

The development of the middle class. The mass migration of Portuguese, Germans, Italians, and other Europeans to Brazil contributed to the nation's modernization by helping to develop an urban middle class. Many immigrants remained in the Brazilian cities, became artisans, civil servants, clerks, and merchants, and married black or mulatto women.

This growing middle class was an unstable alternative to the fixed hierarchy of slaves and masters. In *Dom Casmurro* Bento's neighbors, the family of his sweetheart Capitu, belong to this emerging class. Her father, Padua, is a civil servant who owns his house because of a winning lottery ticket. Lacking monetary resources, Padua turned to Dona Gloria for help after a disastrous flood. His precarious social and economic position, a product of luck and favor, reflects the thin line trod by many in the emerging middle class. A huge social gap existed between the upper class and the middle class. A mid-century marriage across class lines, such as that between Capitu and Bento, was exceptional.

In the second half of the century, the rising numbers of graduates from medical and law schools formed a much more solid middle class that gradually replaced the aristocrats as the most powerful segment of society. Some members of the new urban middle class came from the ranks of the aristocracy, but most were the sons and grandsons of merchants and hard-working immigrants. Upon graduation they took positions of prominence in the professional fields, government, and commerce, and became the social and economic equals of the upper class.

The crucial difference between this powerful new male-led middle-class and the upper-class patriarchs of the fazendas was the former's ready acceptance of contemporary European lifestyles and ideas. The educated middle class participated fully in urban social life, which increasingly imitated that of contemporary European cities. Yet the march of progress conflicted with Brazil's colonial heritage and hierarchy, especially in the contradiction between the slave economy and the principles of European liberalism. The educated middle class formed "a creative element of dissonance" that forced Brazil to break away from its past (Freyre, *Mansions,* p. 361).

The end of the old system. Although the increasingly powerful men of the middle class disagreed with many beliefs and attitudes of the backwoods aristocracy, they recognized the established power of the aristocrats and could not reject them out of hand. Instead there was a peaceful co-existence between the commercial, liberal, urban middle class and the aristocracy, and, throughout the 1850s and 1860s, a "convenient sinking of political differences" (Gledson, p. 92). Brazil's booming economy made this co-existence sweeter, encouraging everyone to ignore the disparity between the nation's slave economy and the liberals' belief in abolition and wage-earning.

The increasing power of the educated middle class finally led to the passage of the Law of the Free Womb in 1871, which declared that all children born of slaves after September 28 of that year would be free. The law was followed in 1888 by the emancipation of all slaves, which cost slave owners dearly. The old aristocrats lost much of their economic power, since they were not compensated for the emancipation. Immigrant wage earners were now the norm in the workplace.

The rise to prominence of the middle class and of institutions other than the fazenda—such as banks, schools, offices, and factories—chipped away at the authority of the patriarchal mansion and changed the social climate of the Brazilian cities. Women took advantage of new opportunities to escape the confines of the home and attend the theater, opera, concerts, and balls. Although marriage and child-bearing still defined their lives, women gained greater choice in selecting a partner. It became possible for them to marry across class and race lines, and an increasing number of young people married for love, rather than to fulfill a familial obligation. Songs of the era proclaimed the importance of love, regardless of one's class and family. The lyrics of a popular song state quite plainly "Quero casar com a mulher do meu amor" (I want to marry the girl I love), conveying a defiance of tradition that mirrored the times (Freyre, *Order and Progress,* p. 72).

The revolution. Gradual changes in the hierarchies of gender, class, economics, and race had an effect on politics in Brazil in 1889. The ailing Emperor had lost the confidence and support of liberal and conservative factions alike. Although he promoted the modernization of Brazil, his reign had never taken the lead in reaching for the future. The powerful middle class grew impatient with his lackluster regime, and a number of prominent figures declared themselves in favor of a republic. Conservatives also chafed under the Emperor because they felt betrayed by the abolition of slavery without compensation. The army disdained the bookish Emperor for his apparent contempt of their ranks. When the Emperor's health faltered and he did not recover after his medical treatment in Europe, all parties grew concerned about the succession. Neither the Princess Isabel nor her French husband were attractive successors. There was not yet a popular cry to replace the empire with a new form of government, but the minority took the reins. Even though they lacked popular civilian support, the armed forces fomented a coup on September 7, 1889, which sent Emperor Dom Pedro II into exile and created the Republic of Brazil. Backed by republican politicians and citizens, General Deodoro da Fonseca proclaimed the country's new status. He proceeded to serve as the first president, while civilian politicians took posts as ministers. They replaced the imperial arms on the Brazilian flag with the slogan "Order and Progress," a motto that formalized the change in the nation's direction.

Reaction to the new regime was tepid. Although people no longer supported the Emperor and thought his removal was beneficial, they were not enthusiastic about the government that replaced him. There was no clean break from the past. Many landowners retained their money and privileges, and many aristocrats, counselors, and dignitaries continued to serve in the political posts that they had held under the monarchy. This old guard formed the new government along with college-educated republicans and military officers who had also begun their political careers under the Emperor. They retained many of the outward appearances of the imperial government. In fact, the new Republic exercised a more authoritarian hold over the nation than the Emperor had. Despite the new regime, the transformation of Brazilian society and its institutions continued at a languid pace.

In the early 1890s a period of economic boom and bust known as the *Encilhamento* ended in a shock wave of severe inflation amid charges of government corruption and culpability. "Speculation became the order of the day. [Brazilians succumbed to] that particular whirlwind of speculation, bogus companies, and unsound financial practices" that makes a nation economically unstable (Burns, pp. 241–42). The crisis rocked the country and undermined the new regime's credibility. The narrator of *Dom Casmurro,* who is writing his memoirs during the 1890s, gives a few astringent asides about the value of money, which most likely refer to this inflationary period.

The first civilian president, Prudente de Morais, took the reins in 1894. "With him, the words "Ordem e Progresso" [began] to take on a concrete meaning" (Freyre, *Order and Progress*, p. xlvi). Under his leadership, the new Republic strove to increase the scope and pace of modernization and to attract further European immigration. Beginning in 1888 industrialization quickened as machines replaced slaves on a large scale. Freed mulattos and blacks learned to operate and service machinery, skills that allowed some to join the middle stratum. Class rather than race became the major criterion of prestige, and a somewhat more egalitarian society emerged in the cities. Technological, political, cultural, and economic changes came to fruition in Brazil during the first decade of the Republic.

The Novel in Focus

Plot summary. The novel opens in the late 1890s in the Engenho Novo suburbs of Rio de Janeiro. The first-person narrator, Bento Santiago, begins by recounting the manner in which he received the nickname "Dom Casmurro," and the reason that he has used the name as the title of his memoirs. Now a retired lawyer, he states that in this book, *Dom Casmurro,* he will tell the real story of his life, a story that begins in 1857, when he is 15. Bento, or Dom Casmurro, frequently interrupts his linear narrative: he addresses his readers directly, comments (often ironically) on the events of the past, interjects other stories from the past, forgets the details of certain incidents, and discusses his present situation in the 1890s. These interruptions are ubiquitous and difficult at times to separate from the plot, which makes Dom Casmurro a sly narrator. This idea is crucial to understanding the novel. His tale begins as 15-year-old Bento is eavesdropping on a conversation between the adults at his widowed mother's home: "that was when my life began . . . now I was to begin my Opera" (Machado de Assis, *Dom Casmurro,* p. 17). In invoking the idea of an "opera" the narrator speaks on two levels: he both marks the start of the major events of his life, and implies that he will be orchestrating his description of the events to follow. Rather than simply narrating the events of his memoir, Dom Casmurro will arrange and stage them for the reader.

The story focuses first on the adolescent Bento, his widowed mother, Dona Gloria, and the dependent of the family, José Dias. José Dias reminds Dona Gloria that after the death of her first child, she had promised God that if she had a male child, he would join the priesthood. José Dias further warns the mother that Bento and Capitu, the 14-year-old girl next door, have fallen in love. If Bento does not go the seminary soon, there will be trouble. José Dias makes his warning with the apparent intention of thwarting a potential marriage, and thus maintaining the family's equilibrium and his own place within it. Dona Gloria, a doting mother, had been ignoring her promise to God, but now resolves to send the boy for holy orders.

OPERA AND THEATER IN RIO DE JANEIRO

The theme of the opera runs throughout *Dom Casmurro.* Machado appears to have had in mind the nineteenth-century German composer Richard Wagner's idea of the opera as a complete work of art, combining scenery, words, music, and theater under the control of a single creative genius. Through his control of the plot, characters, tone, and interpretation, the narrator of *Dom Casmurro* stages an opera in which "appearance is often the whole of truth" (*Dom Casmurro,* p. 21). The author Machado plays a second, or grand, opera in counterpoint to the narrator's, in which the narrator becomes as much a part of the novel as the plot and characters. In truth, opera was very popular in nineteenth-century Rio de Janeiro and other Brazilian cities, as well as in Europe. The Emperor himself supported touring Italian opera companies. In a passage that Machado de Assis cut from the final manuscript of *Dom Casmurro,* he wrote of the Italian opera that "more than one singer had sent our tenderhearted, enthusiastic populace wild" (*Dom Casmurro,* p. xvii). The city's enthusiasm for opera and other theatrical arts from Europe contrasts with the dark and insular world of Bento's boyhood home. His staunchly traditional mother disapproves of the theater, and refuses to allow him to attend until José Dias, a dependent of the family, cajoles her with the plea that "the theater [is] a school of manners" (*Dom Casmurro,* p. 39). Thereafter, Bento becomes a theatergoer, continuing to attend performances throughout his life.

Upon overhearing José's revelation, Bento has a sexual awakening and realizes that he does love Capitu. He visits her, and, after some flirting, reveals what he has overheard. Capitu helps Bento figure out how to keep himself out of the seminary, and recommends that, instead, he attend law school in São Paulo—Brazil's premier school of advanced education. She also proposes that

Bento enlist José Dias's help. As a fellow seeker of favor from the Santiagos—her father is indebted to Dona Gloria—Capitu astutely knows that José Dias will agree to help. If he wishes to retain his position in the family, he has no choice but to follow the direct orders of the young heir.

However, José Dias cannot dissuade Dona Gloria from her pledge. Even though she prefers not to have her beloved son leave her, she does not want to forsake her oath to God. Father Cabral, a family friend, proposes a compromise—if Bento does not develop a desire to join the priesthood after two years in the seminary, he should leave before taking his final vows. José Dias promises to have Bento out in just one year. Capitu and Bento secretly pledge to marry each other.

In the seminary Bento becomes close friends with Escobar, another youth uninterested in the priesthood. Escobar is passionate about commerce. His new friend accompanies Bento to dinner at his mother's home during the weekend furloughs that provide Bento and Capitu with extra opportunities to see each other. After Escobar's departure from his first visit, Capitu speaks from her window to Bento standing in the street. A young gallant on horseback passes by and exchanges looks with Capitu, a common way of flirting. Jealousy overwhelms Bento—"Just try to reason with a burning heart like mine at that moment!" (*Dom Casmurro,* p. 136). This is not his first attack of jealousy and Bento despairs, but the next day Capitu consoles him: there is nothing between her and the horseman. She loves only Bento.

Bento confides the secret of his love affair to Escobar, and their friendship deepens. It is Escobar who finds the solution to the young couple's dilemma: Dona Gloria can provide for an orphan to enter the priesthood in place of her son. This frees Bento to leave the seminary and attend law school in São Paulo for the next five years. Meanwhile, Capitu becomes Dona Gloria's assistant and confidante, while Escobar pursues his love of business.

At the completion of his studies, Bento weds Capitu with the approval of his mother. The couple establish a home where they frequently entertain Escobar, his wife Sancha (Capitu's friend), and later their daughter. Bento serves as a lawyer in a prestigious firm. After a number of disappointing, childless years, Capitu gives birth to a son, Ezequiel. The boy is remarkable for his ability to imitate others, especially Escobar.

The final part of the novel concerns the tragedies that befall the group. First, Escobar drowns while swimming in the ocean. At the funeral Bento is overwhelmed by jealousy at the sight of his wife's parting gaze at the dead man: "There was a moment when Capitu's eyes fixed on the body, like those of the widow though without her tears or cries, but large and wide open, like the waves on the sea out there, as if she wanted to swallow up that morning's swimmer" (*Dom Casmurro,* p. 212). He can barely contain his rage, but it subsides the next day.

Over the following years Bento's jealousy returns, and he comes gradually to convince himself that Ezequiel is actually Escobar's son, that, in Ezequiel, "Escobar began to rise from his tomb" (*Dom Casmurro,* p. 222). No one else questions the boy's paternity, but Bento thinks that the boy's resemblance to Escobar is incontrovertible evidence of his wife's adultery, plain to all. Bento finds the sight of the boy repulsive, and he withdraws from his wife and family life. He sends Ezequiel to boarding school and later considers poisoning himself and then the boy. Tormented, Bento finally confronts Capitu with the charge of adultery. She denies it, exclaiming, "Not even the dead escape your jealousy!" (*Dom Casmurro,* p. 231).

Unmoved, Bento takes his wife and Ezequiel to Switzerland, and provides a place for them there. Bento never sees Capitu again. Although he visits Europe repeatedly, he does not see his family; the trips are merely a pretext, allowing him to pretend to relatives and friends that he has visited them. After the death of his mother and José Dias, Bento has his mother's mansion torn down, and a replica built in the recently developed suburbs of Engenho Novo. Relocation to these suburbs, a less exclusive area than his mother's neighborhood, suggests that he lacks the wealth of his parents.

One day Ezequiel unexpectedly visits—at which point Bento casually inserts into the narrative the fact that Capitu has already died. To Bento's eye, Ezequiel, now a young man, is the spitting image of Escobar. Bento provides the young man with funds for an archaeological expedition to Greece, Palestine, and Egypt while thinking, "I'd rather have paid for a dose of leprosy" (*Dom Casmurro,* p. 242). He is relieved when he hears that Ezequiel died of typhoid in Palestine and has been buried outside Jerusalem. "In spite of everything," he notes, "I dined well and went to the theater" (*Dom Casmurro,* p. 243). He ends his narration by commenting in a voice full of irony that his frequent female guests visit him as they would a retrospective exhibition. He prays that he has successfully proven to the reader that the deceit of his wife had already been part of her character as a teenager, "like the fruit inside its rind" (*Dom Casmurro,* p. 244).

What's in a name? Bento Santiago begins his narrative by describing the circumstances in which a young poet from his neighborhood gave him the sobriquet "Dom Casmurro." Although *casmurro,* an adjective, means "stubborn, headstrong," the narrator admonishes his readers: "Don't look it up in the dictionaries. In this case, *Casmurro* doesn't have the meaning they give, but the one the common people give it, of a quiet person who keeps himself to himself" (*Dom Casmurro,* p. 4). The title *Dom*—used for nobility—associates Bento with the defunct aristocracy, but he quickly explains, "The *Dom* was ironic, to accuse me of aristocratic pretensions" (*Dom Casmurro,* p. 4). By this disarmingly bold adjustment of the truth, the narrator attempts to deceive gullible readers. He freely admits that the title characterizes his memoirs—"I couldn't find a better title for my narrative" (*Dom Casmurro,* p. 4). The narrator's words convey the message that he controls the book and enjoys tweaking the opinion of others with his wit and bile. The words also convey a contrasting message from the author: that the narrator is self-serving and not to be trusted.

Bento is the last remaining member of an aristocratic family. He retains the arch-conservative views of his mid-century upbringing in the staunchly traditional milieu of his mother's home, even though he now lives in the post-Revolution era, when the old aristocratic plantation-owning ruling class has fallen from power. His aim in writing his memoirs—as it was in reconstructing his mother's house—is "to tie the two ends of my life together" (*Dom Casmurro,* p. 5). Just as he builds a replica of his mother's old home on an 1890s foundation, so too his caustic, jaded narrative reconstructs the innocent experiences of his past.

Although the narrator does not directly refer to the changes in the politics, culture, and society of Brazil during his life, those changes are crucial to understanding *Dom Casmurro.* Bento as a youth fantasizes that the Emperor himself will rescue him from the seminary by convincing his mother to let him become a doctor. Similar delusions of haughty self-absorption sustain him as Dom Casmurro in a society without emperors. That he lives in such a different world helps to explain his neighbor's sardonic nickname.

This disinterest in the modernization of Brazil, John Gledson argues, "is something which Machado regarded as typical of his [aristocratic] generation" (Gledson, p. 92). Dom Casmurro, a sophisticated, urban lawyer, is part of the generation that ignored the contradictions of adopting the values and lifestyles of European liberalism while maintaining a slave economy. As a narrator Dom Casmurro is pointedly disinterested in and contemptuous of the new society in which he appears to be "a retrospective exhibition," a reflection of days past (*Dom Casmurro,* p. 243).

THE MEANING OF CASMURRO

Although Portuguese dictionaries at the time of *Dom Casmurro*'s printing defined *casmurro* as "stubborn and headstrong," today the definition has expanded to include the one Bento prefers: "a quiet person who keeps himself to himself" (*Dom Casmurro,* p. 4). This addition to the lexicon reflects the importance of *Dom Casmurro* to Brazilian culture.

The narrative is filled with little details of how society is changing around Dom Casmurro, leaving him a man at odds with and denying the world around him. For example, in his youth, Bento and his mother rode in a carriage through the streets of Rio. Driven by a slave, the carriage, he explains, with its curtain and spy-holes, was a thing of the past. In the narrator's mind the carriage is a metaphor for his "mother's secluded life" and her "faithfulness to old habits, old ways, old ideas, old fashions" (*Dom Casmurro,* p. 155). His love for this outmoded carriage indicates his own devotion to the bygone times. In the 1890s the carriage is a thing of the past, and Bento must join his neighbors on the plebeian train. In the 1890s the narrator can enter the privileged, aristocratic world only through his memory and narration.

Capitu or Desdemona? Critics have pointed out that *Dom Casmurro* is heavily influenced by Shakespeare's *Othello,* which centers on an unjustifiably jealous husband who murders his wife. Knowledge of this influence helps explain the complexities of Bento's self-delusion. Long before Bento suspects that Ezequiel is the son of Escobar, he has begun to interpret Capitu's behavior as evidence of her duplicity. Incidents that

A nineteenth-century depiction of Rio de Janeiro.

as a youth he saw innocently, he now reinterprets according to his conviction about her betrayal. For example, when Capitu's father's voice interrupts a kiss, Bento recounts her abrupt change in demeanor from sweetheart to naive daughter: "In the midst of a crisis which left me tongue-tied, she expressed herself as innocently as could be" (*Dom Casmurro,* p. 75). Her ability to calm her emotions becomes evidence of her guile to the jaded narrator, even though the young Bento could feel only his own embarrassment. According to the old Dom Casmurro, Capitu was a femme fatale with "undertow eyes" that drew him in, hatching plans and deceptions that the innocent young Bento would never have been able to concoct on his own (*Dom Casmurro,* p. 63).

The subtle and ironic voice of the narrator attempts to persuade readers to share his judgement of Capitu. But has Capitu actually deceived and betrayed Bento? Or is she, like *Othello*'s Desdemona, condemned by the mistaken jealousy of her husband? Bento's jealousy of Escobar begins at the man's funeral, when Bento sees the "undertow eyes" that "[want] to swallow up" Escobar, as Capitu takes her last look at the body (*Dom Casmurro,* p. 212). Doubts about Capitu's fidelity swell nine months after the funeral when he gazes at Escobar's face in Ezequiel's visage. Earlier insinuations about Capitu and Escobar come from the vantage of the narrator in the 1890s, who looks back on his memories of what had actually been pleasant times. Although Capitu herself mentions that the child resembles Escobar, no one besides Bento openly shares his conviction regarding the boy's paternity. Since the narrator is known to present his own opinions as facts, it is impossible to gauge objectively whether Capitu has betrayed her spouse, or whether Bento's jealousy has blinded him and turned him into a cruel man.

Outside Bento's mind, in the grand opera that is Machado's novel, what does the story reveal? Capitu does appear to have been a social climber, but that does not mean she betrayed or did not love Bento. By marrying into the Santiago family, she clearly moved up the ladder, gaining tremendously in social prestige and financial security. So she did have more of a motive than love to keep Bento from the seminary. Dom Casmurro insinuates that her parents encouraged the young couple, by allowing them time alone with the intent of seeing their daughter married. The social maneuvering he perceives as he looks back on their love affair becomes another example of Capitu's guilt that justifies his abandoning her; she did not love him, but only used him. Yet in the novel she expresses little but love for Bento.

Even her letters from exile, he concedes, were "submissive, without hatred, affectionate maybe . . . and towards the end full of longing" (*Dom Casmurro,* p. 235). It is in his mind that Capitu's love is doubted; there is little hard evidence.

The novel illustrates social tensions of the day, between men and women, between the old aristocratic upper class and the up-and-coming middle class. Capitu has no recourse to prevent Bento from abandoning her. As a patriarchal husband, he can send her halfway across the world, and pursue other women upon his return to Brazil. His class may have lost strength, but he retains the ability to execute the will of an all-powerful patriarch on Capitu, whether or not she deserves it. Like Capitu, Escobar comes from a milieu different from Bento's. The son of a merchant, he joins the booming commerce of nineteenth-century Brazil. The friendship ends with Escobar's death in 1871, the same year that the Law of the Free Womb was passed. The death of the friendship can be seen as the end of the compromise between the aristocracy and commercial interests in Brazil. The betrayal felt by Dom Casmurro might, from this perspective, reflect the political, economic, and social power lost by the aristocrats to the urban middle class.

Sources and literary context. *Dom Casmurro* does not fit easily with other Brazilian literature written around the same time. In his novels and literary criticism, Machado opposed naturalism, the literary movement that dominated Brazilian letters in the late nineteenth century. Naturalist literature featured the negative consequences of change, the overpowering nature of the sexual drive, and the way that heredity and environment determine the way a person acts.

Machado's works stand out also against the nativist concern in Brazilian literature that strove to portray the national character, since they did not focus on the tradition's main components: local color, the countryside of the "true" Brazil, and heroic tales of Indians and settlers. Instead, the characters of *Dom Casmurro* display an internal type of Brazilianness; they inhabit the changing urban Brazil rather than describe it. The novel reflects certain realistic details of nineteenth-century Rio de Janeiro but creates an independent reality, a separate fictive world, which is the most distinguishing feature between it and other novels of the time.

Although there has been speculation that Machado's own life was another inspiration for *Dom Casmurro,* the author himself would have vigorously denied any connection. Machado deliberately destroyed his personal correspondence and refused to discuss his books in an attempt to hinder any biographical-literary speculation. He wanted *Dom Casmurro* and his other novels to be read for their literary value alone. Rather than seeing his life as a source for his work, Machado believed that his work was his life.

Reviews. Almost all the Brazilian critics received *Dom Casmurro* favorably upon its publication, but none appeared ready for its many innovations and subtleties, particularly the ironic tone of the narrator. In his review of the novel for *Jornal do Commercio,* José Veríssimo wrote that the narrator was a simple, intelligent man who had been deluded by Capitu, and complained that Machado had returned to the "detached intellectual attitude" of his earlier novel *The Posthumous Memoirs of Braz Cubas* (Veríssimo in Caldwell, *Machado de Assis,* p. 153).

Since its publication, the novel's acclaim within Brazil and abroad has risen enormously. The American critic Helen Caldwell was the first to question the truth of Capitu's betrayal, and to recognize the important distinction between narrator and author: "[T]he aim of the fictional author of *Dom Casmurro* and that of the real author are diametrically opposed" (Caldwell, *The Brazilian Othello,* p. 160). While the narrator (or fictional author) portrays himself as a man deceived, the real author depicts Dom Casmurro as a vain curmudgeon out of place in a new society. Machado compounds this author-narrator complexity through the saracastic tone of the 1890s narrator, which overlays his description of his innocent teenage courtship. Keith Ellis praised the novel for its "distinctive use of the first person narrative," which became a central concern of modernist novels in the twentieth century (Ellis, p. 439). A writer ahead of his time, Machado was recognized even by his contemporaries as the greatest living Brazilian novelist.

—John Roleke

For More Information

Burns, E. Bradford. *A History of Brazil.* 3rd ed. New York: Columbia University Press, 1993.

Caldwell, Helen. *The Brazilian Othello of Machado de Assis: A Study of Dom Casmurro.* Berkeley: University of California Press, 1960.

———. *Machado de Assis: The Brazilian Master and His Novels.* Berkeley: University of California Press, 1970.

Candido, Antonio. "The Outline of Machado de Assis." In *On Literature and Society.* Trans. and ed. by Howard S. Becker. Princeton, N. J.: Princeton University Press, 1995.

Ellis, Keith. "Technique and Ambiguity in Dom Casmurro." *Hispania* 45, no. 3 (1962): 436-40.

Fitz, Earl E. *Machado de Assis*. Boston: Twayne Publishers, 1989.

Freyre, Gilberto. *The Mansions and the Shanties: The Making of Modern Brazil*. Ed. and trans. Harriet de Onís. New York: Alfred A. Knopf, 1963.

———. *Order and Progress: Brazil from Monarchy to Republic*. Ed. and trans. Rod W. Horton. New York: Alfred A. Knopf, 1970.

Gledson, John. *The Deceptive Realism of Machado de Assis: A Dissenting Interpretation of Dom Casmurro*. Liverpool: Francis Cairns, 1984.

Machado de Assis, Joaquim Maria. *Dom Casmurro*. Trans. John Gledson. Oxford: Oxford University Press, 1997.

Schwarz, Roberto. *Misplaced Ideas*. London: Verso, 1992.

Doña Barbara

by
Rómulo Gallegos

The acclaim that Rómulo Gallegos (1884–1969) received for his third novel, *Doña Barbara*, was so great that Venezuela's ruling dictator, Juan Vicente Gómez, nominated the Caracas-born author to the nation's senate. Gallegos, however, proudly declined the nomination and departed from Venezuela in self-imposed exile, for to him the Gómez regime was the incarnation of the forces of barbarism that beset Latin America, against which *Doña Barbara* railed. A leader in Venezuela's *Acción Democrática* party, Gallegos supported, in both his political and literary work, the principles of democracy and social justice. His term as elected President of Venezuela in 1948, which lasted less than a year before he was ousted by a military coup, represented one of the few brief interludes of democracy in Venezuelan history.

THE LITERARY WORK

A novel set in Venezuela around 1910; first published in Spanish in 1929, revised current edition published in Spanish in 1930, in English in 1931.

SYNOPSIS

A young man educated in the city returns to his family's rural estate where he struggles against the forces of barbarism.

Events in History at the Time the Novel Takes Place

Civilization and barbarism. *Doña Barbara* concerns the conflict between the forces of civilization and barbarism, a theme that permeates Latin American thought and literature of the nineteenth and early twentieth centuries. First formulated by Domingo Faustino Sarmiento in his 1845 essay ***Facundo*** (also covered in *Latin American Literature and Its Times*), the theme identifies the basic problem of Latin America as barbarism and its solution as civilization. While civilization, according to Sarmiento, emanated from Europe, Latin America was a barbarous land. This barbarism stemmed from the harsh Latin American landscape and its native people who, according to the racist views predominant among intellectuals of Sarmiento's day, were savages incapable of rational thought and ruled by instinct. Because of these barbaric tendencies, Latin America was the scene of constant civil war, dictatorship, and rural backwardness. Gallegos's portrayal of civilization and barbarism, however, is more complex than Sarmiento's. He makes no simple identification of barbarism with Latin America and civilization with Europe and other foreign areas. In *Doña Barbara,* for example, the foreigner from the United States is suggestively named Mr. Danger, and the novel's educated hero, Santos Luzardo, ultimately does not want to go to Europe to study. He would rather remain in the heart of Venezuela, although he recognizes that it still needs to be civilized. Doña Barbara herself is similarly complex, and is not merely a personification of barbarism. Although she wreaks blind vengeance on all who cross her, the novel makes it clear that her actions stem from a traumatic rape and that she does have redeeming qualities. Her daughter, furthermore, is portrayed as the hope of the future.

Order and chaos. In Latin America, independence from Spain was followed largely by anarchy, *caudillismo* (rule by strongmen), civil war, and dictatorship. Sarmiento blamed this fate on native barbarism, but other historians point to the failure of the Latin American colonies to build a solid political and economic base before breaking away from the Spanish Empire. In the early nineteenth century, Spain was suddenly and drastically shaken by the invasion of Napoleon Bonaparte's armies. Its Latin American colonies, though relatively weak and disunited, seized the opportunity to claim independence before they had really attained a strong sense of nationhood. Revolutionary governments seized control in Venezuela and other areas of Latin America in 1810. But their control was tenuous. Having separated from the Spanish imperial government and lacking strong, central governments of their own, the new republics fell into chaos. Individuals could not rely upon the political and legal systems for justice, but had to seek it for themselves, since today's judge or ruling regime might be overthrown tomorrow. A state of relative lawlessness resulted; basically, power could be seized by anyone strong enough to take it.

Between 1908 and 1935 Venezuela was ruled by the dictator Juan Vicente Gómez. Gómez is known for bringing "peace" to Venezuela by replacing a system of rule by regional *caudillos* with a centralized authoritarian government. Yet Gómez himself was, in a sense, the ultimate caudillo. Governing Venezuela as if it were his own personal estate, the dictator relied on cronies and relatives to administrate Venezuelan affairs and constantly rewrote the law to suit his will. Gómez had seized power from the previous dictator, Cipriano Castro, when the latter sailed for Europe to seek medical help, leaving his vice-president, Gómez, in charge. In exchange for the Buchanan Protocol, an agreement absolving U.S. companies from fines they owed to the Venezuelan government, the U.S. government supported Gómez by stationing warships off the South American coast. Their purpose was to prevent Castro from reentering the country.

Under Gómez, all dissent was brutally put down. Those who dared criticize the Gómez regime were swiftly imprisoned, tortured, executed, or exiled. The dictator paid a private secret police force to infiltrate organizations and institutions and to find dissenters. Despite his repressive policies, Gómez gained support among Venezuelan elites because he enriched them; the dictator created an environment favorable to foreign investors by removing all worry about labor strikes or other popular uprisings, and the local elite reaped some of the benefits.

During Gómez's reign, Rómulo Gallegos founded a weekly magazine called *La Alborada* (The Dawn), the title of which was meant to convey the image of emergence from the darkness of tyranny into a brighter future. In essays published in this periodical, Gallegos made a case for a greater respect for law and order, with more power exercised by the legislative and judiciary branches of government. At the time, Gómez was the law. He changed the national constitution so often that university students started referring to their constitutional law courses as "mythology." Gallegos's magazine lasted only three months, but in *Doña Barbara* he continued to stress the importance of a society based on law rather than force.

City and countryside. The forces of law and order held little sway on the *llanos*, the vast, almost treeless plains of the Venezuelan interior. *Doña Barbara* takes place on the llanos, which lie south of the coastal mountain ranges and north of the Orinoco River. Threading through the llanos is a network of rivers and streams that flood in the summer and dry up in the winter, making this region for the most part inhospitable to human settlement. Although the llanos comprises nearly one-third of Venezuela, it contains only about 10 percent of the nation's population. The llanos has been cattle country since colonial times, and up until the early twentieth century, cattle ranches there were not fenced. Free to roam across property lines, the semi-wild herds were managed by *llaneros*, cattlemen whose main duty was to herd the cattle north to high ground during the flood season, and lead them back south toward the Orinoco River when the dry season began.

In the early twentieth century, land in the llanos, as in most of Latin America, was monopolized by a few wealthy owners of immense tracts. These latifundios, or immense tracts, led to the development of a rural society composed of two polarized classes: a very small elite of wealthy landowners, and masses of landless peasants dependent upon the elite for their subsistence. The peasant class of the llanos consisted mainly of pardos, mixed-race descendants of Native Americans, European settlers, and African slaves. As late as 1936 the illiteracy rate in this region was 71 percent.

The desolate, frontier nature of the llanos made these plains a haven for outlaws and for power-wielding strongmen. Hundreds of miles from the coastal city of Caracas, where the central government sat, the large landowners of the llanos were a law unto themselves. Meanwhile, outsiders regarded the region's inhabitants as semi-savages "accustomed from youth to break wild horses, to fight with bulls, to swim the raging rivers and to conquer the alligator and the tiger in solitary combat" (Codazzi in Ewell, p. 16). In sum, in the early twentieth century the llanos was a region of wild nature, sparse population, pardos, and lawlessness. It therefore makes sense that in *Doña Barbara* the llanos is presented as the seat and the source of barbarism.

In contrast, the capital city of Caracas was the Venezuelan bastion of European culture and influence. A dictator from a previous era, Antonio Guzmán Blanco, had spent much time in Paris, and attempted to remake Caracas in that city's image. In *Doña Barbara* Santos Luzardo, the character who represents civilization, is educated in Caracas and attempts to bring the civilizing lessons he has learned in the capital to bear against the barbarism of the llanos. It is the area to which Santos Luazardo feels drawn despite its rusticity; he knows that the llanos is where he belongs.

Europe and America. Although the llanos region in particular was known for its pardo population, Venezuelans on the whole tended to be people of mixed racial heritage, combining elements from Europe, Africa, and America. European explorers and settlers began coming to Venezuela in the sixteenth century, bringing with them African slaves, which led to racially mixed unions. In general, South American attitudes toward interracial marriage and the offspring of such unions have been much more accepting than in the United States.

Nevertheless, racist attitudes that valued European heritage over non-European or mixed heritage were prevalent in Venezuela at the beginning of the twentieth century. Pardos and those of African descent could attain status equal to that of whites, but only if they had already attained exceptional power and wealth. At the time, "whitening" the population was the openly acknowledged aim of Venezuela's elite. Its members sought to increase the numbers of European immigrants, while restricting the entry of non-Europeans into the nation. The belief of Venezuela's elite was that the nation should Europeanize its population through race mixing.

In the minds of Venezuela's leaders, Europe alone had attained the pinnacle of civilization and all non-European peoples were consequently less civilized, more "savage" or "barbaric." The popular view that the Latin American countries had failed to achieve political stability and were instead wracked by violence and anarchy because of their large non-European and hence barbarous population, was articulated in 1919 by Venezuelan author Laureano Vallenilla Lanz. In his *Cesarismo democrático* (Democratic Caesarism), a justification of the dictatorship of Juan Vicente Gómez, Lanz argued that the African, Indian, and mixed-blood portion of the populace was insufficiently civilized to be able to participate in or uphold a democracy. The only way in which Venezuela could progress under these circumstances was to be ruled by a dictator who would maintain order by force. Some-

MEMOIRS OF A PRISONER

In 1929 Josef Rafael Pocaterra, a political prisoner during the Gómez dictatorship, published the book *Gómez: The Shame of America—Fragments from the Memoirs of a Citizen of Venezuela in the Days of Her Decadence,* in which he recounts his prison experience:

> Hunger, thirst, suffocation, the grillos [shackles], we were spared none of these horrors. In the middle of the night the prisoners would be driven from their cells into the middle of the court-yard. There they were beaten and, after having had cold water thrown over them—the poor creatures would be allowed to crawl back to their cells. During certain years there would be three or four deaths a day, deaths due to dropsy, arterio-sclerosis, dysentery, consumption and all the disorders of the digestive and nervous system brought on by the dampness, the lack of proper food, the ill-treatment, the nervous strain of nights spent awaiting tortures which one cannot even recall without feeling nauseated. Flies were thick. The dreadful silence that prevailed in this well of stone was only broken by equally dreadful noises, by shrieks and howls of revolt, by oaths and blasphemies. After each outburst silence would come back and the only sound would be the rattle of the ambulance going back and forth between the prison and the hospital, those twin open sores on the face of the city.
>
> (Pocaterra, p. 151)

A Venezuelan *llanero.*

day, when the people had been sufficiently "whitened," democracy would be possible. As is evident in *Doña Barbara,* Gallegos too was concerned with civilization. His novel's message, though, was that the land needed a Venezuelan civilization; transplanting a European civilization simply would not do.

In Venezuelan literature of the early twentieth century, the mixed-race character who ultimately returns to an innate savagery is a common theme. *Doña Barbara* differs in that it takes into account the travesties visited upon the people of Venezuela and how these travesties encourage barbarism. The character Doña Barbara has been raped (as has, symbolically, the land of Venezuela), an experience that has incited her negative behavior. Nevertheless, the hero Santos Luzardo awakens in both her and her daughter instincts of civilization. Doña Barbara ultimately decides to leave the region, a humane, civilized action that she takes to benefit not herself but her daughter.

Race and the United States. In *Civilization and Barbarism,* Sarmiento looked upon the United States with envy. He admired its civilized achievements, viewing them as a direct result of the lack of racial mixing among European immigrants, native Indians, and African slaves. Venezuelans of the early twentieth century, on the other hand, were for the most part appalled by the racial segregation practiced in the United States. Moreover, they worried that U.S. imperialism, which had already affected Cuba and Puerto Rico, would extend to Venezuela. Venezuelans might then be subjected to U.S. racial standards and be judged inferior. Unlike the notion of race accepted in the United States, where one drop of African blood rendered one "black," the Venezuelan concept of race, though still based on racist precepts, acknowledged many gradations. If one had any European blood, one was considered in some degree "white" and thus racially superior.

What was feared to be the typical U.S. attitude is reflected in the novel by the American character Señor Danger, who regards Venezuelans as "inferior because they did not have light hair and blue eyes" (Gallegos, *Doña Barbara,* p. 139).

The Novel in Focus

Plot summary. Two men travel upstream on the Arauca River that flows through Venezuela's llanos. One is the protagonist, Santos Luzardo, a well-dressed, aristocratic young man, on his way home to his ancestral country estate after a long absence spent in Caracas studying law. The other is a local man of "disturbing aspect," Melquíades Gamarra, also known as "the Wizard" because of his supposed supernatural powers (*Doña Barbara,* p. 4). The juxtaposition of these characters is the first manifestation of the dichotomy between civilization and barbarism that runs through the novel.

These two characters, strangers seemingly thrown together by chance, have actually much to do with each other. Melquíades is chief henchman to Doña Barbara, a woman rancher known as a powerful and evil sorceress. Her ranch, which has been renamed *El Miedo* (fear), lies adjacent to the Luzardo family estate, called *Altamira* (high viewpoint), to which Santos is returning.

The lands of El Miedo and Altamira had once formed a single estate belonging to the Luzardo family until a brother and sister who inherited the property jointly decided to divide the land in two. The brother and sister soon began to dispute the vaguely defined boundary between their lands, and one day the brother killed the sister's husband in a heated argument. Ever since, the two sides of the family—the Luzardos of Altamira and the Barqueros, who named their half of the estate *La Barquereña*—have been at war with each other. Santos Luzardo is the current heir to Altamira, while Lorenzo Barquero, Santos's cousin, would be the current heir to La Barquereña had he not signed his land over to Doña Barbara. She proceeded to rename the place El Miedo.

Doña Barbara is a *mestiza,* a woman of mixed native and European ancestry. She grew up on a riverboat amidst a band of pirates, the captain of which she called "Daddy." At the age of 15 Barbara fell in love with a young man named Hasdrubal who joined the crew as cook. Hasdrubal was killed by order of the captain when he began to suspect Barbara's feelings towards the young man. Soon thereafter, the band of pirates mutinied, slew the captain, and brutally gang-raped Barbara. She escaped with nothing but a deep hatred for and desire to avenge herself against all men. She fled to a Baniba Indian settlement where she sought and received instruction in magic, with particular emphasis on the use of aphrodisiacs and the evil eye.

Lorenzo Barquero was the first victim of Doña Barbara's vengeance. He had been a well-educated young man on the verge of a promising career and a happy marriage in Caracas when he suddenly underwent "a strange moral retrogression" and forsook everything to return to the llanos of his youth (*Doña Barbara,* p. 39). There he met Barbara who, desiring to destroy him, weakened and enslaved him with poisonous aphrodisiacs, and then convinced him to sign over the deed to La Barquereña. As soon as this was accomplished, Barbara evicted Lorenzo along with the child, Marisela, that the two had conceived together. Barbara refused to acknowledge this child as her daughter, for "a child in her womb was to her another victory for the male, a new injury undergone" (*Doña Barbara,* p. 40).

Barbara now spends her time stealing land and cattle from neighboring ranches, principally from Altamira. She bribes the local authorities to overlook or even aid her in her misdeeds, moving boundary lines and rebranding cattle with the El Miedo mark. Meanwhile, Lorenzo Barquero dwells with Marisela in the disputed palm grove that divides Altamira from El Miedo. The heir of the Barquero family spends his days in a drunken stupor in the wretched hut he shares with his daughter, who wears rags and lives like a wild animal.

The history of the Luzardo line has also been troubled. Santos's father murdered his son, Santos's brother Felix, over a political argument, buried the lance with which he had killed the young man in a wall of the house, and then sat staring at the wall wordlessly until he too died. Upon her husband's death, Santos's mother took Santos to Caracas, leaving Altamira in the hands of a string of more or less corrupt overseers. His mother now dead, and his studies in law at the university completed, Santos wishes to move to Europe where the ideal of civilization has been achieved. To raise money for this relocation he wants to sell Altamira, but no one will buy it because no one will have Doña Barbara as a neighbor. Finally, someone offers to buy the ranch, and Santos agrees to meet the prospective buyer at Altamira. As Santos returns to the llanos, his resolve to go to Europe begins to waver. He feels inspired to struggle against the "enemy," whom he conceives of as Doña Barbara—a representative of the region's tyrants—and the countryside itself in its harmfulness and its resistance to civilization. It is in this mood that Santos journeys up the Arauca River where we first meet him.

Upon reaching Altamira, Santos reacquaints himself with the handful of loyal peons who remain on the estate out of love for the Luzardo family. They waver between delight that a Luzardo has returned to set things right and fear that the civilized Santos is too much of a city slicker to meet the challenges of the llanos. Santos soon puts their fears to rest, however, by displaying the skills as a horseman and cattle wrangler that he learned as a boy, and by quickly putting the corrupt overseer, Balbino Paiba, in his place. Balbino, Doña Barbara's current lover, has been enriching her and himself by transferring Altamira cattle to El Miedo and signing over lands to Barbara piecemeal as Santos's representative. Santos bests Balbino verbally, and the overseer flees to El Miedo in shame. Meanwhile, Doña Barbara, who has heard about Santos through her minion Melquíades, is intrigued by the bold newcomer, yet confident she will defeat him.

Santos goes to the palm grove to visit Lorenzo Barquero and sees the wretched condition in which he and his daughter live. Particularly disturbing to Santos is the relationship between them and Señor Danger, an American national who lives on Doña Barbara's land. Danger holds a measure of power over Barbara because he once witnessed a murder she committed. He manages to elude Barbara's attempts to ensnare him in a sexual relationship, and generally holds himself aloof from the populace, whom he regards as racially inferior. Meanwhile, Danger spends his time appropriating the cattle that wander into his domain, and supplying the alcoholic Lorenzo Barquero with whisky. He has developed an interest in Marisela, who is 15 years old and very beautiful. Seeing this distressing situation, Santos insists that Lorenzo and Marisela forget old family rivalries and come to live at Altamira. There, Santos convinces Lorenzo to stop drinking and undertakes the education of Marisela in both manners and academics. She blossoms under his tutelage, yet there is one thing lacking in her makeup that Santos cannot teach her: "Marisela seemed to have the springs of tenderness sealed up in her heart" (*Doña Barbara,* p. 282).

Meanwhile, Santos has resolved to fence his land since "through that the civilizing of the plain would begin" (*Doña Barbara,* p. 137). He sends word to Barbara and Danger announcing his intentions and asking that they participate in a roundup to make sure everyone's cattle ends up on the correct side of the fence. Barbara refuses and Danger produces a document, signed by one of Altamira's corrupt overseers, that requires the pass between Danger's land and Altamira to remain unfenced. Barbara and Santos meet for the first time at the local magistrate's office. Santos demands that she and Danger obey the law or he will take them before a tribunal. Barbara is quite impressed by Santos's courage, eloquence, and appearance. He produces in her "a feeling of respect she had never felt before" and she submits to Santos's demand (*Doña Barbara,* p. 179). Later, at the roundup, she is impressed by his strength and skill with a lasso. She begins to fall in love with him, an emotion she has not experienced since the death of Hasdrubal.

As a token of her admiration, Barbara offers to give Santos back all the lands she has taken from him. She even tells him, "If I had, during my life, met men like you, my story would have been a different one" (*Doña Barbara,* p. 227). In other words, the presence of an authentic civilizing force can help change the ways of the most "barbaric" of characters. Santos admires Barbara's beauty and looks upon this unusual woman with "intellectual curiosity," yet he feels a deep aversion toward her, "not because she was his enemy, but because of something much more intimate and profound" (*Doña Barbara,* pp. 227, 210). Barbara disgusts Santos because of what she represents: barbarism. He asks Barbara to give La Barquereña to her daughter. The mention of Marisela rouses jealousy in Barbara, who insinuates that Santos is sleeping with the girl. Santos leaves El Miedo in a rage and all agreements between him and Doña Barbara are null and void.

In order to raise money to buy fencing supplies, Santos sends two peons to the market to sell heron feathers that have been gathered at Altamira. Balbino Paiba, acting on his own accord, kills the peons and steals the feathers. He does not dare tell Barbara of his deed, for she has changed as a result of her love for Santos and would never countenance this crime. Santos, however, is certain the crime is the work of Doña Barbara and goes to the magistrate to demand justice. When it is not forthcoming, he takes the matter into his own hands, thus abandoning legal avenues and going against his own code of civilized conduct. "I'm being driven to violence, and I'm accepting the direction," he observes (*Doña Barbara,* p. 346). Santos abducts a pair of Barbara's henchmen, the Mondragon brothers, and turns them over to the authorities as the peons' murderers. Barbara, who suspects Balbino's guilt, sends word to Santos to come to a specified, desolate place alone at moonrise if he wants to learn something about the murder. She then sends Melquíades to meet Santos and bring him to her "alive or dead" (*Doña Barbara,* p. 346).

Doña Barbara herself does not understand the object she has in view with these so-called Inscrutable Designs (the name of the chapter in which these plans unfold); she merely acts on instinct.

Pajarote, one of Santos's most loyal peons, follows Santos to the designated spot, where the two wait in hiding. When Melquíades arrives, he is startled by Santos riding out from the hiding place. Assuming that Barbara has betrayed him and sent him here to die, Melquíades draws his gun, but Santos fires before Melquíades can and the latter falls dead from his horse. Santos is utterly demoralized by the realization that he has killed a man, and gives himself up as lost to barbarism. In a state of shock, Santos returns Melquíades's corpse to Doña Barbara. "I knew you'd bring him," Barbara lies, only now interpreting her heretofore "inscrutable" actions as part of a well-formed plan to rid herself of one of the criminals in her service (*Doña Barbara,* p. 401).

Meanwhile, Marisela is nursing her father, who has fallen back into heavy drinking. Through the civilizing instruction of Santos and an awakening love for him, Marisela has finally discovered the tenderness within her, and with it a sense of daughterly duty. She resolves to take her father to San Fernando, a nearby town where she believes he can be cured of his drinking problem. To this end, Marisela sends a demand to Doña Barbara that she give her enough money to go away and never come back. Still jealous, Barbara sends the money to get the girl out of the way, but as Marisela prepares to depart, her father becomes very ill and dies. Seeing lights burning in the palm grove, Santos goes to investigate and finds Marisela sitting with the corpse. In despair, Santos tells Marisela of how he slew Melquíades. From the details of his story, Marisela realizes that it isn't possible that Santos killed Melquíades, but that Pajarote must have fired the fatal shot. Santos is greatly relieved that he is innocent, but what really saves him is Marisela's demonstration of tenderness towards him and her father, and his realization that this new-found compassion is at least in part his work.

At El Miedo, Doña Barbara has turned over a new leaf; she will no longer thwart Santos in any way. After receiving testimony of Balbino's crime, Barbara orders her peons to take their guns and prevent the murderer from absconding with the stolen feathers. In the ensuing struggle Balbino is killed. Barbara takes the feathers to the market on Santos's behalf, and restores to him all the misappropriated lands. When she hears, however, that Marisela and Santos are to marry, her jealousy reasserts itself and she takes her pistol to Altamira. There she sees Santos and Marisela through a window and takes aim at Marisela's heart, but as she continues to gaze upon this scene of domestic bliss her feelings change. She remembers Hasdrubal, and in Marisela sees herself as a young girl. "May he make you happy," she says, before she turns and walks away (*Doña Barbara,* p. 435). Barbara disappears, leaving only a document in which she acknowledges Marisela as her sole heir. Some believe Doña Barbara has killed herself, but others say she just slipped away, and plies the Orinoco and its mysterious tributaries on a riverboat. In the marriage of Santos and Marisela, the divided lands of the Luzardo family are rejoined, and when the fences go up, Señor Danger leaves in defeat.

The barbaric: women, nature, and the supernatural. In *Doña Barbara* barbarism is clearly part of the titular character, a woman whose name is very close to the Spanish word for barbarism, *barbarie.* Civilization, on the other hand, is represented by Santos Luzardo—*luz* being Spanish for "light"; *ardo,* for "I burn." The characterization of civilization and barbarism as male and female respectively is in keeping with historical traditions.

In Latin American tradition, barbarism has been identified with the American land and the people native to it, in whom instinct is presumed to prevail over rationality. Barbarism equals nature. The symbolic equation between women and nature has deep roots in Western culture—consider "Mother Nature" and characterizations of women as intuitive and irrational. Hence, within the civilization/barbarism dichotomy, women are clearly on the side of barbarism. Men, as the representatives of culture, which was for a long time considered to be the concern exclusively of males, are on the side of civilization.

In *Doña Barbara* Santos is a man educated in Caracas, the most civilized place in Venezuela, while Barbara is constantly identified with the countryside. Her soul is "wild and uncouth as the Plain," while her combination of sensuality and hatred for men is likened to the mingling of the Orinoco and Guainía rivers (*Doña Barbara,* p. 227). Her daughter, Marisela, is "open as the prairie" and seems "the spirit of the plain, of its ingenuous, restless soul, wild as the *paraguatán* flower that perfumes the thicket" (*Doña Barbara,* pp. 185, 297). Both women are also compared to animals of the llanos. In the chapter entitled "The Trainers," the education of Marisela parallels the breaking and training of the filly Catira, and when Doña Barbara falls in love with Santos "she felt she wanted to belong to him, although it had to be as one of his cattle, with the Altamira sign burned on their sides" (*Doña Barbara,* p. 220).

KILLING THE CENTAUR

"We must kill the centaur inside every one of us Plainsmen" (*Doña Barbara,* p. 115). When Lorenzo Barquero speaks of the "centaur," he refers to the llanero who spends his life in the saddle and becomes a creature that is half-man/half-horse, referring to the barbarity that this figure represents. Centaurs are creatures of Greek mythology who have the torsos of men and the lower bodies of horses. They are notorious for violent, unruly, and lewd behavior. Though they live in their own land, centaurs make incursions into the lands of men, often in order to abduct and ravish women. Although Lorenzo sees this same sort of bestial wildness in the cattlemen of the plain and wants to destroy it in the name of civilization, there is a positive side to this monster.

Gallegos acknowledged the positive side of barbarism in an earlier novel, *The Last Solar,* when he wrote of "a plant which, deformed by culture, returns to the jungle to recover the vigor of its original savage state" (Gallegos in Ruffinelli, p. 604). In *Doña Barbara* Santos is likened to "a tuft of grass from the plains forced to languish in a flowerpot," and he observes that, "after all . . . barbarism has its enchantment, is something beautiful and worth the trouble of living, in its fullness and intolerance of all limitation" (*Doña Barbara,* pp. 24, 289). Going beyond the bounds of barbarism is portrayed as tantalizing and perhaps even necessary. Not until Santos comes into contact with the barbarism of the llanos is he energized to shake off his malaise and pursue justice there, and not until he reconnects with his rough-and-ready centaurish side—wrangling cattle from horseback and confronting his enemies on their own barbaric terms—can he accomplish his goals.

The relation between civilization and barbarism is, according to the views of those who see the world in these terms, meant to be one of domination. Santos Luzardo looks forward to a time when "the Plain and barbarism will be conquered and retreat" (*Doña Barbara,* p. 138). Just as civilization ought to hold the forces of barbarism in check, so should (to extend the logic of this view) reason control the instincts, people control the land, those of European ancestry control non-Europeans, and men control women.

Not only does the novel align women with nature, it also aligns them with what lies beyond nature—the supernatural. "Civilized" society's conception of the supernatural at the time was largely a product of the philosophy of positivism, which taught that anything beyond the scope of scientific investigation does not exist. Positivism regarded the supernatural as imaginative error made mostly by primitive, uneducated people—people whose innate barbarism had not been civilized. This philosophy of the nineteenth and early twentieth centuries influenced Gallegos's novel, which portrays Barbara's supernatural powers as a deceptive trick played on the superstitious, albeit one that she herself comes to believe. Barbara's "knowledge" of magic comes from the Baniba Indians, a "barbaric" native source, and Barbara succumbs to superstition because she is an irrational being whose "skill lay solely in the ability to derive the best immediate profit from the chance results of her impulses" (*Doña Barbara,* p. 163). In short, the novel presents the supernatural, Doña Barbara's power, and hence the power of barbarism, as sham. One has only to shine the light of reason upon it, and it vanishes, just as Doña Barbara disappears into the landscape at the end of the novel.

Sources and literary context. *Doña Barbara* is one of the three classic *novelas de la tierra,* or Latin American "novels of the land" that were written in the first three decades of the twentieth century. The novela de la tierra (also known as the *novela criollista, novela telúrica,* and the Regionalist novel) represented a turning away from European models towards cultural forms that were rooted in the American landscape and experience. There are three classic examples of this genre, each in a different geographic area: *Doña Barbara* (set in the Venezuelan llanos); *Don Segundo Sombra* by Ricardo Güiraldes (in the Argentine *pampas,* or grasslands); and *La vorágine* (The Vortex) by José Eustasio Rivera (in the Columbian *selva,* or jungle). These novels are an expression of a unique cultural identity conceived as arising in part from the unique Latin American landscape. As the horrors of World War I disillusioned those who looked toward Europe for inspiration, the artistic movement of primitivism inspired a belief that fresh vitality lay in the artistic expression of the "primitive" inhabitants of non-European lands. Latin American authors like Gallegos were stimulated by these trends to formulate a distinctly American art form.

Gallegos wrote his first draft of *Doña Barbara* after a brief visit to the llanos in 1927. He based almost all the characters in the novel (with the notable exception of Santos Luzardo) on people of the La Candeleria region where he had stayed for a mere four days. Some characters, like the peon Antonio Sandoval, were based on people Gallegos actually met, while others, like Doña Barbara and Marisela, were inspired by people of whom he had only heard. The model for Doña Barbara was Francisca Vásquez, also known as Doña Pancha, a woman rancher with a legendary reputation as a skilled llanero and a fierce disputer of property boundaries. Doña Pancha had a daughter and died some years before Gallegos heard her story. There were in fact two families with the names Barqueros and Luzardos engaged in a blood feud. The region had also produced a young man from a fine family who traveled to Caracas, earned a law degree, and returned to run his ranch and help "civilize" the region. After a few successful years, he inexplicably drank himself into an awful state. His traits inspired two characters in the novel—the upstanding Santos Luzardo and the drunken Lorenzo Barquero.

Events in History at the Time the Novel Was Written

Oil and nationalism. In 1930, the year *Doña Barbara* was published, Venezuela paid off its entire national debt with revenues from oil. Over the course of the 27-year dictatorship of Juan Vicente Gómez, Venezuela metamorphosed from an impoverished, primarily agricultural country to the world's greatest exporter, and second greatest producer, of petroleum. Most Venezuelans, however, did not share in the benefits of the oil boom. Three foreign companies (Dutch Shell, Gulf, and Standard Oil) controlled 98 percent of Venezuelan oil. Rights to the oil were sold to these companies by the Gómez regime, and much of the profits from these sales went to strengthen the dictator's army and repressive police force, and to personally enrich Gómez and his friends and relatives. Some of the oil wealth, however, did flow into the populace where it helped to create a middle class. The advent of this middle class reduced the degree of barbarism, as the novel defines it. Middle-class Venezuelans had money enough to educate themselves, and were well-traveled and well-read, qualities associated with civilization in *Doña Barbara*.

The middle class also took an interest in their national history and culture from a global point of view, contributing to a growing wave of nationalism in Venezuela. Meanwhile, the foreign oil companies operated with little concern for the Venezuelan environment, despoiling the countryside and encroaching on the hunting grounds of indigenous inhabitants of the Lake Maracaibo region. Foreigners who came to work in the Venezuelan oil fields received preferential treatment compared to their Venezuelan co-workers, and foreign attitudes toward the native peoples were openly contemptuous. "It is impossible to expect the native mind to conform to the accepted method of living in highly developed countries after centuries of dirt and unsanitary living," wrote William T. Wallace, vice-president of the Venezuelan branch of Gulf Oil in a memo recommending that the company not provide housing for its Venezuelan workers (Wallace in Ewell, p. 64). Such condescension added insult to economic and environmental injuries, and helped foment a new movement against the Gómez dictatorship.

Urban unrest. In 1928 students at the Central University in Caracas protested against Gómez, whom they saw as an unjust dictator and the tool by which foreign powers controlled Venezuela's economy. Gómez promptly had the protest leaders arrested, thereby sparking a much larger student strike throughout the nation. Working-class Venezuelans rallied to support the students, and even some young army officers joined their cause. Different segments of the society banded together for a common purpose, just as in *Doña Barbara* the peons make common cause with Santos Luzardo to battle the forces of barbarism.

In other ways, the situation at the time of the novel's writing contrasts sharply with the time in which it is set. History around 1930 portrays Caracas (represented by Gómez) and foreigners (the oil companies) as promoting discord rather than civilization in Venezuelan society. During the 1928 strike angry crowds filled the streets of Caracas; Gómez's troops responded with gunfire. Gómez then closed the universities and forced the students to work building roads. Those who had participated in the agitation came to be known as "the generation of 1928," and many, like Rómulo Gallegos, fled the country. In 1931 Gallegos went into self-imposed exile rather than

Juan Vicente Gómez

accept (or decline) the post of senator offered him by an admiring Gómez as a reward for his literary success with *Doña Barbara.*

In 1935 the reign of Gómez would end when the dictator died of illness at the age of 79. Gómez's passing left a political vacuum; his tyrannical regime, which remained in power, had silenced political debate and driven future leaders into exile. The response to Gómez's death was riots, arson, and looting in the streets and on the oil fields. Order was soon restored, however, by Gómez's Minister of War, Eleazar López Contreras, who adopted a new, more just constitution to placate the angry population, and offered all exiles a general amnesty. The generation of 1928 came home and formed a variety of leftist political parties, chief among them *Acción Democrática* (AD). One of AD's founding members was Gallegos, who returned to Venezuela in 1936 and began a political career that would result in his election to the presidency in 1947, giving him the opportunity almost two decades after the publication of *Doña Barbara* to put some of his ideas into political action. The experience would prove to be less than happy—a conservative backlash resulted in a military takeover in 1948.

Reviews. When Gallegos published the first edition of *Doña Barbara* in 1929, the novel was a great success. It was named best novel of the month in Spanish by a literary jury, and the Cuban critic Jorge Mañach pronounced it to be the long-awaited Great American Novel. The author, however, was not so pleased with his creation and extensively revised the novel before issuing a second edition in 1930. This revised edition is the novel as we have it today, and is generally conceded to be far superior to its forerunner. *Doña Barbara* is widely considered the best and most important of the novelas de la tierra, as well as its author's most significant work.

After bemoaning the fact that, at the time, the United States often ignored the literature of Latin America, a 1931 reviewer of the English translation gives the novel a warm welcome. "The characters and circumstances . . . go to make up a plot as delicate and credible and psychologically convincing as it is absorbing" (Marsh, p. 7). The review does find fault with the character of Doña Barbara, crediting the novel for its attention to her past but complaining that her "subsequent career is not sufficiently developed"; still, the review praises the novel as a satisfying love story and a landmark work of fiction—"Now for the first time we have a picture of a new and exotic frontier life" (Marsh, p. 7).

Although *Doña Barbara* maintains an undisputed place in Latin American literature, assessment of its merits has undergone a shift in time. Mid- to late twentieth century reviewers sometimes criticize its use of symbolism and commentary as heavy-handed. Yet the novel continues to receive praise for its engaging narrative style and lyrical language. Twenty-five years after it appeared, reviewers were still pointing to the successful balance of elements that made *Doña Barbara* "both realistic and poetic" (Liscano, p. 41).

—Kimberly Ball

For More Information

Ewell, Judith. *Venezuela: A Century of Change.* London: C. Hurst & Company, 1984.

Gallegos, Rómulo. *Doña Barbara.* Trans. Robert Malloy. New York: Peter Smith, 1948.

Hellinger, Daniel C. *Venezuela: Tarnished Democracy.* Boulder, Colo.: Westview Press, 1991.

Liscano, Juan. "'Doña Bárbara,' Novel Extraordinary." *Americas* 6, no. 11 (November 1954): 40-42.

Marsh, Fred T. "Life on the Plains of Venezuela." *The New York Times Book Review,* August 9, 1931, 7.

Masiello, Francine. "Women, State, and Family in Latin American Literature of the 1920s." In *Women, Culture, and Politics in Latin America: Seminar on Feminism and Culture in Latin America.* Berkeley: University of California Press, 1990.

McBeth, B. S. *Juan Vicente Gómez and the Oil Companies in Venezuela, 1908-1935.* Cambridge: Cambridge University Press, 1983.

Pocaterra, Josef Rafael. *Gómez: The Shame of America—Fragments From the Memoirs of a Citizen of the Republic of Venezuela in the Days of Her Decadence.* Paris: André Delpeuch, 1929.

Ruffinelli, Jorge. "Rómulo Gallegos." In *Latin American Writers.* Vol. 2. New York: Charles Scribner's Sons, 1989.

Wright, Winthrop R. *Café con leche: Race, Class, and National Image in Venezuela.* Austin: University of Texas Press, 1993.

Facundo

by
Domingo F. Sarmiento

Domingo Faustino Sarmiento was a man of extremes. During his lifetime, he would be both an exile from his own country (in the 1840s, when he wrote *Facundo*) and president of the Argentine Republic (from 1868 to 1874). Beginning life as an impoverished inhabitant of the frontier, Sarmiento went on to become a powerful politician in the cosmopolitan city of Buenos Aires. His most famous work, known either as *Facundo* or by its original title, *Civilization and Barbarism: Life of Juan Facundo Quiroga,* is likewise an essay of extremes. The essay sets forth a basic opposition—between civilization and barbarism—that has profoundly influenced Latin American thought to the present day. By writing *Facundo,* Sarmiento took vengeance against a figure who had terrorized his own native community of San Juan, yet the author's main targets were the dictator Juan Manuel de Rosas (during whose reign *Facundo* was written) and the phenomenon of *caudillismo.* This phenomenon is one that both Rosas and Facundo represent, in which society submits to the rule of local strongmen (caudillos) rather than to the law.

THE LITERARY WORK

An essay featuring a biography of Argentine historical figure Juan Facundo Quiroga (1788-1836) as a vantage point from which to explore the social and historical situation of the Río de la Plata region after its independence from Spain; published in Spanish in 1845, in English in 1868.

SYNOPSIS

The essay portrays Argentina as the scene of a struggle between two opposing forces: civilization and barbarism, the latter exemplified by Juan Facundo Quiroga, a brutal *caudillo,* or military strongman of the rural plains.

Events in History at the Time of the Essay

Revolution of independence. In 1808 French Emperor Napoleon Bonaparte's troops entered Spain and claimed it as their own, setting up a government under Napoleon's brother, Joseph Bonaparte. This precipitated a Spanish civil war between supporters of Bonaparte and supporters of the deposed Spanish monarch, Charles IV. With the leadership of Spain in question, Spain's South American colonies claimed the right to self-government under Spanish law until a legitimate king should resume the throne. A local government council or *cabildo* already existed in Buenos Aires, and on May 25, 1810, this council claimed temporary autonomy for the Viceroyalty of La Plata—a region including what would become Argentina, Paraguay, Uruguay, and Bolivia.

The Viceroyalty came under Spanish dominion again in 1814 when Ferdinand VII assumed the throne. However, Ferdinand proved to be a foolishly autocratic ruler, and the La Plata region, having tasted sovereignty, declared its complete independence from Spain in 1816. Several years of battle with Spanish royalist troops followed, but by 1824 the autonomy of the Río de la Plata region was uncontested.

Contesting the dominance of Buenos Aires. Buenos Aires was and is the name of both the wealthiest of the Argentine provinces and Argentina's largest and most prosperous city. Because of its coastal and river access, Buenos Aires has proved to be a prime site for trade; accordingly, the city receives goods and capital, as well as immigrants and ideas, from all over the world, making it a place of diversity, activity, and change. In the nineteenth century, much of the influx came from Europe, and Buenos Aires became a city characterized by European culture, dress, and manners--at least among its middle and upper classes. By comparison, other Argentine cities of this era (such as Córdoba, La Rioja, and San Juan) were small, insulated, and impoverished. Thus, a certain antagonism arose between Buenos Aires—which was urban, international, progressive, European, rich, and merchant-oriented—and the rest of Argentina—which was largely rural, parochial, conservative, South American, poor, and rancher-oriented. It is within this context that Sarmiento writes of a struggle between an urban-based "civilization" and a rural-based "barbarism."

Although the Buenos Aires government had claimed independence from Spain in the name of the entire viceroyalty, *porteño* (or Buenos Aires) authority was not widely acknowledged. Paraguay and Bolivia soon claimed autonomous nationhood, and even within Argentina, the several fiercely independent provinces resisted consolidation under Buenos Aires in favor of self-government.

Presidency of Rivadavia. In 1826 an assembly gathered in Buenos Aires in an attempt to establish a national government. Despite its lack of legislative authority, the assembly created the office of the President of the United Provinces of the Río de la Plata (the region of modern Argentina and Uruguay) and elected Bernardino Rivadavia, the current Minister of Government and Foreign Affairs under the Governor of Buenos Aires, to the post. This action roused the ire of the provinces, and civil war was the result.

Support for a strong, centralized Argentine government was based in Buenos Aires, and gave rise to two opposing groups. On the one hand, there were the Unitarians, those favoring centralized government. They tended to be wealthy, educated porteño elites that looked to Europe for cultural and political models. The rest of the country, perhaps fearing porteño domination, tended to favor a looser federation with more autonomy for the individual provinces. They were the opponents of the Unitarians, known as Federalists, who tended to be rural inhabitants, and rejected porteño imitation of European ways. One of the major leaders of the opposition to centralized government was Juan Facundo Quiroga, caudillo of La Rioja province. Sarmiento saw in Facundo an apt representative of the forces of barbarism, which, broadly speaking, he identified with the Federalist countryside. Civilization came from Europe, and thus, in Sarmiento's view, had its firmest foothold in Buenos Aires among the frock-coated Unitarians.

The presidency of Rivadavia, though brief, was highly significant for those who, like Sarmiento, saw in it the model for Argentina's future and even referred to the period of Rivadavia as "The Happy Experience." It was a happy experience for the supporters of Rivadavia, Unitarians who longed for a more civilized, cultured, Europeanized environment. As Minister of Government and Foreign Affairs, Rivadavia had established the European-staffed University of Buenos Aires as well as a public education program for male rural children. He also supported theater and opera groups, publishing houses, and a museum. Such institutions were hailed as civilizing influences by the porteño Unitarians. Less happy were the common laborers whose wages under Rivadavia were subjected to a government cap to ensure "their dependence on daily labor" (Shumway, *The Invention of Argentina,* p. 84). Rivadavia's policies displeased other groups too. More specifically, they upset the provincial military and government employees who were forced to retire on minimal pensions because of Rivadavia's fear of provincial uprisings. Also upset were the *gauchos,* landless inhabitants of the *pampas* who were arrested for vagrancy and forced to work on so-called public projects, usually without pay. Finally, Rivadavia failed to please Catholic conservatives by establishing policies of religious tolerance that appealed to non-Catholic European immigrants.

Dorrego and Lavalle. Beset by Federalist forces (one of the main leaders of which was Facundo Quiroga) and losing a war against Brazil, Rivadavia resigned the presidency in 1827 and the short-lived national government dissolved. Colonel Manuel Dorrego became governor of

Buenos Aires province with the help of fellow Federalist Juan Manuel de Rosas, a wealthy and politically powerful local landowner. Dorrego made peace with Brazil by sacrificing a large piece of disputed territory. Argentine troops, having returned from the war zone, proceeded to overthrow and execute Dorrego, installing their leader, the Unitarian general Juan Lavalle, as governor. Meanwhile, in the city of Córdoba, a similar overthrow of Federalist power was carried out by the forces of another returning Unitarian general, José María Paz.

Lavalle was soon overthrown himself, by a Rosas-led militia composed largely of gauchos. By the end of 1829 the old legislature that Lavalle had disbanded was back in place and had appointed Rosas to the office of governor of Buenos Aires. Paz, however, maintained control over the interior stronghold of Córdoba. Sarmiento saw this as an ironic state of affairs in that the barbaric forces of Federalism were in control of Buenos Aires, the bastion of civilization, while the forces of civilization led by Unitarian General Paz held what had always been the stronghold of barbarism, the Argentine interior.

The Rosas regime. Rosas was granted virtually absolute power over Buenos Aires by the grateful legislature that he had reinstated. The legislators saw in Rosas a bulwark against anarchy, and so condoned his rule as dictator for the next three years. During this time, with the help of Facundo Quiroga and fellow caudillo Estanislao López, he defeated Paz, maintained peace between Buenos Aires and the rest of Argentina, and increased the riches of the wealthy while—thanks to his rural roots—maintaining an undeserved image as champion of the rural poor. In this way, Rosas enjoyed general support until he stepped down from office at the end of his three-year term.

Without the strength of Rosas, the nation soon dissolved into chaos. The provinces were demanding a constitution that would give them a more equitable relationship with Buenos Aires, whose government appeared threatened by Unitarian forces. The assassination of Juan Facundo Quiroga in 1835 promised anarchy; to avert this, the Buenos Aires legislature begged Rosas to resume the governorship on his own terms. His terms were absolute power. Of course, rumors spread that Facundo's assassination had been orchestrated by Rosas, who had so obviously benefited from the death. The charge was never proved, however, and Rosas ruled as dictator for the next 17 years.

The Essay in Focus

Contents summary. The English translation by Mrs. Horace Mann of the third edition of *Facundo* is called neither by this title nor by the full *Civilization and Barbarism: Life of Juan Facundo Quiroga.* Instead it is renamed *Life in the Argentine Republic in the Days of the Tyrants.* The translation can be divided into two main parts: the initial part comprises the first four chapters and provides a geographical, sociological, and historical background for the second part, which tells the life story of Juan Facundo Quiroga. Spanish-language editions of *Facundo* include an introduction and a conclusion that the Mann translation omits. In the introduction, the ghost of Facundo is invoked and commanded to reveal the secret disease (barbarism) that eats away at the Argentine Republic. The conclusion constitutes a direct attack against the Rosas regime and predicts a brighter, more "civilized" future for Argentina.

THE GAUCHO

Gauchos were cattle-wrangling horsemen of the pampas, the vast flat grasslands of Argentina. In the seventeenth century gauchos conducted a brisk contraband trade in the hides of wild pampean cattle (technically owned by the Spanish Crown), which they sold to European traders. Later, when the plains were converted into private property for a few wealthy landowners, gauchos were hired as cowboys to maintain the now privately owned herds on unfenced land. In the nineteenth century, with land being fenced and ranches converted into farms, gauchos lost their place in society. Rivadavia introduced vagrancy laws that criminalized the landless gaucho if he happened to be unemployed; those who were arrested were forced to work, often without pay, on "public" projects that generally served the interests of the land-owning elite.

"Physical contents of the republic." Sarmiento begins by describing the geography of Argentina as vast and empty, dominated by the pampas—immense grassy plains stretching from the Andes to the Atlantic Ocean, unbroken but for the many rivers that join forces finally in the eastern Río de la Plata region. The only part of Argentina to truly benefit from the river system is Buenos Aires, the coastal metropolis where the many waterways meet to empty into the sea—but even

Juan Manuel Rosas

Buenos Aires cannot realize the full potential of its geographical situation, for the sluggish "spirit of the Pampa" has infected her (Sarmiento, *Facundo,* p. 5). As "the only city in the vast Argentine territory which is in communication with European nations," Buenos Aires is Argentina's best hope for civilization, yet she has failed to civilize the rest of the country (*Facundo,* p. 5). Consequently, the barbarism of the provinces has produced Rosas, who in turn has taken control of Buenos Aires.

Why has Buenos Aires, and hence Argentina, failed to achieve civilization? The flatness of the Argentine terrain makes tyrannical domination easy. There is no place to hide, and no defensible place from which to resist. The essay adds that the plains give Argentina "a certain Asiatic coloring" (*Facundo,* p. 8), and for Sarmiento this means "the reign of brute force, the supremacy of the strongest, the absolute and irresponsible authority of rulers, the administration of justice without formalities or discussion"—in a word, barbarism (*Facundo,* p. 9).

Sarmiento next discusses the people of Argentina, who are comprised of three groups: the Spanish, the Indian, and the black African. The first two Sarmiento characterizes as lazy. The black African race possesses "the finest instincts of progress," but, despite its presence, idleness has won out over industry as the defining feature of the Argentine people (*Facundo,* p. 10).

In this land, cities are like islands that harbor the features of civilization, including factories, shops, and schools, as well as "elegance of style, articles of luxury, dress-coats, and frock-coats" (*Facundo,* p. 13). Such dress is emblematic of civilization, and as such exposes its wearer to ridicule and abuse in the barbaric world of the countryside, whose residents hate civilization. Meanwhile the country dwellers of Argentina live in isolation from one another many miles apart in what Sarmiento likens to feudal strongholds. Schools and churches are nonexistent. In summary, Sarmiento asserts that there is no res publica, no sense of commonwealth or community to unite the people and inspire them to acts of citizenship for the common good.

In this first chapter the essay sets forth a fundamental opposition: barbarism, it says, comes from two basic sources, Spain and Latin America, while civilization is a northern European import.

"Originality and peculiarities of the people." Sarmiento now asserts that although the landscape of Argentina has rendered its inhabitants largely barbarous, it has also made them poetic by nature because of the dramatic natural environment in which they dwell. The literature of the Americas should reflect the peculiar situation of these lands, Sarmiento believes; it should describe "the mighty scenes of nature" (*Facundo,* p. 24), and above all should illustrate "the struggle between European civilization and native barbarism, between mind and matter" (*Facundo,* p. 24).

Before proceeding, the essay describes four different types of gaucho: the *rastreador* (tracker); *Baqueano* (path-finder); the outlaw; and the minstrel. According to Sarmiento, an understanding of these different types will elucidate the characters of various Argentine leaders, and the "bloody strife" in which they involve their nation (*Facundo,* p. 45). The leaders to whom Sarmiento refers are the Federalist caudillos, Rosas chief among them, whom Sarmiento sees as brutal, ignorant gauchos elevated to positions of power.

"Association." Sarmiento sums up the character of the Argentine rustic as "independent of every want, under no control, with no notion of government" (*Facundo,* p. 46). Because pastoral existence requires so little labor, and so little cooperation, rural men lead lives of independent idleness. They must find ways to occupy their time, and excuses for socializing, so they turn to the *pulperia,* a combination of country store and saloon, where men pass the greater part of the day drinking and gambling. Here valor is esteemed above all else, and men prove themselves through feats of horsemanship and knife fighting, which can break out at any time. Since the object is only to scar one's opponent, killing happens rarely, but when it does occur, the murderer gains sympathy and renown. He must flee the law, but has become something of a hero of the people. Sarmiento here points out that Rosas's home was once an asylum for murderers like these. Under such conditions are formed the characters of the provincial caudillos. It is therefore understandable that they are barbaric despots.

In order to gain some measure of control over such a lawless populace, repressive tactics are employed. The rural judge must be a brutal tyrant to inspire fear in hardened outlaws, and the military commander can keep order only through tyranny. In any case, the rural leader answers to no law because he is the law. It is true that his official power must be conferred by urban elites, but this makes little difference since power tends to be granted to those most feared. Nothing, then, mitigates the power of the strongest.

Sarmiento now tells his reader that all that has gone before has been a necessary prelude to understand the revolution in which Argentina gained independence from Spain. Before this, according to Sarmiento, Argentina was divided into two opposing societies: "one being Spanish, European, and cultivated, the other barbarous, American, and almost wholly of native growth" (*Facundo,* p. 54). After the revolution, provincial military bands, called *montoneras,* propelled their leaders to political power and this led to "the final triumph, in Facundo Quiroga, of the country over the cities throughout the land" (*Facundo,* p. 55). Facundo paved the way for the government of Rosas, the man who "applied the knife of the gaucho to the culture of Buenos Ayres, and destroyed the work of centuries—of civilization, law, and liberty" (*Facundo,* p. 55).

"The Revolution of 1810." The Argentine Revolution of Independence, like similar revolutions in the United States, France, and Spain, stemmed from European ideas. For this reason, the revolution was incomprehensible to the inhabitants of rural Argentina, who could embrace it only as a throwing-off of authority, which they despised in itself. Only in the cities, which are "a continuation of European civilization," could the ideas shaping the revolution be grasped (*Facundo,* pp. 61-62). The provinces embraced revolution largely because war offered a fitting outlet for the aggressive, brutal nature they had been developing. Unfortunately, in the revolution's aftermath, the rural forces would rise up against the cities, despoiling them of what they could not understand—civilization. Sarmiento is optimistic, however, that European culture will win out in the end, educating Rosas and his ilk and thus civilizing them.

ROSAS: CONTROVERSIAL FIGURE

Rosas has been viewed by some historians as the champion of the people, supporting their interests against those of the elitist Unitarians. Others view him as a bloody tyrant who nevertheless was the only figure strong enough to maintain the fledgling Argentine sovereignty amid constant threats of civil war. This latter view is expressed by British poet John Masefield in his poem *Rosas*:

> So Rosas came to power. Soon his hold
> Gripped the whole land as though it were a horse.
> Church, Money, Law all yielded. . . .
>
> And if the city, terrified to awe,
> Loathed him, as slaves their masters, he was still
> The Gaucho's darling captain; he could draw
> Their hearts at pleasure with his horseman's skill,
> None ever rode like Rosas; none but he
> Could speak their slang or knew their mystery.
>
> (Masefield in Lynch, p. 10)

"Life of Juan Facundo Quiroga." "The man of nature who has not yet learned to restrain or disguise his passions, displays them in all their energy, and gives himself up to their impetuosity" (*History of the Ottoman Empire* in *Facundo,* p. 73). With this quotation, Sarmiento begins his biography of Facundo, a man ruled by his passions and unrestrained by the civilizing force of reason. Juan Facundo Quiroga was the son of a wealthy rural man. He received a minimal education in which he learned to read and write. His youth was marked by rebellion and antisocial behavior; by the age of 15 he was an avid gambler. Despite the prestige of his family, Facundo worked as a common laborer. He gambled away any money or goods with which he was entrusted and soon broke off familial relations entirely—according to one account, by burning down the house in which his parents slept, after taking care to fasten the doors from the outside. This is perhaps the ugliest of the many incidents Sarmiento relates to illustrate Facundo's brutality.

An outlaw drifting between gambling parties and casual slayings, Facundo resolves to join the *montonera*, or military band, of Francisco "Pancho" Ramírez, caudillo of Entre Rios province. En route to join the band, Facundo is captured and sent to prison for one of his many crimes. A group of imprisoned Spanish officers instigates an escape. They open the cells of the common criminals, but when Facundo is released, he kills the Spaniards with an iron bar wrenched from his fetters. For this act, Facundo becomes a hero, and, cleansed in blood, is allowed to reenter society's fold.

Facundo makes his way to the province of La Rioja, where his reputation has preceded him. Whether from fear or esteem, others award him with the post of Sergeant Major of the Militia of the Llanos. He proves himself courageous and fierce in battle, but ultimately betrays his post, and, with the aid of a rebel band he is supposed to subdue, imprisons the government officers and takes over La Rioja. He puts down all opposition instantly by killing his opponents. By intimidation, Facundo increases his wealth, inviting anyone with money to his gambling table, which no one leaves without surrendering everything to him.

Now Facundo has power and wealth, but he hates whatever he cannot attain—"polish, learning, true respectability"—persecuting those who possess them (*Facundo,* p. 105). Facundo displays his contempt for civilization one night by singling out La Rioja's "well-to-do householders and the young men who still had some appearance of culture" (*Facundo,* p. 106). He keeps these men marching all night long, beating them frequently with his sergeant's stick. The result of his depredations on the town of La Rioja is complete devastation. Where once a prosperous town existed, there are now but a few families of beggars huddled amid the ruins.

"Buenos Aires and Cordova." The essay describes two cities of Argentina that illustrate the basic dichotomy of civilization and barbarism: Buenos Aires and Cordova (Sarmiento's spelling for the city of Córdoba). Cordova is essentially a city of the Middle Ages, dominated by the Catholic Church and a university run by Jesuits. Cordova sits cloistered away from the modern world, remaining as stagnant as the artificial lake in its central square. It is, says the essay, the true descendant of Spain, which was considered less civilized than countries in northern Europe. Buenos Aires, on the other hand, is a modern city with strong ties to the more northern country of France and to North America.

"Life of Facundo resumed." In 1825 Rivadavia, then governor of Buenos Aires, summons representatives from the provinces to unite in a congressional body. Facundo arrives as representative of La Rioja and soon receives an assignment to put down a military leader who is overstepping the bounds of his power. Facundo is successful, and at the scene of his victory he raises what will become his trademark flag, a skull and crossbones on a black background.

Sarmiento now contemplates what Facundo's chosen flag represents—"terror, death, hell" (*Facundo,* p. 137)—and contrasts this with the symbolism of the flag of Argentina, the colors of which are blue and white—"the clear sky of a fair day, and the bright light of the disk of the sun: 'peace and justice for all'" (*Facundo,* p. 137).

Under the pressure of heavy opposition from the provinces, Rivadavia resigns the office of governor of Buenos Aires, an act the essay regards as cowardly. He is replaced by Dorrego, a Federalist, but essentially a Buenos Airean who cares little for what becomes of the other provinces. Because of this lack of concern, the essay argues, Buenos Aires fails to bestow its wealth and its civilizing influence on the rest of Argentina. As a result barbarism continues to flourish in the provinces, and eventually takes its vengeance against the port city in the person of Rosas.

The Unitarians revolt, and Dorrego is killed in battle. Moving on to the subsequent battle of Cordova, the essay contrasts Facundo with his opponent, the one-armed General Paz, "a true son of the city, and representative of the power of civilization" (*Facundo,* p. 162). Paz defeats Facundo at Cordova, and Facundo escapes to Buenos Aires, now the stronghold of barbarism since Rosas has seized control of the city. Facundo offers his services to the new governor.

Soon, in a campaign to reclaim the provinces, Facundo, López (caudillo of Santa Fé), and Rosas begin attacking various towns. In quick succession, Facundo conquers Rio Quinto, San Luis, and Mendoza. Finally, Cordova falls, and the Unitarians are driven beyond the boundaries of Argentina. Facundo disbands his army and returns to San Juan, from which he exerts his authority over several other neighboring towns where "Liberty had ceased, and Quiroga's name took the place of law" (*Facundo,* p. 216). But his power is unofficial; Facundo has not been rewarded for his service to Rosas with a governorship.

Facundo eventually returns to Buenos Aires to confront Rosas, towards whom he feels some resentment, and to live amid the luxuries of civilization. In Buenos Aires Facundo seems to assume a new character. He proclaims himself a Unitarian, and speaks of his support for a national constitution. He puts his sons in the best schools and provides them with the European clothing he himself still shuns. But Facundo is all talk; he does not actively support the Unitarians and neither they nor the Federalists embrace him. After a brief chaotic interlude during which Rosas does all he can to undermine the administration of the interim governors, Rosas himself resumes the governorship, this time with the unlimited powers of a despot. He sends Facundo to settle a dispute in the provinces north of Buenos Aires. Despite many warnings, Facundo proceeds on his predetermined route to Cordova without a retinue. His carriage is stopped by armed men, and Facundo is shot dead. The assassins are duly executed, but in Sarmiento's view this is only to hide the true perpetrator of the crime, and Facundo ends with Sarmiento's insistence that "the impartial historian will one day expose the real instigator of the assassination," whom Sarmiento clearly believes to be Rosas (*Facundo,* p. 236).

Racist dichotomies—societies. *Facundo* is a meandering, sometimes confusing essay united by Sarmiento's underlying theme of a single dichotomy: the conflict between civilization and barbarism. This basic dichotomy is manifested in several pairs of opposing entities. Civilization is identified with northern Europe, North America, cities, Unitarians, Paz, and Rivadavia; barbarism is identified with Latin America, Spain, Asia, the Middle East, the countryside, Federalists, Facundo, and Rosas. In general, civilization is the hard-won victory of man over a nature that is both geographical wilderness and human passion. Facundo, whom Sarmiento describes as "only a barbarian, who did not know how to restrain his passions," embodies Argentina, where the forces of law and order have little power over wayward caudillos (*Facundo,* p. 198).

The tendency to divide the world into two opposing categories goes at least as far back as the philosophy of Plato (427?–347? b.c.e.), who posited a radical mind/body dualism. This notion of the separation of mind and matter reached its peak in the Enlightenment or "Age of Reason" of the eighteenth century. Reason, it was said, set the human being above nature and was the force that would save humankind from the ignorance and depravity of superstition.

Jean Jacques Rousseau, a major Enlightenment thinker, spoke of the "noble savage," the primitive man who is pure and vital because uncorrupted by the taint of civilization. This view, known as "primitivism," was countered, however, by another strain of Enlightenment thought that placed the so-called savage on the lowest rung on the ladder of human development, just above animals, while Europeans saw themselves as the pinnacle of mankind. In their view the European had science, while the savage had superstition—a pathetic attempt to gain magical knowledge of and control over a nature that, without science, was mysterious and uncontrollable. *Facundo* is strongly influenced by Enlightenment thought, and in it the gaucho is Sarmiento's savage, who "will lead you into a world of . . . superstitious and vulgar traditions" (*Facundo,* p. 28).

Racist dichotomies—individuals. Although mind and matter were understood to stand in opposition, Enlightenment thinkers, with their emphasis on an orderly and harmonious universe, believed in a correspondence between mind and body. A people who shared physical characteristics were also believed to share mental characteristics. Eighteenth-century German philosopher and poet Johann von Herder developed the concept of *Volksgeist*—the essential spirit of a people. Although Herder wrote of a cultural rather than a racial link between individuals, this notion of essential character could easily be connected to theories of race distinctions. In this vein, it was believed that the character of an individual could be read in the features of his or her head and face—a notion endorsed in the novels of Sir Walter Scott, all of which Sarmiento once claimed to have read. Sarmiento's essay cites the pseudo-sciences of phrenology (study of the skull to determine character traits) and physiognomy (study of the face and its relation to character) to give evidence for the character of Facundo: "There are, in fact, as is proved by phrenology and comparative anatomy, relations between external forms and moral qualities, between the countenance of a man and that of some animal whose disposition resembles his own" (*Facundo,* p. 76). Facundo

Domingo F. Sarmiento

resembles a tiger, in both countenance and character, and since his physical characteristics are certainly beyond his control, one must consider whether Facundo has any choice, in Sarmiento's view, as to his character. In any case, Enlightenment thinkers did not believe that nature must change, but that it must be controlled by the civilizing force of reason, and it is this control over his natural tendencies that Facundo lacks.

The racism inherent in *Facundo* and its links

to phrenology are more fully expressed in the author's last, unfinished work, *Conflict and Harmony in the Races.* In this writing, which was intended as a further elaboration of the theories formulated in *Facundo,* Sarmiento asserts that primitive peoples "all tend to have the same size cranium and all think the same way; that is, they don't think, they feel" (Sarmiento in Earle, p. 166). Sarmiento's presidential policies of encouraging European immigration to supplant the *mestizo,* or mixed-race, population further attest to his racist beliefs.

Literary context. Sarmiento is associated with the "Generation of '37," a Buenos Aires literary society founded by poet and essayist Esteban Echeverría and including such writers as Juan Bautista Alberdi, Juan María Gutiérrez, Miguel Cané, Vicente Fidel López, and José Mármol. Inspired by European revolutionary groups, these young men sought to depose Rosas and to instigate a new era for Argentina through literary and political endeavors. They were influenced by the writings of Enlightenment thinkers George Wilhelm Friedrich Hegel, Jeremy Bentham, John Locke, and John Stuart Mill, as well as by the Romantic poets. (While *Facundo*'s connections to Enlightenment ideas have already been noted, its Romantic tendencies can be seen in its fascination with the figure of the gaucho as a man closer to wild nature and hence innately poetic.) With the notable exception of Alberdi, who was Sarmiento's literary nemesis, the Generation held largely the same views as those presented in *Facundo.* Sarmiento is the most widely read member of the Generation, and *Facundo* is generally considered to be his most important work.

It has been suggested that Sarmiento's writings were self-serving promotions meant to pave the way to political power, yet Sarmiento never abandoned the ideals expressed in *Facundo* to further his career. As President, he undertook nothing less than the civilization of Argentina, instituting schools, museums, libraries, a national bank, and a civil legal code. He also favored the interests of European immigrants, whom he believed to be arbiters of civilization, over those of the native-born mestizo population.

Events in History at the Time the Essay Was Written

The Rosas regime, part II. In the years between the death of Juan Facundo Quiroga and the publication of *Facundo,* Governor Rosas embraced totalitarianism. Every citizen of Buenos Aires was compelled on pain of death to wear a red ribbon, emblematic of support for Federalism and the Rosas regime. All documents, including personal correspondence, had to commence with the phrase, "Long live the Federation and death to the unitarist savages" (Rock, p. 106). The press was censored and the *mazorca,* Rosas's vigilante squad, patrolled the streets on the lookout for the slightest infraction. At any time, Rosas could have anyone arrested and subjected to execution, torture, imprisonment, or exile.

Nonetheless, the Rosas regime continued to enjoy peace and a wide base of support, primarily from ranchers and the rural poor. Then, in 1838, Rosas brought Argentina into conflict with France and Britain over issues of tariffs and the rights of French nationals living in Buenos Aires. European ships blockaded the Buenos Aires harbor, crippling the city's export-based economy and creating an anti-Rosas sentiment amongst those affected. With European support, Rosas's opponents plotted to overthrow the powerful governor, but soon the British and French, dismayed by losses in trade revenue, pulled up their anchors and resumed normal relations with Buenos Aires, leaving the dissidents to face Rosas alone. The dictator overcame his weakened opposition, and, instituting a large standing army, extended the authority of his government over most of Argentina. Troops from Buenos Aires, under the leadership of Manuel Oribe, expanded the realm of porteño power up to the borders of Chile and Bolivia, reclaimed the territory that is modern Uruguay, and conducted a siege against Montevideo, the city across the bay from Buenos Aires, its competitor in trade, and a stronghold of anti-Rosas Unitarians.

To finance his military expeditions, Rosas sought to monopolize trade by blockading the Paraná River against access by other Argentine provinces as well as by Brazil and Uruguay. Eventually this maneuver earned Rosas the powerful opposition that would one day force him to flee to England, where he died in 1877. In 1845, however, as *Facundo* was being published in Chile, where Sarmiento had been exiled for his opposition to the porteño dictator, Rosas's power was at its peak.

Reviews. Upon its publication, sales of *Facundo* were sluggish despite a rave review from Rosas, who reportedly pronounced it "the best thing that has been written against me" (Rosas in Jones, p. 86). Another favorable review, perhaps little more to Sarmiento's liking, appeared in the *Revue des Deux Mondes* in 1846, wherein *Facundo* was praised by the French paper mainly for its picturesque portrayal of an exotic land.

Written by one of the nation's founding fathers, *Facundo* has become a staple of Argentine education, and is considered one of the most important texts for understanding Argentine history. It is not, however, an uncontroversial work. Sarmiento's racial theories as well as what have been called "his creative ways with fact" have been widely criticized (Shumway, *The Invention of Argentina,* p. 181). When he wrote *Facundo,* Sarmiento had never been to the pampas he describes so vividly, and critics protested that he based his biography of Facundo on anecdote and imagination, and that it is therefore largely fictitious.

From a literary perspective, *Facundo* has been characterized as "uneven and sometimes confusing, but rarely dull, rising to the height of poetry on occasion, and always full of energy, keen perception and imagination" (Jones, p. 86). Such a style is well in keeping with Sarmiento's philosophy of action, that "things have to be done. Whether they come out well or not, they have to be done" (Shumway, "The Essay in Spanish South America," p. 584). A number of critics think *Facundo* came out exceedingly well, considering it a literary masterpiece.

So strong was the impact of the essay at the time of its appearance that it instigated a retort; ***The Gaucho Martín Fierro*** (also covered in *Latin American Literature and Its Times*), written by José Hernandez and published during Sarmiento's presidential term, can be read as a pointed response to *Facundo.* A long poem detailing the life of one of the "gaucho outlaws" whom Sarmiento depicted as a type, *Martín Fierro* demonstrates how unjust laws and social conditions benefiting the wealthy landowners and porteño merchants turned the gaucho into an outlaw and drove him beyond the bounds of "civilization."

—Kimberly Ball

For More Information

Criscenti, Joseph T., ed. *Sarmiento and His Argentina.* Boulder, Colo.: Lynne Riener Publishers, 1993.

Earle, Peter G. "Domingo Faustino Sarmiento." In *Latin American Writers.* Vol. 1. New York: Charles Scribner's Sons, 1989.

Jones, C. A. *Critical Guides to Spanish Texts.* Vol. 10. *Sarmiento: Facundo.* London: Grant & Cutler Ltd., 1974.

Lynch, John. *Argentine Dictator: Juan Manuel de Rosas, 1829-1852.* Oxford: Clarendon Press, 1981.

Mosse, George L. *Toward the Final Solution: A History of European Racism.* New York: Howard Fertig, 1978.

Rock, David. *Argentina, 1516-1987: From Spanish Colonization to Alfonsín.* Berkeley: University of California Press, 1987.

Sarmiento, Domingo Faustino. *Life in the Argentine Republic in the Days of the Tyrants.* 3rd ed. Trans. by Mrs. Horace Mann. New York: Hafner Press, 1868.

Shumway, Nicolas. "The Essay in Spanish South America: 1800 to Modernismo." In *The Cambridge History of Latin American Literature.* Vol. 1. Cambridge: Cambridge University Press, 1996.

———. *The Invention of Argentina.* Berkeley: University of California Press, 1991.

Slatta, Richard W. *Gauchos and the Vanishing Frontier.* Lincoln: University of Nebraska Press, 1983.

The Fragmented Life of Don Jacobo Lerner

by
Isaac Goldemberg

One of the most vivid portraits of the world of early twentieth-century Jews in Latin America can be found in the fiction of Isaac Goldemberg. Goldemberg was born to a Jewish father and a Catholic mother on November 15, 1945, in Chepén, a small town in northern Peru where much of *The Fragmented Life of Don Jacobo Lerner* takes place. At the age of eight Goldemberg was brought to Lima by his father, and the boy immersed himself in the unfamiliar ways of the Jewish community there. At age 13 Goldemberg transferred to a dramatically different environment, a military academy in which he was the only Jew and had to defend himself from physical attack. After Goldemberg graduated from Leoncio Prado Military Academy, his father sent him to study in Israel. Goldemberg returned to Peru two years later but had no family left there and no viable means of support, so in 1964 he moved to the United States. Settling in New York, he would draw on his childhood memories to write *The Fragmented Life of Don Jacobo Lerner,* a portrait of the Jewish immigrant experience in Peru in the 1920s and early 1930s.

THE LITERARY WORK

A novel set in Peru between 1923 and 1935; published in Spanish (as *La vida a plazos de Don Jacobo Lerner*) in 1976, in English in 1976.

SYNOPSIS

On his deathbed, a Peruvian Jew looks back upon his life and recalls the events and individuals of significance to him. Intermixed with his perceptions are those of his son, sister-in-law, ex-fiancée, and mistress, as well as chronicles of events in Peru and excerpts from the news journal *Jewish Soul.*

Events in History at the Time the Novel Takes Place

Four centuries in Peru—the Jewish presence. Until 1915 religious toleration did not legally exist in Peru, since its constitution forbade the public practice of any religion other than Catholicism. Yet Jewish communities had appeared and disappeared in the land for the previous four centuries. The Spanish Inquisition, the tribunal assembled to prosecute heresy, had begun in 1492 to investigate Jews in Spain, who were forced to adopt the Catholic faith. Intending to keep the New World free of the "taint" of any Jewish or *converso* (converted Jewish) blood, Spain passed a law prohibiting either of these groups from immigrating to the Americas, but there were loopholes in the law. Crewmen on a ship, for example, did not have to show any special papers or licenses; neither did servants of voyagers. Since a good number of shipowners and captains were Jews themselves, they used these loopholes to assist mostly Portuguese Jews in making a new life for themselves in Peru, away from the hawklike eyes of the Inquisition in Spain and Portugal.

As luck would have it, the refugees did not escape the perils of the Inquisition in the New World, though. The Inquisition's court was imported into Peru in 1570. Despite its vehemence in routing out Judaizers (practicing Jews), it found few offenders at first. The community of immigrant converso Jews actually divided into two groups, those who did and those who did not clandestinely practice the Jewish faith. Together the two groups made a place for themselves in the colonial economy, excelling in trade, growing prosperous, exercising much control in colonial commerce. Their success reinforced a positive stereotype about the acumen of Jews in commerce, which, however, did little to counterbalance the negative image attached to them (discussed below). The Inquisition began over time to rout out more Judaizers, and colonists panicked, thinking about the money or goods they stood to lose if Jewish merchants were burned at the stake. In August 1635 the Inquisition arrested 64 Judaizers, thinking that it had uncovered a so-called grand conspiracy. It took three years to conclude the trials, during which no evidence of any such conspiracy ever came to light. In the end the tribunal had 11 of the prisoners burned to death at the stake, including Lima's most powerful merchant, Manuel Bautista Perez. They perished at a spectacular auto-da-fé, a public performance of the burnings designed to portray Jesus's Last Judgement. On the designated day, garbed in special robes, the prisoners were led from secret cells in the House of the Inquisition to a large platform in Lima's central plaza. Walking alongside them, friars kept exhorting the condemned to believe in Jesus Christ.

After this auto-da-fé the ferocity of the Inquisition's activity against the Jews in Peru declined. Terrorized by the incident, the remaining conversos either fled the area or conformed to surrounding society, finally disappearing altogether. But Peru's anti-Jewish attitudes persisted, even without an identifiable community. The Inquisition came to an official end in Peru only in 1820, and even after that, traces of it remained in, for example, names of streets in Lima, such as *Matar Judios* (Slaughter the Jews) and *Quemados* (the Burnings).

Distinctions are made in Judaism between followers who hail from Central and Eastern Europe (the Ashkenazim) and those from Spain, Portugal, and North Africa (the Sephardim). The original converso community, the one that disappeared, consisted of Sephardim. Next to immigrate to Peru were Ashkenazim, or more exactly, German Jews. Arriving from Central Europe in the 1840s, they developed into a full-blown community with its own burial society and cemetery by the 1870s. Primarily male, these German immigrants were mostly merchants or engineers and were not particularly observant Jews. There were some intermarriages and some conversions, and in the end this community too died out. On the other hand, shortly after the arrival of these German Jews, a Jewish contingent from North Africa immigrated to the Amazon jungle in Peru, and this community endured. It would soon be outnumbered and overshadowed, though, by the next community to surface in Lima. From the late 1800s into the early 1900s, a rising tide of Jews from Eastern Europe made its way into Latin America, at a quickening pace between World War I and World War II. It is to this last group that the novel's Don Jacobo Lerner belongs. Coming from the Russian Ukraine, Bessarabia, Turkey, and Poland, these Eastern Europeans were driven to immigrate for a mix of reasons, the most traumatic being an onslaught of deadly pogroms in the Ukraine. Those who fled to Latin America made their way mainly to Argentina, Brazil, and Uruguay; only a tiny fraction immigrated to Peru, whose total Jewish population would not even exceed 6,000 by the time that the novel was written.

Pogroms—from the Old World to the New. An organized, officially tolerated massacre of Jews, the pogrom was far from a new occurrence in European history. Isolated incidents of such anti-Jewish violence harked back to medieval times, inspired in part by anti-Semitic stereotypes. The Jews, went one groundless accusation, used the blood of Christian children for ritual purposes. They, not the Romans, went another unfounded accusation, had killed Jesus Christ. Actually the first Christian communities behaved in many ways like Jews, congregating in synagogues on the Jewish Sabbath, even in some instances practicing circumcision and observing the dietary laws. A faction of Christians, intent on wiping out these traditions, began to accuse the Jews of all sorts of crimes, including the crucifixion of Jesus Christ (Glassman, pp. 26–27). The accusations mounted until they developed into an exceedingly negative image of Jews, one that painted them as a devilish people with strange accents who exploited peasants, bribed judges, hoarded gold, demoralized women, and lured away Christians from the Church. The destructive consequences of this image waxed and waned over the centuries, culminating in a rash

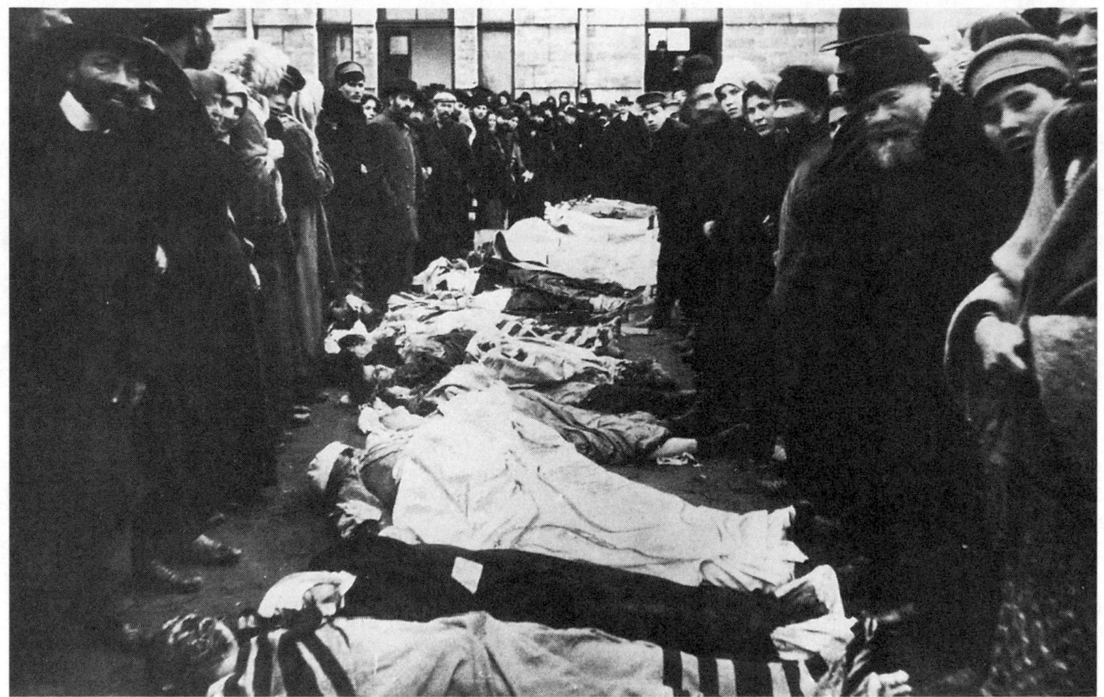

Victims of a Russian pogrom, c. 1905.

of about 2,000 pogroms in Eastern Europe between World War I and II, which ended with a vicious outbreak in the period from 1918 to 1920 (just before Jacobo emigrates from Eastern Europe in the novel).

Pogroms in the Ukraine progressed according to a well-established pattern. On horseback, Cossack soldiers would enter a small town, divide into groups of five or ten, and attack Jews on the streets, beating and sometimes stripping them. The soldiers would barge into one Jewish home after another, demanding a family's valuables. After they were handed over, the soldiers generally destroyed the house and raped its women. Meanwhile, the local peasants waited on the sidelines. In their minds Jews were the enemy. Mostly tradesman and artisans living alongside the largely peasant communities, the Jewish businesspeople represented the outsider who exploited the peasants. The peasants, who harbored this image, were primed to take revenge against their "enemy." Once the Cossacks had done their initial damage, the peasants would make their move, joining in the looting.

In the early part of this century a horrendous civil war was taking place in Russia, bringing with it enormous disarray, giving peasants and Cossack soldiers alike license to kill and loot, and encouraging havoc. The Bolshevik communist party, whose leaders included a few Jews (such as Leon Trotsky), emerged victorious. Meanwhile, another unsubstantiated belief had begun to circulate: the notion that all Jews were communists. Order returned to Russia in 1921 with the Bolshevik victory, after which the pogroms came to a halt. A conservative estimate places their 1918–21 death toll at 35,000 (Jacobo, says the novel, bore witness to a 1919 pogrom; his friend Samuel Edelman's uncle had died in a pogrom incited by Russia's czarist soldiers in 1911). Mostly the Cossacks shot or bayoneted a victim to death, but they burned, hanged, drowned, and buried Jews alive too; scores of victims "were not killed outright but wounded and left to die" (Klier and Lambroza, pp. 299-300). To escape the living nightmare—alone, confused, and dispossessed—thousands of refugees crossed the border into Germany, then proceeded, with help of Jewish relief organizations, to make their way to the New World.

Argentina received the largest influx of Jews to South America in the early twentieth century, taking in nearly 40,000 between 1921 and 1925, when Jacobo Lerner immigrates to Peru. In 1923 Argentina began to restrict Jewish immigration, deflecting newcomers to Uruguay, Chile, Peru, and other nearby countries. Along with the early 1900s immigrants came the anti-Semitic stereotypes, including the misconception that all Jews were communists.

Argentines identified the incoming Jews with Russia's revolutionaries. A pogrom erupted in an episode that has gone down in history as *Semana Trágica* (Tragic Week—January 7–13, 1919). Touching off the crisis was a strike by laborers against an iron works factory. Authorities moved in to crush the strike, workers were killed, and blame was deflected to the Jews. The government portrayed the strike as a Bolshevik plot, part of a revolution being fomented by a Jewish would-be dictator, Pinie Wald. Mobs of reactionary Argentines entered the Jewish neighborhoods of Argentina's capital, Buenos Aires, calling for the death of all Russian Jews. In a manner similar to that of outbreaks in the Ukraine—where that same year anti-Jewish violence erupted—the Argentine rabble rousers physically beat Jews in the Buenos Aires streets, stealing and burning their property in full view of the police. Estimates ascribe 850 to 1,000 deaths to the crisis, including non-Jews as well as Jews (mainly members of another minority, the Catalans, who also figured as scapegoats in the episode) (Elkin, p. 82). In light of these events, the fears of Jacobo's friend in the novel, León Mitrani, that a pogrom would descend on the small town of Chepén in Peru does not seem at all unwarranted. Reference is made also to the depredations visited upon Jews by Germany in the early 1930s, when the Nazi party was preparing to kill all Europe's Jews in the Holocaust of World War II. In the novel Mitrani hears that thousands of Jews in Europe are being dispossessed by Germany, driven from their homes, and mistreated in a manner reminiscent of the pogroms. He worries that the Germans will come to Chepén, an understandable if more farfetched fear, given his earlier pogrom experience.

Peddlers in Peru. In 1925, a few years after immigrating to Peru, Jacobo Lerner, dressed in a felt hat and dark coat, a suitcase full of trinkets on his shoulder, joins his friend Mitrani in the small town of Chepén. Jacobo has been a peddler and aspires now to open a store and stay put. In fact, 90 percent of the Jews who immigrated to Peru in the early 1900s began as peddlers, their long-range goal being to purchase a fixed place of business and give up life on the road. They contributed something of moment to Peru's domestic economy. As yet, no part of the business community had made everyday items accessible to the large mass of peasants who did not have sufficient cash to buy them at a store. The peddler arrived at the peasant's door with an assortment of necessities and other items—matches, scissors, razor blades, cloth, kitchen utensils, religious artifacts—which he sold on credit for a small downpayment and weekly installments. Thereafter, the peddler returned to collect his installments and sell more, taking as much as 100 percent profit, which was considered necessary and fair, given the high risk of doing business without any collateral, on the strength of only a promise. There were three levels through which a peddler might progress:

1) klapper—a "door knocker," who went on the road with his pack to individual homes to peddle and distribute wares;
2) cuentanik—an accounts collector, who built up a clientele and made weekly visits to retrieve the sum owed him;
3) clientelchik—a businessman who, after putting together a few hundred regular customers, hired newer immigrants as klappers and preoccupied himself with collecting on his accounts.

Since Lima was too small to support many Jewish peddlers, some branched out into the provinces, but life on the road was far from easy. Aside from the normal perils of a solitary, unsettled existence, the peddlers faced growing anti-Semitism. Exposed as forgeries in 1921 but nevertheless widely circulated in Europe and the United States, the documents called the *Protocols of the Elders of Zion* suggested that the Jews had set out to conquer all of the non-Jewish world. Newspapers capitalized on the sensationalism of the documents, despite the evidence that they were forgeries, and anti-Semitic tracts appeared that repeated the diabolical notions. Among these tracts was the *International Jew* put out by U.S. automotive maker Henry Ford; as early as 1927 he retracted the anti-Semitic charges, forbidding his name to be linked to them. But the damage had been done; they circulated in a cheap Spanish edition that made its way into Peru.

The Novel in Focus

Plot summary. An amalgamation of excerpts from the newspaper *Jewish Soul,* chronicles of events in Peru, and a narrative told through the viewpoints of Jacobo Lerner; his sister-in-law, Sara; her sister, Miriam; his friend, Samuel Edelman; Jacobo's mistress, doña Juana Paredes; and his son, Efraín, the novel creates a portrait of the small Jewish immigrant community of the 1920s and early 1930s. Its tone is nonjudgmental, although the juxtaposing of the different elements creates moments of humor and irony.

Chronicles of events in Peru, such as the coup against President Augusto B. Leguía and warfare with Colombia, are juxtaposed to news excerpts in the *Jewish Soul* about a picnic, a theatrical event, and medical findings. Reaching into history, other items in the *Jewish Soul* refer to victims of the Inquisition. Still others dwell on the contribution of Jews to the exploration of Peru, declare that there is no anti-Semitism in Peru, and admonish readers to assimilate—"We embrace our new nationality. . . . Jew, become a Peruvian citizen" (Goldemberg, *The Fragmented Life of Don Jacobo Lerner,* p. 34). Letters to the editor share lively opinions and delusions, predicting that the racial mixture of the Indian and Jew will produce a hearty, cunning new breed, in contradistinction to the example in the narrative of the physically and mentally troubled Efraín Lerner.

Written in discontinuous fragments, the narrative concerns the experiences of Jacobo Lerner, from his arrival in Peru in 1923 to his deathbed at the close of 1935. Separated from his childhood friend, León Mitrani, he unexpectedly finds him in Peru. At first Jacobo settles in Lima, where he begins his days as a peddler. Mitrani urges him to open a store in the small town of Chepén, assuring Jacobo that he will grow rich in a short time. Jacobo arrives to find that his friend has become a shell of a man, limping, old before his time, married to a blind woman—and a Catholic at that. But there is difficulty in finding a Jewish woman to wed; as their mutual friend, the traveling peddler Samuel Edelman asks, "Marry a Jewish woman? Fine. And if there aren't any? How long must one wait?" (*The Fragmented Life,* p. 22). Still, Jacobo's ambitions are to find a good Jewish wife—someone like his sister-in-law, Sara, whom he wishes were his—and to prosper. He is consigned, however, to a much grimmer fate. Jacobo has an affair with a local *mestizo,* Bertila Wilson; when she becomes pregnant, he flees. His reaction is both irresponsible and fearful; he is haunted by the specter of Mitrani's vapid existence. She has a son, Efraín.

Jacobo becomes a traveling peddler again, never returning to Chepén. He joins his brother in Lima for a time, where together they run a shoestore. A year later the brother, Moisés, swindles Jacobo and gets away with it. Moisés continues on in the store and becomes the patriarch of Lima's nascent Jewish community. Meanwhile, the deceived Jacobo takes to the road again, but life on the road is perilous, and ultimately he returns to Lima to stay. This time Jacobo invests in a brothel and prospers. With his financial success coming from such a scandalous source, he suffers spiritual deterioration and grows increasingly isolated. Jacobo takes a mistress, a Catholic woman, doña Juana Paredes, who perceives the goodness in him, his generosity to people in need. He almost marries his sister-in-law's sister, Miriam, but the match is broken off by the interference of his mistress's sister. Through the interior monologue of Jacobo and other characters, we learn that he feels conflicted about his son. At one point he asks his sister-in-law, Sara, to take in the boy—whom he himself never meets—but she refuses. Though admired by Jacobo, Sara actually reveals herself to be a mostly vacuous character.

HOW SMALL A MINORITY?

In Lima, where the majority of Peruvian Jews live, the group's population totaled about 300 in 1917; it climbed to 1,500 in 1933, but this still amounted to a tiny fraction of the national population. In 1940 Peru's first census of the century counted a total population of 7 million. Nearly half (46 percent) of the total were Indians and more than half (62 percent) still sustained themselves by raising crops or livestock.

> What madness to have a son with an Indian woman! I really can't let him into my house. What am I going to do with a boy who isn't even one of our people? . . . It wasn't enough that he got involved with her, he had to give her a son. . . . Now he wants his son to come and live with us! Maybe Moisés is happy. Maybe that's the only way he can get Jacobo's money. And the community would speak so well of us if we take care of the child.
>
> (*The Fragmented Life,* p. 117)

Jacobo's mistress, Juana Paredes, offers to raise the boy, but Jacobo rages at the thought of his son being brought up in a non-Jewish household. Yet until now Efraín has been raised in the Catholic household of Bertila, receiving attention only from his religious Aunt Francisca and from the local priest, Father Chirinos, who attempt to raise him as a good Christian. Neither tells him the truth about who his father is or where he lives:

> ". . . [I]s it true that my father was a Jew like Mr. Mitrani?"

"I only know that he didn't believe in our Lord Jesus Christ, as every good Christian should."

"Is it true that the Jews killed Christ?"

"Yes. They tormented him on the cross, without mercy, until he died."

Then I ran crying out of his room and out of the church, and I was still crying when I got home. I couldn't sleep all night thinking of what Father Chirinos had said, and in the morning I asked my grandfather who my father had been, and like other times he told me not to bother him. . . .

(*The Fragmented Life,* p. 109)

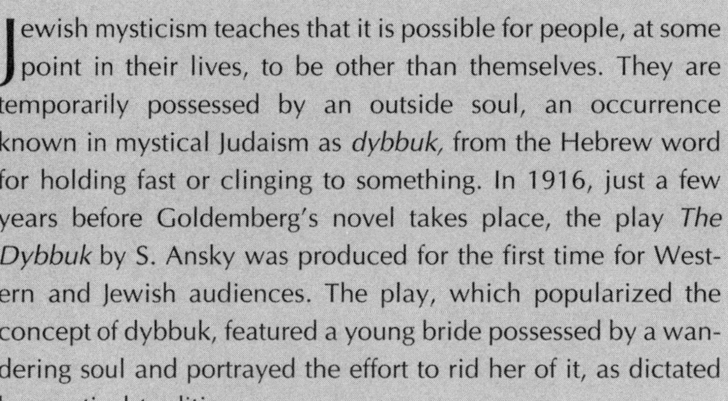

DYBBUK—BELIEFS ABOUT WANDERING SOULS

Jewish mysticism teaches that it is possible for people, at some point in their lives, to be other than themselves. They are temporarily possessed by an outside soul, an occurrence known in mystical Judaism as *dybbuk,* from the Hebrew word for holding fast or clinging to something. In 1916, just a few years before Goldemberg's novel takes place, the play *The Dybbuk* by S. Ansky was produced for the first time for Western and Jewish audiences. The play, which popularized the concept of dybbuk, featured a young bride possessed by a wandering soul and portrayed the effort to rid her of it, as dictated by mystical tradition:

> RABBI AZRAEL: I am filled with profound pity for you, wandering soul! And I will use all my power to save you from the evil spirits. But the body of this maiden you must leave.
>
> (Ansky, p. 110)

He decides not to ask questions of Mitrani, who has informed Efraín that his father is alive and well in Lima, because Aunt Francisca has told him that the Jew grinds up little boys and bakes them. Meanwhile, his mother, Bertila, takes little interest in her son. She travels alone to Lima to unload him on Jacobo, but he throws her out, refusing even to acknowledge Efraín as his own. Abandoned by his father and his mother, barely tolerated by his grandfather, and in time rejected even by his aunt and the priest, the boy endures extreme loneliness. In the end his sense of desolation borders on madness. Efraín winds up in a corner, conversing with a spider, which, in a wrenching scene, he gobbles up. His interior monologue nonetheless conveys information about other characters. Through his debilitating emotional isolation, as well as through the interior monologue of Samuel Edelman, we learn of a riveting event that transpires in the town of Chepén.

Mitrani impresses the townspeople as crazy—he takes to ranting outside the church. One day, with Father Chirinos watching—Efraín spots Chirinos in the main square—they garb him in purple, place a crown of thorns on his head, and dub him King of the Jews. Dragging the purple-cloaked Mitrani into the street, the townspeople proceed to beat him, spit at him, stick him up on a cross and shove a lance into his ribs, leaving him there "with blood dripping down his body while everyone insulted him" (*The Fragmented Life,* pp. 126–27). Mitrani dies and Samuel Edelman has his body sent to Lima for a Jewish burial, but the coffin gets lost, an ominous event that portends trouble for Jacobo. Back in Lima, he begins to feel possessed by his friend's wandering soul. Like Mitrani, Jacobo starts obsessing about pogroms and the coming of the Germans to his house. A rabbi treats him, managing finally to exorcise Mitrani's soul and to reassert Jacobo's sense of self.

Tradition teaches that possessions are never random. A wandering soul enters someone who is ripe to receive it, by invitation or because of a weakened state of mind. People with a tenuous hold on their sense of self are susceptible. In the novel, Jacobo certainly qualifies. After taking ownership of the whorehouse, he cuts himself off from the Jewish tradition that kept him anchored until then. Earlier, his friend, Edelman, had written to the *Jewish Soul,* advocating assimilation in Peru. Jacobo responded, disagreeing with Edelman's views. Assimilation, he warned in his own letter to the editor, threatens us; yes, we can adopt some Peruvian customs, but we must remain Jews in spirit, in religion, in tradition. Given this earlier vehemence, his subsequent abandonment of religious observance is indicative of a weakened soul indeed.

"On the night of the 17th of August [1935], Rabbi Schneider finally succeeded and the spirit of León Mitrani abandoned Jacobo's body through the big toe of his right foot" (*The Fragmented Life,* p. 159). Two months later "Doctor Bernardo Rabinowitz shows up at the house of Jacobo Lerner to tell him that he, Jacobo, is going to die," whereupon Jacobo has the "tangle of memories" that surface in the novel. It closes, though, not with his death but with the pathetic portrait of his son, Efraín, in chilling conversation with his compatriot in the corner, the only one the boy has to talk to—a spider (*The Fragmented Life,* pp. 164, 176).

Mixed messages. In the novel the *Jewish Soul* depicts the Jewish community of Lima as a very philanthropic, paternalistic society concerned about the welfare of all Jewish immigrants, while vehemently proclaiming patriotic adhesion to Peruvian nationality. Although the journal insists upon the social and economic contributions of Jews to Peruvian culture, the only evidence of integration found in its pages are exhortations to acquire Peruvian citizenship and accounts of meetings of the Hebrew Union where members sing both Peruvian and Hebrew songs and dance the Peruvian waltz. The novel's structure lends itself to an ironic interpretation of the official attitude of the Jewish community.

In the Chronicles sections, news of Jewish social gatherings are juxtaposed with reports of major historical events in a period of political turmoil and economic depression for Peru. This narrative strategy suggests the isolation of the Jewish community from surrounding Peruvian society. For example, the Chronicles report the overthrow of President Leguía's government by a military regime headed by Luis Sánchez Cerro and the drive to power of the populist leader Víctor Raúl Haya de la Torre. These events bring the country close to a civil war as it experiences naval mutinies, assassination attempts, and a provincial insurrection. In the Chronicles, these political reports alternate with reports about the actions of the novel's Jewish characters, such as Jacobo Lerner's gift of a Sefer-Tora (a scroll of the first five books of the Hebrew Bible) to the synagogue. Jews and Peruvians seem to live separate, parallel worlds.

The *Jewish Soul* touches on events in Peru only insofar as they relate to the Jews, including items, for example, on the persecution of Jews during the Inquisition and anti-Semitic propaganda in the Peruvian press. The integration into larger society promoted by the *Jewish Soul* appears illusory; through its mix of Chronicles, news items, and interior monologue, the novel shows the identity of the Jewish community to be rooted in European social, religious, and historical traditions with little participation in the larger Peruvian scene. The Jewish community of the 1920s and 1930s lives in its almost air-tight, isolated space.

Torn between two cultures. Jacobo Lerner never recovers from the shock of feeling lost and displaced and remains on the margins of two cultures: the Jewish and the Peruvian. He tries without success to make a place for himself in Peruvian society as a Jew. His first cultural crossover occurs when he is in Chepén, a small town in northern Peru, where he has an affair with Bertila Wilson and sires a Peruvian son. Bertila's father, who refers to Jacobo as "the Jew," welcomes him as a prospective son-in-law because he believes in the stereotype of wealthy Jews, and his devotion is to money. But Jacob rejects marriage to Bertila, because he cares about his Jewish roots and membership in the current Jewish community of Lima:

> He wanted to marry a Jewish woman and have many children. He wanted to live in the capital surrounded by all the luxuries that money could give him. He wanted to go to the synagogue with his friends, to celebrate religious holidays surrounded by his family and to see the bar-mitzvah of his sons. This order of things in his mind was what he leaned on to survive in a country where the way people lived was extremely strange to him. To stay in Chepén now meant giving up all this, to break with the traditional order of his family and his race, in short, to be swirled up in chaos.
>
> (*The Fragmented Life,* pp. 71-72)

There is a defining moment in the novel when Jacobo spends a restless night in a hotel near Chepén. He stands at a crossroads—one path leads to Chepén and his Peruvian family. That he contemplates taking the path to Chepén is evident from a letter he writes to the *Jewish Soul* that night, arguing against the advice of his friend Samuel Edelman to assimilate into Peruvian society, insisting that, while some customs can be adopted, Jews must remain separate in spirit, religion, and tradition. In the end, Jacobo opts not to enter Chepén, to go in another direction that ultimately leads to his final disgrace—partnership with Abraham Singer in the prostitution business. The choice finally brings him financial security and a kind of adaptation to Peruvian society, but ironically it also prompts him to reject his Jewish origins:

> He . . . had cut the umbilical cord that tied him to the universe. Not even in the nervous solitude of his own home did he fulfill his obligations as a Jew, which he had once considered the only source of order in his chaotic life.
>
> (*The Fragmented Life,* p. 149)

Jacobo seems to reject himself for trafficking in prostitution, just as the Jewish community (represented by his sister-in-law) condemns him for the illicit business; his imminent physical death is preceded by this spiritual death. That Jacobo was not the only immigrant who felt trapped and miserable is suggested by other characters mentioned in the novel—the gambler Daniel Abramowitz, who commits suicide, and Lubin, who sets fire to his own store.

COLEGIO LEÓN PINELO

The Jewish school in Peru is named after the Marrano, or secret Jew, León de Pinelo. An important figure in Spanish colonial culture, Pinelo was a poet, theologian, and historian, who documented the experience of the Indians. The Inquisition discovered that in Portugal his family had been accused of practicing Judaism and one of his uncles was burned at the stake. The news threatened Pinelo's safety in Peru, where the intervention of the Archbishop of Lima prevented him from being persecuted, allowing him to escape the Inquisition.

Sources and literary context. There are a few parallels between Efraín's life in the novel and the life of the author. Both of them were born in Chepén to a Catholic mother and a Jewish immigrant father. In contrast to Jacobo Lerner, though, at the age of eight, Goldemberg was taken into his father's house in Lima. There the son immersed himself in his new Jewish environment: "I began to ask myself who am I, what am I" (Goldemberg in Meyer, p. 301). Over the next ten years he read novels that stimulated thoughts and feelings in him about his mixed-race heritage. As a teenager he read the novel ***Deep Rivers*** (also covered in *Latin American Literature and Its Times*) by Peru's José María Arguedas about a boy struggling to reconcile the different cultural strands of his heritage: "This book by Arguedas," Goldemberg has explained, "would be vitally important to me and would spur me to examine a similar problem in my own writings: the cultural and racial crossbreeding in Peru, incorporating history and myth" (Goldemberg in Meyer, p. 303). Other influential readings include *Trilce* (1922), a collection of poems by Peru's César Vallejo about family and the search for lasting values in a changing world. In reference to *The Fragmented Life of Don Jacobo Lerner*, Goldemberg has identified motivations for the writing of it: "Using autobiographical material, it brings together the most important experiences of my childhood: my early Catholic upbringing, the experience of exile, the clash between Jewish and Peruvian culture. . . . To a large degree, the story of the novel . . . is only a backdrop for the recreation of an experience that is at once historical and mythical: the Jewish exile" (Goldemberg in Meyers, p. 304).

Events in History at the Time the Novel Was Written

Peruvian Jewry. Peru in the 1960s and 1970s still claimed a relatively small Jewish community compared to those elsewhere in Latin America:

Population of Latin American Jews*

Argentina	450,000
Brazil	140,000
Uruguay	50,000
Mexico	40,000
Chile	30,000
Venezuela	12,000-15,000
Colombia	11,000
Peru	5,000

*(1960s estimates)

(*Encyclopaedia Judaica* [New York: Keter, 1971], vol. 10, p. 10)

Peru's Jewish population increased only slightly as the decades passed, numbering about 5,300 in 1972, nearly all of whom lived in Lima. Latin American Jewish communities of the time mostly consisted of middle-class families who led comfortable lifestyles and saw to it that their children received fine educations. In Lima, the children attended León Pinelo Jewish day school, Goldemberg's own alma mater.

In other respects, there were changes in the profile of the Jewish community between the setting and writing of the novel. Only a few years after it takes place, in 1939, Peru outlawed peddling, and the Jewish community went through a transitional phase. Subsequent immigrants became wholesalers, importers, and laborers in the textile industry. Their children went on to study in universities, becoming engineers, physicians, and professors.

Relations with Israel have helped reduce the anti-Semitic notions that circulated in Peruvian society over the years. Peru has dispatched specialists to study Israel's cooperative farming; Israel has sent irrigation experts to Peru to conduct experimental work in its desert. More generally, in Latin America as a whole—espe-

Polish Jews bound for South America, 1937. Immigrants from Eastern Europe formed a distinct subcommunity in the Jewish population of Peru in the 1970s, when *The Fragmented Life of Don Jacobo Lerner* was written.

cially in Peru and Chile—key members of the Roman Catholic Church hierarchy have joined with organized Jewish communities to reduce the amount of free-floating anti-Semitism, which has, however, shown resistance to change. In the words of one historian, "the most active manipulators of anti-Semitic attitudes in recent years have been the cults centered around Nazi war criminals who found refuge in Latin America and Arab cadres who have forged a bond between Middle Eastern and Latin American guerrillas" (Elkin, p. 232).

The Jewish community of Peru in the 1970s still retained a separate identity. By then it consisted of three subcommunities: Sephardic, Eastern European, and a new set of German Jews who began immigrating to Peru in the 1930s. Each of the three subcommunities worshipped in its own synagogue under a separate rabbi, but they shared one cemetery and a Central Committee that organized them into a whole. In 1926 the Eastern European community formed a Hebrew union, the *Union Israelita del Peru,* which, beginning in 1931, published the monthly magazine *Nosotros* (transformed in the novel into the newspaper *Jewish Soul*).

In the late 1960s members of Lima's younger Jewish generation showed a keen awareness of their roots. Michael Radzinsky, an Eastern European immigrant who had become a textile manufacturer, passed the reins of community leadership to Azi Wolfenson-Ulanowsky, a dean of the engineering school.

> "I know," said Wolfenson-Ulanowsky, "that I am assuming the leadership of a 400-years-old community. I know where the Inquisition tribunal stood, where our forefathers were burnt at the stake. . . . I . . . am now called upon to be the spiritual heir of these martyrs."
>
> (Wolfenson-Ulanowsky in Beller, p. 139)

Such a declaration bespeaks a strong Peruvian Jewish sense of self, a sense that, in the novel, escapes Jacobo Lerner, one of the immigrants stuck in the flux of an earlier formative era.

Reviews. In the *Times Literary Supplement* (March 10, 1978), Michael Irwin faults *The Fragmented Life of Don Jacobo Lerner* for its narrative complexity, warning that the reader must be constantly on guard to understand and relate the novel's various fragments. He concludes, though, by heralding the work as an unusually promising first novel. In contrast, Lorraine E. Roses is full of praise for the fragmented style of the work:

> The dual structure of the novel—documentary collage and narrative—permits [Goldemberg] to unveil the conditions of underdevelopment that, once again, push Jews to commerce in illegal traffic and dramatize the provincial Catholic fanaticism which goes hand in hand with hatred of any possible plurality. . . . In a more overwhelming way than Pedro Páramo or Artemio Cruz [see ***Pedro Páramo*** and ***The Death of Artemio Cruz,*** also covered in *Latin American Literature and Its Times*], both of whom at one time enjoyed some sort of social position and the warmth of an emotional life, Jacobo Lerner symbolizes . . . sterility without redemption (Roses in Flores, p. 377).

—Jennifer Garson Shapiro and Joyce Moss

For More Information

Ansky, S. *The Dybbuk.* Trans. Henry Alsberg and Winifred Katzin. New York: Liveright Publishing, 1926.

Beller, Jacob. *Jews in Latin America.* New York: Jonathan David Publishers, 1969.

Elkin, Judith Laikin. *Jews of the Latin American Republics.* Chapel Hill: University of North Carolina Press, 1980.

Encyclopaedia Judaica. Vol. 10. Jerusalem: Keter Publishing, 1971.

Flores, Angel. *Spanish American Authors.* New York: H. W. Wilson, 1992.

Glassman, Samuel. *Epic of Survival: Twenty-Five Centuries of Anti-Semitism.* New York: Bloch, 1980.

Goldemberg, Isaac. *The Fragmented Life of Don Jacobo Lerner.* Trans. Robert Picciotto. New York: Peresa, 1976.

Klier, John D., and Shlomo Lambroza, eds. *Pogroms: Anti-Jewish Violence in Modern Russian History.* Cambridge: Cambridge University Press, 1992.

Kristal, Efrain. "Goldemberg: a caballo entres dos culturas." *Huseo húmero* 7 (Octubre-Diciembre 1980): 53-66

Meyer, Doris, ed. *Lives on the Line: The Testimony of Contemporary Latin American Authors.* Berkeley: University of California Press, 1988.

Pike, Fredrick. *The Modern History of Peru.* London: Weidenfeld & Nicolson, 1967.

Gabriela, Clove and Cinnamon

by
Jorge Amado

Born on a cacao plantation in 1912, Jorge Amado was the son of well-to-do landowners in the city of Ilhéus in the state of Bahia. Educated in Bahia, he worked on several student newspapers, and by 1928 he was a police reporter for the *Diário da Bahia*. Amado moved to Rio de Janeiro to finish his studies, entering law school there in 1931. His first novel, *O país do carnaval* (Carnival Land), appeared that same year, followed in 1933 by *Cacau* (Cocoa)—which was confiscated by the Brazilian government for its procommunist inclinations. The two novels mark the start of a prolific career, leading to about 18 more novels by Amado over the next six decades. Aside from writing, Amado was involved in politics early in his career: in 1937 he was arrested for his leftist political activities in opposition to the dictatorial regime of Getúlio Vargas. Upon his release, Amado fled to Argentina and Uruguay. Returning to Brazil in 1941, he was again arrested and ordered to remain in Salvador, a city in Bahia. After the fall of Vargas's government in 1945, Amado was elected to the Brazilian Congress as a Communist candidate. The Communist Party was outlawed in 1947, and Amado moved with his family to Paris, where he remained until 1952. When Amado subsequently returned to Brazil, his political views were more moderate. His later works, including the 1958 *Gabriela, Clove and Cinnamon,* show less interest in politics than in the human comedy and aspects of daily Bahian life.

THE LITERARY WORK

A novel set in Ilhéus, a coastal city in Brazil, in 1925-26; published in Portuguese (as *Gabriela, cravo e canela*) in 1958, in English in 1962.

SYNOPSIS

The on-again off-again romance between Nacib, an Arabic bar owner, and Gabriela, his mulatto cook and wife/mistress, unfolds against a backdrop of social and political developments in a changing Brazilian city.

Events in History at the Time the Novel Takes Place

From monarchy to republic—an overview. *Gabriela, Clove and Cinnamon* is set in Brazil in the last years of the "Old Republic" (1889-1930). A sense of the recent and not-so-recent past pervades Ilhéus, as the elaborate Nativity scene of the Dos Reis sisters demonstrates. Constantly refurbished and extended, this tableau—created by silent, motionless actors as if in a picture—depicts not only the birth of Christ but "a kaleidoscopic, growing world in which the most diverse scenes and figures, from the most divergent periods of history, mingled democratically with one another" (Amado, *Gabriela, Clove and Cinnamon,*

p. 55). One of these figures is Dom Pedro II, Brazil's last emperor; in fact, allusions to the defunct Brazilian monarchy and to the political strife that plagued the republic since its inception appear throughout the novel.

"THE LANGUOR OF OFENÍSIA"

The first chapter of *Gabriela, Clove and Cinnamon,* entitled the "Languor of Ofenísia," traces the infatuation of Ofenísia d'Ávila with the dashing Dom Pedro II. In the novel the Doctor, a scholarly character, devotes his intellectual life to a study of the chaste romance between Dom Pedro II and one of the Doctor's ancestors, Ofenísia d'Ávila, whom the emperor met on a trip to Bahia. Although this alleged love affair consisted only of sighs and glances, the Doctor perpetuates through his writings the image of languid Ofenísia, refusing all men while pining for the emperor and "his black and scholarly beard" (*Gabriela,* p. 27). Photographs and contemporary accounts reveal that Dom Pedro II did indeed have a long and bushy beard. He was also very tall (six-feet four-inches), blue-eyed, and handsome—an undeniably romantic figure.

Brazil had been a Portuguese colony since its "discovery" by the explorer Pedro Álvares Cabral in 1500. Serious colonization efforts did not begin until more than 25 years after Cabral's expedition, and Portugal kept strict control of Brazil's resources and activities. Despite a number of attempts at rebellion, the colony remained under the aegis of Portugal. In 1808 Brazil became a refuge for the Portuguese monarchy when, after failing to persuade Portugal to join his alliance against England, Napoleon Bonaparte sent his armies into Lisbon, Portugal's capital. Dom João, Portugal's regent since his mother, Maria I, had gone insane, decided to remove the entire royal family—the mad queen, himself, his wife, and their six children—to Brazil. Escorted by the British navy, approximately 15,000 people took part in the exodus of the royal court, squeezing aboard some 40 merchant vessels. Along with Dom João came as many treasures as he could transport: art, jewels, and about 60,000 books, which became the foundation of Brazil's national library. Beginning November 29, 1807, the journey lasted 52 days and was, by all accounts, a hideous ordeal, marked by storms, seasickness, and ever-dwindling rations.

The Portuguese royals soon established themselves in Rio de Janeiro, the Brazilian capital, and Dom João set about transforming the colonial city into a place fit for royalty, establishing a national library, an academy of fine arts, a royal school of medicine, a print shop, a national bank, a mint, and botanical gardens. He even oversaw the construction of an aqueduct that would keep the city supplied with fresh water. Altogether these improvements occurred within the relatively short span of 13 years. Dom João loosened Brazil's ties with Lisbon, now controlled by Napoleon, and encouraged British trade.

In 1821, after Napoleon's defeat, Dom João—who had succeeded to Portugal's throne on his mother's death in 1816—was recalled to Portugal. He departed reluctantly, leaving his eldest son, Dom Pedro, in Brazil as its regent. Back in Portugal, a legislative assembly known as the Côrtes attempted to undo Dom João's earlier work and to restore Brazil to its former status as a subservient Portuguese colony. On September 7, 1822, Dom Pedro received a transatlantic directive from the Côrtes, diminishing his authority and ordering him back to Portugal. In response, Dom Pedro reportedly drew his sword and shouted, "Independence or death!" (Page, p. 52). A month later, a Brazilian convention declared him emperor, and he was soon crowned the new nation's constitutional monarch. Within a year, the Brazilian rebels, after a series of battles in which they were aided by the British, achieved the complete withdrawal of Portuguese troops with surprisingly little bloodshed.

Despite his success in making Brazil an independent nation, Pedro I had a troubled reign. The constitution he established in 1824 lasted until 1889, but the emperor's Brazilian subjects resented his "broad powers" as well as his reliance on Portuguese advisors. Revolts and riots broke out frequently, as various regional factions felt their needs were not being addressed. Pedro also made some unpopular foreign policy decisions, paying off part of Portugal's debt in exchange for Portugese recognition of Brazil's independence, and committing Brazil to disadvantageous trade agreements with Great Britain. In 1831, after street demonstrations erupted over a change in the imperial cabinet, Pedro I abdicated the Brazilian throne and returned to Portugal. In 1840, after a regency period, his fifteen-year-old son became Dom Pedro II.

Unlike his father and grandfather, Dom Pedro II was a very popular ruler, "intellectually curious, bookish, thoughtful, genteel, and romantic"

Engraving of Dom Pedro II.

(Page, p. 54). Fluent in many languages, Dom Pedro II was also an indefatigable traveler, whose energy and enthusiasm endeared him to his hosts at home and abroad.

Dom Pedro II's reign was long and, despite a war with Paraguay (1865-70), fairly peaceful. It spanned an important transitional period in Brazil's history—coffee replaced gold and sugar as the country's main resource, massive immigration was encouraged, the pace of industrialization quickened, and slavery was abolished in 1888. However, despite Brazilians' affection for their emperor as an individual and a symbol, many considered their monarchy to be an anachronism. In November 1889 the 63-year-old emperor and his wife were ousted by a military revolt and exiled to Portugal. The empress died less than a month later; Dom Pedro went to France, where pneumonia claimed his life in 1891.

Initially, Brazil's new republican government consisted of an unstable collaboration between the positivists, who dreamed of transforming Brazil into a utopia; the military faction led by Marshal Manuel Deodoro de Fonseca, who became the republic's first president; and the owners of large plantations. The positivists soon severed their connection to the government, their ideals having been thwarted by the reality of practical politics. Eight months into his presidency, the autocratic Marshal Deodoro dissolved the new congress and attempted to rule by decree, sparking a rebellion that forced him out of office in 1891. But his immediate successor, Floriano Peixoto, nicknamed the "Iron Marshal," proved to be even more tyrannical: naval rebellions and a civil war in the South marred his administration. The next president, Prudente de Moraes, from São Paulo, had to deal with a "holy war" in the backlands of Bahia.

Eventually, the new republic stabilized—presidential candidates were selected at meetings of state governments and a candidate who garnered 80-90 per cent of the electoral vote was guaranteed victory. Not surprisingly, the larger states dominated the smaller ones. For many years, the presidency alternated by mutual arrangement between candidates from the states of São Paulo and Minas Gerais. This policy, known as "coffee and milk"—referring to the respective main resources of São Paulo and Minas Gerais—began in 1906 and lasted until 1930.

Brazilians wanted more than stability, though. The First World War (1914-18), and the resulting social agitation, impressed upon them the urgent need for social and political reforms. Universal suffrage, for example, was still denied, which undermined the Republic's claims of democracy. During the 1920s more political factions emerged, and two new rebellions threatened the government. On July 5, 1922, the first centenary of Brazilian independence, 18 idealistic army officers at Copacabana Fort in Rio de Janeiro dismissed their troops and marched alone against government forces. Nearly all were shot and killed on the spot, but their deaths inspired another revolutionary movement in São Paulo on July 5, 1924. The second uprising was also defeated, after which the conspirators split into two groups, one finding asylum in Bolivia, the other in Argentina. The leader of one of the groups, Luiz Carlos Prestes, later became chief of the Brazilian Communists. Though shaken by these revolts, the republic maintained a precarious national stability until another rebellion swept Getúlio Vargas into office in 1930.

Colonels, bandits, and politics. The Vargas regime is still several years away when *Gabriela, Clove and Cinnamon* begins in 1925. In the novel the ambitious, reform-minded Mundinho Falcão faces the greatest opposition to his bid as federal congressman from the local *coronéis* or "colonels" in Ilhéus. While some colonels respond favorably to Falcão's progressive agenda—especially his plan to dredge a channel through the sandbar in the Ilhéan harbor—Ramiro Bastos, the oldest and arguably the most powerful of them, remains violently opposed. Determined to defeat Falcão at all costs, he declares: "No one else is going to rule Ilhéus. . . . There'll be an election a year from now and I'm going to win it . . . even if the whole world turns against me, even if Ilhéus has to become again a land of bandits and killers" (*Gabriela,* p. 242). Bastos is not making idle threats: colonels could—and did—exert a powerful influence over the hotly contested elections of the time.

Although the title of "colonel" apparently originated in the National Guard, the term soon acquired political as well as military connotations. *Coronelismo,* a term for which there is no literal translation, has been defined to reflect the different realms of life into which such a strongman's power extended:

> A monopolistic exercise of power by a coronel whose legitimacy and acceptance are based on and buttressed by his paramount status as the dominant element in social, economic, and political institutions such as prevailed during the transition period from a rural agrarian nation to an urban industrial one.
>
> (Pang, *Bahia in the First Brazilian Republic,* p. 2)

Frequently, though not exclusively, colonels were wealthy landowners who controlled politics, especially elections, at the municipal level, although their actions had significant ramifications at the state and federal levels of government too.

When the social, political, and economic favors that were their stock in trade proved insufficient to win an election, colonels resorted to buying votes, filling out the roster with the names of phantom voters, and even inciting riots that could then be used as an excuse to cancel the results. In Amado's novel, Colonel Bastos considers such strategies after Falcão attracts more supporters and his chances of victory improve. The colonel's supporters plan to take matters into their own hands: "It was suggested that they set up the election in the old way—that is, that they take control of the electoral boards, the voting places, and the record books. An election made to order" (*Gabriela,* p. 301). And if political alliances and tampering with the electoral process still did not achieve the colonels' ends, there was a more permanent solution: assassination.

To eliminate a rival permanently, colonels often hired bandits from Brazil's Northeastern backlands. Drought, poverty, and other socioeconomic pressures had driven many Brazilian peasants into lives of banditry. They were not motivated by a particular political agenda, but by economics. Indeed, the bandits' lack of an ideology made them ideal for the colonels' purposes, especially during the very competitive elections of the 1910s and 1920s:

> As a highly mobile group, bandits became sources of political intelligence for competing coroneis. Bandits were hired out as election enforcers, killed personal as well as public enemies of their employers, and received protection from legal prosecution. This mutually protective system, known as *coiteirismo,* kept the bandits available to but not totally under the control of coroneis.
>
> (Pang, "Agrarian Change," p. 131)

In *Gabriela, Clove and Cinnamon,* Bastos's allies try to assassinate the Mayor of Itabuna when he defects to Falcão's side. Their hired gunman, Fagundes, has traveled with backlander outlaws in the past and is a skilled marksman. Fagundes eludes capture, and his employer, Colonel Tavares, on whose cacao plantation Fagundes works, later tells the outlaw that he will soon be needed for another shooting in Ilhéus.

Racial attitudes in the 1920s. Although slavery in Brazil was abolished in 1888, racial prejudices persisted. Until massive immigration began in the late 1800s, the three main racial strains in Brazil originated from a relatively small percentage of Portuguese colonists, and much larger populations of native Amerindians and African slaves. Contemporary European racist theories argued that a country inhabited by so many "non-white" races could never achieve greatness as a world power. In defense of their nation, Brazilian intellectuals reiterated the "whitening thesis" first proposed by abolitionists in the 1870s: "Abolitionists believed that miscegenation would gradually and inexorably 'whiten' and thereby 'upgrade' the Brazilian population. . . . Ergo: the whiter the better" (Skidmore, p. 9). An unsubstantiated belief that blacks and mulattos had a low reproduction rate lent credibility to the whitening thesis. Large-scale immigration, especially by light-skinned Europeans, was encouraged from 1888 to 1914, in the belief that several generations of miscegenation would result in a "whiter" people.

BRAZIL'S BANDIT KINGS

In the novel the Dos Reis sisters' tableau features one of the most famous Northeastern bandits: Antônio Silvino (1875-1914?), who inspired the popular myth of the "gentleman bandit." After killing two men associated with the murder of his father, Silvino became an outlaw. His fame was rivaled by that of Virgulino Ferreira da Silva (1897-1938), popularly known as Lampião, "the Lantern," because his rifle gave off so much light in his rapid firing of it. Lampião and his two brothers likewise chose lives of crime after their father was shot by the Alagoas state police in 1921. Silvino and Lampião's violent careers ended in 1914 and 1938, respectively. Silvino was wounded and captured by Pernambuco state police; Lampião and his gang were killed in a shootout with an Alagoas *volante* (a special police unit trained to respond quickly to such emergencies). The troops brought the severed heads of Lampião and his wife, Maria Bonita, to the town of Piranhas as proof of their deaths.

World War I helped undermine the prestige of such ideas, leading some Brazilians to consider the possibility, expressed by writers such as Alberto Torres, "that racist thought was in fact an instrument used by industrialized countries to destroy the self-confidence of weaker, darker peoples whose natural resources they wished to plunder" (Skidmore, p. 19). During the early decades of the century, most of the Brazilian elite steered a middle course between enthusiastically embracing the nation's, and sometimes their own,

African heritage—as some of their country's writers were doing—and espousing Nazi Germany's theories of a white Aryan "master race." Still, the whitening ideal remained in place. People expressed their shared belief "that Brazilians were getting whiter and would continue to do so" (Skidmore, p. 19). The *mestiço* (or mixed-race) "problem" thus appeared to be solving itself, a hypothesis seemingly borne out by the results of subsequent population censuses. In comparison to the census of 1940, the 1950 census showed a rise in the *pardo,* or mixed-race, population—from 21.2 percent to 26.5 percent—and a corresponding drop in the black population—from 14.6 percent to 11 percent. There was, nonetheless, a continuation of social distinctions; even today, say historians, there tends to be a correlation between race and social status in Brazil: "[M]ost on top are white, most blacks are on the bottom and mixed-bloods are largely in between," although mulattos, especially those with paler complexions, "have considerable opportunity for upward mobility" (Skidmore and Smith, p. 162).

In Amado's novel a fairly tolerant racial attitude prevails. Fair-skinned women, like Jerusa, Colonel Bastos's blond, pale-complexioned granddaughter, are still prized, but beautiful women of all races are admired. The desirable Gabriela is a "mulatto," a term loosely applied to anyone of partly African heritage. The novel never fully identifies her racial heritage, which ultimately becomes secondary to her beauty, charm, and culinary talents.

The Novel in Focus

Plot summary. *Gabriela, Clove and Cinnamon* is divided into four parts—"The Languor of Ofenísia," "The Loneliness of Gloria," "The Secret of Malvina," and "The Moonlight of Gabriela"—which chronicle the events of a single year in the coastal town Ilhéus.

The novel begins with a leisurely description of a 1925 spring day in Ilhéus, which is dominated by two seemingly unrelated incidents: a powerful colonel fatally shoots his wife and her lover, and a local bar owner finds himself without a cook. Not surprisingly, the first incident attracts more attention as the citizens of Ilhéus argue among themselves about the cuckolded husband's justification. According to the unwritten law of the land, Colonel Jesuíno Mendonça has avenged his honor by killing his betrayers and few in Ilhéus expect him to be punished for his actions.

Nonetheless, the colonel's detractors believe his conduct reflects badly on Ilhéus, which many hope will become a civilized metropolis like Salvador or Rio de Janeiro. Ilhéus's rich history is celebrated by its inhabitants. The scholarly Doctor Pelopidas de Assunção d'Ávila labors to complete a book about the chaste romance between his ancestress, Ofenísia, and Dom Pedro II, while every Christmas the Dos Reis sisters incorporate past and present figures into their ever-expanding Nativity tableau. Once a rural outpost fought over by bandits and lawless landowners, Ilhéus is now showing signs of progress. Although a sandbar in the town's harbor prevents the direct exportation of cacao to foreign markets, new businesses have been founded, local newspapers started, and a bus route between Ilhéus and Itabuna established.

Several "old-time" plantation owners, such as the 82-year-old Colonel Ramiro Bastos, regard these innovations with suspicion. Bastos, who considers himself the unseen power in Ilhéus, is particularly wary of Mundinho Falcão, an ambitious young cacao exporter who advocates further reforms and modernization: "This Mundinho Falcão, recently come from Rio, avoided his control, never came to call on him or consult him, decided matters for himself, did what he damned well pleased. The colonel felt vaguely that the exporter was an enemy who in time would give him trouble" (*Gabriela,* p. 68). Falcão returns from Rio that day with more big plans, which include his running for Congress as Ilhéus's representative.

Compared to Colonel Mendonça's crimes and Falcão's return, the domestic crisis of the bar owner, Nacib Saad, a naturalized Brazilian of Arabic origins, goes almost unnoticed. Nacib, proprietor of the moderately successful Vesuvius Bar, is at his wits' end when his cook, Philomena, goes to live with her son the day before he is to give a big dinner party for 30 people.

In the second part of the novel, news of the murder reaches the house in which Gloria, concubine to an elderly and jealous colonel, is established. Pining for true love, Gloria sees in the tragedy of Mendonça's wife a reflection of her own situation. Meanwhile, a group of migrants, driven from their backland homes by drought, arrive in Ilhéus in search of work. One worker, Clemente, seeks employment on a cacao plantation, hoping that Gabriela, his mulatto lover, will join him. But Gabriela refuses—she plans to become a cook or laundress in Ilhéus. That evening, at the "slave" market, a place where plantation owners and other prospective employers could find cheap sources of migrant labor, Nacib encounters Gabriela. Although dubious of her professed skills as a cook, he hires her on trial.

The events of that spring day shape the course of the next year in Ilhéus, as shown in Part Three of the novel. Two days later Nacib takes Gabriela, who has skin the color of cinnamon and smells alluringly of cloves, as his mistress. Once customers sample Gabriela's splendid Bahian cooking, the Vesuvius Bar prospers. The young woman's sensual beauty, as well as her cooking, attracts admirers, and Nacib grows jealous. Fearful of losing Gabriela as a mistress and a cook, he proposes marriage. Although Gabriela is content with her present situation, she agrees to marry Nacib.

Meanwhile, Falcão pursues his plans to improve Ilhéus, much to the displeasure of the colonels. Bastos is incensed to learn that Falcão has brought an engineer to solve the sandbar problem. The engineer, a married man, creates a scandal when he becomes infatuated with Malvina, Colonel Tavares's intellectual daughter. Tavares ruins the romance, intimidating the engineer into leaving, but he also sparks a rebellion in Malvina, who plans—and later successfully effects—her escape from Ilhéus.

Despite the scandal, the sandbar project is a success. Plans are made to dredge a channel through the sandbar so ships may safely enter the Ilhéan harbor. Bastos and the other planters scheme to undermine Falcão's reputation, paying some plantation workers to set a public bonfire with copies of the *Ilhéus Daily*, a newspaper founded by Falcão. But Falcão scores a coup when several of Bastos's allies offer to support Falcão in his congressional bid.

The last part of the novel focuses on the problems of the newly married Saads. Although Gabriela loves Nacib, she eventually chafes under the restrictions of being a proper, middle-class wife and regrets having changed the situation that suited her so well: "It was lots better before. She could do everything then. . . . What good were all those dresses, shoes, jewels, rings and solid gold earrings, if she couldn't be Gabriela? She hated being Mrs. Saad" (*Gabriela*, pp. 340-41). Tensions mount as Gabriela's discontent and Nacib's disapproval of his wife's nonconformity increase. The political situation likewise grows more volatile—the defection of Aristóteles Pires, mayor of Itabuna and an erstwhile Bastos crony, deals a severe blow to the old man's dominance of Ilhéus. Later, shots ring out when Falcão and Pires meet at the Ilhéan harbor. Falcão escapes unhurt but Pires is seriously wounded and a futile search for the shooter ensues. The gunman, a black man named Fagundes, takes refuge in Gabriela's house. Fagundes, who now works on Colonel Tavares's cacao plantation, was one of Gabriela's fellow travelers on the journey to Ilhéus. Remembering Fagundes's kindness to her on the road, Gabriela helps him escape.

Gabriela and Nacib's marital problems escalate as Gabriela resists her husband's attempts to change her into a docile, conventional wife. The tensions between them come to a head when Nacib learns that, before and after their marriage, Gabriela has taken lovers. When Nacib surprises his wife in bed with Tonico, Colonel Bastos's womanizing son and a man he considered a friend, he hits Tonico and throws him out, then beats Gabriela and throws her out too. Although the unwritten law of the land expects a cuckolded husband to kill his betrayers, Nacib cannot bring himself to do this. An influential friend finds a way to have the Saads' marriage declared invalid. Nacib no longer has to kill Gabriela or Tonico, who is made the scapegoat and pressured to return to his own domineering wife, Olga. Although Nacib fears his neighbors' contempt, the Ilhéans profess their admiration for his ingenious solution to his predicament. His main problem is, once again, the lack of a cook. After a French chef fails to please his customers, Nacib is persuaded to rehire Gabriela, who is pining for her kitchen and for him. With Gabriela reinstated as his cook, Nacib's bar and his new restaurant thrive. Shortly after her return, Nacib and Gabriela resume their sexual relationship.

The mistress of the elderly colonel, Gloria, meanwhile, has discovered true love with a scholar named Josué. Her colonel discovers the affair, but he too deviates from custom by merely evicting his unfaithful mistress and her lover from the house.

On the political front, Colonel Bastos suddenly dies, thus removing the last obstacle from Falcão's path. Colonel Leal, Bastos's main ally, pledges his support to Falcão, agreeing to no longer oppose his candidacy. The novel ends with Falcão about to be swept into office; the completion of the sandbar project and subsequent arrival of a Swedish steamer, the first boat to carry cacao directly from Ilhéus; and the renewal of Nacib and Gabriela's romance. A postscript reveals that a jury later finds the cuckolded husband Colonel Mendonça guilty of murder: "For the first time in the history of Ilhéus, a cacao colonel found himself sentenced to prison for having murdered his adulterous wife and her lover" (*Gabriela,* p. 426).

Women in a changing society. After her marriage ends, Gabriela wonders, "why did men suffer so much when a women with whom they lay, lay also with another man? She couldn't understand it. If Mr. Nacib wanted to, he could have gone to lie with another girl and sleep in her arms. . . . If both of them wanted to, why shouldn't they?" (*Gabriela,* p. 374). Gabriela's sexual philosophy reflects Amado's own repeated advocacy of women's sexual freedom. Indeed, the novel subtly advocates a woman's right to choose her own destiny. Each of its four parts ("The Languor of Ofenísia," "The Loneliness of Gloria," "The Secret of Malvina," "The Moonlight of Gabriela") revolves around a woman, with a verse prologue that details her situation preceding that section. The first chapter evokes the spirit of Ofenísia, the languid maiden who loved Dom Pedro II from afar. Ofenísia refuses her suitors, declaring to her brother, "I want no count or baron, / I want no sugar planter . . . / I want only the beard, / So black, of the Emperor!" (*Gabriela,* p. 4). Deprived of her desire, Ofenísia can only fulfill her threat to "die in this hammock / Of languor" (*Gabriela,* p. 4)

BAHIAN CUISINE

Using ingredients such as dendê palm oil, fresh ginger, dried shrimp, and coconut milk, the African-influenced cuisine of Bahia has attained a fame that is reflected in the novel. The guests at Nacib's restaurant eat "appetizers like those of the old days and wonderful Bahian dishes with seasoning somewhere between the sublime and the divine"; and Gabriela's culinary expertise prompts Mundinho Falcão to declare, "There was no food in the world to compare with the Bahian" (*Gabriela,* pp. 414, 415).

The living women of Ilhéus seem equally trapped and passive. The novel's second part depicts the plight of Gloria, the beautiful concubine of an elderly colonel whose violent jealousy has frightened away rivals. Shut up in a house filled with expensive possessions, Gloria yearns for true love: "I am the colonel's Gloria, / Within my breast a fire; / On snow-white linen sheet / I lie in loneliness" (*Gabriela,* p. 96). Next, Malvina, Colonel Tavares's daughter, voices her discontent with the life she sees being mapped out for her: "Help! they want to marry me, / In a house to bury me . . . / On the bed impregnate me" (*Gabriela,* p. 170). Strong-willed and intelligent, Malvina dreams of independence: "I'll work, I'll find myself / I'll sail away forever" (*Gabriela,* p. 170). The last part of the novel belongs to Gabriela after her marriage. Content and fulfilled as Nacib's cook and mistress, she loses her bloom as a wife. In the prologue to this part, an unnamed speaker laments, "Oh, Sultan, what have you done / With my blithesome girl?" Unmoved by this sultan's boasts of having given Gabriela "a royal palace" and "emeralds and rubies," the speaker exhorts him, "Send her back to her kitchen . . . / To her innocence, / To her sighs in bed. / Why would you change her?" (*Gabriela,* p. 276). Initially free and uninhibited, after her marriage Gabriela becomes as constricted as Gloria and Malvina.

Fortunately the progress that transforms Ilhéus also provides these women with the opportunity to determine their futures. The change in Malvina's situation is the direct result of the town's modernization. Infatuated with the engineer of the sandbar project, Malvina plans to elope with him. Tavares thwarts the romance, but Malvina finds the courage to take control of her own life: "Malvina saw clearly the mistake she had made in thinking that the only way to get away was on the arm of a man, whether husband or lover. . . . Why not leave on her own two feet, alone? That is what she would do" (*Gabriela,* p. 256). Sent away to boarding school, Malvina escapes during the holidays; the Ilhéans later learn she is working and studying in São Paulo.

Subtler but equally significant social changes affect the lives of Gabriela and Gloria. In the case of the former, the mulatto woman's unquenchable spirit helps work a transformation in society. The law that would sentence her to death for betraying her husband is miraculously circumvented to preserve her life without destroying Nacib's honor. Long-established customs yield to reunite Nacib and Gabriela on their old footing, a resolution that would have once been unthinkable. Equally unimaginable to the Ilhéus of the past is the happy conclusion to Gloria's predicament. After the lonely concubine finds true love with a scholar, many expect the worst when their affair is discovered by the colonel. But the old man does nothing more than throw Gloria, her lover, and her belongings out of his house. One Ilhéan attempts to explain the reason for this violent man's nonviolent reaction to his mistress's betrayal: "Why? Because of the bus line, the library of the Commercial Association, the dances at Progress Club. . . . Because of the death of Ramiro Bastos. Because of Mundinho Falcão. . . . Because of Malvina. Because of Nacib" (*Gabriela,* p. 399). No longer passive playthings, the women of Ilhéus have become agents of positive change, a vital part of the new order: "[I]n the end it is they, as much as the planters, merchants and politicians, who effect the social changes requisite for greater material and cultural progress" (Luis, p. 13).

Literary context. *Gabriela, Clove and Cinnamon* grew out of the Regionalist, or social realist, movement in Brazilian literature during the 1930s and 1940s. Like Amado, the New Regionalists, who include Graciliano Ramos (see ***Barren Lives,*** also covered in *Latin American Literature and Its Times*), José Lins do Rego, Rachel de Quierós, and José Américo de Alemeida, described geographic areas, problems, and people they cared about in works that often include hints of the writers' own bittersweet moments in the past, as well as suggestions for social and political reform. In keeping with this focus, *Gabriela, Clove and Cinnamon* has been described as "an appealing three-way mix of politics, sex, and local color" (González Echevarría and Pupo-Walker, p. 177).

Yet, unlike Amado's early novels, *Gabriela, Clove and Cinnamon* de-emphasizes the "political and partisan" in favor of the personal and comedic aspects of Brazilian life. The reasons for Amado's shift in direction have never been fully explained, not even by the author himself. Giorgio Marotti speculates that World War II and Amado's disillusionment with Stalinist communism prompted this change: "Amado . . . saw for himself the reality of the communism he had always dreamt of. . . . [T]he invasion of Hungary by the Soviet Union saw the collapse of many illusions" (Marotti, p. 335). Abandoning his former political orthodoxy, Amado then made "a return to life, to his roots, to mulatto Brazil, to the joy of life" (Marotti, p. 335). Whatever the reason for his change in aesthetics, Amado's decision would help earn him the reputation of being "a great writer who, without losing any of his art, has managed to be popular" (Marotti, p. 325).

Events in History at the Time the Novel Was Written

The end of coronelismo. In 1930, after a flurry of military action in the capital, Getulio Vargas became Brazil's president. In the promising early years of his presidency, Vargas narrowed the gap between rich and poor by establishing a minimum wage, a maximum work week, and equal wages for men and women. He also abolished child labor and set up unions in city factories, endearing himself to the Brazilian masses. In 1932, to appease the democrats who wanted free elections and an end to networks of political bosses, Vargas introduced some electoral reforms—the secret ballot, women's suffrage, and representation of all classes in government. These reforms, along with Brazil's increased urbanization and improved communication and transportation, contributed to the weakening of coronelismo in the New Republic.

Coronelismo did not completely end under Vargas's presidency or even his dictatorship (1937-45). Rather, it survived in a more moderate form. There was, however, a concerted effort by the Vargas regime to confiscate the weapons and ammunition of those colonels who had supported Washington Luiz, Vargas's immediate predecessor. Among these colonels was Horácio de Matos of Bahia, who was assassinated in May 1931, possibly in retaliation for the mysterious shooting of an army officer who had arrested de Matos the previous December. The colonel's death anticipated significant changes for coronelismo in Bahia: "With the death of Horácio, the tradition of violence in politics was gone . . . a new era of politics was ushered in" (Pang, *Bahia in the First Brazilian Republic,* p. 188).

In 1945 Brazil held its first election since 1934, and the nation's new commitment to democracy further weakened the tottering coronelismo power structure. Elaborate systems of voter registration and election supervision kept fraud to a minimum, and as the number of distinct municipalities multiplied (they doubled between 1946 and 1963), power shifted from the old families to other sectors of society (Butler, p. 450). Prominent among these sectors were urban dwellers and those made newly literate by the nation's aggressive (though still inadequate) educational reform policies.

Mid-century modernization. Brazil was motivated to improve its quality of education by the nation's post-World War II desire to modernize. In part linked to the rise of democracy and to a

The *Palacio do Congresso* is a notable example of the modernist architecture that characterizes the Brazilian capital of Brasília.

surge in nationalism, the country experienced an explosive growth in its economy, developing an industrial base and infrastructure that required the training of Brazilian experts to manage it. Meanwhile, along with the rising nationalism and growing economy, came an anti-foreign sentiment. Many Brazilian leaders felt it was necessary to reduce the nation's dependence on outside (mostly North American) capital and goods, and thus encouraged factories and small businesses to produce essential services. Also encouraging Brazil to become economically self-sufficient was the vastly depleted condition of its post-World War II foreign exchange reserves. Vargas reappeared as president (1951-54) and, in line with this trend, established the Brazilian national petroleum company, Petrobrás, in 1953. It joined the National Steel Company (which Vargas had founded while dictator in 1946) in becoming one of the mainstays of the Brazilian economy. Following Vargas's suicide in 1954, and a chain of caretaker governments, Juscelino Kubitschek became president in 1956. Kubitschek, grandson of a Czechoslovakian immigrant, promised Brazil fifty years of progress in five, and generally fulfilled that promise, although graft and overspending marred his term in office. During his administration (1956-61), foreign capital poured in and major industrialization began: an automobile industry developed; new highways connected parts of the country; an international airport was built; and huge dams were constructed to increase Brazil's electrical power supply. Most spectacularly, Brazil constructed a new capital, Brasília, in four years of round-the-clock labor. Completed in 1961, the same year Kubitschek left office, the airplane-shaped city rose on a plateau 600 miles from Rio de Janeiro, a "futuristic city of modernist architecture that captured the imagination of the outside world" (Skidmore and Smith, p. 177). Although Kubitschek failed to solve the chronic problems of poverty—especially in the Northeast—and economic mismanagement, his presidency helped Brazil take its place in the modern world. The major strides made under his leadership may well have influenced aspects of *Gabriela, Clove and Cinnamon,* especially the character of Mundinho Falcão. Like Kubitschek, Falcão is a prosperous businessman with political ambitions, and his drive and determination transform Ilhéus. Also like Kubitschek, Falcão is regarded as an outsider. Kubitschek was the first descendant of an immigrant to serve as Brazil's president; Falcão is a newcomer from Rio whom several colonels regard with hostility because he is not an Ilhéan by birth.

Contemporary women. The Latin American notion of *machismo,* which idealized masculine strength and virility persisted in 1950s Brazil, and continued to be matched by *marianismo* (after the Virgin Mary), which exalted traditionally feminine qualities, such as piety, propriety, and motherhood. Significantly, none of the major female characters in Amado's novel conform to the ideal of marianismo. Ofenísia and Malvina both reject, albeit for different reasons, arranged marriages and domesticity. Gloria, the colonel's concubine, hungers not for wedlock and respectability, but for true love with a man nearer her own age. Finally, Gabriela flourishes as Nacib's mistress but wilts as his wife, and she displays no maternal yearnings. She, like Malvina and Gloria, transcends prevailing social and sexual strictures. In real life, women would find that transcending these strictures in Brazil was a slow process.

By the 1950s, when Amado was writing *Gabriela, Clove and Cinnamon,* women had gained rights such as the vote and equal-wage status with men. However, their progress in society continued to be gradual. Brazil was still considered "a man's country." Upper-class girls whose families could afford to educate them were usually sent to parochial schools, then married off at age 17 or 18 (Bishop, pp. 116-17). The life that Malvina scathingly describes in the novel—"In the kitchen, cooking, / In the rooms, atidying, / At the piano playing, / At the church, confessing" (*Gabriela,* p. 170)—continued to be the lot of most young women of her birth and upbringing. Meanwhile, a small but rising number of middle-class women attended the universities and entered the work force as secretaries, teachers, or clerks. Women organized quasi-political groups, such as the Brazilian Women's Federation, which primarily addressed problems of daily living and grew into a national network that held its first countrywide meeting in 1949. In 1956 President Kubitschek, in response to pressure from conservatives, outlawed this federation and a number of other women's groups. The setback illustrates the halting nature of progress for women in early to mid-twentieth-century Brazil.

Reviews. *Gabriela, Clove and Cinnamon* was described by Juan de Onis as "an exciting and enjoyable romp of a book, rich in literary delights and . . . a record-smashing runaway when it first appeared in Portuguese" (Juan de Onis in Davison, p. 22). The English translation likewise achieved critical and popular success in the United States in 1962. Reviewers praised the colorful setting and exciting plot. Fanny Butcher declared, "[T]he merry-go-round of love, politics, and a Brazilian port's prosperity . . . are sure to make this big, lusty . . . tale welcome in any language" (Butcher in Davison, p. 22). The quality of the translation itself was lauded as well: "The translators have done full justice to the novel's rollicking nimble style—no easy task" (Harriet de Onis in Davison, p. 22).

—Pamela S. Loy

For More Information

Amado, Jorge. *Gabriela, Clove and Cinnamon.* Trans. James L. Taylor and William L. Grossman. New York: Alfred A. Knopf, 1962.

Bishop, Elizabeth, and the editors of *Life. Brazil.* New York: Time Incorporated, 1962.

Butler, E. Bradford. *A History of Brazil.* 2nd ed. New York: Columbia University Press, 1980.

William Luis, ed. *Modern Latin-American Fiction Writers.* 1st series. Dictionary of Literary Biography. Vol. 113. Detroit: Gale Research, 1992.

Davison, Dorothy P. *Book Review Digest 1962.* New York: H. W. Wilson, 1963.

González Echevarría, Roberto, and Enrique Pupo-Walker, eds. *The Cambridge History of Latin American Literature.* Vol. 3. Cambridge: Cambridge University Press, 1996.

Marotti, Giorgio. *Black Characters in the Brazilian Novel.* Trans. Maria O. Marotti and Harry Lawton. Los Angeles: Center for Afro-American Studies, 1987.

Page, Joseph A. *The Brazilians.* Reading, Penn.: Addison-Wesley, 1995.

Pang, Eul-Soo. "Agrarian Change in the Northeast." In *Modern Brazil: Elites and Masses in Historical Perspective.* Eds. Michael L. Conniff and Frank D. McCann. Lincoln: University of Nebraska Press, 1991.

———. *Bahia in the First Brazilian Republic: Coronelismo and Oligarchies, 1889-1934.* Gainesville: University Presses of Florida, 1979.

Skidmore, Thomas E. "Racial Ideas and Social Policy in Brazil, 1870-1940." In *The Idea of Race in Latin America, 1870-1940.* Ed. Richard Graham. Austin: University of Texas Press, 1990.

Skidmore, Thomas E., and Peter H. Smith. *Modern Latin America.* Oxford: Oxford University Press, 1997.

The Gaucho Martín Fierro

by
José Hernández

José Hernández published only two poems: *The Gaucho Martín Fierro* and *The Return of Martín Fierro. The Gaucho Martín Fierro,* popularly known as *La ida* (The Departure), protested the unjust laws and social conditions that forced the gaucho to become an outlaw and led to the demise of his rural way of life. Hernández, who grew up among gauchos on the cattle ranches of Argentina where his father worked as an overseer, committed himself to righting the wrongs they suffered. In addition to producing this poem, perhaps the most widely read piece of Argentinian literature, Hernández supported the gauchos' cause as a political activist, a soldier, a government official, and a journalist.

THE LITERARY WORK

The first of two poems set in rural Argentina in the latter half of the nineteenth century; published in Spanish (as *El gaucho Martín Fierro*) in 1872, in English in 1935.

SYNOPSIS

The gaucho Martín Fierro is conscripted into the military and treated unjustly. He deserts, becomes an outlaw, and teams up with a man named Cruz. Together they seek refuge among the Indians.

Events in History at the Time of the Poem

The rise of the gaucho. *The Gaucho Martín Fierro* takes place in the latter half of the nineteenth century, when gauchos as a recognizable social group were on the decline. In a few short years, the gaucho would be a semi-mythical figure of the past. But who was the gaucho and how did he live before his world began to disintegrate?

Spanish explorers and settlers who arrived in what is now Argentina, beginning in the sixteenth century, brought with them cattle and horses. Some of these animals either escaped from or abandoned the herd, then found their way onto the *pampas,* the vast, flat grasslands of central Argentina that extend from the Andean foothills to the Atlantic Coast. The European animals thrived and reproduced rapidly, multiplying into huge wild herds that roamed the pampas, where they fed on ample grasses. Gauchos were the men of the pampas who exploited these herds, taming and riding the wild horses and slaughtering the cattle. In contrast to the *vaqueros,* or legitimate cowboys, the gauchos were illegal hunters who met the demand for contraband trade to circumvent what colonists felt were unreasonable restrictions placed on them by Spain. Popularly, the gauchos gained a reputation for being cunning as well as passionate and highly independent.

Selling hides and tallow to European traders in the eighteenth century, the gauchos survived on an almost exclusive diet of beef. They typically lived in huts roofed with straw, using cattle skulls as chairs and hides on the floor as beds. Gaucho clothing consisted of a poncho over a *chiripá,* coarse cloth that reached to the knees and was tied at the waist with a sash. The headgear included a headband covered by a narrow-brimmed hat with a strap that fell under the chin. A neckerchief and a long knife, worn in a leather sheath, completed the outfit. Ethnically, most gauchos were probably *mestizos* (descendents of unions between Europeans and natives), but some were black, some white, and some mulatto (of black and white unions). Hernández's poem refers to Martín Fierro not as a mestizo, but as a *criollo.* The term for a white child born in the Americas of European parents, *criollo* also had a looser meaning—it referred to a person who deserves admiration. People credited the criollos with having won independence for Argentina from Spain and for taming the pampas.

Gauchos spent so much time on horseback that others spoke of them as half-man, half-horse, and they were rumored to be permanently bowlegged when out of the saddle. Free of possessions, they owned neither the animals nor the land that they used. They grew into a sizeable group, comprising about one quarter of the Argentinean population prior to the 1870s. But their heyday was short-lived. As a separate class, the gauchos existed for only about 100 years, from 1775–1875.

THE PAMPAS

"The vastness of the horizon, which always looks the same as we advance, as if the whole plain moved along with us, gives one the impression of something illusory in this rude reality of the open country. . . . It is the pampa, the land where man is alone, like an abstract being that will begin anew the story of the species—or conclude it."

(Martínez Estrada, pp. 6-7)

There were gaucho families on the pampas, with women who worked not on horseback, but at domestic tasks: raising children, cooking, cleaning, sewing, and weaving. Because of the lack of clergy on the pampas and the expense and trouble of obtaining a civil ceremony, legal gaucho marriages were rare. Instead, rural men and women performed rituals to establish common-law marriages in the eyes of the community. These rituals failed to satisfy the Church or State, however; children of these unions were regarded as illegitimate, which may explain one interpretation of "gaucho" as being "without a known father" (Carrino, Carlos, and Mangouni in Hernández, p. 93).

The rise of the estancia. By the end of the eighteenth century, the fertile pampas countryside surrounding Buenos Aires and the free herds that roamed it had become private property. The eastern pampas were now divided into *estancias,* huge ranches that each covered hundreds of square miles. These large tracts of land were the currency with which politicians bought support, so that a few powerful families owned virtually everything—a situation known as *latifundismo.*

Gauchos, who were no longer free to use the herds as they wished, were hired by the *estancieros,* owners of the vast estancias, as legitimate ranch hands, to tend the animals they knew so well. On the surface, the life of the gaucho changed little. The estancias were not fenced until 1845, and until then gauchos, for the most part, went where they pleased and picked up work only when they wanted it. Although technically illegal, use by a gaucho of ranchers' cattle was common, so that he never lacked meat or hides.

In this period, gauchos lived in mud huts or lean-tos on or near estancia land, and frequented *pulperias,* all-purpose inns that served as general store, bank, bar, restaurant, and all-around social center. European visitors to the pampas commented on the wretched nature of gaucho dwellings, which were overrun by vermin and, on the wood-poor pampas, furnished with items made from the bones of cattle, a touch that Europeans found macabre. Gauchos were reputed to be lazy and shiftless because they seemingly put so little effort into the betterment and upkeep of their homes, yet they had little incentive to improve their land or dwellings since they did not own them and could be evicted at any time.

In his leisure hours the gaucho was said to be fond of gambling, drinking, and playing the guitar. He was never without his *facón,* his sheathed knife up to 27 inches long that served as a work tool, eating utensil, and weapon. Such a fearsome implement could not have softened his image in the popular imagination of the day, and the representation of the gaucho that comes down to us in literature is that of a wild ruffian living on the fringes of civilization. It is difficult to say to what extent this stereotype is accurate, or what position the gaucho held in the estimation of the peasant populace: gauchos, and the peasant population in general, were largely illiterate, and did not leave a written record of themselves or their

Gauchos from around the turn of the twentieth century.

point of view. But some evidence can be gleaned from other sources; we do know, for example, that knife-fighting was so common among gauchos that the carrying of facóns was repeatedly outlawed.

The estancia was primarily a male world. Ranch hands were discouraged from bringing women and children onto the estancias; many estancieros hired only single men or required workers to leave their families elsewhere. Some women did find employment in estancia homes in traditionally female jobs—working as cook, maid, or wet nurse—and these women received wages that equalled or surpassed those earned by ranch hands. At times women even worked alongside men shearing sheep. Generally, however, the gauchos themselves held sexist views regarding women. A horse ridden by a woman, for example, was considered unfit for a man to ride because a woman's leniency would make the animal unmanageable—and no "real" man would even consider riding a mare.

Buenos Aires and Argentina. For most of the nineteenth century Argentina was a land of separate, self-governing provinces, sometimes united but more often disunited. The first government of the Río de la Plata region to claim independence from Spain was established in Buenos Aires in 1810, and claimed authority over a vast territory, including what is now Argentina, Paraguay, Uruguay, and Bolivia. The outlying areas soon broke away to form their own republics, leaving present-day Argentina unto itself. But disunity persisted, with the provinces in Argentina resisting the hegemony of Buenos Aires. In fact, Argentine history can be roughly understood as a struggle between the wealthy city of Buenos Aires—with its pretensions to European culture—and the rural rest of Argentina.

Buenos Aires is the name of both a city and of the province that contains it. The province contains some of the most productive farmland in the world. Located just off the Atlantic Coast, the city of Buenos Aires has always been Argentina's largest and most prosperous. In the nineteenth century its citizens, known as *porteños,* received an influx of immigration, capital, and culture from Europe that boosted the great pride they took in their European heritage.

The conflict between the city and the countryside is reflected in the two major political factions of nineteenth-century Argentina: the Federalists and the Unitarians. In general, Unitarians can be identified with Buenos Aires; Federalists, with the rural provinces. The Unitarians were the educated elite of Buenos Aires who favored bringing the provinces together under a strong centralized government that they themselves would control. They thought of themselves as the arbiters of "civilization," that is, of society based on current European models and directed by people of European descent. Unitarians were notoriously racist elitists who looked down on anything that came out of Argentina as inferior to the products and people of Europe. On the other hand, the Federalists supported autonomy for the provinces. This could mean championing the rights of the countryside and its largely impoverished population against domination by Buenos Aires, which was the brand of federalism to which the author of *The Gaucho Martín Fierro,* José Hernández, subscribed. It could also mean autonomy for Buenos Aires from the surrounding provinces, a position to which a strong faction of the city subscribed. This vigorous federalist movement flourished in Buenos Aires among those who wanted to maintain their exclusive grip on the lucrative commercial trade flowing in and out of the city's port and who did not want to be taxed to support the less economically viable provinces.

One such porteño Federalist was Juan Manuel de Rosas, governor of Buenos Aires from 1829 to 1852. Rosas was a wealthy landowner of Buenos Aires province and a federalist *caudillo,* a local strongman who attracted the support of gauchos and Indians and who was portrayed by Unitarians as a barbaric warlord. Despite his Federalist political stance, Rosas effectively dominated what was then known as the Argentine Confederation by controlling the nation's trade and foreign affairs. He maintained his power through a combination of popular support, from wealthy landowners as well as the rural poor, and repressive measures carried out by the military, which was a constant presence in the streets of Buenos Aires during his rule. *The Gaucho Martín Fierro* is set sometime after the Rosas dictatorship, and the titular character likens the brutal treatment he receives at a frontier garrison to the injustices dealt out at Palermo, Rosas's headquarters, where Rosas's enemies were tortured and executed. Although he was a Federalist, José Hernández did not support Rosas's authoritarian porteño Federalism.

General Justo José de Urquiza, Federalist caudillo of Entre Ríos province and provincial military commander under Rosas, rebelled and defeated Rosas's troops at Buenos Aires in 1852. In 1854 Urquiza became President of the Argentine Confederation and installed a puppet governor to lead Buenos Aires province. Buenos Aires overthrew this governor and declared itself independent of the Confederation, after which the two governments fought against each other until the Confederation disintegrated in 1861. Buenos Aires assumed dominance over Argentina once again, this time as the seat of a constitutional national government with Bartolomé Mitre as President.

Opposition to the national government flared in the provinces, and federalist caudillos rose to challenge the dominance of Buenos Aires. José Hernández, who had fought under Urquiza, wrote an exalting biography of federalist caudillo General Angel V. Peñaloza, the leader of a remote and impoverished province who resisted unification under Buenos Aires and was defeated and killed in 1863. Hernández also fought under Ricardo López Jordán, the last of the great caudillo rebels, and after defeat, followed Jordán into exile in Brazil in 1871. It was in Brazil that Hernández began work on *The Gaucho Martín Fierro*; he would finish the poem in Buenos Aires when Mitre's successor decreed a general amnesty.

Sarmiento. Domingo Faustino Sarmiento succeeded Mitre as President in 1868 and held the office until 1874. Sarmiento had gained public attention with his 1848 critique of federalism, *Civilization and Barbarism: Life of Juan Facundo Quiroga,* in which he sets forth his diagnosis of the ills plaguing Argentina ("barbarism") and his prescription for a cure ("civilization") (see ***Facundo,*** also covered in *Latin American Literature and Its Times*). In this work the categories of civilization and barbarism are never completely clear, but broadly, barbarism is located in the wild countryside among the gauchos, the native peoples, and the caudillos whose power came from their support. Civilization is centered in the metropolis Buenos Aires, with its strong European heritage and its elite citizens of European descent. Indeed, Sarmiento believed that the only way to civilize the pampas was to import European settlers who would transform the land into an expanse of small farms, displacing the supposedly racially inferior gauchos and Indians. José Hernández was responding to *Civilization and Barbarism* when, during Sarmiento's presidency, he wrote *The Gaucho Martín Fierro,* which locates the source of barbarism not in the gaucho or the countryside, but rather in a corrupt political system benefiting only the Buenos Aires elite.

A massive wave of change swept Argentina in the nineteenth century, transforming it from a backwater colony into a prosperous nation. By mid-century, much had changed, but much remained the same: mule and ox-cart were still the main modes of travel, caudillos still held sway in the rural provinces, bands of indigenous peoples still raided the settlements, and gauchos still roamed the pampas. Fifty years later, at the end of the century, caudillos, the native Indian peoples, and gauchos would all be gone—defeated, pushed aside, or transformed into something more "civilized." Some of the developments that led to the demise of these groups began long before Rosas's fall, but it was expressly the campaign of the post-Rosas unitarian Buenos Aires government to rid Argentina of these last pockets of "barbarism."

Modernization of the estancia. Back on the pampas, as Europe began to demand more beef and mutton, Argentine estancieros marshalled their forces to meet that demand. In the 1820s ranch owners began importing sheep and English cattle to replace the comparatively scrawny pampas cattle. These new herds could not live on the tough pampas grass, however, and necessitated the growing of feed crops. The gaucho, who always worked on horseback, shunned agricultural labor or "foot work" as demeaning. Indeed, such labor might well have seemed backbreaking and tedious compared to the gaucho's traditional task of riding the range and taming wild beasts, work that held an element of danger and required a special skill. Thus the estanciero found few gauchos willing to work in the fields; he had to look elsewhere for peasant laborers.

In addition to livestock, estancieros began to import farmworkers from Europe. European immigrants, primarily from Italy and Spain, came to Argentina seeking a better life. They were valued by the Argentine landowning elite because they had no qualms about farmwork, and also because of racist beliefs that their supposedly superior European blood would "purify" Argentina of its American Indian taint. Like the pampean herds, gauchos found themselves replaced by European imports.

In order to keep the new herds pure, estancieros began to fence their lands in 1845. The arrival of fencing meant the disappearance of the vast unbroken landscape in which the gaucho might freely roam. Fewer gauchos were needed to tend tamer herds on fenced land. In short, the gaucho's traditional work vanished. He found it more difficult to hunt with the fences in place, and estancieros kept a much tighter reign on their profitable European animals than they had on the domestic ones. Yet the gaucho still refused to take up agricultural work. Estancieros had to find other means.

Criminalization of the gaucho. A series of nineteenth-century laws, many of which dealt with the issue of vagrancy, made the terms "gaucho" and "outlaw" synonymous. Gauchos did not own land, so if they were not employed they were considered vagrants. If a rural male could not produce a signed document attesting to his employment, he could be arrested for vagrancy and sentenced to labor without pay on "public works." In 1822 a law went into effect requiring passports for all those traveling between *partidos* (counties) or leaving the province of Buenos Aires. Gauchos, who were mostly illiterate, were now subject to penalties if they lacked documentation they couldn't even read.

The vagrancy laws punished gauchos for maintaining their traditional lifestyle, in which free movement and loose employment relations were important factors. To a certain extent, these same laws benefited the estanciero, who gained the upper hand with gauchos who became his employees. However, the laws also had a countereffect, discussed in the next section, that actually reduced the labor pool on the pampas.

Conscription of the gaucho. From 1806, when its struggles for independence from Spain began, until the publication of *The Gaucho Martín Fierro* in 1872, Argentina was engaged in continuous warfare. It fought against other nations, but mostly the warfare of this period was internal, constituted by civil strife and conflicts with the country's indigenous peoples.

The Argentine government had two main sources of soldiers on which to draw. Foreigners who came to Argentina for a better life joined the armies willingly for pay. The other source stemmed from the rural vagrancy laws of the 1800s, which provided the armed forces with a steady flow of gaucho recruits. Several years of service in the army, often without pay, was the most common sentence for gaucho "crimes" of all sorts, and, with the vagrancy laws in place, there was no shortage of gaucho "criminals." On the frontier, the garrisons, or military outposts from which the government sought to subdue marauding Argentine Indians, were particularly notorious for poor living conditions, lack of pay or even adequate rations for the troops, and brutal punishments for infractions. Corrupt commanders would use the troops for private service, to work their own fields or tend their herds. Conditions for the gauchos were so poor that they often deserted. Some of them even fled to the native peoples they were supposed to combat, joining their raiding parties and engaging in skirmishes against former allies.

Demise of the gaucho. The widespread conscription of gauchos depopulated the countryside, making ranch labor harder to find. Males became scarce in pampean settlements because men were shipped out to the frontier to fight or because they fled such a fate and became outlaws. Long condemned for their "nomadic" ways, gauchos like Martín Fierro were now truly homeless. As outlaw deserters and draft evaders, they were constantly on the run from the law or the recruiter. The only alternatives were to become a farm worker or to move to the city. The gaucho way of life, which centered on freedom and the use of free-roaming herds, was no longer possible; by the end of the nineteenth century the gaucho as independent cattleman of the pampas had disappeared.

The Poem in Focus

The contents. *The Gaucho Martín Fierro* is a long poem in three voices. It begins as a song sung by the titular character, Martín Fierro. In the course of his adventures, Fierro meets up with Cruz, who tells his own story. The author, José Hernández, finishes the poem.

The poem's first voice, Martín Fierro, identifies himself as a *payador*. Payadores were gaucho singers who would improvise lyrics and accompany themselves on guitar. Often they competed with each other in singing contests called *payadas*. In the initial canto of the poem, Martín Fierro issues a challenge to other singers. Thus his song can be understood as a payada performance, an entry in a contest of competing voices, just as the poem, one among several gaucho-themed poems to appear in nineteenth-century Argentina, was a challenge to other literary "voices" of the time.

Indeed, the issue of voice—that is, whose voice is heard and who speaks for whom—is central to the poem, and, in the first canto, Martín Fierro makes it clear that his voice will not be silenced. "Once I set myself to singin', / there's no stopping me," he warns (Hernández, *The Gaucho Martín Fierro,* 12.50–51). The subject of his song is sorrow, a product of the "raw deals" he has received (*Martín Fierro,* 14.108). This is the theme of the poem: the plight of the gaucho in the face of injustice.

After bemoaning his many sufferings and suggesting that through them he has grown wise, Martín Fierro waxes nostalgic for a time when gauchos were "always happy and on good horses and ready to work" (*Martín Fierro,* 18.207-08). In this golden past, "the gaucho was on his land and safe as he could be" (*Martín Fierro,* 19.253-54). Martín Fierro is describing the life of a gaucho working on an estancia, or large ranch, where semi-wild herds of cattle and horses were the responsibility of gaucho keepers. But in this situation, while the gaucho might have considered the land his own, he would not have technically owned it.

The present that Martín Fierro bemoans is a time when the gaucho "spends his life / running away from the law" (*Martín Fierro,* 19.257-58) and "like it or not, / you'll be sent to the frontier or get tossed in a regiment" (*Martín Fierro,* 20.280-82). The landless rural population is subject to harsh laws and a corrupt legal system that in effect make poor men outlaws. For slight infractions, or even nothing at all, one can be arrested and made to serve in the armed forces, a common sentence in the world of Martín Fierro.

After the first two introductory cantos, Martín Fierro begins his own story. In the midst of a peaceful life, he is arrested for getting drunk and singing at a party—for using his voice. Martín Fierro realizes the true cause of his misfortune, however: he failed to vote for the judge in the last election, not because he favored the opposition, but because gauchos "don't give a damn about those things" (*Martín Fierro,* 23.354). The vindictive judge sends Fierro and several others to serve in the army, but promises them that in six months they will be free. Fierro leaves for a frontier garrison, an outpost from which outlying farms are protected from marauding bands of Indians. He takes one of his horses and all his equipment, leaving behind his woman and his children.

Fierro describes the fort as a "rathole" (*Martín Fierro,* 24.384) from which release is improbable. Anyone who dares complain or tries to leave is punished severely. Instead of performing military service, the recruits must work the colonel's fields, a task particularly onerous to the gaucho since he shuns work done on foot (rather than horseback) as demeaning.

When the natives do attack, the gaucho forces are unable to do much with their inadequate equipment—old swords and spears instead of guns—and the substandard mounts the army has issued them. Fierro characterizes the Argentine Indian as a merciless savage who "settles everything / with a spear and a whoop" (*Martín Fierro,*

27.485-86) and tortures women prisoners. In a pitched battle between the ragtag band of recruits and a fierce Argentine Indian posse, Fierro kills a native in self-defense, referring to this act as a "holy deed" (*Martín Fierro,* 31.611).

After two years, Fierro has yet to be released or paid for his service. Moreover, the commandant has taken Fierro's horse for himself, and, on account of a misunderstanding, Fierro is cruelly punished by "staking," a method of torture in which each of the victim's limbs is tied with wet leather strips to stakes in the ground and left in the sun. As the leather dries, it shrinks, and the victim's limbs are pulled tighter and tighter. The incident that brings Fierro to this fate is an encounter with a *gringo*—in Argentine usage an immigrant who speaks poor Spanish. This particular gringo is an Italian immigrant serving in "the regular troops" (*Martín Fierro,* 40.844), made up of soldiers under contract who were privileged above recruits like Fierro. Fierro ridicules the gringo's broken Spanish, then describes his contempt for gringo soldiers as a group:

> I don't know why the government
> sends to the frontier
> a bunch of gringos that don't even
> know how to come up to a horse.
> (*Martín Fierro,* 41.889-92)

Fierro decides to desert. He slips out one night on a stolen horse and returns to his home, where he finds nothing but ruins. He learns that his land and cattle have been confiscated and his sons have been hired out. His wife, Fierro speculates, has taken up with another man who can support her. Fierro determines to become what he has been treated as, an outlaw, swearing to be "as mean as they come" from that day forward (*Martín Fierro,* 45.1014).

He soon gets a chance to act the outlaw. A homeless drifter, Fierro happens upon a dance where he meets up with old friends and gets drunk. A black couple arrives and, for no reason, Fierro insults the woman and then sings a little song about how "the devil made the blacks / as coal for hell's fires" (*Martín Fierro,* 51.1169-70). The black man attacks Fierro with a knife, and the two begin dueling. Fierro kills the black man. The woman starts to cry, and Fierro considers beating her to make her stop, but decides to flee instead. Fierro soon gets into another knife fight, this time with a bullying gaucho in a bar. After severely wounding this opponent, Fierro flees.

Fearing capture, Fierro takes to sleeping out on the pampas, far from human habitation. One night, he is beset by a band of police. He fights them bravely and thus wins the esteem of one of their number, a man named Cruz, who decides to betray his fellow police and join Fierro instead. Cruz and Fierro fend off the rest of the band and then ride off together.

Now Cruz tells his story, which is remarkably similar to Fierro's. Cruz once had a beautiful wife, whom he adored. The commandant admired her too, and that's where Cruz's troubles began. One day he found the commandant and his wife in an amorous embrace. Cruz insulted the commandant, who drew his sword, and, in the ensuing scuffle, Cruz killed one of the commandant's flunkies who tried to interfere. Thus, Cruz became an outlaw and fled to the pampas. Like Fierro, he got into a knife fight at a dance, seriously wounded a man, and ran away before the law arrived. Eventually he was saved from outlaw status by a friend who knew a judge. The judge made Cruz a police sergeant, a post Cruz is now eager to abandon.

ACCUSTOMED TO VIOLENCE

According to one historian, "having busied themselves from childhood in cutting the throats of cattle, [many gauchos] did not hesitate to do the same with men, and this coldly and dispassionately. They set little value on life, and still less did death disturb them. No one ever interfered in another's disputes or quarrels. . . . Gauchos even considered it dishonorable to expose their fellow criminals and not to hide and help them" (Nichols, p. 15).

Cruz suggests to Fierro that the two of them join forces and live as outlaws together. Martín Fierro replies to Cruz that he will head out for Indian territory and live with the heathens rather than continue to skulk around the perimeters of pampa settlements. He would rather live in the wilderness than cling to civilization's edge. "I know that out there the Indian chiefs / take care of Christians," Fierro announces optimistically, "and that they treat them like 'brothers' / when they go there on their own" (*Martín Fierro,* 87.2191-94). Thus, Fierro will join the "savages" for whom he once felt such contempt.

The author then narrates how Martín Fierro at this point finishes his song by smashing his

Although the independent gaucho, tending his free-roaming herds, disappeared by the end of the nineteenth century, the modern gaucho, a paid ranch-hand, nevertheless preserves something of the spirit and dress of his precursor.

guitar against the ground, saying of his instrument:

> No one else is gonna play it,
> you can be damn sure of that;
> since no one else is gonna sing,
> after this gaucho has sung.
> (*Martín Fierro,* 90.2277-80)

Martín Fierro has lost his voice, smashing it to pieces rather than let it be used by another—yet boldly he asserts that he has had the last word. With this act, he surrenders his voice to the author, who is now left to speak for the gaucho, just as sympathetic elites such as the poet José Hernández must now plead the gaucho's cause.

Although Fierro has ended his tale, the author lets us know that Cruz and Fierro indeed headed out for the wilds, and that tears streamed down Fierro's face as he took his last look back at civilization. Maybe the two have been killed in a raid, the author writes, or maybe they are still alive. Society has driven the gaucho away, pushing him into a life of outlawry, wildness, and brutality beyond the pale of civilization. The poem ends on a note of condemnation, having spoken of "wrongs everybody knows about / but no one ever told before" (*Martín Fierro,* 91.2315-16).

Racism and xenophobia. In the course of the poem, Martín Fierro denigrates and exhibits hostility toward three groups: European immigrants, Indians of the pampas, and people of African descent. This hostility raises a question about racism and the fear of foreigners in nineteenth-century Argentina—how did these forces contribute to the gaucho's extinction?

By the middle of the nineteenth century, 4,000 immigrants were arriving in Argentina each year from Europe, mostly from Italy and Spain. Buenos Aires elites encouraged European immigration as a means to "purify" the Argentine population of the taint of Indian blood, which many considered racially inferior. Also, to the unitarians, as exemplified by Sarmiento, Europe represented the source of "civilization"; only through the importation of European ways and ideas would the wild pampas be brought up to the standards of a modern capitalist society. European immigration, in this view, went hand in hand with the modernization of the pampas—with fencing, with farming, with the demise of the gaucho. Gaucho resentment of European settlers is well-documented. This ill will was brutally displayed in the Tandil massacre of 1872, when a band of gaucho zealots swept the pampean countryside before dawn, slaying all the Europeans they could find.

In the military, gaucho resentment of Europeans was based on the fact that, while Europeans joined the army willingly for pay, gauchos were forcibly recruited and often made to serve for years without compensation. In addition to this unjust situation, the Europeans' lack of frontier experience inspired the gauchos' contempt. Horses were the privilege of the wealthy in Europe at this time, so the European poor who immigrated to Argentina tended to have little or no experience on horseback. Gauchos, who equated equestrian skill with manliness, thought the Europeans effeminate and weak, "only fit / to live with sissies" (*Martín Fierro,* 42.915-16), as Fierro judges them.

On the other hand, when Martín Fierro first speaks of the American Indians of the pampas, he characterizes them as "savages," but he also speaks admiringly of their horsemanship and skill with weapons. The native peoples of the pampas were semi-nomadic hunters who conducted frequent raids against settlements, taking livestock and sometimes abducting women and children. Government policy of the nineteenth century sought to push the natives back further and further, claiming their lands for pasturage and farms for wealthy Argentines. By the early 1880s General Julio Roca had virtually cleared the pampas of its original inhabitants.

This racism prevailed, with few exceptions, among nineteenth-century Argentine intellectuals. Indians were widely viewed as brutal savages, a source, if not the source, of Argentine "barbarism." *Mestizo* gauchos (having some Indian blood) were likewise tarnished in the eyes of urban elites, Both gaucho and native were marginalized, dwelling at the edges of "civilization," of which Buenos Aires was the physical and ideal center. Yet gauchos were forced to fight against the indigenous peoples at frontier outposts.

Another dilemma that beset many gauchos stemmed from their mestizo heritage; they were internally divided between the European and Indian, inhabitants of both worlds and of neither. The ambiguity of this situation is reflected in *The Gaucho Martín Fierro,* as Fierro both praises and curses the Indians.

The racism displayed toward blacks is only slightly less than that shown toward Indians in the poem. Africans were abducted and brought to Argentina as slaves beginning officially in 1534 and ending in 1813, when the revolutionary government discontinued the slave trade. The institution of slavery, however, persisted until 1861. Dictator Rosas actively sought the support of Afro-Argentines, the so-called "freed slaves," during his governorship. He managed to gain some support, and the racist unitarians opposing Rosas exaggerated the role Afro-Argentines played in Rosas's regime. Blacks were seen by unitarians as another source of "barbarism," to be eliminated along with the native peoples and the gauchos, pushed aside by those of European ancestry. In the case of Afro-Argentines, as in the case of Argentina's Indians and gauchos, this tactic arguably succeeded. Although blacks constituted about 10 percent of Argentina's population in 1810, by 1887 their numbers had dropped to less than 2 percent, and have continued to drop down to the present day.

Fierro, a wandering outcast stripped of his humanity, lashes out at Indians and blacks in the poem. It is well-documented in history that marginalized groups often turn against rather than aid one another in their common plight. Gauchos, Argentine Indians, and Afro-Argentines were all marginalized groups in the latter half of the nineteenth century. As indicated, there was even internal friction among whites. The European immigrants so wooed by unitarian elites encountered disdain from *criollos,* those born in Argentina, who had to compete with the newcomers for jobs and resources.

The return. In 1879 Hernández published a sequel to *The Gaucho Martín Fierro,* entitled *The Return of Martín Fierro,* popularly known as *La vuelta.* This poem, which is twice the length of its predecessor, describes:

- Tortures inflicted by the Indians on Fierro and Cruz;
- Cruz's death and Fierro's escape from the cruelty of the Indians;
- Fierro's rescue of a white woman and subsequent reunion with his sons;
- The family's encounter with Picardia, the son of Cruz;
- Fierro's verbal duel with a black man, whose brother Fierro killed;
- The peaceful denouement in which Fierro imparts sage advice to his sons and Picardia before everyone goes his separate way.

While *The Gaucho Martín Fierro* was aimed at an urban audience to arouse sympathy for the gaucho's plight, Hernández addressed *The Return of Martín Fierro* to the rural population who had actually claimed *The Gaucho Martín Fierro* as their own. The sequel has a more didactic and condescending tone, and in it Fierro is transformed

ASCASUBI VS. HERNÁNDEZ

In writing *The Gaucho Martín Fierro,* Hernández responded to critics of his day, like Lucio V. Mansilla, who faulted Argentina's poets for treating the gaucho only as a laughable character. Hernández set out instead to portray the ups and downs of gaucho life in eloquent language. One of his predecessors was Hilario Ascasubi, who in 1851 had published *Santo Vega o Los Mellizos de la Flor,* a gaucho poem about the *payador,* or gaucho singer. The poem relates a story that includes dramatic features of gaucho life on the plains. Compare two excerpts by the poets on a common subject of such verse, the Indian attack:

From *Santo Vega*

They charge utter yells
In half-moon formation
Like echoes of hell
Resound, hoarse and confused
Rude trumpets of hide.

From *Martín Fierro*

And beating their palms on their mouths
Their line charge upon us
What yelling! what a din!
How they spurred in mad career!
The whole tribe united
Charged with wild yells
The devils! . . . had us already rushed
Like a wild horse troop

(Ascasubi and Hernández in Holmes, pp. 44–45)

from unrepentant outlaw to law-abiding citizen. Between the two publications, Hernández himself had transformed from an outlaw living on the run to a wealthy businessman, landowner, and politician. Accordingly, this later poem called for assimilation and hard work on the part of the gaucho, advising him to "not forget to pay proper respect to superiors and magistrates" (Hernández in Shumway, p. 285). In 1879 Hernández purchased La Plata bookstore, through which he published *The Return of Martín Fierro* in style rather than as a simple pamphlet, the original format for *The Gaucho Martín Fierro.*

Literary context. *The Gaucho Martín Fierro* belongs to a genre of literature known as "gauchesque poetry," poetry written in the gaucho's voice though never written by a gaucho. This genre arose in the Río de la Plata region in the nineteenth century, just as the actual gaucho began to disappear. Gauchesque poets include Bartolomé Hidalgo, Hilario Ascasubi, and Estanislao del Campo.

The genre can be divided into two main branches: poetry that parodies the gaucho as a crude country bumpkin for the amusement of city-dwellers, and populist poetry that champions the gaucho's cause. *The Gaucho Martín Fierro* clearly falls into the latter category, and this sympathetic view of the gaucho as symbol of Argentine identity has prevailed. Over time, the gaucho has come to represent *Argentinidad,* the essence of Argentine character, in much the same way that the cowboy has become a symbol of American identity: both are understood to represent a spirit of independence and tough self-reliance forged in the vast open spaces of the frontier. In Argentina today, to say that someone is *muy gaucho* is a compliment, tantamount to saying that he or she is the most admirable of persons.

Reviews. The day after *The Gaucho Martín Fierro* was released, a review appeared in the Buenos Aires newspaper *La Prensa* describing the poem as a "palpitating story" (*Martín Fierro,* Introduction, p. 2). The poem was praised by local critics for its accurate use of gaucho dialect and its unsentimental depiction of the gaucho's plight, but *The Gaucho Martín Fierro* found its most receptive audience in the countryside. Copies of the hugely popular poem were stocked in the country stores of the pampas, and those who could not read the poem themselves gathered to hear it read. Rumors spread that Martín Fierro was a real person who someday would come riding into town, returned from the Indians. Many Argentine peasants memorized passages, and some made the tale their own, passing it along to listeners as a sung ballad. A century after the poem's publication, singers in remote areas of Argentina, unaware of any literary source for the song, were still performing versions of *The Gaucho Martín Fierro.*

It has been argued that *The Gaucho Martín Fierro* was shunned by the intellectuals of its day, but, in fact, Argentine and other South American intellectuals showed divided reactions to the poem. Renowned Uruguayan critic Juan María Torres told Argentinians that "*Martín Fierro* is a true creation, of which the literature of your country should be proud" (*Martín Fierro,* Introduction, p. 5). Alberto Navarro Viola, on the other hand, judged the poem to be "an epoch of crimes carefully passed as heroic deeds" (Navarro Viola in Pagés Larraya, p. 236).

Martín Fierro gained wider acclaim in the late nineteenth century when Spanish scholars Miguel de Unamuno and Marcelino Menéndez y Pelayo took notice of it. In 1913 Argentine writer Leopoldo Lugones likened *The Gaucho Martín Fierro* to the *Iliad* and the *Odyssey,* commending it as the national Argentine epic. Today, critics disagree as to whether the poem has its primary (or sole) importance as literary art or as political protest, but scholarly attention to *The Gaucho Martín Fierro* is intense.

—Kimberly Ball

For More Information

Andrews, George Reid. *The Afro-Argentines of Buenos Aires, 1800-1900.* Madison: The University of Wisconsin Press, 1980.

Hernández, José. *The Gaucho Martín Fierro.* Trans. Frank G. Carrino, Alberto J. Carlos, and Norman Mangouni. Delmar, N. Y.: Scholars' Facsimiles and Reprints, 1974.

Holmes, Henry A. *Martín Fierro: An Epic of the Argentine.* New York: Instituto de las Españas, 1923.

Mansilla, Lucio V. *A Visit to the Ranquel Indians.* Trans. Eva Gillies. Lincoln: University of Nebraska Press, 1997.

Martínez Estrada, Ezequiel. *X-Ray of the Pampa.* Trans. Alain Swietlicki. Austin: University of Texas Press, 1971.

Nichols, Madaline Wallis. *The Gaucho: Cattle Hunter, Cavalryman, Ideal of Romance.* Durham, N. C.: Duke University Press, 1942.

Pagés Larraya, Antonio. "José Hernández." In *Latin American Writers.* Vol. 1. New York: Charles Scribner's Sons, 1989.

Rock, David. *Argentina, 1516-1987: From Spanish Colonization to Alfonsín.* Berkeley: University of California Press, 1987.

Shumway, Nicolas. *The Invention of Argentina.* Berkeley: University of California Press, 1991.

Slatta, Richard W. *Gauchos and the Vanishing Frontier.* Lincoln: University of Nebraska Press, 1983.

The Heights of Macchu Picchu

by
Pablo Neruda

Pablo Neruda was born Neftalí Ricardo Reyes Basualto in Parral, Chile, in 1904. He gained fame 20 years later with the publication of his second book of poetry, *Veinte poemas de amor y una cancion desasperada* (*Twenty Love Poems and a Song of Despair,* 1969). By 1946, when he wrote *Alturas de Macchu Picchu,* or *The Heights of Macchu Picchu,* Neruda had become one of the most celebrated Latin American poets. The poem marks a new development in an illustrious career. In it, Neruda fully sheds the private, often surrealistic style of his youth, and assumes the mantle of a public, political poet—a role he would continue to play until his death in 1973.

THE LITERARY WORK

A group of 12 poems set largely in Machu Picchu, Peru, in 1943; published in Spanish (as *Alturas de Macchu Picchu*) in 1946, in English in 1966.

SYNOPSIS

A poet pained by modern life rediscovers a firm sense of purpose upon viewing the Inca ruins of Machu Picchu.

Events in History at the Time of the Poem

Inca Empire—legacy of stone. Although the poem presumably takes place on the day in November 1943 that Neruda visited the ruins of Machu Picchu (which Neruda spells "Macchu Picchu"), it is deeply concerned with a people who lived centuries before the poet was born, and therefore demands some sense of their ancient history. Machu Picchu was built by the Incas, one of the largest and most sophisticated pre-Columbian empires in South America. The Incas called their realm *Tahuantinsuyo,* "the four quarters of the earth"; at its zenith, around 1500, the empire stretched from northwestern Ecuador down to the Maule River in modern Chile. Yet only 300 years earlier, the Incas had been just one of countless small peoples competing for land and resources in the valleys around what is now Cuzco, Peru. Their explosive rise to greatness has been attributed to several factors: a genius for political and social organization; the ability to subjugate and exploit the peoples they conquered; and generous doses of violence and bloodshed.

Inca rulers built their empire by conquest. For hundreds of years, they successfully extracted labor and obedience from dozens of peoples whose population vastly outnumbered that of the Incas themselves. They did this by a combination of military strategy, brute force, and effective social planning. The Incas exploited the fragmented nature of neighboring societies; by forming strategic alliances with other peoples, they kept potential foes from banding against them. When one of the conquered peoples rebelled, the Incas quelled them decisively and violently. However, the Incas depended as much on social reorganization as on bloodshed to maintain control. They pioneered the concept of forced resettlement—

that is, they made defeated tribes move to new territory, and sent tribes long since vanquished to the land just vacated. A people in an unfamiliar environment, surrounded by strangers, found it difficult to muster the cooperation and decisive action necessary for a rebellion. For added security, the Incas deputed numerous governors, many of noble blood, to administer each newly acquired territory. These provincial governors took precise counts of their population, administered the laws, and forestalled discontent. Perhaps most crucially, the provincial governors ensured that each conquered family contributed its share of work and goods to the Incas.

The Incas believed that, by right of conquest, they owned not only the lands but also the labor power of the peoples they defeated. Although they did not quite enforce slavery on these peoples, they squeezed out of them all the labor they could. First, the Incas divided the farmlands of a newly conquered territory. They assigned the largest parts to themselves for practical and religious use; the remainder was reserved for use by the conquered people, who had to produce enough on the downsized territory to feed themselves. The conquered peoples, besides raising enough to sustain themselves, had to labor in the fields of the Incas, tending crops and livestock that would enrich the imperial overlords.

In short, non-Inca peoples lived hard, unpleasant lives in the Inca empire. They did not own the products of their own labor, or the land on which they worked. They were subject to the severe laws of the Incas, which included torture, the death penalty, and exile to the harsh Andean highlands. These laws distinguished between conqueror and conquered; while the Incas were not above the law, a crime committed against them was punished much more severely than the same crime against a non-Inca. Although the Incas allowed a degree of religious liberty, the conquered peoples had to abandon those aspects of their own religion that conflicted with Inca theology. The Incas occasionally required a tribute in the form of human sacrifice; they embarked on nothing of importance without appealing to oracles and engaging in sacrifice, and for major undertakings such as war, their religion required the spilling of childrens' blood.

Thus, when the poet wonders about the workers who built Machu Picchu (in the last four poems of *The Heights of Macchu Picchu*), he correctly assumes that their lives consisted of hard labor and few freedoms. Forced labor—called *mita*—built the Inca Empire. Aside from having to tend the Incas' farms and llama herds, the conquered peoples provided manpower for ambitious public works. Those obligated to provide mita (which included everyone except the Incas themselves) worked the silver mines, chopped and carved wood, served as runners in the messenger service (which united all corners of the empire), carried the litters of the emperors, and fought in the Incas' expansive wars. Almost any job that required brute human labor was executed by the conquered masses. As Neruda's poem makes clear, the common masses, not the emperors, built Machu Picchu; his verse celebrates the ruins not as the remnant of a glorious empire, but as a visible reminder of thousands of dead workers. The ruins do not serve as a symbol of ancient grandeur in the poem; "[r]ather, the ruins serve as a locus for questions about basic human activities: work, survival in nature, community life. . . . Neruda develops a profound meditation on the glory and horror of human achievement" (Bogen, p. 100).

The Incas had no written language; therefore, when Spanish conquistadors pummeled the empire in the 1530s, only traces of it survived in the form of ruins such as Machu Picchu. Beyond this visible evidence, the Incas had committed their history and theology to memory, and, as recorded by the Spanish, these memories fill thick volumes. The majority of Peruvian Indians still speak a version of the Incas' Quechua language. Beyond language is their architecture, which provides perhaps the most impressive remnants of the Incas' civilization. Their fortresses, highways that stretch for thousands of miles, and the temples where they worshipped their gods have endured the ravages of time and the destruction of the Spanish. The structures are comprised of giant, hand-hewn stones, some weighing up to 30 tons, which were dragged to the sites by manpower. Of all known Inca sites, Machu Picchu has been described as the least spoiled and most majestic.

Machu Picchu—the discovery. High in the mountains some 80 miles northwest of Cuzco lies what has been called "perhaps the most moving relic of pre-Columbian civilizations" (Alfred Bingham, p. 210). This site is Machu Picchu, a lost Inca settlement rediscovered in 1911 by Hiram Bingham from the United States. Sponsored by Yale University, Bingham was on his third expedition for Inca sites when an innkeeper at a rural hotel told him of some excellent ruins atop a nearby mountain. At first Bingham responded skeptically; he had listened to such rumors be-

Machu Picchu

fore, only to find a mediocre wall or staircase. His two companions chose not to accompany him: one preferred to study the Peruvian plants near the hotel, while the other wanted to mend his socks. So Bingham set off with just his bodyguard and the innkeeper. After a long and perilous ascent, which required them to cross the Urubamba River, scale some sheer cliffs, and hack through undergrowth, they arrived at the ruins. The find more than justified the climb: this

Inca settlement had remained unknown to most of the outside world for more than three centuries. It was surmised at first that the ruins were those of an Inca city, as reflected in the poem—Neruda calls Machu Picchu "Tall city of stepped stone" (Neruda, *The Heights of Macchu Picchu,* 6.4).

In fact Bingham "discovered" Machu Picchu only in the sense that Christopher Columbus discovered an America in which thousands of people already lived. Neighboring Peruvians knew of these ruins, which stretched between the two peaks of Machu Picchu (Old Picchu) and Huayna Picchu (New Picchu). Bingham found three families scratching out a living on the mountainside below the site, and a Peruvian named Agustín Lizárraga had explored it back in 1902. Now Bingham, by publicizing what he found, initiated a new phase in the life of the ruins; his discovery would ultimately bring tens of thousands of tourists to the site every year.

At first the Peruvian government treated Bingham with ambivalence. On the one hand, they honored him for uncovering part of the nation's heritage; on the other, they distrusted him. Legends of lost Inca gold had circulated throughout South America since the first Spanish invaders. On many occasions, Bingham was delayed or threatened by officials who suspected him of smuggling Inca treasure out of the country. As the years passed, it became evident that Machu Picchu's attractions for tourists far outvalued any mere pile of gold. The Inca city became one of the world's most famous ancient ruins.

Machu Picchu—a description. The ruins of Machu Picchu deserve notice for two reasons: they display Inca architecture at its most impressive—huge walls built on the edge of 3,000-foot cliffs; solid, solemn temples; and hundreds of broad stairways—and they have survived amazingly intact. Although Bingham and his successors had to clear the jungle from some corners of the site, Machu Picchu looked to them almost exactly as it had under the Incas. Only the old thatched roofs had vanished. While other Inca sites disintegrated in warfare or suffered destruction at the hands of enemies, Machu Picchu existed outside history, silent and unseen, for centuries, in an amazingly fine state of preservation.

The reason for its isolation is simple: the site "is in the most inaccessible corner of the most inaccessible section of the central Andes" (Hiram Bingham, p. 177). The Spanish and their colonial successors simply never found the place. No one knows exactly what a settlement built in such an inaccessible location was used for. The site has both temples and living quarters, and is surrounded by the Incas' distinctive terraced farmlands. It was initially suggested that the site was of extreme importance: a holy college perhaps, the hiding place of the last emperors, or even a monument to the mythical home of the first Incas. But later historians have rejected these suggestions. The relative scarcity of human remains indicates that the place was never much used or densely populated. The majority of bones from the site are female, suggesting to some historians that the ruins were a retreat for the Chosen Women, a class of Inca holy women who spent their lives in seclusion, but this surmise remains controversial. Most current historians believe the place was a royal resort, a palace for one of the Inca emperors and his family. Some have suggested that the site may have been abandoned even before the Spaniards arrived. In any case, the current import of the site lies not in its former uses, but in its mute testimony to a vanished civilization.

Chile in the 1940s. Although Machu Picchu sits in present-day Peru, the Inca empire encompassed Neruda's Chile as well. Neruda brought to the ruins a sensibility formed in part by conditions in Chile in the 1940s; his reflections on the lives of Inca laborers were to some extent affected by the plight of Chilean workers at the time the poem was written. As indicated, working-class Indians endured dismal conditions under the Incas and, in certain ways, the Chilean workers of Neruda's day did not live much more easily. Obviously the religious burdens imposed by the Incas no longer existed, and modernization had improved health care and the standard of living. Nevertheless, modern workers had much in common with their Inca forebears. There was in both eras a vast gap between the living conditions of the rich and the poor.

During the 1930s and 1940s Chile was the only country in Latin America to maintain a democracy that included socialist political parties. These parties favored public rather than private ownership and promised to improve conditions for the worker, but they failed to dislodge the conditions responsible for the inequity in Chile. Society consisted of an upper class that amounted to less than 10 percent of the population, a middle class that comprised about 15 percent, and a vast lower class that made up the other 75 percent. In the 1940s the majority of this 75 percent were *campesinos* (rural laborers), and although they sometimes protested against the injustices levied against them, they were far less vocal than miners or urban workers. These more prominent groups suffered miserable conditions, too, yet the miners earned nearly four times and the urban workers three times as much as the campesinos, whose income declined by close to 20 percent during the decade. The campesinos were a promising constituency, then, for socialist political parties, but there were only intermittent attempts to recruit them and they remained mostly removed from politics. From the campesinos to the miners to the urban workers, most laborers endured the same or worse living conditions than in the 1930s, a decade characterized by the economic trauma of a global depression. By the close of the 1940s some 70 percent of the Chilean population—that is, almost all the workers, be they factory laborers, miners, or peasants—were earning less than the wages that the government deemed necessary for survival.

Neruda and the working class. Neruda's father served as a conductor on ballast trains that dumped gravel on the railroad ties to prevent the lines from being washed away in southern Chile's fierce rainstorms. As a boy, Neruda spent much time among the men who performed this demanding, dangerous job. He describes them: "The crew on this type of train had to be made of iron. They came from the fields, from the suburbs, from jails, and were huge, muscular laborers" (Neruda, *Memoirs,* p. 8).

Neruda's affiliation with such workers persisted into his adult years. In 1945 he became a Chilean senator, representing a mining region. His districts, Antofagasta and Tarapacá, lay in the inhospitable north of the country, but were rich in nitrates and silver. In fact, these provinces had belonged to Peru and Bolivia until Chile conquered them in the War of the Pacific (1879–83). As one biographer points out, in reference to *Canto general,* the collection of which *The Heights of Macchu Picchu* is part, "Many of the fieldworkers who elected him to congress are direct descendants of his poem's ancient workers Juan Comefrio, Juan Cortepiedras, Juan Piesdescalzos" (Teitelboim, p. 259).

In his first speech as senator, Neruda protested the miserable living conditions of the miners he represented: he decried the fact that their "hovels are pitifully constructed of trash retrieved from the dump—cardboard boxes, pebbles, tin cans, barrel hoops. With these materials they build a room where fourteen people live one on top of the other" (Neruda in Teitelboim, p. 272). In his memoirs, Neruda speaks with pride of his years as a senator:

> I shall always cherish with pride the fact that thousands of people from Chile's most inhospitable region, the great mining region of copper and nitrate, gave me their vote. . . . They are men with scorched features; their solitude and the neglect they are consigned to has been fixed in the dark intensity of their eyes. . . . But my poetry opened the way for communication, making it possible for me to walk and move among them and be accepted as a lifelong brother by my countrymen, who led such a hard life.
>
> (Neruda, *Memoirs,* p. 167)

MACHU PICCHU: TWO DISCOVERIES

Neruda has been called the second discoverer of Machu Picchu; Hiram Bingham discovered where it was, but Neruda revealed what it meant for modern culture. It is clear that Bingham did not immediately understand the significance of his discovery. In a 1948 account of the expedition, he says that his first reaction to the Inca city was one of ecstacy: "It fairly took my breath away. . . . Surprise followed surprise in bewildering succession. . . . Would anyone believe what I had found?" (Hiram Bingham, p. 165). After examining Bingham's field journal and press releases, however, his biographer (and son, Alfred Bingham) tells a different story: the elder Bingham did not stop for long at Machu Picchu; he continued on his expedition, hoping to find something even more amazing. When he returned to the United States, he spent more time publicizing human bones he had found elsewhere; Machu Picchu was not even the focus of articles he wrote for American magazines (Alfred Bingham, p. 26). As years passed, and Machu Picchu grew in fame, Hiram Bingham retroactively embellished his story, so that the discovery would match the prominence of what was discovered; he had not been able to foresee how much the site might mean to a person such as the Chilean poet Pablo Neruda.

Neruda in the 1940s. The activist tradition of Chile's urban workers profoundly influenced Neruda. While *The Heights of Macchu Picchu* attempts to depict the lives of long-dead Inca workers, the poem's subtext places it squarely in the twentieth century. Neruda visited Machu Picchu in late 1943. Two years later, only a month before writing *The Heights of Macchu Picchu,* Neruda joined the Chilean Communist Party. He believed that only as a communist could he carry out his mission—to unify himself with the working classes and improve the conditions of life for these people.

Clearly, this decision was not made in a day, nor solely as a result of what Neruda saw at Machu Picchu. His political awakening began in Spain in the 1930s. There was a leftist government in power there at the time (during the Second Spanish Republic) and in 1936 right-wing military officers under General Francisco Franco set out to topple it. Supporting them was Nazi Germany and Mussolini's Italy. Neruda worked to mobilize international support for the Republic, wrote poems about the war, and helped Republicans escape persecution after the fascists won. He continued to develop himself politically throughout the early 1940s. On returning to South America in 1943 he had already begun to contemplate writing a "national epic"—the future *Canto general* (1950), which would include *The Heights of Macchu Picchu.*

Some of Neruda's political poetry now seems dated or naive; this is particularly true of his praise for figures like Joseph Stalin and Mao Zedong. It is important to realize that in the 1940s an aura of hope still hung over the Soviet Union. The nation had played a decisive role in defeating Adolf Hitler in World War II, and the crimes of Stalin against his people were not well known. Just as important, the Soviet Union was the chief foe of the United States, and the United States, in the eyes of many Latin Americans, was the chief enemy of their lands, too. U.S. companies stripped Latin America of its natural resources, and the expansionism of the United States had led to its military occupations of Nicaragua, Haiti, the Dominican Republic, and Cuba.

Neruda served the cause of communism faithfully, and not simply as a poet. His role as a senator would soon alter his life profoundly. In 1947 Gabriel González Videla was elected President of Chile as a member of the Radical Party. The Communist Party had played a crucial role in his victory, and he pledged to protect them. However, alarmed by the growing success of the communists, who had garnered a respectable 18 percent of the vote in 1947's municipal elections, González Videla secretly planned to destroy Chile's Communist Party shortly after his election. In 1948, in fact, the Chilean Congress outlawed the Communist Party. Neruda denounced this treachery, then went into hiding to escape government persecution. He fled the country and remained abroad for several years. In 1952 Neruda returned to Chile, where he would remain loyal to the communist cause for the rest of his life. He defended passionately with his poetry one of Chile's subsequent presidents—Salvador Allende, the first Marxist president to be elected in the Western Hemisphere. In 1973, as Neruda was slowly dying of cancer, a U.S.-supported coup overthrew Allende; the poet survived the coup by less than two weeks, leaving behind poetry that embodied his beliefs.

The Poem in Focus

Contents summary. *The Heights of Macchu Picchu* is not a narrative poem: it does not tell a story in the direct way that a novel often does. Instead, it introduces an idea or line of thought, lets it drop for a while, and returns to it later, from a different angle. Passages of description alternate with philosophical or historical questioning. Especially in the first six poems of the 12-poem group, torrents of imagery overwhelm any single interpretation. Thus, it is dangerous to jump to conclusions about the meaning of specific images or lines.

However, in its broader outline the sequence has a fairly clear progression. The first part (poems 1–5) presents a speaker searching for the comprehensive meaning of a desolate world. He is solitary, isolated from his fellow human beings by the grinding and degrading conditions of modern life. He does not probe into the root causes of this isolation, but his images suggest that it is associated with a mercenary impulse:

> Now rage has bled
> the dreary wares of the trader in creatures,
> while, in the plum tree's coronet, the dew
> has left a coat of visitations for a thousand
> years.
>
> (*Macchu Picchu,* 2.16-19)

The second half of the group (poems 6 through 12) deals explicitly with Machu Picchu, and presents answers to the quandaries of the first half. The language becomes simpler and less contorted; the anguish of the first poems gives way, first to awe in the face of the city's (for Neruda believed the ruins to be of a city) ruined splendor, and then to a confident assertion of communion with the long-dead builders of the Inca site. The poet finds an answer to his confusion in this sense of a collective human society, and discovers his duty: to serve as the voice not for an individual but for this community.

In general the cycle charts an arc from loneliness and confusion to fulfillment and faith that the individual life is wrapped up in something larger than itself. The poet's experience of Machu Picchu catalyzes this change. It has been noted that *The Heights of Macchu Picchu* "is a poem of symbolic death and of resurrection in which the poet himself participates as actor, beginning as a lonely voyager and ending with the manifestation of his full commitment to the collectivity, to the American indigenous people" (Durán and Sufir, p. 89).

Within this larger forward movement, some conclusions can be reached about the individual poems. The first opens with the poet searching, "like an empty net," for the "jasmine / of our exhausted human spring": he looks for, but cannot find, a perspective on life that will reconcile him to the suffering and struggle he sees (*Macchu Picchu,* 1.22–23). The shape of this suffering emerges in the second poem, which contrasts the natural world's ability to regenerate itself with the exhausting, depleting frenzy of human life. While a flower develops a seed that in turn becomes a new flower, human life seems to be governed by scarcity and by each individual's need to protect what he or she has:

> . . . for in corridors—air, sea or land—
> who guards his veins unarmed
> like scarlet poppies?
> (*Macchu Picchu,* 2.14-16)

The second poem closes on the question, What is man? "In which of his metallic movements / lived on imperishably the quality of life?" (*Macchu Picchu,* 2.43-44). The next three poems attempt to define this quality by discussing its seeming opposite: death. Neruda asserts that the degrading conditions of modern life fill every day with spiritual death: "Not one death but many came to each, / each day a little death" (*Macchu Picchu,* 3.4-5). These small, metaphorical deaths are contrasted with the grand single death imagined in the fourth poem, which is associated with the poet's love of his fellow man. The poet could accept death if he felt it were shared—that is, if everyone were united in a common cause. But "when, little by little, man came denying me / closing his paths and doors so that I could not touch / his wounded inexistence with my divining fingers," the poet falls back into isolation, "dying of my own death" (*Macchu Picchu,* 4.23–25, 31). The stage is set for the fifth poem. This brief poem is a bleak statement of isolation, ending when the speaker searches his own wounds but finds only cold, empty air: "and nothing did I meet within the wound save wind in gusts / that chilled my cold interstices of soul" (*Macchu Picchu,* 5.12–13). From this point, he can only rise; and rise he does, "through the barbed jungle's thickets" (*Macchu Picchu,* 6.3) to Machu Picchu.

THE POET IN THE CITY

Many of the images of barrenness in *The Heights of Macchu Picchu* originate in the urban experience. From his first days in Santiago, Chile, Neruda had a deeply ambivalent attitude toward cities. The initial two chapters of his memoirs are called "Country Boy" and "Lost in the City." The first deals with his slowly unfolding rural childhood; the second with his college life in the city. The contrast in titles suggests what he thought about cities.

Chile was, and is, a country of great contrasts. The large metropolitan area of Santiago is as chic, fast-paced, and crowded as any capital in the world, but leaving the city for rural Chile is like stepping backwards in time, into a world still dominated by family, community, and the flow of the seasons. Neruda never wholly warmed to the frenetic pace of Santiago, although his experiences there were many and varied. Of his father's railworkers' cape, which Neruda himself wore during his college years, he wrote: "This garment used to stir up the fury of good people and of others who were not so good. . . . These underworld characters, dancers and carpetbaggers, sniggered at our capes and our way of life. We poets fought back hard" (Neruda, *Memoirs,* p. 43).

His early experience as an ambassador for Chile (1927–38) cemented Neruda's attitude about cities. In an early posting, he was sent to the Far East as a diplomat; Neruda was aghast and lonely in the huge Asian metropolises. He himself acknowledged that his isolation in Asia contributed to the desolate mood of his early 1930s poems. Such memories seem also to be in the back of his mind in the first few poems of *The Heights of Macchu Picchu.*

In the sixth poem and beyond, the issues of the first half of the work are revisited and transformed. In his experience of the Inca city, the poet finds the unifying point of the human and natural worlds, which had seemed agonizingly separate in the second poem:

> In you two lineages that had run parallel
> met where the cradle both of man and light
> rocked in a wind of thorns.
> (*Macchu Picchu,* 6.7-9)

In the seventh poem death returns, as the poet ponders the fact that the city is abandoned and lifeless. But instead of the daily deaths of the first half, this is "the true, the most consuming death," which leaves behind "a permanence of stone and language" (*Macchu Picchu,* 7.4,22). Neruda writes:

On the day the clay-colored hand
was utterly changed into clay, and when
  dwarf eyelids closed
upon bruised walls and hosts of battlements,
when all of man in us cringed back into its
  burrow—
there remained a precision unfurled
on the high places of the human dawn,
the tallest crucible that ever held our silence,
a life of stone after so many lives.
(*Macchu Picchu,* 7.28-35)

The next two poems are wholly given over to evoking the loveliness and grandeur of the Andes and the Andean city. The eighth is a lyrical invitation: "Come with me, American love" (*Macchu Picchu,* 8.1). The ninth, a poem of 43 lines, is structured as a chant of descriptions: "Mirror splinters, thunderstorm foundations. / Thrones ruined by the climbing vine" (*Macchu Picchu,* 9.16-17). Human beings, specifically the slaves who built the city, are the subject of the tenth poem. The poet wonders whether the ancient city was a center of pain and suffering: "Macchu Picchu, did you lift / stone above stone upon a groundwork of rags?" (*Macchu Picchu,* 10.24–25). In the eleventh poem, Neruda asserts his sympathy with those buried workers, claiming that they are more important than the architectural grandeur of the city. This recalls the love of humanity expressed in the fourth poem; but here, instead of retreating into isolation, the poet claims not only fellow feeling, but direct kinship with the vanished workers, who are "rising to birth with me, as my own brothers" (*Macchu Picchu,* 11.25). Recalling the nature of Inca society, it is crucial that he align himself, not with the buildings or what they represent of Inca culture or civilization, but rather with what the buildings signify as a product of human labor. Now the stage is set for the concluding poem, which rejects solitude and confusion. The poet will speak for the masses of workers, both past and present, and in this task he has found a purpose that will sustain him. The final lines of *The Heights of Macchu Picchu* ring with a confidence that is the polar opposite of the first poem's empty net:

Give me the struggle, the iron, the volcanoes.
Let bodies cling like magnets to my body.
Come quickly to my veins and to my mouth.
Speak through my speech, and through my
  blood.
(*Macchu Picchu,* 12.42-45)

Connections to communism. Neruda's communist beliefs inform our understanding of *The Heights of Macchu Picchu*. Many communist writers have espoused the doctrine that genuinely great art originates, not in the private mind of an individual artist, but rather, in a direct way, from the people: an artist who cannot draw inspiration from the struggles and hopes of the masses will produce works that express only misery and confusion. As Neruda himself said, "The unhappy writer, the crucified writer are part of the ritual of happiness in the twilight of capitalism. . . . We poets have the right to be happy, as long as we are close to the people of our country and in the thick of the fight for their happiness" (Neruda, *Memoirs,* p. 263). Neruda did not think he ennobled workers by writing about them; he believed his poetry was ennobled and made worthwhile because it was about workers.

This belief is evident in *The Heights of Macchu Picchu*. While Neruda's political convictions suffuse the poems, he does not approach communism as an intellectual or critical exercise. Instead, he focuses his attention as closely as he can on visualizing the real human beings caught up in the historical march of the Inca Empire:

Let me have back that slave you buried here!
Wrench from these lands the stale bread
of the poor, prove me the tatters
on the serf, point out his window.
Tell me how he slept when alive,
whether he snored,
his mouth agape like a dark scar
worn by fatigue into the wall.
(*Macchu Picchu,* 10.29-36)

Part of the twelfth poem is a litany of occupations: farmers, shepherds, grooms, masons, jewelers, and potters are all mentioned in its poetic community. Clearly, Neruda was interested in building a pattern of images that evokes the physical, solid, and tactile qualities of work itself, and not merely impersonal aspects of the political philosophies of capitalism and communism.

Neruda demonstrated this interest not only in writing but also in politics. On his first day in the Chilean Senate (May 30, 1945), he made a

Pablo Neruda

speech about the terrible conditions endured by the miners that he represented. And in 1946, the year in which *The Heights of Macchu Picchu* was published, he delivered a series of lectures on the problems of workers in the North.

Sources and literary context. Neruda spent the first part of World War II as a diplomat in Mexico. In an interview published in 1940 he said, "In Mexico you have some great poets; I would like for Chile's poets to have that special quality that is rooted in form, like poets here. . . . I have purposely attempted to do away with form, that form which is appropriate to Mexico," the implication being that he was trying to help Chile find its own distinct form (Neruda in Teitelboim, p. 249). Mexico intrigued him, and his encounter with its culture clearly influenced his plan to write a great "national epic" of the South American peoples, *Canto general,* of which *The Heights of Macchu Picchu* is the first fruit.

Neruda left Mexico for Chile in September 1943. But, in spite of the fact that he was traveling by airplane, he did not arrive in his homeland until November; his trip was continually interrupted by stays in various capitals, where he was toasted by the intellectual elite of South America. The journey stimulated his desire to learn more about his native surroundings, and this desire resulted in his visit to Cuzco and Machu Picchu in Peru in October 1943.

Neruda's project—to channel the voice of a whole people through his own poetry—owes a good deal to the example of U.S. poet Walt Whitman, who was a lifelong influence on the Chilean poet. Neruda calls him "my comrade from Manhattan" (Neruda, *Memoirs,* p. 262). The Nicaraguan poet Rubén Darío also cast a long shadow over Neruda's career, as Neruda himself acknowledged. Darío wrote at the turn of the twentieth century, and began the *modernismo* movement in Latin America, which ran parallel to European modernism. In a sense, he was the founder of modern Latin American poetry. At a banquet held to honor Neruda and the Spanish writer Federico Garcia Lorca in 1934, the two poets dedicated their honors to Darío. "His luminous name," said Neruda, "should be remembered in its every essence" (Neruda, *Memoirs,* p. 113). Although Neruda and Darío were quite different, and Darío rarely wrote political poetry, their lives reveal some broad similarities. Both traveled to Spain, and were intimately involved with Spanish poetry. Just as important, both were well-traveled in Latin America: Darío even lived in Chile for a time. Both became major figures in the development of poetry in Latin America. Neruda, the later figure, acknowledged his debt to his forerunner:

> Darío was a huge elephant, a music-maker who shattered all the glass windows in the Spanish language to let in the air of the world. . . . Our American stratum is dusty rock, crushed lava, clay mixed with blood. We don't know how to work in crystal. Our elegant poets sound hollow.
> (Neruda, *Memoirs,* p. 261)

When Neruda set out to catch the voice of his continent in *The Heights of Macchu Picchu,* he knew that he was speaking a poetic language revivified by Rubén Darío.

A poet with an energetic social life, Neruda was capable of drawing inspiration from almost anything or anyone. Most of the poets who can be said to have influenced his work were also his personal friends. He is perhaps most like those poets who drew inspiration from the social movements of their time. Like the French poet Paul Éluard, Neruda abandoned the privacy of surrealism for the public commitment of communism. Like the Peruvian poet César Vallejo, Neruda left South America to fight fascism in Europe. The Spanish poet and dramatist Federico Garcia Lorca, whom Neruda met in Argentina in 1932, helped draw Neruda into the struggle against Spanish fascism, an event that profoundly altered Neruda's sense of the poet's public role.

Reviews. To a certain extent, Neruda's literary reputation has been linked to the fortunes of the political causes he espoused. He was widely read in the Soviet Union and China; on the other hand, his fame was slow to spread in the United States, where distrust of communism and dislike for political poetry retarded appreciation for him. Politically motivated criticism was especially common—and virulent—in Latin America, and especially when the poet was still alive: a recurrent figure in his *Memoirs* is that of a critic who attacks him simply because of his political views (attacks that Neruda cherished, because they indicated that his political views were having an impact). In 1946 some newspapers removed his name from advertisements for the first edition of *The Heights of Mac-*

NERUDA AMONG THE RUINS

It is reported that during the visit to Machu Picchu, someone asked Neruda for his immediate impressions, to which he supposedly replied, "I feel that it's the most ideal place to have a barbecue." Although he did not remember having said this, he later commented, "Perhaps when one is struck dumb by a colossal and mysterious phenomenon and he is asked a transcendental question, the first psychological defense of someone who is face-to-face with a moment out of eternity is to grab hold of the most obvious everyday phenomenon in order to affirm his earthly existence" (Neruda in Teitelboim, p. 259).

chu Picchu; he was simply too controversial.

The Heights of Macchu Picchu has long been recognized as a cornerstone of Neruda's work. It has been called "a consummation," as well as a masterpiece (Bizzarro, p. 7). Michael Wood has stated, "It is perhaps the best of all introductions to Neruda, since his gifts receive their full expression there and since it is also a form of spiritual autobiography" (Wood, p. 10). Hernán Loyola has described the poem as "a poetic synthesis, simultaneously a culmination and a doorway" to a new poetry (Loyola, p. 25). M. L. Rosenthal has suggested that the work is marred by a hint of propaganda, "inseparable from the public role Neruda has felt he must play" (Rosenthal, p. 50.) If there has been some disagreement among critics, though, the reaction of the general population has been more unanimous. Neruda "was certainly the most popular of poets, beloved by all classes of Chileans" (Alberti in Poirot, p. 112).

—Jacob Littleton

For More Information

Bingham, Alfred. *Portrait of an Explorer: Hiram Bingham, Discoverer of Machu Pichu.* Ames: Iowa State University Press, 1989.

Bingham, Hiram. *Lost City of the Incas.* New York: Duell, Sloan and Pearce, 1948.

Bizzarro, Salvatore. *Pablo Neruda: All Poets the Poet.* London: Scarecrow Press, 1979.

Bogen, Dan. "An Old-Left Adam." *The Nation* 254, no. 3 (January 27, 1992): 95–99.

Cobo, Bernabe. *Inca Religion and Customs.* Trans. Roland Hamilton. Austin: University of Texas Press, 1990.

Durán, Manuel, and Margery Safir. *Earth Tones: The Poetry of Pablo Neruda.* Bloomington: University of Indiana Press, 1981.

Kofas, Jon V. *The Struggle for Legitimacy: Latin American Labor and the United States, 1930-1960.* Tempe: Arizona State University Press, 1992.

Loyola, Hernán. *Ser y morir en Pablo Neruda.* Santiago, Chile: Editorial Santiago, 1967.

Neruda, Pablo. *The Heights of Macchu Picchu.* Trans. Nathaniel Tarn. New York: Farrar, Straus & Giroux, 1966.

———. *Memoirs.* Trans. Hardie St. Martin. New York: Penguin, 1977.

Poirot, Luis. *Pablo Neruda: Absence and Presence.* New York: Norton and Company, 1990.

Rosenthal, M. L. "*The Heights of Macchu Picchu.*" *Saturday Review* 50 (September 2, 1967): 25.

Teitelboim, Volodia. *Neruda: An Intimate Biography.* Trans. Beverly J. DeLong-Tonelli. Austin: University of Texas Press, 1991.

Wood, Michael. "Pablo Neruda." *The New York Review of Books,* October 3, 1974, 8-12.

The Hour of the Star

by
Clarice Lispector

Clarice Lispector was born in 1920 in the Ukraine to a family of Slavonic-Jewish descent. Her family relocated to Brazil when Clarice was two months old, and she spent a happy childhood in the beautiful but poverty-stricken Northeastern city of Recife. In 1932 her family moved south to Rio de Janeiro, where, after completing law school, Lispector became one of her country's most successful journalists and well-regarded writers. Her first novel, *Close to the Savage Heart,* was published to critical acclaim when Lispector was only 24 years old. The novel took a radical turn from the regional stories popular in Brazil at the time, and with its help Lispector soon became known for her introspective fiction and its exploration of philosophical, universal themes. Because of her preoccupations with language and philosophy, she was accused at times of being indifferent to the actual plight of her fellow Brazilians. Perhaps partly in response to this criticism, Lispector wrote *The Hour of the Star,* which combines her "highly subjective fiction [with] certain sociopolitical themes of urgent importance for Brazil" (Peixoto, p. 89).

THE LITERARY WORK

A novel set in Rio de Janeiro, Brazil, during the 1970s; published (as *A hora de estrela*) in Portuguese in 1977, in English in 1985.

SYNOPSIS

A male narrator struggles to write the story of a poor, uneducated young woman from the rural Northeast who lives in the dockside tenements of Rio de Janeiro. While portraying her bleak existence, he wrestles with his own questions of ethics, meaning, and social justice.

Events in History at the Time the Novel Takes Place

Lispector and Brazilian literature. When Lispector broke onto Brazil's literary scene in the 1940s, it was dominated by realist writers who composed fictions that often featured Brazil's poor, outcasts, criminals, or powerless women. This literary realism dominated Brazil's second stage of modernism, the period from 1930 to 1945. Writers like Jorge Amado (see ***Gabriela, Clove and Cinnamon,*** also covered in *Latin American Literature and Its Times*), Graciliano Ramos (see ***Barren Lives***), Raquell de Queiroz, and José Lins do Rêgo produced documentary-style prose fiction "strongly committed to social justice and national development" and often concerned specifically with the Northeast (Fitz, p. 22). Brazil's modernist literature in general was dominated by two main impulses: the desire to produce innovative new writing in the spirit of Europe's post-World War I avant-garde movements, and the need to locate and create an "authentic Brazilian literature, one based on national themes, forms, and modes of expression" (Fitz, p. 22). Writers sought to discover characters and ideas indigenous exclusively to Brazil. It was the absence of any nationalistic or regional concerns in Lispector's works that marked her fiction as different within the currents of Brazil's literature. Lispector believed that social ills should not merely be fodder for literature—one ought to do something about them. Over the years she sustained a great deal of criticism from those who faulted her for not addressing these ills enough in her stories.

Lispector calls as much attention as possible to the fact that there is always someone *writing* any story, and that in *The Hour of the Star* Macabéa's story is told by a male novelist of a higher social class than his subject. This reflects a real-life phenomenon, that of the socially-conscious authors prominent in Brazil when Lispector made her appearance on the literary scene. Most of these authors were relatively well-off men who wrote from the point of view of an unnamed, omniscient narrator. The narrators' omniscience and invisibility left unexplored any question of his own complicity in the oppression he was describing, or his right in the first place to speak for his subjects.

By highlighting the very processes of creating narratives and characters, Lispector begins to question "how narrative itself [is] implicated in structures of domination and victimization" (Peixoto, p. xx). Her initial novel, *Close to the Savage Heart,* was praised as the first Brazilian work of fiction to make language not just a vehicle but also part of the subject matter (Fitz, p. 24). The 1950s saw the advent of the French *nouveau roman* (new novel), which focused on the relationship between language and reality, and Lispector's work shares some of the new novel's tendencies, though there is no indication that this form influenced her; her fiction shows more concern with the psychology of characters than that of the French writers. In fact, Lispector has been described as somewhat of an anomaly in respect to her novels' preoccupations with language and other universal concerns, which continued to emerge in her fiction of the 1960s and '70s.

Narrating the oppressed. More than any of Lispector's previous fiction, *The Hour of the Star* deals with a specific socioeconomic issue of the time—the plight of the young *Nordestina* (female from the Northeast), who struggles to eke out a living and an identity for herself in the poor tenements of Rio de Janeiro. While the novel evokes the time in which it is set, it is also deeply concerned with the act of writing itself. The male narrator, Rodrigo S.M., takes center stage as he consciously attempts to imagine the Nordestina, Macabéa—her feelings, character, and the events and meanings of her life.

In their migration to urban centers that could barely sustain them, the situation of Brazil's Northeasterners was one of poverty and despair, and the novel reflects this reality; but more than anything it highlights the middle-class male who writes the story of an oppressed Nordestina. Critics who try to explain the use of a male narrator have said that he provides Lispector with a cold distance from which to treat a difficult subject. At the same time, however, "the male mask, by increasing the distance between narrator and character, also points up the outrageous presumption that writing the other, especially the oppressed other, implies"; in this way, "[Lispector] accuses writer, narrator, and reader of participating in and profiting from that oppression" (Peixoto, pp. 92, 89). Addressing the narrator and reader, Lispector, at a loss herself, ends her "Author's Dedication" with a challenge: "[*The Hour of the Star*] is an unfinished book because it offers no answer. An answer I hope someone somewhere in the world may be able to provide. You perhaps?" (Lispector, *The Hour of the Star,* p. 8).

***Nordestinos*—Northeasterners in Brazil.** One of the world's largest countries, Brazil in 1980 had a population of 121 million in an area of 3,286,488 square miles (8,511,965 square kilometers). The vast territory is known for its intense regional diversity. Brazilians throughout history have, in fact, tended to define themselves based on their regional roots. Normally Brazil is divided into five distinct regions: the North, Northeast, South, Southeast, and Central-West. Of these regions the South and Southeast are dominant, while the Northeast is not only the poorest in Brazil but "one of the major underdeveloped areas of the hemisphere"—a region beset by poverty and social problems that seem almost unfixable (Burns, p. 419). Almost two-thirds of the Northeast is made up of the arid, interior *sertão,* an area especially afflicted by poverty, in part because of its irregular rainfall; the remaining third is made up of a transitional semihumid zone and a humid coastal strip where, among other things, planters grow sugar. Plagued by droughts, unemployment, high infant mortality, and illiteracy, the Northeast contained 21 percent of Brazil's population and provided less than 10 percent of the country's national product in 1965 (Burns, p. 420). Most of the region's peasants lived in small clay structures with dirt floors and did not own the land they worked; ownership was instead concentrated in the hands of a few landowners in a manner that recalled the region's colonial roots.

Hunger was common, as were diseases, intestinal parasites, and other health problems.

In the 1950s economists recommended increased capital investment in the Northeast, and Sudene (Superintendency of the Development of the Northeast) was created to produce a development program for the region. The program encouraged industrialization, population dispersal, and increased production in agriculture. Though economic conditions improved in the 1960s as a result of these efforts, the fundamental problems haunting the region (poverty, unemployment, underdevelopment, illiteracy, malnourishment) have for the most part remained unsolved.

The migration south. Urbanization in the 1930s and '40s prompted a massive wave of migration from Brazil's rural areas to its cities. Because of insistent drought and poverty-related diseases like typhoid and tuberculosis as well as underemployment, the unemployed, uneducated, overwhelmingly illiterate refugees from these hinterlands moved cityward and southward in droves. The Northeasterners who migrated southward found themselves at a disadvantage because of their illiteracy and lack of job skills.

Migrants from the Northeast were measured against certain regional stereotypes. They were typically identified with the most underprivileged in society. The general population regarded them as lazy, unmotivated, and backward, guided by a primitive, irrational religiosity and an incurable nostalgia for their native region. In fact, poor Northeastern immigrants of the time had the same aspirations as middle-class city dwellers—better education and financial security for themselves and their children—but their access to the means for realizing these desires was usually far more restricted. Given their heritage of Indian, black, and white racial strains, Northeasterners often differed physically too, sometimes becoming targets of racism in the white-dominated South.

Many Northeastern migrants actually managed to find jobs, but in lowly positions as doormen or construction workers, earning minimum wages or less. Along with other former rural dwellers, they settled into tenements, *favelas* (shanty towns), *cabeças-de-porcos* (rooming houses), or *hospedarias* (flophouses). A few early-to mid-twentieth-century writers portrayed some of the dismal experiences of such lifestyles—Jorge Amado in his novel *Suor* (1934; *Sweat*) about the inhabitants of a tenement in Salvador, and Carolina Maria de Jesus in her diary *Quarto de Despejo* (1960; *Child of the Dark*) about life in a São Paulo favela.

Life in the tenements of Rio. Rio's slums are legendary, some sprawling near the docks; others scrolling up the city's hills. The slums stemmed from an imbalance between urbanization and industrialization. There were not enough jobs for the incoming migrants, but, rather than return to their destitute homelands, the underemployed refugees remained, squeezing into the colonial-style tenements of the dockside slums and, in the 1940s, building shantytowns. Much has been written about Rio's favelas, or shantytowns, less about the tenement slums in which Macabéa lives in the novel. But their populations are demographically similar—overwhelmingly non-white and uneducated. Together the slums and shantytowns formed the basis of Rio's cheap work force. About half of all slum dwellers held jobs outside their own communities. For the most part, they labored to support the lifestyle enjoyed by the white elite, as construction workers, waiters, butlers, and chauffeurs. They constructed "the high rise buildings in which Rio lives and works and in which it takes such pride, and it is they, too who maintain and clean these buildings" (Perlman, p. 29).

POPULATION GROWTH—RIO IN THE SOUTH, RECIFE IN THE NORTHEAST

	1900	1920	1940	1960
Rio de Janeiro	800,000	1,157,000	1,781,000	3,372,000
Recife	113,000	238,000	348,000	707,000

(Adapted from Burns, p. 410)

Working women, whose numbers reached 6.1 million by 1970, held jobs as maids, cooks, nannies, and office or department store clerks. There was little job security for the working poor, since the number of willing laborers far exceeded the quantity of available positions. Many poor women, frustrated with the dearth of job opportunities or lack of control over working conditions, turned to the streets. In 1970s Rio, the dockside slums of Acre Street, where Macabéa lives in the novel, were in fact teeming with prostitutes ready to service the area's sailors.

Some of these real-life prostitutes were mothers. Often at a young age, women in the slums started having many children. Single motherhood became the norm, and even a full-time job might not put enough food on the table for the family. To some of these women, prostitution

Slums of Rio de Janeiro.

seemed to offer the only means of closing the gap.

The Brazilian miracle. Following a military coup in 1964 Brazil experienced a celebrated economic boom, advertised the world over as the "economic miracle." But beneath the glittering sheen of a hyperactive economy, the gap between the country's rich and poor grew ever wider. Of roughly 105 million Brazilians in 1970, the top 10 percent prospered, earning nearly half the nation's wealth, while the bottom 50 percent were by all accounts worse off than ever before, barely garnering 15 percent of the nation's income (Burns, p. 471). During the so-called economic miracle, four out of five Brazilians experienced a decline in income and living standards. At first, many clung to the allure of the "trickle down theory"—the idea that national prosperity would naturally be passed down to petty businesses and poor consumers—but after an oil crisis in 1973 the economy took a sharp turn for the worse, squashing these hopes. By the mid-1970s, when the novel takes place, it was apparent that the military government was placing national industrialization and economic growth above the well-being of Brazil's poor and even its middle class.

The 1964 military coup was backed by the nation's upper and middle classes, the Catholic Church, and the press. The military unseated João Goulart, a liberal whose social reformist politics were alarming the upper and middle classes. Aiming to slow his reforms, his opponents staged rallies, such as the "March of the Family with God and Liberty" in São Paulo on March 19, 1964. Tensions escalated with Goulart reprimanding the army's generals for failing to support him and for lacking discipline. Meanwhile, economic problems proliferated under Goulart's presidency, including a slowdown in growth and repeated labor strikes. Finally, accusing the president of being a communist, the army, with the approval of the U.S. government, moved to overthrow Goulart and marched into Rio to depose him on March 31, 1964.

U.S. influence on cultural values. *The Hour of the Star*'s narrator attributes only a few characteristics to Macabéa, among them her preference for Coca-Cola and her desire to look like Marilyn Monroe. With hundreds of thousands of Brazilian tourists visting the United States, and with U.S.-headed firms dominating advertising in Brazil, status symbols in the two countries became indistinguishable: fancy cars, luxurious apartments with a view, summer homes, designer clothes, and mass-produced home fashions. Affected by advertising and media saturation, many Brazilians avidly consumed nonessential products like cigarettes or cola. Meanwhile, though people mim-

One of the demonstrations mounted in São Paulo against João Goulart, March 21, 1964.

icked the United States in certain respects, they also blamed it for much of what was wrong in Brazil at the time, pointing to its support of the unpopular military regime. As early as 1965 Brazilians grew disenchanted with the regime (Burns, p. 455). Its policies became anathema to workers, intellectuals, and democrats, from its freezing of wages in the face of rising prices, to its censorship, to its increasingly authoritarian rule.

Military dictatorship to democracy. Atrocities committed by the Brazilian military dictatorship (1964–85) did not receive as much worldwide attention as those enacted by its Argentinean or Chilean counterparts, but life under the generals was nonetheless oppressive, particularly in the early 1970s. Censorship and torture were widespread. Left-wing intellectuals were persecuted. While a number of opponents to the regime expatriated to Europe or the United States, others resisted; a violent antigovernment guerrilla opposition formed and, beginning in 1969, staged daring actions, including the kidnapping of foreign diplomats. According to some historians, the guerrillas were trying to provoke the military government into committing such blatant human rights violations that Brazilians would rise up in protest. Gunfire erupted in the streets of Rio in 1970 because of the government-guerrilla conflict; by 1973, however, the guerrilla forces were depleted. The middle class felt betrayed by the military leaders whom it had helped bring to power, but took no organized action. And the poor continued to fester in their already squalid slums. Those who wished to organize in support of the underprivileged met with so much bureaucracy and bad faith at the highest levels of government that their hands were effectively tied. But the situation would not be tolerated in Brazil for much longer.

The Hour of the Star appeared in print at the end of the 1970s during a period of change. The decade brought the slow transition from military rule to democracy, a process denoted by the term *abertura* ("opening," referring to the loosening up of the political and cultural scene). While students were rioting for social justice, clashing violently with the state police at São Paulo's Catholic University in 1977, members of the various underprivileged classes were slowly mobilizing their forces.

> The abertura meant that radical democratic themes—religious, feminist, localist, but chiefly 'humanistic'—were encountered in new ways (or for the first time) as social movements appeared to articulate them. For many people . . . the new social movements provided the first political experience of their lives.
>
> (Yúdice, p. 103)

The year 1978 saw the founding of the *Movimento Negro Unificado Contra Discriminacao Racial* (MNU), Brazil's most important organization of the contemporary black movement. Citizens began pressing for a return to civilian instead of military government. At the same time, the United States under President Jimmy Carter was taking a stand on human rights issues around the world. In Brazil, the seeds of resistance, which had been sown decades earlier, were given new life by international attention. None of this, however, affected the pervasive problems in the Northeast or stemmed the tide of migrants that continued to surge into the urban centers in the decade following the release of the novel (1977–87). Another 15 million rural dwellers crowded hopefully into cities, which were as unequipped to handle them as they had been in the character Macabéa's day (Burns, p. 481).

The Novel in Focus

Plot summary. The novel opens with the discursive musings of its male narrator, Rodrigo S.M., who begins to construct a narrative around "the unremarkable adventures of a girl [from the Northeast] living in a hostile city" (*Hour of the Star,* pp. 12, 15). The narrator is highly self-conscious and involved in much more than a description of his characters and their lives. Discussions of writer's block, creative frustration, and the difficulty of his subject form a significant portion of the book so that Rodrigo S.M. and his own act of writing Macabéa's story becomes as important within the novel as the story he tells. Throughout a long introductory section Rodrigo S.M. muses on words—*God, history, faith, life,* and *death*—that will emerge as the novel's major themes. The story of Rodrigo S.M.'s fictional character Macabéa meanwhile begins, hesitantly, to unfold. Aiming to maintain his "cold impartiality," the narrator tries at times to hide behind the socially enforced division between his situation and Macabéa's—"There are those who have. And there are those who have not. It's very simple: the girl had not. Hadn't what? Simply this: she had not" (*Hour of the Star,* p. 25). Despite these attempts to distance himself, Rodrigo S.M. ends up professing to have merged with his character to such an extent that their lives and deaths intertwine. When he makes the decision to let her die, he claims to have "died" alongside her: "Death is instantaneous and passes in a flash. I know, for I have just died with the girl. Forgive my dying. It was unavoidable" (*Hour of the Star,* p. 85).

This movement of the narrator toward his character appears to occur only after much resistance and struggle. The difficulty Rodrigo S.M. encounters in trying to write Macabéa's story perhaps reflects the difficulty with which society's elites confronted the prospect of leaving their perches and engaging themselves in society as a whole. To some extent, it may also reflect their foolhardiness in speaking for the impoverished. "In order to speak about this girl," writes Rodrigo S.M., "I must acquire dark circles under my eyes from lack of sleep: dozing from sheer exhaustion like a manual laborer . . . to put myself on the same footing as the girl from the North-east" (*Hour of the Star,* p. 19).

As imagined by Rodrigo S.M., Macabéa lives in the tenements of Acre Street, in the heart of Rio's dockside red-light district. Here countless prostitutes, mainly other young Nordestinas like Macabéa, hawk their wares to sailors for the price of a good dinner. Meanwhile, Macabéa takes the bus each day to her job as a typist for a pulley company, a job she performs poorly since she is nearly illiterate. At the opening of the novel, she narrowly escapes being fired when her boss, struck by her docile reception of the bad news that he is letting her go, has a change of heart.

Macabéa and her four roommates (all of whom are called Maria and all of whom work at the local department store) share a small tenement room with thin walls and no hot water. The Marias do not figure prominently in Macabéa's life, except as obstacles to privacy, since the living quarters are so close. Their situation is so common it might be copied from a sociological text—one can only imagine that in the rooms next to theirs are other groups of struggling women, trekking off to work each day either in shops or offices or on the streets to sell their bodies.

In early May, as spring takes its first steps and brides begin shopping for their veils, Macabéa unusually takes a day off work, lying to her employer about a toothache. What freedom awaits her, alone for once at home without the omnipresent Marias! She waltzes around the room to the strains coming from a transistor radio; she begs some instant coffee and boiling water from her landlady, then savors the luxurious liquid as it warms her belly and sweetens her lips. She has never been so happy in her entire life. The following morning, this withered, undernourished virgin awakens, her entire body gripped by "an unforeseen ecstasy" (*Hour of the Star,* p. 42).

That afternoon Macabéa meets her future boyfriend, Olímpico, whom she immediately recognizes as a native Northeasterner. The two share the same unmistakable physical traits; when Olímpico first speaks, his singsong intonation further betrays his origins. They begin a short-lived romance of sorts—she is infatuated; he is aggressively condescending. Their relationship consists largely of walks peppered with frustrating conversation, and characterized by the ever-present downfall of rain.

Olímpico is in many ways a typical Northeastern street thug, of illegitimate birth, with no prospects. Raised by his stepfather to be deceitful and opportunistic, he feels destined to become a politician, but presently labors as a lowly metal worker (a title he inflates in conversation to metallurgist). He harbors two demonstrations of his manliness: a gold tooth, and the secret knowledge of a murder committed in his youth, when he stabbed his rival to death during a backwoods duel. He has a penchant for attending the funerals of strangers and regularly weeps over newspaper obituaries, an act that undercuts his pretended machismo. He also carves wooden statues of Catholic saints, which he cannot bear to sell because they are so well crafted. Nevertheless, the narrator concludes that Olímpico is "wicked to the core" (*Hour of the Star,* p. 47). Macabéa, however, who has never had a boyfriend before, loves him and hopes for a marriage proposal.

Olímpico soon becomes bored with Macabéa, repulsed by her ugliness and annoyed by her constant barrage of questions for which, despite his pretensions to superior knowledge, he has no answers. Their walks become less frequent and their conversations more abusive, until finally Olímpico leaves Macabéa for her seductive officemate Glória. "A cunning vixen but nonetheless goodhearted," Glória is everything that Macabéa is not—lower-middle-class, well-fed, and very aware of her feminine powers (*Hour of the Star,* p. 64). She has fair skin and dyed blond hair, attributes that mark her as a *carioca* (native of Rio), clearly superior to Macabéa in Olímpico's eyes.

When her persistent chest cold proves to be tuberculosis, Macabéa is unfazed by the news. She does not understand what the doctor is telling her, and so informs no one of her condition. So when Glória sends Macabéa to seek the divining skills of a clairvoyante, it is not out of concern for her health but rather out of guilt over taking away her boyfriend, Olímpico.

Armed with a loan from Glória, Macabéa sets out by taxi (the first in her life) to see Madame Carlota. Carlota welcomes Macabéa into her gaudy home with all the ingratiating sweetness befitting a charlatan, but everything she divines about the poor girl's past is remarkably accurate. In fact, she sees the grim facts as being much worse than Macabéa ever imagined, and sends Macabéa into a state of shock: "Macabéa turned pale; it had never occurred to her that her life was that awful" (*Hour of the Star,* p. 75). Up until this point, Macabéa has been sanguine—insofar as she was aware of her hopeless circumstances, she accepted them—and Madame Carlota's description of her wretchedness may be the closest Macabéa has ever come to seeing her position from an outsider's point of view.

Carlota then predicts that Macabéa will be fired from her job after all, and ends up feeling so sorry for the girl she offers to waive her normal fee. But as a dejected Macabéa is about to leave, Carlota suddenly changes her tune, telling Macabéa her luck is actually about to change for the better. Not only will she keep her job and win back Olímpico, but something even better lies in store for her—a rich and handsome foreign gentleman named Hans is about to appear and sweep her off her feet. They will be married and she will have all the satin and velvet she could ever dream of—even a fur coat.

Macabéa, who has made it a habit not to think about the future—"to have a future [is] a luxury"—is beside herself when the prophetic ex-prostitute sends her off to meet her destiny (*Hour of the Star,* p. 58). Within minutes, Macabéa is struck down by a luxurious yellow Mercedes driven by a fair-haired foreigner, who doesn't even look back to acknowledge his victim. Her death is long and drawn out; people gather to watch and Rodrigo S.M. refers to her at this point as "the film-star Macabéa" (*Hour of the Star,* p. 82). In Macabéa's final moments, she remembers the prostitute-lined docks of her slum, and "[t]he docks [go] to the heart of her existence" (*Hour of the Star,* p. 82). When Macabéa dies, the narrator claims to die with her, announcing, "Macabéa has murdered me" (*Hour of the Star,* p. 85). He cannot, in other words, continue telling her story because she is no longer, nor can he prevent her death. At this point, Rodrigo S.M. comes finally to understand the story he has just written: It is the story of "the greatness of every human being" (*Hour of the Star,* p. 85).

Key relationships—author, narrator, and characters. Throughout the novel Rodrigo S.M. constantly forces the reader to acknowledge his presence and status as narrator, and in so doing forms untraditional relationships with both the reader and his own characters. In the same way that imagining Macabéa demands the active participation of the narrator, *The Hour of the Star* requires the active participation of the reader. Especially when he gives in to the temptation to blame Macabéa or to exculpate himself completely, Rodrigo S.M. writes in a way that challenges the reader, often by asking direct questions: "But why should I feel guilty? Why should I try to relieve myself of the burden of not having done anything to help the girl?" (*Hour of the Star*, p. 23).

> [I]t is true that when one extends a helping hand to the lower orders they want everything else; the man on the street dreams greedily of having everything. He has no right to anything but wants everything. Wouldn't you agree?
> (*Hour of the Star*, p. 35)

The emphasis on these twin struggles—that of the writer/narrator and that of the reader—may be Lispector's way of returning some worth and dignity to the lives of girls like Macabéa, who struggle in silence, "for there is no one to listen" (*Hour of the Star*, p. 14). At the same time, Lispector, already calling attention to the narrator's position as a middle-class man writing the story of a lower-class woman, directly implicates the reader in the processes of oppression she sees working both in the social and textual worlds. As Rodrigo S.M. moves from moments of supreme sympathy for Macabéa to others of cold detachment and irony, the reader, who almost assuredly identifies more with this narrator than with Macabéa, is forced into self-consciousness.

Rodrigo S.M. is in an extremely powerful position and has complete control over Macabéa. Not only is he the narrator and she his subject, but he is both a man and an educated member of the middle classes. As he imagines her, Macabéa is almost a nonentity throughout the text—ugly, impoverished, beaten-down, and almost completely devoid of self-awareness. At times Rodrigo S.M. romanticizes her and her plight, imagining her as pure and having found "grace in simple, authentic things," while at others he almost seems to take pleasure in her suffering: "Yes, I adore Macabéa, my darling Maca. I adore her ugliness and her total anonymity for she belongs to no one. I adore her for her weak lungs and her under-nourished body" (*Hour of the Star*, pp. 62, 68). This power relationship between Macabéa and her oppressive narrator is played out within the story itself, in the short-lived affair between Macabéa and Olímpico, who plays "master" to Macabéa's "slave." Though Olímpico is also from the lower classes, he, like the narrator, develops a condescending, exploitive relationship with Macabéa, based, in Olímpico's case, on his gender in a male-dominated society. Thus, Lispector links authorship with class and gender oppression, and even, by using a narrator like Rodrigo S.M., calls into question her own position as an urban female

CLARICE LISPECTOR AND FRENCH FEMINISM

Though Lispector had been an acclaimed writer in Brazil ever since the 1944 publication of her first novel, *Close to the Savage Heart,* only in the late 1970s and early 1980s did she become the "object of extensive international criticism" due, in large part, to the French feminist Hélène Cixous's "celebration of her work as a model of *écriture féminine*" (Peixoto, p. xviii). Cixous is one of many feminists who sought to locate a uniqueness in women's writing, those intrinsic qualities of women's writing that set it off from men's. *Écriture féminine* refers broadly to women's writing, but, more than this, suggests a writing "based on an encounter with another—be it a body, a piece of writing, a social dilemma, a moment of passion—that leads to an undoing of the hierarchies and oppositions that determine the limits of most conscious life" (Conley, p. vii).

Cixous felt that Lispector put into practice exactly this kind of writing. The Frenchwoman imagined a writing that would disrupt social boundaries, and the violence accompanying them, by effacing as much as possible the subject, or self, and instead presenting an emptied-out subject whose contact with the other would be fluid and open. By being always exposed to other people in this fluid relationship, the self is never unified or solid, but, rather, always being born anew. Thus, "Cixous, with Lispector, strives toward a mode of reading, writing, and speaking" in which the other person is "other without being thought of in merely negative or positive terms" relative to oneself (Conley, p. xi). Whereas the self is traditionally defined in opposition to another, then, Cixous sought to blur any solid divide between self and other. She believed that women writing intuitively might be able not only to produce a distinctive women's literature, but also to call into question many of the notions upon which traditional Western culture is founded. By making Lispector a prime example of *écriture féminine,* Cixous positioned the Brazilian writer in the international spotlight; Lispector became required reading for many scholars engaged in women's studies.

writer in relation to a suffering Nordestina. The novel leaves open the question of any one person's being able to form an authentic relationship with another person, especially when class or gender differences structure that relationship.

Sources and literary context. Lispector, like Macabéa, grew up a Nordestina, but differed from her in other ways. The author was not as poor as her character and had both a supportive family and a happy childhood. Lispector always had fond memories of her childhood in Recife, and as she grew older, her nostalgia for the place intensified. This nostalgia, in part, motivated the writing of the novel, and is reflected in the characteristics of the heroine and more explicitly in the musings of its narrator.

As indicated, this novel may also have been a reaction to long-standing criticism of Lispector's work, which claimed that it was not socially relevant enough. The woman whose childhood observations of the Northeast's abject poor caused her "to tremble and rage" was baffled by the remarks of her detractors: "It would indeed be strange if I were to remain indifferent to life in my own country. I may not write about social problems, but I live them intensely" (Lispector, *Discovering the World,* p. 29).

After the onset of the military regime in Brazil in 1964, Lispector and other Brazilian novelists confronted a decade of censorship. When censorship began to end in the mid-1970s, they entered into a period of literature "remarkable for its radical questioning" (González Echevarría and Pupo-Walker, p. 199). Forgoing simple description, novelists wrote stories that highlighted the very act of creating the narrative, as in Ivan Ângelo's ***The Celebration*** (also covered in *Latin American Literature and Its Times*) and Lispector's *The Hour of the Star.*

Reviews. *The Hour of the Star* was published shortly after cancer claimed Lispector's life at the age of 57. Her detractors notwithstanding, Clarice Lispector has always been a critical favorite, winning the prestigious Graça Aranha prize for *Close to the Savage Heart.* Her posthumous novel was no exception to the rule. *The Hour of the Star* was favorably received both in Brazil and in the United States, where the *New York Times* wrote "[Lispector] is studied by the scholars, but has never managed to reach a reading public. *The Hour of the Star* could change all that" (MacAdam, p. 27). John Gledson drew attention to the way in which Lispector captures the true circumstances of her characters by desentimentalizing them:

> Poverty is a difficult subject for anyone. . . . Who could deny its crushing importance and visibility in the continent? Nevertheless, it is easy to feel that, like the Guatemalan earthquake, it has been "sponsored" for consumption at home and abroad. Desentimentalizing is part of Clarice's solution: Macabéa, I suspect, is the poor as no one would want them to be, whatever their political views.
> (Gledson, p. 587)

LISPECTOR'S CONTEMPORARIES

Always a voracious reader, Lispector was influenced by the Brazilian writer Graciliano Ramos among others. Clearly, her innovative conception of *The Hour of the Star* broke drastically from the realism of Ramos. Along with her equally experimental contemporary João Guimarães Rosa (see ***The Devil to Pay in the Backlands,*** also covered in *Latin American Literature and Its Times*), she pushed Brazilian literature into new paths of linguistic and structural innovation as well as philosophical and psychological exploration. Outside Brazil, Lispector was influenced by various foreign writers, including Germany's Hermann Hesse and France's Jean-Paul Sartre.

Writing for the *Luso-Brazilian Review,* Earl E. Fitz commented on the unfulfilled promise of the novel's author: "Given the vigor and innovativeness of what we see here [in *The Hour of the Star*], one must wonder about the wonderful stories we could have expected from Clarice Lispector had she not died so prematurely. With her untimely passing, one of Latin America's most original and powerful voices has been stilled" (Fitz in Olendorf, p. 251).

—Anna Moschovakis and Carolyn Turgeon

For More Information

Burns, E. Bradford. *A History of Brazil.* 3rd ed. New York: Columbia University Press, 1993.

Conley, Verena Andermatt. "Introduction." In *Reading with Clarice Lispector.* Ed. and trans. Verena Andermatt Conley. Minneapolis: University of Minnesota Press, 1990.

Fitz, Earl E. *Clarice Lispector.* Boston: Twayne Publishers, 1985.

Gledson, John. "The Poor As No One Would Want Them to Be." *Times Literary Supplement,* May 30, 1986, 587.

González Echevarría, Roberto, and Enrique Pupo-Walker. *The Cambridge History of Latin American Literature.* Vol. 3. Cambridge: Cambridge University Press, 1996.

Lispector, Clarice. *Discovering the World.* Trans. Giovanni Pontiero. Manchester: Carcanet, 1992.

———. *The Hour of the Star.* Trans. Giovanni Pontiero. New York: New Directions, 1992.

MacAdam, Alfred J. "Falling Down in Rio." *The New York Times Book Review,* May 18, 1984, 27.

Olendorf, Donna, ed. *Contemporary Authors.* Vol. 139. Detroit: Gale Research, 1993.

Peixoto, Marta. *Passionate Fictions: Gender, Narrative, and Violence in Clarice Lispector.* Minneapolis: University of Minnesota Press, 1994.

Perlman, Janice. "Rio's Favelados and the Myths of Marginality." Institute of Urban & Regional Development, University of California Berkeley, 1973. Working paper.

Yúdice, George, ed. *On Edge: The Crisis of Contemporary Latin American Culture.* Minneapolis: University of Minnesota Press, 1992.

A House in the Country

by
José Donoso

Born in Santiago, Chile, in 1924, José Donoso published his first collection of stories, *Veraneo y otros cuentos* (*Summer Vacation and Other Stories*), in 1955 and two years later his first novel, *Coronación* (*Coronation*), for which he won the William Faulkner Foundation Prize for Latin American Literature in 1962. With *Coronación,* Donoso established himself in Chile as the leading novelist of his generation. In 1964 Donoso and his wife, María del Pilar Serrano, left Chile to attend a writers' conference in Mexico. They would not return until 1981. With the publication in 1970 of *El obsceno pájaro de la noche* (*The Obscene Bird of Night*), Donoso achieved an international reputation. *A House in the Country* is his most highly praised novel since *Obscene Bird of Night,* and the first of what some have viewed as a triptych of political texts—including *The Garden Next Door* (1981) and *Curfew* (1986)—that are mindful of how art serves to preserve historical memory when political oppression stifles other forms of expression.

THE LITERARY WORK

A novel set in an undesignated country in South America at an unspecified time; published in Spanish (as *Casa de campo*) in 1978, in English in 1984.

SYNOPSIS

A House in the Country chronicles the games, revolutions, and bloody power struggles that take place among 33 cousins left alone on their parents' estate for a debatable length of time—either one day or one year according to the text.

Events in History at the Time of the Novel

***A House in the Country* as political allegory.** Most commentators agree that *A House in the Country* allegorizes political events in Chile before and during the 1970s, when, under the leadership of Augusto Pinochet, the country suffered one of the most repressive and violent regimes in twentieth-century Latin America. In 1973 a bloody military coup ousted Marxist president Salvador Allende (who died in the process) and installed Pinochet. Overnight the country moved from democratic rule to military dictatorship. This abrupt transition and the events leading up to it are key to understanding *A House in the Country.* Though Donoso's novel makes few direct references to the events, he himself described the novel as political and claimed that he was inspired to write it on September 18, 1973, while he sat listening to the radio and discussing Pinochet's September 11 takeover. As the radio played, he could hear both his and Peruvian author Mario Vargas Llosa's children playing games from which they were supposed to refrain during siesta hour. Through the conjunction of the two events, the novel was born. *A House in the Country* need not be read exclusively as an allegory based on Chile during the 1970s, however, for the novel addresses revolution, repression, and authority as universal issues as well as within a specifically Chilean context. The novel's political basis, in fact, reaches further back into history with allusions to the Spanish conquest of the indigenous population, and the late-nineteenth-century growth of capital and the bourgeoisie. The wealth of the novel's Ventura family, for instance, derives from gold mines worked by the native inhabitants enslaved by the family and parallels the great wealth gathered by the sixteenth-century Spanish conquerors, who enslaved and exploited Chile's native populations. Similarly, the growth of the family's business parallels Chile's economic development of the late nineteenth and early twentieth centuries, while the role of the "foreigners" in the text corresponds to the foreign capital and investors upon which Latin America became increasingly dependent in the early twentieth century.

Salvador Allende—Marxism in Chile. On September 4, 1970, Salvador Allende was voted into the Chilean presidency by the narrowest of margins, backed by the newly formed *Unidad Popular* (Popular Unity), a left-wing political group composed of socialists, communists, and radicals, among others. Many were surprised by Allende's victory. Because Allende had not won by an absolute majority, but, rather, with 36 percent of the votes (as opposed to the National Party's Jorge Alessandri, who had earned 35 percent), he needed to be confirmed as president by Congress. There followed a tense seven weeks of speculation, after which Congress officially selected Allende as president. His party had promised a peaceful transition to socialism, which Allende, who himself had Marxist affiliations, intended to carry out. In the context of the Cold War, the competition between the United States and the Soviet Union for world dominance, the Western Hemisphere's first democratic election of a Marxist president shocked the world.

Allende and his government immediately began implementing their program, raising wages and holding down prices. Like many Latin American countries, Chile had been plagued by inflation and poor economic growth for extended periods of time, but by the middle of 1971 inflation was down 14.5 percent, wages up 40 percent, and, in keeping with Popular Unity's goal of nationalization, most of the country's textile, iron, automobile assembly, and copper industries now belonged to the government. Under Allende's leadership, Chilean factories worked at full capacity for the first time in years; government spending for education, health, and housing increased; large rural properties were split up and redistributed; and national income was similarly redistributed to favor the lower classes. Though the government's program effected rapid change and evoked hostility from much of Chile's electorate, by all accounts Allende's first year in office was a success, and the country's economy seemed to be booming.

By the end of 1971, however, the government faced economic problems and political opposition that would ultimately lead to the undoing of that success, and, two years later, to the government's collapse. First, the parties within Popular Unity became deeply divided on how quickly and widely to bring radical change to Chile. While the radicals and communists supported Allende, the socialists and other revolutionary left-wing groups wanted to hasten the transformation of Chile's economy and society, and to effect a complete overhaul as quickly as possible. To accelerate change, one of these groups, the MIR (Movement of the Revolutionary Left), encouraged peasants and workers to take over estates and factories without waiting for official decrees, and thereby undermined the new government's authority. On the other hand, outside Popular Unity, groups such as the Christian Democrats and the National Party strongly opposed the changes taking place and encouraged resistance and anti-government demonstrations. Allende also faced opposition from the armed forces (the bailiwick of his successor, Pinochet) and from foreign countries such as the United States, whose agenda was imperialist and anti-socialist. Indeed, the U.S. Central Intelligence Agency spent approximately $8 million attempting to undercut the regime by "financing opponents, supplying payments to the opposition press, and initiating a whole variety of 'dirty tricks'" (Caistor, p. 27). The following words by U.S. statesman Henry Kissinger, though expressed after Allende's downfall, capture the U.S. attitude toward early 1970s Chile: "I don't see why we need to stand idly by and watch a country go communist due to the irresponsibility of its own people" (Kissinger in Caistor, p. 27).

In 1972-73, as Allende's administration tried to further implement its program, a host of economic problems surfaced in Chile. The government's short-term successes crumbled under the wary opposition of private industry's capitalist business leaders, who distrusted the new programs and, instead of investing in a socialist future, sold off their inventory, farm machinery, or cattle and invested in foreign currencies. Soon Popular Unity's programs led to shortages, rising prices, and black markets; inflation rose alarmingly, the economy shrank, demand outweighed supply, and foreign investment became scarce. In 1972 alone, inflation rose more than 160 percent, an increase higher than in any other country in the world that year. The government's monetary resources dwindled. Due to rampant opposition, the government could not get new taxes approved by Congress or borrow enough money to cover its deficit. From the U.S. government to the Agency for International Development to the World Bank, outside organizations refused to make loans to Chile. Despite diminishing economic resources, Allende's government refrained from imposing austerity measures on its supporters in the working class. It became harder and harder for the government, under all these financial pressures, to implement its programs of social spending, and it finally proved impossible to prevent the economy from spinning out of control altogether.

Right-wing groups went on the offensive, and, in Popular Unity's last two years in power, forged an alliance with the center. Because these groups had seats in Congress, they were able to block new initiatives, harass Popular Unity officials, and denounce the administration, thus setting the stage for a military takeover. Allende attempted to steady the situation and to placate opposition by appointing military officers and other dissenters to cabinet posts. Unfortunately the military officers, Allende's soon-to-be successors, only grew stronger and more politicized by occupying these posts. Meanwhile, Allende's backers continued to implement their social changes, taking over property and businesses from Chile's landowners, a traditional bastion of power whose fear of and opposition to the government's policies intensified. Strikes and civil disorder increased in almost every economic sector of the nation until civil war seemed imminent.

During the congressional elections of March 1973 the tensions between Popular Unity and its major opponents came to a head. In these elections, the Christian Democrats and National Party won just over half the seats—not enough to do any real damage to Popular Unity—and Allende's government won six extra seats for its members, a small victory that inspired many of Allende's supporters to forge ahead. Not decisive enough to mollify any of these warring groups, the election results led to heightened confrontations, violent street demonstrations, and threats of insurgency; both right-wing and left-wing groups carried arms, and the former began openly soliciting military aid. Popular Unity seemed threatened from all sides, while the threat posed by its policies seems to have placed the party on a dangerous course: "By pursuing an illusion that threatened the livelihood of broad sectors of the population, President Allende's *unidad popular* coalition set the stage for a counterrevolution that imposed upon Chile a regime of coercion, intolerance, and brutality unequaled since the era of conquest" (Loveman, p. 309).

The 1973 coup—from Marxism to military dictatorship. By mid-1973 the economy and government had come to a standstill; inflation had reached 500 percent, and the government was paralyzed. In August 1973 General Augusto Pinochet became minister of defense, and almost immediately—on the night of September 10-11, 1973—launched a swift, violent military coup. By the evening of September 11, the president's Moneda Palace had been bombarded by jets and stormed by infantry, Allende was dead, and a new leader had seized power. There is still some dispute over whether Allende died at Moneda Palace or was removed alive and taken elsewhere to be killed. In any case, hundreds died in the takeover, and thousands more would die in the years to follow.

FROM ALLENDE'S FINAL RADIO BROADCAST

Pinochet's September 11, 1973, coup was bloody and quick. A loyal radio station broadcast Allende's final speech before his death, including these words:

> I have faith in Chile and in its destiny. Other men will overcome this dark and bitter moment, when treason strains to conquer. May you go forward in the knowledge that, sooner rather than later, the great avenues will open once again along which free citizens will march to build a better society. Long live Chile! Long live the people! Long live the workers! These are my last words, but I am sure my sacrifice will not be in vain. I am sure that this sacrifice will constitute a moral lesson that will punish cowardice, perfidy, and treason.
>
> (Allende in Caistor, p. 28)

Riot police surround Moneda Palace after Pinochet's coup.

Instead of restoring Chile to order, the military under Pinochet engaged in a so-called "holy war" against the Marxism that had "infected" the nation: they closed the legislature, curtailed political activity, outlawed organizations that had supported Allende, censored the press, and suspended civil liberties. The military hunted down, tortured, and murdered all "subversives," making any resistance by Allende supporters almost completely futile. Hundreds of thousands of Chileans went into exile; families were torn asunder along political axes, and thousands found themselves jobless. As in Guatemala's and Argentina's so-called dirty wars, government opponents simply and quietly "disappeared," that is, were secreted away by agents of the government. Even Allende supporters who lived outside Chile in foreign cities, such as Buenos Aires, Argentina, and Washington, D.C., were assassinated. Like one of the adults in Donoso's fictional Ventura family, Pinochet justified such actions as being for Chile's own good:

> The greatest possible enforcement and highest respect for Human Rights implies that these must not be exercised by those individuals who spread doctrines or commit acts which in fact seek to abolish them. This makes it necessary to apply restrictions as rigorous as the circumstances may require to those who defy the juridicial norms in force. . . . Our attitude must necessarily remain inflexible for the good of Chile and its people.
>
> (Pinochet in Loveman, p. 311)

Chile's victory over communism, Pinochet maintained, was of international importance, a victory for all against the evils of totalitarian Marxism.

Pinochet in power—an overview. Pinochet once claimed that "there is not a leaf in Chile that stirs without me knowing about it" (Pinochet in Caistor, p. 29). He kept Chile under dictatorial, repressive rule for 16 years, until 1990, when Patricio Aylwin was elected president and Pinochet stepped down to become commander-in-chief of the army, a position he would occupy until May 1998, when he became senator for life. The economic situation Pinochet inherited was dire, and one of the ruling junta's first tasks was to attempt to repair it. Initially, Pinochet's government adopted rigid measures that only increased unemployment and pushed wages down further, but its policies were soon dominated by the ideas of the "Chicago Boys"—a group of economists (most of whom had advanced degrees from the University of Chicago) who promoted radical and aggressive economic reform. Following their advice, the government instituted a conversion to free-market economics; the economy's rapid growth from 1976 to 1981 became known as the "Chilean miracle." Chile's economy was opened to the world, while the role of the state in the country's economy was reduced—a drastic reversal, in effect, of Allende's Marxist program. This transformation was aided, in large degree, by U.S., European, and international banks.

The new economic policies had varying effects on the Chilean people. Because of the government's drastic reduction of public spending, the country's poor were the most affected by the new policies, which resulted in record unemployment and the decline of purchasing power to almost half its 1970 level. At the same time, however, the new free-for-all, capitalist economy allowed large corporations and business-savvy individuals to attain great wealth. Flashy cars, shopping malls, lavish housing developments, computers, and credit cards suddenly became common in Chile, especially in urban centers. Such an extreme and competitive economic situation, with its winners and losers, caused one junta member, Admiral José Toribio Merino, to compare Chile's economy to "a jungle of savage beasts, where he who can kill the one next to him, kills him" (Toribio Merino in Caistor, p. 30).

On other fronts, the government sought to transform all aspects of Chilean life by institutionalizing the military-police state. In higher education, military rectors replaced academics, while humanities and social sciences departments (or any area of study "contaminated" by liberal ideas) were all but wiped out. For Pinochet's first ten years in power—during which time Donoso's *A House in the Country* was written—the military appeared invincible, and only the quietest forms of private protest were possible. As Alfred Stepan explains, "In Chile, eight years of authoritarian rule passed without significant movement out of the initial authoritarian situation: civil society remained debilitated in the face of state strength" (Stepan in Schneider, p. 3). Pinochet would become known worldwide as one of the fiercest, most violent dictators of the twentieth century. In October 1998, 20 years after the publication of *A House in the Country*, the former dictator was arrested in London, England, and charged by the Spanish government with torture and murder.

Social relations under Pinochet. Reactions to the dictatorship varied within every segment of society. Some Chileans prospered under Pinochet and were reassured by the order he brought to a chaotic society; others had their families torn apart and lives crushed. Given the extreme political climate of the time, friendships and family bonds dissolved over political differences. The splits between Allende and Pinochet supporters wreaked havoc in some segments of society, causing marriages to break up, friendships to end, and children to be disinherited.

Many Chileans, convinced that Allende and his policies had almost destroyed their country, "retreated behind the bulwark of modern authoritarianism and became insulated from the suffering of their fellow citizens" (Constable and Valenzuela, p. 11). In contrast, others, resisting the military dictatorship and determined to keep the intellectual and cultural domains alive, created support groups, underground networks, and small academic institutes. Still others, some of the nation's young, embraced the military regime's bold conversion to free-market economics, made their fortunes, and formed a dynamic new entrepreneurial class, roughly equivalent to "yuppies" in the United States (Constable and Valenzuela, p. 205). At the opposite end of the spectrum were the Chileans who became plagued by unemployment and poverty. And the specter of communism still lingered, adding another element to the equation: some Chileans were obsessed with fears of its return; others mourned its failure and hated its polar opposite—the new regime.

Rich and middle-class Chileans, the same classes to which the novel's Ventura family belongs, were in large part unaffected by the coup:

> In tree-lined communities like Providencia and Las Condes, life returned to normal within weeks, and military rule was virtually invisible. Schools reopened; staples reappeared on supermarket shelves. Newsstands bristled with fashion and skiing magazines, and society pages announced the weddings of couples with Basque and British surnames—a reassuring sign that the bonds and values of the elite were passing to a new generation.
>
> (Constable and Valenzuela, p. 142)

Since many of the human rights abuses of the dictatorship were not officially acknowledged, it was possible for an upper-class Chilean to remain ignorant of the gory details, and lead his or her life in relative ease. The average Chilean, however, generally had at least one friend or family member associated with Marxism, and heard news of his or her arrest or disappearance or death. In contrast to the largely static lives of upper- and middle-class Chileans who tolerated or even supported the coup, life changed drastically for liberals on the left side of politics. Because the regime cloaked so many atrocities, rumors circulated, fueling exaggerated ideas that, among other things, tens of thousands of people had been massacred. As one witness observed, "the first years of dictatorship were like putting society in a straightjacket or a psychiatric ward" (Constable and Valenzuela, p. 147). The excited and public political activity of the Allende years ceased: bookstalls shut down, nightlife disappeared, public meetings were banned, and newspapers and magazines closed. The collective sense of failure and disappointment had varying social effects. Some Allende supporters shared their suffering, creating strong bonds of friendship and support. In other cases, the sense of fear and failure undermined relationships between former comrades. As campuses and factories were infiltrated by spies and informants, people sometimes did not know whom to trust and shunned all former acquaintances.

The mood of the poor was also affected by the new government. For many of Chile's poor, the Popular Unity era had offered "an exhilarating new sense of worth—a defiant pride that demanded respect from the rich and a share in their economic power"; under Pinochet this dynamic was reversed (Constable and Valenzuela, p. 223). The high unemployment rate and the cuts in social spending had emotional consequences. Depression afflicted many idled workers, straining domestic relations and encouraging alcoholism. Many of Chile's working men, raised in a culture of *machismo* in which much of a man's identity was tied to work, could no longer support their families. These men were doubly shamed when their wives went to work: women could easily find domestic positions, and thousands did so to ensure their families' survival. Though some men set off valiantly each morning to find whatever work they could, many sank into chronic despair.

A FIRST-PERSON ACCOUNT OF MILITARY VIOLENCE IN PINOCHET'S CHILE

"Every day new bodies arrived, nude and headless. They floated in the river. We were stunned. It wasn't possible. We cried, please no more. They took my husband on the twelfth. A police patrol arrived. My youngest son was only thirteen years old. The wife of my older son was six months pregnant. She was disappeared. Her son still goes to sleep under the bed. In this way we learned that anything was possible."

("Violeta" in Schneider, p. 75)

Literature and Chilean politics. Chilean literature prospered during Allende's presidency, when the government-owned Quimantu Press—the largest publishing conglomerate in Chile—published Chilean literary texts in editions of 100,000 copies. Once Pinochet was in power, however, the military confiscated Quimantu and appointed a general as its new director. Pinochet's government stifled literary and cultural production in Chile. For a time, books by renowned Latin American writers such as Pablo Neruda, Gabriel García Márquez, and Julio Cortázar were banned (see, respectively, ***The Heights of Macchu Picchu, One Hundred Years of Solitude,*** and ***Blow-Up and Other Stories,*** also covered in *Latin American Literature and Its Times*). Most of Chile's artists and intellectuals went into exile, either voluntarily or by force; those who remained confronted censorship and the lack of literary outlets. Literary works from within Chile were published in two ways: either by underground presses, which dealt mostly in testimonials and denunciations, or as government-approved publications, from which emerged heavily coded literature, rife with allegory, symbol, and metaphor. As one literary historian points out, writers within Chile became isolated from the international community, while Chilean writers in exile could reach that community only by being displaced from the land and experiences they sought to describe (Epple, p. x). This sense of loss is expressed further by the writer Antonio Skarmeta:

> Our literature is becoming an exile *obra* [work], and not primarily in the geographic sense. The land missing under our feet—missing not only from under ours but from under those of our compatriots living in Chile as well—is nothing less than life itself, and the concept of life with which we grew up, confidently and spontaneously.
>
> (Skarmeta in Epple, p. x)

Chile's Nobel Prize-winning poet Pablo Neruda was emblematic of the relationship between politics and literature after Pinochet's coup. A member of the Communist Party and an Allende supporter, Neruda was dying of cancer when reports of the coup and its aftermath reached him. Doctors had predicted that the poet still had a couple of years to live, but, heartbroken, in the midst of preparations to flee the country, Neruda died only 12 days after the coup. Almost 2,000 people attended Neruda's funeral, where they sang the socialist anthem in what would be the first public protest against the regime. When they returned from the funeral, Neruda's widow, Matilde, found his home ransacked, with glass covering the floors and most of the valuables stolen. Matilde kept the home as it was. It would be a testimony, she said, to the military's brutality. "We aren't going to hide this. Pablo is here with us, with the broken glass on the floor" (Matilde Neruda in Spooner, p. 54). Though Neruda was not literally killed by the regime, many associated his death with the coup and its promise of repression.

A House in the Country is only one of many subversive Chilean texts responding to dictatorship. Through the use of allegory, symbol, and language-play, these texts not only convey meaning beyond that which is sanctioned by dictatorship, but also highlight the artificiality of the dictatorship's repressive rhetoric. In Donoso's novel, when the character Majordomo, who at least in part represents Pinochet, demands that the Venturas be told the "truth" about a certain event, another character "was about to inquire what truth he had in mind, among the many that power commands" (Donoso, *A House in the Country,* pp. 228-29). Told as a fable and an allegory, *A House in the Country* identifies itself as a subversive text. Late in the novel, the narrator, who is also presented as its author, says quite candidly, "I write as I do so that people like [one of the Venturas] won't recognize themselves—won't admit to it, anyway—or understand what I'm saying about them" (*House in the Country,* p. 283).

The Novel in Focus

Plot summary. The novel opens on a summer day in the country, when all the adults of the large, extremely wealthy Ventura clan have decided to go on a day-long excursion, taking with them every single servant in the house and leaving the children all alone for the first time. There will be a question later about whether the subsequent events transpire over the span of a year or just a day.

The Venturas consist of 13 adults—all related by blood or marriage—and the 33 children among them; throughout the year they live in the city, but spend three months each summer in the country house, located in the fictional Marulanda, in order to monitor the gold mines that provide the family's wealth. On the "day" the novel's story unfolds, the adults set out to a mythical site on their own estate, which we learn was fabricated for them by Arabela, the young girl who lives in the estate's library, in order to get the parents out of the house. Soon after the adults leave, Wenceslao, a ten-year-old boy whose mother dresses him grotesquely in girl's clothing and who is "in a certain sense [the novel's] hero," challenges the myth used by the adults to keep the household in line: the story that the natives outside the estate's walls are dangerous, filthy cannibals (*House in the Country,* p. 262). With this myth and others, the adults have managed to inspire fear in the children and thus to maintain their own power. We learn that Wenceslao's father, Adriano Gomara, was imprisoned by the family for establishing contact with the natives, whose cannibalism supposedly inspired one of his daughters to murder and cook her sister.

The Venturas also keep the household under their control by employing servants, headed by the Majordomo, who have full reign over the estate every night, and who enforce the will of the adults through violence and fear. Though the servants are the adults' lackeys, the older Venturas distance themselves from the servants' actions, preferring to appear the benevolent masters. Throughout *A House in the Country,* the adult Venturas deny reality, cloaking themselves within the elaborate fantasy and artifice that keep their power intact:

> [F]or the Venturas the first commandment was that under no circumstances should anyone confront anything openly, that life was pure allusion and ritual and symbol, which precluded any questions and answers even among the cousins: you could do anything, feel anything, desire anything, embrace anything, so long as it was never spoken of. . . .
>
> (*House in the Country,* pp. 124-25)

When the parents return to the estate, for instance, after what seems to have been one year, they insist they have been gone for only one day. As one of the servants warns another, "Haven't you gotten it into your thick skull that here time does not, has not, *will* not pass, because that is our master's order? Time stopped when they left for the picnic. Woe to him who thinks it will start up again before their return!" (*House in the Country,* p. 232).

In the same vein, throughout the novel the children engage in their favorite activity, participating in the ongoing play, *La Marquise Est Sor-*

tie à Cinq Heures (The Marquise Went Out at Five O'Clock), in which they act out melodramatic roles such as "the Beloved Immortal" and "Mauro the Young Count." The play so permeates their lives that they do not always know when they are in or out of it, or whether what surrounds them is or is not merely illusion—a problem clearly exacerbated by their parents' own unwillingness to see things as they are. Real atrocities can be written off as just another episode in the drama, as when, late in the novel, the Majordomo explains that the tortured, dying Arabela is "only playing *La Marquise Est Sortie à Cinq Heures*" (*House in the Country,* p. 319).

THE PROTAGONIST

According to *A House in the Country*'s narrator, the protagonists of the novel are not the children, servants, or adults. Rather, "pure narrative is the protagonist in a novel that sets out to grind up characters, time, space, psychology, and sociology in one great tide of language":

> The fact remains that Wenceslao, like my other children, is an emblematic figure: the most memorable, perhaps, of a number of boys and girls who, as in a Poussin painting, caper in the foreground, untraceable to any model because they are not portraits, their features unconstrained by any but the most formal lineaments of individuality or passion. They and their games are little more than a pretext for the painting to have a name, because what it expresses does not reside in those quaint games which merely provide a focal point: no, a higher place in the artist's intent has been given to the interaction between these figures and the landscape of rocks and valleys and trees that stretches towards the horizon, where, in golden proportion, it gives way to the beautiful, stirring, intangible sky, creating that unabashedly unreal space which is the true protagonist of the painting.
>
> (*House in the Country,* p. 263)

Once the parents have left, the children release Adriano Gomara, whom the narrator describes as "the man for whom humanity has meaning and can aspire to rational order" (*House in the Country,* p. 210). Upon his release Adriano and his allies quickly modify the kinds of rigid power structures that have been governing the estate. Like Allende, Adriano promises equality for all and establishes friendly relations between himself, the Ventura children, and the natives who live beyond the fence of lances that until now has enclosed the estate. The house is opened to the natives, but soon food and other supplies become scarce. Though idealistic and well-intentioned, Adriano is unable to govern efficiently or practically, and his "rule" soon disintegrates into hostile struggles between warring factions. At the same time, several of the children plot to steal the parents' gold, thus betraying the ill-conceived communist experiment for their own gain.

When the adults, still on their excursion, encounter two children fleeing the estate and, through them, realize how deeply their power is being threatened, they send back their army of servants to stop Adriano. Led by the Majordomo, the servants restore "order" in the house, an order based on fear and terror. The repressive rule of the Venturas restored, the servants terrorize, torture, kill, or "disappear" all dissenters.

When the adults finally return, they bring with them foreigners interested in buying the estate. Two of the children, Juvenal and Melania, have made it appear that Adriano's rise and fall from power, and the children's participation in the short-lived regime, have been just another episode of *La Marquise Est Sortie à Cinq Heures.* Thus, a short period goes by in which nothing seems to have changed (most of the unpleasantness again being attributed to the children's play), though shortly thereafter one of the children, Malvina, along with the foreigners, deceives the adults and escapes into the country with most of their wealth. Many of the adults and servants follow the escapees, and, we are told, die in the thistle storm that plagues the country each year. The remaining adults, children, and servants remain in the ballroom, their barely-alive bodies lying "mingled, resting in each other's laps, on the pillows, muffled in striped blankets," as the elegant figures from the trompe l'oeil overhead watch over them, making sure they do not die "under the choking clouds of thistles" (*House in the Country,* p. 352).

The Mapuche in Allende's Chile. The indigenous peoples of Chile mainly come from the Aracaunian Indian group, which consists of the Picunche, Hiulluche, and the Mapuche, who were once the country's most powerful tribe; the only indigenous people able to partially fend off the Spanish conquerors, the Mapuche were finally subdued in the late nineteenth century (Caistor, p. 14). The Mapuche are the largest Indian group in Chile, making up more than five percent of the total population. They live on the outermost fringes of the social and economic order. As in other parts of the Americas, these native people

A Mapuche woman spinning yarn.

have been persecuted since the time of the Conquest, and today are still regarded by some as inferior to Chileans of Spanish ancestry. As in Donoso's novel, many of these native people were enslaved by and forced to work in the mines of the Spanish conquerors.

Salvador Allende's government attempted to make the Mapuche one of the bulwarks of Chile's Marxist revolution, seeking to mobilize their potential for the good of all Chile, and to activate them politically in their position as an exploited class. However, fully integrating the Mapuche into political life proved difficult. First, Popular Unity's land reform goals were limited because the party did not hold a majority in Congress and had to abide by existing laws. Reform within these laws would not provide enough land to benefit the Mapuche poor, who already had a deep distrust of any "white" government, and who demanded more land, enough at least to sustain themselves. Despite its sympathetic attitude, Allende's government could only do its best within those laws already in place and so could not give the majority of the Mapuche any land at all.

Many left-wing groups sought to hasten Chile's societal overhaul by illegally seizing land themselves—an action sanctioned by some Popular Unity members. One such group, the MCR (Movement of Revolutionary Peasants), initiated a brutal guerrilla campaign in the countryside. Farmers quickly organized their opposition to these guerrillas, which caused the MCR to focus on winning the Indians as allies. Almost half of all the Mapuche lived in Cautin province—outnumbering the whites in that province by over 100,000 people—and the MCR easily set the Indians against the white landowners there by painting the whites as the robbers of Mapuche ancestral lands. In 1972 approximately 1,200 MCR activists lived in Cautin, and gathered the Mapuche together, "[whipping] them into a fury and [launching] them on a *battue* [or hunt] in which the quarry was not bulls but landowners" (Labin, p. 73). In the first four months of Allende's government, there were 57 of these hunts, and in 1971 there were 400 violent seizures of land in Cautin alone (Labin, p. 73). Even these seizures failed to provide the Mapuche with land. The state retained ownership of the deeds, preferring to direct the Indians into state-owned "socialist communities" in which the land was worked collectively, and Indians received training in "class-conscious" political education (Labin, p. 73). Unsurprisingly, the Mapuche soon became disenchanted. All in all, Popular Unity's Indian policies were often confused, scattered, and dictated by legal limitations. Allende's presidency was so brief that a more structured response to the Indian question did not have time to take root.

Sources and literary context. American writer John Barth has called *A House in the Country* a worthy example of postmodernism. Donoso himself has characterized *A House in the Country* in this way, giving a brief definition of postmodernism within his description: "[*A House in the Country*] has all the ingredients: it's eclectic, it's humorous, it apes the forms of classical novels, it is artificial and self-conscious, it is a novel about writing, and there is a spoof in it" (Donoso in Gutiérrez Mouat, p. 17). Many critics have discussed the self-conscious aspect of Donoso's writing. In the Latin American context, such self-conscious writing is often used to explore oppositions—such as truth versus fiction, history versus narrative, or authorized history versus personal history or memory—as many writers responded to chaotic political events and/or repressive regimes like Pinochet's, in which language was manipulated for "official" reasons.

Perhaps the most burning question about *A House in the Country* concerns the precision of its allegory—is it a treatment of events in Chile at the time of Pinochet's coup, or is it meant to elicit memories of a wide variety of Spanish American conquests? Critics are divided. The character Adriano, the leader of the children's revolution, for example, has been regarded in some quarters as a representation of Salvador Allende, although he also shares many characteristics of Cuba's Fidel Castro. Similarly, the presence of cruel and oppressive paramilitary servants that torture and regulate the Ventura children "is one of several elements of the political allegory of [*A House in the Country*] which may just as well apply to, say, pre-revolutionary Cuba, or . . . Peru, as to Chile" (Bacarisse, p. 323). And yet, given the dramatic and bloody events in Chile in the 1970s, it is almost inevitable that the wars and retaliations at the Ventura summer home will resonate as a Chilean struggle. The scholar Lucille Kerr provides a summary of the novel interpreted as Chilean allegory:

A House in the Country	**1970s Chile**
Marulanda	Chile, 1970-73
Ventura adults	The oligarchy
Children	The middle class
Servants	Armed Forces
Majordomo	Augusto Pinochet
Natives	Lower classes or proletariat or Communists
Foreigners	North Americans
Adriano Gomara	Salvador Allende
Rise of Adriano Gomara as leader of one faction of children and natives	Allende's election in 1970
Return of servants and death of Adriano Gomara at their hands	Military coup of 1973

(Adapted from Kerr, p. 150)

As Kerr notes, "within the context of other countries' political history or that of Spanish America as a whole, other equivalents have [also] been suggested: Marulanda could be read as an exemplary Spanish American country during its neocolonial period or as pre-revolutionary Cuba or as Peru in the 1950s; the different groups of characters could be read as generally distinct social classes, the servants as the military forces, and the natives as the lower classes, just as they do in the Chilean model" (Kerr, p. 150).

Reviews. *A House in the Country* was well-received in Chile, even though it appeared when Pinochet was still in power. Outside Chile, critics celebrated—and complained about—the novel's unusual mixture of violence, political allegory, and overt literariness and beauty: "The result will weary some readers with its . . . obliqueness . . . and grind others in studies of literary influence . . . and political reference" (Christ, p. 307). Writing for the *New York Review of Books* (July 18, 1985, p. 33), Michael Wood argued that Donoso's novel should not be read as precise allegory, since it shuns realism as too comfortable, even for expressing harsh truths. In his review, Alexander Coleman called the novel "a gory and splendid romance" that is "lurking with yummy scenes of child cannibalism" and likewise praises its abandonment of the "wretched and meager real" (Coleman, p. 39).

—Carolyn Turgeon

For More Information

Bacarisse, Pamela. "Donoso and Social Commitment: Casa de campo." *Bulletin of Hispanic Studies* 60 (1983): 319-32.

Caistor, Nick. *Chile: A Guide to the People, Politics, and Culture.* New York: Interlink Books, 1998.

Christ, Ronald. "Fictional Diets." *Partisan Review* 52 (1986): 305-08.

Coleman, Alexander. "Evil Pastoral." *Review* 32 (1984): 38-39.

Constable, Pamela, and Arturo Valenzuela. *A Nation of Enemies: Chile under Pinochet.* New York: W. W. Norton and Company, 1991.

Donoso, José. *A House in the Country.* Trans. David Pritchard with Suzanne Jill Levine. New York: Albert A. Knopf, 1984.

Epple, Juan Armando. "Introduction." In *Chilean Writers in Exile.* Trans. Steven White. Ed. Fernando Alegría. Trumansburg, N. Y.: The Crossing Press, 1982.

Gutiérrez Mouat, Ricardo. "Beginnings and Returns: An Interview with José Donoso." *Review of Contemporary Fiction* 12, no. 2 (1992): 11-17.

Kerr, Lucille. "Conventions of Authorial Design: José Donoso's *Casa de campo.*" *Symposium* 42 (1988): 133-52.

Labin, Suzanne. *Chile: The Crime of Resistance.* Surrey: Foreign Affairs Publishing, 1982.

Loveman, Brian. *Chile: The Legacy of Hispanic Capitalism.* New York: Oxford University Press, 1988.

Schneider, Cathy Lisa. *Shantytown Protest in Pinochet's Chile.* Philadelphia: Temple University Press, 1995.

Spooner, Mary Helen. *Soldiers in a Narrow Land: The Pinochet Regime in Chile.* Berkeley: University of California Press, 1994.

Wood, Michael. Review of *A House in the Country. The New York Review of Books,* July 18, 1985, 33.

The House of the Spirits

by
Isabel Allende

Isabel Allende was born in 1946 to Tomás Allende, a Chilean diplomat, and Francisca (Llona Barros) Allende. Twenty-seven years later her uncle, Chilean President Salvador Allende, died in a military coup led by Augusto Pinochet. *The House of the Spirits* was partly a response to this traumatic event: "I think," observed Allende, who had worked in Chile as a journalist, "I have divided my life [into] before that day and after that day" (Allende in Chapman and Dear, p. 14). As a young girl Allende had lived in Chile's capital, Santiago, with her maternal grandparents—a conservative, violent, but endearing grandfather and a spiritualist grandmother whose stories served as Allende's introduction to her family's and her country's past.

THE LITERARY WORK

A novel set from about 1910 to 1973 in a Latin American country resembling Chile; published in Spanish (as *La casa de los espiritus*) in 1982, in English in 1985.

SYNOPSIS

An upper-class family evolves as its country is shaped by social and political changes.

Events in History at the Time the Novel Takes Place

Mining for prosperity. In the early 1900s Chile's economy was growing and its society changing. A war with Bolivia and Peru from 1879 to 1883 had added two nitrate-rich northern provinces to the country, and with the money earned from mining these areas Chile could invest in industry and infrastructure, stimulating the growth of new businesses and creating new jobs. The nitrate mines lured thousands of men north. Between 1880 and 1920 the number of nitrate mine workers grew from 2,800 to 46,200; the U.S.-controlled copper industry, which experienced a boom during World War I (1914-18), also drew men north. Gold and silver mines still attracted occasional fortune-seekers, such as the novel's Esteban Trueba, but were mostly depleted by the early 1900s.

The miner's life was arduous. Not only were explosions and cave-ins common, but the area's medical facilities were so poor that accidents often proved to be fatal and diseases spread rapidly. Men who owned concessions to mines, like Esteban Trueba, shared some of the risks, but generally lived easier lives than the hired workers. In nitrate cities such as Iquique, the business elite occupied luxurious homes and had access to imported delicacies that were beyond the reach of their supposed social inferiors. Resentment over the gross disparities helped fuel a labor movement that would eventually have a major impact on politics in Chile.

The social hierarchy created at the mines was an extension of the hierarchy in Chile's large cities. In Santiago, for example, the growing economy led to more people vying for positions among the business elite; it was difficult for those without an established family name, however, to be adopted into these powerful networks. In fact, upper-class standing (a product of one's family background as much as one's income) was a prerequisite for success in most business transactions. As Esteban explains, it was because of "the prestige of [his] mother's name" that he was able to take out a loan and gain control of a mining business (Allende, *The House of the Spirits,* p. 24). Clearly, Chile's general economic prosperity did not mean that the country enjoyed an equal-opportunity prosperity; upward mobility was not an option for most members of the middle and lower classes.

***Hacendados* and *campesinos*.** In the agricultural regions of Chile, the disparity between rich and poor was even greater than in the mining communities and the cities. In 1930 seven percent of Chile's farms controlled 81 percent of its arable land—these were the huge estates of Chile's rural elite. At the other end of the spectrum, 82 percent of farm owners had to divide up five percent of the remaining farmland. These small-property owners, *minifundistas,* were the most fortunate of Chile's three types of peasants, or *campesinos.* Next came half of Chile's campesinos, the *inquilinos,* peasants who worked for *hacendados* or *patrones,* the owners of the great estates. The third type served as *afuerinos,* migratory laborers wandering from farm to farm seeking work. As was true of Chile's urban elite, the hacendados, Chile's rural elite, were the white-skinned descendants of colonial Spaniards, while the campesinos were mostly *mestizos,* people of mixed indigenous and Spanish ancestry.

In addition to their monopoly on farmland, the hacendados held a virtual monopoly on law and justice. According to one historian, Chile's *haciendas,* or great estates, were "virtually separate fiefdoms where the writ of the hacendado ignored the laws of the land" (Blakemore in Bethell, p. 33). This is clearly the case at the novel's Tres Marías, where Esteban creates his own small society, building houses, hiring a schoolteacher, and doling out supplies and small plots of land for the inquilinos, but also ruling as a tyrant: "Not a girl passed from puberty to adulthood that he did not subject to the woods, the riverbank, or the wrought-iron bed," and when husbands, fathers, and brothers confront him seeking vengeance, he can kill them with impunity (*House of the Spirits,* p. 63).

Mushrooming cities. In the 1930s economic problems in Chile sent large numbers of peasants and miners to the cities in search of work. This trend of internal migration, coupled with a high birth rate and declining death rate, had the most dramatic effect on Santiago, where the population exploded from about 500,000 in the 1920s to more than 2 million by the early 1960s. There were not enough jobs or houses to supply the hordes of new city dwellers, and as a result, shantytowns known as *callampas* (mushrooms) became a common sight around the capital in the 1950s and 1960s. Without electricity, running water, or medical facilities, these callampas were breeding grounds for disease and despair. They were also a reminder to many Chileans of the inadequacy of government support for the country's neediest citizens.

Small steps toward socialism. Spurred by striking mine workers in the first few decades of the 1900s, Chile's labor movement began to move into the cities as the population spread. Workers' aid organizations and trade unions sprouted up throughout urban Chile, with union membership quadrupling between 1932 and 1964. Still, the process of mobilizing workers was slow. Many types of unions were prohibited by law, and powerful Conservative politicians like the novel's Esteban Trueba discouraged membership in those unions that were legal. In 1952 only 13 percent of the Chilean workforce was unionized, a number that fell to ten percent in 1959.

Because of the legal limitations imposed on unions, Chile's workers found that they needed to rely on political parties to achieve many of their goals. Left-wing coalitions like the Popular Front and the People's Action Front pushed some reforms through the legislature, helping to increase government spending on education, health, and social programs. But these reforms tended to help the middle class much more than the working class and the impoverished. In the early 1960s radical change of the sort that might bridge the huge gap between the rich and the poor was still very far from being achieved.

Reform and radicalization. From 1964 to 1970 President Eduardo Frei, elected on the Christian Democrat ticket, set about implementing his party's specific type of social reform. Frei had won the support of many Catholics and some members of the middle and working classes by offering himself as a moderate alternative to the radical right and radical left. He claimed to be situated ideologically between "reactionaries with no conscience" and "revolutionaries with no brains," although the Socialist party labeled him as merely "the new face of the right" (Collier, p. 308). Under Frei the Chilean government established some 20,000 local self-help organizations (such as mothers' centers and youth clubs), built 3,000 new schools, and redistributed more than 1,300 haciendas to groups of peasants. These reforms were an affront to the political right, but for many leftists they did not go far enough. Inspired by Cuba's revolution of 1959, the Movement of the Revolutionary Left (MIR) broke away from the Socialist party, launching a series of bank robberies and bombing attacks while they preached that armed struggle was necessary to eliminate capitalism. Across Chile union membership soared, strikes increased, students (like the novel's Alba) took over university buildings to demand new leadership, local militias formed in the callampas, and farmland was seized by peasants tired of waiting for their share of the land expropriated by the government. These events all helped to push the political right and left farther apart and to splinter political coalitions that had operated for years. However, when a new presidential election loomed ahead, the main parties of the left managed to agree on a common, more radical, platform and on a candidate to represent this platform: Salvador Allende, a Socialist who had run for president unsuccessfully three times before. This time Allende squeaked by with a victory, besting the right's Jorge Allessandri by only 40,000 votes.

The "New Song" movement. While Pablo Neruda supported Allende's platform through his writing, other Chileans supported it through their music. In the mid-1960s a rebirth of interest in traditional folkloric music spread from the neighboring countries of Brazil, Paraguay, Uruguay, and Argentina to Chile, where Violeta Parra gathered, promoted, and produced what became known as *Nueva Canción* (New Song) music. Soon other Chilean musicians began creating their own "new songs" composing songs that both paid homage to their indigenous roots and spoke to their immediate political concerns. Victor Jara, the model for the novel's Pedro Tercero García, was one of the best known of these musicians. The words of his songs, like these lyrics from his 1969 "Prayer to a Worker," call for members of the working class to join together and fight for a more equitable future: "Arise and look at your hands / extend them to your brother so you may grow / together we will go united in blood / Today is the time that could become tomorrow" (Jara in Morris, p. 8).

New Song musicians mobilized many Chileans who otherwise may not have voted for Allende. The musicians accompanied him to political rallies and a couple of them (Claudio Iturra and Sergio Ortega) composed his campaign song, "Venceremos":

POET FOR PRESIDENT

Before the parties of the left united behind Allende, the Communist party rallied behind the famous poet Pablo Neruda (see ***The Heights of Macchu Picchu,*** also covered in *Latin American Literature and Its Times*). The party convinced him to accept its nomination for president. Neruda speaks in his memoirs about his days as a candidate:

> I was in demand everywhere. I was moved by the hundreds and thousands of ordinary men and women who crushed me to them and kissed me and wept. Slum dwellers from the outskirts of Santiago, miners from Coquimbo, men who worked copper in the desert, peasant women who waited for me hours on end with babies in their arms, the neglected and poor from the Bío-Bío River to beyond the Strait of Magellan—I spoke or read my poems to them all in pouring rain, in the mud on streets and roads, in the south wind that sends shivers through each of us.
>
> My enthusiasm was mounting. More and more people were attending my rallies, more and more women coming to them. Fascinated and terrified, I began to wonder what I would do if I was elected President of a republic wholly untamed, patently unable to solve its problems, deeply in debt—and probably the most ungrateful of them all. Its Presidents were acclaimed in the first month and martyred, justly or not, for the remainder of the five years and eleven months of their tenure.
>
> (Neruda, p. 337)

Neruda became an enthusiastic supporter of Allende's candidacy, resigning from the campaign as soon as Allende accepted the nomination for president. He would continue to support Allende throughout his presidency, referring to his work in office as "the most important achievement in the history of Chile" (Neruda, p. 349).

From "Venceremos," or "We Will Triumph"

We will triumph, we will triumph
a thousand chains will have to be broken
we will triumph, we will triumph
we will know how to conquer misery.

Salvador Allende

We will sow the fields of glory
socialism will be the future
together we will make history
carry on, carry on, carry on.

(Iturra and Ortega in Morris, p. 8)

In the novel Pedro Segundo García, father to Pedro Tercero, hears people humming a similarly hopeful song popularized by his son and smiles "at the thought that his son had made more converts with his subversive ballads than with the

Socialist Party pamphlets he so tirelessly distributed" (*House of the Spirits*, p. 175). In real life the popularity of the New Song movement continued during Allende's term, when its best known song, "The People United Will Never Be Defeated," was composed. After Pinochet's coup, when New Song music was outlawed and Victor Jara arrested and murdered, this song became a rallying cry for political dissidents.

Socialism in action. With Salvador Allende's election, Chile's government took the radical turn that many leftists had been hoping for and the right-wing elite had feared. At home and abroad investors were troubled by the prospect of a president with Marxist principles controlling Chile's economy. Shares on the Chilean stock market immediately plunged after his victory, and banks were beseiged by anxious customers emptying their accounts to buy gold or other goods they deemed more valuable than Chilean currency. Surely, they thought, a president who opposed the capitalist system could only weaken his country's financial stability.

Undaunted by the resulting economic chaos in Chile, Allende moved ahead with his socialist program. Greatly increasing the government's social spending, Allende raised the standard of living for many poor Chileans, introduced cultural programs for the masses (many featuring New Song musicians), and inspired teams of volunteers, like Alba in the novel, to work with needy residents of the callampas and the countryside.

Allende also put an end to the hacienda system for good. Any remaining farms of more than 80 hectares were seized by the government, a process that had begun under President Frei. However, unlike Frei, who had redistributed this land to groups of inquilinos only, Allende included afuerinos (the majority of the peasant work-force) in his redistribution plan. He created "agrarian reform centers" from the seized land, farms where former inquilinos and afuerinos worked for a government wage. For many peasants, however, this plan was not the appropriate solution to the problem of rural inequity; it seemed more like replacing patrones with government bureaucrats. As a result many of them worked reluctantly and inefficiently on government plots. Others, with the help of militant radical groups like MIR, seized land from private landowners and worked it as their own. This combination of events, along with bad weather, reduced agricultural production in Chile by one fifth during Allende's term, contributing to food shortages and unrest.

In manufacturing Allende nationalized 80 percent of Chile's industries, starting with copper. Chile's copper industry had been controlled by two U.S. companies for decades, and most Chileans—long resentful of the huge profits these companies were making on their country's copper—supported Allende's nationalization plan. He reclaimed the holdings of the two companies and paid for them with savings bonds, but he ordered the companies to pay back a percentage of the profits they had earned over the years. The companies involved were predictably reluctant to accept Allende's terms. They sued the Chilean government in a number of international courts, weakening the market value of copper. Furthermore, when the companies left, the majority of their technical experts (including many Chileans) left with them, which meant Chile had the copper but little knowledge of how to extract it and refine it efficiently. Similar problems occured with the nationalization of other industries. Often qualified managers and technicians would be passed over for less-qualified, but more politically connected, job candidates. As a result production fell throughout Chile, and the improved standard of living that Allende had brought to so many poor Chileans became harder and harder to support.

Officials and citizens alike began debating

U.S. INTERFERENCE

It was not just U.S. copper companies that resisted Chile's new government and its policies. At the time Allende came to power, the U.S. government was involved in the Cold War—a competition for world leadership with the communist Soviet Union—and a catastrophic war in Vietnam to eliminate communism there. U.S. President Richard Nixon feared that if Allende, the first Marxist president to be elected in Latin America, were successful, communism and socialism might spread throughout the Western Hemisphere. To insure Allende's failure, the U.S. government cut off loans to Chile, blocked loans from the World Bank and Inter-American Development Bank, and granted 8 million dollars to the Central Intelligence Agency to aid the overthrow of Allende. In hopes of fomenting a coup, it funneled money and arms to anti-Allende conspirators among the conservative politicians and military personnel in Chile (Anderson, p. 50).

how to approach these latest challenges, but the army, with urging from conservative politicians, had already made up its mind. On September 11, 1973, it staged a coup that left Allende dead and placed General Augusto Pinochet in absolute power.

The Novel in Focus

Plot summary. *The House of the Spirits* is a novel with two narrators and one narrative collaborator. Although we do not learn this until the Epilogue, the story is told mainly by Alba, who reconstructs the bulk of it from the notebooks of her grandmother Clara (the narrative collaborator). Interspersed with Alba's third-person narrative are her grandfather's remembrances of the events Alba describes. Together, Esteban Trueba and his granddaughter tell a story of four generations of an upper-class family in a city much like Santiago. The story centers on four women: Nívea, a suffragette married to a liberal politician; Nívea's daughter, Clara, a woman with extraordinary spiritual powers and a fierce sense of independence; Clara's daughter, Blanca, whose love for a peasant revolutionary earns him the ire of her father; and Alba, the product of this love, who balances a commitment to socialism with affection for her conservative grandfather.

The story begins with the engagement of Nívea's beautiful daughter, Rosa, to the young Esteban Trueba. Esteban, whose mother's inheritance had been squandered by his alcoholic father, moves north to seek his fortune in a gold mine so that he can marry Rosa as a wealthy man. While he is away, Rosa is accidentally poisoned to death. Heartbroken, Esteban leaves the mine, and after the funeral sets out for his family's dilapidated hacienda, Tres Marías. After restoring the hacienda to working order and establishing himself as its tyrannical patron, Esteban returns to Rosa's family to ask for the hand of Clara, Rosa's younger sister.

The money he has earned from Tres Marías allows Esteban to construct a palatial home in the city as a wedding present for Clara. However, this home and Esteban's desperate love for her barely attract Clara's attention. She dwells in a world apart from Esteban, exercising her magical powers (which include clairvoyance and telekinesis), entertaining the spiritualists, artists, and poets who visit her, going on humanitarian missions to the poor district of the city, and recording family events in her "notebooks that bear witness to life" (*House of the Spirits,* p. 430). Despite her emotional separation from Esteban, Clara gives birth to three children during their marriage, a daughter named Blanca and twin sons, Jaime and Nicolás.

On a series of family stays at Tres Marías, Blanca falls in love with Pedro Tercero García, the overseer's son, a peasant who becomes a protest musician and a revolutionary. Esteban eventually fires Pedro Tercero for preaching socialist ideas to the peasants at Tres Marías and banishes him from the property. Pedro continues his relationship with Blanca, however. When Esteban learns that his daughter is pregnant with Pedro's child, he nearly kills the guitar player but mutilates his hand instead. Clara questions his actions when she learns what has happened; still enraged, Esteban strikes his wife, knocking out two teeth and widening the emotional wall between them. Clara never speaks to him again.

Forced into a marriage her father arranges with an eccentric French count, Blanca escapes in time to give birth to her daughter, Alba, in her parents' house. Alba and her grandfather adore each other; his affection mounts after his beloved Clara dies, when Alba is six. As Alba grows into a student activist and falls in love with a militant Communist, her grandfather becomes a powerful Conservative senator known to non-Conservatives as "a caricature of the picturesque, reactionary oligarch" (*House of the Spirits,* p. 307).

Senator Esteban Trueba's fears of a Marxist takeover are realized. "The Candidate" is elected as president, and Alba rejoices in his victory. She plunges herself into volunteer work for the Socialist cause, helping the hungry victims of her country's food shortage by distributing the crates of food from Tres Marías that her mother had stockpiled. Meanwhile, Tres Marías is seized by the peasants who live there, and when Esteban attempts to take his hacienda back, he is held hostage. After his release an enraged Senator Trueba meets with other Conservative leaders and urges an armed takeover of the new Socialist government, shouting to those who disagree: "Stop acting like a bunch of faggots and take out your guns!" (*House of the Spirits,* p. 349).

When the military acts accordingly, assassinating the president and seizing power, Senator Trueba is ecstatic. However, it soon becomes clear even to this right-wing extremist that the new leaders are instituting a reign of terror, not a Conservative democracy. Esteban's son, Jaime, a confidante of the former president, is assassinated. Blanca and the now nationally famous musician Pedro Tercero are reunited and flee the country to save his life. Alba uses the back rooms of her grandfather's house to hide political fugitives en route to foreign embassies that will help them escape the country; for this crime she is arrested and imprisoned. While in prison she is tortured by her grandfather's illegitimate grandson, the descendent of a raped peasant girl from Tres Marías. Unable to use his own political power to free his granddaughter, Esteban finally turns to a clever prostitute who owes him a favor, finding that her influence with the current regime is greater than his own. When Alba is released, she returns home to her grandfather, who suggests that they record the story that is to become this novel. They discover Clara's notebooks, and with these notebooks and her grandfather's recorded memories, Alba begins to write the story as the novel ends.

Chilean women and the coup. In the novel Alba's great-grandmother Nívea lobbies for women to gain the vote; Alba's grandmother Clara carves out an independent spiritual life and serves as a humanitarian to the poor; Alba's mother chooses her own love, regardless of social class, and plies a trade that earns her money. Going even farther, Alba attends the university and of her own volition becomes involved in the political underground movement, helping smuggle refugees out of Chile.

While the stories of these four women may reflect the progress of women's liberation in Chilean history, they certainly represent more of a vanguard than a typical sample of Chilean women. Even by the time of Pinochet's coup in 1973, most women in Chile wore only skirts or dresses and did not work outside the home. With Pinochet in power, however, many women were forced to reevaluate the roles they played in society. For some whose husbands or fathers were among the newly unemployed, working outside the home was now a necessity to keep their families fed. Others had relatives or friends that had "disappeared" or were missing after being taken by Pinochet's secret police. The missing might be in a cell somewhere, having suffered torture, or might be dead. For their relatives, joining a human rights organization—even if they had never considered such a thing before—seemed the best way to gather the information they needed to help contact or protect their loved ones. Still others who had watched their husbands, brothers, or sons lead political groups found that with so many male leaders murdered or imprisoned, women like themselves were needed to keep opposition politics alive. Their involvement in such groups was tied mostly to their roles as wives and mothers, not as feminists or progressives. In other words, though many Chilean women in the Pinochet era took on non-traditional roles, they did so for traditional reasons—namely, a sense of love and responsibility for their missing loved ones.

When Pinochet seized power in Chile in 1973 he established a number of community organizations with the goal of spreading propaganda that would help to keep him in power. While many of these organizations were geared toward men, two—the National Secretariat of Women and the network of Mothers Centers, both run by Pinochet's wife, Lucía Hiriart de Pinochet—were specifically designed to convey to women what their proper role was to be under Pinochet. According to these organizations, which in the early 1980s numbered some 240,000 members, ideal women were "pillars of the society," characterized by "sacrifice, abnegation, service, honesty, diligence, and responsibility" (Chuchryk, p. 161). Their main role in society was to raise patriotic children who supported the government unconditionally.

While the goal of raising blindly patriotic children clearly bears the mark of Pinochet, the other aspects of ideal womanhood described above were fairly traditional and widespread notions in Chile at the time. Ironically, the characteristics of sacrifice, abnegation, service, diligence, and responsibility are especially evident in dissident women like the novel's Alba, who risks her life and endures torture to help political refugees flee the country and to protect her lover, Miguel. They are also evident in Nívea's tireless campaigning throughout her fifteen pregnancies, in the humanitarian acts of Clara, and in Blanca's decision to hide Pedro in her father's house after the coup. It seems that the four central female characters in *The House of the Spirits,* like the women who became politically mobilized after the coup, are both pioneers and traditionalists in the roles they play. Their personal desire for liberation from society's confining expectations is combined with a love for their families, friends, and all of humanity that leads them to embrace certain traditional notions of womanhood. The successful portrayal of this love and of the optimistic view of humanity that it speaks to seems to have been a central goal of Allende's in the novel. "I write," she explained later, "so that people will love each other more" (Allende in Zinsser, p. 63).

Sources and literary context. *The House of the Spirits* was written some seven or eight years

After the September 1973 coup Santiago's National Stadium was turned into a detention center for members of the political opposition.

after the so-called "Boom" in Latin American literature ended. The Boom was a time of avant-garde writing in the 1960s and early 1970s in which novelists garnered international acclaim for their stylistic experimentation. Gabriel García Márquez's ***One Hundred Years of Solitude*** (also covered in *Latin American Literature and Its Times*) is probably the best known of the Boom novels, famous for its use of magical realism—treating the fantastic as part of the everyday. By the mid-1970s, however, experimental writing and mythical treatments of reality began to seem inappropriate. The rise of right-wing dictatorships in Argentina and Chile and a widespread economic recession across Latin America made many writers focus on the brutal political reality in front of them without referring to magic or fantasy. After the Boom, this no-nonsense approach became widespread, and stories more often featured women and other traditionally marginal members of society.

The House of the Spirits is classified as a post-Boom novel, in accord with the realistic style in which it portrays the coup and the central role that it gives to women. Yet the novel shares many characteristics with *One Hundred Years of Solitude.* Its use of magical realism is evident whenever Clara plays the piano with the lid closed or makes saltshakers slide down the table without touching them, and its ending, which asks the reader to envision the past, present, and future as happening simultaneously, mirrors a similar ending in García Márquez's novel. Nevertheless, its other elements, including the realistic style of its second half, conspire to make *The House of the Spirits* fit some critics' description of the post-Boom novel: it is marked by "greater accessibility" than the Boom novels and by "a relationship to the past based more on a dialogue with history than with myth" (González Echevarría and Pupo-Walker, p. 302).

Living in exile in Venezuela, Isabel Allende began writing the novel as a letter to her dying grandfather, the model for the character of Esteban Trueba. Because he remained in Chile after Pinochet's coup, she had not seen him for years. "I wanted to tell him," she writes, "that he could go in peace because all his memories were with me" (Allende in Zinsser, p. 42). These memories, which came to her through the stories her grandfather had told her years ago, gave her the material to start the novel. Her desire "to survive the terrible experience of exile" and "to keep alive the memory of the past" allowed her to finish it (Allende in Hall, p. 27).

The events and characters in *The House of the Spirits* are truly "memories of the past," that is, they are based largely on real events and characters. Some of the most notable sources are listed below:

Fictional Name	**Historical Source**
The capital	Santiago, Chile
Big house on the corner	Home of Allende's maternal grandparents
Esteban Trueba	Allende's grandfather
Rosa the beautiful	Rose, fiancée to Allende's grandfather
Clara Trueba	Allende's grandmother
Count de Satigny	Allende's father, Tomás Allende
The Poet	Pablo Neruda
The Candidate	President Salvador Allende, Allende's uncle
Gringos	Central Intelligence Agency operatives

Events in History at the Time the Novel Was Written

Chile under Pinochet. The new regime established by the military coup of September 1973 could offer no panacea for Chile's problems. Although Pinochet reversed many of Allende's economic policies—privatizing newly nationalized industries, for example—major difficulties remained, including a high rate of inflation and falling copper prices. Unemployment was officially between 20 and 30 percent, but in a number of poor neighborhoods as many as 80 percent were unable to find jobs. On top of these economic issues, the Chilean military and its secret police instituted a reign of terror. They imprisoned, tortured, and executed thousands of "subversives," and forced hundreds of thousands into exile. The Conservative politicians who had supported the coup and who expected a return to democracy soon discovered that Pinochet had no intention of calling for elections. He was in control and had a watchful army behind him.

Chileans fight back. By 1981, when Allende was starting to write *The House of the Spirits,* Pinochet's regime was so unpopular and Chile's economic trouble so severe that citizens risked imprisonment and torture to speak out against it. The Catholic Church and its cardinal in Santiago criticized the regime's human rights abuses and declared that committing torture was a sin punishable by excommunication, or expulsion from the Church. Musicians who had not been exiled revived the New Song movement under a slightly different name (*Canto Nuevo*), using subtler lyrics than before to call for unity against government oppression. Unions, many now underground, staged strikes, and opposition political parties began to be revived.

Exiled Chileans also contributed to the fight against Pinochet's dictatorship. Musicians from the New Song movement who had been forced out after the coup continued to record and tour internationally, spreading their message about injustice in Chile to a worldwide audience. Politicians living in exile continued to debate the best course for Chile's recovery and to muse about when they might return. And writers in exile, like Isabel Allende, told the story of their country, its past and its disturbing present, to foreign readers, raising international consciousness and concern about its future.

Reviews. Banned in Chile, *The House of the Spirits* was an astounding popular success, and was translated into many languages. Its critical reception was more mixed. Although most reviewers agreed that it was an accessible, engaging story written with a polished technique, some claimed that it simplified complex political issues and failed to give enough depth to some characters. Many critics compared the novel to Gabriel García Márquez's *One Hundred Years of Solitude,* citing its use of magical realism and its family chronicle style. Some regarded Allende's novel as an inferior and unoriginal work because of these similarities, but most who acknowledged its debt to García Márquez's novel pointed to the way Allende sets her book apart by grounding it in history rather than myth. Allende received her most glowing reviews for dealing with issues of gender in the novel. Her rendering of strong, three-dimensional female characters was praised, as was her portrayal of "the patriarchal world of traditional Hispanic society" (Coleman in Hall, p. 30). In the judgment of one critic, this skillful portrayal makes Allende "the first woman to join what has heretofore been an exclusive male club of Latin American novelists" (Coleman in Hall, p. 30).

—Allison Weisz

For More Information

Allende, Isabel. *The House of the Spirits.* Trans. Magda Bogin. New York: Bantam, 1993.

Anderson, Jon Lee. "Profile: The Dictator." *The New Yorker* LXXIV, no. 32 (October 19, 1998): 44–57.

Bethell, Leslie, ed. *Chile Since Independence.* Cambridge: Cambridge University Press, 1993.

Chapman, Jeff, and Pamela S. Dear, eds. *Contemporary Authors New Revision Series.* Vol. 51. Detroit: Gale Research, 1996.

Chuchryk, Patricia M. "Feminist Anti-Authoritarian Politics: The Role of Women's Organizations in the Chilean Transition to Democracy." In *The Women's Movement in Latin America: Feminism and the Transition to Democracy.* Ed. Jane S. Jaquette. Boulder, Colo.: Westview Press, 1991.

Collier, Simon, and William F. Sater. *A History of Chile, 1808-1994.* Cambridge: Cambridge University Press, 1996.

González Echevarría, Roberto, and Enrique Pupo-Walker, eds. *The Cambridge History of Latin American Literature.* Vol. 2. Cambridge: Cambridge University Press, 1996.

Hall, Sharon K., ed. *Contemporary Literary Criticism.* Vol. 39. Detroit: Gale Research, 1986.

Morris, Nancy E. "Canto porque es necesario cantar: The New Song Movement in Chile, 1973-1983." University of New Mexico Latin American Institute Research Paper Series, no. 16 (July 1984).

Neruda, Pablo. *Memoirs.* Trans. Hardie St. Martin. New York: Penguin, 1978.

Zinsser, William, ed. *Paths of Resistance: The Art and Craft of the Political Novel.* Boston: Houghton Mifflin, 1989.

In the Time of the Butterflies

by
Julia Alvarez

Only ten years old in 1960 when her family escaped their homeland, Julia Alvarez fled the brutal "justice" of the Dominican dictator Rafael Leonidas Trujillo Molina. Her father had been active in an anti-Trujillo underground plot that was detected by the Dominican police. Before they could detain him, Alvarez's father fled with his family to New York and remained in the United States thereafter. Alvarez made her fictional debut with *How the García Girls Lost Their Accents*, which is set in the United States. Her second novel, *In the Time of the Butterflies,* takes place in the Dominican Republic and concerns the destiny of three actual anti-Trujillo female activists.

THE LITERARY WORK

A novel set in the Dominican Republic, mostly from 1938 to 1960 but also in 1994; published in English in 1994.

SYNOPSIS

Four sisters grow up to uncover a hoax—that the leader of their country, Rafael Leonidas Trujillo, is not the Great Benefactor he pretends to be. Three of them organize to unseat the viciously cruel dictator and together they suffer a brutal fate.

Events in History at the Time the Novel Takes Place

Dominican overview. An island sits between Puerto Rico and Cuba in the Caribbean Sea. Called Hispaniola or Española, the western third of this island is inhabited by Haiti. On its eastern two-thirds is the Dominican Republic, an area that was controlled mostly by Spain from 1493 to 1822, then by Haiti until 1844. A shaky independence followed, marred by civil strife, periods of U.S. intervention, and 31 years under Rafael Leonidas Trujillo Molina—an allegedly benevolent dictator who, in fact, resorted to torture and thinly disguised murder.

By 1960, the year of the novel's climax, the Republic's population exceeded 3 million (3,047,070). Its cities, primarily Santo Domingo in the south and Santiago in the north, were growing rapidly, although 65 percent of the people still lived in rural areas. The largely agricultural nation boasts a fertile, north-central valley, the *Cibao,* where the novel's Mirabal sisters lived. Farmers like their father often raised cacao in the Cibao. The nation's most profitable crop, sugarcane, grew in the north; cattle were reared in the south.

Poverty was widespread (average per capita income $200), as was illiteracy in 1960 (80 to 90 percent in rural areas). Almost everyone subscribed to the Roman Catholic faith, and people of mixed ancestry dominated the population. But in contrast to other Latin American nations, mulattos (of black and white ancestry) made up the most numerous ethnic group here. The mulattos, along with some mestizos (of Indian and white ancestry), comprised 70 percent of the population, greatly outnumbering a black minority (20 percent) and an even smaller white minority (10 percent) in 1960 (Hanover, p. 66).

In control of government, the economy, education, and social life at the time was the dictator Trujillo, who prided himself on his whiteness (though his family history included some black blood) and kept an all-white corps of elite guards. Obsessed not only with skin color but also with all other aspects of his appearance, Trujillo would fly to New York to purchase whitening cremes, elevator shoes that made him taller, and rare bird feathers for his Napoleon-style bicorne hats. He had a passion for clothes, often outfitting himself in full military dress and draping a plethora of medals across his chest. In a nation that measured 260 miles from its eastern tip to its western border with Haiti, Trujillo owned 12 residences and kept a complete wardrobe in each of them. A mix of dissonant traits, he was charismatic, extremely hard-working, a deft organizer, and an administrator with a keen memory. Trujillo was also arrogant, aloof, a megalomaniac who fed on flattery, and a ruler who ultimately lost touch with reality.

Trujillo's rise. Trujillo's Napoleon-style hats conjure up an appropriate comparison. Certainly he ruled like an emperor, though he took pains to observe the letter if not the spirit of the democracy that his republic was supposed to be. Trujillo has been likened to Joseph Stalin, Adolf Hitler, and, by the novel's María Teresa Mirabal, to Benito Mussolini. The allusions are to Trujillo's political cruelty—his ability to call coldly for the murder of someone he suspected to be an enemy, then to stage a lavish public funeral for the same person without flinching. His dictatorship has been described as the most absolute in Latin America. For 31 years (1930–61), Trujillo ruled with an iron hand, keeping a tight rein on the populace either directly as president himself, or indirectly through a puppet president.

His country was in dire need of stable leadership—there is no doubt about that. It had seen 56 revolutions in the 70 years between 1846 and 1916. The location of the island nation made it strategically important to the United States, which aimed to keep the area stable and out of the clutches of powers from the Eastern Hemisphere. In 1916 the U.S. Navy moved in, occupying and—to the chagrin of the Dominican upper class—administering affairs in the small Caribbean nation. Many upper-class Dominicans were so resentful that they left the country during the U.S. occupation (1916–24), clearing the path for the rise of a Dominican middle class, whose members would, in time, assume the reins of national control.

The U.S. occupiers created the Republic's first modern professional armed forces. In 1919 Trujillo became a lieutenant in the nation's U.S.-created police force. Rumor has it that he rose unethically into position as police chief by leaking news about a rendezvous between his superior (the police chief) and the wife of another man. Forewarned about the rendezvous, the other man killed his wife and the police chief at their meeting place. While there is no evidence to confirm his role in the scandal, Trujillo was quick to take advantage of the vacancy it created. He stepped into office as chief of the police force, a body that he would soon transform into an army. Meanwhile, the population in general grew resentful of the U.S. troops. Their occupation benefited the nation in some ways—in addition to the creation of the first modern police, roads were built, education was expanded, and the nation's debt was reduced. But relations soured between the occupiers and the occupied, with a rash of violent incidents erupting in Santo Domingo and other cities. On one occasion, U.S. troops killed a Dominican who resisted arrest, then murdered an innocent woman and burned some houses in the vicinity. Such misconduct by U.S. servicemen continued, fueling ill-will in the citizenry until anti-American sentiment was nearly universal. Some patriots hid in the hills and fought the U.S. servicemen from there. In the novel, the Mirabals speak admiringly of these rebel patriots.

When the U.S. troops withdrew in 1924 the Dominican Republic reverted to a politically unstable independence. Six years later Trujillo won the presidency in a ruthless election. He ran for office unopposed, after beating, jailing, exiling, or killing his rivals. Both cunning and good fortune seemed to be on his side. Just 18 days after Trujillo took office, a hurricane blasted the island, prompting the Dominican Congress to bestow dictatorial powers on the new president. Trujillo quickly used these powers to eliminate the remaining opposition.

Trujillo's style. In 1931 Trujillo created the "Dominican Party" to replace all other political parties. Over the years, he would maintain the appearance of democracy in the virtually one-party state, rigging elections to produce the desired outcome and making citizens join his Party and attend its local meetings. Invariably the citizens were required to sing Trujillo's praises. He was to be called "Generalissimo Doctor Rafael Leonidas Trujillo Molina, Honorable president of

Rafael Leonidas Trujillo

the Republic, Benefactor of the Fatherland," a title bestowed upon him by the Republic's main university, though Trujillo probably never attended more than elementary school. Less formally, people fell into the habit of referring to him as *El Jefe* (The Boss)—the designation used in *In the Time of the Butterflies*.

As the years passed, Trujillo's honors mounted. January 11 became the Day of the Benefactor, an annual celebration in his honor. The highest peak in the central mountain range was dubbed "Pico Trujillo" (Trujillo Peak). In 1936 the capital city, Santo Domingo, was renamed "Ciudad Trujillo" (Trujillo City); and in 1937 the city celebrated the first anniversary of its renaming with a carnival whose queen was the ravishing Lina Lovatón, one of Trujillo's many mistresses. By then the seemingly insatiable sexual appetite of El Jefe, which would turn to younger and younger girls, had become legendary.

Encouraged by Trujillo himself, the adulation continued as the decades passed. Statues were sculpted in his image; 1955 was declared the Year of the Benefactor; neon signs blazoned *God and Trujillo* in the capital city and a mandatory portrait of El Jefe hung in every home, paying homage to a man who promoted himself as the savior, the hero, the father of his people. After a generation, citizens grew accustomed to praising Trujillo and to having his lackeys monitor their every action. Many Dominicans even accepted and believed in the mythical image of the man, as reflected in the initial regard for him held by the novel's Mirabal sisters. A young girl at the time, María Teresa takes a few moments in the privacy of her diary "to wish El Jefe Happy Benefactor's Day with all my heart. I feel so lucky that we have him for a president" (Alvarez, *In the Time of the Butterflies,* p. 37). Older and a bit wiser, the religious Patria admits that Trujillo is no saint, but reasons that "among the *Bandidos* that had been in the National Palace, this one at least was building churches and schools, paying off our debts" (*Butterflies,* p. 51).

Patria is right. Trujillo's regime did bring improvements—the building of schools, highways, and water systems; repayment of foreign debts; a balanced budget; the end of civil war; and better medical services. But the benefits didn't reach everyone, and there was tremendous graft. Trujillo amassed a personal fortune—about $800 million in a nation that meanwhile remained poverty-ridden. He ranked first among the country's storekeepers, industrialists, and agriculturists, holding 60 to 70 percent of the finest farming and grazing land. Trujillo took a 10 percent cut of everything the government bought or sold, even when it purchased goods from his own firms. He used his economic clout to bully uncooperative businessmen, getting banks to refuse them loans, officials to deny them export permits, gangs to destroy their property. And while such tactics were unethical, they paled beside Trujillo's treatment of citizens who turned against him. In the novel, at the tender age of 12, Minerva learns that Trujillo has murdered her friend Sinita's uncles, father, and brother because the uncles plotted against him. Incredulous, Minerva tries hard to swallow the news that El Jefe does "bad things": "it was as if I had just heard Jesus had slapped a baby" (*Butterflies,* p. 17).

External resistance. Sinita's uncles had planned to "do something to Trujillo"—that is, to oust him from power (*Butterflies,* p. 17). They were not the first, nor would they be the last, although Trujillo and his *calies* (informers) kept a tight rein on the citizenry, first through strong-arm tactics and later by a cloak-and-dagger system of recording devices and spies, along with the manhandling of dissidents in jail until, their spirits broken, they submitted to his regime. Inspiring terror and keeping close tabs on the populace was the *Servicio de Inteligencia Military* (SIM), a military intelligence service that became especially brutal from 1957 to 1960, when it was run by Johnny Abbés Garcia. The SIM made use of two interrogation and torture centers, *La Cuarenta* (in the novel "La 40"), on 40th Street in upper Ciudad Trujillo, and Kilometer Nine on a highway located nine kilometers east of the capital. Among the SIM's instruments were the electric chair, electric cattle prods, and the *pulpo* (which means "octopus"; it was an electric apparatus with tentacles to place on body parts and a cap to screw onto the head).

Outside the torture chambers, the general population lived under the constant surveillance of soldiers and secret policemen. Wherever people congregated, plainclothesmen were there to keep hawklike eyes on them. Mail was censored, phones were wiretapped, and it became prudent to suspect servants of spying for the regime (in the novel, the yardboy Pietro reports all he hears in the Mirabal household for a few pesos and a bottle of rum). It was not only forbidden for citizens to criticize Trujillo, but also to remain silent about him. Young and old, men and women, they all had to sing El Jefe's praises or suffer the consequences.

Of course, an alternative was to go, or to be sent, into exile. With the aid or knowledge of foreign powers, Dominican exiles attempted several times to topple Trujillo.

1947—Invasion of Cayo Confites: Exiles congregate on the deserted island Cayo Confites, near Cuba. Their arsenal consists of three ships, assorted weaponry, and light bombing planes purchased in the United States. The invaders never get outside Cuban waters—a Cuban fleet arrests them for a few hours, then lets them go.

1949—Invasion of Luperón: The invaders plan to leave Guatemala and land in several spots in the Dominican Republic, where they will be joined by dissidents in the country itself. Their only amphibious plane lands in the small port of Luperón, where a Trujillo guard foils their plans by cutting off electric power. In the darkness, the invaders shoot at one another before escaping to the mountains. Trujillo's army hunts them down and kills almost all of them, keeping only a few alive to profess communist support for the plot.

1959—June 14 Invasion: A rash of strongmen have recently been ousted from power in Argentina (Juan Perón), Colombia (Gustavo Rojas Pinilla), Venezuela (Marco Pérez Jiménez), and Cuba (Fulgencio Batista). Encouraged by these successes, Dominican exiles stage a third invasion, landing by boat in two places and by plane in the Constanza Mountain Valley. The invaders are chased by Trujillo's army until all but a few of them have been killed. It is at this point in the novel that Patria, the eldest Mirabal sister, on a religious retreat in the valley, commits herself to the rebel movement.

Internal resistance. Despite talk of human rights abuses, other nations tolerated Trujillo. In truth, U.S. leaders feared a communist takeover of the Dominican Republic more than they feared Trujillo. The ongoing Cold War—the competition between the United States and Soviet Union for world power—encouraged U.S. leaders to tolerate him for years. They finally took a position against him in 1960, having their Central Intelligence Agency (CIA) send over weapons to help oust him from power.

Trujillo's regime had fallen into worldwide disrepute by 1960, a problem El Jefe tried to remedy. In 1955–56 he staged an International Fair of Peace and Brotherhood, a $40 million project that turned out to be a financial disaster. Attracting far fewer than the anticipated 500,000 foreigners, it drew only 24,000, many of whom were flown in by Trujillo, all expenses paid, as part of the effort to repair his badly damaged image.

Some of the exiles (backed by Cuba's Fidel Castro and Venezuela's Rómulo Betancourt) went on to stage the unsuccessful June 14, 1959, invasion. By then, people inside the Republic had begun to form a rebel movement of their own—made up largely of young people, the children of landowners, businessmen, and professionals. Taking their name from the failed invasion, in tribute to its martyrs, the young rebels formed the *Catorce de Junio* (Fourteenth of June Movement). They divided into small groups, secretly building explosives, planning to assassinate Trujillo. It was a goal with which U.S. diplomat Henry Dearborn, who was stationed in the Dominican Republic, heartily concurred: "If I were a Dominican . . . I would favor destroying Trujillo as being the first necessary step in the salvation of my country and I would regard this, in fact, as my Christian duty" (Dearborn in Diederich, p. 47).

Minerva Mirabal's husband, Manolo Tavárez Justo, led this actual Fourteenth of June Movement, which Minerva and her sisters Patria and María Teresa joined. The three sisters would become an inspiration to the underground, which grew to include 30,000-40,000 Dominicans. In her lifetime, Minerva, alias Mariposa (or "Butterfly") #1, showed a defiance that made her their secret heroine. In death, María Teresa and Patria, known as Mariposas #2 and #3, were esteemed as heroines too.

Human rights abuses. The dissidents settled on the time and place to kill Trujillo—January 21, 1960, at a cattle fair. But led by Johnny Abbés, SIM agents cracked down on them before they could execute their plan. Hundreds of Fourteenth of June Movement members were arrested and dragged to the La Cuarenta torture chamber before they were thrown in La Victoria prison. Minerva Mirabal's husband, Manolo, was arrested on January 13, Minerva on the 20th, and María Teresa on the 21st. Patria escaped arrest, but her husband, Pedro, her son Nelson, and María Teresa's husband, Leandro, did not.

Historical accounts indicate that the men were separated from the women and taken to private cells after brutal interrogation. Manolo was tortured in an electric chair, and subjected to beatings and the extraction of his fingernails. Kept in jail by Trujillo, he and the other Mirabal husbands served unbroken prison sentences.

Minerva and María Teresa meanwhile endured two periods of arrest—January 20–21 to February 7, 1960, and May 18 to August 9, 1960. During their first arrest, the women were thrown into small mosquito-ridden rooms and denied adequate food. They received better treatment during the second arrest, by which time the Trujillo regime was feeling the brunt of worldwide pressure. On June 8 a committee of the international Organization of American States (OAS) released a report accusing the Dominican Republic of violating human rights and terrorizing its political prisoners. The regime then committed an international blunder that further soiled its reputation. On June 24, in Caracas, Venezuela, terrorists attempted to assassinate President Betancourt, who was an unremitting critic of Trujillo's rule. The assassins placed a dynamite bomb (whose triggering device was manufactured in the Dominican Republic) in a parked car on a parade route taken by Betancourt's vehicle. The bomb exploded at the proper time, killing a bystander and a presidential aide, and inflicting severe burns on President Betancourt himself. The outraged President blamed Trujillo, after which the OAS broke off diplomatic relations with the Dominican Republic and imposed economic sanctions. OAS nations suspended trade to the Dominican Republic, refusing to sell it weaponry, petroleum, trucks, or spare parts.

The pressure prompted Trujillo to treat his political prisoners better. Minerva and María Teresa were allowed to buy food and were given something to ward off the mosquitoes. Sharing their cell with prostitutes, killers, and other such prisoners, the two were let out to appear at their trial. The court sentenced them to 30 years each, then, on appeal, reduced the sentence to five years each. But, on August 9, 1960, the two were pardoned and released for good, thanks not only to international pressure but also to the Catholic Church.

THE CONSUMMATE SHOWMAN

Trujillo committed atrocities that outraged the world—for example, the massacre of 20,000 workers from Haiti in 1937. Yet he somehow managed to cultivate an image of himself as a proponent of democracy. In the post-World War II era, he shrewdly presented himself as a virulent anticommunist, a ruse that forced him to increase democracy at home in the 1940s, in order to substantiate his image. He even secretly helped found a communist faction in his country, then, in a perverse turnabout snuffed it out of existence during his 1946–47 wave of terror.

Church politics. The Church had long stayed out of politics, but the terror visited on Fourteenth of June Movement prisoners stirred its leaders. No longer willing to stand by and do nothing, the nation's six bishops signed the first of several pastoral letters, public proclamations stating that human rights did not exist in their land and that this was an offense against God. The first letter, read on January 25, 1960, to 624 churches in the Republic, asked Trujillo to halt the "excesses, dry the tears, heal the wounds," and return the human rights to which all Dominican citizens were entitled (Diederich, p. 37). Pastoral letters had preceded the downfall of dictators in Argentina, Venezuela, and Colombia, and the letters about Trujillo enraged him—but he released the female prisoners.

Meanwhile, U.S. emissaries tried persuading Trujillo to change his ways. Senator George Smathers of Florida pleaded with Trujillo, appealing to his vanity. Smathers prophesied, correctly, that all the statues and pictures of Trujillo would be ripped down if he did not transform his government from a dictatorship into a democracy. At the root of his concern was the U.S. fear that if such a transition did not occur, communists would gain the upper hand in the Dominican Republic.

In the end, this fear prompted U.S. agents to break with the Fourteenth of June Movement, whose rebels identified too much with Cuba (and communist notions) for U.S. tastes. Still interested in unseating Trujillo, the United States began making common cause with more conservative conspirators. Toward the end of *In the Time of the Butterflies,* Minerva informs her husband that the U.S. agents have switched their support from the Fourteenth of June Movement to other domestic rebels. The news distresses Manolo, who protests that the *gringos* will take over the revolution, which he is still committed to waging. And, in fact, a revolution of sorts is about to materialize, but not before the three so-called *mariposas,* or butterflies, are caught.

DEFIANT DRAMA

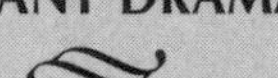

The novel's description of a skit performed by Minerva and her friends recalls an actual historical incident. The actors were older and did not write their own play; but, as in Minerva's case, it was performed for the 1944 centennial. The university's vice-president, Bonilla Atiles, directed some students to enact *La Viuda de Padilla,* a drama about rebels who defied the Spanish Emperor Charles V in the sixteenth century. As in the novel, Trujillo's minions did not detect the play's hidden meaning. Its student-actors went on to join the Democratic Youth and the communist movement, two factions that flourished briefly in 1945 before Trujillo's regime launched a campaign of terror in 1946–47.

The Novel in Focus

The plot. *In the Time of the Butterflies* is a family saga told from the viewpoints of four sisters—Patria, Minerva, María Teresa, and Dedé—all of whom come of age during the course of the novel. It moves from sister to sister, flashing backward and forward in time. The action opens in 1994 with the only surviving sister, Dedé, now a successful life-insurance salesperson. "Everyone wants to buy a policy from the woman who just missed being killed along with her three sisters" (*Butterflies,* p. 5). In the frame-story, Dedé is interviewed by a Dominican American, ostensibly the author herself.

Part 1 (1938–46) introduces the four sisters and their parents, characterizing the girls as sensible (Dedé), smart and rebellious (Minerva), preoccupied with religion (Patria), and naive and romantic (María Teresa). The family lives in rural Ojo de Agua, no place for a girl to get an education, although their father, Enrique, who shows genuine fondness for his daughters, doubts that they really need one, especially since it means sending them away to live at a Catholic school. But his wife convinces him that now that their farm and store are prospering, schooling is part of his family's success.

Away at school, 12-year-old Minerva befriends a waif named Sinita, who turns Minerva's world upside down. Her new friend shares with a horrified Minerva the details of how Trujillo murdered Sinita's uncles. One rude awakening follows another, as the girls watch a beautiful classmate, Lina Lovatón, being whisked off to the capital to become Trujillo's mistress. The school benefits from the affair when El Jefe constructs the Lina Lovatón gymnasium. In 1944, the centennial of the Republic's independence, Minerva and her friends perform a skit in this gym about how their nation gained its freedom from Spain. Written by the girls, their play is a subtle protest against Trujillo's regime, but this is clear only to them. They later perform the skit for Trujillo, and in a hair-raising scene, without warning anyone, Sinita makes the protest more overt. To dodge Trujillo's wrath, the quick-thinking Minerva improvises an ending that honors him. It is the first of many risky moments for her.

In Part 2 of the novel (1948–59), Dedé recalls a romantic rivalry between herself and Minerva over a radical named Virgilio Morales. To escape Trujillo's henchmen, Virgilio fled the country and lived in exile; he returned briefly to the Dominican Republic in the 1940s, when Trujillo made a show of increasing democracy in the country.

Dedé marries a cousin, Jaimito, who refrains from getting involved in politics or anything else that might cause trouble. Falling in step with her husband, she remains detached from the underground, though privately she agrees with her sisters that the regime must be brought down.

Minerva discovers that her father is having an adulterous relationship with a peasant, who has borne him four daughters, a mirror illegitimate family. First outraged, then resigned to the existence of this family, she demands an explanation. "'Cosas de los hombres,' he said. Things a man does" (*Butterflies,* p. 92). She herself falls victim to things that the man Trujillo does when her prosperous family attends a party at which he is the guest of honor. El Jefe picks Minerva as a dance partner. As they dance, she appeals to his vanity, hoping to win permission to attend law school, reasoning that her father will have to let her enroll if Trujillo prescribes it. Minerva reminds Trujillo that he gave women the right to vote, which he did in 1942 to appear democratic. But Trujillo discourages her from enrolling, then makes a vulgar pass at her, whereupon she slaps him. Fortunately, a rainstorm allows the family to escape the outdoor party and head for home. Minerva, however, forgets her purse, which contains incriminating anti-Trujillo letters from the exiled Virgilio. Her father suffers the punishment. He "disappears" (is arrested) and emerges from jail a broken man, proving that those who survive prison are often so ruined physically and mentally that Trujillo need not fear their release.

The novel progresses to the 1950s, a decade covered mostly by María Teresa's diary entries, which are illustrated with occasional diagrams. She enrolls in the university while Minerva is still there and becomes privy to her sister's secret passions—her love for the poetry of José Martí, for example. On vacation, 29-year-old Minerva meets a kindred spirit named Manolo, whom she marries. Still guiding her younger sister, Minerva helps María Teresa prepare a speech when she is elected Miss University, reminding her not to overdo it because the crowd will be restless after the "disappearance" of Galíndez, a former teacher of theirs. As María Teresa's diary explains, her peers are no longer taking such injustices lying down—a national underground is forming, and she has joined it. María Teresa builds grenades and helps run a supply center for the underground; in the process she meets her future husband, a fellow rebel in the underground named Leandro Guzmán Rodriguez.

The action flashes forward to the end of the decade. It is 1959 and the eldest sister, the religious Patria, has now been married to the landowner Pedrito González for 18 years. She stays out of the rebel movement at first, taking care of her son and daughter, but then gets "braver like a crab going sideways. I inched towards courage the best way I could, helping out with the little things" (*Butterflies*, p. 154). Patria goes on a religious retreat to the Constanza Valley, but an invasion of Dominican exiles, the "June 14 Invasion," shatters her peace; the sight of a bloody boy who is her own child's age converts her into a die-hard member of the underground, and her son and husband are also drawn into the movement. Their home becomes a motherhouse; Patria's set of church rebels meets there with Minerva's and Manolo's secular rebels to form the Fourteenth of June Movement, a fledgling group of 40 dissidents whose mission is to effect an internal revolution rather than wait for an outside rescue.

MARTÍ'S COURAGE

A writer and lawyer, José Martí was also the architect of Cuba's revolution for independence from Spain in 1895 (see **"Our America,"** also covered in *Latin American Literature and Its Times*). After spending years in the United States organizing exiled Cubans and their sympathizers, he launched an invasion of Cuba. Martí set out for the invasion from the Dominican Republic, specifically from the port town of Monte Cristi, where Minerva and Manolo are based in the novel. Before the fighting, which would cost Martí his life, he penned a farewell poem. Later rebels, like Minerva Mirabal, could draw courage from poems such as this one by recalling their determined words:

And of me I must say
That following serenely,
Without fear of the lightning and thunder
I am working out the future.

(Martí in Foner, p. 14)

Part 3 of the novel, which focuses on the year 1960, begins with the roundup. Patria remembers how the SIM came to arrest her loved ones. It would be three months before she again saw her husband, her two sisters, or her son. In the meantime, her mentors, the church padres, draft pastoral letters to be read from every pulpit, condemning the regime and throwing in their lot with the people. Her father's other, illegitimate daughters help smuggle supplies to the prison-bound sisters. Minerva wants books, especially José Martí's poems. Even in prison, she shows defiance, forming a school, discussing Martí with her cellmates, singing the national anthem, and refusing to give up her crucifix when the regime retaliates against the Church by confiscating all prisoners' crucifixes. Minerva is punished a few times for her defiance—removed from the cell that she shares with others, and thrown into solitary confinement.

María Teresa, again through diary entries, shares her experience in jail, disclosing the worst of it only after her release from prison. The entry describes her being taken to the torture chamber, stripped to her underclothes, and tortured in front of her husband to make him divulge information.

THE INFLAMMATORY ANTHEM

These lines from the Dominican anthem show why the prisoners offended Trujillo and his guards by singing it:

No country deserves to be free
If it is an indolent and servile slave,
If the call does not grow loud within it,
Tempered by a virile heroism
But the brave and indomitable Quisqueya ["Mother of All Lands"]*
Will always hold its head high,
For if it were a thousand times enslaved,
It would a thousand times regain freedom.

*The Republic's original, Taino Indian, name

(Reed and Bristow, p. 160)

After seven months in prison, the Mirabal sisters are released and placed under house arrest at their mother's home. El Jefe attends a reception at which he speaks of having only two problems—the "damn church and the Mirabal sisters" (*Butterflies*, p. 281). His henchmen tackle the Mirabal problem, transferring Minerva's and María Teresa's husbands to a prison up north in Puerto Plata, reachable only by way of a mountainous road full of hairpin turns. Returning from a visit to the two husbands, Minerva, Patria, and María Teresa are ambushed and killed by Trujillo's henchmen. The husbands are afterwards transferred back to the jail down in the capital.

In the novel's Epilogue, Dedé explains how the truth finally came out in 1962, after Trujillo died, at the trial of the Mirabals' murderers. There were four killers, one each for the three women and their driver, Rufino de la Cruz. As in other cases, the killers made the grisly scene look like an accident, loading the four corpses back into the jeep and shoving it over some sugarcane fields into a ravine. The court sentenced the sisters' killers to 20 or 30 years. But shortly thereafter they were set free in the rash of revolutions that rocked the nation.

Reflecting history—a pivotal "disappearance." When preparing her Miss University acceptance speech, María Teresa is advised by her sister Minerva not to overdo it because the students are "going to be a hard crowd to address after this Galíndez thing" (*Butterflies*, p. 136). The kidnapping and murder of Jesús Galíndez has been described as the turning point in Trujillo's whole evil career. A student and teacher at Columbia University in New York, Galíndez was a Basque from Spain, not a Dominican. But he had lived in the Dominican Republic for six years, working in Trujillo's government and teaching at the main university. Now, at Columbia University, he wrote *The Era of Trujillo* to earn his doctorate. His thesis was a frank but fair disclosure of facts, full of no-nonsense revelations like: "The hard truth is that freedom of speech has not existed [in the Dominican Republic] since May, 1930" (Galíndez, p. 129).

On March 12, 1956, Galíndez suddenly disappeared. He had delivered a lecture at the university, then caught a ride from a student to the New York subway so he could take a train to his lower Fifth Avenue apartment. After walking down some subway stairs, Galíndez was never heard from or seen again. Investigators concluded that he was drugged, placed on a chartered plane, and flown by a 23-year-old American pilot named Gerald Murphy to Trujillo's side. According to one account, the dictator ordered the dazed Galíndez to eat his thesis. When Galíndez failed to respond, Trujillo stalked out, after which the young scholar "was stripped and handcuffed. Then a rope was tied to his feet and led through an overhead pulley. Inch by inch Galíndez was lowered into a vat of boiling water. Sometime later Galíndez's body was fed to the sharks" (Diederich, p. 9). Within a few months, the pilot Murphy was arrested by the SIM, and the next year he was found hanging in a Dominican prison, the victim of a so-called suicide. The U.S. Federal Bureau of Investigation tried to uncover the truth, and the affair grew into a worldwide scandal, badly blighting Trujillo's image.

Sources and literary context. Based heavily on fact, *In the Time of the Butterflies* blends the concerns of four girls growing into womanhood with the grimness of daily existence in a police state. The characters are the creation of the author's imagination, but she has aspired to make them true to the spirit of the real sisters. Alvarez did extensive research, athough she makes no pretense of trying to recreate the Mirabals' characters with exactitude. At times she took liberties with history too, "by changing dates, by reconstructing events, and by collapsing characters or incidents," but Alvarez likewise based the novel's plot on a solid foundation of research (*Butterflies*, p. 324).

The Mirabal sisters became national heroes—monuments and museums were erected, and poems written in their honor. *In the Time of the Butterflies* demythologizes them by portraying them as people rather than as icons. The novel belongs to a growing corpus of Hispanic Caribbean literature written in exile, which harks back to mid-to-late-nineteenth-century writings by Puerto Rican and Cuban exiles such as the already-cited José Martí.

Events in History at the Time the Novel Was Written

From the sisters' murders to the writing of the novel. As indicated, leadership of the conspiracy to unseat Trujillo eventually passed from the June Fourteenth Movement to a more conservative group, made up of military men, professionals, and business leaders. In the end, the United States withheld its support even from these conservatives, concerned that if Trujillo were assassinated there would be a breakdown in law and order and the leftist June Fourteenth Movement would seize power. The Dominican plotters decided to proceed anyhow. By this time, Dominicans were bent on ridding themselves of Trujillo, in part because of the Mirabal murders.

> The cowardly killing of three beautiful women in such a manner had greater effect on Dominicans than most of Trujillo's other crimes. It did something to their machismo. They could never forgive Trujillo this crime. More than Trujillo's fight with the Church or the United States, or the fact that he was being isolated by the world as a political leper, the Mirabals' murder tempered the resolution of the conspirators plotting his end.
>
> (Diederich, pp. 71–72)

The so-called *ajusticiamiento*—just assassination—of Trujillo took 15 minutes. He was on his way to his San Cristobál estate, southeast of the capital, to meet a lover, when two cars of assassins descended on him. They succeeded in killing Trujillo. The killers had planned to afterward seize control of the government, but no coup d'état followed. Instead, Trujillo's family took charge, hunting down and jailing most of the assassins. One of them, General José "Pupo" Roman, suffered barbaric tortures, including the stitching of his eyebrows to his eyelids so his eyes would never close.

THE MIRABAL MURDERS—THE FACTS UNCOVERED

Reports indicate that the Mirabal sisters arrived at Puerto Plata to visit their husbands about 2:00 p.m. on November 25, 1960, stopping at a friend's who was sending food to the jailed men. Manolo and Leandro were happy to see not only their wives but also Patria, whose husband had been left in the jail in the capital, and who had come solely to show her support. The sisters left the men to return home at 4:30 p.m. About three kilometers outside Puerto Plata, a car with SIM agents forced the jeep to a stop and the three women were transferred by the agents into their SIM car. Patria broke away momentarily and tried to alert a passing vehicle without success. Two other SIM agents hopped into the jeep with the Mirabals' driver and made him follow the SIM car. The vehicles took a main road toward a nearby estate of Trujillo's, then veered onto a side road. About 7:30 p.m., a neighbor heard the Mirabal's jeep crash into a ravine. It was later determined that the women died from trauma to the base of the brain and side of the neck. They were apparently strangled after losing consciousness. Multiple fractures indicated that they had also been severely beaten.

Altogether, six men were convicted of murdering Trujillo and sentenced to maximum prison terms, then whisked off and executed illegally by Trujillo's son Ramfis. The Trujillo family remained in power for several months, until a military coup ousted them. This was followed by the 1962 election to power of writer Juan Bosch, referred to in the novel as the "poet president." That same year it became a crime or citizens to praise the dead Trujillo in speech, writing, or art. Statues of him were torn down, as U.S. Senator Smathers had predicted. Turmoil followed. An army coup ousted Bosch within months. Then more coups interrupted presidential terms until there was civil war (April-August 1965) and the U.S. Marines intervened. New elections brought Joaquin Balaguer, president under Trujillo when he died, into power again in 1966, and again in 1994,

The mural "A Song to Liberty," paying homage to the Mirabal sisters, is illuminated during an inauguration ceremony in Santo Domingo on March 6, 1997. The mural was painted on an obelisk that had been constructed by Trujillo.

the year in which Dedé Mirabal ends her story. "I never dreamed that thirty-three years after the fall of Trujillo the Dominican people still wouldn't have a definite democracy" mused one citizen in 1994, the year that *In the Time of the Butterflies* was published (Cambeira, p. 202).

Reviews. Many, but not all, reviews of the novel

have been positive. A critique in the *New York Times* argues that *In the Time of the Butterflies* focuses too much on the sisters' "rather naïve" development into womanhood and includes too many misfortunes (Gonzáles Echevarría, p. 28). On the other hand, a review in *World Literature Today* praises its "strong believable characters" and applauds the literary style as one that "seems to emerge from the core of woman's experience," as evidenced by such descriptions as "'Dedé's courage unraveled like a row of stitches not finished with a good sturdy knot'" (Pritchett, p. 789). Other reviews speak of the novel as a compelling read that manages to balance the personal with the political. More high praise comes from fellow Latino authors such as Rudolfo Anaya (see ***Bless Me, Ultima,*** also covered in *Latin American Literature and Its Times*), who asserts that Alvarez's work "is destined to take its place on the shelf of great Latin American novels" (Anaya in Alvarez, p. iii).

—Joyce Moss

For More Information

Alvarez, Julia. *In the Time of the Butterflies.* New York: Plume, 1994.

Cambeira, Alan. *Quisqueya la Bella: The Dominican Republic in Historical and Cultural Perspective.* Armonk, N.Y.: M. E. Sharpe, 1997.

Diederich, Bernard. *Trujillo: The Death of the Goat.* Boston: Little, Brown, 1978.

Foner, Philip S., ed. *José Marti: Major Poems: A Bilingual Edition.* Trans. Elinor Randall. New York: Homes and Meier, 1982.

Galíndez, Jesús de. *The Era of Trujillo.* Tucson: University of Arizona Press, 1973.

Gonzáles Echevarría, Roberto. "Sisters in Death." *The New York Times,* December 18, 1994, 28:2.

Hanover, Francesca Miller. *Latin American Women and the Search for Social Justice.* Hanover, Mass.: University Press of New England, 1991.

Pritchett, Kay. Review of *In the Time of the Butterflies. World Literature Today* 69, no. 4 (Fall 1995): 789.

Reed, W. L., and M. J. Bristow. *National Anthems of the World.* 8th ed. London: Cassell, 1993.

Iracema, the Honey-Lips: A Legend of Brazil

by

José de Alencar

José de Alencar was born in 1829 in Mecejana, Ceará, in northeastern Brazil. Many years later Alencar would recall that one of the inspirations for *Iracema, the Honey-Lips* was his home state's natural beauty. Because of his Portuguese-born father's political interests, the family moved to the southern city of Rio de Janeiro where the father later became part of the Portuguese royal court. Thanks to these political connections, Alencar was brought up surrounded by the comfort of the court. He attended school in São Paulo, then published his first novel, *Five Minutes* (1856), while working as the editor of a Rio de Janeiro newspaper. The next year he wrote one of his most famous novels, *O guaraní* (1857). After the death of his father in 1860, Alencar embraced politics as a Conservative and served briefly as Emperor Pedro II's minister of justice. This activism lasted for a decade, during which he wrote his masterpiece, *Iracema* (1865). Five years later he grew embittered and left the political world. Alencar died in 1877, a victim of tuberculosis.

THE LITERARY WORK

A novel set in Ceará, Brazil, in the early 1600s; published in Portuguese (as *Iracema*) in 1865, in English in 1886.

SYNOPSIS

The novel recounts the tragic love affair between a Portuguese colonizer, Martim, and a young Tabajara Indian woman, Iracema.

Events in History at the Time the Novel Takes Place

From trading posts to colonies. On April 22, 1500, the Portuguese explorer Pedro Álvares Cabral, who had been blown seriously off the course he had set for the Cape of Good Hope, became the first European to land in what is now Brazil. Approximately 2 to 4 million Indians lived there at the time; the first to be encountered by the Portuguese were the Tupi-speaking peoples, who lived along the coast. Initially, the Portuguese treated their new discovery as a convenient guard post from which to protect the lucrative sea lane to Asia, and as a trading center, from which they shipped boatloads of brazilwood back to Europe, acquired in exchange for trinkets, clothing, ornamental knives, and axes given to the local indigenous peoples (Burns, p. 25). From 1516 to 1519 and 1526 to 1528, a small coast guard patrolled the vast coastline, but this proved inadequate. Although the Portuguese rarely colonized the lands they explored, preferring rather to establish trading centers, foreign incursions by other European powers prompted Portugal's court to begin establishing more permanent colonies in Brazil that would substantiate the court's claim to vast amounts of land.

Given their initial trading-post mentality, the male settlers did not at first bring any Portuguese women with them to colonize Brazil. This shortage of white women accelerated a process—begun by the earliest European settlers (convicts, shipwrecked men, and deserters from the Portuguese fleet)—of Portuguese unions with the local native population and the siring of *mestizo* offspring (Burns, p. 24). After 1538, when African slaves were first brought to the colony, the mulatto population—the offspring of whites and Africans—also increased rapidly. This pattern of miscegenation is at center of *Iracema, the Honey-Lips*.

French activity on the Brazilian coastline. Harassed almost immediately by the Dutch and the French, the Portuguese were obliged to establish agricultural colonies up and down the Brazilian coast to defend their land claims, though their interests in Ceará and similar areas were actually military—that is, defensive, not economic. Later, when it became clear that sporadic agricultural communities could not adequately guarantee their control over the vast Brazilian lands, the Portuguese manned forts in order to discourage the French (who claimed to have discovered Brazil in 1488) or the Dutch from making themselves at home.

The unification of Portugal and Spain between 1580 and 1640 eliminated competition between the two of them for Brazilian land; however, the French and Dutch continued to actively challenge the Portuguese claim to the Brazilian coastline. The fertile lands, so suitable for sugar plantations, as well as vast stands of brazilwood, which was in great demand in Europe (especially at the French court) for its use in manufacturing rich red dyes, inspired these nations to conduct raids and establish their own colonies in Brazil. The French devoted themselves particularly to infiltrating Brazil along the weakly defended northern coast. They traded extensively with the Indians there, and left "interpreters" to live in the Indian villages and organize the felling of brazilwood trees in preparation for the arrival of French boats (Hemming, p. 10). To further their ends, they also encouraged hostilities between the Indians and the Portuguese. France refused to recognize the Treaty of Tordesillas (1494), which divided South America between Portugal and Spain, parceling out to Portugal the eastern half of what is today Brazil. Instead, the French preferred to believe that they owned anything they occupied. They continued to raid the Brazilian coastline in an attempt to break Portugal's monopoly in brazilwood.

In 1555 the French attacked and won control of Rio de Janeiro, establishing what they dubbed the "French Antarctic." It took 12 years before the Portuguese finally banished them from Rio. In 1594, about a decade before the novel takes place, the French made a successful incursion into the northern region of Maranhão and established "Equatorial France." They were expelled in 1615. Afterward the French practiced contraband and piracy, and, in their attempt to root themselves in the region, intermingled with the local Indians, establishing long-lasting, loyal relationships.

Indians in Ceará. *Iracema, the Honey-Lips* takes place in a very specific geography: north and east of the Jaguaribe River and west of the Serrada Ibiapaba. At the time this area was peopled by the coastal Potiguar Indians, whose range extended north into Maranhão and south almost as far as Pernambuco. Also living in the area were the inland Tabajara Indians (or Tobajara), whose territory intersected with the Potiguars' in several places, notably, for the novel, in the vicinity of the Uruburetama Hills. Although the novel's Martim has been befriended by a Potiguar leader, the Potiguar were not always friendly to the Portuguese. In the vicinity of the Paraíba River, for example, a peace treaty was not concluded before 1599; until then, the local Potiguar were fierce enemies, slaying Portuguese settlers and explorers by the hundreds. The Portuguese entered into alliances with the Tabajara, the enemies of the Potiguar along the Paraíba, and together fought the Potiguar and their French allies. In Ceará the situation was different. The Portuguese first entered the area aggressively in 1603, on their way north to discourage the French from establishing themselves in Maranhão. Traveling with the Portuguese was a mixed group of Potiguar and Tabajara. On the verge of starvation, they made their way as far as the Ibiapaba hills, where they were met in early 1604 by a combined force of Tabajara and French. This situation is reflected in the novel's opening pages, which explains that Martim is initially welcomed into Iracema's tribe of Tabajara because her father, the shaman, takes him for yet another Frenchman:

> The Tabajara tribes beyond Ibyapába were full of a new race of warriors, pale as the flowers of the storm, and coming from the remotest shores to the banks of the Mearim [a river in Maranhão]. The old man thought that it was one of these warriors who trod his native ground.
>
> (Alencar, *Iracema, the Honey-Lips,* p. 6)

At the time that Martim shows up on the banks of the Acaraú River, the great Tabajara chief

Although Martim in *Iracema, the Honey-Lips* is befriended by the Potiguar Indians, relations between European and indigenous peoples were not always friendly. Above is a sixteenth-century illustration of native Brazilians attacking a European colony.

Irapúam (Iracema's spurned suitor in the novel) is preparing to lead the Tabajara against the Potiguar. In 1604 Irapúam and other Tabajara in the Ibiapaba region would be conquered by a Portuguese force under Pero Coelho de Sousa, and many hundreds of Indian prisoners—as well, infamously, as Sousa's own Indian allies—would be taken as slaves. They were never sold, thanks to an order of the King, who realized that such action would jeopardize Portuguese colonization of the area. Martim Soares, on whom the novel's protagonist is based, himself started out on the Sousa expedition but got lost.

The Potiguar and the Tabajara both spoke the Tupi language, as did most of the tribes living near or along the coast; this is why Iracema, a Tabajara, and Martim, who has been living among the Potiguar, can communicate. Other cultural aspects were also held in common. The typical weapon was a bow and arrow, which was used on fish, fowl, and beast alike. Both men and women painted their bodies and, before the conquest by the Europeans, wore no clothing to speak of. The native peoples lived in structures of wood and thatch. Until the European arrived with the metal ax, the Indians cleared land with stone axes, cultivating a few plants—including gourds, peanuts, and manioc. They lived in villages, moving every few years when the easily eroded soil would no longer support their rudimentary agriculture. Their primary deity was Tupan, the god of thunder, who was attended by a *pagé*, or shaman. The forest was filled with evil spirits, most notably Anhan (Anhanga in the novel), who was typically blamed for mishaps. The novel also makes mention of "Jurupary," another name for Anhan, whom Araken, Iracema's father, prays will "hide himself, and allow the guest of the Pagé [Martim] to pass unmolested" on his night journey (*Iracema,* p. 25).

Native-Portuguese relations. The Portuguese, like the French, understood the importance of cultivating relationships with the local Indians and benefited hugely from native knowledge and technology, not to mention labor. It would have been difficult, if not impossible, for the Portuguese to exist in Brazil without the Indians' help. The native peoples taught the white men how to cultivate the land, which seeds to plant, and which foods were digestible. To solidify their relationship with the Indians, the Portuguese tended to exploit the network of Indian society. Every tribe consisted of different groups. When one of them wanted to expand its affiliations with other groups in the tribe, a male would enter into a relationship with a woman outside his group; she would then become a member of his group, sharing its work. On the other hand, if a group needed to forge a political alliance with another tribe, it would offer one of its women to this tribe. The Portuguese made use of this custom. After forming an alliance through marriage, the Portuguese would exploit the union, requesting that the woman's group help cut down and haul brazilwood to ships, and provide the ship with supplies for the trip back to Europe.

Two types of relationships prevailed when the Portuguese allied themselves with local Indians. Either the Portuguese lived with the Indians, adopting their customs, or, more commonly, the local Indians offered their women in the belief that this would result in a beneficial alliance. The women then lived with the Portuguese, leaving their Indian group.

Since various Indian tribes practiced polygamy, the Portuguese quickly discovered they could form relationships with a variety of different women, thus multiplying their alliances. However, this strategy was not foolproof, since the Indian tribes were constantly warring against one another. The Portuguese would astutely pick a tribe with which to ally themselves, then identify which tribes were mortal enemies of their allied tribe and declare war on these enemies, a ploy that virtually guaranteed the cooperation of the allied tribe. The wars allowed the Portuguese to expand their landholdings and, eventually, provided a "legitimate" vehicle for gaining Indian slaves.

At first, the Portuguese Crown refused to allow Brazil's Indians to be enslaved; they were to be Christianized, not abused. Eventually however, in the face of the ever-increasing need for labor, as well as a mounting desire for riches, King João III (1521-55) allowed the enslavement of Indians who battled the Portuguese. This leeway was, of course, prone to misuse. In sum, the Portuguese colonized Brazil through both marriage and war. Aside from accelerating the amalgamation of Indian and Portuguese cultures, the marriages produced the mestizos, or mixed-blood Brazilians.

The Novel in Focus

Plot summary. *Iracema, the Honey-Lips* relates the encounter between Martim, a Portuguese explorer in Ceará, and Iracema, a young Tabajara woman. As the novel opens, Martim is leaving Brazil on a raft, accompanied only by a child and a dog. "What left he in that land of exile?" (*Iracema,* p. 2).

As the story unfolds in retrospect, we learn that what Martim left behind was Iracema. He first meets her in the forest. Startled at her bath, the young woman shoots an arrow at the white man, grazing his face. He refrains from attacking her and she quickly repents her action, offering him the broken arrow, a gesture that signified an unbreakable bond in Indian culture. She discovers that he knows her language and leads him to her father's dwelling. Her father, Araken, is a pagé (or shaman) to the god Tupan. When he first sees Martim, he mistakes him for one of the Frenchmen who were living among the Tabajara of the Ibiapaba hills; Martim informs him that he is not French and has, in fact, been living happily among the Potiguar, the traditional enemies of the Tabajara, and is a friend of their famous chiefs Poty and Jacaúna. He is in Tabajara country only by mistake.

Nonetheless, Araken makes him welcome, although he believes that "some bad spirit of the forest . . . blinded the pale-face warrior in the darkness of the wood" (*Iracema,* p. 9). On this ominous note, Araken leaves the dwelling, and Iracema brings Martim serving girls, telling him that she herself cannot attend to him because she guards the secret of the *jurema* (of which Martim will learn more shortly). He leaves the dwelling, noticing that the Tabajara warriors are dancing around a fire; the narrator informs us that Irapúam, the most prominent Tabajara chief in the area, has come to lead them against the Potiguar. Iracema catches up to Martim and persuades him to wait until her brother, Cauby, returns from a hunting trip to lead him safely back to Potiguar territory. He agrees.

Meanwhile, at daybreak, Irapúam is inciting the Tabajara to rise up against the Potiguar (referred to as the Potyuáras in the novel) and the Portuguese, whom he calls the "warriors of fire" (*Iracema,* p. 13). That evening, Martim is pacing morosely in front of Araken's dwelling, feeling homesick. To comfort him, Iracema makes him a liquor of juréma (a hallucinogenic extract of a local acacia plant), which, she tells him, will restore his gladness and perhaps give him a vision of the "bride who expects him" across the ocean (*Iracema,* p. 16). Martim falls into a drugged sleep and sees all he longs for—his parents, his beloved—but finds that what he truly desires is Iracema, to whom he calls in his sleep. She allows him to embrace her briefly, then leaves abruptly. She has perhaps heard Irapúam, whom she finds lurking in the woods. He wants to kill Martim, of whom he is jealous. Iracema makes short work of the chief's romantic overture and he leaves, vowing to take revenge on the white man. Iracema realizes that she is in love with the Portuguese warrior, but when Martim offers to stay among the Tabajara to make her happy, she informs him that she must remain a virgin and keep the secret of the juréma for her tribe and that it is in his best interest to avoid her company: "The brave that shall possess the Virgin of Tupan will die" (*Iracema,* p. 21). They agree that he must leave, but when he tries to do so, he and Cauby, his guide, run into Irapúam and some warriors, who are determined to kill Martim. A battle ensues but before long the Tabajara hear the war-cry of the Potiguars and rush to fend off the enemy. Martim and Iracema escape to Araken's dwelling, trailed by Irapúam, who suspects that the war-cry was somehow a ploy by Iracema to distract the warriors. Irapúam accuses Iracema in front of her father of having given up her sacred virginity to Martim; he hopes that Martim will die for this, but Araken states that, if the accusation is true, Iracema must die. Martim, however, is a guest of the god Tupan and will not be harmed. Iracema hotly defends herself and Irapúam retreats. When Iracema approaches Martim, in joy, he rebukes her harshly, reminding her that her life is at stake. She accuses him of putting her aside because he loves a "white virgin" far away (*Iracema,* p. 33).

In the night they hear the song of the seagull, which Martim knows is the actual war-cry of Poty himself. Iracema rejoices that Martim is to be saved from the Tabajara who are waiting outside the protection of Araken's dwelling to kill him, and vows not to warn her people that Poty is nearby. She goes out alone to call to Poty on Martim's behalf, arranges his rescue, and later leads Martim out of the dwelling via a secret cave. It is a cave in which Araken manipulates the winds to sound like the voice of the god Tupan, which he fortuitously does at this juncture. Irapúam and some drunken warriors arrive at the door but hear the roar of Tupan and retreat. Thereafter, Iracema and Martim meet Poty in the subterranean cave and arrange for Martim to escape during the "Moon of Flowers" celebration, in which the Tabajara warriors all drink jurema and dream. When they return to the dwelling, Iracema again gives Martim some jurema to reduce his sadness in leaving her; this time, however, as she alone knows, she does not shrug off his embrace: "Tupan no longer owned his Virgin in the Tabajara land" (*Iracema,* p. 47).

When it is time for Iracema to leave Martim safely with Poty on the threshold of Tabajara land, she refuses, and claims that Tupan has released her from service because she betrayed the secret of jurema and because Martim's "blood sleeps in her bosom" (*Iracema,* p. 57). Martim is upset but allows her to come along; almost immediately, however, his love for her overcomes him and they begin their lives as husband and wife. The next day, Iracema proves her devotion by shooting her own brother, Cauby, who is among the band of Tabajara pursuing the fugitives. The Tabajara are routed by the Potiguar, and Martim and Iracema settle down with Chief Jacaúna, until the burden of living among her people's enemies becomes too much to bear. Accompanied by Poty, Martim and Iracema build a new home for themselves on a coastal site that Martim believes would be good for Portuguese settlement. He keeps this ambition from Iracema who, four months later, reveals to a joyful Martim that she is pregnant.

His joy dissipates, however, when he sees in the distance sails like those of Portuguese ships and longs for home. Martim tells Poty that he has seen French ships, after which Poty learns that Irapúam and the French are on the move and that Chief Jacaúna is calling for help. Martim and Poty depart at once, without informing Iracema. Instead, they leave her a sign and return to her after the battle, in which the Potiguar were victorious. Martim is content with her for a few short days, but then his ambition and homesickness resurface and his love withers. He considers returning to Portugal but realizes that Iracema would want to go with him, which would be unfair to her, since she would be alienated there and could not take much comfort in his dwindling love. Meanwhile, Iracema realizes that Martim is no longer happy with her and tells him that she will die as soon as their child is born, freeing Martim to return home. This statement elicits a "harsh and bitter" kiss from Martim, who seems to acquiesce to his wife's notion that she must die in order for him to find happiness (*Iracema,* p. 87).

RACIAL MINGLING IN ALENCAR'S INDIANIST NOVELS

A creator of various types of tales, Alencar is perhaps best known for his trio of Indianist novels—*Ubirajara, O guaraní,* and *Iracema*—which examine the historical and mythical roots of Brazilian culture. In this context, the term "Indianism" refers to an ideology in which Brazil's original inhabitants are portrayed as "racially pure," "glorious and brave," and as "honorable and loyal warrior[s] after the fashion of a club-wielding [medieval European] knight" (Reis in Foster, p. 99). In his memoirs, *Como e porque sou romancista* (How and Why I'm a Novelist), Alencar admits that his works idealize the Indian:

> In *O guaraní* the savage is an ideal that the writer attempts to poeticize, stripping off the rough crust the chroniclers wrapped him up in, ripping away from him the ridiculous light that they projected on him, the brutal remainders of an almost extinct race.
>
> (Alencar, *Como e porque sou romancista,* p. 61; trans. A. Potter)

Again Martim spots French sails, and again he and Poty depart. On the day that they celebrate their defeat of the French and their Indian allies, Iracema gives birth, alone, to "the first son born to this Land of Liberty begotten by the blood of the white race" (*Iracema,* p. 90). She names the boy Moacyr, which means "child of pain." One day, Cauby shows up; he and Araken have missed her badly. Cauby decides to wait for Martim's return so that they can be reconciled to each other, but Iracema sends him back to care for their father, who is all alone. He vows to return every year to visit her and her son. Alone again, Iracema loses her will to live and when Martim finally reappears, eight months after he left, she is too weak even to rise. She presents their son to him and dies. He is overcome with love and sorrow.

Martim takes Moacyr to Portugal but returns a few years later with a contingent, has Poty baptized (as Antonio Phelipe Camarão), and founds a settlement. From time to time a bitterly regretful Martim returns to Iracema's grave to contemplate his former happiness.

From romantic love to founding myth. To a modern reader, there is obvious romanticism in Alencar's novel, which presents Iracema as unspeakably beautiful, humble, obedient, sexually uninhibited (once the problem of her sacred virginity is dealt with), and utterly devoted to her white warrior, whom she appears to love from the moment she sets eyes on him. As John Hemming points out, such traits were important elements of the "noble savage" tradition that swept Renaissance Europe in the wake of Portugal's encounter with Brazil's natives; books such as Rabelais's *Pantagruel* and Erasmus's *In Praise of Folly* reacted to or promulgated the image of the Brazilian Indians as supremely uncomplicated, natural, moral, *free,* people. Less theoretically, what turned the explorers' heads were the unabashedly naked Brazilian women. A chronicler aboard Cabral's ship described one such woman:

> [She was] all dyed from head to foot in . . . paint; and indeed she was so well built and so well curved, and her privy part (what a one she had!) was so gracious that many women of our country, on seeing such charms, would be ashamed that theirs were not like hers.
>
> (Caminha in Hemming, p. 4)

Writers of the time remark upon the Indian custom of hospitality, which usually involved the gift of a girl to a man to satisfy his desires; however, this was true only of unattached girls; wives remained faithful to their husbands. Portuguese sailors were astounded when Indian girls visiting their ships "surrendered to the white men with natural innocence" (Hemming, p. 17). People conceived of this natural innocence as a type of purity, which is attached to Iracema in the novel. Given this context, its description of her, which may strike readers as hyperbolic, makes better sense.

Ubirajara, O guaraní, and *Iracema* are all overtly concerned with the idea of Brazil as a hybrid society, the result of inter-marriage between different noble races (in *Iracema* and *O guaraní,* between Europeans and Indians) and different peoples (in *Ubirajara,* between traditionally inimical Indian tribes). However, as Renata Wasserman points out, in each of these novels lasting harmony from such racial and intergroup mingling is possible only in theory. In the first two novels, death and disaster thwart the Indian-European marriages. In *Ubirajara* the intertribal union is mutually beneficial but threatened by the advent of Brazil's violent European conquerors, who are alluded to in the novel's extensive footnotes, though contact has not yet occurred. The suggestion seems to be that, the nobility of Brazil's founding races notwithstanding, only outside of history can harmonious racial mingling be successfully achieved (Wasserman, *Exotic Nations,* pp. 213-16).

In the end, the romantic love in *Iracema* is doomed. The beautiful Indian dies of a broken heart and her Portuguese mate is left with feelings of remorse and longing. Yet the novel closes also with hope in the guise of their son, Moacyr, the mythical first Brazilian, a mixture of Iracema's purity and Martim's colonizing warrior spirit. According to one literary historian, "As Alencar implies," the mother perishes just as Indian America must die, leaving her son, "the symbolic product of all the pain of the Conquest and the first true Brazilian in the care of his Portuguese father" (Haberly in González Echevarría and Pupo-Walker, p. 143).

The real Martim Soares Moreno. *Iracema, the Honey-Lips* was inspired by actual historical events and real people. In mid-1603 an expedition commanded by Pero Coelho de Sousa left Paraíba on the easternmost point of Brazil, in the northern province of Hamaracá, destined for Maranhão, to the north of present-day Ceará. With Coelho de Sousa were 65 white men and 200 Potiguar and Tabajara Indians. At the Ibiapaba hills to the northwest of Ceará the expedition met with the Tabajara in the area, who had the support of seven armed Frenchmen. After much fighting, the Portuguese conquered their opponents, including the famous chief Irapúam, who appears as Iracema's disappointed suitor in Alencar's novel. One of the members of Coelho de Sousa's expedition was 19-year-old Martim Soares Moreno, popularized as the "white warrior" in *Iracema,* the Honey-Lips. Conflicting accounts exist, but apparently he got lost and was adopted by the Potiguar Indians. Certainly he was fast friends with the Potiguar warrior Poty (later baptized as Antonio Phelipe Camarão) and his brother Jacaúna. Soares learned to speak Tupi and assimilated into Indian culture; in 1611 he attacked a French or Dutch ship that tried to land in Ceará, aided by members of the Tremembé tribe. According to sources, he "fought naked, scarred and dyed black with genipapo in the Indian manner" (Hemming, p. 210). Renata Wasserman points out that Alencar knowingly rearranged the chronology of Soares's disappearance into the Brazilian jungle: "the historical model of Martim disappeared for a few years into an Indian tribe; he was next seen, naked and painted, when he was captured with his tribal companions by a Portuguese expedition. It was only after this episode that he went back to the king's service as settler" (Wasserman, *Exotic Nations,* p. 207). Eventually he took back to the Brazilian governor-general a son of his that had been born in Ceará "to prove that the area was peaceful enough for settlement" (Hemming, p. 210). In 1610 or 1611 he was made Captain of Ceará. In 1615, on his way either to Ceará or to Portugal from his base in Maranhão, Soares was blown off course and captured by the French off Santo Domingo. He was sentenced to death in Dieppe, France, for his part in killing Frenchmen in Maranhão. The Spanish ambassador interceded on his part and his life was spared. In 1619 he was named governor of Ceará, and established what is now the city of Fortaleza. Soares died an old man in the land he helped conquer.

Events in History at the Time the Novel Was Written

Father of Brazilian fiction. Published in 1865, *Iracema* was instrumental in the formation of the Brazilian novel. One needs to keep in mind that there were few readers at the time and most of them were male. "Only about 20 percent of Brazilian men could read and write their own names—much less read a novel" (Haberly in Gonzáles Echevarría and Pupo-Walker, p. 139). The handful of Brazilian novelists, then, were males writing for a small male audience. Yet these writers faced a dilemma. They found it impossible to import styles and subjects for their fiction from Europe, for they lived in a traditional slave-owning empire based on different principles than those emerging overseas. In European fiction, for example, characters advanced because they deserved to, that is, because of merit. Such ideas struck Brazilian intellectuals of the period as dangerous, since society in their empire still depended not on merit, but on favor, that is, on the less fortunate finding their way into the good graces of the more fortunate, and staying there.

A sixteenth-century portrait of a family of Tupi-speaking Indians in Brazil.

In any case, the task was to develop a prose fiction suited to Brazil's small cadre of mostly male readers and their environment.

By 1861 Alencar had made considerable progress in this vein with novels about urban life in Brazil and with his first Indianist novel *O guaraní* (1857), which concerned the love between a blond Portuguese woman and a noble Indian in the 1600s. Casting the story in Brazil in a distant and therefore unfamiliar past gave Alencar free rein. He could invent a new reality, apart from Europe's, and not be bound by the circumstances of life in contemporary Rio de Janeiro. The result was the group of three Indianist novels discussed above, which provided Brazil with "a highly original mythology of national genesis" (Haberly in González Echevarría and Pupo-Walker, p. 143).

Romanticism and Brazilianess. Romanticism, the literary movement in Europe from the late 1700s to the mid-1800s, privileged feelings and intuition over reason, and concerned itself with cultural nationalism and national origins. With the help of Alencar's novels, romanticism in Brazil took on characteristics distinct from its European counterparts. In 1853 Domingos José Gançalves de Magalhães published an epic poem, "The Confederation of Tamoios" that, in a classic Greek style, idealized Brazil's past through its Indian culture. In 1856 a young writer submitted an anonymous letter to the newspaper *Diário do Rio de Janeiro* censuring the European epic form chosen by Magalhães, declaring it inadequate to represent Brazilian reality. José de Alencar was the young writer, and he answered his own call with the publication the very next year of *O guaraní.* It was a novel that included what Alencar believed to be the ingredients of Brazilian reality—the idealized Indian, the splendor of Brazilian nature, and the mixture of races. By emphasizing such concepts, he began to differentiate Brazilian from European romantic literature.

When Alencar charged that Magalhães's portrayal of the Indians lacked veracity, he entered into a fray that attempted to define what was, in fact, Brazilian. During these efforts to define a national literature and identity, many novels like *Iracema, the Honey-Lips* promoted the mixture of the races as a positive force that fused the diverse cultures of Brazil. As Renata Wasserman points out, the title of Alencar's novel demonstrates his intention to celebrate the new hybridism of Brazil: "Iracema, the name of the heroine, is a word Alencar invented following rules of word formation in Guarani, the predominant Indian language along the Brazilian coast . . . , and it is also an anagram of America" (Wasserman, "The Red and the White," p. 821).

By idealizing both Martim and Iracema, Alencar joined the ideals of the "noble savage" and innocent Indian culture with the indomitable spirit of the Portuguese adventurer, which, in the character of Martim, is much less violent and greedy than was typical of many actual colonists. In reality Manuel da Nobrega, a Jesuit priest of the time, wrote to the King personally, begging him to send more pure, white women to the colony, as well as more priests to instruct both the colonizers and the Indian population. Alencar reinvents this past with *Iracema, the Honey-Lips,* creating a glorious—if fictitious—history that would help shape Brazil's national identity. By portraying the coupling of the Indian and the Portuguese as the union of noble savage and Christian warrior, the novel created a symbol for the nation that reflected the reality of its already mixed-race population. Such a novel could not idealize the Portuguese alone since Brazil had in 1822 declared independence from Portugal. Similarly the dehumanization to which African slaves were subjected prohibited them from being elevated as a symbol for the nation. The Indians, however, had escaped efforts to turn them into a class of slaves. "It was possible," explains Wasserman, "to take Amerindians for heroes of nationality: their refusal of slavery became a prefiguration of independence" (Wasserman, *Exotic Nations,* p. 195). Furthermore, by Alencar's time, the Indian had for the most part already assimilated into Brazilian society or had fled deep into the forests. So, other than in the colonial past, the Indians whom the novel idealizes did not exist anymore; this meant that any meaning could be safely attached to them and used in the construction of a national identity.

ALENCAR'S LEGACY

"Alencar's influence on the development of the nineteenth-century Brazilian novel cannot be overestimated; he nationalized the genre and made it respectable, he established its peculiar mix of detailed realistic description and romantic ideology, and he largely created its major subgenres."
(Haberly in González Echevarría and Pupo-Walker, p. 144)

Alencar, again relying largely on imagination, went on to invent another type of fiction, the regionalist novel, whose plots took place in various parts of Brazil's interior. In sum, he wrote urban novels, Indianist novels, regionalist novels, and historical novels, all set in the country of his birth.

Reviews. Alencar has been called the "father of Brazilian literature," not only because he dealt so extensively with the cultural and mythic roots of his nation, but because he celebrated the language of Brazilians. *Iracema*'s poetic meter and diction are in part an attempt to incorporate Indian oral tradition into the Portuguese of the mainstream culture. In an 1866 review, Joaquim Maria Machado de Assis, often heralded as Brazil's finest novelist (see ***Dom Casmurro,*** also covered in *Latin American Literature and Its Times*), wrote that *Iracema* is "a model for the cultivation of an American poetry that, please God, will be reinvigorated by works of such superior quality" (Machado de Assis in Wasserman, *Exotic Nations,* p. 187). Apparently other contemporary critics were less generous with their praise, for in an earlier review Machado de Assis complained that *Iracema* had not been given its due attention by the nation's literary critics. More recently, Afrâino Coutinho has been one of a number of Brazilian critics who have agreed that "Alencar created Brazilian fiction, propelling it in the right direction, that of a search for the expression of the nationality" (Coutinho in Wasserman, *Exotic Nations,* p. 187). ***Macunaíma*** (also covered in *Latin American Literature and Its Times*), Mário de Andrade's influential experimental novel that also attempts to define the Brazilian character, is dedicated: "To José de Alencar, father of the living, shining in the vast heavenly field" (Andrade in Castello, p. 201). *Iracema* has, to date, been printed in more than 100 editions in Brazil.

—Anthony Miles Potter

For More Information

Alencar, José de. *Como e porque sou romancista.* São Paulo: Pontes, 1990.

——. *Iracema, the Honey-Lips: A Legend of Brazil.* Trans. Isabel Burton. London: Bickers & Son, 1886.

Burns, Bradford, E. *A History of Brazil.* 3rd ed. New York: Columbia University Press, 1993.

Castello, José Aderaldo. "José de Alencar." In *Latin American Writers.* Vol. 1. Ed. Carlos A. Solé and Maria Isabel Abreu. New York: Charles Scribner's Sons, 1989.

Coutinho, Afrânio. *Enciclopedia de Literatura Brasileira.* Rio de Janeiro: FAE, 1989.

Foster, David William, ed. *Handbook of Latin American Literature.* 2nd ed. New York: Garland, 1992.

González Echevarría, Roberto, and Enrique Pupo-Walker. *Latin American Literature.* Vol. 3. Cambridge: Cambridge University Press, 1995.

Hemming, John. *Red Gold: The Conquest of the Brazilian Indians.* London: Macmillan, 1978.

Macdonald, N. P. *The Making of Brazil: Portuguese Roots, 1500-1822.* Sussex: Book Guild, 1996.

Wasserman, Renata R. Mautner. *Exotic Nations: Literature and Cultural Identity in the United States and Brazil, 1830-1930.* Ithaca, N. Y.: Cornell University Press, 1994.

——. "The Red and the White: The 'Indian' Novels of José de Alencar." *PMLA* 98, no. 5 (October 1983): 815-25.

I, Rigoberta Menchú: An Indian Woman in Guatemala

by
Rigoberta Menchú

THE LITERARY WORK

An autobiography set in Guatemala between 1959 and 1981; published in Spanish in 1983 (as *Me llamo Rigoberta Menchú y así me nació la conciencia*), in English in 1984.

SYNOPSIS

A Quiché Indian woman recounts the difficult and often tragic experiences that led to her becoming an activist for Indian rights.

Born in Chimel, a hamlet in northwestern Guatemala, Rigoberta Menchú was the sixth child of laborers who became Indian rights activists. Her father, Vicente, a founding member of the influential Peasant Unity Committee (Comité Unidad Campesina; CUC), died during a protest at the Spanish embassy in 1980. Menchú's mother and younger brother were tortured and killed by the Guatemalan army in separate incidents. Despite these violent deaths, Menchú carried on her family's work, becoming a leader of the CUC in 1979. In 1981 she was forced to flee to Mexico; the following year, she traveled to Europe to speak on behalf of the Quiché Indians. During that period, she met Elisabeth Burgos-Debray, to whom she related her story in a week-long series of interviews that would become the autobiography *I, Rigoberta Menchú*. Menchú received the Nobel Peace Price in 1992.

Events in History at the Time of the Autobiography

Indians vs. ladinos: an overview. The bitter conflict between Indians—the indigenous people of Guatemala—and *ladinos*—whose ancestors include Spaniards and Europeans—is one of the main themes in the autobiography. Descended from Mayans, Guatemalan Indians comprised more than 60 percent of the country's population in 1996. There are 22 different groups of Guatemalan Indians, including the Quiché, Cakchiquel, Kekchi, and Mam, all of which speak their own languages. Despite their differences, the Indians are united in their distrust of their ladino oppressors, who control most of Guatemala's land and wealth.

As Ann Wright points out in her translation of *I, Rigoberta Menchú,* English offers no exact equivalent for the term *ladino*. Wright herself interprets it as meaning "a person of mixed race or a Spanish-speaking Indian," or, in more general terms, "someone who represents a system which oppresses the Indian" (Wright in Menchú, p. viii). The translator's alternatives highlight the unfixed nature of the term. Others have similar difficulties defining "ladino"—Richard Wilson considers it a synonym for *mestizo* (Wilson, p. 7), while Jean-Marie Simon uses it to refer to "people of mixed Indian and Spanish or European ancestry" (Simon, p. 19). John Hawkins argues that the terms *indígena* (Indian) and *ladino* "exist as a structural set of oppositions" for "groups of people who play out their lives in social institutions derived from the colonial past" (Hawkins, pp. 173-74). After interviewing several groups of Guatemalan high school students, Hawkins concluded that, "Within the general notion of origins, 'Ladino' is associated with Europe, foreign lands, and the nonlocal context, as opposed to 'Indian,' which is associated with particular towns and the local context" (Hawkins, p. 182). The two groups were distinguished not only by different ethnicities but by different languages, occupations, surroundings, and clothing. Literally speaking, ladino is a linguistic category meaning "Latin speaker"; an Indian can, therefore, become a ladino. Menchú's community defines a ladino as "any Guatemalan—whatever his economic position—who rejects, either individually or through his cultural heritage, Indian values of Mayan origin" (Menchú, *I, Rigoberta Menchú,* p. 249).

MARRIAGE IN THE QUICHÉ COMMUNITY

The Quiché observe four marriage customs. In the first—"the open door"—the suitor, his parents, and the village representative approach the family of the girl he wishes to court and request a meeting. Usually several encounters take place before the door is opened for them to enter the girl's house. The couple are given the chance to get to know each other better, while chaperoned by at least one of her parents. If the girl accepts the boy's suit, he kneels to her parents and names the date on which he will come with his parents. During this second ritual, the bride's family holds a fiesta. Both families and the village elders discuss the importance of preserving Indian traditions. The couple joins in the discussion, promising to remain Indian. During the third ritual, the bride and groom make their vows to each other in front of the elders, reaffirming their commitment to their union, the community, and the ways of their people, and rejecting the world of the ladinos. The fourth ceremony is the wedding itself—the *despedida*—during which the bride, after a civil or Catholic Church marriage ceremony, receives her gifts and says goodbye to the community. She then departs with her new husband, and may not visit her parents' house for 15 days.

In her autobiography Menchú writes that her people are committed to preserving the "purity" of their culture, which entails rejecting ladino influences, even in the seemingly harmless guise of basic education and clothing. Menchú's father, for example, refuses to support her when she tells him she wants to learn to read and write, fearing she will become discontented and abandon the community. During Quiché wedding ceremonies, the village elders and the wedded couple commonly discuss, then repudiate, ladino ways: "They say: 'These things may be modern but we mustn't buy the rubbish they have, even if we have the money. We must keep our ways of making our own'" (*Rigoberta Menchú,* p. 71). Fostering understanding between Indians and ladinos without "mixing" cultures becomes an ongoing challenge for Menchú and her people once they begin to organize against their oppressors.

Repression in the Lucas García years. In 1954 the United States sent Central Intelligence Agency (CIA) forces into Guatemala to oust President Jacobo Arbenz Guzmán, whose agrarian reform plan—calling for the expropriation and redistribution of idle lands—threatened the interests of the American-owned United Fruit Company, which had enjoyed tax-exempt export privileges since 1901. Arbenz was forced to resign in order to make way for his successor, Colonel Carlos Castillo Armas (1954-57), who was hand-picked by the United States. Two months after the coup, CIA operatives and the "Committee Against Communism" compiled a blacklist of 70,000 political opponents to the new regime. Over the years many Guatemalans on the list were assassinated while others fled into exile.

The administrations that followed that of Castillo Armas took a similar hard-line stance against communism and those who were considered "enemies of the state." During the 1960s large-scale killings began in response to a growing guerrilla movement led by disaffected young military officers and comprised mostly of university students: "While the Guatemalan guerrillas never numbered more than 500 in the 1960s, they provided the rationale for killing thousands of unarmed civilians" (Simon, p. 23). The 1970s saw an even more dramatic rise in violence during the presidencies of General Kjell Eugenio Laugerud García (1974-78) and his hand-picked successor and defense minister, General Fernando Romeo Lucas García (1978-82). In the last year of Laugerud García's administration, selective assassinations increased and "large-scale army repression" in rural areas began (Simon, p. 29). Outspoken opponents of the Laugerud García regime were abducted and murdered. Amnesty International recorded over 300 cases of "disappeared" Guatemalans between July 1977

A Quiché woman working at a loom.

and June 1978. Victims included students, labor leaders, priests, and Indian peasants. On May 29, 1978, a month before Lucas García's inauguration, Kekchi Indians protesting the expropriation of their land were machine-gunned by army soldiers in Panzós, Alta Verapaz. More than 100 men, women, and children died.

Surpassing the outrages of his predecessor's regime, Lucas García's regime is considered one of the bloodiest and most corrupt in Guatemala's history. His victory in the 1978 elections was widely considered to be fraudulent, but he took office on July 1, 1978, nonetheless. Within the first years of his presidency, repression, abductions, and mass killings increased. Rigoberta Menchú attests: "It was in 1978, when Lucas García came to power with such a lust for killing, that the repression really began in [the province of] El Quiché. It was like a piece of rag in his hands. He set up military bases in many of the villages and there were rapes, tortures, kidnappings. And massacres" (*Rigoberta Menchú*, p. 161).

In 1979 two promising presidential hopefuls—Alberto Fuentes Mohr of the Social Democratic Party (PSD) and Manuel Colom Argueta of the United Front of the Revolution (FUR)—were gunned down within months of each other. A year and a half after Lucas García took office, Amnesty International documented 5,000 "disappearances" and extrajudicial killings. But while instances of urban repression were reported, the atrocities that occurred in the Guatemalan highlands—such as those suffered by Rigoberta Menchú's community—took longer to come to light. Selective killings ballooned into massacres and sometimes into the elimination of entire villages by the Guatemalan army. "In a 1986 interview Interior Minister Juan Rodil Peralta told a foreign reporter that over 25,000 Guatemalans were killed during the four years of the Lucas regime" (Simon, p. 77). In her autobiography, Menchú describes the army massacre of political prisoners at Chajul that claimed her brother's life, the Spanish embassy fire that killed her father, and the torture and killing of her mother—all of which took place under the Lucas García administration.

Like Laugerud García, Lucas García handpicked his successor, General Angel Aníbal Guevara Rodriguez, who "won" easily on March 7, 1982, with the aid of phantom voters and a warehouse of false ballots. But General Guevara never took office. On March 23, 1982, right-wing politicians and 900 dissident army officers staged a military coup, surrounding the National Palace in Guatemala City with tanks and artillery, while army helicopters circled overhead. President Lucas García was forced to resign and General José Efraín Ríos Montt assumed power as the head of a military dictatorship. Although succeeding regimes were themselves marred by violence and corruption, the Lucas García presidency became a collective byword for the worst abuses of power in Guatemalan government. By 1987 a popular adage was, "Well, at least it's not like Lucas" (Simon, p. 81).

Religion, revolution, and the CUC (Peasant Unity Committee). During the mid-1970s peasant organizations began to take shape in Guatemala. Two conservative factions—the Christian Democrat party, formed in 1955, and the Catholic Church hierarchy—contributed to this trend, eagerly supporting groups that "might discourage more radical social change" (Simon, p. 25). The Church was particularly successful, forming "catechist" movements in which rural leaders were trained to carry out community religious work, especially in remote and less accessible areas. In the autobiography Menchú reveals that her father was a catechist and that she herself became one when she was 12, teaching Catholic doctrine to the younger children in the community. The Catholic Action movement, started by Spanish priests in Guatemala, also served to increase social awareness. Based on the principles of Vatican II liberation theology—which promoted the Catholic Church's increased identification with the social and economic needs of the poor—Catholic Action offered concrete as well as spiritual aid but not always on unconditional terms. As a former resident of Chajul recalled, "Catholic Action was a strong movement. They won over converts by offering them benefits. You could only get your cows vaccinated if you belonged to Catholic Action. Almost everyone who participated was younger than thirty-five because then they didn't worry about becoming modernized" (Simon, p. 40).

In many instances programs like Catholic Action and the catechists' movement provided the catalyst for political awakening: "In Marxist terminology, the catechists provided the subjective conditions in which a revolutionary situation could escalate" (Wilson, p. 213). Converts of both Catholic Action and the catechists' movements began to consider not only the welfare of their souls but of their communities too, rejecting passive acceptance of their situation. Menchú writes, "When I first became a catechist, I thought that there was a God and that we had to serve him. . . . But we realized that it is not God's will that we should live in suffering, that God did not give us that destiny, but that men on earth have imposed this suffering, poverty, misery and discrimination on us" (*Rigoberta Menchú,* p. 132). As a consequence of this realization, guerrilla groups and labor movements increased in number and activity, with many Indians taking part in both.

The Comité Unidad Campesina (Peasant Unity Committee) was considered the "largest and most important organization" to emerge from this combined religious/political movement (Perera, p. 67). Rigoberta Menchú attributes the CUC's beginnings to a discussion that her father, Vicente, had with a political prisoner during his incarceration in 1977: "He was someone who defended the peasants and he told my father the peasants should unite and form a Peasants' League to reclaim their lands. . . . [M]y father started to join up with other peasants and discussed the creation of the CUC with them" (*Rigoberta Menchú,* p. 115). Forced to work clandestinely at first, the CUC came out in the open to condemn the Guatemalan army's massacre of the Kekchi Indians in Panzós in May 1978 and to declare its agenda for peasants' rights. Rigoberta Menchú, who joined the CUC in 1979, explains, "Our objectives were: a fair wage from the landowners; respect for our communities; the decent treatment we deserve as people, not animals; respect for our religion, our customs and our culture" (*Rigoberta Menchú,* p. 160). The CUC continued to grow, despite the inevitable targeting of its leaders by the army and the loss of several members in the Spanish embassy fire (see below). In 1980 the CUC organized a series of strikes in the coffee, sugar, and cotton *fincas* (plantations), which paralyzed harvesting and led to the legislation of a minimum wage of 3.20 *quetzals* a day, the first minimum wage in Guatemala's history.

Occupation of the Spanish embassy. One of the pivotal events in Menchú's life is the occupation of the Spanish embassy on January 31, 1980, which claimed the life of her father. Along with other peasants, he had marched to Guatemala City to protest the expropriation of Indian lands and the widespread persecution of Indians and poor ladinos in El Quiché: "The objective was to tell the whole world what was happening in Guatemala and inform people inside the country as well" (*Rigoberta Menchú,* p. 185).

Hoping to attract international attention to their cause, students, laborers, and representatives of such organizations as the newly formed CUC entered the Spanish embassy. The Spanish ambassador, Máximo Cajal, who had seen the Guatemalan killing fields and was disturbed by the murders of several Spanish priests at the hands of the army, was sympathetic to the Indians and willing to discuss their problems. A noon press conference was scheduled at which the protesters would be permitted to air their grievances. A former vice-president of Guatemala, Eduardo Caceres Lehnhoff, arrived to speak with them. The Guatemalan government, however, issued a report that "delinquent subversives" had seized control of the embassy and were holding Cajal hostage. Despite the fact that, according to international law, embassies were considered to be on "foreign soil" and outside Guatemala's jurisdiction, the national police surrounded the embassy compound and launched an attack. Although Cajal shouted from an upstairs window that they were not to enter, the police broke down the door and stormed the embassy. During the attack, the building caught fire and the protesters, trapped inside, were burned to death. Cajal survived by jumping from a window but 39 Guatemalans died in the conflagration, including Menchú's father, Lehrnoff, and the entire embassy staff. One protester, Gregorio Yuja Xona, survived and was taken to a private hospital, supposedly under police protection, to be treated for serious burns. But that same night he was abducted from the hospital and tortured to death; his body was dumped on the grounds of the University of San Carlos the next morning. Spain immediately broke off diplomatic relations with Guatemala for five years.

The Autobiography in Focus

Contents summary. Rigoberta Menchú begins her story several years before her birth, revealing details of her parents' lives and how they came to settle in the mountains of northwestern Guatemala. Her father, Vicente Menchú, and his two younger brothers grew up in the town of Uspantán, also in northwestern Guatemala. Their own father died when they were young children and their mother became a servant to the only rich family in town. Her sons did household jobs for that same family, but eventually their employer said that he could no longer afford to feed them. Menchú's grandmother gave away Vicente, her eldest son, to a ladino family, for whom he worked for nine years, running errands and laboring in the fields. He received no pay and the ladinos did not allow him in their house. When Vicente was 14 he left his situation and went to work in the fincas—plantations—on the south coast. He eventually earned enough money to send for his mother, who had become her employer's mistress. She and her younger sons joined Vicente on the coast and soon all three brothers were working in the fincas. In time they earned enough money to settle in the Altiplano, a mountainous region in northwest Guatemala, and work the land there.

Vicente was the chief breadwinner of the family, but when he reached 18 the army recruited him for a year of military service. When he returned he found his mother ill with a fever, but there was no money to buy medicine or care for her. After her death the brothers separated and found work in different parts of the coast. In the Altiplano Vicente met Menchú's mother, who also came from a poor family, and they got married. They applied for governmental permission to settle in the mountains, then scraped enough money together to pay the fee that would let them clear the land and build a house. After eight years—during which time their children, including Rigoberta, were born—the Menchús' land began to produce. Meanwhile, more people had settled in the mountains and formed a community. At this point the work becomes autobiographical, as Menchú begins to write of her own memories and experiences.

Because their land does not yield much for many years, Menchú's parents have to spend eight months working in the fincas, returning to the mountains only to sow and later harvest their crops of maize and beans. Many children accompany their parents to the fincas. Mothers often strap their infants to their backs as they work, and when the children are old enough they too become coffee and cotton pickers. Working conditions in the fincas are rigorous: a working day begins as early as 3 o'clock in the morning and ends as late as 7 or 8 o'clock at night. The workers themselves must deal with heat, flies, pesticide fumes, stale rations, and the absence of a lavatory: "In the mornings we'd take turns to go off into the scrub and do our business. There are no toilets in the finca. There was only this place up in the hills where everybody went. There were about 400 of us living there" (*Rigoberta Menchú*, p. 35).

At first Menchú's responsibility is merely to watch her younger siblings while her mother works. But when she is eight she starts earning money in the fincas, setting herself to pick 35 pounds of coffee for 20 *centavos* (cents) a day. The overseers of the fincas often find ways to cheat their Indian laborers and avoid paying them their full daily earnings. Nor are the fincas safe for young children. Airplanes spray the crops with pesticide while the Indians labor in the fields; one of Menchú's brothers dies after being exposed to these fumes. Another dies of malnutrition while the family is working in the finca. A fellow laborer helps the Menchús raise money for the tax to bury him in the finca. That night the overseer throws them off the finca for missing a day's work and refuses to pay them for the 15 days they have spent there. Menchú's mother and her surviving children return to the Altiplano for several months.

OCCUPATIONAL HAZARDS

In her autobiography Menchú describes how her brother and later her friend die from pesticide poisoning. The practice of spraying crops while the workers were in the fields was an unfortunate reality in the fincas. DDT, now recognized as one of the most dangerous pesticides, was often used: "In the late seventies, cotton planters out for quick profits regularly sprayed three and four times the presumed 'safe' limit of DDT" (Perera, p. 68). Each year, hundreds of field workers died of liver and lung diseases brought on by exposure to the deadly pesticide.

When Menchú is ten her family has a special ceremony for her, which initiates her into adult life. She assumes more responsibilities, taking over some of her father's duties in the Altiplano community. At the age of 12 she becomes a catechist, teaching Catholic doctrine—which has been brought to her community by the Catholic Action movement—to younger children in the Altiplano and in the fincas. She also takes on the responsibilities of rearing her own livestock and harvesting maize.

Working conditions in the fincas continue to be miserable. As an adolescent Menchú works in the cotton fields. One year a close friend, Maria, dies of poisoning while the planes spray the crops. The workers bury her in the finca and take two days off to mourn her. The overseer, whom Menchú describes as "less criminal than the others," neither fires them nor docks their wages (*Rigoberta Menchú,* p. 89).

Angry and grief-stricken, Menchú searches for a way out of the life she has come to hate. She approaches her father about learning how to read and write but he refuses to support her plans because they would involve her leaving the community: "My father was very suspicious of schools. . . . He gave as an example the fact that many of my cousins had learned to read and write but they hadn't been of any use to the community. They try to move away and feel different when they can read and write" (*Rigoberta Menchú,* p. 89).

During the family's next trip down to the fincas, a landowner offers to hire Menchú as a maid in the capital but her father refuses to allow it. Her elder sister accepts a similar offer but eventually returns, disillusioned by her treatment at the hands of her rich employers. Still intent on gaining an education, 13-year-old Menchú defies her father and decides to try working as a maid.

In Guatemala City Menchú works for a wealthy ladino family, whose members look down on her because she is an Indian. The mistress of the house is abusive towards the servants and withholds their wages at the least excuse. Menchú befriends one of the maids, an Indian who speaks Spanish and has adopted some ladino ways. The other maid tries to persuade Menchú to participate in a resistance campaign against the mistress but Menchú is too afraid to disobey her employers. Just before Christmas the mistress fires the other maid, leaving the burden on Menchú to prepare all the food for the family's holiday feast and to clean the entire house the next day. Menchú works for this family until she has 40 quetzals saved, then gives notice. Just as she announces her departure, one of her brothers arrives with the news that their father is in prison.

For several years Vicente Menchú had been his community's elected representative, thwarting big landowners' attempts to swindle the Indians out of their land or to throw them off their land altogether. He also started traveling to other communities, encouraging Indians to unite against their exploitation by the landowners and establishing contacts with labor unions. When the government became aware of his activities, he was arrested and threatened with a possible sentence of 18 years in the state prison in El Quiché.

Menchú and the rest of her family combine their earnings to hire lawyers and interpreters to help his case, finally obtaining his release 14 months later. Undeterred, Vicente resumes his fight for Indian rights, despite an abduction attempt three months later and a second imprisonment—this time, for 15 days—in 1977. After meeting another political prisoner, Vicente decides to form a peasants' league, an idea enthusiastically accepted by Indian communities, and the CUC is formed. Wanting to protect his family, Vicente Menchú leaves their community and travels to different regions, gathering support for the new organization.

Menchú meanwhile becomes more aware of the exploitation of her race. Not only is her father now a hunted man, but a close female friend of hers is brutally killed for refusing the sexual advances of a wealthy landowner's son. Other female friends are raped by government soldiers during raids on their villages. Menchú's community begins to organize itself against army attacks, using the Bible as inspiration for building weapons of self-defense and traps:

> We tried to relate [Biblical texts] to our Indian culture. We took the example of Moses for the men, and we have the example of Judith. . . . [S]he fought very hard for her people and made many attacks against the king they had then, until she finally had his head. . . . This is how we look for stories and psalms which teach us how to defend ourselves from our enemies. . . . We even got the idea of using our own everyday weapons, as the only solution left to us.
> (*Rigoberta Menchú,* pp. 131-32)

Menchú helps construct the traps and works on learning Spanish from nuns in Guatemala City. She also studies additional Indian dialects to facilitate communication between villages. During one army raid, the Indians succeed in capturing and disarming a soldier. They bring him back to the village and explain their plight to him. The soldier, who is himself Indian, is affected by their words and agrees to take a message about their grievances back to the government. But when he returns to his unit, he is shot as a traitor.

After helping to organize their own village, Menchú and her siblings emulate their father, traveling to different communities to encourage them to unite against their oppressors. One of the villages captures another soldier and tries to inform him of the abuses the Indians have suffered. Like the first soldier, this man is Indian and likewise moved by what he hears. But he is also afraid of his commanding officers, telling the village of the harsh treatment he receives in the Guatemalan army. The Indians release him after he promises not to return to the army and continue killing. The soldier keeps his word and goes into hiding.

In 1979 Menchú's brother, Petrocinio, is captured and tortured by the Guatemalan army. The Menchú family learns that they must come and witness his public punishment or suffer the same treatment. They and the families of other political prisoners travel to the village of Chajul on September 23. The next day the army exhibits their maimed prisoners, then sets fire to them in front of the horrified crowd. The soldiers retreat, holding the Indians off with their guns and shouting political slogans. The Indians try futilely to help the prisoners, who all burn to death. Devastated by their son's death, Menchú's parents increase their efforts in the Indian rights movement, despite the heightened dangers from the Lucas García regime. Meanwhile, Menchú becomes a leader of the CUC and recognizes that poverty and exploitation form common bonds between Indian and ladino workers.

A BRUTAL TRAINING GROUND

Life in the Guatemalan army could be nightmarish, especially for the recruits. The second soldier captured by the Indians describes the abuse to which he was subjected in the barracks: "They gave me a pair of shoes which I found very hard to wear but they beat me into wearing them anyway. They hit me until I got used to them. Then they told me I had to kill the communists from Cuba and Russia . . . and then they gave me a gun" (*Rigoberta Menchú,* p. 148). A young soldier interviewed by Jean-Marie Simon had a similar experience to report about his induction into the army: "[I]t's like going to hell, because you're always hungry; they don't give you much food and if you go out to the store, any soldier can grab you and hit you" (Simon, p. 87). Beatings and torture were commonplace: "What makes recruits scream the most is when they tie your feet behind you with a stick and you have to kneel. They ask you questions like whether you're able to withstand interrogation if you fall into the guerrillas' hands, and whether you would give away the name of your superior. A lot of soldiers cry because the punishment is very harsh, especially those sticks" (Simon, p. 88). By the time basic training ended, many recruits had become as brutal as their commanding officers.

On January 31, 1980, Vicente Menchú participates in an occupation of the Spanish embassy in Guatemala City, which ends in a police attack and a deadly fire. Thirty-nine Guatemalans, including Vicente Menchú, die in the blaze. Four months later—on April 19, 1980—Menchú's mother is abducted by the army and suffers rape, torture, and disfigurement. After the army fails to lure the rest of the family out of hiding, they let Menchú's mother die of her injuries, then leave the body to be eaten by wild animals. The surviving Menchús are grieved by her death but relieved that her suffering is over.

THE INDIANIST

Menchú's life story is interspersed with detailed accounts of Quiché festivals and rituals. She meticulously describes ceremonies of birth, death, and marriage, as well as attempts by the ladinos to repress what they do not understand. While these chapters occasionally disrupt the flow of her narrative—a harrowing account of her brother's death of malnutrition in the fincas, for example, is followed by a lengthy and placid discussion of farming rituals in the Altiplano—they nonetheless present a clear picture of the culture Menchú is committed to preserving. She herself declares, "I'm an Indianist, not just an Indian. I'm an Indianist to my fingertips and I defend everything to do with my ancestors" (*Rigoberta Menchú,* p. 166). Maintaining the rituals and customs of her people is as important to Menchú as securing their freedom from oppressors.

Meanwhile, Menchú continues her work with the CUC, helping to organize a peasants' strike in February 1980. About 80,000 laborers on the sugar and cotton plantations stop work for 15 days, until the government agrees to raise their wages from 75 centavos to 3.20 quetzals per day and improve some of the working conditions. Encouraged, Menchú and her compatriots increase their organization efforts, helping to form the 31st of January Popular Front, in honor of those who died during the Spanish embassy protest. The new union organizes another strike on May 1, 1980—Labor Day in Guatemala—setting up barricades, distributing pamphlets, and closing down factories by phoning in bomb threats. The success of this latest action makes Menchú a hunted woman. After narrowly escaping capture by the army, she flees to Mexico in 1981, returning to Guatemala when the furious search for her subsides. She reunites briefly with her younger sisters, both of whom have joined the guerrillas, and decides to leave the CUC to work for the "Vicente Menchú Revolutionary Christians," combining her Catholic teachings with those of Indian resistance. Renouncing marriage and motherhood, Menchú resolves to dedicate her life to her people's cause.

Breaking down racial barriers. Menchú's autobiography documents not only her political but also her spiritual awakening, especially regarding her attitudes toward Indians and ladinos. Her first visit to "the world of the ladinos" occurs when she is seven and accompanies her father on a visit to Guatemala City: "There were so many interesting things, but also things I didn't want to see, that frightened me. . . . The city for me was a monster, something alien, different" (*Rigoberta Menchú,* p. 32). Although she becomes used to the capital on subsequent visits, she never forgets her first impression of it.

During much of her childhood Menchú accepts the judgments of her elders at face value—the term "ladino" becomes associated in her community with everything bad, cruel, and corrupt. And Indians who adopt ladino ways by discarding their traditional garments in favor of Western dress, speaking Spanish instead of their native dialect, or using machines to grind their maize instead of grinding it by hand—becoming, in Vicente Menchú's words, "ladinized"—are regarded with contempt and disgust: "In the eyes of our community, the fact that anyone should even change the way they dress shows a lack of dignity. Anyone who doesn't dress as our grandfathers, our ancestors, dressed, is on the road to ruin" (*Rigoberta Menchú,* p. 17). Menchú's bitter experiences in the fincas, working for tyrannical overseers and greedy landowners, and her later stint as a maid for a wealthy family only reinforce her hatred of ladinos. Although Menchú sees poor ladino workers in the fincas, they rebuff her attempts to communicate or find common ground, revealing their disdain for Indians and belief in their own racial superiority:

> I said to one one poor *ladino*: "You're a poor *ladino,* aren't you?" and he nearly hit me. He said: "What do you know about it, Indian?" I wondered: "Why is it that when I say poor *ladinos* are like us, I'm spurned?" I didn't know then the same system which tries to isolate us Indians also puts up barriers between Indians and *ladinos.* I knew that all *ladinos* rejected us but I didn't know why. I was more confused. I still thought all *ladinos* were bad.
>
> (*Rigoberta Menchú,* p. 119)

Only after Menchú begins to travel to other communities does she begin to revise her judgments. She attributes much of her new perspective to a ladino who teaches her Spanish and works for the CUC: "[T]he example of my *compañero ladino* made me really understand the barrier that had been put up between the Indian and the ladino, and that because of this same system which tries to divide us, we haven't understood that *ladinos* also live in terrible conditions, the same as we do" (*Rigoberta Menchú,* p. 165). Menchú also learns that the ladinos, as mestizos, are continually in the throes of identity crises: "The *ladinos* try to tear off this shell which imprisons them—being the children of Indians and Spaniards. They want to be something different, not a mixture" (*Rigoberta Menchú,* p. 167). Although the ladinos' belief that they are superior to Indians angers Menchú, she discovers that her own views need adjusting as well: "I identified certain of my attitudes—very rigid ones. Discrimination had made me isolate myself completely from the world of our *compañeros ladinos*" (*Rigoberta Menchú,* p. 168). Increased discussion between the two groups eventually leads to an understanding of their common experiences—poverty, hardship, and exploitation—and their common cause: "To bring about change, we had to unite, Indians and *ladinos*" (*Rigoberta Menchú,* p. 168). At the same time the change in Menchú's behavior also casts doubt on her ability to speak for her people. From this perspective, she experiences not just a gain, but also a loss.

Literary context. Julio Cortázar writes in an epigraph to his novel, *Rayuela* (1963, *Hopscotch*), "Nothing destroys a man more than having to represent his country" (Cortázar in González Echevarría and Pupo-Walker, p. 462). An author's inclination to represent himself or herself as the hero of his own life and to identify himself—perhaps too closely—with the concerns of his country is often denounced as self-serving. This was frequently the case in nineteenth-century autobiographies.

I, Rigoberta Menchú belongs to a slightly different tradition of first-person narratives. Menchú's concerns are more national than literary, more collective than personal. Her account, transcribed from interviews with Elisabeth Burgos-Debray, the book's editor, begins with the stark statement: "This is my testimony. I didn't learn it from a book and I didn't learn it alone. I'd like to stress that it's not only my life, it's also the testimony of my people" (*Rigoberta Menchú,* p. 1). *I, Rigoberta Menchú* does, however, employ some literary devices, including the narrator's withholding of details, her keeping secret what she thinks no one should know. As scholar Doris Sommer points out, Menchú's testimonial, though full of information, consciously holds its readers at "arm's length" (Sommer in Gugelberger, p. 143). The ploy safeguards Menchú's individuality. Finally, Menchú's story fits into the genre of testimonial literature in Latin America, examples of which have been known to manipulate fact, and whose relation to biography has been a matter of debate.

Reviews. Writing for *Choice,* L. B. Metzger praised *I, Rigoberta Menchú* for its depiction of life in the Quiché community: "The excitement of the work lies in its very profound first-person story of childhood, family, and work within the Guatemalan peasant system" (Metzger, p. 734). Stephen Schlesinger, writing for the *Nation,* called the book "a fascinating portrait of the culture of the Quiché tribe" (Schlesinger, p. 538). The political implications of Menchú's story were

THE TRUTH OF THE MATTER?

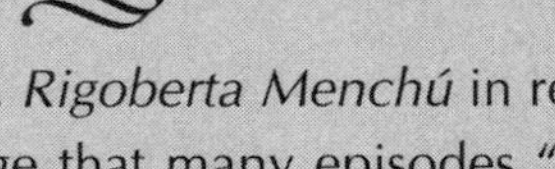

Controversy surrounds *I, Rigoberta Menchú* in respect to its accuracy. Critics charge that many episodes "have either been fabricated or seriously exaggerated," as reported in a recent *New York Times* article (Rohter, p. A1). Points of contention include the following:

- The land dispute depicted as occurring between Indian peasants such as Menchú's father and wealthy European landowners with government ties was actually a family feud between her father and his in-laws.
- The brother whom Menchú professes to have seen burned alive was murdered in different fashion out of her sight.
- In contrast to Menchú's claim that she never had any schooling, she attended two boarding schools on scholarship and attained the equivalent of middle-school education.

The *New York Times* article reports that "local people confirm these discrepancies but point out also that Menchú's father, mother, and two brothers were in fact killed by government forces within a few years of one another (1979-83), even if some of the details have been changed. In a recent book on the matter, David Stoll argues that Menchú drew on the experiences of others in Guatemala, a tactic that suited the revolutionary group 'on whose behalf she was touring Europe when she dictated her life story to Ms. Burgos'" (Rohter, p. A8).

Rigoberta Menchú

similarly lauded. Metzger contended that "it is through the descriptions and discussion of Ladinos and [Menchú's] involvement in political organizing . . . that the reader is provided with the greatest perceptions of the Central American political and social scene" (Metzger, p. 734).

Some critics, however, objected to the structure of *I, Rigoberta Menchú*. Schlesinger found the narrative "marred in places by unnecessary repetitions, lapses in chronology, and a distracting lack of clarity, which could have been avoided by more systematic editing" (Schlesinger, p. 537). Colin Hendry, writing in the *Times Literary Supplement,* lodged a complaint about the content: "It was in Guatemala, after all, with the overthrow of Arbenz in 1954, that the U.S. began its modern wave of intervention against popular movements in Latin America. Menchú herself gives no hint of this history and only a very hazy one of the contemporary political setting" (Hendry, p. 966). This alleged flaw did not, however, stop Hendry from praising *I, Rigoberta Menchú* as "a rare and genuine statement of popular experience 'from below'" that "has the makings of a classic" (Hendry, p. 966).

—Pamela S. Loy

For More Information

Benz, Stephen Connely. *Guatemalan Journey.* Austin: University of Texas Press, 1996.

González Echevarría, Roberto, and Enrique Pupo-Walker. *The Cambridge History of Latin American Literature.* Vol. 2. Cambridge: Cambridge University Press, 1996.

Gugelberger, Georg M., ed. *The Real Thing: Testimonial Discourse and Latin America.* Durham, N.C.: Duke University Press, 1996.

Hawkins, John. *Inverse Images: The Meaning of Culture, Ethnicity and Family in Postcolonial Guatemala.* Albuquerque: University of New Mexico Press, 1984.

Hendry, Colin. Review of *I, Rigoberta Menchú. Times Literary Supplement,* August 31, 1984, 966.

Menchú, Rigoberta. *I, Rigoberta Menchú: An Indian Woman in Guatemala.* Ed. Elisabeth Burgos-Debray. Trans. Ann Wright. London: Verso, 1984.

Metzger, L. B. Review of *I, Rigoberta Menchú. Choice* 22 (January 1985): 734.

Perera, Victor. *Unfinished Conquest: The Guatemalan Tragedy.* Berkeley: University of California Press, 1993.

Rohter, Larry. "Tarnished Laureate." *The New York Times,* 15 December 1998, late edition, A1, A8.

Schlesinger, Stephen. Review of *I, Rigoberta Menchú. The Nation* 240 (May 4, 1985): 537-38.

Simon, Jean-Marie. *Guatemala: Eternal Spring, Eternal Tyranny.* New York: W. W. Norton & Company, 1987.

Wilson, Richard. *Maya Resurgence in Guatemala: Q'eqchi' Experiences.* Norman: University of Oklahoma Press, 1995.

I the Supreme

by
Augusto Roa Bastos

Born June 13, 1917, in the rural Guairá region of Paraguay, Augusto Roa Bastos learned to speak both Spanish and Guaraní at an early age. His family lived near a sugar plantation where his father worked as an administrator. He attended military school, fought in the Chaco War (1932-35) against Bolivia, and worked as a journalist covering the exploitation of laborers in the *yerbales* (maté tea plantations in northern Paraguay). In 1947, though he never belonged to any political party, he was labeled a communist subversive by government authorities and was forced into exile. He moved to Buenos Aires, Argentina, where he wrote all of his major works of fiction, including *Yo el Supremo,* while supporting himself variously as a journalist, teacher, and screenwriter. During the tragedy of Argentina's "Dirty War" (1975-78), unleashed by a neofascist military junta against alleged communist subversives, he was again forced to move and took a teaching position at Toulouse University in France. He returned to Paraguay in 1989 after the fall of the dictator Alfred Stroessner.

THE LITERARY WORK

A novel set in early nineteenth-century Paraguay; published in Spanish in 1974 (as *Yo el Supremo*), in English in 1986.

SYNOPSIS

A dying dictator, José Gaspar Rodríguez de Francia, contemplates the major events of his 26-year rule over Paraguay, and tries to justify his motives and actions.

Events in History at the Time the Novel Takes Place

Colonial Paraguay. Because of its geographic isolation, Paraguay was a politically and economically peripheral Spanish colony. It served as a buffer state protecting the more prosperous colony based in Buenos Aires from hostile Indians and from the rival Portuguese territory of Brazil. Paraguay's colonial economy revolved around the cultivation and export of one crop, *yerba maté,* from which a tea (*maté*) is made. Over-dependence on this single cash crop led to the neglect of staple foods. As a result, Paraguay had to import basic foodstuffs at a high price, which helped to mire common Paraguayans in a state of chronic poverty.

Benefiting the most from this monoculture economy were the two elite groups at the top of Paraguayan society: Spaniards and creoles (Paraguayans of European descent born in Spanish America). Concentrated in the capital, Asunción, Spaniards dominated trade and the higher level positions in the government and military. Although the smallest segment of the society, they wielded the most political and economic power. Below the European-born were the established creole families, who, though wealthy and powerful, lived in a subservient, antagonistic position to the Spaniards.

The majority of the society lived as poor farmers and peasants and were comprised of Guaraní Indians (the main indigenous group in Paraguay), mestizos, blacks, and mulattos. During the seventeenth and eighteenth centuries the Guaraní Indians had thrived under the missionary rule and paternalistic protection of Jesuits throughout southern Paraguay and northern Argentina. The missions had grown in power and wealth until they threatened the power and the commercial enterprise of the colonists. When the Jesuits were expelled from Paraguay in 1767, the missions fell under the control of civil authorities, who exploited the Indians and let the missions diminish in size and power.

DR. FRANCIA'S EARLY YEARS

Born in Paraguay on January 6, 1766, José Gaspar Rodríguez de Francia was the creole son of a career military man and an aristocratic mother. While a student at the University of Córdoba, Francia studied and found inspiration in the work of Enlightenment thinkers such as that of the Frenchman Jean-Jacques Rousseau. (In fact, José Gaspar Rodríguez added "de Francia" to his name as a tribute to his French allegiances.) Enlightenment thinkers celebrated the human ability to reason, promoting the idea that people had control over their fate, which they could improve through education and their ability to reason. The revolutionary philosophies and politics of the Enlightenment fueled the American and French Revolutions, and later contributed to Francia's own absolutist and nationalistic politics.

Francia graduated as a Doctor of Theology and returned to Paraguay to teach Latin. Disputes over his radical religious and political ideas, however, would force him to resign from the seminary of San Carlos several years later. Known as Dr. Francia, he became a lawyer and gained a reputation throughout Asunción for his fearless integrity and protection of Paraguayan peasants. He took only small sums in payment from his poor clients, but demanded large payments from wealthy clients.

Paraguayan independence. In the early 1800s the Spanish Crown was losing its tight grip on its South American colonies. In 1810 the *porteños,* or citizens of the port city of Buenos Aires, rebelled and deposed their royalist governor. An assembly of prominent Paraguayans met to discuss their reaction to this new situation. The porteños controlled the Río de la Plata, which was the only river by which Paraguayans had access to the Atlantic Ocean. Francia shocked the assembly by calling for Paraguayan independence from Spain. Since the Crown did not have the power to govern effectively or to protect the colony from possible porteño domination, he argued, sovereignty reverted to the nation. The Spanish elite rejected Francia's bold suggestion, but did censure the actions of the porteños. In response the Buenos Aires colony blocked Paraguayan trade on the Río de la Plata and sent spies to foment revolt in Asunción.

A porteño army under the command of General Manuel Belgrano moved north to demand Paraguayan submission and met a Paraguayan army in battle. Initially the tide favored the Argentines, and the Spanish officers commanding the Paraguayans fled in panic; in Asunción most Spaniards, including the complacent Governor Bernardo de Velasco, prepared to flee the city. However, in a reversal of fortune, the creole officers rallied the Paraguayan forces to defeat the porteños. From this victory the creole officers realized that the dominance of the Spaniards in Paraguay had come to an end; it was the turn of the creoles to rule. After a second defeat of the porteños, the creoles accepted Belgrano as a kindred spirit against the waning Spanish domination and let him and his army retreat peacefully to Buenos Aires.

The creole officers staged a coup against Governor Velasco on May 14, 1811. In June a five-man junta took his place, with Francia as its most forceful and prominent member. Over the course of the next two years Francia would resign twice from his post to protest the junta's decisions or relations with the army. He used the time to build his popularity with common Paraguayans. At gatherings Francia told the crowds that the revolution had betrayed the people by simply replacing the Spanish elite with a creole elite. A true revolution was necessary.

By November 1812 Francia's leadership abilities were in demand. Continued agitation from the porteños and from Portuguese raiders had combined with internal dissension among the creoles to thrust the government into a crisis. The junta asked him to return to his post, this time with personal control of half the army.

In September 1813 the first popular congress or assembly in Paraguay convened. This congress and the two that followed in 1814 and 1816 represented proportionally all segments of society; in other words, the peasant farmers had a voice that equaled their numerical superiority over the elite, an unheard of example of political egalitarianism in nineteenth-century Latin America. On October 21, 1813, at Francia's instigation, the congress declared Paraguay the first independent republic of South America. Francia had convinced the delegates that the best way to prevent Paraguay from falling into the untrustworthy hands of the porteños was to form a strong independent nation.

Initially the government was ruled by the joint consulship of Francia and Fulgencio Yegros. At the next year's popular congress Francia appealed to his rural supporters to end the shared consulship and declare him dictator. He wanted to streamline the government and said that one absolute ruler would prove more efficient and effective than two, especially when dealing with the civil war that was breaking out in the Río de la Plata region. Over 90 percent of the rural delegates voted for Francia. This victory granted him, for a period of five years, the title and authority of Supreme Dictator of the Republic, from which historians have derived the name "El Supremo" or The Supreme One, though none of Francia's contemporaries referred to him in this way. Opposition to his rule centered in Asunción among the creole and Spanish elite who would suffer the negative effects of the unregulated authority given Francia. In 1816, at the third and last popular congress held before Francia's death, he gained the dictatorship for life.

Nowadays the title "dictator" has only a pejorative association, but in the early nineteenth century a dictator was often seen as a positive leader. Most Latin American republics in the nineteenth century were democracies in name only, with voting restricted to men who held property and/or could read. As a result, typically less than 5 percent of the population voted and had their concerns represented in the government. In contrast the popular congresses that elected Francia as dictator had represented proportionally the entire nation. Francia believed that the congresses had delineated the concerns of the people, and that afterwards it was the dictator's task to enact their will. His reign was to be a popular dictatorship that he would term "enlightened absolutism." His ideas were based on Rousseau's idea of the social contract, in which people give their sovereignty to a government in exchange for protection of their natural rights. In a letter to one of his military commanders about the continual rebellions among the porteños of Buenos Aires, Francia explained:

> These convulsions are the consequence of a nation which still vacillates in its true aims and destiny because it still is not unified, because it does not have a truly popular form. For this very reason, at the time of the institution of the Republic here, I established the great Congresses at periodic intervals to make certain that the nation would join together in the same sentiments and so that we would all advance under a solidly based system.
>
> (Francia in White, p. 76)

El Supremo's reign. Francia distrusted the creole and Spanish elite as a threat to the nation he was building, and he made it a main objective of his reign to crush their power. He issued a law in 1814 that forbade men of European descent from marrying any woman who was not Indian, black, or mulatto. In addition people of European descent could not serve as godparents, an important social bond. This law helped over time to create a society dominated by mestizos. Francia countered the economic power of the creoles by imposing heavy taxes and fines. He nationalized huge ranches and gave the land as homesteads to poor Paraguayans. He attacked one of the most powerful institutions associated with the creoles and Spaniards: the Catholic Church. Francia appointed his own bishops without approval of the Pope, and in 1824 he nationalized Church lands and took fiscal control of Catholic wealth, even while Pope Leo XII ordered the American Church to aid Spain's king in reestablishing his rule over all the former colonies.

The creole elite privately began to voice its dissent to Francia's absolute power early on in his reign and gathered around the only political alternative, the career military man Fulgencio Yegros. Francia, however, during the first stages of his rule, built a state prison system with cells beneath the two largest Asunción military barracks to be used in response to any opposition he might face. Relationships between Francia and the diminishing elite remained tense for the next six years, until they came to a head in February 1820. Francia was informed of an assassination plot against him (by none other than one of its conspirators, Juan Bogarín) that would have resulted in Yegros assuming civil authority. He immediately had all the suspected conspirators arrested, and within a week imprisoned more than 100 members from the elite families. By the end of June 1821, 70 of them had been executed. Francia's reign of terror had begun, and this systematic arrest and murder of his suspected opponents lasted until 1823. He imprisoned even his own mother for conspiracy against him. When the terror finally subsided, Francia had exterminated much of the Spanish and creole elite.

A group of Guaraní women. The Guaraní are the main indigenous group of Paraguay.

He was left, though, with lingering paranoia. In *I the Supreme* this paranoia is conveyed in one of the opening passages, in which Francia suspects his imprisoned enemies of penning an impertinent note even though, as his aide remarks, "They've been confined to utter darkness for years now" (Roa Bastos, *I the Supreme,* p. 5).

Any opponents of Francia's regime—by word, gesture, or action—faced imprisonment, torture, and murder. Foreigners, always regarded as possible spies, had to gain the government's permission to enter, remain in, or leave the country. As English essayist Thomas Carlyle wrote, "Paraguay had grown to be, like some mousetraps and other contrivances of art and nature, easy to enter, impossible to get out of" (Carlyle, p. 551). Already wary of intruders, both foreign and domestic, Francia established unquestionable authority and grew progressively insular in his political and social policies.

Unlike the social elite, however, the common people of Paraguay benefited from this absolute reign. Francia inaugurated Paraguay's first public education system, created a public works program, maintained fiscal stability, reduced taxes to a minimum, and diversified the economy to include cattle ranching and more agriculture. The nation prospered during his relatively stable and tranquil reign, booming in population as refugees from troubled neighboring states fled to Paraguay's comparative peace. In 1798 there were only about 100,000 people in Paraguay, but this number increased almost fourfold, to 375,000, by the late 1830s.

Instead of reserving government positions for members of the elite families—the standard colonial practice—Francia appointed commoners. As a result there was one serious problem: many of the appointees lacked the education necessary to fulfill their duties. The dictator himself attempted to take up the slack, and for most of his reign obsessively managed the government and nation. For example, he frequently audited the ledgers of the state's tax collectors.

Francia devoted himself to his work and lived almost as a hermit in his palace, issuing forth his orders and decrees to the far corners of the land. Unlike most dictators he did not accumulate personal wealth, but lived simply on a small salary. Nor did he ever accept gifts, in contrast to colonial governors who expected lavish presents from favor seekers. Francia's honesty was so well known that it became proverbial.

While his devotion to the nation raised the standard of living and won him great respect in many quarters—the Guaraní Indians referred to him as *Karaí-Guasú* (Great Lord)—he fostered the belief that Paraguayans were politically child-like and incompetent. Only the indispensable dictator was capable of making decisions, no matter how minute, for the country. He never forgave his enemies, and their rage against him outlasted his death and was passed down to their descendants. One historian exclaimed: "To this day it is impossible to hold a rational conversation about Francia with many of the descendants of Paraguay's former upper class" (White, p. 12).

On September 20, 1840, El Supremo became *El Difunto* (The Dead One). Several months after his death, some enemies from among the upper class, not satisfied that he had died, stole his body from the cathedral in Asunción, and it has not been seen since. With Francia gone, his contemporary José Artigas reminded those left behind that the shadow of the man who had proclaimed himself the Perennial Dictator "will long continue to float over Paraguay" (Williams, p. 97).

Foreign relations. Between 1810 and 1880 fighting and civil wars were rife between rival American groups throughout the former Spanish viceroyalty of Río de la Plata, a territory that included modern Argentina, Uruguay, Paraguay, and parts of Bolivia. Brazil also entered into conflicts over control of the Río de la Plata, in which the Uruguay, Paraná, and Paraguay rivers converge and then flow into the Atlantic Ocean. The group that controlled the Río de la Plata had a stranglehold on these rivers and therefore on the interiors of Argentina, Brazil, and Paraguay, since these waterways were the interior states' only connection to the rest of the world. The end of the Cisplatine War (1825-28), fought between Brazil and Argentina, would finish Brazil's ambitions by creating the buffer state of Uruguay in 1828.

The only country that escaped the bloody turbulence of the era was Paraguay; Francia insisted on a strict neutrality in dealing with his neighboring countries. But at the same time, Paraguayan trade in yerba maté depended upon free passage on the rivers, which was often suppressed by hostilities and political pressures. Early in his reign Francia gave preferential treatment to two adventurous Scottish merchant brothers: John Parish Robertson and William Parish Robertson, with the hope that they would convince the British government to guarantee freedom of transport on the Río de la Plata. But in 1815 he saw that the brothers represented interests in the porteño government and would secure no British pledge. He expelled them in retaliation.

Also of concern were the Brazilian raiding parties that threatened the northern frontier of Paraguay. In 1825 the Brazilian envoy Antonio Manoel Correia da Câmara arrived in Asunción to seek Francia's pledge of neutrality in the upcoming Cisplantine War with Argentina. Francia pressed the envoy for an end to Brazilian raids, but despite the envoy's assurances to the contrary, the raids continued. When Correia da Câmara returned to Paraguay in 1827, an outraged Francia did not allow him to enter the nation beyond the border town of Itapúa. Believing that he could not pursue his diplomatic mission in the capital, Correia da Câmara left Paraguay out of frustration in 1829.

Francia maintained a strong defense force and a network of spies on the border out of his fear that Argentina and Brazil would unite to divvy up his small nation. Defense centered on the southern Paraguayan province of Misiones, a beautiful land on the frontier with Argentina and Brazil. Its bountiful crops of yerba maté and tobacco made it an attractive prize for an invading force. Skirmishes with the Argentine province of Corrientes went on for several years in the 1830s. Francia's intent to keep Paraguay isolated and

"POLITICAL CATECHISM"

In the "Political Catechism," which Francia prepared for use in primary schools, the dictator outlined the principles that guided his transformation of Paraguayan society:

Question: What is your country's government?
Answer: The reformed fatherland.

Question: What do you mean by reformed fatherland?
Answer: Its regulation by known and just principles founded in nature, in man's necessities, and the conditions of society.

Question: Who is it that declaims against this system?
Answer: The old Spanish government officials that proposed that we surrender to Bonaparte, and those ambitious for authority.

Question: How can one prove that our system is good?
Answer: By positive deeds.

Question: What are those positive deeds?
Answer: The abolition of slavery without affecting the owners, and to esteem public works as the common burden, with the total suppression of taxes.

(Francia in White, p. 101)

aloof from external conflicts was such that a porteño newspaper at the end of hostilities in 1834 wrote: "Paraguay did not want peace, nor war, with anyone" (White, p. 151).

The Novel in Focus

Plot summary. The plot of *I the Supreme* is deceptively simple: the dying dictator Francia ponders his reign and justifies his policies and opinions against the words of his detractors. The complication is that words and writings are themselves under attack in this ambitious literary experiment. Francia's thoughts and dictations do not follow a linear progression, but travel back and forward in time and place—even into the future. They sometimes contradict, sometimes confirm one another, appearing in a variety of documents written (supposedly) by different hands. In counterpoint to Francia's words are footnotes that contain historical and allegedly historical documents written by his contemporaries and later commentators. These and other explanatory notes—indeed all the manifold texts that comprise the novel—have been brought together by the "Compiler," who claims that the book is a legitimate historical documentary, not a novel.

The following summary details what there is of a storyline, then continues with other elements (descriptions of the characters and documents) that are as key to this novel as its storyline.

Storyline. The main storyline is a word-by-word transcription of Francia's verbal ruminations about himself and his presidency. The setting for this "action" is his palace during the last months of his reign and life. The text varies in tone as Francia's demeanor shifts; it is variously eloquent, impassioned, paranoid, self-aggrandizing, and self-loathing. Francia covers his entire reign along with other events from the past and future. He sometimes telescopes events that occurred at different times into the same moment.

The novel opens with the contents of a note found tacked to the door of the cathedral in Asunción. Signed in the dictator's name, it orders that, upon the death of Francia, his corpse be decapitated, his head be raised on a pike for three days in the main plaza, his military and civil servants be executed, and after the three days his remains be cremated and the ashes thrown into the river. Apparently just handed the note, Francia accuses his enemies of having written it. This event triggers the next 400 pages in which Francia obsessively dictates thoughts on his reign and other topics to his personal secretary.

The point he emphasizes most often is that his decisions were prudent and necessary for the time and place, despite the conflict between his draconian, often brutal, politics and his Enlightenment ideals. This self-justification is aimed against the polemics of his enemies and the denunciations and characterizations of historians. However, a certain amount of self-criticism does appear as Francia doubts his decisions and questions his illusions. As the novel reaches its end, the self-doubts increase exponentially, along with the fragmentation of the texts themselves into smaller and choppier bits and pieces.

Francia's voice finally comes to a halt in the middle of a sentence: "So then, Supreme Deceased, what if we leave you as you are, condemned to perpetual hunger to gobble down an egg, because you didn't know . . ." (*I the Supreme,* p. 424). The implication is that Francia has died even while desperately trying to get everything written down. After this the Compiler has added an appendix full of documents related to a 1961 inquiry into the location of the dictator's corpse. The novel ends with the "Final Compiler's Note," the first lines of which claim to explain the composition of the book:

> The compilation has been culled—it would be more honest to say coaxed—from some twenty thousand dossiers, published and unpublished; from an equal number of other volumes, pamphlets, periodicals, correspondences and all manner of testimony—gleaned, garnered, resurrected, inspected—in public and private libraries and archives. To this must be added the versions collected from the sources of oral tradition, and some fifteen thousand hours of interviews, recorded on tape, filled with inexactitudes and confusions.
>
> (*I the Supreme,* p. 435)

The cast of characters. *José Gaspar Rodríguez de Francia:* the dying Supreme Dictator of Paraguay. The character of Francia enjoys two different temporal perspectives. Primarily he speaks of events from the vantage point of his last year of life in 1840, but occasionally he has knowledge of books that have not yet been written, of events that have not yet occurred—such as the Chaco War between Bolivia and Paraguay in the 1930s—and of devices not yet invented—such as an electric instrument of torture. Apparently in these passages Francia is speaking from the grave, and has the perspective of the author Roa Bastos from the 1970s. This voice beyond the grave amplifies the idea that Francia is literally the Perpetual Dictator, whose reign and ideas still loom over Paraguay in the last quarter of the twentieth century.

Policarpo Patiño: Francia's personal secretary who takes his dictation throughout the novel. Like a machine, he appears to achieve the impossible task of transcribing every word as it is spoken, including his own exchanges with the dictator. Patiño is an uneducated, fearful, and obsequious man, more concerned for his own comforts than his master's great philosophies. Francia eventually sentences him to death.

Juan Parish Robertson: an opportunistic Scottish adventurer who takes advantage of Francia, until the dictator realizes the true nature of the man. Robertson conducts an affair with Francia's octogenarian neighbor, Juana Esquivel, purely out of greed for her lavish gifts. After Robertson and his brother are expelled from Paraguay, they write a scathing account of Francia, depicting his dictatorship as a cruel tyranny.

Pilar the Black: Francia's trusted personal servant who steals from the palace to support his mistress. He goes mad and wears the dictator's clothes, which make the two men indistinguishable. He attacks his employer who is then forced to have him executed, but who suffers thereafter from guilt for Pilar's death.

General Manuel Belgrano: porteño general who led a small army against Paraguay in 1810-11, but was defeated. He later led a diplomatic mission to Asunción and became a friend of Francia, who sees him as an honorable man.

Antonio Manoel Correia da Câmara: underhanded Brazilian envoy who breaks his word to end raids on Paraguay's northern frontier.

Bernardo Velazco: Royalist governor of Paraguay who attacks Francia's policies and personality in a series of letters.

Sultán: Francia's dog and alter ego. He appears as an imaginary voice within Francia's head that mocks the dying dictator for his failures and the loss of his idealism.

The Compiler: neither a traditional character nor a conventional narrator, the Compiler claims to have found, arranged, and annotated the documents that form the novel. From a perspective of the second half of the twentieth century, he claims that the book is an authentic scholarly work of history, containing documents from and about Francia's dictatorship. He makes his presence known through recurrent "Compiler's Notes," or footnotes in the novel, and through parenthetical notes indicating lost pages, burnt text, and marginalia in the old documents; for example, "(*edge of the folio burned*)" (*I the Supreme,* p. 10).

The documents. The Compiler has conjoined several different types of documents to form the pseudo-documentary *Yo el Supremo.* Each has its own particular narrative characteristics.

The main text is the transcription of Francia's verbose dictation to his secretary Patiño. These sections contain Francia's monologue as well as dialogue between him and Patiño about the ongoing dictation. Francia regularly contradicts himself, corrects himself, and lambastes Patiño's stupidity. Although the text appears to catch every word spoken, including those about the dictation itself, without a recording device such a feat is impossible. This impossibility mocks the supposed objectivity of real historical documents and histories.

The entire transcription is a pun with a serious message: the dictator is dictating, an irony not lost upon Francia himself. His aim in dictation is to order events and create a history that affirms his reign in contradistinction to the negative treatment he has received in the words of others. But his own words betray his version of order; out of ignorance or distraction Patiño continually makes errors in his transcription and transposes letters to form inadvertent puns and vulgarities. In his obsession to mull over every aspect of his reign, Francia cannot even prevent factual errors in his own version or refrain from exposing his self-doubts and weaknesses.

Scattered through the novel are selections from Francia's private notebooks written in his hand, which continue the same themes as the main dictation. These selections are joined by a variety of other texts, including what appear to be transcriptions straight from Francia's stream of consciousness, although the Compiler indicates that they were scribbled by the dictator himself. These sections provide the closest view of his inner psyche. Toward the end of the novel Sultán, the dictator's dog, appears in Francia's head as something like an alter ego that accuses and mocks him for his obsession with creating texts.

The novel also features the Perpetual Circular, pronouncements by the dictator on his reign. For example, at the start of one such pronouncement he writes of his detractors, "The pasquinaders consider it beneath my dignity to watch tirelessly as I do over the dignity of the republic in order to safeguard it against those eager to wreak its downfall. Foreign states. Rapacious governments, insatiable grabbers of what belongs to others. Their perfidy and bad faith have long been well known to me" (*I the Supreme,*

p. 76). The idea that such circulars are perpetual signifies both the status of his dictatorship for life and the validity these pronouncements continue to have for Paraguay and Latin America in the twentieth century.

The Compiler has added other documents in footnotes and an appendix, all of which refer to, clarify, or contradict some portion of Francia's testimony. These texts include actual and fictitious documents that are presented as legitimate. Like the opening letter calling for his decapitation, they are illusions that play into the story of Francia. The mix of fact and fiction continues the novel's parody of standard histories.

Enlightened ruler or despotic megalomaniac? Because Francia made enemies of the creole upper class—the group that has written the histories of Paraguay—he has consistently been portrayed as an archetypal despot. Instead of a liberator, he is known as a tyrant who isolated Paraguay to submit its people to his will.

The earliest accounts about Francia for foreign audiences were written by men with whom he had had conflicts. The Robertson brothers, for example, wrote a scathing three-volume portrait, with one volume entitled *Francia's Reign of Terror*. Exotic and often fantastic accounts of the dictator and the far-flung jungles of Paraguay appeared as occasional novelties in the nineteenth-century European press. The creole elite, in addition to allegedly desecrating his corpse, carried out an anti-Francia propaganda campaign that attacked his character in print. Even the dictator's University of Córdoba records have been amended with a pen as follows:

> Afterwards he was President of the Republic of Paraguay, and a very atrocious tyrant who has bloodied the history of that country with a world wide scandal. He was a monster who tore out the entrails of his country.
>
> (A detractor in White, p. 12)

Critical portrayals and personal attacks like these became the source material for later histories of his regime, written by historians who did not take into account the polemical nature of their sources. *I the Supreme* reflects such contemporary works and later histories in the Compiler's footnotes and in Francia's obsessive self-justifications against their words.

Not all opinions about Francia have been negative. Auguste Comte ranked Francia with other great American revolutionaries, such as Simón Bolívar and Benjamin Franklin. In the 1840s the English essayist Thomas Carlyle wrote an essay praising Francia's strong rule of law during a period of social upheaval. Attempts have also been made by some historians to vindicate his reputation. In a move that parallels Roa Bastos's compilation of documents in *I the Supreme,* José Antonio Vázquez put together a compendium of primary sources for the regime with an interlocking narrative. Such efforts, however, have shown little effect.

Roa Bastos in *I the Supreme* gives the fictional Francia, at least, a chance to speak out against the ill treatment to which his memory has been subjected. Throughout the novel Francia differentiates between *He*—the odious tyrant he has been portrayed as—and *I*—the man he sees himself as being. But his verbose self-justifications spiral away from him as much as they clear his name, due to his own self-doubts and to the slippery nature of language, which proves unable to secure the stability and order that he craves. The question of whether his rule was a travesty or triumph remains unanswered, but the novel interrogates history and language in a way that casts into doubt existing evaluations.

THE DICTATOR RESPONDS

Johann Rudolph Rengger, a Swiss doctor whom Francia had refused permission to leave Paraguay for four years, attacked the dictator in *The Reign of Doctor Joseph Gaspar Roderick de Francia.* Francia responded in an article that appeared in a Buenos Aires newspaper on August 21, 1830:

> This is the man who . . . has published a pretended historical essay, of which the object evidently is to undermine the reputation of the Dictator; but the raving and contemptible volume ought rather to have been styled an Essay of Lies. It may, without exaggeration, be affirmed that, as regards Paraguay and its government, it contains not a word of truth.
>
> (Francia, p. 375)

Events in History at the Time the Novel Was Written

Stroessner: a latter-day Francia? After several years of political instability and mass emigration following Paraguay's 1947 civil war, in 1954 General Alfred Stroessner took over as head of state, ruling the country with a totalitarian hand until 1989. A tradition of authoritarian rule in Paraguay had grown since the nineteenth century, beginning with Francia and continuing with dictators Carlos Antonio López (1840-62) and his son Francisco Solano López (1862-70).

Similar to Francia 140 years earlier, Stroessner took charge of a nation that suffered from geographic isolation, economic deprivation, and a political identity crisis caused by years of political in-fighting and civil war. Also like Francia, Stroessner ruled over a Paraguayan population that more readily gave its political support to individual personalities than it did to institutions or ideas. But unlike Francia, Stroessner declared that he was not a dictator, despite his absolute powers and tailoring of laws to harass his opposition, which earned him a horrendous record of human rights violations.

Like Francia's appeals to common Paraguayans, one of Stroessner's first moves was to gain the support of the masses, which he did by converting the *Colorado* party (the major political party of the day) into a popular nation-wide movement. He used this popular support to promote a new political doctrine called *stronismo,* which promised renewed strength and stability in government and gave him unconditional power. For Paraguayans who had suffered under the instability of previous administrations, Stroessner was seen as a comforting paternalistic figure who would guide the nation toward a brighter future. Thanks in part to a media blitz promoted by Stroessner himself, he became a symbol of national solidarity and growth, seen cutting ribbons at ceremonies, distributing graduation diplomas, inaugurating buildings, and meeting with prominent international figures. Stronismo, then, was designed to give Paraguayans a sense of political unity and tranquillity, but its true nature was far more brutal.

Like most authoritarian leaders Stroessner ensured the loyalty of his people through intimidation and a heavy emphasis on law and order. A strong police presence and a record of torture and executions cemented the foundations of stronismo. Given the degree of political violence recently witnessed by the politically unsophisticated Paraguayans, Stroessner's strong-arm tactics were appreciated as a laudable commitment to law and order. Stroessner worked to convince the underprivileged that democratic developments were actually an affront to the established order of stronismo. In other words, anyone who desired a more competitive and responsive political system was acting against the best interests of the nation. In the end, Stroessner's totalitarian society brought more political apathy than genuine support for the regime.

Alfredo Stroessner

Unlike Francia, who sought an end to the economic advantages enjoyed by the upper class at the expense of the poor, Stroessner privileged his country's elite. In fact, under stronismo the gap between rich and poor widened at an accelerated pace. In the 1970s massive construction projects and public works, such as the joint Paraguayan-Brazilian hydro-electric dam at Itaipú, brought a great deal of foreign credit into the country. The wealth lined the pockets of the well-to-do and well connected, and allowed the government to convince Paraguayans of its usefulness and distract them from its inadequacies.

Just the same, Stroessner's repressive and biased policies caused thousands to flee the nation in search of greater economic and political opportunities. The 1980s brought the collapse of Paraguay's credit-flush economy, and popular support for the dictator plummeted as the economy failed. In 1989 a military coup ousted Stroessner from office. Some political exiles, such as Roa Bastos, were able to return to Paraguay for the first time in years.

Literary context. Given the region's political history, it is no surprise that Latin American literature abounds with novels about dictators; Ramón del Balba-Inclán's *The Tyrant* and Miguel Angel Asturias's *The President* (1946) are among the earliest examples. (Asturias's ***Men of Maize*** is covered in *Latin American Literature and Its Times.*) Around 1962 Mario Vargas Llosa (see ***The Storyteller***) and Carlos Fuentes (see ***The Death of Artemio Cruz***) approached a number of Latin American writers—including Gabriel García Márquez (see ***One Hundred Years of Solitude***), Julio Cortázar (see ***Blow-Up and Other Stories***), and Roa Bastos—with the intent of putting together a collection of short stories about dictators. That particular project failed, but each writer agreed to write a novel on the subject. Vargas Llosa produced *Conversation in the Cathedral,* which evokes the regime of Peru's General Manuel A. Odría. García Márquez wrote *The Autumn of the Patriarch,* about a fictional dictator, in 1975. A year earlier, no less than three such works appeared: Alejo Carpentier's *The Recourse of the Method,* Ernesto Sabato's *Abbadón the Exterminator,* and Roa Bastos's *I the Supreme.* (Carpentier's ***The Kingdom of This World*** is covered in *Latin American Literature and Its Times.*) Carpentier did not base his work on an actual dictator but blended facets of many dictators into one, while Sabato chose to depict a dictatorship—the waning days of Argentina's series of military rulers from 1966 to 1973—rather than a lone despot. Added to these are José Lezama Lima's *Paradiso* and Guillermo Cabrera Infante's ***Three Trapped Tigers,*** both novels about dictatorships in Cuba. The majority of these works are set in the twentieth century, which makes Roa Bastos's work stand out in his choice of a nineteenth-century dictator.

Reviews. Soon after its publication, *I the Supreme* received praise as an innovative work. Jean Franco commented that "Roa Bastos's brilliant idea is to let the supreme dictator talk back" while at the same time allowing him to remain at the mercy of what others have written about him (Franco, p. 925). By the time the novel was translated into English, it had gained major international acclaim. Carlos Fuentes described the novel as "an impressive portrait, not only of El Supremo, but of a colonial society in the throes of learning how to swim, or how best to drown, in the seas of national independence" (Fuentes, p. 1). Michiko Kakutani, with a caveat about the often rhetorical and cumbersome feel of the work, exclaimed, "the novel remains a prodigious meditation not only on history and power, but also on the nature of language itself" (Kakutani, p. 25).

—Emerson Spencer Olin and John Roleke

For More Information

Carlyle, Thomas. *Critical and Miscellaneous Essays.* Boston: Phillips, Sampson and Company, 1858.

Foster, David William. *Augusto Roa Bastos.* Boston: Twayne Publishers, 1978.

Francia, José Gaspar Rodríguez de. "Notes Made in Paraguay by El Dictador Francia on the Volume of John Rengger." In *Francia's Reign of Terror.* London: John Murray, Albemarle Street, 1839.

Franco, Jean. "Paranoia in Paraguay." *Times Literary Supplement,* August 15, 1975, 925.

Fuentes, Carlos. Review of *I the Supreme. The New York Times Book Review,* April 6, 1986, 1.

Kakutani, Michiko. Review of *I the Supreme. The New York Times,* April 2, 1986, 25.

Miranda, Carlos R. *The Stroessner Era: Authoritarian Rule in Paraguay.* Boulder, Colo.: Westview Press, 1990.

Roa Bastos, Augusto. *I the Supreme.* Trans. Helen Lane. New York: Alfred A. Knopf, 1986.

White, Richard Alan. *Paraguay's Autonomous Revolution, 1810-1840.* Albuquerque: University of New Mexico Press, 1978.

Williams, John Hoyt. *The Rise and Fall of the Paraguayan Republic, 1800-1870.* Austin: Institute of Latin American Studies, University of Texas at Austin, 1979.

The Kingdom of This World

by
Alejo Carpentier

Alejo Carpentier was born in Havana, Cuba, in 1904, two years after his mother, a Russian pianist and language teacher, and his father, an architect from France, immigrated to Cuba. He received his secondary education in France, and then returned to Cuba to study architecture in Havana. When his father abandoned the family, Carpentier left architecture school and worked as a journalist to support them. Through his work, he traveled widely and became increasingly engaged in anti-imperialist and anti-fascist struggles in the Caribbean and in Europe. He lived for many years in France, Cuba, and Venezuela, returning to Cuba after the 1959 revolution. He published many essays, short stories, poems, and articles, but is perhaps best known for his novels *Music in Cuba* (1946) and *The Kingdom of this World* (1949). *The Kingdom of This World* is remarkable for its introduction of the "marvelous real" into the novel's literary language and content, as well as for its treatment of the politics, culture, and economics of slavery.

THE LITERARY WORK

A novel set in Haiti and Cuba from the 1750s to the early 1820s; published in Spanish (as *El reino de este mundo*) in 1949, in English in 1957.

SYNOPSIS

Told largely from the perspective of Ti Noël, a creole slave on a sugar plantation in the north of Haiti, the novel tracks the massive upheaval caused by the antislavery insurrections, the end of slavery and colonial rule in Haiti, and the nation's early years as an independent republic.

Events in History at the Time the Novel Takes Place

The significance of the Haitian Revolution for Carpentier and for many others in the Caribbean and Latin America cannot be overestimated. While the eighteenth century saw many remarkable revolutionary struggles, this one was distinct in that it not only sought independence from a colonial power, but also freedom from slavery for 80 percent of its population. This achievement meant that, as Franklin Knight argues, the new republic had to destroy and rebuild its entire socioeconomic base, a "high price" for independence (Knight, p. 196).

Colonization of the Caribbean (1492-1780). The island of Hispaniola was the site of the original New World settlement established by Columbus for the Spanish Crown in 1492. In 1509-10, the first sugar mills were built on the island, and by 1615 the first exports of Caribbean sugar reached Spain. In 1595, when the indigenous Carib and Arawak peoples were nearly decimated by disease, exhaustion from their slave labor in the mills, and malnutrition, Spain began to grant *asientos* (agreements) to enslave and import Africans to the Caribbean. By 1640 France had settled the islands of Martinique and Guadeloupe, and most of the Caribbean had fallen under the control of the British, Dutch, French, or Spanish. The latter part of the sevnteenth century saw many conflicts and wars between the European powers. By 1670 Spain had ceded Jamaica and the Cayman Islands to England, and in 1697 it ceded western Hispaniola to France in the Treaty of Ryswick. At this time, the western section of the island was called Saint-Domingue, and the eastern, Santo Domingo. More territorial wars erupted between the European countries from 1739 to 1763, which ended in France's losing control of some areas but managing to retain its hold on Saint-Domingue (later called Haiti).

Saint-Domingue was a very valuable possession. By 1780, several decades after the novel opens, it had become the wealthiest colony in the Caribbean. Joan Dayan writes that Saint-Domingue was "known for its splendor, profligacy and greed" (Dayan, p. 144). During the latter part of the eighteenth century, the French Caribbean surpassed all other exporters of sugar, including the British, exporting 141,089,831 pounds in 1789 alone (Knight, p. 114). The colony produced 40 percent of France's foreign trade, and provided crucial customs revenue. It was also a strategic naval base.

Regional divisions and race relations. Saint-Domingue was governed in three administrative "units" that were divided geographically, politically, and socially: northern, western, and southern. The northern was the most economically powerful region, with the greatest number of large plantations (8,000) and the biggest slave population; it extended across the Plaine du Nord, was separated from the other regions by a mountain chain, and had Cap Français ("Le Cap") as its capital. The western administrative unit was the stronghold of the *petits blancs* or "small whites," and extended across the Artibonite Valley to the town of St. Marc and south to Port-au-Prince. The southern region was the least populous and most rugged of the three regions. It was home to many free persons of color and to a sizable mixed-race population.

By 1791 the total population of the colony was 520,000, of which 452,000 (86 percent of the total) were slaves (the majority of whom were black, with a small minority of mulattos), 28,000 were non-white free persons, and 40,000 were white (Knight, p. 367). The colony of Saint-Domingue was administered by a bureaucracy and a military whose heads answered directly to the French king. There were Provincial Assemblies, but they had to answer to the legislative bodies in France, to which the colonies sent their own deputies.

The late seventeenth century marked the systematization of slavery under the *Code Noir,* or Black Code. Passed by the French King Louis XIV in 1685, it established the legal conditions for the treatment of slaves, who were defined under the Code (and in other legal documents concerning slavery) as property. The Code covered

POLITICAL DESIGNATIONS

Free persons of color (*affranchis*): All persons of black heritage born free or emancipated. They constituted a large and vocal minority in Saint-Domingue, with diverse and changeable political affiliations.

Mulattoes: All those born to a white parent and a non-white parent. The colonial authorities in Saint-Domingue had 128 different designations for the racial composition of those deemed non-white.

Maroons: Those who were never enslaved or who escaped slavery and survived in the mountainous or deserted areas of the island. In 1751 they numbered around 3,000.

***Grands Blancs* (Big Whites):** Owners of large plantations and high functionaries in Saint-Domingue; many were from the French nobility, and a large number of them did not live in Saint-Domingue. They were most frequently pro-monarchy, pro-slavery, and pro-political rights for the free persons of color.

***Petits Blancs* (Small Whites):** The plantation overseers, merchants, and lower functionaries. Mostly middle- to lower-class French or Creole (of French heritage, but born in Latin America), the petit blancs often competed with mulattoes and other free persons for jobs and resources. They were most frequently pro-republican, pro-slavery, and opposed to equality for the free persons of color.

Governor: The head of the bureaucratic administration in Saint-Domingue; answered to the King and oversaw the Assemblies and the Military. He was based in the capital of the Northern Region, Cap Français.

Estates General/National Assembly/National Convention/Constituent Assembly: Legislative bodies of the French government.

The Colonial Assembly: The overarching Assembly within Saint-Domingue. When they drafted a Constitution that broke with the French National Assembly, the regional and social factions within the Colonial Assembly began to pull apart.

such items as the amount of food considered subsistence level for a slave, the "humane punishment" of slaves, and permission to free slaves. This permission was revoked in 1721, after which slaveowners would be charged a heavy fine for emancipations. During the latter half of the eighteenth century, many of the planters openly defied the Code Noir, starving the slaves and devising brutal devices to torture them, including structures specifically designed for the torture of pregnant women or small children.

The most rapidly growing group in Saint-Domingue was that of the free persons of color, who ranged from wealthy plantation owners and merchants to newly freed slaves and subsistence farmers. Along with their status came considerable obstacles, even for the wealthiest free persons of color. Their liberty was often tenuous, and they were much more legally and socially restricted than the poor whites, often their closest competitors for jobs and political power. Free persons of color could inherit property, serve in the colonial militia and the police forces, and marry whites in the earlier part of the eighteenth century. These rights were denied them later in the century, when the community grew in wealth and size and was viewed by the white colonists as a potential economic and political threat. As the white colonists increased their numbers and power, they began proposing more racially discriminatory policies, even suggesting that the "half-castes" be banished to the mountains. In 1758 mulattoes were legally prohibited from wearing European clothes or armor, gaining or using titles, and meeting together, even for weddings or dances.

Murmurs of discontent (1750-91). *The Kingdom of This World* opens in the 1750s. Although the colonists of Saint-Domingue were then at the peak of their economic, social, and political power, a rebel slave movement threatened to undermine the island's prosperity and relative stability. The period from 1754 to 1758, for example, was marked by large-scale poisoning scares linked in part to the slave rebel leader Macandal. Historians are divided about how much these scares reflected actual conditions and how much they were a product of white paranoia. With the public execution of Macandal in 1758, many of the rebels were isolated and the antislavery resistance seemed mortally weakened. Nevertheless, with the stirrings of revolution in the United States, and the dispatch of a mulatto regiment to the American revolutionary war, the colonials continued to fear the possibility of a slave revolution.

France itself had a similar fear—that the colonials would themselves make a bid for independence from France. This constituted a grave economic and political danger for the French, one that prompted them to try to co-opt the free colored community as their barrier against the white planters' ambitions for independence.

In 1788 and then again in May of 1789, France's general assembly convened to make radical changes in the French system of government; this sparked counter-movements for the preservation of the old, monarchic system, both in France and in Saint-Domingue. The French Revolution, which began in 1789, triggered the creation of competing revolutionary and counterrevolutionary militias and governing bodies throughout Saint-Domingue. On August 26th, 1789, the French National Assembly adopted the Declaration of the Rights of Man and of the Citizen. The questions of citizenship and nationality that emerged from this declaration provoked two basic questions for the colonies: First, were the slaves to be defined as human beings or as property? This query stemmed from the inclusion of slaves in the colonists' population estimates, which dictated the number of deputies that would represent them in the French Assembly. Second, what was the legal status of mulattoes? The Declaration of the Rights of Man and the Citizen led to debates over enfranchising mulattoes whose parents were both free, a proposal voted into law on May 15, 1791. In Saint-Domingue, however, the colonists refused to honor this so-called "May Decree," and the colonial deputies broke from the Assembly. Ultimately, the Decree was rescinded under pressure from the colonists and from the French "maritime bourgeoisie."

Revolution in Saint-Domingue (1791-1803). In the midst of the conflict between the colonists and the French government, the slaves of the Northern Plain launched a massive uprising in August 1791. More than 1,000 plantations were burned in just over one month, and, before the colonial militia was able to contain the revolt, hundreds of whites and thousands of slaves had been killed. One of the early leaders of the movement was a slave named Ti Noël from the Lenormand de Mézy plantation in the Northern Plain. Other leaders of this revolt included the former slaves Jean-François and Georges Biassou, the future King Henri Christophe of independent Haiti, and Vincent Ogé, who led a mulatto delegation to Paris in 1791 and returned to Saint-Domingue determined to have the Declaration of the Rights

Toussaint L'Ouverture

of Man and the Citizen apply to the free persons of color. Another rebel slave, Toussaint L'Ouverture, played a critical role in the history of the country. Toussaint was from the North, where he quickly rose to lead the rebel forces there.

In September 1792, when France's Republican Commissioners Léger Felicité Sonthonax and Etienne Polverel arrived in Saint-Domingue to fight the insurrection, they faced two battles. The first, against the rebel slaves, aimed to bolster the system of slavery, which was the economic mainstay of the bourgeoisie who supported the French Revolution. The second, against the royalists, was to ensure the republicans' authority in the colony. The whites and mulattoes were initially united, but, as the news that the French revolutionaries had executed King Louis (January 21, 1793) reached Saint-Domingue, the whites split into royalist and revolutionary factions, with most of the mulattoes siding with Sonthanax, for the moment. Over the dissent of the royalist faction, largely composed of the petits blancs, Sonthanax enforced the May Decree.

Meanwhile, France's enemy, Spain, offered the leaders of the rebel slaves assistance and arms, in exchange for their agreement to fight off the French. Biassou and Jean-François consented, but Toussaint agreed only on the condition that his forces could fight independently and for the French monarchy. Sonthanax thus faced a dual challenge, the force of the counter-revolutionaries and the force of the Spanish-backed slaves. Surrounded in Le Cap, Sonthanax decreed the abolition of slavery on August 29, 1793. Meanwhile, the rebel slaves of Saint-Dominigue used the continuing wars between the European powers that had Caribbean colonies (France, Spain, and England) to strategic effect, managing to gain the equipment, training, and opportunity to challenge the counter-revolutionary forces. In the spring of 1794, after winning many victories for the Spaniards, Toussaint left the Spaniards and joined ranks with the French. He had continued to play all sides, building up his army, and at one point swearing his allegiance to the British forces who had invaded and taken from the French most of the colony's western region, as well as the islands of Martinique, Guadeloupe, and St. Lucia. In mid-1794, after hearing that the French general assembly had passed a decree abolishing slavery, Toussaint turned on Spain and England with his own forces, banding with the French republicans, then under the leadership of Commissioners Etienne Laveaux and Sonthanax. Spain left first in 1795, followed by England in early 1798. After the mulattoes colluded with the royalists to oust the republicans, Toussaint defeated their combined forces and drove out the royalists. In 1796 he was declared Assistant Governor by Laveaux. At this point, Toussaint was in control of the entire north and west of Saint-Domingue, with the mulatto general of the colony's free persons of color, André Rigaud, in control of the south. Fearing that France would attempt to reimpose slavery, Toussaint pushed Laveau and Sonthanax to return to France, which they did over the next year, leaving Toussaint to turn his attentions to the south. By 1800 Toussaint's forces had defeated the French, British, Spanish, and even Rigaud, to gain control of all of Saint-Domingue. In 1801 Toussaint was proclaimed governor-general and began the painful task of reconstruction. His principal assistants in this endeavor were the generals who aided him in battle, Henri Christophe and Jean-Jacques Dessalines.

In the same year Toussaint reached a compromise with France, by which his country would be completely self-governed and yet would still be part of French territory. Fearing that Toussaint was moving towards independence, Napoleon sent his brother-in-law, General Victor-Emmanuel Leclerc, to depose Toussaint, Christophe, and Dessalines. The Napoleonic army captured the ports, but the three Saint-Domingue leaders fought a guerilla-style war, aided by the yellow fever that devastated Leclerc's army. Henri Christophe led the burning of Cap Français and Jean-Jacques Dessalines the burning of St. Marc. Toussaint was soon kidnapped by the French authorities and imprisoned in France, where he died in April 1803. For the others, the news that slavery was to be restored rallied the black population against a weakened and sick Leclerc army. When Leclerc died, the virulently racist General Donatien Rochambeau waged an even more single-minded campaign of "extermination," but ultimately was defeated by Dessalines and his generals. On January 1, 1804, Dessalines declared Saint-Domingue to be independent and renamed it Haiti, after the name given the island by its pre-Columbian inhabitants, Ayti.

Republic of Haiti. Dessalines's declaration of independence had immediate repercussions for antislavery and independence movements throughout Latin America and the Caribbean, though fear of reprisal by the European powers prevented the Haitian leaders from becoming involved in other anticolonial struggles. In October 1804 Dessalines had himself crowned Emperor. In early 1805 he ordered the massacre of many whites in Haiti, possibly because he feared the reinstitution of slavery, possibly as a continuation of the race war begun by Leclerc and Rochambeau, or possibly because of his own racial hatreds. It was Dessalines who made it illegal for whites to own property, declaring that all citizens at the time he took over, whether mulatto or black, were "black." Internationally, his republic was highly regarded for its non-interventionist foreign policy and for its goal of economic autonomy for Haiti, principles that the future King Henri Christophe would attempt to build on in the creation of his new society.

On October 17, 1806, the autocratic Dessalines was ambushed at Pont-Rouge and shot dead, after which Christophe was named acting chief of the government. Determined to instate himself as sole ruler, Christophe denounced mulatto leader Alexandre Pétion's proposal of power-sharing and declared war on him. This conflict marked the beginning of 14 years of civil war. During this discord, the south was again divided from the north and was governed as a Republic, with Pétion as its head of state. The north became a kingdom under Christophe.

For many in both the north and south, post-independence life replicated the structures and conditions of slavery, though now in a society ravaged by wars and disease. The reign of Christophe turned out to be an ill-conceived imposition of European court life upon an impoverished and physically devastated country. After 14 years of civil strife, economic deprivation, and enforced labor conditions that drove many to their death, Christophe's subjects rebelled, marched to the royal palace (called Sans Souci—"without care"), and burned it into ruins. Christophe killed himself in the palace in October 1820, during the worst of the insurrections. Nevertheless, Christophe's attempt to institute a black kingdom based on the European model has been regarded by many as admirable, part of a noble enterprise that had astonishing successes as well as tragic failures.

The Novel in Focus

Plot summary. Alejo Carpentier's *The Kingdom of This World* moves from the early 1750s to 1820, opening in Cap Français (Le Cap), the northern capital and wealthiest city in Haiti. Structured in four parts, the novel depicts the background to the slave revolts and the wars for independence, the Napoleonic invasion of the island by generals Victor-Emmanuel Leclerc and Donatien Rochambeau, the dictatorial reign of King Henri Christophe, and the aftermath of his death. The narrative focuses on the experiences of three characters: Ti Noël, the central protagonist of the novel; Pauline Bonaparte Leclerc, the wife of General Leclerc and the sister of Napoleon; and Pauline's black masseur, Soliman, later a servant to the family of Henri Christophe.

Part One opens as Ti Noël, a slave on the plantation of Monsieur Lenormand de Mézy, escorts his master through Le Cap on a horse-buying trip. Greeted by the governor on his way to the barber shop, Lenormand de Mézy wields the influence and prestige of a large plantation owner, or a *grand blanc* (big white). Barber-shop symbols of the French monarchs are contrasted with the print, on display in the neighboring book shop, of an African king, whose image corresponds to the descriptions of the kings there as warriors whose "precious seed distended hundreds of [women's] bellies with a mighty strain of heroes," descriptions related to Ti Noël by his friend, the Guinean-born slave Macandal (Carpentier, *The Kingdom of This World,* p. 14).

Subsequent chapters deepen this contrast by placing Macandal's evocations of African history and religion alongside the imitation-French society created by the colonists in Saint-Domingue. In these chapters, Macandal conjures the cultural fusion and worldly sophistication of pre-colonial Africa for Ti Noël through descriptions of the metal-workers' art, painted drums, fortresses, and markets. These descriptions are intercut with those of the arduous sugar-mill work being done by Macandal and Ti Noël. As these images of Africa unfold, Macandal's hand is caught in the rollers, dragging his whole arm into the mill. His arm must be amputated, and, now incapacitated for heavier labor, he becomes the cattle pasturer. Macandal takes advantage of his relative freedom and his access to the livestock to test the properties of the plants and fungi he finds. He takes Ti Noël to meet Maman Loi, a Vodou priestess and healer with remarkable powers, who teaches them many of the curative and fatal qualities of the local plants. Macandal then disappears, assuring Ti Noël that it is with a plan in mind.

Later, Ti Noël is alerted by Maman Loi that he must meet Macandal, then learns that Macandal has been planning a full-scale slave revolt. Through drumming, clandestine meeting sites, and call-and-response songs, Macandal has set up a communication network throughout the northern plain and even over the mountains into the Artibonite valley, by means of which the slaves can contact each other and gain spiritual strength for the battle against the white planters. When he returns to the Lenormand de Mézy plantation, Ti Noël begins to poison the animals. The poisoning spreads from plantation to plantation, sending the owners into a panic. Soon many of the plantation owners and their families are mysteriously dying, including Madame Lenormand de Mézy.

Many slaves are tortured by their owners or by vigilantes who are searching for the source of the poisoning. Finally, under torture, a slave gives up Macandal's name, triggering a massive search by the soldiers of the Le Cap army garrison and by some of the planters and their employees. They capture Macandal, then stage his public execution. Believed by the slaves to be capable of conjuring the Vodou gods and of changing his form at will, Macandal becomes a legendary heroic figure on this occasion. After being captured, he is bound to a stake over a roaring fire, from which he momentarily frees himself and escapes into the crowd. Macandal is forced back into the fire but the crowd does not notice this, and is convinced of his "remaining in the Kingdom of this World" (*Kingdom of This World,* p. 52).

Part Two opens 20 years later, in 1791, shortly after the death of the second Madame Lenormand de Mézy, as the master's new lover, the talentless actress Mademoiselle Floridor, is brought to the plantation. The degeneracy of the planter class is suggested through the increased brutality of Lenormand de Mézy's treatment of the slaves and through the alcoholic and malarial ravings of Mademoiselle Floridor. The scene shifts to a gathering at the Bois Caïman [Caiman Woods], a secret meeting spot for the rebel slaves in the woods of Morne Rouge [Red Hill]. The Jamaican revolutionary, Daniel Bouckman, explains that a law has been passed in republican France requiring that Negroes be given their freedom, but that the monarchist landowners of Le Cap have refused to honor the law. Bouckman further declares that a pact has been made between the "great Loas [gods] of Africa" and the "initiated" in the Caribbean to begin a war for freedom from the planters. The group swears their allegiance to Boukman and names the general staff of the revolution, who declare that the signal will be given eight days later.

Reflecting bitterly on the slaves' bid for political freedom, Lenormand de Mézy hears the "Call of the Conch Shells," the signal for the start of the insurrection. As he hides, the slaves overrun his house, drink his wine, and rape his mistress. The rebels are captured and Bouckman is killed. Lenormand de Mézy begs the governor to spare the lives of Ti Noël and his other slaves, intending to sell them in Havana, but the governor calls for the "complete, absolute extermination of the slaves, as well as of the free Negroes and mulattoes" (*Kingdom of This World,* p. 78).

The governor's fears unsettle Lenormand de Mézy, and talk of the "secret religion" of Vodou makes him question every drumbeat and song he hears among the slaves. Gathering his possessions, including his slaves, Lenormand de Mézy boards a ship for Santiago de Cuba, encountering a spectrum of white refugees from Haiti, ranging from French plantation owners like himself to musicians, priests, and artisans. As his master settles into the expatriate life of leisure in Santiago, Ti Noël is drawn to the Cuban churches and culture. He feels greater affinity with the baroque Catholicism and Afro-Cuban influences he encounters there than with those of the French-style churches of Le Cap. From a distance, Ti Noël learns that the struggle against the planters has continued unflaggingly in Haiti, provoking the French to bring in troops and dogs to defeat the revolutionaries.

The perspective then shifts to that of Pauline Bonaparte Leclerc, as she journeys from Europe to the French Caribbean with her husband, the general in charge of the French counter-revolutionary forces. While General Leclerc arrives in Haiti armed with the gunpower and manpower of the Napoleonic army, Pauline comes armed with her own battalion of outfits and accessories, as well as exotic ideas about the Caribbean absorbed through theater outings and stories in France. Pauline's superficial concerns control the action that follows. Her desire to travel overland to the French port city of Brest in a litter delays the departure of the entire army, and once on the ship she basks in the lustful and servile attentions of the male officers. She romanticizes the French Caribbean, focusing on the landscape, the music and dances, and the fruits, while disregarding Leclerc's rising concern about the clashes between slaves and planters. She employs Soliman, a former bath-house attendant, as her masseur, bather, and personal servant. As with the army officers, she stokes Soliman's sexual desire for her. The racial divide between Soliman and those officers is made clear by the difference in her behavior with them, for while she takes several officers as lovers, she allows Soliman only to kiss her feet. Though Pauline's relationship with Soliman is intimate and even dependent, her powerful position as white mistress is tacitly reinforced.

When the plague sweeps through Haiti, General Leclerc sends Pauline, her maids, and Soliman off to the island of Tortuga, where she lives an even more luxuriant life, until Leclerc arrives, seriously ill with the yellow fever. Pauline consults Soliman, and ultimately allows him to take over care of her husband from the European doctor. She participates fully in Soliman's prescribed remedies, praying with him, finding and preparing curative herbs, dedicating all her energies to treating her husband. When he dies, Pauline nearly goes insane. She voyages with his coffin to Rome, carrying an amulet to Papa Legba, Vodou god of the crossroads, from Soliman.

Pauline's departure marks the beginning of the government of French army officer General Donatien Rochambeau, a government dominated by hedonism and corruption. Rochambeau's cruelty shows itself when he publicly tortures and executes blacks, whom he feeds to his dogs, and when he rapes the infant daughters of slaves in order to terrify the population into submission.

Part Three shifts back to Santiago de Cuba, where Ti Noël has purchased his freedom from a Santiago plantation owner who won him in a card game from the now-dead Lenormand de Mézy. He travels back to the now-independent kingdom of Haiti, ruled by King Henri Christophe. Returning to the plantation, he discovers that it is in ruins. Now an old man, Ti Noël stumbles upon the officers of King Henri Christophe's army, dressed in their Napoleonic-style uniforms. He follows them to Sans Souci, the royal residence. Pausing to contemplate it, he is briefly imprisoned, and then forced into labor with other men, pregnant women, and children. The laborers form a long procession of brick-carriers up to the Citadel La Ferrière. Ti Noël remarks to himself that the residence and fortress that he and the other captives are forced to build are "all the product of a slavery as abominable as that he had known on the plantation of M. Lenormand de Mézy" (*Kingdom of This World,* p. 122). Nevertheless, the majority of the Haitians view the fortress as a monument to a king of their own race, and as protection—physical and spiritual—against future military onslaughts by France.

When the building is nearly finished, Ti Noël is allowed to escape and he immediately sets off for his former home. He passes through Le Cap, where he finds the city absorbing the death screams of Corneille Breille, who was Henri Christophe's favored priest until he asked permission to return to France. Henri Christophe sentences Breille to be buried alive in the archbishop's palace.

The scene shifts back to a church service being performed for Henri Christophe, who is palpably anxious. His presentiment is justified when the specter of Corneille Breille can be heard and partially seen. The vision leaves the king paralyzed on the floor, sending him into a fever from which he never fully recovers. Later, in the palace, with the help of Soliman, who is now his valet, the king stands at a window and witnesses his troops in disorder. He moves into the throne room, and from there listens to the sounds of drumming and of the spreading of the fires in his dairies and sugar-cane fields, regretting that he modeled his republic and court life after European examples and repressed the Vodou practices. As Sans Souci burns, and it becomes clear that the drumming communicates the messages of a full-scale revolt, the king shoots himself in the head and dies. The remaining members of the royal family escape to Rome, where Soliman, who has remained with them, dies.

The action now shifts back to Sans Souci, where Ti Noël, having led the sack of the royal

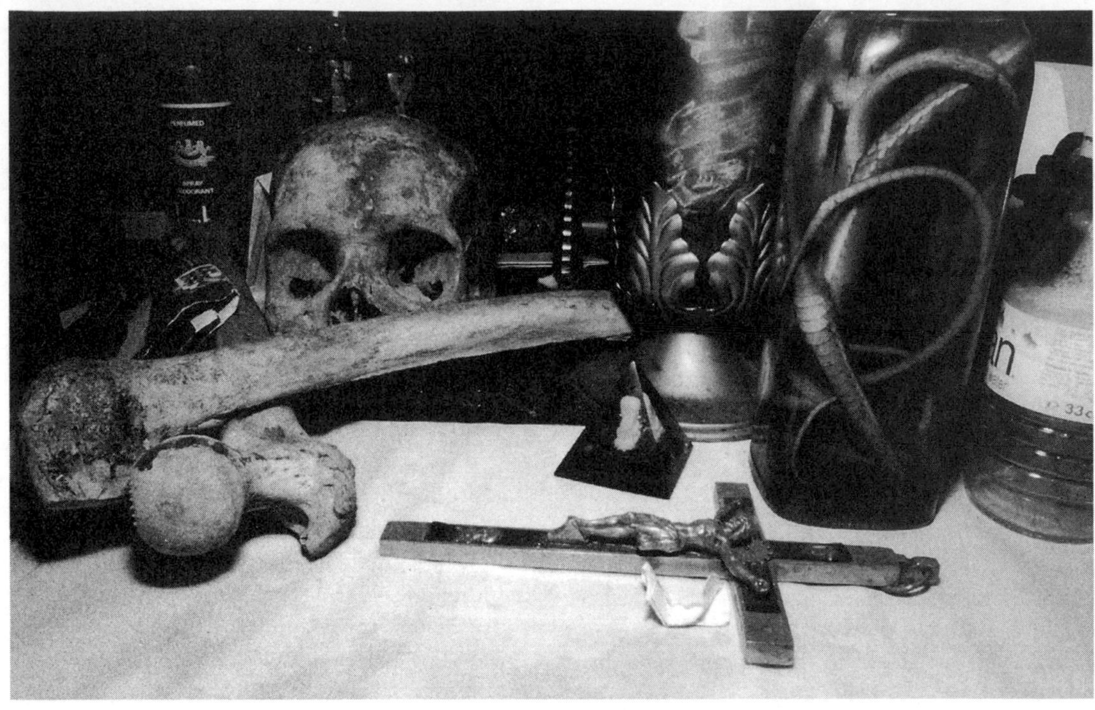

Articles employed in a Vodou ceremony, reflecting the religion's melding of a variety of beliefs and practices.

palace, is furnishing his home with the loot. He wears a green silk coat that belonged to King Henri Christophe and a straw hat folded into a bicorne, and moves about his old master's plantation playing with items snatched from Sans Souci. He talks to himself, believing that he is king and that the animals that wander onto the plantation are gifts from his people.

At this moment, the arrival of surveyors on the property marks the beginning of a new republic. This new republic institutes forced labor, and again makes corporal punishment legal. The republic is run by a new biracial aristocracy that implements the same system of social caste and titles as the Europeans did. Fearing that he will be forced into slavery again, Ti Noël decides to shake off his "human guise," as Macandal used to do, and to turn himself into a series of animals.

In the novel's final chapter, Ti Noël assumes the form of a goose, initially admiring the principle of equality in all geese. However, when he attempts to join the other geese, they shun him. Ti Noël takes this as a sign that he must be brave enough to face the world as a human being. He experiences a revelation, one which impresses upon him the weight of his responsibility to "the Kingdom of this World." Recognizing that it is only in this world that "man finds his greatness, his fullest measure," Ti Noël declares war against the unjust new "masters," then disappears in the "great green wind" that sweeps over the entire plain (*Kingdom of This World,* p. 185).

Vodou and resistance. Many historians link the organization of the Haitian slave revolt to the clandestine meetings at which the slaves practiced their outlawed Vodou rites. They also attribute the strength of the slaves' resistance, both physical and cultural, to the religion's role in the slaves' social organization, as well as to its mythical and spiritual dimensions. Carpentier's treatment of Macandal's escape, presented both as a miracle of transformation and as the collective delusion of a distracted crowd, reveals the role of faith and vision in these events.

Vodou is a dynamic set of religious beliefs and practices, derived from multiple cultural and religious sources in west and central Africa. These beliefs and practices were transformed by the enslaved, who were influenced by Catholicism, Masonic rites, and indigenous American belief systems and practices. As an outlawed set of religious practices for much of the colonial (and even the post-colonial) period, Vodou has by necessity been an improvisational, highly responsive, religion. Altars were often scratched into the ground or built from found objects that could be used to erase their traces as quickly as they created them. In the scenes in which Macandal, and later Bouckman, invoke the spirits, Carpentier accentuates the interaction of Vodou with the natural world. Both Ti Noël and Macandal possess the power to shape-shift into animal forms, reflecting a belief of Vodou practitioners: "In Vodun [Vodou], all beings can take spiritual or physical form at will, and such transformations are under the control of human beings" (Bellegarde-Smith, p. 15). Underlying this belief is the idea that the human and the divine are not sharply divided realms. In fact, in Vodou ceremonies, the spirits of divinities or ancestors may inhabit the body of the participant, called "the horse." The spirit is said to "ride" the person, entering this world from another across the threshold of the body.

Sources and literary context. Carpentier's presentation of the major events and figures in the novel reflects his meticulous historical research. He investigated the minute details of the political, economic, and cultural lives of as many people touched by the Haitian revolution as possible, from the plantation slaves and maroon figures who led the insurrections, to the transient visitors to Le Cap, to the Jesuit priests and Napoleonic army figures. Even in the case of the minor characters or incidental references, the details are often drawn from written historical accounts, sometimes imaginatively redrawn to render certain effects. One historian who is explicitly mentioned in *The Kingdom of This World* is Moreau de Saint-Méry, a leader of the grands blancs, who figures as a fringe character in the novel. His *Description topographique, physique, civile, politique et historique* (originally published in 1797) describes the execution of Macandal:

> les efforts violens que lui faisaient faire les tourments de feu, arrachèrent le piton et il culbuta par-dessus le bucher
>
> [the torment of the fire made him strain violently, uprooting the stake and somersaulting above the fire.]
>
> (Saint-Méry in González Echevarría, p. 133; trans. V. Sams)

Literary critic Roberto González Echevarría compares this passage with Carpentier's description of the dying Macandal: "howling unknown spells and violently thrusting his torso forward. The bonds fell off and the body of the Negro rose in the air, flying overhead" (*Kingdom of This World,* p. 51). González Echevarría discusses many such examples of this "recasting" of historical descriptions, in which Carpentier transforms detail and tone to yield an alternate vision of the "reality" in his nonfiction sources.

Helping to achieve this alternate vision is the baroque style of his prose—in Carpentier's view the proper style for the Latin American novel. Concerned with wordplay and wit, it is also a complex style that gives rise to clever and sometimes purposely ambiguous images. When Ti Nöel transforms himself into a goose, for example, the novel describes his behavior in a way that makes an indirect comment on human nature:

> Ti Nöel employed his magic powers to transform himself into a goose. . . . But, when he attempted to take his place in the clan, he encountered sawtoothed beaks and outstretched necks that kept him at a distance. He was made to keep to the edge of the pasture. . . . In view of this Ti Nöel tried to be circumspect, and not draw too much attention to himself, to approve the decisions of the others. His reward was contempt and a shrugging of wings.
>
> (*Kingdom of This World,* pp. 182–83)

Two authors in particular, Ramiro Guerra y Sánchez and Fernando Ortiz, have profoundly influenced Carpentier (González Echevarría, p. 44). Their work focuses on Cuba's African-based religions and on the economic and cultural aspects of the sugar and tobacco plantations. Carpentier's own research into African-based religious and musical practices frequently explores their historical dimensions and repercussions. It also demonstrates his participation in the primitivist movement of the 1920s and '30s. Involving painters, musicians, writers, and ethnographers, this movement aimed to evoke the primeval essence of national identity. Usually this essence was conceived of in ethnic terms, which put blacks and Indians into the limelight. Whereas before the region's black population, for example, had been thought of as springing from backward societies, it now gained status as an authentic, pulsating force at the forefront of the area's movements for independence.

Lo real maravilloso. *The Kingdom of This World* is held by many to be the first novel of "marvelous realism" (also known as "magical realism") in Latin American literature. Taking the term from art critic Franz Roh, who used it to describe German expressionist art in the 1920s, Carpentier uses the term not to define a "style" of writing, as is widely believed, but a mode of being, or a "marvelous reality" that is unique to Latin

American culture and experience. Since Carpentier was part of the group of Surrealist writers and artists active in Paris in the 1920s and 1930s, his conception of the marvelous has often been aligned with this movement, whose practitioners sought to produce fantastic images in literature by drawing on the unconscious and by juxtaposing words and images in startling ways. However, in his prologue to the first edition of this novel, Carpentier dismisses the Surrealist vision of the "marvelous," which he scathingly describes as a cultivated fusion of random objects and stylistic tics. He argues that the fantastic should be understood as an inherent part of reality, rather than as a subversion of that reality.

CARPENTIER ON "THE MARVELOUS REAL"

"I will say that my first inkling of the marvelous real came to me when, near the end of 1943, I was lucky enough to visit Henri Christophe's kingdom—such poetic ruins, Sans-Souci and the bulk of the Citadel of La Ferrière, imposingly intact in spite of lightning and earthquakes; and I saw the still-Norman Cape Town, the Cap Français of the former colony, where a house with great long balconies leads to the palace of hewn stone inhabited years ago by Pauline Bonaparte. My encounter with Pauline Bonaparte there, so far from Corsica, was a revelation to me."

(Carpentier in Zamora and Faris, p.84)

Events in History at the Time the Novel Was Written

History repeats itself. In 1943 Alejo Carpentier took a trip to Haiti that made a deep and lasting impression upon him. The country was revisiting many of the conflicts that had concerned it 150 years earlier, conflicts that Carpentier would describe in *The Kingdom of This World.* In the novel, for example, Haiti (or Saint-Domingue) was under the political and economic control of a foreign power, France. Similarly, in 1943 Haiti had just emerged from an extended occupation by a foreign power, this time, the United States. The U.S. military presence, which had begun in 1915 (during World War I) in part to counter a sizeable German colony there, and in part to quell civil unrest and establish a U.S. foothold in the Caribbean, did not end until 1934. And it was not until 1941 that U.S. officials in charge of Haitian economics and finance finally left the nation. Most Haitians welcomed their departure.

The much-resented U.S. military occupation of Haiti had important consequences for Haitian political culture well into the mid-20th century. Showing a "marked preference" for mulattos over blacks, the Americans filled the supervised Haitian bureaucracy with mulatto officials and statesmen (Skidmore and Smith, p. 303). This did little to alleviate the racial tensions, familiar to readers of Carpentier's novel, that had plagued Haiti since colonial times. The elevation of the mulattoes by the despised U.S. occupation forces, combined with a pan-Caribbean surge in black nationalism (known as *noirisme,* from *noir,* the French word for "black"), led to the sweeping 1946 political triumph of the black middle class in Haiti. New president Dumarsais Estimé quickly replaced the mulatto political elite with blacks, which outraged Haiti's mulatto population. Accused of exacerbating hostilities between Haitians of different colors, Estimé was ousted in a coup in 1950, the year after Carpentier published *The Kingdom of This World.*

Essential to the *noiriste* movement was a focus on the African heritage of black Haitians. This included the Vodou religion, which both mulattoes in general and the Roman Catholic Church in particular worked hard to suppress. The practice of Vodou had been outlawed in Haiti, in fact, and in 1941-42, the years immediately preceding Carpentier's visit to the country, the Roman Catholic clergy embarked upon a vigorous "anti-superstition" campaign designed to eradicate Vodou entirely. Critics saw this campaign as a Eurocentric attack upon the folk culture of the black majority, the latest attempt by French culture (personified by the mulatto elite) to destroy the African heritage in Haiti. With the rise to power of black national leaders in 1946, the validity of the Vodou tradition in Haitian culture began to be accepted, even by some of the clergy, although it must be said that such acceptance did not mean approval.

Noirisme also directly influenced the way in which Haitians looked back on their history. The mulatto elite had preferred a vision of the hard road to Haitian independence as one built primarily by mulatto heroes, people like Vincent Ogé, Alexandre Pétion, and André Rigaud. The noirists elevated black leaders like Toussaint L'Ouverture, King Henri Christophe, and Jean-Jacques Dessalines. This new recognition encouraged a revival of interest in all forms of black culture in Haiti—Vodou, as mentioned, art, music, and literature.

Reviews. *The Kingdom of This World* was very well received in Latin America and elsewhere, not only by critics but also by other writers. Novelists from Carlos Fuentes (see ***The Death of Artemio Cruz,*** also covered in *Latin American Literature and Its Times*) to Gabriel García Márquez (see ***One Hundred Years of Solitude***) to Salman Rushdie cited it as influential on their work. In France, where the novel was published as *Le Royaume de Ce Monde,* the magazine *Americas* reported that it was rated the "Best Book of the Month" by the Reader's Society (Walker, p. 36). Writing for the *Atlantic,* Phoebe Adams called the language of the novel "poetic" (Adams, p. 84). In his column for the *Saturday Review,* John Cook Wyllie took issue with the vigor of all this applause, arguing that the praise lavished on the book was overzealous. But he went on to describe the novel as having "a nervous and exciting excellence, as of a Haitian drum, high-pitched because of the heat, communicating something of the frenzy as well as the words of the message" (Wyllie, p. 26).

—Victoria Sams

For More Information

Adams, Phoebe. "Revolutions in Tropical Climates." *The Atlantic* 200, no. 2 (August 1957): 82-85.

Bellegarde-Smith, Patrick. *Haiti: The Breached Citadel.* Boulder, Colo.: Westview Press, 1990.

Carpentier, Alejo. *The Kingdom of This World.* Trans. Harriet de Onís. New York: Noonday Press, 1989.

Dayan, Joan. *Haiti, History, and the Gods.* Berkeley: University of California Press, 1995.

González Echevarría, Roberto. *Alejo Carpentier: The Pilgrim at Home.* Austin: University of Texas Press, 1977.

Knight, Franklin. *The Caribbean: Genesis of a Fragmented Nationalism.* New York: Oxford University Press, 1990.

Skidmore, Thomas E., and Peter H. Smith. *Modern Latin America.* 4th ed. New York: Oxford University Press, 1997.

Walker, Kathleen, ed. "Points of View." *Americas* 9, no. 2 (February 1957): 36.

Wyllie, John Cook. "Voodoo Gingerbread." *The Saturday Review* 40 (June 29, 1957): 12, 26.

Zamora, Lois Parkinson, and Wendy B. Faris, eds. *Magical Realism: Theory, History, Community.* Durham, N. C.: Duke University Press, 1995.

Kiss of the Spider Woman

by
Manuel Puig

Born December 28, 1932, in General Villegas, a town in the province of Buenos Aires, Manuel Puig Delledonne developed an early love of storytelling when his mother began taking him to the movies at the age of four. Twenty years later, after attending the school of architecture at the University of Buenos Aires, Puig was awarded a scholarship to study filmmaking at the Centro Sperimentale di Cinematografia in Rome. Discovering that he was not temperamentally suited for the occupation, Puig began to write film scripts while dividing his time between Europe and New York. He moved back to Argentina in 1967 and turned some of these screenwriting attempts into his initial pieces of literary fiction. In 1968 he published his first novel, *The Betrayal of Rita Hayworth,* which launched him onto the international literary scene. *Betrayal* was followed by *Heartbreak Tango, The Buenos Aires Affair,* and *Kiss of the Spider Woman,* the novel that established him as a major Latin American writer. During the 1970s and 1980s Puig continued to write novels while living in Mexico, New York, and Brazil; he died July 22, 1990, in Cuernavaca, Mexico.

THE LITERARY WORK

A novel set in an Argentine prison in 1975; published in Spanish (as *El beso de la mujer araña)* in 1976, in English in 1978.

SYNOPSIS

A gay male and a political revolutionary become friends while sharing an Argentine prison cell during a period of domestic military violence.

Events in History at the Time of the Novel

The decline of Argentina: an overview. After World War II Argentina struggled to regain its economic position as the most productive Latin American nation. It had slipped to third place behind Brazil and Mexico by the 1970s, and was fighting massive inflation. Society became polarized between the wealthy elite, whose assets were safely in foreign banks, and an increasingly impoverished majority. The nation's steady economic decline toppled regime after regime—Argentina had 13 different governments between 1944 and 1976—spawning violence in the streets and halls of power. It was a rapid, embarrassing descent into chaos for a nation aspiring to European sophistication and international repute.

Kiss of the Spider Woman takes place against the violent backdrop of mid-1970s Argentina, but the terror and unrest of the period had its roots in the earlier government of Juan Domingo Perón (1946-55). Perón rose to power in the aftermath of World War II and during a period of economic crisis, when much of the country, especially its working class, had still not recovered from the Great Depression. Together with his charismatic second wife, María Eva Duarte, or "Evita," Perón empowered Argentina's urban

DOCTRINE OF NATIONAL SECURITY

To understand the long-standing and strident opposition of Onganía and the Argentine military in general to left-wing "subversive" politics and Marxist union activity, it is necessary to recognize the influence of U.S. foreign policy during the Cold War (the competition between the United States and Soviet Union for world leadership). The United States saw global politics as a battle between capitalist democracy and communism, and took care to train and assist military personnel in Latin American countries, including Argentina, in battling Marxist "subversion." Argentine military leaders, anxious to prove themselves loyal to powerful U.S. interests, believed that vigilance against communism excused leaders from observing democratic procedure. This became known as the "Doctrine of National Security." The Doctrine of National Security justified the imprisonment of leftists by the military throughout post-World War II Argentina; it would also excuse the torture and murder of thousands of Argentines during the "Dirty War" that was to engulf the nation by the mid-1970s.

labor interests—increasing wages, enforcing labor legislation, supporting and creating unions—at the expense of the nation's aristocratic and industrialist classes. His government also nationalized many important industries and services. Perón accomplished much in his years as president, allowing the underprivileged a chance to prosper in ways they never had before. At the same time, however, his generosity towards the country's poorer classes not only alienated the country's wealthy, but also sparked the worst inflation in decades and, some claimed, led to a shattered economy. Furthermore, in the eyes of his many detractors, Perón was a fascist dictator who resorted to force to quiet opposition; many of his opponents suffered exile, imprisonment, and torture. Once his regime began to lose control of the economy, increased class strife followed. A confrontation with the powerful Catholic Church as well as the death of the popular Evita also contributed to Perón's fall. In 1955 he resigned from office rather than face an inevitable coup or civil war, leaving workers vulnerable to concerted military efforts to eradicate their recent political and economic gains. Despite his exile in Madrid, Perón's voice was heard for the next 14 years, as Argentines wrestled with his legacy, and as he prepared to return.

Military oppression and guerrilla terrorism. In 1966 the right-wing General Juan Carlos Onganía took control of Argentina as the result of a military coup that deposed Arturo Illia, Argentina's fifth president in the years following Perón's resignation and exile. Unlike his predecessors, whose governments had been provisional, Onganía initiated a heavy-handed program of reform and proclaimed the arrival of "The Argentine Revolution." He closed Congress, suspended legal guarantees, routed the universities of his ideological opponents, suppressed political parties, got rid of his political enemies, and made aggressive overtures to foreign capital. Most of all, he tried to stifle Argentina's troublesome labor movement, the bastion of Peronism, a vaguely defined philosophy of social democracy and workers' rights that looked nostalgically to the reign of the former president. In 1967 Onganía instituted a two-year wage freeze.

Onganía's attempts to stifle all leftist movements, in the vociferous unions and elsewhere, may have contributed to the rise of guerrilla terrorism in the country. Deprived of a legitimate political outlet to express its discontent, the Left struck back against government violence with violence of its own. By early 1970 a Peronist guerrilla group, the Montoneros, was gaining strength in the Buenos Aires area; their first major act of terrorism was to kidnap and assassinate former president Pedro Aramburu on May 29, 1970—debate is ongoing about whether the government itself killed Aramburu to frame the Left, and whether the Montonero leaders were in reality government agents in the first place. Whoever actually committed the crime, this assassination spelled the end of Onganía's presidency. More

Police use tear gas to disperse a crowd of demonstrators in Buenos Aires during the turbulent summer of 1969.

importantly, however, it marked the beginning of the increasing political violence and terrorism that would characterize 1970s Argentina:

> It was not only the labor opposition that doomed Onganía's regime. There was also a shocking rise in political violence, such as clandestine torture and execution by the military government and kidnapping and assassination by the revolutionary left. . . . A deadly toxin had entered the Argentine body politic. There was now a revolutionary left, committed to traumatizing the nation by violence against those they identified as the oppressors: the military and the police, along with their collaborators, the well-tailored executives of the multinationals. And the government struck back with violence of its own. Civil war had broken out.
>
> (Skidmore and Smith, p. 99)

Automotive union unrest. In *Kiss of the Spider Woman,* Valentín is arrested in 1972 for "promoting disturbances with strikers at two automotive assembly plants" (Puig, *Kiss of the Spider Woman,* p. 148). Valentín's imprisonment makes little sense without the knowledge that the Argentine automotive unions were hotbeds of civic unrest and Marxist agitation, and that the Argentine government saw these unions as distinct threats. It seems clear that many of the lower-class workers were not Marxists—Marxist ideas were brought to the movement by middle-class leaders, radical Catholic priests, and serious revolutionaries. In Puig's novel, the middle-class student Valentín fits the mold of an actual dangerous political agitator rather well.

While 1972, the year of Valentín's arrest, saw no major labor unrest in Argentina's automotive industry, the years immediately prior to it had; at the city of Córdoba, strikes by disgruntled autoworkers drew the attention of the entire nation. The Argentine automotive industry began its major growth in 1954 at Córdoba when the company Industrias Kaiser Argentina (IKA) started to manufacture automobiles rather than just assemble them. Four years later another Argentine company, SIAM Di Tella, a large steel manufacturer, also began to produce cars. The 1958 election of Argentine president Arturo Frondizi brought to the nation the new policy of encouraging foreign investment, and the two automakers were quickly joined by a host of European and U.S. manufacturers, including Citröen, FIAT, and Ford. Over the years, the automobile workers' unions grew more and more militant and powerful, and waged at times what amounted to economic war against the nation's industrial and multinational business elite.

The first strike at Córdoba occurred at the IKA

On November 18, 1972, a crowd estimated at more than 100,000 gathers outside Perón's home in suburban Buenos Aires, urging his return to the Argentine presidency.

plant in 1959 over pay raises. This was followed by another in 1963, in which workers protesting layoffs took some of the administrative staff hostage and seized control of the factory. IKA's U.S.-born president acceded instantly to the strikers' demands to rehire those laid off, and the hostages were released; he then retaliated immediately by locking the workers out for ten days and firing those responsible for the strike. A similar situation transpired at SIAM. SIAM automotive workers enjoyed good working conditions and were extremely well paid by Argentine standards, but the workers protested when SIAM tried to pay them in company bonds during the 1962-63 recession. Attempts at meeting some sort of agreement failed—the Peronist-inspired workers refused to give way and at one point resorted to destroying factory equipment—and eventually the company let go half its workers and shut down many of its branch plants. In 1966, during a serious downturn in sales, there was more trouble at the IKA plant and once again the workers seized control in protest over staff reductions. Argentina was facing a recession at the time, and IKA was adamant about reducing the number of its employees. Some of those who were ultimately laid off set bombs and pelted the houses of IKA executives.

In 1969 a major labor dispute at Córdoba grew to national proportions. Including all the associated industries that sprang up around the manufacture of cars, buses, and railroad cars, the automotive industry in Córdoba employed around 50,000 people at the time of the *cordobazo,* as the unrest came to be known. That number was down significantly from what it might have been; at the beginning of the decade, Córdoba made half of all the cars produced in Argentina, but ten years later it made only one-fifth. Part of the reason for this shift was that union leaders and members in the city had a reputation for being aggressive Marxists; manufacturers preferred to take their business elsewhere rather than deal with this element.

Many of the autoworkers were young and ambitious—especially the students working in the factories—and saw their jobs in the factories as stepping-stones to higher education and better prospects; when hard times hit, these workers tended to be resentful of their thwarted ambitions. Some were already unhappy about the foreign ownership of many of the factories and had their eyes on revolution.

The cordobazo began on May 19, 1969, as some 14,000 workers and students took to the streets. Ignited by specific policies, such as management's decision to do away with the "English Saturday" (by which workers were paid for 48 hours of work but worked 44, staying only until noon on Saturday), the outbreak is usually seen more generally as the expression of a "restlessness and aggression nurtured by a generation of inflation and mistrust for government" (Rock, p. 350). For two days, rioters and military police battled in the streets, and 16 people died before order was more or less restored. These deaths were a discredit to the army, which was perceived as having acted too hastily in firing on the crowd. The federal government played up the unrest, calling Córdoba a city under siege and, in the eyes of certain Peronists, trying to scare the middle class with tales of potential civil war: "State-controlled television channels kept showing the same few burning buildings and exaggerated the reports of street clashes" (Lewis, p. 380). There were, however, some legitimate reasons for the military complaints—a number of autoworkers had been devising Molotov cocktails and other weapons in the plants, preparing for violent protest. The cordobazo frightened the government because it demonstrated, among other things, the power of the masses and the extent of their discontent. The fallout contributed to a mood that cost military strongman and president Juan Carlos Onganía his job.

> For the labour movement it [the cordobazo] represented a culmination of a long history of popular insurrections in Argentina. . . . The police were forced to retreat in the face of mass violence, and had the arming of the masses been ensured, a revolutionary situation could have resulted. Within the popular camp the Cordobazo acted as a catalyst for radical transformations and the emergence of solid politico-military organizations. New forms of struggle were popularized and a democratic anti-bureaucratic consciousness became widespread. In short, it led to the formation of a new mass vanguard.
>
> (Munck et al., p. 174)

A "second cordobazo" (known popularly as the "viborazo") hit the city the following year on March 12. This time workers at the city's five FIAT plants were the primary agitators, and were joined by the utilities union, whose members blacked out the city, adding greatly to the confusion. Heavily armed policemen were called in to stop the looting and violence in the darkened city, an act that again weakened support for the president. The uproar contributed to the fall of Onganía's successor, General Roberto Levingston. General Alejandro Lanusse, the new president, called in the army to deal with the October 1971 unrest and took steps to suppress the troublesome unions. His government lasted only months and was replaced by that of the democratically elected Héctor Cámpora, who made it clear that he would serve as a stand-in until Juan Perón was ready to run for president. Perón was elected in 1973, to the delight of the unions.

UNREST IN ARGENTINA: THE MAJOR PLAYERS

GUERRILLA MOVEMENTS

Montoneros. Leftist/Peronist, until Perón threw them out in May 1974; derived support from urban centers in east Argentina, especially around the capital. After the split with Perón, attacked right-wing military and political figures, as well as leaders of the federally-authorized union (CGT, below), which diverged from its constituent labor movements; in some circles, held to have been controlled by Argentine intelligence forces.

ERP (People's Revolutionary Army). Non-Peronist; based in Córdoba; derived support from workers, students, and peasants from interior of country; kidnapped FIAT's director in 1971 and demanded that $1 million in food and clothing be given to Córdoba's poor and unemployed in return for his release.

MILITARY ORGANIZATIONS

AAA (Argentine Anticommunist Alliance). Right-wing; indirectly supported by federal police; responsible for disproportionately large number of killings and disappearances.

Mano (Hand). Right-wing, formed around 1970, allegedly by off-duty police; engaged in kidnappings and executions of diplomats and of Peronist and leftist-affiliated civilians.

UNIONS

CGT (General Worker's Confederation). Labor organization established in 1930; by 1954 was the most powerful union in the country and the bureaucratic mainstay of Perón's political authority; in 1970s closed ranks with Perón regime against left; weakened after death of Perón in 1974, the CGT was abolished after the military coup of 1976 but was reinstated in 1981.

SITRAC-SITRAM. Largest radical, non-Peronist alliance of autoworkers based in Córdoba.

CGE (General Economic Confederation). Federally established organization of employers convened to bargain collectively with the CGT; established as sole representation for employers and consolidated under Peronist authority in 1951; later closed ranks with Perón and CGT in 1974 purging of left.

Perón's swan song. Between 1970 and 1975, during which period the events in *Kiss of the Spider Woman* take place, Perón regained his influence in Argentine politics, at first through his ideological sponsorship of left-wing union, student, and other protest movements, and then through the office of president, which he held from 1973 to 1974. In 1970 the still-exiled Perón told the French magazine *Africasia* that he had authorized his followers to begin a violent revolution in Argentina: "Violence already reigns and only more violence can destroy it" (Perón in Sobel, p. 13). Many of the various guerrilla movements that sprang to life in the 1970s called themselves "Peronist," and the former leader openly sponsored several of them. Perón's 1973 return to power only escalated the level of violence in Argentina. In an attempt to "purify" the movement, right-wing and left-wing Peronists assassinated one another in rapid succession and wreaked havoc throughout the country with their bombs and kidnappings. Perón tried to put an end to this with an anti-terrorism bill, passed on January 25, 1974, that "virtually doubled prison sentences for convicted kidnappers, conspirators and armed extremists, and turned over internal security functions to the federal police rather than local law enforcement officers" (Sobel, p. 103). He also outlawed several prominent guerrilla movements and sponsored crackdowns on left-wing organizations and publications. After his death in 1974, when his wife and vice-president, María Estela (Isabel) Martínez Peron, became president, guerrilla warfare on both sides grew so pervasive that she declared a state of siege. She was ousted in 1976 by armed forces whose military regime would prove one of the cruelest in the world.

Descent into hell: 1976. The ouster of Isabel Perón in 1976—the year in which *Kiss of the Spider Woman* was published—signaled the beginning of what came to be known as Argentina's "Dirty War." Under General Jorge Rafael Videla, the military tortured and killed at least 9,000 people, though many sources say that the real total is easily three times that number. Most of these people simply "disappeared," and their fates remain unknown to this day. Discoveries of mass graves and underwater burials, and tales of both living and dead people being thrown out of airplanes into the ocean testify to the horror of the time. Puig's tale of two prisoners—one tortured, the other fatally betrayed—during the early stages of this reign of terror gives individual expression to likely victims of this dirty war.

Prison life. The novel's prisoners, Molina and Valentín, share a tiny cell, survive on miserable food, sleep on cardboard mattresses, and must be taken to the bathroom. Because their chance of survival was greater, they were fortunate compared to those imprisoned after the 1976 coup. For many post-coup prisoners in the *pozos* (pits) or jails of Argentina, life became an unbearable horror, relieved only by death.

The experience typically began when the captives, kidnapped from their homes or workplaces by groups of heavily armed federal agents, entered the prison wearing hoods over their heads. These hoods would remain in place for the duration of the incarceration, a condition known as being "walled-up" (Argentine National Commission, p. 56). Confused, terrified, and vulnerable to attack at all times, the hooded prisoners suffered psychological torture every bit as rending as the physical torture that they endured:

> The psychological torture of the "hood" was as bad or worse than the physical, although the two cannot be compared since whereas the latter attempts to reach the limits of pain, the hood causes despair, anxiety and madness. . . .
>
> (Cubas in Argentine National Commission, p. 57)

Prisoners were often handcuffed or chained around their feet; they were attached to one another, to the walls, floors, or, sometimes, to the beams of their prisons. Identified only by number, they were fed un-nourishing and sometimes utterly unhealthy foods (like uncooked offal meats). They slept on infested mattresses soaked through with bodily fluids—their own and those of former prisoners—and suffered from such pestilence as maggots and lice.

Most prisoners were tortured at some point during their incarceration. Typically, they were tied to metal beds and given electrical jolts. Women reported multiple rapes; pregnant women were sometimes tortured until they miscarried, or given Caesarean sections, after which their children were spirited away forever. Beatings were a matter of course; Valentín's sorry condition at the end of the novel—beaten and delirious—was shared by most prisoners. One cannot say with certainty how many people were tortured to death as opposed to "merely" killed outright, but the condition of the many corpses that turned up—at the bottom of rivers, in the ocean, and in mass graves—indicate that even those slated to die were tortured.

The Novel in Focus

Plot summary. *Kiss of the Spider Woman* synthesizes several narrative elements: conversations between two prisoners, Luis Alberto Molina and Valentín Arregui Paz; interrogations of Molina by the warden; scholarly footnotes with citations from various psychoanalysts and intellectuals; a report on Molina's fate; and a closing stream-of-consciousness passage from Valentín's perspective after he has been tortured in prison. The story unfolds through dialog without surrounding description. Molina is an apolitical gay window dresser jailed on a "corruption of minors" charge; Valentín is a heterosexual socialist engaged in the revolutionary struggle against the Argentine government of the mid-1970s. As the novel opens, Molina is recounting Jacques Tourneur's 1942 film, *Cat People*.

Initially scornful of Molina's love of campy melodramas and erotic horror films, Valentín, listening to Molina recount the films, soon finds himself engaged by their suspense and eager to hear how they end. Nevertheless, he repeatedly attempts to establish his commitment to revolutionary ideals, ideals that in his mind exclude any enjoyment of sensual pleasure or decadence. When Molina presses him to "live for the moment," Valentín responds:

> There's no way I can live for the moment, because my life is dedicated to political struggle, or, you know, political action, let's call it. Follow me? I can put up with everything in here, which is quite a lot. . . . But it's nothing if you think about torture . . . because you have no idea what that's like. . . . Anyway, I put up with all of it . . . because there's a purpose behind it. Social revolution, that's what's important, and gratifying the senses is only secondary.
>
> (*Spider Woman*, pp. 27-28)

Hurt by Valentín's strident rejection of his attempts to make their imprisonment more bearable, Molina counters that "if men acted like women there wouldn't be any more torturers" (*Spider Woman*, p. 29). From this early conversation, the two men infer that despite their physical (and, later, emotional) closeness, their political and social outlooks divide them. This distance reveals itself in the contradictory identifications each man feels with different characters in the films. For instance, in the first film Molina recites, Valentín identifies with the macho psychiatrist and is attracted to the male protagonist's female co-worker, while Molina identifies with the elegant and sensitive heroine and is attracted to her gentle architect husband.

Until now, Valentín has treated Molina with varying degrees of condescension and suspicion, but Molina's acute sensitivity to Valentín's arguments gradually seems to win the other man's respect. Valentín reveals that, despite his identification with the underclass, he pines for his ex-girlfriend, who comes from a bourgeois family.

At this point Molina launches into another film recitation (of a Nazi propaganda film about a love affair between a German soldier and a French singer in occupied France), which Valentín interrupts to criticize Molina for his escapist enjoyment of Nazi propaganda, and for his identification with the privileged heroine and the implicit ethics of Nazism. Provoked to tears, Molina discloses his love for a married heterosexual waiter. The object of his affection grew up in Buenos Aires, a good student who was forced for economic reasons to quit school and work in a factory. When workers without connections to organized crime or to the government started getting laid off, Molina's friend tried to help them get their jobs back. The union bosses told him to leave it alone or risk getting fired. Instead, he quit in protest of union favoritism. After months of unemployment he finally found work as a waiter, a position lower-paying than the factory job and far below his youthful ambitions. Molina explains that he was incredibly attracted to an individual who would go to such lengths on principle alone.

Valentín identifies with Molina's friend and begins a passionate tirade about the importance of free schooling in a liberated society. He argues that the social elite locks Argentine workers into believing that they do not deserve an education, and makes an analogy with the small, cramped

STUCK BY MISTAKE

Like Molina, Puig himself turned to the movies to escape from life's harsh realities. Growing up in a small *pampas* town, early on he began to identify with the heroes of Hollywood films of the 1930s and '40s: "Little by little I changed the terms: that which was reality changed into a class Z movie in which I had been stuck by mistake. Reality . . . was what happened in the movies, not what happened in town . . ." (Puig in Matuz, p. 263).

cell that he and Molina share: "reality . . . isn't restricted by this cell we live in. If you read something, if you study something, you transcend any cell you're inside of, do you understand what I'm saying?" (*Spider Woman,* p. 78).

A later film summary picks up these threads of loyalties and elitist escapism. The film plot focuses on a young car-racing fanatic from a wealthy Latin American family who enters a race in Le Mans, France. An unjust disqualification and the destruction of his car trigger a crisis of conscience, and he must decide whether to indulge his dream of racing in Europe or return to his country and take an active part in a revolution for economic justice. The novel shifts mid-scene from this story to Valentín's thoughts:

> a European woman, a bright woman . . . a woman with a knowledge of Marxism . . . a woman who understands the problems of Latin America, a European woman who admires a Latin American revolutionary . . . a fellow who hates the colonialists in his country, a fellow ready to sacrifice his life in defense of principles, a fellow who cannot comprehend the exploitation of the workers . . . a fellow with an unshakable faith in the precepts of Marxism, a fellow with his mind made up to enter in contact with guerrilla organizations, a fellow who from up in the sky observes the mountains certain of his forthcoming meeting with the liberators of his country, a fellow who's afraid of being taken for an oligarch.
>
> (*Spider Woman,* pp. 124-26)

This sequence suggests that Molina's story has triggered a similar crisis of conscience in Valentín, as he seems to be repressing both his privileged background and his love for a girl from his former social circle. Molina wakes Valentín and tells him that he had cried out in his sleep. After some hesitation, Valentín explains that he has been thinking about a different woman, not his current girlfriend. When he receives a letter the next day from the current girlfriend, who is a fellow revolutionary, he is wracked with guilt.

Molina falls ill, complaining of stomach cramps, and a day or so later, Valentín also becomes violently ill. For the next few days, Molina takes care of his cellmate, wiping up Valentín's vomit and diarrhea, putting cool washcloths on his forehead, and preparing teas and elixirs. During this time the men become increasingly attached to one another; Molina constantly recites stories from films, and Valentín opens up bit by bit about his fears and desires.

Molina soon begins receiving visits from his mother. After seeing her, he always returns to the cell with two brown bags of goods that he shares with a grateful Valentín. What the reader knows, unlike Valentín, is that Molina's "visits" are actually meetings with the prison warden, who has promised Molina an early release in exchange for any information he can extract from Valentín regarding the actions and whereabouts of his fellow militants. The illness that plagued them both proves to have been food poisoning; the warden is trying to break Valentín's defenses by making him sick, and Molina fell victim by eating the food, too. Small acts of generosity on Molina's part, such as sharing his provisions or cooking their meals, induce Valentín to become less guarded and more likely to share information with his cellmate. As weeks pass, however, Molina seems more ambivalent about his task, asking the warden to give him more time.

Molina's sexual orientation and Valentín's radicalism are placed in a sociopolitical context through a footnote that falls between an emotionally charged scene in the cell and Molina's second interview with the prison warden. Here, the novel reproduces a long passage by the scholar J. C. Flugel:

> In . . . *Man, Morals and Society,* [Flugel] claims with respect to those who during infancy have strongly identified themselves with paternal or maternal figures of a particularly stern disposition, that as they grow up they will embrace conservative causes and will be fascinated by authoritarian regimes. . . . On the other hand, those who in infancy somehow reject—on an unconscious, emotional or rational level—such rules of parental conduct will favor radical causes, repudiate distinctions of class and treat understandingly those who exhibit any unconventional inclinations: homosexual, for example.
>
> (*Spider Woman,* p. 195)

The novel goes on to cite the work of social theorist Herbert Marcuse, who argued that the social function of the homosexual is analogous to that of the critical philosopher, since the homosexual's presence is a continual reminder of the repressed elements in society. Homosexuals, states the footnote, have been placed on the sidelines of movements for class liberation and political action. These theories complement the dynamics of Molina and Valentín's relationship, and aspects of their personalities, but at the same time these dynamics defy the clinical explanations offered in the footnote.

When Molina learns that he may be moved or released, he nearly reveals his growing concern for Valentín to the warden. When he returns to the cell, he expresses his mixed feelings about being pardoned and leaving the cell, as well as his fears for Valentín's welfare. His kindness and his sadness move Valentín, and they begin to caress each other tenderly. They make love that evening, and again on several other nights. The police soon release Molina under close surveillance. Valentín has persuaded Molina to take a message to his comrades, assuring him that he will definitely not get caught.

The novel switches to the surveillance log being written on Molina—the government has tapped his phone and watches his every move. When he waits at a street corner for a suspicious length of time, he is approached by two police agents, who begin to arrest him, but he is shot by an unidentified person from a passing car before they can finish the arrest. In the final scene of the novel, Valentín has been tortured and, in a drugged haze, he engages in an imaginary dialogue with his ex-lover Marta, in which he describes an erotic encounter with an island "native" on a deserted beach. In addition to other images, the "man's shirt" tied across the native's chest suggests that Valentín is recalling his sexual intimacy with Molina, and that the "island" represents their cell. Just as Molina claimed that he had felt himself become Valentín after making love with him, Valentín here takes on Molina's role as storyteller for his imaginary listener, Marta. His final description is of a "spider woman" with threads emerging from her waist that he claims disgust him, and he pities her for being trapped in her own web. While he characterizes "the island" as a beautiful place, Valentín ends by expressing his desire to leave the place once he is strong enough, to join his comrades again.

Censorship of film and literature in Argentina. Puig's use of film narratives in *Kiss of the Spider Woman* illustrates his knowledge of and appreciation for the medium, as well as the significant role that film has had in Argentina's socio-cultural evolution. Argentine popular culture of the 1970s was an amalgam of many influences: European, U.S., and other Latin American film, music, and television competed for Argentine audiences. In the novel, Molina's film tastes include an international repertoire of Hollywood and other "B" movies, and a penchant for decidedly anti-intellectual escapism. In contrast, Argentine film of the time set its creative sights on the nation's immediate social and political situation. For Argentina, the period from the late 1950s to the early 1960s was a time of artistic and intellectual experimentation following the ousting of Juan Perón. Fernando Birri, for example, who founded the country's first film school, made a documentary in 1958, *Tire dié* (Throw Us a Dime), that explored unpleasant Argentine realities, such as shantytown youngsters begging for coins.

Under the military governments of 1966-73, some filmmakers fled the country, while others remained and struggled against the government in cultural pursuits. Expressions like the "Third World" and "the people" took on a positive, Latin American spin, with the help of films such as Octavo Getino's and Fernando Solanas's *La hora de los hornos* (The Hour of the Furnaces), a four-hour documentary conveying the idea that conditions in Argentina sprang from past dependency on Europe. Completed in 1968, by which time censorship was a fact of everyday life in Argentina, the film was screened secretly in businesses and homes.

Perón's return to power in 1973 brought a liberalization of censorship in film, which led to increased production (54 films in the first year of his term in office alone) and audience attendance (up by some 40 percent that same year). The most successful films—such as *La Patagonia, Rebelde* (Rebellion in Patagonia), *Quebracho, Juan Moreira, La tregua* (The Truce), and *La Raulito* (Tomboy Paula)—were anti-imperialist. This liberalization quickly ended, however, with the death of Perón in 1974. In the terror-filled political vacuum that followed, filmmakers like Solanas received death threats and were eventually forced into exile. After the 1976 military coup, the quality and quantity of cinema as well as other arts in Argentina rapidly declined. The military attempted to create a sanctioned, conservative, anticommunist culture, founded on Christian and family values. To this end, it would terrorize and blacklist journalists, teachers, and other uncooperative professionals.

There were public burnings of writings by Mao Zedong, Vladimir Lenin, Argentina's own Ernesto "Che" Guevara, and even early letters by a radical Perón, and in their place arose fascist-sounding publications like *The SS in Action* and *Maybe Hitler Was Right.* Radio, television, and newspapers were shut down or purged of any content deemed offensive to the military's political and moral sensibilities. Publishing houses and bookstores were looted and shut down as well, authors were banned, and theaters were closed indefinitely. Cinema especially came under fire by censors, who had to approve a project before it could receive funding and who screened each finished film before it was released to the public. The military's Censorship Board hired film reviewers to weed out any material with even remotely subversive content. In 1976 and 1977 no fewer than 180 titles were banned, including, for example, Argentine (*The Hour of the Furnaces*), Italian (*Silence the Witness*), and U.S. motion pictures (*Ode to Billy Joe, Breaking Point*) whose plot lines were objectionable because they resembled events in Argentina.

Homosexuality and dictatorships in Latin America. According to one observer, "the military governments that came to power in Latin America beginning in the mid-1960s were committed, among other things, to a moral cleansing of the body politic that included a reform of sexual mores, most specifically the homosexual presence" (Foster, p. 77). These military dictatorships made persecution of gay males by gangs of thugs an integral part of absolute social control.

Literature of the Southern Cone responded to this tyrannical agenda by creating characters whose "quest for gay liberation [was] not only the generalized struggle against a variety of self-serving intolerances, but also . . . an effort to counter forms of political repression." (Foster, p. 74). During and after the experiences of dictatorship, Latin American writers produced daring works that challenged the authority of the military state, such as David Viñas's *Los hombres de a caballo* (Men on Horseback, 1967), Carlos Arcidiácono's *Ay de mí Jonathan* (Woe Is Me, Jonathan, 1976), and Oscar Hermes Villordo's *Con la brasa en la mano* (With the Burning Coal in His Hand, 1984). Their stories both criticized the rise in military authority and supported the gay experience in a newly redemocratized, post-military dictatorship Argentina. The stories held political as well as social oppression up to scrutiny, the belief of the authors being that sexual liberation equaled political liberation, and that "any movement of political freedom that does not take into account the sexual rights of the individual cannot in good faith promise release from tyranny" (Foster, p. 76).

Sources and literary context. Puig himself always insisted that the major artistic influences upon him were cinematic and not literary: "I don't have obvious literary models, because, I think, there are no great literary influences in my life. This space is filled by the influence of the movies" (Puig in Matuz, p. 266). An aficionado of all forms of motion pictures, he unashamedly wrote stories that would simultaneously entertain the masses and succeed as critically acclaimed works of art. Interested in using popular culture to address traditionally taboo subjects, he did so with an eye for their commercial appeal. *Kiss of the Spider Woman,* for instance, concerns the taboo subject of sexual orientation and simultaneously incorporates storylines from films, drawing on a number of real-life Hollywood features, including *Cat People* (1942), *I Walked with a Zombie* (1943), and *The Enchanted Cottage* (1945).

With the novel's emphasis on film, Puig helped inaugurate a new trend in Latin American literature—the post-Boom novel, which moved away from all-inclusive stories like Gabriel García Márquez's ***One Hundred Years of Solitude*** (also covered in *Latin American Literature and Its Times*). The post-Boom novel showed more direct concern for politics and social conditions of the moment and for mass media and popular culture. It furthermore sought to eliminate from its stories the narrative voice—with its particular authorial point-of-view—and to reach a widespread audience.

Reviews. Largely due to Puig's ability to strike a balance between high art and pulp fiction, *Kiss of the Spider Woman* was well received by critics as well as by the general public in Latin America and elsewhere. The novel has been adapted into a play, a musical, and a film. In fact, *Kiss of the Spider Woman* received so much positive critical attention that many judge 1976—the year of its publication—to be the key moment in Puig's career and in Latin American "post-Boom" literature.

Not surprisingly, critics focused on the novel's treatment of Hollywood film and homosexuality. Not all of the reviews were complimentary. Writing for the *New York Times Book Review,* Robert Coover complained about the contents: "Most of the book is a frail little love story that Mr. Puig's fans will perhaps find thin and disappointing. . . . It is Mr. Puig's fascination with old movies that largely provides substance and ultimately defines its plot, its shape" (Coover, pp. 15, 31). Others were more generous in their praise. An anonymous reviewer for *Choice* stated that the relationship between Valentín and Molina "manages to surmount the inherent clichés of sacrificial gay and self-doubting revolutionary; and in the end, what Molina and Valentín have established manages to triumph—for the book ends on a replacement of ugly reality with a satisfying and romantic movie fantasy" (*Choice,* p. 844). Writing in the *Hudson Review,* Clara Clairborne Park lauded Puig's masterful use of pop culture: "In a paradoxical rebuke to all us snobs of culture, the tawdry, sentimental art is seen to have nourished not only the life of the imagination, but real affection, and, at length, heroic self sacrifice" (Park in Stine, p. 371).

—Emerson Spencer Olin and Victoria Sams

For More Information

Argentine National Commission on the Disappeared. *Nunca Más: The Report of the Argentine National Commission on the Disappeared.* New York: Farrar Straus Giroux, 1986.

Coover, Robert. "Old, New, Borrowed, Blue." *The New York Times Book Review,* April 22, 1979, 15, 31.

Foster, David William. *Sexual Textualities: Essays on Queering Latin American Writing.* Austin: University of Texas Press, 1997.

Lewis, Paul H. *The Crisis of Argentine Capitalism.* Chapel Hill: University of North Carolina Press, 1990.

Matuz, Roger, ed. *Contemporary Literary Criticism.* Vol. 65. Detroit: Gale Research, 1991.

Munck, Ronaldo, Ricardo Falcon, and Bernardo Galitelli. *Argentina: From Anarchism to Peronism. Workers, Unions and Politics, 1855-1985.* London: Zed Books, 1987.

Puig, Manuel. *Kiss of the Spider Woman.* Trans. Thomas Colchie. New York: Vantage International, 1991.

Review of *Kiss of the Spider Woman. Choice* 16 (Spring 1979): 844.

Rock, David. *Argentina, 1516-1987.* Berkeley: University of California Press, 1987.

Skidmore, Thomas E., and Peter H. Smith. *Modern Latin America.* 4th ed. Oxford: Oxford University Press, 1997.

Sobel, Lester, ed. *Argentina & Peron, 1970-75.* New York: Facts on File, 1975.

Stine, Jean C., ed. *Contemporary Literary Criticism.* Vol. 28. Detroit: Gale Research, 1984.

The Labyrinth of Solitude

by
Octavio Paz

Octavio Paz was born in Mexico City in 1914 in the midst of the Mexican Revolution. His father, a journalist and lawyer deeply involved in the Revolution, was rarely home, so Paz was raised mainly by his mother, aunt, and grandfather, whose library of Mexican writers and European classics supplemented his education in a French Catholic school. In 1943, after establishing himself as a poet, Paz left Mexico for 11 years, living first in the United States and then in Paris, France, as a diplomat. It was during this time that he wrote *The Labyrinth of Solitude,* his best-known essay. In the post-war desolation of France, Paz confronted Mexico's history of uprootedness and alienation and sought to escape from the solitude that then seemed to have encompassed the world.

THE LITERARY WORK

An essay about Mexico; published in Spanish in 1950 (as *El laberinto de la soledad: Vida y pensamiento de México*; revised in 1959), in English in 1961.

SYNOPSIS

Octavio Paz reflects on the character of Mexicans, the history of Mexico, and the long search for a Mexican identity.

Events in History at the Time of the Essay

From the conquest and colonialism to Paz. In 1519 Hernán Cortés, who had been living in Cuba, landed off the coast of present-day southeastern Mexico with some 500 Spanish soldiers. His goal was to conquer the natives, convert them to Christianity, and fill his coffers with their gold in the process. These natives included a number of different Latin American Indian tribes with their own beliefs and languages, among whom the Aztecs, led by Moctezuma II, were the most dominant in the area at the time. By allying themselves with tribes that had been terrorized by the Aztecs, by exploiting Moctezuma's initial belief that the Spaniard Cortés was a god, and by involuntarily spreading European diseases to which the natives had no immunity, the Spaniards were able to conquer the Aztec empire in 1521 and to establish a Catholic Spanish colony in its place. As neighboring lands were conquered, the colony expanded to include all of present-day Mexico, parts of the southwestern United States, and most of Central America.

The conquered area, renamed "New Spain," was quickly organized according to the principles of Spanish government. While some Aztec nobles retained local leadership as *caciques* (chiefs), Spaniards were clearly the privileged class. Land that had been held communally by groups of Indians was seized by the Spanish Crown, and, while most of it was granted back to Indians for farming, Spanish settlers gradually began claiming the land for themselves. A local tax and welfare practice known as the *encomienda* system was also established. Under this system, a Spaniard would be assigned to protect the inhabitants of an Indian village and to convert them to Christianity. In exchange, the villagers paid this *encomendero* (grantee) a tax, or tribute, in goods or services, often in the form of forced labor. Those Indians without an encomendero paid their tax directly to the Spanish Crown. Only those tribes who had supported Spain during the conquest were exempt from either tax.

Since the Aztecs had been accustomed to paying a regular tribute to their overlords before the conquest, this new system proved fairly easy to establish. It was also a necessary source of income for many Spanish colonists, who needed encomienda funds to offset the heavy taxes and duties they were required to pay to the Church and the Spanish Crown. However, by the 1560s the Spanish government had grown uneasy about the power held by encomenderos and the increase in forced labor as a form of tribute payment. The Spanish government seized a number of encomiendas, or Indian territories assigned to individual colonists, and abolished the policy of allowing personal service in lieu of tribute. Thereafter, Indians were directed to pay a standard tribute, essentially a head tax, directly to the colonial government.

The encomienda system was just one element in a network of municipal, regional, and village governments that stretched across New Spain. While the primary purposes of this network were to maintain Spanish rule, spread Spanish culture, and fill the Spanish treasury, it also served to unify an area previously fragmented by separate tribes with their own languages and social structures. As Paz explains in Chapter Five of *The Labyrinth of Solitude,* "The Conquest, then, whether considered from the native or the Spanish point of view, must be judged as an expression of a will to unity. Despite the contradictions that make it up, it was a historical act intended to create unity out of the cultural and political plurality of the pre-Cortesian world" (Paz, *The Labyrinth of Solitude,* p. 100).

Mexican Catholicism—from its inception, to Sor Juana, to Paz. The unity imposed by Spanish rule also extended to religion. In fact, although some Indians initially resisted conversion to Catholicism, ultimately the Spanish missionaries succeeded in creating a Catholic Mexico. Part of this success stemmed from the Indians' willingness to blend Aztec religious symbols with Catholic ones. For example, in 1531 an Indian who had recently been converted reported an encounter with the Virgin Mary at the site of a shrine to the Aztec mother goddess, Tonantzín. Identifying herself as the Virgin of Guadalupe, this figure had dark skin and Indian features. When news spread of her appearance, thousands of Indians embraced the Catholic faith and made the Virgin of Guadalupe the religion's uniquely Mexican symbol.

Another reason that native Mexicans found Catholicism so appealing was the social status it conferred. If all Christians were considered equal in the eyes of God, they reasoned, then surely the Christian Indian must be entitled to fairer treatment from the Spanish than the pagan Indian. The Spanish clergy's paternalist approach to Indian converts made it clear that truly equal status was not attainable in New Spain, but at least the principle of Christian equality offered converted Indians a tool with which to resist social injustice. As Paz points out, this was a tool unavailable to native North Americans in their confrontations with colonial Protestants, who had no interest in converting them.

In the end, however, the Indians' acceptance of Catholicism was as much an act of desperation as it was a rational choice. Despite their willingness to condone some symbolic links between Indian deities and their own religious figures (such as Tonantzín/the Virgin of Guadalupe), the Spanish simply refused to allow the practice of any religion in New Spain except Catholicism. From the time of Cortés's arrival, Aztec pyramids were uniformly replaced with churches and pre-Christian idols and religious records were destroyed.

Spanish clergy members meanwhile sought to ensure that pagan beliefs would fare no better than these physical emblems of paganism. Exploiting the Aztecs' suspicion that they had been betrayed by their gods during the Conquest, one Spanish friar wrote a widely distributed tract explaining that the Aztecs' old gods were devils who had tricked them and should be condemned. In the face of such rhetoric and in the midst of a cultural upheaval that left them searching for any source of spiritual comfort, it is not surprising that so many native Mexicans embraced Catholicism in the colonial era.

While Catholicism continued to gain fresh converts in New Spain, the rise of Protestantism reduced the membership of the Catholic Church in Europe. Focused on the outside threat of the Protestant Reformation, Spanish clergy devoted little energy to revitalizing their own religious life. In fact, in both Spain and New Spain, the Tribunal of the Inquisition, an authority dedicated to maintaining the orthodoxy of Catholic

Sor Juana Inés de la Cruz

doctrine, sought to establish a strict, uniform code of religious belief and behavior, denouncing not only suspected Protestants and Jews, who might be burned at the stake, but any Catholics who strayed from the Inquisition's definition of orthodoxy.

Needless to say, New Spain in the 1500s and 1600s was not a place where the free exchange of ideas—especially religious ideas—was encouraged. Nevertheless, one writer managed to flourish in the midst of this restrictive atmosphere. Born in 1648, Sor Juana Inés de la Cruz was a child prodigy who became a nun and an accomplished poet and also dabbled in music, science, and philosophy. Her secular interests and unconventional opinions elicited harsh criticism from her fellow nuns and a local bishop, who wrote under an assumed name—Sor Philotea. In a 1691 reply to this bishop (see **"Reply to Sister Philotea,"** also covered in *Latin American Literature and Its Times*), Sor Juana defended her intellectual exploits, explaining that she enhanced her knowledge of God by learning about His creations. This unapologetic response, however, earned her even harsher criticism. Finally in 1694, ostracized and defeated, Sor Juana stopped defending herself and spent the next year of her life, her last, performing acts of penance to atone for her putatively sinful ideas. For Paz, Sor Juana's story evokes the following conclusion about Mexican colonial life: "It was a world open to participation, was even a living cultural order, but it was implacably closed to all personal expression and all adventure; it was

Miguel Hidalgo y Costilla, the "Father of Mexican Independence."

a world closed to the future" (*Labyrinth of Solitude,* p. 116).

The independence movement. In the three centuries following the defeat of the Aztecs, Spain continued to reap the riches of New Spain through restrictive trade policies and heavy taxes. However, in the 1700s and early 1800s the Spanish government found itself embroiled in a number of wars and other expensive military operations, some in Europe and others in the Americas. To subsidize these activities, Spain's monarchs raised taxes to an even higher level and added new import duties, including extra taxes on tobacco, wine, and even ice. By the early 1800s only one-half of the income received from New Spain was applied to the colony itself; one-third went to Spain. Furthermore, in 1804 the Spanish king extended to New Spain a Royal Law of Consolidation. This law forced Church institutions to auction off their property and loan the proceeds to the Spanish government. In addition to undermining the power of the Church, this law threatened to destroy the credit system in New Spain because almost all colonial businesses were indebted to the Church to some degree. Mexicans of all classes were adversely affected by the Law of Consolidation, and many staged desperate protests calling for its repeal. Finally, in 1808 the law was suspended.

While most colonists coped grudgingly with the Spanish Crown's burdensome financial policies in the first decade of the 1800s, some became increasingly discontented. At the same time, certain Enlightenment ideas about natural rights and social equality—the same ideas that had helped to spur revolutions in the North American colonies and in France—began to circulate among the intellectuals of New Spain. Frustrated *criollos* (colonists of Spanish descent born in Mexico), who were ineligible for high-ranking Church or state positions because they were not born in Spain, resented being treated as second-class citizens by *gachupines* (a derogatory term for Spaniards or colonists born in Spain) and added this injustice to their list of complaints against the Spanish government.

Despite frustrations with the policies of their mother country, however, very few colonists of New Spain thought seriously about following the revolutionary example of the North American colonies until 1808, when Napoleon Bonaparte invaded Spain and proclaimed his brother, Joseph, its new king. The subsequent period of instability in Spain was seen as a window of opportunity by colonists interested in establishing self-rule. In 1808 New Spain's colonial leader tried to set up an independent colonial government but was ousted and imprisoned by a group of Spaniards; in 1809 a plot to launch a revolution against Spain—led by a group of criollo clergymen and local government officials—was foiled. It was not until September of 1810 that Father Miguel Hidalgo y Costilla, a criollo parish priest in his 60s, gave the *Grito de Dolores* (Cry from Dolores—the priest's village), the call to arms that began the Mexican War for Independence.

With some 60,000 rebels backing him, Father Hidalgo fought to end "bad government" (a reference to Spanish colonial leaders and Napoleon, not the exiled Spanish king, Ferdinand VII), slavery, and the Indian tribute system. These goals gained him much support from Indians and *mestizos* (Mexicans of mixed Spanish and Indian ancestry), who saw the war as an opportunity to take revenge on the middle and upper class criollos and gachupines who had oppressed them, be they encomenderos, land-grabbing hacienda owners, royal officers, or exploitative mine owners. Father Hidalgo's war was about social revolution far more than independence; in fact, it was perceived as too radical by most of New Spain's criollos, even those convinced of the need for Mexico to free itself from Spanish control.

Although Father Hidalgo is widely hailed as the "Father of Mexican Independence," his troops were defeated by royalist forces only six months after the Grito de Dolores; he was soon executed as a traitor. From 1811 to 1819 various other revolutionaries struggled unsuccessfully for Mexican independence.

In 1820, however, the independence movement took a fascinating turn. Back in Spain, the year marked a radical change in government. The by-now reinstated King Ferdinand VII was forced by a military revolt to uphold the provisions of a liberal constitution—provisions that included the establishment of a constitutional monarchy, freedom of the press, and limits on the power of the Church. Horrified by this course of events, Mexican conservatives and high-ranking Church and government officials—the same group that had always opposed Mexican independence—now began plotting to free Mexico from the corrupting influence of a liberal Spain. Once this group of conservative revolutionaries had formed an alliance with their former enemies, little fighting was necessary to secure Mexico's independence from Spain. Liberals or conservatives, criollos, mestizos, or gachupines, most of New Spain's colonists and colonial officials agreed it was time to become Mexicans, and in 1821 they did.

From political independence to cultural independence. In 1821 Mexico was no longer a colony of Spain, but in many ways it was still Spanish. The conservative leader of the independence movement, General Agustín de Iturbide, made himself emperor, and he set to work creating an elaborate royal court and distributing busts of himself in public buildings. Emperor Agustín's Spanish-style monarchy, however, failed to address serious Mexican problems, chief among them the economic instability caused by the devastation of the war. As a result, only ten months after his reign began, Agustín was forced out of power by a group of military leaders.

Soon the monarchy was replaced by a republic modeled on the United States (though Catholicism was still the only religion permitted). This new form of government was not a guarantee of stability, however. A rift quickly developed between two political groups within the new republic. Liberals supported states' rights, freedom of the press and religion, public education free of Church control, and equal rights for Mexicans of all classes and races. Conservatives, on the other hand, wanted a strong central government, a censored press, an exclusively Catholic country, Church-run education, and a class system that preserved the rule of the elite. As these two groups struggled for control of Mexico, economic problems persisted. Few solutions could be effectively implemented because as soon as one group gained power, it would replace all government personnel and rewrite laws and parts of the constitution to reflect its views. For most of the 1800s this political instability continued, although the Reform movement of the 1850s produced a liberal constitution, the Constitution of 1857, with more staying power than previous ones.

The Mexican Revolution. The liberal reforms detailed in the Constitution of 1857 promised more to Mexico's citizens than was delivered. Toward the end of the century, under the 34-year rule of Porfirio Díaz, a president-cum-dictator who claimed to be a liberal, the Catholic Church retained most of its power, the free exchange of ideas was violently suppressed, and grave social inequalities persisted. While Díaz was able to bring economic stability to the country, the benefits of this stability did not extend to large numbers of Mexicans.

In November 1910 Francisco Madero, a liberal-minded hacienda owner, called for a national uprising against Díaz. Tired of Díaz's abuses of power and anxious for reform, Mexicans gradually joined the fight. For some, the Revolution was about improving public education, curtailing Church power, or enacting fair labor laws. For others, like the peasants who fought behind agrarian reformer Emiliano Zapata, it was about getting back their land from the government-sponsored criollos who had seized it.

The many different goals of the Revolution made it long, devastating, and complicated. As they came to power, rebels would seize the presidency and implement some of the changes they had fought for, but these changes were never sufficient to quell the fighting of remaining factions, and the government changed hands frequently. When the fighting finally stopped in 1920, 15 million people had died, and much of the country was in ruins. During the next two decades, however, more of the ideas they had died for—those legislated in the Constitution of 1917—were implemented by the Mexican government.

The Ateneo confronts positivism. The driving force behind the Díaz dictatorship (1876-1910) was the philosophy of positivism. Based on the work of the French thinker August Comte, who stressed notions of order and progress, Díaz's brand of positivism extolled the use of science to explain and solve all manners of social and financial problems in Mexico. Thus, his advisors became known as *científicos* (scientists). While the science of economics certainly aided Díaz's efforts to bring financial stability to Mexico, the social science that his regime subscribed to was more suspect. Along with Comte's ideas, the científicos adopted the internationally popular social Darwinist notions of Herbert Spencer. Citing the doctrine of "survival of the fittest," the ciéntificos justified the marginalization of Indian peasants. The ciéntificos argued that Indians were genetically inferior to criollos and therefore destined to die out eventually, so the government should not waste its resources on educating them or protecting their supposed rights. Given this attitude, it comes as no surprise that during the Díaz regime powerful criollos continued to seize land from Indians and to otherwise mistreat them.

PACHUCOS AND THE ZOOT-SUIT RIOTS

While Mexico was establishing friendlier relations with the United States, relations between many Mexican Americans and Anglo Americans in the United States were strained. One common target of Anglo criticism at this time was the *pachuco*—the rebellious Mexican American teenage type who dressed in a flashy zoot suit. The pachuco is described by Paz in the first chapter of *The Labyrinth of Solitude*; though not detailed in his essay, the zoot suit ensemble consisted of colorful tailored shirts, tapered coats, baggy pants that narrowed at the ankles, shiny shoes, wide-brimmed porkpie hats, and ducktail haircuts. In the summer of 1943 pachucos in Los Angeles, considered by many local police to be innately violent, or predisposed "to kill, or at least to let blood" (Ayres in Gutiérrez, p. 125), became involved in a series of violent encounters with American servicemen that became known as the "Zoot-Suit Riots." Although scores of Mexican American young men were arrested during these encounters for disturbing the peace, it was later discovered that the servicemen had initiated the violence.

Little more than a year before the Mexican Revolution began, a group of young scholars formed the "Ateneo de la Juventud," or "Youth Atheneum," to promote a philosophical alternative to positivism. Disturbed by the abuses perpetrated by Díaz in the name of positivism and by the científicos's reliance on foreign modes of thought, the Ateneo sought to return Mexican culture to its Indian and Spanish origins and to change education policy to reflect this return. Including such figures as artist Diego Rivera and essayists José Vasconcelos, Alfonso Reyes, and Antonio Caso, the Ateneo was encouraged by Justo Sierra, Diaz's anti-positivist minister of public instruction and fine arts; thanks to Sierra's influence, this group had a major impact on the direction of Mexican arts and education in the 20th century.

Mexico in 1950. When Paz writes in *The Labyrinth of Solitude* about "present day" Mexico, he is speaking of a country caught between an agrarian past and an increasingly industrial future, and also a country experiencing major social changes. In the 1940s the Mexican government invested heavily in resources in industry and infrastructure, adding new refineries, pipelines, and wells to Pemex, the national oil company, and extending national rail and highway networks considerably. Irrigation projects under President Miguel Alemán (1946-52) converted thousands of hectares of desert into farmland and used dams to triple Mexico's production of electrical energy. On the social front, a literacy initiative brought the percentage of illiterate Mexicans down from 58 to 42.5. And in 1943 President Manuel Ávila Camacho established Mexico's first social security system.

Despite this progress, however, problems remained. Mexico's agricultural production could not match the rate of population increase; food shortages in 1943 and 1944 led to riots. Political corruption on the local, state, and national levels was common, with bribes and payoffs influencing government policy and contracts.

Another major change in 1940s Mexico, for better or for worse, was its increased involvement in foreign affairs. After the bombing of Pearl Harbor in 1941, Mexico ended diplomatic relations with Japan, and in 1942, after a German submarine attack on two of its tankers, Mexico entered World War II on the side of the United States and other Allied powers. This act was just one example of Mexico's increasing cooperation with the United States. In 1943 President Ávila Camacho initiated the *bracero* (hired hand) program with U.S. President Franklin D. Roosevelt. This program brought Mexican laborers to the United States to perform agricultural and railroad jobs left vacant because of the war. Many Mexican businesses were also stimulated by the war, supplying Allied military forces with necessary raw materials such as copper and rubber. Not every business arrangement between Mexico and the United States was a fair deal, however, nor were the profits of all Mexican businesses justly distributed. During the 1940s, despite a growing middle class, a significant gap between Mexico's rich and poor remained.

The Essay in Focus

Contents summary. *The Labyrinth of Solitude* consists of nine chapters. In chapters 1 through 4 the essay illustrates Paz's concept of the Mexican character and introduces some universal notions about history and existence that reappear throughout the piece. Chapters 5 through 8 trace Mexico's history, from the conquest of the Aztecs by Cortés to the status of Mexico in the Cold War era—that is, in the post-World War II era of struggle between the United States and the Soviet Union for world leadership. The final chapter, added in the second (1959) edition, explains the full significance of Paz's concept of solitude. Overall, the essay analyzes the collective "unconscious" of Mexico, notions engrained in the people, of which they may be unaware.

In the first chapter of *The Labyrinth of Solitude,* "The *Pachuco* and Other Extremes," Paz introduces the subject of Mexican identity by describing the pachuco, a type of Mexican American adolescent of the 1930s and 1940s who dressed in flashy clothes and rebelled against both his Mexican heritage and his adopted American culture. "His whole being is sheer negative impulse," Paz writes, "a tangle of contradictions, an enigma" (*Labyrinth of Solitude,* p. 14). While the pachuco represents an extreme, Paz nevertheless uses him to symbolize the alienation and uprootedness of Mexicans in general. After sketching a few differences between the North American and the Mexican character, Paz concludes the chapter with some thoughts about solitude, hope, and the search for meaning—thoughts he applies not just to Mexico but to all of humanity.

In the next three chapters, "Mexican Masks," "The Day of the Dead," and "The Sons of La Malinche," Paz describes some fundamental aspects of the Mexican's hidden character. Gradually the following picture of the Mexican man emerges: he is distant, guarded, disingenuous, and suspicious, and speaks in metaphors and unfinished phrases to protect himself from being understood too well. He represses his true feelings until moments of explosion, such as fiestas or acts of passion or violence. His greatest fear is that he might be "opened," or violated, by someone else, as his symbolic mother, La Malinche (Cortés's Indian mistress), was violated by Cortés. Because of La Malinche's betrayal of her Indian culture by coupling with a Spaniard, the Mexican man rejects her and thus must confront life as an orphan, separated from his origins. Under a mask of stoicism, he "locks himself up in" the resulting solitude (*Labyrinth of Solitude,* p. 64).

In Chapters 5 through 8 of *The Labyrinth of Solitude,* Paz's focus shifts from psychological description to historical analysis. In an attempt to understand how Mexicans' solitude came about and "how we have attempted to transcend our solitude" (*Labyrinth of Solitude,* p. 88), Paz considers the significance of major events in Mexican history in regard to the Mexican psyche.

In Chapter 5, "The Conquest and Colonialism," Paz traces the Mexican sense of orphanhood to the Aztecs' betrayal by the gods when they were conquered by Cortés. He goes on to defend some aspects of Spanish colonialism in Mexico, especially its ability to unite previously diverse cultures under a common government and religion. But he also critiques the "sterility" of Spanish colonial Catholicism by telling the story of Sor Juana Inés de la Cruz's persecution by the Church for her intellectual endeavors. The experience of Sor Juana taught Mexicans, he concludes, that "to be ourselves, we had to break with [the] exitless [colonial] order, even at the risk of becoming orphans" (*Labyrinth of Solitude,* p. 116).

In Chapter 6, "From Independence to the Revolution," Paz describes the break with colonial traditions as a long, difficult process that extended far beyond the moment in which Mexico gained its political independence from Spain. Although the War for Independence began primarily as a class war, Paz explains, its goals were essentially reversed when the conservative opponents of newly liberalized Spain chose to make it their war as well; rather than reducing inequalities between the classes, the separation from Spain actually helped to preserve the status quo of class power in Mexico. In the decades following independence, other elements of colonial society also proved difficult to relinquish. Liberal reformers, attempting to create a Mexico modeled on the United States, fought against conservatives, who looked to the traditions of Europe for guidance. In the end, Paz explains, the reform movement gave "true meaning" to the independence movement by negating Mexico's Spanish heritage, its pre-colonial past, and its Catholicism; Mexicans were orphaned again, this time by a "necessary matricide" (*Labyrinth of Solitude,* p. 126). In addition, their own social tensions remained, leading inevitably to the Mexican Revolution, "an explosive and authentic revelation of our real nature"—an "opening out" (*Labyrinth of Solitude,* p. 135).

In Chapter 7, "The Mexican Intelligentsia," Paz discusses the history of Mexican writing about Mexico, describing the contributions of the republic's great thinkers to an understanding of Mexican identity and to the nation's ongoing attempt to transcend its historical solitude. Paz determines that "the Mexican intelligentsia has not been able to resolve the conflict between the insufficiencies of our tradition and our need and desire for universality" (*Labyrinth of Solitude,* p. 168). However, in the emotional aftermath of World War II people of all nations now confront a common alienation and must invent a common future.

Chapter 8, "The Present Day," begins with some reflections on the accomplishments and failures of the Mexican Revolution and the persistent problem of rural poverty in Mexico. Paz then describes the changes in Mexico's economy and society in recent years and explains the challenges that his country faces in its attempt to reduce the financial gap between itself and the "advanced" nations of the world. Finally, Paz discusses the current worldwide political situation, stressing the increasing importance of formerly peripheral countries in determining the course of world history. For the first time in more than 300 years, he declares, Latin Americans are ceasing to be the objects and starting to be the agents of historical change.

In the final chapter, "The Dialectic of Solitude," Paz develops his thoughts about solitude into a treatise on love, history, and myth. "Solitude is the profoundest fact of the human condition," he begins. "[Man's] nature . . . consists in his longing to realize himself in another" (*Labyrinth of Solitude,* p. 195). It is solitude that makes love possible, for if we did not feel alone we would not seek companionship. Love relationships require a constant motion between self and other, a cycle of departure from one world to the creation or re-creation of another (a process akin to the Mexican man opening himself). This cycle is mirrored, Paz contends, in the history of all societies. According to one myth, he writes, "we have been expelled from the center of the world and are condemned to search for it through jungles and deserts or in the underground mazes of the labyrinth" (*Labyrinth of Solitude,* p. 209). Societies' attempts to save themselves from the real nightmares of history are often predicated on the dream of returning to this "center of the world," where time stops and history becomes myth. However, until such a return is possible, Paz concludes, contemporary society must find a new way of participating in the world.

An ongoing debate. Though Paz's essay on the Mexican personality joins others by previous essayists, such as Samuel Ramos (who will be discussed later), it goes beyond their attempts to define Mexicanness by concerning itself also with the Mexican connection to the universal human condition. A sentence in the seventh chapter shows this concern: "The whole history of Mexico, from the Conquest to the Revolution, can be regarded as a search for our own selves, which have been deformed or disguised by alien institutions, and for a form that will express them" (*Labyrinth of Solitude,* p. 166). Just a few pages later, Paz concludes the chapter with the following thought:

> Ever since World War II we have been aware that the self-creation demanded of us by our national realities is no different from that which similar realities are demanding of others. The past has left us orphans, as it has the rest of the planet, and we must join together in inventing our common future.
>
> (*Labyrinth of Solitude,* p. 173)

Together, these two quotes seem puzzling. If, on the one hand, Mexicans have been seeking for years to free themselves from foreign influence, or "alien institutions," why would Paz propose that Mexico "join together" with other countries to invent a common future? These ostensibly contradictory concepts reflect a central tension within Paz's essay—a tension between "Mexicanism" and universalism.

In the decades following the Mexican Revolution, a wave of nationalism spread across Mexico, sweeping up many intellectuals in its path. In order to help rebuild their war-torn country, "many who might have been complacent office holders or 'pure' intellectuals or alienated reformers were thrust into public roles of improvisation and reconstruction" (Morse in Bethell, p. 35). Those who did write fiction wrote mainly about Mexico—novels about the Mexican Revolution were especially popular—and writers like the *Contemporáneos* group (see "Literary context") who expressed an interest in the literary experimentation going on in Europe and the United States were dismissed as elitist, Europeanizing, and sometimes even "effeminate" (Morse in Bethell, p. 36).

Octavio Paz was a young poet in Mexico in the 1930s, and it is clear that even then he was confronting the tension between nationalism and universalism. He collaborated for a while with the Contemporáneos and learned a great deal from them about poetry; as he became increasingly involved in Mexican politics, however, he broke with them, determining that he could not separate his poetry from his Mexican nationalism.

When Paz began writing *The Labyrinth of Solitude* in Paris a decade later, in the 1940s, he was a more mature poet with an attachment to the universal ideas of Surrealism about love and poetry. He was also a Mexican who had lived outside his country for many years. Whatever effect these circumstances had on his essay, the result was a careful synthesis of nationalistic ideas about Mexicanism and universal ideas about humankind. In the end, the essay connects the two sets of ideas with the notion that, by confronting one's Mexicanness, one can reach the universal: Although the identities of Mexico and of Mexicans are unique, both consist of a series of masks, added to by the passing of history. When the series of masks are removed and Mexicans and their country must face their nakedness, they will discover their true universality. In Paz's words, "Mexicanism will become a mask, which, when taken off, reveals at last the genuine human being it disguised" (*Labyrinth of Solitude,* p. 171). It follows that this would relieve the solitude Paz perceives as plaguing Mexicans in his own time.

Surrealism in post-war France. Although Paz writes about 1940s Mexico in *The Labyrinth of Solitude,* he actually saw very few of the changes he describes. From 1945 to 1951, after spending two years in the United States, Paz lived in Paris, where he worked as a cultural attaché. The Paris of this time was a demoralized place; it had survived the Nazi occupation and bombing attacks of World War II, but a feeling of desolation pervaded the city. Paz was not immune to this feeling; fortunately he befriended a Parisian poet who helped him to cope. This poet, André Breton, was at the center of a literary and artistic movement known as Surrealism. In an attempt to convey the workings of the subconscious, the Surrealists experimented with techniques such as "automatic writing" (writing devoid of conscious thought) and produced art with fantastic, dreamlike images. For the Surrealists, poetry and love had an almost religious power; each had an ability to restore one's inner life—an ability that was especially necessary in postwar France. While the Surrealists acknowledged that poetry and love could not change the world, they were convinced that both could save them from despair. As Breton writes in a 1948 poem, "The poetic embrace / like the flesh embrace / as long as it lasts / forbids all fall into the world's misery" (Breton in Wilson, p. 40).

Paz's involvement with Breton's Surrealist group in France had an obvious impact on the concept of poetry and love in the essay's final chapter, "The Dialectic of Solitude." Just as Breton envisioned poetry and love as a means of preventing those who create them from falling into the world's misery, Paz's essay describes love (or "true erotic communion") as a transformative experience that we must struggle to find in the face of society's and history's attempts to frustrate it. The essay's debt to Breton is clear when it explains how poetry and love both provide exits from the labyrinth of solitude.

Literary context. Octavio Paz drew on the work of Mexican and European writers in composing *The Labyrinth of Solitude.* Essays on Mexican identity were common in the era of the Ateneo scholars, and Paz discusses the work of two Ateneo essayists, José Vasconcelos and Alfonso Reyes, in his chapter on the Mexican intelligentsia. Another group of young men that helped to establish Mexico's essayistic tradition was known as the Contemporáneos Group. Writing in the journal *Contemporáneos* in the 1920s, these young men, including Jorge Cuesta, argued for a cosmopolitan Mexican literature that did not lose sight of its Mexican roots but also reflected some of the literary experiments and innovation going on at the time in Europe and the United States. Paz likely had the work of this group in mind when he wrote *Labyrinth.*

More influential, however, was the work of Samuel Ramos. In constructing his essay, Paz borrows most substantially from Ramos's 1934 *Profile of Man and Culture in Mexico.* Ramos's book is a psychological exploration of Mexican character that discusses the Mexican's inferiority complex and "masked" identity. The similarities between Ramos's and Paz's approaches led one critic writing in 1959 to accuse Paz of neglecting to credit Ramos sufficiently for his ideas. Paz does mention Ramos's work often in *The Labyrinth of Solitude,* but usually as a starting point for his own observations. In a response to this critic, Paz explains the main difference between their work as follows: Ramos "does not touch Mexican history or the Mexican's vital relationship with certain universal ideologies. . . . He is not interested in situating us in the world" (Paz in Wilson, p. 52).

Reviews. The year in which the first edition of *The Labyrinth of Solitude* appeared (1950), Mexico was still in the midst of a nationalist revival, so Paz's universalist notions were not well received. Mexican critics pointed to a trend in Paz's poetry and prose toward obscurity, elitism, and Europeanization.

When the English translation of the second edition was published in 1961, however, the book received more positive international reviews. One British critic praised the "lucid, thoughtful, provocative" history in the book while faulting the "psycho-literary generalities" in which Paz indulges to "cover his uncertainty" about whether he can accurately define his country (Wood in Foster and Ramos Foster, pp. 173-74). But other reviewers responded to the essay with more wholehearted applause. One critic writing in the journal *Américas* shared the sentiments of many when he described the essay as "some of the most profound pages that have been written about the soul of [Paz's] people" (Durand in Foster and Ramos Foster, p. 170). Another critic praised the essay's blend of myth and concrete reality, explaining that the image of Mexico that Paz creates is "truer than the profound truths it reveals for presenting them in a mythos made entirely beautiful" (Christ in Foster and Ramos Foster, p. 177). Its beauty and power were recognized again in 1990, when *The Labyrinth of Solitude* was cited as one of the major reasons for awarding Paz the Nobel Prize for Literature.

—Allison Weisz

For More Information

Aguilar Camín, Héctor, and Lorenzo Meyer. *In the Shadow of the Mexican Revolution: Contemporary Mexican History, 1910-1989.* Trans. Luis Alberto Fierro. Austin: University of Texas Press, 1993.

Bethell, Leslie, ed. *The Cambridge History of Latin America.* Vol. 10. Cambridge: Cambridge University Press, 1995.

Foster, David William, and Virginia Ramos Foster, eds. *Modern Latin American Literature: A Library of Literary Criticism.* Vol. 2. New York: Frederick Ungar, 1975.

Gutiérrez, David G. *Walls and Mirrors: Mexican Americans, Mexican Immigrants, and the Politics of Ethnicity.* Berkeley: University of California Press, 1995.

MacLachlan, Colin M., and Jaime E. Rodriguez O. *The Forging of the Cosmic Race: A Reinterpretation of Colonial Mexico.* Berkeley: University of California Press, 1980.

Miller, Robert Ryal. *Mexico: A History.* Norman: University of Oklahoma, 1985.

Paz, Octavio. *The Labyrinth of Solitude and Other Writings.* Trans. Lysander Kemp, Yara Milos, and Rachel Phillips Belash. New York: Grove Press, 1985.

———. *Sor Juana or, The Traps of Faith.* Trans. Margaret Sayers Peden. Cambridge, Mass.: Harvard University Press, 1988.

Werner, Michael S., ed. *Encyclopedia of Mexico: History, Society, and Culture.* 2 vols. Chicago: Fitzroy Dearborn, 1997.

Wilson, Jason. *Octavio Paz.* Boston: Twayne, 1986.

Like Water for Chocolate

by
Laura Esquivel

> **THE LITERARY WORK**
>
> A novel set in Coahuila, on the U.S.-Mexico border, from 1910 to 1934; published in Spanish (as *Como agua para chocolate*) in 1989, in English in 1992.
>
> **SYNOPSIS**
>
> A middle-class Mexican woman at the time of the Revolution subverts traditional skills to achieve her desires.

Born in 1950 in Mexico, Laura Esquivel began her career as a screenwriter in partnership with her husband at the time, the director Alfonso Arau. *Like Water for Chocolate* was Esquivel's first novel, and it almost immediately propelled her to international fame, with translations into over 30 languages and some 3 million copies sold worldwide. The 1992 film based on the book, whose screenplay was written by Esquivel herself, became the largest grossing foreign film ever released in the United States. Simultaneously defending traditional female activities while subverting stereotypical notions of femininity, *Like Water for Chocolate* shows how revolutionary historical processes can also resonate in everyday life.

Events in History at the Time the Novel Takes Place

The Mexican Revolution. The Mexican Revolution (1910-20) brought profound political and economic change to Mexico. The revolution was rooted in the changes created by rapid economic growth under the dictatorship of Porfirio Díaz (1876-1911). During this period, economic development was achieved at the cost of brutal repression, foreign control of most industries, and increasing social polarization. Burgeoning middle classes sought political and economic advancement from which they were largely barred by the entrenched political establishment of the Porfirian regime. The rural poor suffered too. Rising land values motivated rich landowners to expand their holdings and push small landholders off their property. An 1883 land law that required proof of land ownership resulted in the seizure of millions of acres of private and communal lands by government-supported land companies. *Haciendas,* or large privately owned estates, grew at the expense of small holders, turning many of them into peasants who labored on a hacienda for wages. Their payment might consist of advances in food and clothing or of a lease on land to work for themselves on their time off, for which they became indebted. By 1910 over one-half of all Mexicans worked in debt peonage on the haciendas, or large estates, of a few wealthy families (Meyer and Sherman, pp. 457-58). A worldwide depression from 1907 to 1909, followed by Díaz's decision to remain in the presidency after having promised to step down, pushed the crisis to the boiling point. The revolution began in late 1910 in the northern states but soon extended to the entire country. Díaz abdicated and went into exile in 1911, but the coalition of revolutionary forces soon broke down into factions. By the time the fighting finally began to subside in the 1920s, all the major leaders had been killed and some 1.5 to 2 million Mexicans had also died—one in every eight people. Many more were wounded, and tens of thousands migrated to the United States. On a single day in October 1913, more than 8,000 refugees crossed the border from Piedras Negras, Coahuila, to Eagle Pass, Texas (Meyer and Sherman pp. 552, 554). Civilian populations were often caught in the crossfire, and it was not uncommon for the women who were left behind to be targets of rape, as shown in the novel (Esquivel, *Like Water for Chocolate,* p. 129). In many ways difficult, the period was also the defining moment for Mexican history, in which the people were finally able to forge a truly national identity.

LIKE WATER FOR CHOCOLATE

Hot chocolate, often made with water and not milk in Mexico, has been consumed in the area at least since the thirteenth century, having been part of the indigenous diet long before the arrival of the Spaniards. The expression "like water for chocolate" translates roughly as "water at the boiling point" and describes a situation so tense that it is on the verge of exploding. In *Like Water for Chocolate* this expression is mostly related to frustrated passion. However, the fact that the novel takes place precisely on the Mexican-U.S. border between Piedras Negras and Eagle Pass, and that the story begins in the crucial year of 1910, also suggests a society at the boiling point.

A changing role for women. Although harshly criticized in the popular press, a small number of Mexican women by the 1890s had entered previously male-dominated fields, such as dentistry, medicine, law, pharmacy, higher education, and journalism. A commercial school for women opened in 1903 and its classes filled immediately. Despite such advances, however, the official rhetoric of domesticity encouraged women to limit their sphere of activity to the home. Legally, moreover, women were considered inferiors with no constitutional rights. They were idealized in women's magazines and sentimental literature, but treated as non-citizens outside the home. Under the 1884 Civil Code, Mexican women had no rights; they could not even legally move from one city to another without the permission of a male guardian: father, husband, brother, or son.

When the Revolution swept the country, thousands of women left their homes and joined the struggle as spies, arms smugglers, and, most importantly, as soldiers' companions, or *soldaderas.* The soldaderas were an essential support for revolutionary troops: they cooked, cleaned, nursed the wounded, and buried the dead. Many women served in the ranks and in a few cases became officers and leaders. As Michael Meyer notes, "in an oblique and unintended sort of way the Revolution contributed to the emancipation of the Mexican woman" (Meyer and Sherman, p. 557). Although in reality soldaderas were never fully integrated into post-revolutionary society, the female revolutionary was romanticized and immortalized in song and popular culture. Films, often based on these folk ballads, or *corridos,* further consolidated the popular mythology of the female soldier, and it is this image to which Esquivel most obviously makes reference in her novel; classic images of the soldadera portrayed by María Felíx appeared in the films *La escondida* (1955), *Cafe Cólón* (1958), *La cucaracha* (1958), and *La generala* (1970).

The sentimentalization of womanhood. *Like Water for Chocolate* is divided into 12 chapters, each preceded by a recipe corresponding to the action that follows. This structure is derived from the tradition of women's magazines that first came into vogue during the mid-nineteenth century. These periodicals, sometimes called "calendars for young ladies," included, like Esquivel's novel, recipes, home remedies, and, often, serialized sentimental novels in monthly installments. As María Elena Valdés points out, these novels usually had a domestic setting and were "highly coded in an authentic woman's language of inference and reference to the commonplaces of the kitchen and the home" (Valdés, p. 81). Although these formulaic stories were never considered "literature" by the cultural establishment, such publications conserved and transmitted women's experiences. At the same time, however, these magazines fostered an attitude towards women that further limited their role since the primary purpose of such publications was to instruct women "in minute detail on how to be and act, what to do and think, and, especially, what they as superior beings might never aspire to" (Aldaraca, p. 63). During this time, writers, both male and female, promulgated a "sentimentalization of womanhood" whereby women were

Soldaderas cooking for revolutionary troops, 1913.

ostensibly elevated as the moral guardians of the home. For middle-class men, to have a wife at home was a way to keep up appearances, an entrance into polite society. In a more general sense, the sentimentalization of womanhood was designed to prevent women's entrance into public spheres of influence, the margins of which they had increasingly come to challenge by the mid-nineteenth century.

In *Like Water for Chocolate* the superficiality of this cult of domesticity is typified by Tita's mother, Elena, and her older sister, Rosaura, who, although by all appearances conform to the roles expected of them, become caricatures due to their blind acceptance of the imposed regulations on female behavior. Elena, who rules her home with an iron fist and has a set phrase memorized for every occasion, is far more concerned with the "proper" way of performing tasks than with the actual creativity involved in making the product. In an early episode, when Tita sews without basting first, her mother makes her rip out the stitches and start again, even though her creation "was the most perfect" (*Like Water for Chocolate,* p. 12). For her part, although she is genuinely upset when her husband Pedro refuses to make love to her, Rosaura's primary concern is with the appearance of decency. While Rosaura's resistance to change literally causes her to rot from within and eventually die, her sisters, Gertrudis and Tita, both respond to the revolutionary changes around them in their own ways. Sexually liberated Gertrudis leaves the home and takes an active role in the Revolution. Tita's revolution, in contrast, is more personal, and is, in fact, not fully realized until the next generation of women, represented by her niece. Rosaura insists that she will continue a family tradition and retain her only daughter as her caretaker until the end of her days; in fact, she even considers naming her daughter after Tita. But Tita envisions a different future for the child and names her Esperanza (Hope). As Esquivel notes in an interview, Esperanza represents "our collective hope, [she] was going to the university to study, she was going to have it all" (Esquivel in Loewenstein, p. 604). Significantly, it is for Esperanza, and not for Tita, that the traditional happy ending is reserved.

Cookbooks and the discourse of nationalism. The relationship between cooking and national identity was most marked during the first century of Mexican independence. Mexican cookbooks written during the nineteenth century—primarily by male authors—were nationalistic both in their narrative and in the recipes included. Authors ostensibly sought to differentiate Mexican cuisine from European cooking. Nonetheless, the elite classes continued to prefer

European dishes over native foods. Jeffrey Pilcher reports that in one book supposedly "accommodated for the Mexican palate" not a single recipe for tamales, enchiladas, or quesadillas was included, and, in fact, a popular 1845 publication actually condemned the consumption of tamales as immoral, since this food belonged to the "lower orders" (Pilcher in Bower, pp. 207-08). This passion for European (and, especially, French) cuisine reached an ironic apex under Porfirio Díaz when, among the scores of state celebrations and banquets in honor of the centennial of Mexican independence, not a single national dish was included on the menu. Cookbooks by women, in contrast, were considerably less concerned with class and ethnic lines. One woman's cookbook from 1912 gave more recipes for enchiladas than for any other dish; and Vicenta Torres's widely distributed 1896 cooking manual included pre-Hispanic recipes, promising her readers that these "secrets of the indigenous classes" would be appropriate for any social occasion (Pilcher in Bower, pp. 202-05, 213). In this way women brought traditional Mexican cooking into the mainstream, anticipating, in a way, the radical recuperation of the indigenous past that would later form the foundation of the Mexican cultural revolution.

A REVOLUTION IN THE KITCHEN

"Nineteenth century Mexican elites . . . used instructional literature to attempt to mold a patriarchal nation based on Western European models. Cooking manuals contributed to this identity by assigning women to a domestic role within the nation and spelling out acceptable cultural (eating) practices. But standards of domestic morality and national identity created by male authors did not necessarily reach a complaisant female audience. Indeed, community cookbooks produced by women in Porfirian Mexico imagined an alternate vision of the nation and of the female place within it."

(Pilcher in Bower, p. 209)

The Novel in Focus

Plot summary. *Like Water for Chocolate* takes place on a ranch in northern Mexico at the time of the Revolution. Just as the country is in a state of flux, the De la Garza family must also adapt to changing times. Fifteen-year-old Tita is in love with Pedro Múzquiz, but, as the youngest daughter, an idiosyncratic family tradition dictates that she must care for her mother, Elena. Unable to marry Tita, Pedro weds her older sister, Rosaura, to be close to his beloved. Gertrudis, the middle sister, runs off with a revolutionary soldier and is disowned by her mother when she is discovered working in a brothel; she subsequently distinguishes herself on the battlefield and becomes a revolutionary general. Rosaura, the oldest sister, is the least sympathetic of the three De la Garza sisters. Although she ostensibly conforms to societal expectations, she can neither nurse nor care for her children and is a disaster in the kitchen. When Rosaura is unable to care for her newborn son, Roberto, Tita assumes caretaking responsibilities for the child, and miraculously produces milk from her own breast. The birth of Roberto brings Pedro and Tita closer together and, sensing the charged atmosphere, Elena insists that Pedro and Rosaura relocate to San Antonio, Texas. Separated from the aunt who has been feeding him, the child dies, and Tita suffers an emotional breakdown. The family doctor, John Brown, is summoned to take the girl to an asylum. But, because he is secretly in love with Tita, rather than complying with Elena's request, he brings her to live with him, and she eventually recovers.

Meanwhile, the ranch has been caught in revolutionary crossfire, leaving Elena paralyzed. Tita returns home to care for her mother, but Elena, who believes that Tita is trying to slowly poison her dies soon after from a self-induced attack of vomiting. Going through her mother's belongings, Tita discovers that Elena too had a tragic love affair and had been forced to marry someone she did not love. Tita also discovers that her sister, Gertrudis, is the product of this forbidden love. Tita vows that she will never renounce love, and thinks for a time that she will marry John Brown, but, after Elena's death, Pedro and Rosaura have returned to the ranch with a second child, Esperanza, and Tita secretly consummates her love with Pedro. In the final chapter, the action of the novel shifts to several years later. Rosaura has died of flatulence and her daughter, Esperanza, is marrying Alex, the son of John Brown. After the wedding guests have left, Pedro and Tita openly give full rein to their pleasure for the first time. Pedro dies at the moment of climax, and to join him Tita must rekindle the flame of passion. To do so, she swallows some candles (in the English translation; in the Spanish original, she swallows matches). Their bodies grow so inflamed at the moment of her death that the entire ranch burns. When Esperanza returns from her honeymoon, she recovers Tita's recipe book, which is also the story of her life. Esperanza's daughter, the narrator of the novel, inherits this book upon her mother's death.

Recipes for reading. Esquivel situates her novel during the Revolution, at a specific historical moment (1910) in which the nineteenth-century values of Porfirian Mexico were overturned. The narration clearly privileges the ancient oral tradition of female knowledge bequeathed to Tita by Nacha, the indigenous woman who serves as the family's cook, over the artificial rules of conduct upheld by Elena and reproduced by Rosaura. Tita, unable to marry the man she loves due to an outdated rule of conduct, battles throughout the novel with imposed conventions and her own desires: "[S]he couldn't resist the temptation to violate the oh-so-rigid rules her mother imposed in the kitchen . . . and in life" (*Like Water for Chocolate,* p. 198). That Tita feels circumscribed by this textually mediated tradition is indicated by her vehement rejection of Manuel Antonio Carreño's *Manual de urbanidad y buenas maneras* (Manual of Courtesy and Good Manners), a popular manual on etiquette that demarcates proper behaviors in every detail of human activity. "Damn good manners!" she complains. "Damn Carreño's etiquette manual! Both were to blame that her body was hopelessly destined to wither away, little by little" (*Like Water for Chocolate,* p. 58). There is a concern here for individual desire over social propriety that positions Tita's discourse as a kind of alternate "formula" that lies outside the "recipes" dictated by society.

The pleasure of the text. Esquivel has said that she wrote *Like Water for Chocolate* through the eyes of a camera, and this visual dimension is clearly evident in the novel (Esquivel in Loewenstein, p. 595). The author invites the reader to reassess conventional approaches to literature and to experience a pleasure in reading, through flagrant sight-gags, such as when Tita drops the apricots on Pedro's head, the huge quilt she knits, and especially by the scents, tastes, colors, and textures of food (*Like Water for Chocolate,* pp. 31-32). Food functions as a narrative device in the novel, transporting both the characters and the reader into a sensual dimension of reality. Esquivel's playful approach to food is further underscored as Tita describes her emotional and physical state in terms of culinary metaphors that make fun of both the "seriousness" of canonized discourse and the time-worn metaphors of popular literature: "[I]t was then that she understood how dough feels when it is plunged into boiling oil"; "She felt so lost and lonely! One last chile in walnut sauce left on the platter after a fancy dinner couldn't feel any worse than she did" (*Like Water for Chocolate,* pp. 16, 57-58). At the same time, these metaphors from the kitchen, along with the recipes and household remedies that frame the narrative, have a more serious aim. With them Esquivel is able to rescue the neglected oral tradition of female discourse by creating a chain of characters through which the story (and the recipes) have been handed down. Thus, although the novel revolves around a love story, Tita's awakening as a woman does not depend on men but, rather, upon her own realization of this ancient legacy. But Tita does something more than continue tradition: she invents her own recipes and she writes them down, along with the story of her life. In this way the novel shows that, just as there are exterior revolutions that can change the course of a nation, there are interior revolutions that each person can create for him or herself. For the narrator, the recipient of this written inheritance, her great-aunt Tita's culinary creations are nothing short of

NINETEENTH-CENTURY ETIQUETTE

Manuel Antonio Carreño's *Manual de urbanidad y buenas maneras* dictated proper behavior for men and especially for women, upon whom the reputation of the family resided.

> The woman contains in her being all that is beautiful and interesting in human nature. . . . But nature has conceded her this privilege at the cost of great deprivations and sacrifices, and exceedingly serious obligations to morality and to society; and while it is true that in her the qualities of good breeding may shine with greater brilliance, it is also true that . . . even insignificant defects that may pass unnoticed in a man stand out in her like the slightest stain on crystal. . . . And so, young women who are cultured . . . must draw sustenance only from that knowledge which is most useful for such a precious ornament; that her heart, born to make men happy, must proceed to its noble destiny on the path of religion and honor.
>
> (Carreño, p. 49; trans. K. Ibsen)

A Mexican kitchen from around the turn of the century.

poetry. Associating domestic activities with the act of writing forces us to recognize the importance of these tasks while at the same time opening a "feminine" space of discourse. As Cecelia Lawless explains:

> Tita . . . uses the kitchen and the recipe to expand the confines of the site and to set up her own discursive territoriality from which to voice herself as subject. She makes the private become a realm for the public by sharing her recipes with those in the house and outside of it, as well as with the readers of her story. Through the reusing of space—the kitchen—and language—the recipe—Tita builds community.
>
> (Lawless in Bower, p. 228)

Sources and literary context. As Esquivel explains, the novel's focus on the art of cooking and the sensorial dimension of food mirrors her own background. She fondly recalls the aromas of her grandmother's and her mother's kitchens. Although the fictional De la Garza family tradition of the youngest daughter becoming the mother's caretaker is not drawn from real life, concern with female-centered traditions is. Esquivel describes herself as someone who protested rules that she thought unfair to women.

> We weren't allowed to wear pants in school, so we fought to be able to wear them. And we thought that was change. But, I tell you, in all of that I did sometimes forget some essential elements and that's when I had to rediscover all that was happening in the home. . . . [I]t was my own experiences that I wanted to transmit when I wrote *Like Water for Chocolate*.
>
> (Esquivel in Loewenstein, p. 603)

In contrast to other novels set during the Mexican Revolution, *Like Water for Chocolate* centers on a woman, Tita. That this personal perspective is posited as an alternative to official historical discourse, is demonstrated by the chapter in which Gertrudis escapes with a revolutionary. The episode differs from literary precursors about such relationships in that it is a parody: Esquivel plays not only with the almost supernatural sexual potency that other Latin American novelists have imagined for their male protagonists but also with the consecrated—and highly masculine—tradition of literature about the Mexican Revolution. Tita is, in effect, writing her own version of history. From her perspective, the romantic encounter is more important than the events taking place on the battlefield, even though she knows that official history will remember the incident differently: "Tita saw the incident from a completely different perspective than the rebel soldiers. She watched the whole thing from the patio as she was washing dishes" (*Like Water for Chocolate,* p. 56). By recontextualizing history from Tita's point of view, the novel suggests that social transformation took place not only in the military engagements recorded in history books on the Mexican Revolution, but also in more subtle, personal, and even hidden ways.

Popular influences. Sentimental novels of the Mexican nineteenth century were written principally by women and for a female public. Esquivel's novel rescues these marginalized literary forms and reinforces the idea of a community of women. In addition, since many of the typical elements of women's novels from the nineteenth century have been continued in twentieth-century romance novels (*novelas rosas*) and serialized television programs (*telenovelas*), the conventions Esquivel has appropriated from popular discourse will be easily recognized by present-day readers. Nonetheless, and although *Like Water for Chocolate* seemingly replicates popular forms on the surface, a deliberate inversion of roles has been effected that allows the author to appropriate and challenge elements from this genre. One obvious variation from the norm is that, unlike the characters in standard romance fiction, in which passivity is considered a virtue, in Esquivel's novel the female characters are stronger and more decisive than their male counterparts. The head of the family is a woman, one of the sisters becomes a general in the revolution, and it is Tita, not Pedro, who eventually dares to stand up to her mother and to Rosaura as well. Pedro, in contrast, is portrayed as weak and indecisive and, even as an adult, subject to petty jealousies. Although he loves Tita, he does not challenge her mother's decision that Rosaura be his bride. As if there were any doubt that the playful inversion of masculine and feminine characteristics is intentional, Pedro refuses to consummate his relation with Rosaura until months after the wedding, and when he finally relents, he recites to God: "Lord this is not lust nor lewdness, but to make a child to serve you" (*Like Water for Chocolate,* p. 40). John Brown also incarnates certain characteristics more generally associated with women. He is patient, nurturing, and long-suffering. His intuition surprises Tita on more than one occasion, and like the stereotypical self-sacrificing woman, he waits a lifetime for Tita only to ultimately give her up to Pedro. Even in the traditionally female domain of the kitchen, Esquivel questions the rigidity of conventional roles. Since recipes are a code to which only women normally have access, it is possible to speak of a female variety of language suggested by culinary discourse. Nonetheless, Esquivel is careful to note that such language is not biologically determined but learned through oral tradition. Thus, when Gertrudis attempts to read a recipe, although she is a woman she is unable to decipher its code: "Gertrudis read the recipe as if she were reading hieroglyphics" (*Like Water for Chocolate,* p. 192). In a further inversion of anticipated gender roles, it is a man under her command, Sargent Treviño, who manages to decode the words and successfully prepare the desired product.

SOR JUANA INÉS DE LA CRUZ ON THE ART OF COOKING

Although Sor Juana Inés de la Cruz (1651-95) was a brilliant intellectual and the greatest poet of her time, she was restricted by authorities who disapproved of women's entrance into the traditionally male domain of learning (see **"Reply to Sor Philothea,"** also covered in *Latin American Literature and Its Times*). When a pious abbess did not allow Sor Juana to read or write, she found renewed inspiration and creativity in everyday life, discovering cooking ("women's work") to be an art and a science of monumental import.

> What could I not tell you . . . of the secrets of nature I have discovered while cooking! That an egg holds together and fries in fat or oil, and that, on the contrary, it disintegrates in syrup. That to keep sugar liquid, it suffices to add the tiniest bit of water in which a quince or some other fruit has soaked. But . . . what is there for us women to know, if not bits of kitchen philosophy? . . . And I always say, when I see these details: If Aristotle had been a cook, he would have written much more.
>
> (Juana Inés de la Cruz, pp. 225-26)

As Cecelia Lawless notes, we rarely see men at work in the novel (Lawless in Bower, p. 233). Indeed, the male characters in *Like Water for Chocolate* are of such secondary importance that they are never described in physical detail, whereas the female body is frequently lauded. The fact that details of the male anatomy are excluded from the narration is perhaps consistent with a more feminine vision of romance that privileged idealistic or spiritual attraction over graphic explicitness. A careful reading of the text, moreover, reveals that every instance in which the female body is described in hyperbolic detail represents a moment in which the perspective of the episode has shifted to a male character. In such passages, Esquivel evokes the male gaze by which a female is converted into "woman"; her parody of the overwrought nineteenth-century prose is at its most exaggerated at these times. For example, it is through Juan's gaze that the nude Gertrudis is evoked as "an angel and devil in one woman" and when Pedro inadvertently walks in on a bare-breasted Tita nursing his child it is his vision that transforms her into "Ceres herself, goddess of plenty" (*Like Water for Chocolate,* pp. 55, 76). Bridget Aldaraca notes that one of the results of the sentimentalization of womanhood during the nineteenth century was, precisely, that women became "often perceived not as individual but as genre" (Aldaraca, p. 66). Esquivel has adroitly taken this tradition and used it to differentiate between the textually mediated archetypes of "woman" and the real experiences of women. Real women, the novel shows, may have "masculine" attributes such as strength and courage, just as real men may show "feminine," nurturing sides. It is this balance, the novel suggests, that allows each individual to break free of societal restrictions and stereotypic gender roles.

Events in History at the Time the Novel was Written

Evolution of women's rights. Founded in Mexico City in 1935, the United Front for Women's Rights counted a membership of over 50,000 by 1940. With the support of President Lázaro Cárdenas (1934-40), women won the right to vote in many states, although national suffrage was not granted until 1955. Mexico guaranteed women equal job opportunities, salaries, and legal standing in 1974, but traditional attitudes toward women continued to lag behind these constitutional victories. Significantly, the action of *Like Water for Chocolate* ends with Tita's death in 1934, the year Cárdenas came to power. Cárdenas's presidency represented perhaps the highest moment of revolutionary change but also the time in which the one-party rule of the *Partido Revolucionario Institucional* (Institutional Revolutionary Party, or PRI) was fully consolidated.

Late-twentieth-century literary currents. When *Like Water for Chocolate* was first published in 1989, Mexico was in the midst of another important period of change. With the formation in 1988 of the *Partido Democrático Revolucionario* (Revolutionary Democratic Party, PRD) by Cárdenas's son, Cuáhtemoc Cárdenas, Mexico's ruling party, PRI, faced its first major threat since 1968, when student protests had ended in a massacre in the plaza of Tlatelolco (see Elena Poniatowska's ***Massacre in Mexico,*** also covered in *Latin American Literature and Its Times*). In literature this renewed questioning of the established order in the 1980s and early 1990s focused less on larger political issues and more on the defense of individual rights. In the same way, many women writers sought another angle that was subversive but not overtly political, that was feminine but not necessarily feminist. As in *Like Water for Chocolate,* in novels such as Poniatowska's *Querido Diego, te abraza Quiela* (1978, translated as *Dear Diego*) and, especially, Ángeles Mastretta's *Arráncame la vida* (1985, translated as *Mexican Bolero*), official history functions as a backdrop but not as the central focus of the novel. These novels also share with Esquivel's text the integration into literary discourse of popular or private discourses specifically associated with women (the sentimental novel, boleros, recipes, letters). Laura Esquivel has said that inside every recipe there is a piece of the personal history of a family. In *Like Water for Chocolate,* recipes have the symbolic function of being a personal record of history from the perspective of the periphery.

At the same time, by situating her novel in the revolutionary period, Esquivel looks nostalgically at the early idealism of the Revolution at a time when President Carlos Salinas de Gortari (1988-94) was dismantling its sacred icons and pressing the nation to become part of the capitalist world order. The election of Salinas in 1988 and the subsequent implementation of the North American Free Trade Agreement (NAFTA) between Mexico, Canada, and the United States in 1994 brought to a head the modernizing economic policies of the Mexican government that had increasingly encouraged foreign investment at the expense—many believed—of the Mexican people and their traditions. The tension between tradition and modernity experienced by Tita is not unlike the choices faced by modern-day Mexico as it is forced to compromise revolutionary ideals and historic traditions in favor of U.S.-style capitalism. The economic crisis, urban violence, and continued unrest in the indigenous communities of the southern state of Chiapas all bear witness to the difficulties this transition has entailed.

Reviews. The initial reaction to *Like Water for Chocolate* in Mexico was largely negative. Typical of the often hostile reception within the Mexican cultural press, Antonio Marquet condemned the novel as "simplistic," "infantile," and "full of banal conventionalisms" (Marquet, p. 58). Marquet believed the novel's main purpose was to satisfy "feminine sexual fantasies" such as matricide, prostitution, and exhibitionism (Marquet, pp. 64-65). For his part, Guillermo Fadanelli criticized the novel's "overworked and facile phrases," which he attributed to the author's "inability to create anything better" (Fadanelli, p. 4). Some of the academics in Mexico dismissed the work as a poor imitation of the male canon.

In contrast, the novel was generally well-received by critics in the United States. Writing for the *Los Angeles Times Book Review,* Karen Stabiner described *Like Water for Chocolate* as a wondrous and romantic tale. James Polk, in a review for the *Chicago Tribune,* hailed it as "an inventive and mischievous romp" (Polk, p. 8). In like manner, other U.S. reviewers described the novel as a joyful reading experience.

Despite its precarious beginning, *Like Water for Chocolate* has continued to attract the interest of scholars. By 1998 it had been the subject of some 40 academic articles, an impressive response to a Mexican novel published less than ten years earlier.

—Kristine Ibsen

For More Information

Aldaraca, Bridget. "El ángel del hogar: The cult of domesticity in nineteenth-century Spain." In *Theory and Practice of Feminist Literary Criticism.* Ed. Gabriela Mora and Karen S. Van Hooft. Ypsilanti, Mich.: Bilingual Press, 1977.

Bower, Anne L., ed. *Recipes for Reading: Community Cookbooks, Stories, Histories.* Amherst: University of Massachusetts Press, 1997.

Carreño, Manuel Antonio. *Manual de urbanidad y buenas maneras, para uso de la juventud de ambos sexos.* New York: Appleton, 1854.

Esquivel, Laura. *Like Water for Chocolate: A Novel in Monthly Installments with Recipes, Romances and Home Remedies.* Trans. Carol and Thomas Christensen. New York: Doubleday, 1992.

Juana Inés de la Cruz, Sister. *A Sor Juana Anthology.* Trans. Alan Trueblood. Cambridge, Mass.: Harvard University Press, 1988.

Fadanelli, Guillermo. "La literatura a la que estamos condenados." *Unomásuno* (April 28, 1990): 4.

Ibsen, Kristine. "On Recipes, Reading and Revolution: Postboom Parody in *Como agua para chocolate.*" *Hispanic Review* 63, no. 2 (1995): 133-46.

Loewenstein, Claudia. "Revolución interior al exterior: An Interview with Laura Esquivel." *Southwest Review* 79, no. 4 (1994): 592-608.

Marquet, Antonio. "La receta de Laura Esquivel: ¿Cómo escribir un best-seller?" *Plural* 237 (1991): 58-67.

Meyer, Michael C., and William L. Sherman. *The Course of Mexican History.* 4th ed. New York: Oxford University Press, 1991.

Polk, James. Review of *Like Water for Chocolate. Chicago Tribune,* October 18, 1992, 8.

Stabiner, Karen. Review of *Like Water for Chocolate. Los Angeles Times Book Review,* November 1, 1992, 6.

Valdés, María Elena de. "Verbal and visual representation of women: *Como agua para chocolate/Like Water for Chocolate.*" *World Literature Today* 69, no. 1 (1995): 78-83.

Macho Camacho's Beat

by
Luis Rafael Sánchez

Luis Rafael Sánchez was born on November 17, 1936, in Humacao, Puerto Rico. Sánchez spent his childhood in Humacao and his adolescence and youth in San Juan. After receiving a bachelor's degree from the University of Puerto Rico and a master's degree from New York University, Sánchez went to Spain where he obtained his Ph.D. from the Complutense University of Madrid. Having established himself as one of Puerto Rico's most prominent intellectuals and successful playwrights during the 1960s and 1970s, Sánchez first ventured into novels with *Macho Camacho's Beat,* which breaks away from earlier Puerto Rican texts in its experimental form and exploration of the island's sociopolitical conflicts. It achieves this largely through a focus on the role of mass media (radio, cinema, television, advertisements) and on the plurality and instability of language (Spanish, English, local Spanglish) in everyday Puerto Rican life.

THE LITERARY WORK

A novel set in San Juan, Puerto Rico, during the early 1970s; published in Spanish (as *La guaracha del Macho Camacho*) in 1976, in English in 1980.

SYNOPSIS

The novel intertwines vignettes about several characters from different social classes with the voice of a disc jockey who reminds readers about the popularity of a new *guaracha* tune by musician Macho Camacho, the main refrain of which is "Life is a Phenomenal Thing." The vignettes take place simultaneously on a Wednesday afternoon around 5:00 p.m. during a traffic jam in which two of the main characters are trapped.

Events in History at the Time the Novel Takes Place

A short history of colonialism in Puerto Rico. In 1493, during his second journey to the Americas, Christopher Columbus claimed Puerto Rico—then called Borikén by its native Taíno Indian inhabitants—for the Spanish empire. Like most of the rest of Latin America, Puerto Rico underwent processes of conquest and colonization that included the exploitation of its natural resources, the extinction of its native inhabitants, and the importation of African slaves to replace the extinct natives.

Many of the national and cultural characteristics of today's Puerto Rico emerged during the four centuries of Spanish domination (1493-1898). Although some of these characteristics can be seen as Spain's exclusive legacy (e.g., the Spanish language and the predominance of Catholicism), it is crucial to remember that they are part of a hybridization process involving the various cultures that converged on the island during this period—primarily, but not exclusively, the African, the Spanish, and to a lesser degree the Taíno cultures. After the extinction of the Indians, the concept that Spaniards and other whites were superior continued to dominate the island, as manifested in the racism towards African slaves or dark-skinned citizens, and in the "official" culture's contempt for African traditions.

The year 1898 marked a shift in Puerto Rico's status as a colony. This shift, however, did not signify the independence of the island; it represented only a change in the colonizing power. As a result of the Spanish-American War, Puerto Rico—along with Guam, the Philippines, and, until 1902, Cuba—became a colonial territory of the United States. Once more Puerto Rico's social, political, and economic structures were transformed, this time to accommodate the exigencies of the United States.

After Puerto Ricans had lived for almost two years under a military government, the U.S. Congress passed the Foraker Act, which instituted a civil government in Puerto Rico. This act allowed Puerto Ricans to elect a resident commissioner, who would represent their interests in the United States; in 1904 this commissioner became a nonvoting delegate in the U.S. House of Representatives. In 1902 the Official Languages Act stated that both English and Spanish could be used as official languages in all official and public activities.

Puerto Rico became a U.S. military bastion: the most prominent U.S. military bases in the Caribbean were established on the island because of its strategic geographic location. In 1917, in view of the possibility that it would be participating in World War I, the United States granted Puerto Ricans U.S. citizenship through the Jones Act. This maneuver made it possible for the United States to draft Puerto Rican islanders into the U.S. military. The Jones Act also changed Puerto Rico's governmental structure, introducing the separation of the executive, legislative, and judicial branches. While the governor and other official functionaries would be named by the U.S. president, Puerto Ricans had the right to choose those who were to belong to two newly created legislative bodies: the Senate (19 elected members) and the House of Representatives (39 elected members). The Jones Act did not make any mention of the island's political status.

In the 1940s and 1950s Puerto Ricans migrated in massive numbers to the continental United States in an attempt to improve their economic situation; over 100,000 made their way to the mainland from 1950 to 1954, when there was a high demand for labor and too few hands because of U.S. involvement in the Korean War. Back in Puerto Rico manufacturing surpassed agriculture as the main source of income in 1955. Prompting this pivotal change was an industrial and social development program known as "Operation Bootstrap," which provided special tax breaks to commercial companies from the United States who wanted to relocate in Puerto Rico, and attracted small, labor-intensive industries to the island. This rapid industrialization led to rapid urbanization, which, in turn, encouraged the adoption of a city-oriented lifestyle. With it came an increasing focus on consumerism. Because there was an insufficient number of jobs to absorb the working-age population, the rural-to-urban shift led also to widespread unemployment on the island.

Related to Operation Bootstrap was Puerto Rico's controversial political status. Ultimately the controversy would surround three positions: should Puerto Rico become independent of the United States, assume the status of statehood within the United States, or have an in-between status? Political events of the late 1940s and early '50s showed an increase in autonomy for Puerto Rico:

1946: Puerto Rico has its first native governor, Jesús T. Piñero, who is nevertheless appointed by the U.S. president.

1947: Through a special amendment to the Jones Act approved by the U.S. Congress, Puerto Ricans are allowed to choose their own governor.

1948: Luis Muñoz Marín (1898-1980) becomes the island's first elected governor and inaugurates the Operation Bootstrap program; he will remain in office until 1964.

1950: The U.S. Congress approves Law 600, which authorizes Puerto Ricans to be governed by their own constitution, which still had to be submitted to the U.S. president and Congress for approval.

1951: A referendum demonstrates Puerto Ricans' acceptance of Law 600, which also establishes Puerto Rico's status as an associate territory of the United States.

1952: The Puerto Rican Constitution is approved. It ratifies the separation of the three governmental branches and expands the numbers in the Senate (from 19 to 27) and House of Representatives (from 31 to 51). Puerto Rico's governor now has the right to select the heads of all the island's departments, which increases autonomy from the United States.

The island continued in the 1950s and 1960s to experience rapid industrialization and urbanization. Puerto Rico's economic development up until today—through North American investment, tourism, and U.S. federal aid—has consolidated the island as a consumerist society, and makes it the "promised land of opportunities" for other Caribbean islanders, like Haitians and Dominicans, whose countries are in less advantageous economic situations and whose citizens end up illegally migrating to Puerto Rico.

Puerto Rico in the late 1960s and early 1970s. The end of the 1960s marked another pivotal turn of events in Puerto Rico's history. A plebiscite to decide the island's status—independence, statehood, or commonwealth—took place in 1967. In the end, the majority (60.5 percent) of the island opted to remain a commonwealth. In 1968 Puerto Rico's first pro-statehood governor, Luis A. Ferré, was elected. While in office, Ferré openly condemned any group that was not politically aligned with a pro-U.S. ideology—in other words, any group that favored independence. The islanders continue to show a preference for remaining a commonwealth, most recently in a plebiscite of December 1998.

Student movements. Student movements at Puerto Rico's universities have long been connected to, though not exclusively determined by, pro-independence ideals. The desire for political and cultural autonomy from the United States has found its way into the many demonstrations staged at Puerto Rican universities. In 1948 students' rights to engage in political activities at the University of Puerto Rico (UPR) were suspended because of disturbances that occurred after university officials banned a campus speech by Pedro Albizu Campos, one of Puerto Rico's most important nationalist leaders (Trillin, p. 124). The suspension of these rights remained in force until 1970.

By the end of the 1960s and the beginning of the 1970s, the majority of students at the various UPR campuses (as well as at other private universities and community colleges) had organized to protest U.S. intervention in Vietnam, the mandatory draft of Puerto Rican youth for this unpopular war, and the presence of the Reserve Officers' Training Corps (ROTC) on UPR campuses. One of the more vocal groups in these demonstrations was the FUPI or *Federación Universitaria Pro-Independencia* (Pro-Independence University Federation), which had been created in 1956. At the UPR's main campus, which is located in Río Piedras, part of San Juan's larger metropolitan area, the student movement's main center of activity during this time had moved from the College of Humanities to the College of Social Sciences—hence, the reference in *Macho Camacho's Beat* both to the FUPI and a bombing in this part of the Río Piedras campus (Trillin, p. 124).

DEFINING THE COMMONWEALTH

As a commonwealth Puerto Rico retains control of its internal affairs, in which the United States may not intervene. It is exempt from U.S. tax laws but has only limited representation in Congress. Puerto Rico does not have a representative in the U.S. Senate and, while it sends a Puerto Rican Resident Commissioner to the U.S. House of Representatives, this commissioner does not enjoy full voting privileges. Similarly Puerto Ricans themselves do not have full voting privileges in U.S. elections; they can vote in national party primary elections but not in presidential elections. Executive power in Puerto Rico resides in its governor, who is elected for four years, and rules with the help of a cabinet of 17 appointed secretaries and Puerto Rico's two-house legislature.

Social conditions. In 1970 a total of 2,712,022 people inhabited the 3,435 square miles that constitute the island of Puerto Rico. This figure would go up almost 18 percent during the next decade (to 3,196,520 inhabitants). By 1970 more Puerto Ricans lived in urban areas than in rural ones. As the 1980 census indicated, 67 percent of the population, or 2 of every 3 people, lived in cities (Silvestrini and Luque de Sánchez, p. 580). The rapid industrialization that took place after the 1950s, the decay of agriculture, and the high unemployment rate in the interior of the island explain much of the rural-urban migration. Unfortunately in many cases such migration did not lead to economic progress. The lack of employment and material alternatives in the cities as well as the emphasis that urban life placed on consumerism and the use of imported products (by 1980 the total amount of money spent on imported products was $2,450 million out of which $300 million was spent on cars and $1,041 million on food) accelerated the growth of slums and other areas of extreme poverty (Silvestrini and Luque de Sánchez, pp. 582, 586-87). By the early 1970s close to half of all city houses were new structures (built since 1960) and equipped with conveniences such as

Students jailed after disturbances at the University of Puerto Rico in 1948. The students had been demanding the resignation of Jaimé Benitez, the school's dean. As a result of such incidents, students' rights to engage in political activities were suspended for over two decades.

electricity, refrigerators, and indoor toilets, although only about 33 percent of the homes in cities had telephones at this point. Making up about 10 percent of the population, middle- and upper-class members earned $10,000 or more a year. Meanwhile, close to another half of the homes in Puerto Rico were substandard dwellings, and 42 percent of the island's families earned less than $3,000 a year (Wagenheim, p. 177). Such families would rent shacks in one of the slum areas for about $23 a month. "Despite poverty and high levels of violence," notes one historian, "the general mood in [the slum] La Perla is one of gaiety. There is constant noise from radios, jukeboxes, and television sets" (Wagenheim, p. 179).

Popular culture and mass media in Puerto Rico. *Macho Camacho's Beat* explores the role of popular culture in everyday life and the pervasiveness of mass media in Puerto Rican society. The novel constantly refers to cultural phenomena, such as the fictional *guaracha* of Macho Camacho as well as "real" television shows (*El hijo de Ángela María, El Show de Iris Chacón*), actors (Bette Davis, Libertad Lamarque, Madeline Willemsen), singers (Tom Jones, Juan Manuel Serrat, Danny Rivera), newspapers (*El Mundo, El Nuevo Día*), and magazines (*Time, Vea, Estrellitas*).

Associated with the question of national identity, how to define Puerto Rican culture, especially popular culture, has been a subject of constant debate. The earliest examples of Puerto Rican popular culture were related to Afro-Caribbean groups. These expressions of popular culture were eventually substituted for another kind of "whiter" popular culture, connected to the *jíbaro* (or the rural farm worker) and nostalgia for an agrarian past. Puerto Rican cultural and governmental institutions adopted the jíbaro as the official spokesman of popular culture, displacing other cultural legacies, especially those related to Afro-Caribbean cultures.

The appearance of *salsa* as a popular musical genre during the 1960s reclaimed and brought to the foreground Afro-Caribbean cultural manifestations in Puerto Rico. Of Cuban origin, this popular style of music (see description below) incorporated Puerto Rican elements as it evolved. Salsa illustrated how forms of popular culture were coming together with mass media at the time. The fusion was apparent not only in the way radio and television stations heavily incorporated salsa into their programming to broaden their audiences, but also in the creation of a new musical industry with its own labels (such as Fania Records) dedicated to salsa (Manuel, pp.

73-74). Salsa's close relationship with other Afro-Caribbean rhythms, such as the Cuban *son* and Puerto Rican *bomba* and *plena,* and to the marginalization experienced by Puerto Ricans in New York, who greatly influenced this music, made it particularly popular among certain sectors of society, such as the lower classes.

Guaracha and salsa music. Guaracha music originated in Spanish theater as an accompaniment to a dance performed by one dancer. It is thought that guaracha's appearance in Puerto Rico is linked to frequent visits of Cuban *bufo* theater companies to the island during the nineteenth century. Generally speaking, guaracha is "an up-tempo genre of Cuba and, subsequently, Puerto Rico, originally with a light, often satirical or bawdy text and verse-chorus form" (Manuel, p. 250). Its fast and lively pace and rhythmic structure are similar to those of the son, another kind of Cuban music that emerged from a mixture of Spanish-derived and Afro-Cuban elements (Manuel, p. 36). The similarity between son and guaracha is important since both eventually became the foundation for salsa music. By the late 1960s and early 1970s salsa and its performers were taking over the Puerto Rican musical scene (as well as those of other places, such as Venezuela), after having emerged as "a new musical movement that could at once embrace Puerto Rican tradition and capture the spirit of the [New York Latino] barrio in all its alienated energy and heightened self-awareness" (Manuel, p. 73). For example, in 1968 one of Puerto Rico's most popular radio stations, WKAQ, changed its format from news broadcasting to only salsa. Salsa singers resurrected guaracha music and played it either in its original form or as an adaptation that incorporated various elements tied to the musical genre that was emerging during that time.

The Novel in Focus

Plot summary. *Macho Camacho's Beat* opens with a note that establishes the repetition (of words, phrases, and sounds) that recurs throughout the novel. It also provides a brief explanation of what the book is about:

> *Macho Camacho's Beat* tells the story of the flattering success of Macho Camacho's guaracha *Life is a Phenomenal Thing,* according to information received from disk jockeys, announcers, and microphoniacs. It also tells of some of the miserable and splendid ups and downs in the lives of certain supporters and detractors of Macho Camacho's guaracha *Life is a Phenomenal Thing.* Furthermore, as an appendix to *Macho Camacho's Beat,* transcribed in its entirety is the text of Macho Camacho's guaracha *Life is a Phenomenal Thing,* so as to afford unsurpassed delight to collectors of all-time musical hits.
>
> (Sánchez, *Macho Camacho's Beat,* p. 3)

After this note, the novel is divided into 20 short sections that give readers the perspectives of the main characters: Mother/Heathen Chinky; her son, the Kid; her neighbor, Doña Chon; her lover, The Old Man/Senator Vicente Reinosa; his wife, Graciela Alcántara y Lopéz de Montefrío; and their son, Benny. Each section is divided into short paragraphs that revolve mainly around a particular character but that can nevertheless include the intervention of other characters as well as the narrator. Every section includes a constant play of first-person point of view, through which readers gain insight into the characters' lives, with third-person narration that comments on the characters. Between the sections is a short paragraph that represents the voice of a radio announcer/disc jockey. Invariably the paragraph concerns Macho Camacho and his guaracha: how popular the song is, how talented the artist is, how incomparable he is in relation to other artists of the moment, and so forth. For example: "AND LADIES AND gentlemen, friends, this man sits down one day and writes a guaracha that is the

THE MARTÍN PEÑA CHANNEL

By the early 1970s one of the most notorious slums in Puerto Rico was located along the Martín Peña Channel in San Juan. The area, characterized by marshes and stagnant waters, housed more than 71,000 people in 14,000 tightly packed homes (Wagenheim, p. 178). Though the slum's existence harked back to the Depression of the 1930s, it grew rapidly in the 1950s. Most of Martín Peña's scrap wood and metal shacks were built illegally on public land, and most lacked indoor sanitary facilities. The area was inaccessible to garbage pickup trucks, so refuse and human waste filled the channel. Such conditions partly explain why by the early 1970s "the Martín Peña slum [had San Juan's] highest infant mortality rate, the greatest number of welfare cases, the highest rates of tuberculosis, pneumonia, delinquency, and violence" (Wagenheim, p. 178). Three of the characters in *Macho Camacho's Beat,* Heathen Chinky, the Kid, and Doña Chon, live in the Martín Peña slum area.

mother of all guarachas, sweet, neat, a treat. And that guaracha because it's so true is going up to the heaven of fame, into the first rank of popularity . . ." (*Macho Camacho's Beat,* p. 79). The overall novel has five different storylines that are intertwined throughout the book.

Storyline #1. Heathen Chinky waits for her lover, The Old Man, to arrive. Segments 1, 6, 11, and 16 present a view of Heathen Chinky's world, including her poor house in the Martín Peña Channel, her sexual prowess, and her passion for popular culture, especially for dancer Iris Chacón and for Macho Camacho's guaracha. This storyline discloses her perspective on her relationship with Senator Vicente Reinosa (whom she always calls The Old Man). For the last six months they have been meeting to have sex every Monday, Wednesday, and Friday during the afternoon. She thinks about this relationship more as a desirable business transaction than as prostitution: "The Old Man passes me pesos but people who pass me pesos are people I want to pass me pesos" (*Macho Camacho's Beat,* p. 9). Although she does not like the situation, her survival depends on maintaining it: "I'll get out of debt and I'll tell him to. One more month and" (*Macho Camacho's Beat,* p. 169). She dreams of becoming a rich and famous entertainer with the name of The Lobster Lady. While waiting for The Old Man, Heathen Chinky drinks *cubalibres* (rum and coke) and has two different erotic fantasies. The first concerns an early sexual encounter (while she was still a pre-adolescent) with her three cousins Hughie, Louie, and Dewey; the second concerns her recent accidental encounter with one of her cousins and the sexual adventures that ensued.

Storyline #2. Senator Vicente Reinosa is caught up in traffic on his way to a sexual encounter with his lover, Heathen Chinky. Through segments 2, 7, 12, and 17, readers get to know the character of Vicente, a 45-year-old Puerto Rican senator who thinks that "elegance, oratory and women are his forte" (*Macho Camacho's Beat,* p. 22). Much to his dismay, at some point Vicente finds himself humming Macho Camacho's guaracha while stuck in traffic. What he considers to be an embarrassing moment is interrupted by news that a bomb has exploded at the Social Science Building of the University of Puerto Rico. The episode exposes the senator's contempt for people with strong nationalist views as well as his desire for more power: he wants to become the governor of Puerto Rico.

Storyline #3. Graciela Alcántara y Lopéz de Montefrío sits in the waiting room of her psychiatrist, Dr. Severo Severino. In segments 3, 8, 13, and 18, the focus of the story is on Graciela as she awaits her psychiatric session. Not much happens during these segments. She glances at *Time* magazine and becomes fascinated with a photograph of Elizabeth Taylor and Richard Burton's house in Puerto Vallarta, Mexico. This photograph reminds her of how miserable she feels about living in Puerto Rico after having studied in Switzerland. She looks down upon everything outside the realm of her high-class life, especially Macho Camacho's guaracha, a song she deems to be the lowest of the low. When she finally goes in to talk to Dr. Severino, she asks him if he likes this guaracha. Much to her dismay, he answers "yes."

Storyline #4. Doña Chon and The Mother talk about life while The Kid is being tormented by other children in a park. These four segments—4, 9, 14, 19—are set in two different places: The Mother's house, where she spends time with her neighbor, Doña Chon, and a nearby park, where The Mother has left her mentally challenged three-year-old son, The Kid, sunbathing to see if he gets better. The action in The Mother's house takes place in the kitchen where The Mother and Doña Chon talk about food, life, money, motherhood, and the injustices that poor people like them have to endure. By the end of their conversation, The Mother, who has an appointment with The Old Man, asks Doña Chon if she could go to the park and bring The Kid back. Meanwhile, in the park, The Kid is being tormented by other children who taunt and abuse him since he cannot fight back. At some point, one of the children takes a mirror and puts it in front of The Kid's face. Horrified at his image, The Kid runs away from the park.

Storyline # 5. In his Ferrari, Benny is caught in the same traffic jam as his father. In segments 5, 10, 15, and 20, the novel focuses on the senator's son, a rich, arrogant teenager whose main concerns revolve around his new Ferrari. He contemplates the lack of good race tracks in Puerto Rico for cars like his. As he gets more frustrated with the traffic jam, Benny condescendingly thinks about the futility of studying, especially about his experience at the University of Puerto Rico, where professors want to make him think critically. Benny also reminisces about two of his evil adventures with friends Bonny, Billy, and Willy. The first involves the bombing of the "offices of the separatists, antisocial scum, the offices and workshops where they print and do their presswork, poisoning nordophilic sentiments" (*Macho Camacho's Beat,* p. 156). The second adventure involves burning a prostitute's genitals and how that action, which landed them in court but not in jail, became the reason that his parents gave him a Ferrari (as a way of making him feel better about having had to go to court). At some point, Benny finds an opening in the traffic and starts to drive away from it by using small surface streets. Traveling 80 miles an hour on one of these narrow streets, he runs over The Kid while Doña Chon screams at the sight. The segment ends with Benny thinking about having to wash the blood of this child off his Ferrari.

The novel closes with the full text of Macho Camacho's guaracha:

> LIFE IS A PHENOMENAL THING
> Life is a phenomenal thing,
> frontwards or backwards, however you swing.
> But life is also a groovy street, it's coffee for
> breakfast and bread that you eat.
> Oh, yes, life is a nice chubby chick
> spoiling herself in a Cadillac trick.
> The trumpet breaking up the ball,
> don't let the maracas back down,
> the drums heard way across town,
> the thing can't have any stop,
> black women want sweat to mop,
> black women are getting hot.
> (*Macho Camacho's Beat,* p. 211)

Type characters. In an interview Luis Rafael Sánchez explains that *Macho Camacho's Beat* has "type characters . . . all of them physically, morally and spiritually off the wall" (Sánchez, Interview, p. 39). Roughly speaking, the novel's six principal characters can be divided into two main groups: the Mother/Heathen Chinky, the Kid, and Doña Chon, all of whom belong to the Island's lower class, while Senator Vicente Reinosa/the Old Man, Graciela, and Benny are part of Puerto Rico's wealthy and powerful sector. These characters represent certain social characteristics extant in everyday life on the island in the early 1970s that relate to "the spiritual decomposition of Puerto Rico; a condition revealed in the inability to communicate our most inner feelings" (Sánchez, Interview, p. 39). In the novel the various ways in which each of the characters relates to Macho Camacho's guaracha serve as markers of their social differences.

The upper-class characters. Broadly speaking, Senator Vicente Reinosa/The Old Man represents a number of disagreeable behaviors: machismo, greed, materialism, political hypocrisy, abuse of power, and colonial mentality or acquiesence to colonial perceptions of hierarchy. His fetish for black and mulatto women exposes the persistence of some of the biases inherited from Spanish and American colonialism, which explain why a powerful man like him is married to a fair-skinned woman and takes a mulatto woman as his lover.

Senator Vicente Reinosa's political views demonstrate how reactionary he has become; he shows a preference for U.S. colonial domination. Anything related to understanding Puerto Rico as a country with its own national identity is out of the picture for him. The most difficult part of his political career has been to feign a liking for those toward whom he feels contempt: poor people. He displays his true colors in response to Macho Camacho's guaracha (the anthem of the disenfranchised in Puerto Rico): to him, the tune is "repulsive . . . a tiara of vulgarity, a headdress of trash, a banner of the rabble" (*Macho Camacho's Beat,* p. 77).

The senator's wife, Graciela Alcántara y Lopéz de Montefrío, is a repressed, frigid woman whose life centers upon social appearances, the acquisition of material commodities, and an extreme hatred for anything that deviates from her social class and her education in Switzerland. Her displeasure with Puerto Rico and its lower class exemplifies her colonized mentality. Everything related to Europe or a life of opulence is acceptable to her; anything else falls out of her ideal conception of the world. In keeping with this attitude, Graciela cannot stand Macho Camacho's guaracha, a song she calls "a street-corner hymn, a repulsive hymn, a hymn of the mob" (*Macho Camacho's Beat,* p. 185). She even prohibits her servants from playing it in her house. Although her husband agrees with her about how repulsive the song is, he reprimands her for expressing her class-conscious views out loud, since those who have elected him are, in fact, poor people who live in slums.

From the start, Benny, son to Graciela and the senator, is presented as a rich, spoiled teenager who has no respect for humankind. Acknowledging his own selfishness, Benny says, "don't ask me for anything because I'm not the giving type" (*Macho Camacho's Beat,* p. 101). His inhumanity surfaces especially at the end of the novel, when he runs over The Kid and does not even stop to see what happened:

> It wasn't my fault to some brains splattered on the door of the Ferrari and to some eyes plopped in the gutter like the yolks of half-fried eggs. Benny doesn't hear frights. Benny doesn't

A slum district in San Juan.

> hear laments. Benny doesn't feel the afternoon breathing with difficulty. . . . Benny asks, rusty, hurried by his hurry: I mean when will I be able to wash my Ferrari?: the voice shrill and rancor hurting him.
>
> (*Macho Camacho's Beat,* pp. 209-10)

Like his parents, Benny cares mainly about appearances and material goods, especially his new Ferrari. He is obsessed with his car and totally devoid of knowledge about Puerto Rican culture or society. He wants only to "have my Ferrari to feel at home in Puerto Rico" (*Macho Camacho's Beat,* p. 106). His insensitivity surfaces in his attitude toward Macho Camacho, whom he calls "that monkey-faced nigger" (*Macho Camacho's Beat,* p. 58). The slur demonstrates Benny's bigoted mentality and his prejudiced upbringing.

The lower-class characters. The Mother/Heathen Chinky, a poor mulatto woman, is the main focus through which readers can question issues related to marginalization in terms of race, gender, and class. Her nickname, Heathen Chinky, comes from the lyrics of the popular singer Felipe Rodríguez (*Macho Camacho's Beat,* p. 47). For The Mother, sex and other activities that directly involve her body (e.g., eating, dancing) are vital ways of enjoying and experiencing life to the maximum: "My thing is to eat and to ball" (*Macho Camacho's Beat,* p. 146). Specifically, The Mother takes immense pleasure from hearing Macho Camacho's guaracha: "When that guaracha says that life is a phenomenal thing, that's when my brain goes wildest" (*Macho Camacho's Beat,* p. 91).

Doña Chon provides a counterpoint to The Mother at many levels. Doña Chon is not only older and less attractive than Heathen Chinky, but she does not like the expressions of popular mass culture admired by The Mother. Although their moral values are different, Doña Chon is always willing to help The Mother out by taking care of The Kid. Doña Chon's life experiences as a poor woman with a son in jail for drug trafficking become the basis of her particular understanding of life. She is aware of how social class militates against breaks for the poor in matters such as getting caught selling drugs: "For the rich they look the other way. The rich selling grass under the government's nose, offering stuff to everybody and his cousin. . . . For poor people, seven years in the dark" (*Macho Camacho's Beat,* p. 199). Rather than believing that "Life is a Phenomenal Thing," as The Mother does, Doña Chon comes up with her own axiom: "Life is like a bundle of dirty clothes but it's a bundle of problems" (*Macho Camacho's Beat,* p. 147).

The novel does not provide the reader with an insight into The Kid's point of view. Everything about him is conveyed through what other characters and the narrator say about The Kid.

He is almost a nonentity, which is reinforced by the fact that in the novel no relationship whatsoever is established between The Kid and Macho Camacho's guaracha.

The guaracha, then, serves as a fulcrum for various attitudes exposed by characters who are at times almost caricatures. Their separate responses to the guaracha help crystallize Sánchez's conception of several approaches to life that he perceived as existing in 1970s Puerto Rico.

Sources and literary context. The publication of *Macho Camacho's Beat* formed part of the larger cultural transformation that was taking place in Puerto Rico during the 1970s. Artists, writers, critics, and historians of the decade questioned the monolithic culture promoted by Puerto Rican governmental institutions. They intended instead to show the complex realities that coexisted on the island, including the views of traditionally marginalized groups such as women, gays and lesbians, members of the working class, and illegal immigrants. Sánchez sees himself as part of a group of writers who were "undertaking a complete revamping of the novel as a literary form" by legitimizing the language of the people (Sánchez, Interview, p. 41). This acknowledgment of the language of the people as grist for the artistic mill is a means of bridging the gap between "high culture" and "popular cultural forms," also achieved by marrying the genre of the novel to the popular music of the guaracha. The novel, unlike its character Graciela, questions the boundaries between high and popular cultures in Puerto Rico, just as Manuel Puig's ***Kiss of the Spider Woman*** (also covered in *Latin American Literature and Its Times*) did this same year in regard to the two forms of culture in Argentina.

Puerto Rican scholar Carmen Vázquez Arce locates Sánchez as part of a larger generation of Latin American writers known as the *novísimos* (the newest ones) or the *contestatarios del poder* (contesters of power), terms coined by the late Uruguayan critic Ángel Rama. In respect to content, the characteristics that link Sánchez and *Macho Camacho's Beat* to this generation are an examination of the often complex and contradictory contemporary realities of Latin American urban spaces; how these realities might be influenced by U.S. culture; an open exploration of the role of sexuality in society; and the impact of mass media. In respect to style, Vázquez Arce points to Sánchez's use of humor in *Macho Camacho's Beat,* especially through parody and irony (Vázquez Arce, pp. 21-28).

Reviews. *Macho Camacho's Beat* was unanimously praised as an important literary work in Puerto Rico and Latin America. Luis M. Arrigoitia called the novel "the literary event of the year" in Puerto Rico because of its popularity with both critics and readers, who were buying copies of the novel so fast that it was difficult to find it in stores (Arrigoitia, p. 71; trans. G. Blasini).

LANGUAGE IN *MACHO CAMACHO'S BEAT*

In a very literal sense, the Spanish and English languages are both sources for the text of *Macho Camacho's Beat.* Language has been one of the most contested issues in twentieth-century Puerto Rican society. The U.S. takeover in 1898 brought with it the imposition of English as an official language along with Spanish; English eventually became a required second language in schools. Although it is not generally an everyday language, English has been integrated into colloquial Spanish on the island. For example, a person can be *friquiao* (freaking out) or *jangiando* (hanging out). The novel in its Spanish original reflects the mixture in lines like "Foot note sin el foot" [footnote without the foot] (Sánchez, *La guaracha del Macho Camacho,* p. 42). The rhythm created by the language, a conscious attempt to imitate music, is more apparent in the Spanish original than in the English version. The first sentence of the novel, for example, uses 27 "a" sounds in Spanish, but only nine in the English translation (Guinness, p. 107). Beyond its rhythm, language is used in a way that illustrates the condition of Puerto Rican society at the time. "In the novel," explains Sánchez, "you begin to see language in a state of decay. It is an attempt to portray the spiritual decomposition of Puerto Rico; a condition revealed in many of us in our inability to communicate our most intimate feelings" (Sánchez, Interview, p. 39).

Various critics compared Sánchez's novel to James Joyce's *Ulysses* and Virginia Woolf's *Mrs. Dalloway*. Like these novels, *Macho Camacho's Beat* takes place in one day and includes shifting perspectives and a fragmentary structure whose separate elements are not always immediately obvious.

Although they deemed *Macho Camacho's Beat* to be an important novel and a great contribution to Latin American literature, some reviewers were critical of the English version. For example, even though Jerome Charyn stated that *Macho Camacho's Beat* is "a funny, mordant first novel about modern-day Puerto Rico," he ended his review by saying, "I suspect that the music of *Macho Camacho's Beat* is impossible to catch in translation" (Charyn, p. 12). Gerald Guinness echoed Charyn when he stated that "[translator Gregory] Rabassa's English-language version of *La guaracha* fails to convey the feel and texture of the original" (Guinness, p. 121). These questions and comments about the translation mainly revolved around the particular localisms included in the novel. Nevertheless, as Robert Houston observed, *Macho Camacho's Beat* still works for audiences in the United States for two main reasons. In the first place, "the book does that most difficult of things for novels to do. It creates, movingly and vividly, a particular time, a particular place and the people who inhabit that time and place" (Houston, p. 642). In the second place, "*Macho Camacho's Beat* is full of life. And not just the kind of life that is intelligible only to a Latin or Puerto Rican audience. . . . The voices that sing are eminently human, are clearly recognizable, are ours, too" (Houston, p. 644).

—Gilberto M. Blasini

For More Information

Arrigoitia, Luis M. "Una novela escrita en puertorriqueño: *La guaracha del Macho Camacho* de Luis Rafael Sánchez." *Revista de Estudios Hispánicos* 5 (1978): 71-89.

Charyn, Jerome. "Swinging through San Juan." *The New York Times Book Review,* January 18, 1981, 12.

Guiness, Gerald. "*La guaracha* in English: Traduttore Traditore?" *Revista de Estudios Hispánicos* 8 (1981): 107-22.

Houston, Robert. "'Life is a Phenomenal Thing . . .'." *The Nation* 232, no. 20 (May 23, 1981): 642-44.

Manuel, Peter, with Kenneth Bilby and Michael Largey. *Caribbean Currents: Caribbean Music from Rumba to Reggae.* Philadelphia: Temple University Press, 1995.

Sánchez, Luis Rafael. Interview with Helen Calaf Agüera. *Review* 28 (1981): 39-41.

——. *La guaracha del Macho Camacho.* Buenos Aires: Ediciones La Flor, 1976.

——. *Macho Camacho's Beat.* Trans. Gregory Rabassa. New York: Pantheon Books, 1980.

Silvestrini, Blanca G., and María Dolores Luque de Sánchez. *Historia de Puerto Rico: Trayectoria de un pueblo.* San Juan: Cultural Puertorriqeuña, 1987.

Trillin, Calvin. "U.S. Journal: San Juan, Puerto Rico: House of Studies." *The New Yorker* XLV, no. 52 (February 14, 1970): 124-29.

Vázquez Arce, Carmen. *Por la vereda tropical: notas sobre la cuentística de Luis Rafael Sánchez.* Buenos Aires: Ediciones De La Flor, 1994.

Wagenheim, Kal. *Puerto Rico: A Profile.* 2nd ed. New York: Praeger, 1975.

Macunaíma

by
Mário de Andrade

Born on October 9, 1893, Mário de Andrade lived in São Paulo, Brazil, for most of his life, during which the city turned from a backwater into a vibrant center of culture, industry, and commerce. Andrade participated in many of the initiatives that brought the city to cultural prominence. He was a graduate of the Conservatory of Drama and Music, an art critic, and a professor of musicology and aesthetics at the Conservatory. In 1922 he published a landmark book of poetry, *Hallucinated City,* and played an important role in the city's "Modern Art Week," a series of lectures, poetry readings, musical performances, and art exhibits that rocked Brazil's staid literary, artistic, and critical establishment. Andrade helped found the city's Department of Culture and the Brazilian society for Ethnography and Folklore, both of which he headed for a time. He chaired Art History at the newly established University of Rio de Janeiro, and became director of its Art Institute in 1938. Two years later Andrade returned to São Paulo, where he died on February 25, 1945. From his knowledge as a Brazilian musicologist, folklorist, linguist, and poet came his best-known work today, *Macunaíma.*

THE LITERARY WORK

An experimental work set in Brazil in mythic time and in the 1920s; published in Portuguese (as *Macunaíma, o herói sem nenhum caráter*) in 1928, in English in 1984.

SYNOPSIS

Macunaíma, the hero, loses a talisman his wife gave him before she died; to retrieve it, he leaves his native Amazon forest and travels to São Paulo. He kills a giant, recovers the talisman, returns home, and dies, turning into the constellation of the Big Dipper.

Events in History at the Time of the Novel

Brazil in the 1920s. In Brazil, as in the United States, the 1920s was a heady, prosperous period. The city of São Paulo was growing rapidly, and new industries were establishing themselves in and around it, supported by the high prices of coffee, growing entrepreneurship on the part of both traditional landowners and immigrants, and a large population of urban, industrial workers from European countries. In 1920, 17 percent of Brazil's workers were immigrants; the majority of them lived in the south-central part of the country, whose most important city was São Paulo (Topik, p. 173). In the half century between 1871 and 1920 Brazil received around 3.5 million immigrants, the bulk of whom went to the state of São Paulo and the city of Rio de Janeiro; Italians went mostly to São Paulo, where they formed the largest immigrant community and, by the 1920s, a significant percentage of the city's population (Maram, pp. 178-79). The giant from whom Macunaíma must retrieve his talisman is a cannibal industrialist, who is said to be Peruvian of Florentine (Italian) descent; his name and occupation seem to tap into anxiety about massive immigration and the economic modernization that equipped the city with factories and skyscrapers. (An Italian industrialist built Brazil's first skyscraper, known as the Martinelli building; it opened in 1929 and was the highest structure in Latin America at the time.) In the novel, modes of public transportation, telephones, and other technical wonders also intrigue and frighten Macunaíma when he arrives in the big city.

Regional diversity and amalgamation. Between 1889 and 1930 the Brazilian economy was to a large extent fueled by exports, 80 per cent of which were Amazonian rubber and coffee from São Paulo (Topik, p. 6). Yet the Amazonian region remained sparsely populated; though many workers had moved there to extract rubber, they tended to work alone. Some cities, like Manaus, grew and became rich, but the region remained mostly uninhabited. And though there were clashes between rubber extractors and the Indian tribes whose territories they invaded, many Indian groups continued to live in isolation. Anthropologists, however, managed to meet with and study some of these Indian groups. That was the case of the German Theodor Koch-Grünberg, whose study *Vom Roraima zum Orinoco* inspired Mário de Andrade to write *Macunaíma*; its hero is named after a mythic figure of the Taulipang tribe described by the German anthropologist. Many of the stories Macunaíma tells in the Amazon, and many of his adventures there as well as some in the city, derive from the mythology Andrade found in that study. Yet Andrade did not write an anthropological work. His hero is a composite of different Indian tribes and other Brazilian ethnicities; he is meant to be a representative of the Brazilian people, formed by what has been called "the most ample and profound process of miscegenation in the history of humanity" (Brum, p. 24).

In transporting Macunaíma from the Amazon to São Paulo, Andrade makes him suffer an extreme cultural and geographic dislocation from the Neolithic or Stone Age to a twentieth-century city. (According to ethnographers, the Amazon tribes live in a Neolithic material culture, that is, they live as human beings are thought to have lived in the Neolithic era, features of which are the use of stone tools, a nomadic or seminomadic existence, and rudimentary agriculture, if any.) In truth, while not that extreme, the difference between Brazilian cities and most of the rest of the country, where at that time about 84 percent of the population lived, was considerable (Topik, p. 8). Most larger cities (São Paulo being an interesting exception) were ports and export centers, oriented toward Europe both economically and culturally; they did not have at the time a noticeable modernizing influence on the rural part of the country. On his way to São Paulo Macunaíma travels through the rest of Brazil; he covers places in no particular geographic order, described in terms of various characters' locations and traits, in what Andrade calls "degeographication." In the characterization of the country, as in that of his hero, Andrade jumbles together regionalisms and nationalisms, creating an early manifestation of our own time's "globalization." He places plants and animals in areas where they are not native; he says Macunaíma visits a farm in one location, when in reality that farm is situated in another location, and so forth.

Though the novel's geographical mixture sacrifices strict local accuracy for a truer general image of the country, individual details are factual. Andrade provides much ethnographic information in his description of activities in Macunaíma's tribe's daily life: the men hunt game and fish by casting *timbó*, a liana (or vine) whose extract paralyses their prey; the women weave mats, pound manioc root to make flour, and adorn themselves with stones, feathers, and woven and braided strips; men and women paint themselves with juices from Amazonian plants; they groom each other and clean themselves and each other of a number of insects and parasites. The novel furthermore exposes the unromantic details of living in the tropics: throughout the book the characters casually swat mosquitoes, are bitten by ants, and are attacked by ticks, lice, and other pests. Sometimes in a "natural" way and sometimes in revenge, Macunaíma and his brothers are castigated by Vei, the burning, tropical Sun, who lashes their backs.

The novel's description of Brazil's cities, despite its mythological trappings, is factually precise. In São Paulo Macunaíma plausibly encounters elevators, vehicles known as Hupmobiles, and foreign-born prostitutes. The location of the giant's house is precisely identified and described in terms of actual locations, and, though Englishmen did not, as the novel tells us, grow guns and whisky on trees, it is true that transportation and communication systems were foreign-built and controlled (mostly by the English), and that imported manufactured goods dominated the market. The Afro-Brazilian *macumba* ceremony that Macunaíma attends in Rio is also rendered with ethnographic precision.

Members of the Borra tribe of Amazonian Indians. Though Andrade is not specific as to Macunaíma's tribe, much of the detail he provides is ethnographically factual.

On the other hand, little Indian boys are not born black, like Macunaíma, or blessed by African tribal kings. With these extraordinary shifts in place and combinations of racial and cultural traits, Andrade's novel builds an image of Brazil and Brazilians as culturally and racially mixed, and neutralizes regional and other differences while not denying them. The novel attempts to bring all that is Brazilian into the tale of Macunaíma, the "hero of our people," who cannot tell buildings from palm trees because he perceives modern structures according to the primitive conceptions acquired by him in the Amazon. In the process, the novel also examines the relation between the rest of Brazil and its richest and most modern city, São Paulo.

Brazilian folklore and national identity. Andrade takes the name of his hero directly from Koch-Grünberg's account of an Indian trickster figure, Maku/naima. The name can be translated from its original language as "The Great Evil One"—though a misunderstanding led missionaries to use it as a translation of the word "God" into the languages of Amazonian Indians (Proença, p. 15). Luis da Câmara Cascudo, the great Brazilian folklorist, records a similarly named Maíua, or Maa-aíua among many Indian tribes, a "mysterious being from whom all evil comes" (Cascudo, pp. 444-45). It is easy to conflate this mischievous spirit with the Pedro Malasartes figure of Iberian folklore, who was brought to Brazil by the Portuguese. Described as "cunning, cynical, . . . without scruples or remorse," Pedro Malasartes wins the reader over by his cleverness and his way of cheating the rich and the pompous, even though he is—and one recognizes Andrade's subtitle—"a hero without character" (Cascudo, p. 445). Macunaíma also resembles the African trickster god Exu, a mischief-maker who has to be propitiated before any other African god can be invoked, whose help is invaluable and without whom nothing can be done because, unappeased, he spoils everything. In this sense too, Andrade's Macunaíma is a composite figure, a combination of trickster figures from the three "races" traditionally conceived as the formative parts of a Brazilian national identity.

In the novel Macunaíma attends an Afro-Brazilian ceremony in Rio de Janeiro, invokes Exu, and gets his help. Andrade's novel documents the ceremony itself and the way in which Brazilian culture takes for granted that anyone, regardless of background, may attend it and ask the gods for help in love or against enemies. These ceremonies, called *candomblé* in the northern state of Bahia, and *macumba* in Rio, combine elements of various African cultures, adapted to

American climatic conditions (in which growing and harvesting seasons differ from those of Africa), and to Brazilian laws (which prescribe that the dead be buried within 24 hours instead of the three days of African ritual). They are also syncretic with Christianity: many of the African gods are worshipped under the guise and on the feast days of Catholic saints. In certain parts of Brazil African cults likewise became syncretic with Indian religious practices, a phenomenon of which Andrade was aware; the presence of his Indian hero at an Afro-Brazilian ceremony is therefore plausible. This fusion affirms a view of Brazilian identity as composite, as a combination of racial and cultural elements that themselves have changed because of their interaction.

In the forest Macunaíma encounters adventures and beings from Indian mythologies, like the Curupira, a spirit that protects game animals by leading hunters into grave danger. Curupira tries to eat Macunaíma, who eludes the spirit with his trickster's ways and escapes because he is too lazy to follow the spirit's treacherous advice. Macunaíma also obeys Indian rituals in the forest. When, in another adventure, he kills his own mother, who had turned into a doe, he and his brothers wrap her in a hammock and bury her, then "fast . . . for a time in accordance with the tribal rules" (Andrade, *Macunaíma,* p. 15).

Away from the forest Macunaíma consistently describes São Paulo in terms that conflate nature and modern civilization; the city is a savanna covered with palm trees that have plumes of smoke on top instead of leaves; city lights are crazy, careering stars (*Macunaíma,* p. 33). He applies the name "machine" not only to the mechanical and technological objects new to his Amazonian experience, but also to natural phenomena like the moon and human beings. In fact, at the beginning he asks to sleep with the Machine Goddess, in order to become the Emperor of Machines, just as he had become the Emperor of the Forest after sleeping with Ci, Mother of the Forest (*Macunaíma,* p. 35). The city is also described in terms of natural features associated with the Brazilian forest or countryside: the giant lives in the *noruega* of Pacaembu—Pacaembu being an old, elegant quarter of the city, and noruega the cool, damp, south-facing side of a mountain that does not receive the sun. The giant himself is a conflation: Italian or Peruvian, he is an industrialist, a figure of Indian mythology, and a cannibal.

Macunaíma hunts tapirs in front of the Commodities Exchange, causing a riot; he has to be told that the panthers roaming the roads are actually called "Fords, Hupmobiles, Chevrolets, Dodges" (*Macunaíma,* p. 34). Though Andrade destabilizes staid notions of Brazilian history, folklore, and even geography throughout the book, it is in its hero himself that he creates a new model for Brazilian identity. It is impossible to classify Macunaíma in terms of moral standards or cultural or even racial characteristics. As we follow his adventures, he displays inconsistent moral and psychological traits, and conforms to, or directly opposes, the norms of a number of cultures. The novel's opening describes Macunaíma as "hero of our people"; if this description is taken seriously, it must be acknowledged the portrait is often more critical than patriotic. Andrade's novel disputes the Romantic view of the Indian as heroic ancestor of the Brazilian nation (as promoted by José de Alencar's ***Iracema, the Honey-Lips*** [also covered in *Latin American Literature and Its Times*]), and proposes instead an image of Brazilianness that shows resilience and inclusiveness but also incorporates uncertainty and contemplates failure. The uncertainty is a consequence of Macunaíma's contradictory qualities. He cannot be pinned down; one is always uncertain about who he really is and therefore how Brazilianness should be defined. The question of failure is raised by the way in which the novel plays out: Macunaíma fails to make a name or place for himself in the city, he loses his talisman on the way home, and his friends and family, even his heir, perish.

Modern Art Week in São Paulo, Brazil. In 1922, 100 years after Brazilian independence, a group of artists rented the posh Municipal Theater in São Paulo, and, sponsored by the widely circulating daily *Jornal do Commercio,* organized a "Week" in which they could showcase their works. Most had spent time in Europe, especially in France, whose cultural influence on Brazil was very strong, but also in Italy and Germany, where they had come into contact with new movements like dada, futurism, and surrealism, and with writers like Guillaume Apollinaire, Paul Verlaine, and Stéphane Mallarmé.

The "Week" aimed to jolt a provincial public into modernity, and to attack an establishment of artists and critics whom it claimed was out of touch both with the modern world and with the national and popular roots of Brazilian culture. To a full house, participants in the "Week" recited poetry that broke rules of meter and rhyme, and used colloquial words formerly banned from proper literary expression. They read artistic and political manifestoes that attacked established

Brazilian cultural authorities; showed paintings and sculptures whose glaring colors and contorted shapes defied academic standards of beauty and identified with the "primitive" and tropical; and played dissonant music that incorporated popular tunes and the sounds of machines in the modern city. Together these artists set patterns that would dominate much of the Brazilian intellectual scene in subsequent decades. The public applauded and booed and was delighted or indignant and shocked, and the old guard suffered noisily this onslaught of the young. Mário de Andrade played an important part in this movement, and the preface to his book of poetry, *Hallucinated City,* is one of the manifestoes of this revolutionary movement.

The "Week of Modern Art" can also be seen in many ways as a continuation of previous cultural developments in Brazil. Almost a century earlier, Brazilian writers had adapted European Romanticism to their efforts to develop a literature of Brazilian national identity. Similarly, in 1922 Brazilian artists adapted European—and to a lesser extent, North American—modernism to their own efforts. They formed an iconoclastic movement, Brazilian modernism, that would last from 1922 to 1945 and include a rash of regional fiction set in northeastern, central, and southern Brazil. Like the Romantics before them, the modernists were attracted by the Europeans' bold experiments in language and in form as well as their interest in the primitive and the non-European. These models justified and inspired the Brazilians in their attack on the local cultural establishment, and their immersion in what they saw as a more authentically Brazilian culture of native shapes and colors, music and beliefs. Andrade returns to the Romantic image of the Amerindian, which, because it was associated with nature and represented an alternative to European civilization, was so important to the earlier construction of Brazilian identity, but he changes that image radically. Unlike the "noble savages" of the widely read mid-nineteenth-century stories by José de Alencar, Macunaíma is in no way admirable. Also included in Andrade's image of Brazilian identity is the Afro-Brazilian contribution, a factor de-emphasized in earlier definitions.

The Novel in Focus

Plot summary: an overview. The plot of *Macunaíma* is simple, like a fairy tale's. The hero is born, "sired by the Terror of the Night," and "black as calcined ivory," to an Indian woman (*Macunaíma,* p. 3). He is lazy, irresponsible, and lecherous. He seduces his brother's wife, accidentally kills his mother, and marries a warrior woman of the forest, who gives him a magic stone, called a *muiraquitã,* and confers on him the title of Emperor of the Amazons before she dies and becomes a star. He loses the stone, learns it is in the possession of a giant/industrialist in the city of São Paulo, and with his two brothers goes in search of it.

His adventures make him crisscross Brazil from north to south and east to west; he traverses rivers, mountains, forests, and shrub-covered plains, cities, farms, and ranches. Like heroes in fairy tales, he gets supernatural help, and sometimes he performs wonders. Unlike such heroes, he usually bungles his adventures and wastes the helpful efforts of his friends. He transforms himself and his brothers into various objects and animals, and in the course of his travails turns from a very black sprite into a handsome blond youth.

When he arrives in São Paulo, Macunaíma attempts to trick the giant into giving him the magic stone, but is too clumsy to succeed. Eventually, however, he kills the giant, recovers the stone, and returns to the forest, where, again unlike the heroes of fairy tales, he is sick, lonely and most unhappy. Finally a star takes pity on him and transforms him into the constellation of the Big Dipper. A small parrot to whom he has told his story repeats it to the narrator, who tells it to us.

Plot summary: the story in detail. At birth Macunaíma is seen as exceptional; when he is introduced to the tribe, "King Nagô," a Brazilian folk figure of African origin, states his approval of him; the combination of Indian and African sets the syncretic mode that Andrade uses throughout the book (*Macunaíma,* p. 2). As a child Macunaíma is remarkable for playing tricks, for showing a premature interest in sex, and for refusing to talk until he is six. One of his early tricks is to make his mother order his sister-in-law into the forest to play with him; there he turns into a beautiful prince and seduces her. Then, and throughout the book, Andrade uses "play" to mean lovemaking, but Macunaíma's play is not necessarily benevolent, and often includes violence:

> Macunaíma began to pelt her with pebbles; Sofará [his sister-in-law] yelped with excitement on being wounded and in turn decorated his body with drips of blood. At last a stone split the corner of her mouth and knocked out three teeth. She leaped from the branch and landed

> astride the hero's belly with a great crash. He wrapped his body around hers, and howling with relish, they made love ["played around," in the original] again.
>
> (*Macunaíma*, p. 7)

Macunaíma's brother Jiguê witnesses one of these trysts and gives Macunaíma an epic beating, then returns his wife to her parents and gets himself another wife. Macunaíma arranges to "play" with his brother's second wife, the beautiful Iriqui, as well. A famine follows. Macunaíma's clumsy attempts at hunting lead him to the Curupira, who protects animals by disorienting and sometimes killing hunters; our hero avoids his traps but kills his own mother, whom Curupira has misleadingly turned into a doe. After burying his mother, Macunaíma and his two brothers leave their village.

THE AMAZONS

In ancient Greek legend, the Amazons were warrior women who cut off their right breast so it would not interfere with their ability to draw a bow. The Amazon river, forest, and region are so named because early Spanish explorers understood—or imagined—that somewhere in that enormous wilderness there lived a race of strong and valiant women who, like their legendary Greek counterparts, not only did without men—whom they invited over once a year for procreation—but would kill any man who came near their territory. Various Spanish explorers, particularly Cristóbal de Acuña, reported on the existence of Amazons in the Amazon, though none of them actually encountered any of these women.

In their first adventure, the hero encounters Ci, Mother of the Forest, whom he recognizes as an Amazon warrior woman by her withered right breast.

Macunaíma engages in a ferocious battle with Ci, who is about to win when he calls on his brothers for help. They overwhelm her and as they pin her down, Macunaíma "plays" with her. After that Ci and Macunaíma enjoy many hours of intense pleasure. She bears him a son. However, while Macunaíma sleeps off a drunk, a black serpent attacks the unprotected Ci and sucks her other breast dry. Since brother Jiguê has not been able to impregnate any of Ci's Amazon subjects, there is no untainted milk for the child; he nurses from Ci's snake-poisoned milk, and dies. From his grave the medicinal plant guaraná is born. Tired of life, Ci gives Macunaíma a green stone as a talisman, then she rises into the sky and turns into the star Beta Centauri (*Macunaíma*, p. 21). Macunaíma perforates his lip to carry the stone as a labret.

The brothers wander "throughout the forests over which Macunaíma held sway," followed by a "retinue of scarlet macaws and parakeets," eventually meeting up with a monster (*Macunaíma*, p. 22). In perfectly non-heroic fashion, Macunaíma vanquishes it by luck and cuts off its head. The head follows him, desiring to be his slave, but our hero is afraid and in headlong flight loses the labret, which is swallowed by a fish that is sold to the São Paulo industrialist Venceslau Pietro-Pietra, also known as the giant Piaiman. Macunaíma decides to go to São Paulo to retrieve the talisman. His brothers go with him, for he needs looking after.

Now that Ci is no longer alive, her consort Macunaíma, Emperor of the Forest, inherits a fortune in cocoa pods. (The Brazilian state of Bahia is one of the largest producers of cacao—the seeds from which chocolate is made—in the world.) With this fortune in cocoa pods, he travels to São Paulo, which he calls the *maloca* (an Indian word for village) on the banks of the Tietê River. On the way he bathes in a pool on a rock in the middle of a river and turns white. His brothers attempt to achieve the same effect, but since Macunaíma has used up and muddied the water, one of them turns copper-colored and the other has only enough water left to wash the palms of his hands and the soles of his feet. The three brothers are now the color of the three predominant races (white, Indian, black) in the Brazilian population.

Macunaíma is confused by the noises and the bustle of the city, but regains his bearings when he realizes that what he had taken for a cage operated by a monkey that transported him to his perch on a very tall tree, are only the "machine" called elevator in the "machine" called hotel; he learns to turn his brother into the machine telephone when he wants to communicate with someone, and into the machine taxi when he wants to go somewhere. All of that, however, uses up his resources—cocoa had made him rich in the forest, but melts away quickly to buy the fascinating machines and the women of the city, who don't give themselves away, but have to be wooed with the lobster and champagne machines.

Dona Vitoria Umbarana dos Santos, a macumba priestess like Aunt Ciata in *Macunaíma*.

He does find the giant Piaiman, in whose house there is a permanently bubbling, huge pot of *polenta* (a typical Italian, corn-based porridge) seasoned with human flesh. Disguised as a "French" prostitute, Macunaíma successfully awakens Piaiman's sexual interest, but cannot convince him to hand over the talisman. After several unsuccessful attempts to cheat or wrest the talisman from the giant, Macunaíma goes to Rio de Janeiro for a macumba session held by the unparalleled Aunt Ciata. The ritual begins slowly, building up to great intensity as the gods descend into their initiates, particularly into a blond Polish girl. The girl is made to embody the giant Piaiman and is mercilessly beaten by the god Exu at the request of Macunaíma. Anything done to her reflects on the giant whom she embodies. It is, we read, "horrifying" (*Macunaíma,* p. 58). Macunaíma becomes a "son" of Exu in a chapter that firmly links the Amerindian and the West African trickster gods. The giant is fully incapacitated by the beating, and has to look for a cure in Europe.

While he is gone, the Sun takes a shine to Macunaíma and, even though he has been defecated on by vultures and smells very bad, chooses him as a husband for one of her daughters. She bids him wait a day while they make their round, and promises immortality and eternal youth as a dowry, as well as France, Europe, and Bahia (*Macunaíma,* p. 64). Instead, Macunaíma wanders off, finds a Portuguese fishwife washerwoman who cleans him up, and delightedly "plays" with her. Once again he throws away proffered help and goods. In another adventure he takes over a celebration of the Southern Cross, the constellation that occupies the place of honor on the Brazilian flag, and tells the assembled crowd the real—that is, the Indian—story of the constellation, who used to be Paui-Podole, the Crested Curassow. He is very pleased with his oratory, and the reader is left in doubt about whether he is a patriot with original views on what is really national or just another demagogic windbag.

When the giant returns from Europe, Macunaíma is waiting for him, and there is a Homeric fight. Half tricked, half wrestled, Piaiman falls into his own cooking pot and boils to death. Victorious, Macunaíma recovers his talisman and starts toward home. He once more crisscrosses the country, pursued and rescued along the way, reciting folk rhymes and proverbs, carelessly losing his talisman for good, and cheating or being cheated by friends and enemies. He is protected from the vengeful Sun (for whose daughter Macunaíma did not wait around) by a cloud of parrots who follow and shade him. Finally, he finds the village of his birth and his old house; they are in ruins. One by one his brothers and his friends succumb to disease, and he is left alone, the Sun on his back, his wife and only son dead, the forest inhospitable. He tells his story to a companionable parrot, and begs heavenly bodies to take him to them. Most refuse, because of their unpleasant memories of him. Finally the Crested Curassow takes pity on him, and he is turned into the Big Dipper.

The parrot finds the narrator of the book and tells him the tale of Macunaíma, and this is how we learn about it.

The "Letter to the Amazons" and literary tradition. At the center of *Macunaíma* Mário de Andrade placed the "Letter to the Amazons" (*Macunaíma,* pp. 67-79), a discussion of the hero's adventures in the big city, and a parody of every bit of patriotic exaggeration and Latin-misquoting pedantry that could ever pass for literary language and learned discourse. It mocks what Andrade implies is a pseudo-patriotism that translates the national character into foreign "science," as in the philological discussion of the proper spelling of *muiraquitã* (*Macunaíma,* p. 68). It also criticizes the replacement of what is Brazilian—imperfect as it may be—by corrupt foreign imports, as when Macunaíma suggests that his "subjects" should learn how to behave from French prostitutes. And it reproaches the wasteful exploitation of natural resources for the acquisition of foreign luxuries: the purpose of the letter is to request that the Amazons send Macunaíma more cocoa to spend on champagne, lobsters, and prostitutes.

In Macunaíma's letter, the novel ridicules all the traditional ways of speaking about Brazil, from the letter written in 1500 reporting the discovery of Brazil to the King of Portugal, through the Romantic novels and poems that created a national literature after Independence, through the literature and oratory that the Modern Art Week attacked. In any case, the letter's addressees, Macunaíma's subjects, belong to a nonliterate culture; they could not read this letter from their leader, who is cut off from them.

At the time it was written, the main impact of *Macunaíma* was not political but cultural. It was shocking because it used a colloquial Brazilian idiom that had not been considered good enough for literature, and did not pay attention to language rules imposed by Portugal that were based on Portuguese, not Brazilian, usage. It was also shocking because of its casual, ill-bred excursions into the sexual and the "dirty" and because of its attitude toward enshrined literary forms like the nineteenth-century novel. It shook up the literary world and forced people to think of Brazilianness as including new elements (those derived from the African heritage) and speaking a separate variety of language. But although—or perhaps because—the novel refers more to historical processes than to specific events, it continues to resonate in Brazilian culture. Forty years after its publication, in the middle of a military dictatorship that lasted from 1964 into the 1980s, Joaquim Pedro de Andrade (no relation to the author) directed a film based on the book, in which the giant stood for the foreign and internal capital that was cannibalizing ordinary Brazilian people, represented by Macunaíma. The hero's sufferings were those of citizens oppressed by dictators and their foreign supporters; his resilience was that of the Brazilian people, and his sadness that of a nation repeatedly victimized by internal and external exploitation. In a very different vein, its rambunctious validation of popular culture also caused it to be chosen in 1974 as the theme for one of the corporations, or samba schools (associations of expert dancers and musicians), participating in the yearly Carnival parade in Rio.

Sources and literary context. Andrade says that he was so moved by Koch-Grünberg's study of Amazonian Indians, he wrote *Macunaíma* in a week in 1926 (Andrade, *Macunaíma, o herói,* p. 401). He published it at his own cost in 1928. Andrade called the work a "rhapsody," rather than a novel, and in an influential study (*O tupi e o alaúde*; meaning "The Tupy Indian and the Lute"), Gilda de Mello e Souza analyses it in terms of its musical structure. Critics call the work a novel because it is written in prose and has something like a plot, but, as Andrade's classification indicates, the book's loose structure, folk motifs, emotional charge, and roots in an individual as well as a national unconscious are meant to undermine distinctions within genres and among the arts.

In its combination of formal experimentation and probing of national identity, *Macunaíma* carries out the program of the Modern Art Week. It appeared the same year as the "Anthropophagist Manifesto," in which Andrade and other modernists—especially Oswald de Andrade (no relation)—proposed that Brazilian culture should, and does, cannibalize foreign influences and metabolize them into an essentially national body of works and being. Mário de Andrade's elaborate and often scatological fabric of puns and allusions, his references to Indian and African rituals, folk motifs, Indian legends, popular sayings and proverbs, and musical forms, does not sound like anything written before it. It achieves this uniqueness by using the full resources of Brazilian Portuguese. At the same time, the work confronts head-on the Romantic conception of Brazilianness as rooted in a lush and benevolent tropical nature that gives birth, unproblematically, to a noble Indian. Andrade's concept of a tri-racial Brazilian rakishness questions that nobility while cannibalizing artistic movements that changed the European cultural scene in the first three decades of this century.

The modernists' interest in the problem of nationality assigned their works a political dimension many of them had not sought. A number of writers, prominent among whom was Jorge Amado (see ***Gabriela, Clove and Cinnamon,*** also covered in *Latin American Literature and Its Times*), pointed out that the modernist revolution in artistic forms avoided and ignored economic and social aspects of Brazilian life, like poverty, inequality, and exploitation, which were at least as endemic and far more urgent than a perceived backwardness in literature, painting, and music. This controversy has not lost its importance. In fact, one way of defining *Macunaíma* is to say that it is mostly about how important art is in defining national character. *Macunaíma* attempts this definition by means of inclusiveness and its consequence, paradox. Macunaíma's "lack of character" actually comprises countless contradictory traits: cowardice and courage; sensuality and disenchantment; optimism and melancholy; playfulness and violence; innocence and perversion; cleverness and stupidity. Any "national identity" he represents is multiple and self-contradictory. In the end, Andrade even undermines the argument for considering Macunaíma a specifically Brazilian character. In a letter to Manuel Bandeira, of December 12, 1930, he conceives of the possibility that the book, rather than being about a distinct Brazilian identity, might be a "more universal satire to contemporary man, particularly from the point of view of this wandering detachment, these moral notions created on the spur of the moment, that I feel and see so much in contemporary man" (*Macunaíma, o herói,* p. 412; trans. R. Wasserman, here and elsewhere). The climate of melancholy and disenchantment with which the novel ends counters the optimism of earlier works on national identity and of the national self-glorification fashionable at the turn of the century. At the same time the novel self-consciously places literature in the equation. It is ultimately the literary element that prevails in *Macunaíma,* the parrot who knows the story and the author from whom we learn it.

The translation. Though the English translation is careful and at times felicitous, *Macunaíma* is probably a translator's nightmare. One example is the hero's refrain "Ai! . . . Que preguiça!" which translates roughly and literally as "Oh! . . . What sloth!" or "Oh! . . . I feel so lazy!" In Portuguese the first word, *ai,* is an exclamation, yet it is also the Indian word for the three-toed sloth, an animal named for its very slow movements (*Macunaíma, o herói,* p. 6). Considering Macunaíma's laziness, the pun becomes clear. The refrain is a bilingual pun presented as characterization of the hero. Macunaíma utters the exclamation on a number of occasions when he has just been offered help or an opportunity to improve his situation—he even says it at times when he is invited to have sex. In those cases the expression becomes an ironic commentary on one view of people from the tropics as "lazy." Since Macunaíma is the "hero of our people," a representative of "Brazilianness," his "laziness" becomes an unrepentant acceptance of one explanation for why Brazil has not reached the level of material development of England or the United States, whose people deplore laziness without acknowledging its positive side, and who also supply many of the objects the hero needs or desires in industrial São Paulo. Macunaíma's refrain characterizes the "Brazilian" hero as dedicated to the pleasure of doing nothing, portrayed in the novel as a positive trait, except that it means he must depend on foreigners for guns and whisky, since they do not really grow on trees. Otherwise his laziness is connected to his disdain for the rat-race and portrayed mostly as cute. The translator renders "Ai! . . . Que preguiça!" as "Oh! What a fucking life!" which hints at the sexual appetites of the hero, but loses the other connotations.

A similar problem arises in connection with Andrade's consistent use of "play" to mean lovemaking; in ordinary Portuguese the word does not have the erotic connotation, which is given entirely by the context. The translator chose the literal and somewhat technical "making love" for the playful and metaphorical "play," and lost Andrade's freedom with language, as well as the lack of solemnity with which Macunaíma approaches the erotic.

Mário de Andrade's use of Indian words presents another difficulty for the translator. Andrade often breaks into epic lists of Brazilian plants and animals, many of which have preserved their original Indian names. They sound familiar in Portuguese even if the reader does not know what exactly they mean, but neither the names nor the familiarity are readily available in any other language. When Macunaíma encounters the agouti, an animal that throws the poisonous juice of manioc on him and makes him grow from a rickety child into a beautiful young man, he swerves away from the liquid, which washes over his body but misses his head. In the original, his head remains that of a *piá,* the Indian word for "child"; which is the word used in the translation (*Macunaíma,* p. 13). The word is known to ordinary Brazilians and is used in the everyday language of certain regions; this interweaving of elements from European and non-European languages and cultures is, for Andrade, an important part of the national character and of the Brazilian difference, but it is difficult to translate culturally or linguistically.

Reviews. Andrade's letters show the interest he took in what critics were saying about the book—and many of the best-known critics wrote about it. Of Tristão de Athayde's mostly favorable reaction, Andrade wrote that he should have been more severe, particularly since de Athayde always judged books by how Catholic they were: he thought the criticism "sort of dumb. He did not take a position. As a Catholic, he should have been more censorious. . . . It is an injustice to state that the language of the book is like *candomblé*" (*Macunaíma, o herói,* p. 405). In another letter, he mentioned two reviews, diametrically opposed to each other, one comparing him to Rabelais, the other calling him an idiot (*Macunaíma, o herói,* p. 421). He also heard of a Rio paper that published a wonderful review, in 1945, and asked a friend to send him a copy (*Macunaíma, o herói,* p. 421).

By the time *Macunaíma* was published in English, it was well established in Brazilian literature; American reviewers were aware of this fact. Paul West in the *Nation* called the book "a classic" (West, p. 7). Alexander Coleman in the *New York Times Book Review* discussed the importance of the book in Brazilian modernism, "a new wave that created a national past into which Brazilian art could be born" (Coleman, p. 2). V. B. Landers in *Choice* noted that *Macunaíma* is a "masterpiece of the Brazil modernist movement" (Landers, p. 1637). The critics praised the richness of the work, and found irresistible a confessedly impossible attempt at summarizing it. The translation came in for qualified praise, but, critics noted, Britishisms (in the translation of a text that declares the independence of Brazilian Portuguese from that of Portugal), outdated slang, and "Oh! What a fucking life" do not quite convey the linguistic inventiveness of Andrade's language.

—Renata Wasserman

For More Information

Andrade, Mário de. *Aspectos da literatura brasileira.* São Paulo: Martins, 1972.

———. *Hallucinated City.* Bilingual edition. Trans. Jack E. Tomlin. Nashville: Vanderbilt University Press, 1968.

———. *Macunaíma, o herói sem nenhum caráter.* Critical Edition. Ed. Telê Ancona Lopez. Florianópolis: Editora da Universidade Federal de Santa Catarina, 1988.

———. *Macunaíma.* Trans. Edward Arthur Goodland. New York: Random House, 1984.

Brum, Argemiro J. *O Desenvolvimento econômico brasileiro.* Petrópolis: Editora Vozes, 1983.

Cascudo, Luís da Câmara. *Dicionário do Folclore Brasileiro.* 2nd ed. Vol. 2. Rio de Janeiro: Instituto Nacional do Livro/Ministério da Educação e Cultura, 1962.

Coleman, Alexander. "A Hero of Enormous Appetites." *The New York Times Book Review,* March 3, 1985, 13.

Johnson, John Randall. *Macunaíma: From Modernism to Cinema Novo.* Austin: University of Texas Press, 1977.

Landers, V. B. Review of *Macunaíma,* by Marío de Andrade. *Choice* 22 (July 1985): 1637-38.

Maram, Sheldon L. "The Immigrant and the Brazilian Labor Movement, 1890-1920." In *Essays Concerning the Socioeconomic History of Brazil and Portuguese India.* Eds. Dauril Alden and Warren Dean. Gainesville: The University Presses of Florida, 1977.

Martins, Wilson. *The Modernist Idea: A Critical Survey of Brazilian Writing in the Twentieth Century.* New York: New York University Press, 1970.

Proença, Cavalcanti. *Roteiro de Macunaíma.* São Paulo: Anhembi, 1955.

Topik, Steven, *The Political Economy of the Brazilian State, 1889-1930.* Austin: University of Texas Press, 1987.

Wasserman, Renata R. Mautner. *Exotic Nations: Literature and Cultural Identity in the United States and Brazil, 1839-1930.* Ithaca: Cornell University Press, 1994.

West, Paul. Review of *Macunaíma,* by Marío de Andrade. *Nation* 241 (July 20, 1985): 52.

The Mambo Kings Play Songs of Love

by
Oscar Hijuelos

The son of pre-Revolutionary Cuban immigrants, Oscar Hijuelos was born in the Upper West Side of New York City in 1951. He received his Bachelor's and Master's degrees at the City College of New York. While his first novel, *Our House in the Last World,* met with high acclaim but little commercial success, his second novel, *The Mambo Kings Play Songs of Love,* became an international bestseller, garnered the 1990 Pulitzer Prize, and was adapted into a popular Hollywood film. Focusing on aspects particular to the experience of individual Cuban Americans, the novel manages also to convey universal truths: "These two brothers, clothed in flamboyant and elegiac prose, are ordinary human beings with complex inner lives—no stereotypes here. . . . [The novel is] about Cubans and music but . . . also . . . about . . . the way that the memory works—like a spinning record, a TV rerun—that occurs again and again" (Hijuelos in Ryan, p. 256).

THE LITERARY WORK

A novel set in New York and Cuba from 1918 to 1980; published in English in 1989.

SYNOPSIS

Two brothers from Cuba, César and Nestor Castillo, find success as mambo musicians in New York City in the 1950s. Told reflectively when César is an old man, the novel recalls his experiences in the nightclubs of New York and studios of Hollywood, his many love affairs, and his volatile relationship with his beloved brother.

Events in History at the Time the Novel Takes Place

Cuba and the United States. The relationship between Cuba and the United States has always been volatile and complex. The formal political relationship dates to the end of the Spanish-American War in 1898, when the U.S. military occupied the island. For the next 60 years, the United States wielded a powerful influence, directly and indirectly, over the island nation. Much of this influence was in the economic sector. Before the 1959 Revolution, Cuba conducted approximately 70 percent of its trade with the United States; this trade consisted largely of sugar exports, on which the Cuban economy is based (Rudolf, p. 139). The United States arranged to purchase Cuba's entire sugar crop at fixed rates, which helped to stabilize the fragile economy; in return, the United States gained military bases in Cuba, and U.S. corporations were allowed to operate and acquire land there. By 1929, in fact, U.S. interests had acquired more than $1.5 billion in Cuban real estate. The United States also invested heavily in Cuban business enterprises, such as public utilities, telephones, electricity, and transportation, and supplied the island with manufactured goods. By 1930 investments totaled $1.2 billion and U.S. corporations provided 75 percent of Cuba's imports.

In 1954 Cuba had the largest number of

Cadillacs per capita of any nation in the world (Pérez, p. 297). Virtually all machinery on the island was U.S.-made, and, though there was a substantial variety of Cuban-made programs at the time, television and radio shows broadcast from the United States also permeated the airwaves. The city streets were filled with U.S. department and dime stores, supermarkets, ice cream parlors, and movie theaters showing first-run Hollywood films. "Except that everyone speaks Spanish," said one woman in 1958, "I wouldn't know I'd left the U.S. Oh sure, Havana has some old Spanish buildings, but then so do San Antonio [Texas] and St. Augustine [Florida]" (Smith, p. 63).

The borders between Cuba and the United States were wide open during these years, with an average 50,000–100,000 Cubans traveling to Florida and New York annually, maintaining houses and community ties in both nations. Cubans felt very much at home in the United States, as illustrated by their investments: by 1955 Cuban real estate investments in New York and Florida totaled more than $150 million (Pérez, p. 299).

THE MAMBO AND CHA-CHA-CHA CRAZE

Mambo music is a complex blend of Spanish guitar-based folk, European brass band, and African percussion and rhythms. It is filled with conga drums, flutes, violins, chants, melodies, spirited singing, dueling horns, and saxophones, and it accompanies an equally dramatic and lively dance style. The mambo became extremely popular in New York City in the late 1940s and '50s, a period in which musicians like Tito Puente, Machito, and Pérez Prado became superstars. In the mid- to late 1950s the mambo's popularity in America was eclipsed by the simpler cha-cha-cha.

Playground or purgatory? In the mid-1950s Cuba was the playground of the United States. Its stunning tropical beauty and more than 200 natural harbors lured tourists, while its lack of government controls enticed entertainment moguls to set up nightclubs and casinos, including the world-famous Tropicana and Copacabana. Induced by brazenly corrupt dictator Fulgencio Batista—known for embezzling money and soliciting bribes in exchange for power and influence—U.S. gangsters, such as Santos Trafficante, controlled most of the nightclubs, casinos, and major hotels in Havana after 1953 (Smith, p. 74). Americans flocked by the thousands from the United States to Cuba's shimmering shores to party and play. There was some merging of U.S. and Cuban culture. The mambo beat that pulsated from Cuba's bandstands became extremely popular in the urban United States, brought there by inspired tourists and eager musicians—like the novel's César and Nestor Castillo—who hoped to gain fame and riches in the States.

Beneath the glittering surface, there was a vigorous underworld in Cuba in the 1950s. Cuba's gambling revenues in 1957 totaled $500,000 a month, and prostitution flourished on the island. According to one estimate, Havana alone had 270 brothels and 11,500 prostitutes at the time. Though gangsters and the upper classes were growing wealthier, 62 percent of the island's 5.8 million people earned less than $75 a month (Pérez, p. 305). Inequity grew. Crime, the homeless population, and suicide rates increased dramatically as unemployment jumped from 8.9 to over 18 percent. Sociologist Lowry Nelson described the scene in 1958: "It would be impossible to give even a rough estimate of the beggar population of Cuba, but it is considerable, as anyone who has visited Cuban cities can testify. Large numbers are women" (Nelson in Pérez, p. 304). Showing dismay at the actions of fellow visitors, U.S. journalist Arthur Schlesinger Jr. added, "My fellow countrymen reeled through the streets, picking up 14-year-old Cuban girls and tossing coins to make men scramble in the gutter" (Schlesinger Jr. in Pérez, p. 305).

Corruption on the streets and in the government reached epic proportions. As the wallets of the amoral grew fatter, the anger and resentment of the lower, working classes swelled. Some emigrated from Cuba to the United States to find work, while others, who stayed behind, began to stage an uprising.

***Auténtico/Ortodoxo*/military governments in Cuba.** The Cuban *Auténtico* party, which originally took power in the 1930s, ruled through 1952. Associated strongly with *gangsterismo* or terror, violence, and corruption, Auténtico politicians typically robbed the government and exploited their own political positions at every opportunity (Pérez, p. 284). They more than doubled the government payroll and used 80 percent of the 1949-50 budget to pay their own salaries. Various leaders were charged with embezzlement, including President Grau San Martín (1944–48), who was accused of stealing $174 million. In 1947 Senator Eduardo Chibas formed an opposition party, *Ortodoxo,* committed to "public integrity, administrative honesty, and national reform" (Pérez, p. 287). Chibas offered the Cuban people hope for an accountable government, but his suicide in 1951 left the population more cynical, disillusioned, and resigned than ever. When Fulgencio Batista, who had ruled previously from 1934-44, staged a coup d'état in 1952, circumventing the elections and establishing a military dictatorship, Cubans' worst fears were realized. Instead of reforms, they were to be subject to the most corrupt government in the history of their nation. Batista imprisoned his opponents, closed all presses and universities (centers of opposition), suspended the constitution, and dissolved Congress. The May 26, 1957, issue of the weekly news magazine *Carteles* reported that Batista's government included 20 members, each of whom had a Swiss bank account with more than $1 million on deposit; and Batista openly "donated" $1 million monthly to the government-tied press (they had only praise for the leader), $1.3 million to labor unions, and $1.6 million to the Catholic Church (Pérez, pp. 303–04). Simultaneously the Cuban economy all but collapsed as sugar prices fell and the nation's inability to support such lavish spending became painfully evident.

The legacy of the Ortodoxo movement and Batista's usurpation of power spawned a revolutionary movement in 1950s Cuba. A young lawyer by the name of Fidel Castro Ruz was a member of the Ortodoxo party and, outraged by the coup d'état and events that followed, quickly organized forces to overthrow Batista. In July 1953 he staged his first action: an attack on a military outpost. The attack failed, but it catapulted Castro into the national—and international—spotlight and inspired other disgruntled citizens to join his cause. In 1955 "Civic Dialogue" discussions were held to urge Batista to hold new elections. He refused. In 1957 Castro-backed forces tried unsuccessfully to assassinate him. Though his initial bids to topple Batistia failed, Castro built a reputation of bold leadership and garnered a strong support base, especially among the peasants, who would prove to be key to a successful revolution.

1950s New York. Meanwhile, prosperity grew in the United States during the 1950s. It was a decade characterized by firm belief in the American Dream of attaining material and social success. For many—including recent immigrants from Cuba—the dream was coming true.

New York hosted the highest population of Cuban immigrants in this era; it was a decade during which "every Cuban knew every Cuban" (Hijuelos, *The Mambo Kings Play Songs of Love,* p. 36). Almost any Cuban who arrived in the city could stay with relatives and easily found work through friends in the community. But the novel makes it clear that not everything was right for newcomers in the United States after World War II. "At this time in New York there was a bit of malevolent prejudice in the air, postwar xenophobia" (*Mambo Kings,* p. 36). The brothers in the novel, César and Nestor Castillo, are warned not to speak Spanish to each other on some streets. Yet this lingering racism does not make them angry or bitter. Generally speaking, Cuban immigrants of the period tried to fit in with their surroundings, to assimilate. For the most part, they felt they were welcome immigrants, not exiles, and had no desire to return to their lives in Cuba but wanted rather to seize the opportunities available in the United States. The novel illustrates this attitude. César and Nestor read books on English grammar, study newspapers, and learn street slang from African American musicians. For Cubans in New York at this time, "the better one's English, the higher his status" (*Mambo Kings,* p. 38). The 1950s, then, was a decade in which the atmosphere in the United States was largely receptive to Cubans. Average citizens, especially in New York City where nightclubs flourished, were wild about Cuban music, and the Cuban entertainer Desi Arnaz was at the height of his popularity with the *I Love Lucy* television show. Both the music and the

I LOVE LUCY

Filmed in Hollywood but set in New York City, *I Love Lucy* premiered on October 15, 1951. It became the most-watched show on television by the new year. Because Desi Arnaz, the Cuban bandleader who was married in real life to Lucille Ball, had a heavy accent and was just coming off a failed radio show, *Your Tropical Trip,* televison executives were uneasy with casting him as Ball's on-screen spouse. But Ball insisted, and Arnaz was cast as Ricky Ricardo, Cuban bandleader at Manhattan's Tropicana nightclub. The pair were a hit; they formed perhaps the first TV family to be embraced by the entire nation (Castleman and Podrazik, p. 66).

Desi Arnaz

show bred goodwill in the United States, opening doors that brought the Cuban and mainstream communities closer together.

Castro's revolution. Meanwhile in Cuba, political opposition was escalating. By the late 1950s Castro had built a strong base of support aimed at ridding the Cuban people of the tyranny and repression of the Batista regime. The "26th of July Movement," as the rebels were known, succeeded in overthrowing Batista in December

1958—a defining moment in Cuban history that has had repercussions to this day. At first the Revolution was a popular success. Ernesto "Che" Guevara, a hero of the Revolution, marched triumphantly into Havana January 1, 1959, to declare victory. The entire city celebrated.

However, as the novel puts it, the rose of revolution soon "sprouted a thorn" (*Mambo Kings*, p. 259). Castro's government nationalized major firms in Cuba in 1960, from textile businesses to banks and department stores. In 1961 Castro declared Marxism-Leninism to be Cuba's official ideology and fused his movement with Cuba's Communist Party. These policies incited the upper classes to flee en masse: an estimated 200,000 middle- and upper-class Cubans immigrated to the United States from 1960 to 1962. Eventually Castro seized 80 percent of the nation's private property and nationalized every industry, including banks. U.S. businesses were thrown out of Cuba and bank debts erased. In retaliation, the United States broke off relations with the country and imposed an economic embargo. Once the largest trading partner of Cuba, the United States was replaced in this role by the Soviet Union. This more than alarmed U.S. leaders—especially in light of the Cold War, the ongoing competition between the United States and the Soviet Union for world leadership. The thought of a communist military base just miles from the U.S. coastline created abundant anxiety in the U.S. administration. The situation came dangerously close to total catastrophe during the Cuban Missile Crisis in October 1962.

The Bay of Pigs and the Cuban Missile Crisis. The immediate precursor to the Missile Crisis was the disastrous U.S.-sponsored invasion by Cuban exiles at the island's "Bay of Pigs" (after the Spanish name of the inlet, Bahía de Cochinas). In March 1960 President Dwight D. Eisenhower authorized the Central Intelligence Agency (CIA) to train a paramilitary group of Cuban exiles whose mission was to invade Cuba and restore U.S. interests. Eisenhower's successor, President John F. Kennedy, inherited the plan and gave it lukewarm support. Meanwhile, U.S. agents mistakenly believed that Castro was so unpopular in Cuba that the invasion of a small army would touch off a coup d'état. On April 17, 1961, 1,400 CIA-trained anti-Castro Cubans landed on the beach at the Bay of Pigs. (In Cuba, the invasion is known as *Playa Girón,* the name of the beach where most of the exile forces landed.) Some 1,200 were immediately captured or killed and 100,000 suspected sympathizers on the island were imprisoned. The invasion was a major fiasco for the United States both militarily and politically. After the victory of "David" (little Cuba) over "Goliath" (the U.S. superpower) Castro became more popular than ever in his own country and in other parts of Latin America.

The U.S. government was humiliated by the Bay of Pigs and more wary than ever of Castro. The U.S. government monitored Cuban activity closely and in mid-1962 spy planes took pictures of what were determined to be missile silos in Cuba, outfitted by the Russians, perhaps with nuclear warheads. Alarm bells sounded in the minds of U.S. leaders. Right-wing forces—including most of the Cuban exiles in the United States—urged President John F. Kennedy to immediately launch an air strike against Cuba. Fearful that such a strike would touch off World War III, and fully cognizant of the failure of the Bay of Pigs, Kennedy decided instead to create a naval blockade of the island that would prevent Soviet ships carrying missiles from reaching it. It was a tense six days from October 22 to 28, as Soviet Premier Nikita Khrushchev and U.S. President Kennedy played a deadly game of chess on a world scale. To both leaders' credit, however, an agreement was reached before any military engagement occurred. Krushchev turned his ships back toward the Soviet Union and, in return, Kennedy agreed that the United States would never invade Cuba. The world has probably never been as close to nuclear war as during those six days.

Radicalism of Cuban immigrants. Kennedy's promise to stay out of Cuba enraged many Cuban immigrants in the United States. In their eyes, he had betrayed them and they were despondent over the fact that they could never return to their homeland. Cubans in America were now exiles, unable to reunite with their families or friends in the place of their birth if they so desired. In the novel, the famous mambo band leader Ernesto Lecouna is so distraught that his Cuba no longer exists that it interferes with his musical ability. César Castillo is also terribly upset because he can no longer just board an airplane to visit his family there.

Despite Castro's resilience and popularity in Cuba, Cubans in the United States continued to fight for his overthrow throughout the 1960s and 1970s. They formed active exile groups, such as the Cuban American National Foundation led by Miami businessman Jorge Mas Canosa. These exile groups conducted "Freedom Flights" of refugees from Cuba, which were organized by the administration of President Lyndon B. Johnson. Also, with the aid of the U.S. government, the exiles began sending anti-Castro messages through the airwaves to Cuba on Radio Martí and TV Martí, broadcast out of Miami, Florida. (These media were named after José Martí, the famous nineteenth-century Cuban exile and revolutionary [see **"Our America,"** also covered in *Latin American Literature and Its Times*]). Cuban exiles aligned themselves with the Republican Party and heavily supported Presidents Richard Nixon, Ronald Reagan, and George Bush. Over the years, Mas Canosa and others continued to lobby the U.S. legislature against ending the economic embargo against Cuba, even after Cuba stopped receiving Soviet support and evidence substantiated the fact that the embargo was damaging only the people of Cuba, not Castro's government.

"SONGS OF LOVE"

Although the brothers in the novel call their band the Mambo Kings, their bestselling "Beautiful Maria of My Soul" is a bolero, a love song. The brash mambos are primarily fast-paced instrumentals. In contrast, boleros are characterized by their mournful lyrics "bemoaning unhappiness in love, [and] questioning the injustice of fate" (Pérez Firmat in Luis and González, p. 153). According to the critic and historian Gustavo Pérez Firmat, the theme of the entire novel comes down to the single question, "Is life mambo or bolero?"

The Novel in Focus

Plot summary. *The Mambo Kings Play Songs of Love* begins as a story told by César Castillo to his nephew Eugenio Castillo, son of César's brother, Nestor. César is relating the turbulent tale of the Mambo Kings, the band he and Nestor formed in the 1950s in New York City. Now 62 and near death, César lies in the bed of a decrepit hotel in Harlem, New York, and reminisces about his life. His memories, dreams, and fantasies comprise the plot of the novel, which unfolds in a non-linear style. The novel begins in the 1980s, then flashes backward. There are scenes of César's childhood and adolescence in Cuba but the story really begins when César and Nestor arrive in New York City in the winter of 1949.

The two brothers wear thin-soled shoes and flimsy jackets and have never before seen snow nor experienced cold weather. César and Nestor have left Cuba not because of political repression but simply for better economic opportunity; full of U.S.-backed nightclubs and casinos, Havana in 1949 was extremely competitive for musicians. A family friend quickly sets them up with room and board and a job at a meat-packing plant. New York was the center of Latin music in the United States. César and Nestor form the Mambo Kings band with fellow Cubans at the meat-packing plant and begin playing at clubs all over town. While César quickly establishes himself as an incorrigible ladies' man—as he was known to be in Cuba—Nestor is less able to adapt to U.S. society. He is terribly lovesick over Maria, a woman with whom he had a brief but passionate affair in Cuba. Nestor writes her love letter after love letter, but receives no reply. Then he writes a bolero: a poignant, bittersweet song called "Bellísima María de mi Alma" ("Beautiful Maria of My Soul"). César realizes immediately that this song will become the Mambo Kings' trademark.

Nestor's life in America improves greatly when he meets a young Cuban woman, Delores Fuentes. Delores watches the Mambo Kings play one night and is instantly smitten with Nestor. They quickly marry when Delores becomes pregnant—though, it is clear, Nestor is not in love with Delores. He is still pining for Maria. Two children, Eugenio and Leticia, are born within three years.

Meanwhile, the brothers' musical career is taking off. They make it to number five on the *Brooklyn Herald* popularity poll of local mambo bands. (Famous mambo artists like Tito Puente and Machito are ahead of them.) But the money from playing gigs all over New York is not enough to feed Nestor's growing family or to support César's spending habits. Both brothers play mambo music at night and work by day at the meat-packing plant. Their fortunes take a turn for the better when they meet Desi Arnaz, co-star of the *I Love Lucy* television show. César and Nestor fawn over Arnaz, the most famous Cuban in America, and he is taken with them. Arnaz loves the "Beautiful Maria" song and asks the brothers to play it on his show. After the event, César invites Arnaz and Lucille Ball over to his and Nestor's apartment. Delores cooks everyone a Cuban feast, and César realizes that he and Arnaz both used to play with César's musical mentor in Cuba.

Three months later, Arnaz sets up Nestor and César with a first-class trip to Hollywood for the filming of an episode of *I Love Lucy*. They play their song on the show and even speak a few lines of dialogue. Afterwards, they party with a few would-be starlets at the pool of the Garden of Allah Hotel. César, the consummate womanizer, seduces two of them and one also takes a liking to Nestor. Nestor, who's already wracked with guilt and melancholy over being in love with Beautiful Maria and not his wife, has a one-night stand with the woman. The experience leaves him guilt-ridden.

César and Nestor become local celebrities in their New York neighborhood when the *I Love Lucy* episode airs. Their song becomes a minor national hit and rises to number eight on the charts. Desi Arnaz even sings the song on the Ed Sullivan television show. César and Nestor travel the country on a "Mambo U.S.A." tour. Mambo is at the peak of its popularity at this time and César enjoys wine, women, and song in every town he visits. On the other hand, Nestor's melancholy deepens. He constantly broods over Beautiful Maria and feels guilty that he lacks affection for his loving wife. One fateful night in New Jersey, Nestor drives César and his girlfriend, Vanna Vane, to New York City after a show. It's late and Nestor is a little drunk. The car hits a patch of ice and smashes into a tree. Nestor dies immediately. César and Vanna are barely hurt.

Nestor's death changes César: "That was the end, he supposed, the end of his happy and carefree life" (*Mambo Kings,* p. 191). César begins brooding over his brother's death, acting much like Nestor himself did. Obsessed with guilt and remorse, César stops playing music, gets horribly drunk every night, and makes lewd passes at Nestor's widow, Delores. In an effort to collect himself, César decides to travel to Cuba. He visits his ex-wife and daughter in Havana. His daughter, Mariela, is now 13 and has not seen her father since she was five. In fact, she does not even think of him as her father. He also visits his mother, father, and brothers back on their farm. Tormented by memories of abuse at the hands of his father, César spends a few tense moments with him. As usual, César drinks to excess during his visit; his mother laments over her "poor drunkard of a son" (*Mambo Kings,* p. 218).

Feeling lost, César decides to join the Merchant Marine. He travels around the Mediterranean and the Caribbean for 18 months, enjoying the journey, especially the drunken nights in exotic places like Marseilles, France, and Tangiers, Morocco. But César still has trouble dealing with his brother's death. He also suffers from seasickness. He ages rapidly during his travels.

When César returns to New York, he learns that Delores has married a shy accountant, Pedro. Now an uncomfortable presence in the crowded household, César moves to an apartment downstairs. He charms the elderly landlady and becomes the building's superintendent but also develops terrible health problems. Placed in a hospital, he learns that his liver and kidneys are failing and his body is incapable of processing alcohol.

By this time, 1961, the Cuban Revolution has turned irrevocably towards communism. César receives letters from relatives complaining about losing their jobs, food shortages, and rationing of clothes and needed supplies. He attends meetings of fiery Cuban exiles who are planning invasions to depose Castro and in letters tries to convince his daughter, whose stepfather is a Castro official, of the evils of communism. In order to raise money to help his family in Cuba, César decides to resume his musical career. He hooks up with his old musician friends and plays at weddings and seedy bars.

César laments the changes of the 1960s in music and fashion. The mambo disappears and is replaced by the pachanga, the bossa nova, and the bugaloo. He believes that "elegance had gone

THE DECLINE OF MAMBO

Mambo music was emblematic of 1950s glamour. Both women and men would shop for the most fashionable clothes and primp for hours to get ready for a night out dancing. However, the great societal changes of the 1960s brought an end to the mambo's popularity. Massive open-air rock concerts like the Monterey Pop festival and Woodstock were the "in" places to gather, and swank nightclubs were considered passé. But Latin and Cuban music did not fade away completely. Rather, it fused with American forms: the bugaloo, for example, was a hybrid of Latin music, soul, and blues; Carlos Santana combined Latin percussion with a wildly inventive guitar rock sound; in the 1970s salsa took established Latin sounds and gave them a synthesized disco beat; and in Florida, salsa became the "Miami Sound," which was a 1980s blend of rock guitars, conga drums, synthesizers, and popular lyrics.

down the toilet . . . it was bell bottomed trousers, paisley jackets and impossibly wide-collared shirts" (*Mambo Kings,* p. 293).

At this point in the novel, César experiences a series of setbacks and small triumphs. He finds steady work as a musician. His job as a superintendent, fixing sinks and performing other handy work, is not too taxing. Then he finds that his local bar is up for sale and decides to buy it. He takes a loan from a gangster and transforms the Irish pub into "Club Havana." Opening night is a huge success; the entire neighborhood turns out to dance the mambo all night long. But César continues to drink and his health is in a shambles. "In the name of the mambo, the rumba, and the cha-cha-cha he ignored all this [his poor health]" (*Mambo Kings,* p. 321).

César relishes his role as the club's generous *patron,* allowing his old musician friends to jam there and setting up newly arrived Cuban exiles with jobs and places to live. He goes out of his way in his charity and hires far too many workers. Although the club does a good business, César is unable to make payments to the gangster. Local hoods start to sell drugs in the bar and César witnesses the decline of the neighborhood into a violent, drug- and disease-ridden place. Sadly, he sells his stake in Club Havana, then presses on.

César falls in love with a pretty 28-year-old woman, Lydia. He showers her and her young daughter with gifts and sweeps Lydia off her feet. César cannot believe that a young woman like her would become involved with a *viejito,* an old man, but she does. She calls him *viejito lindo,* good-looking old man, which reminds him of his days as a dashing ladies' man. They are happy for a few months but César's jealousy of Lydia's young male admirers becomes overwhelming and they part ways.

César, now 62, sees his health deteriorate rapidly. He is diagnosed with complete systemic failure. Doctors advise him that if does not give up drinking immediately, take a battery of different pills, and stick to a regimented diet, he will die very soon. César decides to accept death sooner rather than later. He says his good-byes to family and friends and checks into the Hotel Splendour, his favorite trysting spot in the city. Reviewing his life, he finishes his thoughts by carefully remembering every woman he ever loved or lusted after. It is an extremely long list. César ends the night by writing down the lyrics to "Beautiful Maria of My Soul." He dies in his sleep.

The novel closes with a meeting between Eugenio and Desi Arnaz in California. Arnaz is now an old man, but he remembers the brothers fondly and is kind to Eugenio. Eugenio imagines himself on the *I Love Lucy* show with a young Desi and Lucy. Then César and Nestor magically appear and warmly greet Eugenio. They play "Beautiful Maria of My Soul" and César's big heart transforms into the trademark pink satin heart logo of the *I Love Lucy* show and flies away. César, Nestor, Desi, and Eugenio are at peace.

Memory and loss among the *Gallegos.* Hijuelos describes César, Nestor, and Desi Arnaz as *Gallegos.* The term originally referred to natives of Galicia, a cold region of northern Spain, but later, throughout Latin America, it came to mean any immigrant from anywhere in Spain. According to the novel, Gallegos were known as the "the most hard working and honest Cubans, ambitious, strong-willed, and proud . . . [with] a taste for fierce battle and sometimes a melancholic outlook" (*Mambo Kings,* p. 132). Spain's early twentieth-century dictator Francisco Franco, as well as Fidel Castro's father and César's father in the novel, are Gallegos. In Spain, Gallegos are normally linked with the mood of melancholy.

In the first half of the novel, Nestor fits the description of the classic melancholic Gallego: he is consumed by the sadness of the love he left behind in Cuba. Nestor is still functional—he supports his family and takes pride in his music—but he is never able to let go of his obsession with the past. In the novel, Desi Arnaz comments that Nestor's sad state is a product of his being a Gallego.

While Arnaz and César are more often jovial than Nestor, their smiles mask similar pains of memory and loss. Hijuelos writes of Arnaz: "sometimes you can see that same Cuban melancholy breaking through Ricky Ricardo's expressions, at once vulnerable and sensitive" (*Mambo Kings,* p. 176). Once Nestor dies, César takes on many of his brother's Gallego personality traits. He broods alone for hours, unable to take his mind off the night of his brother's death. He finally comes to the paradoxical understanding that he feels happy when he is suffering.

César's struggle to deal with the pain of memory and loss is reflected in the lives of many Cuban exiles. For example, a Cuban painter in Miami, Arturo Rodriguez, always portrays himself with a missing or disjointed leg. A nation that

Antonio Banderas and Armand Assante, in a scene from the 1992 film adaptation of *The Mambo Kings*.

has been ravaged, burned, and controlled from the inside or outside for most of its existence, Cuba has given rise to particular feelings in its people, among which is a sense of displacement and betrayal. In the novel, this sense is portrayed at first through Nestor, then César. The melancholic longing of the brothers suggests the longing of Cuban exiles for a homeland they tend to call their own but that has, for most of its history, not been fully theirs.

Sources and literary context. *The Mambo Kings Play Songs of Love* is one of a few recent Latin

American and Latino works of fiction to focus on music: others are Guillermo Cabrera Infante's ***Three Trapped Tigers*** and Rafael Sánchez's ***Macho Camacho's Beat*** (both also covered in *Latin American Literature and Its Times*). Hijuelos incorporates in the novel his own knowledge of music and nostalgia for musical genres that have lost popularity during his lifetime. A jazz musician who despised rock-and-roll, he projected some of his personal sentiments into the outlook of his characters, particularly César, who also despises modern music (Dear, p. 193). As mentioned, some of the novel's characters—for example, Desi Arnaz, Tito Puente, and Ernesto Lecouna—are based on genuine musicians of the era. Like the mambo dance and the Mambo Kings band, the characters rise quickly to stardom and as quickly fade away. The novel is a replay, a rerun of experience, told in hindsight, with all the realism, delusion, and melancholy that a retrospective entails.

Events in History at the Time the Novel Was Written

The Cuban miracle. Since 1959 more than one million people, or one-eighth of Cuba's population, have immigrated to the United States. Though initially many were despondent over their inability to return to their homeland, they have adjusted extremely well to U.S. life and have become one of the nation's most successful immigrant communities. According to the 1990 U.S. census, Cuban Americans have the lowest unemployment rate (5.8 percent) and the highest per capita income ($33,500) of any Latino group. In fact, many Cubans have achieved more success in the United States than they did in Cuba even before Castro. "No group of newcomers in the United States had ever moved so quickly from penury to prosperity" (Shorris, p. 68). Their success has been labeled "the Cuban miracle" and as a group they are characterized as self-sufficient, politically powerful, and culturally influential. Although they represent just 5 percent (1.2 million) of all Latinos in the United States, Cubans make up the majority of doctors in the Latino population, have played a large role in running the Hispanic Cultural Association, and fill seats of government. In 1985, for example, Xavier Suarez became the first Cuban-American mayor of Miami.

The Mariel Boatlift. In the 1980s, the period in which the novel ends and was written, relations between the Cuban and U.S. governments remained strained. Though some diplomatic ties had been renewed in 1977, several events refroze the thaw that had been occurring. First, in April of 1980, Cuban leader Fidel Castro gave all Cubans who wished to immigrate to the United States the chance to leave from the port of Mariel, Cuba. In six months, 124,779 people emigrated from Cuba, including—along with political protestors—prisoners, prostitutes, drug addicts, and mental patients. This influx of "undesirables" created a public backlash in the United States against the Mariel Boatlift. Neither mainstream American society nor the Cuban American community welcomed the *Marielitos,* as these Cuban immigrants were called. Public perception of these people was not helped by the fact that 40 percent were black: both the United States and Cuba have long racist histories. Prior to Mariel, less than 2 percent of Cuban immigrants were Afro-Cuban.

Throughout the 1980s, with U.S. President Ronald Reagan in office, matters worsened between Cuba and the United States. Castro and Reagan refused to negotiate face-to-face over political or territorial disputes. Castro's stance was that "principles are not negotiable. . . . [U.S. leaders] will see that they will never bring us to our knees" (Castro in Pérez, p. 381). In the mid-1970s through the early 1980s, Cuba sent troops to Angola to fight against South Africa, an ally of the United States. Then, in the early '80s, Reagan backed the counter-revolution against the Sandinista government in Nicaragua, a government that Cuba supported. Castro backed the independence movement of Puerto Rico, a U.S. commonwealth (Rudolf, p.143). Reagan flexed the U.S. military muscle in 1983 by invading Grenada and ousting its president, a close friend of Castro. In this particular confrontation, U.S. forces fought directly against the Cubans and arrested many—both in and out of the military. This tit for tat went on through Reagan's tenure in office. By 1989, at the time of the novel's publication, George Bush had replaced Reagan as president. He declared to a Miami audience that the United States "could not think of improving relations with Cuba until it saw some sign of change in Cuba's foreign and domestic policies" (Bush in Smith, p. 179). Thus the embargo continued.

Many have speculated about the political leanings of *The Mambo Kings Play Songs of Love.* The novel is not overtly opinionated, though it exposes some deleterious effects of communism in Cuba through the letters César receives from relatives and through his correspondence with his daughter. Interestingly, the novel was published in a pivotal era. The communist regime of the Soviet Union had begun to dissolve, along with its sway over nations in Eastern Europe. Cuba was one of the lone communist strongholds left in the world.

Reviews. *The Mambo Kings Play Songs of Love* received almost universal acclaim upon its publication in 1989. The *New York Times* called it "street smart and lyrical, impassioned and reflective" (Kakutani, p. 26). But, as with all great works, innovation breeds controversy. Earl Shorris admired Hijuelos's style but found his portrayal of the ultra-macho César "dangerously close to stereotypes" (Shorris, p. 390). Others were offended by the sexually explicit passages throughout the book. But the vast majority of critics described it as "a remarkable new novel" and lauded its original style and bravado on all levels (Kakutani in Ryan, p. 256). In *Newsweek* Cathleen McGuigan praised the book, calling it "the sweatiest read of the summer. . . . Fortunately, Hijuelos has a tender touch with his characters, and César is more than a stereotype. . . . Like an album of mambo tunes, some of the sequences begin to sound alike, but the rhythms and colors are hard to resist" (McGuigan, p. 60).

—Diane R. Sneva

For More Information

Castleman, Harry, and Walter J. Podrazik. *Watching TV: Four Decades of American Television.* New York: McGraw-Hill, 1982.

Dear, Pamela S., ed. *Contemporary Authors New Revision Series.* Vol. 50. Detroit: Gale Research, 1996.

Hijuelos, Oscar. *The Mambo Kings Play Songs of Love.* New York: Farrar, Straus and Giroux, 1989.

Kakutani, Michiko. Review of *The Mambo Kings Play Songs of Love. The New York Times,* August 4, 1989, C26.

Luis, William, and Ann González, eds. *Modern Latin-American Fiction Writers.* 2nd series. Dictionary of Literary Biography. Vol. 145. Detroit: Gale Research, 1994.

McGuigan, Catherine. Review of *The Mambo Kings Play Songs of Love. Newsweek* 114 (August 21, 1989): 60.

Pérez, Louis A. Jr. *Cuba: Between Reform and Revolution.* New York: Oxford University Press, 1988.

Pérez Firmat, Gustavo. *Life on the Hyphen: The Cuban-American Way.* Austin: University of Texas Press, 1994.

Rudolf, James D., ed. *Cuba: A Country Study.* Washington, D.C.: American University Press, 1985.

Ryan, Bryan, ed. *Hispanic Writers.* Detroit: Gale Research, 1991.

Shorris, Earl. *Latinos: A Biography of the People.* New York: W. W. Norton, 1992.

Smith, Wayne S. *Portrait of Cuba.* Atlanta: Turner, 1991.

Massacre in Mexico

by
Elena Poniatowska

Elena Poniatowska Amor was born in Paris, France, in 1932, the daughter of Paulette Amor Iturbe, an aristocratic Mexican nationalist, and Jean Evremont Poniatowski Sperry, a French citizen of royal Polish ancestry, descended from King Stanislaus II, the last king of Poland. Elena and her younger sister were raised in France, where they began their primary education. In 1942 their mother took her children to Mexico, where Poniatowska has lived ever since. She began her literary career as a journalist for the Mexican daily *Excelsior*. After a year she joined the newspaper *Novedades*, where she continued writing about social and cultural events, and honed her skills at what would become her preferred genre: the interview. Poniatowska first achieved literary renown with the publication in 1969 of *Hasta no verte Jesús Mío* (*Until We Meet Again*), a testimonial novel based on the life of Jesusa Palancares, a poor Mexican woman who recounts her role as a *soldadera* (soldier's female companion) in the Mexican Revolution from the perspective of a slum on the outskirts of Mexico City. For this work Poniatowska received the Mazatlán Prize, a Mexican national book award, in 1970. *Massacre in Mexico,* one of the first and most widely read accounts of the student uprisings that culminated tragically at the Plaza of the Three Cultures in Tlatelolco, was published the following year. It has sold more than 250,000 copies and has been translated into Polish, Czech, and English. For this work she was awarded the coveted Xavier Villaurrutia literary prize, which she refused, asking the president of Mexico: "Who is going to award a prize to those who fell at Tlatelolco in 1968?" (personal communication by the author).

THE LITERARY WORK

A testimonial account of the student movement in Mexico City from July 22 to October 31, 1968; published in Spanish (as *La noche de Tlatelolco)* in 1971, in English in 1975.

SYNOPSIS

The testimonies of students, teachers, housewives, soldiers, and politicians, as well as fragments of newspaper articles, documentary photos, and slogans, are woven together to create a literary montage attesting to events surrounding the massacre of students at the Plaza of the Three Cultures in Tlatelolco, a Mexico City neighborhood, on the evening of October 2, 1968.

Events in History at the Time the Testimony Takes Place

The 1960s. Although essentially a domestic conflict, the events documented in *Massacre in Mexico* were profoundly influenced by world affairs of the late 1960s. The assassination of United States civil rights leader Martin Luther King in April 1968, as well as that of presidential candidate Robert Kennedy in June of the same year, galvanized Mexico along with the rest of the international community. The U.S. civil rights movements of the 1960s, whose goals included guaranteeing the vote to blacks, also touched the hearts of people in Mexico, where social and economic oppression had victimized people too. Mexicans watched their television screens in horror as riots broke out in many U.S. cities, and peaceful demonstrations were met with guns and billy clubs across the southern United States.

The ebb and flow of the era's communist movements also affected Mexicans. First there was the influence of Cuba's 1959 revolution, whose champions, Fidel Castro and Ernesto "Che" Guevara, quickly became symbols of anti-imperialist movements that swept universities from Mexico to Argentina, culminating in massive demonstrations that repudiated the United States' foreign policy, particularly in terms of its political, economic, and military intervention in Latin America and other developing nations.

The philosophies of Karl Marx and Herbert Marcuse were highly influential in international and Mexican ideological circles; Marcuse's theory of "the great refusal" discouraged the individual from accepting the existing social order and encouraged the masses to rise up against repression and the status quo without necessarily waiting for a revolution. Demonstrations of such philosophies frequently met with strong government repression, as in the killing of four students on the campus of Kent State University in Ohio in 1970. The student protest at Kent State resembled others that erupted in the 1960s, not only in the United States but in countries such as France as well. Through widespread access to mass communications, Mexicans were made aware of the May 1968 demonstrations by French students, who took to the streets of Paris in droves and were violently confronted by governmental forces.

Given this global ferment, when faced with the first student outbursts in the summer of 1968, the Mexican ruling party (known as the PRI, or the Institutional Revolutionary Party) attempted to depict the disturbances as the work of foreign infiltrators, particularly veterans of the May insurrection in Paris.

> To that end, several young foreign tourists were snatched by the police as they walked through the streets. Mexicans with foreign-sounding last names were featured prominently in press releases on the arrests, and the police went so far as to record Mexican names like Emilio, Antonio, or Maria Antonieta as Emile, Antoine, and Marie Antoinette, with duly gallicized [French sounding] last names.
>
> (Hellman, p. 176)

During the early months of student unrest in Mexico, it was also purported that the U.S. Central Intelligence Agency, members of the Communist Party, Cuban revolutionaries, and even enemies of Mexico's president Gustavo Díaz Ordaz were responsible for manipulating students. The students, however, emphatically denied that they were being guided by foreign agitators and foreign ideologies. They made a point of associating themselves and their cause with such domestic heroes as Emiliano Zapata, Pancho Villa, and Benito Juárez. "Clearly expressing the position of the movement was the slogan, 'We are not the agitators. Hunger and misery are the agitators'" (Hellman, p. 178). In the view of the students, there were fundamental problems that their government, run by "various power figures" who were "accustomed to wheeling and dealing . . . behind the scenes," had not managed to solve (Paz in Poniatowska, p. ix). They essentially wanted to democratize their republic—and thus sought a dialogue with Mexico's power brokers.

In 1964 the PRI had selected as its presidential candidate Gustavo Díaz Ordaz, who was considered by some to be the most conservative, if not reactionary, candidate in the history of the ruling party. He had served as Secretary of the Interior in the previous presidential cabinet and was "badly tinged with policy decisions reform-minded groups could not stomach. It had been he who applied the laws of 'social dissolution' against David Alfaro Siqueiros and other radicals" (Meyer and Sherman, p. 664). Siqueiros was one of the "big three" Mexican muralists who, along with José Clemente Orozco and Diego Rivera, had covered thousands of square feet of Mexico's public buildings with revolutionary images taken from the country's violent past.

Upon inheriting the presidency from his predecessor, Adolfo López Mateos, Díaz Ordaz appointed Carlos Madrazo, a liberal-minded member of the party, as president of the PRI. Quickly Madrazo initiated substantial changes within the ruling party. These changes promoted the internal democratization of the PRI, which increased general civilian participation, and brought more women into government positions, while reducing the historically unlimited power of local political bosses, or *caciques* (Meyer and Sherman, p. 664). Not surprisingly Madrazo met with an enormous wave of disapproval from those whose traditional powers and privileges were being questioned. Also not surprisingly members of Mexico's elite demanded his dismissal. Díaz Ordaz quickly fired the reform-minded politician

The year 1968 was one of ferment throughout the world, and the Olympic Games in Mexico City became a venue for promoting political views. Here, American sprinters Tommie Smith (center) and John Carlos (right) turn the awards stand into a political platform as they give a "Black Power" salute while receiving their medals for the 200-meter dash.

and, among other anti-democratic gestures, annulled elections in states where opposition parties had, he claimed, won because of unspecified "irregularities" in the election process.

The 1968 Olympic games. The fact that student uprisings reached a critical point in the year that the Olympics were to be held in Mexico City is not coincidental. Since it was the first time that the Olympic games would be held in a developing country, the PRI was anxious that the country present itself to the rest of the world as a nation on the rise. To that end, it invested millions of pesos in the construction of athletic facilities, housing for foreign visitors, and a modern subway system modeled after that of Paris. Workers labored around the clock and, to the surprise of many, all was ready by October 12, when the games were scheduled to begin. The eyes of the world would be focused on the nation's capital for a period of three weeks, and the administration was intent on creating an image of progress and stability to impress the world community. However, not everyone was so easily persuaded. To some, the cost of staging the games—between $150 and $200 million—seemed far too high for a developing nation to bear. The student movement seized the opportunity to point out the disparity between the government's carefully controlled image of Mexico and reality.

> [T]he repressive measures applied by the Mexican government to assure that the games would be staged without disruption, provided immediate focus for the [student] movement. The movement's symbols and slogans centered on the Olympiad and highlighted the irony of claiming 1968 as the "Year of Peace" in Mexico. . . . The signs underscored the brutality of the regime that was playing host to the world's athletes: "Mexico will win the gold medal for repression"—"Welcome to Mexico, site of the Olympic Butchery, 1968." Others depicted the Olympic dove of peace with a knife in its breast, the five-ring Olympic symbol as five smoking grenades, and a riot policeman racing along with his club held aloft like a flaming Olympic torch.
>
> (Hellman, pp. 178-79)

The Mexico City student movement. The student movement in Mexico City was born on July 22, 1968. Student groups from two rival Mexico City high schools, or *preparatorias,* clashed in the first conflict of a movement that would be brutally crushed less than four months later. Although the exact motives of this outbreak remain unclear, it is rumored that it resulted from tension between two neighborhood gangs: "The Spiders" and "The Ciudadelans" (inhabitants of the Ciudadela neighborhood). Receiving a call for help from one of the high school's principals, the mayor of Mexico City, General Alfonso Corona del Rosal, immediately dispatched the locally feared and hated *granaderos,* a paramilitary squadron used to disperse rioters. The granaderos broke up the crowd and stopped the confrontation, their actions politicizing much of Mexico's student population against the government (Meyer and Sherman, p. 667).

"LETTER FROM A MOTHER TO HER SON IN THE RIOT SQUAD"

Dear Son:

. . . You have no idea how terrified I was when I read the papers; I realized the grave dangers you had been exposed to, all for love of [President] Díaz Ordaz. The big hard heads of those savage students might have damaged your nice rifle. I've heard that some of them are such brutes that they might even go so far as to smash their faces against that billy club of yours that you take such loving care of. . . .

Hoping that you will continue to kill students and teachers with the same furious passion,

Love,
Mom
"La Poquianchis Mayor,"
Women's house of detention,
Santa Marta Acatitla

[An ironic] leaflet collected at the August 27, 1968, student demonstration and read in the Manuel M. Ponce Auditorium on September 6, 1968, during the lecture series "Storytellers Meet the Public," sponsored by the INBA [National Institute of Fine Arts]

(*Massacre in Mexico,* pp. 58–59)

Four days later, on July 26, students supporting Fidel Castro gathered to celebrate the anniversary of the Cuban Revolution at the Benito Juárez monument in downtown Mexico City. The granaderos were again dispatched, and a full scale riot ensued. Eyewitnesses noted that the litter containers along the street were curiously filled with stones, "right there at hand should some charitable soul wish to make use of them. Since when have the residents of Mexico City been in the habit of throwing stones into litter containers?" (Poniatowska, *Massacre in Mexico,* p. 326). During the following weeks, many similar incidents occurred between students and granaderos, and barricades and heavy artillery appeared in the center of the city. During one particularly violent confrontation, the granaderos demonstrated their authority and their ignorance of history by blowing up the seventeenth-century baroque doors of the school of San Ildefonso in an attempt to capture students who were hiding inside.

The beginning of the end. Massive student demonstrations escalated as the city's government officials worked around the clock to finish up the myriad of preparations for the Olympics, which were scheduled to begin in October. Among the most forceful demonstrations were those held on the campuses of the National Polytechnic Institute (IPN) and the National Autonomous University (UNAM). On Sunday, July 28, student delegates from the UNAM and IPN met at the IPN School of Economics to discuss the idea of organizing a strike, scheduled to take place unless the following six demands were met:

1) The dissolution of rightist student groups supported by the government and its ruling party, the PRI;
2) The expulsion of students who were members of these groups as well as of the ruling party (PRI);
3) Indemnities paid to families of the dead and those wounded in skirmishes with the granaderos;
4) Immediate release of all jailed students;
5) The disbanding of the granaderos and other repressive police units;
6) The derogation of Article 145 of the Penal Code, which allowed for imprisonment based on the crime of "social dissolution."

As Judith Hellman points out, "these demands were neither radical nor revolutionary. . . . The student movement was essentially calling for the recognition of constitutional guarantees and the protection of civil liberties provided by the constitution" (Hellman, p. 180). In other words, the students recognized that Mexico was not ready for a revolutionary alternative and—at least in terms of their demands—stayed well within the boundaries of the country's political establishment, essentially respecting its overriding authority.

The Secretary of the Interior (and Mexico's future president), Luis Echeverría, agreed to debate with student leaders, but the talks broke down when the latter demanded that the dialogue be broadcast on public radio and television, a long-time time bastion of unconditional PRI support.

On August 27 the National Student Strike Committee held a demonstration in the Zócalo, Mexico City's main square, which attracted an estimated 500,000 participants and constituted the most massive antigovernment demonstration in Mexico's history. The demonstration lasted into the night, and, when the granaderos were sent into the square with heavy artillery, the first verified student death in the student movement occurred (Meyer and Sherman, p. 668).

President Díaz Ordaz's State of the Union Address on September 1, 1968, was not a typical speech full of heady rhetoric and golden predictions of Mexico's economic future. In light of the impending Olympic Games, he was obliged to directly address the issues at hand. He stated that the students did not act alone in their clashes with the government, and claimed that Article 145 of the Penal Code could not, as the students demanded, be abolished, because this was beyond the power of the President. Not surprisingly, the president's analysis of current events in Mexico on the eve of the Olympic Games was far from positive:

> We have caused Mexico to appear in the eyes of the world as a country in which the most reprehensible events may take place; for the unfair and almost forgotten image of the Mexican as a violent, irascible gunman to be revived; and for slander to be mixed with painful truth in the same news reports.
>
> (Díaz Ordaz in Meyer and Sherman, p. 669)

The students regarded the President's statement as just another governmental ploy to postpone any confrontation—or any conciliation—until after the Olympic Games, when, of course, the students would no longer have the benefit of world attention directed towards their country and, it was hoped, their cause. In the middle of September, the President sent in 10,000 troops to occupy the UNAM. They arrested approximately 500 demonstrators. The recently appointed rector of the university, Javier Barrios Sierra, resigned in protest at the blatant undermining of his institution's autonomy. In the weeks that followed, bands of discontented students demonstrated in the streets, painting slogans on walls, and occasionally burning public buses in protest against the government's unilateral actions.

The night of Tlatelolco. On the afternoon of October 2, 1968, members of the National Student Strike Committee organized another meeting. This time, it was held at the Plaza of the Three Cultures, an archaeological site-cum-residential neighborhood, that owes its name to the three cultures that it represents. The site preserves the ruins of a pre-Hispanic settlement and a Franciscan colonial monastery (which was also the first college in Mexico). These remains are juxtaposed with a series of ultramodern high-rises designed by celebrated local architects. Involving from 5,000–10,000 people, the meeting was not as massive as those that had preceded it. The student leaders assembled themselves on a balcony of the Chihuahua apartment building and began their speeches. Although the harangues were emotional, the demonstration itself was orderly and peaceful.

FRAGMENT OF THE POEM "IN MEMORY OF TLATELOLCO" BY ROSARIO CASTELLANOS

An accomplished poet, novelist, and dramatist, Rosario Castellanos (1925-74) distinguished herself as one of Mexico's foremost writers of the 20th century. She died tragically in an accident with an electrical appliance while serving as Mexico's ambassador to Israel, six years after the events commemorated in her poem on Tlatelolco:

> Darkness breeds violence
> and violence seeks darkness
> to carry out its bloody deeds.
> That is why on October 2 they waited for nightfall
> so that no one would see the hand
> that held the gun, only its sudden lightning flash.
> [. . .]
> Don't search for something there are no signs of now:
> traces of blood, dead bodies,
> because it was all an offering to a goddess,
> the Eater of Excrement.
>
> (Castellanos in Poniatowska, p. 171)

At approximately 6:10 in the evening, under a light rainfall, several green flares were spotted in the air. As bystanders and participants looked up at the sky, granaderos and other representatives of authority, heavily armed with tanks, bazookas, cannons, and other heavy artillery moved in on the demonstrators trapped in the Plaza.

There are many versions of the violent events that ensued. The government version, which appeared in local newspapers the following day, claimed that terrorists in the surrounding apartment buildings began firing on the police. Many participants and bystanders, however, insisted that the police opened fire without being provoked, and only at that point did snipers begin to shoot from the buildings. Whatever the truth may be, thousands of innocent people were caught in the crossfire as the government moved in on the plaza in a pincher formation. In the mayhem that followed, many soldiers were killed or injured as well, including one of the commanding officers, General Hernández Toledo. Official government statistics initially claimed that only 8, then 18, and finally 43 deaths had occurred, but other sources place the death count at at least 400, while some 2,000 were jailed. Sócrates Campus Lemus, an arrested student leader who was accused by many members of the student organizations of being coopted by the government, claimed that the killings had been carefully orchestrated by ambitious opposition politicians, including one of Mexico's most respected economists, Víctor Urquidi, in the interest of bringing down the government for personal gain (Meyer and Sherman, p. 671).

The Testimony in Focus

Contents summary. *Massacre in Mexico* is divided into two sections that are separated by a photo layout of captioned images. Generally speaking, Section 1, "Taking to the Streets," reflects the students' euphoria before the events of October 2, while Section 2, "The Night of Tlatelolco," explores the aftermath of the confrontation between government forces and student demonstrators. The former is constructed through a selection of quotes from interviews with professors, students, parents, and political activists, complemented by slogans taken from student banners, chants, and street posters. In one particular instance, a father shares his approbation of the protest: "If the one thing the Student Movement has accomplished is to strip the Mexican Revolution bare, to show that it was a filthy, corrupt old whore, that alone is enough to justify it" (*Massacre in Mexico,* p. 147). Comprising the second section are testimonies from parents of the dead and wounded as well as survivors, along with newspaper clippings that detail the events that transpired. The testimonies consist not only of descriptions but also of snippets of conversation at the demonstration. At one point, for example, a sister panics by the side of her fallen sibling: "Little brother, speak to me. . . . Please, somebody get him a stretcher! I'm right here, Julio . . . a stretcher!" (*Massacre in Mexico,* p. 225).

Cumulatively the book achieves its effect through its compilation of the different impressions, chants, dialogue, news stories, banners, poems attributed to various teachers, students, prisoners, parents, politicians, and bystanders:

> WE DON'T WANT OLYMPIC GAMES! WE WANT A REVOLUTION!
>
> —Chant by students at a number of meetings
>
> ***
>
> We try not to let our political differences affect our daily life here in prison.
>
> —Luis González Sánchez, member of the Communist Youth, prisoner in Lecumberri
>
> ***
>
> We have been so tolerant that we have been criticized for our excessive leniency, but there is a limit to everything, and the irremediable violations of law and order that have occurred recently before the very eyes of the entire nation cannot be allowed to continue.
>
> —Gustavo Díaz Ordaz, Fourth Annual Presidential Message to the National Congress, September 1, 1968
>
> ***
>
> TO THE PEOPLE OF MEXICO:
> You can see that we're not vandals or rebels without a cause—the label that's constantly been pinned on us. Our silence proves it.
>
> —Handbill at the September 13 demonstration [a silent march]
>
> ***
>
> Tlatelolco? I hear it's always been a place where human sacrifices were offered [by the ancient Aztecs].
>
> —Francisca Ávila de Contreras, eighty-year-old resident of the Calle de Neptuno, near the Nonoalco-Tlatelolco Bridge
>
> ***
>
> The dead bodies were lying there on the pavement, waiting to be taken away. I counted lots and lots of them from the window, about seventy-eight in all. They were piling them up there in the rain. . . . I remember that Carlitos, my son, had been wearing a green corduroy jacket, and I thought I recognized his dead body every time they dragged another one up. . . .
>
> —Margarita Nolasco, anthropologist (*Massacre in Mexico,* pp. 12, 44, 45, 55, 124, 210)

Social unrest in Mexico. At a demonstration on August 13, 1968, students chanted "Vallejo, Vallejo, Vallejo, Freedom!"; they also chanted "Che-Che-Che-Guevara" (*Massacre in Mexico*, p. 150). Why chant these names, the first belonging to a Mexican railway worker, the second to a doctor-guerrilla leader who helped Fidel Castro take over Cuba?

In 1958 the workers of Mexico's national railways organized a series of strikes that were violently broken by government forces. These strikes are generally held to be symbolically tied to the student uprisings ten years later, and perhaps to constitute their most tangible stimulus. The long-term incarceration of two of the union's most conspicuous leaders, Demetrio Vallejo (12 years) and Valentín Campa (11 years) gave the students something specific to fight for. However, as Octavio Paz is quick to point out, the students "failed to see the difference in objectives and tactics and above all the different class structures involved in the two movements, and hence did not appreciate the entirely different significance of these two episodes" (Paz in Poniatowska, p. ix).

Nevertheless, the students identified with Vallejo's victimization by Mexico's power mongers. Similarly they took inspiration from the memory of Che Guevara. After helping Fidel Castro overthrow Cuba's dictatorship in 1959, Guevara had gone on in the 1960s to stage agrarian insurrections that fired the imagination of protestors everywhere. "We chose Che as our symbol of demonstrations from the very first. Che was our link with student movements all over the world!" (*Massacre in Mexico,* p. 32). Not yet 40, Guevara died tragically on October 8, 1967, in guerrilla warfare in Bolivia, after which youth everywhere turned the rebel into an icon. "Young men all over Mexico wanted to be like him. He was . . . the symbol of the new man, the pure and incorruptible hero" (Krauze, p. 692). Mexican youth plastered his face on the walls of Mexico's National Palace, regarding him as champion of the downtrodden and an agent of light; opposing him were agents of darkness—the exploiters who wielded power in business and government and the U.S. imperialists. Mexico's student movement, however, did not include only such absolute views; it also encompassed the views of more moderate activists who agreed with the students that change in Mexico was imperative: "The teachers were the most moderate group in the entire Movement. . . . They supported the students, but also did their best to keep them from acting on impulse" (*Massacre in Mexico,* p. 94). The presence of such mature activists underscored the legitimacy of the student's demands and also foreshadowed the riveting impact that the massacre was to have on Mexican writers of the era.

Sources and literary context. Writers responded to the massacre with a spate of novels, plays, short stories, poems, and essays. Carlos Fuentes (see ***The Death of Artemio Cruz,*** also covered in *Latin American Literature and Its Times*) referred to the deadly event in his drama *All Cats Are Gray in the Night* (1968), and so did Octavio Paz in his essay *Posdata* (1970). "In the extensive and powerful literary response to Tlatelolco," observes one literary historian, "is captured not only historical data but also the intense and often anguished psychological reality underneath the facts and statistics" (Foster, p. 273). Within this outpouring, Poniatowska's *Massacre in Mexico* has achieved singular renown for its portrayal of the massacre: "The distinction of having written the most dramatic, most widely read, and most unusual account of the event belongs to Elena Poniatowska [and] . . . her unique *La noche de Tlatelolco*" (Foster, p. 330). Authors would continue to invoke the event in later works (Gustavo Sainz in *Brother Wolf,* 1978; Poniatowska herself in *Silence Is*

PAZ ON *MASSACRE IN MEXICO*

Referring to the tone as well as the material in Poniatowska's book, poet and essayist Octavio Paz (see ***The Labyrinth of Solitude,*** also covered in *Latin American Literature and Its Times*) describes its contents:

> The mood at the beginning is one of joyous enthusiasm and euphoria: on taking to the streets, the students discover the meaning of collective action, direct democracy, and fraternity. Armed with these weapons alone, they fight repression and in a very short time win the support and the loyalties of the people. Up until this point, Elena Poniatowska's account is the story of the civic awakening of an entire generation of young people. This story of buoyant collective fever soon takes on darker overtones, however: the wave of hope and generous idealism represented by these youngsters breaks against the wall of sheer power, and the government unleashes its murderous forces of violence; the story ends in a bloodbath.
>
> (Paz in Poniatowska, p. viii)

The August 13, 1968 student demonstration in Mexico City.

Strong, 1980; and Fuentes in *Christopher Unborn,* 1987). In fact, the massacre is said to have rechanneled Mexican literature away from experiments in "time and space and point of view" toward a direct focus on the nature of power in Mexico; the massacre brought a sobering end to the "illusion of democracy" in the nation, and writers responded accordingly (Foster, p. 245).

Traditionally, Poniatowska's work has been described as "testimonial literature," a genre that demonstrates "an explicit commitment to denounce repression and abuse of authority, raise the consciousness of its readers about situations of political, economic, and cultural terror, and offer an alternative view to official, hegemonic history" (Jörgensen, p. 68). Testimonial literature is often considered a hybrid genre, because it incorporates both historical and literary qualities, straddling the areas of fiction and nonfiction.

In an interview Poniatowska has described how she was informed about the events that transpired in Tlateloco by several "hysterical" women who came to her home on the night of the tragedy. Moved by their horrible tales of murder and destruction, she visited the Plaza of the Three Cultures on the following day:

> I went on October 3 to see Tlatelolco. It shocked me to see the piles of empty shoes, to see the tanks there and the traces of machine gun fire all over the place. Then I said to myself, what happened here? (Because when the women came to tell me on the night of October 2, I thought they were hysterical.) I even saw blood on the wall, bloody handprints, and all the windows broken out. I saw that there had been a real battle there. After that I kept track of the testimonies of the people who told me their experiences, and that's how I put together the book.
>
> (Poniatowska in Jörgensen, p. 77)

The testimony is a tricky genre to define, because the question of authority is always a point of great debate. Who actually is the author of *Massacre in Mexico*? Elena Poniatowska, who orchestrated many voices in her polyphonic narrative, or the informants, without whose testimonies the work would not exist? Whatever the case may be, the undeniably literary characteristics of the work stem precisely from its very humanity and mystery:

> As with all historical events, the story of what took place in 1968 in Mexico is a tangled web of ambiguous facts and enigmatic meanings. These events really happened, but their reality does not have the same texture as everyday reality. Nor does it have the fantastic self-consistency of an imaginary reality such as we find in works of fiction.
>
> (Paz in Poniatowska, p. viii)

Reviews. In a book-length interview with Esteban Ascencio, Elena Poniatowska recalls the almost nonexistent reaction to the publication of her work in 1971:

> The only review that was published about the book when it came out was by José Emilio [Pacheco]. It was as if it didn't exist. Its promotion—if it could be called that—was from mouth to mouth, which is the best of all. I especially recall Don Tomás Espresate [founder of Ediciones ERA, the company that published the book]. . . . They threatened to put a bomb in the offices of his publishing house and he responded that he had been in the Spanish Civil war until 1939 and that he was afraid neither of bombs nor of anonymous threats.
>
> (Ascensio, p. 44; trans. M. Schuessler)

In a review published on March 31, 1971, in the news magazine *Siempre!* José Emilio Pacheco—the highly respected author and literary critic who had helped to edit the book—denounced the government's actions and underscored the transcendence of Poniatowska's work: "No other publication has expressed the atrocious enormity of the crime in all of its dimensions as does this multiple narration of its survivors" (Pacheco, p. x; trans. M. Schuessler). At the end of his review, Pacheco demands that the government clarify the many mysteries surrounding the tragedy: "Elena Poniatowska's book, which is also the book of those who are imprisoned and of the mothers who lost their children in one of the worst killings in a history as violent and sad as ours, provides the opportunity to demand that the government publicly investigate and punish those responsible—whoever they may be" (Pacheco, p. xi; trans. M. Schuessler).

—Michael Schuessler

For More Information

Ascensio, Esteban. *Me lo dijo Elena Poniatowska.* México, D.F.: Ediciones del Milenio, 1997.

Foster, David William, ed. *Mexican Literature: A History.* Austin: University of Texas Press, 1994.

García Pinto, Magdalena. *Women Writers of Latin America: Intimate Histories.* Trans. Trudy Balch and Magdalena García Pinto. Austin: University of Texas Press, 1991.

Hellman, Judith Adler. *Mexico in Crisis.* 2nd ed. New York: Holmes and Meier, 1983.

Jörgensen, Beth E. *The Writing of Elena Poniatowska: Engaging Dialogues.* Austin: University of Texas Press, 1994.

Krauze, Enrique. *Mexico: Biography of Power.* Trans. Hank Heifetz. New York: HarperCollins, 1997.

Meyer, Michael C., and William L. Sherman. *The Course of Mexican History.* New York: Oxford University Press, 1979.

Pacheco, Jose Emilio. "Tlatelolco Dos de Octubre." *Siempre,* March 31, 1971, x-xi.

Poniatowska, Elena. *Massacre in Mexico.* Trans. Helen R. Lane. New York: The Viking Press, 1975.

Men of Maize

by
Miguel Ángel Asturias

Miguel Ángel Asturias was born in Guatemala City in 1899. No stranger to oppression, Asturias lived much of his life abroad in order to avoid political persecution at home. During his stay in Paris in the 1920s, he studied surrealism and, under the tutelage of Professor Georges Reynaud, translated the *Popol Vuh,* a sacred book of the Maya Indians of Guatemala. Asturias's first novel, *El Señor Presidente* (1946), explored political corruption and discontent in Guatemala—subjects that would reappear in many of his later works, including the "Banana Trilogy," a fiercely polemical exposé of the United Fruit Company that included the novels *Viento fuerte* (1949; Strong Wind), *El Papa verde* (1954; The Green Pope), and *Los ojos de los enterrados* (1960, The Eyes of the Interred). Although his popularity never rivaled that of later Latin American authors, in 1967 Asturias became the first Latin American writer to receive the Nobel Prize for Literature—one year after he was awarded the International Lenin Peace Prize by the Soviet Union. *El Señor Presidente* was arguably Asturias's most popular work during his lifetime, but since his death in 1974, critics have widely acclaimed *Men of Maize* as his masterpiece.

THE LITERARY WORK

A novel set in Guatemala beginning in 1898 and spanning approximately 50 years; published in Spanish (as *Hombres de maíz*) in 1949, in English in 1975.

SYNOPSIS

Six separate yet interwoven stories explore the plight of native people of Guatemala, who fight to maintain their cultural identity in the face of the forces of change.

Events in History at the Time the Novel Takes Place

The importance of maize. Asturias's use of maize (corn) as the central motif in the novel corresponds to the myth of creation in the *Popol Vuh,* the sacred book of the Quiché Maya Indians. In the *Popol Vuh* human beings are created from yellow and white maize, ground nine times by the Xmucane (Grandmother of Light), and from water, which becomes human fat when worked by several mythic beings called "Bearer, Begetter, Sovereign Plumed Serpent":

> the making, the modeling of our first mother-father
> with yellow corn, white corn alone for the flesh,
> food alone for the human legs and arms
> for our first fathers, the four human works
> [first four human beings].
>
> (Tedlock, p. 164)

Asturias echoes the *Popol Vuh* at the beginning of *Men of Maize* as Gaspar Ilóm reflects upon his reason for fighting the maizegrowers: "The [maizegrowers'] maize impoverishes the earth and makes no one rich. . . . Sown to be eaten it is the sacred sustenance of the men who were made of maize. Sown to make money it means

A Guatemalan woman cooks tortillas for her family. Corn-based tortillas form an essential part of the Guatemalan diet.

famine for the men who were made of maize" (Asturias, *Men of Maize,* p. 11). Generations later, an old woman that Hilario Sacayón, another of the novel's characters, meets on his journey reiterates: "[W]e can feed on maize, which is the flesh of our flesh on the cobs . . . but everything will end up impoverished and scorched by the sun, by the air, by the clearing fires, if we keep sowing maize to make a business of it, as though it weren't sacred, highly sacred" (*Men of Maize,* p. 192).

In Indian communities, the sowing and harvesting of maize are tasks that combine the ritualistic and the practical. Rigoberta Menchú (see ***I, Rigoberta Menchú,*** also covered in *Latin American Literature and Its Times*), a late twentieth-century Quiché Indian woman, describes the ceremony performed before maize is sown:

> We choose two or three of the biggest seeds and place them in a ring, candles representing earth, water, animals and the universe. . . . The seed is honoured because it will be buried in something sacred—the earth—and because it will multiply and bear fruit the next year.
>
> (Menchú, p. 32)

Another Indian recalls, "When you plant [maize], you throw four seeds into the ground, no more, no less. . . . Each group of corn has four stalks, four plants. . . . [W]e cut down any other plant growing next to the corn because it robs it of its strength" (Simon, p. 38).

Theological implications notwithstanding, maize is essential to Indian life. "[T]heir primary food is the corn-based tortillas which furnishes one-half the calories in the average daily diet. A family of six consumes 150 tortillas daily. . . . Guatemala produces over 500,000 tons of corn each year" (Simon, p. 22). In the novel Ilóm invites the Machojón family to a feast in which maize-based tamales constitute much of the menu: "Large tamales, red ones and black ones, . . . and smaller ones like acolytes in white maize-leaf surplices . . . and tamales with aniseed and tamales with green maize-ears, like the soft unhardened flesh of little maize boys" (*Men of Maize,* p. 22).

Racial tensions. Asturias does not furnish the reader with an exact time frame for *Men of Maize,* but most critics agree that, roughly speaking, the action begins in 1898, a year before Asturias was born, and ends in the mid-1940s, about the time the novel was written. This was a particularly turbulent period for Guatemala, which had been plagued by ethnic division and social unrest since its independence from Spain on September 15, 1821. Between 1821 and 1847 Guatemala was part of a federation of Central American states (including Nicaragua, Honduras, Costa Rica, and El Salvador, for example), which together adopted some social reforms of Spanish traditions during these years. Many of Guatemala's social and political problems stemmed from the uneasy relationship between the indigenous people, of Mayan Indian descent, and the *ladinos*. A loose category, the term *ladino* refers to everyone who has adopted the clothing and behaviors of Western culture. Ladinos may be European, Indian, mestizo (a mix of the two), or black; a ladinized Indian is one who has adopted Spanish traits. Since the Spanish conquest in 1524, ladino descendants of the original *conquistadores* (conquerors) have controlled the wealth and resources of Guatemala, as they do when the novel begins.

The ongoing conflict between Indians and ladinos acquires a personal dimension at the start of *Men of Maize*. Gaspar Ilóm, an Indian chieftain, and his tribe battle the ladino planters who cut down their trees to plant maize for profit: "The maizegrower sets fire to the brush and does for the timber in a matter of hours. And what timber. The most priceless of woods. . . . Different if it was to eat. It's to make money" (*Men of Maize*, p. 11). Tomás Machojón, who used to be one of Ilóm's men, is caught in the middle of this struggle because he is married to a ladino woman, Vaca Manuela. Interracial marriages have, in fact, been frowned upon in Guatemala: "Throughout the highland Mayan region, in Mexico and Guatemala, Ladinos believe themselves to be superior, treat Indians as inferiors and shun mixed marriages" (Brintnall, p. 20). In the novel Vaca Manuela is the "supreme authority" in the Machojón's marriage; she persuades her husband to betray the Indians and adopt the planters' cause.

> Señor Tomás . . . was an Indian but his wife, Vaca Manuela Machojón, had turned him into a Ladino. Ladino women have iguana's spittle, which hypnotizes men. Only by hanging them by their ankles can you extract those viscous mouthfuls of flattery and servility which get them their way in everything. That was how Vaca Manuela won Señor Tomás over for the maizegrowers.
>
> (*Men of Maize*, p. 18)

It is through ladino treachery—as personified by Tomás and Vaca Manuela—that the Indian Ilóm is poisoned and his men slaughtered by Colonel Godoy. This betrayal of the Indians by the ladinos resonates throughout the novel in the form of a curse that dooms all the betrayers.

Nineteenth-century Guatemalan politics—an overview. Historically, political alliances in Guatemala have been divided into two factions, Conservative and Liberal. For the most part, Conservatives have adopted a "live and let live" strategy in dealing with the indigenous people, who are too poor to wield any real political power but too numerous to ignore completely. Liberal politics, which favor the more mercantile interests of the ladinos, are in ascendancy when the novel begins. This period of Liberal ascendancy began in 1873 when Justo Rufino Barrios, known as the "Reformer," became president of Guatemala. During his 12 years in office (1873-85), Barrios implemented many of the sweeping economic and political changes that provide the backdrop for Asturias's novel.

THE UNITED FRUIT COMPANY IN GUATEMALA

A major economic and political force in Guatemala until recent years, the United Fruit Company was a multinational corporation founded in 1899 by three enterprising U.S. citizens: a ship captain, a fruit importer, and a railroad developer. In 1906 Guatemalan President Manuel Estrada Cabrera made critical concessions to the North Americans so that they would bring their business to Guatemala instead of to another Latin American country with similar resources; among other things, he granted them the exclusive right to operate Guatemala's central railway line. While the wealthy elite of Guatemala prospered from this relationship, the Indian people were forced to leave their homes in the highlands and to work as peons on the plantations. Forcing the Indians to work against their will was nothing new in Guatemala. In 1877 the Liberal government issued an edict, the *Reglamento de Jornaleros* (Law of the Day Laborers), which permitted coffee growers to recruit a certain number of Indians for a limited time from communities in the highlands, even against their will. The system remained in effect through the early 1900s, although over time the government took some steps on behalf of the forced laborers—for example, the setting of minimum wages. Such measures hamstrung exploiters to a degree but certainly did not stop them. The monopolies granted to United Fruit by Estrada Cabrera and his successors allowed the company to exploit the people and the land of Guatemala—creating a reserve of resentment in the indigenous population that would fuel future conflicts.

Determined to "modernize" Guatemala, Barrios and his supporters embarked upon a program of progressive reform that included establishing a strong, centralized national government

Manuel Estrada Cabrera

and seeking foreign capital to invest in Guatemala's economy. To attract investors (both ladino and foreign) the government legalized the sale of uncultivated Indian land to the highest bidder and forced the Indian people to toil on privately owned plantations, often in a form of debt peonage. Commerce was likewise under non-Indian control; much of it wound up in the hands of foreigners because Indian culture discouraged the accumulation of goods beyond what was necessary to live. In the novel, the presence of the two foreign shop owners in remote San Miguel Acatán (the Bavarian Don Deferic and the anonymous "Chinaman") suggests the success of Barrios's Liberal policies in reaching even the most rural sections of Guatemala.

Barrios's plan to centralize and consolidate government authority resulted in the construction of new roads, railways, and telegraph lines, which made formerly remote villages (like Pisiguilito in the novel) increasingly accessible to outsiders and more susceptible to government control. The Indians were no longer permitted to govern themselves, and instead were obliged to adopt a system in which tribal elders functioned solely in an advisory or ceremonial capacity—only the ladino *alcade* (mayor) with the support of government troops wielded any real power. In the story of Gaspar Ilóm, for example, the Indian elders are ill-defined figures who step out of the shadows only when custom demands that they take part in the ceremonies welcoming Colonel Godoy to Pisiguilito.

Indian insurrections in the highlands. Not surprisingly Barrios had trouble implementing many of his ideas without the use of force. In fact, under Barrios's rule the military became a tool of political oppression for the first time in Guatemala. When the Indians protested government policies (such as forced labor on the plantations) with weapons instead of words, troops were dispatched to force them into submission. Hidden in the hills, the Indian insurrectionists presented a real threat to planters and townspeople alike. The novel's Colonel Godoy points out to the townspeople of Pisiguilito: "If we hadn't arrived here last night the Indians would have come down from the mountains this morning and not one of you slobbering bastards would have lived to tell the tale" (*Men of Maize,* p. 14). What Godoy leaves unsaid, however, is the part that Liberal policies played in fostering the acrimonious relationship between ladinos and Indians.

A system of oppression. These tensions did not disappear when Manuel Estrada Cabrera became president in 1898. A ruthless dictator, Estrada Cabrera not only expanded upon the policies (both good and bad) that Barrios had implemented, but persecuted anyone—ladino or Indian—who questioned his authority. When Asturias's father, for example, a district judge, dismissed a case against political opponents of the dictator, he lost his job and nearly lost his life. Estrada Cabrera accomplished some good—he substantially improved the public health and education systems, for example—but his rule has been remembered much more for its tyranny and oppression. In 1920 Estrada Cabrera was finally deposed, after being declared insane by a government assembly.

EL SEÑOR PRESIDENTE

Manuel Estrada Cabrera provided the model for Asturias's first, and arguably most popular, novel, *El Señor Presidente.* This is the complex story of a corrupt dictator who manipulates and destroys the lives of his people. Asturias wrote the novel over a period of 24 years, finally publishing it in 1946. Any reluctance to release such an indictment of despotism is not surprising given the atmosphere of deceit and intrigue that persisted in Guatemala during the presidency of Jorge Ubico (1931-44).

The Novel in Focus

Plot summary. The narrative of *Men of Maize* unfolds on two levels, sometimes simultaneously: the magical realm of Mayan myth and the factual, everyday reality of the ladinos. "Men crisscrossed with cartridge belts" and wielding machetes share the same space with firefly wizards who sow "sparkling lights in the black air of the night" and who dwell "in tents of virgin doeskin" (*Men of Maize,* p. 19). The narrative often shifts abruptly from one perspective to the other, offering multiple interpretations of passing events, leaving the reader to decide which world—that of the Indian or the ladino—makes more sense. The plot is divided into six parts—"Gaspar Ilóm," "Machojón," "The Deer of the Seven-Fires," "Colonel Chalo Godoy," "María Tecún," and "Coyote-Postman"—covering an indefinite span of years. The second, third, and fourth sections all take place seven years after the events of the first part, addressing the consequences of an Indian massacre brought about by treachery. Still more time has passed in the last two sections, both of which deal with the disappearance of a beloved wife and the Indians' loss of cultural identity.

"Gaspar Ilóm." At the turn of the century, deep in the highlands of Guatemala, Gaspar Ilóm and his men battle ladino planters and state troops in an attempt to reclaim the land of their Mayan ancestors. Government-sponsored planters have destroyed the forests and exhausted the fields of the Indians in order to cultivate high-yield crops for financial gain. This abuse of the earth controverts the religious reverence with which the indigenous people hold the natural world. "We are made of maize," a character will say later in the novel, "and we can't make a business out of what we're made of, out of what our flesh is" (*Men of Maize,* p. 192).

MAIN CHARACTERS IN *MEN OF MAIZE* (IN ORDER OF APPEARANCE)

Gaspar Ilóm: Leader of the Indian guerillas who are determined to reclaim the homeland of their ancestors from the maizegrowers, by violent means if necessary. He is married to **La Piojosa Grande** (translated in the novel as "great fleabag," but more traditionally as "the great filthy one," a reference to the Aztec Great Earth Mother). She runs away after Ilóm is poisoned.

Tomás Machojón: Once a member of Gaspar Ilóm's band, now married to **Vaca Manuela,** a ladino woman who urges him to betray his former leader.

Colonel Gonzalo Godoy: The head of the government troops ordered to track down and kill Gaspar Ilóm and his guerilla band.

Zacatone: Apothecary who sells the poison used to kill Gaspar Ilóm.

The Tecún Brothers: Seven brothers who take revenge on Zacatone and his family for bewitching their grandmother.

Curer/Deer of the Seven-Fires: Indian shaman who can assume the shape of a deer (his *nahual* double) at will. He counsels the Tecún brothers when their grandmother falls ill.

Goyo Yic: Blind beggar who regains his sight and becomes a peddler in order to wander the world in search of his runaway wife.

María Tecún: Supposedly the only member of the Zacatone family to survive the Tecún brothers' wrath; the runaway wife of Goyo Yic.

Nicho Aquino: Postman for San Miguel Acatán whose wife has disappeared without a trace.

Hilario Sacayón: Muleteer sent by the people of San Miguel Acatán to trace the path of the broken-hearted postman.

Gaspar's guerrilla tactics have proven so effective that the nearby townspeople refuse to leave their houses before midday for fear of being shot by "Indians with rainwater eyes" (*Men of Maize,* p. 12). Finally it is only through deceit that Colonel Chalo Godoy can bring down the "invincible" Gaspar Ilóm. With the aid of Ilóm's former comrade, Tomás Machojón, Godoy poisons the unsuspecting chieftain. La Piojosa Grande, Ilóm's wife, runs away with their son when she realizes that her husband is poisoned. While Ilóm rushes to the river to purge himself, Godoy massacres Ilóm's men. Ilóm survives the poison but drowns himself when he realizes the fate of his companions.

"Machojón." Stories begin to circulate within the Indian community that the firefly wizards—godlike figures who seem to change shape at will—have vowed to "extinguish" Ilóm's murderers and all of their descendants. Seven years after Ilóm's death, Machojón, the only son of Tomás Machojón (who is now the prosperous owner of a large *hacienda*), mysteriously disappears one day while riding into town to court his beloved. The reader knows that Machojón has been attacked by the firefly wizards, who have mourned the death of Gaspar Ilóm and laid a curse on those involved. It may be that the disappeared Machojón has been turned into a star:

> The fireflies beat against the straw hat pulled down around his ears, like golden hailstones with wings on. . . . The horse, the packsaddle, the sheep-skin cover . . . everything was on fire, without giving off either flame, smoke, or any smell of burning. The candle glow of the fireflies streamed down from his hat, behind his ears, over the collar of his embroidered shirt, over his shoulders, up the sleeves of his jacket, down the backs of his hairy hands, between his fingers, like frozen sweat, like the light at the beginning of the world, a brightness in which everything could be seen, but without definite form. . . . He sat himself upright, with his face uncovered, to confront the enemy who was dazzling him. . . . As long as he stayed in the saddle he would be a star up in the sky.
>
> (*Men of Maize,* p. 31)

Machojón's body is never found, and no one knows whether he was swallowed by the earth, has gone to travel the world, or was consumed by a fiery "swarm of locusts" (*Men of Maize,* p. 31). His father and Colonel Godoy, however, believe that he was gunned down by Indian guerrillas. Soon Indian *peons* (field laborers) claim to see the figure of "Machojón" outlined in the glow of the burning fields. Desperate for work, the Indians gamble that Don Tomás will allow them to first burn and then cultivate his land so that he might catch a glimpse of his lost son in the flames. The chapter ends when a catastrophic fire consumes the lives of all those involved in the destruction of the land.

"The Deer of the Seven-Fires." With the Machojón family dead, the curse of the firefly wizards descends that same year upon the Zacatones, the family of the apothecary who supplied the poison used on Ilóm. This section, however, revolves around the Tecún brothers, who have played no previous part in the story, and their connection to the Zacatones is revealed only belatedly.

When their grandmother falls ill with "cricket hiccups," the Tecún brothers seek help from the healer or "curer," a practitioner of Indian remedies, and, some believe, a firefly wizard in human form. (Later in this chapter, the curer will be identified as the human "double" of the mysterious Deer of the Seven-Fires). Informed that the Zacatones have bewitched their grandmother, the brothers retaliate with terrifying swiftness: before the night is out, every member of the Zacatone family, except for María Tecún, is dead.

In an unexpected twist, the healer himself is found with a bullet through his head at approximately the same moment that Gaudencio Tecún shoots and kills a splendid deer. Was the healer killed by government troops or by the hand of Gaudencio Tecún? No one knows for sure. But Gaudencio grounds his explanation on the Mayan belief of *nahualism*: "The curer and the deer . . . were one and the same person. I fired at the deer and did in the curer, because they were one and the same, identical" (*Men of Maize*, p. 56).

"Colonel Chalo Godoy." While riding on patrol, Colonel Godoy and his men are trapped in a mountain cirque (a steep crater) by a mysterious forest fire. Only Godoy stands his ground when his terrified soldiers break rank and attempt to scale the steep walls of the cirque. Many manage to escape the flames only to be shot and killed by the Tecún brothers, who await them at the top of the hill. The guerilla tactics of the Tecún brothers suggest that they, too, have joined the struggle against the maizegrowers and the government troops who support them. Later, Eusebio Tecún tells his brother that it was the curer, now transformed into the Deer of the Seven Fires, who came back to life to take revenge on Colonel Godoy for the murder of Gaspar Ilóm. After telling Eusebio his story, the resurrected deer "set off running downhill. Soon after, the fire could be seen" (*Men of Maize*, p. 98). Colonel Godoy's death ends the first part of the novel. At least one of his men, and therefore the curse of the firefly wizards, survives.

"María Tecún." When Goyo Yic, the blind beggar, is deserted by his wife—María Tecún—and family, he tries to resume the familiar routine of his life by returning to the foot of an Amate tree to beg for alms. Without the support of his family, however, he lacks the endurance to continue: "The blind man wearied of hearing so many people passing by him all day and all night and of repeating unto nausea his prayers for alms" (*Men of Maize*, p. 107). Goyo turns to a practitioner of Indian remedies (in this case, an herbalist) to restore what he has lost: first his eyesight, and then, he hopes, his wife.

NAHUALISM

The sacred books of Mayan religion tell of the Indian's unique relationship with his or her animal double, or *nahual*. This animal is the Indian's special protector and, in certain circumstances, an extension of the Indian. There are various ways to pick a nahual; it is often determined by the closeness or the action of an animal on the person's birthday. The fates of the person and nahual are believed to be linked. For example, Goyo Yic, the peddler, spends his days searching for his missing family; his nahual is an opossum: "The moonlight changed him from a man into an animal, an opossum, a female possum, with a pouch in front of him to carry the babies in" (*Men of Maize*, p. 124). The connection between a man and his nahual is so strong that when Goyo becomes distracted from his search by the charms of pretty women and drink, the pet opossum he adopted runs away.

Through a combination of religious ritual and surgical skill, the herbalist removes the cataracts from Goyo's eyes. Yet Goyo's hope soon turns to despair when he realizes that his eyes cannot help him to find a wife that he has never seen. What is worse, the inner vision he once relied on is now obscured by the ever-changing spectacle of the world around him.

Becoming first a peddler of trinkets, then a vendor of alcohol, Goyo sadly admits to Mingo, his friend and partner, that his search for his wife has lasted too long: "I don't feel anything. Before compadre, I searched to find her; now I search so as not to find her" (*Men of Maize,* p. 137). Goyo takes refuge in alcohol, drinking away his profits until one day he and Mingo become so drunk that they lose their liquor license and are arrested for smuggling. Transported to an island prison, Goyo now has no hope of seeing his family again. Ironically, it is at this moment, when the future appears the darkest, that Goyo's luck will begin to change.

"Coyote-Postman." The tale of the coyote-postman is, in some ways, the culmination of the five stories that precede it. Many of the lingering questions and unsolved mysteries from earlier portions of the novel find resolution in this final chapter—a chapter which, not surprisingly, is longer than the first five combined.

Some years have passed and the story of Goyo Yic and his errant wife has become a part of local legend—now any woman who deserts her husband is called a *tecuna,* after María Tecún, Goyo's wife. In this final section the deserted husband is Señor Nicho Aquino, the postman for San Miguel Acatán, "a small town built on a shelf of golden stone above abysses where the atmosphere is blue" (*Men of Maize,* p. 154). Once again the narrative unfolds on two levels—the everyday reality of the townspeople and the magical reality of Mayan mythology. Nicho, the coyote-postman, has a foot in both worlds, and, as his story progresses, he finds it increasingly difficult to keep the two separate. In fact, early in the narrative, Nicho assumes the shape and inhabits the world of his nahaul double, the coyote.

After an arduous trip delivering mail to the capital, which is many miles and many mountains away, Nicho returns home to San Miguel Acatán, eager for the company of his beautiful wife, Isabra. To his dismay, he finds his *rancho* deserted; the fire is cold and his bed is empty. After drowning his sorrows in drink at the local bar, he is arrested for drunkenness, dosed with camphorated oil to rid him of the alcohol, then flogged.

Nicho is far from recovered—either emotionally or physically—when he sets out three weeks later on his normal route to the capital. Gamely shouldering two heavy sacks laden with mail, he sets off for his destination via the now infamous Tecún Pass. He reaches the inn of Nana Moncha at the village of Tres Aguas, where he meets a strange old man with blackened hands: a firefly wizard in human guise. Traveling together, they veer from the "high road" and enter the mythological realm of Nicho's ancestors. Here the postman undergoes a series of trials, journeys through fantastic landscapes (a cavern of firefly wizards that leads to an aerial plain suspended from branches over the earth and dimly lit grottos), reviews the secrets of the past and, ultimately, discovers the tragic fate of his missing wife.

Meanwhile, Hilario Sacayón, a muleteer, has been sent by the people of San Miguel Acatán to locate the missing postman. Although aware of the legends of runaway wives and the men who die in search of them, Sacayón remains skeptical of their veracity. He himself has contributed to the propagation of one local myth about a tragic romance between a traveling sewing-machine salesman named O'Neill and a nonexistent girl, Miguelita of Acatán. An old woman he meets on the road assures him, "When you tell a story that no one else tells anymore, you say: I invented this, it's mine. But what you're really doing is remembering—you, through your drunkenness, remembered what the memory of your forefathers left in your blood" (*Men of Maize,* p. 204). Sacayón remains a skeptic, however, until he meets, on María Tecún Ridge, a coyote that seems very familiar:

> Was it or was it not a coyote? How could he doubt that it was, when he saw it so clearly. But that was it, he clearly saw it and saw that it wasn't a coyote, because as he looked he had the impression that it was a person and a person he knew. . . . They'll laugh in my face if I tell them I arrived in good time at María Tecún Ridge and saw Aquino the postman in the form of a coyote.
>
> (*Men of Maize,* p. 210)

Thoroughly shaken by his experience, Sacayón keeps his encounter with the coyote-postman a secret.

Meanwhile, Nicho emerges from the cavern and realizes that there is no going back to the world he left behind; one of the conditions of his passage through the mythic realm was that he destroy the bags of mail he had carried from San Miguel Acatán. Traveling to the coast, he finds work doing odd jobs in a rat-infested hotel. One of Nicho's jobs is to ferry guests of the hotel out to the Harbor Castle prison on an island just off the coast. It is during one of these trips to the island that he encounters María Tecún, on her way to visit her oldest son, who was recently imprisoned in Harbor Castle. It is here that the paths of the remaining characters converge. Goyo Yic, also imprisoned in Harbor Castle, is reunited first with his son, then with his runaway wife, who explains her flight: she feared having too many children by him and not being able to provide for them. Believing Goyo Yic to be dead, María Tecún has married Benito Ramos, a sterile survivor of the massacre of Gaspar Ilóm's tribe so many years before. The epilogue to *Men of Maize* reveals that Nicho eventually inherits the hotel from the original owner, the Boss Lady. Meanwhile, Goyo Yic and María Tecún reconcile after Benito Ramos's death and return to Pisiguilito, where they build a rancho big enough for their children and grandchildren to live with them: "Wealth of men, wealth of women, to have many children. Old folk, young folk, men and women, they all became ants after the harvest, to carry home the maize" (*Men of Maize,* p. 306).

Myth: the key to social and political identity. Recurring throughout *Men of Maize* is the loss of cultural identity for the Indian whose lifestyle and traditional beliefs are in danger of being absorbed by ladino society. Both the peddler, Goyo Yic, and the postman, Nicho Aquino, have allowed themselves to be subsumed into a materialistic culture that venerates profit over a heritage with roots that extend deep into the earth itself. Ariel Dorfman (author of ***Death and the Maiden*** [also covered in *Latin American Literature and Its Times*]) argues that in such cases "human beings . . . possess their myths only in order to orient themselves in the darkness, to understand their essence which is scattered in time" (Dorfman in Asturias, p. 411).

The interpolation of Mayan legend into the narrative is one of the ways that Asturias underscores the importance of myth in Indian society. René Prieto argues that in order "to paint a picture of hope and renewal, Asturias looks back to the ancient myths of Mesoamerica" (Prieto, pp. 132-33). More importantly, perhaps, Asturias allows his characters to generate their own mythology—a collection of stories that interpret the uncertainties of life according to traditional standards. The local legend of the tecuna (runaway wife), for example, makes sense of a phenomenon that threatens to disrupt the core of domestic society in San Miguel Acatán.

Not surprisingly, therefore, it is in the subterranean cavern of firefly wizards, where Nicho observes the stories and history of his people, that he first understands "the emblems of a rich tradition that defines and sustains him" (Prieto, p. 145). By choosing his Indian heritage over the privileges and power of the ladino world, Nicho passes the test that most other characters (Tomás Machojón, Goyo Yic) have failed up until now; when confronted with adversity and self-doubt, Nicho listens to the voice of his ancestors. The problems plaguing Nicho do not magically disappear when he leaves the cavern—he is never reunited with his wife and never returns to San Miguel Acatán. He does, however, become the agent through which the now chastened Goyo Yic can recapture the future he had lost.

Sources and literary context. For much of the mythological details in *Men of Maize,* Asturias drew upon the sacred books of Mayan religion: the *Popol Vuh,* the *Annals of the Cakchiquels,* and the books of the *Chiiam Balam.* Interestingly, his familiarity with the literature of the indigenous people of the Maya can be traced back to his stay in Paris in the early 1920s—it was under the guidance of the French scholar Georges Raynaud that he helped translate the *Popol Vuh* into Spanish. It was also during this period that Asturias came into contact with the work of the French Surrealists. He would later adopt and incorporate into his own work many of the innovations of the Surrealists—their emphasis on the alternative reality of the dream state and non-chronological time, for example, are key components in each of the sections of *Men of Maize.*

In his seminal study, *Miguel Ángel Asturias,* Richard Callan details the parts that Aztec as well as Greek mythology play in Asturias's work. The ancient Aztecs inhabited the same general region—Mexico and Central America—as the Mayans. Widespread contact in the region over the centuries led to similarities in mythologies.

> Several gods from the Aztec pantheon are discernible in the first section. Gaspar Ilóm . . . is Huitzilopochtli, the sun and fertility god; his wife, la Piojosa Grande (literally, the Great Filthy One), is the Great Earth Mother, Tlazolteotl, whose name in Nahuatl means "Goddess of Filth." From their union was born Martín who is actually referred to as corn in the novel . . . in view of the Indians' belief that they were Corn Men.
>
> (Callan, p. 66)

Events in History at the Time the Novel Was Written

The end of the Liberal regime. Asturias's manipulation of time in *Men of Maize* makes it difficult to speculate at exactly what point in Guatemala's history the novel ends (one character will race from infancy to mature adulthood in the time it will take another to travel from adolescence to middle age). It is almost as difficult to pinpoint when the novel was written. According to Gerald Martin (who translated *Men* of *Maize* into English), Asturias began working on the novel "without knowing it" while living abroad in the mid-1920s. Martin notes that "fully recognizable fragments of parts one, three and six appeared between 1925 and 1933 in newspapers and magazines in France and Latin America" (Martin in Asturias, p. xv). Yet the majority of *Men of Maize* was almost certainly written after Asturias returned home in 1933—two years after General Jorge Ubico had been elected president of Guatemala.

Life for the Indian people did not improve under Ubico's regime. Although he did away with the system of debt peonage, Ubico implemented a vagrancy law that made any Indian without a job vulnerable to periods of enforced labor. The laborers were often sent miles away from their families to work on the large coffee plantations on the coast, and were paid barely enough to survive from season to season. Ironically, Ubico, the man responsible for separating the members of countless families, encouraged the Indians to refer to him as *Tata,* or Papa. Within three years of assuming office, he passed a decree that obliged all Indian men to pay a tax or to work for two weeks of the year without pay. In June 1944 disgruntled workers called a general strike that successfully forced Ubico from office.

"Ten Years of Spring." The years before the publication of *Men of Maize* (1949) brought a number of changes to Guatemala. President Juan José Arévalo Bermejo (1945-50), an idealistic university professor, supported a program of labor reform that dispensed with Ubico's vagrancy law of 1934 and replaced it with a system that protected the rights of all workers. In 1952 President Jacobo Arbenz Guzmán (1950-54) dismantled the Liberal legacy one step further by sponsoring an agrarian reform act redistributing large tracts of public and privately owned land. Many of the new social and political reforms would not last ten years (a period that would subsequently be referred to nostalgically as "The Ten Years of Spring"). Yet the optimistic note upon which the novel concludes reflects the climate of promise prevailing in Guatemala when Asturias was writing *Men of Maize*—a novel he could never have hoped to publish in his homeland just five short years before.

Changing cultural identities. When Asturias was writing *Men of Maize*, race relations between Indians and ladinos continued to be strained (and are to this day), although the years since the 1940s saw minute social changes in the way indigenous people are treated. In the decades between the publication of *Men of Maize* in 1949 and its translation into English in 1975, some of the more blatant discriminatory practices were abolished. Indians were no longer forced to walk in the streets instead of on public sidewalks or expected to remove their hats and look down on the ground when addressed by a ladino. Ladinos, however, continued to speak to Indians as inferiors: "[I]t is still the rule that Ladinos address Indians, no matter what their age and position, as children by using the informal *tú* or *vos*. Titles of respect, such as *don, doña, señor* and *señora* are almost never used with Indians, except as a joke" (Brintnall, p. 19).

In contrast to the novel, in which recognition of their common culture ultimately unites such diverse characters as Goyo Yic, Hilario Sacoyón, and Nicho Aquino, many Indians abandoned their heritage through "ladinoization." Hoping to achieve a higher level of social status and acceptance in the ladino world, these Indians reshaped their cultural identities by changing the way they dressed, learning to speak Spanish, or, like Tomás Machojón in the novel, marrying a ladino. This trend was a fairly minor occurrence in the highlands: "[I]t is generally recognized that it is almost impossible for an Indian to Ladinoize without leaving the community where he was born" (Brintnall, p. 21). But Indians who relocated to the city were often able to adapt: "Ladinoization does occur on a massive scale, but generally among Indians who have become part of the permanent labor force on large commercial plantations . . . or who have entered the ranks of the urban poor" (Brintnall, p. 21).

Reviews. Although critics in the United States hailed *Men of Maize* as a "richly textured work," most of them acknowledged that the complex novel might be difficult going for a reader unfamiliar with the "myth-haunted Mayan landscape" (Perera in Samudio, p. 55). What to one reader was the work of "an innovator of language and an individual stylist," was dismissed as "feverish overwriting" by another (*Choice* in Samudio; Allen in Samudio, p. 55). More recently, Mario Vargas Llosa (author of ***The Storyteller*** [also covered in *Latin American Literature* and *Its Times*]) noted that the "temporal confusion and chronological arbitrariness" have proven to be troublesome obstacles for all but the most "stubborn and determined readers" (Vargas Llosa in Asturias, p. 445).

Despite the difficulties of its style, the novel has enjoyed a long life in print. Seven different editions have been published in Spanish and the novel has been translated into the major European languages.

—Deborah Kearney and Pamela S. Loy

For More Information

Asturias, Miguel Ángel. *Men of Maize: The Critical Edition.* Trans. Gerald Martin. Pittsburgh: University of Pittsburgh Press, 1993.

Brintnall, Richard. *Revolt Against the Dead: The Modernization of a Mayan Community in the Highlands of Guatemala.* New York: Gordon and Breach, 1979.

Brinton, Daniel G., ed. *Annals of the Cakchiquels.* Trans. Daniel G. Brinton. Philadelphia: Brinton, 1885.

Callan, Richard. *Miguel Ángel Asturias.* New York: Twayne, 1970.

Menchú, Rigoberta. *I, Rigoberta Menchú: An Indian Woman in Guatemala.* Ed. Elisabeth Burgos-Debray. Trans. Ann Wright. London: Verso, 1984.

Prieto, René. *Miguel Asturias' Archeology of Return.* Cambridge: Cambridge University Press, 1993.

Samudio, Josephine, ed. *The Book Review Digest, 1976.* New York: H. W. Wilson, 1977.

Simon, Jean-Marie. *Guatemala: Eternal Spring, Eternal Tyranny.* New York: W. W. Norton, 1987.

Tedlock, Dennis, trans. *Popol Vuh: The Mayan Book of the Dawn of Life.* New York: Simon and Schuster, 1985.

Watanabe, John M. *Maya Saints and Souls in a Changing World.* Austin: University of Texas Press, 1992.

One Hundred Years of Solitude

by
Gabriel García Márquez

Born in 1928 in Aracataca, Colombia, Gabriel García Márquez began publishing short stories in the 1940s, after moving to Bogotá to study law. An indifferent student, García Márquez began working as a journalist for various newspapers, establishing friendships with other young writers, and, eventually, publishing his first novel, *La hojarasca* (*Leaf Storm*) in 1955. By 1955 he was one of the most renowned newspapermen in Colombia. He moved the next year to Paris, France, as the European correspondent for *El Espectador,* the more liberal of the nation's two major newspapers. When the newspaper shut down, García Márquez stayed in Paris to write fiction full-time, achieving moderate success with his early short stories and novels. In 1964 García Márquez had a sudden inspiration, and was able to imagine "word by word" the text of *One Hundred Years of Solitude,* the novel he'd been trying to get out since 1942 (García Márquez in Bell-Villada, p. 56). He was by now living in Mexico, where he wrote the novel obsessively, accumulating thousands of dollars of debt in order to support his family and continue his work. The phenomenal success of *One Hundred Years of Solitude* took the writer by surprise; he suddenly found himself in the limelight, an uncomfortable but useful position for him in that he was able to use this global success to benefit the left-wing causes he fervently supported. The novel went on to become an international bestseller, and to help him win, among other awards, the Nobel Prize for Literature in 1982.

THE LITERARY WORK

A novel set somewhere in South America at an unspecified time; published in Spanish (as *Cien años de soledad*) in 1967, in English in 1970.

SYNOPSIS

One Hundred Years of Solitude chronicles 100 years and six generations of the Buendía family, who live in the mythical community of Macondo from its founding to its destruction.

Events in History at the Time the Novel Takes Place

***One Hundred Years of Solitude* and Colombia.** Millions of readers have delighted in *One Hundred Years of Solitude* with little or no knowledge of the Colombian backdrop so important to the novel. As Stephen Minta points out, however, García Márquez "is a writer who is profoundly concerned with the past of his continent, and, more specifically, with the history of his native land, Colombia" (Minta, p. 1). Many Colombians have felt that *One Hundred Years of Solitude,* with its assortment of Latin character types—who are haunted by solitude, incest, war, ghosts, and tormenting passions—captures the spirit of the national character. What may be seen as merely "magical" and beautiful by those who read the novel in translation in actuality derives "in great measure from the lived fabric of Latin American experience" (Bell-Villada, p. 12). In addition,

Colombian troops in 1902, at the time of the War of a Thousand Days.

many of the novel's events are carefully correlated to actual Colombian history, including the series of civil wars in the nineteenth and twentieth centuries, the 1899-1902 War of a Thousand Days, military repression, labor strikes, and the banana massacre of 1928. While many characters are based on García Márquez's friends and family, one of the novel's protagonists, Colonel Aureliano Buendía, is drawn from the actual Liberal general Rafael Uribe Uribe, a key figure in the War of a Thousand Days. García Márquez has long been a political activist, and a man deeply concerned with the fate of the Latin American peoples. Far more than merely fanciful, his novel reflects an intricate history of political and social phenomena that informs the reader's comprehension of characters and plot. This history, however, is only one ingredient that informs the novel, which manages to transform traditional linear discourse into a more diffuse depiction of reality. The novel does not tell a straightforward story but rather plays with chronology and other elements, describing extraordinary events as if they were ordinary and mixing time periods, as suggested by the novel's first sentence, which refers to the past, the present, and the future: "Many years later, as he faced the firing squad, Colonel Aureliano Buendía was to remember that distant afternoon when his father took him to discover ice" (García Márquez, *One Hundred Years of Solitude*, p. 1).

The civil wars. Colombia won independence from Spain in 1819 as part of the larger territory called Gran Colombia. In the first century of its independence, the country was dominated by two major political parties, the Liberals and the Conservatives, both of which emerged out of the political turmoil of the post-independence period. Once Colombia was free from Spanish domination, political power fell to a group of landowners, merchants, and clergy of Spanish descent but born in Spanish America, all of whom, though wealthy, had been excluded from the colonial government and considered inferior to Spanish-born colonizers. The question of how to restructure and modify the new nation's government and economy dominated the post-independence period. One group, the future Liberal party, wanted reform—free trade, greater federalism, religious freedom, civil marriage, secular education, and separation of Church and state—while those who would become Conservatives wanted to maintain the traditional order, with its protectionist trade policies, centralized government, and ties between Church and state (Minta, p. 12). Both of these groups developed into mass political parties, essentially dividing the population between them. Both parties have always been multiclass, so any member of society could conceivably be either a Liberal or Conservative. Initially promoting clearly separate programs, the two parties were almost constantly in conflict with each other.

Colombia saw eight civil wars in the nineteenth century alone. The incessant conflict stemmed from the fact that the two parties placed themselves in total opposition to each other; if one party was in power, the other was almost always completely excluded from it. "The group that did not control the state could expect only discrimination from it, whereas those persons politically connected with the party in power could expect to monopolize state decision making and the benefits to be derived from state power" (Oquist in Minta, p. 13). Each of the parties was able to retain control for long periods, which inspired unrest among its opposition. Elections often led to violence as each of the parties vied for this total power. The party in power was able to control the country in other ways as well, by appointing mayors, police chiefs, judges, and public school teachers. Control would alternate between the two parties for more than 100 years at a time: after 1850 the Liberals were in power, consolidating their position in the civil wars between 1858 and 1863, until the Conservatives wrested this power away in 1885 and maintained it until 1930, at which point the Liberals returned to office, only to lose power again in 1946.

These civil wars were bloody and were accompanied by many smaller revolts throughout

THE POPULARITY OF GABRIEL GARCÍA MÁRQUEZ

By the early 1970s Gabriel García Márquez had attained the level of popularity usually reserved for movie stars or other beloved public figures in Latin America. People from all social classes were acquainted with his novels; for instance, a group of peasants chatting with García Márquez cried out "Macondo!" when told he'd written *One Hundred Years of Solitude.* The news of his Nobel Prize win in 1982 was greeted with "spontaneous outpourings of public sentiment and jubilation," which included an entire elementary school student body arriving at García Márquez's home to greet him, strangers honking their horns, and people celebrating in the streets (Bell-Villada, pp. 6-7). As Gene H. Bell-Villada points out, García Márquez has become "a mass phenomenon, a special kind of public figure whose work inspires not only admiration and respect but personal warmth and affection from most all. Seldom in our time does the higher art of literature gain so broad a following" (Bell-Villada, p. 7).

the country. As the nineteenth century progressed, the parties' initial ideological platforms became less and less relevant, while factionalism within parties grew more prevalent. Since both parties were multiclass, members of the two parties had similar backgrounds and lifestyles, and did not establish firm positions on most issues. Though disputes over the relations between Church and state remained fiery and ideological, most of the conflicts revolved almost solely around power, rather than around concrete issues. As *One Hundred Years of Solitude*'s Colonel Aureliano Buendía wryly remarks, "The only difference today between Liberals and Conservatives is that the Liberals go to mass at five o'clock and the Conservatives at eight" (*One Hundred Years,* p. 248).

The War of a Thousand Days. The longest and most violent of the wars between the two parties was the War of a Thousand Days, which lasted from 1899 to 1902, and caused perhaps 100,000 deaths in all. The conflict began when a group of Liberals attempted to unseat the Conservative government. Though few expected the war to last as long as it did, longstanding disputes between the two parties, as well as "the development of a highly lucrative speculative business within the war economy," led to a protracted, increasingly violent campaign (Minta, pp. 16-17). The Liberals scored some initial victories, but the Conservatives eventually proved themselves to be stronger. The 1900 Conservative government victory at Palonegro should have been decisive; some 15,000 government troops were able to defeat 14,000 rebels in the war's bloodiest battle. The Liberals continued to fight, however, abandoning traditional warfare for savage guerrilla tactics that alarmed party leaders on both sides. Attempts were made by each of the parties to end the war. Some Liberal rebel troops, like those of *One Hundred Years of Solitude*'s Colonel Aureliano Buendía, nevertheless continued to fight, and the war dragged on until 1902. By that point the country and its economy were devastated.

One of the most notable figures of the war was the Liberal general Rafael Uribe Uribe, whom García Márquez used as a model for *One Hundred Years of Solitude*'s Colonel Aureliano Buendía. Uribe Uribe began his career fighting for the Liberal government against a 1876 Conservative rebellion, then, in 1885, served as a colonel in an armed conflict between two Liberal factions. Defeated by the more conservative faction of the Liberal party, Uribe Uribe was briefly jailed. In the 1890s he moved to Bogotá and played an active role within Liberal politics. Defeated in another insurrection and again imprisoned, he began earning a reputation as a Liberal hero, and, in the 1896 elections, was the only Liberal who gained a congressional seat. At around the same time, Uribe Uribe began planning for war, attempting to enlist Liberal support from Nicaragua and Guatemala. He became a key player in the Liberal preparations for the failed 1899 coup, and then fought tirelessly through the War of a Thousand Days. Unrelenting and unwilling to compromise, he gave up only in 1902, less than one month before the war officially ended. Uribe Uribe capitulated on October 24, 1902, and, just like his fictional counterpart, signed the Treaty of Neerlandia. This treaty marked the end of the military ambitions of Rafael Uribe Uribe.

An incredibly popular war hero even today, Uribe Uribe was defeated in battle after battle. As Stephen Minta observes, "Perhaps the strangest aspect of Uribe Uribe's life and military career was the way in which he was able to preserve a glorious reputation unscathed through a wealth of defeats" (Minta, p. 14). In all his years of fighting, Rafael Uribe Uribe was never able to achieve anything for the Liberal party, and yet, 100 years after Uribe Uribe's birth, the revolutionary was honored with these words: "Everything was against him. But his romantic figure grew in adversity, like the cactus in the sand of the desert" (Eduardo Santa in Minta, p. 15). Similarly, Colonel Aureliano Buendía fights tirelessly throughout *One Hundred Years of Solitude,* "[fighting] thirty-two civil wars and [losing] them all" and is so popular that 17 women send 17 daughters to him, hoping to make more venerable the blood of their heirs (*One Hundred Years,* p. 415).

The United Fruit Company. At the end of the nineteenth century, while the country was at war, the United Fruit Company entered Colombia. Colombia's banana industry had begun developing in the 1880s, with the help of the newly built Santa Marta railroad route. The United Fruit company—a conglomerate of several U.S. companies—soon dominated the fledgling banana industry. By the mid-1920s Colombia had become the largest exporter of bananas in the world; by the 1930s, 60 percent of the industry and 75 percent of the banana-producing land had fallen under the control of the United Fruit Company. This near-monopoly allowed the company to manipulate the price of fruit by, for example, leaving large tracts of land uncultivated (to create less supply, which would cause more demand, leading to higher prices). Some estimated that up to 85 percent of the company's land was left fallow—this in a country where many people were undernourished for want of land and food. Such tactics were bound to inspire controversy.

Colombia's banana production peaked in the 1920s, a decade known as the "Dance of Millions" because of Colombia's rapid economic growth. Private investment from the United States increased, leading to large-scale construction projects in Colombia and the employment of much cheap Colombian labor. Thousands of Colombians worked for these exploitative U.S. companies, and became increasingly organized, forming radical political groups and staging workers' strikes. Four major strikes against the United Fruit Company took place between 1918 and 1934, but it is the bitter strike of 1928 that plays a central role in *One Hundred Years of Solitude.* Workers made nine demands, presented in a legal fashion to the company by a small delegation. One of these demands was that the company acknowledge its legal position as an employer; by hiring workers through independent contractors, the United Fruit Company had been able to bypass all existing labor laws. The company refused to negotiate, so the workers went on strike.

The government sided with the company and sent in military troops to arrest the workers. Soon after, the company resumed full-scale production. As the confrontation escalated, the military banned all meetings between three or more people. Strikers gathered in Ciénaga, and refused to move when the new decree was read. In response, soldiers fired into the crowd and killed an unknown number of strikers. The conflict lasted for months, with the military continuing to use brutal and repressive force against the workers. Ultimately, a great number of people were killed in what is known as the Ciénaga massacre. As in *One Hundred Years of Solitude,* few people afterwards wanted to discuss the violence that had taken place and "something like a conspiracy of silence developed" (Minta, p. 169).

Gypsies in the New World. In *One Hundred Years of Solitude* Gypsies play a part in Macondo life from the time Macondo is first founded and settled by the Buendías; only later will the Arabs, the Italian Petro Crespi, and other outside groups join the community. In fact, Gypsies have a long history in the New World. Gypsy culture, which originated in India, was (and is) nomadic; many Gypsies were not citizens of any country or members of any Church, but instead wandered Europe independently. Anti-Gypsy prejudice proliferated in Europe, making Gypsies the constant victims of persecution. Many countries used the New World as a safety valve to rid themselves of undesired immigrants such as the Gypsies, whose "powerless status made them prime candidates for New World expansion and settlement" (Sway, p. 45).

By the end of the seventeenth century, every European country with connections to the New World began deporting Gypsies to the Americas. England deported Gypsies to Barbados in the West Indies. In the sixteenth century hundreds of Gypsies were sent from Portugal to Brazil, and, at the same time, Spain began sending Gypsies to its colonies in South America. From 1801 to 1803 Napoleon sent hundreds of France's unwanted Gypsies to Louisiana. Hundreds of Gypsies would eventually arrive in colonial North America, where they formed thriving communities despite the antipathy of previously arrived settlers; much of the present U.S. Gypsy population arrived in the late 1800s. After 1924, when the United States passed restrictive immigration laws, Eastern European Gypsies began immigrating to all parts of Latin America; "this alternative immigration strategy explains why so many Gypsies living in the United States today speak Spanish and have ties to various Latin American countries" (Sway, p. 39). Though Gypsies were used for purposes of colonization, they were never properly colonized into a fixed settlement. Then as now, Gypsies were able to survive by exploiting markets for their skills and services, travelling constantly in order to insure a fresh demand for their products and talents.

The Novel in Focus

Plot summary. *One Hundred Years of Solitude* chronicles six generations of the Buendía family, beginning with the founding of Macondo by the family's patriarch, José Arcadio Buendía, and his wife Úrsula—a pair of cousins "joined till death by a bond that was more solid than love: a common prick of conscience" (*One Hundred Years,* p. 20). When the couple had first decided to marry, their relatives tried to stop them, warning that "those two healthy products of two races [two families] that had interbred over the centuries would suffer the shame of breeding iguanas" (*One Hundred Years,* p. 20). Previous intermarriages between the two families had led to dire consequences. The precedent of a child born with a pig's tail haunts Úrsula and compels the young bride to stay a virgin throughout her marriage's first year, until one day José Arcadio is forced to kill, for honor's sake, a man who publicly questions his virility. After the murder, the couple not only consummate their marriage, but become plagued by the murdered man's ghost, whose presence finally drives them out of their ancestral village and over the mountains to Macondo, "the land that no one had promised them" (*One Hundred Years,* p. 23).

Accompanied by adventurous friends and in search of the sea, the Buendías found Macondo when, during one of their nightly stops, José Arcadio dreams of "a noisy city with houses having mirror walls" rising up on the exact spot; even the name "Macondo" is revealed to the patriarch in his dream (*One Hundred Years,* p. 24). In its first years, Macondo is a "truly happy village where no one was over thirty years of age and where no one had died" (*One Hundred Years,* p. 9). This edenic world is "so recent that many things lacked names" (*One Hundred Years,* p. 1). Every year a Gypsy group passes through, bringing with them astonishing inventions from the outside world—including ice, magnets, flying carpets, fake teeth, and magnifying glass. The leader of these Gypsies, Melquíades, is said to possess the keys of Nostradamus (or the mysteries of the universe) and later resurrects himself from the dead because "he could not bear the solitude" (*One Hundred Years,* p. 50). José Arcadio Buendía becomes so entranced by the wonders brought by Melquíades that he becomes utterly isolated within the realm of his own feverish scientific pursuits and ultimately goes crazy. Melquíades moves into the house, writes a series of manuscripts, and, after becoming the first person to die in Macondo, haunts the room in which he has lived.

Úrsula, "that woman of unbreakable nerves who at no moment in her life had ever been heard to sing" (*One Hundred Years,* p. 9), is left to raise the couple's children—Aureliano, Amaranta, José Arcadio, and Rebeca, the Indian orphan girl who arrives one day on their doorstep and is adopted into the family. All the children are afflicted, in various ways, by strange passions and solitary natures. Aureliano eventually falls in love with and marries the pre-pubescent Remedios, daughter of the magistrate Don Apolinar Moscote, the first in a series of government outsiders to impose his authority in Macondo. After Remedios's early death Aureliano becomes Colonel Aureliano Buendía, famous Liberal fighter in a series of bloody and ill-fated civil wars against the Conservatives, battling in 32 civil wars and losing them all. Meanwhile, Amaranta becomes an implacable, eternal virgin nourished throughout her life by her hatred for Rebeca and unyielding jealousy over Rebeca's happiness with Pietro Crespi, the Italian musician beloved by both women. Rebeca discards Pietro when José Arcadio, who ran off with the Gypsies as a boy, returns to Macondo an enormously well-endowed, tattoo-covered, flatulent beast of a man—a mix of attributes Rebeca finds irresistible.

Outside their loves and marriages, both Aureliano and the massive José Arcadio father children by Pilar Ternera, the local prostitute/fortune-teller who provides sexual solace to the village men. (Aureliano will, in addition, father 17 men by 17 women during the war.) José Arcadio's son with Pilar, whose name is Arcadio, becomes a cruel tyrant over Macondo during a period of Liberal victory, and lusts after Pilar, whom he does not know is his own mother. In a similarly illicit fashion, Aureliano's son with Pilar, whose name is Aureliano José, desires his aunt, Amaranta, who returns his feelings but, despite some incestuous dabblings, keeps her virginity intact. Arcadio, in turn, fathers three children—the twins Aureliano Segundo and José Arcadio Segundo, and Remedios. Aureliano Segundo becomes a fun-loving, gluttonous man, who marries the most frigid, beautiful woman the town has ever seen, Fernanda del Carpio, then spends all his days with the lusty Petra Cotes, whose influence causes his animals to breed at such a fantastic rate that he is able to amass a fortune because of it. José Arcadio Segundo becomes interested in inventions and politics, and eventually locks himself up in Melquídes's old room, determined to decipher the strange manuscripts left by the Gypsy. Remedios—a devastating beauty who will paint the walls with her own excrement if not properly supervised—becomes one of the novel's odder characters, living in a world of her own making until one day she ascends straight to heaven while folding sheets in the yard.

Aureliano Segundo fathers three children with Fernanda: Meme, José Arcadio, and Amaranta Úrsula. Macondo has changed dramatically since its founding, and now immigrants fill the village and shops line its streets. The railroad has reached Macondo and brings with it the first American visitors, one of whom samples the local bananas and soon establishes a huge banana company just outside town. Meme becomes the first Buendía to learn English and to associate with the children from the United States, who, like all the Americans associated with the banana company, live within a fenced settlement. Soon Meme falls terribly in love with a young mechanic, whose death compels her to live the rest of her life in silent mourning. Meme gives birth to one of the last Aurelianos (Amaranta Úrsula also gives birth to an Aureliano), the child of her dead lover. Meanwhile, the abused and exploited banana company workers, led by José Arcadio Segundo, decide to hold a strike; military retaliation leads to the violent massacre of 3,000 workers, a catastrophe then utterly denied by the government, which claims that "nothing has happened in Macondo. . . . This is a happy town" (*One Hundred Years,* p. 316). Indeed, this official version of events is spread throughout the country so thoroughly that it finally becomes accepted. To compound the tragedy, a heavy rain then devastates the town for five years straight. Soon after the sun reappears, Amaranta Úrsula and her nephew Aureliano fall passionately in love; "secluded by solitude and love and by the solitude of love . . . Aureliano and Amaranta Úrsula were the only happy beings, the most happy on the face of the earth" (*One Hundred Years,* pp. 409-10). Though they are, in fact, the only Buendías to find perfect happiness through love, they produce a child born with a pig's tail, finally confirming the fears of their ancestors. "All the ants in the world" devour the child at the same moment that Aureliano, who has taken up his grandfather's project, finally deciphers Melquíades's manuscripts (*One Hundred Years,* p. 420):

> right there, standing, without the slightest difficulty, as if they had been written in Spanish and were being read under the dazzling splendor of high noon, he began to decipher them aloud. It was the history of the family, written by Melquíades, down to the most trivial details, one hundred years ahead of time.
>
> (*One Hundred Years,* p. 421)

A "biblical," wrathful hurricane appears just as Aureliano has his moment of greatest lucidity, and thus the novel ends:

> Before reaching the final line, however, he had already understood that he would never leave that room, for it was foreseen that the city of mirrors (or mirages) would be wiped out by the wind and exiled from the memory of men at the precise moment when Aureliano Babilonia would finish deciphering the parchments, and that everything written on them was unrepeatable since time immemorial and forever more, because races condemned to one hundred years of solitude did not have a second opportunity on earth.
>
> (*One Hundred Years,* p. 422)

Solitude and Latin America. *One Hundred Years of Solitude* ends with a violent, apocalyptic hurricane that destroys Macondo and all of its inhabitants. In García Márquez's 1982 Nobel Prize acceptance speech, he points out that this is only one of several possibilities for the fate of Latin America:

> Face to face with a reality that overwhelms us, one which over man's perceptions of time must have seemed a utopia, tellers of tales who, like me, are capable of believing anything, feel entitled to believe that it is not yet too late to

FERNANDA DEL CARPIO AND COLOMBIA'S *CACHACOS*

One Hundred Years of Solitude's Fernanda del Carpio is described as "a woman who was lost to the world":

> [Fernanda] had been born and raised in a city six hundred miles away, a gloomy city where on ghostly nights the coaches of the viceroys still rattled through the cobbled streets. Thirty-two belfries tolled a dirge at six in the afternoon. In the manor house, which was paved with tomblike slabs, the sun was never seen.
>
> (*One Hundred Years,* pp. 210-11)

This representation is not idiosyncratic, but reflects regional differences in Colombia and the various attitudes of its people. Fernanda hails from the city of Bogotá, or someplace close by it in the chilly, rainy Andean region (or highlands) of Colombia. People from this region, called *cachacos,* are considered formal, rigid, and haughty by Colombia's Caribbean coastal dwellers, the *costeños,* who include both García Márquez and the fictional residents of Macondo. In contrast to the cachacos, costeños come from a sunny, laid-back world, where the spoken language is informal, and the population more racially mixed (due, in part, to the slave trade once common in this region). García Márquez has called his first visit to Bogotá "the most terrible experience in the whole of my youth," and the city itself "that remote and unreal city that was the centre of gravity of the power which has been imposed on us since our earliest times" (García Márquez in Bell-Villada, p. 39). His unflattering portrait of Fernanda del Carpio, who "imposes the standards of a reactionary colonial culture and the observances of the most repressive form of Catholicism" on the family, clearly reflects García Márquez's disdain for Colombia's highland culture and his identification with his own costeño roots (Minta, p. 159).

> undertake the creation of a minor utopia: a new and limitless utopia for life wherein no one can decide for others how they are to die, where love really can be true and happiness possible, where the lineal generations of one hundred years of solitude will have at last and forever a second chance on earth.
>
> (García Márquez in McGuirk and Cardwell, p. 211)

In this light, the solitude that affects the entire Buendía line is not merely melancholic or romantic, but an expression of García Márquez's concerns for the future of Latin America. As Stephen Minta puts it, for García Márquez solitude is

> an expression of the collective isolation of Latin American people, a people for whom history has seemed a process to be endured rather than created, people divorced from a sense of history because theirs has been written by outsiders, a people condemned to a peripheral role in relation to a greater world whose limits have been defined elsewhere.
>
> (Minta, p. 31)

The Buendías' solitude, then, is symbolic of "the inward-looking nature of their town, their culture, their continent, all locked into a permanent state of underdevelopment, unable to relate to the world outside on terms other than those of a deeply felt and crippling inferiority" (Minta, pp. 148-49).

Not only is Latin America isolated from the rest of the world, but Colombia itself is an underdeveloped country with regions geographically isolated from each other, a place in which many have remained ignorant of even the most horrifying events occurring around them. Throughout his Nobel Prize speech, entitled "The Solitude of Latin America," García Márquez speaks of Latin America's stormy recent past, which he sums up as a "highly unusual state of affairs," one that includes dictatorships, wars, coups, assassinations, disappearances, genocide, imprisonments, missing children, exiles, and 20 million Latin American children dying before their second birthday (García Márquez in McGuirk and Cardwell, p. 209). Europeans, he says, are without the proper means of interpreting Latin Americans:

> One realizes this when they insist on measuring us with the same yardstick with which they measure themselves, without recalling that the ravages of life are not the same for all, and that the search for one's own identity is as arduous and bloody for us as it was for them. To interpret our reality through schemas which are alien to us only has the effect of making us even more unknown, even less free, even more solitary.
>
> (García Márquez in McGuirk and Cardwell, p. 209)

Thus, the fate of the Buendía family—with its perpetual unhappiness, vulnerability, self-insulation, solitude, and eventual annihilation—represents the saddest destiny possible for the Latin American people as a whole. It is for the future of Latin America, then, that García Márquez puts forth the possibility of a second, utopian opportunity on earth—one that will bypass the fate of his own unhappy characters.

Sources and literary context. *One Hundred Years of Solitude* is usually seen as a key text of the 1960s Latin American "Boom," a period in which Latin America's literary output was for the first time internationally perceived to be modern, frenzied, rich, and experimental. Coinciding with the Cuban Revolution, and motivated by both impatience and despair, writers like Carlos Fuentes (see ***The Death of Artemio Cruz,*** also covered in *Latin American Literature and Its Times*), Julio Cortázar (see ***Blow-Up and Other Stories***), Mario Vargas Llosa (see ***The Storyteller***), and José Donoso (see ***A House in the Country***) revitalized the novel, revealing its possibilities at the same time critics were calling the novel a dead form. Novels of the Boom were notoriously self-conscious and concerned with expanding and re-evaluating traditional notions of history, narrative, truth, and reality—themes especially crucial given the ways repressive political regimes in Latin America consistently manipulated language and truth for "official" reasons.

One Hundred Years of Solitude has also been seen as the prototypical "magic realism" novel. In basic terms magic realism refers to a mode of writing that blends magical and real events without giving any special attention to the fantastic-seeming events it describes. Instead, the narrator speaks of fantastic events as if they were unsurprising, even banal, everyday occurrences. Nonetheless, García Márquez claims that every line of *One Hundred Years of Solitude* is based in reality. As Kathleen McNerney notes:

> At first glance that might seem preposterous: yellow butterflies constantly flitting around [Meme's lover]; a line of blood that winds its way through town to find the mother of the victim; a young woman being assumed into

Colombian troops take up positions in Bogotá after President Mariano Ospina declares a state of emergency, November 11, 1949.

> heaven wrapped in expensive sheets; a man who disappears and another who returns from the dead.
>
> (McNerney, p. 19)

From a Latin American perspective, however, myth, folktale, legend, and other commonly discounted forms of nontraditional knowledge (especially usual in countries like Colombia, with its Indian and African roots) are viable aspects of a reality that could at the same time include the disappearances and genocide mentioned above, and a violent banana massacre subsequently denied by the goverment responsible for it. *One Hundred Years of Solitude* achieves a fusion of these nontraditional forms and linear history that was inspired by the oral abilities of García Márquez's grandmother. He set out, when crafting the novel, to replicate her storytelling skills.

Events in History at the Time the Novel Was Written

***La Violencia*: 1946-66.** *La Violencia* was a chaotic 20-year period marked by violence and conflict in Colombia. Though never directly referred to in *One Hundred Years of Solitude,* la Violencia covers the period in which García Márquez conceived of and wrote the novel, and colors the text throughout; some critics claim that, in addition to the previous century's civil wars, la Violencia provides the background for over half the novel (de Valdés, p. 4). An estimated 250,000 people died during this 20-year period, which began with the 1946 government elections. In these elections the Liberals were split between moderate and dissident left-wing candidates. The Conservative candidate, backed by his party in full, won the presidency. In the next couple of years, there were sporadic clashes between members of the two parties—events that might have been relatively minor were it not for the April 9, 1948, assassination of Liberal leader Jorge Eliécer Gaitán in a crowded Bogotá street. The gunman—a fanatical Conservative—was quickly beaten to death by an angry mob. Liberals then began rioting in a "spontaneous orgy of violence": sacking the Capitol and other official buildings, setting fire to the Conservative newspaper, looting stores, and trashing churches (Bell-Villada, p. 25). The army could do nothing in the face of such chaos. By that evening Bogotá's main district was in shambles and as many as 2,500 people had died in the course of a day that would come to be known as *el bogotazo.*

El bogotazo sparked political violence that spread rapidly throughout Colombia, especially in rural areas. The bloodiness of this violence was extreme:

> Virulent hatred quickly became a normal component of rural interparty strife. Assassinations and armed clashes were to be routinely climaxed by decapitations and castrations, drawings and quarterings, with pregnant women and whole families hacked to pieces.
>
> (Bell-Villada, p. 26)

Some gunmen achieved wide notoriety for their extreme levels of violence; Teófilo Rojas "Chispas," for example, became famous for assassinating an average of two people every day. Land-theft became common practice in the countryside, where anyone with a gun could force a family off its own property. Some landowners retained armed bands to help them increase their holdings by stealing people's property; in the areas where police still existed, officers often participated in these takeovers. In the end, at least 2 million peasants were forced from their homes and into the cities.

The government participated in the chaos. In 1949 Conservatives in Congress took to blowing whistles to drown out opposing voices; during one stormy session Conservative party members actually shot the Liberal who had the floor. In the same year the Conservative president, Mariano Ospina, responded to Liberal talk of his impeachment by dissolving Congress and declaring a state of siege. Ospina's successor, Laureano Gómez, who took power in 1950, "unleashed against the Liberals a war of repression comparable to that of any military dictatorship" (Bell-Villada, p. 26). In retaliation, Liberals began killing Conservatives and torching their homes. Vast areas of the country fell into rebel hands. In this way, the state effectively collapsed.

In 1957 the period called the National Front began, under which both party leaders agreed to come together in unity. This meant an equal distribution of power between the Conservatives and Liberals—other parties, like the Communists, were ignored. There followed a period of relative calm, punctuated by intermittent acts of banditry and other violence that extended into the 1960s. The lasting effects of la Violencia have long been debated, with some arguing that they persist even today in the kidnappings and "common violent crime that affects most Colombian cities" (Oquist in Minta, p. 23).

Reviews. *One Hundred Years of Solitude* has been and continues to be a phenomenal success around the world. When the novel first came out, its Argentine publisher projected gradual sales of 10,000 copies or so, followed by a drop in interest. Instead the first printing—of 8,000 copies—sold out within one week. The novel took all of Latin America by storm, and by now has sold many millions of copies in the Spanish-speaking world alone. Earning García Márquez instant and universal fame, *One Hundred Years of Solitude* has been translated into more than 30 languages worldwide. Even in Soviet Russia the novel quickly sold a million copies, causing such amazement that there is a story often cited by García Márquez of "the elderly Soviet woman who copied out the entire text of the novel word by word, in order to make sure she had really read what she had read" (Bell-Villada, p. 4). The novel received numerous awards, including Italy's Chianchiano Prize, the title of best foreign book of the year in France, and the Rómulo Gallegos Prize, which is the most prestigious Latin American literary prize.

As one might expect, reviews were almost unanimously positive. Early Latin American reviewers called it "the best Colombian novel of all time," "the great novel of America," and "one of the literary masterpieces of the twentieth century" (Fiddian, p. 12). In an influential review for an Argentine journal, Tomás Eloy Martínez (author of ***Santa Evita*** [also covered in *Latin American Literature and Its Times*]) praised the novel—"everything that occurs in *One Hundred Years of Solitude* is important"—but located its "one Achilles' heel" in the great beauty of its language: "the perfect arrangement of the words sweetens the experience of reading, slows it down periodically, and finally anaesthetizes our sense of taste and smell" (Martínez, pp. 36-37). Writing in Spanish for *Hispania,* Gabriela Mora-Cruz pointed out that Márquez's fictional world, like real life, includes everything from love to cruelty to births, deaths, violence, superstition, politics, and comedy. The novel, she concluded, for all its magical realism, reproduces the very rhythm of existence.

—Carolyn Turgeon

For More Information

Bell-Villada, Gene H. *García Márquez: The Man and His Work.* Chapel Hill: The University of North Carolina Press, 1990.

Bushnell, David. *The Making of Modern Colombia: A Nation in Spite of Itself.* Los Angeles: University of California Press, 1993.

de Valdés, María Elena, and Mario J. Valdés. *Approaches to Teaching Gabriel García Márquez's One Hundred Years of Solitude.* New York: The Modern Language Association of America, 1990.

Fiddian, Robin, ed. *García Márquez.* New York: Longman, 1995.

García Márquez, Gabriel. *One Hundred Years of Solitude.* Trans. Gregory Rabassa. New York: Harper Perennial, 1970.

Martínez, Tomás Eloy. "America: the Great Novel." In *García Márquez.* Ed. Robin Fiddian. New York: Longman, 1995.

McGuirk, Bernard, and Richard Cardwell, eds. *Gabriel García Márquez: New Readings.* Cambridge: Cambridge University Press, 1987.

McNerney, Kathleen. *Understanding Gabriel García Márquez.* Columbia: University of South Carolina Press, 1989.

Minta, Stephen. *Gabriel García Márquez: Writer of Colombia.* London: Jonathan Cape, 1987.

Mora-Cruz, Gabriela. Review of *Cien años de soledad,* by Gabriel García Márquez. *Hispania* 51 (1968): 914-18.

Sway, Marlene. *Familiar Strangers: Gypsy Life in America.* Chicago: University of Illinois Press, 1988.

Wood, Michael. *Gabriel García Márquez's One Hundred Years of Solitude.* Cambridge: Cambridge University Press, 1990.

"Our America"

by
José Martí

José Martí was born January 28, 1853, in Havana, Cuba, to lower-middle-class Spanish parents. The man who would become known as the "Apostle," and adored by Cubans of all political persuasions was only 17 when he was convicted of treason and sentenced to six years' hard labor for agitating for Cuba's independence from Spain. Martí spent his adult life in exile, most of it in New York City, a situation that he grew to think of as his "cup of poison" (Ronning, p. 8). While in exile, Martí wrote prolifically for Spanish-language Latin American newspapers, mostly about the United States and the necessity of defending and nurturing Latin American culture, and he organized what he hoped would be the revolutionary army that would at last free Cuba. His essay "Our America" speaks not just to Cuba but to the whole region now known as Latin America. The essay strives to create a new commonality among the people of Latin America, to encourage a sense of unity and self-determination in the face of growing U.S. expansionism. (It should be noted that Martí did not use the term "Latin America," which would become common only in the twentieth century; rather he spoke of the "Americas" and "Our America." For clarity, this entry employs the twentieth-century term.)

THE LITERARY WORK

An essay written in New York City in January 1891; published (as "Nuestra América") in the newspapers *La Revista Illustrada* (New York City) on January 10, 1981, and *El Partido Liberal* (Mexico City) on January 30, 1891.

SYNOPSIS

A seminal work of Latin American nationalism, "Our America" argues for the rejection of European and United States cultural values in the forging of racially harmonious and politically stable Latin American nations.

Events in History at the Time of the Essay

José Martí: biography. José Martí was born in 1853 in Havana to a Spanish father and mother, Mariano Martí and Leonor Pérez. His father had first come to Cuba with the Spanish army and held minor government posts most of his life. In 1865 Martí was enrolled in the Escuela Superior Municipal de Varones, a boys' school under the direction of Rafael María de Mendive. Mendive, who believed fervently in Cuba's right to independence from Spain, encouraged the young Martí's growing revolutionary philosophies. Many members of the Cuban population were, in fact, discontented with Spanish rule. The wealthy plantation owners desired more Cuban political control over Cuban economics, and greater representation in Madrid, Spain, in exchange for their extremely high taxes; this class of Cubans, however, did not as a whole support open rebellion. That was the agenda of the island's smaller planters, who generally resented the superior attitude of the Spaniards sent to govern Cuba, the unfair taxation of Cubans, which paid for Spanish bureaucracies and war machines in Spain and Puerto Rico, and the continuing enslavement of Africans. (There were as many as 367,350 slaves in Cuba in 1860 [Bethell, p. 21].)

On October 10, 1868, Carlos Manuel de Céspedes, a small sugar planter in Oriente province, freed his slaves and issued the "*Grito de Yara*" (Cry from Yara), which launched a major Cuban independence and antislavery insurrection that grew to be known as the Ten Years' War. Spain reacted by tightening its grip; Mendive and his supporters, in turn, became more vocal in their protests. In January 1869 Mendive underwrote the publication of two patriotic journals that Martí produced. Weeks later, Mendive was arrested and deported for his political views; in October of the same year, Martí was sentenced to six years' hard labor when he was caught in the act of writing a letter critical of Spanish rule. At age 17 he began his sentence. In chains, under a blazing sun, he toiled in a Havana rock quarry not far from his parents' home. Within six months, his health was permanently destroyed; authorities commuted his sentence from hard labor to exile, and he was deported to Spain in January of 1871.

In Madrid Martí became involved in Spanish revolutionary politics and studied law at the university. Spain itself was in the midst of social upheaval. Advocates of individual and political freedom came to power, but even they did not seriously consider extending such privileges to Cubans. Martí took his cause to newspapers and leaflets, and once wrote a letter to the Spanish prime minister. None of it came to any avail, and Martí left Spain.

From Madrid, he travelled restlessly from France to Mexico, to Cuba (under an assumed name), to Guatemala, and then back to Cuba in 1878. During his prolonged absence, the Ten Years' war had been waged, at the cost of 50,000 Cuban lives, 208,000 Spanish lives, and $300 million in damage that the Cubans were expected to repay. A "peace" was reached in February 1878, but no Cuban with any nationalist tendencies could live with its terms—which included keeping Cuba under Spanish rule and its slaves in bondage. Martí quickly became a leader of "La Guerra Chiquita" (The Little War), an August 1879 uprising of black and white Cubans, including slaves, against the Spanish. He headed the movement's central committee in Havana until Spanish authorities found that he was becoming too vocal a critic and deported him once again to Spain. Almost immediately, he returned to the Americas, where he became president of the Cuban Revolutionary Committee in New York City. In New York, he supplemented his activism with a constant stream of writing, largely for Spanish American newspapers, and began organizing the manpower and materials needed for a final, successful Cuban revolution. During this period, he wrote "Our America" and other essays (many on life in the United States) that made him famous throughout the Americas. Martí warned his Latin American readers of rapacious U.S. imperialism, and chastised U.S. politicians and writers for their ignorance and greed concerning Latin America. Always he preached tolerance, justice, and respect. In 1890 both Argentina and Paraguay made him their U.S. Consul, and Uruguay asked him to represent its national interests at the International Monetary Conference, held that year in Washington, D.C.

As of 1891, the year "Our America" was published, Martí began to divest himself of responsibilities not immediately associated with the revolution. He travelled widely through North, South, and Central America, encouraging Cuban exiles and revolutionaries in Cuba itself, drawing together discordant factions, and collecting the money and materials necessary for the planned revolution. In 1894 all seemed finally ready. Martí was practically penniless and quite ill; nonetheless, he travelled to Florida around Christmas to finalize preparations. In mid-January, he and other leaders of the revolution suffered a terrible blow: the U.S. federal government, pressured by the Spanish, seized in Florida three loaded ships, the product of years of work, that were to carry the exiled Cubans to war.

Recovery from such a catastrophe could not have been easy, yet, with what resources they could muster, Martí and his supporters began the insurrection on February 25, 1895, as revolutionaries in Cuba were given the go-ahead to launch simultaneous anti-Spanish actions at sites across the land.

On March 25 Martí and Máximo Gómez, a seasoned Dominican warrior who had long been intimately involved in Cuban revolutionary groups, issued the "Montecristi Manifesto." This document set out the principles guiding the Cuban insurrectionaries: during the war, peaceful Spaniards would not be harmed, Cuban blacks (absolute emancipation had occurred in 1886) would be welcome compatriots, and private property would be respected in the rural areas. Once the rebellion was complete, the "new Cuba" would enjoy economic prosperity for all and an end to the feudal social structure, in which Cubans labored almost exclusively for the benefit of their Spanish overlords (Simons, p. 159). Martí himself landed on April 11 with his chief military advisors. In the minds of many Cuban nationalist fighters, he was to have been the first president of the free Cuba.

The revolution went badly, however, and was rapidly put down in many areas of the island. Martí died on May 19, riding (some say foolishly) against Spanish soldiers. Although his companions tried to stop them, the Spaniards took his body from the field and buried it in Santiago de Cuba.

The Monroe Doctrine and its aftermath. In 1891, when he wrote "Our America," Martí could look back upon nearly a century of open U.S. desire to take over the rich but troubled Spanish colony of Cuba and to control trade and politics throughout the Americas.

> **1808:** Thomas Jefferson suggests that the United States would buy Cuba from Spain, if Spain proved unable to maintain its hold on the island.
>
> **1823:** U.S. President James Monroe asserts what would become known as the "Monroe Doctrine," signaling U.S. desire to exercise economic and ideological control over the Americas: "The American continents . . . are henceforth not to be considered as subjects for future colonization by any European powers" (Monroe in Foner and Garraty, p. 743).
>
> **1848:** After winning the Mexican-American War (1846–48), the United States annexes Texas and takes New Mexico and California from Mexico in the Treaty of Guadalupe Hidalgo; U.S. President James Polk tentatively offers Spain $100 million for Cuba but is turned down.
>
> **1850:** U.S. volunteers, especially Southerners anxious to annex Cuba and thus tilt the national scales in favor of slave-owning states, back Cuban revolutionary Narciso López; the attempt fails, U.S. volunteers die or are executed by Spanish authorities, and U.S. citizens speak of war against the Spaniards in Cuba.
>
> **1854:** U.S. President Franklin Pierce sponsors the Ostend Manifesto, which declares that if Spain refuses to sell Cuba to the U.S., "by every law, human and divine, we shall be justified in wresting it from Spain if we possess the power" (Buchanan et al., in Simons, p. 170).
>
> **1857:** U.S. President James Buchanan's inaugural speech includes the following expansionist rhetoric: "[W]e have never acquired any territory except by fair purchase or, as in the case of Texas, by the voluntary determination of a brave, kindred, and independent people. . . . No nation shall have a right to complain if we shall still further extend our possessions" (Buchanan in Smith, p. 1047).

José Martí

During the years leading up to the U.S. Civil War, discussions about when and how—rarely whether—to conquer or annex Caribbean and Central American nations were commonplace in U.S. journals and newspapers. Both pro- and antislavery factions were eager to extend U.S. territory southward. Even after the 1861–65 Civil War—many years after, in fact—the issue consistently surfaced. Martí responded angrily to one such article, entitled "Do We Want Cuba?" which appeared in the *Philadelphia Manufacturer* on March 16, 1889, and was reprinted in the *New York Evening Post*. The article concluded that, no indeed, the U.S. should not take Cuba, despite its riches, because, among other things, Cubans were lazy and effeminate and unworthy of the honor: "The only hope we could possibly have to equip Cuba for the dignity of being one of our United States is to Americanize it totally, covering it with people of our own race" (*Philadelphia Manufacturer* in Kirk, p. 54). Martí's six-page reply, "Vindication of Cuba," published in the *Evening Post* on March 21, 1889, castigates U.S. imperialism and arrogance, and marks a turning point in Martí's attitude toward the United States. Whereas before he was annoyed by its selfish foreign policy and alarmed by its encroachments into Latin America, in the spring of 1889, "Martí's frustration with the United States finally exploded" (Kirk, p. 54).

IN THE ENTRAILS OF THE MONSTER

On March 18, 1895—the day before his death—José Martí began a letter to his friend Manuel Mercado, in which he explains that the Cuban revolution that he leads will not only overthrow the Spanish, but, equally importantly, will thwart U.S. expansion in Latin America. Thus "David" will bring down "Goliath":

> [E]very day now I am in danger of giving my life for my country and my duty (I understand this and I have the courage to fulfill it) to prevent in time—with the independence of Cuba—the United States from spreading throughout the Antilles, and with this added strength falling then on our Latin American countries. All that I have done until today, and all that I will continue to do, is toward this goal. . . . Our objective is to close off this route, which we are stemming with our blood, preventing the annexation of the nations of our America by the unruly and brutal North which despises them. I lived in the monster and know well its entrails—and my sling is that of David.
>
> (Martí in Kirk, p. 170)

International conferences: 1889-91. In the two years immediately preceding his writing of "Our America," Martí attended two important international conferences, both of which firmed his resolve to fight U.S. imperialism in Latin America. The first, the inaugural Pan-American Congress, was held in Philadelphia and Washington, D.C., and—at the invitation of the United States—was attended by representatives from nearly all American nations. The congress was convened to discuss issues such as banking, common currency, and common systems of law, including a tribunal to arbitrate disputes between American nations. Martí was deeply suspicious of this conference's underlying rationale; he believed that close ties with the United States would not, contrary to U.S. assurances, be beneficial to Latin America nations. Martí wrote a series of five articles on the Congress for the prestigious Buenos Aires newspaper *La Nación*. In the third of these articles, published on December 19 and 20, he wrote:

> For all of Latin America, from independence to the present, there was never any matter that required as much good sense, and vigilance, or that demanded a more minute, thorough examination, than this invitation of the United States. . . . The invitation is to the other, less powerful nations of Latin America . . . and its intention is to form a cartel against Europe and the rest of the world. Spanish America was able once to save itself from the tyranny of Spain. Now, after seeing with judicial eyes the antecedents, causes, and purpose of this invitation, it is necessary to say . . . that the time has arrived for Spanish America to declare her second independence.
>
> (Martí in Kirk, pp. 56-57)

Martí perceived the Pan-American Congress to be a glorified public relations stunt for the United States, by which that country, with its wealth and power, would woo the smaller Latin American nations into its sphere of dominance. In his opinion, to be thus seduced would mean the end of Latin American sovereignty and self-determination.

In 1891 Washington again hosted an international congress, the International Monetary Conference; Martí represented Uruguay. This time, the United States was trying to convince the Latin American nations to accept the premise of "bimetallism," by which silver would be circulated as money on the same terms as gold. The United States produced more silver than any other nation in the world, and the basic idea seems to have been to encourage Latin America to break off its ties with Europe (which, of course, opposed bimetallism) and trade almost exclusively with the United States. Martí was on two important committees during this conference, at which the United States's bimetallist project failed.

Cuban community at Key West. José Martí had been a lifelong supporter (and instigator) of Cuban independence. However, he was appalled by the personal aspirations of certain Cuban military leaders, both on the island and in exile, and dedicated himself to the formation of a civil (as opposed to military) egalitarian Cuban state; Martí had removed himself in 1884 from the revolutionary planning of Antonio Maceo and Máximo Gómez because he could not support their preference for military control of Cuba. He incurred much anger and resentment for his action—as leader of the Cuban exiles in New York City, his support was crucial, and there would be no revolution in 1884 because of his resignation from the effort. He spent the next seven years writing and teaching, and planning a revolution based on the principles of democracy, racial equality, and social justice. In 1891, the year in which he wrote "Our America," he traveled to Florida to speak with the emigré communities there. In Tampa, Florida, where many anti-Spanish, exiled Cuban tobacco workers lived, he and leaders of the Cuban community drafted the "Resoluciones tomadas por la Emigración Cubana de Tampa" ("Resolutions taken by the Cuban Emigrants of Tampa"); two months later, in Key West, Florida, home to the largest Cuban community in the United States (more than 7,000 out of a total of 25,000), these resolutions were solidified as the basic tenets of the Cuban Revolutionary Party. In April 1892 Martí was elected "Delegate" (meaning President) of the Party. The Cubans of Key West were as much responsible for the formation of the Revolutionary Party as was the famous Martí. The city had for years been the eye of the revolutionary storm; its inhabitants were relatively well-off, thanks to the thriving cigar industry, could afford to support revolutionary activities, and included many experienced and influential soldiers. Cuba was physically nearby, and the Florida revolutionaries were in close proximity to other Cuban communities scattered throughout the Caribbean and Central America. In contrast to the Cuban community in New York City, which consisted largely of political refugees from Cuba (especially intellectuals and artists like Martí), Key West Cubans had fled largely for economic reasons; many of them were black or mulatto factory workers and therefore highly receptive to Martí's focus on class rights and racial equality. The Key West emigré community was the most tightly knit of the major refugee centers, as historians point out (Ronning, p. 23). In the words of a key Cuban military man, Martí chose to establish his revolutionary base there because "the legendary Key was already consecrated by the history of patriotism, as the cradle of our liberties, because all the *caudillos* (military men) had proclaimed it as the patriotic center of the greatest power" (Figueredo in Ronning, p. 38). Less poetically, in Key West Martí found a community eager to hear his message of hope: the new Cuba would be a brotherhood of dignified workers, joined by love and a common desire to build a nation of racial harmony on sturdy Latin American foundations.

The Essay in Focus

Contents summary. "Our America" begins by ringing an alarm: "What remains of the village in America must rouse itself. These are not times for sleeping in a nightcap, but with weapons for a pillow . . . weapons of the mind, which conquer all others" (Martí, "Our America," p. 84). The nations of Latin America ("our" America, as opposed to the United States of America) must unite as brothers against the threat of unidentified invaders, "giants with seven-league boots" ("Our America," p. 84).

Against this giant, all of Latin America must "go forward in close order, like silver in the veins of the Andes" ("Our America," p. 85). To do this successfully, Latin Americans must ship back to Europe those born in America who are ashamed of the mother who reared them "because she wears an Indian apron" ("Our America," p. 85). The first step in guaranteeing sovereignty is to encourage pride in what is indigenous to Latin America, and to create a system of government that grows naturally from the specific history of the place. Foisting the legislative apparatus of U.S. or French systems of government, for example, on Latin American nations can lead only to failure, to economic and political stagnation. "The government must originate in the country. The spirit of the government must be that of the country. Its structure must conform to rules appropriate to the country" ("Our America," p. 87).

Accordingly, in Latin American nations the Europeanized white elite must give way to "the natural man" (the Indian, the African, the *mestizo*), who knows how to govern better than anyone the land that produced him. National institutions—governments, universities, the media —must encourage people in the knowledge of what is specifically Latin American: "The European university must bow to the American university. The history of America, from the Incas to the present, must be taught in clear detail and to the letter, even if the Archons of Greece are overlooked. . . . Nationalist statesmen must replace the foreign statesmen. Let the world be grafted onto our republics; but the trunk must be our own" ("Our America," p. 88).

“Our America”

Martí proceeds to reflect on the Latin American colonies' bid to achieve nationhood, mentioning the revolutions in Mexico, Central America, Venezuela, and Argentina, and the bitter and prolonged in-fighting that immediately followed. As Martí's essay states, “Hate was attempted” (“Our America,” p. 91). The essay alludes to the way in which factions in leading cities fought for power, while in the countryside regional strongmen, like Argentina's Facundo Quiroga, for example, exercised autocratic rule. The essay also discusses the unsatisfactory aftermath of nationhood across Latin America, when, all too often, “[t]he bookworm redeemers failed to realize that the revolution succeeded because it came from the soul of the nation”; the “soul” the essay refers to is the non-European rural, or natural, population (“Our America,” p. 89). Martí's writing posits that, to protect the new nations from familiar oppression by new leaders, it is necessary to change the spirit, and not merely the form of the government. Replacing one oppressor with another, home-grown though he be, is not what the Latin American revolutions were about. The predatory tiger, which represents the power-hungry violence lodged most prominently in colonialism, must be killed. The best way to kill that tiger, according to Martí, is to “try love” (“Our America,” p. 91). This solution seems only logical for fledgling Latin American nations that fell into the traps of intra-national struggle when they adopted European or U.S. models of government. They are a people “[e]xhausted by the senseless struggle . . . between the city and the country, weary of the impossible rule by rival urban cliques over the natural nation tempestuous or inert by turns (“Our America,” p. 91). Out of this exhaustion comes a kind of brotherhood and a commitment to innovate, to leave behind the tired and useless institutions that led to such an antagonistic state in the first place.

Martí comes now to the moral high point of the essay, exhorting Latin Americans to attend to the needs of the poor and downtrodden, to heal one another's wounds, and to create a Latin American culture for and by Latin Americans: “Playwrights bring native characters to the stage. Academies discuss practical subjects. . . . In the Indian respublics, the governors are learning Indian” (“Our America,” p. 92). Having painted a portrait of Latin American nations at peace with themselves and other nations, Martí returns to the issue of danger from without. Latin America must work to counter the “tradition of expansion or the ambitions of some powerful leader” of North America, by which Martí means the United States (“Our America,” p. 93). A Latin America divided, at war, unsettled, is prey; strong and confident, no longer burdened by colonial institutions and divisive political theories, Latin America can “confront and dissuade” the possibility of U.S. aggression (“Our America,” p. 93). Martí insists that “[t]he scorn of our formidable neighbor who does not know us is Our America's greatest danger. . . . Through ignorance, it might even come to lay hands on us” (“Our America,” p. 93).

“Our America” closes with an ecstatic vision of peace and unity. Racial hatred is not really

BARBARITY AND CIVILIZATION

In the early parts of “Our America,” Martí states that the struggle between “the natural man” and “learned, artificial men” is “not between civilization and barbarity, but between false erudition and Nature” (“Our America,” p. 87). In this statement he is no doubt referring to the ideas of Domingo Sarmiento, an Argentine writer and politician who wrote ***Facundo*** (1845; also covered in *Latin American Literature and Its Times*), a sociological examination of what Sarmiento saw as the constant Argentine struggle between civilization and barbarism. To Sarmiento, who was Argentina's president from 1868 to 1874, civilization was represented by urban culture that allied itself with Europe, barbarism by the rural mestizo and Indian culture. *Facundo* in part tells the story of a gaucho-outlaw who turned into a politician, Facundo Quiroga, the so-called “tiger of the plains.” It is from this image that Martí draws the image of the tiger of violent opposition that “lurks behind each tree, lying in wait at every turn” (“Our America,” p. 90).

Such strident rhetoric aside, it is important to note that Martí himself was to a large extent involved with the Europeanized elite against which he seems to write in “Our America.” Many of the points that he makes in the essay—from the grin-and-bear-it drinking of sour-tasting wine made from the home-grown bananalike plantain, to the rejection of Greek history in favor of American history—are meant to be read metaphorically. “The wine is made from plantain, but even if it turns sour, it is our own wine!” writes Martí (“Our America,” p. 92). Since Chile and Argentina grew grapes at the time, it would have been possible to suggest using them, but the effect would have been less dramatic.

possible because souls have no color; in "the justice of Nature," "man's universal identity springs forth from triumphant love and the turbulent hunger for life" ("Our America," p. 94). The project of nation-building, however, encourages acquisitiveness and greed; the United States, "the continent's fairskinned nation," is not evil inherently, but does not understand its southern neighbors and therefore thinks it can dominate them unopposed ("Our America," p. 94). The "immediate unity in the continental spirit" will help solve this problem; indeed, "the hymn is already being sung . . . from the Río Grande to the Straits of Magellan" ("Our America," p. 94).

"Seven-league boots." "Our America" opens with a warning: Latin America must be attentive to dangers that threaten it from the outside. "Giants with seven-league boots," the essay begins, recalling a pan-European fairytale motif, are on the verge of falling upon the parochial and complacent Latin American people ("Our America," p. 84). The image of the booted giant or the monster recurs throughout Martí's work, invariably in reference to the United States of America. Much has been written on the subject of Martí's anti-U.S. stance (notably by post-revolution Cuban communists). When he first arrived in New York in 1880 Martí was liberal in his praise of U.S. democratic traditions and the morality of the nation's founding fathers; over time, however, his view soured, thanks mostly to the U.S. "tradition of expansion [and] the ambitions of some powerful leader" ("Our America," p. 93). His missives to Latin American newspapers and journals regularly warned of the U.S. imperialist designs on Latin America, and grew so vehemently critical of the U.S. domestic and foreign policies that some of those papers edited his work severely or simply refused to publish his articles at all. Martí did not change his opinions, but he did soften his tone. Thus, the warning that opens "Our America" is not of a new danger but of a renewed threat. The U.S. tradition of desiring to dominate or annex Latin American nations continues unbroken, and it is time for those nations to put a decisive end to it. Martí was especially sensitive to the issue because the United States had long dreamed of annexing Cuba, his homeland.

Exactly how Martí felt about the United States is open to debate. Critics on both sides of the political divide have claimed him, arguing that he was openly hostile to the nation or that he was warmly receptive to many of its philosophies. Part of the problem is that Martí occupied both positions at different times in his life, and his political reservations did not necessarily extend to U.S. culture in general; he was a deep admirer of the scholar Ralph Waldo Emerson and the poet Walt Whitman, for example. Cer-

MARTÍ ON RACE

Throughout "Our America," José Martí emphasizes that there should be no place for racial hatred in the new Latin American nations, or anywhere, for that matter: "Whoever foments and spreads antagonism and hate between races, sins against humanity" ("Our America," p. 94). The theme is an old one with Martí. At age nine, he went to live with his father in the small Cuban town of Hanábana and saw something there that profoundly affected him for the rest of his life. Hanábana was surrounded by plantations dependent on the labor of African slaves, and the young boy witnessed the cruel treatment meted out there: "And the blacks? Who has ever seen a friend physically whipped and does not consider himself forever in that man's debt? I saw it, I saw it when I was a child, and I can still feel the shame burning on my cheeks" (Martí in Kirk, p. 24). Martí, who is as famous for his poetry as his prose, published a verse collection, *Versos Sencillos,* in 1891, the same year that "Our America" appeared. One of the poems in this volume conjures what he had witnessed at the plantation, and its lasting effect on him:

El viento, fiero, quebraba
Los almácigos copudos
Andaba la hilera, andaba,
de los esclavos desnudos.
[. . .]
Rojo, como en el desierto
Salió el sol al horizonte:
Y alumbró a un esclavo muerto,
Colgado a un seibo del monte.

Un niño lo vio: temblo
De pasión por los que gimen:
¡Y, al pie del muerto, juró
Lavar con su vida el crimen!

[The fiery winds were breaking up the bushy plantation trees; and the line of naked slaves was moving, moving. . . .

Scarlet as in the desert, the sun rose in the horizon; it shone upon a dead slave, hanging from a mountain ceiba.

A child saw him and shook with passion for those that suffer. And beneath the dead man he swore to expiate with his life the crime.]

(Martí in Fernández Retamar, p. 4)

Simón Bolívar

tainly Martí was too complex a man to opt wholeheartedly for either a positive or negative attitude. It is worth noting, however, that, in the last piece of writing we have before his death, the letter to his friend Manuel Mercado, he refers to the United States as a "monster," and declares that he has dedicated his life to ensuring that it does not trample upon Latin America (Martí in Kirk, p. 170).

Sources and literary context. Martí claimed that the most important political influence on him was that of the Venezuelan nationalist Simón Bolívar, whom he called "father of the Americas" (Martí in Fernández Retamar, p. 2). Bolívar was born in 1783 in Caracas and educated in Spain. In Europe, he became acquainted with the Enlightenment (an eighteenth-century European movement that focused on the individual's power to reason and on a person's natural rights, including the rights to life and liberty). Bolívar returned to Venezuela and advocated freedom for its people. In 1811, urged by Bolívar as well as others, Venezuela declared its independence, but the Spanish monarchy refused to give up its hold on the land and Bolívar was forced to flee. Although he realized it was unlikely, he was hoping to unite all of Spanish America into a single nation, and travelled widely across South America, urging different Spanish colonies to band together. He failed in his hopes and died young, of tuberculosis, at age 47. Bolívar is famous for having said: "Do not adopt the best system of government, but the one which is most likely to succeed" (Bolívar in Skidmore and Smith, p. 30). Giving an address to the Hispanic American Literary Society in October 1893, Martí said of Bolívar: "He burned with our own desire for freedom; he spoke with the voice of our own natures, his zenith was our continent's finest hour, his fall strikes at the heart" (Martí, pp. 98-99).

Three years earlier, Martí had written a dramatic piece about his 1881 trip to Venezuela in the children's journal, *La Edad de Oro* (which he himself published), demonstrating the depth of Bolívar's influence on him:

> They tell how a traveller arrived one day at Caracas at dusk. Without shaking off the dust of the road, he did not ask where he could eat or sleep, but how he could find the statue of Bolívar. . . . [He] wept before the statue, that for him seemed to come to life, moving just as a father when his son comes near. The traveller did well, because all the peoples of the Americas must love Bolívar as a father.
>
> (Martí in Fernández Retamar, p. 2)

Martí is Cuba's most famous political and cultural essayist, but the island produced at least three other important nineteenth-century practitioners of the genre. Félix Varela y Morales (1787-1853), a Catholic priest, was a proponent of Cuban independence in the 1820s. Condemned by the Spanish to death, Father Varela, like José Martí some 50 years later, fled to the United States. Between 1824 and 1826 he published the newspaper *El Ilabanero,* a pro-independence journal that was smuggled into Cuba. The other two best-known Cuban essayists are José Antonio Saco (1797–1879), who wrote in support of the abolition of slavery, and José de la Luz y Caballero (1810–62), who lobbied for Cuban independence.

"Our America" has been compared to another landmark essay, "Ariel" (1900), by the Uruguayan writer José Enrique Rodó. Both urge Latin Americans to beware of the United States and to assert their separateness. Rodó's essay, however, foresees a European-style Latin America, without a mix of contradictory beliefs and lifestyles, while Martí's asks Latin America to stop perceiving life through the eyeglasses of France or the United States. "Our America" instead advocates acknowledging the region's distinctiveness; in a highly rhetorical moment in the essay, the European-educated Martí, who himself knew a great deal about ancient Greek civilization and the European tradition that it stands for, writes that it is preferable for Americans to study the Incas, even if that means ignoring classical Greece.

Impact. The Chilean poet Gabriela Mistral once wrote in the autograph book of a Cuban girl: "Don't forget, if you have a brother or son, that the purest man of our Latin race, José Martí, lived in your country. Try to form your little friend in the image of Martí, at the same time a fighter and as pure as an archangel" (Mistral in Kirk, p. 166). Other Latin American writers have joined Mistral in their praise of Martí. For example, Rubén Darió, the Nicaraguan poet, wrote that all Cubans should emulate Martí, and lamented his death as a loss to all Latin Americans: "Oh, Cuba! . . . [T]he blood of Martí was not yours alone; it belonged to an entire race, to an entire continent; it belonged to the powerful young that loses in him the first of its teachers; he belongs to the future" (Darió in Fernández Retamar, p. 1). Martí's writings and public performances greatly influenced generations of Latin Americans; an observer of his Key West speeches noted: "[Martí] continued more and more to fire the patriotic spirit in his oratorical displays, with phrases so touching that the people believed them as an article of faith. . . . And since all people create their own idol, it was Martí whom they worshipped as the Indians worshipped the sun" (Arnao in Ronning, p. 136).

The modern cult of Martí. After his death at the Battle of Dos Ríos on May 19, 1895, José Martí suffered a period of obscurity for some 25 years. Since that time, however, he has emerged as the most influential symbol of Cuban nationalism for future generations. As one critic states, Martí plays a "sacramental role" in Cuban politics: "Cubans in and outside the island revere Martí as the very spirit of their national identity, and they search in his works, as they would in a sacred text, for the keys that either justify the current revolutionary government or make sense of the reality of exile" (Santí, p. 14). Fidel Castro, the communist dictator, has made it amply clear, both in his speeches and in the official government propaganda that his regime sponsors, that Martí is his hero, his intellectual role model; whether or not this stance is merely politically expedient is not as clear.

As John Kirk points out, the name of Martí is ubiquitous throughout the island. The Havana airport is officially named the Aeropuerto José Martí; the national library is the Biblioteca José Martí; the city's central square is the Plaza José Martí; Martí's face appears on postage stamps and on Cuban currency; his portrait hangs in every school; and almost every village has erected some sort of public monument to the man (Kirk, p. 3). In Cuba interpretation of his substantial body of writings—27 volumes—has varied widely through the decades. Martí has served, at various times, as an idol of anti-U.S. sentiment, a confirmed Marxist, and, more recently, as a "democratic revolutionary" (Kirk, p. 16). Outside Cuba the situation is not much different. Exiled Cubans in particular have tended to keep alive the image of Martí that flourished in Cuba before 1959; in this view, Martí was a prophet of peace, harmony, and freedom: a second Christ. Despite volumes of work to the contrary, the Cuban exiles in the United States have sometimes tried to gloss over Martí's anti-U.S. writings. The truth lies somewhere between the two interpretations. What is certain is that Martí's life and writings have been a battleground of ideology on both sides of the 1959 Revolution, as demonstrated by the following example:

> The Marxist regime of Fidel Castro heralds [Martí] as the ideological author of its revolution and accords him a veneration not second to that given the founders of Marxism-Leninism itself, whilst at the other end of the political spectrum, Martí's name has been appropriated by a Florida radio station set up by the [1980s] Reagan administration to churn out anti-Castro propaganda.
>
> (Turton, p. 1)

—Lorraine Valestuk

For More Information

Bethell, Leslie, ed. *Cuba: A Short History*. Cambridge: Cambridge University Press, 1993.

Fernández Retamar, Roberto. "The Modernity of Martí." In *José Martí: Revolutionary Democrat*. Eds. Chrisopher Abel and Nissa Torrents. Durham, N. C.: Duke University Press, 1986.

Foner, Eric, and John A. Garraty, eds. *The Reader's Companion to American History*. Boston: Houghton Mifflin, 1991.

González Echevarría, Roberto, and Enrique Pupo-Walker. *The Cambridge History of Latin American Literature*. Vol. 1. Cambridge: Cambridge University Press, 1996.

Kirk, John M. *José Martí, Mentor of the Cuban Nation*. Tampa: University Presses of Florida, 1983.

Martí, José. "Our America." In *Our America by José Martí: Writings on Latin America and the Struggle for Cuban Independence.* Ed. Philip S. Foner. Trans. Elinor Randall, with additional translations by Juan de Onis and Roslyn Held Foner. New York: Monthly Review Press, 1977.

Ronning, C. Neale. *José Martí and the Emigre Colony in Key West: Leadership and State Formation.* New York: Praeger, 1990.

Santí, Enrico Mario. "José Martí and the Cuban Revolution." In *José Martí and the Cuban Revolution Retraced.* UCLA Latin American Studies. Vol. 62. Los Angeles: UCLA Latin American Center Publications, 1986.

Simons, Geoff. *Cuba: From Conquistador to Castro.* London: MacMillan, 1996.

Skidmore, Thomas E., and Peter H. Smith. *Modern Latin America.* 4th ed. New York: Oxford University Press, 1997

Smith, Page. *The Nation Comes of Age: A People's History of the Ante-bellum Years.* Vol. 4. New York: Penguin, 1984.

Turton, Peter. *José Martí: Architect of Cuba's Freedom.* London: Zed Books, 1986.

Pedro Páramo

by
Juan Rulfo

Juan Rulfo (1917-86) was born in Jalisco, Mexico, where, as a child, he experienced the violence of the government-Church conflict that escalated into the Cristero rebellion (1926-29). Losing both of his parents at an early age, Rulfo lived in a Franciscan orphanage before studying at the University of Guadalajara. In 1942 he began contributing to the journal *America* and in 1945 published the first in a series of *cuentos*, or short stories, that would form part of what is now considered his only other significant work, *El Llano En Llamas* (The Burning Plains). In 1954 Rulfo published fragments of *Pedro Páramo,* which appeared in its entirety in 1955 and distinguished itself as remarkable for its innovative style and intimate look at rural village life.

THE LITERARY WORK

A novel set in rural Mexico from the late nineteenth century to the 1940s; first published in Spanish in its entirety in 1955, in English in 1959.

SYNOPSIS

A man's search for his father leads him to Comala, a ghost town filled only with voices and the dead, from whom he learns the tragic history surrounding his father's death and the decline of the village.

Events in History at the Time the Novel Takes Place

Rural Mexico in the late nineteenth century. Towards the end of the nineteenth century Mexico was a predominantly rural and agricultural country in which feudalistic *haciendas* still prevailed. Self-enclosed and self-governing, these large estates manufactured their own products and paid their laborers extremely low wages that the peasants had no choice but to accept—private jails and terror kept the work force in line. On the hacienda "exploitation had deep, centuries-old roots and entailed the lifelong and hereditary serfdom of laborers forever indebted to their 'master'" (Krauze, p. 219). Rural Mexico had been dominated by the hacienda and its predecessor, the *encomienda,* since colonial times, and not much had changed for the average peasant between Mexico's independence from Spain (1820s) and the turn of the century.

During the regime of President Porfirio Díaz, who assumed power in 1876 and, by continuously reelecting himself, maintained his political hold until 1910, the situation took a turn for the worse. After a new land law was enacted in 1883, land concentration became more acute. Many of the rural Mexicans who had inherited ancestral lands but could not prove legal title to them lost their holdings to large land companies. In the five years after the enactment of the law, these companies gained almost 70 million acres of rural land; by 1894 one-fifth of Mexico's territory had been absorbed by land companies. Whole communities as well as individual landowners had to forfeit territory. Because, by the turn of the century, most villages had lost their *ejidos* (comunally owned village lands) to either land companies or to the haciendas of a few hundred wealthy families, employment on haciendas became necessary for the villagers' survival. Mexican peasants found themselves totally dependent for sustenance on the *hacendado* (hacienda owner), who might also be the local *cacique* (political strongman) making the political decisions that affected the daily lives of the peasants. In Rulfo's novel the hacendado Pedro Páramo is also the local cacique, and has complete economic and political control over the village of Comala.

Under President Díaz Mexico experienced some economic growth and modernization, but these benefits came only to a privileged few. He updated the railway system and electrified much of Mexico, bringing the country together in these ways. Still, the vast majority of Mexicans remained illiterate and impoverished, suffering poor working conditions on the haciendas and in the cities. This would not be radically changed by the revolution that was about to occur. By 1910, 45 percent of the inhabitants in the principal agricultural regions lived on haciendas. "The rest were relegated to a sharply reduced area of inferior land, often arid or on steep hillsides, where they made up an impoverished mass that could be drawn upon by the ordinary haciendas of Mexico . . . for casual labour" (Bauer in Bethell, p. 132). Although the labor of the rural peasants fueled the nation, the benefits of modernization did not filter down to these landless people. The rural masses living on or near the haciendas suffered greatly:

> The contrast between the hacendado and those who worked the hacienda and made it live is so stark as to be absurd. . . . Within a mile of the grand hacienda house were miserable, one-room, floorless, windowless adobe shacks. . . . Twice a day a few minutes would be set aside to consume some tortillas wrapped around beans and chile. . . . Infant mortality on many haciendas exceeded 25 percent.
>
> (Meyer, p. 464)

During Díaz's regime the Mexican peasant earned low wages (about 35 cents a day, making him 12 times poorer than a contemporary U.S. farm worker); he was frequently forced into debt by the hacendado, who made all the decisions and orchestrated almost every part of the peasants' lives. In control not only of the land but also the water supply and the local store, the hacendado often subjected his rural peasants, who had no real judicial rights, to corporal punishment. Aside from administering "justice," he exercised control over other domains of the mini-society on his estate. He paid the local priest, maintained the local school, controlled the forces of law and order, provided medical attention, and imported domestic and foreign merchandise. Like the majority of rural Mexicans, the villagers in *Pedro Páramo* depend on the landed elite for their meager survival.

Caciques. The cacique—rooted in the indigenous tradition of the Aztec *tlatoani* (speaker)—arose as a prominent force in the years following the Wars for Independence, won in 1821. As Mexico was being shaped into a nation, the cacique filled a political vacuum created by years of fighting and political instability. Because of the vastness and geographic isolation of Spanish America, these political strongmen were able to establish strong nuclei of local power within rural Mexico. Since the colonial period the term "cacique" has "conveyed the idea of absolute—almost theocratic—authority" (Krauze, p. 132). Caciques had to be extremely wealthy in order to wield this kind of power, and so, like Pedro Páramo, were usually hacendados as well, passing their power on to their heirs and establishing dynasties that cemented their authority. By sustaining the surrounding community through his wealth and provisions (in exchange for hard labor), the cacique was able to create a dependent situation that, coupled with violence and terror, might allow him and his family, in effect, to enslave the peasants on his hacienda, or those in his village, indefinitely.

A 1729 Spanish dictionary defined caciques in this way: "the first of his village or republic, the one who has more authority or power and who because of his pride wants to make himself feared and obeyed by all his inferiors" (Chevalier, p. 30). This definition applies also to the *caudillo,* who functioned like the cacique, but on a national, rather than local, scale. While a cacique ruled men, caudillos ruled men and caciques. Both types of strongmen functioned as dictators, the only difference between them being one of station. The caudillo would often try to incorporate a cacique into his own government—if he found the cacique limiting his own power, however, he might attempt to destroy him. As the nation became more unified, a president like Díaz protected and invigorated these mostly petty tyrants in order to centralize his own political control. Díaz, in fact, came to be acknowledged as the "Great Cacique" (Chávez Orozco in Chevalier, p. 39).

A meeting of Pancho Villa (front row, second from left) and Álvaro Obregón (front row, third from left) in 1914.

The Mexican Revolution. Two significant historical events, the Mexican Revolution and the Cristero rebellion, provide some of the backdrop to *Pedro Páramo.* The Mexican Revolution began as a reaction to the conditions of inequality, peasant exploitation, and land concentration that had been perpetuated and exacerbated under the Díaz regime. In the summer of 1906 Mexican intellectuals met and devised the Liberal Plan, which, among other things, called for the redistribution of lands. Under this plan the state would redistribute all uncultivated lands to the peasants, and restore the ejido lands that had been taken away from the native Indian communities. When Francisco I. Madero, a wealthy northerner, published *The Presidential Succession in 1910*—a document calling for both an end to reelection of the same president and the formation of an opposition party—he set into motion the events that would lead to the outbreak of revolutionary violence in 1910. After President Díaz managed to reelect himself yet again in 1910, Madero published another text, the *Plan of San Luis Potosi,* which declared the election "illegal" and called for citizens to "rise in arms" against the "tyranny that oppresses them" (Madero in Meyer and Sherman, p. 499). Fighting soon broke out as rebel armies and peasant mobs took up weapons. At this point all the rebels had one thing in common: they were convinced that getting rid of Díaz would be a change for the better.

Díaz's federal armies reacted to the peasant uprisings, but their efforts to quell the outbreaks were generally unsuccessful. Unlike the federal army, the small rebel units had the sympathy of the people. Many of these peasants rallied under the leadership of charismatic regional leaders like Pancho Villa, Venustiano Carranza, and Álvaro Obregón—all of whom are mentioned in *Pedro Páramo*. After Díaz resigned in 1910 most of these leaders' physical and political fighting became directed primarily towards each another, and the revolution deteriorated into factionalism.

Support for individual rebel leaders not only came from idealists but also (and perhaps more often) from opportunists, who would side with the faction that seemed most likely to win. *Pedro Páramo* alludes to this trend of opportunism when the titular character dines with a faction of rebels and co-opts them by providing them with men, money, and a new leader, El Tilcuate. Páramo tells El Tilcuate to join sides with whomever is winning, and, though Páramo's men initially join Pancho Villa's faction, they then switch over to the faction led by Carranza and Obregón, who have only recently "made peace" with each other (Rulfo, *Pedro Páramo*, p. 115). This "peace" is probably a reference to the fallout from the Convention of Aguascalientes, held in 1914 by the leaders of the military factions to determine Mexico's future course. Ironically, the convention only crystallized the battle between the camps of Villa and Carranza. A month after the convention General Obregón opted to side with Carranza, becoming the military spearhead of his contingent. Outside of this rivalry but still a formidable presence was Emiliano Zapata's southern-based agrarian reform faction.

In 1916 the rebels, attempting to legitimize the Revolution, organized a congress for the purpose of designing a new constitution, which was proclaimed in early 1917. The Constitution included articles that foreshadowed the direction the domestic in-fighting would take in the 1920s and '30s. Anticlerical and pro-land reform, the Constitution called for, among other things, a reduction of Church powers and the restoration of lands taken from the peasants during the Díaz regime. The ideals that the Constitution attempted to realize, however, would not materialize under the presidency of Carranza, newly elected in 1917. His government practically ignored the land reform promised in Article 27 (a mere 450,000 acres of land were distributed) and responded to workers' strikes by having them violently put down. Many of the revolutionary groups in Mexico grew extremely disillusioned; the *zapatistas* were especially affected after their charismatic leader was assassinated in 1919. Zapata never saw the mass land distribution called for in his famed *Plan de Ayala* (with which he hoped to free peasants from the tyranny of the hacienda) and life for the great majority of Mexicans failed to improve in the unstable years directly following the onset of the Revolution. Carranza himself was assassinated in 1920, and real land reform did not materialize until the presidency of Lazaro Cardenas, who assumed office in 1934. Many hacendados remained largely untouched in the decades following the Revolution. For the fictional Pedro Páramo, the Revolution is but a minor nuisance, and he easily remains unaffected by it.

The Cristero rebellion. Another important historical event that affected the life of the author and inspired events in *Pedro Páramo* is the relatively short-lived Cristero rebellion, which took place in Mexico between 1926 and 1929. In 1926, after a period of escalating tensions between Church and state, the archbishop of Mexico, José Mora y del Río, stated that Roman Catholics should not accept the new, anticlerical Constitution. Mexican president Plutarco Calles, a long-time enemy of the Church, reacted forcefully, introducing even more anticlerical measures, such as the deportation of foreign priests, the forbidding of religious teaching, and the mandatory registration of priests with the government before they could work. In a countermove the archbishop of Mexico in July 1926 declared a strike, and all Catholic baptisms, weddings, and masses came to a halt for the first time in four centuries.

Catholic leaders began organizing the peasants, especially in Juan Rulfo's native state of Jalisco, and these Catholic guerrillas, or *Cristeros*, rebelled violently against the government. "For them, the 'cause' was clear: They were fighting to bring back masses, they were fighting to defend religion" (Krauze, p. 422). The Cristeros burned government schools, murdered teachers, dynamited trains, and staged other acts of violence in support of their cause. Of course, the violence was far from one-sided. In their efforts against the Cristeros, the government's federal troops contributed to the destruction by burning villages, killing lay people, and sometimes hanging priests. More than 70,000 lives were lost in the *Cristiada* (another name for the rebellion), agricultural production dropped by almost 40 percent, and over half a million rural Mexicans fled to the cities or to the United States. In 1928 newly elected president Álvaro Obregón was assassinated by José de León Toral, a Cristero. An impending peace agreement was postponed by the assassination, but was eventually concluded in 1929.

The Novel in Focus

Plot summary. *Pedro Páramo* follows the journey of Juan Preciado, who, at his dying mother's request, travels to the hot and arid town of Comala in search of his father. Comala, he slowly realizes, is a lifeless town populated by ghosts, voices, and murmurs, where the memories and whispers of the dead fill the streets. Juan Preciado has three guides on this morbid journey: Abundio, who leads him into Comala; Doña Eduviges, who offers Juan Preciado a spare room for the night; and Damiana, who arrives at Doña Eduviges's home and invites Juan Preciado to accompany her. More than guides, these three companions are storytellers, sharing their memories with Juan Preciado and offering insights into his family's and Comala's past. All three guides, Juan Preciado realizes after each has left, are dead.

From Abundio, Juan Preciado learns that his father, Pedro Páramo, is dead, as are the rest of Comala's former inhabitants. Juan Preciado's guides narrate the story of his deceased father and of Comala, explaining why and how it has become the deserted ghost town that it is. Interspersed between their narrations are the thoughts of the deceased Pedro Páramo, snippets of conversations between other deceased townspeople, and their memories of key events in the town's history—all presented in fragments sprinkled throughout the narrative. Juan Preciado himself dies in Comala of sheer terror: the voices of the lingering souls that remain in Comala, transforming it into a worldly purgatory, are enough to kill him. Juan therefore learns much of this tragic story of Comala posthumously, while sharing a coffin with a female companion, Dorotea, who states that she had died of hunger after the onset of the Cristiada.

Pedro Páramo's story begins with his childhood love for Susana, who left Comala as a youngster. Never forgetting Susana, the dead Pedro even now reminisces about their childhood games. The story continues with the death of Pedro Páramo's father, after which Pedro begins his own economic ascension by absorbing, through violent coercion, intimidation, marriage, and even murder, the lands surrounding his hacienda. Juan Preciado learns that Pedro married his mother, Dolores, because of her large property and in order to cancel a substantial debt that he owed her family.

As Pedro's hacienda grows, so does his political and social authority as local cacique. His power appears limitless and he is able to act with impunity. He proceeds, among other things, to make free use of women of the area for his own sexual satisfaction, fathering many an illegitimate child (including Juan Preciado's first guide, Abundio, who leads him into Comala). The town priest, Father Rentería, delivers one of the illegitimate children, Miguel, to Pedro Páramo.

Juan Preciado learns that Father Rentería becomes guilt-ridden about having delivered this bad seed to Pedro and feels responsible for the decline of Comala. When Miguel accidentally dies, the priest at first refuses to give him the needed blessing because Miguel killed the priest's brother and seduced his niece. Yet Pedro's power is so all-encompassing that he is able to persuade the priest to offer the blessing, paying him a handsome sum in exchange. The priest, overwhelmed by shame, weeps as he realizes that he too is a sinner for having accepted the bribe of a rich man, while at the same time denying many of the poorer people's requests for absolution: "My fault. I've betrayed everybody who loves me, and they still trust in me and ask me to intercede for them with God" (*Pedro Páramo,* p. 28).

Candles, food, and flowers adorn a Mexican home for a celebration of the Day of the Dead.

When Pedro's wife, Dolores, leaves Comala one day to visit her sister, Pedro is content to be rid of her and never invites her back, leaving her fate and that of their child, Juan Preciado, in God's hands. Eventually Pedro Páramo's childhood sweetheart, Susana, returns to Comala because "there were strange winds blowing in those days. It was said that a revolution had broken out" (*Pedro Páramo,* p. 81). Her father, fearing for her safety in the desolate mountains where they had been living, returns her to Comala. Pedro then weds the widowed Susana, who, stricken by grief and madness, is nothing like the child Pedro remembers and reveres.

It is at the height of Pedro's power that the Mexican Revolution erupts. After his foreman dies at the hands of rebels threatening to take his land, Páramo shrewdly offers the rebels money and men in support of their cause. With this offer he is able to avoid any violence, and immediately wins the rebels' favor:

> "We've rebelled against the government and against people like you because we're sick of putting up with you. Because the government is rotten and because you and your kind are just stupid crooks and bandits. I won't say any more about the government because we're going to do our talking with bullets."
>
> "How much do you need for your revolution?" Pedro Páramo asked. "Maybe I can help you."
>
> (*Pedro Páramo,* p. 97)

And thus the Revolution passes over Pedro Páramo, so to speak; his hacienda and his position of power as cacique are left intact. His power, in this respect, is greater than that of the Church, the state, or the Revolution.

Comala's ruin is brought about when Susana dies, and the solemn tolling of the bells prompts the villagers to throw a party, complete with circus and musicians. Whether or not the townspeople misinterpret the tolling or indeed celebrate Susana's death is ambiguous. However, Pedro—enraged at this festive display—vows revenge on the town: "'I'll fold my arms and Comala will starve to death.' And that was what he did" (*Pedro Páramo,* p. 115). One day a drunken Abundio comes to ask Pedro for money for his own wife's funeral. Pedro refuses and Abundio, it seems, stabs him to death.

The wandering souls of Comala are unable to find rest, Juan Preciado learns, because they are full of sin, and the prayers of the living survivors are not enough to grant them forgiveness and lead them out of purgatory. Besides, the living themselves are too full of sin to be of any help;

the only survivors Juan Preciado encounters before his death are an incestuous brother and sister living as a couple. As noted, even the town priest, Father Rentería, had fallen from God's grace while Comala was still "alive." Because his own hands "aren't clean enough" either, a priest in neighboring Contla denies Rentería absolution for the sin of having "sold his soul" (*Pedro Páramo,* p. 69).

Lingering souls. Popular Catholic belief holds that, when a person dies, a prayer session is necessary to allow the dead person's soul to rise to heaven. In Mexico this prayer session, the *Novenario* (nine continuous days of prayer), normally takes the form of a religious mass conducted by a priest. At the time of the novel, it was not uncommon for the deceased to be dressed in a habit so that he or she would resemble a saint as closely as possible; such clothing, many believed, would help shorten the soul's stay in purgatory (the limbo between heaven and hell where worldly sins are purged through suffering) and bring it closer to heaven. Like *Pedro Páramo*'s Father Rentería, many priests were known to deny services of absolution, or pardon, to the poor who could not afford to buy a mass. In such cases the relatives would pray the Novenario at home to help the soul of the deceased bypass purgatory and go straight to heaven. Popular belief held that prayer had the power to lead the soul out of purgatory; the number of people praying for a particular soul was especially important—the more people praying, the less time the soul would spend in purgatory.

In *Pedro Páramo* Comala becomes a worldly purgatory for the lingering souls who sometimes approach the living to ask for their prayers. As Damiana, though dead herself, says,

> Just tonight I came across a wake. I stopped to say a paternoster [Our Father], and while I was saying it a woman left the others and came over to me. "Damiana! Pray for me, Damiana!" She opened her rebozo and I saw she was my sister Sixtina . . . you wouldn't know, but my sister Sixtina died when I was twelve years old.
>
> (*Pedro Páramo,* p. 40)

The burden of their sins condemns the lingering souls of Comala to remain in this worldly purgatory. One Comala survivor has resigned herself to sharing her town with the dead:

> There's so many of them, and so few of us, we don't even try to pray for them so their souls can rest. Our prayers aren't enough for all of them. Perhaps a bit of the paternoster might reach them, but it wouldn't do them any good. We're too full of sin. There isn't one of us living here who's in the grace of God. We can't even raise our eyes without feeling them burn with shame. And shame doesn't cure anything. At least that's what the bishop said when he came by here a while back for the confirmations. I went up to him and confessed everything. "That can't be pardoned," he said.
>
> (*Pedro Páramo,* p. 50)

Race in post-colonial Mexico. Since the time of the colonial regime, when Spaniards distinguished between people born of Indian and European blood, Mexicans have been divided along racial lines. Colonial Mexicans—whites, mestizos, Indians—experienced variable treatment. There was even a distinction between different kinds of whites—*peninsulares,* who were born in Spain (or elsewhere in Europe) and creoles, who were the children of Europeans born in the New World. The most privileged positions were reserved for the peninsulares. More generally, in respect to the three racial groups, only whites and mestizos had substantial access to power and property.

By the late eighteenth century, the term "Indian" did not refer simply to an ethnic group, but, more generally, to many Mexicans of low socioeconomic status. During the Díaz regime, "'racial' labels were still applied," even though "all Mexicans stood as formally equal citizens before the law" (Knight, "Racism," p. 73). In fact, most Mexicans were mestizos of mixed ancestry, but the labels "white" and "Indian" were loosely and subjectively applied and based mainly on non-biological characteristics like language, social class, culture, and economic status. Those considered "white"—a race associated historically and economically with ownership, wealth, and power—maintained the real privileges. In the socio-symbolic order of the early twentieth century, "white" Mexicans still enjoyed a preferred status.

In *Pedro Páramo,* for example, Pedro Páramo's lawyer explains how he deals with the village women who have borne Miguel Páramo's children: he simply explains that they "ought to be glad [their babies will] have light skin" (*Pedro Páramo,* p. 103). In order to understand the significance of this statement, it is necessary to know that the whiteness of Páramo's offspring may have indeed carried with it some form of privilege, symbolic if not always concretely socioeconomic. The illegitimate children are considered lucky by the lawyer precisely because they descend from a rich, powerful hacendado.

Sources and literary context. *Pedro Páramo* stands out in literary history not only because of its themes—it has been described as an offshoot of the "novels of the Revolution"—but also because of its radical departure from traditional narrative form and style. *Pedro Páramo* relies not on one narrator's unified and chronological account of events, but, rather, on a series of narrative voices—both first-person and third-person—told in discontinuous fragments of time. The novel is furthermore based upon a series of stories threaded together by Juan Preciado's guides, who in many ways function as oral storytellers.

The reader is transported in time by these various storytellers as they chat with Juan Preciado before and after his death. However, *Pedro Páramo* does not present time as a straightforward totality, but relies rather on the scattered memories and recollections of the individual storytellers. Reality itself is fragmented and ambiguous, and boundaries between it and the imagination fade so that there is no clear contrast between life and death, or between the physical and spiritual worlds.

These apparent contradictions, which contribute to the original and fantastic flare of *Pedro Páramo,* are based on Mexican mythological traditions rooted in pre-Columbian as well as Catholic beliefs. Juan Rulfo's literary vision incorporates Aztec mythology and popular culture, both of which hold that death is merely the continuation of life, and therefore not final.

Some of the events depicted in *Pedro Páramo* are loosely based on historical events and characters in Juan Rulfo's life. The Cristero rebellion, for example, had a direct impact on the life of Juan Rulfo and made a significant mark on his childhood. In fact, some have said that Rulfo was first exposed to literature when a Catholic priest was forced to hide Church books in Rulfo's childhood home. Also, the name Media Luna, given to Pedro Páramo's hacienda, is taken from a real-life hacienda, as are the names of Damiana Cisneros, whom Juan knew as child, and of the village Sayula, which is the city where Rulfo's birth is registered. Perhaps coincidentally, an actual community named Comala exists near Colima; this community is not necessarily the setting of the novel.

MEXICO'S DAY OF THE DEAD

Mexicans traditionally spend the first day of November celebrating their dead relatives who, it is believed, return to their earthly homes at this time. This Day of the Dead is one of the most important celebrations of the Mexican year, especially in rural areas where months are spent in preparation for it. Though the occasion has a public aspect—shops fill with materials for the rituals, and skeleton figures decorate windows and the streets—it is essentially a private affair, celebrated in private by individual families who create huge altarpieces to honor their dead ancestors. Families set up cloth-covered tables framed by suspended arches decorated with green leaves, flowers, and fruits. On the tables are incense, more flowers, food, drink, pictures of religious figures, and, most prominently, photographs of deceased relatives. The deceased return to their homes on this day in order to enjoy the lavish feasts, or offerings, their living relatives have prepared for them. Often the tables will be covered with the dead relatives' favorite foods, as well as sugar figures, candied fruits, meats, and other delicacies. The conviction is that although the dead cannot eat the food, they are able to enjoy its essence before returning to the other world. The families consume the feast in a loud celebration. In this way communal ties are reaffirmed and relatives are kept alive in memory. According to popular lore if one fails to honor his or her dead relatives, the outcome might be sickness or death.

Many writers have discussed what they see as Mexico's special relationship to death, evidenced in large part by this annual celebration. Octavio Paz (see ***The Labyrinth of Solitude,*** also covered in *Latin American Literature and Its Times*), for instance, argues that death is not the same source of terror to modern Mexicans that it is to other cultures:

> To the inhabitant of New York, Paris, or London death is a word that is never uttered because it burns the lips. The Mexican, on the other hand, frequents it, mocks it, caresses it, sleeps with it, entertains it; it is one of his favourite playthings and his most enduring loves.
>
> (Paz in Carmichael and Sayer, p. 10)

Events in History at the Time the Novel Was Written

Mexico during the 1950s. When *Pedro Páramo* was first published in 1954, Mexico was enjoying a period of relative economic prosperity and growth. The Revolution had been abandoned, and the government had redefined itself in a move away from rural agrarianism and towards urbanization and industrial growth. The presidency of Miguel Alemán, who assumed office in 1946, was significant in this shift from agrarian land reform to urbanization. Alemán's administration funded urban development, industry, and tourism, and Mexico experienced an impressive industrial growth accompanied by an unprecedented rise in population, much of which was absorbed by the urban centers. Drawn by the promises of industry, rural Mexicans flocked to the cities by the hundreds of thousands in search of work during the 1950s, and many a rural village and hacienda was depopulated. In Rulfo's novel, however, only Pedro Páramo's revenge leads to the ruin and depopulation of Comala:

> Some say it was because he was tired, and others because he was disillusioned, but the one sure thing is that he sent everybody away. . . . After that the fields all went to ruin. . . . That was when people began to leave. The men went first, to look for other work.
>
> (*Pedro Páramo,* p. 78)

By 1960 Mexico had become a predominantly urban nation, with more than half of its population living in cities. Both the hacienda system and the rural cacique had declined. As the twentieth century progressed, political stabilization, federal controls, urbanization, and the decline of the hacienda system all contributed to the cacique's decline. Under the presidency of Aldolfo Ruiz Cortines, *caciquismo* took its last breaths. Ruiz Cortines "quieted them all, he attracted them all to him, he kept them calm, and he made them collaborators of the government" (Aguilar in Krauze, p. 613). Many critics suggest that *Pedro Páramo,* published during the administration of Ruiz Cortines, traces this decline of caciquismo in Mexico.

Reviews. Although *Pedro Páramo* was not well received initially by some critics because of its unusual narrative structure, reviewers eventually recognized the novel as a masterpiece. By 1967 *Pedro Páramo* had received almost universal acclaim. Critics emphasized its originality, describing the novel as a refreshing work that breaks away from the traditional novels of the Mexican Revolution (novels that typically feature realistic character types in straightforward chronological time). Above all, *Pedro Páramo* won acclaim for its poetic language and revolutionary technique, and is now widely recognized as a major influence on subsequent Latin American literature.

More than one U.S. critic compared Juan Rulfo to William Faulkner, mainly because of the "magically realistic" tendencies of *Pedro Páramo.* Other critics, including Carlos Fuentes (see ***The Death of Artemio Cruz,*** also covered in *Latin American Literature and Its Times*), discussed *Pedro Páramo*'s links with Greek mythology. Still others praised the novel as social commentary, noting how it traces the decline of Mexican caciquismo, comments on the failures of the Revolution, and illustrates the significance of death in Mexican society. "A book as truly original as this one is," acknowledged one reviewer "is perhaps bound to make special demands on the reader . . . [and] it rewards those demands. . . . It exerts, throughout, a powerful fascination; its episodes are vivid and haunting; its style is a triumph" (Wickenden in Davison, p. 1160).

—Olivia Treviño

BRACEROS

During World War II Mexico collaborated with U.S. President Franklin D. Roosevelt in allowing Mexican *braceros* —temporary manual laborers—to work in the agricultural region of the southwestern United States. When the work force in the United States was depleted because of the draft, Mexicans stepped in to harvest the crops. They were recruited by U.S. labor agents, who looked to Mexico for the thousands of workers needed by U.S. farmers. Begun in 1942 and formally sanctioned by legislation in 1951, the bracero program drew an average 350,000 workers from Mexico to the United States before its end in 1964, despite an interval (1954-58) in which several million U.S. residents of Mexican descent were deported. The resulting ghost towns, explains the author, helped spark the idea for *Pedro Páramo*:

> The town where I discovered solitude, because everyone goes away as braceros, is called Tuxcacuesco, but it might be Tuxcacuesco and it could be another one. . . . I hit on a realism that doesn't exist, on people who never existed.
>
> (Rulfo in Benítez, pp. 13-18)

For More Information

Bethell, Leslie, ed. *Latin America: Economy and Society, 1870-1930.* New York: Cambridge University Press, 1989.

Benítez, Fernando. "Interview with Juan Rulfo." In *Inframundo: The Mexico of Juan Rulfo.* Mexico: Ediciones del Norte, 1983.

Carmichael, Elizabeth, and Chloë Sayer. *The Skeleton at the Feast: The Day of the Dead in Mexico.* Austin: University of Texas Press, 1991.

Chevalier, François. "The Roots of Caudillismo." In *Caudillos: Dictators in Spanish America.* Ed. Hugh M. Hamill. Norman, Oklahoma: University of Oklahoma Press, 1992.

Davison, Dorothy P., ed. *The Book Review Digest, 1960.* New York: H. W. Wilson, 1961.

Knight, Alan. "Racism, Revolution, and Indigenismo: Mexico, 1910-1940." In *The Idea of Race in Latin America, 1870-1940.* Ed. Richard Graham. Austin: University of Texas Press, 1990.

——. "Popular Culture and the Revolutionary State in Mexico, 1910-1940." *Hispanic American Historical Review* 74, no. 3 (1994): 393-444.

Krauze, Enrique. *Mexico: Biography of Power.* New York: HarperCollins, 1997.

Meyer, Michael, and William Sherman. *The Course of Mexican History.* New York: Oxford University Press, 1991.

Rulfo, Juan. *Pedro Páramo.* New York: Grove Press, 1959.

Schwartz, Kessel. *A New History of Spanish American Fiction.* Vol. 2. Miami: University of Miami Press, 1971.

Rebellion in the Backlands

by
Euclides da Cunha

> **THE LITERARY WORK**
>
> A narrative that fuses elements of history, biography, fiction, travel literature, geography, and anthropology; set in northeastern Brazil from 1893 to 1897; published in Portuguese (as *Os Sertões*) in 1902, in English in 1944.
>
> **SYNOPSIS**
>
> After years of wandering the backlands of Brazil, the mystic pilgrim Conselheiro founds the town of Canudos. Perceiving Conselheiro's theocracy as a threat to the Republic of Brazil, the federal government sends four expeditions against it, the last of which massacres its population and razes the town.

Euclides da Cunha was born in 1866 in the Brazilian state of Rio de Janeiro. Having lost his mother when he was three, he was raised by relatives and in boarding schools. He completed high school at the Colégio Aquino in Rio de Janeiro and entered the Polytechnic School and later the Military School, where he was trained as a military engineer. From 1893 on da Cunha was engaged in building trenches, sanitary works, bridges, and barracks. In fact, he wrote *Rebellion in the Backlands* while directing work on a bridge in the state of São Paulo. Simultaneously, he worked as a reporter, which led to his visiting the Canudos front in this capacity. The success of *Os Sertões* in 1902 caused da Cunha's election to the Brazilian Academy of Letters, and he followed it with other publications on regions of Brazil and on Latin American questions. As a result of a domestic triangle, da Cunha was shot and killed by another army officer in 1909.

Events in History at the Time of the Narrative

The siege of Canudos. By the time Euclides da Cunha reached the front lines in mid-September 1897, government troops had encircled Canudos, a remote town in the interior of Bahia, Brazil, cutting off supply lines and the escape routes of its defenders, followers of the mystic Antônio Macíel (called *Conselheiro,* the Counselor). The rebels of Canudos were called *jagunços* after an old term for the hired gunmen who constituted the private armies of ranchers. The jagunços, in turn, had nicknames for their enemy, the government soldiers: weakness of the government; Republicans; Masons; Protestants; and Dogs, little dogs working for the big Dog; the Beast 666; or the Antichrist, which had come to destroy their New Jerusalem.

Every so often the enemy captured a jagunço. After interrogation, which inevitably invoked the answer *não sei* (I don't know), the prisoners were asked to shout *Viva a República* (Long live the Republic). They responded with *Viva o Bom Jesus!* (Long live the Good Jesus), then were given the "red necktie." That is, they were decapitated by having a scythe-like knife drawn rapidly across their throats.

The jagunços had previously repelled three government-sponsored military expeditions.

Attacking a town like Canudos was difficult for a conventional army. First of all, it lay in a remote, desert-like area of the interior of the state of Bahia, called the *sertão.* Water and provisions were at a premium, and none of the four expeditions made adequate logistical plans. As a result, Canudos is one of the rare instances in which those inside a besieged town were better supplied than the besiegers. Once they arrived at the front, the army faced all the classical difficulties inherent in fighting a guerrilla force. The jagunços fortified and dug trenches within their mud huts, which meant that every one of the 2,000 or more houses in Canudos was a site of potential ambush.

SOME KEY EVENTS RECOUNTED IN *REBELLION IN THE BACKLANDS*

1893: Town of Canudos is founded by religious leader Antônio Conselheiro and his followers.

1895: Two Capuchin friars urge people to leave Canudos and return to orthodox Catholicism; the friars' mission fails.

1896 (October): Officials of the city of Juazeiro send an urgent telegram to the Bahian capital, asking for protection against an expected invasion from Canudos.

1896 (November): The first expedition (116 soldiers) sent by the governor to defend Juazeiro is defeated at Uauá.

1897 (January): The second expedition (550 soldiers) sent to pacify Canudos must retreat because of lack of provisions and ammunition, as well as fierce resistance from the town's defenders.

1897 (March): The third expedition (1,200 soldiers), led by Moreira César, becomes the first to actually attack Canudos. Moreira César and the second-in-command are both killed, and the expedition is routed. Canudos is the subject of intense national concern.

1897 (June): The fourth expedition (4,283 soldiers), under Arthur Oscar, begins the siege of Canudos.

1897 (September): Euclides da Cunha stays a little over two weeks in Canudos as a newspaper reporter. Antônio Conselheiro, the leader of Canudos, dies.

1897 (October 5): The last defenders of Canudos are killed; the town is demolished; Conselheiro's body is exhumed and his head sent to Salvador.

By the time da Cunha arrived in September 1897, the conflict between the Brazilian government and the millenarian religious movement in the northeastern backlands had passed its climax. Federal troops had been besieging the backland community for almost 90 days when the defenders lost their leader, Antônio Conselheiro, to dysentery on September 22. Canudos was run as a religious dictatorship, and the loss of its spiritual leader was a crushing blow. Shortly afterwards, a contingent of Canudos's minor leaders fled the town, giving up on the cause of constructing a just society free from the interference of powerful elites. Nonetheless, a formidable fighting force remained, popularizing a saying that allegedly began with their new military commander, Marciano de Sergipe: "If our Counselor has died, then I want to die too." Some days later, on October 1, a large group of prisoners, mostly women, old men, and children, surrendered to the federal troops. Basing his description on others' accounts, da Cunha gives the impression that he witnessed the horrific spectacle of haggard, wounded women and children limping into camp in the first voluntary surrender:

> Our men viewed them with a mournful eye. They were at once surprised and deeply moved. In the course of this fleeting armistice the settlement *in extremis* was here confronting them with a legion of disarmed, crippled and mutilated, famished beings in an assault that was harder to withstand than any they had known in the trenches under enemy fire. It was painful for them to admit that all these weak and helpless ones—so many of them!—should have come out of those huts which had been bombarded for three whole months. As they contemplated those swarthy faces, those filthy and emaciated bodies whose gashes, wounds, and scars were not concealed by the tattered garments they wore—as they viewed all this, the longed-for victory suddenly lost its appeal, became repugnant to them.
>
> (da Cunha, *Rebellion in the Backlands,* p. 471)

Da Cunha had been sent to Canudos by a newspaper, the *Estado de São Paulo.* Compared to other reporters, such as Manoel Benício, who stayed for most of the campaign from June to October, da Cunha hardly cut an imposing figure there. He spent much of his time behind the lines dining with the commander of the expedition, Arthur Oscar, and rarely visited the front. His dispatches to the newspaper were sporadic. Due to ill health, he left Canudos no later than October 1, and did not witness the fall of the town four days later. If the *Estado* had invested travel expenses in hopes of obtaining a "scoop" in the Canudos affair, it must have been disappointed with the meager results. Five years later, however, da Cunha wrote *Os Sertões,* which for decades would remain the final word on what happened at Canudos, and which would transform the incident into a premier example of millenarianism.

On October 5 the last defenders of Canudos were eliminated. The army gathered in front of the town's "new church," a fortress-like building with crude Gothic towers, which had been constructed by the followers of the Conselheiro and leveled by army cannonballs. Immediately opposite it was the site of the old church. Miraculously, a large cross in front of this church had not been hit and is still preserved today in a small chapel. A band played Brazil's national anthem, after which the army applied kerosene everywhere, to corpses and houses, and burned the town of Canudos to the ground. The army was fulfilling a directive: stone should not remain on stone. Obediently it reduced the town, estimated by some to be the second-largest in the state of Bahia, into wasteland.

"The Counselor." Antônio Vicente Mendes Maciel (or Marciel), "the Counselor," was born in the state of Ceará in 1830. After failing at a number of endeavors, including schoolteaching and marriage, he disappeared from public view for three years, from 1871 to 1874. This disappearance took the form of a hermitage, a solitude in the desert like Christ's or St. Anthony's. By 1874 Maciel had remade himself into a *peregrino,* or religious pilgrim, discarding normal clothing for a simple blue tunic, letting his hair grow, and adopting the nomadic existence of a mendicant or beggar. The English word *pilgrim* and its Portuguese cognate both derive from the Latin *peragro,* which means "to wander." And indeed, Maciel's only job now was to cross and recross the sertão of Bahia and nearby Sergipe, finding water and food in the roots of the *umbuzeiro* tree, taking his rest in the shade of the *juazeiro* tree, stopping at the towns of the region to preach, to act as godfather for infants and marriages, and to encourage the inhabitants to practice personal, Catholic decency and to build churches or little chapels of the *via sacra* ("sacred path," alluding to the route taken by Jesus from Jerusalem to Golgotha, where he was crucified).

Maciel was known by several nicknames and titles, among them *conselheiro,* or counselor. This title meant that Maciel was the lay equivalent of a *padre,* or priest, performing all of the priest's functions except for the ministration of the sacraments. With the usual Brazilian preference for nicknames over given names, Maciel has entered the annals of history under the alias "Antônio Conselheiro."

Such counselors were not unusual in the Brazilian sertão. They fulfilled an important function in a region where only one in three dioceses enjoyed the direction of a parish priest. Given the absence of a well-defined Church infrastructure, the Catholicism of the backlander was mediated not through a priest, but through sacred images and actions—such as fasting, pilgrimage, flagellation, and reciting prayers to achieve spe-

MILLENARIAN MOVEMENTS IN THE AMERICAS

Millenarian movements are based on the Christian belief that Jesus Christ will return to earth and reign for 1,000 years. Broadly, they concern themselves with a vision of the near future and are associated with expectations of apocalyptic destruction and utopian renewal. Because they envision a utopian society, such movements tend to draw a hostile reaction from governments. Brazil has hosted several millenarian movements over time. Even as events were unfolding at Canudos, another religious movement was gathering strength in the nearby state of Ceará (birthplace of the Conselheiro himself). Cicero Romão Batista, a Catholic priest who allegedly performed miracles, drew a large number of backlands peasants to himself in a hamlet called Joaseiro. His following grew in the 1890s, as did Joaseiro, which people believed to be the holy location chosen for the second coming of Jesus Christ. On a pretext of rooting out bandits, government forces attacked Joaseiro in 1913, whereupon its defenders retaliated and brought down the state government at the capital, Fortaleza. The United States had a similar movement around the time of the Canudos rebellion—the Ghost Dance religion of the American Indian tribes. Inspired by the prophet Wovoka in Nevada, the religious movement involved a dance and divine songs that would allegedly lead to the disappearance of the white man, the restoration of Indian hunting grounds and a reunion with the dead. The religion spread from one tribe to the next. At Pine Ridge Reservation in South Dakota, white troops, perceiving the movement as a threat, confronted some Ghost Dance followers. The result was the Wounded Knee massacre of 1890, which killed nearly 300 Indians, many of whom were women and children.

A statue of Conselheiro in Monte Santo, Brazil.

cific results. Holy texts in the sertão derived primarily from the *Missão Abreviada* (Abbreviated Missal)—a compilation of digests of the four gospels, lives of the saints, prayers, meditations, and instructions. Conselheiro, who was himself a kind of wandering image for the people of the interior to invoke and adore, preferred a particular missal, authored by José Gonçalves Couto, a missionary to the Portuguese areas of India, in 1873. The missal, which the Counselor chose above milder versions, such as the "Hours of Mary," emphasizes the apocalyptic elements of Christianity and portrays Christ's agony and death as in keeping with divine retribution for human depravity.

In retrospect, it is easy to trace the growing conflict between Conselheiro and the authorities that would lead both to the founding of Canudos and to its destruction. Conselheiro's following grew quite large, and began to be perceived as a threat. Its initial mobility and lack of fixed abode disturbed the authorities. Also, the retinue was racially heterogeneous. The Conselheiro himself was opposed to slavery, and freedmen flocked to him after abolition in 1888. Lacking faith in the labor potential of their own local population, landowners had joined with government leaders to promote immigration from Europe and shut the freedmen out of the labor market. These freedmen formed only one part of a huge underclass with no land and little or no employment. The economy of the Brazilian northeast, including the sertão, was latifundarian, which means that a few individuals from the higher social echelons owned and controlled everything, and a combination of free artisans, peasants, and slaves or former slaves worked for them. An independent, landed peasantry did not exist in the backlands; instead, huge cattle ranches with absentee landlords were the rule. Individuals who wished to improve their way of life were forced either to become bandits, or to migrate to the coffee industry of São Paulo and other southern states. In a society in which less than 5 percent of the population owned the land on which they lived, Antônio Conselheiro represented a kind of freedom from economic constraints.

Conselheiro's group also disturbed the authorities because it defied basic structures of sertão life: the economy, by which hired laborers toiled for absentee landowners; the clan or extended family, which required loyalty and obedience; and the Catholic Church, whose leaders asked increasingly for members to practice religious orthodoxy and submit all questions about the faith to the nearest priest—however distant he might be from his flock. Recognizing the threat, a group of landowners and churchmen concentrated, from the outset, on squashing the Counselor's campaign.

In June 1876 the Counselor was arrested on the charge that he had murdered his mother and his ex-wife. The authorities had him taken to Salvador, where he was beaten, shorn of his long hair, led through the jeering crowds, and put on a boat for Ceará. In his hometown no one spoke against him, and it became public knowledge that his mother had died when he was three and that his wife was living as a prostitute. The Conselheiro was freed, and he returned to his followers.

Antônio Conselheiro continued his nomadic existence for another 17 years, during which Brazil became (in 1889) a republic ruled by a military dictatorship instead of an empire ruled by a monarch. Conselheiro, like many citizens of Brazil at the time, preferred the monarchy to the Republic, which he considered the more corrupt system of the two. The official shift gave the authorities new grounds for moving against the Counselor—now they could brand him as an enemy of the Republic. The truest element of this accusation was Conselheiro's opposition to civilian marriage, which was republican law. For him, as for most backlanders, marriage could only be a Church sacrament. The authorities also accused him of encouraging people not to pay taxes to the Republic; this, in all probability, was a distortion of his real stance, that taxes of any kind were a way of robbing the poor to pay the rich. In da Cunha's work Conselheiro is characterized as "combative" in relationship to the Republic:

> [H]e looked upon the Republic with an evil eye and consistently preached rebellion against the new laws. . . . [T]he chambers of the various localities in the interior of Baía had posted up on the traditional bulletin boards . . . the regulations governing the collection of taxes and the like. [Conselheiro] did not like the new taxes and planned an immediate retaliation. . . . He gathered the people and . . . had them make a bonfire of the bulletin boards in the public square. . . . [H]e began openly preaching insurrection against the laws of the country.
>
> (*Rebellion,* p. 141)

The founding of Canudos. The police clashed with the *Conselheiristas* on several occasions, the last time in 1893 in Masseté, where deaths occurred. Conselheiro and his followers realized that they would have greater security from government harrassment if they could found a permanent community in a defensible position. Some assert that the idea of founding the town of Canudos occurred much earlier than 1893. In the first work of fiction about the Conselheirista movement, *Os jagunços,* novelist Afonso Arinos portrayed the decision as messianic; years before founding Canudos, the Counselor has a vision:

> That piece of land was nothing if not the New Canaan. That people had been called upon to

> realize God's work. And he would call them together, would reveal to them the high destiny which God had in store for them. He would take them to the construction of the holy city. The missionary's face was transfigured. Grandiose and sublime ideas bubbled in the brain illuminated by the divine ray. The vision of future days passed in front of his fiery eyes.
> (Arinos, p. 50; trans. T. Beebee)

Da Cunha accepted Arinos's interpretation, and, with the help of contemporary psychological theories on the delusion of crowds, depicted the Counselor and his followers as religious fanatics suffering from collective psychosis. Others, however, have argued that the decision to found Canudos was more pragmatic, due to the Counselor's advancing age—in 1893 he was 63—and the need for a permanent defensive position against attack.

MEDIEVAL STANDARDS

Was the Counselor insane? He was portrayed as such at the time of the conflict, and in almost all the literature on Canudos for decades after the war. Da Cunha accepts these judgments without question, adopting their vocabulary of "madman" and "fanatic." Nevertheless, unlike lesser authors on the conflict he is aware of the need to explain the fact that thousands of followers did not consider their leader insane and shared his goals and ideals. How would he account for this? Da Cunha goes beyond the facile, ill-defined, and unsatisfying notion of "collective insanity" to the thesis that Antônio Conselheiro was a product of his social environment, and that he stood out against that backdrop only in the vehemence of his vision. The sertão, da Cunha argues, was a society that was still living by the medieval standards according to which it was founded. Behavior that had seemed normal in the middle ages looked like insanity in the nineteenth century.

In any case, Canudos grew quickly, not only because of the Counselor's fame and the attractive (to his followers) prospect of building a mud-hut Jerusalem, but also because of the town's favorable location near a relatively constant source of water (the river Vasa-Barris), the relative ease with which the jagunços could construct their simple houses from the vegetation of the region, and, above all, the availability of free land and freedom from elite authority. According to official army records, when Canudos was destroyed, it consisted of 5,200 huts, which would make it the second-largest city in Bahia. Eyewitnesses, however, reported 2,000 huts, for a total population of around 10,000. Indians who had lost their traditional homelands as well as ex-slaves and former bandits joined the population at Canudos, refuge of the dispossessed and poorest of the poor. Interestingly, the accounts of Canudos are full of names of ex-bandits of the region, men with fearsome reputations who apparently were willing to "go straight" under the leadership of the Counselor. Canudos acquired its own police force or civic guard, paid no taxes, and, of course, conducted no civil marriages. Prostitution and alcohol, both endemic to the ordinary life of the backlander, were forbidden there. The town was free of the colonels, large landowners who, directly or indirectly, ruled every other town in the region. But in the end, the erection of Canudos would intensify rather than diminish conflict with the authorities. A pocket of freedom in a freedomless desert, the town had to be annihilated at all costs.

Canudos and the Republic. Abolition in 1888 marked the end of the northeastern sugar oligarchies, the economic backbone of Brazil's monarchy. The Brazilian army, meanwhile, which traditionally played no role in politics, had gained prestige and influence in a protracted war fought against Paraguay (1865-69). During this war members of the middle and lower classes who composed the army ranks came into contact with republics such as Argentina, and subsequently had less sympathy for the old Empire than did other segments of the population. Even though it lacked popular civilian support, the armed forces fomented a coup on September 7, 1889, which sent the Emperor Dom Pedro II into exile and created the Republic of Brazil.

The most contested issue in the new Republic was local versus centralized government. Strong local political bosses in various regions of Brazil demanded a weak federal government, and went into revolt at various times to defend their interests. The longest and bloodiest of these conflicts was the so-called "Federalist Revolt," in which the three southernmost states, Paraná, Santa Catarina, and Rio Grande do Sul, were forcibly repatriated by federal troops (1893-95). Colonel Moreira César, who would lead the ill-fated third expedition against Canudos, gained fame through his ruthless repression of the rebels in this war. His attitude towards Canudos seemed to be the same as that towards the southern rebels, even though the two situations were completely different, since Canudos never claimed independence nor formulated its own constitution.

The fragility of the new government led to a climate of suspicion, fear, and repression that made Canudos, a relatively insignificant town in the wasteland of a long-ignored region, appear to threaten the stability of the whole Republic. Wild rumors circulated to explain the defeats of the military expeditions sent to subdue the town. According to one of these rumors, Canudos was receiving financial aid and arms from European monarchies in order to overthrow the Republic and restore the Emperor in Brazil. Whatever their personal convictions, politicians were forced to support the campaign against Canudos at the risk of being labeled crypto-monarchists.

Canudos housed a remarkable cross-section of the common people of rural Brazil—peasants, petty merchants, and religious fanatics, as well as ex-bandits, freedmen, and at least one Indian tribe. Opposing this cross-section was an alliance of Brazilian elites: the Catholic Church, which wanted to see the heretical views of the Counselor stamped out; the local landowners, who felt their monopoly on land and labor being threatened by Canudos; the army, which saw itself as the defender of the Republic wherever challenged; and the politicians, who drew support from the first three groups and had nothing to gain from taking sides with a peasant rebellion.

The conflict erupts. The only attempt at negotiating peace with Canudos came in the form of a mission of two priests, who arrived in May 1895 to preach to its people. The townspeople, the priests said, must leave Canudos; they must abandon their adoration of the Counselor as a miracle-worker and an incarnation of Jesus; and they must renounce the medieval customs they had adopted—prolonged fasting, flagellation, and other extreme forms of penance—along with the idolatry, fetishism, and other practices absorbed from indigenous and African religions. The mission failed, and the priests' published report, ghost-written by another priest who had not been with them, took on an aggressive tone, fanning the flames of hatred against Canudos. The report described a "deplorable situation of fanaticism and anarchy [that] must cease for the honor of the Brazilian people" (Marciano, p. 19; trans. T. Beebee). Perhaps this explains why in October 1897 not a single protest emerged from the Catholic Church against the decapitations, rapes, and kidnappings that were perpetrated on the population of Canudos.

In 1896 the Conselheiristas bought wood in the city of Juazeiro. A local deputy there, an old enemy of the Conselheiro, pressured the seller not to deliver the product. The deputy then sent telegrams to the governor of Bahia predicting that Juazeiro would soon be invaded by the angry Conselheiristas. In order to avoid the reputation of being a crypto-monarchist, the governor acceded to the demand for support, and in November 1896 sent 116 men to protect Juazeiro. When the attack did not materialize, the company proceeded to the town of Uauá, where they met a force of Conselheiristas. A battle ensued, in which eight soldiers died, as did 150 jagunços, who fought with scythes, clubs, and blunderbusses. Despite their superior re-

ORTHODOX VS. "FOLK" CATHOLICISM IN BRAZIL

In the late nineteenth century there was an "orthodox," Rome-based Brazilian Catholic practice, administered by priests for the minority living on the coast, and there was another, syncretic "folk" Catholicism practiced by the majority in the interior and administered mostly by men like the Counselor. Three reasons contributed to this: Rome, the source of official Catholic doctrine, was very far away; there were insufficient priests for the population (the ratio was estimated at one priest for every 20,000 people); and the racial mixing of the population brought indigenous and African practices and beliefs into contact with those derived from Europe. The isolation of the sertão also allowed the survival of medieval religious practices and beliefs, such as flagellation and Sebastianism (the belief that the Portuguese emperor Dom Sebastião, missing and presumably killed in action against the Moors in the fifteenth century, would return as the messiah of his people). Folk Catholicism in the sertão was characterized by penitence, self-castigation, the presence of the unquiet souls of the dead, fear of hell and damnation, and an emphasis on ritual, image, fetish, and prayers for the achievement of specific effects. Nothing is more expressive of the differences between the practices of the official Church and that of the backlanders than the failed mission of two Church emissaries to Canudos. When one of them told the residents of Canudos that it was Church doctrine that they should not take their fasting to the point of physical pain, and that the drinking of coffee was allowed during a fast, he was greeted with the derisive comment: "That is not fasting; that is feasting" (Marciano, trans. T. Beebee, p. 15).

sults, the soldiers retreated to Juazeiro. The battle hardened positions on both sides. The soldiers' retreat meant that the backlanders had won their first real victory. New inhabitants streamed into Canudos.

A second expedition of 550 soldiers, and a third of 1,200 were defeated in January and March of 1897, respectively. The death of the commander and vice-commander of the third expedition made Canudos a national concern, a threat to the fledgling Republic. The town was rumored to have extraordinary armaments, the only explanation for its amazing resistance in the minds of those unfamiliar with the local conditions; the arms, they said, were supplied by foreign powers interested in restoring the monarchy. Monarchist newspapers were destroyed, and monarchist sympathizers were lynched by angry mobs as far away as Rio de Janeiro and São Paulo.

DA CUNHA'S PERSPECTIVE

An eyewitness to part of the fourth expedition, Euclides da Cunha had conceived a profound respect for the people of the backlands, and also wished to counter the simplistic ideas of the war that the public had been fed. He furthermore viewed Canudos on a grander scale than had any previous author. Canudos was, for him, symptomatic of the problems of Brazil and of Latin America in general: the imposition of European models and ideas on an American reality that failed to fit those models. Da Cunha's text thus enlarges Canudos to the scale of apocalypse. Canudos was, argues *Rebellion in the Backlands,* a war between two stages of civilization for which no one could be blamed, but in which the Republic betrayed its own ideals in destroying genuine Brazilian culture that had developed from the land and had not been imported from Europe. To place the Canudos conflict within this framework meant drawing a mental map of Brazil, on the grandest of scales. Such a map would correlate the physical placement and movement of people with their cultural and social development. It would, according to da Cunha, associate coastal Brazil, which in the late nineteenth century contained all of the country's major population centers, with a Europeanizing influence, and concomitantly with an inauthentic or incomplete Brazilianness. The vast, nearly empty backlands, on the other hand, were the scene of a mixing of the races that produced a truly unique Brazilian culture.

The fourth expedition, which eventually involved half of the Brazilian army, could and would not fail. Having learned from the rout of the third expedition the foolhardiness of a direct assault on Canudos, the fourth expedition carefully established its preliminary siege line on June 27, but succeeded in totally encircling the town only on September 23. Repeated assaults by government forces, combined with bombardment, gradually drew the net tighter, until Canudos fell to the government forces on October 5, 1897.

The Narrative in Focus

Contents summary. *Rebellion in the Backlands* is divided into three parts: "The Land" (ca. 50 pp.); "Man" (ca. 120 pp.); and "The Conflict" (ca. 300 pp.). In the narrative da Cunha follows a line of Darwinist reasoning that the Canudos war was a case in which advanced forces of civilization inevitably crushed a retrograde form of life. This reasoning is in keeping with the notions of scientist Charles Darwin about the survival of the fittest. The three divisions of the narrative may reflect the author's Darwinist philosophy: first, geography and climate influence the mode of life of the backlands inhabitants; second, that way of life gives rise to the forms of social organization and religious messianism characteristic of Canudos; third, both the land and the people who live there determine the conditions of the conflict described in the balance of the book's pages.

Da Cunha's text delays its narration of the war in order to show that the residents of Canudos were the people of the earth, thus allowing the space of Brazil to generate the tragic narrative. In "The Land," the text gives an extensive description of the geology, climatology, flora, and fauna of the sertão. The first sentence of *Rebellion in the Backlands* constructs topographically the continuity and completeness that da Cunha and his fellow Republicans so ardently sought in Brazil's political life:

> The central plateau of Brazil descends, along the southern coast, in unbroken slopes, high and steep, overlooking the sea; it takes the form of hilly uplands level with the peaks of the coastal mountain ranges that extend from the Rio Grande to Minas. To the north, however, it gradually diminishes in altitude, dropping eastward to the shore in a series of natural terraces which deprive it of its primitive magnitude, throwing it back for a considerable distance in the direction of the interior.
>
> (*Rebellion,* p. 3)

The former site of Canudos, now submerged.

"Completeness" is demonstrated by the physical integrity shown in this sweeping, bird's-eye description of the national territory. Everything is accounted for in this largest of overviews: starting with the whole of the coast, then traveling from south to north, Rio Grande to Minas Gerais. Once the physical description moves to the sertão, or backlands, it begins to fail: "Our best maps, conveying but scant information, show here an expressive blank, a hiatus, labeled *Terra Ignota,* a mere scrawl indicating a problematic river or an idealized mountain range" (*Rebellion,* p. 9). The sertão, excluded from Brazilian cultural memory, nevertheless expresses itself in Brazilian life—the result is a tragedy that could have been avoided if Brazilians had paid attention to the needs of the backlanders. The subtext is that regional rebellions must be suppressed but also that all Brazilians must be identified with the nation—da Cunha repeats several times that the Republic had a duty to bombard the people of Canudos with education rather than cannonballs.

Later chapters return to the theme of landscape, and it plays an important role in the description of the struggle between backlanders and government forces: "The *caatingas* [scrub forests] are an incorruptible ally of the *sertanejo* [backwoodsman] in revolt, and they do in a certain way enter into the conflict. They arm themselves for the combat, take the offensive. For the invader they are an impenetrable wilderness; but they have numerous paths by which they are accessible to the backwoodsman, who was born and grew up there" (*Rebellion,* p. 191). The activity and aggression of the caatinga in this brief description typify the way da Cunha uses landscape in his text.

The economy, customs, and appearance of the sertanejo are the subject of the second part of the book, which treats the mixed racial origins and retrograde civilization of the people of the interior. In the wildness of the sertão Africans, Europeans, and Indians interbred without the inhibitions against racial mixing found in the more "civilized" areas of Brazil. The three best-known "types" to emerge from this miscegenation were the mulatto (white and black); the mestizo (white and Indian); and the *cafuso* (black and Indian), but these are only the simplest of the various racial mixtures to be found in the backlands.

In the late nineteenth century Darwinism had been pressed into the service of Eurocentrism in the view that the white races were more highly evolved than others. Da Cunha shared the abhorrence of miscegenation that this view supported—despite the fact that his personal background was not entirely European. He posits in *Rebellion in the Backlands* that the apparently indiscriminate racial mixing of the sertão has caused the region's backwardness. At the same time, he recognizes that miscegenation has produced the true Brazilian: "the bedrock of our race," as he calls the sertanejos (*Rebellion,* p. 464). Da Cunha's text suggests that he is torn between the racialist notions of European theorists, which associated miscegenation with inferiority, and his own admiration for the sertanejos, who are able to survive under the most adverse conditions in an inhospitable environment. Notable passages of this section describe the terrible effects of drought, and the sertanejo as a "Hercules-Quasimodo" (*Rebellion,* p. 89). Da Cunha's striking oxymoron points to the backlander as the union of opposites: the Greek hero Hercules, an image of strength, power, and masculine beauty, with the antihero of Victor Hugo's *The Hunchback of Notre Dame,* an image of deformity and weakness. Da Cunha characterizes Conselheiro as a product of his environment: "when all is said, [the Counselor] was doing no more than to condense the obscurantism of three separate races. And he grew in stature until he was projected into history" (*Rebellion,* p. 129). The Counselor and his followers are described in vivid terms that testify to equal measures of fascination and repugnance in the author.

TRAVESTIES AT CANUDOS

The final image in *Rebellion in the Backlands,* of the so-called civilized victors in joyous frenzy over the sight of the Counselor's head, probably says more about the dialectic of barbarism and civilization than would a hundred other details that could be drawn from history. In real life, after the fall of Canudos, a host of travesties were visited upon the defeated: the burning of the corpses of jagunços with wood from the very homes they had defended; alleged rapes carried out on female prisoners; and perhaps most poignant of all, the separation of children from their surviving parents and their subsequent "donation" to soldiers, "good" families of Salvador, and bordellos of the region. As in the narrative, the Counselor's head was severed from his exhumed body. Dr. Nina Rodriguez and other members of the Faculty of Medicine at the University of Bahia examined his brain for evidence of propensity to crime and madness, in keeping with the philosophy of physiological psychology at the time. They claimed to have found it.

The last section, "The Rebellion," tells the story of the armed conflict from the sending of troops to Juazeiro to the examination of the deceased Counselor's brain by the doctors of Salvador. In this section, fictionalized scenes from the lives of the Canudos residents give way to portrayals of the soldiers sent against them. The Counselor virtually disappears from the story in this last section; the text assumes the viewpoint of the federalists almost exclusively. Da Cunha narrates the wearisome march to Canudos and the retreat of the wounded from the battle site by following an imaginary band along the route. His account uses this typical band to convey the feelings and experiences of the government soldiers: "In these brief periods of repose, an obsessing idea would lay hold of them, shattering their peace of mind—supposing the jagunços should attack them! Here they were, helpless, impoverished, ragged, repulsive-looking . . . livid with hunger, being swept across the desert like so many useless dead weights" (*Rebellion,* p. 377). In contrast, the text tells in more neutral terms of the repeated assaults on Canudos and of the jagunços' counter-attacks. Readers are likelier to gain a lasting impression from the section's descriptions of the dead and wounded, of the soldiers' hunger and suffering, and of the treatment of prisoners, than from its descriptions of combat. Several times the text describes the corpses of fallen soldiers, speculating on exactly how they died without reconstructing the actual scene of combat. The section also includes descriptions of the third expedition's attack on Canudos, the guerrilla tactics of the jagunços, and the fearful losses of the fourth expedition shortly after arriving on Favela Hill, where the soldiers are in an exposed position. There are some vivid, agonizing passages describing the fate of the rebel prisoners: the "red necktie"—decapitation with a knife especially shaped to the purpose. In the book's concluding incident, the victors carried the Counselor's head to Salvador, "where it was greeted by delirious multitudes with carnival joy" (*Rebellion,* p. 476).

Sources and literary context. Da Cunha apparently used, but did not cite, several published accounts of the war at Canudos. Most of these, such as Dantas Barreto's *Last Expedition to Canudos* (1898), were written by soldiers and included eyewitness information. The first account to be published, that of Afonso Arinos, depended, in fact, on second-hand information. Afonso Arinos was an author with monarchist sentiments and a profound interest in the culture and geography of the sertão. His novel, *Os Jagunços* (1898), invents a fictitious jagunço, Luís Pachola, whom it follows through the course of the war. Arinos made the landscape responsible for the difficulties encountered by the army in fighting against the jagunços, and hinted that an ecological determinism shaped the society engaged in the conflict, which was the approach da Cunha took in *Rebellion in the Backlands*. However, Arinos's fiction does not agree with da Cunha's text on how absolute the destruction was. Arinos's character Pachola and a few others manage to escape through underground tunnels to the river. In contrast, da Cunha's version says that Canudos fought until the last male survivor: "Canudos did not surrender. The only case of its kind in history, it held out to the last man" (*Rebellion*, p. 475). Not only was Canudos not the only case of defenders holding out to the last man—the Roman siege of the Jews at Masada is but one example—but *Rebellion in the Backlands* also chooses not to mention that there was a large exodus from Canudos following the death of the Conselheiro on September 22, and not to relate the aftermath of the final clash. Real-life survivors suggest that this version of the tragedy is misleading.

Another important source for *Rebellion in the Backlands* was Manoel Benício's 1899 *O Rei dos Jagunços* (King of the Jagunços). Benício was not a monarchist but an army colonel who accompanied the fourth expedition as a journalist and was nearly executed for his severe criticisms of the army's actions. Rather than focus on the individual psychology of an idealized jagunço, Benício inserts the story of Canudos into the history of interpersonal relationships in the sertão. He begins with a detailed recounting of a family feud between the Araújos, a prominent family of the Ceará sertão, and the Maciels generations before the Counselor's birth. Da Cunha weaves many of these same details into the second section of *Rebellion in the Backlands*.

Benício's book portrays the end of Canudos as the surrender of Beatinho (the religious leader who succeeded the Counselor upon his death) and the immediate decapitation of the prisoners. It takes every opportunity to counter the official view of Canudos as a redoubt of banditry and mysticism. The book concludes that if the Counselor was a bad Catholic, he was also a true martyr who died, like Jesus, for his faith. Thus, while da Cunha presented his text as a "book of revenge" for the atrocities committed by the military at Canudos, his critical attitude was preceded by that of Benício. Arinos, Benício, and da Cunha all intended their texts to have a particular impact. Arinos's account attempted to create an emotional empathy with the jagunço; Benício's text blamed both sides for inflexibility and barbarism; and da Cunha's used the tragedy to promote Brazilian nationhood.

CANUDOS AND BRAZILIAN LITERATURE

Canudos has served as the source for more literary works than any other single incident of Brazilian history. These works embrace a variety of genres, from ballad to epic to novel. The embers of Canudos were still aglow after the town's destruction by government forces in 1897, when Brazilian authors began setting pen to paper in an effort to recount and explain the most significant millenarian event in Brazil, and possibly in the Americas. The significance of Canudos was in large part shaped by its reception and transformation in the Brazilian imagination. During the war itself, Canudos was interpreted—contradictorily—as a redoubt of religious fanatics and bandits, and as a counter-revolutionary state-within-a-state, financed by the substantial number of monarchists remaining in Brazil. Almost immediately after the war, a counter-memory of Canudos began to be constructed by such authors as Afonso Arinos, Manoel Benício, and Euclides da Cunha. The war of bullets has produced a war of words, in which basic concepts of Brazilianness, modernity, and social justice have been debated under the pretext of getting the Canudos story "right." Lori Madden expresses the trajectory of Canudos historiography when she writes that the conflict "has stimulated the imagination of diverse writers of alternative points of view since it affords evidence to be viewed as a political rebellion, a civil war, a problem of ethnicity, a messianic movement, a social movement, and other phenomena. It has become a mirror to the manipulations of its interpreters to such a degree that Canudos historiography, studied over time, tells a story of the evolution of ideas" (Madden, p. 6). Fiction, along with other genres, has played an important role in that evolution.

The preoccupation of *Rebellion in the Backlands* with the backlands of Brazil undoubtedly has something to do with the prevalence of that region in subsequent Brazilian literature, a prevalance which is disproportionate to the region's population or economic importance. Rachel

Quiroz's *O quinze* (1930), Graciliano Ramos's *Vidas secas* (1938; **Barren Lives** [also covered in *Latin American Literature and Its Times*]); and Bernardo Guimarães Rosa's *Grande sertão: veredas* (1956; ***The Devil to Pay in the Backlands***) are all Brazilian novels set in more or less the same region as *Rebellion in the Backlands,* and they deal with many of the same issues. The most obvious and famous reworking of *Rebellion in the Backlands,* however, is *La guerra del fin del mundo* (1981; *The War of the End of the World*) by the Peruvian novelist Mario Vargas Llosa (see ***The Storyteller***). This long fiction, which tells the Canudos story from a variety of points of view, quickly outsold *Rebellion in the Backlands,* and became the single most important medium by which people all over the world came in contact with the Canudos story. Vargas Llosa has paid a fitting tribute to Euclides da Cunha in this novel by making him into a major character—the nearsighted journalist—in this retelling.

The genres of *Rebellion in the Backlands.* From its first appearance, the generic status of *Rebellion in the Backlands* has been hotly disputed. An entire critical tradition, from José Veríssimo to Afrânio Coutinho, has defined it as a work of fiction, in categories varying from novel to tragedy to epic. For example, that all the feared *capangas* (gunslingers) of Canudos would have gathered for the Counselor's sermons, and simultaneously succumbed to religious ecstasy, as depicted in *Rebellion in the Backlands,* is highly unlikely. Certainly da Cunha himself never witnessed such an episode. He not only fictionalizes events, but also admits that he is doing so, and implies that the participants themselves fictionalized their own situation, as if they were actors in a tragic drama. At a crucial moment in the fighting, says the narrative,

> all the huts adjacent to the engineering commission constituted an enormous theater pit from which to view the drama that was taking place. Focusing their binoculars through all the crevices in the walls, the audience stamped, applauded, shouted bravos, and hissed. In their eyes the scene before them—real, concrete, inescapable—was a stupendous bit of fiction which was being acted out on that rude stage.
>
> (*Rebellion,* p. 432)

This element of the writing has been ascribed (by Luiz Costa Lima) to the incompatability between literary models such as tragedy, and da Cunha's belief in positivism. Positivism, the conviction that using the scientific method would create social progress, became a leading ideology in Brazilian universities and military academies such as the ones da Cunha attended in his formative years. This philosophy of science and progress might allow for realistic genres, such as the modern novel or "problem play," whose purpose was to critique social vices, but had little sympathy for forms like myth and tragedy, which presupposed a universe ruled by fate rather than by scientific principles. Da Cunha very carefully describes the landscape of the sertão so that it may carry the weight of explanation, meanwhile eliminating the notions of fate and destiny that are typical ingredients in tragic fiction.

Da Cunha seems to feel that history, as a genre, was reserved for the great events of Europe, and could not possibly be used to describe the slaughter of peasants in a remote part of Latin America. He even explains the morally repugnant behavior of the Federalists in executing their prisoners as a consequence of this absence of history. Did they not fear the judgment of posterity? No, responds da Cunha: "History would not go as far as that. Concerned with the fearful physiognomy of peoples amid the majestic ruins of vast cities, against the supremely imposing background of cyclopic coliseums, with the glorious butchery of classic battles and the epic savagery of great invasions, History would have no time for the crude slaughter pen" (*Rebellion,* p. 443). In other words, history takes as its objects grand battles affecting the course of civilizations. Its wars are fought in the classical mode, with two armies confronting each other in vast arrays that decide the fate of nations in a single day. Therefore, argues da Cunha, Canudos could not become the subject of history. Another genre, still unnamed, had to be found to narrate the Canudos story. The confused generic status of *Rebellion in the Backlands* brings to mind da Cunha's central thesis about the inability of Latin American reality to correspond to preconceived European models. In literature, as in other endeavors, new models would have to emerge from the reality of Latin America.

Reviews. The day after its publication in 1902, *Os Sertões* was reviewed by José Veríssimo, one of the most noted Brazilian critics of the period. Veríssimo seemed most impressed by the book's all-embracing, interdisciplinary nature. For Veríssimo *Os Sertões* was at once the work "of a man of science, a geographer, a geologist, an ethnographer; of a man of thought, a philosopher, a sociologist, a historian; and of a man of feeling, a poet, a novelist, an artist, who knows how to see and to describe, who thrills and feels just as much in the face of nature as he does from contact with people" (Veríssimo, p. 45). Veríssimo's opinion has been restated and confirmed by most of the Brazilian literati ever since. Enthusiastic praise for the book caused the original 1,000 copies to sell out quickly. On the basis of this one book alone, da Cunha was elected several years later to the prestigious Brazilian Academy of Letters. Sometime after the author's death in 1909 the work was canonized as "Brazil's greatest book," as Samuel Putnam called it in the preface to his 1944 English translation.

—Thomas O. Beebee

For More Information

Arinos, Afonso. *Os Jagunços.* 1898. 3rd ed. Rio de Janeiro: Philobiblion, 1985.

Beebee, Thomas O. "*Os Sertões* Illustrated." *TAXI* 4 (July 1997). Available <http://www2c.meshnet.or.jp/~taxi/07-97/sertao/sertoes1.html>.

Benício, Manoel. *O rei dos jagunços.* Rio de Janeiro: Jornal do Comércio, 1899.

Costa Lima, Luiz. *Control of the Imaginary.* Trans. Ronald W. Sousa. Minneapolis: University of Minnesota Press, 1988.

Cunha, Euclides da. *Rebellion in the Backlands.* Trans. Samuel Putnam. Chicago: University of Chicago Press, 1944.

Hilton, Ronald. "Positivism in Latin America." In *Dictionary of the History of Ideas.* Vol. 3. New York: Scribner's, 1973.

Levine, Robert M. *Vale of Tears: Revisiting the Canudos Massacre in Northeastern Brazil, 1893-1897.* Berkeley: University of California Press, 1992.

Madden, Lori. "The Canudos War in History." *Luso-Brazilian Review* 30, no. 2 (Winter 1993): 5-22.

Marciano, João Evangelista de Monte. *Relatório apresentado ao Arcebispado da Bahia sobre Antônio Conselherio no seu séquito no Arraial de Canudos.* 1895. Rpt. Salvador: Centro de Estudos Baianos da Universidade Federal da Bahia, 1987.

Torres, Victor F. *The Canudos War Collection.* Albuquerque: Latin American Institute of the University of New Mexico, 1990.

Vargas Llosa, Mario. *The War of the End of the World.* Trans. Helen R. Lane. New York: Farrar, Strauss & Giroux, 1984.

Veríssimo, José. "A Campanha de Canudos. Pelo Sr. Euclides da Cunha." In *Estudos de Literatura Brasilaeira.* 5a série. Belo Horizonte: Itataia, 1977.

Recollections of Things to Come

by
Elena Garro

Elena Garro (1920–98) was born in Puebla, Mexico, to a Mexican mother and a Spanish father, but she spent most of her childhood in the nearby southern state of Guerrero. As a young woman she worked briefly as a reporter and took on the cause of society's poor and marginalized. Garro showed particular concern for Mexico's Indian population and, for one notable story, even had herself incarcerated in a women's prison in order to expose the substandard living conditions endured by the inmates. In 1937 Garro married the Mexican writer and diplomat Octavio Paz, with whom she spent much of the 1940s and 1950s abroad, traveling through Europe and the United States. It was sometime around 1950, while weathering an illness in Switzerland, that Garro wrote *Recollections of Things to Come.* Set after the Mexican Revolution of the 1910s and during the *Cristero* rebellion, the novel draws on history as well as myth, distinguishing itself especially in its portrayal of women caught in the circumstances of the era.

THE LITERARY WORK

A novel set in Mexico in the 1920s; published in Spanish (as *Los recuerdos del porvenir*) in 1963, in English in 1969.

SYNOPSIS

A small town in southern Mexico is gradually decimated by the forces of revolution and rebellion.

Events in History at the Time the Novel Takes Place

The *Porfiriato*. In the first part of *Recollections of Things to Come,* the people of the southern Mexican town of Ixtepec debate and reconsider the long series of intrigues, assassinations, and betrayals that resulted from the 1910 overthrow of president Porfirio Díaz, an event that signaled the formal beginning of the Mexican Revolution. The predicaments of the townspeople (caught in the murderous grip of a northern general) and of the agrarian Indians (who are hanged regularly from the town's trees) stem from the complicated political struggle that had occupied Mexico for well over a decade by the time the novel begins. Díaz's regime, referred to as the *Porfiriato,* was essentially a dictatorship. He had been in office almost continuously since 1877, ignoring his own revolutionary call for "Valid Voting, No Reelection" by getting himself reelected seven times. He ruled over a period of vast industrialization and economic growth spurred on by foreign investment. Under Díaz 12,000 miles of railroad, built mostly with foreign money, crisscrossed the nation by 1900. He also encouraged the development of mineral resources (gold, silver, copper, and zinc) in Mexico, and opened the way for foreign investors to build factories there. Trade with other nations (especially the United States) increased exponentially.

These improvements, however, benefited only the very rich, leaving different factions of the nation's middle and upper classes at odds with one another. Mexico's resources, such as oil, sugar, and ore, were being exported by foreign investors, and as much as one-fifth of Mexico's land was sold to non-Mexicans. Ultimately the Porfiriato satisfied neither the wealthy nor the poor. According to one study, "average purchasing power in 1910 was only one-quarter the 1810 level; this figure is probably much too low, but nevertheless points to the enormity of the economic problems plaguing Mexico" (Skidmore and Smith, p. 233). Illiteracy and infant mortality were certainly very high, and peasants who lost their land to large commercial concerns or to railroad development were left with few resources for self-support. Other sorts of laborers (miners and railroad workers, for example) staged bitter strikes to protest their exploitative working conditions. The stage was set for a revolution in the 1910s. Garro's novel reflects on the revolution and traces the political and social ramifications of its aftermath in the 1920s.

The Revolution begins: Francisco Madero. Spiritualist, friend to the poor, tireless author of politico-historical books on Mexico's past—Francisco Madero was responsible for deposing Díaz. The son of a wealthy *hacienda* owner who had political ties to Díaz's government, Madero advocated a more equitable distribution of political power and publicly opposed the government's anti-democratic measures; in particular, he upheld the principle upon which Díaz had trampled: "Valid Voting, No Reelection." Madero had been educated abroad (in Paris, France, and at Berkeley, California) and had learned Christian philosophy, which inspired him to improve the lives of all Mexicans. Voicing revolutionary rhetoric from his San Antonio, Texas, headquarters, where he was living in exile after Díaz jailed him for a time, he instigated uprisings across the country and captured a major Mexican city (Ciudad Juárez). Díaz, at this point, recognized his imminent downfall, so he resigned in May 1911 and left the country. Francisco León de la Barra served briefly as interim president until Madero became president in November 1911, "through the freest election in Mexican history" (Krause, p. 263).

Although he started out as a hugely popular leader, Madero was soon much reviled in several quarters. Because of his agrarian reform platform, the nation's elite hated and feared him, and he soon alienated the poor as well. He made a fatal mistake at the very beginning of his term: out of respect for the Mexican Constitution, he left Díaz's "elected" officials in power. Although Madero instituted major changes in his brief presidency—he encouraged freedom of the press (in which, paradoxically, he was savaged), created new schools, built new highways, legalized labor unions, and instituted universal and direct voting throughout Mexico—he failed to attend fast enough to the issue of agrarian reform. Spurred on by a hostile press, strong opponents rose against him from the peasant class and accused him of ignoring their plight; how, they argued, could a wealthy and privileged man such as he understand or care about the predicament of the poor and exploited? That he had retained Díaz's old cronies pointed directly to his reluctance to help the masses, or to recognize their political will, they argued. Led by Emiliano Zapata, the rural protest escalated into its own revolution. However, this revolution would not for long be directed at Madero, who, with the help of U.S. Ambassador Lane Wilson, was overthrown, assassinated, and then replaced by General Adolfo de la Huerta in February 1913.

Agrarian reform: Emiliano Zapata. Emiliano Zapata hailed from a relatively privileged Mexican Indian background. Beginning with a small local revolution in the southern state of Morelos, in which he reclaimed ancestral land, Zapata devoted his life to pressing for the return of appropriated land to the Indians who had farmed and lived on it for generations. When the Revolution first began in earnest, he led his troops in support of Madero against Díaz. Eventually, though, he began to distrust Madero's commitment to agrarian reform and to the welfare of the Indians. When Madero finally reacted with hostility to the latest of Zapata's many demands for the return of land, Zapata drafted his *Plan de Ayala,* which was issued in December of 1911. The Plan called for the restoration of ancestral lands and denounced Madero as a traitor to the people of Mexico. When the *zapatistas* (as Zapata's followers were known) backed up their threats with violence all over the southern state of Morelos, Madero responded with force. Towns such as the one Garro describes in her novel were caught in the crossfire of the two warring factions. As the novel opens, old Dorotea recounts how her house was burned by the Zapatistas; despite this fact, however, she is loyal to their memory, especially because the alternative—the federal soldiers represented in the novel by Francisco Rosas and his men—have proven so much worse.

The zapatistas continued their resistance to the Mexican government during Huerta's regime and during the U.S.-supported rebellion that forced Huerta to resign on July 15, 1914, and then to disappear into exile. However, it was primarily Zapata's less idealistic northern counterpart, Pancho Villa, and future presidents Venustiano Carranza and Álvaro Obregón, none of whom Zapata fully trusted, who led the Mexican Revolution. Indeed, when Carranza took over the presidency later in 1914, he and Zapata found themselves immediately at odds to such an extent that Carranza set out to crush Zapata's agrarian movement. Even more disheartening for Zapata, though, was the internal dissent that threatened to destroy the zapatista movement from within. Now that they faced other revolutionaries rather than a dictator's troops in battle, Zapata's followers became less committed to and more discouraged by the fighting. By April 1919 much of the zapatistas' battling was internal, as key leaders of the movement assassinated each other. Zapata himself was assassinated in an ambush by Carranza's federal army. After his death, as shown in *Recollections of Things to Come,* his revolutionary troops continued their activities.

The Northerners. Venustiano Carranza, Zapata's nemesis, was born in 1859 and raised in wealth in the northern state of Coahuila. Carranza showed little interest in social or economic reform, which he argued would impede individual rights and a free-market economy. After Huerta's defeat, however, Mexico's leaders were as divided as ever. To appease the zapatistas, Carranza approved the Decree of January 6, 1915, which allowed villages to buy back a few parcels of land from the hacienda owners who had benefited from land seizures begun in 1856. The reform was limited in that the decree applied only to those haciendas that abutted villages, and the dispossessed hacienda owners, unlike the peasants who had originally lost the lands, were to be compensated for their losses. Of course, Zapata was not satisfied with these concessions and so continued his battles. It is perhaps the feud between Carranza's government and southerners such as the zapatistas that brings Francisco Rosas to Ixtepec in the novel; earlier in the Revolution of the 1910s Rosas had served under Carranza, switching allegiances to him from the popular northern general Pancho Villa.

Carranza's regime oversaw the drafting and partial implementation of the Constitution of 1917, which, in addition to introducing land reform, addressed the continuing problems of labor unrest and government conflict with the powerful Catholic Church. Carranza himself shied away from making any truly radical changes, but those who attended the constitutional conference that he called (in May 1917) had other ideas, and redrafted the Mexican Constitution in significant ways. Article 123 sought to free peasant workers from labor conditions of near enslavement. It put limits on the length of a workday, established a minimum wage, health

LONG NIGHT OF EXPIATION

At least one prominent historian has pointed out that Francisco Madero was the victim of wide-ranging and venal plots by the military and the Díaz-era political elite, aided and abetted by such forces as the national press, the U.S. ambassador, and the surging tide of agrarian resentment in the South (Krauze, pp. 264-73). At heart, however, Madero's policies were just, his intentions respectful of the Constitution, and his overall philosophy one of confidence in and optimism for Mexico's future. He furthermore deserved credit for overthrowing the dictator Díaz. It is not surprising, then, that he was a controversial figure in life and death, and that Mexicans in the immediate aftermath of his slaying struggled to assign meaning to his presidency. In *Recollections of Things to Come,* the townspeople of Ixtepec are at odds about Madero's legacy:

> "Our troubles began with Madero," [doña Elvira] said. . . .
>
> "The forerunner of Francisco Rosas [the general who has occupied the fictional Ixtepec] is Francisco Madero," said Tomás Segovia sententiously. . . .
>
> "Since we assassinated Madero we have had a long night of expiation," Martín Moncada exclaimed, still with his back to the group.
>
> His friends looked at him virulently. Hadn't Madero been a traitor to his own people? He belonged to a wealthy creole family, and yet he had headed the rebellion of the Indians. His death was not only just but necessary. He was to blame for the anarchy that prevailed in the country. The years of civil war that followed his death had been atrocious for the mestizos who resisted the hordes of Indians fighting for rights and lands that did not belong to them.
>
> (Garro, *Recollections of Things to Come,* pp. 64-65)

The people of Ixtepec are precisely those who stood to gain the most from many of Madero's new policies; that some of them mouth the idea of his being "a traitor" illustrates how successfully those responsible for his downfall convinced the nation of their own legitimacy.

insurance, and employer liability for accidents, and prohibited child labor. For the first time in Mexican history, workers were permitted the right to organize and strike.

NORTH VS. SOUTH

In *Recollections of Things to Come,* the southern Catholic town of Ixtepec is occupied by a troop of contemptuous federal troops, led by the northerners Francisco Rosas and Justo Corona, who enforce the Calles government's shutting of churches and execute Indians and other agrarian reformers. As historians point out, there was a vast difference between northerners and southerners in 1920s Mexico. In the South, in "old Mexico," the mestizos and Indian peasants were generally devout Catholics who lived traditional lives; in the North, particularly in the state of Sonora, people lived more secular lives and, perhaps because they lived on the recently created U.S. border (1868), had a more warlike and international perspective:

> They described themselves as the Californians of Mexico, who wished to transform their country into another California. Once they took on the gigantic task of controlling national resources of water and land, they were astonished to find that the centre and the south of the country were quite different from their own far north-west. . . . [W]hen they realized what kind of life was led by the peasants of traditional Mexico, they decided that the peasants were not men in the true sense of the term, as they kissed the hands of the great landowners and the priests, did not understand the logic of the marketplace, and frittered away what money they had on alcohol and fireworks.
>
> (Bethell, pp. 155-56)

In the novel such sentiments are uttered by Colonel Justo Corona, who complains of the people of Ixtepec: "Up north we're different. Since childhood we've known what life is and what we want out of it. That's why we're open and aboveboard. But the people around here are dishonest. You never know how you stand with them" (*Recollections,* p. 103).

The most controversial articles of the new constitution moved to limit the influence of the Church by declaring it subject to civil authority and by forbidding it to provide elementary education. An inflammatory new provision, Article 130, defined priests as professionals who were subject to secular law. Though these articles would not be enforced for several more years, they set a hostile tone for government-Church relations. As *Recollections of Things to Come* demonstrates, this hostility would erupt in widespread violence in the second half of the 1920s, in the conflict called the Cristero rebellion.

Despite Carranza's attempts to legislate reform, his popularity was eroded by Zapata's assassination and by his own failure to sponsor revolutionary change. When the President's term expired in 1920, Álvaro Obregón clearly intended to run for the office, but Carranza wanted to pick his own successor. Instead of acquiescing to this, Obregón, a former garbanzo-bean farmer who had seen his family's business prosper under his direction, took his campaign on the road. He formed alliances with labor and the zapatistas, and gained popular support. Once Carranza realized the strength of his opposition, he agreed to step down and proceeded to flee, only to be assassinated by his own former guards as he tried to evade federal troops on his way into exile.

Obregón was elected almost unanimously and served out his full term (1920–24), with policy changing very little from the days of Carranza. The major accomplishments of Obregón's regime include the hiring of new teachers, particularly in rural areas, and the implementation of programs designed to foster literacy. He encouraged a revolution in the arts that displayed the new Mexican nationalism. Indian and mestizo features rather than European ones emerged in paintings and murals, many of which depicted the Revolution itself. Among the most notable of these artists were Diego Rivera, José Clemente Orozco, and David Alfaro Siqueiros, whom the government employed to fulfill the objective.

Obregón's personally selected successor was Plutarco Elías Calles, a former school teacher, an avowed atheist, and an unpopular member of Obregón's cabinet who was known for his inflexibility and his lack of humor. In effect, this business of hand-picking one's successor violated the Revolutionary promise of a return to "Valid Voting, No Reelection," and some legislators of the time refused to tolerate it. Prompted by the matter of Obregón's successor, Obregón's secretary of the treasury, Adolfo de la Huerta, led a rebellion that began in December 1923, and gained some popular support. Obregón, however, had the help of the United States and ultimately put down the rebellion, forcing de la Huerta to flee into exile. On December 1, 1924,

Members of the *Brigadas Femininas,* 1911.

Calles, the illegitimate son of a Sonoran landowner and a former schoolteacher, became Mexico's president, remaining in office until 1928, with Álvaro Obregón continuing to wield influence from behind the scenes. As the narrator of *Recollections of Things to Come* notes, "in those days the fatherland bore the double name of Calles-Obregón" (*Recollections,* p. 255).

The *Cristero* rebellion. The Constitution of 1917 greatly limited the power of the Catholic Church, but the government did not strictly enforce the constitution's anti-clerical provisions at first. By 1926, however, Church-state antagonism had grown to unprecedented levels. Among other positions, the deeply conservative Church vehemently and publicly opposed the increasing socialism of the federal government and supported the de la Huerta rebellion against the openly atheist Calles. Calles, who had always resented the social and political power of the Catholic Church, and who, as governor of Sonora, had expelled all priests from the state, resolved to assert the government's authority, and began to apply Article 130. Before July 2, 1926, schoolchildren were often taught by priests or nuns according to Catholic doctrine; on this date the nation's elementary schools became secularized. Moreover, all priests had to register with the government so that it could enforce a ratio of one priest for every 5,000 inhabitants. The authorities deported foreign priests and nuns, and closed monasteries and convents. Church land and the buildings on it were declared to be the property of the Mexican government. In response, the Church immediately ceased all religious services and urged Catholics to "paralyze in every way possible the social and economic life of the country" by purchasing only bare necessities (Soto, p. 114). Armed conflict followed shortly after. The *Cristiada* (War for Christ) had begun.

As *Recollections of Things to Come* demonstrates, women played a major role in the Cristiada, most famously in the *Brigadas Femininas* (Feminine Brigade). The Brigadas Femininas, whose membership at its height reached 10,000, mostly unmarried working-class women, fought on the side of the primarily rural, generally poor *Cristeros* (Catholic guerrillas)—the main contribution of these women was to carry munitions and other supplies to the men at war (Soto, p. 115). The amount of female support garnered by the Cristeros was enough to make the federal government reluctant to pursue women's suffrage and other equal rights legislation. Women were deemed to be in the thrall of the Catholic Church and hence not trustworthy of the vote.

Recollections of Things to Come

Both sides of the Cristiada committed atrocities. *Recollections of Things to Come* records the violence done to protesting churchgoers by government forces: "Under the almond trees there were women whose heads had been shattered by gun-butts and men whose faces were mangled by kicking" (*Recollections*, p. 157). The federal army burned villages, executed priests, and hanged suspected Cristeros. The Cristeros, too, committed violent crimes, attacking government-appointed teachers, destroying government buildings, and on one occasion dynamiting a train and killing 100 people on board. By the rebellion's end, as many as 70,000 had died in the fighting.

NUNS AND ASSASSINS

In 1928 a young man named José de León Toral shot and killed Álvaro Obregón just before he was to serve a second term as Mexican president. Toral had been inspired by Madre María Concepción Acevedo de la Llata, or "Madre Conchita," as she was known. Madre Conchita was the abbess of a convent in Mexico City, and often held anti-government meetings at her home, including gatherings at which Catholics discussed how to assassinate either Calles or Obregón. The nuns were embittered by such policies as the Calles government's closing of the convents, which put many nuns at risk not only of deportation, but of physical abuse and even death. They also knew that Obregón was very likely to carry on Calles's policies, as the men were ideologically so close. At one gathering of Cristeros at Madre Conchita's home, conspirators are known to have discussed the following assassination scenario: "A hypodermic needle containing poison was the planned instrument of death. The assassination plan called for a girl with a needle hidden in a bouquet to dance with one of the men, and then to inject the poison" (Soto, p. 116). The eventual slaying of Obregón was, in fact, much simpler: Toral shot the president-elect at a restaurant. Garro's novel reports that "the death of Álvaro Obregón, which left him slumped over his plate at a greasy banquet, gave us great joy" (*Recollections,* p. 151). Madre Conchita and 20 nuns were arrested for the crime along with Toral. While he was condemned to death, it was illegal to execute a woman in Mexico, so Madre Conchita received a 20-year prison sentence. Eventually, she married a fellow prisoner.

In March 1928 Calles sought to resolve the conflict by drawing up an agreement sanctioned by the Vatican in Rome. Obregón's assassination derailed the plan and, although the "official" end of the Cristiada came in June 1929, with the reopening of churches, in fact Church-state relations remained inimical well into the 1930s.

Women's struggle for equal rights. The women in Garro's novel live under the thumb—sometimes the heel—of the men in Ixtepec. Isabel and Conchita wait about listlessly for marriage; Julia Andrade is beaten by her lover; doña Elvira reflects on the oppressive years of her marriage and rejoices in her widowhood. Their situations were in many ways typical for women in 1920s Mexico. In retrospect, women contributed greatly to the Revolution—they risked their lives carrying supplies to battlefields, traveled with revolutionary armies, sometimes engaged in battle, published and wrote newspaper articles, organized protests, and acted as spies and couriers. Yet the rights of women to vote and exercise other rights as citizens were denied them by the very parties and politicians that they had so vigorously and courageously supported. Chauvinism had much to do with this, but so did basic political expediency. Liberal factions did not wish to allow women—assumed to be unthinkingly loyal to the Catholic Church—to swell the ranks of Mexico's conservatives. Thus, at the Constitutional Congress of 1917, called by President Carranza (himself the beneficiary of massive female support), women's suffrage was hardly discussed. Worldwide, the women's rights movement was gaining ground (women in the United States, for example, would gain the vote in 1920), but Mexican women remained without many basic rights of citizenry. Wives, for instance, had to obtain the consent of their husbands before taking up a profession, and unmarried women under the age of 30 could not leave their father's house without approval.

This is not to say that women were neglected by revolutionary legislation altogether. The Decree of December 29, 1914, legalized divorce as well as a woman's right to own property. The 1917 Constitutional Congress ratified Article 123 of the Constitution, giving working women rights and benefits pertaining to hours worked, maternity leave, and minimum wage. (The article, however, often inconsistently enforced and misinterpreted, did little for many female workers.) The Law of Domestic Relations (April 9, 1917) allowed married women to enter into contracts and legal suits and gave them equal rights in matters relating to child custody. However, largely because of the Cristero rebellion and the events leading up to it, little attention was paid to women's rights legislation in the 1920s, when *Recollections of Things to Come* is set. There were health and education programs that attempted to improve conditions for Mexico's women, and four Mexican states granted women's suffrage (two of them revoked this right before the decade's end) in their elections, but a combination of tradition and fear kept women from making much progress. It was not until 1953 that Mexican women would finally achieve national suffrage.

Mexico and race. "If only we could exterminate all the Indians! They are the disgrace of Mexico!" is the sentiment among much of Ixtepec's mestizo, or mixed Spanish-Indian, population (*Recollections*, p. 21). The novel explains that the mestizos hate the Indians because the Indians make them feel a kind of self-loathing based on the idea that the mixed-race people "were without a country and without a culture, leaning on some artificial forms that were nourished only by ill-gotten gain" (*Recollections*, p. 21). Only Nicolás Moncada is unashamed of his Indian blood. When he tries to make others acknowledge the plain fact that all mestizos have Indian blood, they deny it in bitter anger. It takes the hanging death of Ignacio, a fixture in Ixtepec, and a well-liked person, to make some of the townsfolk reconsider their hatred of the Indians.

The existence of the mestizo class in Mexico dates back to 1522 when Princess Malintzin, the Indian mistress chosen by the Spanish conqueror Hernán Cortés, bore one of the first mixed-race children. The newborn Martín Cortés would be acknowledged, at least symbolically, as the very first. Thereafter, the pure Indian population decreased steadily, and the new mestizo racial strain grew exponentially. Meanwhile, the Spanish conquerors declared themselves privileged because of their fairer skin, which, to their minds, indicated racial purity. They created a hierarchy based largely upon skin color that would persist in forthcoming centuries.

While some Spanish fathers legitimized their mestizo children, many did not. Mestizo children enjoyed fewer social and economic opportunities than children with fairer skin. However, there was far less discrimination against the mestizos than against the Indians, who lived mostly in rural poverty. The sale of lands during Díaz's pre-1910 dictatorship had deprived many Indian peasants of their homes and work, leaving them vulnerable to exploitation. Some landowners forced Indian laborers to work not for wages but just for inadequate food and shelter. Such marginalization encouraged the Indians to keep their own cultures intact; there was no incentive for them to attempt assimilation into the world of the Spaniards. Their having being dispossessed by Díaz also encouraged them to join the Revolution against him in massive numbers.

"THE TURK"

In the novel doña Elvira takes a look at a picture of Calles in the newspaper and says: "What a face! What a face! See? He never smiles. He was born to read death sentences! . . . What can you expect of a Turk like Calles?" (*Recollections,* pp. 150-51). Rumor had it that Calles was a Moslem—a Syrian, actually—and he never addressed the question, because he was ashamed of his illegitimacy. He was not, incidentally, a "Turk" (the general name that Mexicans gave to all people from the Middle East), but was the son of a down-at-the-heels member of the once-prosperous Elías family of the northern state of Sonora (Krauze, p. 412). As for the deaths to which doña Elvira alludes, they were legion. Beginning in 1926 Calles rid himself of 25 opposing generals and had 150 other opponents shot (Krauze, p. 435). He had the reputation of an iron-willed killer.

In the 1920s, when *Recollections of Things to Come* is set, skin color and wealth still determined social standing (and still does to a great degree). The Indians in the novel are all poor members of the peasantry, while mestizos comprise the upper and middle classes of Ixtepec. The breakdown reflects a widely held belief of the time that people of European heritage were favored genetically, thereby explaining their greater wealth and education. While this belief was not universally shared, it allowed some Europeans and mestizos to justify their distinctive treatment, or mistreatment, of Indians, and the exclusion of dark-skinned peoples from the upper reaches of Mexico's government.

The Novel in Focus

Plot summary. Garro's tale is told in two distinct but closely related parts. Part One takes place in the 1920s, after the height of the fighting in the Mexican Revolution, and concerns the strife between federal troops and the town from which they intend to weed agrarian reformers and sympathizers. Part Two takes place in the midst of the Cristero rebellion that pitted the government against the Church and its sympathizers in the late 1920s. Each half is narrated by a voice that is the collective memory of the southern Mexican town of Ixtepec, in which the novel is set.

The opening of the novel introduces the children of the Moncada family. Isabel Moncada and her two brothers, Nicolás and Juan, are the indulged yet thoughtful children of increasingly impoverished, though genteel, mestizo parents, doña Ana and don Martín. Martín, who has the clocks in their home turned off at night, sees his life as suspended between two kinds of time. On the one hand, there is anecdotal or linear time—the time charted on calendars and recorded by clocks; on the other hand, there is circular or mythical time, which allows both lived and collective memories to free people from the insubstantiality of immediate experience. As the novel relates, "[i]n that time one Monday was all Mondays, words became magic, people changed into incorporeal personages, and landscapes were transmuted into colors" (*Recollections*, p. 15).

TIME AND HISTORY

"[Garro] understands memory as related to both past and future and emphasizes the repetitive nature of human action" (Muncy, p. 268). In other words, Garro understands that time exists in more than one category. What many critics have called "pre-Hispanic" or, sometimes, "mythical" time, is more eternal than linear time and encompasses not just the present, but the past (what is recalled) and the future (what is to come) as well—hence Garro's title, *Recollections of Things to Come.* Incorporated in her novel is the notion that the past and the future are always already part of our everyday experience.

The brooding and violent northerner, General Francisco Rosas, dominates Ixtepec. With his government troops, he has come to impose "order" on the town. In other words, he is there to quash any incipient rebellion and to ferret out suspected revolutionaries still loyal to the zapatista cause of agrarian reform. Before the arrival of the government forces, Ixtepec was occupied and looted by zapatistas. Most of the townspeople lament the replacement of these local revolutionaries with the much more brutal and oppressive government troops. Dorotea, the old lady who lives next to the Moncados, says of the zapatista forces that once rampaged in Ixtepec: "They were very poor and we hid our food and money from them. That is why God sent us Rosas, so we could miss them. You have to be poor to understand the poor" (*Recollections,* p. 10). Now familiar with much worse oppression, the townsfolk have idealized the zapatistas and long for them to return and drive away the new occupiers who decorate the town's trees with hanged agrarian reformers.

General Rosas himself is a surprisingly young man who controls the town through fear. His murderous rampages are worse when he drinks and after he fights with his mistress, the beautiful Julia, whom the people of Ixtepec blame for Rosas's actions. She and the mistresses of the other officers are kept in rooms at the local hotel, where they cannot talk to the townspeople. Some envy them and some pity them, but most are fascinated by these women who were either abducted from their homes or chose of their own free will to live as kept women. Julia is the most aloof of them. She acquiesces to Rosas's wishes, but she does not offer him the affection and interest that he craves. His frustration often culminates in murderous rages.

One day a mysterious stranger arrives in Ixtepec and heads for the hotel where he speaks with Julia, who does not seem surprised to see him. When Rosas arrives, he immediately drives the stranger away with a lash of his whip. The man, whose name is Felipe Hurtado, is befriended by Juan Cariño, a kind but mentally unbalanced man who lives in the local brothel and insists upon being called "Mr. President." Cariño directs Hurtado to the home of Joaquín and Matilde Meléndez, the Moncado children's aunt and uncle. Don Joaquín and doña Matilde take Felipe in, despite the fact that he has put himself in danger by talking to Julia. Hurtado seems to have known Julia before—he knows her last name, "Andrade"—and the townsfolk whisper among themselves that he has come to Ixtepec for her. He soon charms much of the town, including Isabel Moncado, whose brothers have left Ixtepec to work in the nearby mines. Hurtado listens to the voices of the townspeople who complain about the Indian rebels as well as landowners like their own Rodolfito Goríbar, who uses the corrupt government to increase his holdings, having the Indians who used to live on them hanged as agrarian reformers. Hurtado's response to these complaints is to introduce theater to Ixtepec—he believes that people are happier when they have illusion.

Meanwhile, Rosas's relationship with Julia becomes more and more frustrating for him; he hears the rumors about Julia and Hurtado, and steps up violence against Ixtepec's peasant population, whom he accuses of treason. As he becomes increasingly jealous, Rosas savagely beats Julia for looking at Hurtado in public and is suspected of having one of his officers shot when he fears that the drunken man may be planning to abduct her. Finally Julia flees her hotel prison and seeks out Hurtado at the Meléndez home. They spend a dangerously long time together before Julia returns to the hotel to face Rosas, who immediately sets out to murder Hurtado. But, before he is able to capture the stranger, "time stopped dead" (*Recollections,* p. 138). Ixtepec is frozen in night even while day has broken all around it, and into this strange timelessness Hurtado escapes. The people of Ixtepec later learn that he was last seen riding out of the dark town into the daylight with Julia in his arms.

As Part Two begins, the town and General Rosas mourn the loss of the beautiful Julia but are soon distracted. Calles's government has entered into a period of seriously strained relations with the Catholic Church and has begun to enforce anti-clerical constitutional measures, which has led to a suspension of all religious services. The general and his troops burn the church's statues and take over the building. Meanwhile the priest, Father Beltrán, mysteriously disappears. One night two soldiers viciously stone don Roque, the sacristan, in front of doña Matilde's house but his body cannot be found the next morning. The people of Ixtepec blame the government for using religious repression to divert attention from the issue of land redistribution. Still, they slyly revolt on behalf of the Church.

> We did not want to let the church fall into the hands of the soldiers. What would we do without it, without its feast days, without its statues that listened patiently to our laments? And would they condemn us . . . to die like stray dogs, without a whimper, after living a miserable life?
>
> "It's better to die fighting!" a man shouted throwing his hat into the air.
>
> (*Recollections,* p. 153)

Soldiers are killed during the night and the Cristero slogan: "Long Live Christ the King!" begins appearing in windows.

Rosas and his men are desperate to assert their power, so they search the Meléndez home and others for the body of don Roque, but find him nowhere. They strengthen their resolve and place the town under constant surveillance. One day three townswomen appear at Rosas's office. He and his soldiers think that they have had enough and are going to return don Roque's body, but instead they offer a token of peace, and invite Rosas and his officers to a fiesta planned in their honor at the home of the town doctor. They claim to seek reconciliation; General Rosas warily accepts.

The fiesta is preceded by calm in the town of Ixtepec while elaborate preparations are made. On the night of the party, Isabel and some other young women are sent to escort the officers to the doctor's home. Once there, they dance with the men, and the people of the town join in the revelry. Suddenly, however, the festive mood becomes tense as General Rosas and his men try to leave against the protests of their hostess. Rosas insists that the party continue until he returns, allowing only Isabel, with whom he shares an attraction, and her family to go home. So, with one of the officers enforcing the general's orders, the party continues. The band plays, and the guests dance well into the next day, until one of the musicians finally collapses. Exhausted, the townsfolk are forced to stay and suffer the heat until Rosas returns. He has uncovered the plot that the fiesta was designed to disguise. Four of the partygoers are arrested and, along with Nicolás Moncada, Father Beltrán, and Juan Cariño, are charged with treason and sedition. On the night of the fiesta, they had conspired in the escape of the priest and the sacristan. Juan Moncado, Dorotea, and the owner of the brothel died in the attempt. Soldiers had searched the houses of the conspirators and seized Cristero documents and posters as evidence of sedition.

As he leaves the party for the second time, General Rosas calls to Isabel Moncado, making it clear that she is to accompany him back to his room; in this way he asserts that his will reigns supreme in the town. After they spend the night together, she takes Julia's place in the hotel. The town hopes that she is trying somehow to trick Rosas but fears that she has betrayed them by becoming his mistress. In fact, although she hates herself for it, Isabel does love Rosas. Rosas, however, immediately regrets having made Isabel his lover, and considers her a poor substitute for Julia, whom he still loves. It slowly maddens him to even look at Isabel because, with eyes so similar to those of his prisoner, her brother Nicolás, she is a reminder of his own cruelty.

Illustration from an early manuscript showing La Malinche (center) acting as intermediary between Hernán Cortés (seated) and Aztec emissaries (right).

The prisoners are prosecuted and most, including Nicolás, are sentenced to death. At the last moment, Isabel pleads with Rosas for her brother's life, even as Nicolás determines to die for the Cristero cause. Rosas gives in to Isabel and orders her brother set free, but Nicolás refuses the pardon and is executed with the others.

When Isabel learns of this, she allows Gregoria, the Indian servant who has tended to her since her arrival at the hotel, to bring her to the shrine of the Virgin Mary to absolve her sins. They walk for hours but before they arrive, Isabel flees in order to be with Rosas. She loses her way and falls. By the time that Gregoria finds her, Isabel has been transformed into a stone onto which Gregoria carves her tragic story.

Sources and literary context. *Recollections of Things to Come* is one in a long series of Mexican novels to examine the social and political ramifications of the Mexican Revolution. The tradition began with the 1915 serial newspaper publication of Mariano Azuela's *Los de abajo* (The Underdogs), which deals in part with the defeat of Pancho Villa and the victory of Carranza; Azuela also wrote a 1937 novel about the Cristero rebellion, *El camararda Pantoja* (Comrade Pantoja). Garro may have been influenced by the many truth-speaking madmen that people Azuela's novels when she created the character of Juan Cariño, who, imagining himself to be the president of Mexico, stands up to Rosas (Foster, p. 267). Other prominent Mexican writers to treat the Revolution include Martín Luis Guzmán, whose *The Eagle and the Serpent* (1928) examines the cruelty and lust for power of the generals Villa and Obregón, whom the author himself knew. Like the roughly contemporary (1955) ***Pedro Páramo*** by Juan Rulfo (also covered in *Latin American Literature and Its Times*), Garro's novel infuses the historical recounting of the Revolution and Cristiada with magic—both novels play with time, the dead, and unconventional narrators. Agustin Yarez in *The Edge of the Storm* (1947) uses the trope of the collective narrator to tell his tale, as Garro does in her 1963 novel. *Recollection of Things to Come,* however, stands out from all of these others in its attention not only to the forces of history and the violence of men, but also to the effects of such forces on the lives of women.

La Malinche and her heirs. One of 20 women baptized and given to Spanish men to fulfill their sexual needs, the mistress of the Spanish conqueror Hernán Cortés is known by many names—Princess Malintzin, doña Marina, and the most enduring epithet, La Malinche. She played a pivotal role as middle woman between the Spaniards and Aztecs, serving as translator and diplomat, facilitating communication and relations between the two groups. Among her other roles, she gave birth to a mestizo (Indian-Spanish) child with Córtes, who gave her some property and married her off to one of his soldiers, Juan Jaramillo. She died at the tender age of 24.

Through time, La Malinche would become greatly maligned. In the 1500s the Indians portrayed her as powerful, serious, beautiful, loyal, and well respected. It was an image that would do a 180-degree turnabout when the Mexicans won independence from Spain in 1821. La Malinche suddenly became a scapegoat for 300 years of exploitive Spanish rule, attaining a reputation as the Indian woman who sold out to the white men. "In a wink she was demoted from crucial interpreter and counselor to wily lover and mistress, traitor of her race, mother of the mestizo" (Schroeder, Wood, and Haskett, p. 297). Thereafter, La Malinche became ensconced in the Mexican consciousness as a symbol of deceit, an image that endured to the time of Garro's novel. In keeping with this image, in 1926, a year in which the novel takes place, the Mexican artist José Clement Orozco painted Córtez and Malinche naked with the corpse of an Indian beneath her feet. The painting, in other words, holds her partly responsible for their deaths.

Garro uses the figure of La Malinche to elaborate and complicate themes of deceit, betrayal, and gender politics in *Recollections of Things to Come.* Both Julia and Isabel, mistresses of the stranger who has "conquered" Ixtepec, bear the brunt of the townspeople's anger and hatred toward Rosas and his troops. Julia is held responsible for her lover's murderous rages and military cruelties; when men are found hanging from trees, the deaths are called "more sins for Julia," even though she clearly has neither the power nor the political will to have ordered such actions (*Recollections,* p. 8). Yet Julia serves not only as the scapegoat for the miserable and oppressed of Ixtepec, but also as the focus of their love and admiration for her great beauty. This paradox, points out Sandra Messinger Cypess, is inherent to the La Malinche legend, for, although she is viewed as a traitor, she is also the archetypal sexual object, mother of Mexico (Cypess, p. 118).

Isabel Moncada, too, takes on the La Malinche role when she replaces Julia as Rosas's mistress. She, even more obviously than her predecessor, is a "traitor," who betrays her family for love of the enemy. The townspeople are never certain whether they ought to think of her as a whore, complicit with the deaths of her brothers, or as a heroine who will redeem Nicolás by giving herself to Rosas. Gregoria, however, is certain: on the stone that was once Isabel Moncado, she inscribes: "I caused the unhappiness of my parents and the death of my brothers Juan and Nicolás" (*Recollections,* p. 288). Recent history has shown similar uncertainty about La Malinche. Was she indeed a traitor or was she a heroine? In some circles, La Malinche has begun to re-emerge as a positive figure, a woman whose cooperation with the Spaniards helped preserve her race. Like the female characters in *Recollections of Things to Come,* hers is a perplexing image.

Events in History at the Time the Novel Was Written

Church and state in the early 1960s. *Recollections of Things to Come* focuses on the battle between Church and state in the 1920s. In the early 1960s, when the novel was written, these two factions were again engaged in political struggle, although by no means as serious or as deadly a struggle as the predecessor. In places like Puebla and Morelia, cities with strong Catholic traditions, Catholic interests, which tended to be associated with wealth and with business, were challenged in riots by socialist-leaning students and educators. These protesters and others like them were impassioned by Fidel Castro's successful Cuban Revolution in 1959, and began to unite behind the idea that the Mexican Revolution had benefited only the wealthy.

The Church, however, was not entirely the stodgy bourgeois institution it was portrayed to be. While firmly opposed to Soviet-style communism and wary of Marxism in general, it was nonetheless moving to the left. This situation can be attributed to some extent to the events of the Cristero rebellion; given the anti-clerical measures imposed by President Calles, future Mexican priests were trained abroad (mostly in the United States and Italy). This training exposed them to the populist philosophies of Vatican II (an international Church council that tried to address the spiritual needs of the modern world) and worldwide leftist politics in general. Out of such exposure came the birth of "liberation theology" in Latin America, which attended to the spiritual, economic, and political needs of the poor. A new clerical focus on Mexico's peasants, rather than the wealthy, began to influence the balance of political power throughout the nation.

The Revolution revisited. Some 50 years after the Mexican Revolution began, its vestigial traces could still be seen in Mexican national politics. In 1962, a year before *Recollections of Things to Come* appeared, Mexico saw agrarian revolt and suppression as in the 1920s. In Emiliano Zapata's home state of Morelos, government forces murdered Rubén Jaramillo. A Methodist preacher and agrarian reformer, Jaramillo was an outspoken critic of the government and *caciques* (local political strongmen), and demanded that land be redistributed to the peasants who had a right to it. Jaramillo began to organize the peasants, forming a Committee for the Defense of the Sugarcane Workers, whereupon the government tried to reason with him, offering him fields of his own and money. Nothing, however, weakened his commitment to the cause of returning lands to the peasants. In the end, he and his family were killed, by consent of then-president Adolfo López Mateos, on March 23, 1962 (Krauze, p. 642). Contemporary novelist Carlos Fuentes, whose ***The Death of Artemio Cruz*** (also covered in *Latin American Literature and Its Times*) is also set during the Revolution, wrote an exposé of the murder in the journal *Siempre!* López Mateos went on to redistribute land to Mexico's rural poor: 16 million hectares in all. His critics, however, pointed out that he had not distributed useful or arable land, but only "mountains and crags" (Krauze, p. 658).

Reviews. *Recollections of Things to Come* was well received in its Spanish-language edition, earning Garro the prestigious Xavier Villaurrutia prize in 1963. One critic called it a great accomplishment, "a novel of reality and unreality, of life and death. What the reader understands of these circumstances comes from the extended, magical communication that Garro achieves" (Brushwood, pp. 52-53). This same author, however, critiqued Garro's use of the town as narrator as striking a false note. Jean Franco, however, defended the strategy:

> The choice of this collective protagonist has the advantage of giving voice to all the marginalized elements of Mexico—the old aristocracy, the peasantry (and former supporters of the assassinated revolutionary leader Zapata), the indigenous, and women; in sum, all those left behind by modernization and the new nation.
>
> (Franco, p. 134)

In their praise, reviewers deemed the novel to be "a masterful portrayal of the aftermath of the Mexican Revolution as seen through women's experience"; turning to its prose, they complimented the mix of "passages of haunting lyricism and beauty" with "sharp, monstrous evocations of violence and death" (Pope in González Echevarría, p. 244; Gyurko in Foster, p. 266).

—Amy Garawitz and Lorraine Valestuk

For More Information

Bethell, Leslie, ed. *The Cambridge History of Latin America*. Vol. 5. Cambridge: Cambridge University Press, 1986.

Brushwood, John S. *Mexico in its Novel: A Nation's Search for Identity*. Austin: University of Texas Press, 1966.

Cypess, Sandra Messinger. "The Figures of La Malinche in the Texts of Elena Garro." In *A Different Reality: Studies on the Work of Elena Garro*. Ed. Anita K. Stoll. Lewisburg, Penn.: Bucknell University Press, 1990.

Foster, David William. *Mexican Literature: A History*. Austin: University of Texas Press, 1994.

Fowler-Salamini, Heather, and Mary Kay Vaughn, eds. *Women of the Mexican Countryside, 1850-1990*. Tucson: University of Arizona Press, 1994.

Franco, Jean. *Plotting Women: Gender and Representation in Mexico*. New York: Columbia University Press, 1989.

Garro, Elena. *Recollections of Things to Come*. Trans. Ruth L. C. Simms. Austin: University of Texas Press, 1969.

González Echevarría, Roberto, and Enrique Pupo-Walker, eds. *The Cambridge History of Latin American Literature*. Vol. 2. Cambridge: Cambridge University Press, 1996.

Krauze, Enrique. *Mexico: Biography of Power*. Trans. Hank Heifetz. New York: HarperCollins, 1997.

Schroeder, Susan, Stephanie Wood, and Robert Haskett, eds. *Indian Women of Early Mexico*. Norman: University of Oklahoma Press, 1997.

Skidmore, Thomas E., and Peter H. Smith. *Modern Latin America*. 4th ed. Oxford: Oxford University Press, 1997.

Soto, Shirlene. *Emergence of the Modern Mexican Woman*. Denver: Arden Press, 1990.

"Reply to Sor Philothea"

by
Sor Juana Inés de la Cruz

Juana Ramírez de Asbaje was born on the *hacienda* of San Miguel Nepantla, near Mexico City, the capital of New Spain, probably in 1648. The out-of-wedlock daughter of Isabel Ramírez de Santillana and Pedro Manuel de Asbaje y Vargas Machuca, the young Juana Inés was raised at the hacienda of her maternal grandfather Pedro Ramírez de Santillana, where she quickly demonstrated prodigious talents and exceptional intellectual ability. Upon her grandfather's death in 1656 Juana's mother sent her to live in Mexico City with her aunt, and in 1664 she became a lady-in-waiting to and protégée of the Viceroy's wife, doña Leonor María Carreto, the Marquise de Mancera. Although she enjoyed many favors during her life at court, after five years she joined the Carmelite convent in Mexico City, which she was forced to leave for reasons of ill health. Once recuperated, she entered the Convent of San Jerónimo in 1668 where she professed on February 24, 1669, under the religious name Sor Juana Inés de la Cruz. A collection of her poetry, *Inundación Castálida* (Castalian Inundation), was published in Spain in 1689. According to many scholars, Sor Juana, who became known as the "Mexican Phoenix" and "Tenth Muse," was the greatest poet of the Spanish language in this era. Her death from the plague on April 17, 1695, contributed to the demise of the Baroque era in Spanish-American literature. In addition to sonnets and many other types of verse, Sor Juana penned several plays (dealing with both the religious and the mundane), composed songs, and wrote prose that was revolutionary for the time, such as her "Reply to Sor Philothea."

THE LITERARY WORK

A letter written by Sor Juana Inés de la Cruz in the Convent of San Jerónimo in Mexico City; dated March 1, 1691; published posthumously in Spanish (as "Respuesta a sor Filotea de la Cruz") in 1700, in English in 1981.

SYNOPSIS

A defense of women's right to study secular and religious texts, the "Reply to Sor Philothea" offers a unique look into the life and views of the most important writer of New Spain.

Events in History at the Time of the Letter

The Baroque in Latin America. From the middle of the sixteenth century until the end of the seventeenth century, first in Italy, Germany, and Holland, and then in Spain and its American colonies, "the Baroque" was the dominant style in the creative arts. The Baroque is characterized by ideological, semantic, and syntactic asymmetry. Other features are extravagance, intricacy, and a sense of artificiality—in contrast to the art of the Renaissance, which it followed chronologically and which strove for harmony, order, and verisimilitude. Some historians see the Baroque period in art as a direct response to unsettling pan-European events such as the Protestant Reformation and Catholic Counter-Reformation, and to scientific discoveries, predominantly in as-

The Baroque interior of the Church of Santo Domingo in Oaxaca, Mexico.

tronomy, that unseated traditional ideas of knowledge and reality.

Baroque literary works generally have a dynamic form and an indeterminate vision of reality; they are objects in constant transformation. Unlike the Renaissance ideal, which strove to closely represent reality, Baroque works tend to hide an intellectual mystery that must be revealed; as such, the Baroque may be considered the art of that which is unfinished. As the Mexican novelist Carlos Fuentes (see ***The Death of Artemio Cruz,*** also covered in *Latin American Literature and Its Times*) observes, the great distances between the promises and realities of the Renaissance are filled by the Baroque (Fuentes, p. 206; trans. M. Schuessler). The Baroque also juxtaposed different media—architecture and landscape, painting and poetry, music and theatre—creating a multifaceted, kaleidoscopic, and splendid artistic whole.

El desengaño. In literature, and especially in poetry, the Spanish Baroque's distinguished trait is that of the *desengaño*, that is, the sudden realization that what one sees or believes is not necessarily real or true. Desengaño is the psychological state produced upon uncovering this shell of illusion and deceit (Wardropper, p. 6). As appearances continually deceive us, the corollary of desengaño is the admission that the world is irrational—the unjust govern the just, and evil triumphs over good (Wardropper, p. 6). Carlos Fuentes sees desengaño illustrated in the enormous distances between the utopian ideal and historical reality, the noble savage and the incarcerated slave, the idea of law and the way it is enforced, the ancient gods and the modern one—all of which create a desperate feeling of emptiness that is filled by the Baroque (Fuentes, pp. 205-24). In Latin America, the Baroque enjoyed a full and original adoption, due, perhaps, to the strange political and cultural relationship between native and European civilizations there, along with the natural exuberance of the American environment: its enormous rivers, impenetrable jungles, never-before-imagined animals, and birds of resplendent plumage. This is seen clearly in the architecture of Latin America's colonies, which was carried to extraordinarily original extremes. The churches of Santo Domingo in Oaxaca, Mexico, and Santa María Tonanzintla in Puebla, Mexico, are examples of an esthetic hybrid, in keeping with a continent in which the biological mixing of races produced the *mestizo,* or individual of mixed American Indian-European heritage. Sor Juana demonstrates such an influence in the abundance of indigenous terms throughout her writing, especially those referring to native delicacies; in one of her dramatic compositions, she even includes a *tocotín;* (Indian dance form), accompanied by the words of this ritual written in the Nahuatl language.

The epoch was one of great contradictions and Sor Juana may be considered their embodiment: she was both religious and pagan, a woman and an intellectual, scholastic and hermetic, a nun and scholar. Such paradoxes helped to set what Octavio Paz has called the "traps of faith," in which Sor Juana became ensnared towards the end of her life (Paz, p. 387). Although claiming to want no trouble with the Holy Office, she nonetheless exceeded the established limitations of the epoch. Sor Juana became ensnared because she applied herself to secular investigations while openly opposing the religious hierarchy of her time.

The convent. In seventeenth-century New Spain, there were two principal career paths for middle and upper-class *criolla* women (Spanish American woman of European descent). The first and most common was that of a wife and mother; the second—less common—was that of a nun.

According to the Italian traveler Antonio Gemelli Carreri, there were 29 religious communities of monks and 22 of nuns in the capital of New Spain at the end of the seventeenth century (Paz, p. 117). Sor Juana believed—mistakenly—that the convent's atmosphere of peace and calm would allow her to dedicate all her time to intellectual and literary endeavors.

In the convent of San Jerónimo, Sor Juana lived a restricted existence. She was not allowed to leave the community's premises, although she had daily contact with the outside through the *locutorium* (from the Latin *loquor,* "I speak"), a room in the convent where the nuns were allowed to receive their relatives and friends—with their faces veiled, and protected from their visitors by a metal screen. In this space Sor Juana conversed daily with her learned friend the university professor Carlos de Sigüenza y Góngora about intellectual and scientific matters, and received visits from her beloved friends and protectors, the two Vicereines—Lenor María Carreto, the Marquise de Mancera, and María Luisa Manrique de Lara, the Marquise de la Laguna and Countess of Paredes.

Although one might believe that austerity ruled within the world of the convent, Sor Juana lived in relative comfort. Her cell was actually a kind of two-level apartment, complete with a maid. In her spare time, in the privacy of her quarters, Sor Juana was able to read from her extensive library—said to contain more than 5,000 volumes—study the stars and the movements of the heavens with her astronomical instruments, compose poetry and drama, play her musical instruments, and engage in an extensive correspondence, most of it lost to time.

The "Letter Worthy of Athena": crucial context. The "Reply to Sor Philothea" was written in response to a disconcerting missive sent to the author by the Bishop of Puebla, Manuel Fernández de Santa Cruz, who used the traditional female pseudonym of Sor Philothea (in Greek, *philothea* means "love of God") to admonish the poet for her apparent lack of religious devotion, as evidenced by her excessive interest in the study of earthly matters.

TIMETABLE OF EVENTS LEADING TO THE WRITING OF THE "REPLY"

1650: Sermon delivered by the famous Jesuit priest Antonio Vieyra that refutes earlier authorities about Christ's expressions of love just before he died.

1690: Publication of the letter by Sor Juana (the "Letter Worthy of Athena") that, in turn, refutes Vieyra's opinion.

1691: Letter from Sor Philothea (the Bishop of Puebla) that admonishes Sor Juana for her audacity.

1691: Sor Juana's reply in defense of her position.

In order to better understand the content of Sor Juana's "Reply," it is necessary to review a series of events that began with the publication, during the last days of November, 1690, of a pamphlet entitled "Letter Worthy of Athena by Sister Juana Inés de la Cruz, a Professed Nun in the Most Spiritual Convent of San Jerónimo. . . . Printed and Dedicated to That Same Sister by Sister Philothea de la Cruz, Her Studious Follower in the Convent of the Most Holy Trinity in Puebla de Los Angeles." The reference to Athena, the Greek goddess of wisdom, reflects the effusive—if not entirely sincere—praise being showered upon its author by Sor Philothea. Essentially, the "Letter Worthy of Athena" is a superbly reasoned critique by Sor Juana of a sermon given some 40 years before by a highly respected Portuguese Jesuit, Antonio Vieyra, in which he presents his interpretation of a phrase attributed to Christ in the gospel of John: "A new commandment I give unto you: that you love one another as I have loved you." In Sor Juana's opinion, Christ's love differs from that of humans, who wish love to be returned for their own sakes. Christ wishes to be loved not for his sake but for the sake of others, that is, for the sake of the people who love him. It follows, as Sor Juana saw it, that Christ desires a person to love others for his or her own sake, not for the return love it might bring. This contradicts the opinion set forth by Father Vieyra.

THE CATHOLIC PRINCES OF NEW SPAIN

Sor Juana's fate was determined by her difficult relationship with three important figures of New Spain's religious hierarchy: the misogynist Francisco de Aguiar y Seijas, Archbishop of Mexico, whose religious fervor included bodily mutilation and other excesses; Manuel Fernández de Santa Cruz, Bishop of Puebla, the person who incited Sor Juana to write the polemic "Letter Worthy of Athena" that sparked the events that led to the "Reply"; and Antonio Núñez de Miranda, her spiritual advisor and confessor, who personally instigated Sor Juana's entry into the Hieronymite convent and, on the eve of her profession, lit the candles on the church's altar. He would abandon his spiritual daughter after the composition of her "Reply," leaving her in the hands of the two aforementioned bishops. Physically and morally weakened by their actions and reactions, Sor Juana became more vulnerable to the pestilence that swept Mexico City the year of her death.

Although Sor Juana claims that she was asked to write the critique of Vieyra's sermon by a high-ranking religious authority (generally accepted to be Manuel Fernández de Santa Cruz), she does not miss the opportunity to express her own premonitions regarding the negative impact her critique would soon have on its readers, all of them male and many of them members of the Society of Jesus, such as the misogynist Archbishop of Mexico, Francisco de Aguiar y Seijas. In the words of Octavio Paz:

> It is not difficult to deduce from all this that the person who might feel affected by Sor Juana's critique was not Vieyra, absent and far removed from it all, but Archbishop Francisco Aguiar y Seijas. An attack on Vieyra was an oblique attack on Aguiar. It was also a confrontation with influential friends of the Archbishop.
>
> (Paz, p. 402)

This is clearly evidenced in a fragment of the letter in which Sor Juana appears to foresee its negative reception, but nonetheless insists on her argumentative ability, even though she is a woman: "It is no faint chastisement, for one who believed there was no man who dared reply to him, to see that an arrogant woman dares, one for whom study of this nature is so foreign, and so remote from her gender." (Sor Juana in Paz, p. 391).

Not surprisingly, Sor Juana's letter set off widespread criticism and debate, both in America and Europe, as it was seen as a veiled attempt to attack the theology of the Jesuits, the most powerful religious order in seventeenth-century New Spain. According to Octavio Paz, Sor Juana would be destroyed in the struggle between two princes of the Roman Catholic Church: Manuel Fernández de Santa Cruz, the Bishop of Puebla, and his rival the Jesuit Archbishop Aguiar y Seijas (Paz, p. 403). In order to mask his role in prompting her to write the initial letter, the Bishop of Puebla represents himself as "Sor Philothea" when he chastises Sor Juana for the ideas expounded in the "Letter Worthy of Athena." His brief missive precedes Sor Juana's text, and starts with high praise: "[I]n spite of the fact that in his sermon Vieyra had soared 'above himself like a second Eagle of the Apocalypse,' Sor Juana had 'sharpened her quill to a finer point,' and the Portuguese scholar could 'glory in seeing himself refuted by a woman who is the honor of her sex'" (Sor Philotea in Paz, p. 396).

After praising Sor Juana's intellect and calling her "the honor of her sex," Sor Philothea proceeds to admonish Sor Juana for not applying such a privileged (and God-given) intellect to the pursuit of religious knowledge:

> Any science that does not light the way to Salvation God regards as foolishness. . . . What a pity that such a great intellect should so lower itself by unworthy notice of the Earth as to have no desire to penetrate what comes to pass in Heaven; and, having already stooped to the Earth, may it not descend farther to consider what comes to pass in Hell.
>
> (Sor Philotea in Paz, p. 396)

This chastisement triggers Sor Juana's "Reply to Sor Philothea de la Cruz," in which she argues, based upon her own life experience and that of other women in history, that women have the right and ability to learn. Essentially, the "Reply" is a self-defense of the author's life and her interest in intellectual matters generally consigned to the public, masculine sphere. In it Sor

Juana also explains that in order to understand theology, the "queen of sciences," it is necessary to comprehend all of the lesser, worldly sciences. She cites numerous examples of Catholic saints, such as St. Augustine and St. Jerome—the patron saint of her order—who found their way to Heaven precisely through the concerted study of the mysteries of life on Earth. Indeed, the fourth-century St. Jerome himself was a literary scholar, who dedicated his life to the translation of the Bible into Latin, producing the *Vulgate,* which became for centuries the cornerstone of Catholic liturgy. Ironically, St. Jerome battled famously with his love for secular literature, especially the works of Cicero—and eventually renounced all literature that was not sacred.

The Letter in Focus

Contents summary—pre-convent days. "The Reply to Sor Philotea" begins with Sor Juana explaining why her response to Sor Philothea has been delayed as long as it has. She claims that she has not known how to reply to "your most learned, prudent, pious, and loving letter" (Sor Juana, "Reply to Sor Philotea," p. 205), or how to thank Philothea for publishing her original work, the "Letter Worthy of Athena." According to Sor Juana, the publication of this letter was unforeseen by her, and had disconcerted and shocked her:

> It is no affectation of modesty on my part, Madam, but the simple truth of my entire soul, to say that when the letter that you chose to call Athenagoric ["worthy of Athena"] came into my hands, I burst into tears of embarrassment, something I do not very easily do.
>
> ("Reply," p. 206)

Regarding Sor Philothea's chastisement of her intellectual activity, Sor Juana explains that she has been reluctant to write about sacred subjects, not because she does not wish to, but because she feels herself to be unworthy.

Sor Juana next turns to the story of her life, beginning with her inclination to write:

> From my first glimmers of reason, my inclination to letters was of such power and vehemence, that neither the reprimands of others—and I have received many—nor my own considerations—and there have been not a few of these—have succeeded in making me abandon this natural impulse which God has implanted in me.
>
> ("Reply," p. 210)

Before she was three years old, she had learned to read by accompanying her elder sister to class. She also recalls that, as a child, "I refrained from eating cheese, because someone had told me it made you stupid, and my urge to learn was stronger than my wish to eat, powerful as this is in children" ("Reply," p. 211). When she was six or seven, young Juana discovered that in Mexico City there was a university where one could study many different things. She begged her mother to dress her as a boy in order that she might attend. Her request was, not surprisingly, denied, and she returned to her self-directed study of the books in her grandfather's library. After she arrived in Mexico City, where she lived with her maternal aunt, "people were astonished, not so much at my intelligence as at the memory and store of knowledge I had at an age at which it would seem I had scarcely had time to learn to speak" ("Reply", p. 211).

So assiduous was the young Juana in her studies and so uncanny her abilities, that she claims to have learned Latin in less than 20 lessons. She confesses that she was so studious that, at an age

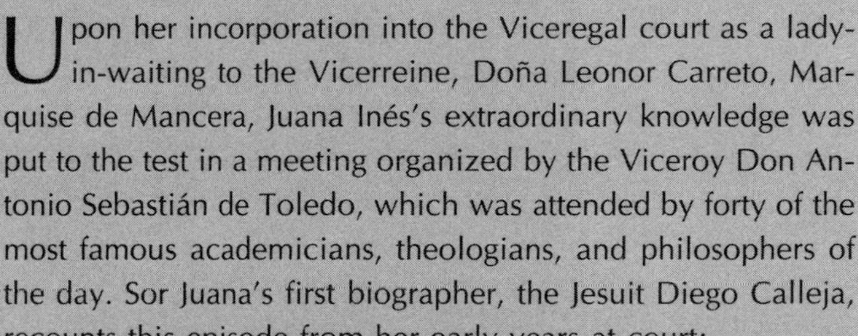

A CURIOUS COMPETITION

Upon her incorporation into the Viceregal court as a lady-in-waiting to the Vicerreine, Doña Leonor Carreto, Marquise de Mancera, Juana Inés's extraordinary knowledge was put to the test in a meeting organized by the Viceroy Don Antonio Sebastián de Toledo, which was attended by forty of the most famous academicians, theologians, and philosophers of the day. Sor Juana's first biographer, the Jesuit Diego Calleja, recounts this episode from her early years at court:

> The honorable Marquis de Mancera . . . wanted to ascertain the truth and to learn whether such amazing wisdom was innate or acquired . . . and so he gathered together one day in his palace all the men of letters in the university and city of Mexico. They numbered some forty, of varied professions, such as theologians, scripturists, philosophers, mathematicians, historians, poets, humanists. . . . So on the appointed day they gathered for this curious and remarkable competition, and the honorable Marquis testifies that the human mind cannot conceive what he witnessed, for he says that "in the manner that a royal galleon . . . might fend off the attacks of a few canoes, so did Juana extricate herself from the questions, arguments, and objections these many men, each in his specialty, directed to her."
>
> (Calleja in Paz, p. 98)

Sor Juana Inés de la Cruz

when most young women were very self-conscious about their hair and how it was arranged, she habitually cut hers off:

> I used to cut four or five fingers' width from mine, keeping track of how far it had formerly reached, and making it my rule that if by the time it grew back to that point, I did not know such-and-such a thing which I had set out to learn as it grew, I would cut it again as a penalty for my dullness . . . for I did not consider it right that a head so bare of knowledge should

> be dressed with hair, knowledge being the more desirable ornament.
>
> ("Reply," pp. 211-12)

Contents summary—convent life. Sor Juana Inés confesses that her entry into the convent was due more to necessity than divine inspiration. As an out-of-wedlock daughter of a poor criolla family, her hopes for a good marriage were not promising. The fact that her own mother never married and her experiences growing up with half-brothers and half-sisters may also have shaped her negative view of married life. She confesses that various aspects of convent life repelled her; she desired to live alone, in peace, and to have no other occupation than studying. Just the same, becoming a nun seemed the "least unreasonable and most becoming choice" she could make, given how little marriage interested—or was possible for—her ("Reply," p. 212). She discovered, once she had taken her vows, that the convent, which kept her from studying her books whenever she liked, only increased her zeal to learn. In fact, says Sor Juana, this desire "exploded like gunpowder" ("Reply," p. 212). Sor Juana's intellectual appetite was voracious, as she reveals upon attempting to excuse her forays into non-sacred learning:

> I went on, continually directing the course of my study . . . toward the eminence of sacred theology. To reach this goal, I considered it necessary to ascend the steps of human arts and sciences, for how can one who has not mastered the style of the ancillary branches of learning hope to understand that of the queen of them all?
>
> ("Reply," p. 213)

She backs up her argument by presenting examples in which a lack of worldly knowledge would render impossible the interpretation and appreciation of religious texts.

In the same vein, Sor Juana also laments that she never had a teacher during the long hours of her self-directed and isolated study and that her studies were interrupted by her duties at the convent, where she was treasurer and archivist for many years, as well as by the daily distractions of convent life—quarrels between servants, the idle chatter of fellow sisters, and the well-intentioned visits of friends. She also mentions the jealousy and wrath brought about by her literary acclaim. Such jealousy "has even gone so far as a formal request that study be forbidden me" ("Reply," p. 224). Indeed this did occur at least once during the years Sor Juana spent at the convent of San Jerónimo. An overzealous female prelate succeeded in prohibiting Sor Juana from consulting her books during the three months that the individual resided at the convent. However, even such insistence by a figure of authority couldn't stop her natural inclinations: "[A]lthough I did not study from books, I did from everything God has created, all of it being my letters, and all this universal chain of being my book" ("Reply, " p. 224). She observed the pattern traced on the ground by a top, and discovered many secrets of nature while in the kitchen, noting how an egg keeps together when fried in oil but disintegrates in syrup, wryly pointing out that "if Aristotle had been a cook, he would have written much more" ("Reply," p. 226). In other words, though deprived of her books, she probably learned as much by observing phenomena in the kitchen as she had from studying books.

As proof that other women scored achievements outside the domestic sphere, Sor Juana enumerates examples of the many learned women who played decisive roles in biblical history: Deborah, who drew up military and political laws; the Queen of Sheba, who dared to challenge the wisdom of the wisest and who became the judge of nonbelievers; Abigail, who held the gift of prophecy; and Esther, who was blessed with a supreme persuasiveness, among many others. After her discussion of Hebraic heroic figures, she recalls those of the Ancients: the mythological sibyls, curiously described as "chosen by God to prophesy the principal mysteries of our faith"; the Roman goddess of wisdom, Minerva; the Roman poet Lucan's wife, Polla Argentaria, who reportedly helped her husband with the correction of his epic, *Pharsalia*; and the oracle Nicostrata, held by some to have invented Latin letters ("Reply," p. 227). Sor Juana ends her compendium by mentioning an influential and admired woman of her own time: Christina Alexandra, Queen of Sweden, who had famously converted to Catholicism in the mid-seventeenth century, and who was deeply interested in the arts and sciences.

Having liberally demonstrated the invaluable role of women throughout history, Sor Juana turns to another question: should women be prohibited from study? According to her argument, the idea that they should is based upon a historical misinterpretation of a phrase in St. Paul's first letter to the Corinthians: "Let women keep silence in the churches, for it is not permitted them to speak" (1 Cor. 14:34). Sor Juana concludes that Paul means that women should not lecture publicly, nor should they preach. Studying, writing, and teaching privately, however, are not only permissible, but are in fact desirable. Of course this is only the case of a select few, because not everyone is worthy of such a pursuit, not even men:

> [T]he interpretation of Holy Scripture should be forbidden not only to women, considered so very inept, but to men, who merely by virtue of being men consider themselves sages, unless they are very learned and virtuous, with receptive and properly trained minds.
> ("Reply," p. 230)

Practically, too, educating women makes sense: learned older women would become the instructors for the younger female generation, thus avoiding the "dangerous medium of male masters" ("Reply," p. 233).

Towards the end of her "Reply," Sor Juana returns to the ill-fated "Letter Worthy of Athena" that landed her in such trouble. Sor Juana challenges Sor Philothea/de Santa Cruz to answer a series of succinct questions that go to the heart of the theological and political stakes behind their fraught correspondence:

> If the crime is the Athenagoric Letter, was there anything more to that than simply setting forth my views without exceeding the limits our Holy Mother Church allows? If she with her most holy authority does not forbid my doing so, why should others forbid it? Was holding an opinion contrary to Vieyra an act of boldness on my part, and not [his] holding one opposing the three holy Church Fathers [Augustine, Thomas Aquinas, and John Chrysostom]? Is not my mind, such as it is, as free as his, considering their common origin? Is his opinion one of the revealed precepts of Holy Faith, that we should have to believe it blindly?
> ("Reply," pp. 236-37)

Sor Juana ends her "Reply" by promising that anything she writes in the future will "ever seek sanctuary at your feet and safety through your correction" ("Reply," p. 243). In this way, although the nun offers to present her works to the Bishop's censor, she does not, in fact, agree to give up her studies and composition entirely. Nonetheless, the furor caused by her "Reply" was so great that she abjured secular pursuits, such as writing verse and reading nonreligious texts, and devoted herself entirely to the care of the ill in 1692.

As a postscript, recent scholarly research has found documentation that Sor Juana Inés de la Cruz did eventually return to her intellectual pursuits. Indeed, she had begun to rebuild her library and replace her scientific instruments, sold at the command of her clerical superiors, before her death in 1695.

Literary context. The "Reply to Sor Philothea" occupies an important position in the development of literature in Spanish, and of women's literature in general: "[T]he document is an impassioned, carefully reasoned, occasionally pedantic, defense of the historical and spiritual rights of women to study, to teach, and to write" (Peden in de la Cruz, *Poems,* p. 7). It is furthermore one of the first such defenses in the Western hemisphere. The sociohistorical and autobiographical content of the "Reply" gives us a glimpse into the world of seventeenth-century New Spain, and serves as a compendium of the knowledge—philosophical, historical, scientific, and otherwise—of the age. The "Reply" also illuminates many obscure passages in Sor Juana's literary production, and is an invaluable resource for interpreting such lyric masterpieces as the *First Dream,* as well as some of her dramatic and prose pieces. The only truly self-descriptive text by Sor Juana, it helps explain, for example, the wide scope of her learning, which came not from the convent but rather from her early readings of the many books in her grandfather's library.

Impact. The "Reply to Sor Philothea" was not published until 1700, when it was included in the anthology entitled *Fama y obras póstumas* (Fame and Posthumous Works) and received no attention from literary critics for 200 years. We do know that Bishop Manuel Fernández de Santa Cruz did not deem Sor Juana's defense worthy of reply, as, according to Octavio Paz, "the Bishop of Puebla could not have been happy with her response; he had wanted a frank and unequivocal renunciation of secular letters, not a reasoned defense" (Paz, p. 426). Indeed, in 1692 Sor Juana was forced to give up her books and musical and scientific instruments, which were auctioned off by Bishop Aguiar y Seijas in order to raise money for the poor. This was followed two years later by a statement of self-condemnation, which she signed in her own blood. She denied that she had existed before becoming a nun, defended with her blood the doctrine of the Immaculate Conception (which states that the Virgin Mary was begotten without sin), and turned to penance and self-sacrifice. Several months before her death she had written in the convent's Book of Professions:

> In this place is to be noted the day, month, and year of my death. For the love of God and his Most Holy Mother, I entreat my beloved sisters the nuns, who are here now and who shall be in the future, to commend me to God, for I have been and am the worst among them. Of them I ask forgiveness, for the love of God and his Mother. I, worst of the world, Juana Inés de la Cruz.
>
> (Sor Juana in Paz, pp. 464-65)

Since the mid-twentieth century, a time of controversy and renewed progress in the global arena of woman's rights, hundreds of books and articles have been written on Sor Juana's literary work. One of the pioneer scholars of this renewed interest and celebration of the life and works of Sor Juana Inés de la Cruz, Dorothy Schons, considers Sor Juana "the first feminist of America," an epithet justified by her "Reply" (Schons in Paz, p. 486).

—Michael Schuessler

For More Information

Fuentes, Carlos. *El espejo enterrado.* Mexico City: Fondo de Cultura Económica, 1994.

Juana Inés de la Cruz, Sister. "The Reply to Sor Philotea." In *A Sor Juana Anthology.* Trans. Alan Trueblood. Cambridge, Mass.: Harvard University Press, 1988.

——. *Poems, Protest, and a Dream: Selected Writings / Sor Juana Inés de la Cruz.* Trans. Margaret Sayers Peden. New York: Penguin, 1997.

——. *The Answer / La respuesta. Including a Selection of Poems.* Critical edition. Trans. Electa Arenal and Amanda Powell. New York: CUNY, The Feminist Press, 1994.

Menim, Stephanie, ed. *Feminist Perspectives on Sor Juana Inés de la Cruz.* Detroit: Wayne State University Press, 1991.

Paz, Octavio. *Sor Juana or, The Traps of Faith.* Trans. Margaret Sayers Peden. Cambridge, Mass.: Harvard University Press, 1988.

Wardropper, Bruce. "Temas y problemas del barroco español." In *Historia crítica de la literatura española.* Barcelona: Editorial Crítica, 1991.

Santa Evita

by
Tomás Eloy Martínez

Born in Argentina in 1934, Tomás Eloy Martínez immigrated to the United States in 1983. He had been forced to leave Argentina by President Isabel Perón's government and had lived in exile in Venezuela for eight years, continuing to do so because of Argentina's military dictatorship. A journalist and writer, Martínez's many Spanish-language nonfiction books include *Sagrado* (1969), *La pasión según Trelew* (1973), *Lugar común la muerte* (1979), and *Las memorias del general* (1996). Most of these deal with Argentine history and/or Peronism in some form. To date, Martínez has published three works of fiction: *La novela de Perón* (translated into English as *The Peron Novel* in 1987); *La mano del amo* (1991; The Hand of the Master), and *Santa Evita* (retained this title—which means "Saint Evita"—in the English translation). According to Martínez, both *La novela de Perón* and *Santa Evita* resulted from years of research and interviews; the stories he gathered, however, could only be told through fiction. In a 1996 review in the *New York Times Book Review* Nicolas Shumway writes, "With these two books, [Martínez] affirms his place among Latin America's best writers" (Shumway, p. 27).

THE LITERARY WORK

A novel set mainly in Buenos Aires from 1952 to 1956, and including flashbacks from the lifetime of Eva Perón; published in Spanish in 1995, in English in 1996.

SYNOPSIS

Santa Evita follows the strange odyssey of Eva Perón's corpse, which becomes a powerful political symbol in post-1955 Argentina.

Events in History at the Time the Novel Takes Place

Argentina before Perón. *Santa Evita* begins with the death of Eva Perón, and then traces the movements of her corpse, using flashbacks to tell the story of her rise to power and her marriage to Juan Domingo Perón. The most influential Argentine leader of the twentieth century, Juan Domingo Perón was elected president in February 1946, three years after a military coup ended a period of Conservative rule. The time was ripe for a leader like Perón, who championed the working classes, composed largely of immigrants whose sense of class-awareness had been steadily increasing since the 1880s. In the 50 years before Perón came to power, Argentina had developed a large export economy, shipping beef and grain around the world, and experiencing periods of great prosperity enjoyed by the landowning classes. The introduction of foreign capital also helped develop the economy, as European and American investors, banks, and insurance companies contributed to the building of railroads and the handling of Argentina's growing overseas trade.

For many Argentines the turn of the twentieth century had been a "Golden Age," and although the new wealth did not trickle down to many workers, it lured hundreds of thousands of European immigrants to Argentina. Argentina's economy before World War I was, however, a dependent one. Much of the beef and grain money had to be used to import large amounts of manufactured goods that were not produced in Argentina. What was needed was the development of an industrial sector that could produce many of these goods itself, but most of Argentina's leaders before Perón were either neutral or openly hostile to such development. Until 1916 power remained in the hands of Conservative leaders, politicians aligned with the landowners whose wealth depended upon the export trade. The Radical party was elected into office in 1916 and maintained power for 14 years, but it had no clear economic vision, and little was done to industrialize the nation. In 1930 the Conservatives overthrew the Radical party, an ominous beginning to what became the "infamous decade," or the "era of economic fraud," throughout which elections were rigged to keep the Conservative party in power. Its leaders remained hostile to Argentina's wider economic development and to the working classes.

FROM HUMBLE BEGINNINGS: THE ORIGINS OF JUAN DOMINGO PERÓN

Perón was born on a small pampas farm in 1895. At five he moved with his family to Patagonia, in the cold south of the country, where he grew up in the manner of the cowboy-like gaucho: "breaking wild horses, lassoing ostriches . . . fording icy streams in sub-zero weather, riding the stony mesa, spurs strapped to his bare feet, his poncho streaming in the wind" (Barnes, p. 26). At 16 he went off to military college, becoming one of the army's best shots, a fencing champion, and a fierce fighter with his fists.

During the 1930s Argentina faced economic crisis. The worldwide Great Depression had a disastrous effect on its economy, prices on exports dropped, and the imports upon which the country depended became much less accessible. Thus, despite government reticence, national industries expanded in these years, and large numbers of rural Argentines moved to urban centers, joining the workers already involved in manufacturing. Many of these workers were by now second-generation immigrants who had risen into the new middle class and had rejected the more radical ideas of socialism or anarchism brought over by their European parents. By Perón's time Argentina was far less advanced than other Latin American countries in labor and social legislation. Unlike Argentina, most of these other countries had passed labor laws that regulated conditions for workers and that recognized workers' unions. Thus, any leader championing the cause of the workers would be poised to win vast support from a large segment of society ignored by most previous leaders.

Perón's rise to power. In 1943 the Conservative government was overthrown in a coup led by a band of army rebels called the Group of United Officers, which included the young colonel Juan Domingo Perón. Perón was immediately appointed undersecretary of war and, soon after, secretary of labor; both positions would be crucial in his rise to power. Perón began cultivating the support of the working classes; he increased wages, enforced labor legislation, and helped form new trade unions while expanding those that already existed. As historians have pointed out, "by 1945 his Labor Secretariat was the nation's sole collective bargaining agency, and under [Perón's] auspices unions were virtually certain to attain whatever they sought" (Madsen and Snow, p. 46). Coming from an immigrant, middle-class background himself, Perón identified with the workers and widely publicized his pro-labor stance. Although many wealthy Argentines had recovered from the effects of the depression, many of the nation's poor still suffered, especially since overflowing labor pools in the cities kept wages at depression levels. For obvious reasons Perón soon gained a mass following. By 1945 he also held the positions of minister of war and vice-president.

In October 1945 a group of military officers who opposed Perón's pro-labor stance—and wanted to harness his ambition—arrested him. Two weeks later a few hundred thousand people, mostly workers, demonstrated in front of the Government House in Buenos Aires, and many smaller demonstrations took place outside the city—all for the release of Perón. Some scholars argue that Perón's lover, Eva Duarte, whom he had met in 1943, mobilized these forces herself and sent them marching downtown; others claim that labor leaders spread word of Perón's arrest. In either case, Perón was released around midnight, after which he addressed the crowd from the Government House balcony in a speech "in-

Juan and Eva Perón

terrupted constantly by a clamorous dialogue of love that established, definitively, a bond between the leader and his people" (Luna in Madsen and Snow, p. 49). Within days union leaders formed the Labor Party, which nominated Perón as its presidential candidate for the February elections. During his campaign the charismatic Perón inspired frenzy in his followers, even causing women to faint; in February he won the election with ease.

Perón in power—an overview. Perón first ruled Argentina from 1946 until 1955, when he was unseated by a military coup, and he returned to power from 1973 to 1974. The deep influence of Peronism on Argentine politics continues today. Though notoriously difficult to define, Peronism is at base a worker's movement, with strong Argentine nationalist themes running throughout its various political philosophies. Perón promised his country a "New Argentina" based on social justice, political self-determination, and economic independence: a combination of philosophies that constituted the "third position, the golden mean between heartless capitalism and godless Marxism" (Poneman, p. 64). Officially his party was called the "Justicialist Party"; through the official doctrines of *justicialismo* Perón attempted to transfer class and corporate allegiances to a more general national allegiance, in part by protecting each according to his or her needs and opposing undeserved wealth and power. As mentioned, Perón reformed and improved life for Argentina's working classes, whom he called *masas descamisadas*, or the "shirtless masses." In addition to increasing wages and expanding labor unions, he placed controls on child and female labor, created employment agencies, annual bonuses, and vacation resorts, subsidized legal services and housing, and regulated working hours, as well as implementing many other labor reforms (Rock, p. 262). By 1955 the CGT, or *Confederacion General del Trabajo* (General Confederation of Labor), had 2.3 million members and was one of the country's most powerful organizations. For many Argentines, Perón was a hero.

Perón's other accomplishments include the construction of 500,000 new homes as well as new schools, hospitals, clinics, and recreational facilities; the decreasing of foreign investment, interpreted by Peronists as a newfound economic independence for Argentina; the promotion of women's rights, including the right to vote; and the creation of a large number of businesses and manufacturing firms that decreased dependence on foreign trade.

Perhaps his greatest accomplishment, however, was to marry Eva Perón in 1946. She not only maintained her husband's working-class support but broadened it with her powerful personality, impassioned speeches, and overwhelming charity. Her Eva Perón Foundation provided housing and hospitals for the poor, and every week she would hold personal audiences with the masses of people lined up outside, usually granting whatever aid they requested. She became famous for such charity, handing out money, medicine, and toys, becoming known as "Lady Bountiful," "Standard-Bearer of the Poor," "Lady of Hope," and even as "Saint Evita."

Juan Perón was not a perfect leader, however, and his critics have been many. Some of them regarded his political philosophy of justicialismo as ill-defined, an uneasy blend of national, social, and Christian elements that allowed Perón to seem all things to most people, and in this way to manipulate the masses more easily. Secondly, wage increases and Perón's seemingly generous charity sparked the worst inflation in decades, almost depleted foreign reserves, and, some claimed, led to a completely shattered economy. The largesse reserved for party supporters, mainly the workers and the military, caused the rest of the community to suffer. In economic development, industrial growth was mostly limited to small businesses, while larger firms showed little growth; businesses employing fewer than ten workers made up more than 80 percent of the nation's industrial firms (Rock, p. 265). Perón often resorted to force in order to temper resistance, squelching his opponents through exile, imprisonment, threat, and torture. His was a dictatorship in which the government, presses, and judiciary system were purged of all dissent. According to one critic Perón "destroyed anyone in his path, including supporters who did not bow low enough" (Poneman, p. 69). To many of Perón's detractors he was a fascist ruler who did much to stunt the growth of the economy and prevent the possibility of democracy in Argentina.

Peronists and anti-Peronists present clashing versions of Perón, viewing him alternately as a hero and as a tyrant. The extent to which he was either is open to debate. What seems clear is that, while Perón did much to advance the cause of women, the working classes, and others, allowing them to prosper in ways they never had before, many of his achievements came at great cost to Argentine society as a whole.

Eva Perón—background. During her husband's presidency, Eva Perón became one of the most powerful women in the world. Even before their marriage and his presidency she began to involve herself in government affairs, taking on minor duties and rousing support for Perón. Soon she represented him at ceremonial functions, delivering speeches that moved crowds of workers. Her accessibility and continual interaction with the common people provided a link between the people and Perón, who was less interested in day-to-day administration. Although Evita, as she was called, would soon transform herself into a glamorous, blonde beauty, she never lost the traces of her working class background, the "tackiness" of which her detractors accused her, or her anger toward the upper classes. Evita always presented herself to the common people as one of them, a fellow worker from the provinces.

Evita Perón was born María Eva Ibarguren in 1919 in Los Todos, a village 150 miles west of Buenos Aires on the pampas, a "dreary, squalid, little pueblo, built on the site of a long-forgotten Indian encampment" (Barnes, p. 11). Her mother, Juana Ibarguren, had been a cook at the Duarte farm in the community of Chivilcoy, where she began a long-term affair with the married Juan Duarte. Juana had five illegitimate children by Duarte, including Evita. Although Duarte visited the children until his death, they all experienced the stigma of illegitimacy; when Duarte died (Evita was seven), for example, the children were not allowed inside the widow's home to see their father for the last time. Without Duarte's help, money became scarce, so Juana and her daughters began working as cooks at the local estates. Indeed, all that Duarte left his and Juana Ibarguren's children was the right to bear his name, whereupon Eva Ibarguren became Eva Duarte. When she was ten the family moved to Junín, and at age 15 she left for Buenos Aires. Some say she left with the tango singer Agustín Magaldi when he passed through town; others, that she went alone. For a young Argentine girl with dreams of becoming an actress, however, Buenos Aires was the only place for her to go.

Evita appears to have been rather lucky in those early Buenos Aires years, for she seemed to get enough acting roles to support herself. Some biographers contend that she worked as a prostitute and/or had a series of brief affairs that advanced her career or position in some way; others argue that such claims are groundless. Much of her early life remains cloudy and inaccessible to us, especially because she herself later had many records destroyed or documents changed, and, therefore, her biographers often disagree. By all accounts, however, she was not a particularly gifted stage or film actress, although by 1942 she seemed to have found her niche in radio dramatizations—most successfully in a weekly series in which she acted out the lives of famous women, including England's Queen Elizabeth I and the French actress Sarah Bernhardt. This series was successful enough that Eva Duarte began appearing on magazine covers and making more money than she ever had before. In addition to working in radio, from 1937 on Evita appeared in a small number of films, usually in minor roles; indeed, Evita's roles were so small that in only one, *La pródiga,* could she actually be seen (Dujovne Ortiz, p. 80).

In 1944 an earthquake almost completely destroyed the Argentine town of San Juan. Subsequent fund-raising efforts included a variety show at which Eva Duarte, one of the many actresses there, met Juan Perón. Again, events are unclear. Some accounts portray Eva Duarte as crafty and calculating, slipping into the seat next to the man rumored to be one of the most powerful in the new military government; others present their meeting as more random. In her autobiographical *La Razón de mi Vida* (My Mission in Life), Evita says she placed herself next to Perón and declared, "If, as you say, the cause of the people is your own cause, however great the sacrifice I will never leave your side until I die" (Perón in Barnes, p. 25). In *Santa Evita* she simply says, "Thanks for existing" (Martínez, *Santa Evita,* p. 176), and with these carefully chosen words she changes her destiny. Whatever the exact circumstances of their meeting, Eva Duarte and Juan Perón left with each other that night, married two years later, and stayed together until her death in 1952.

Like her husband, Eva Perón has been both loved and reviled, and, again like her husband, seemed to earn both responses. As the head of the Eva Perón Foundation, she oversaw fantastic displays of charity for the poor, but, as we see in *Santa Evita,* she could abuse her almost unlimited power in ways that were cruel and ruthless. Her foundation was unregulated, kept no financial accounts, and received generous state subsidies, CGT donations, and tax exemptions, all of which created suspicion among her detractors and fanned rumors that she was siphoning off foundation funds. The work she did was heavily publicized and a powerful element of Peronist propaganda. Everyone was aware of how grateful they should be to the Peróns, who became the "smiling parents" of an entire nation of children in this "benign but authoritarian" version of the New Argentina (Fraser and Navarro, p. 131). Almost everything the foundation produced—from hospital beds to clothing to vaccines—had Evita's initials stamped or painted on it. Joseph A. Page states the obvious criticism: "[Evita] never explained why the Peronist government did not attempt to use the powers at its disposal to eliminate the causes of social and economic injustice, rather than dispense palliatives" (Page, p. 19). Since her death, an entire mythology has surrounded Evita. She is remembered variously as a saint, a revolutionary, a harlot, and a petty tyrant.

THE GENEROUS WOMAN

Evita's last film was *The Generous Woman,* or *La pródiga,* in which she played the title role. Many of her biographers have noted the uncanny similarities between this 1945 role and the role she was beginning to play in real life. In the film, her character—called "Mother of the Poor" and "Sister of the Sad"—is always helping the less fortunate. All prints of this film were thought to have been destroyed, most likely on Evita's orders, until a print was found in the 1980s.

Political instability after Perón. In 1952 Eva Perón died of cancer. The whole country went into an enforced yet generally sincere mourning for her, which is described in detail in the beginning of *Santa Evita.* Many feel that Evita's death, at least partially, led to Perón's fall three years later because she had eclipsed him in popularity and as the embodiment of Peronism. Several other factors contributed to his fall, however, including the damaged economy, which had been affected by bad harvests, inflation, and overspending; his persecution of dissenters, which had increased social unrest; and a fatal confrontation with the powerful Catholic Church. Unwilling to wait for a coup or to start a civil war, Perón resigned from office and left the country.

The military leaders who came into power after Perón had not only a vexed relationship to Peronism, but also a slew of social problems and a damaged economy to confront. These leaders were mainly liberals and nationalists, and each group of them had different ideas about how to deal with Perón's legacy. Most liberals called for total suppression of Peronist materials, unions, and influences, while Perón's first successor, General Eduardo Lonardi, had a more conciliatory approach that was supported by the nationalists. But Lonardi's presidency quickly gave way to that of the liberal-minded General Pedro Aramburu, who immediately assaulted Peronism in all its forms. Many Peronist organizations, unions, and laws were eliminated. Perón's political party was dissolved, and the CGT appropriated. The government also forbade people from mentioning Perón's name, or displaying Peronist signs or slogans. The names of both Evita and Juan Perón could be mentioned only through insults like "the fugitive tyrant" or "the whore." It was at this time that Evita's corpse disappeared from the CGT—a central event in *Santa Evita.*

SAINT EVITA?

After Evita's death, some Argentine labor leaders made an official request to the Vatican for Evita's canonization. The Vatican denied this request, but images of Evita as saint became widespread while Perón retained power. The following lines are from a prayer in a 1953 children's schoolbook:

> . . . Evita, I promise to be as good as you wish me to be,
> respecting God, loving my country;
> taking care of General Perón; studying
> and being towards everyone the child
> you dreamed I would be; healthy, happy,
> well-educated and pure in heart.
>
> (Fraser and Navarro, p. 170)

The primary goal of this new military government was to remain in power long enough to destroy all vestiges of Peronism and to set the stage for a civilian government. The Peronists, however, established a resistance movement; new generations of Peronists succeeded the old and took over labor unions. In short, Peronism remained a vital force in Argentina for many years, inspiring passions on both sides and preventing any kind of consensus or political order. Meanwhile, the economy continued to perform poorly, and recessions and inflation prevented industrial progress. Unemployment affected all major social groups. The standard of living, even for the wealthy, decreased dramatically. At the same time military rule became increasingly repressive. By the 1970s "Argentina had become notorious for its political violence and repression" (Rock, p. 321).

The Novel in Focus

Plot summary. The novel opens during the last hours of Eva Perón's life, as she lies dying of uterine cancer, reviewing her days and remembering her last request to Perón: "Don't let them forget me" (*Santa Evita,* p. 7). After her death the country is grief-stricken: 500,000 mourners line up to kiss her coffin. True to his wife's wishes, Perón has had Evita embalmed on the night of her death, and she has become a work of art, her body now incorruptible, immortal. The embalmer, Dr. Pedro Ara, from whose actual memoirs Martínez quotes, calls his creation "a statue of supreme beauty, like the Pietà; or the Victory of Samothrace" (*Santa Evita,* p. 20). After the public viewing of her corpse, Evita's body is moved to the CGT, where a special laboratory has been set up for Dr. Ara to finish his embalming, and where the corpse lies almost forgotten in the political turmoil following Evita's death. This is 1952.

Three years later Juan Perón has fled the country, the corpse remains with Dr. Ara, and the new government wants Evita dead "like any other" (*Santa Evita,* p. 16). Colonel Carlos Eugenio de Moori Koenig is appointed head of the Intelligence service and given the job of disposing of Evita's corpse properly. In a country divided by political turmoil, Evita's corpse is a dangerous political symbol. A tomb or grave would too easily become a sacred spot, inspiring political fervor in followers of Perón and possible rebellion against the new government. As the Colonel himself says, "Heaven only knows how the useless dead body of Eva Duarte came to be confused with the country. . . . Whoever has the woman has the country in the palm of their hand" (*Santa Evita,* p. 25).

The main narrative of *Santa Evita* follows the corpse's bizarre journey across two continents, as again and again the new Argentine powers hide the body, only to have it discovered by avid Peronists hot on its trail. Illicit photographs of the corpse are delivered to the Colonel when it has been kept under strictest cover, and flowers and candles appear near the cadaver even when men are on watch. Three copies of the body had been made by an Italian sculptor before Evita's death, so the Colonel and other members of the Intelligence service attempt to bury the fake bodies to confuse the enemy, while transferring Evita's real body to a warehouse. A fire breaks out, and the real corpse is placed in an army truck parked outside the Intelligence service, for lack of a better place. Flowers appear by the truck. The Colonel hides the body behind the screen at a local movie house, but again the flowers appear and the owner's daughter mistakes Evita's body for a doll. The Colonel moves the body to the house of one of his men, Arancibia, but, like Ara and the Colonel, Arancibia also becomes obsessed with Evita. When he catches his wife around the corpse, Arancibia kills her, claiming he thought she was a thief. Finally Evita's body is transferred to Italy, where, under a false name, it remains buried for 16 years. The Colonel, however, is now crazy, and mistakenly follows a copy of the corpse to Germany, tricked by other members of the Intelligence service because he knows too much. The corpse is eventually returned to Perón in 1971. He now lives outside Madrid with his third wife, Isabel Perón, who would become Argentina's president upon Peron's death in office in 1974. In 1976 Evita finally receives a proper burial in Recoleta Cemetery, Argentina's most prestigious burial ground.

Santa Evita moves back and forth in time, from the corpse of Evita to Evita in life—as a girl, as an actress, as Perón's partner, and so on. She is remembered and reconstructed in interviews, documents, screenplays, and testimonies. Martínez, who claims to be as accurate as possible in this reconstruction, speaks directly to the reader about the novel he is writing—citing sources, describing interviews, and musing on the nature of his own project. "The sources on which this novel is based are not altogether reliable," he tells us, "but only in the sense that this is true of reality and language as well: lapses of memory and imperfect truths have found their way into them" (*Santa Evita,* p. 126). The author's narration is central to the novel, as Martínez's own story becomes wrapped up in Evita's. "If I don't try to know her by writing her, I'm never going to know myself," Martínez concludes, implying that he, like all Argentines, is inextricably tied to his country and its past (*Santa Evita,* p. 368). That past, that history, is furthermore elusive. History, like literature, says the novel, is always a "search for the invisible, or the stillness of what flies" (*Santa Evita,* p. 54).

Argentina and the dead. At the center of *Santa Evita* is the dead body of Eva Perón. Colonel de Moori Koenig and his peers must hide the corpse so that others cannot use it as a political tool; meanwhile, the very men surrounding the corpse become obsessed with it, and are haunted by Evita, just as Martínez's narrator is haunted by her. "The fascination for her dead body began even before her illness, in 1950," this narrator tells us, when Julio Cortázar's novel *The Test* imagined multitudes of people coming from all over Argentina to worship a bone and having their hearts broken by a woman in white (*Santa Evita,* p. 180). This is the image of Evita that literature is leaving us, the narrator says: that of her dead body. Indeed at one point the narrator compares his novelistic project to the project of an embalmer: "both try to immobilize a body or a life in the pose in which eternity is to remember it" (*Santa Evita,* p. 140). Dr. Ara, within and without the novel, published a book documenting his painstaking embalming of Evita, his masterpiece. In both Ara's book and his own, the narrator says, "the biographer is at once the embalmer, and the biography is also the autobiography of his funerary art" (*Santa Evita,* p. 140).

In an interview with Calvin Sims, Martínez compared the embalmed body of Evita to the country of Argentina. "[Evita's body] is the embalmed body of a beautiful woman who has not yet been resuscitated. In the same way Argentina is a country of hope and promise that has never been fulfilled. This is the melancholy nature of Argentina" (Martínez in Sims, p. 3). The powerful symbolic value of Evita's corpse also "points towards [Argentina's] tendency toward necrophilia" (Martínez in Sims, p. 3). For, as the Colonel is told in *Santa Evita,* "every time a corpse enters the picture in this country, history goes mad" (*Santa Evita,* p. 16).

Indeed, as Sims points out, Argentina has a long history of using corpses for political purposes. Spanish settlers of the sixteenth and seventeenth centuries used to smear their bodies with their victims' blood, and parade the corpses through town. Juan Perón's hands were sawed off 13 years after his death, when vandals broke into his tomb; this event prompted a Peronist demonstration of around 50,000 people. In 1989 President Carlos Saúl Menem shipped the body of Juan Manuel de Rosas, the notorious dictator from the nineteenth century, back to Argentina from England. None of these cases could match, however, the case of Eva Perón, and the bizarre wandering of the corpse that might have inspired either worship or revolution.

Sources and literary context. Martínez's novel can be categorized in different ways. First, Martínez himself discusses the long line of "Evita texts" that preceded his: works by Julio Cortázar, Juan Carlos Onetti, Jorge Luis Borges, Rodolfo Walsh, Copi, and Néstor Perlongher (*Santa*

Evita, pp. 180-85). (Cortázar's ***Blow-Up and Other Stories*** and Borges's **"The South"** are also covered in *Latin American Literature and Its Times.*) Biographers of Eva Perón proliferate, and, of course, Evita has received even more attention worldwide through Andrew Lloyd Weber and Tim Rice's musical opera *Evita,* and the Alan Parker film adaptation. *Santa Evita* has a place, then, in the context of all these imaginings of Eva Perón—some comic, some tragic, some wildly inaccurate, and others, like Martínez's, careful blends of history and fiction. Martínez lists his own sources—interviews, rumors, archives, old film clips, and so on—throughout the novel. But where history begins and fiction ends is never entirely clear. As Martínez puts it:

> If history—as appears to be the case—is just another literary genre, why take away from it the imagination, the foolishness, the indiscretion, the exaggeration, and the defeat that are the raw material without which literature is inconceivable?
>
> (*Santa Evita,* p. 129)

According to Gustavo Pellón, two of the three main currents in the recent Spanish American novel have been the documentary novel, which "exists in a constant tension between fiction and non-fiction," and the historical novel, which often comments "on the process whereby history is constructed" (Pellón, pp. 282, 288). In *Santa Evita* and *La Novela de Perón,* Martínez straddles both of these genres. The two novels use documents to reconstruct particular events and people, while seeking the roots of traumatic events associated with Peronism, and engaging in the revision of history common in current Latin American fiction. Among Martínez's influences is Jorge Luis Borges, without whom, says Martínez, "my novel would not have appeared" (Martínez in Bach, p. 14).

Events in History at the Time the Novel Was Written

Striving for democracy. Since 1983, when President Raúl Alfonsín took office, Argentina has been undergoing a democratic rebirth. Alfonsín defeated the Peronists and neutralized the authoritarian and revolutionary extremes—all of whom had been discredited by the violent chaos of the 1960s and '70s. The country was filled with relief; "casting aside the shackles of censorship and repression, dramatists, filmmakers, poets, and artists joined together in an outburst of creative energy and cultural vitality" (Rock, p. 390). It seemed at the time that the legacies of militarism and Peronism would be put to rest, but by the late 1980s it was clear that the conditions from which dictatorship had sprung—mainly economic—were not so easily surmounted. Although he had freed a country long repressed, Alfonsín was unable to lead it into a "new future" (Rock, p. 403).

In 1989 Carlos Saúl Menem became president, and has remained in office through the writing of *Santa Evita* and into the present day. Under Menem's leadership, the phase of consolidated democracy began. Faced with his country's economic collapse, Menem made the economy central to his neoliberal political project, and reduced inflation to an annual 3.5 percent in his first term in office. Seen as an "economic miracle," this achievement helped Menem win a second term in 1995, the year in which *Santa Evita* was published. Menem has also helped reconcile Peronism and liberalism, the forces that divided Argentina for so long. Many Argentines, however, have become disenchanted with politics, feeling their nation lacks a parliament committed to making democracy work and to representing the will of the people. In addition, Menem has been criticized for signing amnesties for those convicted of military crimes. The amnesty excused military violence like that seen in the "Dirty War" (1976-83)—a brutal, indiscriminately repressive domestic war that followed the collapse of Peronism, during which all due process of law vanished and some 30,000 people disappeared. Civilian courts had found guilty and sentenced the perpetrators. Menem's granting of amnesty implied that such violence could be seen as a judicial act. Martínez himself has commented on the matter, noting cynically that Menem wants to prove that Argentina has made peace with barbarism.

When Menem first campaigned for the presidency, he fashioned himself a populist, charismatic leader in the style of Perón, made use of Peronist iconography, and spouted rhetoric reminiscent of Perón's. Within the first months of his term, however, he began introducing the kinds of neoliberal policies traditionally considered within Peronism as antinational, thus turning the search for Argentina's identity away from Peron's "mystic nationalism" and towards an easier, more pragmatic approach to Argentina's problems. Some argue that Menem's policies are, in effect, undoing Perón's legacy, but Peronism does not

Eva Perón

seem so easily quelled. In the 1995 elections Menem's strongest opposition came from José Bordón, a dissident Peronist who took 29.2 percent of the vote. Clearly, Peronism is still a vital force in Argentine politics, though it has not been unified as a movement since Perón's first presidency. Still ill-defined, Peronism has come to signify different meanings to different political groups. Even so, in 1987 Daniel Poneman was able to write:

> Perón's speeches blare from cassette-players at street-corner stands where Perón badges, books, photographs, and calendars are on sale. Many Argentines automatically vote Peronist, without even knowing who is running.
>
> (Poneman, p. 79)

Evita—the enduring myth. Just as Peronism has had many faces and been used for strikingly different purposes, so has the myth of Eva Perón. To traditional Peronists Evita has been pure and saintly, to anti-Peronists she has been an impure social climber, and to the Montoneros (or the leftist guerrilla group of Peronists who emerged in 1969), she was a violent revolutionary, inspiring them to storm supermarkets, kidnap billionaires, and then distribute their booty in the shantytowns (Dujovne Ortiz, p. 298). As Martínez himself has said:

> Her image is already installed in history with such force and with as many lights and shadows as that of Henry the VIII, Marie Antoinette or JFK. The immortality of great personages begins when they become a metaphor with which people can identify. Evita is already several metaphors: she is the Robin Hood of the twentieth century, she is the Cinderella of the tango and the Sleeping Beauty of Latin America. Broadway musicals and Hollywood films enrich those meanings, they don't erase them.
>
> (Martínez in *New Perspectives Quarterly,* p. 32)

Indeed, the proliferation of Evitas in film and literature has led to rivalries and controversies, as artists, like the various Peronist factions, attempt to pinpoint and present the "real" Evita. *Evita,* the U.S. musical opera, has been banned in Argentina; like many others, Menem called *Evita* "a total and absolute disgrace" for presenting Evita as a tramp who exchanged sex for social advancement (Menem in Schrieberg, p. 55). During the production of Alan Parker's 1996 film version of *Evita,* starring U.S. actress Madonna, the Argentine people had mixed reactions. Some were thrilled to be extras, but many protested the filming (and Menem refused to give it government cooperation or approval).

Reviews. Upon its publication in Buenos Aires in 1995 *Santa Evita* became the "buzz of Argentina" and an immediate bestseller. Visitors to Evita's tomb "could be seen clutching well-thumbed copies of it" (Fraser and Navarro, p. 198).

One foreign reviewer thought it was "a pity that the novel wasn't better"; "it gives the reader neither a visceral sense of Evita's life nor an understanding of the powerful hold she exerted over her country's imagination" (Kakutani, p. C31). This critic furthermore did not like the translation. But for the most part, reviews have been glowing. The writer Gabriel García Márquez called it "the novel I always wanted to read," while Mario Vargas Llosa (see ***The Storyteller,*** also covered in *Latin American Literature and Its Times*) admitted that "*Santa Evita* defeated me from the first page" (García Márquez and Vargas Llosa in Bach, p. 14). Echoing this admiration, Nicolas Shumway called Martínez a "superb craftsman" and one of Latin America's best writers: "In recent years few have confronted their countries' past with the wit, style and candor that Mr. Martínez shows in 'Santa Evita'" (Shumway, p. 27).

—Carolyn Turgeon

For More Information

Bach, Caleb. "Tomas Eloy Martínez: Imagining the Truth." *Americas* (English edition) 50, no. 3 (June 1998): 14.

Barnes, John. *Evita First Lady: A Biography of Eva Perón.* New York: Grove Press, 1978.

Dujovne Ortiz, Alicia. *Eva Perón.* Trans. Shawn Fields. New York: St. Martin's Griffin, 1996.

"Evita or Madonna: Whom Will History Remember?" *New Perspectives Quarterly* 14, no. 1 (winter 1997): 32–33.

Fraser, Nicholas, and Marysa Navarro. *Evita: The Real Life of Eva Perón.* New York: W. W. Norton, 1996.

Kakutani, Michiko. "The Legend of Evita as Latin Gothic." *The New York Times Book Review,* September 20, 1996, C31.

Madsen, Douglas, and Peter G. Snow. *The Charismatic Bond: Political Behavior in Time of Crisis.* Cambridge, Mass.: Harvard University Press, 1991.

Martínez, Tomás Eloy. *Santa Evita.* Trans. Helen Lane. New York: Alfred A. Knopf, 1996.

Page, Joseph A. "Introduction." In *In My Own Words: Evita,* by Eva Perón. New York: New Press, 1996.

Pellón, Gustavo. *The Cambridge History of Latin American Literature.* Vol. 2. Cambridge: Cambridge University Press, 1996.

Poneman, Daniel. *Argentina: Democracy on Trial.* New York: Paragon House, 1987.

Rock, David. *Argentina, 1516-1987.* Berkeley: University of California Press, 1987.

Schrieberg, David. "Don't Cry for Menem." *Newsweek* 126, no. 12 (September 25, 1997): 55.

Shumway, Nicolas. "Body Guards," *The New York Times Book Review,* September 29, 1996, 27.

Sims, Calvin. "Eva Perón's Corpse Continues to Haunt Argentina." *The New York Times,* 30 July 1995, sec. 1, p. 3.

A Short Account of the Destruction of the Indies

by
Friar Bartolomé de las Casas

> **THE LITERARY WORK**
>
> A brief personal account written in 1542; published in Spanish (*as Brevissima relación de la destrucción de las Indias*) in 1552, in English in 1583.
>
> **SYNOPSIS**
>
> Bartolomé de las Casas reports to the King of Spain on the atrocities and injustices that Spanish soldiers have committed against the native people of the Americas.

Born in Seville, Spain, in 1474, Bartolomé de las Casas was among the first wave of Spanish missionaries in the New World. From 1502 on, he lived almost continually in the New World. Although initially an owner of native slaves, he was always uneasy with the Spanish treatment of Native Americans. He experienced a spiritual turning point upon attending a sermon delivered by the Dominican friar Antonio de Montesinos, which convinced him of the injustice being wrought upon native peoples of the Americas, particularly in the Caribbean. Beginning in 1511 he raised his voice on their behalf, using his power as a Dominican friar (and eventual Bishop of Chiapas) to condemn Spanish atrocities. This effort reaches its climax in *A Short Account of the Destruction of the Indies*, a renowned description of a genocidal nightmare.

Events in History at the Time the Account Takes Place

The perils of empire. When Columbus returned from his first voyage to the New World, he did more than simply reshape the European conception of the world. As profoundly as his discovery affected science and philosophy, it made its first and most devastating impact in the fields of politics and power.

In 1492 Spain was already among Europe's principal kingdoms, wielding its power from the Netherlands to the Vatican to the Mediterranean. The news that Columbus had discovered a "New World" must have seemed like a gift from heaven: if it could exploit and export the riches of these new lands, Spain would rise, from being one kingdom among many, to undisputed preeminence in Europe. For the next century, this is precisely what happened. Competition from Portugal, France, and England was quick to arise, yet, despite this competition, by 1550 Spain was reaping the treasures of an empire that stretched from present-day California to the southernmost tip of South America. The Spanish gained wealth and power on an unprecedented scale, establishing an empire that lasted into the nineteenth century. But there was a wrinkle in the fabric of the empire: the lands that Spain had conquered were already inhabited. To benefit from the wealth of Columbus's discoveries, Spanish settlers would have to find a way to subjugate the numerous peoples and empires of the Americas.

Today it is generally assumed that the Spaniards' preferred method was simple, unmitigated brutality. Hernán Cortez's conquest of the Aztecs and Francisco Pizarro's of the Incas are only the most famous incidents in a long tragedy of greed, murder, and enslavement. There is, of course, a great deal of truth to this picture; but it is not the whole truth. Especially in the first 50 years after 1492, the Spaniards were deeply concerned that their conquest be justified, both legally and religiously. The Spanish kings, searching for a way to justify their endeavors, encouraged open debate on the subject of the Native Americans. For the first few decades, at least, it seemed possible to reconcile concern for the natives (and, especially, concern for Christianizing them) with desire for gold. This conflict is summed up in the words of Bernal Díaz, a foot soldier of the time: "We came here to serve God, and also to get rich" (Díaz in Hanke, p. 32).

A NEW WORLD?

Of course, the Western Hemisphere was "new" from the vantage point only of the Europeans, not the natives who lived there. In fact, Christopher Columbus died believing he had discovered a more efficient passage to the East Indies, not a "new" world. Subsequent voyages by Americo Vespucci confirmed that indeed Columbus had stumbled upon lands previously unknown to the Europeans, who called these lands the "Indies," "West Indies," or "New World." An account in 1507 of Vespucci's travels used "America" to designate South America and the West Indies, which others soon applied to the whole New World.

Spain's moral dilemma cannot be separated from the very source of its so-called "right" to dominance of the New World: Christianity. In the *Inter caetera,* a papal bull signed May 4, 1493, Pope Alexander VI decreed that Spain could colonize the New World, as long as it conquered in the name of Jesus Christ. In other words, Spain had lawful dominion over Native Americans but was obligated to attend to its new subjects' souls by making real efforts to convert them to Christianity. *Inter caetera* was not simply a hypocritical attempt to put a Christian face on naked greed. God spoke, it was widely believed, through the Pope's mouth; failure to obey his orders meant risking damnation after death, and dire consequences for Spain in this world. (In the *Short Account* Las Casas repeatedly warns that Spain's crimes against Native Americans will cause God to punish the nation.)

Thus, Spain had to answer two questions. First, and most urgently, it had to discover the most effective means of converting Native Americans to Christianity. Second, it had to decide how to justify declaring war on native peoples who refused to convert. From the modern perspective, it may seem as if the Spaniards decided simply to ignore the Pope's edict, as the centuries of conquest would suggest. However, in the first 50 years of Spanish presence in the Americas, this serious moral dilemma led to an open, and important, debate on the nature of Native Americans and their rights under Christian law. Las Casas is only the most famous of various defenders of native peoples.

The *encomienda* system. As soon as they arrived in the Americas, the Spanish conquerors needed to organize a system that would begin the process of Christianization ordered by the Pope. They responded to this need in a way typical of their conflicted mixture of greed and evangelism: they created the *encomienda* system.

The roots of the encomienda system lay in the 1502 proclamation of Queen Isabella of Spain, which authorized the governor of Hispaniola (present-day Haiti) to "compel and force" the natives to grow crops, construct buildings, and mine gold—for a fair wage (McAllister, p. 157). This led to the creation of encomiendas: large estates whose land was owned by the Crown, but whose peoples were entrusted to a colonist, the *encomendero.* Encomiendas were granted to those who served the King, and encomenderos were expected to care for their natives and educate them in Christianity. In reality, as Las Casas points out repeatedly, the encomenderos exploited and even tortured native peoples, and "produced little Christianity" among them (McAllister, p. 166). Las Casas reports that natives were literally worked to death by the encomendero, and killed as soon as they were too weak to work. There were encomenderos who, to enforce discipline or discover the whereabouts of gold, had natives burned at the stake or roasted on spits. The natives were essentially slaves; along with such torture, the brutal working conditions and epidemic diseases (like smallpox) brought over by the Europeans quickly killed off the once numerous populations of the New World.

Always, the Spanish were most concerned with the mining of silver and other precious metals. Crops were grown almost solely for subsis-

Spaniards torturing Indians. Engraving by Theodore de Bry for a sixteenth-century edition of *A Short Account of the Destruction of the Indies.*

tence: mining, diving for pearls, and even conducting raids on other native tribes were the chief duties of the native workers.

Moral backlash. In 1511 an almost unknown Dominican friar named Antonio de Montesinos preached a sermon in the colonial capital of Santo Domingo (in present-day Dominican Republic). In this sermon Montesino fulminated against the slave-holding Spanish: "This voice says that you are in mortal sin, that you live and die in it, for the cruelty and tyranny you use in dealing with these innocent people. Tell me, by what right or justice do you keep these Indians in such cruel and horrible servitude?" (Montesino in Hanke, p. 17). The colonists were outraged, and demanded that Montesino be punished. But while both the head of the Dominican Order in Spain, and King Ferdinand himself, threatened to punish the rebellious preacher, the sermon led directly to the first attempt to relieve the suffering of the Indians: the Laws of Burgos.

Enacted in 1512, the Laws of Burgos attempted to normalize relations between settlers and natives. The laws did not abolish slavery, but they did regulate how much work slaves could be forced to do, how they could be punished, and how they must be treated. They also defined the slaveowners' obligation to provide food, rest, and (most important) religious education. One of the laws prohibits a Spaniard "from calling an Indian 'dog' or any other name unless it is his real name"

(Hanke, p. 25). The debate over the laws established the terms of the argument for the rest of the century. One side claimed that the natives were naturally servile, and could be brought to know God only by force and labor, which justified almost anything the Spanish did to keep them in line. The other side argued that, although obligated to serve the King and God, the natives were in all other respects free and equal to Spaniards, and should be treated with no more severity than any of the King's European subjects.

THE *REQUERIMIENTO*

Perhaps no document better captures the conflict between the high ideals of the Spanish court and the sordid reality of conquest as practiced by the brutal Spanish soldiers, than the *Requerimiento.* This document was drafted in 1513, as the largest Spanish fleet yet assembled for America lay waiting in port. Designed to clarify the conditions under which the Spanish could make war on, and enslave, native peoples, it finds its justification in the Christian imperative of *Inter caetera.* One historian writes, "It begins with a brief history of the world since its creation and an account of the establishment of the Papacy, which leads naturally to a description of the donation by Alexander VI of 'these isles and Tierra Firme' to the Kings of Spain" (Hanke, p. 33). (Alexander VI is the pope who allowed Spain to settle the New World in 1493; "isles and Tierra Firme" refer to the Indies and to mainland South and Central America.) The Indians are then commanded to convert to Christianity at once, and to accept the King as their ruler. Any native who resists can be killed or enslaved.

These demands are troubling enough to modern sensibilities; but the way Spanish soldiers carried out the Requerimiento dismayed many even in the sixteenth century. Almost invariably, the document was read in Latin to uncomprehending natives. Frequently it would be read miles from a village as a sneak attack was prepared, or even from the deck of a Spanish ship. Bent on capturing Indians, soldiers on the ship would read the Requerimiento while still at sea to legalize whatever they did to the natives when they landed. In short, "the sight of Spanish swords and dogs and of their own dwellings in flames was often the first knowledge the Indians had of the presence of Christians in their midst" (Hanke, p. 34). Thinking of the Requerimiento, Las Casas said that he did not know whether he should laugh or cry.

The Laws of Burgos were an important milestone in the Conquest. For the first time, the Spanish court recognized that Native Americans had rights, and attempted to protect those rights. However, it is uncertain to what extent the laws were ever enforced. Many of the settlers were adventurers, speculators, and even convicts; they came to the New World to enjoy the kind of wealth that Spain's rigid class structure denied them at home. Living thousands of miles from the Spanish court, many undoubtedly continued to do what they pleased.

The Laws of Burgos, then, did little to stem the everyday brutality of the Conquest. But if the Laws did not stop conquistadors from slaughtering and enslaving, neither did they quiet the increasingly vocal opponents of Spanish actions. For the next 30 years, the debate continued to rage, in letters sent between the colonies and Spain; in strife between soldiers and missionaries; and in councils held at the court city of Valladolid. Over the course of these decades, the voice of Las Casas became preeminent in the defense of the natives.

Las Casas—his moral journey. Las Casas did not come to the New World to defend its native peoples. A member of the secular clergy (as opposed to a full member of a religious order), he owned a number of Indians by 1510. He was in Hispaniola when Montesino delivered his indictment, but he was not immediately convinced. He accompanied Diego Velázquez on the latter's invasion of Cuba in 1512, and was granted a fairly large encomienda. He prospered, but the seeds of discontent had been sown, in part by Montesino's speech. The massacres that accompanied the conquest of Cuba haunted Las Casas; and although he treated his slaves well, he was troubled by the severity of his fellow encomenderos.

He made a decisive break with his past in 1515. Meditating on a biblical text that condemns oppression and hypocrisy, he came to believe that "everything which had been done to the Indians in the Indies was unjust and tyrannical" (Griffin in Las Casas, p. xxii). He freed his slaves and traveled to Spain, where he informed King Ferdinand of all the atrocities he had seen. From this time on, he acted as a continual thorn in the side of the Spanish settlers, by appealing to the conscience of the Spanish court. Twice, in 1521 and from 1545 to 1560, he attempted to establish peaceful, noncoercive settlements of natives and priests; these efforts eventually succumbed to the violence and turbulence of the world outside. In the case of the second settlement (called Verapaz), the missionaries started out well, but the natives in their sphere were attacked by a band of soldiers. Not differentiating among Europeans, the natives assumed the missionaries were in league with the soldiers, and, fearing massacre, the missionaries fled. More famous than these ventures was Las Casas's writing of letters, arguments, debates, a history, a description of native cultures, and the impassioned, violent, propagandistic *A Short Account of the Destruction of the Indies.*

New Laws of 1542—first (and last) fruits. In short, Las Casas played a part in the struggles of his time far more direct and effective than that of a mere observer. He could boast of powerful allies, especially in Spain: in 1544, despite opposition from colonists, he was named Bishop of Chiapas (in southern Mexico). The most direct evidence of his impact on the debate over the Conquest are the New Laws, a sweeping (if only briefly enacted) reform of the Conquest, the encomienda system, and relations between colonist and native. These laws, passed in 1542 and repealed three years later, are generally considered to be at least partly the result of Las Casas's ceaseless agitation.

At the heart of the New Laws were two main issues: the organization of the colonial government and the treatment of native peoples. The New Laws "revoked or limited the right of the Spaniards to service and tribute from Indians, who would ultimately be put under the crown and administered by paid royal officials" (Hanke, p. 83). Another law prohibited the granting of encomiendas, and stated that all present encomiendas would revert to the Crown upon the death of the present encomendero. Thus, in terms of colonial organization, the New Laws were intended to abolish the encomienda system. They were similarly radical in their treatment of Indians: they restated the Laws of Burgos in even firmer terms, outlawed the enslavement of natives in any circumstances, and provided for punishment of any encomendero who mistreated his natives.

Las Casas, who agitated for these reforms in person, must have felt both vindication and relief. By the same token, he must not have been surprised when the inevitable happened. Encomenderos from Mexico to Peru protested loudly, unanimously, and (in the end) effectively that their rights were being trampled. In 1545 the most radical of the laws relating to the encomiendas was overturned, and following years saw further regression. Although the encomienda system was crippled in the long run, in Las Casas's time the slaveowners were the ones who won. As one historian writes, "No further attempt was made to change radically the laws and basic institutions that had been established in these fateful fifty years" (Hanke, p. 105).

Missionaries and Indians. A papal bull of 1493 allowed for the establishment of religious orders in the New World. Soon, the Franciscans, Augustinians, Jesuits, and Dominicans began to send groups across the ocean to begin evangelical activities. The Jesuits focused on native self-sufficiency and improvement through education. The Franciscans and Augustinians started the first universities. The Dominicans, Las Casas among them, recognized and emphasized the rationality of the natives and their aptitude for Christianity.

Native peoples generally accepted the missionaries because of their peaceful demeanor, their acceptance of native traditions, and their skill as healers (the Franciscans in particular held this distinction). Las Casas notes that missionaries who could preach without interruption from soldiers were welcomed with open arms. However, the relationship followed a downward pattern. At first, the clergy made concessions to the natives, and learned their languages and customs in order to better preach the gospel. Focusing on children, the missionaries fostered a teacher-student relationship, but allowed native practices to continue as long as they did not breach the basic tenets of Christianity. Conflict began when priests questioned native practices such as incest and bigamy. "Initially, Indians tended to allow missionaries to get a foot in the door. Often that was followed within a generation or two by rebellion intended to expel priest and civilians alike" (Deeds, p. 78). Las Casas himself blames not the priests, but the intrusions of Spanish soldiers for the disintegration of trust and respect. On more than one occasion, he bemoans the fate of missions, like his own Verapaz, that were sabotaged by the greed of roving Spaniards. He predicts that "the Indians would turn against them [the missionaries at Verapaz] once more, especially since it was no longer possible to preach the word of God without incidents caused by the wicked Spaniards" (Las Casas, *A Short Account of the Destruction of the Indies,* p. 86).

The Account in Focus

Contents summary. *A Short Account of the Destruction of the Indies* is a brief yet highly repetitious book. After three dedications (designed to secure the book a royal audience), Las Casas starts the text proper with its unvarying pattern: the description of an area and when it was conquered, followed by graphic descriptions of the brutal actions of the Spanish there. He holds to this pattern for 19 chapters, following the path of conquest from Hispaniola to Peru. While details vary from region to region, the larger picture never changes: the natives of a region were peaceful and virtuous, welcoming the Spaniards in all hospitality; the Spaniards responded with unprovoked fury, massacring, torturing, and enslaving their hosts. Driven by a lust for gold and pearls, the Spaniards not only ignored their duty to spread Christianity; they also forgot how to be Christians themselves, committing the worst acts of blood lust as casually as they would eat dinner.

Las Casas uses two kinds of evidence to illustrate Spanish atrocities. The first is statistical. He estimates that at least 12 million Native Americans were killed in the first 40 years of conquest, and suggests that the real number may be closer to 15 million. He peppers his account with reports of 30,000 natives killed in a single massacre, or of whole islands depopulated in a matter of months. While such numbers are only approximate, they undoubtedly convey a sense of the grand scale of Spanish brutality. However, it is Las Casas's other type of evidence—anecdotal—that most moves the reader. The majority of the book is taken up by tales of unconscionable violence. Las Casas reports Spaniards raping, roasting, impaling Native Americans—not only men in battle, but also women and children. He reports that Spaniards would often crowd a house with the leaders of a tribe, on the pretext of a feast, and then set the house on fire, hacking to death anyone who attempted to escape. He repeatedly deplores the vicious mastiffs trained to hunt the natives who fled into the mountains; often, he claims, Indian-hunting became a sport as popular as fox-hunting. One of the most famous incidents described by Las Casas involves four or five nobles tortured over an open fire. Their screams disturbed the Governor's nap: he ordered the torturer to cease. But the torturer, unwilling to loose his captives, stuffed bungs in their mouths to stop their cries, and continued the torture.

Las Casas contrasts these horrors with the peacefulness and hospitality of the Indians. Here he follows a pattern common to many chroniclers and propagandists of the time: he exaggerates details to create the image of a utopia in the New World. Partly to refute those conquistadors who justified their terror by accentuating the sloth and viciousness of Native Americans, he paints a picture of the natives as nearly perfect: kind, gentle, hospitable, and ripe to hear the word of God. He writes, "These people are the most guileless, the most devoid of wickedness and duplicity, the most obedient to their native masters and to the Spanish Christians whom they serve" (*Short Account*, p. 28). On the few occasions in which he mentions a native rebellion, he always points out that it is more than justified by native grievances. Against this background, the greed of the Spaniards shines even darker. The Spaniards, Las

HATUEY, A CUBAN LEADER

Las Casas repeatedly asserts that the Spanish in the New World have forgotten God, and now worship only gold. He compares them to Jeroboam, the Jewish king of the Old Testament book of I Kings who ordered his people to worship golden calves. To emphasize the effect this lust for wealth has on the natives, Las Casas recounts the story of Hatuey. This Arawak leader moved his people from Hispaniola (now Haiti) to Cuba, hoping to escape the terrors of the Spanish. When he learned that the Spanish were mounting an expedition to Cuba, he addressed his people. Las Casas reports the speech as follows:

> "They have a God whom they worship and adore, and it is in order to get that God from us so that they can worship Him that they conquer us and kill us." He had beside him as he spoke a basket filled with gold jewelry and he said, "Here is the God of the Christians. . . . Mark you: if we keep this God about us, they will kill us in order to get their hands on him. Let us throw Him into this river."
>
> (*Short Account*, pp. 27-28)

Hatuey's assumption, based on the behavior of the Spanish, was that they worshipped gold as a god and wanted to take his tribe's gold so that they could have more to worship. Overall, the story encapsulates the tragic irony of the Conquest: the Spaniards lost all sense of devotion to Christian ethics, even though they used Christ to justify their bloody deeds. Thus, in their treatment of the natives, they emulated the demons of Christian hell, and were doomed to damnation themselves according to the terms of their own religion.

Hatuey was eventually captured and condemned to be burned alive. In an effort to save his soul, a friar explained heaven, hell, and God to him. The chief asked if Christians went to heaven, and when told that they did, he said he chose hell, so as never to have to see a Christian again.

Casas claims, begin their slaughters instantly, without provocation, and for no other reason than to strike terror into the hearts of the survivors. And even though those survivors remain obedient to their oppressors, their nightmare does not end. In slavery, they are worked mercilessly in gold mines or in the fields. They are chained around the neck; when a slave collapses, unable to work anymore, he is instantly beheaded so that the chain need not be broken. Perhaps most horrific is the fate of the pearl diver. These slaves lived in water from dawn until dusk, diving 30 feet and more to claw at oysters on the sea floor. Those who did not fall prey to sharks died in a few weeks anyway, as the stress of repeated diving caused fatal hemorrhaging, and the cold water caused pneumonia.

It is undeniable that the *Short Account* fed anti-Spanish sentiment from the 1550s until modern times. In the sixteenth century, it was translated into numerous European languages, often accompanied by lurid illustrations. The book was reprinted as recently as the Spanish American War of 1898, for purposes of propaganda. However, this denigration of Spain had nothing to do with Las Casas's own intentions. In his time, Spain, arguably the most important country in Europe, was engaged in countless political and religious struggles with all its neighbors. Thus, the European interest in the *Short Account* had less to do with concern for Native Americans than with a desire to blacken Spain at any cost. Las Casas himself was motivated by a deep concern for Spain's welfare, which he feared was threatened by the nation's own evil actions. He gave orders that his final book (a critical history of Spain in the New World) not be published until 40 years after his death, and then only if its publication would not harm Spain in any way. The book was not published until the 1850s.

Although descriptions of these inhumanities take up the majority of the *Short Account,* they are not the essence of Las Casas's narrative. He wants the bloodshed to stop; but he wants it to stop so that true Christianity can take root in the New World. Las Casas reminds his readers again and again that the natives are ready to hear the word of Christ, and that only the greed and violence of the Spanish hold them back. Even more than the hellish physical torture they suffered in this world, Las Casas laments the eternal torture natives would suffer as non-Christians. Most of them were killed before they even had a chance to hear of the faith that Las Casas believes would have assured them of heaven.

Worse, they were killed by the very people responsible for converting them. Las Casas does not doubt that the Spaniards deserve to possess the New World. He even affirms that they deserve some authority over native peoples. But this authority is based on the fact that the Spanish are Christians, and thus the authority must be exercised in a Christian way. Not only must the Spaniards attempt to gain converts; more basically, they are required to treat Native Americans as fellow human beings, entitled to life and property and protected by law and justice. Instead, Las Casas insists, the Spanish have conducted nothing more than a naked grab for power, gold, and prestige. He warns that such misdeeds destroy natives and doom the conquerors to hell; the wrongdoings also threaten to draw God's wrath upon Spain itself. Thus, he implores the Spanish Crown to order an end to the bloodshed before it is too late.

THE BLACK LEGEND

Despite his strenuous objections to his country's conduct in the New World, Las Casas remained a loyal subject of Spain and its King. Thus, he would have been dismayed to learn that his *Short Account* became the critical document in the *Leyendo Negro,* the Black Legend. One historian defines the Leyendo Negro as "traditional literature that criticizes the people, history, and national character of Spain, in part for cruelty in the conquest of native America, and in part for bigotry, pride, hypocrisy, and other more or less undesirable attributes" (Gibson, p. 4). The theory of the Leyenda Negra was developed by Spanish historians early in this century; invariably, they pointed to Las Casas as the first and most important figure in the creation of the legend.

The great debate of Sepúlveda and Las Casas. Deep behind Las Casas's assertion of Native American nobility lies what was, for European Christians, a debatable question: what kind of humans were the newly discovered peoples? For Las Casas and his supporters, the answer was simply that Native Americans were human, and lacked only knowledge of Christ to make them equal to Europeans. This side seems to have been supported by Pope Paul III's 1537 bull *Sublimis Deus,* which declared that Indians were created by God with human souls. However, the situa-

Bartolomé de las Casas

tion was more complex. Other clerics and lawyers, finding support in Aristotle and some Church Fathers, advanced a more negative view of Indians. (In *Politics,* Aristotle speculates that there may be in the world "natural slaves," or humans so base and ignorant that they are fit only to serve better humans.) Without denying the natives' basic humanity, these clerics and lawyers propounded a view of the natives as vicious, animalistic humans. The Native Americans, they argued, were slaves by nature; the only way for Spaniards to convert them was to drag them forcibly from their own sloth. These two sides waged a running battle throughout the first half of the sixteenth century, beginning with the debate over the Laws of Burgos. One of the most famous incidents in this battle was the debate between Las Casas and Juan Ginés de Sepúlveda, the chaplain to the King of Spain. This debate took place in 1551 in the Junta of Valladolid, a kind of court for judging grievances and points of law in Valladolid, Spain. Although it had little practical effect on Spain's policies, the debate stands as a cultural and historical lightning rod. One historian writes, "For the first time in history, a nation and her king initiated discussions concerning the justice of a war that was being waged" (Losada, p. 279). In addition, his experience in the Junta seems to have prompted Las Casas to publicly print his *Short Account* the following year. It had been read to the King in 1542, but apparently the friar now came to realize that it needed a wider audience.

The debate was extremely intellectual, but it originated as much in personal grudges as in Aristotelean theory. In 1548 Sepúlveda's book *The Second Democrates; Or, the Just Causes of the War Against the Indians* was refused the royal license that all books in Spain needed before publication. Sepúlveda suspected, probably correctly, that Las Casas had campaigned to have his book refused. Sepúlveda complained to the Council of the Indies, which organized a debate between the two men in 1550. This was not a debate in modern terms: the two men were never in the same room at the same time. They took turns, several months apart, presenting their cases to a panel of judges, and then replying to a summary of the other's arguments.

Each session filled several days of long, abstract, highly learned arguments. But the basic argument was simple. Sepúlveda claimed that the Indians were the natural slaves hypothesized by Aristotle: this class of people was fit only to serve better people. War against the natives was justified, because only by war could they be forced to accept Christianity. Finally, war was urgently needed to end the vile practices of cannibalism, human sacrifice, and idolatry that Sepúlveda claimed were endemic to South America. All of his more rarefied philosophical arguments boiled down to the belief that the natives were "homunculi in whom hardly a vestige of humanity remains . . . pigs with their eyes always fixed on the ground" (Sepúlveda in Las Casas, p. xxviii).

Las Casas's reply was equally simple; but, in the process of making it, he advanced a number of ideas that were remarkably progressive, and all but unspeakably radical for his time. His first complaint was that Sepúlveda, who had never been to the New World, relied for his knowledge of the Indians on the accounts of conquistadors and slaveowners. Thus, he himself, Las Casas, is eminently more qualified to judge the nature of the natives. He rejects the assertion of their natural slavery first by his own reading of Aristotle, and then by recourse to his personal experience. According to Aristotle, says Las Casas, the number of humans who fall in the category of natural slaves is very small; Native Americans are too numerous and prosperous to fit this category. In other words, they are not natural slaves. They therefore deserve the same rights of sovereignty that Aristotle says should be given to all peoples, even those that are conquered. Las Casas asserts that war is justified only in extreme circumstances, and that nothing in America has met those circumstances. Most startling, he offers a defense of native practices that foreshadows the cultural relativism of modern times. He admits that cannibalism and human sacrifice exist, although he denies their prevalence; but he also argues that even these horrendous practices do not justify slaughter.

> Clearly one cannot prove in a short time or with a few words to infidels, especially the Indians, that to sacrifice men to God is contrary to nature; consequently neither anthropophagy nor human sacrifice constitutes just cause for making war. . . . [T]hey are not obliged to abandon the religion of their forefathers until they come to know another which they find better.
>
> (Las Casas in Losada, p. 297)

The answer, as always for Las Casas, is peaceful preaching.

The Junta was remarkably inconclusive. It did not affect Spanish policy in the least. Both sides claimed victory; although, inasmuch as Sepúlveda's book was never licensed, he was perhaps the loser. Exactly what prompted Las Casas to publish his own book the following year is uncertain. He may have felt the time was ripe for swaying public opinion, that given the debate, he would be striking at a moment when the Court was favorably disposed to his view. In any case, his book was licensed in 1552.

Literary context. Las Casas's book is at once unique and extremely traditional. His boldness in criticizing his own country's policies, and especially his recognition of Native American culture and achievement, are fairly unusual. In addition, his courage in pressing his complaint to the King, and eventually even publishing his book, are noteworthy. However, precisely because Las Casas is so well remembered, it is easy to forget that he did not operate alone. A fairly large group of clerics, both in the New World and in Spain, agreed with him, including, for example, Fray Juan Fernandez de Angulo, Marcos de Niza, and Juan del Valle. Las Casas was always the most vocal, but never the only, proponent of Indian rights. And, inasmuch as his complaints frequently found a sympathetic royal ear, we may conclude that all but his most radical assertions played on the conscience of the Spanish court. In other words, he was simply expressing unequivocally an issue that the court was concerned with in a more ambivalent way: the justice of its actions in the Americas. To understand this, it is necessary to remember an aspect of sixteenth-century Spain that is all but forgotten now: its obsession with legalism. This was a country in which a powerful, politically vital fleet was held in port for weeks while lawyers drafted the Requerimiento; a country in which the court would listen to the most subtle philosophical and religious arguments for days on end. It is in this context that Las Casas tendered his *Short Account*. In many ways, his thought prefigures that of the twentieth century; in just as many ways, it would have been at home in the twelfth century. Las Casas was heir to a long tradition of extremely sophisticated argumentation, developed by scholars from Aristotle to St. Thomas Aquinas, and practiced with the utmost sincerity by a whole class of clerics and lawyers.

Events in History at the Time the Account Was Written

After the New Laws of 1542. For an all too brief period after the New Laws of 1542, it must have seemed as if the disastrous side-effects of the Conquest could be reversed: Spain appeared to have come to its senses and to be accentuating the more altruistic side of its mission to the New World. It was a tack that would last only as long as it took the colonists to remind the King of their importance, both as subjects and as creators of wealth. The sections of the New Laws that regulated treatment of natives were never revoked, but the central laws that might have permanently altered the situation (such as the abolition of encomiendas or the punishment of abusive slaveowners) were. Las Casas lived his last decades without being rewarded for his efforts. He continued to agitate and wrote two voluminous scholarly books on the New World. But as the tumultuous sixteenth century drew to a close, it became increasingly apparent that the Conquest would follow, if in a somewhat mitigated fashion, the furious pattern of its first half century. In the end, the encomienda system would expire, not because of Las Casas's efforts, but rather because of the greed of the settlers themselves—native populations dwindled and the precious metals dried up, becoming harder to find.

Impact. In retrospect, however, Las Casas was hardly a failure. His effect on the course of Spain's endeavors cannot be overstated. Ironically, the man who spent his life vindicating the humanity of Native Americans has become, for history, the figure who vindicates the humanity of Spaniards. Without his presence, an already black history would appear utterly bleak. He has been called the true conscience of the Conquest: "For many, both in Spain and beyond, his presence seems, somehow, to redeem the inescapable complicity of all Europe in the Spanish conquest" (Griffin in Las Casas, p. xiii). This is undoubtedly overstated: nothing can erase the slaughter of the conquistadors. But his memory should remind modern readers that, however sad the actual events of the Conquest are, for at least a little while Europe was able to pause and consider the injustice and impropriety of its invasion. Its motives were never simple, unalloyed greed.

Since his death, Las Casas's reputation has grown in Latin America and elsewhere. He was the unwitting servant of anti-Spanish propagandists in the sixteenth and seventeenth centuries. During South America's wars of independence from Spain in the nineteenth century, he was often cited as a prophetic figure, one who insisted on the rights of indigenous peoples to govern themselves. Even today, as much of Latin America struggles with the long after-effects of colonialism, he is cited in this regard. His insistence on the virtues of peace, humility, and poverty have made him a hero to many liberation theologians—those modern Christians who attempt to reconcile Christianity with social justice. He is, in brief, one of those writers whose memory looms so large not only because of what he wrote, but also because of how he lived. The eighteenth-century French philosopher Denis Diderot proposed a statue of Las Casas whose legend would read: "In a century of ferocity, Las Casas, whom you see before you, was a benevolent man" (Diderot in Las Casas, p. xiv). It is a simple statement of an almost impossible feat for the time. Las Casas achieved it through personal action, eloquent debate, and largely through writing.

—Soraya Alamdari and Jacob Littleton

For More Information

Biermann, Benno M. "Bartolomé de Las Casas and Verapaz." In *Bartolomé de Las Casas and History*. Ed. Juan Friede and Benjamin Keen. DeKalb: Northern Illinois Press, 1971.

Deeds, Susan M. "Indigenous Responses to Mission Settlement in Nueva Vizcaya." In *The New Latin American Mission History*. Ed. Erick Langer and Robert H. Jackson. Lincoln: University of Nebraska Press, 1995.

Gibson, Charles. *The Black Legend: Anti-Spanish Attitudes in the Old World and the New*. New York: Alfred A. Knopf, 1971.

Hanke, Lewis. *The Spanish Struggle for Justice in the Conquest of America*. Boston: Little, Brown, 1965.

Keen, Benjamin. *Essays in the Intellectual History of Colonial Latin America*. Boulder, Colo.: Westview Press, 1998.

Las Casas, Bartolomé de. *A Short Account of the Destruction of the Indies*. Trans. Nigel Griffin. London: Penguin, 1992.

Losada, Angel. "The Controversy Between Sepúlveda and Las Casas in the Junta of Valladolid." In *Bartolomé de Las Casas in History*. Ed. Juan Friede and Benjamin Keen. DeKalb: Northen Illinois Press, 1971.

McAllister, Lyle N. *Spain and Portugal in the New World, 1492-1700*. Minneapolis: University of Minnesota Press, 1984.

"The South"

by
Jorge Luis Borges

Born in Buenos Aires, Argentina, on August 24, 1899, to middle-class parents of Spanish and English descent, Jorge Luis Borges would become the undisputed giant of Latin American letters. Shy and bookish, a librarian by profession, Borges reflected throughout his career on the lives of his heroic Argentine relatives and on the myths and realities of the nation's (often violent) character. When "The South" appeared in the two-volume 1956 edition of *Ficciones* (in the volume *Artifices*), Borges wrote in the preface that the story was perhaps his finest to date. It achieves a dreamlike, romanticized treatment of elements embedded in the Argentine sense of national heritage, namely of the violence and cruelty attached to the traditional rural lifestyle. In the mid-twentieth century Argentina was testing different versions of nationalism. One view holds that the story reflects tensions and fears felt by many Argentine citizens at the time.

THE LITERARY WORK

A short story set in the city of Buenos Aires and in the Argentine countryside in 1939; published in Spanish (as "El Sur") in the Buenos Aires newspaper *La Nación* on February 8, 1953, and in the two-volume *Ficciones* edition of 1956; first published in English in 1962 in the collection *Ficciones*.

SYNOPSIS

A man who prides himself on being Argentine appears to recover his cultural past at the expense of his life.

Events in History at the Time the Short Story Takes Place

"La década infame." In 1939, on the eve of World War II, Argentina was witnessing the end of the so-called "infamous decade" of the 1930s, in which conservative politicians consistently rigged elections to keep themselves in power. The decade was characterized by, among other things, burgeoning and competing philosophies of Argentine nationalism and the political expressions thereof. In 1930, in a bloodless coup, a coalition of conservative and nationalist politicians overthrew the Radical government of Hipólito Yrigoyen. The new leader of the nation, General José Félix Uriburu, courted European-style fascism, which relied on rule by a military-backed dictator and which elevated nation and race over the individual. Fascism had steadily been gaining political ground in Italy and Germany, and it took root in Argentina as well. The period of Uriburu's rule (1930-32) oversaw a shift in political power from Argentina's middle-class to its growing and sometimes ruthless political-military machine. Foreigners lived under the threat of deportation; anti-government activists were in danger of arrest, torture, and even execution.

In 1932 the conservatives overpowered the nationalists and General Agustín Justo became president. Justo favored the wealthy landowners and exporters from the pampas (Argentina's fertile grasslands), and instituted a number of juntas, or regulatory boards, to support rural agricultural producers. In response to pressure from such outlying areas of its empire as Australia and South Africa, Great Britain—Argentina's most significant trading partner—had threatened to cut off or greatly reduce its importation of Argentine beef. Justo responded quickly to this threat. In the Roca-Runciman agreement of 1933 (and again in the Eden-Malbrán treaty of 1936), the two nations arrived at a settlement whereby Argentina would continue to export beef to Britain at the same levels as always, and Britain would gain important concessions for British businesses (notably the railroads) operating in Argentina (Rock, pp. 224-25). Heated opposition rose up against the concessions granted to the beef industry in the Roca-Runciman treaty; some opponents protested that Britain was being offered outrageously advantageous terms, while others claimed that this settlement was merely a way of protecting the wealthy ranchers who backed Justo's government (Rock, p. 227). As will be discussed below, these ranchers did not share their wealth with the workers who labored for them.

The resentment about the clout that Britain enjoyed in Argentina played into a new manifestation of nationalism that emerged mid-decade to join the more radical right-wing strain represented by Uriburu. Characteristics of this nationalism were its championship of the Church (clericalism) and of all things Argentine (nativism), as well as policies of anti-Semitism, antianarchism, and fierce anticommunism. In 1934 the U.S. oil company Standard Oil became embroiled in a price war with Argentina's national oil company, Yacimientos Petrolíferos Fiscales (YPF); Justo's government had to bail out YPF, which had difficulty competing with Standard Oil, and protest erupted over this perceived instance of U.S. imperialism. (A noticeable anti-U.S. resentment had first emerged in Argentina in the late 1920s, also tied to the business practices of American oil interests.) Eventually, in 1937, Justo gave YPF a monopoly over all oil imported into the nation, and made it illegal for any oil to be exported (Lewis, p. 55). Meanwhile, politicians and historians were examining what they perceived as the destructive influence of Britain in Argentine history, drawing attention to such things as "the British invasions of 1806-1807, Britain's role in the foundation of Uruguay in the late 1820s, its seizure of the Falkland Islands in 1833, the blockades under Rosas, the later collaboration between the ruling oligarchy and British business interests"; the upshot of such public discourse was that the pro-Britain Justo felt himself challenged by pro-nationalists, some of whom were vocal members of the Argentine army (Rock, p. 230).

In fact, Justo did support nationalist, militaristic organizations. He financially and politically backed two that had been created by his predecessor, Uriburu; the first, the Special Section, a branch of the federal police, hired tough men to "beat up and torture the government's opponents"; the second, the Argentine Civic Legion, which modeled itself on and wore the same distinctive brown shirts as the German stormtroopers, announced that Argentina was destined to dominate South America (Lewis, p. 119). Under the guidance of General Juan Bautista Molina, who had strong Nazi leanings and who took over the organization in 1936, the Civic League grew to have as many as 10,000 members (Lewis, p. 119). In Borges's short story "The South," violence overtakes an average citizen at the hands of uncouth rural thugs. In fact, in the time at which the story is set, violence, or the threat thereof, was percolating throughout Argentine society and would remain pervasive in 1953, when Borges first published the tale. Such violence was not new to Argentina society. A hundred years earlier, the dictator Juan Manuel de Rosas (ruled 1835 to 1852) had "a band of spies and thugs" torture, murder, and imprison his enemies (Shumway, p. 120). Subsequent outbreaks of brutality in Argentina are seen as a return to this original violence.

The Argentine South. In "The South" Juan Dahlmann boards a 7:30 a.m. train in downtown Buenos Aires and travels south, through the city's suburbs, around small farms, and into the nation's preeminent ranching district, disembarking at sunset. Such a journey would have taken him into the heart of the pampas, which comprise most of the Argentine provinces of Buenos Aires and La Pampa. Vast, treeless, stoneless, relentlessly flat, and incredibly fertile, the pampas form "a near semi-circle roughly five hundred miles in radius from the River Plate estuary" (Rock, p. 2). Although the pampas also stretch north of the city of Buenos Aires and into Uruguay, the majority of Argentina's grassy plains are to the city's south. Because of the area's economic importance, railroads and roads crisscross the countryside, which is home to the cowboylike *gauchos* that figure in fact and legend.

The Argentine pampas.

On the eve of World War II, when the short story is set, the Argentine South was experiencing rapid change. At the national level, in a trend begun in the late 1930s, for the first time industrial production started to surpass agriculture; industry finally became the most valuable component of the Argentine economy in 1943 (Rock, p. 232). As the economy changed so did demographics; migrants poured out of the rural areas (an average of 70,000 per year between 1937 and 1943), mostly from the pampas, into the cities. "Before 1946, an estimated two-thirds of the migrants came from the pampas, perhaps as much as 40 percent of them from the province of Buenos Aires alone" (Rock, p. 235).

The pampas dwellers flooded into the cities for various reasons—chief among them was economic hardship. Many of the workers on the pampas were itinerant laborers, who would move from place to place as jobs opened up. Their wages amounted to much less—up to four times less—than those of city laborers (Rock, p. 236).

Also reflected in the short story is the prevalence of absentee landlords on the pampas. The protagonist Juan Dahlmann owns a ranch in the South that he has but rarely visited; in this regard, he resembles 62 percent of the actual landlords in the South at the time (Rock, p. 237). Some 20,000 of these landlords, most of whom rarely or never appeared, owned nearly three-quarters of the pampas. "The South" is vague as to just how much land Dahlmann owns, but the story refers to his "ranch." Given the fact that there were large ranches on the pampas that sometimes covered hundreds of square miles, Dahlmann's may have been sizable. Such ranches thrived on the hard laborer of the workers, who in many cases harbored resentment against the wealthy absentee landlords. Such festering resentment helps explain the tension between the rough-looking rural laborers and Dahlmann in the story.

The gaucho and *Argentinidad*. In much the same way that the cowboy has become an enduring symbol of the United States, particularly of the nation's rugged individualism, so has the gaucho become an important symbol of *Argentinidad*—that which is perceived as being essentially Argentine. The gauchos, a largely mestizo population, traditionally roamed the pampas, living off free-range cattle, which they would avail themselves of as needed. Without license to do so, they rode wild horses and slaughtered the cattle to meet demands for their byproducts. Under Spanish colonial rule, the gauchos ran what was essentially a black market in tallow, hides, and beef. They lived in small ramshackle houses constructed of and furnished with whatever materials were at hand. The gaucho developed a reputation for cunning and violence; he typically carried a long (up to 27 inches) dagger, or *facón*. In "The South," a slumped-over ancient gaucho throws this archetypal weapon to Juan Dahlmann. In real life, gauchos frequented *pulperías*—a combination general store, restaurant, and tavern, not unlike the establishment at which Juan Dahlmann will meet his destiny.

When the pampas were fenced in 1845 and individual ranches became clearly demarcated, the free-wheeling life of the gauchos drew to a close. Their itinerant lifestyle became criminalized and many were either forced to do the staid agricultural—as opposed to ranching—work that they despised, or were conscripted into the Argentine army to fight the native peoples, who resisted being pushed from their traditional homelands by the flood of incoming European ranchers. In the last quarter of the nineteenth century the traditional gauchos disappeared; they were replaced by a straggling population of demoralized and exploited ranch-hands. The gaucho that Juan Dahlmann in 1939 calls "outside time" was by then a figure of the mythic past (Borges, "The South," p. 178).

The gaucho's transformation into a heroic icon is indebted largely to the publication of José Hernández's 1872 poem ***The Gaucho Martín Fierro*** (also covered in *Latin American Literature and Its Times)*. Hernández wrote sympathetically of the plight of the gaucho civilization, doomed as it was by the political machinations, economic greed, and overt racism of Argentina's elite classes in the nineteenth century. "I have tried," he wrote, "to present a type who personifies the character of our gauchos . . . the impetuousness of his pride, excessive to the point of crime; and all the drive and tumult found in children of nature who remain unpolished and unrefined by education" (Hernández in Shumway, p. 265). Hernández's poem instantly became central to rural Argentine culture—people could recite long passages of it, the gauchos adopted it as part of their own heritage, and the poem cemented the formation of a type of gaucho national literature. Preceding the poem were other gauchesque works by writers such as Bartolomé Hidalgo, Hilario Ascasubi, and Estanislao del Campo. Argentine culture as a whole was divided about the value of these works, but by the time of Borges's short story, even the cultural elite had begun to hold up Hernandez's poem as an example of the essentially heroic Argentine character. The wild ruffian haunting the borders of civilization became valorized as an important symbol of what it meant to be Argentine: fiercely independent, self-reliant, and possessed of a distinctively non-European culture. This certainly is what city-dweller and intellectual Juan Dahlmann of "The South," who embraces rural traditions that are only partly his own, sees in the poem. All this must be viewed in the context of the nationalist sentiments that were on the rise in Argentina at the time. But even now, to say of a man in Argentina that he is *muy gaucho* is to heap praise upon that person.

BORGES AND THE GAUCHO TRADITION

In a 1951 lecture (first published in the magazine *Sur* in 1955) entitled "The Argentine Writer and Tradition" Borges claims that so-called *gauchesque* poetry (which was never written by the gauchos themselves, who were usually illiterate) is an utterly fabricated literary tradition defined more by propaganda and artificial language than by any genuine rendering of the gaucho lifestyle, and that the gaucho himself is the embodiment of Argentine provincialism, of its lack of sophistication and polish. For Borges, the genre, which he admits has produced admirable works, is too self-consciously preoccupied with "being Argentine." "Nationalists pretend to venerate the capacities of the Argentine mind but want to limit the poetic exercise of that mind to a few impoverished local themes," writes Borges. "As if we Argentines could only speak of *orillas* [outbacks] and *estancias* [ranches] and not of the universe" (Borges, *Labyrinths,* p. 182). Borges points out that Argentine nationalists often hold up Ricardo Güiraldes's renowned 1926 novel *Don Segundo Sombra* as a model of the gauchesque tradition, and yet this work draws heavily on the references to India in Rudyard Kipling's *Kim,* which was, in turn, influenced by Mark Twain's Mississippi River novel *Huckleberry Finn.* For Borges, influences across space and time lead to a literary tradition more than any obsession with local color or national culture. As demonstrated by "The South," Borges himself found Argentine issues and settings compelling subjects, but he refused to limit his stories to this locally tinged content. Rather his strength lies in bringing to light the universality in what was Argentine and in relating Argentina to subjects and settings outside its own particular sphere.

A modern-day gaucho at work.

The Short Story in Focus

Plot summary. Juan Dahlmann, civic librarian, considers himself to be "profoundly Argentine" ("The South," p. 174). He descends from the Germanic Johannes Dahlmann, a minister, who arrived in Buenos Aires from Europe in 1871. However, he more greatly values his mother's *criollo* (Spanish Argentine) lineage. (More broadly, *criollo* is a term for a person of Spanish descent born in the Americas). Her father, Francisco Flores, served as a soldier who died fighting the Indians on the border of Buenos Aires province, probably in 1874. From this heroic grandfather Dahlmann has developed a notion of his "Argentinization," the prime elements of which include "an old sword, a locket containing the daguerreotype of a bearded, inexpressive man, the joy and courage of certain melodies, the habit of certain verses in *Martín Fierro,* the passing years, a certain lack of spiritedness, and solitude" ("The South," p. 174). As part of this romantic idea about the Argentine past and his own place in the progression of history, Dahlmann has retained his maternal family's ranch, although he has not been there in years.

In February 1939, while intently reading *The Arabian Nights,* Dahlmann runs into the corner of a casement window in his building; the wound becomes infected and a fever sets in. Eventually the librarian is taken to a sanatorium by his physician, and undergoes a myriad of painful and humiliating treatments to cure the septicemia (blood poisoning) that has nearly killed him. It is arranged for him to travel to his ranch in the South to complete his recuperation. He takes *The Arabian Nights* with him on the train as a talisman to remind him that the forces of evil have been thwarted by his recovery in the sanatorium, but he soon puts it down to enjoy the sights of the countryside through which he is passing, and to "allow himself simply to live" ("The South," p. 176). As he whisks through the landscape (complete with horsemen, lakes, pastures, and glowing clouds) made dreamlike and ideal by his nostalgia, he finds that he recognizes even the vegetation, although he could not name the things he sees—"his direct knowledge of the country was considerably inferior to his nostalgic, literary knowledge" ("The South," p. 177). In the growing solitude, which he senses is "perhaps hostile," Dahlmann begins to feel as though he were traveling not only deeper into the southern countryside, but retreating into the past as well: "In fact," explains one literary interpreter, "when he thinks he is going south, to the estancia, to recover his health, he is really going south to recover an image of his past" (Sarlo, p. 46).

As he nears his destination Dahlmann learns that the train will not stop at its usual station; he welcomes this potentially annoying information as an opportunity to have an adventure. He waits at a small local store/restaurant, outside of which there are horses tied up, for a ride to his country home. His fellows there are "rough-looking young men" and an ancient gaucho in authentic costume who "seemed to be outside time" ("The South," p. 178).

> Dahlmann was warmed by the rightness of the man's hairband, the baize poncho he wore, his gaucho trousers, and the boots made out of the skin of a horse's leg, and he said to himself, recalling futile arguments with people from districts in the North, or from Entre Rios, that only in the South did gauchos like that exist anymore.
>
> ("The South," p. 178)

Over a simple dinner Dahlmann becomes gradually aware of the drunken antagonism of these characters toward him and eventually one of them, "the young thug with the Indian-looking face," challenges him to a knife fight outside ("The South," p. 179). As the shopkeeper protests that Dahlmann is unarmed, the old gaucho suddenly throws the sick man a dagger. When he instinctively picks it up, Dahlmann realizes that this action has more or less committed him to fighting the other man. He also realizes that "the weapon would serve less to defend him than to justify the other man's killing him" ("The South," p. 179). As the story ends, Dahlmann goes outside with the man, prepared to die:

> They went outside, and while there was no hope in Dahlmann, there was no fear, either. As he crossed the threshold, he felt on that first night in the sanatorium, when they'd stuck that needle into him, dying in a knife fight under the open sky, grappling with his adversary, would have been a liberation, a joy, and a fiesta. He sensed that had he been able to choose or dream his death that night, this is the death he would have dreamed or chosen.
>
> Dahlmann firmly grips the knife, which he may have no idea how to manage, and steps out into the plains.
>
> ("The South," p. 179)

This climactic scene, a knife fight with a stranger, is a romantic, gauchesque way to die, a fate far worthier of an Argentine than blood poisoning. It is as out of kilter with the rest of the story as a sprinkling of other details: the clothing on the old gaucho, which is typical of the nineteenth, not the twentieth, century and the facts that the shopkeeper calls the unidentified stranger, Señor Dahlmann, by name, and that this shopkeeper reminds Dahlman of the personnel at the sanatorium.

Borges as the Argentine writer. The 1950s were a heady and traumatic decade for the middle-aged Borges. He achieved international acclaim in 1951 upon the publication of two short story collections (the first in Buenos Aires under the title *Death and the Compass*; the second in Paris under the title *Ficciones*). In 1953 a third collection (called *Labyrinths*) was included in *La Croix du Sud* (The Southern Cross), a French series on Latin American literature. Meanwhile, back in Argentina, scholars began publishing articles on Borges's writings.

At the same time Borges became the focus of a vigorous debate on the proper cultural and political role for Argentine writers. At issue was whether writers ought to address the circumstances of their place and time in history, as literary critics of the time suggested and as readers began to demand. Committed to literature for its own sake rather than for the sake of realism or social commentary, Borges could not have been more inimical to this demand. His fictions tended to feature characters in search of themselves

KNIFE FIGHTS

In "The South" Juan Dahlmann takes a cup of coffee "a few yards from Yrigoyen's house"; the brief reference here is undoubtedly to one-time Argentine President Hipólito Yrigoyen, who died in 1933, imprisoned under house arrest in the city of Buenos Aires ("The South," p. 176). This reference lends credence to one interpretation of the story, which posits that Juan Dahlmann, hero of "The South," does not in fact die in a knife fight on the pampas at sundown, but "imprisoned in a sanatorium and subjected to methodical attentions," he dreams a heroic death for himself as, in truth, he dies under the surgeon's knife in the hospital ("The South," pp. 176-77). Supporting this interpretation is the fact that in the story the owner of the pulpería reminds Dahlmann of the sanatorium personnel. Borges himself suggests that an alternate reading is possible in his Foreword to the 1956 publication of *Artifices,* where he writes: "Of 'The South,' which may be my best story, I shall tell the reader only that it is possible to read it both as a forthright narration of novelistic events and in quite another way, as well" (Borges, "Foreword to Artifices," p. 129).

rather than characters trying to come to grips with their social mileau. This did not prevent Borges from inserting traces of contemporary reality in stories such as "The South," with its allusions to nationalism and violence. It also did not prevent him from taking political stands, as he did against Argentine dictatior Juan Domingo Perón, or participating in events of his times. His example offered much grist for the mill of debate—Borges was both detached from and involved in his environment.

In an article published in *Sur* (October 1951), H. A. Murena complained about the eclectic nature of Borges's literary work, which, Murena charged, makes Argentine writers the heirs of all societies rather than their own particular society. Other critics of the time accused Borges of creating an alienated, aristocratic, superfluous kind of literature, and of representing the oligarchy. Condemning his anti-Peronism, these critics identified Borges with the enemy, describing him as an artist apart, out of touch with the national reality. In "The Argentine Writer and Tradition" Borges argued that William Shakespeare never doubted his right to create *Hamlet,* a play set in remote Denmark. Similarly, Argentine writers should not be afraid of being insufficiently Argentine, but should concentrate on successful writing rather than on local color, trusting that whatever does succeed will become part of Argentine literary tradition. This certainly is the case with Borges's own literary works, which sometimes reflected his own social environment and sometimes did not. That he followed his own advice in embracing a wide array of settings is clear from his writings, as is his simultaneous attachment to and concern for the development of Argentine literature.

Sources and literary context. "The South" opens with an episode similar to one that occurred in Borges's own life and that he claimed opened the door to his serious writing of fiction. In 1938 he cut his head on a freshly-painted window; life-threatening blood poisoning set in and Borges lost the ability to speak. When this faculty returned to him over the course of his recovery, he was worried that his mind had been weakened, so he persuaded his mother to read to him to test whether or not he could understand her. He could and, according to the story, decided to see whether he could fulfill a new literary project as further proof of his sanity and health. Thus he began to write short fiction, having already written poetry and essays. Borges's biographers point out, however, that in fact he had begun his fiction writing career well before this incident (Alazraki, p. 851). His first short story, "Hombre de la esquina" (Streetcorner Man), appeared in 1933.

Other similar elements between Borges's life and that of the protagonist are the ethnic heritage of their parents, their occupation as librarians, and the setting for the short story. Borges based the setting on another real-life experience; in 1934 he visited relatives on the Uruguay/Brazil border, which, in his words, "seems to have impressed me far more than all the kingdoms of the world and the glory of them" (Borges in Rodríguez Monegal, p. 259). "The South" is redolent with the memories of this trip: "the stone fences, the longhorn cattle, the horses' silver trappings, the bearded gauchos, the hitching posts"—all of which made the trip "more a journey into the past than a journey through space"—reappear in the short story that Borges would write some 20 years later. Significantly, on this 1934 excursion Borges also witnessed a casual murder in a rural bar. Actually the rough backland setting recurs in much of Borges's short fiction. He touches also on the gauchos and their environment in other short stories, such as "Tlon, Ugbar, Orbis Tertius," "The Shape of the Sword," and "The Dead Man."

SYMBOL OF RESISTANCE

In 1946 Borges, already hailed as one of Argentina's leading intellectuals and artists was, because of his open criticism of Perón, transferred from his post as assistant at the Miguel Cané municipal library to that of Inspector of Poultry and Rabbits in the Buenos Aires public market. He refused the dubious honor and in a public statement denounced the "subservience . . . cruelty . . . [and] stupidity" of the Perón dictatorship (Rodríguez Monegal, p. 393). This turn of events did not go unnoticed by the city's other intellectuals, and Borges became "the symbol of Argentina's resistance to totalitarianism" (Rodríguez Monegal, p. 393). However, while the intelligentsia continued to voice concern over Peronist tyranny, it was able to offer but little in the way of viable resistance.

Events in History at the Time the Short Story Was Written

The dictatorship of Juan Perón. Juan Domingo Perón was elected president of Argentina in

1946. Perón's successful political strategy was to unite the interests of Argentine labor—both workers and managers—and the military and set them against the nation's cultural elite, big business, and the intelligentsia. The U.S. Department of State denounced him for his fascist tendencies, as did others in his own nation, but none of this blocked the dictator's magnificent rise to power, a rise that Borges would publicly lament until Perón's death in 1974.

PROFOUNDLY ARGENTINE

In "The South" Juan Dahlmann believes himself to be "profoundly Argentine," thanks mostly to the fact that he is related on his mother's side to a minor military hero ("The South," p. 174). By such standards Borges himself would have been one of the most "Argentine" people in the nation's history. The nineteenth-century dictator Juan Manuel de Rosas was his great-great-great-uncle (Alazraki, pp. 845-46). His great-grandfather, Colonel Isidoro Suárez, fought Spanish forces at the head of a Peruvian cavalry unit in 1820 at Junín and was exiled to Uruguay at the time of the Rosas dictatorship. His mother's father, Isidoro Acevedo, also fought against Rosas in the civil war. His other grandfather, Colonel Francisco Borges, died in 1874 in the civil strife at La Verde. Another relative, on his mother's side, was Francisco Narciso de Laprida, who presided at the 1816 Congress of Tucumán, at which Argentina became independent of Spain. The heroic past is present in much of Borges's work, including one poem written in the early 1950s, "A Page to Commemorate Colonel Suárez, Victor at Junín," which compares the struggle of his famous ancestor against Rosas with the struggle of ordinary Argentines against another "tyrant" (unnamed, but obviously Perón):

> His great-grandson is writing these lines,
> and a silent voice comes to him out of the past,
> out of the blood:
> "What does my battle at Junín matter if it is only
> a glorious memory, or a date learned by rote
> for an examination, or a place in the atlas?
> The battle is everlasting and can do without
> the pomp of actual armies and of trumpets.
> Junín is two civilians cursing a tyrant
> on a street corner
> or an unknown man somewhere, dying in prison."
> (Borges in Rodríguez Monegal, p. 427)

Upon his succession to power Perón did his best to silence his opposition. He purged the universities of his critics, terminated the tenure of nearly all Supreme Court judges, and restricted freedom of the press (Rock, pp. 280-81). In 1951 he expropriated the leading newspaper, *La Prensa,* which had long been critical of his regime, and turned it into a state mouthpiece. He instigated a new "contempt law" to prevent what he called "libel, slander, or defamation against public authorities" (Rock, p. 303). By 1953 (the year "The South" was published) many of Borges's literary friends and relatives had been in jail (his own aged mother and his sister had been arrested briefly for singing the national anthem and passing out anti-Perón pamphlets); apart from his removal from his position at the Miguel Cané municipal library, however, the authorities did not interfere with Borges himself in any way.

Perón promised his country a "New Argentina" based on social justice, political self-determination, and economic independence. Coming from an immigrant, middle-class background himself, he identified himself with the nation's workers and widely publicized his pro-labor stance. In the eyes of many he became a savior, a leader who "stood up for the common people, who put the anti-Argentinian oligarchy in its place, who defended national sovereignty against foreign capitalism, who made workers feel good about themselves, who safeguarded the country's Catholic traditions, and protected the family" (Shumway, p. 298).

In fact, Argentine workers saw in Perón a leader who "stood for something every Argentine politician since 1930 manifestly failed to offer: the charismatic possibility of achieving a new order without bloodshed or corruption" (Woodall, p. 133). As Borges and other liberals saw it, however, Perón was leading Argentina down a dangerous path towards fascism; "a great number of Argentines are becoming Nazis without being aware of it," Borges wrote (Woodall, p. 133). Such warnings, however, went for naught given the power and popularity of Perón and the champion of his cause, his wife Eva (or "Evita" as she was popularly known).

Although Borges had no way of knowing it, Perón's power was already on the wane by the time "The South" appeared in print in 1953. Evita had died of cancer in 1952, and without her charisma the dictator lost substantial influence. Gradually the Argentine economy had spun out of his control, and an ill-conceived battle with the Catholic Church finally gave his opponents in the military the chance for which they had been waiting. In 1955 Perón went quietly into exile, where he would remain until his return in 1972 and a brief resurgence of power before his death in 1974.

Reviews. Borges himself wrote in the preface to the 1954 collection *Artifices,* which features "The South," that the story "may be my best story" (*Collected Fictions,* p. 129). In an article for the *London Review of Books,* John Sturrock concurred, writing that "The South" is among Borges's "finest stories" and praising it for its "heroic ingenuity" (Sturrock in Hall, p. 362). Writing for the *New York Review of Books,* J. M. Coetzee called the story "haunting" and saw it, along with the many other works by Borges about confronting death, as "reveal[ing] the attractions of a life of action for their bookish and rather timid author" (Coetzee, p. 82). Critics the world over have praised Borges as one of the masters of modern literature, pointing out the dense allusions and overt references in his fiction to the works of other international writers. Nonetheless, using a phrase from "The South" itself, the critic Peter Witonski argued in the *National Review* that Borges is a "profoundly Argentine" writer:

> His many references to the literature and culture of his native land may be missed by the reader unfamiliar with Argentina. Borges the bookman is drawn to the literature of the world, which he enjoys citing with mock-pedantry; but Borges the man is drawn to what he has called "the implacable pampas" of Argentina. . . . His many references to the knife-play and philosophy of the gaucho serve to emphasize this point.
>
> (Witonski in Marowski and Matusz, p. 36)

—Emerson Spencer Olin and Lorraine Valestuk

For More Information

Alazraki, Jaime. "Jorge Luis Borges." In *Latin American Writers.* Eds. Carlos A. Solé and Maria Isabel Abreu. Vol. 2. New York: Charles Scribner's Sons, 1989.

Borges, Jorge Luis. "The South." In *Collected Fictions.* Trans. Andrew Hurley. New York: Viking, 1998.

———. *Labyrinths: Selected Stories and Other Writings.* Eds. Donald A. Yates and James E. Irby. New York: Modern Library, 1983.

Coetzee, J. M. "Borges's Dark Mirror." *The New York Review of Books,* October 22, 1998, 80-82.

Hall, Sharon K., ed. *Contemporary Literary Criticism: Yearbook 1986.* Vol. 44. Detroit: Gale Research, 1987.

Lewis, Paul H. *The Crisis of Argentine Capitalism.* Chapel Hill: University of North Carolina Press, 1990.

Marowski, Daniel G., and Roger Matuz, eds. *Contemporary Literary Criticism.* Vol. 48. Detroit: Gale Research, 1988.

Rock, David. *Argentina, 1516-1982: From Spanish Colonization to the Falklands War.* Berkeley: University of California Press, 1985.

Rodríguez Monegal, Emir. *Jorge Luis Borges: A Literary Biography.* New York: E. P. Dutton, 1978.

Shumway, Nicolas. *The Invention of Argentina.* Berkeley: University of California Press, 1991.

Woodall, James. *The Man in the Mirror of the Book: A Life of Jorge Luis Borges.* London: Hodder & Stoughton, 1996.

The Storyteller

by

Mario Vargas Llosa

> **THE LITERARY WORK**
>
> A novel set in Peru and Florence, Italy, from circa 1953 to 1985; published in Spanish (as *El hablador*) in 1987, in English in 1989.
>
> **SYNOPSIS**
>
> A Peruvian writer composes a novel about a friend from the past who abandons his modern-day life and his study of ethnology to become a storyteller in an Amazonian tribe.

The Storyteller is the tenth published novel by Peru's best-known living author, Mario Vargas Llosa (1936-). Though his fiction contains political and social commentary, for Vargas Llosa the novel is first and foremost a work of art. Vargas Llosa's career can be divided into three periods according to major changes in his political outlook. In the 1960s he was a Marxist who enthusiastically supported the Cuban revolution. In the 1970s, after witnessing the authoritarianism of Castro's government as well as the authoritarian tendencies of the left in Peru, Vargas Llosa became disillusioned with the Latin American left in general. Accordingly, he entered a neo-liberal phase during which he sought to strengthen artistic, political, and economic freedoms by actively supporting democracy and free market economics. *The Storyteller* was written during this phase and exemplifies his rejection of utopian notions of all stripes. After his failed bid for the Peruvian presidency in 1990, Vargas Llosa entered a third phase marked by a seeming pessimism on his part about the effectiveness of political action in the face of human frailty.

Events in History at the Time of the Novel

Peru and the world of the Machiguengas. Peru is a nation divided into three very different regions: the desert coast where the crowded city of Lima overflows with nearly a third of the national population; the high Andes in which the descendants of the Incas farm their terraced hillside plots and the Amazon river has its source; and the *montaña,* or Amazon rainforest, that covers the eastern half of Peru. It is this mysterious jungle that is the focus of *The Storyteller.*

Home to indigenous tribes, the jungle is divided into two regions: the *ceja de la montaña* (eyebrow of the jungle) formed by the eastern slopes of the Andes, and the lower montaña or jungle proper. The sheer slopes of the ceja form a formidable geographic barrier between the lower montaña and the rest of Peru. In addition, torrential rains, dense vegetation, and an abundance of disease-bearing insects make the montaña resistant to exploration and colonization. Thus throughout Peru's history, the montaña has been the nation's great frontier, believed to hold untold riches in a variety of forms. As a source of gold, oil, lumber, rubber, cocaine, farmland, and new converts to Christianity, the jungle has attracted much attention in the centuries since Spanish conquest, yet due to its impenetrability

A young Machiguenga woman stirring manioc.

it has remained largely untouched by "civilization." Indeed, the contrast between the jungle and the rest of Peru is so stark that one might conceive of them as two distinct worlds sharing a national territory.

Within the jungle live the Machiguengas, one of the 65 distinct ethnic groups known to inhabit the Peruvian rainforest. In 1982 they numbered about 10,000 among the estimated 300,000 denizens of the jungle, which contains only about

10 percent of Peru's population, even though it covers more than half the national territory. The Machiguengas live along the banks of the river tributaries that thread through the jungle and form the principal routes of transportation. Traditionally, they reside in simple bamboo huts, dress in cotton tunics (*kushmas*) dyed with tree bark, and subsist on slash-and-burn agriculture, bow-and-arrow hunting, and fishing. Their staple crop is manioc, a starchy root vegetable from which they brew *masato*, manioc beer. They live in small groups of one to three families, forming a fixed settlement for a time and relocating every few years to find better hunting grounds or richer farmland. The Machiguengas do not regard any region as their exclusive territory. An egalitarian people without hierarchy or formal leadership, they do not engage in communal activities.

Machiguenga worldview. To understand the culture, one must become familiar with its worldview. In Machiguenga belief, the universe consists of five different levels or realms arranged in a vertical hierarchy, much like the Christian conception of the three realms of heaven, earth, and hell. As in the Christian worldview, conditions are better at the top and worse at the bottom. The Machiguengas inhabit the middle realm, known as *Kipatsi*. The realm directly above Kipatsi is *Menkoripatsi*, and is perceived from Kipatsi as the sky. Here dwell the *saangarite*, perfect beings who occasionally come down to Kipatsi and can protect humans from demons. The spirits of exceptionally enlightened Machiguenga shamans, known as *seripigari*, come here after death. The next realm up is *Inkite*, visible from Kipatsi as the stars. These upper realms enjoy continual daylight from their own sun, *Kyenti*, which is permanently fixed in the sky. They are happy places where the land is fertile, the people are beautiful, and the masato is plentiful. Below Kipatsi is twilit *Kamabiria*, where live the spirits of most Machiguenga dead who look up to Kipatsi as their sky. This realm has no sun of its own, but must rely on what little light filters down from *Poriatsiri*, the sun of Kipatsi. At the very bottom lies *Gamaironi*, realm of monsters and demons. Gamaironi has its own sun, which is excessively hot, rendering this realm scorched and stark. The spirits of exceptionally wicked Machiguengas come here after death. In the lower realms, life is hard; the land is rocky, there are no fish, and there is no masato.

It is important to note that these realms are not conceived as being distinct from one another, but are contiguous parts of a single physical universe. The Machiguengas, like many other tribal peoples, do not share the modern conception of two distinct categories of "natural" and "supernatural." Gods, demons, and other strange and powerful beings are just as natural as the plants and animals of the jungle, or as the Machiguengas themselves. Likewise, plants, animals, and human beings have properties and powers many of us would consider supernatural.

The Machiguengas have two creator gods: *Tasorinchi* and *Kyentibákori* (Tasurinchi and Kientibakori in the novel). Whatever Tasorinchi creates is perfect, while Kyentibákori can produce only imperfection. In this way, the Machiguengas account for the existence of good and evil in the universe. As recounted in *The Storyteller*, the Machiguengas were created by Tasorinchi, and thus were once perfect beings. This changed when a Machiguenga man asked Tasorinchi to give his people such things as hunger, sickness, and death. Offended by this lack of appreciation for perfection, Tasorinchi granted the man's wish, then retired to Inkite, taking all his perfect creations with him. The good things remaining in Kipatsi are but shadows of what Tasorinchi took away, while the bad things (stinging insects, poisonous fruits, demons, and so on) are the work of Kyentibákori, who dwells in Gamaironi.

The dichotomy between perfection and imperfection is central to the Machiguenga worldview. All things are judged according to where they fall on a continuum between these two extremes, with the Machiguengas and their world, Kipatsi, lying precisely in the middle. Machiguengas are sometimes good and sometimes bad, and both sáangaríte and demons visit Kipatsi. Significantly, perfection and imperfection are not moral qualities; what matters is not so much what one does, but how perfect one *is*. Perfection and imperfection are, furthermore, contagious. If one associates with the perfect sáangaríte one becomes more perfect oneself, while contact with demons is degrading.

Linked to the perfection-imperfection distinction is the notion of purity. The Machiguengas regard the human body and its functions as impure, and regard the female human body and its functions as particularly impure. Menstrual blood is feared by Machiguenga men as a dangerous and polluting substance and menstruating Machiguenga women are sequestered in special "bleeding houses" so that others might not come into contact with the blood or even have to look upon the bleeding women. Demons and other imperfect beings are attracted to such impurity, while the perfect sáangaríte, who subsist on fragrances and reproduce asexually, avoid it. Because women are so impure, they attract demons and repel the sáangaríte, thus becoming through contagion ever less perfect and never more perfect. Women are therefore considered inherently inferior to men in Machiguenga society.

According to the anthropological literature, the Machiguengas lack the concept of individuality. Certainly individuality is less important to the Machiguengas than to modern Western society. The human body, the Machiguengas believe, merely houses temporarily the true inner being, or *iseire,* of a person, and can host different spirits at different times and even metamorphose into animal forms. Thus identity for the Machiguengas is fluid rather than fixed; this perhaps accounts for why they have personal names but traditionally do not use them in conversation, rather referring to a person by way of the relationship in which he or she currently stands to the speaker. In *The Storyteller* Vargas Llosa conveys this lack of concern for individuality by having all Machiguengas refer to one another as "Tasurinchi," distinguishing individuals with such epithets as "Tasurinchi, the blind one," or "Tasurinchi, the one who lives at the bend in the river . . ." (Vargas Llosa, *The Storyteller,* pp. 57, 45). Machiguengas, in fact, do not call each other "Tasurinchi"; this is Vargas Llosa's invention, one of many in a novel by an author whose main concern was not anthropological accuracy, but artistic creation inspired by anthropology. Vargas Llosa uses Machiguenga lore throughout the novel; he writes of Tasorinchi and Kyentibákori, of seripigari and sáangaríte, of Inkite and Gamaironi. He is often faithful to the Machiguenga tradition, but not always. Like any good storyteller, Vargas Llosa bends tradition to his purpose, thus creating something new.

> The novel is not, nor does it pretend to be an accurate portrayal of the Machiguengas. . . . *The Storyteller* . . . does not purport to document the complex historical, political, or anthropological reality of the Peruvian Indians.
>
> (Vargas Llosa in Kristal, p. 158)

From "discovery" to independence. Despite the vast disparity that separates the world of the Machiguengas from modern Peru, the two are not distinct—one world impinges upon the other. The Machiguengas were first contacted by Spanish Catholic missionaries centuries ago. Yet up until the latter half of the twentieth century, the Machiguenga way of life remained essentially unaltered from its prehistoric form. *The Storyteller* begins in the mid-twentieth century, but it is important to understand the forces in preceding centuries that transformed Peru, and the conditions that protected the Machiguengas and other Amazonian tribes from this transformation.

In 1528, when Spanish explorers first came to the region now known as Peru, the land was already controlled by the powerful Inca empire. The Incas were a Quechua people from Cusco, a region in southern central Peru. Although they had neither writing nor the wheel, beginning in the thirteenth century the Incas expanded their control to eventually cover a vast area extending

MACHIGUENGA ORAL TRADITION

> There was a man who used to get drunk all the time, and went off to drink by himself, leaving his wife home alone. He said he did not want his wife to have children because he wanted her to work only for him. One night, when the woman was alone, *Narani* [a demonic night bird] appeared in human form and called to her. She was afraid he would kill her, but then she told him to come and give her a child. Narani entered and spent the night until her husband returned. Then Narani assumed his bird shape and flew out. . . .
>
> (Yokari in Johnson, pp. 8–10)

This typical Machiguenga folktale ends badly for everyone. The selfish husband drives his wife into the arms of a demon who impregnates her, breaking her in the process. Before she dies, her husband slits her belly open, exposing thousands of demon babies. Afterwards, the husband is beset by angered demons who fatally pollute him with their contagious imperfection and he dies a miserable death. The "moral" of this story, scholar Allen Johnson suggests, is that strong emotions are fatal and must be avoided. In a study of Machiguenga folktales, Johnson determined that the single most popular subject for such tales is the dangerous nature of strong emotions. Living as they do, in small isolated groups without a formal legal or political system for resolving conflicts, the Machiguengas are especially threatened by strong emotional outbursts that could lead to aggression. Accordingly, great emphasis is placed upon controlling one's emotions and maintaining calm and courteous relations with others. Machiguenga folktales, Johnson observes, reflect this preoccupation by focusing on conflicts between the strong desires of individuals, which lead to physical hostility and tragedy.

from southern Colombia to northern Chile, and from the Pacific coast in the west to the jungle's edge in the east. In the sixteenth century, a small party of Spanish adventurers led by Francisco Pizarro made short work of conquering the Incan empire. The Incas were divided by civil war at the time and, terrified by the Spaniards' muskets and bizarre appearance, they offered little initial resistance. Later they did resist, but by then they had been weakened by diseases caught from the Spaniards against which they had no immunity. Millions of Incas died in the years following the Spanish invasion, while those who survived the epidemics were enslaved by the Spaniards and forced to work in the silver mines under horrific conditions.

Because of the jungle's relative impenetrability, the Machiguengas and other Amazonian tribes (who are distinct from the Quechua peoples) never came under Incan control. For the same reason, the Spanish invasion did not have much impact on the people of the montaña. The few Spanish missionaries who did penetrate the jungle made contact with various tribes, including the Machiguengas, but did not remain for long.

Although Spaniards and others of European descent began to intermarry with indigenous people shortly after initial contact, a racist hierarchy favored those of the "purest" European descent while relegating indigenous people to the lowest status as *gente sin razón,* "people without reason." Native Americans were widely considered barbaric savages to be civilized, or at least controlled, by the more advanced Europeans. In the twentieth century the legacy of European domination was still apparent in Peru's ruling class—for the most part composed of *blanquitos,* people of exclusively European heritage—and in the fact that many Peruvians still spoke of an "Indian problem," that is, how to fit the Indians, who according to the 1940 census formed at least 46 percent of the nation's population, into modern Peruvian society.

When worlds collide. Like the rest of South America, Peru achieved independence from Spain in the early nineteenth century. To most of the population, however, independence brought little change. Power continued to be concentrated in the hands of a *criollo* (Spanish-descended) urban elite, and thus Spain, in a sense, continued to dominate. After independence, the new nations began to dispute boundaries of the former Spanish territories, and the montaña in particular became a contested area among Peru, Ecuador, Bolivia, and Brazil. In order to strengthen claims to this largely uncharted region, the Peruvian government reestablished missions among the native tribes and colonized some portions of the ceja de montaña in the mid-nineteenth century.

Another factor that increased incursions into the jungle in the middle of the nineteenth century was the discovery there of cinchona trees, the bark of which contains quinine—a substance with the ability to mitigate malarial fever. Outsiders came into the jungle to collect cinchona bark, which was then sold as an export. Later in the century, many more entrepreneurs invaded the jungle during the "rubber boom." With the popularity of the bicycle and later the automobile came an increased demand for rubber with which to make tires, so Peruvians and foreigners alike took to the jungle to collect the sap of rubber trees. The allure of great profits, combined with the remoteness of the jungle from the rule of law, resulted in often nefarious business practices and the capture and enslavement of natives who were forced to tap the rubber trees. In *The Storyteller* Machiguenga characters recount again and again the terrible times of kidnap and enslavement during the "tree-bleeding," and in fact tales about the horrors of this era (1880s–1920) figure prominently in Machiguenga oral tradition.

Between 1878 and 1883 Peru fought Chile in the War of the Pacific. Seeing her profitable guano islands (source of bat-droppings used as fertilizer) and southern coast threatened by Chilean invasion, Peru looked to the jungle as a more secure and relatively untapped national resource. In addition to rubber and quinine, it was hoped the jungle would yield a navigable waterway to the Atlantic coast. Perhaps even more significantly for the Machiguengas, the jungle was envisioned as a virtually limitless source of arable land. Such a resource, it was believed, would provide valuable cash crops for export and would be the solution to *latifundia,* the monopolization of large tracts of land by a small group of wealthy landowners that is characteristic of Latin America. Such high hopes fueled many a jungle development program in the century to follow, yet the harvest has been scant. Clearing large sections of jungle to be used as permanent farmland irreparably damages segments of the rainforest and does not significantly enrich the Peruvian people. The soil of the rainforest is actually quite poor and not suitable for permanent agriculture; the plant life that flourishes there does so only through an intricate balance that has developed over millions of years of evolution. The farming practices of the Machiguengas, who use a plot for a short time, then let it lie fallow for many years, are much more in keeping with the requirements of the jungle environment.

In addition to changes wrought through governmental and economic activity, another, perhaps more important, influence on the Machiguengas has been a new breed of Christian (largely Protestant) missionaries who in this century have encouraged the Machiguengas to relocate into large permanent communities and to engage in communal agriculture to produce cash crops.

Democracy, dictatorship, and jungle development. *The Storyteller* begins in the 1950s, when, according to the novel, Peru "was moving from the spurious peace of General Odría's dictatorship to the uncertainties and novelties of the return to democratic rule in 1956" (*The Storyteller*, p. 12). Peruvian politics throughout the twentieth century was a tug of war between democracy and dictatorship in which free market advocates like Manuel A. Odría, backed by the nation's wealthy elites, alternated with reform-minded leftists who sought to rectify Peru's extreme economic inequities. Both sides resorted to authoritarian tactics to achieve their ends, and both sides turned to the jungle for solutions to the nation's woes.

In 1963 Peruvians elected as president Fernando Belaúnde Terry, founder of the moderate Popular Action party. In order to quell uprisings of landless Andean peasants, Belaúnde undertook some ambitious projects including colonization of the montaña with Quechua farmers and, to facilitate jungle agriculture, the construction of a highway running north and south along the entire length of the jungle's fringe. These expensive programs did not significantly improve the plight of the Andean peasants, but they did worsen the situation of the jungle Indians. As previously noted, large-scale agriculture does irreparable harm to the jungle ecosystem. The jungle highway has more often been used as a landing strip for the airplanes of drug traffickers than as a transport route for market crops. Through these failed projects, Belaúnde squandered vast sums of money and greatly increased Peru's foreign debt.

Belaúnde was removed from office by military coup and replaced by General Juan Velasco, a genuine populist. Velasco insisted that his would be a "revolutionary" government that would benefit the poor. Like Belaúnde, Velasco sought to help the landless poor with an ambitious program to colonize the rainforest. Velasco planned to convert some 1,200,000 acres of jungle into farmland for peasant settlers. At the same time, in an effort to soften the impact of such settlement on the native Amazonian tribes, the Velasco government instituted the Law of Native Communities and Agricultural Promotion for the Jungle Region—affirming the rights of tribal Indians to enough land to continue their traditional methods of hunting and agriculture. This law established *comunidades nativas,* rainforest communities with a prescribed form of political organization foreign to the traditional Machiguenga way of life. Each community is represented by a popularly elected *presidente*. The Machiguengas, however, do not seem to place much stock in this leader since they traditionally conceive of leadership as something that cannot be bestowed or taken away, but is inherent in the individual or built up over a lifetime. Given this view, if community members disagree with a decision of their presidente, they simply choose not to go along with it, and if necessary will leave the community.

In 1975 Velasco succumbed to a bloodless coup effected by more moderate-minded military officers. General Morales Bermúdez succeeded Velasco and passed a new law in 1978 that undid many of the provisions of Velasco's law concerning the comunidades nativas. The new law barred indigenous peoples from having full title to any lands the government defines as suitable for forestry or agricultural exploitation, and the government reserves the right to award these lands, if currently used by indigenous peoples, to businesses who might "require" them. As one might expect, agribusinesses as well as logging and mining companies have been the beneficiaries of this law, which has awarded them large tracts of jungle.

In 1980 Belaúnde took office for a second term and continued the policy of giving more and more jungle land to large privately owned companies. In the following decade, Peru experienced a gold boom that has proven anything but lucrative for those living on the land where gold was found. The government sold mineral concessions, mostly to foreign companies, for lands occupied by tribal peoples. Even though the tribal peoples held title to these lands, mining companies were allowed to excavate them in order to extract gold dust, leaving only piles of gravel in their wake. In addition, the Peruvian government has been busy granting oil concessions in the jungle despite the fact that drilling for oil entails pollution of the environment, detonation of explosives that frightens away wildlife, and the building of roads through indigenous lands. Indigenous rights groups complain that the Peruvian government and the companies it sponsors act as though the jungle were uninhabited. The chemicals used by such companies to deforest the land contaminate it, poisoning the wildlife and polluting the rivers. Widespread deforestation leads to erosion of the soil, which leads to waterways clogged with silt and deadly flooding during the rainy season. As the most lucrative species of trees are eliminated from the jungle, the plants and animals that depend on them are threatened with extinction, and indigenous hunters are deprived of fish and game. In addition, massive destruction of the Amazon rainforest could result in climatic changes due to acceleration of the greenhouse effect, the increase of solar radiation in the atmosphere because of more gases like carbon monoxide. Meanwhile, tribal peoples struggle to maintain a viable existence as their world continues to disintegrate.

The Novel in Focus

Plot summary. A Peruvian writer vacationing in Florence, Italy, in the year 1985 happens upon a photography exhibition entitled "Natives of the Amazon Forest." The writer, who is also the narrator of much of this novel and is never named, enters and discovers that the natives are none other than the Machiguengas, a tribal people in whom the writer has a special interest. The writer recognizes many of the faces in the photographs, and is particularly struck by one picture of a man addressing a rapt audience. "Yes," he marvels, "No doubt whatsoever about it. A storyteller" (*The Storyteller,* p. 7). Thus the novel begins. It will also end in Florence in 1985, after all the implications of this photography exhibit for the Peruvian writer have been made clear. In between, the novel consists of six chapters, three in the Peruvian writer's voice, and three in the voice of a Machiguenga storyteller. The two voices alternate, the Peruvian writer providing a fairly linear account of his life from college days to the present (1985), while the storyteller weaves a tapestry of Machiguenga myth, legend, and stories of daily life.

In the "Peruvian writer" chapters, the novel takes us back to the Peru of the 1950s and introduces us to Saúl Zuratas, a friend from the Peruvian writer's college days. Saúl is "the ugliest lad in the world; but he was also a likable and exceptionally good person" (*The Storyteller,* p. 8). He has bright red hair, a giant purple birthmark that covers half his face, for which he is known as *Mascarita* (Mask Face), and a parrot named Gregor Samsa. His mother is Christian; his father, Jewish; and Saúl is an atheist by conviction. At the university he studies law to please his father and ethnology to please himself. The stares and taunts of ill-mannered people do not raise his ire, but one day the Peruvian writer becomes enraged when the Saúl is the butt of rude remarks at a local bar.

Afterwards Saúl sends the Peruvian writer a present, a small bone with an elaborate design engraved on it. In an accompanying note, Saúl explains that the design represents the universal order, which is distorted by anger. It is a Machiguenga artifact, and the Peruvian writer is fascinated by it and by Saúl's recounting of Machiguenga myths and beliefs, in which serenity is held as the supreme good while violent emotion is the force that can destroy the world. Obviously Saúl himself is fascinated with the Machiguengas; his interest, perceives the Peruvian writer, is "something more than 'ethnological'" (*The Storyteller,* p. 16). Saúl visits the Machiguengas in the rainforest at every opportunity, and gradually comes to feel more at home in their world than the outside world. Like his biblical namesake who became a Christian on the road to Damascus, "Saúl experienced a conversion. In a cultural sense and perhaps in a religious one also" (*The Storyteller,* p. 19).

Upon graduation Saúl receives a prestigious fellowship to continue his studies in France. He turns it down, however. His professors say it is because he has begun to have ethical misgivings about ethnology; Saúl says it is his duty to stay with his elderly father who has no one else in the world.

Meanwhile, the Peruvian writer has been developing a Machiguenga obsession of his own. On a trip to the Amazon jungle in 1958 he encounters the Schneils, a married couple with the Summer Institute of Linguistics, a missionary group doing fieldwork among the Machiguengas. From them the Peruvian writer learns of the Machiguengas' nomadic existence, their practice of wandering in small family units over a vast region, and of their fatalistic outlook. Suicide is common, and tribal members resign themselves to death at the first sign of illness.

From the Schneils the Peruvian writer hears for the first time of the Machiguenga *hablador*—the word is Spanish for "speaker," and is the clos-

Mariano Vicente, a Machiguenga man renowned for telling stories.

est translation of the Machiguenga word that the Schneils can offer. The hablador is a mysterious figure of whom the Machiguengas will say little. The Schneils conjecture that the hablador is a messenger and news-bringer facilitating communication between the widely separated members of the Machiguenga community. He may also fulfill the role of tribal historian, keeping alive the old stories—a function similar to that of the medieval troubadour. The Peruvian writer is fascinated with the idea of the hablador, an individual who was "the living sap that circulated and made the Machiguengas into a society" (*The Storyteller,* p. 93). As a writer, the Peruvian finds the notion that storytelling can serve such an essential function in human life extraordinarily moving.

The Peruvian writer meets with Saúl one last time before leaving for Spain to continue his studies. In this final conversation, Saúl claims to know nothing of Machiguenga habladores and then proceeds to criticize the Summer Institute, asserting that the Machiguengas must be respected, and that "the only way to respect them is not to go near them" (*The Storyteller,* pp. 98-99). From Spain, the Peruvian writer sends letters to Saúl, but Saúl never writes back. Over the years, the Peruvian writer's obsession with the hablador figure grows. He reads whatever he can find, which isn't much. He attempts a book on Machiguenga storytellers, but to no avail. In 1963 the Peruvian writer runs into one of his former professors from Lima who relates a startling piece of news: Saúl has moved to Israel with his father and joined a kibbutz.

The narration leapfrogs forward to 1981. The Peruvian writer is now producing a program called "Tower of Babel" for Peruvian television. The program is a hodgepodge of segments having to do with "culture," anything the Peruvian writer and his team find interesting, and the Peruvian writer uses the opportunity to produce a segment on the Machiguengas. When the television team travels to the jungle, the Peruvian writer reconnects with the Schneils, who have lived among the Machiguengas all these years.

Things have changed considerably during this time. About half of the wandering Machiguengas have, at the behest of the Institute and other groups who believe it is for the Machiguengas' own good, settled down in large communities. The Peruvian writer is disturbed by his conversations with Machiguenga tribal leaders who endlessly quote the Bible and seem to have become the zombies that Saúl accused the Institute of wanting to make them. He is also disappointed by the refusal of all Machiguengas to speak of the hablador, although he does see this as an indication of the hidden depths of Machiguenga culture still untouched by the missionaries. He brings up the subject of habladores with the Schneils, and Edwin Schneil tells of two habladores he has seen during his time with the Machiguengas. The first was an old man, the second a young man, an "albino," with bright red hair and a purple birthmark covering half his face.

The Peruvian writer is certain the storyteller must be Saúl and believes he now understands the reason behind the taboo against speaking of the hablador. The Machiguengas were hiding Saúl, protecting him from discovery, probably because he had asked them to do so. The Peruvian writer asks a friend with ties to the Peruvian Jewish community to find out what he can about a certain Zuratas family. Had they really gone to Israel? No, he finds out. The father died in Peru and as for the son, no one but the Peruvian writer knows what became of him.

***

In the parallel "storyteller" chapters, the storyteller addresses us, his audience, directly. The writing style conveys a mythic sense of reality in which time is divided into a "before" and "afterwards." The principle myth (invented by Vargas Llosa) of the Machiguengas tells of the event that forever divided time in two: the falling of the sun. When the sun fell, the Machiguengas began walking—this was the only way to keep the sun in the sky and to stay alive. For this reason, the Machiguengas must continue to walk, never settling in one place for too long. When bad things happen, it is an indication that it is time to move on, and thus for the Machiguengas a nomadic life is required.

The storyteller relays many things. He tells the tale of Tasurinchi and Kientibakori, the two creator gods. Besides recounting myths and legends, he speaks of his own experiences walking amongst the Machiguengas with no steady companion but his parrot. He describes trips to *seripigaris,* holy men who visit other worlds under the influence of the hallucinogenic plant ayahuasca. He recalls the time of the "tree-bleeding." He relates how he became a storyteller. Throughout, the storyteller does not presume; he constantly qualifies his story with the words "perhaps," and "at least that is what I have learned" (*The Storyteller,* p. 38). The storyteller is clearly Saúl, an outsider to Machiguenga culture; and in a sense, all storytellers are outsiders, the ones who find their world remarkable because they never quite feel a part of it. Yet paradoxically storytellers are also the ultimate insiders, the ones who go everywhere and get into everybody's business, the ones who create the world by naming it.

The storyteller speaks about the plight of those in Machiguenga society who are rejected because of innate flaws. He speaks about the Machiguenga babies who are drowned by their mothers in the river because they are born "imperfect," physically deformed in some way—an actual Machiguenga custom. He chides the Machiguengas for the infanticide they commit on account of an imperfection as small as a birthmark, asking, "Do you think I'm a devil? Is that what my face means?" "No, no, no," the Machiguengas reply, ". . . You're Tasurinchi, the storyteller" (*The Storyteller,* p. 212). The storyteller relates what a seripigari once told him: "Being born with a face like yours isn't the worst evil; it's not knowing one's obligation" (*The Storyteller,* p. 214). Saúl implies that such is the plight of modern humanity. We do not know what it is we are supposed to be doing, unlike the Machiguengas, who must walk.

The hablador tells the story of a group of outsiders, people forced to move constantly from one place to another, like the Machiguengas. He tells them the story of the tribe to which he used to belong, the Jews, though he does not call them by name. That tribe "lived very far from here, in a place that had been its own and no longer was, belonging now to others"; eventually a child was born among them who claimed: "I am the breath of Tasurinchi, I am the son of Tasurinchi, I am Tasurinchi. I am all three things at once" (*The Storyteller,* p. 215). The tribe immediately recognized this child as a hablador. He told them to abandon their beliefs and follow him, but the tribe decided not to, saying, "Aren't we what we believe, the stripes we paint on ourselves, the way we set our traps?" (*The Storyteller,* p. 216). They decided to stay who they were: "What would keep them together if they became the same as everybody else? Nothing, nobody" (*The Storyteller,* p. 216). Like the Jews, the Machiguengas live in a land that was theirs and is now claimed by others. Like the Jews, the Machiguengas' identity as a people is threatened by those who would have them abandon their ways and beliefs.

Toward the end of the novel, the storyteller offers his audience a new story, the story of "Gregor-Tasurinchi, who was changed into a buzz-buzz bug" (*The Storyteller,* p. 220). By now we can be certain that the storyteller is Saúl. His story is a retelling of Franz Kafka's *The Metamorphosis,* in which a character named Gregor Samsa is transformed, in a degenerate variation on the classic mythological theme, into a giant cockroach. *The Metamorphosis* resonates with *The Storyteller* in many ways, but Saúl offers one possible moral to this tale: "We'd best be what we are" (*The Storyteller,* p. 220). When we lose our humanity, we can become something monstrous. Perhaps modern "civilized" human beings have lost their humanity and have become something monstrous when compared to people like the Machiguengas who "have a deep and subtle knowledge of things that we've forgotten. The relationship between man and Nature, for instance. . . . Man and God, as well" (*The Storyteller,* p. 100).

***

Back in Florence, it is 1985 and the Peruvian writer once more ponders the picture in the photography exhibition. The storyteller is distant and obscure. The right side of his face, the side on which Saúl had his birthmark, is darkened, but it could just be a shadow. There is no way the Peruvian writer will ever know for sure, yet he decides at this moment that the storyteller in the photograph is Saúl. It seems to fit, like the last piece in a puzzle, and indeed with this decision *The Storyteller* feels complete. The novel has set up contrasting voices, and they are linked. On one hand, there is the Machiguenga storyteller; on the other, there is the Peruvian writer, a modern-day novelist of the Western world. In fact, there is a third presence too, albeit in the background, the creator of *The Storyteller* in its entirety, the novelist Vargas Llosa.

The Peruvian writer speculates on what might have led Saúl to pursue such an extraordinary life. Perhaps because he was Jewish, the Peruvian writer conjectures, Saúl felt a special affinity with the wandering tribe. Perhaps his birthmark, which made Saúl "a marginal among marginals," allowed him to understand this marginalized people in a way most Westerners could not, and made him belong more in their world than in his own (*The Storyteller,* p. 243).

The ethics of missionization. "Those apostolic linguists of yours are the worst of all. They work their way into the tribes to destroy them from within, just like chiggers. Into their spirit, their beliefs, their subconscious, the roots of their way of being" (*The Storyteller,* p. 95). In *The Storyteller,* Saúl rails eloquently against all those who would try to change the Machiguengas, but he reserves his fiercest criticism for the Summer Institute of Linguistics (SIL), a Protestant missionary group whose purpose is to translate the New Testament into every language in the world in order to facilitate conversion to Christianity. Established in the United States in 1934, the Summer Institute of Linguistics is funded by churches in the United States and England as well as the governments of nations that host SIL projects.

Currently SIL has about 2,000 members in more than 50 countries working to interpret 6,500 languages in order to gain converts. Translation of the Christian scripture into the Machiguenga language is one of few projects completed to date.

SIL is a controversial organization, just as missionary work in general is a controversial undertaking. Missionary groups and those who support them contend that missionaries, in addition to their religious endeavors, provide valuable services to the world's marginal peoples. Missionaries often set up schools, health care centers, worker cooperatives that facilitate participation in the greater economy, and transportation routes to remote areas. SIL in particular has as its first priority community development, and pursues this goal through such means as helping indigenous people gain legal title to their lands.

On the other hand, some contend that missionaries actually weaken or even destroy the communities they are supposed to serve. Missionaries often work to assimilate tribal peoples into the greater national culture and economy, which entails promoting the sort of individualism necessary for survival in a modern capitalist society, but foreign to many tribal peoples who must cooperate extensively to survive. With such individualism comes hierarchy based upon one's ability to earn cash, and this can be devastating to an egalitarian culture such as that of the Machiguengas. For SIL, such assimilation is an explicit goal. Both SIL and Catholic missionaries have worked among the Machiguengas since 1947 with marked results. The traditional Machiguenga pattern of living in small semipermanent communities scattered over a wide area has been abandoned by many upon the urging of the missionary groups. By gathering this dispersed people into larger permanent settlements, missionaries are able to reach a greater number of Machiguengas, who, the missionaries argue, are better off for living in communities where they can collectively produce cash crops and benefit from missionary-provided services. In the mid-1970s SIL established a Machiguenga cooperative for production and marketing of crops and livestock and for collective purchasing of various supplies. The co-op was not very lucrative for the Machiguengas, and some argue that the gathering of Machiguengas into large communities as well as the redirection of much of their time and energy into the production of goods for sale has seriously worsened the Machiguenga quality of life. The traditional Machiguenga lifestyle provides each member with a more than adequate diet in exchange for only 1.5 to 3.3 hours of work per day. In contrast, the typical Machiguenga household in the SIL co-op contributed 183 hours of work in 1980 for an annual income of $6. Also, the permanently settled communities must spend more time in subsistence food production; since an area's resources are more quickly depleted by the larger population, the inhabitants must travel farther and farther afield to find and grow food.

Saúl rants about the SIL at a café: "Learn the aboriginal languages! What a swindle! What for? To make the Amazonian Indians good Westerners, good modern men, good capitalists, good Christians of the Reformed Church? Not even that. Just to wipe their culture, their gods, their institutions off the map and corrupt even their dreams" (*The Storyteller,* pp. 96-97). It has also been argued that missionaries undermine a people's confidence in themselves and destroy their culture by encouraging them to renounce their traditional beliefs and practices in favor of Christianity. Though it was forced on them in the past, today's indigenous peoples are free to choose whether they will accept this religion. But perhaps, as Saúl avers, "our culture is too strong, too aggressive" for many to resist, and Christianity is hard to reject when it is accompanied by airplanes, and modern medicine (*The Storyteller,* p. 99).

In the novel the Schneils are perplexed by the Machiguenga storyteller, failing to understand the importance of this figure (invented by Vargas Llosa) because, after all, he is not "religious," according to their notions. Yet each story that the storyteller tells, whether mythological or anecdotal, is infused with the Machiguenga worldview, with its morality, aesthetics, and yes, religion—a religion in which "God is air, water, food, a vital necessity, something without which life wouldn't be possible" (*The Storyteller,* p. 101). The invention of the storyteller helps raise a question that reflects a real-life dilemma related to the missionary phenomenon: by replacing the stories of indigenous peoples with stories of Christianity, are missionaries depriving already marginalized groups of their identities as peoples at a time when these groups are most under threat?

Literary context. Vargas Llosa wrote *The Storyteller* during his neo-liberal period, a time in which the writer came to reject the socialism he had embraced in the 1960s in favor of free-market capitalism. In *The Storyteller,* the Peruvian writer first embraces then rejects socialist *indi-*

genismo, the position that the traditional social systems of Peru's indigenous peoples are closely akin to socialism and that instituting socialism on a national level will allow indigenous peoples "at one and the same time, [to] be able to adopt modern ways and to preserve their essential traditions and customs" (*The Storyteller,* p. 78). Socialist indigenismo is presented as a naive, utopian non-solution to the plight of Peru's indigenous peoples in *The Storyteller.*

In 1958 Vargas Llosa journeyed to the Amazon rainforest where he met Wayne Snell and Betty Elkins-Snell, a couple who lived among and studied the Machiguengas, and who obviously provided his inspiration for the novel's Schneils. Like Saúl and the Peruvian writer, Vargas Llosa became fascinated by the Machiguengas and their tragic approach to life. He read the anthropological and linguistic studies of the Machiguengas, but used them selectively for *The Storyteller,* at times adhering to and at times deviating from documented Machiguenga myths and characteristics. The people are not, as the novel suggests, perpetually on the move, and "the figure of a storyteller who walks through the jungle . . . to share stories and gossip does not exist" (Kristal, p. 165). On the other hand, the fatalistic worldview does, as do other elements, such as the poem "Sadness is looking at me" from an anthropological transcription of a real Machiguenga song (Kristal, p. 164).

Turning to literary precedents, Vargas Llosa's novel most closely evokes "The Ethnographer" by Jorge Luis Borges, a short story in which a student abandons the pursuit of anthropology after being accepted into a North American Indian tribe.

Reviews. Acclaimed science fiction writer Ursula K. Le Guin, an apt reviewer for a novel that has to do with the meeting of two worlds, pronounced *The Storyteller* to be Vargas Llosa's "most engaging and accessible book, for the urgency of its subject purifies and illuminates the writing" (Le Guin, p. 1). Dean Flower, on the other hand, wrote that *The Storyteller* "is not Vargas Llosa's most approachable fiction, partly because it's a story he refused to falsify by turning into a well-made story" (Flower, p. 314). Both critics seem to agree (and this is a recurring theme in the novel's reviews) that in *The Storyteller,* a commitment to the subject matter, to the story, transcends writing technique. Whether or not this improves or detracts from one's opinion of the novel depends upon what one thinks of Vargas Llosa's writing technique overall. Though the author's innovative style—documenting a single conversation in a two-volume novel, interspersing many different points of view in one novel—is widely admired, a few reviewers have found it distracting, feeling it takes away from the development of the characters and from the story. The most consistent factor in reviews of *The Storyteller,* however, is praise for Vargas Llosa's uncompromising struggle to portray another world and another experience with integrity and humanity.

—Kimberly Ball

For More Information

Baksh, Michael George. "Cultural Ecology and Change of the Machiguenga Indians of the Peruvian Amazon." Ph.D. diss., University of California at Los Angeles, 1984.

Elkin, Judith Aiken. *Jews of the Latin American Republics.* Chapel Hill: The University of North Carolina Press, 1980.

Fins, Stephanie. "Missionization and the Machiguenga." *Cultural Survival Quarterly* 7, no. 3 (fall 1983): 24-27.

Flower, Dean. "Story Problems." *The Hudson Review* 43, no. 2 (summer 1990): 311–18.

Hudson, Rex A., ed. *Peru: A Country Study.* Library of Congress, Federal Research Division. 1993.

Johnson, Allen. "The Political Unconscious: Stories and Politics in Two South American Cultures." In *Political Psychology: Cultural and Cross Cultural Perspectives.* Ed. S. Renshon and J. Duckitt. MacMillan: In press. Photocopy.

Kristal, Efraín. *Temptation of the Word: The Novels of Mario Vargas Llosa.* Nashville, Tenn.: Vanderbilt University Press, 1998.

Le Guin, Ursula K. "Feeling the Hot Breath of Civilization." *The New York Times Book Review,* October 29, 1989, 1, 49-50.

Llosa, Mario Vargas. *The Storyteller.* Trans. Helen Lane. New York: Penguin, 1990.

Rosengren, Dan. *In the Eyes of the Beholder: Leadership and the Social Construction of Power and Dominance Among the Matsigenka of the Peruvian Amazon.* Etnologiska Studier #39. Göteborg: Göteborgs Etnografiska Museum, 1987.

Sponsel, Leslie E., ed. *Indigenous Peoples and the Future of Amazonia: An Ecological Anthropology of an Endangered World.* Tuscon: The University of Arizona Press, 1995.

Werlich, David P. *Peru: A Short History.* Carbondale: Southern Illinois University Press, 1978.

Three Trapped Tigers

by
Guillermo Cabrera Infante

Born in 1929 in Gibara, Cuba, and raised on the island, Guillermo Cabrera Infante founded the Cuban Film Archive in 1951. He worked as a fiction editor in the mid-1950s for the magazine *Carteles,* in which he published works of his own (stories and film criticism) that won him a following. After the Cuban Revolution of 1959 Cabrera Infante took posts in the new government. He served as Cuban cultural attaché in Belgium from 1962 to 1964, and then as chargé d'affaires until 1965. He then moved to Madrid for a short time, after which he was forced out by the government for writing critically about the dictator Francisco Franco. In 1968, having lived in London for two years, Cabrera Infante publicly denounced the government of Fidel Castro in Cuba, officially becoming a dissident exile. He was declared a traitor by the Cuban government, which stifled public reception of his writings in Cuba. Outside Cuba many critics and writers characterized his 1967 work, *Three Trapped Tigers,* as one of the most radically experimental Latin American novels of all time.

THE LITERARY WORK

A novel set in Havana, Cuba, during the summer of 1958; published in Spanish (as *Tres tristes tigres*) in 1967, in English in 1971.

SYNOPSIS

Multiple narrators take the reader through the cultures and subcultures of Havana in the summer of 1958.

Events in History at the Time the Novel Takes Place

The Batista era. The work opens in Havana in the summer of 1958, six months before the famous New Year's Eve flight from Cuba by Fulgencio Batista, the latest of a series of repressive and authoritarian Cuban leaders. Havana, the largest city in the Caribbean, is a port city and the center of Cuban commerce. By this time, Havana had also become the locus of world-famous tourism, gambling, and prostitution industries. Though ironic and unsentimental, *Three Trapped Tigers* evokes a sense of nostalgia for this dynamic era in Cuban history. The work presents swiftly moving currents of thought and emotion running within and among a wide range of characters. Through a complicated network of personal and cultural allusions, the novel links the fantasies and disenchantment of its characters to larger forces that have shaped Cuban culture.

At the time, Cuba was just a couple of generations away from having been a colony (it won independence in 1902), and only a few more from being a slave society (Cuba abolished slavery in 1886). The economy had only recently begun to shift away from its heavy dependence upon sugar production and was still largely agricultural and non-industrial. While the city afforded greater economic and social opportunities for all Cubans than before, racial hierarchies and social stratification were still firmly entrenched. In 1911 the government passed the Morua Law (prohibiting the formation of political associations based on color or race). Popular protest against the law brought a government response that resulted in the loss of over 3,000 Afro-Cuban lives in 1912, and the stifling of Afro-Cuban political participation until the 1958 revolution. The social fabric of *Three Trapped Tigers* reflects this legacy. Many moments in the novel suggest prejudices; the doorman, for example, rushes suspiciously toward the mulatto musician Eribo as he enters the apartment building of the young heiress Vivian Smith-Corona, and all of the servants who figure in the novel are black or mulatto. The privileges of being light-skinned are continually evoked by the characters, while having darker skin and hair is treated by many of the figures in the novel as socially disadvantageous and as indicative of sensuality and primitiveness. Afro-Cuban musical forms, such as *rumba* and *son,* were being celebrated in the nightclubs of Havana, and even in the United States by such shows as *I Love Lucy,* yet the Afro-Cuban cultures from which this music originated were simultaneously being denigrated.

FULGENCIO BATISTA

Together with his predecessor, Gerardo Machado, Fulgencio Batista was one of the dictators of Latin America, who, like Augusto Pinochet of Chile and Rafael Leonidas Trujillo of the Dominican Republic, assumed and maintained power through armed force as well as the cultivation of strong ties with the United States and with local economic elites. A sergeant in the Cuban military at the time, Batista was the key organizer of an uprising in 1933 that ousted the increasingly unpopular Machado. By January 14, 1934, Batista had risen to the position of chief of the army, and had garnered enough support within Cuba and from the United States to also oust the current president—the leftist, reform-minded Ramón Grau San Martín. Between 1934 and 1952 Batista and his appointees dominated the political scene, with several short-lived exceptions. He ruled directly from 1940 to 1944 and otherwise through puppet presidents.

In 1952, with the populace split between candidates from the incumbent *Auténticos* and the opposition *Ortodoxos* parties, Batista presented himself as the third candidate in a bid for his former office, but proceeded to ignore electoral protocol and to stage a coup d'état three months prior to the election. He installed himself as president. (Ironically, a then little-known political activist, Fidel Castro Ruz, had been invited to run as an Ortodoxo candidate for the Chamber of Deputies in the ill-fated 1952 election.) Batista's regime grew increasingly repressive and corrupt, courting the financial investment of known figures in U.S. organized crime, such as Meyer Lansky, expanding the national lottery, conceding favored syndicates a portion of the take, and allowing the police to collect an unauthorized "tax" and to collude with drug traffickers and gambling institutions (Schwarz, p. 55). In exchange for such favors, the police were expected to crack down on any potential opposition to Batista. Gamblers, in other words, became part of the sanctioned structure of the Cuban economy and society.

Cabrera Infante's insistence that the novel has been written in Cuban, rather than Spanish, makes sense in view of the island's abundance of dialects and sociolects pertinent to various cultural groups. Language is the principal indication of social status in Cuba. In *Three Trapped Tigers* a character's use of language can make or break a job interview, a social encounter, or a reputation. Accents and dialects can distinguish a Havanan from a provincial, and one's manner of speaking can reflect class and educational background. In the 1950s, as tourism and other industries expanded, many Cubans migrated from the provinces to the cities, mainly to Havana. In the novel many of the characters come from Oriente, the eastern rural province of Cuba, and their accent often reflects their origins. Cabrera Infante uses phonetic spelling and idiomatic expressions to suggest a character's geographical birthplace and social status in Cuban society, as with Beba Longoria, the social-climbing mistress of Colonel Cipriano Suarez Damera. In a witty telephone conversation with an unnamed friend, she alludes to her lover's good fortune, revealing their social aspirations and the corrupt complicity of the army with the Batista regime:

> He couldn't be better off. In the top aichilongs as he says. I don't know if you heard but they given him a concession in the market La Lisa. Well, darling, not *a* stall, of course, but the market *intotal*, as he say.
>
> (Cabrera Infante, *Three Trapped Tigers,* p. 34)

Similarly, much is revealed about the more educated or well-read characters, such as the actor Arsenio Cué, the would-be writer Silvestre, and the photographer Códac, through their adept wordplay. Their punning brings alive the double-entendre-filled language of *choteo,* described by the novel's translator as a language that forms an integral part of Havanan conversation. A provocative form of speech, choteo uses humor and irony to play one sense of a word off another, often with sexual innuendoes.

In the novel such double entendres are perhaps most clearly found in the work of the deceased literary lion, Bustrofedón. The photographer Códac recalls Bustrofedón's improvisation on world culture, a playful undercutting of the seriousness and reverence given to history and high culture in society.

Bustrofedón's litany enumerates his canon of celebrated figures: "Amerigoes Prepucci and Hareun al-Hashish and Nevertitty, and Antigreppine the mother of Nehro and . . . Sheets and Kelly and Fuckner and Scotch Fitzgerald and Somersault Mom and Julius Seizure and Bertold Bitch and Alexander the Hungrate and . . . George BricaBraque and Elder de Broiler and Gerónimo Ambusch and Versneer . . ." (*Three Trapped Tigers,* p. 223). Literary in-jokes are frequently traded between characters in these raunchy and hilarious exchanges. In scenes of ferocious one-upmanship, the characters seem to want to subvert the literary traditions that have shaped them and, at the same time, to display their own erudition.

In another scene, Arsenio's "fiancée," Sibila, speaks to him and to Vivian in French, the language of cultural refinement in many mid-century Latin American societies. Whereas French was the language of high culture, English was the language of commerce and popular culture, as the influx of American tourists and film in the twentieth century transformed Cuban society.

U.S. tourism in Cuba. Cuba's climate, affordable luxury, and paradisal image has attracted tourists from the United States since the latter part of the nineteenth century. In fact, most of the tourism from then on was from the United States, where images of Cuba as a hedonist's playground circulated widely in popular travel magazines and in film. According to the 1925 travel journal of writer Frank Carpenter, Havana "thronged with sightseers from the United States" at the time, while the "Havana Country Club offered memberships to wealthy North Americans in the 1920's" (Schwarz, p. 3). Seductive images of "Latin" culture emerged in the United States when Cubans, Spaniards, and Argentines were portrayed by such actors as Rudolph Valentino, Theda Bara, and even Greta Garbo.

On New Year's Eve, 1926, the Gran Casino Nacional opened in Havana, with celebrities giving toasts with champagne, then outlawed in the United States because of the Prohibition amendment. In 1939 Cuba's largest nightclub, the Tropicana (where *Three Trapped Tigers* begins), opened, featuring performers like the African-American dancer Josephine Baker and the Brazilian singer Carmen Miranda. The club could seat 1,200-1,400 people and was built in the gardens of a mansion in the posh Marianao neighborhood. By the 1950s, when the novel takes place, Havana boasted several nightclubs nearly as large, a string of luxury hotels and casinos, and many restaurants and bars, as well as an internationally recognized ballet company, a symphony orchestra, and a museum of fine arts.

The rise of tourism and the investment of U.S. capital in other sectors of the Cuban economy (such as mining, public utilities, and oil) have been pinpointed as significant factors in Cuba's shift from exclusive dependence on sugar (Pérez-Stable, p. 34). In any case, the shift had only a limited effect on the population. Much of the economic development of this period benefited the foreign investors and local elites more than the general populace. While these local elites in-

WORDPLAY IN *THREE TRAPPED TIGERS*

While most of the novel is rife with puns and linguistic play, nowhere is it as relentless as in the passages that involve Bustrofedón. Here are some of his renamings of famous figures from the past:

Figures from History	Figures in the Novel
Amerigo Vespucci	Amerigoes Prepucci
Haroun Al-Rashid	Hareun al-Hashish
Nefertiti	Nevertitty
Agrippina	Antigreppine
Nero/Nehru	Nehro
Keats and Shelley	Sheets and Kelly
Somerset Maugham	Somersault Mom
Georges Bracque	George BricaBraque
Pieter Bruegel ("the Elder")	Elder de Broiler
Hieronymus Bosch	Gerónimo Ambusch
Vermeer	Versneer

Cuban tourism poster from the 1940s, aimed at visitors from the United States.

cluded many Cubans, they also included immigrants who hailed from the United States and from Spain after the Civil War there. Beginning in the late 1940s children of these elites and of professionals in Cuba gravitated into the tourist economy, which afforded greater economic opportunities than jobs in the professions. Youth from the lower classes were also attracted to the tourist industry by relatively high wages and potential for climbing the social ladder.

By the 1950s other industries such as advertising, fashion, and entertainment were also growing, as reflected in *Three Trapped Tigers* by the burgeoning careers of the fashion photographer Códac, the singer Cuba Venegas, and the publisher Viriato Solaun. The rapidly developing recording careers of artists such as bandleader Beny Moré (a fixture on the Havana club scene and a peripheral character in *Three Trapped Tigers*) and the Trio Matamoros band, reflect the development of a symbiotic relationship between these clubs, the radio industry, and record companies in Cuba. By this time, U.S. popular culture had so pervaded Cuba that most films shown in the cinemas were American, and many American film stars were recognizable to Cubans (Chanan, p. 48).

Ironically, at the same time as the music, film, gambling, and tourist industries were booming, and prostitution was on the rise, the Batista regime maintained a tight grip on the public morals of Cuban society by censoring politically objectionable or sexually explicit publications (Cabrera Infante himself was imprisoned for writing stories that contained "English profanities"). Other tactics by which Batista's government controlled public morality were closure of radio stations and schools. Unwilling, among other circumstances, to be hampered by censors, writers like Alejo Carpentier (see ***The Kingdom of This World,*** also covered in *Latin American Literature and Its Times*) left Cuba and had their works published elsewhere.

The United States and Cuba—proximity and profit. The Platt Amendment of 1901 established "an organic link between Cuba and the United States in which U.S. authority was grafted onto the Cuban national consciousness by appending the amendment to the Cuban Constitution and ultimately drafting the statute into the Permanent Treaty" (Pérez, p. 12). The amendment authorized U.S. intervention for the "preservation of Cuban independence, [and/or] the maintenance of a government adequate for the protection of life, property, and individual liberty" (Pérez, pp. 12-13). Cuban soldiers were increasingly trained and educated in the United States, where they were also often furnished with equipment and supplies.

By 1929 the United States was the dominant investor in nearly every industry in Cuba: sugar, tobacco, railways, utilities, mining, banking, fruit, and tourism. U.S. investors controlled 70-75 percent of all Cuban sugar production (Morley, p. 32).

After World War II, with the advent of the Cold War (the competition between the United States and the Soviet Union for world leadership), Cuba became strategically important. The island figured in U.S. plans to protect itself from any military conflicts in the Caribbean. In 1948 nations of the western hemisphere formed the Organization of American States (OAS), with the active support of the United States, whose leaders hoped the organization would give them a freer hand in Latin America than the United Nations had. It was thought that U.S. dominance of the OAS, which assumed control of economic affairs in the region, would allow U.S. investors and diplomats greater latitude, particularly in Cuba.

Throughout this period, and especially during Batista's 1950s presidency (1952-58), U.S. support for the Cuban leader remained constant, with no change in policy or strategy until the last year of Batista's rule. In addition to the growing investments in gambling and tourism, private U.S. investment in industry in Cuba was booming, with Texaco Oil, Goodyear, International Telephone and Telegraph, and other corporations increasing their presence on the island. U.S. business revenues by the end of 1958 were higher in Cuba than in any other Latin American nation.

Cultural fusion and social division. While African and, to a lesser degree, Asian cultures have had a profound influence on Cuban culture, from its music and literature to its food and religion, control of the Cuban economic, political, and major social institutions has largely been in the hands of Cubans of European descent and U.S. residents. In colonial Cuba Spanish-born *peninsulares* (a reference to the Iberian peninsula, on which Spain is located) were privileged over the locally born *criollos* (descendants of Spaniards), and U.S. and European residents likewise occupied privileged positions. As in many Caribbean societies, there has been an internalized racism in Cuban society; those Cubans who rise to the upper classes and attain high-level political, professional, and commercial positions are almost exclusively light-skinned. Batista's rise to military and political power, as a mulatto from a lower-class background, stands as a rare exception to the rule. The novel *Three Trapped Tigers* underscores the internalization of these racist values in the entertainment and fashion industry, as well as through interactions among characters. For instance, an exchange between the mulatto musician Eribo and Vivian

Smith-Corona, the wealthy blonde heiress that he is trying to seduce, illustrates a fusion of racial and class prejudices. When Eribo mixes his wit with sexual innunendo, Vivian responds coldly:

> [VIVIAN:]—That's really dirty. It's the sort of thing Balbina would say.
> [ERIBO:]—The *servant,* I said.
> [VIVIAN:]—What's wrong with that? It would be worse if I called her a maid.
> [ERIBO:]—Is she a Negro?
> [VIVIAN:]—What are you talking about?
> [ERIBO:]—Is she black or isn't she?
> [VIVIAN:]—All right, yes.
> [ERIBO:]—I didn't say anything.
> [VIVIAN:]—No, she's not black. She's Spanish.
> [ERIBO:]—It's always one or the other.
> [VIVIAN:]—You're neither one nor the other.
> [ERIBO:]—You just don't know how right you are, sweetie.
> (*Three Trapped Tigers,* p. 101)

Vivian aligns her boyfriend Eribo's uncouth comment with Balbina; his questions draw out the presumptions behind her response. The scene suggests that social status is defined by both racial hierarchies and by determining others' perception of one's race.

The Novel in Focus

Plot summary. *Three Trapped Tigers* defies any attempt to impose a chronology or linear structure upon it. However, three undercurrents and their antitheses seem to run through the work as a whole: illusion and disillusion, violence and repression (social and psychological), dynamic verbal exchanges and total noncommunication. While the novel's plot is nonlinear, its movement could be summarized as follows: wandering through Havana at a near-manic pace, a photographer and his friends, mainly artists and writers, randomly connect with several models and actresses, a blues singer about to be "discovered," and other unfixed fixtures in the city nightlife. The novel derives its energy from the verbal and physical dynamism of its characters, from their movement from squalor to luxury and back, from sheer adrenaline-filled sequences of flirtatious and decadent conversation while on the road, and from changes in location from barstool to backstage to diner booth. The central characters of the work are Silvestre, a would-be writer; Arsenio, an actor and aspiring television writer; Eribo, a drummer and advertising typesetter; Códac, a press photographer; Magalena Cruz, Beba Longoria, and Laura Díaz, models and actresses; Bustrofedón, a writer we meet only through a posthumously played recording of his work; and Mr. Campbell, an established writer from the United States.

Three Trapped Tigers pays homage to the legendary nightlife of a complex city, or a complexed city, if the sequence of psychoanalysis sessions (with an unnamed female subject) are any indication. In these psychoanalytic sessions and in the work as a whole, there is an implicit tension between the subconscious and self-conscious responses of the characters, individually and collectively, to a society on the brink of radical transformation.

The book opens in the celebrated Tropicana nightclub, with a "Prologue" in which the emcee introduces the coming spectacle. In this introduction, he addresses his audience bilingually, echoing or emphasizing his statements by switching between Spanish and English, as evident in his welcoming statement:

> our ENORMOUS American audience of glamorous and distinguished tourists who are visiting the land of the gay senyoritas and brave caballerros . . . as we say in our romantic language, the language of colonizadors and toreros (bullfighters) and very, very, but verry (I know what I say) beautiful duennas.
> (*Three Trapped Tigers,* p. 4)

The English language included in the introduction in the original Spanish version underscores the impact of tourism and U.S. cultural influence on Cuban society. As the novel's translator, Suzanne Levine, writes: "English, for Latin America . . . represents both the detested language of an imperial presence and the desired language of economic and cultural power" (Levine, p. 91). The emcee introduces the reader to the guests at the nightclub that evening, and in so doing, he presents some of the main characters of *Three Trapped Tigers.* The collective and public drama of the nightclub introduction is then refracted into individual "scenes," subconsciously or self-consciously performed by the characters.

The opening sets the reader up for the multiplicity of speakers, languages, and audiences that the work will encompass. Each subsequent section is narrated in the first person, occasionally by an unnamed narrator, as in the psychoanalytic sessions that punctuate the entire work. The collection of "voices" that are presented in the novel provides a panoramic view of Havana as a metropolitan and magnetic attraction for Cubans and for people from the United States. In addition to the range of perspectives these "voices" reflect, a similarly wide range of tones is set, both within and between the different sections of the work.

The "Beginners" section, which follows the "Prologue," presents various characters' reflections on their childhood or their introduction to Havana in a relatively intimate and confessional tone. Their stories contain the familiar elements of early sexual curiosity, provincial fascination with the capital city, youthful rebellion and adult disapproval, and desire for actual or vicarious escape from poverty and parochialism. Silvestre, for example, gives a seemingly nostalgic account of sneaking into Western movies at the local cinema, which takes a dramatically different turn upon his accidental witnessing of a murder outside the theater. In this case, the threads of violence and illusion converge. Violence is an integral part of other tales of initiation too; Arsenio, new to Havana and an aspiring writer and actor, is shot in the shoulder by an older actor. Laura Díaz recounts her simultaneous sexual and theatrical initiation as a young girl, when she and a friend are caught watching a couple surreptitiously having sex and then proceed to tell the story to friends and neighbors. She learns the thrill of holding an audience's attention, but her story is charged with guilt, for having driven the couple apart by exposing their secret and for not revealing her own reason for hiding where she did, which was so that she and her friend could masturbate undisturbed.

The work's extraordinary sensitivity to the rhythms, inflections, puns, and expressions of everyday speech and literary language brings each of these characters to life sharply. Catch the rhythm of the drummer Eribo's homage to the bandleader Beny Moré: "Remembering Beny made me remember a common past, that is music: a *danzón* [musical style] titled "Isora" in which the *tumbadora* [drum] repeats a double beat of the double bass filling the bar and beating the most accomplished dancer, who has to put up with or dive under the swaying mean measure of the rhythm" (*Three Trapped Tigers,* p. 88). The pun-happy idioms of Bustrofedón, Silvestre, and the others are given twists and turns in allusive sentences charged with double and triple meanings that infuse the already-rich Cuban language with the narrators' personal styles. For instance, Códac recalls a lunch with Bustrofedón, describing how their raucous behavior drove the waiter to refuse to serve them. The description incorporates figures from Greek mythology (Icarus, Poseidon, Nausicaa) and an allusion to a well-known newspaper (the *Herald Tribune*) among other puns:

> . . . and the fellouch refuses to serve us and gets off our cloud to plunge icariously into the horizontal chasm of thiseatery and starts bellyaching in the backroom to the Poseidowner and we're still there in the hearafter drowning of laughter on the shores of the tablecloth, almost nausicated, with this unbelievable public proclaimer Bustrophone herald tribunely crying out loud.
>
> (*Three Trapped Tigers,* p. 208)

Much of the novel's remarkable accomplishment lies in its evocation of the history, music, language, and spirit of an extraordinarily complex cultural moment, and it manages this largely through a dizzying, dynamic use of language. For instance, through phonetic spelling, it manages to present the verbal rhythms of the straightforward though parochial Delia Doce, as she would translate them to writing. Delia writes a letter to her friend Estelvina, whose daughter, Gloria Pérez, left their hometown to live in Havana. Delia recounts Gloria's disastrous stay with her, characterizing her rise to fame as being accompanied by a moral fall, and ends with this moral observation:

> As I was saying this daughter of yours turned out a right good for nothing hear in Havana which is a very dangeroused city for young peeple from the Country without any experience on life whatso ever.
>
> (*Three Trapped Tigers,* p. 19)

Delia's language and her attempt to render a formal account of events reflect her lack of education and comically reveal her naiveté in the process. In the monologue by aspiring actress and model Magalena Cruz that follows Delia's section, a very different tone is set, as the language of this passage captures the rhythms of casual phone conversation. Here again, the novel uses phonetic spelling to replicate Magalena Cruz's colloquial speech, as well as creative punctuation to capture the idiosyncrasies of her speaking style and her personality. Her perspective is nearly directly opposed to Delia's, as she recounts a fight with her older and morally judgmental hostess-housemother from the point-of-view of a young but streetwise model: "and so I pick up my stylish stole and my bitchy bag and I take one mean step, yeah, then two mean steps, yeah yeah (*Three Trapped Tigers,* p. 14). Our perspective on Magalena's tough talk alters dramatically when it is later intimated that she had repeatedly been exposed to violence, and possibly suffered a breakdown and endured shock therapy.

Puns serve as a deferral or an evasion of pain, as much as a tactic of seduction. Many of the characters furthermore use humor to deflate myths, whether these myths are about Cuban or American history, or about origins, or about (often apocalyptic) endings. Similarly, humor and parody both pay homage to and subvert the writers that comprise the canon of Cuban literature. Examine, for instance, the life spans attributed to each writer. Alejo Carpentier's years are given as 1904-1882, 22 years lived in the wrong direction (an allusion to his novella *Journey to the Source*). Similarly, Virgilio Piñera is fictively killed off with the year of death given as 1966 (he was alive at the time of the book's publication); the latter move could be a not-so-subtle dismissal of the value of Piñera's later literary production.

While the novel as a whole takes the reader on a linguistic and narrative journey through Havana, the parodist-ventriloquist Bustrofedón leads his reader/listener on another journey in the section titled "The Death of Trotsky as Described by Various Cuban Writers, Several Years After the Event—or Before." This section is a transcription of a recording of Bustrofedón's literary creation, an imaginary collection of written accounts of the murder of Leon Trotsky. The collection contains descriptions by José Martí, poet and leader in the struggle for Cuba's independence (see **"Our America,"** also covered in *Latin American Literature and Its Times*); Virgilio Piñera, the aforementioned poet/playwright; and others, from the celebrated poet/novelist José Lezama Lima to the poet Nicolás Guillén. Two sections in particular illustrate the humor of Bustrofedón's mimicry of the lauded writers, those "by" the ethnologist Lydia Cabrera and the novelist Alejo Carpentier. The section by Cabrera mocks the anthropologist-as-interpreter mode that she employs in her writing, with a comical "translation" of the murder of Trotsky as an Afro-Cuban ritual. In this section, Bustrofedón provides the "original" language in parentheses, the humor of which is evident when one thinks of common English words associated with the phonetic sounds of these terms: "What a difficult situation! There remained (*Ol-lef*) no other (*nozingelsu*) solution (*Ungawa!*) than to go away (*fokkoffo*)!" (*Three Trapped Tigers*, p. 250). Carpentier's literary style is lampooned with an ironic replication of his baroque language and of the self-conscious erudition of his novel *The Lost Steps*, here parodied as "Lot's Steps." In this description of Trotsky's reflections, Carpentier's self-conscious erudition is reproduced in burlesque:

> He walked down steeply sloping bifid paths bordered by volcanic rubble and gazed at the imposing *château-fort* which already towered above him. He was facades that mingled a delirium of styles, where Bramante and Vitruvius disputed the primacy with Herrera and Churriguera and where traces of early Plateresque were fused with a bold display of late Baroque.
>
> (*Three Trapped Tigers*, pp. 260-61)

These parodies reveal the primacy of style in these writers' efforts to relay meaning. This section of the novel presents storytelling as a process, and exposes the subjectivity of supposedly "factual" accounts, as does the section in which Mr. Campbell tells and retells his "story of the stick," a fictional account of the loss of a cane purchased on his visit to Cuba. His account is retold by the fictional Mrs. Campbell in a "corrected" version, which is followed by Mr. Campbell's response to her edits. All of these scenes reveal Cuba, and particularly Havana, as a textual world. In it, places, events, people, and speech are all filtered through the visual and verbal language of film and literature. Not only do the characters often talk in Hollywood film-speak and allude to literature and popular culture, but Havana emerges in *Three Trapped Tigers* as a city experienced through the images of literature and film.

Havana: Cabrera Infante's Paradiso/Inferno. The depiction in *Three Trapped Tigers* of the cultures and subcultures of Havana in 1958 relies heavily on the evocative use of language and of cultural references, as well as on the unique perspective of an exile. Unlike the majority of Cuban exiles, Cabrera Infante moved from being an advocate of the revolution and an insider in the cultural institutions of the early revolutionary government to being one of the earliest dissident exiles of that government. While Mario Vargas Llosa (see ***The Storyteller***, also covered in *Latin American Literature and Its Times*) claims that Cabrera Infante's vision of Havana "owes much more to the writer's fantasy than to his memories," he then says of this version of Havana:

> There it is now, spirited into reality, more real than the one that served as its model—living almost exclusively by night, in those convulsive, pre-revolutionary years, shaken by tropical rhythms, smoky, sensual, virulent, journalistic,

The Casino Español in Havana.

> bohemian, jocose and gangsterish, in its savory eternity of words.
>
> (Vargas Llosa, p. 56)

Such a notion of spiriting Havana into reality coincides with Cabrera Infante's repeated assertions that his books are not really novels. As the author himself states:

> I don't take a map of the city with me because everywhere I go I have Havana on my mind. . . . My contention is that by remembering I can

> rebuild Havana, brick by word, word by word, all guided by my memory. . . . I use nostalgia to form and inform what I write. She is actually the whore of memory but I've married her the way some people marry money. Call me Mr. Memory.
> (Cabrera Infante in Levine, p. 24)

While perhaps not brick by brick, Cabrera Infante reconstructs Havana street by street, as the characters' routes through the city take the reader along actual streets such as the coastal Malecon and the grand Quinta Avenida, through the Parque Central and through the posh neighborhoods of Miramar and Marianao. Many of the landmarks of *Three Trapped Tigers* are familiar places to readers of the English novelist Graham Greene, whose writing invokes the Hotel Inglaterra and the Tropicana Cabaret, or to fans of U.S. writer Ernest Hemingway, who preferred El Floridita bar and the Bar Celeste. In *Three Trapped Tigers* Silvestre's story of sneaking into movies with his brother mentions the Majestic and the Alcázar, two of the more than 20 movie houses in Havana alone, which showed primarily films from the United States. Constant references to street names and numbers, beaches, clubs, and bars, locate the characters in a precisely Havanan landscape. Such references even place the characters in their social milieu, such as when Códac refers to Vivian's friends as people who frequent the clubs and casinos of high society—they are "Havana Yacht Club types, or Vedado Tennis, or Casino Español" (*Three Trapped Tigers,* p. 89).

Sources and literary context. Cabrera Infante has stated in a number of interviews that he drew inspiration from James Joyce's novels, particularly *Ulysses* (a 24-hour odyssey through Dublin, with real and fictitious local specificity), for his depiction of the world of *Three Trapped Tigers.* As the Spanish-language translator of Joyce's *Dubliners,* Cabrera Infante certainly has an intimate understanding of how Joyce renders the geography, rhythms of speech, history, and culture of Dublin, and the fact that Joyce wrote from self-imposed exile compounds the parallels one could draw between their works. Likewise, Cabrera Infante also acknowledges a literary debt to Roman author Petronius's *Satyricon* (an account of two students journeying through Italy in the age of Nero), and to Lawrence Sterne's *Tristram Shandy.*

While *Three Trapped Tigers* draws on too many films to identify, U.S. westerns, film noir, and gangster films of the 1940s and '50s (such as *The Treasure of the Sierra Madre*) figure most prominently in the dialogues of the protagonists of Cabrera Infante's novel. Likewise, a number of Cuban personalities mentioned in the work, such as the bandleader Beny Moré and the critic Rine Leal, were celebrated figures in Havana at that time. The character La Estrella, who so captivates Códac with her voice, is said to be modeled after Frédy, a popular Havanan singer. Coupled with the censorship of Saba Cabrera's film *P.M.* (see below), the news of Frédy's death in 1961 prompted Cabrera Infante to begin writing *Three Trapped Tigers* (Levine, pp. 70-71).

The surreal quality of the novel is attributed to Cabrera Infante's evocation of Lewis Carroll, as suggested in the epigraph to the novel: "And she tried to fancy what the flame of a candle looks like after the candle is blown out," a quotation from *Alice in Wonderland* (*Three Trapped Tigers,* epigraph). The central "Mirrormaze" section in *Three Trapped Tigers,* which uses inversion and reflection (literally by the mirroring of a page of text onto the facing page), suggests a parallel with another Carroll work, *Through the Looking Glass.* Similarly, there is a parody of Edgar Allan Poe's poem "The Raven" that evokes Carroll's "Jabberwockey" in its nonsensical language: "While I nodled, noodled, nundled, trundlingly I come unsundered, / As if someone howsomever, rapping, crapping at my do'er" (*Three Trapped Tigers,* p. 212).

The epilogue to the novel, a rambling monologue by an anonymous woman, is said by Cabrera Infante to have been drawn from the speeches of a homeless woman whom he had encountered often in downtown Havana. In this final moment of *Three Trapped Tigers,* racism, religious chauvinism, hunger, and violence are alluded to in an outpouring of apocalyptic fervor. Her speech impresses on the reader a sense of fatality and desperation in the face of the corruption and violence of Batista's regime.

Events in History at the Time the Novel Was Written

Revolutionary history. The fall of Batista in 1958 left a political vacuum in Cuba, according to several historians, with the populace deprived of any access to traditional institutions of political decision making. On July 18, 1959, after a five-month interim with an anti-communist president, Castro and his close friend and ally Osvaldo Dorticós Torrado installed themselves as prime minister and president, respectively. Their revolutionary government stepped into the vacuum, and they immediately set about creating their own revolutionary institutions, replacing, for example, the military forces with the Rebel Army. Cabrera Infante took an active part in these new institutions in their early days, serving as editor of the national daily newspaper's cultural weekly, titled *Lunes de Revolución.* This journal featured pieces by well-known Cuban writers like José Lezama Lima and Virgilio Piñera, and in addition to fiction, included articles and reviews of film and art.

By 1961 Castro had launched major literacy and health care campaigns (with impressive results), and early that year he publicly declared Cuba a socialist country and himself a Marxist-Leninist. Castro demanded that the United States dramatically cut back the size of its Havana embassy, and U.S. President Dwight D. Eisenhower broke off diplomatic relations with Cuba on January 3, 1961. By February 2 the new U.S. President, John F. Kennedy, had authorized an April 17th invasion of Cuba. This attack, known in the U.S. as the "Bay of Pigs" invasion (in Cuba it is called "Playa Girón"), went forward with disastrous results, traceable to a lack of enthusiasm for it in Cuba and to Kennedy's own lukewarm support. The Cuban counter-revolutionaries were defeated, many U.S. soldiers were captured (though freed by Christmas of that year), and the stakes were raised in the conflict between the United States and Cuba. Cabrera Infante served as a war correspondent for *Revolución* during the "Bay of Pigs" invasion.

However, six weeks after the invasion, upon the censorship of a film made by his brother, Saba, Cabrera Infante's relationship to the Castro government changed dramatically. In May 1961 the film, entitled *P.M.,* concerning the nightlife of pre-revolutionary Havana, was televised in Cuba. When the filmmakers applied for permission to exhibit the film in theaters, they were asked to send it to the government's film institute. Expecting no objections, they sent the film to ICAIC (the national film institute), where, over the protests of more than 200 writers and artists, Guillermo Cabrera Infante among them, it was quickly banned from any further public exhibition and confiscated. Soon after, and most likely because of the protest, the cultural weekly edited by Cabrera Infante was shut down. The reason given for banning the film was its irresponsibility to the ideals of the revolution, most likely because its treatment of pre-revolutionary nightlife in Havana diverged from the prescribed social realist style and content called for in documentaries produced in the revolutionary era (Chanan, p. 102).

Soon after, Cabrera Infante was appointed cultural attaché to Belgium, and left Cuba for Brussels, where he lived for the next four years, shifting from cultural attaché to chargé d'affaires before making a visit home for his mother's funeral in 1965. Detained for four months in Havana, Cabrera Infante then left Cuba for good, resigning from his post and moving to Madrid in that same year. While in Europe he wrote a manuscript for *Three Trapped Tigers,* focusing on the period and the context treated in his brother's film. In several interviews, Cabrera Infante cites the movie—and its censorship—as an inspiration for the novel. After his prize-winning manuscript received numerous "recommended" cuts from the censors in Spain, then under dictator Francisco Franco, Cabrera Infante began the rewriting process. The censors' primary objections were to his references to sexuality and homosexuality and their association with military figures and institutions in the work. Cabrera Infante retained much of the sexual content of the novel, but reworked it by shifting its focus to literary parody rather than politics. He then published the novel with the Seix Barral publishing house, the company that sponsored one of the prizes (the Biblioteca Breve prize) earned by his manuscript. Eventually forced out of Madrid in 1967 for writings that were critical of Franco, Cabrera Infante moved to London. Keeping a low profile, but growing increasingly discontented with reports of escalating censorship and repression by the Cuban government, Cabrera Infante publicly denounced the Castro regime for the first time in 1968. In the meantime, *Three Trapped Tigers* was gaining international acclaim, though Cabrera Infante was then censored from the left as well as the right for his denunciation of Castro. His books were (and continue to be) banned in Cuba, though people there paid high prices for copies smuggled into the country.

Reviews. Though his books are banned in Cuba, several reviews of his work written by Havana-based writers have been published by the Free Press Agency of Cuba (APIC) and in several Cuban-American journals and papers. One such review, by journalist David Bacallao Velez, describes the style of *Three Trapped Tigers* as "concise, with tremendous aesthetic and compositional rigor" (Bacallao Velez, p. 1; trans. V. Sams). Peruvian writer Mario Vargas Llosa states that Cabrera Infante's prose "is one of the most personal and unusual creations in our language: an exhibitionistic, luxurious, musical and intrusive prose," and he declares Cabrera Infante's 1997

Cervantes Prize well deserved (Vargas Llosa, p.56). Leland Guyer rounds out the chorus of praise by calling *Three Trapped Tigers* "a wondrous novel" (Guyer, p. 358).

—Victoria Sams

For More Information

Bacallao Velez, David. "El Proyecto Prensa Libre." *APIC,* February 8, 1998.

Cabrera Infante, Guillermo. *Three Trapped Tigers.* Trans. Donald Gardner and Suzanne Jill Levine in collaboration with the author. New York: Marlowe and Company, 1971.

Chanan, Michael. *The Cuban Image: Cinema and Cultural Politics in Cuba.* Bloomington: Indiana University Press, 1985.

Dominguez, Jorge I. *Cuba: Order and Revolution.* Cambridge, Mass.: Harvard University Press, 1978.

Guyer, Leland. "Guillermo Cabrera Infante: Two Islands, Many Worlds." *World Literature Today* 71, no. 2 (spring 1997): 358.

Levine, Suzanne Jill. *The Subversive Scribe: Translating Latin American Fiction.* Saint Paul: Graywolf Press, 1991.

Lumsden, Ian. *Machos, Maricones, and Gays.* Philadelphia: Temple University Press, 1996.

Morley, Morris H. *Imperial State and Revolution: The US and Cuba, 1952-1986.* Cambridge: Cambridge University Press, 1987.

Pérez, Louis A., Jr. *Army Politics in Cuba: 1898-1958.* Pittsburgh: University of Pittsburgh Press, 1976.

Pérez-Stable, Marifeli. *The Cuban Revolution: Origins, Course, Legacy.* New York: Oxford University Press, 1993.

Schwarz, Rosalie. *Pleasure Island: Tourism and Temptation in Cuba.* Lincoln: University of Nebraska Press, 1997.

Vargas Llosa, Mario. "Touchstone." *The Nation* 266, no. 17 (May 11, 1998): 56-62.

Woman Hollering Creek and Other Stories

by
Sandra Cisneros

Sandra Cisneros was born in Chicago in 1954 to a Mexican father and a Mexican American mother, the only daughter among seven children. Her upbringing was marked by the constraining influence of her brothers—because they insisted that she play a traditional female role, she often felt like she had "seven fathers" (Cisneros in Matuz, p. 150). She also contended with the displacement caused by her family's frequent moves between the United States and Mexico. So, from an early age Cisneros confronted the questions about her identity as a female and a Mexican American that would become central to her writing as an adult. Cisneros has dealt with many of these questions in books of poetry and in her widely acclaimed collection of vignettes, *The House on Mango Street* (1985). In *Woman Hollering Creek,* written mainly while Cisneros was living in San Antonio, Texas, she focuses on the varied experiences of girls and women with a Mexican heritage—characters who are distinguished by their different levels of income, education, independence, and Americanization, but united by similar histories, needs, and desires.

THE LITERARY WORK

A collection of 22 short stories and vignettes set in Mexico and the southwestern United States between the early 1900s and the late 1980s; published in English in 1991.

SYNOPSIS

A series of mostly female Mexican and Mexican American narrators share snapshots of their lives and reflect on their identities, cultures, and relationships.

Events in History at the Time of the Short Stories

Some of the events included in this section take place before the action of the stories, but the effects of these events have proved long-lasting. They play a significant role in twentieth-century Mexican and Mexican American culture, and their impact resonates in the lives of Cisneros's characters.

Guadalupe and Mexican Catholicism. When Hernán Cortés conquered the Aztec Empire in 1521, he brought with him the religion of his native Spain, Catholicism. Spanish missionaries came to Mexico during and after the Conquest, eager to Christianize—and, in their view, civilize—the natives. However, before Cortés's arrival the Aztecs and other cultures in Mexico had long practiced their own religions. Therefore, many of these natives, although forced to convert, initially resisted the teachings of Catholicism. Just the same, the missionaries were ultimately quite successful at gaining converts.

Part of the missionaries' success was due to a reported miracle that allowed the Aztecs to conceive of Catholicism as linked to their own native religion. In December 1531 the Virgin Mary is said to have appeared outside Mexico City, at the hill of Tepeyac—a site that was a shrine to Tonantzín, the Aztec mother goddess. The Virgin Mary sup-

Painting of the Virgin of Guadalupe by Juan de Villegas.

posedly spoke here to a native convert to Catholicism named Juan Diego, asking him to tell the bishop of Mexico of her wish that a church be built here in her honor. When the bishop rebuffed him, demanding some proof that this request had come from the Virgin Mary, Juan Diego returned to the hill. This time the Virgin told him to pick some flowers, which grew nearby in a place where flowers normally did not grow and were out of season. He was to place them in his cloak, and open it in front of the bishop. When Juan Diego opened his cloak for the bishop, the flowers fell to the floor and imprinted on the cloak was a picture of the Virgin as she had appeared, with brown skin and dark hair. Juan Diego afterward returned home to find that his uncle had also been visited by the Virgin, who told him that the church was to be dedicated to "the ever Virgin Saint Mary of Guadalupe," afterwards known simply as the Virgin of Guadalupe (Laso de la Vega in Poole, p. 28).

After hearing of the Virgin of Guadalupe's appearance, thousands of Indians agreed to be converted. Indians and Spanish colonists alike embraced her as a source of comfort and a symbol of a uniquely Mexican religion and identity—a Catholicized Tonantzín. She came to represent the blending of European and Indian societies, the rebirth of the native goddess Tonatzín as the Virgin of Guadalupe. The cult of Guadalupe is still a powerful force in Mexican and Mexican American life, as Cisneros's stories "Tepeyac," "Anguiano Religious Articles . . . ," and "Little Miracles, Kept Promises" indicate. The Virgin is regarded by many not just as a symbol of Mexican heritage, but as a source of strength, a confidante, and a granter of miracles. In fact, the Mexican poet Octavio Paz (see ***The Labyrinth of Solitude***, also covered in *Latin American Literature and Its Times*) once observed, "The Mexican people, after more than two centuries of experiments and defeats, have faith only in the Virgin of Guadalupe and the National Lottery" (Paz in Lafaye, p. xi). Demonstrating this faith, millions of pilgrims every December visit the site where the Virgin of Guadalupe is said to have appeared.

The Chicano in America. In 1848 a war between Mexico and the United States ended with the signing of the Treaty of Guadalupe Hidalgo, in which Mexico was forced to sell the present-day states of Arizona, California, New Mexico, Utah, Nevada, and parts of Colorado to the United States for $15 million. Texas, also a former Mexican territory, had been annexed by the United States in 1845, a move that helped ignite the war. In the course of just a few years, Mexico had lost about one-half of its land.

Although Mexico no longer owned the territory that became the southwestern United States, many Mexicans (between 86,000 and 116,000) remained on the land after the war. The U.S. government allowed these original Mexican Americans—Chicanos—to choose the citizenship they preferred, and promised to protect their political, land, and property rights. It failed, however, to honor their property claims, tolerating flagrant wrongdoing by newcomers from more established parts of the United States. Many Chicanos found that their unfamiliarity with American language, culture, and laws made it easy for them to be exploited by the growing numbers of Anglo Americans that were settling among them, and also by a few wealthy and powerful members of the Chicano elite.

The California gold rush of 1849 and the promise of work building railroad lines in the 1860s brought more Mexicans to the United States. At the end of these events, some returned home, but many settled in California, Texas, and other formerly Mexican lands. Immigration continued from the 1860s into the twentieth century, when political turmoil and economic trouble in Mexico—as well as recruitment efforts by U.S. agriculture interests—heightened the appeal of crossing the border. By 1990 Chicanos in the United States, including recent immigrants and those whose ancestors lived in the Southwest when it had been Mexico, numbered 14.5 million.

Emiliano Zapata and the Mexican Revolution. In Mexico the three decades following the Treaty of Guadalupe Hidalgo were marked by instability, including a series of internal conflicts and a brief period of rule by the French-installed Emperor Maximilian (1864-66). Staging a coup d'état in 1876, Porfirio Díaz began a 34-year pres-

ZAPATA'S LOOK

Emiliano Zapata, bandit-hero of the Revolution, was a peasant. Nonetheless, he cut an impressive figure, as described by one historian:

> In tight black pants with giant silver buttons along the outer seam of each leg, an embroidered leather or cotton jacket, a silk handkerchief tied loosely around his neck, silver spurs, a pistol at his waist and, to top it off, a wide felt sombrero with a flowered border, Zapata was impressive and clearly more than a little vain. Somewhat taller than the average villager and of a normal build, he had a long, thick moustache that curled up slightly at the ends, dark skin, dark eyes, and a penetrating gaze. . . . He wasted little time with talk; when he did speak[,] his words—emerging in "rushes and sparks"—betrayed the nervous energy he had had since childhood.
>
> (Brunk, p. 23)

Emiliano Zapata

idency (1876-80 and 1884-1911) that ended this instability, though at a great cost. Before he came to power, Díaz had aligned himself with the Liberal Party of Mexico, a group that sought to lessen some of the country's economic inequalities. The party drafted a constitution that limited the special privileges of the wealthy Catholic Church and the military, and provided a bill of rights similar to that of the United States. Once his presidency began, however, Díaz left many of his liberal principles behind and became a dictator.

One of Díaz's early supporters was José Zapata, a farmer and soldier from the town of Anenecuilco in the southern state of Morelos. Zapata's support for Díaz hinged on a promise Díaz had made before he came to power: he would see to it that the people of Anenecuilco, whose land had been seized illegally by *hacendados*—hacienda owners, many of whom descended from 16th-century Spanish colonists—would have their land titles honored by the new government. This promise was one of many that Díaz did not keep, but Zapata's family did not forget it.

In 1910 Porfirio Díaz was still in power, and frustration with his dictatorship was widespread. Mexicans across the country wanted reform and were willing to fight for it. Some called for protective labor laws, some for an improved public education system, others for a curtailment of Church power; ironically, many of these grievances had been rallying points decades earlier for the Liberals whom Díaz ostensibly supported. When Francisco Madero, a liberal-minded hacendado, called for a national uprising on November 20, 1910, Mexicans across the country slowly began to respond.

In Morelos the battle cry was for land redistribution. Not only did the peasants of Morelos seek to regain the land José Zapata had spoken of—the land that was seized illegally by hacendados—they now had even greater losses to contend with. In an attempt to weaken the economic power of the Catholic Church, the Liberals had banned corporate landholding in their 1857 constitution. Incidentally, this ban also affected land that was held communally by groups of peasants. Putting the ban into practice, the government auctioned off, usually to the highest hacendado bidder, any land that was still communally held in Morelos in the mid-nineteenth century.

By the spring of 1911 a horse trader, farmer, and village council president named Emiliano Zapata had decided that his people's legal and political attempts to regain their land had been exhausted. It was time to enter the Revolution in quest of justice. Zapata was to become a hero to the peasants of Morelos and neighboring states and a bandit to hacienda owners and a succession of Mexican presidents. For almost nine years, Zapata led the fight for "Land and Liberty"—the goal of his ancestor, José Zapata, and of generations of Morelos's inhabitants.

The Revolution was long, devastating, and complicated. Presidential power shifted often, as did alliances among rebel groups. It was difficult for those involved to know whom to support and whom to trust. This was especially true for Emiliano Zapata, who counted many former allies among his enemies as the war progressed. Although Zapata and his rebels fought first against President Díaz's federal troops, or *federales,* their opponents later included the liberal hacendado Francisco Madero, who had failed to deliver on a promise of land reform after winning the presidency; General Victoriano Huerta, who ousted Madero and terrorized rebel strongholds like Morelos; and Venustiano Carranza, whom Zapata denounced as a corrupt politician after he won the presidency, though they had fought against a common enemy only a month before. Zapata trusted almost no one outside of Morelos during the war, and trusted outsiders even less when they gained the power of the presidency. "Revolutions will come and revolutions will go," he said in 1914, "but I will continue with mine" (Zapata in Womack, pp. 197-98).

Zapata's revolution was about land. His "Plan of Ayala," written in November 1911, called for the immediate return of land to the citizens and villages that held title to it, and for the seizure of remaining hacienda properties held by those who opposed his movement; these lands were to be donated to needy peasants who had no legitimate claims to land.

Zapata never saw the Plan of Ayala enacted, although the peasants of Morelos did have a portion of their land returned to them in the 1920s. He continued to fight stubbornly, however, even after suffering a major defeat at the hands of the *Carrancistas* (Carranza's forces) in 1915. In the years following this defeat, his troops and the people of Morelos suffered from food shortages and a plague of deadly diseases. In 1918, in fact, the population of Morelos dropped an astounding 25 percent. Still, Zapata continued to lead the fight until April 1919, when the rebel who trusted no one was deceived by a federal colonel whose soldiers shot him dead at point-blank range.

In "Eyes of Zapata," Inés speaks of "the hard man's work I do clearing the field with the hoe and the machete, dirty work that leaves the clothes filthy, work no woman would do before the war" (Cisneros, *Woman Hollering Creek and Other Stories,* p. 86). Throughout the Revolution, women were forced to take on many roles formerly relegated to men. Some, like Inés, worked the fields because their husbands were away fighting. Others, *soldaderas,* traveled with bands of soldiers, and in addition to cooking and cleaning for them, took charge of medicine, munitions, mail, and train dispatches, and often spied behind enemy lines. *Soldadas* (female soldiers) actually fought alongside the men. Although most women returned to traditional ways of life after the Revolution, the roles they played during this period helped pave the way for an improvement of the Mexican woman's position in the late twentieth century.

THE DESTRUCTION OF MORELOS

Only three years into the war, Zapata's home state of Morelos had already been burned and looted almost beyond recognition by Huerta's soldiers. The balladeer Marciano Silva, who traveled with Zapata's forces during this time, describes its appearance:

> Our pueblos only plains
> White ashes, pictures of horror
> Sad deserts, isolated places
> Where only sorrow stirs. . . .
> (Silva in Brunk, p. 148)

"Mericans" or Mexicans? One of the issues raised repeatedly in *Woman Hollering Creek* is the clash between Mexican and American culture in the Chicano communities of the United States. In "Mericans," for example, a young girl tells of her "awful grandmother" who prays in a church for "the grandchildren born in that barbaric country [the United States] with its barbarian ways" while the girl and her brothers play "B-Fifty-two bomber" and "Flash Gordon" outside (*Woman Hollering Creek,* pp. 18-19). The contrast between the grandmother's traditional, religious lifestyle and the carefree, Americanized lifestyle of the children illustrates a larger trend in Chicano society during the 1940s and 1950s.

The World War II era was a period of great change in Mexican American history. With a large number of Americans (including some 400,000 Chicanos) fighting overseas, many Mexican American men and women were able to fill vacant jobs at home. Often these jobs—especially the ones producing weapons and equipment for the war—paid higher salaries than previous jobs, allowing Mexican American workers to improve their position in society. As their social positions improved, they began to move out of the barrios and rural areas they had shared with other Mexican Americans and into more diverse urban areas, often leaving behind much of their Mexican culture in the process.

At the same time that World War II was improving the lot of Mexican Americans, Mexican immigration to the United States was dropping significantly. Whereas 44 percent of Mexican Americans in 1930 had been born in Mexico, only 17 percent were Mexican-born in 1950. This change also contributed to the increasing Americanization of Mexican American society, since those born in the United States tended to identify more strongly with American culture than with Mexican culture.

FAR FROM HIS FATHER'S FOOTSTEPS

Although Zapata never veered from his fight for "Land and Liberty," he did not display the same steadfastness in his relationships with women. In fact, at the time of his death Zapata had fathered at least eight children by a number of different women; his first two children, Nicolás and María Elena, were the children of Inés Aguilar, the inspiration for the narrator in Cisneros's "Eyes of Zapata." As a sad final chapter to Zapata's story, his son Nicolás would gain considerable power in Morelian politics in the 1930s and 1940s because of his father's name, only to abuse it by seizing land from the people of Anenecuilco for himself and his cronies. Ironically, Nicolás's actions made his father's famous words about politicians, spoken about 25 years before, ring true: "They're all a bunch of bastards!" (Zapata in Womack, pp. 205-06).

Of course, a large number of Mexican Americans—regardless of their birthplace—remained ambivalent about their cultural identities and loyalties. Furthermore, ill treatment by members of white society continued, no matter whether one identified more strongly with American or Mexican culture. Like African Americans, Mexican Americans were forced to confront segregation in schools, restaurants, hotels, and movie theaters in the 1940s and 1950s; whether or not they felt American, they knew that signs reading "No Dogs or Mexicans Allowed" applied to them (Gutiérrez, p. 131).

Chicanos vs. *vendidos*. The 1960s were a time of profound social change in the United States, and the Mexican American community contributed to this change. In the 1950s most Mexican American political leaders sought to integrate their community peacefully into mainstream American society, but, by the early 1960s, many young Mexican Americans were frustrated by the lack of cultural pride and political power in their community. They identified themselves proudly as "Chicanos"—a formerly disparaging term for rural Mexican immigrants—and spoke of the unity of all people of Mexican origin, glorifying Mexican historical figures and embracing Mexicans and Mexican Americans of all classes in a struggle to build a political platform and inspire a cultural renaissance.

Although the Chicano movement had a good deal of support among young people and students, many Mexican Americans thought it was a mistake, preferring the gradual process of reform to the cultural revolution that was being proposed. In 1969 Mexican American activist José Angel Gutiérrez and San Antonio congressman Henry B. González debated the validity of the movement in a famous discussion. González, who had gained esteem for his legislative work on civil rights issues, prided himself as a representative of all groups in his district, not just Mexican Americans. He labeled Gutiérrez and other Chicano activists as "professional Mexicans" who were trying "to stir up the people by appeals to emotion [and] prejudice in order to become leader[s] and achieve selfish ends." He claimed that their movement was based on "a new racism [that] demands an allegiance to race above all else" (González in Gutiérrez, p. 186).

Gutiérrez, on the other hand, accused González of behaving like a *gringo,* a white American, and claimed that González and any other Mexican Americans whose goal was assimilation into mainstream culture were *vendidos,* or sellouts, who were contributing to the oppression of their people. According to Gutiérrez, what the Chicano people needed was "social change that will enable La Raza [literally, "The Mexican Race"] to become masters of their destiny, owners of their resources, both human and natural, and a culturally separate people from the gringo" (Gutiérrez in Gutiérrez, p. 187).

Although the Chicano movement did revitalize Mexican identity and culture within the United States in the 1960s and early 1970s, its goal of creating a "culturally separate people" within American society was not realized. In fact, despite the attempts by its leaders to gloss over their group's class differences, the fact remains that the lives of working class and impoverished Mexican Americans were largely unaffected by the movement. Nonetheless, it did leave a permanent mark on American society. Many students, artists, and intellectuals continued to embrace the themes of the Chicano movement well into the 1990s, although it never regained the broad appeal it had enjoyed earlier. As the 1980s approached, most Mexican American members of the middle and working classes seemed more interested in finding a permanent place in the mainstream workforce than in exploring their cultural identities.

Chicanas break with tradition. While male activists and politicians debated the best way to increase the Chicano community's political power, many Mexican American women struggled to gain power in their personal lives. Traditionally, Mexican women were expected to be passive, subordinate homemakers, faithful to their husbands but accepting of their husbands' infidelity, much like Cleófilas at the beginning of the short story "Woman Hollering Creek."

One way in which Chicanas, or female Mexican Americans, were able to step beyond the confines of this traditional role was by working outside the home. Between 1960 and 1970 the number of employed Mexican American wives aged 14 to 54 rose from 24 to 35 percent. By 1980 the percentage of Chicanas in the labor force almost equalled that of white women. Although a number of these Chicanas took jobs out of economic necessity, many gained a sense of freedom and independence from their role as breadwinner and claimed greater authority at home over how money was spent.

Not all Mexican American women found work outside the home liberating, however. For many, the competing demands of home and work were a major source of stress and anxiety. While some working Chicanas found that their spouses were willing to share household chores, a large number had to contend with husbands resentful of their wives' role as breadwinner and therefore even more insistent that they fulfill all of their traditional marital responsibilities. The tension and conflict that arose out of such situations helped contribute to a growing divorce rate among Mexican Americans and to an increase in Chicana-headed households.

By the 1980s more and more Chicana women—like the narrator of "Never Marry a Mexican"—had rejected the traditional Mexican-style marriage in search of a lifestyle that balanced family responsibilities with personal fulfillment. In Mexico itself in recent years, the status and lifestyles of women have changed in similar, though less extreme, ways. Although traditional ideas of womanhood still weigh heavily on their lives, many Mexican women have begun to work outside the home and to question the dominant influence men have had over their public and private lives.

CÓMO SE LLAMA? (WHAT'S YOUR NAME?)

Since their first incarnation as a group in 1848, Mexican Americans have called themselves by a number of different names, all charged with special significance. First-generation immigrants often identify themselves as *Mexicanos,* while the terms "Spanish" and "Hispanic" have been associated with those seeking to assimilate into white culture or downplay their Mexican heritage. Cisneros writes in "La Fabulosa": "She likes to say she's 'Spanish,' but she's from Laredo like the rest of us" (*Woman Hollering Creek,* p. 61). In 1983 the *Los Angeles Times* surveyed the Mexican American population of Los Angeles and found that most Mexican Americans born in the United States preferred the term "Mexican American." "Latino," a term referring to the entire Spanish-speaking community, was the second choice, and "Hispanic" was third, though especially popular among the middle class. Only four percent of those surveyed identified themselves as "Chicano."

The Short Stories in Focus

Plot summary. The 22 stories in *Woman Hollering Creek* are broken into three sections. The first section deals with childhood on both sides of the Mexican-United States border and includes the stories "My Lucy Friend Who Smells Like Corn," "Eleven," "Salvador Late or Early," "Mexican Movies," "Barbie-Q," "Mericans," and "Tepeyac." The young narrators of these stories describe moments of happiness, sadness, shame, and confusion, while raising issues to which Cisneros returns throughout the collection. In "Eleven," for example, 11-year-old Rachel tells of the embarrassment she feels when her teacher, Mrs. Price, forces her to wear an ugly sweater that was left behind in the classroom. Although Rachel tells the teacher that the sweater is not hers, Mrs. Price insists, and it is not until "stupid" Phyllis Lopez remembers that she owns the sweater that Rachel is allowed to take it off (*Woman Hollering Creek,* p. 9). This is the first of many times that one of Cisneros's female characters struggles against another character's controlling influence to assert her own desires.

The second section consists only of two stories, "One Holy Night" and "My *Tocaya,*" both of which deal with love, deception, and the confusion of adolescence. In "One Holy Night," an eighth-grade girl in a Southwestern town falls in love with a Mexican man, Chaq Uxmal Paloquín, or "Baby Boy," who enchants her with stories about his royal Mayan ancestry. After she is "initiated" as his Queen, the girl is not ashamed but excited to finally find out how sex feels, and is even tickled that "it wasn't a big deal" (*Woman Hollering Creek,* p. 30). When the girl's grandmother learns what has happened, she goes searching for the man responsible, only to find that he has left town. A few weeks later, the girl discovers that she is pregnant. While she spends the last months of her pregnancy living with relatives in Mexico, her family contacts Baby Boy's sister, who reveals that his words to the girl have been lies. His name is Chato, meaning "fat-face," and he has no Mayan blood. This revelation—and the newspaper clippings his sister sends that suggest he has been involved in rape or murder—does not change the girl's feelings, however. She stares at the face in the clippings and muses about the children she will have and the man she loves.

The third section of stories deals primarily with grown women, all of Mexican heritage but from very different walks of life. "Little Miracles, Kept Promises" is a collection of letters requesting help from above or giving thanks for help granted. In one letter, college-educated Barbara Ybañez of San Antonio asks San Antonio de Padua for "a man who isn't a pain in the *nalgas.* . . . Someone please who never calls himself 'Hispanic' unless he's applying for a grant from Washington, D.C." (*Woman Hollering Creek,* p. 117). After a fire has destroyed her home, Adelfa Vásquez from Escobas, Texas, asks San Martín de Porres to send "clothes, furniture, shoes, dishes . . . anything that don't eat" and to convince her daughter to quit school so she can stay home and help her parents (*Woman Hollering Creek,* p. 117). Leocadia Dimas of San Marcos, Texas, writes to thank Don Pedrito Jaramillo, the Healer of Los Olmos, for "THE GOOD DOCTORS THAT DID THEIR JOB WELL" while operating on the cancer in her granddaughter (*Woman Hollering Creek,* p. 119). Finally, Rosario De Leon, who has just cut off her hair to give to the Virgin of Guadalupe, sorts through the web of emotions that led her, after years of resistance, to embrace Guadalupe and what she represents:

> I don't know how it all fell into place. How I finally understood who you are. No longer Mary the mild, but our mother Tonantzín. . . . That you could have the power to rally a people when a country was born, and again during civil war, and during a farmworkers' strike in California made me think maybe there is power in my mother's patience, strength in my grandmother's endurance.
>
> (*Woman Hollering Creek,* p. 128)

Rosario's struggle to accept the nurturing aspects of her culture while rejecting its oppressive elements is a struggle faced by other characters in *Woman Hollering Creek,* though some face more extreme oppression than others. In the title story, a young Mexican woman, Cleófilas, marries a Mexican man and moves with him across the border to the United States, where she discovers desolation in traditional married life. Beaten by her husband and isolated from society except for her widowed neighbors, Dolores (meaning "pain") and Soledad (meaning "solitude"), Cleófilas withdraws into a fantasy world of *telenovelas* (soap operas) and romance novels. Meanwhile, while watching her infant son laugh, she muses about what the name of the creek near her house—La Gritona, or "Screaming Woman"—might signify. She concludes that it may be a reference to "La Llorona," the "weeping woman" of Mexican folklore who kills her own child. When Cleófilas subsequently breaks down in a doctor's exam room, a sympathetic woman there arranges for a friend to drive Cleófilas to a bus station so she can escape from her husband and return to Mexico. Felice, the Chicana woman driving her to freedom (whose name means "happiness"), is a revelation to Cleófilas. She is brash, independent, irreverent, and single, and when she drives over La Gritona Creek, she lets out a "holler like Tarzan" in honor of its name (*Woman Hollering Creek,* p. 55). Amazed at Felice's behavior and at her own realization that the name of the creek might represent a woman hooting in joy instead of howling in pain, Cleófilas discovers that she herself is laughing, released for a moment from her pain by this woman hollering next to her.

The remaining pieces in the third section of *Woman Hollering Creek* share some issues with the pieces above and also introduce new subjects. They include stories of personal discovery, conflicting cultural loyalties, broken hearts, and gossip, and are told by a number of different voices, including an artist who has an affair with her white teacher and, later, his son ("Never Marry a Mexican"); a common-law wife of Zapata who transforms herself into a bird so she can transcend the limits of space and time to relive the moments spent with him ("Eyes of Zapata"); a working-class Chicana incensed at the "crab ass" owner of a religious store ("Anguiano Religious Articles Rosaries Statues Medals Incense Candles Talismans Perfumes Oils Herbs"); and an artist who falls in love with her exterminator, a poet who looks like an Aztec god, only to be left by him after he reveals that he is married and has four children ("Bien Pretty").

Redefining Guadalupe and La Malinche. At the end of the title story of *Woman Hollering Creek*, two women meet. Cleófilas, a Mexican, is the wounded product of an oppressive marriage. Felice, a Chicana, is a free-spirited, independent woman. Discussing the creek they're driving over, which is called "La Gritona," or "Screaming Woman," the Chicana says to the Mexicana "Did you ever notice . . . how nothing around here is named after a woman? Really. Unless she's the Virgin. I guess you're only famous if you're a virgin" (*Woman Hollering Creek*, p. 55).

In another story in this collection, "Little Miracles, Kept Promises," a young woman explains to the Virgin of Guadalupe how the woman was treated when she rejected the Virgin because of the "self-sacrifice" and "silent suffering" she represented:

> Don't think it was easy going without you. Don't think I didn't get my share of it from everyone. Heretic. Atheist. *Malinchista. Hocicona.* But I wouldn't shut my yap. My mouth always getting me in trouble. Is that what they teach you at the university? *Miss High-and-Mighty. Miss Thinks-She's-Too-Good-for-Us.* Acting like a bolilla, a white girl. Malinche.
>
> (*Woman Hollering Creek*, pp. 127-28)

These two excerpts refer to two central paradigms by which women in Mexican and Mexican American society have been judged. The Virgin of Guadalupe represents purity, unselfish sacrifice, motherhood, and, to many, passivity verging on martyrdom, characteristics echoed darkly by the broken life of Cleófilas. La Malinche, on the other hand, is the incarnation of cultural betrayal: the Indian woman who, with the Spaniard Cortés, is credited with creating the first *mestizo* child—and may have killed him. Felice attests to the ubiquity of the Virgin in Mexican and Mexican American culture. She is, as Felice explains, the only woman things are named for in her part of Texas. The name of Malinche likewise surfaces quite often in Mexican and Mexican American culture, but only when insults are being hurled, as Rosario of "Little Miracles, Kept Promises" can attest.

LA MALINCHE/LA LLORONA

Cortés may have brought Catholicism to Mexico, but he is probably better known in Mexico for being the first to mix Indian blood with European. The legend relates that his Indian mistress, Malinche (also called Doña Marina), was a willing perpetrator of what some have described as a crime of cultural betrayal. She is said to have given birth to the first mestizo child, the mixed European-Amerindian issue of her union with Cortés. In fact, Malinche served as a translator and go-between for the Indians and Spaniards, a border figure who linked the two cultures in other ways besides having a mestizo child. Legend, however, overpowers history in the matter of this original birth. In some versions of the legend, La Malinche rejects her role as a mother, stabbing her child to protest Cortés's decision to return to Spain and then becoming a "weeping woman" ("La Llorona") who forever laments what she has done. However, Chicana writers tend to separate the figures of La Malinche and La Llorona. They associate La Llorona with creating as well as destroying life, connecting her particularly to changeable nature, especially to water, death by drowning, and forces cloaked by night. Her weeping they associate with a mourning for their lost selves, lost because of the discrimination and violence pressing in on them, and because of the assimilation of their children into the overpowering mainstream American culture. In other words, La Llorona has become associated with a search for one's self, taking on a positive dimension. In this way, Sandra Cisneros, in *Woman Hollering Creek*, "can play on the folklore surrounding La Llorona and turn her into an active heroine" (Rebolledo and Rivero, p. 194).

These two paradigms for womanhood appear repeatedly in *Woman Hollering Creek*. They are part of the cultural heritage with which Cisneros's characters must wrestle. Rather than accept Guadalupe as the paragon of womanhood and Malinche as the embodiment of evil, however, these characters tell stories that help to redefine the significance of each figure. In the process, Cisneros's women help to redefine themselves.

When Rosario decides to accept the Virgin of Guadalupe into her life, she does so strictly on her own terms. To her, Guadalupe now represents the birth of Mexican culture, a tie to her Indian heritage, the power and unity of her people, and the strength of her mother and grandmother. Similarly, when Cleófilas joins Felice in laughter, she is choosing to put a positive spin on an ambiguous figure. La Gritona may be "La Llorona/La Malinche," crying because she has betrayed her society by rejecting the traditional role of motherhood, but she could also be a hollering woman, like the cheerful, liberated Chicana at Cleófilas's side. Rosario and Cleófilas—two women from different countries (the United States and Mexico, respectively) and radically different circumstances—have both learned to start shaping for themselves the models of womanhood that Mexican culture has bequeathed to them.

The story's reinterpretation of traditional role models is part of a larger literary trend. Other Chicana writers have modified their estimation of the Virgin of Guadalupe, acknowledging her goodness but viewing her tendency to accept and endure as a negative rather than a positive quality, and condemning what they deem to be her failure to act on her own behalf. Similarly, while the reaction of Chicano writers to the traditionally traitorous La Malinche is "varied and complex," many think of her as a survivor, "a woman who, with a clairvoyant sense, cast her lot with the Spaniards in order to ensure survival of her race. . . . It was often because of Malinche's diplomacy and intelligence that a more total annihilation of the Indian tribes of Mexico did not occur" (Rebolledo and Rivero, pp. 192-93).

Literary context. Sandra Cisneros is one of the three or four best known Latina writers in the United States and probably the best known Chicana writer. Set in Chicago, her first major success, *The House on Mango Street* (1985), has been translated into a number of languages and is used widely in American classrooms from middle school to graduate school. Such far-reaching acclaim for an American Latina writer would have been unheard of before the early 1980s. Although some magazines and journals that grew out of the Chicano movement printed Latina literature in the 1970s, it was not until 1983 that established Latina writers began to emerge. Cisneros has explained that she began writing because of what was missing in the literature around her. "She couldn't see herself in the novels and stories she was reading" (Stavans, p. 74). In essence, her stories or "verbal photographs" in *Woman Hollering Creek* help fill the vacuum by bringing to life recognizable females, ones that defy old stereotypes. "Cisneros's intention isn't only to explain a trauma or to re-create a certain flavor of childhood, but to offer a persuasive portrait of Chicanas as aggressive and independent" (Stavans, p. 74). According to at least one scholar, she has "inherited the mantle of Tomás Rivera" (see ***. . . and the earth did not part,*** also covered in *Latin American Literature and Its Times*). She did not speak in Spanish, however; she was the next generation; she had an authentic Mexican American voice (Shorris, p. 390).

Reviews. *Woman Hollering Creek* was received by Mexican American and mainstream critics as a huge success. It won a number of awards and was praised for its emotional power, its range of characters, and the originality of its style, which was described as "poetic descriptions" into which Cisneros "breathes narrative life" (Prescott and Springen in Mooney, p. 348).

Chicano scholar Ilan Stavans spoke of Cisneros's "breathtaking prose" and described *Woman Hollering Creek and Other Stories* as a "candid, engaging" work. "Cisneros's major contribution to Latino letters," this critic declared, "can be found in her strength of approaching the Hispanic experience north of Rio Grande in a non-apologetic, authentic fashion" (Stavans, pp. 16, 74). Similarly, the scholar Earl Shorris applauded *Woman Hollering Creek and Other Stories* as a superior work. Shorris preferred it to Cisneros's *House on Mango Street*; in his estimation, "the style and tone often wobbled, but the book contained some beautifully realized stories, characters that the reader married and remarried at the end of the paragraph" (Shorris, p. 390).

—Allison Weisz

For More Information

Brunk, Samuel. *Emiliano Zapata: Revolution and Betrayal in Mexico.* Albuquerque: University of New Mexico Press, 1995.

Cisneros, Sandra. *Woman Hollering Creek and Other Stories.* New York: Vintage Books, 1991.

Gutiérrez, David G. *Walls and Mirrors: Mexican Americans, Mexican Immigrants, and the Politics of Ethnicity.* Berkeley: University of California Press, 1995.

Lafaye, Jacques. *Quetzalcoatl and Guadalupe: The Formation of Mexican National Consciousness, 1531-1813.* Trans. Benjamin Keen. Chicago: University of Chicago Press, 1974.

Matuz, Roger, ed. *Contemporary Literary Criticism.* Vol. 69. Detroit: Gale Research, 1992.

Mooney, Martha T., ed. *The Book Review Digest, 1991.* New York: H. W. Wilson, 1992.

Poole, Stafford, C. M. *Our Lady of Guadalupe: The Origins and Sources of a Mexican National Symbol, 1531-1797.* Tucson: The University of Arizona Press, 1995.

Rebolledo, Tey Diana, and Eliana S. Rivero, eds. *Infinite Divisions: An Anthology of Chicana Literature.* Tuscon: The University of Arizonia Press, 1993.

Shorris, Earl. *Latinos: A Biography of Power.* New York: W. W. Norton, 1992.

Stavans, Ilan. *The Hispanic Condition: Reflections on Culture and Identity in America.* New York: HarperCollins, 1995.

Womack, John Jr. *Zapata and the Mexican Revolution.* New York: Knopf, 1969.

"The Youngest Doll"

by
Rosario Ferré

THE LITERARY WORK

A short story set in post-1950s Puerto Rico; published in Spanish (as "La muñeca menor") in the collection *Papeles de Pandora* (Pandora's Roles) in 1976, in English in 1991.

SYNOPSIS

An aunt creates a series of dolls for her nieces, the last of which literally becomes her youngest niece and exacts revenge upon the niece's husband for her own and her aunt's mistreatment.

Born in Ponce, Puerto Rico, in 1942 to a sugar industrialist family, Rosario Ferré grew up in a politically charged household. Her father, Luis, an engineer by trade, was one of the framers of the Puerto Rican Constitution (1950) and served as governor of the island from 1968 to 1972. After earning a Master's degree from the University of Puerto Rico and a doctorate from the University of Maryland, Ferré herself became politically active. She founded the Puerto Rican literary journal *Zona de carga y descarga* (Loading and Unloading Zone), which from 1970 to 1976 served as a forum for young Puerto Rican authors. Published in 1976, her first collection of short stories, *Papeles de Pandora,* included "The Youngest Doll." Ferré's fiction focuses on the inferior status of women in Puerto Rico and their dual role as nurturer (wife and mother) and temptress (like Pandora, the dangerous female from mythical Greece who tempted a man into opening a box that released the world's troubles). Ferré is credited with starting the feminist movement in Puerto Rico, of which she became, "if not its only voice, one of its most resonant and forceful spokespersons" (Rivera in Chapman, p. 168). "The Youngest Doll" tells the story of a woman seizing power in patriarchal Puerto Rico and describes the class and gender barriers that Ferré's literature seeks to change.

Events in History at the Time of the Short Story

Operation Bootstrap. Shortly after World War II Puerto Rican society underwent a dramatic transformation. The U.S. government, which had managed Puerto Rico as a protectorate since 1898, implemented a far-reaching economic plan to reduce Puerto Rico's dependence on agriculture and to build the island's industrial economy. Up to that point Puerto Rico's main industries were sugar, coffee, and tobacco, and the country was subject to the extreme volatility of those markets. Enacted in 1947, "Operation Bootstrap," as the economic plan was called, provided significant tax incentives to all new industries. Specifically, it allowed any new business tax-free status for ten years. Many U.S. corporations quickly seized this opportunity and relocated manufacturing sites to Puerto Rico, creating a sea of sweatshops and employing thousands of former farmworkers, women, and children. As industries sprang up, cities grew and the population of Puerto Rico doubled to 2 million by 1960. Workers earned from 60¢ to $1.00 per day

Luis Muñoz Marín, the first native-born governor of Puerto Rico.

and initially appreciated the steady paychecks; the factory jobs offered welcome stability from the seasonal and erratic employment patterns of farm labor. According to one historian, "In the United States, the sweatshop is recognized as a menace to workers and consumers; in Puerto Rico it is thought of as the bearer of a kind of industrial salvation, and is welcomed by the government, business organizations and the unemployed" (Wagenheim, p. 148).

But industrialization came with a heavy price. Almost overnight wealth shifted dramatically from native sugar-, coffee-, and tobacco-producing families to foreign-owned companies, which severely altered the social structure of Puerto Rico. Landed families, such as that of the protagonists in "The Youngest Doll," lost their income and influence. Women of this class were especially hard hit because they no longer had a role in society: they were neither members of the aristocracy nor part of the working class and found themselves, as the niece does in the story, without outlet for their creative or professional skills.

Further consequences of Puerto Rico's transformation into an industrialized nation included severe environmental destruction due to lack of pollution controls on manufacturing and a total dependence on imports for basic daily necessities because farmers no longer grew foodstuffs but instead were encouraged to raise cattle for export. Puerto Rico essentially became "a trading post where we import what we consume and export what we produce" (Benítez in Fernández, p. 230). In fact, according to the U.S. Commerce Department, by the 1960s Puerto Rico had become the world's largest purchaser per capita of mainland U.S. goods. The industrialization project acquired a sardonic name, "Urbanization Campbell," because the people lived mostly on Campbell's soup (Wagenheim, p. 223).

As Ferré's short story indicates, all classes were affected by Operation Bootstrap—and not just economically. "As one class lost its economic base and went into a state of decline, another was created: a dependent professional and commercial elite whose business ethos found expression in such sayings as 'time is money' and 'everything has its price'" (Vélez, p. 4). The protagonists in "The Youngest Doll" are from the old sugar-producing aristocracy and are rapidly losing their wealth and position in society. They are being replaced by men such as the young niece's doctor-husband, who was so materialistic and superficial that the niece "began to suspect that it wasn't just her husband's silhouette that was made of paper, but his soul as well" (Ferré, "The Youngest Doll," p. 5).

Public Law 600. Initially, however, the changes in Puerto Rico appeared to be very positive. The nation seemed to be gaining independence and stepping into the modern age. The United States had gained control of Puerto Rico after the Spanish-American War in 1898, making its inhabitants U.S. citizens in 1917 and imposing a half century of English education on them. Their status was ambiguous, however. In 1950 Public Law 600 enabled Puerto Rico for the first time to draft its own constitution. Its extremely popular and first-ever native governor, Luis Muñoz Marín (in office 1948–64), oversaw the framing of the constitution; Luis Ferré, Rosario's father,

SPLIT PERSONALITY

As Puerto Rico became more intertwined with and reliant upon the mainland United States—economically, politically, and socially—a split personality or identity crisis developed among many Puerto Ricans. Puerto Ricans speak Spanish but are citizens of an English-speaking country. They are part of the wealthiest, most powerful nation on earth but remain the poorest community of the United States, with unemployment at 16 percent and an average annual income of $6,200—half that of Mississippi, the poorest state in the union (Novas, p. 176; statistics for the early 1990s, when "The Youngest Doll" appeared in English). Puerto Ricans, especially those who migrate from the island to the mainland and back, receive mixed signals from both places, and maltreatment abounds:

> They [Puerto Rican migrants] had been reminded in the United States that they were Puerto Rican, but here [in Puerto Rico] they are told that they speak Spanish with an English accent, that "you are not really one of us." The young Puerto Rican may well ask himself, not only "Where am I going—" but "Who am I?"
>
> (Maldonado in Wagenheim, p. 283)

The fractured personality extends to politics as well. Many, such as Ferré's father, have favored Puerto Rico's becoming a state, while others have lobbied for national independence. However, Puerto Rico's tax-exempt status and heavy reliance on duty-free trade with the United States, not to mention public assistance (75 percent of the population receives food stamps), make independence seem virtually impossible. But the debate remains heated, as it has been since the end of the Spanish-American War, when Puerto Rico was independent for less than a week. In 1993 Puerto Ricans voted on whether to remain a commonwealth, to become a state, or to seek independence. The results indicated that 48 percent preferred to remain a commonwealth, 46 percent favored statehood, and just 4 percent voted for independence.

was one of its authors. Meanwhile, the status of Puerto Rico changed. Neither a colony nor a state, it was a protectorate until 1952, when it became a commonwealth of the United States, gaining much greater autonomy.

While the constitution, native governorship, and commonwealth status allowed Puerto Rico to govern its internal affairs, ultimate authority remained with the government of the United States. While Puerto Ricans technically became citizens of the United States and were subject to the military draft, they did not have any congressional representation and could not vote in U.S. elections. They were exempt from taxation, however, and could work and travel freely in the United States, which millions began doing from the 1960s onward. According to the U.S. Census, 887,662 Puerto Ricans lived in the United States in 1960 and by 1970 that number had jumped to 1,391,463. In 1973 close to 5 million were traveling to and from the mainland for work, with approximately one-fifth settling there permanently (Thernstrom, p. 860).

Welfare state—the 1970s. Running on a pro-*jíbaro* statehood platform, Luis Ferré was elected governor in 1968. The Puerto Rican economy was in shambles. Operation Bootstrap had failed abominably at making Puerto Rico more independent and instead had created an economy entirely dependent on the United States. In the process, unemployment shot up to nearly 20 percent and many manufacturing jobs moved from Puerto Rico to Malaysia, where wages were lower and land less expensive. Taking advantage of the tax-free opportunities, pharmaceutical companies moved in to take the garment manufacturers' place, but employed a mere 3,000 workers, compared to the tens of thousands that had been laboring in sweat shops. Adding to the unemployment problem, the population soared to 2.7 million by 1970 and kept climbing to 3.1 million by 1980. Governor Ferré turned to U.S. President Richard Nixon for help with Puerto Rico's ailing economy, and Nixon agreed to extend the newly created food stamp program to Puerto Ricans. About 75 percent of the population qualified. But instead of helping people on their feet again and moving the economy forward, the food stamp program encouraged the growth of an underground economy in which people worked "under the table" without reporting income so that they would not lose their benefits (Fernández, p. 224).

By this time Operation Bootstrap was seen as a "dismal failure" by nearly everyone familiar with Puerto Rican society (Fernández, p. 226). Agricultural and manufacturing work declined sharply, and Puerto Rico became wholly reliant on the United States for jobs, public assistance, and basic necessities. Chaos was the order of the day. Ferré lost the 1972 election and political leadership changed hands at every subsequent election. There was no long-range, coherent economic plan put forth, and continual debate over the statehood/commonwealth/independence issue only added to the disarray. In 1973 the gross national product began to decline two percent a year and net federal disbursements rose from $608 million in 1970 to a whopping $2.38 billion in 1977 (Morales Carrión, p. 313). The oil crisis and worldwide recession of the 1970s hit Puerto Rico hard, resulting in "inflation, and a deterioration in the quality of life, punctuated by an increase in crime and violence, drug abuse, environmental pollution, and a decay in public service" (Morales Carrión, p. 313). As "The Youngest Doll" indicates, society was literally crumbling: "In those days, the family was nearly ruined; they lived surrounded by a past that was breaking up around them with the same impassive musicality with which the crystal room chandelier crumbled on the frayed linen cloth of the dining-room table" ("The Youngest Doll," p. 2).

Puerto Rican women's movement. At the time "The Youngest Doll" was written (1976) the women's movement on the U.S. mainland was firmly established and its impact was being felt worldwide. The National Organization for Women (NOW), formed in 1967, was petitioning Congress for an Equal Rights Amendment and in 1973 the Supreme Court (*Roe v. Wade*) legalized abortion, which some saw as a major victory for women's rights. Women were sharing stories and rewriting history from their unique perspectives, effecting political and cultural change through the printed word. Ferré read the essays and prose of European and U.S. feminists, including Virginia Woolf, Simone de Beauvoir, and Betty Friedan. Sharing their revolutionary spirit, Ferré spread the women's rights message across Puerto Rico in the 1970s through writings like "The Youngest Doll," which gave women a public voice, and control at least in fiction over their environment—two privileges clearly absent from their patriarchal society up to that point. By telling a story that exposed women's limited role in society and promoted the notion of overcoming barriers, Ferré became a "forceful spokesperson" for the women's movement in Puerto Rico; she became one of the writers "who

Men working on a Puerto Rican sugar plantation.

are re-writing Puerto Rican history from the perspective of the oppressed classes: workers, peasants, women" (Vélez, p. 4). Her efforts complemented the founding in 1972 of Puerto Rico's first modern feminist organization, *Mujer Integrate Ahora* (MIA, "Woman, Become Involved Now, or Woman, Get Yourself Together Now" [Lovler, p. 18]). Its initial successes consisted of a report on the status of women in Puerto Rico and the founding of a commission to stop gender discrimination. Between the early 1970s, when "The Youngest Doll" appeared in Spanish, and the 1990s, when it appeared in English, MIA sponsored lectures on women and work, established consciousness-raising groups, and campaigned for abortion reform. With a spirit resembling the one conveyed by Ferré's story, members of the feminist group bandied the slogan "Soy MIA"; a declaration of independence of sorts, the expression not only means "I am a member of MIA," but also "I am mine" (Loveler, p. 18).

Like most of the world, Puerto Rico has been a patriarchal society in which men serve as the leaders in private as well as public life. Patriarchy in Puerto Rico has been punctuated by a "machismo" or "macho" attitude that conveys strength, bravery, and power; typified by a tough man who "struts his stuff and takes no guff" (Novas, p. 125). In this atmosphere, sexism has, for much of the twentieth century, been accepted and promoted. Men are to work and be the public figures, women are to stay at home and sacrifice their personal ambitions for the family. Except for lower-class women who must work, women have not been encouraged to hold jobs. Extremely high birthrates through the 1960s, '70s, and '80s made professional careers for women difficult to maintain. In the late 1980s, 59 percent of all Puerto Rican women over 16 were unemployed and many were overtly encouraged to stay in their "place" (Vélez, p. 3). Ferré's story, along with works by other Puerto Rican authors (Carmen Lugo Filippi, Mayra Montero, Carmen Valle, and Ana Lydia Vega) challenge these attitudes. "The Youngest Doll" shows a woman who exacts revenge on those who try to prevent her from living fully. Through its heroine the story challenges patriarchal hierarchies and suggests that Puerto Rican females must empower themselves.

In fact, the history of women in Puerto Rico shows that their status has been in transition since the publication of "The Youngest Doll." A 1980s study on Puerto Rican women identifies some of the basic myths that have been foisted on colonized peoples: belief in the supremacy of male authority and high esteem for sacrifice and selflessness in the female, who sublimates her own desires to serve as daughter, wife, and mother. "The last three decades [1960s–90s]," reports the study, "have brought considerable social and economic changes" that have been "altering traditions, norms, and values within Puerto Rican society" (Margarida Juliá in García Coll and de Lourdes Mattei, p. 119). Some scholars protest that the change is minimal; in many families, women still have no control over their personal growth. But the study in question reports that as many as half the women in its sample voiced their commitment to fulfilling their own ambitions, even if this created friction in the home, and the report furthermore indicates that their families were adjusting to this commitment.

The Short Story in Focus

Plot summary. The setting of "The Youngest Doll" is a decaying sugar plantation in rural Puerto Rico, where an aging dollmaker lives with her nine nieces. She is a member of the "extinct sugarcane aristocracy" and the story takes place as her family's social position and wealth are rapidly disappearing ("The Youngest Doll," p. 6). One day when the aunt, then a young woman, bathed in the river, she was bitten by a river prawn. The doctor treated her wound superficially, then told her that the prawn had embedded itself in her leg and that it would take years for him to treat the wound, which might never heal.

Once the prawn takes up residence in her body, the beautiful young woman refuses to see any male callers and devotes her life to helping raise her nieces. To fill her time she starts making dolls for each of them, one for each year of their lives until they marry and leave home. At first her dolls are quite plain and simplistic but as she improves at her craft the dolls become more ornate and lifelike. She makes molds of the girls' faces to make the dolls absolutely realistic and constructs them of the finest mikado china and luxurious materials. She makes all of the components herself, except for the glass eyes, which she imports from Europe. However, she does not place the eyes in the dolls until she soaks them for a few days in the river where she was bitten "so that they would learn to recognize the slightest stirring of the prawn's antennae" ("The Youngest Doll," p. 3).

One by one the girls marry and leave home. Eventually the youngest is the only niece left. About this time the doctor who has been treating the aunt's leg for so many years brings his son, who has just graduated from medical school, to see the aunt. The elder doctor shows his son her leg and the young man is greatly surprised upon seeing her affliction. He tells his father that he could have cured her immediately. The doctor replies: "That's true . . . but I just wanted you to come and see the prawn that has been paying for your education these twenty years" ("The Youngest Doll," p. 4).

The young doctor is attracted to the niece and begins calling upon the aunt in place of his father. He courts "the youngest," bringing her flowers and drinking tea with her on the porch in the afternoons. He is a member of the new professional class in Puerto Rico that is replacing the old aristocracy to which she belongs, and she is intrigued by that. The youngest agrees to marry him, and for the occasion, the aunt makes the youngest her last doll. This doll is incredibly lifelike—more than all the others the aunt has made. She puts her niece's baby teeth in it, places diamond studs in the eyes, and fills the doll with honey. The youngest takes it with her to her new home in the city.

She places the doll on the piano and each day her husband makes her sit on the balcony "so that passersby would be sure to see he had married into high society" ("The Youngest Doll," p. 5). She begins to suspect that her husband is very materialistic and shallow and soon her suspicions are confirmed. He sells her doll's eyes for a gold pocket watch and plans to sell the porcelain hands and face also but the youngest thwarts his plot. She says that ants discovered that the doll was filled with honey and devoured her.

Over the years the doctor becomes a millionaire and the youngest remains locked away in her apartment, sitting in a rocking chair on the balcony; she is an ornament that helps her husband acquire clientele who wanted "to see a genuine member of the extinct sugarcane aristocracy up close" ("The Youngest Doll," p. 6). The doctor is quite happy, but one day he notices that, although he is aging, his wife is not. He goes into her room to examine her while she is sleeping. Her chest is not moving so he places his stethoscope on it. Suddenly her eyes open and hundreds of prawns' antennae emerge from her hollow sockets.

From the doll to larger society. "The Youngest Doll" portrays Puerto Rican society after Operation Bootstrap from a woman's perspective, showing the effects of industrialization and its attendant materialism on certain women's lives. It illustrates this using a familiar literary convention: the doll. But, instead of the women being dolls manipulated by men, as in Heinrick Ibsen's play *The Doll House,* Ferré's dolls are made and ultimately controlled by women.

Aside from promoting female empowerment, the story points to the ill effects industrialization and colonization have had on all Puerto Rico. Ferré's story portrays a crumbling society in contemporary Puerto Rico. The sugarcane aristocracy is becoming "extinct" in a society deeply divided and confused by the myriad influences exerted upon it throughout history. For centuries the Spanish controlled Puerto Rico, heavily affecting language, cuisine, culture, and religion. Then, in 1898, just as Puerto Rico broke free of its Spanish overlords, the United States took control. Once Puerto Rico became part of the United States, it underwent rapid change. Puerto Ricans were "Americanized," inundated with U.S. products and encouraged to migrate to and from the mainland. The combination of Spanish roots and U.S. modernization made it difficult for Puerto Ricans to recognize their own particular cultural identity. Puerto Ricans have been dominated by forces that impose on the islanders the ideals and languages of others. The time of the story, post-1950s Puerto Rico, finds them in disarray.

The decay of society is prevalent in the imagery of the story: the crumbling chandelier, the aunt's rotting leg (which could be fixed by the wealthy and newly middle-class doctor but is not because then he would not make money on it—a clear analogy of the relationship between the United States and Puerto Rico), the sightless doll, whose diamond eyes have been despoiled by the money-grubbing doctor. There is also the image of ants devouring parts of the honey-filled doll, alluding perhaps to the destruction wrought by industrialization and Operation Bootstrap on Puerto Rico's old sugar aristocracy and social structure.

Describing the disarray of Puerto Rico in the modern age is nothing new—everyone from Governor Marín to U.S. President Gerald Ford openly admitted the failure of Operation Bootstrap. But an illustration of the disarray as perceived by a woman and of its effects on a certain class of women is revolutionary. The niece in "The Youngest Doll" is nothing more than a relic, a symbol of the regal past who has no future. She sits on her balcony all day so people can see that her husband married well but she herself has no occupation and no money. She dies within this confined space and is replaced by the doll, but it takes her husband years and years to notice the switch. The suggestion is that women like the niece have no role in the new industrial society and that their plight has been ignored and overlooked. However, the story also suggests that women themselves can change the situation. The niece loses her identity by becoming a doll, then seizes it back by defying her husband, a revolutionary prescription that promises hope to female readers, as fantastic tales of Puerto Rican folklore often do.

Puerto Rican folklore. In "The Youngest Doll," Ferré writes a fantastic tale that in many ways resembles folklore, drawing on the reality of Puerto Rican society and conveying revolutionary ideas to conquer the "evils"—sexism and materialism—in it. Written in Spanish (not English, the much-resented language of instruction in public schools from 1898 to 1948), Ferré's story can be viewed as a traditional folktale, told by a late-twentieth-century woman, which makes a strong political statement to a society very familiar with the genre.

Derived from the original Taino inhabitants, African slaves, and Spanish colonists, and handed down through the generations, folklore is a strong component of Puerto Rican culture. Stories abound that incorporate the beauty of the land and people, and the dreams and longings of a conquered nation. The stories concern the oppression of the poor peasant, or *jibaro,* and the search for identity, a particular concern of Ferré who, shortly after publishing her first short stories, published a few collections of folktales for children. One of the tales, "Arroz con Leche," concerns the inequality between women and men. A man searches for a wife, testing candidates by asking them impossible questions. They are all unable to provide answers, but one clever candidate responds with an impossible question of her own that stumps the prospective groom. He takes her as his wife, but the marriage is unhappy because he focuses on material possessions and she wants love. In the end he plans to murder her because she outsmarted him, but the wife kills him first in self-defense. Based on a children's rhyme that is popular in Puerto Rico and comes from a Spanish ballad, "Arroz con Leche" is a tale of good versus evil in which the good triumphs, as is typically the case in such folklore. Such tales not only give voice to the oppressed; they also bolster hope that change can occur in the future. They are a "complex working out of wishes" that promote social change and enable the underclasses to vent frustrations (Vélez, p. 2).

Sources and literary context. There are similarities between Ferré's story and "Las Hortensias," a 1949 tale by Felisberto Hernández of Uruguay. "Las Hortensias" features a man who creates dolls modeled on his wife; they are life-size and can even satisfy his sexual desires. In contrast to "Las Hortensias," "The Youngest Doll" has women, not men, make the dolls. The nineteenth-century novel *La muñeca* (The Doll) by a Puerto Rican woman, Eulalia Sanjujo, may have also been an influence.

The influence on Ferré of feminist writers of her era has already been noted, as has the influence of folklore. When she was young, her father and her nurse used to tell her Puerto Rican tales, which would later find their way into her children's books. Her adult tale, "The Youngest Doll," takes the myth of Pandora and sets it on its ear. According to Greek mythology, when Pandora's Box is opened, it lets loose a torrent of misfortunes and misery on mankind. Ferré's story lets loose a torrent of emotion and ideas from a female perspective, challenging patriarchal conventions and female stereotypes not only by her characters and plot lines but also by being the work of a female writer of short stories. "For women in Latin America, setting down a short story is like screaming out loud; it breaks the rules, violates the code of silence into which we were born" (Correas de Zapata, p. 5).

Ferré was the first Puerto Rican woman—and among the first of all Latin American women—to challenge through literature the patriarchal models of social behavior. Until her work was published, Puerto Rican literature, with very few exceptions, had been male-dominated. "The world was run by men and written about by men who, consequently, wrote us, our role and our place in their world" (Correas de Zapata, p. 5). Due to Ferré's work and that of others like her, characterizations of Latin American women are now more varied and their stereotypes have been replaced with realistic portraits of multi-faceted human beings.

Reviews. The publication of "The Youngest Doll" in 1976 greatly advanced the feminist movement in Puerto Rico. The story was hailed as "defiant magic feminism [that] challenges all our conventional notions of time, place, matter and identity" and rewrites "Puerto Rican history from a woman's perspective" (Hart and Rivera in Chapman, p. 168).

A translator of her own stories, Ferré supports writing in English. The defiance of her tales, however, has been described as more passionate in the Spanish versions than the English translations. In Spanish, the stories subvert language, especially vulgarities used by men in reference to women; the vulgarities become a tool used by the heroines to break down the patriarchal society and liberate themselves from it. The English versions are thus remarkable, but less so than their Spanish equivalents, in part because cleaner substitutions were made for the vulgarities, originally included by Ferré to turn everyday sexual insults against Puerto Rico's brazen biases (Ferré in Luis and González, p. 133).

—Diane R. Sneva

For More Information

Chapman, Jeff, ed. *Contemporary Authors New Revision Series*. Vol. 55. Detroit: Gale Research, 1997.

Correas de Zapata, Cela, ed. *Short Stories by Latin American Women*. Houston: Arte Publico Press, 1990.

Fernández, Ronald. *The Disenchanted Island*. New York: Preager, 1992.

Ferré, Rosario. "The Youngest Doll." In *The Youngest Doll*. Trans. Rosario Ferré and Diana Vélez. Lincoln: University of Nebraska Press, 1991.

García Coll, Cynthia T., and María de Lourdes Mattei, eds. *The Psychosocial Development of Puerto Rican Women*. New York: Praeger, 1989.

Hintz, Suzanne S. *Rosario Ferré: A Search for Identity*. New York: Peter Lang, 1995.

Lovler, Ronnie. "I Am Mine." *Ms.* 3, no. 8 (February 1995): 18.

Luis, William, and Ann González, eds. *Modern Latin-American Fiction Writers*. 2nd series. Dictionary of Literary Biography. Vol. 145. Detroit: Gale Research, 1994.

Morales Carrión, Arturo. *Puerto Rico: A Political and Cutural History*. New York: W. W. Norton, 1983.

Novas, Himilce. *Everything You Need to Know About Latino History*. New York: Plume, Penguin, 1994.

Thernstrom, Stephan, ed. *Harvard Encyclopedia of American Ethnic Groups*. Cambridge, Mass.: Harvard University Press, 1980.

Vélez, Diana, ed. *Reclaiming Medusa*. San Francisco: Spinsters/Aunt Lute, 1988.

Wagenheim, Kal, ed. *The Puerto Ricans*. New York: Praeger Publishers, 1973.

Index

A

B

C

D

E

H

I

J

K

L

M

N

Index

O

P

Q

R

S

T

W

Y

Z